MW01697544

About Pearson

Pearson is the world's learning company, with presence across 70 countries worldwide. Our unique insights and world-class expertise comes from a long history of working closely with renowned teachers, authors and thought leaders, as a result of which, we have emerged as the preferred choice for millions of teachers and learners across the world.

We believe learning opens up opportunities, creates fulfilling careers and hence better lives. We hence collaborate with the best of minds to deliver you class-leading products, spread across the Higher Education and K12 spectrum.

Superior learning experience and improved outcomes are at the heart of everything we do. This product is the result of one such effort.

Your feedback plays a critical role in the evolution of our products and you can contact us – reachus@pearson.com. *We look forward to it.*

MANAGEMENT INFORMATION SYSTEMS

MANAGING THE DIGITAL FIRM

FIFTEENTH EDITION

MANAGEMENT INFORMATION SYSTEMS

MANAGING THE DIGITAL FIRM

FIFTEENTH EDITION

Kenneth C. Laudon

New York University

Jane P. Laudon

Azimuth Information Systems

Adapted by

Sahil Raj

School of Management Studies, Punjabi University, Patiala

Pearson

Authorized adaptation from the global edition, entitled *Management Information Systems: Managing The Digital Firm, 15th Edition*, ISBN 9781292211756 by Kenneth C. Laudon and Jane P. Laudon, published by Pearson Education, Inc, Copyright © 2018.

Indian Subcontinent Adaptation

ISBN 978-93-528-6547-5

First Impression, 2018
Second Impression,2019

This edition is manufactured in India and is authorized for sale only in India, Bangladesh, Bhutan, Pakistan, Nepal, Sri Lanka and the Maldives. Circulation of this edition outside of these territories is UNAUTHORIZED.

Published by Pearson India Education Services Pvt. Ltd, CIN: U72200TN2005PTC057128.

Head Office: 15th Floor, Tower-B, World Trade Tower, Plot No. 1, Block-C, Sector 16, Noida 201 301, Uttar Pradesh, India.
Registered Office: 4th Floor, Software Block, Elnet Software City, TS-140, Block 2 & 9, Rajiv Gandhi Salai, Taramani, Chennai 600 113, Tamil Nadu, India.
Fax: 080-30461003, Phone: 080-30461060
in.pearson.com; Email: companysecretary.india@pearson.com

Printed in India at India Binding House

About the Authors

Kenneth C. Laudon is a Professor of Information Systems at New York University's Stern School of Business. He holds a B.A. in Economics from Stanford and a Ph.D. from Columbia University. He has authored 12 books dealing with electronic commerce, information systems, organizations, and society. Professor Laudon has also written more than 40 articles concerned with the social, organizational, and management impacts of information systems, privacy, ethics, and multimedia technology.

Professor Laudon's current research is on the planning and management of large-scale information systems and multimedia information technology. He has received grants from the National Science Foundation to study the evolution of national information systems at the Social Security Administration, the IRS, and the FBI. Ken's research focuses on enterprise system implementation, computer-related organizational and occupational changes in large organizations, changes in management ideology, changes in public policy, and understanding productivity change in the knowledge sector.

Ken Laudon has testified as an expert before the United States Congress. He has been a researcher and consultant to the Office of Technology Assessment (United States Congress), the Department of Homeland Security, and the Office of the President, several executive branch agencies, and Congressional Committees. Professor Laudon also acts as an in-house educator for several consulting firms and as a consultant on systems planning and strategy to several Fortune 500 firms.

At NYU's Stern School of Business, Ken Laudon teaches courses on Managing the Digital Firm, Information Technology and Corporate Strategy, Professional Responsibility (Ethics), and Electronic Commerce and Digital Markets. Ken Laudon's hobby is sailing.

Jane Price Laudon is a management consultant in the information systems area and the author of seven books. Her special interests include systems analysis, data management, MIS auditing, software evaluation, and teaching business professionals how to design and use information systems.

Jane received her Ph.D. from Columbia University, her M.A. from Harvard University, and her B.A. from Barnard College. She has taught at Columbia University and the New York University Graduate School of Business. She maintains a lifelong interest in Oriental languages and civilizations.

The Laudons have two daughters, Erica and Elisabeth, to whom this book is dedicated.

Brief Contents

Complete Contents

Business Cases And Interactive Sessions

Here are some of the business firms you will find described in the cases and Interactive Sessions of this book:

Chapter 1: Information Systems in Global Business Today

Rugby Football Union Tries Big Data
Employee Pick-ups and Drop-offs at Convergys
ETM's Re-Routing KSTRC
The Domino's PULSE™ System: Reading the Pulse of the Customer

Chapter 2: Global E-Business and Collaboration

Azure Medical System: Integrating Departments Using Enterprise System
HDFC Banking on Business Intelligence and Analytics Technology
Collaboration for Improved Services at eClerx
Ranbaxy: Taking the ERP Pill

Chapter 3: Information Systems, Organizations, and Strategy

AirAsia: Saving on Operational Costs through Effective Information Systems
Securing Flipkart
Smart Products, Smart Companies
Deutsche Bank: The Cost of Legacy Systems

Chapter 4: Ethical and Social Issues in Information Systems

The Dark Side of Big Data
Ethical Issues of Google Earth
Are We Relying Too Much on Computers to Think for Us?
Facebook Privacy: What Privacy?

Chapter 5: IT Infrastructure and Emerging Technologies

EasyJet Flies High with Cloud Computing
Establishing Global Classrooms through WebEx
Building Virtualization Infrastructure at NTT
BYOD: Business Opportunity or Big Headache?

Chapter 6: Foundations of Business Intelligence: Databases and Information Management

BAE Systems
The Gym Database
Societe Generale Builds an Intelligent System to Manage Information Flow
Lego's Enterprise Software Spurs Growth

Chapter 7: Telecommunications, the Internet and Wireless Technology

Wireless Technology Makes Dundee Precious Metals Good as Gold
The Global Battle over Net Neutrality
Monitoring Employees on Networks: Unethical or Good Business?
RFID Enabled Weighbridge Automation

Chapter 8: Securing Information Systems

Hackers Attack Singapore's Telecom Infrastructure
SAS Helping SEBI Check Equities-Trading Malpractices
BYOD: A Security Nightmare?
Securing Information: The HSBC Way

Chapter 9: Achieving Operational Excellence and Customer Intimacy: Enterprise Applications

Alimentation Couche-Tard Competes Using Enterprise Systems
Optimizing Operations at QuarkCity: A Move Away from Legacy Systems
McDonald's Serving Hot and Fresh
Customer Relationship Management Helps Celcom Become Number One

Chapter 10: E-commerce: Digital Markets, Digital Goods

Uber Storms Europe: Europe Strikes Back
Zomato Scripting Success With E-Com
Social Media Analytics in Indian Politics
Paytm Cashing on Demonetization

Chapter 11: Managing Knowledge

Connecting Unisys Globally Through Social Collaboration Information Systems
KMS Empowering Capella University
Will Robots Replace People in Manufacturing?
Knowledge Management and Collaboration at Tata Consulting Services

Chapter 12: Enhancing Decision Making

Roche: Changing Medical Care with Mobile Technology and Big Data
Singapore Sports Institute Uses Analytics for SEA Games
Britain's National Health Service Jettisons Choose and Book System
GE Bets on the Internet of Things and Big Data Analytics

Chapter 13: Building Information Systems

Angostura Builds a Mobile Sales System
Centralization of Operations at Tata Power
Developing Mobile Apps: What's Different
ConAgra's Recipe for a Better Human Resources System

Chapter 14: Managing Projects

Intuit Counts on Project Management
Can the National Health Service Go Paperless?
Reliance Installing the 4G Project in India
A Shaky Start for Healthcare.gov

Chapter 15: Managing Global Systems

The Bel Group: Laughing All the Way to Success
Indian E-commerce: Obstacles to Opportunity
One Organization, One Data, One Information: ONGC's Global System
Crocs Clambers to Global Efficiency

Preface

The Global Edition is written for business school students in Europe, the Middle East, South Africa, Australia, and the Pacific Asian region. Case studies and examples focus on how firms in these regions use information systems. We wrote this book for business school students who wanted an in-depth look at how today's business firms use information technologies and systems to achieve corporate objectives. Information systems are one of the major tools available to business managers for achieving operational excellence, developing new products and services, improving decision making, and achieving competitive advantage. Students will find here the most up-to-date and comprehensive overview of information systems used by business firms today. After reading this book, we expect students will be able to participate in, and even lead, management discussions of information systems for their firms.

When interviewing potential employees, business firms often look for new hires who know how to use information systems and technologies for achieving bottom-line business results. Regardless of whether you are an accounting, finance, management, operations management, marketing, or information systems major, the knowledge and information you find in this book will be valuable throughout your business career.

What's New in This Edition

Currency

The 15th edition features all new opening, closing, and Interactive Session cases. The text, figures, tables, and cases have been updated through September 2016 with the latest sources from industry and MIS research.

New Topics

- **Big Data and the Internet of Things:** In-depth coverage of big data, big data analytics, and the Internet of Things (IoT) in Chapters 1, 6, 7, and 12. Includes big data analytics, analyzing IoT data streams, Hadoop, in-memory computing, non-relational databases, and analytic platforms.
- **Cloud Computing:** Updated and expanded coverage of cloud computing in Chapter 5 (IT infrastructure) with more detail on types of cloud services, private and public clouds, hybrid clouds, managing cloud services, and a new Interactive Session on using cloud services. Cloud computing also covered in Chapter 6 (databases in the cloud), Chapter 8 (cloud security), Chapter 9 (cloud-based CRM and ERP), Chapter 10 (e-commerce), and Chapter 13 (cloud-based systems development).
- **Social, Mobile, Local:** New e-commerce content in Chapter 10 describing how social tools, mobile technology, and location-based services are transforming marketing and advertising.

- **Social Business:** Expanded coverage of social business, introduced in Chapter 2 and discussed in throughout the text. Detailed discussions of enterprise (internal corporate) social networking as well as social networking in e-commerce.
- BYOD and mobile device management
- Smart products
- DevOps
- Zero-day vulnerabilities
- Machine learning
- Chatbots
- Near field communication (NFC)
- Native advertising
- Windows 10
- Microsoft Office 365
- Zero-day vulnerabilities
- Platforms
- Software-defined storage (SDS)

The 15th Edition: The Comprehensive Solution for the MIS Curriculum

Since its inception, this text has helped to define the MIS course around the globe. This edition continues to be authoritative but is also more customizable, flexible, and geared to meeting the needs of different colleges, universities, and individual instructors. Many of its learning tools are now available in digital form. This book is now part of a complete learning package that includes the core text, and Learning Tracks.

The core text consists of 15 chapters with hands-on projects covering the most essential topics in MIS.

The CORE Text

The core text provides an overview of fundamental MIS concepts using an integrated framework for describing and analyzing information systems. This framework shows information systems composed of management, organization, and technology elements and is reinforced in student projects and case studies.

Chapter Organization

Each chapter contains the following elements:

- A Chapter Outline based on Learning Objectives
- Lists of all the Case Studies
- A chapter-opening case describing a real-world organization to establish the theme and importance of the chapter

A diagram accompanying each chapter-opening case graphically illustrates how management, organization, and technology elements work together to create an information system solution to the business challenges discussed in the case.

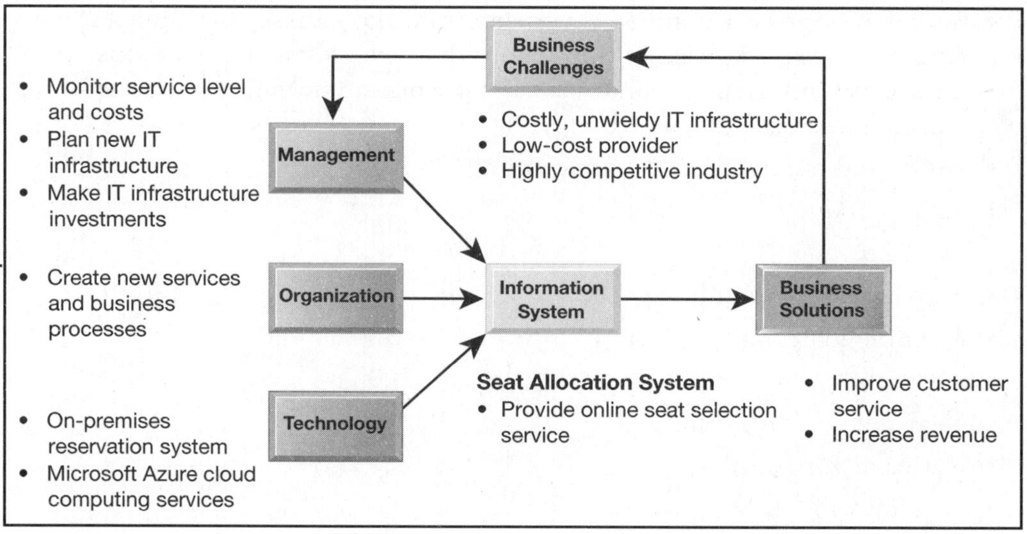

- A diagram analyzing the opening case in terms of the management, organization, and technology model used throughout the text
- Two Interactive Sessions with Case Study Questions
- A Review Summary keyed to the Student Learning Objectives
- A list of Key Terms that students can use to review concepts
- Review questions for students to test their comprehension of chapter material
- Discussion questions raised by the broader themes of the chapter
- A series of Hands-on MIS Projects consisting of two Management Decision Problems, a hands-on application software project, and a project to develop Internet skills
- A Collaboration and Teamwork Project to develop teamwork and presentation skills with options for using open source collaboration tools
- A chapter-ending case study for students to apply chapter concepts
- Two assisted-graded writing questions with prebuilt grading rubrics
- Chapter references

Key Features

We have enhanced the text to make it more interactive, leading edge, and appealing to both students and instructors. The features and learning tools are described in the following sections.

Business-Driven with Real-World Business Cases and Examples

The text helps students see the direct connection between information systems and business performance. It describes the main business objectives driving the use of information systems and technologies in corporations all over the world: operational excellence, new products and services, customer and supplier intimacy, improved decision making, competitive advantage, and survival.

In-text examples and case studies show students how specific companies use information systems to achieve these objectives.

We use only current (2016) examples from business and public organizations throughout the text to illustrate the important concepts in each chapter. All the case studies describe companies or organizations that are familiar to students, such as Nike, Rugby Football Union, Facebook, Walmart, Fiat, Unilever, and GE.

Interactivity

There's no better way to learn about MIS than by doing MIS! We provide different kinds of hands-on projects where students can work with real-world business scenarios and data and learn firsthand what MIS is all about. These projects heighten student involvement in this exciting subject.

- **Interactive Sessions.** Two short cases in each chapter have been redesigned as Interactive Sessions to be used in the classroom (or on Internet discussion boards) to stimulate student interest and active learning. Each case concludes with case study questions. The case study questions provide topics for class discussion, Internet discussion, or written assignments.

INTERACTIVE SESSION: TECHNOLOGY

Getting Social with Customers

Businesses of all sizes are finding Facebook, Twitter, and other social media to be powerful tools for engaging customers, amplifying product messages, discovering trends and influencers, building brand awareness, and taking action on customer requests and recommendations. Half of all Twitter users recommend products in their tweets.

About 1.6 billion people use Facebook, and more than 30 million businesses have active brand pages, enabling users to interact with the brand through blogs, comment pages, contests, and offerings on the brand page. The "like" button gives users a chance to share with their social network their feelings about content and other objects they are viewing and websites they are visiting. With like buttons on millions of websites, Facebook can track user behavior on other sites and then sell this information to marketers. Facebook also sells display ads to firms that show up in the right column of users' home pages and most other pages in the Facebook interface such as photos and apps.

Twitter has developed many new offerings to interest advertisers, like "promoted tweets" and "promoted trends." These features give advertisers the ability to have their tweets displayed more prominently when Twitter users search for certain keywords. Many big advertisers are using Twitter's Vine service, which allows users to share short, repeating videos with a mobile-phone app or post them on other platforms such as Facebook.

Lowe's is using Facebook mobile video and Snapchat image messaging to help first-time millennial home buyers learn home improvement skills. The home improvement retailer launched a new series of social videos in April 2016 to showcase spring cleaning and do-it-yourself projects. Lowe's believes this

Lowe's "In-a-Snap" Snapchat series tries to inspire young homeowners and renters to undertake simple home improvement projects such as installing shelves to build a study nook. During the Lowe's Snapchat story, users can tap on the screen to put a nail in a wall or chisel off an old tile. Lowe's is working on another series of video tutorials on Facebook and Instagram called "Home School" that uses drawings from chalk artists to animate maintenance projects.

Lowe's social media activities have helped increase brand engagement. Although the company's social campaigns are designed to teach first-time homeowners or young renters about home improvement, the company is also hoping they will encourage consumers to think differently about the brand beyond its products and services. Management believes millennials who are becoming first-time homeowners want to know the deeper meaning of what a company is trying to stand for, not just the products and services it offers.

An estimated 90 percent of customers are influenced by online reviews, and nearly half of U.S. social media users actively seek customer service through social media. As a result, marketing is now placing much more emphasis on customer satisfaction and customer service. Social media monitoring helps marketers and business owners understand more about likes, dislikes, and complaints concerning products, additional products or product modifications customers want, and how people are talking about a brand (positive or negative sentiment).

General Motors (GM) has 26 full-time social media customer care advisers for North America alone, covering more than 150 company social channels from GM, Chevrolet, Buick, GMC, and Cadillac, and

Each chapter contains two Interactive Sessions on Management, Organizations, or Technology using real-world companies to illustrate chapter concepts and issues.

- **Hands-On MIS Projects.** Every chapter concludes with a Hands-On MIS Projects section containing three types of projects: two Management Decision Problems; a hands-on application software exercise using Microsoft Excel, Access, or web page and blog creation tools; and a project that develops Internet business skills.
- **Collaboration and Teamwork Projects.** Each chapter features a collaborative project that encourages students working in teams to use Google Drive, Google Docs, or other open source collaboration tools. The first team project in Chapter 1 asks students to build a collaborative Google site.

Case Study Questions encourage students to apply chapter concepts to real-world companies in class discussions, student presentations, or writing assignments.

CASE STUDY QUESTIONS

1. Assess the management, organization, and technology issues for using social media technology to engage with customers.
2. What are the advantages and disadvantages of using social media for advertising, brand building, market research, and customer service?
3. Give an example of a business decision in this case study that was facilitated by using social media to interact with customers.
4. Should all companies use social media technology for customer service and marketing? Why or why not? What kinds of companies are best suited to use these platforms?

Two real-world business scenarios per chapter provide opportunities for students to apply chapter concepts and practice management decision making.

Management Decision Problems

11-8 U.S. Pharma Corporation is headquartered in New Jersey but has research sites in Germany, France, the United Kingdom, Switzerland, and Australia. Research and development of new pharmaceuticals is key to ongoing profits, and U.S. Pharma researches and tests thousands of possible drugs. The company's researchers need to share information with others within and outside the company, including the U.S. Food and Drug Administration, the World Health Organization, and the International Federation of Pharmaceutical Manufacturers & Associations. Also critical is access to health information sites, such as the U.S. National Library of Medicine, and to industry conferences and professional journals. Design a knowledge portal for U.S. Pharma's researchers. Include in your design specifications relevant internal systems and databases, external sources of information, and internal and external communication and collaboration tools. Design a home page for your portal.

11-9 Canadian Tire is one of Canada's largest companies, with 50,000 employees and 1,100 stores and gas bars (gas stations) across Canada selling sports, leisure, home products, apparel, and financial services as well as automotive and petroleum products. The retail outlets are independently owned and operated. Canadian Tire has been using daily mailings and thick product catalogs to inform its dealers about new products, merchandise setups, best practices, product ordering, and problem resolution, and it is looking for a better way to provide employees with human resources and administrative documents. Describe the problems created by this way of doing business and how knowledge management systems might help.

Students practice using software in real-world settings for achieving operational excellence and enhancing decision making.

Store & Region Sales Database

I	Store N	Sales Regic	Item N	Item Descripti	Unit Pri	Units So	Week Ending	Click to Add
1	1	South	2005	17" Monitor	$229.00	28	10/27/2016	
2	1	South	2005	17" Monitor	$229.00	30	11/24/2016	
3	1	South	2005	17" Monitor	$229.00	9	12/29/2016	
4	1	South	3006	101 Keyboard	$19.95	30	10/27/2016	
5	1	South	3006	101 Keyboard	$19.95	35	11/24/2016	
6	1	South	3006	101 Keyboard	$19.95	39	12/29/2016	
7	1	South	6050	PC Mouse	$8.95	28	10/27/2016	
8	1	South	6050	PC Mouse	$8.95	3	11/24/2016	
9	1	South	6050	PC Mouse	$8.95	38	12/29/2016	
10	1	South	8500	Desktop CPU	$849.95	25	10/27/2016	
11	1	South	8500	Desktop CPU	$849.95	27	11/24/2016	
12	1	South	8500	Desktop CPU	$849.95	33	12/29/2016	
13	2	South	2005	17" Monitor	$229.00	8	10/27/2016	
14	2	South	2005	17" Monitor	$229.00	8	11/24/2016	
15	2	South	2005	17" Monitor	$229.00	10	12/29/2016	
16	2	South	3006	101 Keyboard	$19.95	8	10/27/2016	
17	2	South	3006	101 Keyboard	$19.95	8	11/24/2016	
18	2	South	3006	101 Keyboard	$19.95	8	12/29/2016	
19	2	South	6050	PC Mouse	$8.95	9	10/27/2016	
20	2	South	6050	PC Mouse	$8.95	9	11/24/2016	
21	2	South	6050	PC Mouse	$8.95	8	12/29/2016	
22	2	South	8500	Desktop CPU	$849.95	18	10/27/2016	

Record: 1 of 96 No Filter Search

Improving Decision Making: Using Web Tools to Configure and Price an Automobile

Software skills: Internet-based software
Business skills: Researching product information and pricing

3-11 In this exercise, you will use software at car websites to find product information about a car of your choice and use that information to make an important purchase decision. You will also evaluate two of these sites as selling tools.

You are interested in purchasing a new Ford Escape (or some other car of your choice). Go to the website of CarsDirect (www.carsdirect.com) and begin your investigation. Locate the Ford Escape. Research the various Escape models, and choose one you prefer in terms of price, features, and safety ratings. Locate and read at least two reviews. Surf the website of the manufacturer, in this case Ford (www.ford.com). Compare the information available on Ford's website with that of CarsDirect for the Ford Escape. Try to locate the lowest price for the car you want in a local dealer's inventory. Suggest improvements for CarsDirect.com and Ford.com.

Each chapter features a project to develop Internet skills for accessing information, conducting research, and performing online calculations and analysis.

Assessment and AACSB Assessment Guidelines

The Association to Advance Collegiate Schools of Business (AACSB) is a not-for-profit corporation of educational institutions, corporations, and other organizations that seeks to improve business education primarily by accrediting university business programs. As a part of its accreditation activities, the AACSB has developed an Assurance of Learning Program designed to ensure that schools do in fact teach students what they promise. Schools are required to state a clear mission, develop a coherent business program, identify student learning objectives, and then prove that students do in fact achieve the objectives.

We have attempted in this book to support AACSB efforts to encourage assessment-based education. The back end papers of this edition identify student learning objectives and anticipated outcomes for our Hands-On MIS projects. The authors will provide custom advice on how to use this text in colleges with different missions and assessment needs. Please e-mail the authors or contact your local Pearson representative for contact information.

For more information on the AACSB Assurance of Learning Program and how this text supports assessment-based learning, please visit the website for this book.

Customization and Flexibility: Learning Track Modules

Our Learning Tracks feature gives instructors the flexibility to provide in-depth coverage of the topics they choose. This supplementary content takes students deeper into MIS topics, concepts, and debates; reviews basic technology concepts in hardware, software, database design, telecommunications, and other areas.

Author-Certified Test Bank and Supplements

- **Author-Certified Test Bank.** The authors have worked closely with skilled test item writers to ensure that higher-level cognitive skills are tested. Test bank multiple-choice questions include questions on content but also include many questions that require analysis, synthesis, and evaluation skills.
- **Annotated Slides.** The authors have prepared a comprehensive collection of 50 PowerPoint slides for each chapter to be used in your lectures. Many of these slides are the same as used by Ken Laudon in his MIS classes and executive education presentations. Each of the slides is annotated with

teaching suggestions for asking students questions, developing in-class lists that illustrate key concepts, and recommending other firms as examples in addition to those provided in the text. The annotations are like an Instructor's Manual built into the slides and make it easier to teach the course effectively.

Student Learning-Focused

Student Learning Objectives are organized around a set of study questions to focus student attention. Each chapter concludes with a Review Summary and Review Questions organized around these study questions, and each major chapter section is based on a Learning Objective.

Career Resources

The Instructor Resources for this text include extensive Career Resources, including job-hunting guides and instructions on how to build a Digital Portfolio demonstrating the business knowledge, application software proficiency, and Internet skills acquired from using the text. The portfolio can be included in a resume or job application or used as a learning assessment tool for instructors.

Instructor Resources

At the Instructor Resource Center, http://www.pearsoned.co.in/KennethCLaudon/, instructors can easily register to gain access to a variety of instructor resources available with this text in downloadable format. If assistance is needed, our dedicated technical support team is ready to help with the media supplements that accompany this text. Visit http://support.pearson.com for answers to frequently asked questions and toll-free user support phone numbers.

The following supplements are available with this text:

- Instructor's Resource Manual
- Test Bank
- TestGen® Computerized Test Bank
- PowerPoint Presentation
- Lecture Notes

Learning Tracks

Chapter	Learning Tracks
Chapter 1: Information Systems in Global Business Today	How Much Does IT Matter? Information Systems and Your Career The Mobile Digital Platform
Chapter 2: Global E-business and Collaboration	Systems From a Functional Perspective IT Enables Collaboration and Teamwork Challenges of Using Business Information Systems Organizing the Information Systems Function Occupational and Career Outlook for Information Systems Majors 2014–2020
Chapter 3: Information Systems, Organizations, and Strategy	The Changing Business Environment for IT

Chapter	Learning Tracks
Chapter 4: Ethical and Social Issues in Information Systems	Developing a Corporate Code of Ethics for IT
Chapter 5: IT Infrastructure and Emerging Technologies	How Computer Hardware Works How Computer Software Works Service Level Agreements The Open Source Software Initiative Comparing Stages in IT Infrastructure Evolution Cloud Computing
Chapter 6: Foundations of Business Intelligence: Databases and Information Management	Database Design, Normalization, and Entity-Relationship Diagramming Introduction to SQL Hierarchical and Network Data Models
Chapter 7: Telecommunications, the Internet, and Wireless Technology	Broadband Network Services and Technologies Cellular System Generations Wireless Applications for Customer Relationship Management, Supply Chain Management, and Healthcare Introduction to Web 2.0 LAN Topologies
Chapter 8: Securing Information Systems	The Booming Job Market in IT Security The Sarbanes-Oxley Act Computer Forensics General and Application Controls for Information Systems Management Challenges of Security and Control Software Vulnerability and Reliability
Chapter 9: Achieving Operational Excellence and Customer Intimacy: Enterprise Applications	SAP Business Process Map Business Processes in Supply Chain Management and Supply Chain Metrics Best-Practice Business Processes in CRM Software
Chapter 10: E-commerce: Digital Markets, Digital Goods	E-commerce Challenges: The Story of Online Groceries Build an E-commerce Business Plan Hot New Careers in E-Commerce E-commerce Payment Systems Building an E-commerce Website
Chapter 11: Managing Knowledge	Challenges of Knowledge Management Systems
Chapter 12: Enhancing Decision Making	Building and Using Pivot Tables
Chapter 13: Building Information Systems	Unified Modeling Language Primer on Business Process Design and Documentation Primer on Business Process Management Fourth-Generation Languages
Chapter 14: Managing Projects	Capital Budgeting Methods for Information Systems Investments Enterprise Analysis (Business Systems Planning) and Critical Success Factors Information Technology Investments and Productivity

Acknowledgments

The production of any book involves valued contributions from a number of persons. We would like to thank all of our editors for encouragement, insight, and strong support for many years. We thank our editor Samantha McAfee Lewis and project manager Katrina Ostler for their role in managing the project.

Our special thanks go to our supplement authors for their work. We are indebted to Robin Pickering for her assistance with writing and to William Anderson and Megan Miller for their help during production. We thank Diana R. Craig for her assistance with database and software topics.

Special thanks to colleagues at the Stern School of Business at New York University; to Professor Werner Schenk, Simon School of Business, University of Rochester; to Professor Mark Gillenson, Fogelman College of Business and Economics, University of Memphis; to Robert Kostrubanic, Indiana-Purdue University Fort Wayne; to Professor Lawrence Andrew of Western Illinois University; to Professor Detlef Schoder of the University of Cologne; to Professor Walter Brenner of the University of St. Gallen; to Professor Lutz Kolbe of the University of Gottingen; to Professor Donald Marchand of the International Institute for Management Development; and to Professor Daniel Botha of Stellenbosch University who provided additional suggestions for improvement. Thank you to Professor Ken Kraemer, University of California at Irvine, and Professor John King, University of Michigan, for more than a decade-long discussion of information systems and organizations. And a special remembrance and dedication to Professor Rob Kling, University of Indiana, for being our friend and colleague over so many years.

We also want to especially thank all our reviewers whose suggestions helped improve our texts. Reviewers for Managing the Digital Firm include:

Charles Wankel, St. John's University
Ahmed Kamel, Concordia College
Deborah E Swain, North Carolina Central University
Jigish Zaveri, Morgan State University
Robert Gatewood, Mississippi College
James Drogan, SUNY Maritime College
Amiya Samantray, Marygrove College
John Miles, Keuka College
Werner Schenk, University of Rochester
Shuyuan Mary Ho, Florida State University
Brian Jones, Tennessee Technological University
Robert Fulkerth, Golden Gate University
Osman Guzide, Shepherd University

Pearson gratefully acknowledges and thanks the following people for their contribution to the Global Edition:

Daniel Ortiz Arroyo, Aalborg University
June Clarke, Sheffield Hallam University
Andy Jones, Staffordshire University
Sahil Raj, Punjabi University
Neerja Sethi, Nanyang Technological University
Vijay Sethi, Nanyang Technological University

K.C.L.
J.P.L.

Preface to The Indian Edition

Information systems are one of the major tools available to business managers for achieving operational excellence, developing new products and services, improving decision making, and achieving competitive advantage. There is a whole new world of doing business using new technologies for managing and organizing. What makes the MIS field the most exciting area of study in schools of business is the continuous change in technology, management, and business processes. A continuing stream of information technology innovations are transforming the traditional business world. Some of the examples include the emergence of cloud computing, the growth of a mobile digital business platform based on smartphones and tablet computers, the use of social networks by managers to achieve business objectives and so on. Most of these changes have occurred in the last few years.

New cases that have been added to this edition are: ETMs re-routing KRSTC, collaboration for improved services at eClerx, NTT Datacenter, RFID enabled weighbridge automation, managing the supply chain to deliver at McDonald's, Zomato scripting success with e-commerce, PayTM cashing on demonetization, and KMS empowering Capella.

Compared to the industrial organization of the previous century, the new fast-growing 21st century business firms are less concerned about hierarchy and structure, and lay more emphasis on employees taking on multiple roles and tasks. They use social media to enter into conversations with consumers and demonstrate a greater willingness to listen to them, in part because they have no choice. They show a better understanding of the importance of information technology in creating and managing business firms and other organizations. Organizations and business firms demonstrate these characteristics to an extent that they are 21st century digital firms.

Acknowledgment

I earnestly thank the editorial team of Pearson particularly Varun Goenka and Sailza. Both Varun and Sailza were great support as they were very much involved in this project. Also special thanks to Shivinder Kaur for her active involvement in the revised edition of this book.

About the Adapter

Sahil Raj is a faculty member at School of Management Studies, Punjabi University, Patiala. His main area of interest is the application of information systems in business organizations. Prior to his present organization, he had worked in Ranbaxy Laboratories Ltd. He holds an engineering degree as well as an MBA and a Ph.D. Sahil Raj has been regularly contributing research papers to national and international journals and has presented research papers in many national and international conferences. He has already authored three books which includes Management Information System on Pearson Publication. He also actively contributes in various global edition books of Pearson. Presently, he is guiding research projects in the areas of artificial neural networks, business intelligence, strategic information systems, expert systems and big data analytics.

PART **ONE**

Organizations, Management, and the Networked Enterprise

PART ONE introduces the major themes of this book, raising a series of important questions: What is an information system, and what are its management, organization, and technology dimensions? Why are information systems so essential in businesses today? Why are systems for collaboration and social business so important? How can information systems help businesses become more competitive? What broader ethical and social issues are raised by widespread use of information systems?

CHAPTER

1 Information Systems in Global Business Today

Learning Objectives

After reading this chapter, you will be able to answer the following questions:

1-1 How are information systems transforming business, and why are they so essential for running and managing a business today?

1-2 What is an information system? How does it work? What are its management, organization, and technology components? Why are complementary assets essential for ensuring that information systems provide genuine value for organizations?

1-3 What academic disciplines are used to study information systems, and how does each contribute to an understanding of information systems?

CHAPTER CASES

Rugby Football Union Tries Big Data
Employee Pick-ups and Drop-offs at Convergys
ETM's Re-Routing KSTRC
The Domino's PULSE™ System: Reading the Pulse of the Customer

Rugby Football Union Tries Big Data

In 1871, twenty-one English clubs decided that their sport, officially called rugby union but commonly referred to simply as rugby, needed an administrative body. The clubs formed The Rugby Football Union (RFU), which today manages the English national team (England Rugby) in partnership with Premier Rugby Limited. Responsible for the promotion of rugby at all levels, the RFU organizes the Six Nations Championship, the unofficial northern hemisphere championship featuring teams from England, Scotland, Wales, Italy, Ireland, and France, and the Heineken Cup, its club-level counterpart. Owned by its member clubs, the RFU's mission is to maximize profits from international ticket sales and vending so that it can support the more than 60,000 volunteers who organize matches and seminars, help secure loans and insurance policies, fundraise, write grant proposals, provide medical advice and support, and perform the clerical duties that keep the lower-level clubs operating.

To succeed in this complicated mission, the RFU entered into a five-year deal with IBM to capture and analyze Big Data that will be useful to both fans, and later—it is hoped—the players themselves. The system is called TryTracker. In rugby, a try, worth five points, is the highest scoring opportunity. Teams get possession of the ball through a scrum, a contest for the ball where eight players bind together and push against eight players from the other team. The outcome determines who can control the ball. To score a try, a team must break through the opposition's defenses, move into their in-goal area, and "ground" the ball. This is done in one of two ways. A player

©Michal Sanca/Shutterstock

can either hold the ball in one or both hands or arms and then touch it to the ground in the in-goal area, or exert downward pressure on a ball already on the ground using one or both hands or arms or the upper front of the body (from the neck to the waistline).

The IBM TryTracker does not just track tries, however. It uses predictive analytics to track three categories of data: keys to the game, momentum, and key players. TryTracker uses over 8,000 measures of performance. Traditional rugby statistics on team and individual performance as well as live text commentary complement the TryTracker data. The keys to the game are determined ahead of a specific contest by analyzing a historical database of past matchups between a pair. For example, in 2015 England's key was to average at least 3.2 meters per carry in the forwards; attempt an offload from 10 percent of opposition tackles; and make more than 66 percent of total line-breaks in the match. Fans can use their mobile devices to keep track of how their favorite team is faring, concentrating on game elements that will increase its winning chances. Key players for each team are selected after the game by comparing a single score compiled using different criteria for each position. Goal scoring is currently excluded so as not to overvalue kickers and undervalue players who contribute to creating scoring opportunities.

Like the IBM SlamTracker used at the Grand Slam tennis tournaments, the goal of TryTracker is to provide data visualization and real-time statistics to draw in fans. To compete with more popular sports such as Premier League football, the RFU hopes that enhanced communication will increase fan engagement. In 2015, IBM TryTracker was an ever-present fixture of EnglandRugby.com's extensive match coverage. As their understanding of game mechanics and emotional investment in what their team needs to do in order to prevail grows, casual fans will become dedicated fans who return again and again. Beyond marketing strategy, the long-term potential of predictive analysis is that it may provide tactical insights to players and coaches that will improve match play and thus the overall product offered to fans.

In 2016 IBM has deployed the same predictive analytics technology to the Australian New South Wales Waratahs Rugby team with an emphasis on predicting player injuries based on their general health, and performance data on the field generated from GPS sensors that players wear.

Sources: IBM, "Building a Solid Foundation for Big Data Analytics," IBM Systems Thought Leadership Paper, 2016; IBM, "IBM Predictive Analytics Reduces Player Injury and Optimises Team Performance for NSW Waratahs Rugby Team," IBM.com, accessed November 14, 2016; IBM, "3 Ways Big Data and Analytics Will Change Sports," by Preetam Kumar, IBM Analytics, ibmbigdatahub.com, December 17, 2015; Simon Creasey, "Rugby Football Union Uses IBM Predictive Analytics For Six Nations," ComputerWeekly.com, 2016; "About Us," rfu.com, accessed December, 14, 2015; "TryTracker: Rugby Data Analysis," *Telegraph*, November 19, 2015; Oliver Pickup, "How Does TryTracker Work," *Telegraph*, November 19, 2015; Simon Creasey, "Rugby Football Union Uses IBM Predictive Analytics for Six Nations," *ComputerWeek*, September 2015; "IBM Rugby Insight Summer 2015," MSN.com/sports, September 3, 2015; "Live England vs. Scotland with IBM TryTracker," www.englandrugby.com, March 15, 2015; "IBM TryTracker Confirms Performance," www.englandrugby.com/ibmtrytracker/, November 29, 2014; IBM UK, "IBM TryTracker Rugby

Insight: QBE Internationals 2014 England vs. Australia," *IBM Rugby Insight,* November 27, 2014; Oliver Pickup, "IBM TryTracker: How Does It Work?" *Telegraph,* October 31, 2013.

The challenges facing the RFU demonstrate why information systems are so essential today. The RFU is classified as a "Friendly Society," somewhere between a true company and a charity. It receives both government support and corporate sponsorship money. But it must maximize revenues from ticket sales, hospitality and catering, television rights, and its travel company in order to support both grassroots and elite rugby in England.

The chapter-opening diagram calls attention to important points raised by this case and this chapter. The RFU entered into a strategic partnership with IBM to educate and engage fans. Using the data collected by sports data company Opta and the analytics developed by IBM, it may also be able to improve coaching and game performance as an additional way of cultivating customers. IBM is also helping the RFU to develop a customer relationship management (CRM) system integrated with its Web site.

Here are some questions to think about: What role does technology play in the RFU's success as the administrative head of rugby union in England? Assess the contributions which these systems make to the future of RFU.

1-1 How are information systems transforming global business, and why are they so essential for running and managing a business today?

It's not business as usual in the global economy anymore. Information systems and technologies are transforming the global business environment. In 2015, global firms and governments spent about €3.4 trillion on information

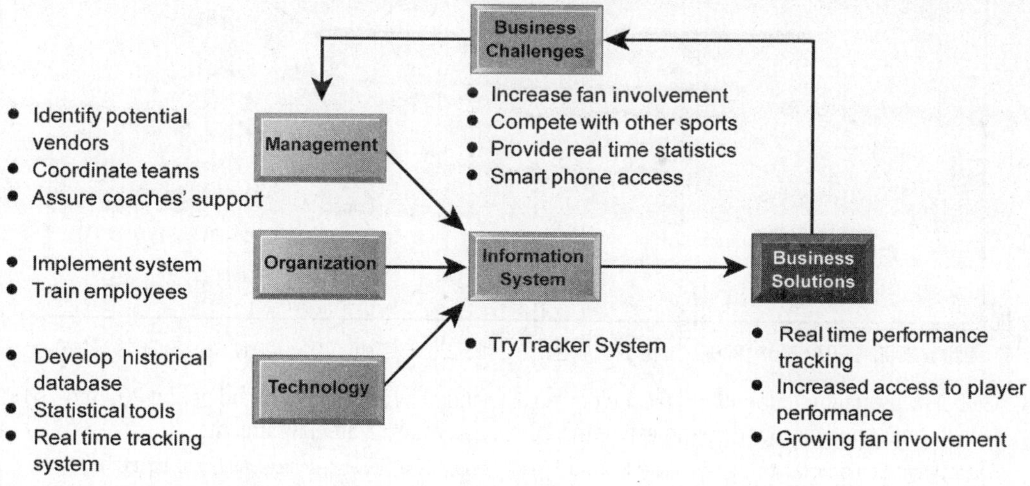

systems hardware, software, and telecommunications equipment. In addition, they spent another €544 billion on business and management consulting and services—much of which involves redesigning firms' business operations to take advantage of these new technologies (Gartner, 2016; IDC 2016; Shumsky, 2016). In fact, most of the business value of IT investment derives from these organizational, management, and cultural changes inside firms (Saunders and Brynjolfsson, 2016). It is not simply the technology that is changing. Figure 1.1 shows that between 2005 and 2015, global investment in information technology consisting of hardware, software, and communications equipment grew from €2.43 trillion to €3.18 trillion and is expected to expand to €3.55 trillion by 2020. While America and Europe account for an estimated 70 percent of this investment, 30 percent is occurring in Asia Pacific, Latin America, the Middle East and North Africa, and Eastern Europe. (Accelerance, 2016; IDC, 2016).

As managers, most of you will work for firms that are intensively using information systems and making large investments in information technology. You will certainly want to know how to invest this money wisely. If you make wise choices, your firm can outperform competitors. If you make poor choices, you will be wasting valuable capital. This book is dedicated to helping you make wise decisions about information technology and information systems.

How Information Systems Are Transforming Business

You can see the results of this large-scale spending around you every day by observing how people conduct business. Changes in technology and

FIGURE 1.1 INFORMATION TECHNOLOGY CAPITAL INVESTMENT

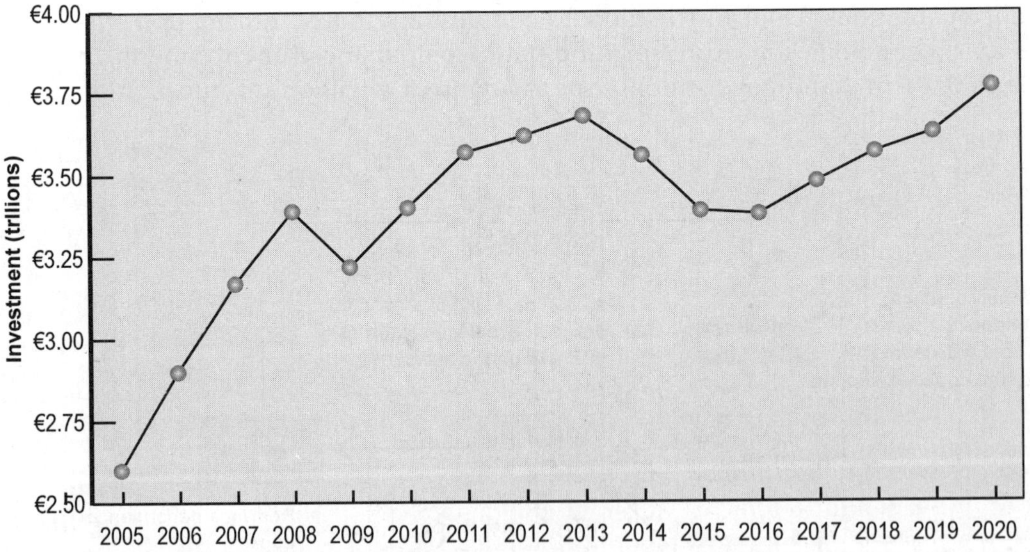

Global investment in information technology has expanded by 30 percent in the period 2005 to 2015. IT investment now accounts for an estimated 20 percent of all capital investment.

Source: World Economic Outlook, International Monetary Fund, October 2016; industry sources; author estimates.

new, innovative business models have transformed social life and business practices. Some 2.8 billion people worldwide have smartphones (50 percent of the world's population), and an estimated 1.26 billion use their smartphones for Internet access. More than 1 billion people use tablet computers, about 15 percent of the global population. In developing and emerging countries, phones and tablets are the primary means of access to the Internet (Pew Research, 2016; eMarketer, 2015). An estimated 2.34 billion people now use social networks, with Facebook accounting for 1.7 billion people alone. Messaging services like WhatsApp, Facebook Messenger, and Twitter collectively have over 2 billion monthly users. Smartphones, social networking, texting, e-mailing, and webinars have all become essential tools of business because that's where your customers, suppliers, and colleagues can be found (eMarketer, 2016a).

By June 2015, more than 150 million businesses worldwide had dot-com Internet sites registered (Curtis, 2015). In 2016 1.62 billion Internet users will purchase online, generating $1.9 billion in sales. Half of these sales will be from mobile devices. While still only 8 percent of total retail global sales, online commerce is growing at 6 percent annually, three times the growth of traditional offline retail (eMarketer, 2016a). In 2015, FedEx moved about 11.5 million packages daily in 220 countries and territories around the world, mostly overnight, and the United Parcel Service (UPS) moved more than 18 million packages daily. Businesses are using information technology to sense and respond to rapidly changing customer demand, reduce inventories to the lowest possible levels, and achieve higher levels of operational efficiency. Supply chains have become more fast-paced, with companies of all sizes depending on just-in-time inventory to reduce their overhead costs and get to market faster.

In comparison with the 2.7 billion people who read a print newspaper, online newspapers are read by one billion people, growing at 10 percent annually, far faster than print newspapers (WPT, 2016; Conaghan, 2015). An estimated 1.7 billion people watch videos and feature films online, 100 million post to a blog everyday, and 250 million read a blog, creating an explosion of new writers and new forms of customer feedback that did not exist five years ago. Social networking site Facebook attracted more than 1.7 billion monthly visitors worldwide. Nearly all of the *Fortune* 2000 global firms now have Facebook pages, Twitter accounts, and Tumblr sites.

Global e-commerce and Internet advertising continue to expand. Google's online ad revenues surpassed €80 billion in 2016, and Internet advertising continues to grow at more than 20 percent a year, reaching more than €194 billion in revenues in 2016 (eMarketer, 2016c). That's about one-third of all advertising in the world.

These changes in information technology and systems, consumer behavior, and commerce have spurred the annual growth of digital information to over 5 exabytes every few days, roughly equivalent to all the libraries in existence (Pappas, 2016). A recent study concluded that the value of information flowing between countries has grown 45 times since 2005, and the value of this information now exceeds the value of goods and finance exchanged (McKenzie, 2016).

What's New in Management Information Systems

Plenty. In fact, there's a whole new world of doing business using new technologies for managing and organizing. What makes the MIS field the most exciting area of study in schools of business is the continuous change in technology, management, and business processes. Five changes are of paramount importance.

IT Innovations. A continuing stream of information technology innovations is transforming the traditional business world. Examples include the emergence of cloud computing, the growth of a mobile digital business platform based on smartphones and tablet computers, big data, business analytics, and the use of social networks by managers to achieve business objectives. Most of these changes have occurred in the past few years. These innovations are enabling entrepreneurs and innovative traditional firms to create new products and services, develop new business models, and transform the day-to-day conduct of business. In the process, some old businesses, even industries, are being destroyed while new businesses are springing up.

New Business Models. For instance, the emergence of online video services like Netflix for streaming, Apple iTunes, Amazon, and many others for downloading video has forever changed how premium video is distributed and even created. Netflix in 2016 attracted more than 75 million subscribers worldwide to what it calls the "Internet TV" revolution. Netflix has moved into premium TV show production with 30 original shows such as *House of Cards* and *Orange Is the New Black*, challenging cable and broadcast producers of TV shows, and potentially disrupting cable network dominance of TV show production. Apple's iTunes now accounts for 67 percent of movie and TV show downloads and has struck deals with major Hollywood studios for recent movies and TV shows. A growing trickle of viewers are unplugging from cable and using only the Internet for entertainment.

E-commerce Expanding. E-commerce generated about $600 billion in revenues in 2016 and is estimated to grow to nearly $900 billion by 2020. E-commerce is changing how firms design, produce, and deliver their products and services. E-commerce has reinvented itself again, disrupting the traditional marketing and advertising industry and putting major media and content firms in jeopardy. Facebook and other social networking sites such as YouTube, Twitter, and Tumblr along with Netflix, Apple Beats music service, and many other media firms exemplify the new face of e-commerce in the twenty-first century. They sell services. When we think of e-commerce, we tend to think of selling physical products. While this iconic vision of e-commerce is still very powerful and the fastest-growing form of retail in the United States, growing up alongside is a whole new value stream based on selling services, not goods. It's a services model of e-commerce. Growth in social commerce is spurred by powerful growth of the mobile platform: 80 percent of Facebook's users access the service from mobile phones and tablets. Information systems and technologies are the foundation of this new services-based e-commerce. Mobile e-commerce hit $130 billion in 2016 and is growing at more than 30 percent a year.

INTERACTIVE SESSION: MANAGEMENT

Employee Pick-ups and Drop-offs at Convergys

Convergys is a leading provider of customer management solutions for organizations across India. It started business in 2009, when the Business Process Outsourcing (BPO) industry was still in its infancy. But owing to the sky-rocketing prices of real estate in Delhi, it decided to build its center outside the city. The Delhi National Capital Region (NCR) was still developing at that time and property prices were significantly more economical in Gurgaon as compared to Delhi. So, the firm decided to set up its main Indian headquarters in Gurgaon. But limited connectivity to this new place, coupled with poor residential facilities, proved to be a challenge for the employees of Convergys, who had to commute from Delhi to work. This led the management to announce pick-up and drop-off facilities for all its workers.

Coordinating the logistics of the pick-ups and drop-offs went well initially. But over a decade of aggressive expansions in operations, staff (now over 10,000 strong) as well as centers (with three facilities in Gurgaon, and one each in Bangalore, Thane, and Pune), Convergys had to arrange around 200 pick-ups and drops-offs every day.

In addition to the cost burden of this activity, the company had to deal with the challenges of managing the pick-ups and drop-offs. The transport desk manually decided on the shortest route for every ride so that employees could reach the offices in time for work. But with over 1,000 cabs sourced from 40 vendors, managing 44 different shift timings was a herculean task. Ipinder Singh, the technical director at Convergys, tried looking into some off-the-shelf software to see if they could meet his company's requirements. But even with the deployment of these software, Singh found that a lot of the tasks would have to be done manually. He finally decided to design a solution in-house.

In order to automate tasks, the processes involved with running the existing system needed to be understood. Every week, supervisors (over 100 in number) would send complete information about their team's shift timings, addresses, contact numbers, and leave status for the following week to the transport department. The team at this department sorted through the sheets they received and made a plan for the coming week. The whole process was time consuming. Once the plan was frozen, no changes could be made unless the whole plan was overhauled. This meant that in case an employee took an unexpected leave, there was a problem. Moreover, if there was a change in the employee's address or phone number, or if an employee quit in the middle of a week, the pick-up vans would keep waiting for that employee, adding to the company's transportation expenses.

Ipinder Singh's team of developers built an automated application that had all the parameters and metrics preloaded in the system, so that it could generate costs by department and employee. He integrated the transport application with the human resource information system. This helped him get updated information regarding change in address, phone number, leave, or resignation status of employees. Further, Convergys automated a lot of the transport department's manual tasks. For example, earlier, cab drivers were required to fill out a sheet after every trip, stating the distance covered. The transport department would then enter this information into Excel sheets to compute the costs for the different types of vehicles. This function is now handled almost entirely by the new application.

In spite of all these developments, one pressing issue still remained. How to find the most optimal route for each of the cabs so that the staff can reach the office on time? There are two aspects to this question. First, considering that the vendors charge on the basis of the kilometers covered by their cars, going a longer route significantly increases the costs to company. Second, late arrival of employees to work translates to losses for the firm. So, it was imperative that Singh find a solution to the optimal route challenge as quickly as possible.

Ipinder Singh decided to buy a generic routing solution with 10–12 built-in algorithms, and layered it with a digital version of the Eicher world maps. The software was further customized by feeding in additional information about the cab capabilities, average speed on various roads, locations of employees, and so on. With all this done, the software could now select the optimum route, as well as reschedule the ride in case an employee fell sick. In doing so, Convergys was able to save 30 to 40 percent of its transportation costs.

The firm now also allows employees to change or cancel the status of their pick-up or drop-off through a self-service portal. This has reduced dependency on the transport helpdesk. Using this portal, employees can also get information about their routes and pick-up time without any delay or difficulty.

Sources: Roy, Debarati: "Convergys Boosts its Fleet Management", Cio.In (2012). Retrieved from http://www.cio.in/case-study/convergys-turns-course-its-fleet-management; Convergys. Retrieved from http://www.convergysindia.in/

CASE STUDY QUESTIONS

1. Why did Convergys need an information system to manage the transportation of employees?
2. What were the problems in the manual process of fleet management?
3. What was the benefit of integrating human resource data with the transportation information system?
4. Discuss the role of the routing solution and self-service portals.

Management Changes. The management of business firms has changed: With new mobile smartphones, high-speed wireless Wi-Fi networks, and tablets, remote salespeople on the road are only seconds away from their managers' questions and oversight. Business is going mobile, along with consumers. Managers on the move are in direct, continuous contact with their employees. The growth of enterprise-wide information systems with extraordinarily rich data means that managers no longer operate in a fog of confusion but instead have online, nearly instant access to the really important information they need for accurate and timely decisions. In addition to their public uses on the web, wikis and blogs are becoming important corporate tools for communication, collaboration, and information sharing.

Changes in Firms and Organizations. Compared to industrial organizations of the previous century, new fast-growing twenty-first-century business firms put less emphasis on hierarchy and structure and more emphasis on employees taking on multiple roles and tasks and collaborating with others on a team. They put greater emphasis on competency and skills rather than position in the hierarchy. They emphasize higher speed and more accurate decision making based on data and analysis. They are more aware of changes in technology, consumer attitudes, and culture. They use social media to enter into conversations with consumers and demonstrate a greater willingness to listen to consumers, in part because they have no choice. They show better understanding of the importance of information technology in creating and managing business firms and other organizations. To the extent organizations and business firms demonstrate these characteristics, they are twenty-first-century digital firms.

You can see some of these trends at work in the Interactive Session on Management. Millions of managers rely heavily on the mobile digital platform to coordinate suppliers and shipments, satisfy customers, and manage their employees. A business day without these mobile devices or Internet access would be unthinkable.

iPhone and iPad Applications for Business

1. Salesforce1
2. Cisco WebEx Meetings
3. SAP Business One
4. iWork
5. Evernote
6. Adobe Acrobat Reader
7. Oracle Business Intelligence Mobile
8. Dropbox

Whether it's attending an online meeting, checking orders, working with files and documents, or obtaining business intelligence, Apple's iPhone and iPad offer unlimited possibilities for business users. A stunning multi-touch display, full Internet browsing, and capabilities for messaging, video and audio transmission, and document management make each an all-purpose platform for mobile computing.

Globalization Challenges and Opportunities: A Flattened World

In 1492, Columbus reaffirmed what astronomers were long saying: the world was round and the seas could be safely sailed. As it turned out, the world was populated by peoples and languages living in isolation from one another, with great disparities in economic and scientific development. The world trade that ensued after Columbus's voyages has brought these peoples and cultures closer. The "industrial revolution" was really a worldwide phenomenon energized by expansion of trade among nations and the emergence of the first global economy.

In 2005, journalist Thomas Friedman wrote an influential book declaring the world was now "flat," by which he meant that the Internet and global communications had greatly reduced the economic and cultural advantages of developed countries. Friedman argued that the United States and European countries were in a fight for their economic lives, competing for jobs, markets, resources, and even ideas with highly educated, motivated populations in low-wage areas in the less developed world (Friedman, 2007). This "globalization" presents both challenges and opportunities for business firms.

A significant percentage of the global economy depends on imports and exports. In 2015, about 57 percent of the worlds €74 trillion GDP resulted from imports and exports (World Bank, 2016). Many *Fortune* 1000 global firms derive more than half their revenues from foreign operations. Tech companies are particularly dependent on offshore revenue: 85 percent of Intel's revenues in 2015 came from overseas sales of its microprocessors, while Apple earned 60 percent of its revenue outside of the United States. Eighty percent of the toys sold in the United States are manufactured in China, while all iPhones and about 90 percent of the PCs assembled in China use American-made Qualcomm, Intel or AMD chips.

It's not just goods that move across borders; jobs do too, some of them high-level jobs that pay well and require a college degree. In the past decade, the United States lost 5 million manufacturing jobs to offshore, low-wage producers. But manufacturing is now a very small part of U.S. employment (less than 12 percent of the labor force and declining). Manufacturing jobs in the last decade have been replaced by service and retail jobs even as the value of manufactured goods made in the U.S. has soared by 20 percent in the same period, largely due to highly automated factories and enterprise information systems (Casselman, 2016). In a normal year in the United States, about 300,000 service jobs move offshore to lower-wage countries. On the plus side, the global labor force expanded from 3.2 billion to 3.4 billion during the 2010 – 2015 period, an expansion of 200 million new jobs. The U.S. economy creates more than 3.5 million new jobs in a normal, non-recessionary year. Although only 1.1 million private sector jobs were created due to slow recovery in 2011, by 2015 the U.S. economy was adding more than 2 million new jobs annually for the third straight year. Employment in information systems and the other service occupations is expanding, and wages in the tech sector are rising at 5 percent annually. Outsourcing may have accelerated the development of new systems worldwide as new systems could be developed and maintained in low-wage countries. In part this explains why the job market for MIS and computer science graduates is growing rapidly in the United States as well as Europe, the Middle East, and Asia Pacific.

The challenge for you as a business student is to develop high-level skills through education and on-the-job experience that cannot be outsourced. The challenge for your business is to avoid markets for goods and services that can be produced offshore much less expensively. The opportunities are equally immense. Throughout this book, you will find examples of companies and individuals who either failed or succeeded in using information systems to adapt to this new global environment.

What does globalization have to do with management information systems? That's simple: everything. The emergence of the Internet into a full-blown international communications system has drastically reduced the costs of operating and transacting on a global scale. Communication between a factory floor in Shanghai and a distribution center in Rapid City, South Dakota, or Antwerp, Belgium, is now instant and virtually free. Customers can now shop in a worldwide marketplace, obtaining price and quality information reliably 24 hours a day. Firms producing goods and services on a global scale achieve extraordinary cost reductions by finding low-cost suppliers and managing production facilities in other countries. Internet service firms, such as Google, Netflix, Alibaba, and eBay, are able to replicate their business models and services in multiple countries without having to redesign their expensive fixed-cost information systems infrastructure. Briefly, information systems enable globalization.

The Emerging Digital Firm

All of the changes we have just described, coupled with equally significant organizational redesign, have created the conditions for a fully digital firm. A digital firm can be defined along several dimensions. A **digital firm** is one in which nearly all of the organization's *significant business relationships* with customers, suppliers, and employees are digitally enabled and mediated. *Core business processes* are accomplished through digital networks spanning the entire organization or linking multiple organizations.

Business processes refer to the set of logically related tasks and behaviors that organizations develop over time to produce specific business results and the unique manner in which these activities are organized and coordinated. Developing a new product, generating and fulfilling an order, creating a marketing plan, and hiring an employee are examples of business processes, and the ways organizations accomplish their business processes can be a source of competitive strength.(A detailed discussion of business processes can be found in Chapter 2.)

Key corporate assets—intellectual property, core competencies, and financial and human assets—are managed through digital means. In a digital firm, any piece of information required to support key business decisions is available at any time and anywhere in the firm.

Digital firms sense and respond to their environments far more rapidly than traditional firms, giving them more flexibility to survive in turbulent times. Digital firms offer extraordinary opportunities for more flexible global organization and management. In digital firms, both time shifting and space shifting are the norm. *Time shifting* refers to business being conducted continuously, 24/7, rather than in narrow "work day" time bands of 9 a.m. to 5 p.m. *Space shifting* means that work takes place in a global workshop as well as within national boundaries. Work is accomplished physically wherever in the world it is best accomplished.

Many firms, such as Cisco Systems, 3M, and GE (see the Chapter 12 ending case), are close to becoming digital firms, using the Internet to drive every aspect of their business. Most other companies are not fully digital, but they are moving toward close digital integration with suppliers, customers, and employees.

Strategic Business Objectives of Information Systems

What makes information systems so essential today? Why are businesses investing so much in information systems and technologies? In the United States, more than 57 million managers and 120 million workers in the information and knowledge sectors in the labor force rely on information systems to conduct business. Information systems are essential for conducting day-to-day business in most advanced countries as well as achieving strategic business objectives.

Entire sectors of the economy are nearly inconceivable without substantial investments in information systems. E-commerce firms such as Amazon, eBay, Google, and E*Trade simply would not exist. Today's service industries—finance, insurance, and real estate as well as personal services such as travel, medicine, and education—could not operate without information systems. Similarly, retail firms such as Walmart and Sears and manufacturing firms such as General Motors, Volkswagen, Siemens, and GE require information systems to survive and prosper. Just as offices, telephones, filing cabinets, and efficient tall buildings with elevators were once the foundations of business in the twentieth century, information technology is a foundation for business in the twenty-first century.

FIGURE 1.2 THE INTERDEPENDENCE BETWEEN ORGANIZATIONS AND INFORMATION SYSTEMS

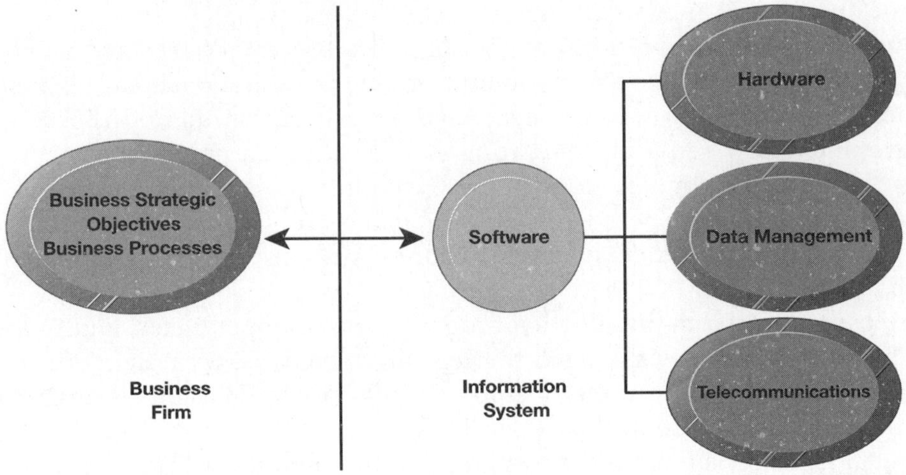

In contemporary systems, there is a growing interdependence between a firm's information systems and its business capabilities. Changes in strategy, rules, and business processes increasingly require changes in hardware, software, databases, and telecommunications. Often, what the organization would like to do depends on what its systems will permit it to do.

There is a growing interdependence between a firm's ability to use information technology and its ability to implement corporate strategies and achieve corporate goals (see Figure 1.2). What a business would like to do in five years often depends on what its systems will be able to do. Increasing market share, becoming the high-quality or low-cost producer, developing new products, and increasing employee productivity depend more and more on the kinds and quality of information systems in the organization. The more you understand about this relationship, the more valuable you will be as a manager.

Specifically, business firms invest heavily in information systems to achieve six strategic business objectives: operational excellence; new products, services, and business models; customer and supplier intimacy; improved decision making; competitive advantage; and survival.

Operational Excellence

Businesses continuously seek to improve the efficiency of their operations in order to achieve higher profitability. Information systems and technologies are some of the most important tools available to managers for achieving higher levels of efficiency and productivity in business operations, especially when coupled with changes in business practices and management behavior.

Walmart, the largest retailer on earth, exemplifies the power of information systems coupled with state of the art business practices and supportive management to achieve world-class operational efficiency. In fiscal year 2016, Walmart achieved $499 billion in sales—nearly one-tenth of retail sales in the United States—in large part because of its Retail Link system, which digitally links its suppliers to every one of Walmart's stores. As soon as a customer purchases an item, the supplier monitoring the item knows to ship a replacement to the shelf. Walmart is the most efficient retail store in the industry, achieving sales of more than $600 per square foot, compared with its closest competitor, Target, at $425 a square foot and other large general merchandise retail firms producing less than $200 a square foot.

New Products, Services, and Business Models

Information systems and technologies are a major enabling tool for firms to create new products and services as well as entirely new business models. A **business model** describes how a company produces, delivers, and sells a product or service to create wealth.

Today's music industry is vastly different from the industry a decade ago. Apple Inc. transformed an old business model of music distribution based on vinyl records, tapes, and CDs into an online, legal distribution model based on its own iPod technology platform. Apple has prospered from a continuing stream of innovations, including the iTunes music service, the iPad, and the iPhone.

Customer and Supplier Intimacy

When a business really knows its customers and serves them well, the customers generally respond by returning and purchasing more. This raises revenues and profits. Likewise with suppliers, the more a business engages its suppliers, the better the suppliers can provide vital inputs. This lowers costs. How to really know your customers or suppliers is a central problem for businesses with millions of offline and online customers.

The Mandarin Oriental hotel group which operates hotels in Asia, Europe, and the Americas, exemplifies the use of information systems and technologies to achieve customer intimacy. These hotels use computers to keep track of guests' preferences.When a customer arrives at one of these hotels, the system automatically changes the room conditions, such as dimming the lights, setting the room temperature, or selecting appropriate music, based on the customer's digital profile. The hotels also analyze their customer data to identify their best customers and to develop individualized marketing campaigns based on customers' preferences.

Large national retailers in Europe, the U.S., and Asia exemplify the use of information systems to enable supplier and customer intimacy. Every time a dress shirt is bought at a store the record of the sale appears immediately on computers of suppliers like TAL Apparel Ltd. in Hong Kong, a contract manufacturer that produces one in eight dress shirts sold in the United States and Europe. TAL runs the numbers through a computer model it developed and then decides how many replacement shirts to make and in what styles, colors, and sizes. TAL then sends the shirts directly to retail stores, completely bypassing retailers' warehouses (European Commission, 2014).

Improved Decision Making

Many business managers operate in an information fog bank, never really having the right information at the right time to make an informed decision.

Instead, managers rely on forecasts, best guesses, and luck. In the past decade, information systems and technologies have made it possible for managers to use real-time data from the marketplace when making decisions.

For instance, Privi Organics Ltd., a leading Indian company that manufactures, supplies, and exports aroma chemical products worldwide, uses the Oracle Human Capital Management system for real-time insight into individual employee information—including performance rating and compensation history. The system helps managers make faster human resource decisions, such as promotions or transfers, by integrating all employee records across the organization. Managers are able to quickly review employee performance ratings for the previous three years and drill down into more details.

Competitive Advantage

When firms achieve one or more of these business objectives—operational excellence; new products, services, and business models; customer/supplier intimacy; and improved decision making—chances are they have already achieved a competitive advantage. Doing things better than your competitors, charging less for superior products, and responding to customers and suppliers in real time all add up to higher sales and higher profits that your competitors cannot match. Apple Inc., Walmart, and the Mandarin Group are industry leaders because they know how to use information systems for this purpose.

Survival

Business firms also invest in information systems and technologies because they are necessities of doing business. Sometimes these "necessities" are driven by industry-level changes. Today, most national banks in the world have ATMs and link to national and international ATM networks, such as CIRRUS. Providing ATM services to retail banking customers is simply a requirement of being in and surviving in the retail banking business.

Most nations have statutes and regulations that create a legal duty for companies and their employees to retain records, including digital records. For instance, the European Council REACH law and the U.S. Toxic Substances Control Act (1976) regulate the exposure of workers to more than 75,000 toxic chemicals and require firms to retain records on employee exposure for 30 years (European Commission, 2007). Financial regulatory agencies such as the U.S. Securities and Exchange Commission (SEC), Financial Conduct Authority (FAC UK), Financial Services Agency (FSA Japan), and the China Securities Regulatory Commission (CSRC People's Republic of China) require certified public accounting firms that audit public companies to retain audit working papers and records, including all e-mails, for five years or longer. Many other pieces of national and regional legislation in health care, financial services, education, and privacy protection impose significant information retention and reporting requirements on global businesses. Firms turn to information systems and technologies to provide the capability to respond to these record management requirements.

1-2 What is an information system? How does it work? What are its management, organization, and technology components? Why are complementary assets essential for ensuring that information systems provide genuine value for organizations?

So far we've used *information systems* and *technologies* informally without defining the terms. **Information technology (IT)** consists of all the hardware and software that a firm needs to use in order to achieve its business objectives. This includes not only computer machines, storage devices, and handheld mobile devices but also software, such as the Windows or Linux operating systems, the Microsoft Office desktop productivity suite, and the many thousands of computer programs that can be found in a typical large firm. "Information systems" are more complex and can be best understood by looking at them from both a technology and a business perspective.

What Is an Information System?

An **information system** can be defined technically as a set of interrelated components that collect (or retrieve), process, store, and distribute information to support decision making and control in an organization. In addition to supporting decision making, coordination, and control, information systems may also help managers and workers analyze problems, visualize complex subjects, and create new products.

Information systems contain information about significant people, places, and things within the organization or in the environment surrounding it. By **information** we mean data that have been shaped into a form that is meaningful and useful to human beings. **Data**, in contrast, are streams of raw facts representing events occurring in organizations or the physical environment before they have been organized and arranged into a form that people can understand and use.

A brief example contrasting information and data may prove useful. Supermarket checkout counters scan millions of pieces of data from bar codes, which describe each product. Such pieces of data can be totaled and analyzed to provide meaningful information, such as the total number of bottles of dish detergent sold at a particular store, which brands of dish detergent were selling the most rapidly at that store or sales territory, or the total amount spent on that brand of dish detergent at that store or sales region (see Figure 1.3).

Three activities in an information system produce the information that organizations need to make decisions, control operations, analyze problems, and create new products or services. These activities are input, processing, and output (see Figure 1.4). **Input** captures or collects raw data from within the organization or from its external environment. **Processing** converts this raw input into a meaningful form. **Output** transfers the processed information to the people who will use it or to the activities for which it will be used. Information systems also require **feedback**, which is output that is returned

FIGURE 1.3 DATA AND INFORMATION

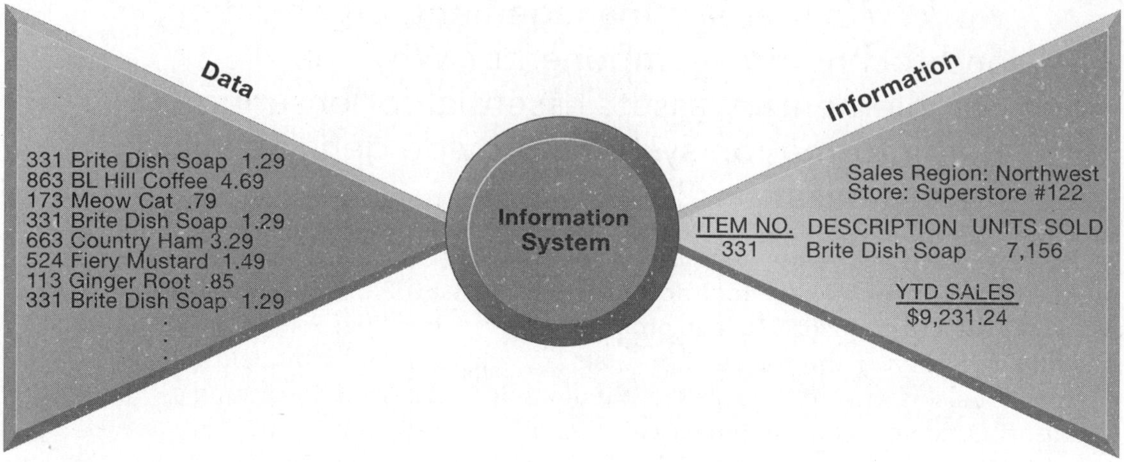

Raw data from a supermarket checkout counter can be processed and organized to produce meaningful information, such as the total unit sales of dish detergent or the total sales revenue from dish detergent for a specific store or sales territory.

FIGURE 1.4 FUNCTIONS OF AN INFORMATION SYSTEM

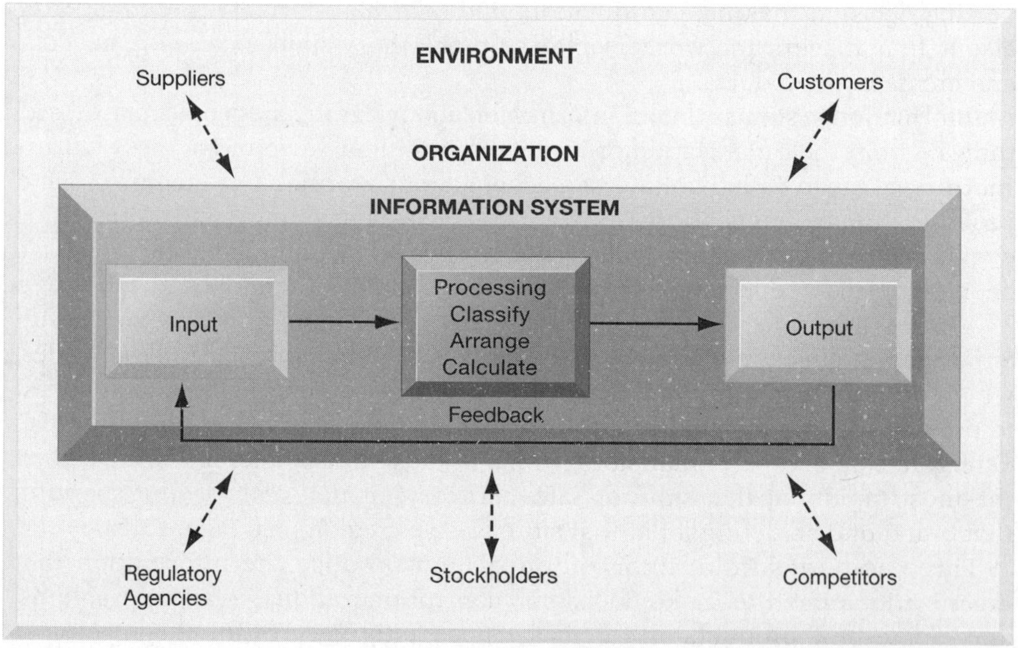

An information system contains information about an organization and its surrounding environment. Three basic activities—input, processing, and output—produce the information organizations need. Feedback is output returned to appropriate people or activities in the organization to evaluate and refine the input. Environmental actors, such as customers, suppliers, competitors, stockholders, and regulatory agencies, interact with the organization and its information systems.

to appropriate members of the organization to help them evaluate or correct the input stage.

In a professional sports team's system for selling tickets, the raw input consists of order data for tickets, such as the purchaser's name, address, credit card number, number of tickets ordered, and the date of the game for which the ticket is being purchased. Another input would be the ticket price, which would fluctuate based on computer analysis of how much could optimally be charged for a ticket for a particular game. Computers store these data and process them to calculate order totals, to track ticket purchases, and to send requests for payment to credit card companies. The output consists of tickets to print out, receipts for orders, and reports on online ticket orders. The system provides meaningful information, such as the number of tickets sold for a particular game or at a particular price, the total number of tickets sold each year, and frequent customers.

Although computer-based information systems use computer technology to process raw data into meaningful information, there is a sharp distinction between a computer and a computer program on the one hand and an information system on the other. Computers and related software programs are the technical foundation, the tools and materials, of modern information systems. Computers provide the equipment for storing and processing information. Computer programs, or software, are sets of operating instructions that direct and control computer processing. Knowing how computers and computer programs work is important in designing solutions to organizational problems, but computers are only part of an information system.

A house is an appropriate analogy. Houses are built with hammers, nails, and wood, but these do not make a house. The architecture, design, setting, landscaping, and all of the decisions that lead to the creation of these features are part of the house and are crucial for solving the problem of putting a roof over one's head. Computers and programs are the hammers, nails, and lumber of computer-based information systems, but alone they cannot produce the information a particular organization needs. To understand information systems, you must understand the problems they are designed to solve, their architectural and design elements, and the organizational processes that lead to the solutions.

Dimensions of Information Systems

To fully understand information systems, you must understand the broader organization, management, and information technology dimensions of systems (see Figure 1.5) and their power to provide solutions to challenges and problems in the business environment. We refer to this broader understanding of information systems, which encompasses an understanding of the management and organizational dimensions of systems as well as the technical dimensions of systems, as **information systems literacy**. **Computer literacy**, in contrast, focuses primarily on knowledge of information technology.

The field of **management information systems (MIS)** tries to achieve this broader information systems literacy. MIS deals with behavioral issues as well as technical issues surrounding the development, use, and impact of information systems used by managers and employees in the firm.

FIGURE 1.5 INFORMATION SYSTEMS ARE MORE THAN COMPUTERS

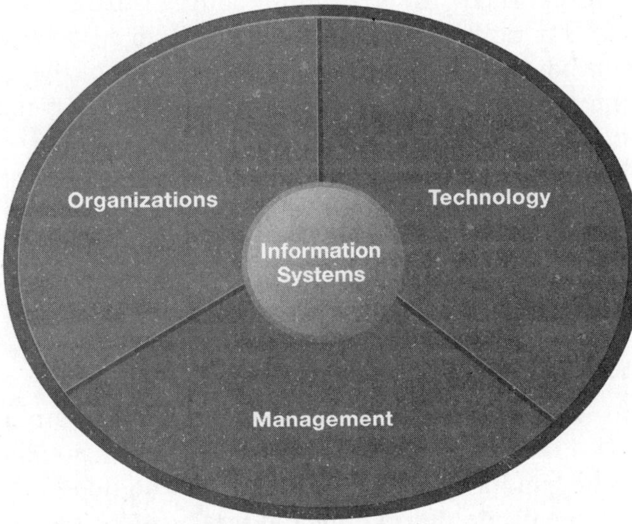

Using information systems effectively requires an understanding of the organization, management, and information technology shaping the systems. An information system creates value for the firm as an organizational and management solution to challenges posed by the environment.

Let's examine each of the dimensions of information systems—organizations, management, and information technology.

Organizations

Information systems are an integral part of organizations. Indeed, for some companies, such as credit reporting firms, there would be no business without an information system. The key elements of an organization are its people, structure, business processes, politics, and culture.We introduce these components of organizations here and describe them in greater detail in Chapters 2 and 3.

Organizations have a structure that is composed of different levels and specialties. Their structures reveal a clear-cut division of labor. Authority and responsibility in a business firm are organized as a hierarchy, or a pyramid structure. The upper levels of the hierarchy consist of managerial, professional, and technical employees, whereas the lower levels consist of operational personnel.

Senior management makes long-range strategic decisions about products and services as well as ensures financial performance of the firm. **Middle management** carries out the programs and plans of senior management, and **operational management** is responsible for monitoring the daily activities of the business. **Knowledge workers**, such as engineers, scientists, or architects, design products or services and create new knowledge for the firm, whereas **data workers**, such as secretaries or clerks, assist with scheduling and communications at all levels of the firm. **Production or service workers** actually produce the product and deliver the service (see Figure 1.6).

FIGURE 1.6 LEVELS IN A FIRM

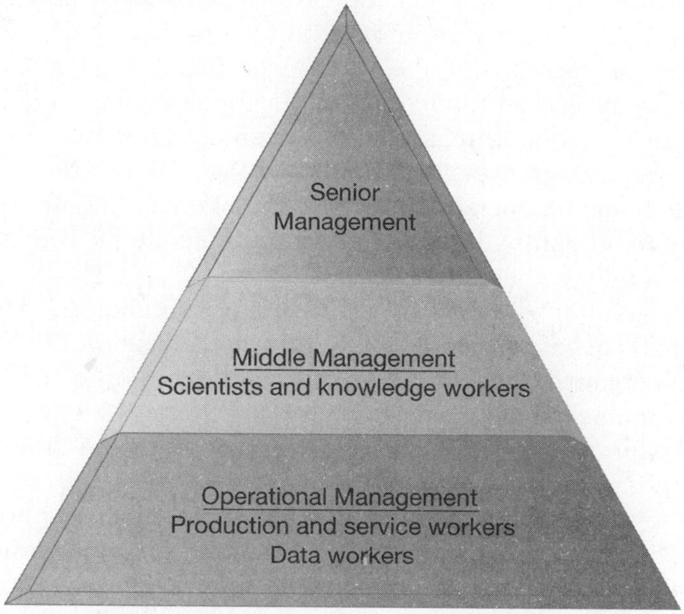

Business organizations are hierarchies consisting of three principal levels: senior management, middle management, and operational management. Information systems serve each of these levels. Scientists and knowledge workers often work with middle management.

Experts are employed and trained for different business functions. The major **business functions**, or specialized tasks performed by business organizations, consist of sales and marketing, manufacturing and production, finance and accounting, and human resources (see Table 1.1). Chapter 2 provides more detail on these business functions and the ways in which they are supported by information systems.

An organization coordinates work through its hierarchy and through its *business processes.* Most organizations' business processes include formal rules that have been developed over a long time for accomplishing tasks. These rules guide employees in a variety of procedures, from writing an invoice to responding to customer complaints. Some of these business processes have been written down, but others are informal work practices, such

TABLE 1.1 MAJOR BUSINESS FUNCTIONS

FUNCTION	PURPOSE
Sales and marketing	Selling the organization's products and services
Manufacturing and production	Producing and delivering products and services
Finance and accounting	Managing the organization's financial assets and maintaining the organization's financial records
Human resources	Attracting, developing, and maintaining the organization's labor force; maintaining employee records

as a requirement to return telephone calls from coworkers or customers, that are not formally documented. Information systems automate many business processes. For instance, how a customer receives credit or how a customer is billed is often determined by an information system that incorporates a set of formal business processes.

Each organization has a unique **culture**, or fundamental set of assumptions, values, and ways of doing things, that has been accepted by most of its members. You can see organizational culture at work by looking around your university or college. Some bedrock assumptions of university life are that professors know more than students, that the reason students attend college is to learn, and that classes follow a regular schedule.

Parts of an organization's culture can always be found embedded in its information systems. For instance, UPS's first priority is customer service, which is an aspect of its organizational culture that can be found in the company's package tracking systems, which we describe later in this section.

Different levels and specialties in an organization create different interests and points of view. These views often conflict over how the company should be run and how resources and rewards should be distributed. Conflict is the basis for organizational politics. Information systems come out of this cauldron of differing perspectives, conflicts, compromises, and agreements that are a natural part of all organizations. In Chapter 3, we examine these features of organizations and their role in the development of information systems in greater detail.

Management

Management's job is to make sense out of the many situations faced by organizations, make decisions, and formulate action plans to solve organizational problems. Managers perceive business challenges in the environment, they set the organizational strategy for responding to those challenges, and they allocate the human and financial resources to coordinate the work and achieve success. Throughout, they must exercise responsible leadership. The business information systems described in this book reflect the hopes, dreams, and realities of real-world managers.

But managers must do more than manage what already exists. They must also create new products and services and even re-create the organization from time to time. A substantial part of management responsibility is creative work driven by new knowledge and information. Information technology can play a powerful role in helping managers design and deliver new products and services and redirecting and redesigning their organizations.Chapter 12 treats management decision making in detail.

Information Technology

Information technology is one of many tools managers use to cope with change. **Computer hardware** is the physical equipment used for input, processing, and output activities in an information system. It consists of the following: computers of various sizes and shapes (including mobile handheld devices); various input, output, and storage devices; and telecommunications devices that link computers together.

Computer software consists of the detailed, preprogrammed instructions that control and coordinate the computer hardware components in an information system.Chapter 5 describes the contemporary software and hardware platforms used by firms today in greater detail.

Data management technology consists of the software governing the organization of data on physical storage media.More detail on data organization and access methods can be found in Chapter 6.

Networking and telecommunications technology, consisting of both physical devices and software, links the various pieces of hardware and transfers data from one physical location to another. Computers and communications equipment can be connected in networks for sharing voice, data, images, sound, and video. A **network** links two or more computers to share data or resources, such as a printer.

The world's largest and most widely used network is the **Internet**. The Internet is a global "network of networks" that uses universal standards (described in Chapter 7) to connect millions of networks in more than 230 countries around the world.

The Internet has created a new "universal" technology platform on which to build new products, services, strategies, and business models. This same technology platform has internal uses, providing the connectivity to link different systems and networks within the firm. Internal corporate networks based on Internet technology are called **intranets**. Private intranets extended to authorized users outside the organization are called **extranets**, and firms use such networks to coordinate their activities with other firms for making purchases, collaborating on design, and other interorganizational work. For most business firms today, using Internet technology is both a business necessity and a competitive advantage.

The **World Wide Web** is a service provided by the Internet that uses universally accepted standards for storing, retrieving, formatting, and displaying information in a page format on the Internet. Web pages contain text, graphics, animations, sound, and video and are linked to other web pages. By clicking on highlighted words or buttons on a web page, you can link to related pages to find additional information and links to other locations on the web. The web can serve as the foundation for new kinds of information systems.

All of these technologies, along with the people required to run and manage them, represent resources that can be shared throughout the organization and constitute the firm's **information technology (IT) infrastructure**. The IT infrastructure provides the foundation, or *platform*, on which the firm can build its specific information systems. Each organization must carefully design and manage its IT infrastructure so that it has the set of technology services it needs for the work it wants to accomplish with information systems. Chapters 5 through 8 of this book examine each major technology component of information technology infrastructure and show how they all work together to create the technology platform for the organization.

For instance, UPS operates the largest global package delivery system in the world. UPS invests heavily in information systems technology to make its business more efficient and customer oriented. It uses an array of information technologies, including bar code scanning systems, wireless networks, large

INTERACTIVE SESSION: TECHNOLOGY

ETM's Re-Routing KSTRC

Karnataka State Road Transport Corporation or KSRTC is a state-owned road transportation company. It provides public transportation by plying a fleet of 7,000 interstate and intra-state buses and by managing 60 depots. The corporation transports 2,500,000 passengers daily, with the help of 33,000 workers. The passengers are charged as per the normal fare table which is based on the distance traveled. The route for a particular journey is divided into stages and the fare table contains fee computation for each stage. Some variants on normal fares are half for children; there is a 10 percent hike in ticket price in the peak season months of April, May, June, and October, and a 10 percent discount in lean season months (July, August, and September). Since 2004, KSRTC has been using Electronic Ticketing Machines (ETMs) for fare collection.

An ETM is a hand-held device which has a keypad, thermal printer, multi-line display, memory, battery, and a port for data transfer integrated into it. This device is issued to a conductor at the depot, at the start of his shift. The ETM machine number, conductor's number, and driver's number are entered in the KSRTC server, and a unique number for the trip is generated. This number appears on all tickets, waybill, and reports for this trip. The conductor then prints a start-of-shift report displaying all accumulators set to zero. The machine supports several functions through its menus. The conductors can access different menus to set up a route, fare table, and other data which are related to the trip; for example, they can issue printed tickets, record information regarding passes, enter transactional data, view trip details and totals, and print reports. The inspectors, who utilize the device for audit purposes, use another menu.

The fare information, referred to as reference data, is generated daily in the KSRTC server, and uploaded in the ETM before issuing it to the conductor. For issuing the tickets, the conductor turns on the machine, and selects the route for the trip and the direction of travel. By default, the first stage of a trip is set. The conductor then enters the destination's section number and presses the ticket issue key, which leads to the generation of a printed ticket to be given to passengers. As the journey proceeds, the conductor increments the stage number in the machine and accordingly tickets are issued to passengers boarding the bus from places other than that of the origin. Different keys are used for issuing half-fare and luggage tickets. One printed ticket contains identification number for the trip generated at the time of issuing ETM, unique ticket number, date and time of issue, route and boarding stage, destination stage, and fare basis. One ticket can display all these details for a maximum of nine passengers in English and the regional language. A specific option on ETM allows the conductor to even close the trip.

Besides this, some additional information can be entered in the ETM using specific menu options such as entry for police warrants; payments made such as bridge fee, tollgate fee, bus stand fee; diesel issue entries; and the number of window bookings (from advanced reservation system through the Internet or mobile phones). At the end of shift, the conductor generates a collection report and an end-of-shift report which depict the total number and value of tickets sold and the amount to be paid at the depot. Around one percent of the total revenue generated from a trip is given to the drivers and conductors, which is automatically deducted from the pay-in amount. After this, the ETM machine is returned to the depot, and the data from the machine is transferred to the KSRTC server. The conductor also hands in the waybill which has handwritten information of the dispatcher signature, manual tickets booked in case of ETM problem, kilometers operated, window number of bookings, and other data related to work. If manual tickets were issued on the route, they are also entered into the server at this time.

The data transferred from an ETM to server is then used for further analysis and reporting. An ETM can generate status report which is basically a summary of the entire trip containing the date and time of issuing report, an ETM number, unique trip identification number, current value of various tickets, cash value totals, and route and trip information. Another report is the trip report which can be printed at any time within the trip, and contains details specific to that trip such as unique shift number, conductor number, driver number, an ETM number, route and schedule number, trip identifier and start time, current ticket number and total value of cash and tickets till that time. The other options for trip report are for all trips stored in that machine, for current trip or any specific trip during that shift. In the event of breakdown of a bus or some similar situation, if passengers are to be transferred to another bus, a trip report is used to inform the receiving bus conductor about passengers with and without a ticket. Another report, Ticket Details Report, provides summary of issued ticket by ticket type (adult ticket, child ticket, luggage ticket, police warrant ticket, etc.) or trip. The collection report, start-of-shift report, and end-of-shift report are also generated through ETMs. In addition to this, the conductor can print a list of all routes uploaded in the ETM memory containing route number, origin, and destination; the number of stops; and fare tables for individual routes containing name and stage number of each stop on route, kilometers covered, and fare. The back-office systems use these reports to detect anomalies, and investigation is carried out manually.

Other than the ETM, KSRTC also offers booking, sales, and distribution for tickets off vehicle. An initiative by the KSRTC and the Karnataka government, AWATAR (Any Where Any Time Advanced Reservation System), allows the customers to book tickets online to any destination from any place where KSRTC plies its buses. This is the first state transport undertaking facility which lets its customers make advance reservations through one of the three modes: mobile phones, the Internet, or Wide Area Network (WAN) of about 600 counters. Earlier KSRTC only deployed WAN to make advance reservations which led to numerous issues such as advance booking could be made only 10 days before the journey, from the corporation's counters at the place of boarding. Sometimes, return tickets were not available from many destinations. Through AWATAR, customers can make 30 days advance reservations, cancel e-tickets, issue duplicate tickets, view bus services for different routes, check availability of seats, see the list of pick-up points, check fares, etc. For this, the customer has to first register on the KSRTC website. This customer information is stored in KSRTC data center which, at present, has 1,60,000 registered customers' database, transaction database, and payments or billing information database. The system AWATAR has also been applauded by international travelers because it also allows them to make hotel bookings as well. To facilitate customers in rural and remote areas of Karnataka, the government has planned to launch kiosks which will provide AWATAR services in these areas.

The use of ETMs and the introduction of AWATAR have made numerous benefits available to the corporation and the general public. Not only has it improved the company's image, it has also reduced possibilities of fraud and misuse. It also provides accurate and timely information. The corporation replaces these ETMs after every five years, which is equal to the accounting book life of these devices. KSRTC is now looking for other probable developments in the future, such as, using GSM for data transfer and equipping the devices with RFID.

Sources: Retrieved from http://www.cxotoday.com/story/online-awatar-for-travel-agents/; Retrieved from https://www.ssatp.org/sites/ssatp/files/publications/Toolkits/Fares%20Toolkit%20content/case-studies/karnataka-india.html; Retrieved from http://egov.eletsonline.com/2006/04/ksrtc-to-introduce-e-ticketing-facility/; Retrieved from http://www.thehindu.com/todays-paper/tp-national/tp-karnataka/ksrtc-to-introduce-eticketing-facility/article3145486.ece.

CASE STUDY QUESTIONS

1. Discuss how ETMs are used for issuing tickets to passengers. How is the data from ETMs used for report generation and analysis at the KSRTC?
2. How does AWATAR enable off-vehicle advance reservation? List other benefits of AWATAR.
3. Can a similar device be used for collecting student fees? How? Think of other probable areas where such a device would be useful.

mainframe computers, handheld computers, the Internet, and many different pieces of software for tracking packages, calculating fees, maintaining customer accounts, and managing logistics.

Let's identify the organization, management, and technology elements in the UPS package tracking system we have just described. The organization element anchors the package tracking system in UPS's sales and production functions (the main product of UPS is a service—package delivery). It specifies the required procedures for identifying packages with both sender and recipient information, taking inventory, tracking the packages en route, and providing package status reports for UPS customers and customer service representatives.

The system must also provide information to satisfy the needs of managers and workers. UPS drivers need to be trained in both package pickup and delivery procedures and in how to use the package tracking system so that they can work efficiently and effectively. UPS customers may need some training to use UPS in-house package tracking software or the UPS website.

UPS's management is responsible for monitoring service levels and costs and for promoting the company's strategy of combining low cost and superior service. Management decided to use computer systems to increase the ease of sending a package using UPS and of checking its delivery status, thereby reducing delivery costs and increasing sales revenues.

The technology supporting this system consists of handheld computers, bar code scanners, desktop computers, wired and wireless communications networks, UPS's data center, storage technology for the package delivery data, UPS in-house package tracking software, and software to access the World Wide Web. The result is an information system solution to the business challenge of providing a high level of service with low prices in the face of mounting competition.

Using a handheld computer called a Delivery Information Acquisition Device (DIAD), UPS drivers automatically capture customers' signatures along with pickup, delivery, and time card information. UPS information systems use these data to track packages while they are being transported.

It Isn't Just Technology: A Business Perspective on Information Systems

Managers and business firms invest in information technology and systems because they provide real economic value to the business. The decision to build or maintain an information system assumes that the returns on this investment will be superior to other investments in buildings, machines, or other assets. These superior returns will be expressed as increases in productivity, as increases in revenues (which will increase the firm's stock market value), or perhaps as superior long-term strategic positioning of the firm in certain markets (which produce superior revenues in the future).

We can see that from a business perspective, an information system is an important instrument for creating value for the firm. Information systems enable the firm to increase its revenue or decrease its costs by providing information that helps managers make better decisions or that improves the execution of business processes. For example, the information system for analyzing supermarket checkout data illustrated in Figure 1.3 can increase firm profitability by helping managers make better decisions as to which products to stock and promote in retail supermarkets.

Every business has an information value chain, illustrated in Figure 1.7, in which raw information is systematically acquired and then transformed through

FIGURE 1.7 THE BUSINESS INFORMATION VALUE CHAIN

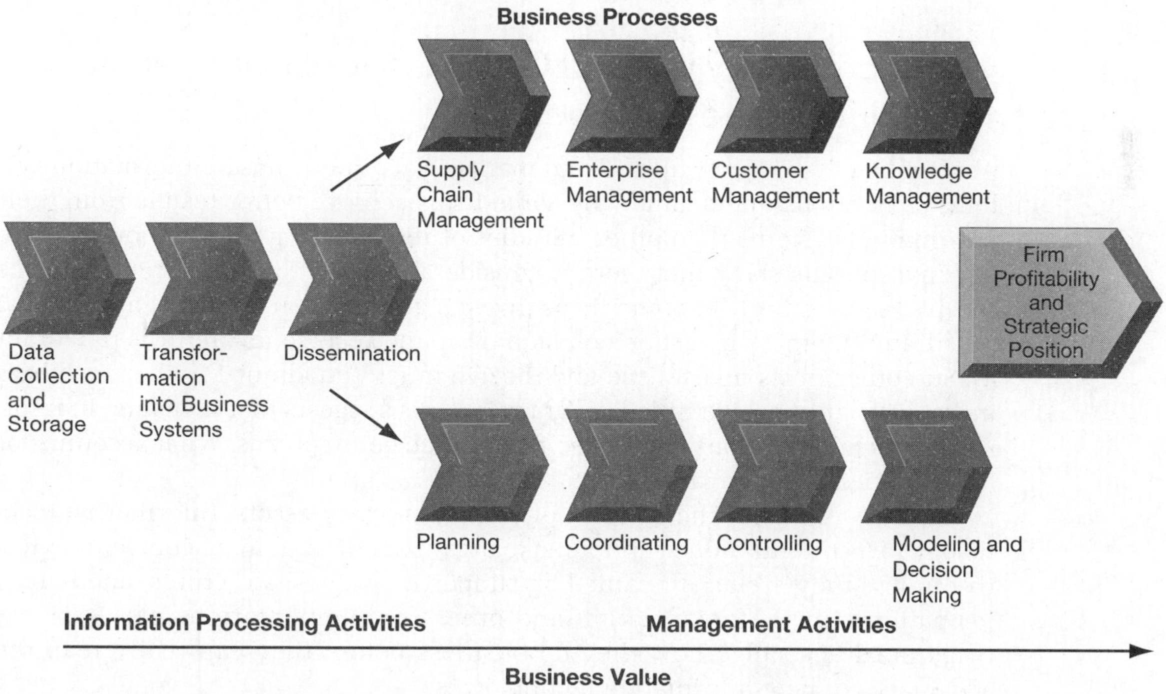

From a business perspective, information systems are part of a series of value-adding activities for acquiring, transforming, and distributing information that managers can use to improve decision making, enhance organizational performance, and, ultimately, increase firm profitability.

various stages that add value to that information. The value of an information system to a business, as well as the decision to invest in any new information system, is, in large part, determined by the extent to which the system will lead to better management decisions, more efficient business processes, and higher firm profitability. Although there are other reasons why systems are built, their primary purpose is to contribute to corporate value.

The business perspective calls attention to the organizational and managerial nature of information systems. An information system represents an organizational and management solution, based on information technology, to a challenge or problem posed by the environment. Every chapter in this book begins with a short case study that illustrates this concept. A diagram at the beginning of each chapter illustrates the relationship between a business challenge and resulting management and organizational decisions to use IT as a solution to challenges generated by the business environment. You can use this diagram as a starting point for analyzing any information system or information system problem you encounter.

Review the diagram at the beginning of this chapter. The diagram shows how the Rugby Football Union's systems solved the business problem presented by the need to generate revenue in a highly competitive industry. These systems created a solution that takes advantage of opportunities that new digital technology and the Internet provided. They opened up new channels for selling tickets and interacting with customers, optimized ticket pricing, and used new tools to analyze player performance. These systems were essential in improving the rugby teams' overall business performance. The diagram also illustrates how people, technology, and organizational elements work together to create the systems.

Complementary Assets: Organizational Capital and the Right Business Model

Awareness of the organizational and managerial dimensions of information systems can help us understand why some firms achieve better results from their information systems than others. Studies of returns from information technology investments show that there is considerable variation in the returns firms receive (see Figure 1.8). Some firms invest a great deal and receive a great deal (quadrant 2); others invest an equal amount and receive few returns (quadrant 4). Still other firms invest little and receive much (quadrant 1), whereas others invest little and receive little (quadrant 3). This suggests that investing in information technology does not by itself guarantee good returns. What accounts for this variation among firms?

The answer lies in the concept of complementary assets. Information technology investments alone cannot make organizations and managers more effective unless they are accompanied by supportive values, structures, and behavior patterns in the organization and other complementary assets. Business firms need to change how they do business before they can really reap the advantages of new information technologies.

Complementary assets are those assets required to derive value from a primary investment (Teece, 1998). For instance, to realize value from automobiles requires substantial complementary investments in highways, roads, gasoline

FIGURE 1.8 VARIATION IN RETURNS ON INFORMATION TECHNOLOGY INVESTMENT

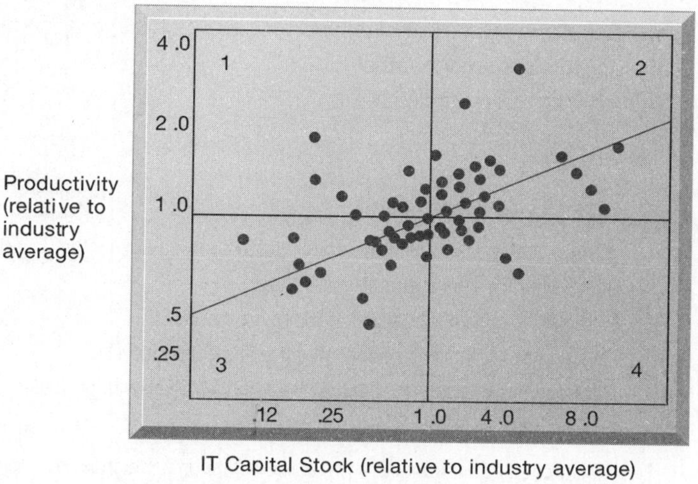

Although, on average, investments in information technology produce returns far above those returned by other investments, there is considerable variation across firms.

Source: Based on Brynjolfsson and Hitt (2000).

stations, repair facilities, and a legal regulatory structure to set standards and control drivers.

Research indicates that firms that support their technology investments with investments in complementary assets, such as new business models, new business processes, management behavior, organizational culture, or training, receive superior returns, whereas those firms failing to make these complementary investments receive less or no returns on their information technology investments (Brynjolfsson, 2005; Brynjolfsson and Hitt, 2000; Laudon, 1974). These investments in organization and management are also known as **organizational and management capital**.

Table 1.2 lists the major complementary investments that firms need to make to realize value from their information technology investments. Some of this investment involves tangible assets, such as buildings, machinery, and tools. However, the value of investments in information technology depends to a large extent on complementary investments in management and organization.

Key organizational complementary investments are a supportive business culture that values efficiency and effectiveness, an appropriate business model, efficient business processes, decentralization of authority, highly distributed decision rights, and a strong information system (IS) development team.

Important managerial complementary assets are strong senior management support for change, incentive systems that monitor and reward individual innovation, an emphasis on teamwork and collaboration, training programs, and a management culture that values flexibility and knowledge.

Important social investments (not made by the firm but by the society at large, other firms, governments, and other key market actors) are the Internet and the supporting Internet culture, educational systems, network and computing standards, regulations and laws, and the presence of technology and service firms.

TABLE 1.2 COMPLEMENTARY SOCIAL, MANAGERIAL, AND ORGANIZATIONAL ASSETS REQUIRED TO OPTIMIZE RETURNS FROM INFORMATION TECHNOLOGY INVESTMENTS

Organizational assets	Supportive organizational culture that values efficiency and effectiveness
	Appropriate business model
	Efficient business processes
	Decentralized authority
	Distributed decision-making rights
	Strong IS development team
Managerial assets	Strong senior management support for technology investment and change
	Incentives for management innovation
	Teamwork and collaborative work environments
	Training programs to enhance management decision skills
	Management culture that values flexibility and knowledge-based decision making.
Social assets	The Internet and telecommunications infrastructure
	IT-enriched educational programs raising labor force computer literacy
	Standards (both government and private sector)
	Laws and regulations creating fair, stable market environments
	Technology and service firms in adjacent markets to assist implementation

Throughout the book we emphasize a framework of analysis that considers technology, management, and organizational assets and their interactions. Perhaps the single most important theme in the book, reflected in case studies and exercises, is that managers need to consider the broader organization and management dimensions of information systems to understand current problems as well as to derive substantial above-average returns from their information technology investments. As you will see throughout the text, firms that can address these related dimensions of the IT investment are, on average, richly rewarded.

1-3 What academic disciplines are used to study information systems, and how does each contribute to an understanding of information systems?

The study of information systems is a multidisciplinary field. No single theory or perspective dominates. Figure 1.9 illustrates the major disciplines that contribute problems, issues, and solutions in the study of information systems. In general, the field can be divided into technical and behavioral approaches. Information systems are sociotechnical systems. Though they are composed of machines, devices, and "hard" physical technology, they require substantial social, organizational, and intellectual investments to make them work properly.

Technical Approach

The technical approach to information systems emphasizes mathematically based models to study information systems as well as the physical technology and formal

FIGURE 1.9 CONTEMPORARY APPROACHES TO INFORMATION SYSTEMS

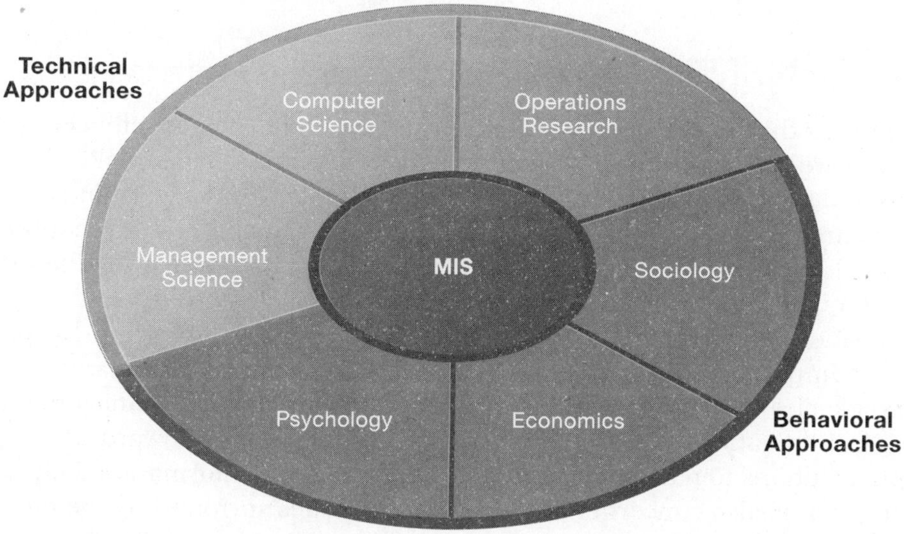

The study of information systems deals with issues and insights contributed from technical and behavioral disciplines.

capabilities of these systems. The disciplines that contribute to the technical approach are computer science, management science, and operations research.

Computer science is concerned with establishing theories of computability, methods of computation, and methods of efficient data storage and access. Management science emphasizes the development of models for decision-making and management practices. Operations research focuses on mathematical techniques for optimizing selected parameters of organizations, such as transportation, inventory control, and transaction costs.

Behavioral Approach

An important part of the information systems field is concerned with behavioral issues that arise in the development and long-term maintenance of information systems. Issues such as strategic business integration, design, implementation, utilization, and management cannot be explored usefully with the models used in the technical approach. Other behavioral disciplines contribute important concepts and methods.

For instance, sociologists study information systems with an eye toward how groups and organizations shape the development of systems and also how systems affect individuals, groups, and organizations. Psychologists study information systems with an interest in how human decision makers perceive and use formal information. Economists study information systems with an interest in understanding the production of digital goods, the dynamics of digital markets, and how new information systems change the control and cost structures within the firm.

The behavioral approach does not ignore technology. Indeed, information systems technology is often the stimulus for a behavioral problem or issue. But the focus of this approach is generally not on technical solutions. Instead, it concentrates on changes in attitudes, management and organizational policy, and behavior.

Approach of This Text: Sociotechnical Systems

Throughout this book you will find a rich story with four main actors: suppliers of hardware and software (the technologists); business firms making investments and seeking to obtain value from the technology; managers and employees seeking to achieve business value (and other goals); and the contemporary legal, social, and cultural context (the firm's environment). Together these actors produce what we call *management information systems*.

The study of management information systems (MIS) arose to focus on the use of computer-based information systems in business firms and government agencies. MIS combines the work of computer science, management science, and operations research with a practical orientation toward developing system solutions to real-world problems and managing information technology resources. It is also concerned with behavioral issues surrounding the development, use, and impact of information systems, which are typically discussed in the fields of sociology, economics, and psychology.

Our experience as academics and practitioners leads us to believe that no single approach effectively captures the reality of information systems. The successes and failures of information systems are rarely all technical or all behavioral. Our best advice to students is to understand the perspectives of many disciplines. Indeed, the challenge and excitement of the information systems field are that it requires an appreciation and tolerance of many different approaches.

The view we adopt in this book is best characterized as the **sociotechnical view** of systems. In this view, optimal organizational performance is achieved by jointly optimizing both the social and technical systems used in production.

Adopting a sociotechnical systems perspective helps to avoid a purely technological approach to information systems. For instance, the fact that information technology is rapidly declining in cost and growing in power does not necessarily or easily translate into productivity enhancement or bottom-line profits. The fact that a firm has recently installed an enterprise-wide financial reporting system does not necessarily mean that it will be used, or used effectively. Likewise, the fact that a firm has recently introduced new business procedures and processes does not necessarily mean employees will be more productive in the absence of investments in new information systems to enable those processes.

In this book, we stress the need to optimize the firm's performance as a whole. Both the technical and behavioral components need attention. This means that technology must be changed and designed in such a way as to fit organizational and individual needs. Sometimes, the technology may have to be "de-optimized" to accomplish this fit. For instance, mobile phone users adapt this technology to their personal needs, and as a result manufacturers quickly seek to adjust the technology to conform with user expectations. Organizations and individuals must also be changed through training, learning, and planned organizational change to allow the technology to operate and prosper. Figure 1.10 illustrates this process of mutual adjustment in a sociotechnical system.

FIGURE 1.10 A SOCIOTECHNICAL PERSPECTIVE ON INFORMATION SYSTEMS

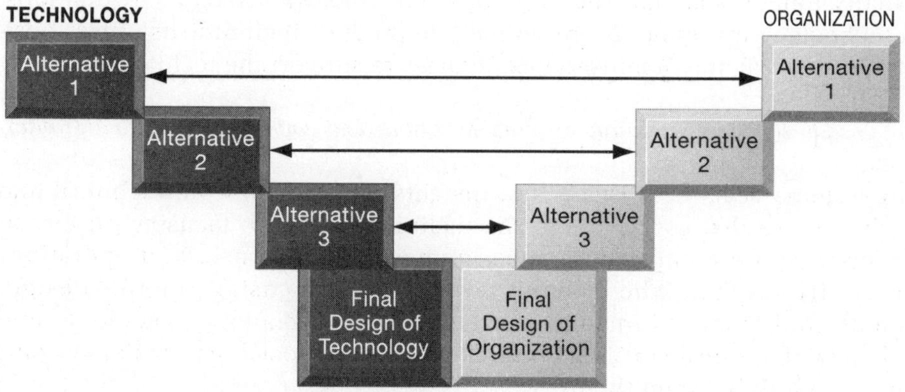

In a sociotechnical perspective, the performance of a system is optimized when both the technology and the organization mutually adjust to one another until a satisfactory fit is obtained.

Review Summary

1-1 ***How are information systems transforming business, and why are they essential for running and managing a business today?***

E-mail, online conferencing, smartphones, and tablet computers have become essential tools for conducting business. Information systems are the foundation of fast-paced supply chains. The Internet allows many businesses to buy, sell, advertise, and solicit customer feedback online. Organizations are trying to become more competitive and efficient by digitally enabling their core business processes and evolving into digital firms. The Internet has stimulated globalization by dramatically reducing the costs of producing, buying, and selling goods on a global scale. New information system trends include the emerging mobile digital platform, big data, and cloud computing.

Information systems are a foundation for conducting business today. In many industries, survival and the ability to achieve strategic business goals are difficult without extensive use of information technology. Businesses today use information systems to achieve six major objectives: operational excellence; new products, services, and business models; customer/supplier intimacy; improved decision making; competitive advantage; and day-to-day survival.

1-2 *What is an information system? How does it work? What are its management, organization, and technology components? Why are complementary assets essential for ensuring that information systems provide genuine value for organizations?*

From a technical perspective, an information system collects, stores, and disseminates information from an organization's environment and internal operations to support organizational functions and decision making, communication, coordination, control, analysis, and visualization. Information systems transform raw data into useful information through three basic activities: input, processing, and output.

From a business perspective, an information system provides a solution to a problem or challenge facing a firm and represents a combination of management, organization, and technology elements. The management dimension of information systems involves issues such as leadership, strategy, and management behavior. The technology dimension consists of computer hardware, software, data management technology, and networking/telecommunications technology (including the Internet). The organization dimension of information systems involves issues such as the organization's hierarchy, functional specialties, business processes, culture, and political interest groups.

In order to obtain meaningful value from information systems, organizations must support their technology investments with appropriate complementary investments in organizations and management. These complementary assets include new business models and business processes, supportive organizational culture and management behavior, and appropriate technology standards, regulations, and laws. New information technology investments are unlikely to produce high returns unless businesses make the appropriate managerial and organizational changes to support the technology.

1-3 *What academic disciplines are used to study information systems, and how does each contribute to an understanding of information systems?*

The study of information systems deals with issues and insights contributed from technical and behavioral disciplines. The disciplines that contribute to the technical approach focusing on formal models and capabilities of systems are computer science, management science, and operations research. The disciplines contributing to the behavioral approach focusing on the design, implementation, management, and business impact of systems are psychology, sociology, and economics. A sociotechnical view of systems considers both technical and social features of systems and solutions that represent the best fit between them.

Key Terms

Business functions, 21
Business model, 15
Business processes, 13
Complementary assets, 28
Computer hardware, 22
Computer literacy, 19
Computer software, 23
Culture, 22
Data, 17
Data management technology, 23
Data workers, 20
Digital firm, 12
Extranets, 23
Feedback, 17
Information, 17
Information system, 17
Information systems literacy, 19
Information technology (IT), 17
Information technology (IT) infrastructure, 23
Input, 17
Internet, 23
Intranets, 23
Knowledge workers, 20
Management information systems (MIS), 19
Middle management, 20
Network, 23
Networking and telecommunications technology, 23
Operational management, 20
Organizational and management capital, 29
Output, 17
Processing, 17
Production or service workers, 21
Senior management, 30
Sociotechnical view, 32
World Wide Web, 23

Review Questions

1-1 How are the information systems transforming businesses, and why are they so essential for running and managing a business in the present times?

- Discuss the ways in which firms can use information system to implement corporate strategies.
- Why are the firms moving towards digitization these days?
- Discuss a few examples to demonstrate how changes in technologies and business models have transformed business practices.
- List the changes in doing business which is supported by information technology.
- What is the relation between globalization and information systems?

1-2 What is an information system? How does it work? What are its management, organization and technology components? Why are complementary assets essential for ensuring that information systems provide genuine value for organizations?

- Using an analogy, explain how information systems differ from computers and software programs.

- Discuss the function of information systems and the way they bring about value addition for the firm.
- Discuss the role of organization levels and organization culture in the development of information systems.
- List and describe the technologies that constitute the information technology infrastructure of a firm.
- Briefly describe the role of complementary assets in the reaping of optimal returns from information technology investments.
- What is meant by organization and management capital? List a few major complementary investments.

1-3 What academic disciplines are used to study information systems? How do each of them contribute to an understanding of information systems?

- How are information systems socio-technical? Why there is a need to adopt socio-technical perspective to understand and implement information systems?
- What does the technical approach emphasize on?
- Although behavioral approach deals with issues arising from technology, how is it different from technical approach?

Discussion Question

1-4 What does it mean to describe the world as "flat"?

1-5 If you were setting up the website for a competitive rugby team, what management, organization, and technology issues might you encounter?

Hands-On MIS Projects

The projects in this section give you a hand-on experience in analyzing financial reporting and inventory management problems, using data management software to improve management decision making about increasing sales, and using Internet software for researching job requirements.

Management Decision Problems

1-6 Warbenton Snack Foods is a manufacturer of potato crisps and savoury snacks in the U.K. Warbenton's financial department uses spreadsheets and manual processes for much of its data gathering and reporting. Warbenton's financial analyst would spend the entire final week of every month collecting spreadsheets from the heads of various departments. She would then consolidate and re-enter all the data into another spreadsheet, which would serve as the company's monthly profit-and-loss statement. If a department needed to update its data after submitting the spreadsheet to the main office, the analyst had to return the original spreadsheet and then wait for the department to resubmit its data before finally submitting the updated data in the consolidated document. Assess the impact of this situation on business performance and management decision making.

1-7 Rabatt operates deep-discount stores offering housewares, cleaning supplies, clothing, health and beauty aids, and packaged food throughout Germany, with most items selling for 1 euro. Its business model calls for keeping costs as low as possible. The company has no automated method for keeping track of inventory at each store. Managers know approximately how many cases of a particular product the store is supposed to receive when a delivery truck arrives, but the stores lack technology for scanning the cases or verifying the item count inside the cases. Merchandise losses from theft or other mishaps have been rising and now represent over 3 percent of total sales. What decisions have to be made before investing in an information system solution?

Improving Decision Making: Using the Internet to Locate Jobs Requiring Information Systems Knowledge

Software skills: Internet-based software
Business skills: Job searching

1-8 Visit a job-posting website such as Monster.com. Spend some time at the site examining jobs for accounting, finance, sales, marketing, and human resources. Find two or three descriptions of jobs that require some information systems knowledge. What information systems knowledge do these jobs require? What do you need to do to prepare for these jobs? Write a one- to two-page report summarizing your findings.

Collaboration and Teamwork Project

Selecting Team Collaboration Tools

1-9 Form a team with three or four classmates and review the capabilities of Google Drive and Google Sites for your team collaboration work. Compare the capabilities of these two tools for storing team documents, project announcements, source materials, work assignments, illustrations, electronic presentations, and web pages of interest. Learn how each works with Google Docs. Explain why Google Drive or Google Sites is more appropriate for your team. If possible, use Google Docs to brainstorm and develop a presentation of your findings for the class. Organize and store your presentation using the Google tool you have selected.

The Domino's PULSE™ System: Reading the Pulse of the Customer

CASE STUDY

Domino's is an international pizza-delivery franchise, headquartered in Ann Arbour, Michigan, in the United States. Founded in 1960, Domino's Pizza has more than 10,000 corporate and franchise stores in 70 countries across the world. Domino's was sold to Bain Capital in 1998 and went public in 2004. The company started operations in India in 1996. It subsequently changed its name to Jubiliant FoodWorks Limited in 2009. Due to the sluggish growth of the U.S. economy, the company started spreading its operations aggressively to other nations. More than half of Domino's revenues come from its overseas businesses. It sells more pizzas in India than anywhere else outside the US. With four lakh pizzas every day, and more than 12 crore pizzas every year, Domino's sells nearly twice the number of burgers that McDonald's sells in India.

Owing to an aggressive expansion of operations and growing order counts from customers, the information system employed by Domino's plays an important role in increasing the operating efficiencies of the pizza chain. It provides the management with accurate information at any given point of time. Right from the time a customer places an order to when the management wants to track sales, the information system supplies the data in real time.

Domino's PULSE™ Point-of-Sale (PoS) system is a graphical user-interface and touch-screen based computerized information system that manages ordering, inventory, and reporting at Domino's Pizza. It has been implemented in over 50 percent of the international stores. More than one-third of the stores' orders originate from online sources; so to efficiently manage orders, the firm decided to roll out its new PoS system at all its domestic stores.

The PULSE™ user-interface is kept simple: it gives information about menu, functions, and customers. A Domino's employee selects a menu item (based on the customer's choice) from a list of available items appearing as tabs on the screen. When a customer orders or calls Domino's for a pizza, the representative enquires about some basic information of the customer (such as their name and contact number and the address they are calling from), which serves as a primary input for processing the order. For returning callers, the contact number is used to identify the customer and retrieve their account details. Whenever Domino's receives a call, the customer's number flashes on the screen. Since all previous orders are saved in PULSE™, the representative knows whether the call is from a new or existing customer. The employee makes suggestions to the customer based on their order history.

Once an order is placed, be it via phone, online, or at the counter, it automatically gets transferred into a centralized computer and the main servers. This enables the management to plan their operations effectively. When a manager sees that a particular customer has not ordered for some time, he or she personally calls the customer with a special offer to encourage them to come back.

Domino's has also successfully deployed Voice over IP (VoIP). Using this facility, the pizza chain has been able to allocate a particular number to a specific region or geographic area. When a customer calls the pizza chain, VoIP automatically detects the location of the caller and intelligently routes the call to their nearest store location. This way, the customer does not need to memorize more than one number for different store locations. For the firm too, this system eliminates the need to maintain multiple analog lines for each number, thereby saving costs. Since VoIP transmits voice calls over the Internet by converting voice into packet data, there is a significant reduction in telecommunication expenses for the company.

Additionally, Domino's maintains hosting agents or virtual call centers along with its VoIP services. When the incoming load at the store is at its peak, such as during weekends or holidays, the calls are routed to these agents who professionally take orders and transmit them to the nearest pizza chain, where they are processed and delivered. Domino's PULSE™ even manages the refund process in case a customer is not satisfied with the product, the wrong order is delivered, or the delivery is not made within the stipulated time.

Considering the volume of orders received by Domino's, a back-up server has been installed at each store to increase the speed of processing of the orders. The operating system has also been upgraded from Windows XP to Windows Server 2008 R2, which has a Hyper-V virtualization technology built into it. This has not only increased the performance of the PoS system, but also lowered the IT costs.

To provide additional comfort to its online customers, Domino's Pizza launched a new initiative: a mobile phone application for both Android and iOS devices. This application allows the user to browse through all products on the menu and also access their promotional coupons. Besides this, the app lets the consumer design their own pizza. The interface of the app is user-friendly—it displays the order at the top of the screen while the user is navigating through other content. The payment and delivery options can also be selected by the user. The app fetches the account details whenever the user logs into the application. The success of this app is also due to the fact that Domino's focuses strongly on SMS marketing. The user who receives a lucrative offer via SMS now does not have to call or visit the Domino's website to redeem it. The user can redeem the offer by ordering using the mobile app.

Due its large presence over multiple geographical areas, internal communication among the employees within the chain was a key challenge for Domino's. The solution to this was provided by eConnect, a subsystem within PULSE™. Through eConnect, a branch manager can contact any of the other branches or even the headquarters. For evaluating the performance of the stores, managers can generate reports from PULSE™. Each store prepares a monthly report using this system, which helps determine the consolidated performance of the store. Some of the items which the report contains are:

- Net sales of the present month, net sales for this month last year, net sales of the last month, and expected sales
- Growth rate and achievement over budget for the month
- Orders delivered

These reports help compare the past sales for different months with the current month. This can be used to make future projections and check the growth or decline in sales for each branch. These reports are then forwarded to the senior management with the help of the 'push' facility within PULSE™. In a similar manner, any data can be accessed from the information system using the 'pull' feature. Reports of daily services, inventory, and even the guidelines from superiors are issued via the push–pull feature.

No firm can run without having an efficient evaluation and tracking system in place. In order to keep an eye on the sales of a Domino's store, its manager analyzes the store sales every week. The manager assesses the order frequencies and also identifies the areas from where new orders are coming. On the basis of the data collected, the manager divides the areas into three main sectors discussed below:

1. **Yellow:** The localities from where new customers have started ordering pizzas are categorized as yellow. These are 5 to 10 percent of total orders. In order to encourage these customers to order more frequently, the manager initiates distribution of pamphlets in these localities, that contain a few of the basic, inexpensive pizzas from Domino's.
2. **Green:** The localities from where the orders are coming at a steady rate are categorized as green. These are 10 percent to 30 percent of the total orders. In order to increase the orders in this segment, the manager orders distribution of pamphlets containing medium-range pizzas.
3. **Red:** The localities from where the store receives the maximum orders are categorized as red. These are 60 percent of the total orders. The order frequency in this segment is higher than that of any other area, and so the manager orders distribution of pamphlets containing the store's specialized range of pizzas. The most costly items are promoted in these areas.

PULSE™ also aids in inventory management. The details of the inventory at each branch are regularly prepared in a worksheet. Each item of raw material which is used to make the finished products is described in this sheet. The used quantity of each item is compared against available quantity and ideal usage. Then variance is calculated to identify whether products are being optimally utilized. This helps conduct wastage analysis at each branch, and the reports are then collated at the head office to see the comparative wastage at different branches.

These are some of the ways in which the information system at Domino's Pizza has been able to provide a competitive edge to the chain. It has ensured real-time data processing, efficient communication, consistent reporting for decision making, and effective management of store operations. In a nutshell, it has guaranteed customer satisfaction.

Sources: Domino's PULSE™ point-of-sale system" (2009). Retrieved from http://www.wikinvest.com/stock/Domino's_Pizza_(DPZ)/Dominos_Pulse_Point-of-sale_System; "Nortel Enables Advanced Communications for Smaller Companies, Branch Offices; Domino's Pizza, Others Lower Costs, Improve Customer Service with Nortel BCM 50.", The Free Library (2014). Retrieved from http://www.thefreelibrary.com; "Domino's Pizza and Breakaway rollout new Pulse POS system" (2003). Retreived from http://www.pizzamarketplace.com/; Phi, Hoang, "Domino's Pizza tailoring to local tastes", The Saigon Times (2012). Retrieved from http://english.thesaigontimes.vn/; "Domino's Pizza and Breakaway Complete Corporate Rollout of New POS System" (2003). Retrieved from http://www.prnewswire.com/; Alfs, Lizzy, "What's next for Domino's Pizza? CEO Patrick Doyle outlines some goals", The Ann Arbor News (2013). Retrieved from http://www.annarbor.com/, (Navigation > Home > Business Review > Article), as accessed on 02 November 2017 at 2pm IST; "Domino's Android App". Retrieved from http://www.dominospizza.co.nz/corporate/android-app; "Dominos Pizza, Inc.'s Annual Report Persuant to Section 13 or 15(d) of the Securities Exchange Act of 1934", United States Securities and Exchange Commission (2013). Retrieved from http://www.sec.gov/, (Navigation/Home > Archives > Edgar > Data), as accessed on 02 November 2017 at 2pm IST; Bhushan, Ratna,"India emerges as Domino's biggest market outside US", The Economic Times (2014). Retrieved from http://articles.economictimes.indiatimes.com/.

CASE STUDY QUESTIONS

1-10 How does the Domino's PULSE™ system help manage customers' orders? Is there a system in place to identify the new customers?

1-11 How does PULSE™ help the manager to segregate the areas of customer orders and use appropriate targeting strategies?

1-12 As a senior manager, discuss how you would conduct wastage analysis in Domino's stores through PULSE™.

1-13 Discuss the eConnect and reporting feature of the Domino's PULSE™ system.

1-14 How does VoIP help Domino's serve its customers in an efficient manner?

1-15 Share your experience of an unique customer service at Domino's and try to link that service with the features of the PULSE™ system.

Chapter 1 References

Brynjolfsson, Erik and Lorin M. Hitt. "Beyond Computation: Information Technology, Organizational Transformation, and Business Performance." *Journal of Economic Perspectives* 14, No. 4 (2000).

Brynjolfsson, Erik. "VII Pillars of IT Productivity." *Optimize* (May 2005).

Bureau of Economic Analysis. *National Income and Product Accounts*. www.bea.gov, accessed April 19, 2016.

Carr, Nicholas. "IT Doesn't Matter." *Harvard Business Review* (May 2003).

Chae, Ho-Chang, Chang E. Koh, and Victor Prybutok. "Information Technology Capability and Firm Performance: Contradictory Findings and Their Possible Causes." *MIS Quarterly* 38, No. 1 (March 2014).

Conaghan, Jim. "Newspaper Digital Audience Grew Twice as Fast as the Internet in the Past 12 Months." Newspaper Association of America (October 9, 2015).

Curtis, Sophie. "Dot-com at 30: Will the World's Best-Known Web Domain Soon Be Obsolete?" Telegraph.co.uk (March 15, 2015).

Dedrick, Jason, Vijay Gurbaxani, and Kenneth L. Kraemer. "Information Technology and Economic Performance: A Critical Review of the Empirical Evidence." Center for Research on Information Technology and Organizations, University of California, Irvine (December 2001).

eMarketer. "eMarketer Numbers for: Blogging, 2014–2018." (2016).

eMarketer. "Worldwide Retail E-commerce Sales." (2016a).

eMarketer. "Tablet Users to Surpass 1 Billion Worldwide in 2015." (January, 2015a).

eMarketer. "US Adults Spend 5.5 Hours with Video Content Each Day." (April 16, 2015b).

eMarketer. "US Digital Ad Spending, 2013–2019." (March 2015c).

FedEx Corporation. "SEC Form 10-K for the Fiscal Year Ended May 31, 2015."

Friedman, Thomas. *The World Is Flat*. New York: Picador (2007).

Garretson, Rob. "IT Still Matters." *CIO Insight* 81 (May 2007).

Hughes, Alan and Michael S. Scott Morton. "The Transforming Power of Complementary Assets." *MIT Sloan Management Review* 47. No. 4 (Summer 2006).

Lamb, Roberta, Steve Sawyer, and Rob Kling. "A Social Informatics Perspective of Socio-Technical Networks." http://lamb.cba.hawaii.edu/pubs (2004).

Laudon, Kenneth C. *Computers and Bureaucratic Reform*. New York: Wiley (1974).

Lev, Baruch. "Intangibles: Management, Measurement, and Reporting." The Brookings Institution Press (2001).

McKinsey Global Institute. "Digital America: A Tale of the Haves and Have-Mores (December 2015).

Mithas, Sunil and Roland T. Rust, "How Information Technology Strategy and Investments Influence Firm Performance: Conjecture and Empirical Evidence." *MIS Quarterly* (March 2016).

Nevo, Saggi and Michael R. Wade. "The Formation and Value of IT-Enabled Resources: Antecedents and Consequences of Synergistic Relationships." *MIS Quarterly* 34, No. 1 (March 2010).

Otim, Samual, Kevin E. Dow, Varun Grover, and Jeffrey A. Wong. "The Impact of Information Technology Investments on Downside Risk of the Firm: Alternative Measurement of the Business Value of IT." *Journal of Management Information Systems* 29, No. 1 (Summer 2012).

Ren, Fei and Sanjeev Dewan. "Industry-Level Analysis of Information Technology Return and Risk: What Explains the Variation?" *Journal of Management Information Systems* 21, No. 2 (2015).

Ross, Jeanne W. and Peter Weill. "Four Questions Every CEO Should Ask About IT." *Wall Street Journal* (April 25, 2011).

Sabherwal, Rajiv and Anand Jeyaraj. "Information Technology Impacts on Firm Performance: An Extension of Kohli and Devaraj (2003)." *MIS Quarterly* (December 2015).

Sampler, Jeffrey L., and Michael J. Earl. "What's Your Information Footprint?" *MIT Sloan Management Review* (Winter 2014).

Saunders, Adam and Erik Brynjolfsson. "Valuing Information Technology Related Intangible Assets." *MIS Quarterly* (March 2016).

Shanks, Ryan, Sunit Sinha and Robert J. Thomas. "Managers and Machines, Unite!" Accenture (2015).

Stats-Wordpress. "Wordpress Global Statistics," https://wordpress.com, accessed April 22, 2016.

Teece, David. *Economic Performance and Theory of the Firm: The Selected Papers of David Teece*. London: Edward Elgar Publishing (1998).

U.S. Bureau of Labor Statistics. *Occupational Outlook Handbook*. (December 17, 2015).

Weill, Peter and Jeanne Ross. *IT Savvy: What Top Executives Must Know to Go from Pain to Gain*. Boston: Harvard Business School Press (2009).

CHAPTER

2 Global E-business and Collaboration

Learning Objectives

After reading this chapter, you will be able to answer the following questions:

2-1 What are business processes? How are they related to information systems?

2-2 How do systems serve the different management groups in a business, and how do systems that link the enterprise improve organizational performance?

2-3 Why are systems for collaboration and social business so important, and what technologies do they use?

2-4 What is the role of the information systems function in a business?

CHAPTER CASES

Azure Medical System: Integrating Departments Using Enterprise System
HDFC Banking on Business Intelligence and Analytics Technology
Collaboration for Improved Services at eClerx
Ranbaxy: Taking the ERP Pill

Azure Medical System: Integrating Departments Using Enterprise System

Azure Medical Systems is the leading manufacturer of X-ray field equipment in north India and the second-largest producer of high-end X-ray machines after Meditronics (Phillips). It has a manufacturing facility in Punjab and Baddi (Himachal Pradesh), with its corporate offices in Chandigarh, and 29 sales and services centers across India. The company has an annual turnover of about ₹200 crore with a well-established market in Asia, South America, the Arabic countries, and South Africa. Azure has a total workforce of nearly 1,000 employees, most of whom are in the marketing and services departments. The firm lays a lot of emphasis on forecasting, planning to locate potential markets, and innovating products.

At the start of the manufacturing cycle, the Production Planning and Control (PPC) department first makes a list of materials required for manufacturing a specified equipment, checks what is available in-house, and places an order for the rest of the material. The PPC department then generates a Bill of Material (BOM) and releases the orders to the store, and the production, purchase, vendor development, quality, and logistics departments. In case of special orders, which are made to the customer's specifications, the process is slightly altered. Information of the order is given to the PPC unit and the in-house R&D department is consulted for viability, timelines, and costing.

Earlier, the various departments coordinated over e-mails, and the hard copies of all the decisions were filed. This resulted in a duplication of data and drawings, and it took hours to locate a specific BOM. To solve this issue, the company has now developed an Oracle-based enterprise system which runs all applications for the different functional departments. The system keeps a dump of all the BOMs, indents, purchase orders, Gate Receiving Slips (GRS), bills, quality reports, vendor reports, suggestion forms, codes, and vendor and drawing numbers. All this data can be accessed using an employee ID.

All the reports within a period of six months can be directly accessed through a special permission. Once an order is confirmed, the concerned departments give their feedback to the PPC division with the time period required to process the order. If there is any deviation from the actual, expected time, the company has processes in place to overcome the gaps in scheduling, both at the customer and manufacturer ends. Using a uniform tracking system, all departments can plan their work to achieve one common goal of delivering the product to the customer.

The PPC department uses the enterprise system to integrate the various departments so that they can work with one another better. Earlier, to create an indent, a hard copy was required to be generated and personally approved by the various authorized personnel. But now, an executive simply needs to put in the name or code of the item into the enterprise system, and its various specifications, cost, vendors, and inventory status can be fetched at a moment's notice. Departments can now order the required raw material from a centralized store and make indents. If the store does not have adequate quantities of the required material, it knows exactly when to release purchase orders to procure those materials from outside.

The store is the major user of the enterprise system, with thousands of items in its listing. Materials are categorized into semi-finished and finished products. The company outsources its pre-paint assemblies and assembles the semi-finished materials inside the plant. The finished products include every item, from screws to finished assemblies. The store keeps a record of all these items and assigns a unique code to each. Whenever a new product is added to the system, a BOM is raised for it and circulated among all the departments. As the company is ISO-certified, every new revision of the BOM and the drawings is highlighted and re-circulated for approval. Moreover, dynamic conditions and stiff competition demand regular modification in the designs and constant re-engineering of the product. This calls for a constant change in specifications and costs. The enterprise system takes care of this without sweat: all the store manager needs to do is make modification, and the changes are communicated to every functional department that has access to the BOM.

Sources: Ackermanns & Helden, v., 2002. *Critical success factors concerning ERP systems implementation*. s.l.:s.n; Al-Mashari, M., Zairi, M. & Al-Mudimigh, A., 2010. ERP Implementation: An Integrated Methodology. *European Center for best practice management*; Bancroft, N., Seip, H. & Sprengel, A., n.d. *Implementing SAP R/3: How to introduce a large system into a large organization*. S.l.: Manning Publication Co., USA1998; Berry, B., 2008. *Aligning Enterprise Architecture and ERP*. Oregon: s.n; Chang, S. -I., 2004. ERP *Life cycle Implementation, Management and Support: Implications for Practice and Research*. Hawaii, 37th Hawaii International Conference on System Sciences; Davenport, T., 1998. *Putting the Enterprise into the Enterprise System*. S.l.: Harvard Business Review; Davenport, T. H., 2000. *Mission Critical: Realizing the Promise of Enterprise Systems*. 1st Ed. S.l.: Harvard Business Press; Gibson, N. & Holland, C. a. L. B., 1999. A Case Study of a fast Track SAP R/3 Implementation at Guilbert. *Electronic Markets*, Issue June, pp. 190–193; Ginzberg, M., 1981. Early Diagnosis of MIS Implementation Failure: Promising Results and Unanswered Questions. *Management Science*, 27(4), pp. 459–476; Gupta, A., 2000. Enterprise Resource Planning: the emerging organizational value systems. *Industrial Management and data systems*, 100(3), pp. 114–118; Holland, C. & Light, B.,

1999. A Critical Success Factors Model for ERP implementation. *IEEE Software*, May/ June, pp. 30–35; *How CISCO IT upgraded Its ERP Purchasing Module* (1992-2007) Cisco System, Inc.; Idorn, N., 2008. *A business process management approach to ERP implementation. A study of ERP implementation in the light of third wave of Process Management*. s.l.:s.n; Jarrar, Y., Al-Mudimmigh, A. & Zairi, M., 2000. ERP implementation critical success factors–the role and impact of business process management. *Management of Innovation and Technology*, Volume I, pp. 122-127; Johansson, B. & Sudzina, F., 2009. How factors affecting selection of implementation approach influence ERP system implementation costs. *17th European Conference on Information Systems*; Klaus, H., Rosemann, M. & Gable, G., 2000. What is ERP?. *Information Systems Frontiers*, II(2), pp. 141–162; Koen, H. & Noordveld, P., n.d. *BPM based ERP Implementation*. s.l.:s.n; Mabert, V., Soni, A. & Venkataraman, M., 2003. The impact of organizational size on ERP implementation in the U.S. manufacturing sector. *Omega*, 20(2), pp. 235–246; Mandal, P. & Gunasekaran, A., 2003. Issues in implementing ERP: A Case Study. *European Journal of Operational Research*, Volume 146, pp. 274–283; Martin, M., 1998. An ERP Strategy. *Fortune*, pp. 149–151; Prouty, K., 2011. *ERP much better off with than without (Analyst Insight)*, s.l.: Aberdeen Group; Sadagopan, S., 1999. ERP: *A Managerial Perspective*. s.l.:Tata McGraw Hill Education Private Limited; Sage, 2011. *White paper on ERP - Building on the Basics*, s.l.: Sage; Seranmadevi, R. & Natarajan, M. L., 2009. Extended Enterprise Application Software - An Indian Perspective - "Zeal to Zenith". *Journal of Computer Applications*, II(3); Sheikh, K., 2001. An Introduction to ERP: Arcitecture, Implementation and Cases. In: *Manufacturing Resource Planning (MRP II) with introduction to ERP, SCM and CRM*. New Delhi: Tata McGraw Hill, pp. 494–537; Sumner, M., 1999. Critical Success Factors in *Enterprise Wide Information Management Systems Projects*. s.l., AMICS; Wagle, D., 1998. The case for ERP systems. *The McKniseys Quarterly (2)*, pp. 130–138; Welti, N., 1999. *Successful SAP R/3 Implementation: Practical Management of ERP projects*. USA: Addison Wesley Longman Limited; Yusuf, Y., Gunasekaran, A. & Abthorpe, M. S., 2004. Enterprise Information System Project Implementation: A Case Study of ERP in Rolls Royce. *International Journal of Production Economics*, Volume 87, pp. 251-266.

The experience of Azure Medical Systems illustrates how much organizations these days rely on information system to improve their performance and remain competitive. It also shows how much system supporting collaboration and coordination between departments can make a difference in improving the efficiency of operations at a manufacturing plant.

The chapter-opening diagram calls for attention to important points raised by this case and this chapter. Azure is a leading manufacturer of X-ray field equipments with a clear focus on forecasting, accurate planning, and innovating, but it was hampered by outdated processes for managing information that prevented various departments from working efficiently and effectively. Hence, the company decided to move away from the conventional email system to enterprise system through which various departments could coordinate their activities. The Oracle-based enterprise system ran all the applications for different departments, and as a result of which Azure is able to solve problems posed by conventional email system. The enterprise system helped Azure Medical Systems integrate all the key activities of the manufacturing cycle. Apart from managing the key operations of the PPC department, the enterprise system also helped Azure to efficiently manage the items in the store department. With this system, a store manager at Azure can now communicate all the changes in costing and specifications to every functional department because of the fact that every department is seamlessly integrated applying enterprise system.

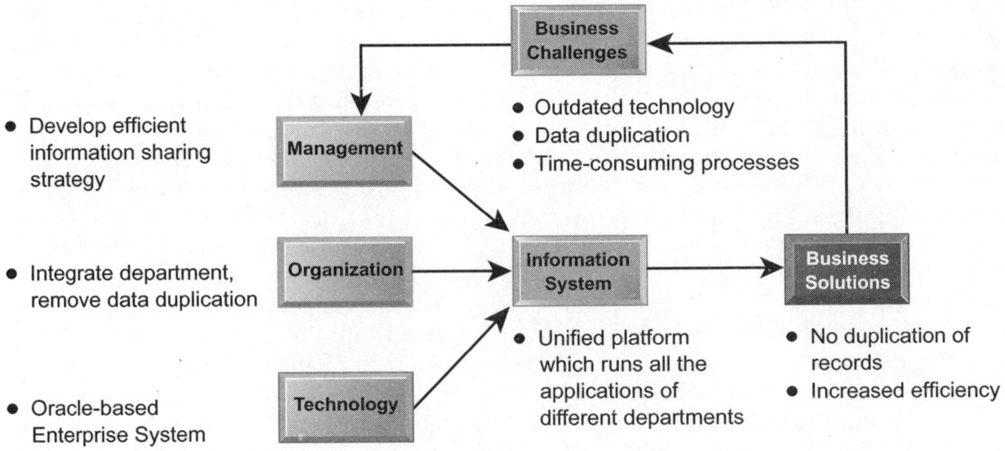

2-1 What are business processes? How are they related to information systems?

In order to operate, businesses must deal with many different pieces of information about suppliers, customers, employees, invoices, and payments, and of course their products and services. They must organize work activities that use this information to operate efficiently and enhance the overall performance of the firm. Information systems make it possible for firms to manage all their information, make better decisions, and improve the execution of their business processes.

Business Processes

Business processes, which we introduced in Chapter 1, refer to the manner in which work is organized, coordinated, and focused to produce a valuable product or service. Business processes are the collection of activities required to produce a product or service. These activities are supported by flows of material, information, and knowledge among the participants in business processes. Business processes also refer to the unique ways in which organizations coordinate work, information, and knowledge and the ways in which management chooses to coordinate work.

To a large extent, the performance of a business firm depends on how well its business processes are designed and coordinated. A company's business processes can be a source of competitive strength if they enable the company to innovate or to execute better than its rivals. Business processes can also be liabilities if they are based on inefficient ways of working that impede organizational responsiveness and efficiency. The chapter-opening case describing Azure's improvements in processes used for collaboration and communication clearly illustrates these points, as do many of the other cases in this text.

Every business can be seen as a collection of business processes, some of which are part of larger encompassing processes. For instance, uses of mentoring, wikis, blogs, and videos are all part of the overall knowledge management process. Many business processes are tied to a specific functional area.

TABLE 2.1 EXAMPLES OF FUNCTIONAL BUSINESS PROCESSES

FUNCTIONAL AREA	BUSINESS PROCESS
Manufacturing and production	Assembling the product Checking for quality Producing bills of materials
Sales and marketing	Identifying customers Making customers aware of the product Selling the product
Finance and accounting	Paying creditors Creating financial statements Managing cash accounts
Human resources	Hiring employees Evaluating employees' job performance Enrolling employees in benefits plans

For example, the sales and marketing function is responsible for identifying customers, and the human resources function is responsible for hiring employees. Table 2.1 describes some typical business processes for each of the functional areas of business.

Other business processes cross many different functional areas and require coordination across departments. For instance, consider the seemingly simple business process of fulfilling a customer order (see Figure 2.1). Initially, the sales department receives a sales order. The order passes first to accounting to ensure the customer can pay for the order either by a credit verification or request for immediate payment prior to shipping. Once the customer credit is established, the production department pulls the product from inventory or produces the

FIGURE 2.1 THE ORDER FULFILLMENT PROCESS

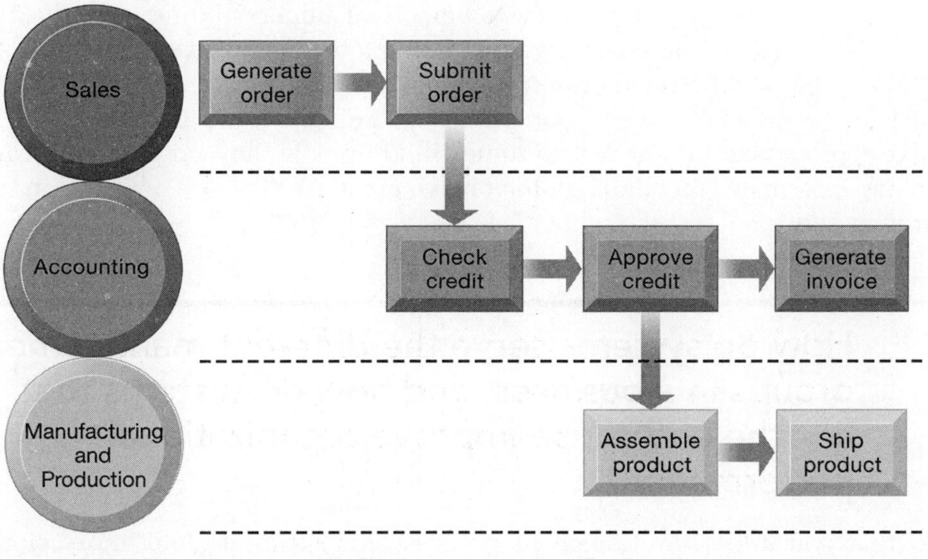

Fulfilling a customer order involves a complex set of steps that requires the close coordination of the sales, accounting, and manufacturing functions.

product. Then the product is shipped (and this may require working with a logistics firm, such as UPS or FedEx). A bill or invoice is generated by the accounting department, and a notice is sent to the customer indicating that the product has shipped. The sales department is notified of the shipment and prepares to support the customer by answering calls or fulfilling warranty claims.

What at first appears to be a simple process, fulfilling an order, turns out to be a very complicated series of business processes that require the close coordination of major functional groups in a firm. Moreover, to efficiently perform all these steps in the order fulfillment process requires a great deal of information. The required information must flow rapidly within the firm from one decision maker to another; with business partners, such as delivery firms; and with the customer. Computer-based information systems make this possible.

How Information Technology Improves Business Processes

Exactly how do information systems improve business processes? Information systems automate many steps in business processes that were formerly performed manually, such as checking a client's credit or generating an invoice and shipping order. But today, information technology can do much more. New technology can actually change the flow of information, making it possible for many more people to access and share information, replacing sequential steps with tasks that can be performed simultaneously, and eliminating delays in decision making. New information technology frequently changes the way a business works and supports entirely new business models. Downloading a Kindle e-book from Amazon, buying a computer online at Best Buy, and downloading a music track from iTunes are entirely new business processes based on new business models that would be inconceivable without today's information technology.

That's why it's so important to pay close attention to business processes, both in your information systems course and in your future career. By analyzing business processes, you can achieve a very clear understanding of how a business actually works. Moreover, by conducting a business process analysis, you will also begin to understand how to change the business by improving its processes to make it more efficient or effective. Throughout this book, we examine business processes with a view to understanding how they might be improved by using information technology to achieve greater efficiency, innovation, and customer service.

2-2 How do systems serve the different management groups in a business, and how do systems that link the enterprise improve organizational performance?

Now that you understand business processes, it is time to look more closely at how information systems support the business processes of a firm. Because there are different interests, specialties, and levels in an organization, there are different kinds of systems. No single system can provide all the information an organization needs.

A typical business organization has systems supporting processes for each of the major business functions—sales and marketing, manufacturing and production, finance and accounting, and human resources. You can find examples of systems for each of these business functions in the Learning Tracks for this chapter. Functional systems that operate independently of each other are becoming a thing of the past because they cannot easily share information to support cross-functional business processes. Many have been replaced with large-scale cross-functional systems that integrate the activities of related business processes and organizational units. We describe these integrated cross-functional applications later in this section.

A typical firm also has different systems supporting the decision-making needs of each of the main management groups we described in Chapter 1. Operational management, middle management, and senior management each use systems to support the decisions they must make to run the company. Let's look at these systems and the types of decisions they support.

Systems for Different Management Groups

A business firm has systems to support different groups or levels of management. These systems include transaction processing systems and systems for business intelligence.

Transaction Processing Systems

Operational managers need systems that keep track of the elementary activities and transactions of the organization, such as sales, receipts, cash deposits, payroll, credit decisions, and the flow of materials in a factory. **Transaction processing systems (TPS)** provide this kind of information. A transaction processing system is a computerized system that performs and records the daily routine transactions necessary to conduct business, such as sales order entry, hotel reservations, payroll, employee record keeping, and shipping.

The principal purpose of systems at this level is to answer routine questions and to track the flow of transactions through the organization. How many parts are in inventory? What happened to Mr. Smith's payment? To answer these kinds of questions, information generally must be easily available, current, and accurate.

At the operational level, tasks, resources, and goals are predefined and highly structured. The decision to grant credit to a customer, for instance, is made by a lower-level supervisor according to predefined criteria. All that must be determined is whether the customer meets the criteria.

Figure 2.2 illustrates a TPS for payroll processing. A payroll system keeps track of money paid to employees. An employee time sheet with the employee's name, social security number, and number of hours worked per week represents a single transaction for this system. Once this transaction is input into the system, it updates the system's master file (or database—see Chapter 6) that permanently maintains employee information for the organization. The

FIGURE 2.2 A PAYROLL TPS

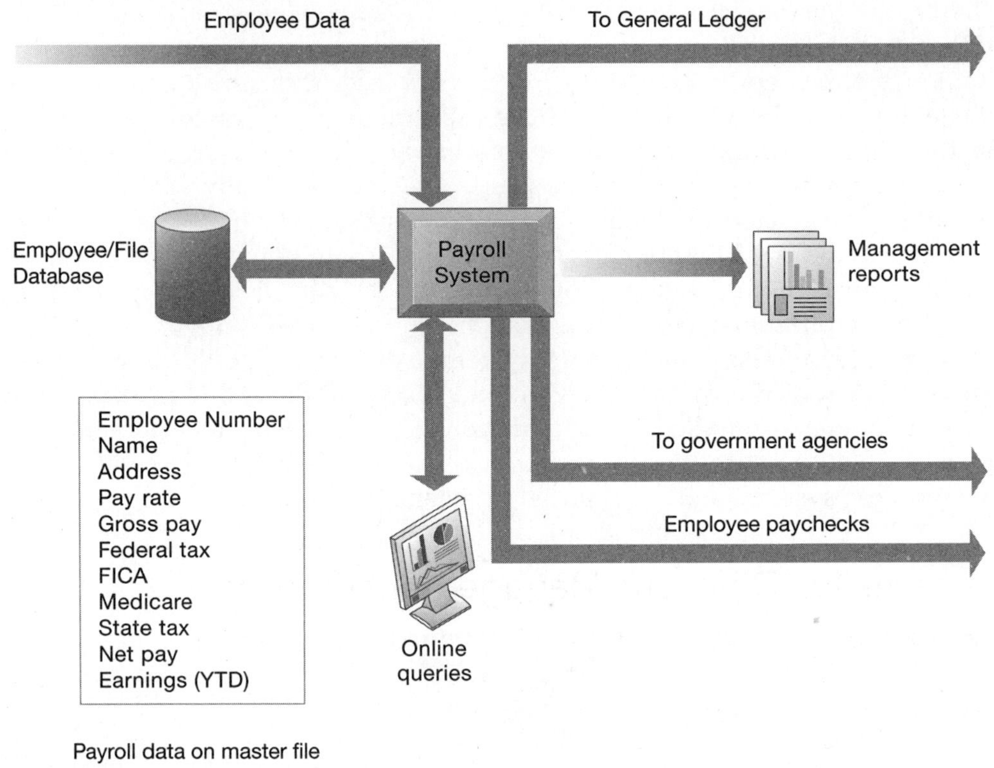

A TPS for payroll processing captures employee payment transaction data (such as a time card). System outputs include online and hard-copy reports for management and employee paychecks.

data in the system are combined in different ways to create reports of interest to management and government agencies and to send paychecks to employees.

Managers need TPS to monitor the status of internal operations and the firm's relations with the external environment. TPS are also major producers of information for the other systems and business functions. For example, the payroll system illustrated in Figure 2.2, along with other accounting TPS, supplies data to the company's general ledger system, which is responsible for maintaining records of the firm's income and expenses and for producing reports such as income statements and balance sheets. It also supplies employee payment history data for insurance, pension, and other benefits calculations to the firm's human resources function and employee payment data to government agencies such as the U.S. Internal Revenue Service and Social Security Administration.

Transaction processing systems are often so central to a business that TPS failure for a few hours can lead to a firm's demise and perhaps that of other firms linked to it. Imagine what would happen to UPS if its package tracking system was not working! What would the airlines do without their computerized reservation systems?

Systems for Business Intelligence

Firms also have business intelligence systems that focus on delivering information to support management decision making. **Business intelligence** is a contemporary term for data and software tools for organizing, analyzing, and providing access to data to help managers and other enterprise users make more informed decisions. Business intelligence addresses the decision-making needs of all levels of management. This section provides a brief introduction to business intelligence. You'll learn more about this topic in Chapters 6 and 12.

Business intelligence systems for middle management help with monitoring, controlling, decision-making, and administrative activities. In Chapter 1, we defined management information systems as the study of information systems in business and management. The term **management information systems (MIS)** also designates a specific category of information systems serving middle management. MIS provide middle managers with reports on the organization's current performance. This information is used to monitor and control the business and predict future performance.

MIS summarize and report on the company's basic operations using data supplied by transaction processing systems. The basic transaction data from TPS are compressed and usually presented in reports that are produced on a regular schedule. Today, many of these reports are delivered online. Figure 2.3 shows how a typical MIS transforms transaction-level data from inventory, production, and accounting into MIS files that are used to provide managers with reports. Figure 2.4 shows a sample report from this system.

FIGURE 2.3 HOW MANAGEMENT INFORMATION SYSTEMS OBTAIN THEIR DATA FROM THE ORGANIZATION'S TPS

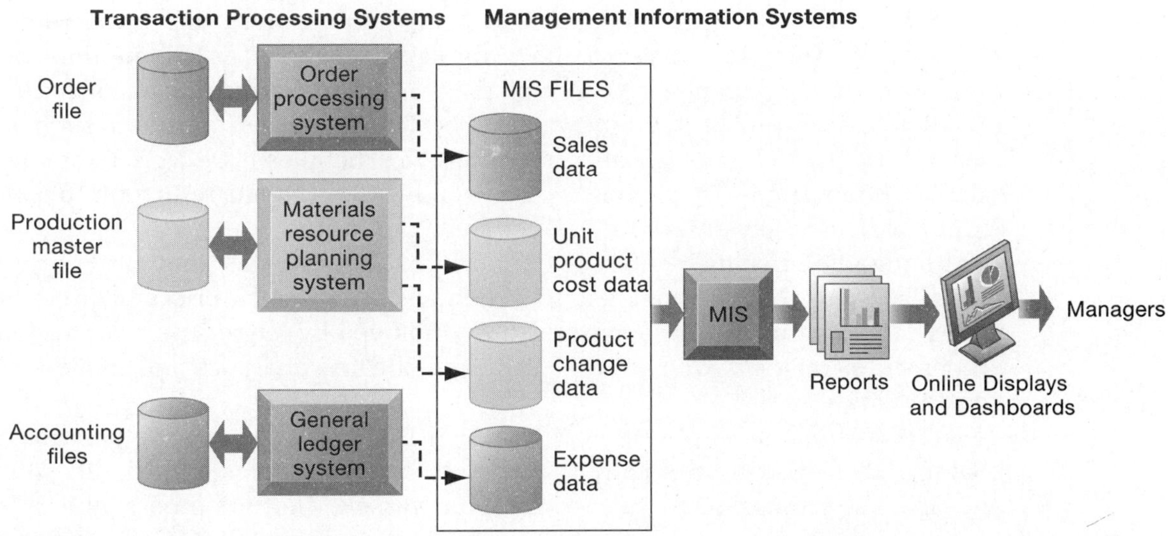

In the system illustrated by this diagram, three TPS supply summarized transaction data to the MIS reporting system at the end of the time period. Managers gain access to the organizational data through the MIS, which provides them with the appropriate reports.

FIGURE 2.4 SAMPLE MIS REPORT

Consolidated Consumer Products Corporation Sales by Product and Sales Region: 2017

PRODUCT CODE	PRODUCT DESCRIPTION	SALES REGION	ACTUAL SALES	PLANNED	ACTUAL versus PLANNED
4469	Carpet Cleaner	Northeast	4,066,700	4,800,000	0.85
		South	3,778,112	3,750,000	1.01
		Midwest	4,867,001	4,600,000	1.06
		West	4,003,440	4,400,000	0.91
	TOTAL		16,715,253	17,550,000	0.95
5674	Room Freshener	Northeast	3,676,700	3,900,000	0.94
		South	5,608,112	4,700,000	1.19
		Midwest	4,711,001	4,200,000	1.12
		West	4,563,440	4,900,000	0.93
	TOTAL		18,559,253	17,700,000	1.05

This report, showing summarized annual sales data, was produced by the MIS in Figure 2.3.

MIS typically provide answers to routine questions that have been specified in advance and have a predefined procedure for answering them. For instance, MIS reports might list the total pounds of lettuce used this quarter by a fast-food chain or, as illustrated in Figure 2.4, compare total annual sales figures for specific products to planned targets. These systems generally are not flexible and have little analytical capability. Most MIS use simple routines, such as summaries and comparisons, as opposed to sophisticated mathematical models or statistical techniques.

Other types of business intelligence systems support more non-routine decision making. **Decision-support systems (DSS)** focus on problems that are unique and rapidly changing, for which the procedure for arriving at a solution may not be fully predefined in advance. They try to answer questions such as these: What would be the impact on production schedules if we were to double sales in the month of December? What would happen to our return on investment if a factory schedule were delayed for six months?

Although DSS use internal information from TPS and MIS, they often bring in information from external sources, such as current stock prices or product prices of competitors. These systems are employed by "super-user" managers and business analysts who want to use sophisticated analytics and models to analyze data.

An interesting, small, but powerful DSS is the voyage-estimating system of a large global shipping company that transports bulk cargoes of coal, oil, ores, and finished products. The firm owns some vessels, charters others, and bids for shipping contracts in the open market to carry general cargo. A voyage-estimating system calculates financial and technical voyage details. Financial calculations include ship/time costs (fuel, labor, capital), freight rates for various types of cargo, and port expenses. Technical details include a myriad of factors,

FIGURE 2.5 **VOYAGE-ESTIMATING DECISION-SUPPORT SYSTEM**

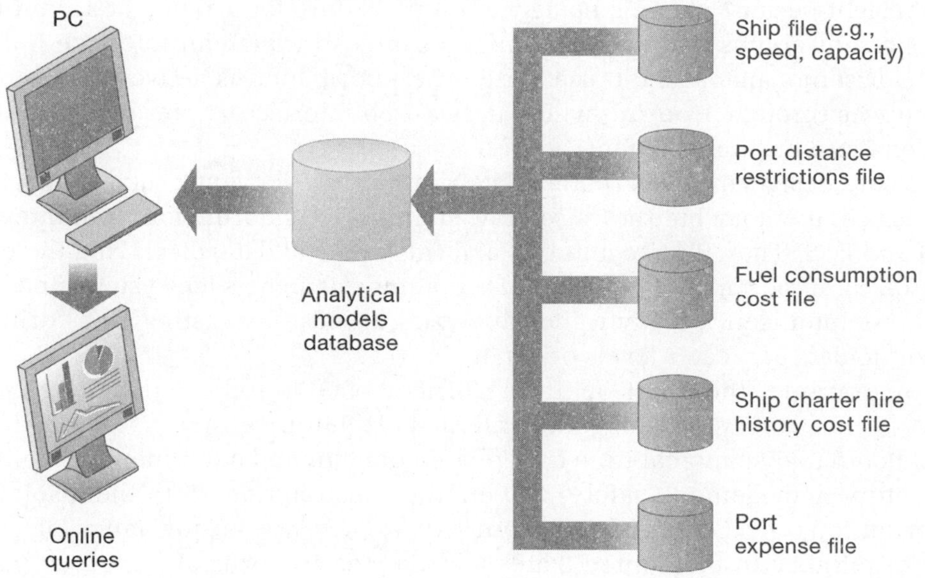

This DSS operates on a powerful PC. It is used daily by managers who must develop bids on shipping contracts.

such as ship cargo capacity, speed, port distances, fuel and water consumption, and loading patterns (location of cargo for different ports).

The system can answer questions such as the following: Given a customer delivery schedule and an offered freight rate, which vessel should be assigned at what rate to maximize profits? What is the optimal speed at which a particular vessel can optimize its profit and still meet its delivery schedule? What is the optimal loading pattern for a ship bound for the U.S. West Coast from Malaysia? Figure 2.5 illustrates the DSS built for this company. The system operates on a powerful desktop personal computer, providing a system of menus that makes it easy for users to enter data or obtain information.

The voyage-estimating DSS we have just described draws heavily on models. Other business intelligence systems are more data-driven, focusing instead on extracting useful information from very large quantities of data. For example, large ski resort companies such as Intrawest and Vail Resorts collect and store large amounts of customer data from call centers, lodging and dining reservations, ski schools, and ski equipment rental stores. They use special software to analyze these data to determine the value, revenue potential, and loyalty of each customer to help managers make better decisions about how to target their marketing programs.

Business intelligence systems also address the decision-making needs of senior management. Senior managers need systems that focus on strategic issues and long-term trends, both in the firm and in the external environment. They are concerned with questions such as: What will employment levels be in five years? What are the long-term industry cost trends? What products should we be making in five years?

Executive support systems (ESS) help senior management make these decisions. They address nonroutine decisions requiring judgment, evaluation, and insight because there is no agreed-on procedure for arriving at a solution. ESS present graphs and data from many sources through an interface that is easy for senior managers to use. Often the information is delivered to senior executives through a **portal**, which uses a web interface to present integrated personalized business content.

ESS are designed to incorporate data about external events, such as new tax laws or competitors, but they also draw summarized information from internal MIS and DSS. They filter, compress, and track critical data, displaying the data of greatest importance to senior managers. Increasingly, such systems include business intelligence analytics for analyzing trends, forecasting, and "drilling down" to data at greater levels of detail.

For example, the chief operating officer (COO) and plant managers at Valero, the world's largest independent petroleum refiner, use a Refining Dashboard to display real-time data related to plant and equipment reliability, inventory management, safety, and energy consumption. With the displayed information, the COO and his team can review the performance of each Valero refinery in the United States and Canada in terms of how each plant is performing compared to the production plan of the firm. The headquarters group can drill down to from executive level to refinery level and individual system-operator level displays of performance. Valero's Refining Dashboard is

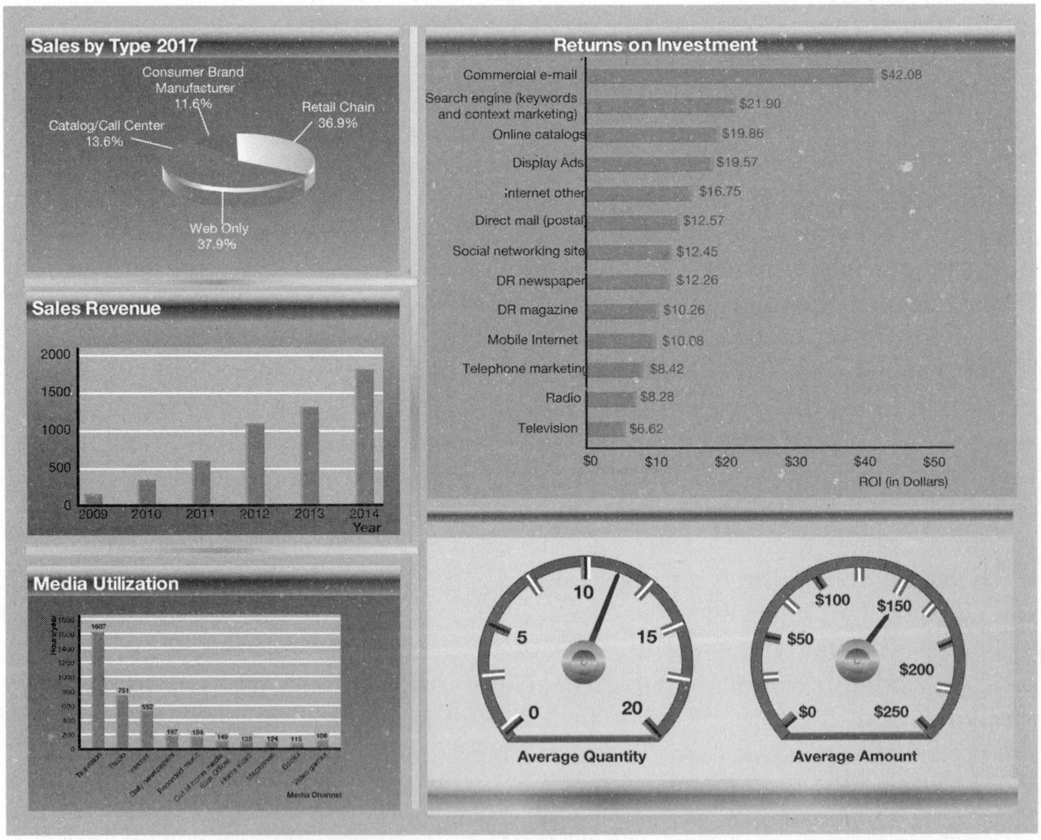

A digital dashboard delivers comprehensive and accurate information for decision making, often using a single screen. The graphical overview of key performance indicators helps managers quickly spot areas that need attention.

Management

an example of a **digital dashboard**, which displays on a single screen graphs and charts of key performance indicators for managing a company. Digital dashboards are becoming an increasingly popular tool for management decision makers.

The Interactive Session on Technology describes real-world examples of several of these types of systems used by an organization with employees and staff members working all over the world. Note the types of systems illustrated by this case and the role they play in improving both operations and decision making.

Systems for Linking the Enterprise

Reviewing all the different types of systems we have just described, you might wonder how a business can manage all the information in these different systems. You might also wonder how costly it is to maintain so many different systems. And you might wonder how all these different systems can share information and how managers and employees are able to coordinate their work. In fact, these are all important questions for businesses today.

Enterprise Applications

Getting all the different kinds of systems in a company to work together has proven a major challenge. Typically, corporations are put together both through normal "organic" growth and through acquisition of smaller firms. Over a period of time, corporations end up with a collection of systems, most of them older, and face the challenge of getting them all to "talk" with one another and work together as one corporate system. There are several solutions to this problem.

One solution is to implement **enterprise applications**, which are systems that span functional areas, focus on executing business processes across the business firm, and include all levels of management. Enterprise applications help businesses become more flexible and productive by coordinating their business processes more closely and integrating groups of processes so they focus on efficient management of resources and customer service.

There are four major enterprise applications: enterprise systems, supply chain management systems, customer relationship management systems, and knowledge management systems. Each of these enterprise applications integrates a related set of functions and business processes to enhance the performance of the organization as a whole. Figure 2.6 shows that the architecture for these enterprise applications encompasses processes spanning the entire organization and, in some cases, extending beyond the organization to customers, suppliers, and other key business partners.

Enterprise Systems Firms use **enterprise systems**, also known as enterprise resource planning (ERP) systems, to integrate business processes in manufacturing and production, finance and accounting, sales and marketing, and human resources into a single software system. Information that was previously fragmented in many different systems is stored in a single comprehensive data repository where it can be used by many different parts of the business.

INTERACTIVE SESSION: TECHNOLOGY

HDFC Banking on Business Intelligence and Analytics Technology

Housing Development Finance Corporation Limited (HDFC) was among the first financial bodies to receive an in-principle approval from the Reserve Bank of India (RBI) to set up a bank in the private sector. This was part of RBI's liberalization plan for the Indian banking industry in 1994. The bank was incorporated in August 1994 as HDFC Bank Limited, with its registered offices in Mumbai. HDFC Bank commenced operations as a scheduled commercial bank in January 1995. It was the first bank in the country to adopt new-age technology in its banking operations. More than 65 percent of its current customers conduct banking transactions through online direct channels.

HDFC partnered with the Statistical Analysis System (SAS) Institute to apply business intelligence and analytics technology in order to take vital decisions in the diverse areas of banking. As a first step, it integrated its CRM solution with the SAS analytics suite. In this manner, SAS analytics could be deployed on the entire customer database. This gave HDFC a greater insight into customer behavior and encouraged the bank to cross-sell. For example, bank executives were easily able to figure out if a customer had an active account or just a salary account. Besides, they could also determine if the customer used the HDFC account as a primary account.

Since the SAS analytics suite was implemented on top of the bank's data warehouse, it offered the bank a consolidated, 360-degree view of its customers—relating to all the customer interactions with the bank, be it for the credit card facility, fixed deposits, or asset accounts. The analytics allowed for the segmentation of customers and the identification of "imperia customers". These were customers who ranked high in the bank's value chain because of the high profit margins they represented. The bank's executives could aggressively target these customers, who were said to bring in great profits at comparatively lower costs to the bank.

The SAS tool also provided suggestions for the kind of products that should be sold to specific customers. Based on the customer's profile, behavior, and lifecycle, SAS identified the products that the customer was most likely to find viable or attractive. Based on the advanced statistical models, a solution for customer acquisition, customer retention, and value management was generated. This reduced the turnaround time and increased the response rate for each marketing campaign. More than 70 percent of HDFC's credit cards have been sold to customers with existing savings or salary accounts with the bank. This has proven the effectiveness of the SAS model, which has been able to utilize customer data and assign buying and spending propensities to each customer.

The SAS tool has also enabled the bank to identify suspicious activities in banking transactions such as large cash deposit, sudden withdrawals in otherwise dormant accounts, movement of money into multiple accounts (called "layering"), or opening several accounts within a short period of time. All this is part of the Anti-Money Laundering (AML) regulations. Similarly, the bank is also KYC-complaint. The SAS application cleanses customer data and classifies each profile into good or bad. This way, when a customer opens an account with the bank, the SAS analytics tool can identify the bad profiles with ease. The identification of suspicious activity by the SAS tool is so comprehensive and reliable that these records are valuable even to the Financial Intelligence Unit.

HDFC has implemented a fast-track retail loan (home, car, or personal) process for amounts of less than five lakh rupees. Customers can now track the status of their loan application online within minutes of applying (the same process took 24 hours earlier). Given that HDFC processes eight to ten thousand loan applications in a span of eight hours, a speedy credit approval process has proved to be a blessing and has been made possible due to the robust and dependable technology offered by SAS. When a customer applies for a loan online, the SAS analytics tool verifies the customer's identity. The analytical models are then run on top of the customer's data to generate certain metrics, such as the application score and propensity to default. Loan approvers have all the information they need to make their decision within minutes. The customers can also determine the loan amount and tenure of repayment that they are eligible for based on their current income, among other factors.

For wholesale credit approval, a slightly different approach is followed. Using the specific analytical models developed for each segment of wholesale credit (such as those for large corporates, SME-manufacturing, SME-services, and so on) risks for each segments are assessed. These might be individual risk, business risk, management risk, and financial risk. Based on the output from each of the four categories, the weighted aggregate is computed and the application is rated on a scale of 1 to 10, where 1 is the best score and 10, the worst.

Using the SAS application, HDFC can identify the debt exposure of each customer. Each month, HDFC rejects up to 2 percent of the loan applications because of the applicant's record of defaulting on repayment. This way, the bank has been able to reduce its losses by nearly 1 percent.

The bank rightly credits its power of effective decision making to the success of the SAS tool. HDFC has ambitious plans for the future. It aims to inculcate analytics in its strategic decisions as well. The bank is also working on using analytics to measure channel efficiency and allocate resources. Since customers can now be reached through a variety of channels such as phones, e-mail, social networks, and so on, this analysis will help examine the different parameters of costs, usage, or efficiency for each channel. It will be useful in identifying the best channel through which a customer can be reached. Also, it will allow the bank to determine how much should be spent on each channel to optimize the profits.

Sources: "Improve cross-selling capabilities". Retrieved from http://www.sas.com, (Navigation > Home > English-US > Customer > HDFC), as accessed on 02 November 2017 at 2pm IST; "HDFC Bank signs Analytics Service Agreement", *Money Control*. Retrieved from http://www.moneycontrol.com/, (Navigation > Home > News > Business > Article), as accessed on 02 November 2017 at 2pm IST; Shah, Aatash, "Banking on Big Data analytics" (2014). Retrieved from http://www.edvancer.in as accessed on 02 November 2017 at 2pm IST; "Credit Risk", *WikiInvest*. Retrieved from http://www.wikinvest.com as accessed on 02 November 2017 at 2pm IST; "HDFC Bank uses SAS analytics to streamline cross-selling" (2010). Retrieved from https://www.youtube.com as accessed on 02 November 2017 at 2pm IST.

CASE STUDY QUESTIONS

1. What are the benefits of integrating the SAS analytics suite with the HDFC Bank's CRM?
2. How does the SAS analytics ensure that HDFC Bank is compliant with the Anti-Money Laundering (AML) regulations?
3. Discuss the use of SAS analytics in loan processing at the HDFC Bank.
4. What do you understand by debt exposure and the role of analytics in determining it?
5. What is the future of analytics at HDFC Bank?

For example, when a customer places an order, the order data flow automatically to other parts of the company that are affected by them. The order transaction triggers the warehouse to pick the ordered products and schedule shipment. The warehouse informs the factory to replenish whatever has been depleted. The accounting department is notified to send the customer an invoice. Customer service representatives track the progress of the order through every step to inform customers about the status of their orders. Managers are able to use firmwide information to make more precise and timely decisions about daily operations and longer-term planning.

Supply Chain Management Systems Firms use **supply chain management (SCM) systems** to help manage relationships with their suppliers. These systems help suppliers, purchasing firms, distributors, and logistics companies share

FIGURE 2.6 ENTERPRISE APPLICATION ARCHITECTURE

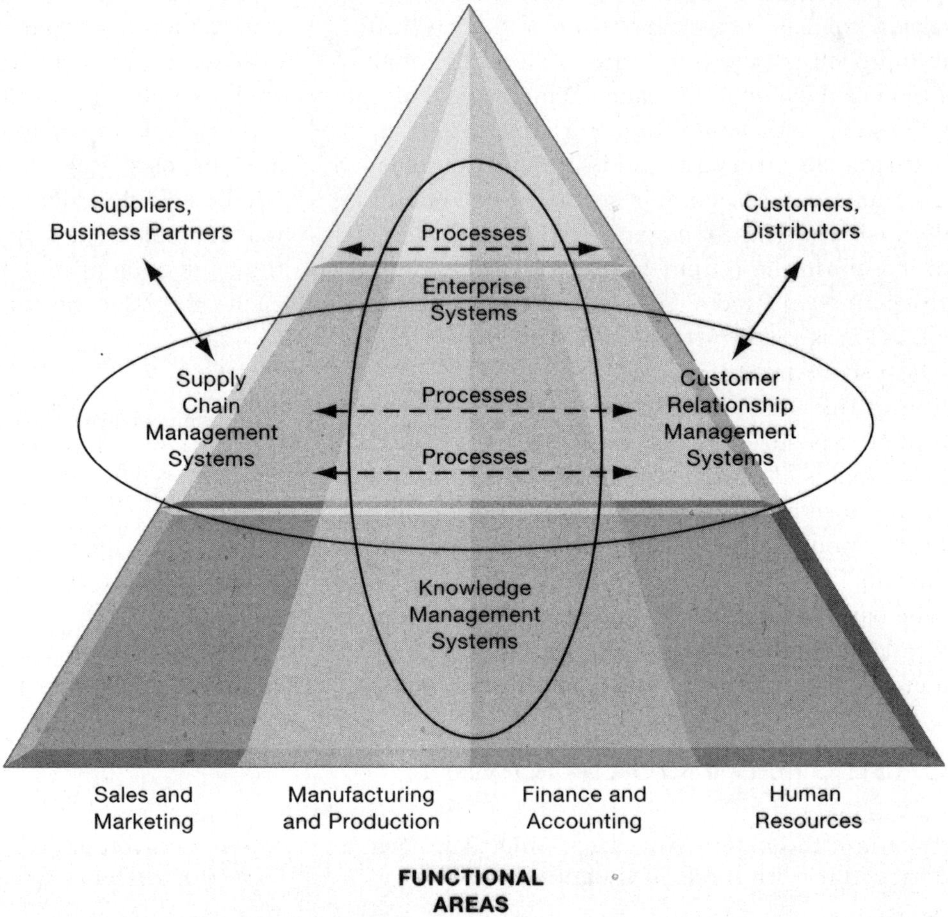

Enterprise applications automate processes that span multiple business functions and organizational levels and may extend outside the organization.

information about orders, production, inventory levels, and delivery of products and services so they can source, produce, and deliver goods and services efficiently. The ultimate objective is to get the right amount of their products from their source to their point of consumption in the least amount of time and at the lowest cost. These systems increase firm profitability by lowering the costs of moving and making products and by enabling managers to make better decisions about how to organize and schedule sourcing, production, and distribution.

Supply chain management systems are one type of **interorganizational system** because they automate the flow of information across organizational boundaries. You will find examples of other types of interorganizational information systems throughout this text because such systems make it possible for firms to link digitally to customers and to outsource their work to other companies.

Customer Relationship Management Systems Firms use **customer relationship management (CRM) systems** to help manage their relationships with their customers. CRM systems provide information to coordinate all of the business processes that deal with customers in sales, marketing, and service to optimize revenue, customer satisfaction, and customer retention. This information helps firms identify, attract, and retain the most profitable customers; provide better service to existing customers; and increase sales.

Knowledge Management Systems Some firms perform better than others because they have better knowledge about how to create, produce, and deliver products and services. This firm knowledge is unique, is difficult to imitate, and can be leveraged into long-term strategic benefits. **Knowledge management systems (KMS)** enable organizations to better manage processes for capturing and applying knowledge and expertise. These systems collect all relevant knowledge and experience in the firm and make it available wherever and whenever it is needed to improve business processes and management decisions. They also link the firm to external sources of knowledge.

We examine enterprise systems and systems for supply chain management and customer relationship management in greater detail in Chapter 9. We discuss collaboration systems that support knowledge management in this chapter and cover other types of knowledge management applications in Chapter 11.

Intranets and Extranets

Enterprise applications create deep-seated changes in the way the firm conducts its business, offering many opportunities to integrate important business data into a single system. They are often costly and difficult to implement. Intranets and extranets deserve mention here as alternative tools for increasing integration and expediting the flow of information within the firm and with customers and suppliers.

Intranets are simply internal company websites that are accessible only by employees. The term *intranet* refers to an internal network, in contrast to the Internet, which is a public network linking organizations and other external networks. Intranets use the same technologies and techniques as the larger Internet, and they often are simply a private access area in a larger company website. Likewise with extranets, which are company websites that are accessible to authorized vendors and suppliers and are often used to coordinate the movement of supplies to the firm's production apparatus.

For example, Six Flags, which operates 18 theme parks throughout North America, maintains an intranet for its 1900 full-time employees that provides company-related news and information on each park's day-to-day operations, including weather forecasts, performance schedules, and details about groups and celebrities visiting the parks. The company also uses an extranet to broadcast information about schedule changes and park events to its 30,000 seasonal employees. We describe the technology for intranets and extranets in more detail in Chapter 7.

E-business, E-commerce, and E-government

The systems and technologies we have just described are transforming firms' relationships with customers, employees, suppliers, and logistic partners into digital relationships using networks and the Internet. So much business is now enabled by or based upon digital networks that we use the terms *electronic business* and *electronic commerce* frequently throughout this text.

Electronic business, or **e-business**, refers to the use of digital technology and the Internet to execute the major business processes in the enterprise. E-business includes activities for the internal management of the firm and for coordination with suppliers and other business partners. It also includes **electronic commerce**, or **e-commerce**.

E-commerce is the part of e-business that deals with the buying and selling of goods and services over the Internet. It also encompasses activities supporting those market transactions, such as advertising, marketing, customer support, security, delivery, and payment.

The technologies associated with e-business have also brought about similar changes in the public sector. Governments on all levels are using Internet technology to deliver information and services to citizens, employees, and businesses with which they work. **E-government** refers to the application of the Internet and networking technologies to digitally enable government and public sector agencies' relationships with citizens, businesses, and other arms of government.

In addition to improving delivery of government services, e-government makes government operations more efficient and also empowers citizens by giving them easier access to information and the ability to network electronically with other citizens. For example, citizens in some states can renew their driver's licenses or apply for unemployment benefits online, and the Internet has become a powerful tool for instantly mobilizing interest groups for political action and fund-raising.

2-3 Why are systems for collaboration and social business so important, and what technologies do they use?

With all these systems and information, you might wonder how is it possible to make sense of them. How do people working in firms pull it all together, work toward common goals, and coordinate plans and actions? Information systems can't make decisions, hire or fire people, sign contracts, agree on deals, or adjust the price of goods to the marketplace. In addition to the types of systems we have just described, businesses need special systems to support collaboration and teamwork.

What Is Collaboration?

Collaboration is working with others to achieve shared and explicit goals. Collaboration focuses on task or mission accomplishment and usually takes place in a business or other organization and between businesses. You collaborate with a colleague in Tokyo having expertise on a topic about which you know nothing. You collaborate with many colleagues in publishing a company blog. If you're in a law firm, you collaborate with accountants in an accounting firm in servicing the needs of a client with tax problems.

Collaboration can be short-lived, lasting a few minutes, or longer term, depending on the nature of the task and the relationship among participants. Collaboration can be one-to-one or many-to-many.

Employees may collaborate in informal groups that are not a formal part of the business firm's organizational structure, or they may be organized into formal teams. **Teams** have a specific mission that someone in the business assigned to them. Team members need to collaborate on the accomplishment of specific tasks and collectively achieve the team mission. The team mission might be to "win the game" or "increase online sales by 10 percent." Teams are often short-lived, depending on the problems they tackle and the length of time needed to find a solution and accomplish the mission.

Collaboration and teamwork are more important today than ever for a variety of reasons.

- *Changing nature of work*. The nature of work has changed from factory manufacturing and pre-computer office work where each stage in the production process occurred independently of one another and was coordinated by supervisors. Work was organized into silos. Within a silo, work passed from one machine tool station to another, from one desktop to another, until the finished product was completed. Today, jobs require much closer coordination and interaction among the parties involved in producing the service or product. A report from the consulting firm McKinsey & Company estimated that 41 percent of the U.S. labor force is now composed of jobs where interaction (talking, e-mailing, presenting, and persuading) is the primary value-adding activity. Even in factories, workers today often work in production groups, or pods.
- *Growth of professional work*. "Interaction" jobs tend to be professional jobs in the service sector that require close coordination and collaboration. Professional jobs require substantial education and the sharing of information and opinions to get work done. Each actor on the job brings specialized expertise to the problem, and all the actors need to take one another into account in order to accomplish the job.
- *Changing organization of the firm*. For most of the industrial age, managers organized work in a hierarchical fashion. Orders came down the hierarchy, and responses moved back up the hierarchy. Today, work is organized into groups and teams, and the members are expected to develop their own methods for accomplishing the task. Senior managers observe and measure results but are much less likely to issue detailed orders or operating procedures. In part, this is because expertise and decision-making power have been pushed down in organizations.
- *Changing scope of the firm*. The work of the firm has changed from a single location to multiple locations—offices or factories throughout a region, a nation, or even around the globe. For instance, Henry Ford developed the first mass-production automobile plant at a single Dearborn, Michigan, factory. In 2015, Ford employed 199,000 people at about 67 plants worldwide. With this kind of global presence, the need for close coordination of design, production, marketing, distribution, and service obviously takes on new importance and scale. Large global companies need to have teams working on a global basis.
- *Emphasis on innovation*. Although we tend to attribute innovations in business and science to great individuals, these great individuals are most likely

working with a team of brilliant colleagues. Think of Bill Gates and Steve Jobs (founders of Microsoft and Apple), both of whom are highly regarded innovators and both of whom built strong collaborative teams to nurture and support innovation in their firms. Their initial innovations derived from close collaboration with colleagues and partners. Innovation, in other words, is a group and social process, and most innovations derive from collaboration among individuals in a lab, a business, or government agencies. Strong collaborative practices and technologies are believed to increase the rate and quality of innovation.

- *Changing culture of work and business.* Most research on collaboration supports the notion that diverse teams produce better outputs faster than individuals working on their own. Popular notions of the crowd ("crowdsourcing" and the "wisdom of crowds") also provide cultural support for collaboration and teamwork.

What Is Social Business?

Many firms today enhance collaboration by embracing **social business**—the use of social networking platforms, including Facebook, Twitter, and internal corporate social tools—to engage their employees, customers, and suppliers. These tools enable workers to set up profiles, form groups, and "follow" each other's status updates. The goal of social business is to deepen interactions with groups inside and outside the firm to expedite and enhance information sharing, innovation, and decision making.

A key word in social business is *conversations*. Customers, suppliers, employees, managers, and even oversight agencies continually have conversations about firms, often without the knowledge of the firm or its key actors (employees and managers).

Supporters of social business argue that, if firms could tune into these conversations, they would strengthen their bonds with consumers, suppliers, and employees, increasing their emotional involvement in the firm.

All of this requires a great deal of information transparency. People need to share opinions and facts with others quite directly, without intervention from executives or others. Employees get to know directly what customers and other employees think, suppliers will learn very directly the opinions of supply chain partners, and even managers presumably will learn more directly from their employees how well they are doing. Nearly everyone involved in the creation of value will know much more about everyone else.

If such an environment could be created, it is likely to drive operational efficiencies, spur innovation, and accelerate decision making. If product designers can learn directly about how their products are doing in the market in real time, based on consumer feedback, they can speed up the redesign process. If employees can use social connections inside and outside the company to capture new knowledge and insights, they will be able to work more efficiently and solve more business problems.

Table 2.2 describes important applications of social business inside and outside the firm. This chapter focuses on enterprise social business—its internal corporate uses. Chapters 7 and 10 describe social business applications relating to customers and suppliers outside the company.

TABLE 2.2 APPLICATIONS OF SOCIAL BUSINESS

SOCIAL BUSINESS APPLICATION	DESCRIPTION
Social networks	Connect through personal and business profiles
Crowdsourcing	Harness collective knowledge to generate new ideas and solutions
Shared workspaces	Coordinate projects and tasks; co-create content
Blogs and wikis	Publish and rapidly access knowledge; discuss opinions and experiences
Social commerce	Share opinions about purchasing or purchase on social platforms
File sharing	Upload, share, and comment on photos, videos, audio, text documents
Social marketing	Use social media to interact with customers; derive customer insights
Communities	Discuss topics in open forums; share expertise

Business Benefits of Collaboration and Social Business

Although many articles and books have been written about collaboration, nearly all of the research on this topic is anecdotal. Nevertheless, there is a general belief among both business and academic communities that the more a business firm is "collaborative," the more successful it will be, and that collaboration within and among firms is more essential than in the past. A global survey of business and information systems managers found that investments in collaboration technology produced organizational improvements that returned more than four times the amount of the investment, with the greatest benefits for sales, marketing, and research and development functions (Frost and Sullivan, 2009). McKinsey & Company consultants predict that social technologies used within and across enterprises could potentially raise the productivity of interaction workers by 20 to 25 percent (McKinsey Global Institute, 2012).

Table 2.3 summarizes some of the benefits of collaboration and social business that have been identified. Figure 2.7 graphically illustrates how collaboration is believed to affect business performance.

Building a Collaborative Culture and Business Processes

Collaboration won't take place spontaneously in a business firm, especially if there is no supportive culture or business processes. Business firms, especially large firms, had a reputation in the past for being "command and control" organizations where the top leaders thought up all the really important matters and then ordered lower-level employees to execute senior management plans. The job of middle management supposedly was to pass messages back and forth, up and down the hierarchy.

Command and control firms required lower-level employees to carry out orders without asking too many questions, with no responsibility to improve processes, and with no rewards for teamwork or team performance. If your work group needed help from another work group, that was something for

TABLE 2.3 BUSINESS BENEFITS OF COLLABORATION AND SOCIAL BUSINESS

BENEFIT	RATIONALE
Productivity	People interacting and working together can capture expert knowledge and solve problems more rapidly than the same number of people working in isolation from one another. There will be fewer errors.
Quality	People working collaboratively can communicate errors and corrective actions faster than if they work in isolation. Collaborative and social technologies help reduce time delays in design and production.
Innovation	People working collaboratively can come up with more innovative ideas for products, services, and administration than the same number working in isolation from one another. Advantages to diversity and the "wisdom of crowds."
Customer service	People working together using collaboration and social tools can solve customer complaints and issues faster and more effectively than if they were working in isolation from one another.
Financial performance (profitability, sales, and sales growth)	As a result of all of the above, collaborative firms have superior sales, sales growth, and financial performance.

FIGURE 2.7 REQUIREMENTS FOR COLLABORATION

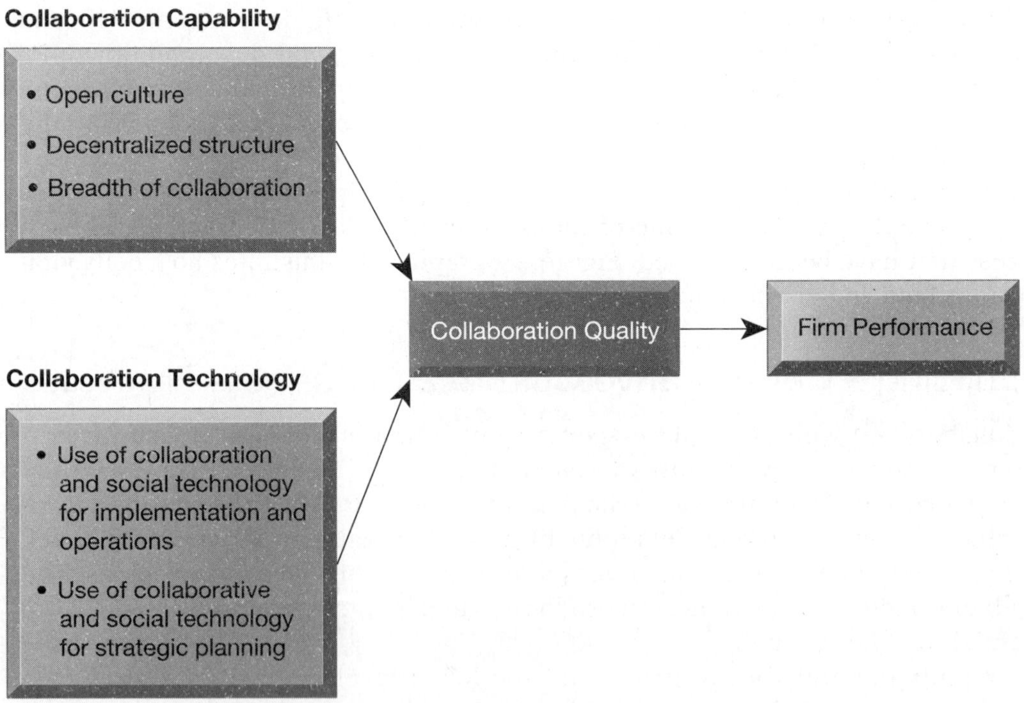

Successful collaboration requires an appropriate organizational structure and culture along with appropriate collaboration technology.

the bosses to figure out. You never communicated horizontally, always vertically, so management could control the process. Together, the expectations of management and employees formed a culture, a set of assumptions about common goals and how people should behave. Many business firms still operate this way.

A collaborative business culture and business processes are very different. Senior managers are responsible for achieving results but rely on teams of employees to achieve and implement the results. Policies, products, designs, processes, and systems are much more dependent on teams at all levels of the organization to devise, to create, and to build. Teams are rewarded for their performance, and individuals are rewarded for their performance in a team. The function of middle managers is to build the teams, coordinate their work, and monitor their performance. The business culture and business processes are more "social." In a collaborative culture, senior management establishes collaboration and teamwork as vital to the organization, and it actually implements collaboration for the senior ranks of the business as well.

Tools and Technologies for Collaboration and Social Business

A collaborative, team-oriented culture won't produce benefits without information systems in place to enable collaboration and social business. Currently there are hundreds of tools designed to deal with the fact that, in order to succeed in our jobs, we are all much more dependent on one another, our fellow employees, customers, suppliers, and managers. Some of these tools are expensive, but others are available online for free (or with premium versions for a modest fee). Let's look more closely at some of these tools.

E-mail and Instant Messaging (IM)

E-mail and instant messaging (including text messaging) have been major communication and collaboration tools for interaction jobs. Their software operates on computers, mobile phones, and other wireless devices and includes features for sharing files as well as transmitting messages. Many instant messaging systems allow users to engage in real-time conversations with multiple participants simultaneously. In recent years, e-mail use has declined, with messaging and social media becoming preferred channels of communication.

Wikis

Wikis are a type of website that makes it easy for users to contribute and edit text content and graphics without any knowledge of web page development or programming techniques. The most well-known wiki is Wikipedia, the largest collaboratively edited reference project in the world. It relies on volunteers, makes no money and accepts no advertising.

Wikis are very useful tools for storing and sharing corporate knowledge and insights. Enterprise software vendor SAP AG has a wiki that acts as a base of information for people outside the company, such as customers and software developers who build programs that interact with SAP software. In the past, those people asked and sometimes answered questions in an informal way on SAP online forums, but that was an inefficient system, with people asking and answering the same questions over and over.

Virtual Worlds

Virtual worlds, such as Second Life, are online 3-D environments populated by "residents" who have built graphical representations of themselves known as avatars. Companies like IBM, Cisco, and Intel Corporations use the online world for meetings, interviews, guest speaker events, and employee training. Real-world people represented by avatars meet, interact, and exchange ideas at these virtual locations using gestures, chat box conversations, and voice communication.

Collaboration and Social Business Platforms

There are now suites of software products providing multifunction platforms for collaboration and social business among teams of employees who work together from many different locations. The most widely used are Internet-based audio conferencing and video conferencing systems, cloud collaboration services such as Google's online services and tools, corporate collaboration systems such as Microsoft SharePoint and IBM Notes, and enterprise social networking tools such as Salesforce Chatter, Microsoft Yammer, Jive, Facebook at Work, and IBM Connections.

Virtual Meeting Systems In an effort to reduce travel expenses and enable people in different locations to meet and collaborate, many companies, both large and small, are adopting videoconferencing and web conferencing technologies. Companies such as Heinz, GE, and PepsiCo are using virtual meeting systems for product briefings, training courses, strategy sessions, and even inspirational chats.

A videoconference allows individuals at two or more locations to communicate simultaneously through two-way video and audio transmissions. High-end videoconferencing systems feature **telepresence** technology, an integrated audio and visual environment that allows a person to give the appearance of being present at a location other than his or her true physical location. Free or low-cost Internet-based systems such as Skype group videoconferencing, Google+ Hangouts, Zoom, and ooVoo are of lower quality, but still useful for smaller companies. Apple's FaceTime is useful for one-to-one videoconferencing. Some of these tools are available on mobile devices.

Companies of all sizes are finding web-based online meeting tools such as Cisco WebEx, Skype for Business, and Adobe Connect especially helpful for training and sales presentations. These products enable participants to share documents and presentations in conjunction with audioconferencing and live video via webcam.

Cloud Collaboration Services Google offers many online tools and services, and some are suitable for collaboration. They include Google Drive, Google Docs, Google Apps, Google Sites, and Google+. Most are free of charge.

INTERACTIVE SESSION: TECHNOLOGY

Collaboration for Improved Services at eClerx

Collaboration is an important component for success for firms nowadays. This inculcates collaborating not just within but outside the firm as well, which fetches unparalleled business benefits. When companies have to harness ideas from diverse groups such as employees, customers, general public or other firms, they need to share content and media, or people in the organization need to connect using different platforms from different locations; in such a situation, collaboration provides the solution. One such example is of an organization called eClerx which managed its massive growth through collaborative solutions. eClerx is a leading knowledge process outsourcing company based in Mumbai, and caters to large global firms. Founded in the year 2000, the company outsources its services – front- and back-end operations support to firms transforming rapidly but facing issues of scalability. It has five delivery centers spread across India, over 9,000 employees, and a huge client base including 30 *Fortune 500* companies. In 2012, its *Fortune 500* clientele contributed over US$ 2 trillion towards its annual revenue. This client base alone has more than 5.5 million employees worldwide, supported by eClerx to collaborate and carry out their operations. This, in turn, requires that eClerx offers a scalable 24 × 7 delivery model for its clients which is available for all days of a year. In addition to this, it has client relationship offices in India and abroad (in cities like New York, Singapore, London, Dublin, and so on).

The entire portfolio of services offered by eClerx and its rapid growth required a collaborative culture. For this reason, eClerx conducts weekly review meetings with stakeholders where a number of participants connect from different offices in remote locations. Some of these stakeholders require only audio connectivity, while others require both audio and video connectivity for content sharing. Some of them also connect through Skype and PSTN (Public Switched Telephone Network) for B2B and B2C communications. Many times, these meetings are marred by the quality of connections. They are also limited by the number of users that could connect at one time. Besides this, for a outsourcing firm which enables back-end and front-office operations of large global clients, regular collaboration becomes a necessity both within the company and outside with clients and other stakeholders. Not only is eClerx required to increase call capacity but also the quality of user experience. With this, the firm would be able to ensure higher level of service to its customers and shorter lead times. So, in a bid to facilitate face-to-face meetings of staff and clientele across continents, eClerx turned to Polycom collaboration solutions to build a unified communications environment. Polycom, a pioneer in video conferencing solutions, was founded in 1990 in San Francisco. It offers video, voice, and content collaboration and communication technology and employs around 3,800 people. It provides collaborative solutions for healthcare where doctors and patients connect through videos, video collaboration for crew members on the sets of movie, video collaboration and internet telephony for educators among many others. Polycom has been ranked as a leader in web and video conferencing by premier industry analysts such as Aragon Research, Gartner, and IDC Market Space.

The deployment of Polycom at eClerx was carried out in two phases. The first phase consisted of deployment of products offered by Polycom, and in the second phase, capacity addition was carried out. The first product deployed was Polycom RealPresence Collaboration Server. This application allowed multiple people to connect and exchange videos, voice, and content. It supports almost all devices for connecting and lets people collaborate at the highest quality and at the lowest cost, irrespective of their location. The other innovative technology by Polycom is NoiseBlock which provides unparalleled video experience by eliminating unwanted background noise. Sanjay Kukerja, CIO, eClerx too confirms the benefits of deploying Polycom's technologies by asserting that they have been able to serve their customers better and promote a stronger teamwork culture in their firm by conducting face-to-face conversations globally. The Polycom RealPresence Collaboration Server also allows video sharing between existing systems at a firm and Skype for business videos. Another product selected by eClerx was Polycom RealPresence Distributed Media Application (DMA). DMA is available as a hardware or as a network-based virtualization application which manages and distributes calls across collaboration networks. It allows 75,000 devices to register simultaneously and can support 25,000 concurrent calls. User accounts and personal meeting rooms are also automatically created through DMA virtually. This eliminates the need for administrative involvement and maintenance of redundant databases for user support. Besides this, the backup by DMA is maintained at geographically distributed locations which overcome the issue of single points of failure such as loss of connection in virtual meetings. The application can integrate with existing corporate database, directory, and IT setup leading to removal of process or data duplication. Additionally, the option of recording live streaming videos is also made available through DMA.

Finally, Polycom RealPresence Content Sharing Suite was also deployed at eClerx. This tool allows the sharing of content across Skype for business and traditional (non-Skype) video systems. It can handle disparate devices and networks. It allows sharing and displaying the content in proper format. An easy and consistent experience of this application drives the rate of adoption of technology among users. Irrespective of location or time zone, teams present in India or anywhere across the globe can easily share documents, presentations, and videos through any of these channels of collaboration – video conferencing, virtual meeting, Skype for business client, or web browsers.

Each of these products can be availed as a standalone solution or as part of multiple products in one subscription. The solution can therefore be hosted as a standalone solution, as a hybrid solution or delivered through cloud. At eClerx, the first phase of the technology deployment had been a tremendous success and the firm was able to recover the investment within 12 months of deployment. This is also a testament to the necessity of collaboration at eClerx because it demonstrates just how fast the rate of adoption of these collaborative technologies at the firm was. The second phase catered to a capacity addition for video and content, and it had to be launched within six months of the first phase. Through this technology deployment, eClerx has been able to secure B2B and B2C connections, which has also enabled the firm to take faster decisions and be more efficient and productive.

Source: As accessed on 02 November 2017 at 2pm IST—Retrieved from http://www.eclerx.com; Retrieved from http://www.polycom.co.in, (Navigation > Home > Company > About Us > History of Innovation); Retrieved from http://www.cxotoday.com; http://www.polycom.co.in; Retrieved from http://www.polycom.co.in, (Navigation > Home > Customer Stories > Eclerx Services).

CASE STUDY QUESTIONS

1. What factors accounted for the necessity of a collaboration solution at eClerx?
2. Discuss the features of Polycom's technologies as a tool for collaboration. What were the benefits of implementing these at eClerx?
3. Do all organizations require collaborative solutions? Justify your response.

Google Drive is a file storage and synchronization service for cloud storage, file sharing, and collaborative editing. Such web-based online file-sharing services allow users to upload files to secure online storage sites from which the files can be shared with others. Microsoft OneDrive and Dropbox are other leading cloud storage services. They feature both free and paid services, depending on the amount of storage space and administration required. Users are able to synchronize their files stored online with their local PCs and other kinds of devices with options for making the files private or public and for sharing them with designated contacts.

Google Drive and Microsoft OneDrive are integrated with tools for document creation and sharing. OneDrive provides online storage for Microsoft Office documents and other files and works with Microsoft Office apps, both installed and on the web. It can share to Facebook as well. Google Drive is integrated with Google Docs, a suite of productivity applications that offer collaborative editing on documents, spreadsheets, and presentations. Google's cloud-based productivity suite for businesses (word processing, spreadsheets, presentations, calendars, and mail) called Google Apps for Business also works with Google Drive.

Google Sites allows users to quickly create online team-oriented sites where multiple people can collaborate and share files. Google+ is Google's effort to make these tools and other products and services it offers more "social" for both consumer and business use. Google+ users can create a profile as well as "Circles" for organizing people into specific groups for sharing and collaborating. "Hangouts" enable people to engage in group video chat, with a maximum of 10 people participating at any point in time.

Microsoft SharePoint and IBM Notes Microsoft SharePoint is a browser-based collaboration and document management platform, combined with a powerful search engine that is installed on corporate servers. SharePoint has a web-based interface and close integration with productivity tools such as Microsoft Office, including Office 365, Microsoft's online web-based version of these tools offered as a subscription service. SharePoint software makes it possible for employees to share their documents and collaborate on projects using Office documents as the foundation.

SharePoint can be used to host internal websites that organize and store information in one central workspace to enable teams to coordinate work activities, collaborate on and publish documents, maintain task lists, implement workflows, and share information via wikis and blogs. Users are able to control versions of documents and document security. Because SharePoint stores and organizes information in one place, users can find relevant information quickly and efficiently while working together closely on tasks, projects, and documents. Enterprise search tools help locate people, expertise, and content. SharePoint now features social tools.

Southern Valve & Fitting USA (SVF) provides wholesalers with plumbing, irrigation, and utility valves and fittings. The company had initially used EMC Documentum eRoom and Google Docs for document sharing but encountered integration problems. SVF ported its documents and team sites to Microsoft SharePoint Online, which is integrated with Office 365. This solution combines multiple programs for communication and collaboration into a single online service. Employees can access documents from anywhere in the world using a standard Internet connection and make light edits to documents using Microsoft Office 365 productivity tools. Everything is accessed from a single platform. An order placed in China is handled as a SharePoint project, and all the sales order data and paperwork are shared throughout company (Microsoft Corporation, 2015).

IBM Notes (formerly Lotus Notes) is a collaborative software system with capabilities for sharing calendars, e-mail, messaging, collective writing and

TABLE 2.4 ENTERPRISE SOCIAL NETWORKING SOFTWARE CAPABILITIES

SOCIAL SOFTWARE CAPABILITY	DESCRIPTION
Profiles	Ability to set up member profiles describing who individuals are, educational background, interests. Includes work-related associations and expertise (skills, projects, teams).
Content sharing	Share, store, and manage content including documents, presentations, images, and videos.
Feeds and notifications	Real-time information streams, status updates, and announcements from designated individuals and groups.
Groups and team workspaces	Establish groups to share information, collaborate on documents, and work on projects with the ability to set up private and public groups and to archive conversations to preserve team knowledge.
Tagging and social bookmarking	Indicate preferences for specific pieces of content, similar to the Facebook Like button. Tagging lets people add keywords to identify content they like.
Permissions and privacy	Ability to make sure private information stays within the right circles, as determined by the nature of relationships. In enterprise social networks, there is a need to establish who in the company has permission to see what information.

editing, shared database access, and online meetings. Notes software installed on desktop or laptop computers obtains applications stored on an IBM Domino server. Notes is web-enabled and offers an application development environment so that users can build custom applications to suit their unique needs. Notes has also added capabilities for blogs, microblogs, wikis, RSS aggregators, help desk systems, voice and video conferencing, and online meetings. IBM Notes promises high levels of security and reliability and the ability to retain control over sensitive corporate information.

Enterprise Social Networking Tools The tools we have just described include capabilities for supporting social business, but there are also more specialized social tools for this purpose, such as Salesforce Chatter, Microsoft Yammer, Jive, and IBM Connections. Enterprise social networking tools create business value by connecting the members of an organization through profiles, updates, and notifications similar to Facebook features but tailored to internal corporate uses. Table 2.4 provides more detail about these internal social capabilities.

Although companies have benefited from enterprise social networking, internal social networking has not caught on as quickly as consumer uses of Facebook, Twitter, and other public social networking products. The chapter-ending case study addresses this topic.

Checklist for Managers: Evaluating and Selecting Collaboration and Social Software Tools

With so many collaboration and social business tools and services available, how do you choose the right collaboration technology for your firm? To answer

FIGURE 2.8 THE TIME/SPACE COLLABORATION AND SOCIAL TOOL MATRIX

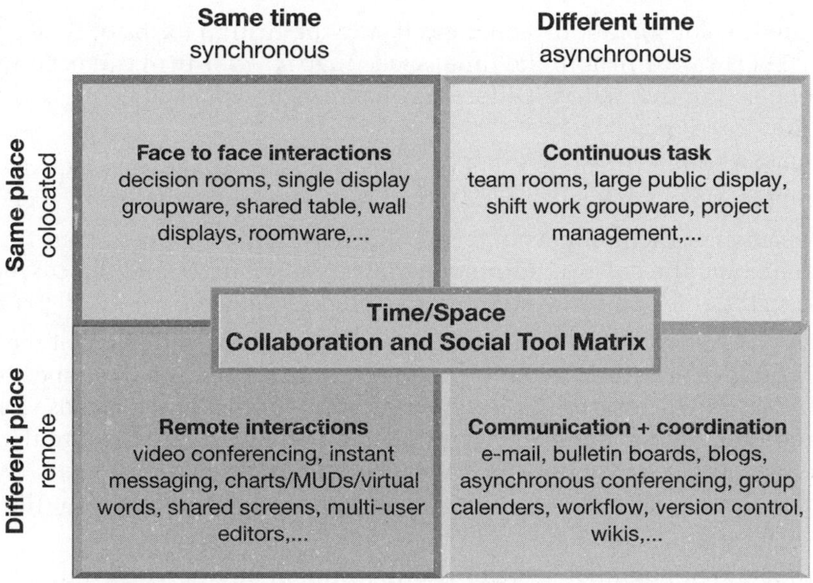

Collaboration and social technologies can be classified in terms of whether they support interactions at the same or different time or place and whether these interactions are remote or colocated.

this question, you need a framework for understanding just what problems these tools are designed to solve. One framework that has been helpful for us to talk about collaboration tools is the time/space collaboration and social tool matrix developed in the early 1990s by a number of collaborative work scholars (Figure 2.8).

The time/space matrix focuses on two dimensions of the collaboration problem: time and space. For instance, you need to collaborate with people in different time zones, and you cannot all meet at the same time. Midnight in New York is noon in Bombay, so this makes it difficult to have a videoconference (the people in New York are too tired). Time is clearly an obstacle to collaboration on a global scale.

Place (location) also inhibits collaboration in large global or even national and regional firms. Assembling people for a physical meeting is made difficult by the physical dispersion of distributed firms (firms with more than one location), the cost of travel, and the time limitations of managers.

The collaboration and social technologies we have just described are ways of overcoming the limitations of time and space. Using this time/space framework will help you to choose the most appropriate collaboration and teamwork tools for your firm. Note that some tools are applicable in more than one time/place scenario. For example, Internet collaboration suites such as IBM Notes have capabilities for both synchronous (instant messaging, meeting tools) and asynchronous (e-mail, wikis, document editing) interactions.

Here's a "to-do" list to get started. If you follow these six steps, you should be led to investing in the correct collaboration software for your firm at a price you can afford and within your risk tolerance.

1. What are the collaboration challenges facing the firm in terms of time and space? Locate your firm in the time/space matrix. Your firm can occupy more than one cell in the matrix. Different collaboration tools will be needed for each situation.
2. Within each cell of the matrix where your firm faces challenges, exactly what kinds of solutions are available? Make a list of vendor products.
3. Analyze each of the products in terms of its cost and benefits to your firm. Be sure to include the costs of training in your cost estimates and the costs of involving the information systems department, if needed.
4. Identify the risks to security and vulnerability involved with each of the products. Is your firm willing to put proprietary information into the hands of external service providers over the Internet? Is your firm willing to expose its important operations to systems controlled by other firms? What are the financial risks facing your vendors? Will they be here in three to five years? What would be the cost of making a switch to another vendor in the event the vendor firm fails?
5. Seek the help of potential users to identify implementation and training issues. Some of these tools are easier to use than others.
6. Make your selection of candidate tools, and invite the vendors to make presentations.

2-4 What is the role of the information systems function in a business?

We've seen that businesses need information systems to operate today and that they use many different kinds of systems. But who is responsible for running these systems? Who is responsible for making sure the hardware, software, and other technologies used by these systems are running properly and are up-to-date? End users manage their systems from a business standpoint, but managing the technology requires a special information systems function.

The Information Systems Department

In all but the smallest of firms, the **information systems department** is the formal organizational unit responsible for information technology services. The information systems department is responsible for maintaining the hardware, software, data storage, and networks that comprise the firm's IT infrastructure. We describe IT infrastructure in detail in Chapter 5.

The information systems department consists of specialists, such as programmers, systems analysts, project leaders, and information systems managers. **Programmers** are highly trained technical specialists who write the software instructions for computers. **Systems analysts** constitute the principal liaisons between the information systems groups and the rest of the organization. It is the systems analyst's job to translate business problems and requirements into information requirements and systems. **Information systems managers** are leaders of teams of programmers and analysts, project managers, physical facility managers, telecommunications managers, or database specialists. They are also managers of computer operations and data entry staff. Also, external specialists, such as hardware vendors and manufacturers, software firms, and consultants, frequently participate in the day-to-day operations and long-term planning of information systems.

In many companies, the information systems department is headed by a **chief information officer (CIO)**. The CIO is a senior manager who oversees the use of information technology in the firm. Today's CIOs are expected to have a strong business background as well as information systems expertise and to play a leadership role in integrating technology into the firm's business strategy. Large firms today also have positions for a chief security officer, chief knowledge officer, chief data officer, and chief privacy officer, all of whom work closely with the CIO.

The **chief security officer (CSO)** is in charge of information systems security for the firm and is responsible for enforcing the firm's information security policy (see Chapter 8). (Sometimes this position is called the chief information security officer [CISO] where information systems security is separated from physical security.) The CSO is responsible for educating and training users and information systems specialists about security, keeping management aware of security threats and breakdowns, and maintaining the tools and policies chosen to implement security.

Information systems security and the need to safeguard personal data have become so important that corporations collecting vast quantities of personal data have established positions for a **chief privacy officer (CPO)**. The CPO is responsible for ensuring that the company complies with existing data privacy laws.

The **chief knowledge officer (CKO)** is responsible for the firm's knowledge management program. The CKO helps design programs and systems to find new sources of knowledge or to make better use of existing knowledge in organizational and management processes.

The **chief data officer (CDO)** is responsible for enterprise-wide governance and utilization of information to maximize the value the organization can realize from its data. The CDO ensures that the firm is collecting the appropriate data to serve its needs, deploying appropriate technologies for analyzing the data, and using the results to support business decisions. This position arose to deal with the very large amounts of data organizations are now generating and collecting (see Chapter 6).

End users are representatives of departments outside of the information systems group for whom applications are developed. These users are playing an increasingly large role in the design and development of information systems.

In the early years of computing, the information systems group was composed mostly of programmers who performed highly specialized but limited technical functions. Today, a growing proportion of staff members are systems analysts and network specialists, with the information systems department acting as a powerful change agent in the organization. The information systems department suggests new business strategies and new information-based products and services and coordinates both the development of the technology and the planned changes in the organization.

In the next eight years to 2024, IS/MIS will add about 500,000 jobs and will grow 50 percent faster than the average job growth for the economy as a whole. Out of 114 occupations, MIS is ranked 15th in terms of salaries. In 2016 the median wage for IT/MIS jobs is about $80,000, twice the level for all occupations. While all IT/IS occupations show above-average growth, the fastest-growing occupations are computer support specialists (12 percent), database administrators (11 percent), systems analysts (21 percent), information security analysts (18 percent), software engineers (17 percent), and information systems managers (15 percent) (Bureau of Labor Statistics, 2015). Unexpectedly, computer programmers will lose 8 percent in this period, in part because the process of creating computer programs is becoming increasingly efficient with the growth of online software services and cloud computing. In general, the management of IT occupations IS showing faster expansion than the technical occupations in IT. With businesses and government agencies increasingly relying on the Internet for computing and communication, system and network security management positions are especially in demand. See the Learning Track for this chapter titled "Occupational and Career Outlook for Information Systems Majors 2012–2018" for more details on IS job opportunities.

Organizing the Information Systems Function

There are many types of business firms, and there are many ways in which the IT function is organized within the firm. A very small company will not have a formal information systems group. It might have one employee who is responsible for keeping its networks and applications running, or it might use consultants for these services. Larger companies will have a separate information systems department, which may be organized along several different lines, depending on the nature and interests of the firm. Our Learning Track describes alternative ways of organizing the information systems function within the business.

The question of how the information systems department should be organized is part of the larger issue of IT governance. **IT governance** includes the strategy and policies for using information technology within an organization. It specifies the decision rights and framework for accountability to ensure that the use of information technology supports the organization's strategies and objectives. How much should the information systems function be centralized? What decisions must be made to ensure effective management and use of information technology, including the return on IT investments? Who should make these decisions? How will these decisions be made and monitored? Firms with superior IT governance will have clearly thought out the answers.

Review Summary

2-1 *What are business processes? How are they related to information systems?*

A business process is a logically related set of activities that defines how specific business tasks are performed, and it represents a unique way in which an organization coordinates work, information, and knowledge. Managers need to pay attention to business processes because they determine how well the organization can execute its business, and they may be a source of strategic advantage. There are business processes specific to each of the major business functions, but many business processes are cross-functional. Information systems automate parts of business processes, and they can help organizations redesign and streamline these processes.

2-2 *How do systems serve the different management groups in a business, and how do systems that link the enterprise improve organizational performance?*

Systems serving operational management are transaction processing systems (TPS), such as payroll or order processing, that track the flow of the daily routine transactions necessary to conduct business. Management information systems (MIS) produce reports serving middle management by condensing information from TPS, and these are not highly analytical. Decision-support systems (DSS) support management decisions that are unique and rapidly changing using advanced analytical models. All of these types of systems provide business intelligence that helps managers and enterprise employees make more informed decisions. These systems for business intelligence serve multiple levels of management and include executive support systems (ESS) for senior management that provide data in the form of graphs, charts, and dashboards delivered via portals using many sources of internal and external information.

Enterprise applications are designed to coordinate multiple functions and business processes. Enterprise systems integrate the key internal business processes of a firm into a single software system to improve coordination and decision making. Supply chain management systems help the firm manage its relationship with suppliers to optimize the planning, sourcing, manufacturing, and delivery of products and services. Customer relationship management (CRM) systems coordinate the business processes surrounding the firm's customers. Knowledge management systems enable firms to optimize the creation, sharing, and distribution of knowledge. Intranets and extranets are private corporate networks based on Internet technology that assemble information from disparate systems. Extranets make portions of private corporate intranets available to outsiders.

2-3 *Why are systems for collaboration and social business so important, and what technologies do they use?*

Collaboration is working with others to achieve shared and explicit goals. Social business is the use of internal and external social networking platforms to engage employees, customers, and suppliers, and it can enhance collaborative work. Collaboration and social business have become increasingly important in business because of globalization, the decentralization of decision making, and growth in jobs where interaction is the primary value-adding activity. Collaboration and social business enhance innovation, productivity, quality, and customer service. Tools for collaboration and social business include e-mail and instant messaging, wikis, virtual meeting systems, virtual worlds, cloud-based file-sharing services, corporate collaboration systems such as Microsoft SharePoint and IBM Notes, and enterprise social networking tools such as Chatter, Yammer, Jive, and IBM Connections.

2-4 *What is the role of the information systems function in a business?*

The information systems department is the formal organizational unit responsible for information technology services. It is responsible for maintaining the hardware, software, data storage, and networks that comprise the firm's IT infrastructure. The department consists of specialists, such as programmers, systems analysts, project leaders, and information systems managers, and is often headed by a CIO.

Key Terms

Business intelligence, 49
Chief data officer (CDO), 71
Chief information officer (CIO), 71
Chief knowledge officer (CKO), 71
Chief privacy officer (CPO), 71
Chief security officer (CSO), 71
Collaboration, 58
Customer relationship management (CRM) systems, 56
Decision-support systems (DSS), 50
Digital dashboard, 53
Electronic business (e-business), 58
Electronic commerce (e-commerce), 58
E-government, 58
End users, 71
Enterprise applications, 53
Enterprise systems, 53
Executive support systems (ESS), 52
Information systems department, 70
Information systems managers, 71
Interorganizational system, 57
IT governance, 72
Knowledge management systems (KMS), 57
Management information systems (MIS), 49
Portal, 52
Programmers, 70
Social business, 60
Supply chain management (SCM) systems, 55
Systems analysts, 70
Teams, 59
Telepresence, 64
Transaction processing systems (TPS), 47

Review Questions

2-1 What are business processes? How are they related to information systems?

- List and describe some functional business processes in an organization.
- Is the role of information system limited to automation of business processes? Discuss.

2-2 How do systems serve the different management groups in a business, and how do systems that link the enterprise improve organizational performance?

- Discuss the necessity of Transaction Processing Systems (TPS) and which level of management do they serve? Can a firm function without TPS?
- Explain the role played by Management Information System (MIS) in business. How does MIS obtains its data from TPS?
- Which business intelligence functions does Decision Support Systems (DSS) support? What kind of information flows into DSS?
- How does the information needs of senior management differ from that of the lower and middle levels of management? Which information system serves them?
- Define enterprise applications and discuss their role in increasing the business productivity.
- Discuss enterprise application architecture. Which enterprise application serves business processes outside the organization and how?
- Explain e-business, e-commerce, and e-government. What functions do they perform?

2-3 Why systems for collaboration and social business are so important and what technologies do they use?

- List and describe some applications of social business and the changes which have led to the proliferation of the same.
- Discuss the business areas which have reaped maximum benefits from the implementation of collaboration and social business.
- Describe the role of organization structure, culture, and appropriate technology for the success of collaboration.
- Describe time/space matrix. How can it be used to choose collaboration and social technologies?

2-4 What is the role of the information systems function in a business?

- Compare the roles played by programmers, systems analysts, information systems managers, the chief information officer (CIO), the chief security officer (CSO), the chief data officer (CDO), and the chief knowledge officer (CKO).
- What is IT governance and what type of questions does it resolve for a firm?

Discussion Questions

2-5 How could information systems be used to support the order fulfillment process illustrated in Figure 2.1? What are the most important pieces of information these systems should capture? Explain your answer.

2-6 Identify the steps that are performed in the process of selecting and checking out a book from your college library and the information that flows among these activities. Diagram the process. Are there any ways this process could be changed to improve the performance of your library or your school? Diagram the improved process.

Hands-On MIS Project

The projects in this section give you a hands-on experience analyzing opportunities to improve business processes with new information system applications, using a spreadsheet to improve decision making about suppliers, and using Internet software to plan efficient transportation routes.

Management Decision Problems

2-7 Fulbert Timber Merchants in Brixton, UK, features a large selection of building supplies, including timber, fencing and decking, mouldings, hardwood flooring, sheet materials, windows, doors, ironmongery, and other materials. The prices of building materials are constantly changing. When a customer inquires about the price on fixtures, fittings, hangings, and other items, sales representatives consult a manual price sheet and then call the supplier for the most recent price. The supplier in turn uses a manual price sheet, which has been updated each day. Often, the supplier must call back Fulbert's sales reps because the company does not have the newest pricing information immediately on hand. Assess the business impact of this situation, describe how this process could be improved with information technology, and identify the decisions that would have to be made to implement a solution.

2-8 Quincaillerie is a small family hardware store in Paris, France. The owners must use every square foot of store space as profitably as possible. They have never kept detailed inventory or sales records. As soon as a shipment of goods arrives, the items are immediately placed on store shelves. Invoices from suppliers are only kept for tax purposes. When an item is sold, the item number and price are rung up at the cash register. The owners use their own judgment in identifying items that need to be reordered. What is the business impact of this situation? How could information systems help the owners run their business? What data should these systems capture? What decisions could the systems improve?

Achieving Operational Excellence: Using Internet Software to Plan Efficient Transportation Routes

Software skills: Internet-based software
Business skills: Transportation planning

2-9 In this exercise, you will use Google Maps to map out transportation routes for a business and select the most efficient route.

You have just started working as a dispatcher for Trans-Europe Transport, a trucking and delivery service based in Brussels, Belgium. Your first assignment is to plan a shipment of paintings from the Museum Aan de Stroom in Antwerp, Belgium, to the Royal Museums of Fine Arts of Belgium in Brussels. To guide your trucker, you need to know the most efficient route between the two cities. Use Google Maps to determine the route that is the shortest distance between the two cities, the route that takes the least time, and the estimated fuel cost for both routes. Compare the results. Which route should Trans-Europe Transport use?

Collaboration and Teamwork Project

Identifying Management Decisions and Systems

2-10 With a team of three or four other students, find a description of a manager in a corporation in *Business Week*, *Forbes*, *Fortune*, the *Wall Street Journal*, or another business publication or do your research on the web. Gather information about what the manager does and the role he or she plays in the company. Identify the organizational level and business function where this manager works. Make a list of the kinds of decisions this manager has to make and the kind of information the manager would need for those decisions. Suggest how information systems could supply this information. If possible, use Google Docs and Google Drive or Google Sites to brainstorm, organize, and develop a presentation of your findings for the class.

Ranbaxy: Taking the ERP Pill

CASE STUDY

Ranbaxy Laboratories Ltd started its operations in 1961. It is one of the leading pharmaceutical companies in India, and also has significant presence the world over. Before the implementation of the ERP package, SAP, Ranbaxy used legacy systems to run its various operations. Tally was used by the finance department, while the inventory and product planning departments used MRP-I and MRP-II for material requirement planning and to schedule the inventory processes and activities of various departments. MRP-II also focused on the processes related to product planning, inventory management, and manufacturing. There were several issues with these legacy systems, the major problem being that of disconnection among all of them. Tally, the accounting software, was used by the finance teams only. It had no link to the processes followed by the other departments. As a result, it was difficult for managers to avail a streamlined flow of information. The MRP systems kept stock at Ranbaxy at a very rudimentary level, leading to frequent ordering of materials.

In order to integrate the processes of various departments, Ranbaxy decided to implement the SAP ERP package. Since Ranbaxy is a manufacturing organization and works in a competitive market, it is important that it increases organizational efficiency, controls its inventory levels through proper planning, reduces cost, increases profits, and streamlines its business flow. With SAP, the information generated by these departments is more accurate and available in real time. Each project manager is responsible for the exact planning, forecasting, and budgeting for a particular project. All the other departments work according to the plan for the project, or products and services. All functional departments have the clearest understanding of the operations to be performed, right from procurement to finance, project management, and sales.

SAP divides a single process into smaller sub-processes. For example, the process for stocking the store is further divided into generation of item codes, assigning item codes to the appropriate location, defining the stock levels, receipt and delivery of materials, and so on. Keeping track of every sub-process is important, especially since coordination between so many different departments may cause delays if proper tracking systems are not in place. The activity or department that slows down performance is identified early, and appropriate decisions are taken in order to enhance the efficiency of that department.

Maintaining the quality of the medicines and heatlhcare products is of utmost importance at

Ranbaxy. SAP focuses on each process involved in the manufacturing of medicines, and identifies the processes that are responsible for defects. Through this information, the management takes effective decisions to overcome problems, thereby ensuring the quality of medicines. SAP has also helped reduce various kinds of costs. It has enhanced organizational productivity. Over time, labor costs have been minimized. Ranbaxy now also uses standard processes to raise purchase orders. Unlike the MRP systems that placed orders haphazardly, the orders in SAP are placed in accordance with the min–max plan of the inventory department. This has reduced the ordering and transportation costs of the company to a great extent. SAP has also integrated the various suppliers or vendors. Communication among different departments and the vendors has improved vastly.

Information is the backbone of an organization. Accurate, timely information helps the management take decisions at the right time. SAP provides timely information related to inventory, project planning, project costs, sales, and production.

The processes followed at Ranbaxy after the implementation of the SAP ERP are as follows:

1. Project planning and forecasting: The SAP helps managers plan the manufacturing process effectively. It lets them know the exact quantity of the medicines to be manufactured along with the date of exhaustion of stock.

2. Raising indent: Whenever there is a need to procure material for manufacturing, the manager raises an indent using SAP. The indent contains the exact purpose for which the material is requisitioned and the location at which it is needed. This indent is forwarded to the store manager for approval, after which the procurement teams go ahead with the purchase of the material.

3. RFQ (request for quotation): This module of SAP sends requests for quotations to the various approved suppliers. The procurement department compares these quotations and selects the best supplier after taking into consideration cost, quality, time, shipment, and other relevant factors.

4. Creation of purchase orders (POs): Once the quotation is finalized, the purchase department generates a PO for the approved indent. This PO contains the terms and conditions laid out by the legal department. A copy of this PO is forwarded to the finance department through the notification summary feature in the SAP for approval.

5. Receiving and delivering material: The ordered material is finally received, inspected, and delivered to the store. The store generates a receipt in the SAP to acknowledge the successful delivery of material.

6. Manufacturing requests: The material needed by the manufacturing personnel is issued through a move-order request. After obtaining the necessary approvals for the move, the material is issued to the requester.

7. Invoice creation: Finally, the SAP generates invoices for the finance department and records the entries into the GL (general ledger).

This is how SAP has been successfully implemented to achieve integration among all the functional departments at Ranbaxy and increase the efficiency of the business processes.

Sources: Aladwani, A.M., "Change management strategies for successful ERP implementation", *Business Process Management Journal*, Vol. 7, No. 3, pp. 266–75 (2001); Atkinson, H., "ERP software requires good planning", *Journal of Commerce*, p. 14 (1999); Burns, M., "ERPs: a buyers' market", *CAmagazine*, Vol. 132, No. 7, pp. 37–45 (1999); "Keebler sharpens demand planning processes with my SAP", *Business Wire* (2001); Caldwell, B., "GTE goes solo on SAP R/3", *Information Week*, No. 685, p. 150 (1998); Campbell, S., "Merisel gets powered by SAP ERP", *Computer Reseller News*, p. 66 (1999); Collett, S., "Rayovac charges into SAP with a big bang", *ComputerWorld*, p. 56 (1999); Collett, S., "SAP gets stuck in the spin cycle", *Computer World*, p. 1 (1999); Davenport, T., "Mission Critical—Realizing the Promise of Enterprise Systems", *Harvard Business School Publishing*, Boston, MA (2000); Dong, L., "Modeling top management influence on ES implementation", *Business Process Management Journal*, Vol. 7 No. 3, pp. 243–50 (2001); Geishecker, L., "ERP vs best of breed", *Strategic Management*, pp. 63–66 (1999); Huang, Z. and P. Palvia, "ERP implementation issues in advanced and developing countries", *Business Process Management Journal*, Vol. 7, No. 3, pp. 276–84 (2001).

CASE STUDY QUESTIONS

2-11 Discuss the flow of information before the implementation of the ERP system at Ranbaxy.

2-12 Discuss how the SAP has helped Ranbaxy overcome its previous problems.

2-13 Discuss the process flow after the implementation of the SAP ERP system.

Chapter 2 References

Aral, Sinan, Erik Brynjolfsson, and Marshall Van Alstyne. "Productivity Effects of Information Diffusion in Networks," MIT Center for Digital Business (July 2007).

Banker, Rajiv D., Nan Hu, Paul A. Pavlou, and Jerry Luftman. "CIO Reporting Structure, Strategic Positioning, and Firm Performance." *MIS Quarterly* 35, No. 2 (June 2011).

Bernoff, Josh and Charlene Li. "Harnessing the Power of Social Applications." *MIT Sloan Management Review* (Spring 2008).

Boughzala, Imed and Gert-Jan De Vreede. "Evaluating Team Collaboration Quality: The Development and Field Application of a Collaboration Maturity Model." Journal of Management Information Systems 32 No. 3 (2015).

Bughin, Jacques, Michael Chui, and Martin Harrysson. "How Social Tools Can Reshape the Organization." McKinsey Global Institute (May 2016).

Bureau of Labor Statistics. "Occupational Outlook Handbook." Bureau of Labor Statistics (December 2015).

Compare Products. "Videoconferencing Trends of 2016." (2015).

Dimension Data. "2016 Connected Enterprise Report." (2016).

Forrester Consulting. "Total Economic Impact of IBM Social Collaboration Tools" (September 2010).

Forrester Research. "Social Business: Delivering Critical Business Value" (April 2012).

Frenkel, Karen A. "How the CIO's Role Will Change by 2018." *CIO Insight* (January 31, 2014).

Frost and Sullivan. "Meetings Around the World II: Charting the Course of Advanced Collaboration." (October 14, 2009).

Gast, Arne, and Raul Lansink. "Digital Hives: Creating a Surge Around Change." *McKinsey Quarterly* (April 2015).

Greengard, Samuel. "Collaboration: At the Center of Effective Business." *Baseline* (January 24, 2014).

__________. "The Social Business Gets Results." *Baseline* (June 19, 2014).

Guillemette, Manon G. and Guy Pare. "Toward a New Theory of the Contribution of the IT Function in Organizations." *MIS Quarterly* 36, No. 2 (June 2012).

Johnson, Bradford, James Manyika, and Lareina Yee. "The Next Revolution in Interactions," *McKinsey Quarterly* No. 4 (2005).

Kane, Gerald C. "Enterprise Social Media: Current Capabilities and Future Possibilities." *MIS Quarterly Executive* 14, No. 1 (2015).

Kane, Gerald C., Doug Palmer, Anh Nguyen Phillips, and David Kiron. "Finding the Value in Social Business. *MIT Sloan Management Review* 55, No. 3 (Spring 2014).

Kiron, David, Doug Palmer, Anh Nguyen Phillips, and Nina Kruschwitz. "What Managers Really Think About Social Business." *MIT Sloan Management Review* 53, No. 4 (Summer 2012).

Kolfschoten, Gwendolyn L., Fred Niederman, Robert O. Briggs, and Gert-Jan De Vreede. "Facilitation Roles and Responsibilities for Sustained Collaboration Support in Organizations." *Journal of Management Information Systems* 28, No. 4 (Spring 2012).

Li, Charlene. "Making the Business Case for Enterprise Social Networks." Altimeter Group (February 22, 2012).

Malone, Thomas M., Kevin Crowston, Jintae Lee, and Brian Pentland. "Tools for Inventing Organizations: Toward a Handbook of Organizational Processes." *Management Science* 45, No. 3 (March 1999).

Maruping, Likoebe M. and Massimo Magni. "Motivating Employees to Explore Collaboration Technology in Team Contexts." *MIS Quarterly* 39, No.1 (March 2015).

McKinsey & Company. "Transforming the Business Through Social Tools." (2015).

McKinsey Global Institute. "The Social Economy: Unlocking Value and Productivity Through Social Technologies." McKinsey & Company (July 2012).

Microsoft Corporation. "Customer Stories: Southern Valve." (January 18, 2015).

Mortensen, Mark. "Technology Alone Won't Solve Our Collaboration Problems." *Harvard Business Review* (March 26, 2015).

Poltrock, Steven and Mark Handel. "Models of Collaboration as the Foundation for Collaboration Technologies." *Journal of Management Information Systems* 27, No. 1 (Summer 2010).

Ricards, Tuck, Kate Smaje, and Vik Sohoni. "'Transformer in Chief': The New Chief Digital Officer." *McKinsey Digital* (September 2015).

Saunders, Carol, A. F. Rutkowski, Michiel van Genuchten, Doug Vogel, and Julio Molina Orrego. "Virtual Space and Place: Theory and Test." *MIS Quarterly* 35, No. 4 (December 2011).

Siebdrat, Frank, Martin Hoegl, and Holger Ernst. "How to Manage Virtual Teams." *MIT Sloan Management Review* 50, No. 4 (Summer 2009).

Tallon, Paul P., Ronald V.Ramirez, and James E. Short. "The Information Artifact in IT Governance: Toward a Theory of Information Governance." *Journal of Management Information Systems* 30, No. 3 (Winter 2014).

Violino, Bob. "What Is Driving the Need for Chief Data Officers?" *Information Management* (February 3, 2014).

Weill, Peter and Jeanne W. Ross. *IT Governance*. Boston: Harvard Business School Press (2004).

CHAPTER

3 Information Systems, Organizations, and Strategy

Learning Objectives

After reading this chapter, you will be able to answer the following questions:

3-1 Which features of organizations do managers need to know about to build and use information systems successfully?

3-2 What is the impact of information systems on organizations?

3-3 How do Porter's competitive forces model, the value chain model, synergies, core competencies, and network economics help companies develop competitive strategies using information systems?

3-4 What are the challenges posed by strategic information systems, and how should they be addressed?

CHAPTER CASES

AirAsia: Saving on Operational Costs through Effective Information Systems
Securing Flipkart
Smart Products, Smart Companies
Deutsche Bank: The Cost of Legacy Systems

AirAsia: Saving on Operational Costs through Effective Information Systems

AirAsia India is a leading Indo-Malaysian low-cost ailrine. It began its operations in 1996 and now (as on 2017) has a fleet of 221 aircrafts (including subsidiaries of AirAsia Group), flies to 165 domestic and international destinations covering 25 countries, and is the largest low-cost airline carrier. AirAsia India was launched in 2013 as a joint venture between AirAsia Berhad, Tata Sons, and Telestra Tradeplace. As in 2017, in India, it currently operates in 17 destinations. The airline's success can be traced back to the time when Tim Fernandes purchased the company, became the CEO, and restructured the organization. At a time when every other airline was offering tickets at comparable prices with the same facilities, he came up with the concept of a no-frills, hassle-free, low-cost airline. Although the concept had already been implemented in Southwest Airlines in the U.S., applying the same strategy in India was a challenge. Since Indian customers are generally price-sensitive, Tim saw a huge potential in offering low-cost services here. "Being an unproven model, the low-cost, long-haul business is rather risky ... When we first started, many people thought it was a crazy idea to offer low fares as it was not economically viable. Especially with an airline with high acquisitions like us, we were expected to fail. However, with strong persistence and right strategies we persevered and we are now the leading and largest low-cost carrier in Asia," says Tim.

Airlines face several challanges while trying to provide services at low costs. When reducing the price, the quality of service cannot be compromised, and this is especially true for airlines where passenger safety is of utmost importance. AirAsia implemented the low-cost carrier strategy in two different ways. It first amended the basic facilities provided to passengers and then reduced the operational expenses of the company. AirAsia brought about a no-frills service policy, by which it meant that no free meals would be provided on board flights. This helped the company reduce both the number of employees required to cater to and serve passengers and the turnaround time needed to clear the airplane for the next destination. While the airlines that provided meals on board took about an hour to leave the airport, AirAsia took only 30 minutes. This helped AirAsia fly 20 to 30 percent more flights than its competitors. The airline started flying economy class passengers exclusively, which helped them seat 20 percent more people on a single flight.

© Gts. Shutterstock

To save on the operational costs, AirAsia implemented effective information systems in the following manner:

1. **Yield management system:** Ticketing and routes are two of the most important aspects of an airline business. A yield management system helps sell tickets at the most appropriate price and optimally manage the routes. AirAsia has managed to sell the same type of seats on the same route at different prices because of its yield management system. The system charges passengers based on the time of the reservations. Passengers who reserve tickets in advance are charged less for the same seat as compared to a passenger who reserves a seat closer to the date of flying. This helped AirAsia reap maximum profit from tickets and also motivate passengers to book in advance. The system of advance booking has helped AirAsia know the occupancy status of flights. Moreover, it has enabled the company to figure out the routes on which the demand is high.
2. **Customer reservation system:** AirAsia discontinued the conventional system of booking tickets through travel agents, thereby reducing the airline's total expenses by 11 to 15 percent. The airline also implemented its own customer reservation system, a web-enabled online reservation suite provided by Navitaine Open Skies Technology. This system allows the passengers to book tickets directly, without using the services of travel agents. By doing so, it also saved on the cost of printing paper tickets, since the system provided the customer with the option to print tickets at their end. This whole process has helped AirAsia reduce its operational expenses by 40 to 45 percent.
3. **Operators management software:** As the operations of AirAsia grew exponentially, the company implemented an airline operators management software, merlot.aero, to forecast, organize, and report on the airline and crew activities. AirAsia can now easily manage the crew requirements. Crew members can inform the management about their absence from duty using their personal mobile phones, and the software automatically helps find the best possible replacement for the absent employee. The software also provides the schedule and other necessary flight information to all the concerned parties. This keeps AirAsia connected to all the important stakeholders. Finally, this software helps manage critical activities such as flight scheduling, network planning, aircraft portal and maintenance, and crew payroll management, among others.

Sources: Alexander, Keith L. (2004). The Economics of Low Cost Carriers – All the Numbers Add Down for the Nation's Low-Cost Carriers. Washington Post, Feb 29, 2004; Economist, The (2004). Low Cost Airlines – Turbulent Skies. Economist Print Edition – July 89, 2004; http://www.economist.com/business/displaystory.cfm?story_id=2897525; Hecker, JayEtta Z. (2004, June 3). COMMERCIAL AVIATION – Despite Industry Turmoil, Low-Cost Airlines are Growing and Profitable; United States General Accounting Office – Testimony Before the Subcommittee on Aviation, Committee on Transportation and Infrastructure, House of Representatives;Kong, Ying & Le Dressay, Andre (2003); Spinning off low cost cariers – when does it make sense? Journal of the Academy of Business and Economics, April 2003; Schneiderbauer, Dieter & Fainsilber, Olivier (2004). Impact of low cost airlines – Summary of Mercer Study; Mercer Management Company; John Carney: "The man who bought AirAsia for 50 CENTS when it had just two aircraft and turned it into a hugely successful budget airline... now it's his 'worst nightmare'", December 29, 2014; accessed on December 2, 2015 (http://www.dailymail.co.uk/news/article-2889449/Meet-multi-millionaire-bought-AirAsia-50-cents-thirteen-years-ago-just-two-aircraft-turned-hugely-successful-budget-airline.html); AirAsia: AirAsia wins Airline Strategy Award 2008; Accessed on December 2, 2015 (https://www.facebook.com/notes/airasia/airasia-wins-airline-strategy-award-2008/19413023741); "AirAsia is best Asian low-cost airline"; accessed on December 2, 2015 (http://www.eturbonews.com/5559/airasia-best-asian-low-cost-airline); http://www.academia.edu/9150463/Air_asia_marketing_strategies

The AirAsia case illustrates some of the ways through which information systems help businesses compete as well as the challenges of finding the right business strategy and how to use technology in that strategy.

The airline industry is an extremely crowded playing field with large number of players operating and vying for the same customers. Even though AirAsia is an established player in the industry, it has many competitors, and it is searching for a way to use the information system that will work with its particular business model. The chapter-opening diagram calls attention to important points raised by this case and this chapter. AirAsia has been a leading airline player which operates more than 400 flights everyday. The present business model is being challenged by the fact that many players in the market are offering tickets at comparable prices with the same facilities. Tim Fernaedes, CEO of AirAsia, thought of a new business model of having a no-frills and low-cost airline service especially for the Indian customers. Accordingly, a new strategy was implemented in which apart from reducing the basic facilities offered to the customers, information system was also implemented in order to curtail the operational costs.

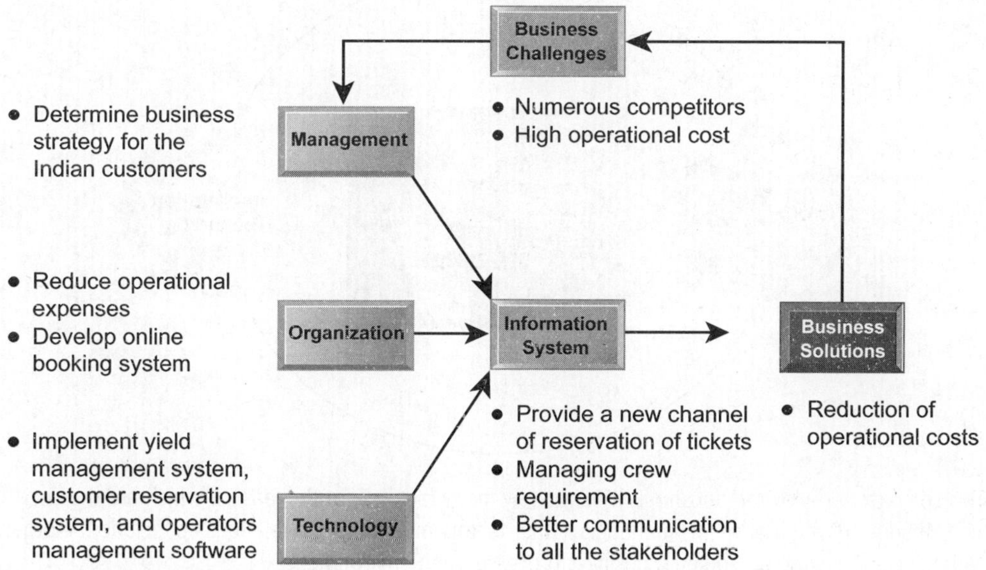

Here are some questions to think about: What role does technology play in AirAsia's success? Assess the contribution of the systems described in the case study.

3-1 Which features of organizations do managers need to know about to build and use information systems successfully?

Information systems and organizations influence one another. Information systems are built by managers to serve the interests of the business firm. At the same time, the organization must be aware of and open to the influences of information systems to benefit from new technologies.

The interaction between information technology and organizations is complex and is influenced by many mediating factors, including the organization's structure, business processes, politics, culture, surrounding environment, and management decisions (see Figure 3.1). You will need to understand how information systems can change social and work life in your firm. You will not be able to design new systems successfully or understand existing systems without understanding your own business organization.

As a manager, you will be the one to decide which systems will be built, what they will do, and how they will be implemented. You may not be able to anticipate all of the consequences of these decisions. Some of the changes that occur in business firms because of new information technology (IT) investments cannot be foreseen and have results that may or may not meet your expectations.

FIGURE 3.1 THE TWO-WAY RELATIONSHIP BETWEEN ORGANIZATIONS AND INFORMATION TECHNOLOGY

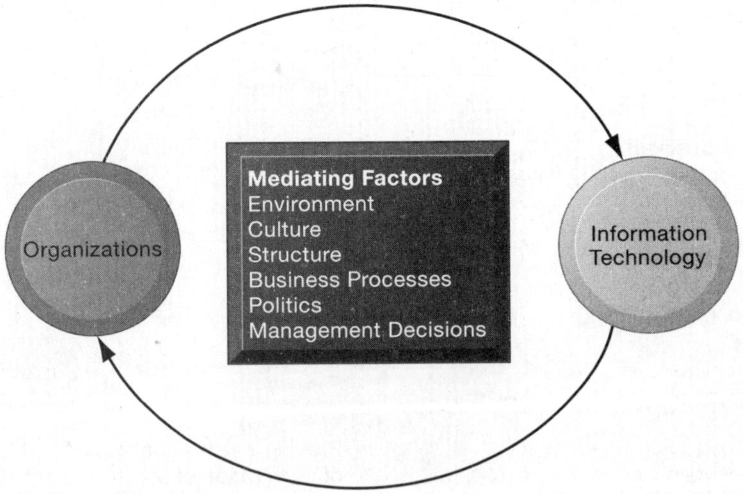

This complex two-way relationship is mediated by many factors, not the least of which are the decisions made—or not made—by managers. Other factors mediating the relationship include the organizational culture, structure, politics, business processes, and environment.

FIGURE 3.2 THE TECHNICAL MICROECONOMIC DEFINITION OF THE ORGANIZATION

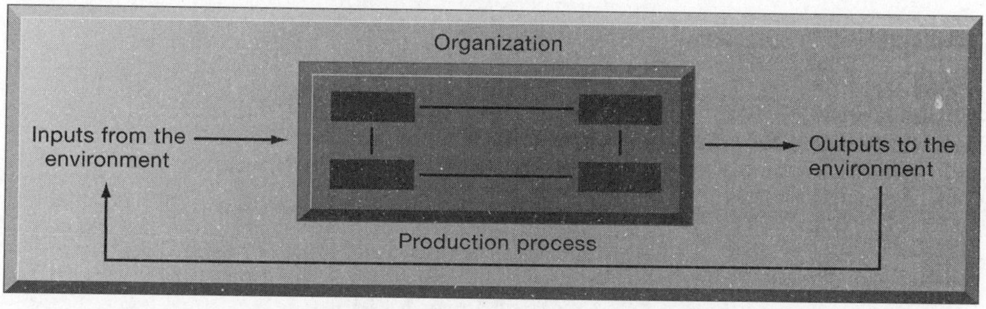

In the microeconomic definition of organizations, capital and labor (the primary production factors provided by the environment) are transformed by the firm through the production process into products and services (outputs to the environment). The products and services are consumed by the environment, which supplies additional capital and labor as inputs in the feedback loop.

Who would have imagined 15 years ago, for instance, that e-mail and instant messaging would become a dominant form of business communication and that many managers would be inundated with more than 200 e-mail messages each day?

What Is an Organization?

An **organization** is a stable, formal social structure that takes resources from the environment and processes them to produce outputs. This technical definition focuses on three elements of an organization. Capital and labor are primary production factors provided by the environment. The organization (the firm) transforms these inputs into products and services in a production function. The products and services are consumed by environments in return for supply inputs (see Figure 3.2).

An organization is more stable than an informal group (such as a group of friends that meets every Friday for lunch) in terms of longevity and routineness. Organizations are formal legal entities with internal rules and procedures that must abide by laws. Organizations are also social structures because they are a collection of social elements, much as a machine has a structure—a particular arrangement of valves, cams, shafts, and other parts.

This definition of organizations is powerful and simple, but it is not very descriptive or even predictive of real-world organizations. A more realistic behavioral definition of an organization is a collection of rights, privileges, obligations, and responsibilities delicately balanced over a period of time through conflict and conflict resolution (see Figure 3.3).

In this behavioral view of the firm, people who work in organizations develop customary ways of working; they gain attachments to existing relationships; and they make arrangements with subordinates and superiors about how work will be done, the amount of work that will be done, and under what conditions work will be done. Most of these arrangements and feelings are not discussed in any formal rulebook.

FIGURE 3.3 THE BEHAVIORAL VIEW OF ORGANIZATIONS

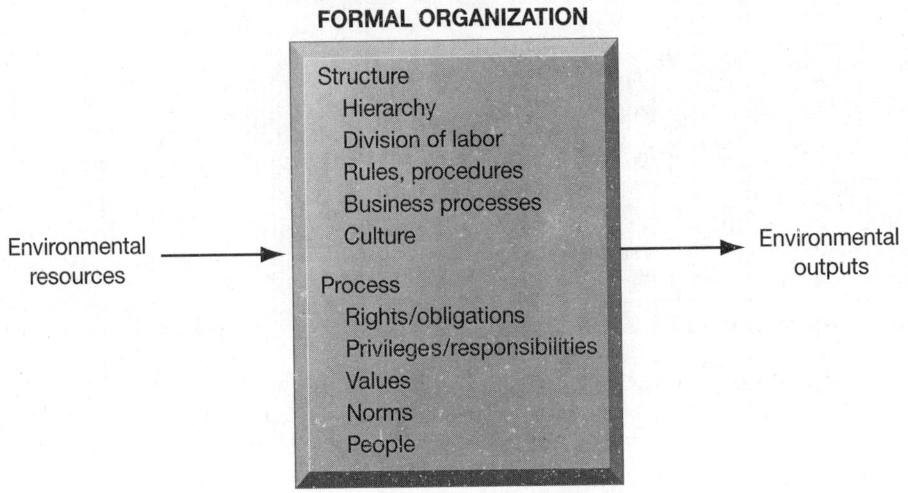

The behavioral view of organizations emphasizes group relationships, values, and structures.

How do these definitions of organizations relate to information systems technology? A technical view of organizations encourages us to focus on how inputs are combined to create outputs when technology changes are introduced into the company. The firm is seen as infinitely malleable, with capital and labor substituting for each other quite easily. But the more realistic behavioral definition of an organization suggests that building new information systems, or rebuilding old ones, involves much more than a technical rearrangement of machines or workers—that some information systems change the organizational balance of rights, privileges, obligations, responsibilities, and feelings that have been established over a long period of time.

Changing these elements can take a long time, be very disruptive, and requires more resources to support training and learning. For instance, the length of time required to implement a new information system effectively is much longer than usually anticipated simply because there is a lag between implementing a technical system and teaching employees and managers how to use the system.

Technological change requires changes in who owns and controls information, who has the right to access and update that information, and who makes decisions about whom, when, and how. This more complex view forces us to look at the way work is designed and the procedures used to achieve outputs.

The technical and behavioral definitions of organizations are not contradictory. Indeed, they complement each other: The technical definition tells us how thousands of firms in competitive markets combine capital, labor, and information technology, whereas the behavioral model takes us inside the individual firm to see how that technology affects the organization's inner workings. Section 3-2 describes how each of these definitions of organizations can help explain the relationships between information systems and organizations.

Features of Organizations

All modern organizations share certain characteristics. They are bureaucracies with clear-cut divisions of labor and specialization. Organizations arrange specialists in a hierarchy of authority in which everyone is accountable to someone and authority is limited to specific actions governed by abstract rules or procedures. These rules create a system of impartial and universal decision making. Organizations try to hire and promote employees on the basis of technical qualifications and professionalism (not personal connections). The organization is devoted to the principle of efficiency: maximizing output using limited inputs. Other features of organizations include their business processes, organizational culture, organizational politics, surrounding environments, structure, goals, constituencies, and leadership styles. All of these features affect the kinds of information systems used by organizations.

Routines and Business Processes

All organizations, including business firms, become very efficient over time because individuals in the firm develop **routines** for producing goods and services. Routines—sometimes called *standard operating procedures*—are precise rules, procedures, and practices that have been developed to cope with virtually all expected situations. As employees learn these routines, they become highly productive and efficient, and the firm is able to reduce its costs over time as efficiency increases. For instance, when you visit a doctor's office, receptionists have a well-developed set of routines for gathering basic information from you, nurses have a different set of routines for preparing you for an interview with a doctor, and the doctor has a well-developed set of routines for diagnosing you. *Business processes*, which we introduced in Chapters 1 and 2, are collections of such routines. A business firm, in turn, is a collection of business processes (Figure 3.4).

Organizational Politics

People in organizations occupy different positions with different specialties, concerns, and perspectives. As a result, they naturally have divergent viewpoints about how resources, rewards, and punishments should be distributed. These differences matter to both managers and employees, and they result in political struggle for resources, competition, and conflict within every organization. Political resistance is one of the great difficulties of bringing about organizational change—especially the development of new information systems. Virtually all large information systems investments by a firm that bring about significant changes in strategy, business objectives, business processes, and procedures become politically charged events. Managers who know how to work with the politics of an organization will be more successful than less-skilled managers in implementing new information systems. Throughout this book, you will find many examples where internal politics defeated the best-laid plans for an information system.

Organizational Culture

All organizations have bedrock, unassailable, unquestioned (by the members) assumptions that define their goals and products. Organizational culture

FIGURE 3.4 ROUTINES, BUSINESS PROCESSES, AND FIRMS

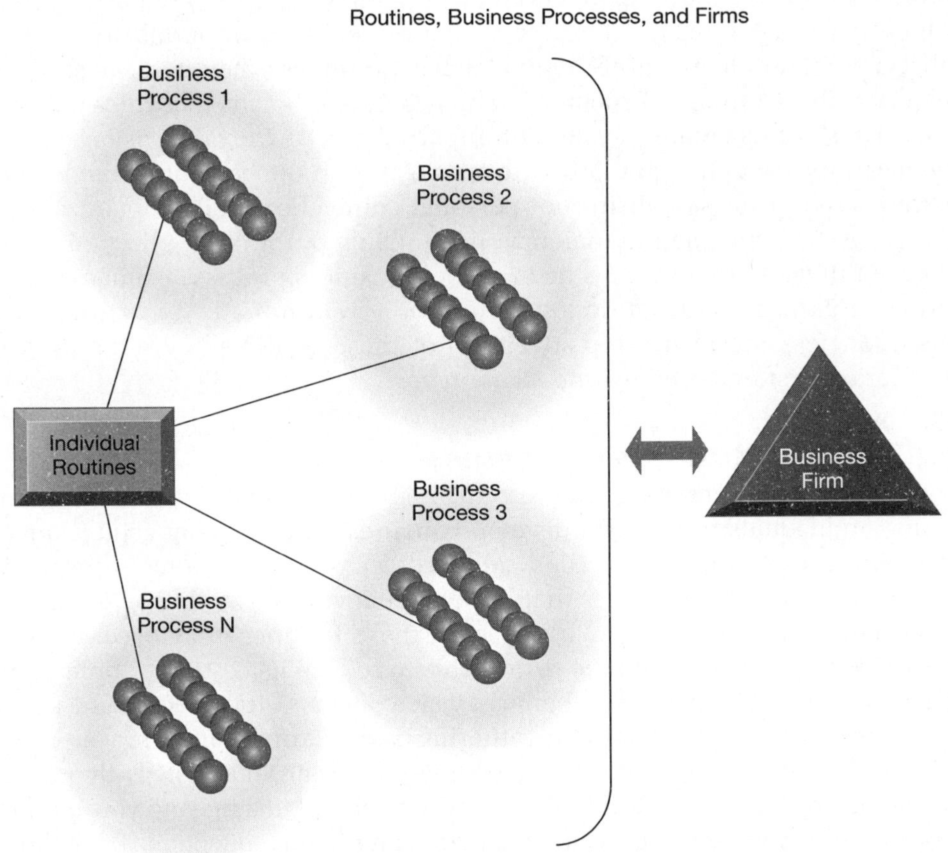

All organizations are composed of individual routines and behaviors, a collection of which make up a business process. A collection of business processes make up the business firm. New information system applications require that individual routines and business processes change to achieve high levels of organizational performance.

encompasses this set of assumptions about what products the organization should produce, how it should produce them, where, and for whom. Generally, these cultural assumptions are taken totally for granted and are rarely publicly announced or discussed. Business processes—the actual way business firms produce value—are usually ensconced in the organization's culture.

You can see organizational culture at work by looking around your university or college. Some bedrock assumptions of university life are that professors know more than students, the reason students attend college is to learn, and classes follow a regular schedule. Organizational culture is a powerful unifying force that restrains political conflict and promotes common understanding, agreement on procedures, and common practices. If we all share the same basic cultural assumptions, agreement on other matters is more likely.

At the same time, organizational culture is a powerful restraint on change, especially technological change. Most organizations will do almost anything to avoid making changes in basic assumptions. Any technological change that threatens commonly held cultural assumptions usually meets a great deal of resistance. However, there are times when the only sensible way for a firm to move forward is to employ a new technology that directly opposes an existing organizational culture. When this occurs, the technology is often stalled while the culture slowly adjusts.

Organizational Environments

Organizations reside in environments from which they draw resources and to which they supply goods and services. Organizations and environments have a reciprocal relationship. On the one hand, organizations are open to and dependent on the social and physical environment that surrounds them. Without financial and human resources—people willing to work reliably and consistently for a set wage or revenue from customers—organizations could not exist. Organizations must respond to legislative and other requirements imposed by government as well as the actions of customers and competitors. On the other hand, organizations can influence their environments. For example, business firms form alliances with other businesses to influence the political process; they advertise to influence customer acceptance of their products.

Figure 3.5 illustrates the role of information systems in helping organizations perceive changes in their environments and also in helping organizations act on their environments. Information systems are key instruments for *environmental scanning*, helping managers identify external changes that might require an organizational response.

FIGURE 3.5 ENVIRONMENTS AND ORGANIZATIONS HAVE A RECIPROCAL RELATIONSHIP

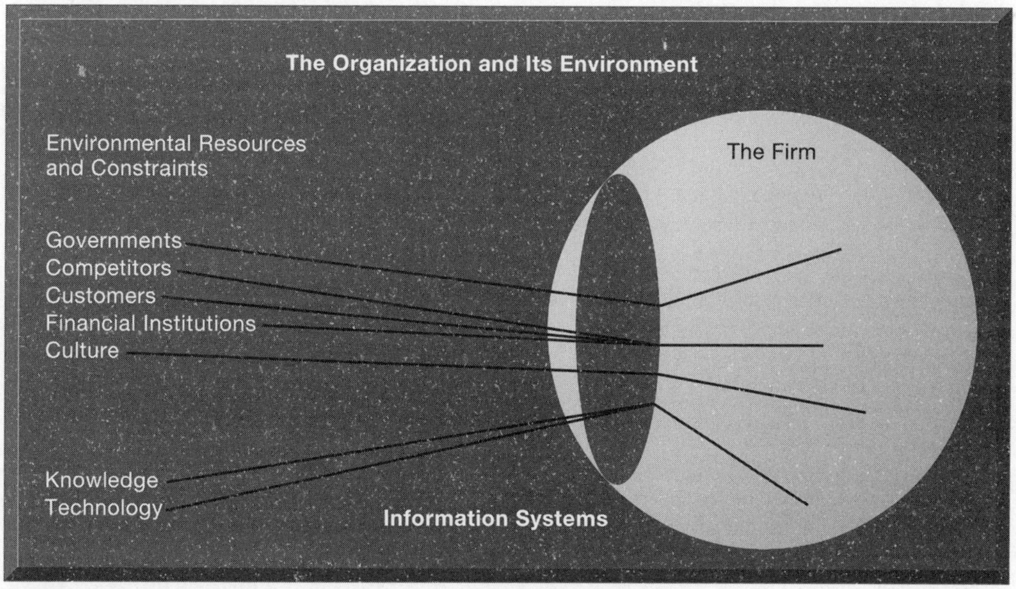

Environments shape what organizations can do, but organizations can influence their environments and decide to change environments altogether. Information technology plays a critical role in helping organizations perceive environmental change and in helping organizations act on their environment.

Environments generally change much faster than organizations. New technologies, new products, and changing public tastes and values (many of which result in new government regulations) put strains on any organization's culture, politics, and people. Most organizations are unable to adapt to a rapidly changing environment. Inertia built into an organization's standard operating procedures, the political conflict raised by changes to the existing order, and the threat to closely held cultural values inhibit organizations from making significant changes. Young firms typically lack resources to sustain even short periods of troubled times. It is not surprising that only 10 percent of the *Fortune* 500 companies in 1919 still exist today.

Disruptive Technologies: Riding the Wave Sometimes a technology and resulting business innovation come along to radically change the business landscape and environment. These innovations are loosely called "disruptive" (Christensen, 2003; Christensen, Raynor, and McDonald, 2015). What makes a technology disruptive? In some cases, **disruptive technologies** are substitute products that perform as well as or better (often much better) than anything currently produced. The car substituted for the horse-drawn carriage, the word processor for typewriters, the Apple iPod for portable CD players, and digital photography for process film photography. Table 3.1 describes just a few disruptive technologies from the past.

TABLE 3.1 DISRUPTIVE TECHNOLOGIES: WINNERS AND LOSERS

TECHNOLOGY	DESCRIPTION	WINNERS AND LOSERS
Microprocessor chips (1971)	Thousands and eventually millions of transistors on a silicon chip	Microprocessor firms win (Intel, Texas Instruments), while transistor firms (GE) decline.
Personal computers (1975)	Small, inexpensive, but fully functional desktop computers	PC manufacturers (HP, Apple, IBM) and chip manufacturers prosper (Intel), while mainframe (IBM) and minicomputer (DEC) firms lose.
Digital photography (1975)	Using CCD (charge-coupled device) image sensor chips to record images	CCD manufacturers and traditional camera companies win; manufacturers of film products lose.
World Wide Web (1989)	A global database of digital files and "pages" instantly available	Owners of online content and news benefit, while traditional publishers (newspapers, magazines, and broadcast television) lose.
Internet music, video, TV services (1998)	Repositories of downloadable music, video, TV broadcasts on the web	Owners of Internet platforms, telecommunications providers owning Internet backbone (ATT, Verizon), and local Internet service providers win, while content owners and physical retailers (Tower Records, Blockbuster) lose.
PageRank algorithm	A method for ranking web pages in terms of their popularity to supplement web search by key terms	Google is the winner (it owns the patent), while traditional key word search engines (Alta Vista) lose.
Software as web service	Using the Internet to provide remote access to online software	Online software services companies (Salesforce.com) win, while traditional "boxed" software companies (Microsoft, SAP, Oracle) lose.

In these cases, entire industries were put out of business. In other cases, disruptive technologies simply extend the market, usually with less functionality and much less cost than existing products. Eventually they turn into low-cost competitors for whatever was sold before. Disk drives are an example: Small hard disk drives used in PCs extended the market for disk drives by offering cheap digital storage for small files. Eventually, small PC hard disk drives became the largest segment of the disk drive marketplace.

Some firms are able to create these technologies and ride the wave to profits; others learn quickly and adapt their business; still others are obliterated because their products, services, and business models become obsolete. They may be very efficient at doing what no longer needs to be done! There are also cases where no firms benefit and all the gains go to consumers (firms fail to capture any profits). Moreover, not all change or technology is disruptive (King and Baatartogtokh, 2015). Managers of older businesses often do make the right decisions and find ways to continue competing. Disruptive technologies are tricky. Firms that invent disruptive technologies as "first movers" do not always benefit if they lack the resources to exploit the technology or fail to see the opportunity. The MITS Altair 8800 is widely regarded as the first PC, but its inventors did not take advantage of their first mover status. Second movers, so-called "fast followers," such as IBM and Microsoft, reaped the rewards. Citibank's ATMs revolutionized retail banking, but they were copied by other banks. Now all banks use ATMs, with the benefits going mostly to the consumers.

Organizational Structure

All organizations have a structure or shape. Mintzberg's classification, described in Table 3.2, identifies five basic kinds of organizational structure (Mintzberg, 1971).

The kind of information systems you find in a business firm—and the nature of problems with these systems—often reflects the type of organizational structure. For instance, in a professional bureaucracy such as a hospital, it is not unusual to find parallel patient record systems operated by the administration, another by doctors, and another by other professional staff such as nurses and social workers. In small entrepreneurial firms, you will often find poorly designed systems developed in a rush that often quickly outgrow their usefulness. In huge multidivisional firms operating in hundreds of locations, you will often find there is not a single integrating information system, but instead each locale or each division has its set of information systems.

Other Organizational Features

Organizations have goals and use different means to achieve them. Some organizations have coercive goals (e.g., prisons); others have utilitarian goals (e.g., businesses). Still others have normative goals (universities, religious groups). Organizations also serve different groups or have different constituencies, some primarily benefiting their members, others benefiting clients, stockholders, or the public. The nature of leadership differs greatly from one organization to another—some organizations may be more democratic or authoritarian than others. Another way organizations differ is by the tasks they perform and the technology they use. Some organizations perform primarily

TABLE 3.2 ORGANIZATIONAL STRUCTURES

ORGANIZATIONAL TYPE	DESCRIPTION	EXAMPLES
Entrepreneurial structure	Young, small firm in a fast-changing environment. It has a simple structure and is managed by an entrepreneur serving as its single chief executive officer.	Small start-up business
Machine bureaucracy	Large bureaucracy existing in a slowly changing environment, producing standard products. It is dominated by a centralized management team and centralized decision making.	Midsize manufacturing firm
Divisionalized bureaucracy	Combination of multiple machine bureaucracies, each producing a different product or service, all topped by one central headquarters.	*Fortune* 500 firms, such as General Motors
Professional bureaucracy	Knowledge-based organization where goods and services depend on the expertise and knowledge of professionals. Dominated by department heads with weak centralized authority.	Law firms, school systems, hospitals
Adhocracy	Task force organization that must respond to rapidly changing environments. Consists of large groups of specialists organized into short-lived multidisciplinary teams and has weak central management.	Consulting firms, such as the Rand Corporation

routine tasks that can be reduced to formal rules that require little judgment (such as manufacturing auto parts), whereas others (such as consulting firms) work primarily with nonroutine tasks.

3-2 What is the impact of information systems on organizations?

Information systems have become integral, online, interactive tools deeply involved in the minute-to-minute operations and decision making of large organizations. Over the past decade, information systems have fundamentally altered the economics of organizations and greatly increased the possibilities for organizing work. Theories and concepts from economics and sociology help us understand the changes brought about by IT.

Economic Impacts

From the point of view of economics, IT changes both the relative costs of capital and the costs of information. Information systems technology can be viewed as a factor of production that can be substituted for traditional capital and labor. As the cost of information technology decreases, it is substituted for labor, which historically has been a rising cost. Hence, information technology should result in a decline in the number of middle managers and clerical workers as information technology substitutes for their labor.

As the cost of information technology decreases, it also substitutes for other forms of capital such as buildings and machinery, which remain relatively expensive. Hence, over time we should expect managers to increase their investments in IT because of its declining cost relative to other capital investments.

IT also affects the cost and quality of information and changes the economics of information. Information technology helps firms contract in size because it can reduce transaction costs—the costs incurred when a firm buys on the marketplace what it cannot make itself. According to **transaction cost theory**, firms and individuals seek to economize on transaction costs, much as they do on production costs. Using markets is expensive because of costs such as locating and communicating with distant suppliers, monitoring contract compliance, buying insurance, obtaining information on products, and so forth (Coase, 1937; Williamson, 1985). Traditionally, firms have tried to reduce transaction costs through vertical integration, by getting bigger, hiring more employees, and buying their own suppliers and distributors, as both General Motors and Ford used to do.

Information technology, especially the use of networks, can help firms lower the cost of market participation (transaction costs), making it worthwhile for firms to contract with external suppliers instead of using internal sources. As a result, firms can shrink in size (numbers of employees) because it is far less expensive to outsource work to a competitive marketplace rather than hire employees.

For instance, by using computer links to external suppliers, automakers such as Chrysler, Toyota, and Honda can achieve economies by obtaining more than 70 percent of their parts from the outside. Information systems make it possible for companies such as Cisco Systems and Dell Inc. to outsource their production to contract manufacturers such as Flextronics instead of making their products themselves.

As transaction costs decrease, firm size (the number of employees) should shrink because it becomes easier and cheaper for the firm to contract for the purchase of goods and services in the marketplace rather than to make the product or offer the service itself. Firm size can stay constant or contract even as the company increases its revenues. For example, when Eastman Chemical Company split off from Kodak in 1994, it had $3.3 billion in revenue and 24,000 full-time employees. In 2015, it generated more than $9.6 billion in revenue with only 15,000 employees.

Information technology also can reduce internal management costs. According to **agency theory**, the firm is viewed as a "nexus of contracts" among self-interested individuals rather than as a unified, profit-maximizing entity (Jensen and Meckling, 1976). A principal (owner) employs "agents" (employees) to perform work on his or her behalf. However, agents need constant supervision and management; otherwise, they will tend to pursue their own interests rather than those of the owners. As firms grow in size and scope, agency costs or coordination costs rise because owners must expend more and more effort supervising and managing employees.

Information technology, by reducing the costs of acquiring and analyzing information, permits organizations to reduce agency costs because it becomes easier for managers to oversee a greater number of employees. By reducing overall management costs, information technology enables firms to increase revenues while shrinking the number of middle managers and clerical workers. We have seen examples in earlier chapters where information technology expanded the power and scope of small organizations by enabling them to perform coordinating activities such as processing orders or keeping track of inventory with very few clerks and managers.

Because IT reduces both agency and transaction costs for firms, we should expect firm size to shrink over time as more capital is invested in IT. Firms should have fewer managers, and we expect to see revenue per employee increase over time.

Organizational and Behavioral Impacts

Theories based in the sociology of complex organizations also provide some understanding about how and why firms change with the implementation of new IT applications.

IT Flattens Organizations

Large, bureaucratic organizations, which primarily developed before the computer age, are often inefficient, slow to change, and less competitive than newly created organizations. Some of these large organizations have downsized, reducing the number of employees and the number of levels in their organizational hierarchies.

Behavioral researchers have theorized that information technology facilitates flattening of hierarchies by broadening the distribution of information to empower lower-level employees and increase management efficiency (see Figure 3.6). IT pushes decision-making rights lower in the organization because lower-level employees receive the information they need to make decisions without supervision. (This empowerment is also possible because of higher educational levels among the workforce, which give employees the capabilities to make intelligent decisions.) Because managers now receive so much more accurate information on time, they become much faster at making decisions, so fewer managers are required. Management costs decline as a percentage of revenues, and the hierarchy becomes much more efficient.

These changes mean that the management span of control has also been broadened, enabling high-level managers to manage and control more workers spread over greater distances. Many companies have eliminated thousands of middle managers as a result of these changes.

Postindustrial Organizations

Postindustrial theories based more on history and sociology than economics also support the notion that IT should flatten hierarchies. In postindustrial societies, authority increasingly relies on knowledge and competence and not merely on formal positions. Hence, the shape of organizations flattens because professional workers tend to be self-managing, and decision making should become more decentralized as knowledge and information become more widespread throughout the firm.

Information technology may encourage task force–networked organizations in which groups of professionals come together—face-to-face or electronically—for short periods of time to accomplish a specific task (e.g., designing a new automobile); once the task is accomplished, the individuals join other task forces. The global consulting firm Accenture is an example. Many of its 373,000

FIGURE 3.6 FLATTENING ORGANIZATIONS

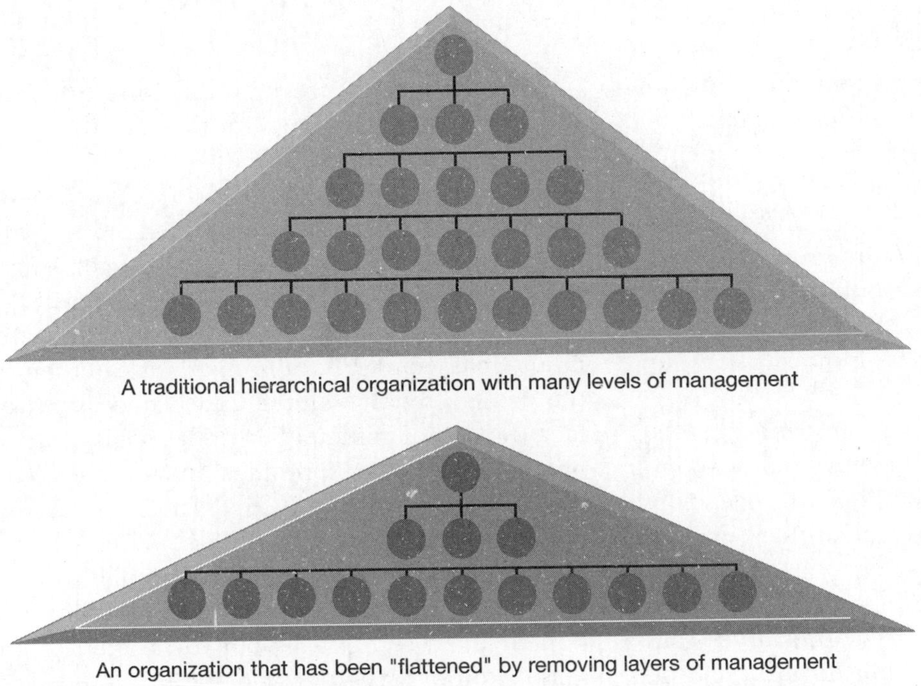

Information systems can reduce the number of levels in an organization by providing managers with information to supervise larger numbers of workers and by giving lower-level employees more decision-making authority.

employees move from location to location to work on projects at client locations in more than 56 different countries.

Who makes sure that self-managed teams do not head off in the wrong direction? Who decides which person works on which team and for how long? How can managers evaluate the performance of someone who is constantly rotating from team to team? How do people know where their careers are headed? New approaches for evaluating, organizing, and informing workers are required, and not all companies can make virtual work effective, as described in the Interactive Session on Technology.

Understanding Organizational Resistance to Change

Information systems inevitably become bound up in organizational politics because they influence access to a key resource—namely, information. Information systems can affect who does what to whom, when, where, and how in an organization. Many new information systems require changes in personal, individual routines that can be painful for those involved and require retraining and additional effort that may or may not be compensated. Because information systems potentially change an organization's structure, culture, business processes, and strategy, there is often considerable resistance to them when they are introduced.

INTERACTIVE SESSION: TECHNOLOGY

Securing Flipkart

Flipkart is one of the leading eCommerce companies in India. Located in Bangalore, it started its operation in 2007 by selling books online. Gradually, it widened its array of offerings to include a host of other products including electronics and lifestyle goods. In order to manage its growing business, Flipkart also had to increase the number of delivery partners. Prompt delivery of the products has never been more important than in the context of online retail.

The logistical challenge of such a business is huge. Every single order must be delivered, without fail. It is this realization that led Flipkart to develop an online logistics application called eKart, which is a part of W.S. Retail Services Private Limited, the business-to-customer wing of Flipkart. With the help of this information system, delivery executives can get vital information on their mobile devices. Since a large part of Flipkart's operations involve movement of goods, the relevance of a mobile application cannot be overstated. However, organizations need to be cautious when deploying sensitive business data to employees and other trade partners over mobile applications. Flipkart realized that in order to manage the flow of information to so many people in their delivery channels, it would need to come up with an effective way of monitoring the devices on which delivery information was shared. Vendors like XenMobile, Mobilerin, AirWatch, and Fiberlink came up with solutions to Flipkart's challenges. After an extensive analysis of all these applications, Flipkart decided to go with the Fiberlink MaaS360 Mobile Data Management (MDM) solution. This application offered a competitive advantage to Flipkart and demonstrated an ability to work towards helping Flipkart achieve its goals.

MaaS360, an IBM company, is a leader in mobile management and security solutions for organizations. The solutions developed by MaaS360 help organizations securely manage and integrate mobile technology to their businesses. In 2013, MaaS360 won the SIIA CODiE award for the best mobile device application for enterprises.

As more and more organizations are following the Bring Your Own Device (BYOD) policy, concerns about mobile data confidentiality are increasing. The MDM solution developed by MaaS360 addresses this issue. This application, which is available for all the major operating systems (Android, Windows, and iOS), registers the official devices and authenticates them using a unique password. The administrator can then track the device, receive alerts, and if necessary, even lock the device remotely or reset its password. The homepage of MDM provides an interactive dashboard showing all the devices, users, documents, applications, and location of the device.

MaaS360's AppSecurity feature enables organizations to share and manage confidential information. It even sets a time-out for a single sign-on session on a particular application. It provides a threat management facility that allows administrators to detect applications with malware and uninstall those applications remotely. MaaS360 Secure Mail allows only authorized users to access confidential email. Organizations can restrict the forwarding, copying, pasting, and screen capture options in such emails.

A large host of features such as these makes MaaS360 a good choice for a mobile data management application for Flipkart. The eCommerce company operates in more than a dozen delivery hubs across India. Using MaaS360's MDM solution, it can seed all the devices at one centralized location, thus eliminating the need for decentralized IT teams at each of the delivery hubs. This centralization of devices has helped Flipkart save costs. Delivery executives get the information of where to deliver the parcels on their official mobile devices. In addition, MaaS360 enables Flipkart to track the physical location of the delivery executives and ensure that they follow the recommended routes, which helps save both time and cost. MaaS360 also ensures that all the devices get remote updates from Flipkart's in-house logistics program application, so that everyone is using the latest version of the application.

All these features of MDM technology have enabled Flipkart to be a leading provider of online retail services in India.

Sources: MaaS360. Retrieved from http://www.maas360.com; "Raising Efficiency While Reducing Administrative Burdens for Flipkart". Retrieved from http://content.maas360.com/www/content/cs/cs_maas360_mdm_flipkart.pdf; Nair, Radhika P., "Flipkart to throw open its logistics arm 'eKart' to deliver packages of competitors", The Economic Times (2014). Retrieved from http://articles.economictimes.indiatimes.com/2014-02-13/news/47305247_1_logistics-arm-payzippy-sachin-bansal.

CASE STUDY QUESTIONS

1. Do you think Flipkart was in need of MDM technology? How is it adding value to the firm?
2. How are the employees benefiting from this technology? How is the management benefiting from the deployment of this technology?
3. Discuss the key features of MDM as provided by IBM's MaaS360.
4. Do you think the technology provides any competitive edge to Flipkart?

There are several ways to visualize organizational resistance. Research on organizational resistance to innovation suggests that four factors are paramount: the nature of the IT innovation, the organization's structure, the culture of people in the organization, and the tasks affected by the innovation (see Figure 3.7). Here, changes in technology are absorbed, interpreted, deflected, and defeated by organizational task arrangements, structures, and people. In this model, the only way to bring about change is to change the technology, tasks, structure, and people simultaneously. Other authors have spoken about

FIGURE 3.7 ORGANIZATIONAL RESISTANCE TO INFORMATION SYSTEM INNOVATIONS

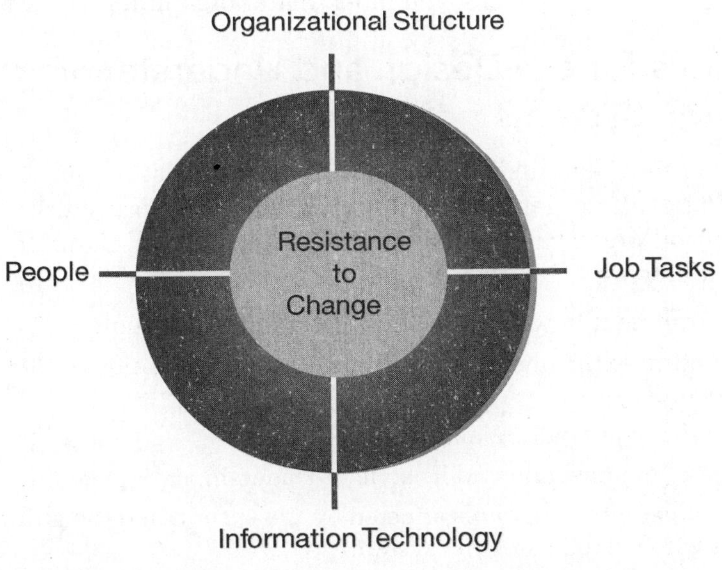

Implementing information systems has consequences for task arrangements, structures, and people. According to this model, to implement change, all four components must be changed simultaneously.

the need to "unfreeze" organizations before introducing an innovation, quickly implementing it, and "refreezing" or institutionalizing the change (Kolb and Frohman, 1970).

Because organizational resistance to change is so powerful, many information technology investments flounder and do not increase productivity. Indeed, research on project implementation failures demonstrates that the most common reason for failure of large projects to reach their objectives is not the failure of the technology but organizational and political resistance to change. Chapter 14 treats this issue in detail. Therefore, as a manager involved in future IT investments, your ability to work with people and organizations is just as important as your technical awareness and knowledge.

The Internet and Organizations

The Internet, especially the World Wide Web, has an important impact on the relationships between many firms and external entities and even on the organization of business processes inside a firm. The Internet increases the accessibility, storage, and distribution of information and knowledge for organizations. In essence, the Internet is capable of dramatically lowering the transaction and agency costs facing most organizations. For instance, brokerage firms and banks in New York can now deliver their internal operating procedures manuals to their employees at distant locations by posting them on the corporate website, saving millions of dollars in distribution costs. A global sales force can receive nearly instant product price information updates using the web or instructions from management sent by e-mail or text messaging on smartphones or mobile laptops. Vendors of some large retailers can access retailers' internal websites directly to find up-to-the-minute sales information and to initiate replenishment orders instantly.

Businesses are rapidly rebuilding some of their key business processes based on Internet technology and making this technology a key component of their IT infrastructures. If prior networking is any guide, one result will be simpler business processes, fewer employees, and much flatter organizations than in the past.

Implications for the Design and Understanding of Information Systems

To deliver genuine benefits, information systems must be built with a clear understanding of the organization in which they will be used. In our experience, the central organizational factors to consider when planning a new system are the following:

- The environment in which the organization must function
- The structure of the organization: hierarchy, specialization, routines, and business processes
- The organization's culture and politics
- The type of organization and its style of leadership
- The principal interest groups affected by the system and the attitudes of workers who will be using the system
- The kinds of tasks, decisions, and business processes that the information system is designed to assist

3-3 How do Porter's competitive forces model, the value chain model, synergies, core competencies, and network economics help companies develop competitive strategies using information systems?

In almost every industry you examine, you will find that some firms do better than most others. There's almost always a standout firm. In the automotive industry, Toyota is considered a superior performer. In pure online retail, Amazon is the leader; in off-line retail, Walmart, the largest retailer on earth, is the leader. In online music, Apple's iTunes is considered the leader with more than 60 percent of the downloaded music market, and in the related industry of digital music players, the iPod is the leader. In web search, Google is considered the leader.

Firms that "do better" than others are said to have a competitive advantage over others: They either have access to special resources that others do not, or they are able to use commonly available resources more efficiently—usually because of superior knowledge and information assets. In any event, they do better in terms of revenue growth, profitability, or productivity growth (efficiency), all of which ultimately in the long run translate into higher stock market valuations than their competitors.

But why do some firms do better than others, and how do they achieve competitive advantage? How can you analyze a business and identify its strategic advantages? How can you develop a strategic advantage for your own business? And how do information systems contribute to strategic advantages? One answer to that question is Michael Porter's competitive forces model.

Porter's Competitive Forces Model

Arguably, the most widely used model for understanding competitive advantage is Michael Porter's **competitive forces model** (see Figure 3.8). This model provides a general view of the firm, its competitors, and the firm's environment. Earlier in this chapter, we described the importance of a firm's environment and the dependence of firms on environments. Porter's model is all about the firm's general business environment. In this model, five competitive forces shape the fate of the firm.

Traditional Competitors

All firms share market space with other competitors who are continuously devising new, more efficient ways to produce by introducing new products and services, and attempting to attract customers by developing their brands and imposing switching costs on their customers.

New Market Entrants

In a free economy with mobile labor and financial resources, new companies are always entering the marketplace. In some industries, there are very

FIGURE 3.8 PORTER'S COMPETITIVE FORCES MODEL

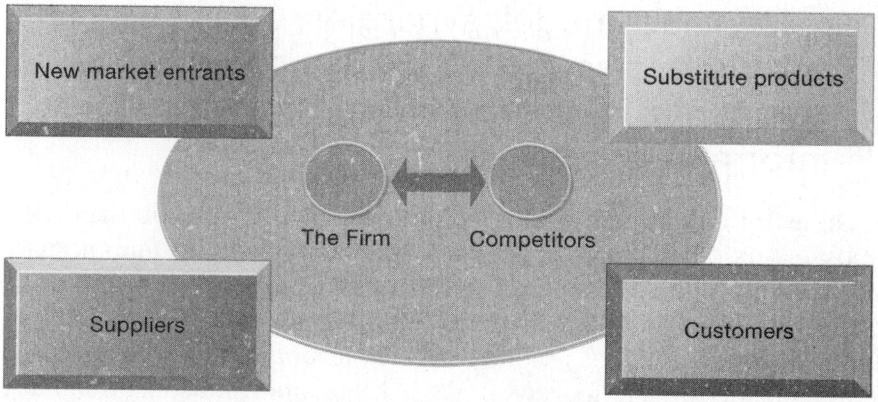

In Porter's competitive forces model, the strategic position of the firm and its strategies are determined not only by competition with its traditional direct competitors but also by four other forces in the industry's environment: new market entrants, substitute products, customers, and suppliers.

low barriers to entry, whereas in other industries, entry is very difficult. For instance, it is fairly easy to start a pizza business or just about any small retail business, but it is much more expensive and difficult to enter the computer chip business, which has very high capital costs and requires significant expertise and knowledge that are hard to obtain. New companies have several possible advantages: They are not locked into old plants and equipment, they often hire younger workers who are less expensive and perhaps more innovative, they are not encumbered by old worn-out brand names, and they are "more hungry" (more highly motivated) than traditional occupants of an industry. These advantages are also their weakness: They depend on outside financing for new plants and equipment, which can be expensive; they have a less-experienced workforce; and they have little brand recognition.

Substitute Products and Services

In just about every industry, there are substitutes that your customers might use if your prices become too high. New technologies create new substitutes all the time. Ethanol can substitute for gasoline in cars; vegetable oil for diesel fuel in trucks; and wind, solar, coal, and hydro power for industrial electricity generation. Likewise, Internet and wireless telephone service can substitute for traditional telephone service. And, of course, an Internet music service that allows you to download music tracks to an iPod or smartphone has become a substitute for CD-based music stores. The more substitute products and services in your industry, the less you can control pricing and the lower your profit margins.

Customers

A profitable company depends in large measure on its ability to attract and retain customers (while denying them to competitors) and charge high prices. The power of customers grows if they can easily switch to a competitor's products and services or if they can force a business and its competitors to compete on price alone in a transparent marketplace where there is little **product differentiation** and all prices are known instantly (such as on the Internet). For instance, in the used college textbook market on the Internet, students (customers) can find multiple suppliers of just about any current college textbook. In this case, online customers have extraordinary power over used-book firms.

Suppliers

The market power of suppliers can have a significant impact on firm profits, especially when the firm cannot raise prices as fast as can suppliers. The more different suppliers a firm has, the greater control it can exercise over suppliers in terms of price, quality, and delivery schedules. For instance, manufacturers of laptop PCs almost always have multiple competing suppliers of key components, such as keyboards, hard drives, and display screens.

Information System Strategies for Dealing with Competitive Forces

What is a firm to do when it is faced with all these competitive forces? And how can the firm use information systems to counteract some of these forces? How do you prevent substitutes and inhibit new market entrants? There are four generic strategies, each of which often is enabled by using information technology and systems: low-cost leadership, product differentiation, focus on market niche, and strengthening customer and supplier intimacy.

Supermarkets and large retail stores such as Walmart use sales data captured at the checkout counter to determine which items have sold and need to be reordered. Walmart's continuous replenishment system transmits orders to restock directly to its suppliers. The system enables Walmart to keep costs low while fine-tuning its merchandise to meet customer demands.

Low-Cost Leadership

Use information systems to achieve the lowest operational costs and the lowest prices. The classic example is Walmart. By keeping prices low and shelves well stocked using a legendary inventory replenishment system, Walmart became the leading retail business in the United States. Walmart's continuous replenishment system sends orders for new merchandise directly to suppliers as soon as consumers pay for their purchases at the cash register. Point-of-sale terminals record the bar code of each item passing the checkout counter and send a purchase transaction directly to a central computer at Walmart headquarters. The computer collects the orders from all Walmart stores and transmits them to suppliers. Suppliers can also access Walmart's sales and inventory data using web technology.

Because the system replenishes inventory with lightning speed, Walmart does not need to spend much money on maintaining large inventories of goods in its own warehouses. The system also enables Walmart to adjust purchases of store items to meet customer demands. Competitors, such as Sears, have been spending 24.9 percent of sales on overhead. But by using systems to keep operating costs low, Walmart pays only 16.6 percent of sales revenue for overhead. (Operating costs average 20.7 percent of sales in the retail industry.)

Walmart's continuous replenishment system is also an example of an **efficient customer response system**. An efficient customer response system directly links consumer behavior to distribution and production and supply chains. Walmart's continuous replenishment system provides such an efficient customer response.

Product Differentiation

Use information systems to enable new products and services or greatly change the customer convenience in using your existing products and services. For instance, Google continuously introduces new and unique search services on its website, such as Google Maps. By purchasing PayPal, an electronic payment system, in 2003, eBay made it much easier for customers to pay sellers and expanded use of its auction marketplace. Apple created the iPod, a unique portable digital music player, plus iTunes, an online music store where songs can be purchased for $0.69 to $1.29 each. Apple has continued to innovate with its multimedia iPhone, iPad tablet computer, and iPod video player.

Manufacturers and retailers are using information systems to create products and services that are customized and personalized to fit the precise specifications of individual customers. For example, Nike sells customized sneakers through its NIKEiD program on its website. Customers are able to select the type of shoe, colors, material, outsoles, and even a logo of up to eight characters. Nike transmits the orders via computers to specially equipped plants in China and Korea. The sneakers take about three weeks to reach the customer. This ability to offer individually tailored products or services using the same production resources as mass production is called **mass customization**.

Table 3.3 lists a number of companies that have developed IT-based products and services that other firms have found difficult to copy—or at least taken a long time to copy.

TABLE 3.3 IT-ENABLED NEW PRODUCTS AND SERVICES PROVIDING COMPETITIVE ADVANTAGE

Amazon: One-click shopping	Amazon holds a patent on one-click shopping that it licenses to other online retailers.
Online music: Apple iPod and iTunes	The iPod is an integrated handheld player backed up with an online library of more than 43 million songs.
Golf club customization: Ping	Customers can select from more than 1 million different golf club options; a build-to-order system ships their customized clubs within 48 hours.
Online person-to-person payment: PayPal	PayPal enables the transfer of money between individual bank accounts and between bank accounts and credit card accounts.

Focus on Market Niche

Use information systems to enable a specific market focus and serve this narrow target market better than competitors. Information systems support this strategy by producing and analyzing data for finely tuned sales and marketing techniques. Information systems enable companies to analyze customer buying patterns, tastes, and preferences closely so that they efficiently pitch advertising and marketing campaigns to smaller and smaller target markets.

The data come from a range of sources—credit card transactions, demographic data, purchase data from checkout counter scanners at supermarkets and retail stores, and data collected when people access and interact with websites. Sophisticated software tools find patterns in these large pools of data and infer rules from them to guide decision making. Analysis of such data drives one-to-one marketing that creates personal messages based on individualized preferences. For example, Hilton Hotels' OnQ system analyzes detailed data collected on active guests in all of its properties to determine the preferences of each guest and each guest's profitability. Hilton uses this information to give its most profitable customers additional privileges, such as late checkouts. Contemporary customer relationship management (CRM) systems feature analytical capabilities for this type of intensive data analysis (see Chapters 2 and 9).

Credit card companies are able to use this strategy to predict their most profitable cardholders. The companies gather vast quantities of data about consumer purchases and other behaviors and mine these data to construct detailed profiles that identify cardholders who might be good or bad credit risks. We discuss the tools and technologies for data analysis in Chapters 6 and 12.

Strengthen Customer and Supplier Intimacy

Use information systems to tighten linkages with suppliers and develop intimacy with customers. Fiat Chrysler Automobiles LLC uses information systems to facilitate direct access by suppliers to production schedules and even permits suppliers to decide how and when to ship supplies to Chrysler and Fiat factories. This allows suppliers more lead time in producing goods. On the customer

TABLE 3.4 FOUR BASIC COMPETITIVE STRATEGIES

STRATEGY	DESCRIPTION	EXAMPLE
Low-cost leadership	Use information systems to produce products and services at a lower price than competitors while enhancing quality and level of service	Walmart
Product differentiation	Use information systems to differentiate products, and enable new services and products	Uber, Nike, Apple
Focus on market niche	Use information systems to enable a focused strategy on a single market niche; specialize	Hilton Hotels, Harrah's
Customer and supplier intimacy	Use information systems to develop strong ties and loyalty with customers and suppliers	Toyota Corporation, Amazon

side, Amazon keeps track of user preferences for book and CD purchases and can recommend titles purchased by others to its customers. Strong linkages to customers and suppliers increase **switching costs** (the cost of switching from one product to a competing product) and loyalty to your firm.

Table 3.4 summarizes the competitive strategies we have just described. Some companies focus on one of these strategies, but you will often see companies pursuing several of them simultaneously. For example, Starbucks, the world's largest specialty coffee retailer, offers unique high-end specialty coffees and beverages but is also trying to compete by lowering costs.

The Internet's Impact on Competitive Advantage

Because of the Internet, the traditional competitive forces are still at work, but competitive rivalry has become much more intense (Porter, 2001). Internet technology is based on universal standards that any company can use, making it easy for rivals to compete on price alone and for new competitors to enter the market. Because information is available to everyone, the Internet raises the bargaining power of customers, who can quickly find the lowest-cost provider on the web. Profits have been dampened. Table 3.5 summarizes some of the potentially negative impacts of the Internet on business firms identified by Porter.

The Internet has nearly destroyed some industries and has severely threatened more. For instance, the printed encyclopedia industry and the travel agency industry have been nearly decimated by the availability of substitutes over the Internet. Likewise, the Internet has had a significant impact on the retail, music, book, retail brokerage, software, telecommunications, and newspaper industries.

However, the Internet has also created entirely new markets; formed the basis for thousands of new products, services, and business models; and provided new opportunities for building brands with very large and loyal customer bases. Amazon, Alibaba, eBay, iTunes, YouTube, Facebook, Travelocity, and Google are examples. In this sense, the Internet is "transforming" entire industries, forcing firms to change how they do business.

TABLE 3.5 IMPACT OF THE INTERNET ON COMPETITIVE FORCES AND INDUSTRY STRUCTURE

COMPETITIVE FORCE	IMPACT OF THE INTERNET
Substitute products or services	Enables new substitutes to emerge with new approaches to meeting needs and performing functions
Customers' bargaining power	Availability of global price and product information shifts bargaining power to customers
Suppliers' bargaining power	Procurement over the Internet tends to raise bargaining power over suppliers; suppliers can also benefit from reduced barriers to entry and from the elimination of distributors and other intermediaries standing between them and their users
Threat of new entrants	Internet reduces barriers to entry, such as the need for a sales force, access to channels, and physical assets; it provides a technology for driving business processes that makes other things easier to do
Positioning and rivalry among existing competitors	Widens the geographic market, increasing the number of competitors and reducing differences among competitors; makes it more difficult to sustain operational advantages; puts pressure to compete on price

Smart Products and the Internet of Things

The growing use of sensors in industrial and consumer products, often called the Internet of Things (IoT), is an excellent example of how the Internet is changing competition within industries and creating new products and services. Nike, Under Armour, Gatorade, and many other sports and fitness companies are pouring money into wearable health trackers and fitness equipment that use sensors to report users' activities to remote corporate computing centers where the data can be analyzed (see the Interactive Session on Technology). Farm tractors from John Deere, Kubota, and Mahindra are loaded with field radar, GPS transceivers, and hundreds of sensors keeping track of the equipment, as described in the Chapter 1 ending case. GE is creating a new business out of helping its aircraft and wind turbine clients improve operations by examining the data generated from the many thousands of sensors in the equipment (see the Chapter 12 ending case). The result is what are referred to as "smart products"—products that are a part of a larger set of information-intensive services sold by firms (Gandhi and Gervet, 2016; Davis, 2015; Porter and Heppelmann, 2014; Iansiti and Lakhani, 2014).

The impact of smart, Internet-connected products is just now being understood. Smart products offer new functionality, greater reliability, and more intense use of products while providing detailed information that can be used to improve both the products and the customer experience. They expand opportunities for product and service differentiation. When you buy a wearable digital health product, you not only get the product itself, you also get a host of services available from the manufacturer's cloud servers. Smart products increase rivalry among firms that will either innovate or lose customers to competitors. Smart products generally raise switching costs and inhibit

INTERACTIVE SESSION: TECHNOLOGY

Smart Products, Smart Companies

If you don't use a smart product yet, you soon will. Your shoes, your clothing, your watch, your water bottle, and even your toothbrush are being redesigned to incorporate sensors and metering devices connected to the Internet so that their performance can be monitored and analyzed.

What difference does that make? Take Nike, the world's biggest sports footwear and apparel company. Nike has created a series of information technology–based products and an ecosystem of gadgets and services built around measurable personal improvement through exercise. The Nike+ ecosystem links Nike's corporate computer system to smart devices such as the Nike+ SportWatch GPS, the Nike+ FuelBand, and the Nike+ Running App on Apple and Android mobile devices. This enables Nike to analyze individual performance and activity data collected by the devices to help users train and work out more effectively. It also adds value to Nike products and a reason to stay with the brand.

The Nike+ SportWatch GPS keeps track of your location, pace, distance, laps, calories burned, and (with the Polar Wearlink+) heart rate. The Nike+ Running App tracks your route, distance, pace, calories burned, and time using your phone or another Nike-partnered device, giving you audio feedback as you run. The Nike+ FuelBand activity tracker is worn on the wrist and used with an Apple iPhone or iPad. The FuelBand enables wearers to track their physical activity, steps taken daily, and amount of calories burned. The information it collects is integrated into the Nike+ online community and phone application, allowing wearers to set their own fitness goals, monitor their progress on the device LED display, and compare themselves to others within the Nike community.

Nike's proprietary software turns all tracked movement from Nike's smart devices into NikeFuel points, which can show achievements, can be shared with friends, or can be used to engage others in competition. NikeFuel is Nike's universal way for measuring movement for all kinds of activities using a metric that enables comparisons—no matter what height, weight, gender, or activity—to past performances, another person, or a daily average (which Nike defines as 2,000 Fuel points.) Users of multiple Nike+ devices can visit the nikeplus.com site to access all their data—including lifetime NikeFuel points accumulated from all their Nike+ devices.

Nike is developing other fitness technology products to integrate with Nike+. The more people measure their activity with NikeFuel, the more they are locked in to the Nike ecosystem and the harder it will be to switch to other companies' products. Nike's integration of information and technology into its products keeps people coming back to Nike's own website and apps.

Nike believes that technology is revolutionizing its relationship with consumers, turning it into a company that provides services as well as products. In the past, when you bought a product, that was the end of the relationship with the company. Now, the purchase of any Nike product has become the beginning of the company's relationship with the consumer. The deeper the relationship, the more consumers will embrace and stay loyal to the Nike brand.

Under Armour, noted for performance clothing using technologically advanced material, is making its products smarter as well. The company has spent $710 million to scoop up mobile apps such as MyFitnessPal, MapMyFitness, and Endomondo, which enables it to tap into the world's largest digital health and fitness community. Under Armour can generate revenue from in-app ads, including ads from other companies, and purchases from app which the users referred to for its products. The platform delivers an unprecedented depth of information and insight about fitness-and health-oriented consumers, creating numerous opportunities for Under Armour and other brands to engage with potential and existing customers. For example, MapMyFitness collects data about a user's name, e-mail address, birth date, location, performance, and profile if the user connects to the app using social media. Under Armour does not sell identifiable personal data about individuals to third parties but does provide advertisers with aggregate information about app users. Under Armour is hoping that the daily use of its smartphone apps will build stronger ties to customers that will lead to stronger sales of its own apparel, footwear, and other athletic gear.

Under Armour has teamed up with e-commerce retailer Zappos to send users a pop-up notification when their sneakers need replacement, based on workout data logged in MapMyFitness apps. The brand visualizes clothes themselves to eventually become the means to track movement and biorhythms. Under Armour developed its own smart footwear called UA SpeedForm Gemini 2 Record Equipped, which tracks a runner's time and date, duration, distance, and splits without the need for other devices. The company also partnered with HTC to develop UA HealthBox, a $400 red box that includes a Wi-Fi scale (for measuring weight and body fat), a heart rate chest strap and removable sensor, and a shower-proof dimpled fitness band to track workouts and sleep. The data these devices collect are stored on an Under Armor Record app on an iPhone or Android phone.

Gatorade, with a 78 percent share of the $7.21 billion sports-drinks market, is developing a microchip-fitted "smart cap" bottle that communicates digitally with a bandage-like sweat patch to provide athletes and fitness buffs constant updates on how much they should drink. According to Gatorade, individual hydration needs differ, with sweat loss ranging from half a liter to more than two liters per hour of exercise. The company is planning to launch as many as a dozen different formulas for electrolytes and carbohydrates in small pods that snap on to bottles.

Gatorade began testing the smart-cap bottle with Brazil's national soccer team ahead of the 2014 World Cup and is testing a new version with the Boston Celtics basketball team and FC Barcelona soccer squad. In the field-tested prototypes, flashing lights tell players when they need to hydrate. Users can customize the smart caps with their name, team logo, and number.

According to Xavi Cortadellas, Gatorade's senior director of global innovation and design, personalized nutrition and integrating technology in sports are the next frontier of performance. Gatorade's parent company, PepsiCo, is actively attempting to expand into areas outside of sugary sodas, and such technology-enabled products provide opportunities.

Sources: Kate Taylor, "Gatorade Is Developing a 'Smart Cap' That Keeps Track of Hydration," *Business Insider*, March 21, 2016; Mike Esterl, "Gatorade Sets Its Sights on Digital Fitness," *Wall Street Journal*, March 10, 2016; Edward C. Baig, "Under Armour and HTC Team Up on Connected Fitness," *USA Today*, January 5, 2016; www.underarmour.com, accessed April 20, 2016; www.nike.com, accessed April 19, 2016; John Kell, "Why Under Armour Is Making a Costly Bet on Connected Fitness," Fortune, April 21, 2016; and Jared Linzdon, "The Rise and Fall of Wearable Fitness Trackers," *The Globe and Mail*, January 5, 2015.

CASE STUDY QUESTIONS

1. What are the different competitive strategies that are being pursued by the companies mentioned in the case?
2. How are information technology and smart products related to these strategies? Describe the role of information technology in these products.
3. Are there any ethical issues raised by these smart products such as their impact on consumer privacy? Explain your answer.

new entrants to a market because existing customers are trapped in the dominant firm's software environment. Finally, smart products may decrease the power of suppliers of industrial components if, as many believe, the physical product becomes less important than the software and hardware that make it run.

The Business Value Chain Model

Although the Porter model is very helpful for identifying competitive forces and suggesting generic strategies, it is not very specific about what exactly to do, and it does not provide a methodology to follow for achieving competitive advantages. If your goal is to achieve operational excellence, where do you start? Here's where the business value chain model is helpful.

The **value chain model** highlights specific activities in the business where competitive strategies can best be applied (Porter, 1985) and where information systems are most likely to have a strategic impact. This model identifies specific, critical leverage points where a firm can use information technology most effectively to enhance its competitive position. The value chain model views the firm as a series or chain of basic activities that add a margin of value to a firm's products or services. These activities can be categorized as either primary activities or support activities (see Figure 3.9).

Primary activities are most directly related to the production and distribution of the firm's products and services, which create value for the customer.

FIGURE 3.9 THE VALUE CHAIN MODEL

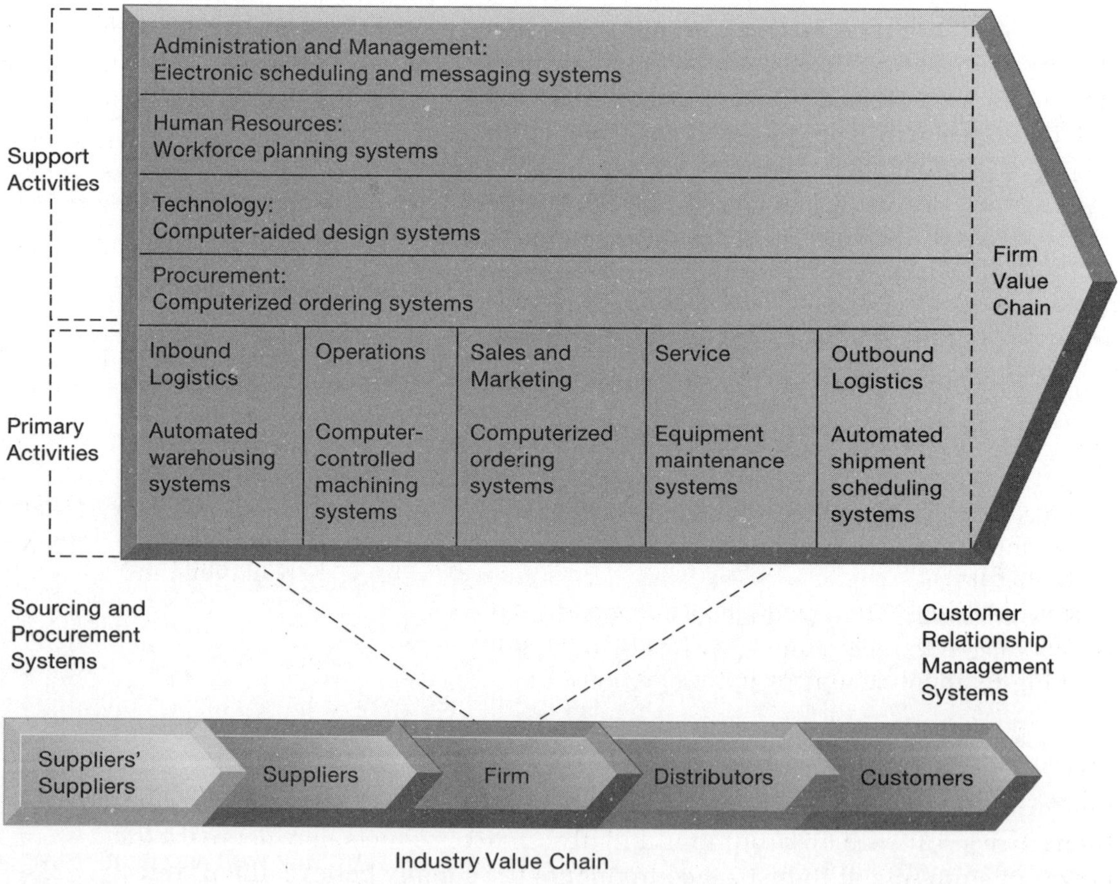

This figure provides examples of systems for both primary and support activities of a firm and of its value partners that can add a margin of value to a firm's products or services.

Primary activities include inbound logistics, operations, outbound logistics, sales and marketing, and service. Inbound logistics includes receiving and storing materials for distribution to production. Operations transforms inputs into finished products. Outbound logistics entails storing and distributing finished products. Sales and marketing includes promoting and selling the firm's products. The service activity includes maintenance and repair of the firm's goods and services.

Support activities make the delivery of the primary activities possible and consist of organization infrastructure (administration and management), human resources (employee recruiting, hiring, and training), technology (improving products and the production process), and procurement (purchasing input).

Now you can ask at each stage of the value chain, "How can we use information systems to improve operational efficiency and improve customer and supplier intimacy?" This will force you to critically examine how you perform value-adding activities at each stage and how the business processes might be improved. You can also begin to ask how information systems can be used to improve the relationship with customers and with suppliers who lie outside the firm's value chain but belong to the firm's extended value chain where they are absolutely critical to your success. Here, supply chain management systems that coordinate the flow of resources into your firm and customer relationship management systems that coordinate your sales and support employees with customers are two of the most common system applications that result from a business value chain analysis. We discuss these enterprise applications in detail later in Chapter 9.

Using the business value chain model will also cause you to consider benchmarking your business processes against your competitors or others in related industries and identifying industry best practices. **Benchmarking** involves comparing the efficiency and effectiveness of your business processes against strict standards and then measuring performance against those standards. Industry **best practices** are usually identified by consulting companies, research organizations, government agencies, and industry associations as the most successful solutions or problem-solving methods for consistently and effectively achieving a business objective.

Once you have analyzed the various stages in the value chain at your business, you can come up with candidate applications of information systems. Then, once you have a list of candidate applications, you can decide which to develop first. By making improvements in your own business value chain that your competitors might miss, you can achieve competitive advantage by attaining operational excellence, lowering costs, improving profit margins, and forging a closer relationship with customers and suppliers. If your competitors are making similar improvements, then at least you will not be at a competitive disadvantage—the worst of all cases!

Extending the Value Chain: The Value Web

Figure 3.9 shows that a firm's value chain is linked to the value chains of its suppliers, distributors, and customers. After all, the performance of most firms depends not only on what goes on inside a firm but also on how well the firm coordinates with direct and indirect suppliers, delivery firms (logistics partners, such as FedEx or UPS), and, of course, customers.

How can information systems be used to achieve strategic advantage at the industry level? By working with other firms, industry participants can use information technology to develop industrywide standards for exchanging information or business transactions electronically, which force all market participants to subscribe to similar standards. Such efforts increase efficiency, making product substitution less likely and perhaps raising entry costs—thus discouraging new entrants. Also, industry members can build industrywide, IT-supported consortia, symposia, and communications networks to coordinate activities concerning government agencies, foreign competition, and competing industries.

Looking at the industry value chain encourages you to think about how to use information systems to link up more efficiently with your suppliers, strategic partners, and customers. Strategic advantage derives from your ability to relate your value chain to the value chains of other partners in the process. For instance, if you are Amazon.com, you want to build systems that:

- Make it easy for suppliers to display goods and open stores on the Amazon site
- Make it easy for customers to pay for goods
- Develop systems that coordinate the shipment of goods to customers
- Develop shipment tracking systems for customers

Internet technology has made it possible to create highly synchronized industry value chains called value webs. A **value web** is a collection of independent firms that use information technology to coordinate their value chains to produce a product or service for a market collectively. It is more customer driven and operates in a less linear fashion than the traditional value chain.

Figure 3.10 shows that this value web synchronizes the business processes of customers, suppliers, and trading partners among different companies in an industry or in related industries. These value webs are flexible and adaptive to changes in supply and demand. Relationships can be bundled or unbundled in response to changing market conditions. Firms will accelerate time to market and to customers by optimizing their value web relationships to make quick decisions on who can deliver the required products or services at the right price and location.

Synergies, Core Competencies, and Network-Based Strategies

A large corporation is typically a collection of businesses. Often, the firm is organized financially as a collection of strategic business units and the returns to the firm are directly tied to the performance of all the strategic business units. Information systems can improve the overall performance of these business units by promoting synergies and core competencies.

Synergies

The idea of synergies is that when the output of some units can be used as inputs to other units or two organizations pool markets and expertise, these relationships lower costs and generate profits. Bank and financial firm mergers such as

FIGURE 3.10 THE VALUE WEB

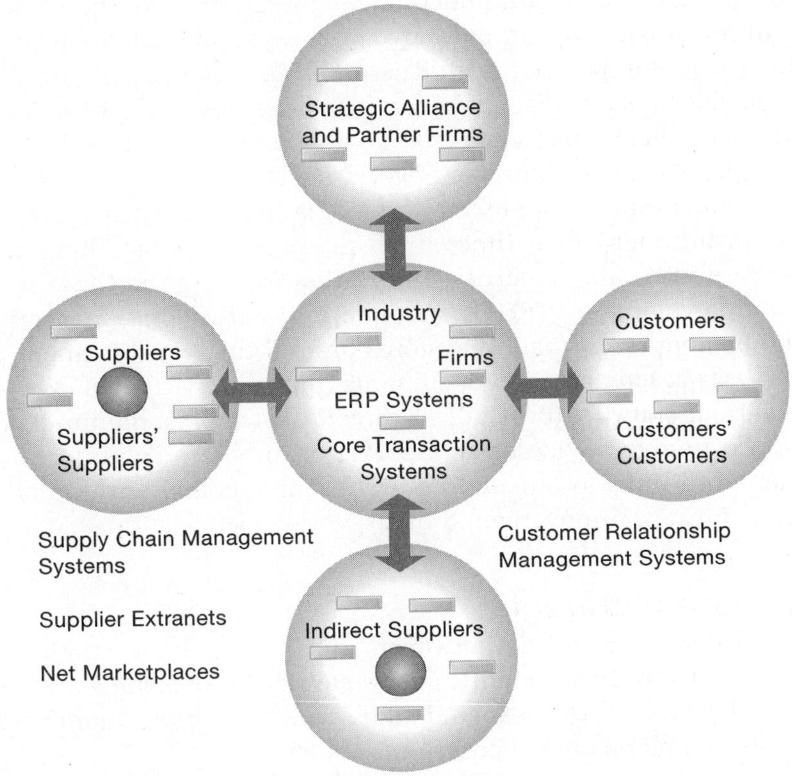

The value web is a networked system that can synchronize the value chains of business partners within an industry to respond rapidly to changes in supply and demand.

the merger of JPMorgan Chase and Bank of New York as well as Bank of America and Countrywide Financial Corporation occurred precisely for this purpose.

One use of information technology in these synergy situations is to tie together the operations of disparate business units so that they can act as a whole. For example, when large national banks acquire mortgage originating firms they are able to tap into a large pool of new customers who might be interested in its credit card, consumer banking, and other financial products. Information systems would help the merged companies consolidate operations, lower retailing costs, and increase cross-marketing of financial products.

Enhancing Core Competencies

Yet another way to use information systems for competitive advantage is to think about ways that systems can enhance core competencies. The argument is that the performance of all business units will increase insofar as these business units develop, or create, a central core of competencies. A **core competency** is an activity for which a firm is a world-class leader. Core competencies may involve being the world's best miniature parts designer, the best package delivery service, or the best thin-film manufacturer. In general, a core competency relies on knowledge that is gained over many years of practical field experience with a technology. This practical knowledge is typically supplemented with a long-term research effort and committed employees.

Any information system that encourages the sharing of knowledge across business units enhances competency. Such systems might encourage or enhance existing competencies and help employees become aware of new external knowledge; such systems might also help a business leverage existing competencies to related markets.

For example, Procter & Gamble, a world leader in brand management and consumer product innovation, uses a series of systems to enhance its core competencies. An intranet called InnovationNet helps people working on similar problems share ideas and expertise. InnovationNet connects those working in research and development (R&D), engineering, purchasing, marketing, legal affairs, and business information systems around the world, using a portal to provide browser-based access to documents, reports, charts, videos, and other data from various sources. It includes a directory of subject matter experts who can be tapped to give advice or collaborate on problem solving and product development and links to outside research scientists and entrepreneurs who are searching for new, innovative products worldwide.

Network-Based Strategies

The availability of Internet and networking technology has inspired strategies that take advantage of firms' abilities to create networks or network with each other. Network-based strategies include the use of network economics, a virtual company model, and business ecosystems.

Network Economics Network economics refers to market situations where the economic value being produced depends on the number of people using a product. For certain products and markets, the real economic value comes from the fact that other people use the product. In these situations, "network effects" are at work. For instance, what's the value of a telephone if it is not connected to millions of others? Email has value because it allows us to communicate with millions of others. Business models which are based on network effects have been highly successful on the Internet, including social networks, software, messaging apps, and on-demand companies like Uber and Airbnb.

In traditional economics—the economics of factories and agriculture—production experiences diminishing returns. The more any given resource is applied to production, the lower the marginal gain in output, until a point is reached where the additional inputs produce no additional outputs. This is the law of diminishing returns, and it is the foundation for most of modern economics.

In some situations, the law of diminishing returns does not work. For instance, in a network, the marginal costs of adding another participant are about zero, whereas the marginal gain is much larger. The larger the number of subscribers in a telephone system or the Internet, the greater the value to all participants because each user can interact with more people. It is not much more expensive to operate a television station with 1,000 subscribers than with 10 million subscribers. The value of a community of people grows with size, whereas the cost of adding new members is inconsequential. The value of Facebook to users increases greatly as more people use the social network.

From this network economics perspective, information technology can be strategically useful. Internet sites can be used by firms to build communities of users—like-minded customers who want to share their experiences. This builds customer loyalty and enjoyment and builds unique ties to customers. eBay, the giant online auction site, is an example. This business is based on a network of millions of users, and has built an online community by using the Internet. The more people offering products on eBay, the more valuable the eBay site is to everyone because more products are listed, and more competition among suppliers lowers prices. Network economics also provides strategic benefits to commercial software vendors. The value of their software and complementary software products increases as more people use them, and there is a larger installed base to justify continued use of the product and vendor support.

Virtual Company Model Another network-based strategy uses the model of a virtual company to create a competitive business. A **virtual company**, also known as a virtual organization, uses networks to link people, assets, and ideas, enabling it to ally with other companies to create and distribute products and services without being limited by traditional organizational boundaries or physical locations. One company can use the capabilities of another company without being organizationally tied to that company. The virtual company model is useful when a company finds it cheaper to acquire products, services, or capabilities from an external vendor or when it needs to move quickly to exploit new market opportunities and lacks the time and resources to respond on its own.

Global fashion companies, such as LVMH, GUESS, Ann Taylor, Levi Strauss, and Reebok, enlist Hong Kong–based Li & Fung to manage production and shipment of their garments. Li & Fung handles product development, raw material sourcing, production planning, quality assurance, and shipping. Li & Fung does not own any fabric, factories, or machines, outsourcing all of its work to a network of more than 15,000 suppliers in 40 countries all over the world. Customers place orders with Li & Fung over its private extranet. Li & Fung then sends instructions to appropriate raw material suppliers and factories where the clothing is produced. The Li & Fung extranet tracks the entire production process for each order. Working as a virtual company keeps Li & Fung flexible and adaptable so that it can design and produce the products ordered by its clients in short order to keep pace with rapidly changing fashion trends.

Business Ecosystems and Platforms The Internet and the emergence of digital firms call for some modification of the industry competitive forces model. The traditional Porter model assumes a relatively static industry environment; relatively clear-cut industry boundaries; and a relatively stable set of suppliers, substitutes, and customers, with the focus on industry players in a market environment. Instead of participating in a single industry, some of today's firms are much more aware that they participate in industry sets—collections of industries that provide related services and products (see Figure 3.11). **Business ecosystem** is another term for these loosely coupled but interdependent networks of suppliers, distributors, outsourcing firms, transportation service firms, and technology manufacturers (Iansiti and Levien, 2004).

The concept of a business ecosystem builds on the idea of the value web described earlier, the main difference being that cooperation takes place across

FIGURE 3.11 AN ECOSYSTEM STRATEGIC MODEL

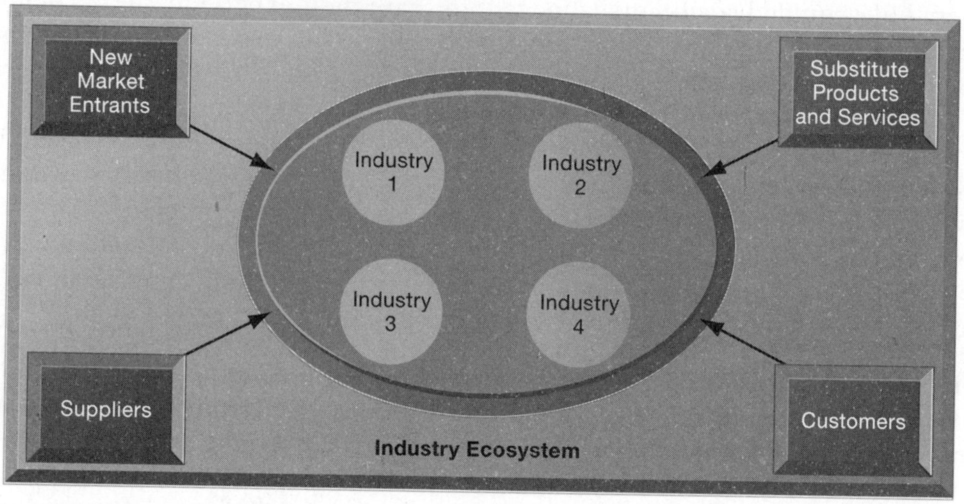

The digital firm era requires a more dynamic view of the boundaries among industries, firms, customers, and suppliers, with competition occurring among industry sets in a business ecosystem. In the ecosystem model, multiple industries work together to deliver value to the customer. IT plays an important role in enabling a dense network of interactions among the participating firms.

many industries rather than many firms. For instance, both Microsoft and Facebook provide **platforms** composed of information systems, technologies, and services that thousands of other firms in different industries use to enhance their own capabilities (Van Alstyne et al., 2016).

Microsoft has estimated that more than 40,000 firms use its Windows platform to deliver their own products, support Microsoft products, and extend the value of Microsoft's own firm. Facebook is a platform used by billions of people and millions of businesses to interact and share information as well as to buy, market, and sell numerous products and services. Business ecosystems can be characterized as having one or a few keystone firms that dominate the ecosystem and create the platforms used by other niche firms. Keystone firms in the Microsoft ecosystem include Microsoft and technology producers such as Intel and IBM. Niche firms include thousands of software application firms, software developers, service firms, networking firms, and consulting firms that both support and rely on the Microsoft products.

Information technology plays a powerful role in establishing business ecosystems. Obviously, many firms use information systems to develop into keystone firms by building IT-based platforms that other firms can use. In the digital firm era, we can expect greater emphasis on the use of IT to build industry ecosystems because the costs of participating in such ecosystems will fall and the benefits to all firms will increase rapidly as the platform grows.

Individual firms should consider how their information systems will enable them to become profitable niche players in larger ecosystems created by keystone firms. For instance, in making decisions about which products to build or which services to offer, a firm should consider the existing business ecosystems related to these products and how it might use IT to enable participation in these larger ecosystems.

A powerful, current example of a rapidly expanding ecosystem is the mobile Internet platform. In this ecosystem there are four industries: device makers (Apple iPhone, Samsung Galaxy, Motorola, LG, and others), wireless telecommunication firms (AT&T, Verizon, MTN [South Africa], STC Group [Saudi Arabia], Vodafone [UK], Orascom [Egypt], and others), independent software applications providers (generally small firms selling games, applications, and ring tones), and Internet service providers (who participate as providers of Internet service to the mobile platform).

Each of these industries has its own history, interests, and driving forces. But these elements come together in a sometimes cooperative and sometimes competitive new industry we refer to as the mobile digital platform ecosystem. More than other firms, Apple has managed to combine these industries into a system. It is Apple's mission to sell physical devices (iPhones) that are nearly as powerful as yesterday's supercomputers. These devices work only with a high-speed broadband network supplied by the wireless phone carriers. In order to attract a large customer base, the iPhone had to be more than just a cell phone. Apple differentiated this product by making it a "smart phone," one capable of running more than a million different, useful applications. Apple could not develop all these applications itself. Instead, it relies on thousands of generally small, independent software developers to provide these applications, which can be purchased at the iTunes store. In the background is the Internet service provider industry, which makes money whenever iPhone users connect to the Internet. These four different industries together form an ecosystem, creating value for consumers that none of them could acting alone.

3-4 What are the challenges posed by strategic information systems, and how should they be addressed?

Strategic information systems often change the organization as well as its products, services, and operating procedures, driving the organization into new behavioral patterns. Successfully using information systems to achieve a competitive advantage is challenging and requires precise coordination of technology, organizations, and management.

Sustaining Competitive Advantage

The competitive advantages that strategic systems confer do not necessarily last long enough to ensure long-term profitability. Because competitors can retaliate and copy strategic systems, competitive advantage is not always sustainable. Markets, customer expectations, and technology change; globalization has made these changes even more rapid and unpredictable. The Internet can make competitive advantage disappear very quickly because virtually all companies can use this technology. Classic strategic systems, such as American

Airlines's SABRE computerized reservation system, Citibank's ATM system, and FedEx's package tracking system, benefited by being the first in their industries. Then rival systems emerged. Amazon was an e-commerce leader but now faces competition from eBay, Walmart, and Google. Information systems alone cannot provide an enduring business advantage. Systems originally intended to be strategic frequently become tools for survival, required by every firm to stay in business, or they may inhibit organizations from making the strategic changes essential for future success.

Aligning IT with Business Objectives

The research on IT and business performance has found that (a) the more successfully a firm can align information technology with its business goals, the more profitable it will be, and (b) only one-quarter of firms achieve alignment of IT with the business. About half of a business firm's profits can be explained by alignment of IT with business (Luftman, 2003).

Most businesses get it wrong: Information technology takes on a life of its own and does not serve management and shareholder interests very well. Instead of businesspeople taking an active role in shaping IT to the enterprise, they ignore it, claim not to understand IT, and tolerate failure in the IT area as just a nuisance to work around. Such firms pay a hefty price in poor performance. Successful firms and managers understand what IT can do and how it works, take an active role in shaping its use, and measure its impact on revenues and profits.

Management Checklist: Performing a Strategic Systems Analysis

To align IT with the business and use information systems effectively for competitive advantage, managers need to perform a strategic systems analysis. To identify the types of systems that provide a strategic advantage to their firms, managers should ask the following questions:

1. What is the structure of the industry in which the firm is located?
   - What are some of the competitive forces at work in the industry? Are there new entrants to the industry? What is the relative power of suppliers, customers, and substitute products and services over prices?
   - Is the basis of competition quality, price, or brand?
   - What are the direction and nature of change within the industry? From where are the momentum and change coming?
   - How is the industry currently using information technology? Is the organization behind or ahead of the industry in its application of information systems?
2. What are the business, firm, and industry value chains for this particular firm?
   - How is the company creating value for the customer—through lower prices and transaction costs or higher quality? Are there any places in the value chain where the business could create more value for the customer and additional profit for the company?
   - Does the firm understand and manage its business processes using the best practices available? Is it taking maximum advantage of supply chain management, customer relationship management, and enterprise systems?

- Does the firm leverage its core competencies?
- Is the industry supply chain and customer base changing in ways that benefit or harm the firm?
- Can the firm benefit from strategic partnerships, value webs, ecosystems, or platforms?
- Where in the value chain will information systems provide the greatest value to the firm?

3. Have we aligned IT with our business strategy and goals?

- Have we correctly articulated our business strategy and goals?
- Is IT improving the right business processes and activities to promote this strategy?
- Are we using the right metrics to measure progress toward those goals?

Managing Strategic Transitions

Adopting the kinds of strategic systems described in this chapter generally requires changes in business goals, relationships with customers and suppliers, and business processes. These sociotechnical changes, affecting both social and technical elements of the organization, can be considered **strategic transitions**—a movement between levels of sociotechnical systems.

Such changes often entail blurring of organizational boundaries, both external and internal. Suppliers and customers must become intimately linked and may share each other's responsibilities. Managers will need to devise new business processes for coordinating their firms' activities with those of customers, suppliers, and other organizations. The organizational change requirements surrounding new information systems are so important that they merit attention throughout this text. Chapter 14 examines organizational change issues in more detail.

Review Summary

3-1 *Which features of organizations do managers need to know about to build and use information systems successfully?*

All modern organizations are hierarchical, specialized, and impartial, using explicit routines to maximize efficiency. All organizations have their own cultures and politics arising from differences in interest groups, and they are affected by their surrounding environment. Organizations differ in goals, groups served, social roles, leadership styles, incentives, types of tasks performed, and type of structure. These features help explain differences in organizations' use of information systems. Information systems and the organizations in which they are used interact with and influence each other.

3-2 *What is the impact of information systems on organizations?*

The introduction of a new information system will affect organizational structure, goals, work design, values, competition between interest groups, decision making, and day-to-day behavior. At the same time, information systems must be designed to serve the needs of important organizational groups and will be shaped by the organization's structure, business processes, goals, culture, politics, and management. Information technology can reduce transaction and agency costs, and such changes have been accentuated in organizations using the Internet. New systems disrupt established patterns of work and power relationships, so there is often considerable resistance to them when they are introduced.

3-3 *How do Porter's competitive forces model, the value chain model, synergies, core competencies, and network economics help companies develop competitive strategies using information systems?*

In Porter's competitive forces model, the strategic position of the firm and its strategies are determined by competition with its traditional direct competitors, but they are also greatly affected by new market entrants, substitute products and services, suppliers, and customers. Information systems help companies compete by maintaining low costs, differentiating products or services, focusing on market niche, strengthening ties with customers and suppliers, and increasing barriers to market entry with high levels of operational excellence.

The value chain model highlights specific activities in the business where competitive strategies and information systems will have the greatest impact. The model views the firm as a series of primary and support activities that add value to a firm's products or services. Primary activities are directly related to production and distribution, whereas support activities make the delivery of primary activities possible. A firm's value chain can be linked to the value chains of its suppliers, distributors, and customers. A value web consists of information systems that enhance competitiveness at the industry level by promoting the use of standards and industrywide consortia and by enabling businesses to work more efficiently with their value partners.

Because firms consist of multiple business units, information systems achieve additional efficiencies or enhance services by tying together the operations of disparate business units. Information systems help businesses leverage their core competencies by promoting the sharing of knowledge across business units. Information systems facilitate business models based on large networks of users or subscribers that take advantage of network economics. A virtual company strategy uses networks to link to other firms so that a company can use the capabilities of other companies to build, market, and distribute products and services. In business ecosystems, multiple industries work together to deliver value to the customer. Information systems support a dense network of interactions among the participating firms.

3-4 *What are the challenges posed by strategic information systems, and how should they be addressed?*

Implementing strategic systems often requires extensive organizational change and a transition from one sociotechnical level to another. Such changes are called strategic transitions and are often difficult and painful to achieve. Moreover, not all strategic systems are profitable, and they can be expensive to build. Many strategic information systems are easily copied by other firms so that strategic advantage is not always sustainable.

Key Terms

Review Questions

3-1 Which features of organizations do managers need to know to build and use information systems successfully?

- Discuss the two way relationship between organization and IT from both technical and behavioral perspective.
- Describe the role of IS and disruptive technologies in aiding organizations in perceiving and managing environment changes.

3-2 What is the impact of information systems on organizations?

- How does information technology help in reducing transaction costs and internal management costs? Explain.
- Discuss the behavioral consequences of introducing new information technology applications in organizations.
- How should the change brought about by the introduction of information technology be managed to curb organizational resistance?
- Which organizational factors should be considered while planning for a new information system?

3-3 How do Porter's competitive forces model, the value chain model, synergies, core competencies, and network economics help companies develop competitive strategies using information systems?

- Define Porter's competitive forces model and explain how it works.
- Describe what the competitive forces model explains about competitive advantage.
- List and describe four competitive strategies enabled by information systems that firms can pursue.
- Describe how information systems can support each of these competitive strategies and give examples.
- Explain why aligning IT with business objectives is essential for strategic use of systems.
- Define and describe the value chain model.
- Explain how the value chain model can be used to identify opportunities for information systems.
- Define the value web and show how it is related to the value chain.
- Explain how the value web helps businesses identify opportunities for strategic information systems.
- Describe how the Internet has changed competitive forces and competitive advantage.
- Explain how information systems promote synergies and core competencies.
- Describe how promoting synergies and core competencies enhances competitive advantage.
- Explain how businesses benefit by using network economics and ecosystems.
- Define and describe a virtual company and the benefits of pursuing a virtual company strategy.
- Define and describe business ecosystems and platforms.

3-4 What are the challenges posed by strategic information systems, and how should they be addressed?

- Discuss the need for strategic system analysis and the role of structure, goal alignment, and value chains in this.
- Define strategic transitions. Why do they need to be managed?

Discussion Questions

3-5 It has been said that there is no such thing as a sustainable strategic advantage. Do you agree? Why or why not?

3-6 What is meant by the phrase "IT should flatten hierarchies?"

3-7 What are some of the issues to consider in determining whether the Internet would provide your business with a competitive advantage?

Hands-On MIS Projects

The projects in this section give you hands-on experience identifying information systems to support a business strategy and to solve a customer retention problem, using a database to improve decision making about business strategy, and using web tools to configure and price an automobile.

Management Decision Problems

3-8 Marks & Spencer Group is a leading department store chain in the United Kingdom. Its retail stores sell a range of merchandise. Senior management has decided that Marks & Spencer should tailor merchandise more to local tastes, and that the colors, sizes, brands, and styles of clothing and other merchandise should be based on the sales patterns in each individual store. How could information systems help management implement this new strategy? What pieces of data should these systems collect to help management make merchandising decisions that support this strategy?

3-9 T-Mobile has launched aggressive campaigns to attract customers with lower mobile phone prices, and it has added to its customer base. However, management wants to know if there are other ways of luring and keeping customers. Are customers concerned about the level of customer service, uneven network coverage, or data plans? How can the company use information systems to help find the answer? What management decisions could be made using information from these systems?

Improving Decision Making: Using Web Tools to Configure and Price an Automobile

Software skills: Internet-based software
Business skills: Researching product information and pricing

3-10 In this exercise, you will use software at car websites to find product information about a car of your choice and use that information to make an important purchase decision. You will also evaluate two of tnese sites as selling tools.

You are interested in purchasing a new Vauxhall Corsa (or some other car of your choice). Go to the Web site of AutoTrader.co.uk (www.autotrader.co.uk) and begin your investigation. Locate the Vauxhall Corsa. Research the various models, choose one you prefer in terms of price, features, and safety ratings. Locate and read at least two reviews. Surf the Web site of the manufacturer, in this case Vauxhall (www.vauxhall.co.uk). Compare the information available on Vauxhall's Web site with that of Autotrader.co.uk for the Vauxhall Corsa. Try to locate the lowest price for the car you want in a local dealer's inventory. Suggest improvements for Autotrader.co.uk and Vauxhall.co.uk.

Collaboration and Teamwork Project

Identifying Opportunities for Strategic Information Systems

3-11 With your team of three or four other students, select a company described in the *Wall Street Journal*, *Fortune*, *Forbes*, or another business publication or do your research on the web. Visit the company's website to find additional information about that company and to see how the firm is using the web. On the basis of this information, analyze the business. Include a description of the organization's features, such as important business business processes, culture, structure, and environment as well as its business strategy. Suggest strategic information systems appropriate for that particular business, including those based on Internet technology, if appropriate. If possible, use Google Docs and Google Drive or Google Sites to brainstorm, organize, and develop a presentation of your findings for the class.

Deutsche Bank: The Cost of Legacy Systems

CASE STUDY

Deutsche Bank AG, founded in 1870, is one of the world's top financial companies, with 2,790 branches in 70 countries. It offers a range of financial products and services, including retail and commercial banking, foreign exchange, and services for mergers and acquisitions. The bank provides products for mortgages, consumer finance, credit cards, life insurance, and corporate pension plans; financing for international trade; and customized wealth management services for wealthy private clients. Deutsche Bank is also the largest bank in Germany, with 1,845 retail branch locations, and plays a central role in German economic life. In many ways, Deutsche Bank is the embodiment of the global financial system.

Deutsche has the world's largest portfolio of derivatives, valued at around $46 trillion. A financial derivative is a contract between two or more parties whose value is dependent upon or derived from one or more underlying assets, such as stocks, bonds, commodities, currencies, and interest rates. Although Deutsche Bank had survived the 2008 banking crisis, which was partly triggered by flawed derivatives, it is now struggling with seismic changes in the banking industry, including recent regulatory change and fears of a global economic downturn. The bank was forced to pay $7.2 billion to resolve U.S. regulator complaints about its sale of toxic mortgage securities that contributed to the 2008 financial crisis. In addition, the Commodity Futures Trading Commission (CTFC) complained that Deutsche Bank submitted incomplete and untimely credit default swap data, failed to properly supervise employees responsible for swap data reporting, and lacked an adequate business continuity and disaster recovery plan. A credit default swap is a type of credit insurance contract in which an insurer promises to compensate an insured party (such as a bank) for losses incurred when a debtor (such as a corporation) defaults on a debt and which can be purchased or sold by either party on the financial market. Credit default swaps are very complex financial instruments.

Deutsche Bank is in trouble with U.S. regulators for its inability to fulfill swap reporting requirements under the Commodity Exchange Act and CFTC Regulations. The CFTC complained that on April 16, 2016, Deutsche Bank's swap data reporting system experienced a system outage that prevented Deutsche Bank from reporting any swap data for multiple asset classes for approximately five days. Deutsche Bank's subsequent efforts to end the system outage repeatedly exacerbated existing reporting problems and led to the discovery and creation of new reporting problems,

For example, Deutsche Bank's swap data reported before and after the system outage revealed persistent problems with the integrity of certain data fields, including numerous invalid legal entity identifiers. (A Legal Entity Identifier [LEI] is an identification code to uniquely identify all legal entities that are parties to financial transactions.) The CFTC complaint alleged that a number of these reporting problems persist today, affecting market data that is made available to the public as well as data that is used by the CFTC to evaluate systemic risk throughout the swaps markets. The CFTC complaint also alleged that Deutsche Bank's system outage and subsequent reporting problems occurred in part because Deutsche Bank failed to have an adequate business continuity and disaster recovery plan and other appropriate supervisory systems in place.

In addition to incurring high costs associated with coping with regulators and paying fines, Deutsche Bank was a very unwieldy and expensive bank to operate. The U.S. regulators have pointed out Deutsche Bank's antiquated technology as one reason why the bank was not always able to provide the correct information for running its business properly and responding to regulators. Poor information systems may have even contributed to the financial crisis. Banks often had trouble untangling the complex financial products they had bought and sold to determine their underlying value.

Banks, including Deutsche Bank, are intensive users of information technology and they rely on technology to spot misconduct. If Deutsche Bank was such an important player in the German and world financial systems, why were its systems not up to the job?

It turns out that Deutsche Bank, like other leading global financial companies, had undergone decades of mergers and expansion. When these banks merged or acquired other financial companies, they often did not make the requisite (and often far-reaching) changes to integrate their information systems with those of their acquisitions. The effort and costs required for this integration, including coordination across many management teams, were too great. So the banks left many old systems in place to handle the workload for each of their businesses. This created what experts call "spaghetti balls" of overlapping and often incompatible technology platforms and software programs. These antiquated legacy systems were designed to handle large numbers of transactions and sums of money, but they were not well-suited to managing large bank operations. They often did not allow information to be shared easily among departments or provide senior management with a coherent overview of bank operations.

Deutsche Bank had more than one hundred different booking systems for trades in London alone, and no common set of codes for identifying clients in each of these systems. Each of these systems might use a different number or code for identifying the same client, so it would be extremely difficult or impossible to show how the same client was treated in all of these systems. Individual teams and traders each had their own incompatible platforms. The bank had employed a deliberate strategy of pitting teams against each other to spur them on, but this further encouraged the use of different systems because competing traders and teams were reluctant to share their data. Yet the Bank ultimately had to reconcile the data from these disparate systems, often by hand, before trades could be processed and recorded.

This situation has made it very difficult for banks to undertake ambitious technology projects for the systems that they need today or to comply with regulatory requirements. U.S. regulators criticized Deutsche Bank for its inability to provide essential information because of its antiquated technology. Regulators are demanding that financial institutions improve the way they manage risk. The banks are under pressure to make their aging computer systems comply, but the IT infrastructures at many traditional financial institutions are failing to keep up with these regulatory pressures as well as changing consumer expectations. Deutsche Bank and its peers must also adapt to new innovative technology competitors such as Apple that are muscling into banking services.

In July 2015 John Cryan became Deutsche Bank's CEO. He has been trying to reduce costs and improve efficiency, laying off thousands of employees. And he is focusing on overhauling Deutsche Bank's fragmented, antiquated information systems, which are a major impediment to controlling costs and finding new sources of profit and growth. Cryan noted that the bank's cost base was swollen by poor and ineffective business processes, inadequate technology, and too many tasks being handled manually. He has called for standardizing the bank's systems and procedures, eliminating legacy software, standardizing and enhancing data, and improving reporting.

Cryan appointed technology specialist Kim Hammonds as Chief Operating Officer to oversee the re-engineering of the bank's information systems and operations. Hammonds had been Deutsche Bank's Global Chief Information Officer and, before that, Chief Information Officer at Boeing. Hammonds observed that Deutsche Bank's information systems operated by trial and error, as if her former employer Boeing launched aircraft into the sky, watched them crash, and then tried to learn from the mistakes.

In February 2015 Deutsche announced a 10-year multi-billion dollar deal with Hewlett-Packard (HP) to standardize and simplify its IT infrastructure, reduce costs, and create a more modern and agile technology platform for launching new products and services. Deutsche Bank is migrating to a cloud computing infrastructure through which it will run its information systems in HP's remote data centers. HP will provide computing services, hosting, and storage. Deutsche Bank will still be in charge of application development and information security technologies, which it considers as proprietary and crucial for competitive differentiation. Deutsche Bank will most likely build mobile, Web, and other applications tailored to its customers' banking preferences, as well as computer-based trading software.

Deutsche Bank is withdrawing from high-risk client relationships, improving its control framework, and automating manual reconciliations. To modernize its IT infrastructure, the bank will reduce the number of its individual operating systems that control the way a computer works from 45 to 4, replace scores of outdated computers, and replace antiquated software applications. Thousands of its applications and functions will be shifted from Deutsche Bank's mainframes to HP cloud computing services. Automating manual processes will promote efficiency and better control. These improvements are expected to reduce "run the bank" costs by 800 million Euros. Eliminating 6,000 contractors will create total savings of 1 billion Euros.

Deutsche Bank is not the only major bank to be hampered by system problems. IT shortcomings were one reason Banco Santander's U.S. unit in 2016 failed the U.S. Federal reserve's annual "stress tests," which gauge how big banks would fare in a new financial crisis. According to Peter Roe, Research Director with TechMarketView LLP in the UK, banks now spend about 75 percent of their IT budgets on maintaining existing systems and operations, and only 25 percent on innovation.

A 2015 Accenture consultants report found that only 6 percent of board of director members and 3 percent of CEOs at the world's largest banks had professional technology experience. More than two-fifths (43 percent) of the banks have no board members with professional technology experience. Since many of the biggest challenges facing banking are technology-related, that means that many banks lack sufficient understanding of technology required for making informed technology decisions. Financial technology innovations, security, IT resilience, and technology implications of regulatory changes are now all critical issues for bank boards of directors, but many lack the expertise to assess these issues and make decisions about strategy, investment, and how best to allocate technology resources.

Sources: Geoffrey Smith, "Things You Should Know About the Deutsche Bank Train Wreck," *Fortune*, September 28, 2016; Hayley McDowell, "System Outage Sees Deutsche Bank Charged over Reporting Failures," The Trade News, August 19, 2016; Derek du Preez, "US Regulator Charges Deutsche Bank over Multiple Systems Failures," Diginomica, August 19, 2016; Kat Hall, "Deutsche Bank's Creaking IT Systems Nervously Eyeing Bins," The Register, October 27, 2015; Martin Arnold and Tom Braithwaite, "Banks' Ageing IT Systems Buckle Under Strain," *Financial Times*, June 18, 2015; Martin Arnold, "Deutsche Bank to Rip Out IT Systems Blamed for Problems," *Financial Times*, October 26, 2015; Ben Moshinsky, "Deutsche Bank Has a Technology Problem," Business Insider, October 20, 2015; Edward Robinson and Nicholas Comfort, "Cryan's Shakeup at Deutsche Bank Sees Tech Restart," Bloomberg, December 20, 2015; Accenture, "Bank Boardrooms Lack Technology Experience, Accenture Global Research Finds," October 28, 2015.

CASE STUDY QUESTIONS

3-12 Identify the problem described in this case study. What people, organization, and technology factors contributed to this problem?

3-13 What was the role of information technology at Deutsche Bank? How was IT related to the bank's operational efficiency, decision-making capability, and business strategy?

3-14 Was Deutsche Bank using technology effectively to pursue its business strategy? Explain your answer.

3-15 What solution for Deutsche Bank was proposed? How effective do you think it will be? Explain your answer.

Chapter 3 References

Amladi, Pradip. "The Digital Economy: How It Will Transform Your Products and Your Future." *Big Data Quarterly* (March 25, 2016).

Attewell, Paul, and James Rule. "Computing and Organizations: What We Know and What We Don't Know." *Communications of the ACM* 27, No. 12 (December 1984).

Bernstein, Ethan, John Bunch, Niko Canner, and Michael Lee."Beyond the Holocracy Hype." *Harvard Business Review* (July–August 2016).

Bresnahan, Timothy F., Erik Brynjolfsson, and Lorin M. Hitt, "Information Technology, Workplace Organization, and the Demand for Skilled Labor." *Quarterly Journal of Economics* 117 (February 2002).

Cash, J. I., and Benn R. Konsynski. "IS Redraws Competitive Boundaries." *Harvard Business Review* (March–April 1985).

Ceccagnoli, Marco, Chris Forman, Peng Huang, and D. J. Wu. "Cocreation of Value in a Platform Ecosystem: The Case of Enterprise Software. *MIS Quarterly* 36, No. 1 (March 2012).

Chen, Daniel Q., Martin Mocker, David S. Preston, and Alexander Teubner. "Information Systems Strategy: Reconceptualization, Measurement, and Implications." *MIS Quarterly* 34, No. 2 (June 2010).

Christensen, Clayton M. *The Innovator's Dilemma: The Revolutionary Book That Will Change the Way You Do Business.* New York: HarperCollins (2003).

Christensen, Clayton. "The Past and Future of Competitive Advantage." *Sloan Management Review* 42, No. 2 (Winter 2001).

Christensen, Clayton M., Michael E. Raynor, and Rory McDonald. "What Is Disruptive Innovation?" *Harvard Business Review* (December 2015).

Clemons, Eric. "The Power of Patterns and Pattern Recognition When Developing Information-Based Strategy. *Journal of Management Information Systems* 27, No. 1 (Summer 2010).

Coase, Ronald H. "The Nature of the Firm." (1937). In Putterman, Louis and Randall Kroszner. *The Economic Nature of the Firm: A Reader*. Cambridge University Press, 1995.

Davis, Euan. "The Rise of the Smart Product Economy." Cognizant (2015).

Drucker, Peter. "The Coming of the New Organization." *Harvard Business Review* (January–February 1988).

Feintzeig, Rachel." So Busy at Work, No Time to Do the Job." *Wall Street Journal* (June 28, 2016).

Gandhi, Suketo and Eric Gervet. "Now That Your Products Can Talk, What Will They Tell You?" *MIT Sloan Management Review* (Spring 2016).

Gurbaxani, V. and S. Whang, "The Impact of Information Systems on Organizations and Markets." *Communications of the ACM* 34, No. 1 (January 1991).

Hagiu, Andrei and Simon Rothman. "Network Effects Aren't Enough." *Harvard Business Review* (April 2016).

Hitt, Lorin M. "Information Technology and Firm Boundaries: Evidence from Panel Data." *Information Systems Research* 10, No. 2 (June 1999).

Hitt, Lorin M., and Erik Brynjolfsson. "Information Technology and Internal Firm Organization: An Exploratory Analysis." *Journal of Management Information Systems* 14, No. 2 (Fall 1997).

Iansiti, Marco and Karim R. Lakhani. "Digital Ubiquity: How Connections, Sensors, and Data Are Revolutionizing Business." *Harvard Business Review* (November 2014).

Iansiti, Marco, and Roy Levien. "Strategy as Ecology." *Harvard Business Review* (March 2004).

Jensen, M. C. and W. H. Meckling. "Specific and General Knowledge and Organizational Science." *In Contract Economics*, edited by L. Wetin and J. Wijkander. Oxford: Basil Blackwell (1992).

Jensen, Michael C. and William H. Meckling. "Theory of the Firm: Managerial Behavior, Agency Costs, and Ownership Structure." *Journal of Financial Economics* 3 (1976).

Kane, Gerald C., Doug Palmer, Anh Nguyen Phillips, and David Kiron. "Is Your Business Ready for a Digital Future?" *MIT Sloan Management Review* (Summer 2015).

Karimi, Jahangir and Zhiping Walter. "The Role of Dynamic Capabilities in Responding to Digital Disruption: A Factor-Based Study of the Newspaper Industry." *Journal of Management Information Systems* 32, No. 1 (2015).

Kauffman, Robert J. and Yu-Ming Wang. "The Network Externalities Hypothesis and Competitive Network Growth." *Journal of Organizational Computing and Electronic Commerce* 12, No. 1 (2002).

King, Andrew A. and Baljir Baatartogtokh. "How Useful Is the Theory of Disruptive Innovation?" *MIT Sloan Management Review* (Fall 2015).

King, J. L., V. Gurbaxani, K. L. Kraemer, F. W. McFarlan, K. S. Raman, and C. S. Yap. "Institutional Factors in Information Technology Innovation." *Information Systems Research* 5, No. 2 (June 1994).

Kling, Rob. "Social Analyses of Computing: Theoretical Perspectives in Recent Empirical Research." *Computing Survey* 12, No. 1 (March 1980).

Kolb, D. A., and A. L. Frohman. "An Organization Development Approach to Consulting." *Sloan Management Review* 12, No. 1 (Fall 1970).

Kraemer, Kenneth, John King, Debora Dunkle, and Joe Lane. *Managing Information Systems*. Los Angeles: Jossey-Bass (1989).

Lamb, Roberta and Rob Kling. "Reconceptualizing Users as Social Actors in Information Systems Research." *MIS Quarterly* 27, No. 2 (June 2003).

Laudon, Kenneth C. "A General Model of the Relationship Between Information Technology and Organizations." Center for Research on Information Systems, New York University. Working paper, National Science Foundation (1989).

__________. "Environmental and Institutional Models of Systems Development." *Communications of the ACM* 28, No. 7 (July 1985).

__________. *Dossier Society: Value Choices in the Design of National Information Systems*. New York: Columbia University Press (1986).

Laudon, Kenneth C. and Kenneth L. Marr, "Information Technology and Occupational Structure." (April 1995).

Leavitt, Harold J. "Applying Organizational Change in Industry: Structural, Technological, and Humanistic Approaches." In *Handbook of Organizations*, edited by James G. March. Chicago: Rand McNally (1965).

Leavitt, Harold J. and Thomas L. Whisler. "Management in the 1980s." *Harvard Business Review* (November–December 1958).

Ling Xue, Gautam Ray, and Vallabh Sambamurthy. "Efficiency or Innovation: How Do Industry Environments Moderate the Effects of Firms' IT Asset Portfolios." *MIS Quarterly* 36, No. 2 (June 2012).

Luftman, Jerry. *Competing in the Information Age: Align in the Sand* (2nd ed.). Oxford University Press USA (August 6, 2003).

March, James G. and Herbert A. Simon. *Organizations*. New York: Wiley (1958).

McAfee, Andrew and Erik Brynjolfsson. "Investing in the IT That Makes a Competitive Difference." *Harvard Business Review* (July/August 2008).

McFarlan, F. Warren. "Information Technology Changes the Way You Compete." *Harvard Business Review* (May–June 1984).

McLaren, Tim S., Milena M. Head, Yufei Yuan, and Yolande E. Chan. "A Multilevel Model for Measuring Fit Between a Firm's Competitive Strategies and Information Systems Capabilities." *MIS Quarterly* 35, No. 4 (December 2011).

Mintzberg, Henry. "Managerial Work: Analysis from Observation." *Management Science* 18 (October 1971).

Piccoli, Gabriele and Blake Ives. "Review: IT-Dependent Strategic Initiatives and Sustained Competitive Advantage: A Review and Synthesis of the Literature." *MIS Quarterly* 29, No. 4 (December 2005).

Porter, Michael E. *Competitive Advantage*. New York: Free Press (1985).

__________. *Competitive Strategy*. New York: Free Press (1980).

__________. "Strategy and the Internet." *Harvard Business Review* (March 2001).

__________. "The Five Competitive Forces That Shape Strategy." *Harvard Business Review* (January 2008).

Porter, Michael E. and James E. Heppelmann. "How Smart, Connected Products Are Transforming Competition." *Harvard Business Review* (November 2014).

Porter, Michael E. and Scott Stern. "Location Matters." *Sloan Management Review* 42, No. 4 (Summer 2001).

Shapiro, Carl and Hal R. Varian. *Information Rules*. Boston, MA: Harvard Business School Press (1999).

Starbuck, William H. "Organizations as Action Generators." *American Sociological Review* 48 (1983).

Tallon, Paul P. "Value Chain Linkages and the Spillover Effects of Strategic Information Technology Alignment: A Process-Level View." *Journal of Management Information Systems* 28, No. 3 (Winter 2014).

Van Alstyne, Marshall W., Geoffrey G. Parer, and Sangeet Paul Choudary. "Pipelines, Platforms, and the New Rules of Strategy." *Harvard Business Review* (April 2016).

Tushman, Michael L. and Philip Anderson. "Technological Discontinuities and Organizational Environments." *Administrative Science Quarterly* 31 (September 1986).

Weber, Max. *The Theory of Social and Economic Organization*. Translated by Talcott Parsons. New York: Free Press (1947).

Williamson, Oliver E. *The Economic Institutions of Capitalism*. New York: Free Press, (1985).

Zhu, Feng and Nathan Furr. "Products to Platforms: Making the Leap." *Harvard Business Review* (April 2016).

CHAPTER

4 Ethical and Social Issues in Information Systems

Learning Objectives

After reading this chapter, you will be able to answer the following questions:

4-1 What ethical, social, and political issues are raised by information systems?

4-2 What specific principles for conduct can be used to guide ethical decisions?

4-3 Why do contemporary information systems technology and the Internet pose challenges to the protection of individual privacy and intellectual property?

4-4 How have information systems affected laws for establishing accountability and liability and the quality of everyday life?

CHAPTER CASES

The Dark Side of Big Data
Ethical Issues of Google Earth
Are We Relying Too Much on Computers to Think for Us?
Facebook Privacy: What Privacy?

The Dark Side of Big Data

Organizations today are furiously mining big data, looking for ways to benefit from this technology. There are many big data success stories. For example, the Berg biopharmaceutical company is mining big data on patient tissue samples, clinical history, and demographic characteristics to pinpoint potential biomarkers for pancreatic cancer so that it can be detected much earlier and treated more effectively. The city of Barcelona has reduced its annual water bill by 25 percent by analyzing data from sensors installed in local parks to monitor soil moisture.

But there's a dark side to big data, and it has to do with privacy. We can now collect or analyze data on a much larger scale than ever before and use what we have learned about individuals in ways that may be harmful to them. The following are some examples.

Predictive policing In February 2014, the Chicago Police Department sent uniformed officers to make custom notification visits to individuals—especially gang members—whom a computer system had identified as likely to commit a crime in the future. The intent was to prevent crime by providing the targeted individuals with information about job training programs or informing them

© Sangoiri/123RF

about increased penalties for people with certain backgrounds. Many community groups protested the practice as another form of racial profiling.

Insurance rates Auto insurance companies such as Progressive offer a small device to install in your car to analyze your driving habits, ostensibly to give you a better insurance rate. However, some of the criteria for lower auto insurance rates are considered discriminatory. For example, insurance companies like people who don't drive late at night and don't spend much time in their cars. However, poorer people are more likely to work a late shift and to have longer commutes to work, which would increase their auto insurance rates.

Deloitte Consulting LLP developed a predictive modeling system for insurance applicants that predicts life expectancy by using data about individual consumers' buying habits as well as their personal and family medical histories. The company claims it can accurately predict whether people have any 1 of 17 diseases, including diabetes, tobacco-related cancer, cardiovascular disease, and depression, by analyzing their buying habits. What you pick up at the drugstore might increase your health insurance rates.

Computerized hiring More and more companies are turning to computerized systems to filter and hire job applicants, especially for lower-wage, service-sector jobs. The algorithms these systems use to evaluate job candidates may be preventing qualified applicants from obtaining these jobs. For example, some of these algorithms have determined that, statistically, people with shorter commutes are more likely to stay in a job longer than those with longer commutes or less reliable transportation or those who haven't been at their address for very long. If asked, "How long is your commute?" applicants with long commuting times will be scored lower for the job. Although such considerations may be statistically accurate, is it fair to screen job applicants this way?

Targeting financially vulnerable individuals Data brokers have been around for decades, but their tools for collecting and finely analyzing huge quantities of personal data grow ever more powerful. These data brokers now sell reports that specifically highlight and target financially vulnerable individuals. For example, a data broker might provide a report on retirees with little or no savings to a company offering reverse mortgages, high-cost loans, or other financially risky products. Very few rules or regulations exist to prevent targeting of vulnerable groups. Privacy laws and regulations haven't caught up with big data technology.

Sources: Brian Brinkmann, "Big Data Privacy: What Privacy?" Business2Community, March 2, 2016; Bernard Marr, "The 5 Scariest Ways Big Data Is Used Today," *DataInformed*, May 20, 2015; Victoria Craig, "Berg Hopes Big Data Will Lead to Breakthrough for Pancreatic Cancer, *Fox Business*, June 11, 2015; and "Police Gang-warning Tactic of 'Custom Notifications' Is Working," *Chicago Sun-Times*, March 27, 2014.

The challenges of big data to privacy described in the chapter-opening case show that technology can be a double-edged sword. It can be the source of many benefits, including the ability to combat disease and crime and to achieve major cost savings and efficiencies for business. At the same time, digital

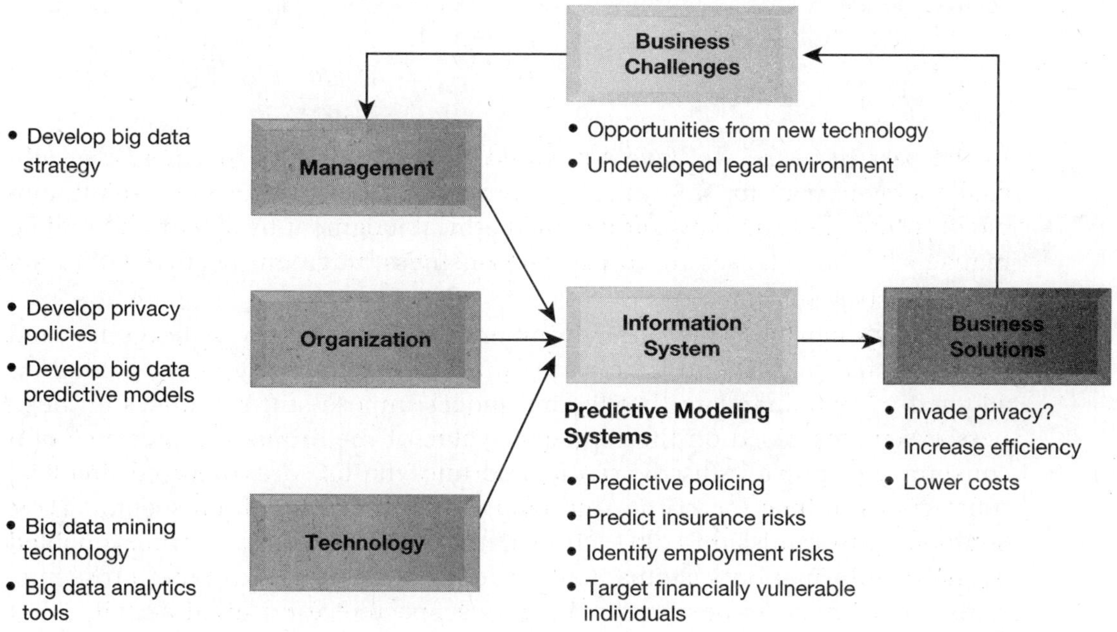

technology creates new opportunities for invading your privacy and using information that could cause you harm.

The chapter-opening diagram calls attention to important points this case and this chapter raise. Developments in data management technology and analytics have created opportunities for organizations to use big data to improve operations and decision making. One popular use of big data analysis is for predictive modeling—sifting through data to identify how specific individuals will behave and react in the future. The organizations described here are benefiting from using predictive modeling to fight crime, select the best employees, and lower insurance and credit lending risks. However, their use of big data is also taking benefits away from individuals. Individuals might be subject to job discrimination, racial profiling, or higher insurance rates because organizations have new tools to assemble and analyze huge quantities of data about them. New privacy protection laws and policies need to be developed to keep up with the technologies for assembling and analyzing big data.

This case illustrates an ethical dilemma because it shows two sets of interests at work, the interests of organizations that have raised profits or even helped many people with medical breakthroughs and those who fervently believe that businesses and public organizations should not use big data analysis to invade privacy or harm individuals. As a manager, you will need to be sensitive to both the positive and negative impacts of information systems for your firm, employees, and customers. You will need to learn how to resolve ethical dilemmas involving information systems.

Here are some questions to think about: Does analyzing big data about people create an ethical dilemma? Why or why not? Should there be new privacy laws to protect individuals from being targeted by companies analyzing big data? Why or why not?

4-1 What ethical, social, and political issues are raised by information systems?

In the past 10 years, we have witnessed, arguably, one of the most ethically challenging periods for U.S. and global business. Table 4.1 provides a small sample of recent cases demonstrating failed ethical judgment by senior and middle managers. These lapses in ethical and business judgment occurred across a broad spectrum of industries.

In today's new global legal environment, managers who violate the law and are convicted may spend time in prison. U.S. federal sentencing guidelines adopted in 1987 mandate that federal judges impose stiff sentences on business executives based on the monetary value of the crime, the presence of a conspiracy to prevent discovery of the crime, the use of structured financial transactions to hide the crime, and failure to cooperate with prosecutors (U.S. Sentencing Commission, 2004). International treaties and Interpol, enabled by global information systems, have made it possible to extradite, prosecute, arrest, and imprison business managers suspected of criminal activity on a global basis.

TABLE 4.1 RECENT EXAMPLES OF FAILED ETHICAL JUDGMENT BY SENIOR MANAGERS

Volkswagen (2015)	Volkswagen agrees to pay $14.7 billion to consumers and agencies in the U.S. and replace nearly 500,000 diesel cars with faulty emission software. Faces additional fines worldwide.
General Motors Inc. (2015)	General Motors CEO admits the firm covered up faulty ignition switches for more than a decade, resulting in the deaths of at least 114 customers. More than 100 million vehicles worldwide need to be replaced.
Takata Corporation (2015)	Takata executives admit they covered up faulty airbags used in millions of cars over many years. To date, 100 million cars need airbags replaced.
Citigroup, JPMorgan Chase, Barclays, UBS (2012)	Four of the largest money center banks in the world plead guilty to criminal charges that they manipulated the LIBOR interest rate used to establish loan rates throughout the world.
SAC Capital (2013)	SAC Capital, a hedge fund led by founder Steven Cohen, pleads guilty to insider trading charges and agrees to pay a record $1.2 billion penalty. The firm was also forced to leave the money management business. Individual traders for SAC were found guilty of criminal charges and were sentenced to prison.
GlaxoSmithKline LLC (2012)	The global healthcare giant admitted to unlawful and criminal promotion of certain prescription drugs, its failure to report certain safety data, and its civil liability for alleged false price reporting practices. Fined $3 billion, the largest healthcare fraud settlement in U.S. history and the largest payment ever by a drug company.
McKinsey & Company (2012)	CEO Rajat Gupta heard on tapes leaking insider information. The former CEO of prestigious management consulting firm McKinsey & Company was found guilty in 2012 and sentenced to two years in prison.

Although business firms would, in the past, often pay for the legal defense of their employees enmeshed in civil charges and criminal investigations, firms are now encouraged to cooperate with prosecutors to reduce charges against the entire firm for obstructing investigations. These developments mean that, more than ever, as a manager or an employee, you will have to decide for yourself what constitutes proper legal and ethical conduct.

Although these major instances of failed ethical and legal judgment were not masterminded by information systems departments, information systems were instrumental in many of these frauds. In many cases, the perpetrators of these crimes artfully used financial reporting information systems to bury their decisions from public scrutiny in the vain hope they would never be caught.

We deal with the issue of control in information systems in Chapter 8. In this chapter, we will talk about the ethical dimensions of these and other actions based on the use of information systems.

Ethics refers to the principles of right and wrong that individuals, acting as free moral agents, use to make choices to guide their behaviors. Information systems raise new ethical questions for both individuals and societies because they create opportunities for intense social change and, thus, threaten existing distributions of power, money, rights, and obligations. Like other technologies, such as steam engines, electricity, the telephone, and the radio, information technology can be used to achieve social progress, but it can also be used to commit crimes and threaten cherished social values. The development of information technology will produce benefits for many and costs for others.

Ethical issues in information systems have been given new urgency by the rise of the Internet and e-commerce. Internet and digital firm technologies make it easier than ever to assemble, integrate, and distribute information, unleashing new concerns about the appropriate use of customer information, the protection of personal privacy, and the protection of intellectual property.

Other pressing ethical issues that information systems raise include establishing accountability for the consequences of information systems, setting standards to safeguard system quality that protects the safety of the individual and society, and preserving values and institutions considered essential to the quality of life in an information society. When using information systems, it is essential to ask, "What is the ethical and socially responsible course of action?"

A Model for Thinking About Ethical, Social, and Political Issues

Ethical, social, and political issues are closely linked. The ethical dilemma you may face as a manager of information systems typically is reflected in social and political debate. One way to think about these relationships is shown in Figure 4.1. Imagine society as a more or less calm pond on a summer day, a delicate ecosystem in partial equilibrium with individuals and with social and political institutions. Individuals know how to act in this pond because social institutions (family, education, organizations) have developed well-honed rules of behavior, and these are supported by laws developed in the political sector that prescribe behavior and promise sanctions for violations. Now toss a rock into the center of the pond. What happens? Ripples, of course.

FIGURE 4.1 THE RELATIONSHIP BETWEEN ETHICAL, SOCIAL, AND POLITICAL ISSUES IN AN INFORMATION SOCIETY

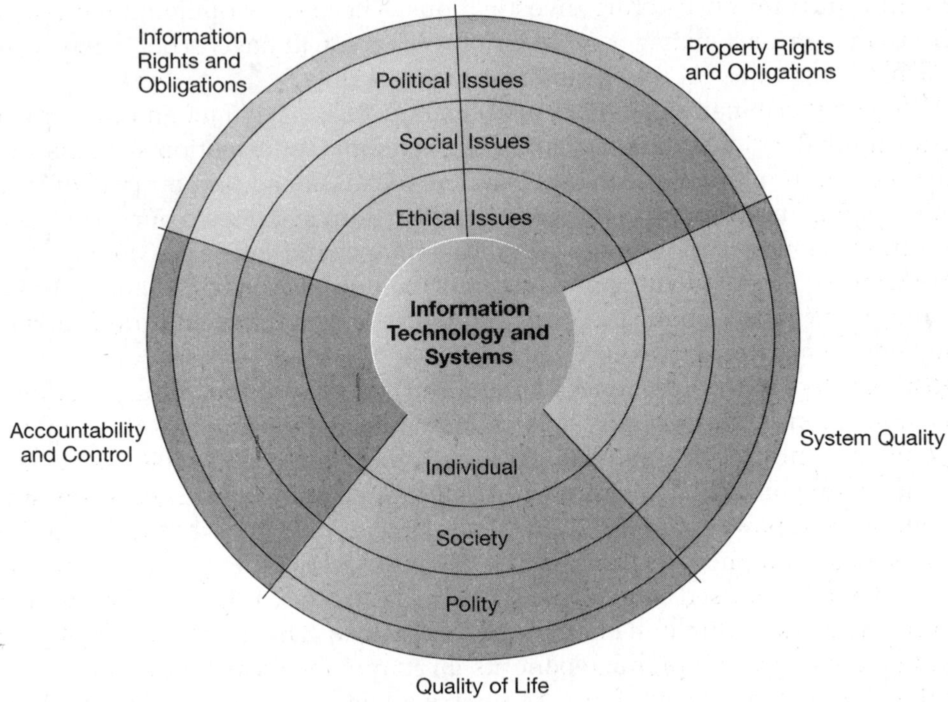

The introduction of new information technology has a ripple effect, raising new ethical, social, and political issues that must be dealt with on the individual, social, and political levels. These issues have five moral dimensions: information rights and obligations, property rights and obligations, system quality, quality of life, and accountability and control.

Imagine instead that the disturbing force is a powerful shock of new information technology and systems hitting a society more or less at rest. Suddenly, individual actors are confronted with new situations often not covered by the old rules. Social institutions cannot respond overnight to these ripples—it may take years to develop etiquette, expectations, social responsibility, politically correct attitudes, or approved rules. Political institutions also require time before developing new laws and often require the demonstration of real harm before they act. In the meantime, you may have to act. You may be forced to act in a legal gray area.

We can use this model to illustrate the dynamics that connect ethical, social, and political issues. This model is also useful for identifying the main moral dimensions of the information society, which cut across various levels of action—individual, social, and political.

Five Moral Dimensions of the Information Age

The major ethical, social, and political issues that information systems raise include the following moral dimensions.

- *Information rights and obligations* What **information rights** do individuals and organizations possess with respect to themselves? What can they protect?

- *Property rights and obligations* How will traditional intellectual property rights be protected in a digital society in which tracing and accounting for ownership are difficult and ignoring such property rights is so easy?
- *Accountability and control* Who can and will be held accountable and liable for the harm done to individual and collective information and property rights?
- *System quality* What standards of data and system quality should we demand to protect individual rights and the safety of society?
- *Quality of life* What values should be preserved in an information- and knowledge-based society? Which institutions should we protect from violation? Which cultural values and practices does the new information technology support?

We explore these moral dimensions in detail in Section 4.3.

Key Technology Trends that Raise Ethical Issues

Ethical issues long preceded information technology. Nevertheless, information technology has heightened ethical concerns, taxed existing social arrangements, and made some laws obsolete or severely crippled. Five key technological trends are responsible for these ethical stresses, summarized in Table 4.2.

The doubling of computing power every 18 months has made it possible for most organizations to use information systems for their core production processes. As a result, our dependence on systems and our vulnerability to system errors and poor data quality have increased. Social rules and laws have not yet adjusted to this dependence. Standards for ensuring the accuracy and reliability of information systems (see Chapter 8) are not universally accepted or enforced.

Advances in data storage techniques and rapidly declining storage costs have been responsible for the multiplying databases on individuals—employees, customers, and potential customers—maintained by private and public organizations. These advances in data storage have made the routine violation of individual privacy both inexpensive and effective. Enormous data storage systems for terabytes and petabytes of data are now available on-site or as online services for firms of all sizes to use in identifying customers.

TABLE 4.2 TECHNOLOGY TRENDS THAT RAISE ETHICAL ISSUES

TREND	IMPACT
Computing power doubles every 18 months	More organizations depend on computer systems for critical operations and become more vulnerable to system failures.
Data storage costs rapidly decline	Organizations can easily maintain detailed databases on individuals. There are no limits on the data collected about you.
Data analysis advances	Companies can analyze vast quantities of data gathered on individuals to develop detailed profiles of individual behavior. Large-scale population surveillance is enabled.
Networking advances	The cost of moving data and making it accessible from anywhere falls exponentially. Access to data becomes more difficult to control.
Mobile device growth impact	Individual cell phones may be tracked without user consent or knowledge. The always-on device becomes a tether.

Credit card purchases can make personal information available to market researchers, telemarketers, and direct mail companies. Advances in information technology facilitate the invasion of privacy.

© Andriy Popov/123RF

Advances in data analysis techniques for large pools of data are another technological trend that heightens ethical concerns because companies and government agencies can find out highly detailed personal information about individuals. With contemporary data management tools (see Chapter 6), companies can assemble and combine the myriad pieces of information about you stored on computers much more easily than in the past.

Think of all the ways you generate digital information about yourself—credit card purchases; telephone calls; magazine subscriptions; video rentals; mail-order purchases; banking records; local, state, and federal government records (including court and police records); and visits to websites. Put together and mined properly, this information could reveal not only your credit information but also your driving habits, your tastes, your associations, what you read and watch, and your political interests.

Companies purchase relevant personal information from these sources to help them more finely target their marketing campaigns. Chapters 6 and 12 describe how companies can analyze large pools of data from multiple sources to identify buying patterns of customers rapidly and suggest individual responses. The use of computers to combine data from multiple sources and create digital dossiers of detailed information on individuals is called **profiling**.

For example, several thousand of the most popular websites allow DoubleClick (owned by Google), an Internet advertising broker, to track the activities of their visitors in exchange for revenue from advertisements based on visitor information DoubleClick gathers. DoubleClick uses this information to create a profile of each online visitor, adding more detail to the profile as the visitor accesses an associated DoubleClick site. DoubleClick creates a detailed dossier of a person's spending and computing habits on the web that is sold to companies to help them target their web ads more precisely.

LexisNexis Risk Solutions (formerly ChoicePoint) gathers data from police, criminal, and motor vehicle records, credit and employment histories, current and previous addresses, professional licenses, and insurance claims to assemble and maintain dossiers on almost every adult in the United States. The company sells this personal information to businesses and government agencies.

Demand for personal data is so enormous that data broker businesses such as Risk Solutions are flourishing.

A data analysis technology called **nonobvious relationship awareness (NORA)** has given both the government and the private sector even more powerful profiling capabilities. NORA can take information about people from many disparate sources, such as employment applications, telephone records, customer listings, and wanted lists, and correlate relationships to find obscure connections that might help identify criminals or terrorists (see Figure 4.2).

NORA technology scans data and extracts information as the data are being generated so that it could, for example, instantly discover a man at an airline ticket counter who shares a phone number with a known terrorist before that person boards an airplane.

Finally, advances in networking, including the Internet, promise to reduce greatly the costs of moving and accessing large quantities of data and open the possibility of mining large pools of data remotely by using small desktop machines, mobile devices, and cloud servers, permitting an invasion of privacy on a scale and with a precision heretofore unimaginable.

FIGURE 4.2 NONOBVIOUS RELATIONSHIP AWARENESS (NORA)

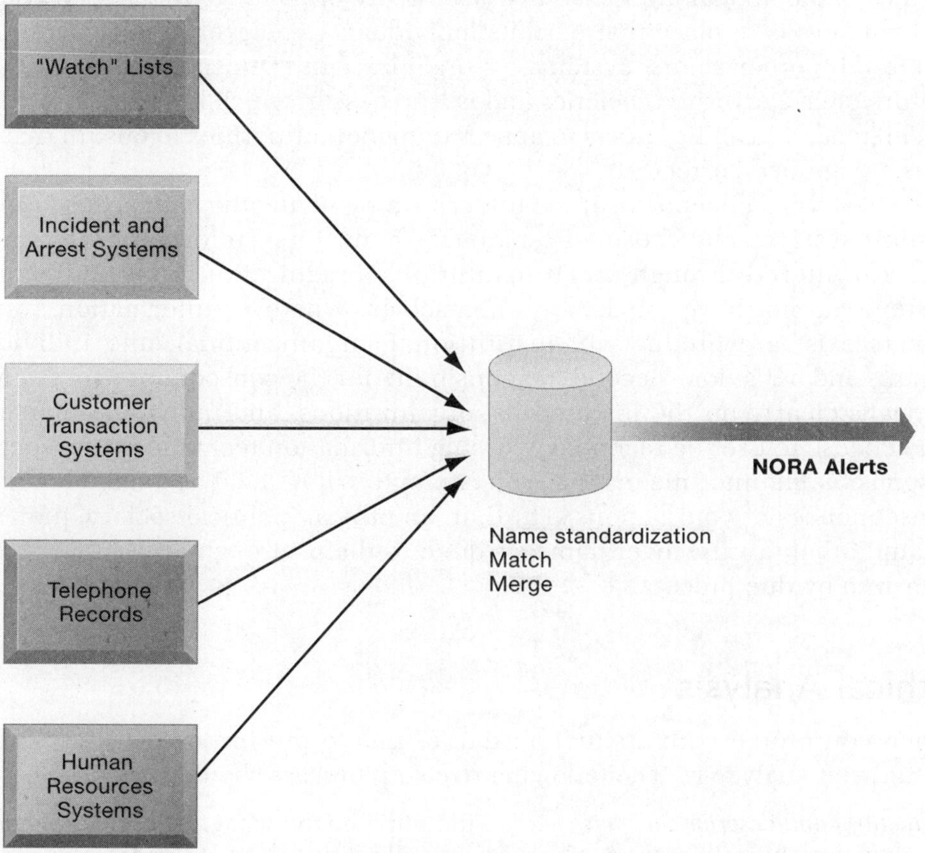

NORA technology can take information about people from disparate sources and find obscure, nonobvious relationships. It might discover, for example, that an applicant for a job at a casino shares a telephone number with a known criminal and issue an alert to the hiring manager.

4-2 What specific principles for conduct can be used to guide ethical decisions?

Ethics is a concern of humans who have freedom of choice. Ethics is about individual choice: When faced with alternative courses of action, what is the correct moral choice? What are the main features of ethical choice?

Basic Concepts: Responsibility, Accountability, and Liability

Ethical choices are decisions made by individuals who are responsible for the consequences of their actions. **Responsibility** is a key element of ethical action. Responsibility means that you accept the potential costs, duties, and obligations for the decisions you make. **Accountability** is a feature of systems and social institutions; it means that mechanisms are in place to determine who took action and who is responsible. Systems and institutions in which it is impossible to find out who took what action are inherently incapable of ethical analysis or ethical action. **Liability** extends the concept of responsibility further to the area of laws. Liability is a feature of political systems in which a body of laws is in place that permits individuals to recover the damages done to them by other actors, systems, or organizations. **Due process** is a related feature of law-governed societies and is a process in which laws are known and understood, and ability exists to appeal to higher authorities to ensure that the laws are applied correctly.

These basic concepts form the underpinning of an ethical analysis of information systems and those who manage them. First, information technologies are filtered through social institutions, organizations, and individuals. Systems do not have impacts by themselves. Whatever information system effects exist are products of institutional, organizational, and individual actions and behaviors. Second, responsibility for the consequences of technology falls clearly on the institutions, organizations, and individual managers who choose to use the technology. Using information technology in a socially responsible manner means that you can and will be held accountable for the consequences of your actions. Third, in an ethical, political society, individuals and others can recover damages done to them through a set of laws characterized by due process.

Ethical Analysis

When confronted with a situation that seems to present ethical issues, how should you analyze it? The following five-step process should help.

1. *Identify and describe the facts clearly* Find out who did what to whom and where, when, and how. In many instances, you will be surprised at the errors in the initially reported facts, and often you will find that simply getting the facts straight helps define the solution. It also helps to get the opposing parties involved in an ethical dilemma to agree on the facts.

2. *Define the conflict or dilemma and identify the higher-order values involved* Ethical, social, and political issues always reference higher values. The parties to a dispute all claim to be pursuing higher values (e.g., freedom, privacy, protection of property, and the free enterprise system). Typically, an ethical issue involves a dilemma: two diametrically opposed courses of action that support worthwhile values. For example, the chapter-opening case study illustrates two competing values: the need to make organizations more efficient and cost-effective and the need to respect individual privacy.
3. *Identify the stakeholders* Every ethical, social, and political issue has stakeholders: players in the game who have an interest in the outcome, who have invested in the situation, and usually who have vocal opinions. Find out the identity of these groups and what they want. This will be useful later when designing a solution.
4. *Identify the options that you can reasonably take* You may find that none of the options satisfy all the interests involved but that some options do a better job than others. Sometimes arriving at a good or ethical solution may not always be a balancing of consequences to stakeholders.
5. *Identify the potential consequences of your options* Some options may be ethically correct but disastrous from other points of view. Other options may work in one instance but not in similar instances. Always ask yourself, "What if I choose this option consistently over time?"

Candidate Ethical Principles

Once your analysis is complete, what ethical principles or rules should you use to make a decision? What higher-order values should inform your judgment? Although you are the only one who can decide which among many ethical principles you will follow, and how you will prioritize them, it is helpful to consider some ethical principles with deep roots in many cultures that have survived throughout recorded history.

1. Do unto others as you would have them do unto you (the **Golden Rule**). Putting yourself in the place of others, and thinking of yourself as the object of the decision, can help you think about fairness in decision making.
2. If an action is not right for everyone to take, it is not right for anyone (**Immanuel Kant's categorical imperative**). Ask yourself, "If everyone did this, could the organization, or society, survive?"
3. If an action cannot be taken repeatedly, it is not right to take at all. This is the **slippery slope rule**: An action may bring about a small change now that is acceptable, but if it is repeated, it would bring unacceptable changes in the long run. In the vernacular, it might be stated as "once started down a slippery path, you may not be able to stop."
4. Take the action that achieves the higher or greater value (**utilitarian principle**). This rule assumes you can prioritize values in a rank order and understand the consequences of various courses of action.
5. Take the action that produces the least harm or the least potential cost (**risk aversion principle**). Some actions have extremely high failure costs of very low probability (e.g., building a nuclear generating facility in an urban area) or extremely high failure costs of moderate probability (speeding and automobile

accidents). Avoid actions which have extremely high failure costs; focus on reducing the probability of accidents occurring.

6. Assume that virtually all tangible and intangible objects are owned by someone else unless there is a specific declaration otherwise. (This is the **ethical no-free-lunch rule**.) If something someone else has created is useful to you, it has value, and you should assume the creator wants compensation for this work.

Actions that do not easily pass these rules deserve close attention and a great deal of caution. The appearance of unethical behavior may do as much harm to you and your company as actual unethical behavior.

Professional Codes of Conduct

When groups of people claim to be professionals, they take on special rights and obligations because of their special claims to knowledge, wisdom, and respect. Professional codes of conduct are promulgated by associations of professionals such as the American Medical Association (AMA), the American Bar Association (ABA), the Association of Information Technology Professionals (AITP), and the Association for Computing Machinery (ACM). These professional groups take responsibility for the partial regulation of their professions by determining entrance qualifications and competence. Codes of ethics are promises by professions to regulate themselves in the general interest of society. For example, avoiding harm to others, honoring property rights (including intellectual property), and respecting privacy are among the General Moral Imperatives of the ACM's Code of Ethics and Professional Conduct.

Some Real-World Ethical Dilemmas

Information systems have created new ethical dilemmas in which one set of interests is pitted against another. For example, many companies use voice recognition software to reduce the size of their customer support staff by enabling computers to recognize a customer's responses to a series of computerized questions. Many companies monitor what their employees are doing on the Internet to prevent them from wasting company resources on nonbusiness activities. Facebook monitors its subscribers and then sells the information to advertisers and app developers (see the chapter-ending case study).

In each instance, you can find competing values at work, with groups lined up on either side of a debate. A company may argue, for example, that it has a right to use information systems to increase productivity and reduce the size of its workforce to lower costs and stay in business. Employees displaced by information systems may argue that employers have some responsibility for their welfare. Business owners might feel obligated to monitor employee e-mail and Internet use to minimize drains on productivity. Employees might believe they should be able to use the Internet for short personal tasks in place of the telephone. A close analysis of the facts can sometimes produce compromised solutions that give each side half a loaf. Try to apply some of the principles of ethical analysis described to each of these cases. What is the right thing to do?

4-3 Why do contemporary information systems technology and the Internet pose challenges to the protection of individual privacy and intellectual property?

In this section, we take a closer look at the five moral dimensions of information systems first described in Figure 4.1. In each dimension, we identify the ethical, social, and political levels of analysis and use real-world examples to illustrate the values involved, the stakeholders, and the options chosen.

Information Rights: Privacy and Freedom in the Internet Age

Privacy is the claim of individuals to be left alone, free from surveillance or interference from other individuals or organizations, including the state. Claims to privacy are also involved at the workplace. Millions of employees are subject to digital and other forms of high-tech surveillance. Information technology and systems threaten individual claims to privacy by making the invasion of privacy cheap, profitable, and effective.

The claim to privacy is protected in the United States, Canadian, and German constitutions in a variety of ways and in other countries through various statutes. In the United States, the claim to privacy is protected primarily by the First Amendment guarantees of freedom of speech and association, the Fourth Amendment protections against unreasonable search and seizure of one's personal documents or home, and the guarantee of due process.

Table 4.3 describes the major U.S. federal statutes that set forth the conditions for handling information about individuals in such areas as credit reporting, education, financial records, newspaper records, and electronic and digital communications. The Privacy Act of 1974 has been the most important of these laws, regulating the federal government's collection, use, and disclosure of information. At present, most U.S. federal privacy laws apply only to the federal government and regulate very few areas of the private sector. There were 20 major privacy bills before Congress in 2015, although few of them are likely to be passed in the near future (Kosseff, 2014).

Most American and European privacy law is based on a regime called **Fair Information Practices (FIP)** first set forth in a report written in 1973 by a federal government advisory committee and updated most recently in 2010 to take into account new privacy-invading technology (Federal Trade Commission [FTC], 2010; U.S. Department of Health, Education, and Welfare, 1973). FIP is a set of principles governing the collection and use of information about individuals. FIP principles are based on the notion of a mutuality of interest between the record holder and the individual. The individual has an interest in engaging in a transaction, and the record keeper—usually a business or government agency—requires information about the individual to support the transaction. After information is gathered, the individual maintains an interest in the record, and the record may not be used to support other activities without the

TABLE 4.3 FEDERAL PRIVACY LAWS IN THE UNITED STATES

GENERAL FEDERAL PRIVACY LAWS	PRIVACY LAWS AFFECTING PRIVATE INSTITUTIONS
Freedom of Information Act of 1966 as Amended (5 USC 552)	Fair Credit Reporting Act of 1970
Privacy Act of 1974 as Amended (5 USC 552a)	Family Educational Rights and Privacy Act of 1974
Electronic Communications Privacy Act of 1986	Right to Financial Privacy Act of 1978
Computer Matching and Privacy Protection Act of 1988	Privacy Protection Act of 1980
Computer Security Act of 1987	Cable Communications Policy Act of 1984
Federal Managers Financial Integrity Act of 1982	Electronic Communications Privacy Act of 1986
Driver's Privacy Protection Act of 1994	Video Privacy Protection Act of 1988
E-Government Act of 2002	The Health Insurance Portability and Accountability Act (HIPAA) of 1996 Childrens Online Privacy Protection Act (COPPA) of 1998 Financial Modernization Act (Gramm-Leach-Bliley Act) of 1999

individual's consent. In 1998, the Federal Trade Commission (FTC) restated and extended the original FIP to provide guidelines for protecting online privacy. Table 4.4 describes the FTC's Fair Information Practice principles.

The FTC's FIP principles are being used as guidelines to drive changes in privacy legislation. In July 1998, the U.S. Congress passed the Children's Online Privacy Protection Act (COPPA), requiring websites to obtain parental permission before collecting information on children under the age of 13. The FTC has recommended additional legislation to protect online consumer privacy in advertising networks that collect records of consumer web activity to develop

TABLE 4.4 FEDERAL TRADE COMMISSION FAIR INFORMATION PRACTICE PRINCIPLES

Notice/awareness (core principle). Websites must disclose their information practices before collecting data. Includes identification of collector; uses of data; other recipients of data; nature of collection (active/inactive); voluntary or required status; consequences of refusal; and steps taken to protect confidentiality, integrity, and quality of the data.
Choice/consent (core principle). A choice regime must be in place allowing consumers to choose how their information will be used for secondary purposes other than supporting the transaction, including internal use and transfer to third parties.
Access/participation. Consumers should be able to review and contest the accuracy and completeness of data collected about them in a timely, inexpensive process.
Security. Data collectors must take responsible steps to ensure that consumer information is accurate and secure from unauthorized use.
Enforcement. A mechanism must be in place to enforce FIP principles. This can involve self-regulation, legislation giving consumers legal remedies for violations, or federal statutes and regulations.

detailed profiles, which other companies then use to target online ads. In 2010, the FTC added three practices to its framework for privacy. Firms should adopt privacy by design, building products and services that protect privacy, firms should increase the transparency of their data practices, and firms should require consumer consent and provide clear options to opt out of data collection schemes (FTC, 2012). Other proposed Internet privacy legislation focuses on protecting the online use of personal identification numbers, such as social security numbers; protecting personal information collected on the Internet that deals with individuals not covered by COPPA; and limiting the use of data mining for homeland security.

In 2012, the FTC extended its FIP doctrine to address the issue of behavioral targeting. The FTC held hearings to discuss its program for voluntary industry principles for regulating behavioral targeting. The online advertising trade group Network Advertising Initiative (discussed later in this section), published its own self-regulatory principles that largely agreed with the FTC. Nevertheless, the government, privacy groups, and the online ad industry are still at loggerheads over two issues. Privacy advocates want both an opt-in policy at all sites and a national Do Not Track list. The industry opposes these moves and continues to insist that an opt-out capability is the only way to avoid tracking. Nevertheless, there is an emerging consensus among all parties that greater transparency and user control (especially making opting out of tracking the default option) is required to deal with behavioral tracking. Public opinion polls show an ongoing distrust of online marketers. Although there are many studies of privacy issues at the federal level, there has been no significant legislation in recent years. A 2016 survey by the Pew Research Center found 91 percent of Americans feel consumers have lost control of their personal information online and 86 percent have taken steps to protect their information online.

Privacy protections have also been added to recent laws deregulating financial services and safeguarding the maintenance and transmission of health information about individuals. The Gramm-Leach-Bliley Act of 1999, which repeals earlier restrictions on affiliations among banks, securities firms, and insurance companies, includes some privacy protection for consumers of financial services. All financial institutions are required to disclose their policies and practices for protecting the privacy of nonpublic personal information and to allow customers to opt out of information-sharing arrangements with nonaffiliated third parties.

The Health Insurance Portability and Accountability Act (HIPAA) of 1996, which took effect on April 14, 2003, includes privacy protection for medical records. The law gives patients access to their personal medical records that healthcare providers, hospitals, and health insurers maintain and the right to authorize how protected information about themselves can be used or disclosed. Doctors, hospitals, and other healthcare providers must limit the disclosure of personal information about patients to the minimum amount necessary to achieve a given purpose.

The European Directive on Data Protection

In Europe, privacy protection is much more stringent than in the United States. Unlike the United States, European countries do not allow businesses to use personally identifiable information without consumer's prior consent. On October 25, 1998, the European Commission's Directive on Data Protection went into effect, broadening privacy protection in the European Union (EU) nations. The directive requires companies to inform people when they collect information about them and disclose how it will be stored and used. Customers must provide their **informed consent** before any company can legally use data about them, and they have the right to access that information, correct it, and request that no further data be collected. Informed consent can be defined as consent given with knowledge of all the facts needed to make a rational decision. In 2009, the European Parliament passed new rules governing the use of third-party cookies for behavioral tracking purposes, and required website visitors to give explicit consent to be tracked by cookies. Websites are required to have highly visible warnings on their pages if third-party cookies are being used (European Parliament, 2009). The Directive developed a **safe harbor** transborder data framework for non-European firms that allowed them to move data across borders for storage and processing. A safe harbor is a private, self-regulating policy and enforcement mechanism that meets the objectives of government regulators and legislation but does not involve government regulation or enforcement.

In 2015 Europe's highest court struck down the safe harbor agreement, in large part because of revelations that U.S. intelligence agencies had gained access to EU personal data stored in the U.S. The European Council subsequently approved the EU General Data Protection Regulation (GDPR) to replace the existing Data Protection Directive. The concept of safe harbor was replaced by a policy now called Privacy Shield. When it takes effect, the GDPR will apply across all EU countries, rather than the current situation in which each member-state regulates privacy matters within its own borders. Facebook and Google, for instance, currently base their European operations in Ireland, where privacy protections are minimal. The GDPR will apply to any firm operating in any EU country, require unambiguous consent to use personal data for purposes like tracking individuals across the Web, limit the ability to use data for purposes other than those for which it was collected (tertiary uses, such as constructing user profiles), and strengthen the right to be forgotten, specifically, by allowing individuals to remove personal data from social platforms like Facebook and prevent them from collecting any new information. Companies operating in the EU will have to delete personal information once it no longer serves the purpose for which it was collected. In addition, an independent ombudsman was created to investigate complaints and enforce the policy. The new regulation was finally signed in 2016 and does not interfere with transborder dataflows.

Internet Challenges to Privacy

Internet technology has posed new challenges for the protection of individual privacy. Information sent over this vast network of networks may pass through many computer systems before it reaches its final destination. Each of these systems is capable of monitoring, capturing, and storing communications that pass through it.

Websites track searches that have been conducted, the websites and web pages visited, the online content a person has accessed, and what items that person has inspected or purchased over the web. This monitoring and tracking of website visitors occurs in the background without the visitor's knowledge. It is conducted not just by individual websites but by advertising networks such as Microsoft Advertising, Yahoo, and Google's DoubleClick that are capable of tracking personal browsing behavior across thousands of websites. Both website publishers and the advertising industry defend tracking of individuals across the web because doing so allows more relevant ads to be targeted to users, and it pays for the cost of publishing websites. In this sense, it's like broadcast television: advertiser-supported content that is free to the user. The commercial demand for this personal information is virtually insatiable. However, these practices also impinge on individual privacy. **Cookies** are small text files deposited on a computer hard drive when a user visits websites. Cookies identify the visitor's web browser software and track visits to the website. When the visitor returns to a site that has stored a cookie, the website software searches the visitor's computer, finds the cookie, and knows what that person has done in the past. It may also update the cookie, depending on the activity during the visit. In this way, the site can customize its content for each visitor's interests. For example, if you purchase a book on Amazon.com and return later from the same browser, the site will welcome you by name and recommend other books of interest based on your past purchases. DoubleClick, described earlier in this chapter, uses cookies to build its dossiers with details of online purchases and examine the behavior of website visitors. Figure 4.3 illustrates how cookies work.

Websites using cookie technology cannot directly obtain visitors' names and addresses. However, if a person has registered at a site, that information can be combined with cookie data to identify the visitor. Website owners can also combine the data they have gathered from cookies and other website monitoring

FIGURE 4.3 HOW COOKIES IDENTIFY WEB VISITORS

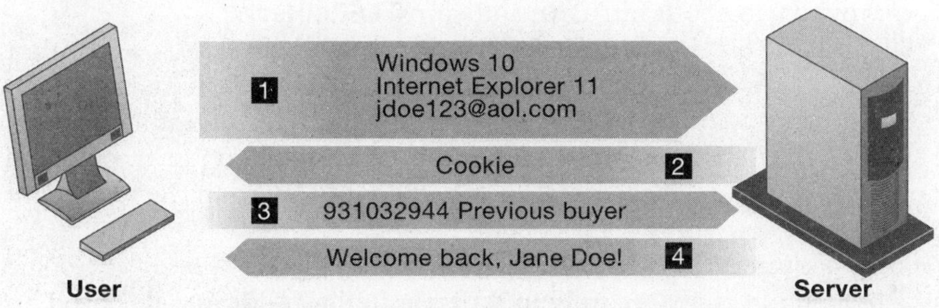

1. The Web server reads the user's web browser and determines the operating system, browser name, version number, Internet address, and other information.
2. The server transmits a tiny text file with user identification information called a cookie, which the user's browser receives and stores on the user's computer hard drive.
3. When the user returns to the website, the server requests the contents of any cookie it deposited previously in the user's computer.
4. The Web server reads the cookie, identifies the visitor, and calls up data on the user.

Cookies are written by a website on a visitor's hard drive. When the visitor returns to that website, the web server requests the ID number from the cookie and uses it to access the data stored by that server on that visitor. The website can then use these data to display personalized information.

tools with personal data from other sources, such as offline data collected from surveys or paper catalog purchases, to develop very detailed profiles of their visitors.

There are now even more subtle and surreptitious tools for surveillance of Internet users. So-called super cookies or Flash cookies cannot be easily deleted and can be installed whenever a person clicks a Flash video. Flash uses these so-called local shared object files to play videos and puts them on the user's computer without his or her consent. Marketers use web beacons as another tool to monitor online behavior. **Web beacons**, also called *web bugs* (or simply tracking files), are tiny software programs that keep a record of users' online clickstreams. They report this data back to whomever owns the tracking file invisibly embedded in e-mail messages and web pages that are designed to monitor the behavior of the user visiting a website or sending e-mail. Web beacons are placed on popular websites by third-party firms who pay the websites a fee for access to their audience. So how common is web tracking? In a path-breaking series of articles in the *Wall Street Journal*, researchers examined the tracking files on 50 of the most popular U.S websites. What they found revealed a very widespread surveillance system. On the 50 sites, they discovered 3,180 tracking files installed on visitor computers. Only one site, Wikipedia, had no tracking files. Two-thirds of the tracking files came from 131 companies whose primary business is identifying and tracking Internet users to create consumer profiles that can be sold to advertising firms looking for specific types of customers. The biggest trackers were Google, Microsoft, and Quantcast, all of whom are in the business of selling ads to advertising firms and marketers. A follow-up study found tracking on the 50 most popular sites had risen nearly fivefold due to the growth of online ad auctions where advertisers buy the data about users' web-browsing behavior.

Other **spyware** can secretly install itself on an Internet user's computer by piggybacking on larger applications. Once installed, the spyware calls out to websites to send banner ads and other unsolicited material to the user, and it can report the user's movements on the Internet to other computers. More information is available about intrusive software in Chapter 8.

Nearly 80 percent of global Internet users use Google Search and other Google services, making Google the world's largest collector of online user data. Whatever Google does with its data has an enormous impact on online privacy. Most experts believe that Google possesses the largest collection of personal information in the world—more data on more people than any government agency. The nearest competitor is Facebook.

After Google acquired the advertising network DoubleClick in 2007, Google began using behavioral targeting to help it display more relevant ads based on users' search activities and to target individuals as they move from one site to another to show them display or banner ads. Google allows tracking software on its search pages, and using DoubleClick, it can track users across the Internet. One of its programs enables advertisers to target ads based on the search histories of Google users, along with any other information the user submits to Google such as age, demographics, region, and other web activities (such as blogging). Google's AdSense program enables Google to help advertisers select keywords and design ads for various market segments based on search histories such as helping a clothing website create and test ads targeted at teenage females. A recent study found that 88 percent of 400,000 websites had at least one Google tracking bug.

Google also scans the contents of messages users receive of its free web-based e-mail service called Gmail. Ads that users see when they read their e-mail are related to the subjects of these messages. Profiles are developed on individual users based on the content in their e-mail. Google now displays targeted ads on YouTube and Google mobile applications, and its DoubleClick ad network serves up targeted banner ads.

The United States has allowed businesses to gather transaction information generated in the marketplace and then use that information for other marketing purposes without obtaining the informed consent of the individual whose information is being used. These firms argue that when users agree to the sites' terms of service, they are also agreeing to allow the site to collect information about their online activities. An **opt-out** model of informed consent permits the collection of personal information until the consumer specifically requests the data not to be collected. Privacy advocates would like to see wider use of an **opt-in** model of informed consent in which a business is prohibited from collecting any personal information unless the consumer specifically takes action to approve information collection and use. Here, the default option is no collection of user information.

The online industry has preferred self-regulation to privacy legislation for protecting consumers. The online advertising industry formed the Online Privacy Alliance to encourage self-regulation to develop a set of privacy guidelines for its members. The group promotes the use of online seals, such as that of TRUSTe, certifying websites adhering to certain privacy principles. Members of the advertising network industry, including Google's DoubleClick, have created an additional industry association called the Network Advertising Initiative (NAI) to develop its own privacy policies to help consumers opt out of advertising network programs and provide consumers redress from abuses.

Individual firms such as Microsoft, Mozilla Foundation, Yahoo, and Google have recently adopted policies on their own in an effort to address public concern about tracking people online. Microsoft's Internet Explorer 11 web browser was released in 2015 with the opt-out option as the default, but by 2016 Microsoft removed this feature in large part because most websites ignore the request to opt out. Other browsers have opt-out options, but users need to turn them on, and most users fail to do this. AOL established an opt-out policy that allows users of its site to choose not to be tracked. Yahoo follows NAI guidelines and allows opt-out for tracking and web beacons (web bugs). Google has reduced retention time for tracking data.

In general, most Internet businesses do little to protect the privacy of their customers, and consumers do not do as much as they should to protect themselves. For commercial websites that depend on advertising to support themselves, most revenue derives from selling customer information. Of the companies that do post privacy policies on their websites, about half do not monitor their sites to ensure that they adhere to these policies. The vast majority of online customers claim they are concerned about online privacy, but fewer than half read the privacy statements on websites. In general, website privacy policies require a law degree to understand and are ambiguous about key terms (Laudon and Traver,

2015). In 2016, what firms such as Facebook and Google call a privacy policy is in fact a data use policy. The concept of privacy is associated with consumer rights, which firms do not wish to recognize. A data use policy simply tells customers how the information will be used without any mention of rights.

In one of the more insightful studies of consumer attitudes toward Internet privacy, a group of Berkeley students conducted surveys of online users and of complaints filed with the FTC involving privacy issues. Some of their results show that people feel they have no control over the information collected about them, and they don't know who to complain to. Websites collect all this information but do not let users have access, the website policies are unclear, and they share data with affiliates but never identify who the affiliates are and how many there are. Web bug trackers are ubiquitous, and users are not informed of trackers on the pages they visit. The results of this study and others suggest that consumers are not saying, "Take my privacy, I don't care, send me the service for free." They are saying, "We want access to the information, we want some controls on what can be collected, what is done with the information, the ability to opt out of the entire tracking enterprise, and some clarity on what the policies really are, and we don't want those policies changed without our participation and permission." (The full report is available at knowprivacy.org.)

Technical Solutions

In addition to legislation, there are a few technologies that can protect user privacy during interactions with websites. Many of these tools are used for encrypting e-mail, for making e-mail or surfing activities appear anonymous, for preventing client computers from accepting cookies, or for detecting and eliminating spyware. For the most part, technical solutions have failed to protect users from being tracked as they move from one site to another.

Because of growing public criticism of behavioral tracking, targeting of ads, and the failure of industry to self-regulate, attention has shifted to browsers. Many browsers have Do Not Track options. For users who have selected the Do Not Track browser option, their browser will send a request to websites requesting the user's behavior not be tracked, but websites are not obligated to honor their visitors' requests not to be tracked. There is no online advertising industry agreement on how to respond to Do Not Track requests nor, currently, any legislation requiring websites to stop tracking. Private browser encryption software or apps on mobile devices provide consumers a powerful opportunity to at least keep their messages private.

Property Rights: Intellectual Property

Contemporary information systems have severely challenged existing laws and social practices that protect **intellectual property**. Intellectual property is considered to be tangible and intangible products of the mind created by individuals or corporations. Information technology has made it difficult to protect intellectual property because computerized information can be so easily copied or distributed on networks. Intellectual property is subject to a variety of protections under three legal traditions: trade secrets, copyright, and patent law.

Trade Secrets

Any intellectual work product—a formula, device, pattern, method of manufacture, or compilation of data—used for a business purpose can be classified as a **trade secret**, provided it is not based on information in the public domain. Protections for trade secrets vary from state to state. In general, trade secret laws grant a monopoly on the ideas behind a work product, but it can be a very tenuous monopoly.

Software that contains novel or unique elements, procedures, or compilations can be included as a trade secret. Trade secret law protects the actual ideas in a work product, not only their manifestation. To make this claim, the creator or owner must take care to bind employees and customers with nondisclosure agreements and prevent the secret from falling into the public domain.

The limitation of trade secret protection is that, although virtually all software programs of any complexity contain unique elements of some sort, it is difficult to prevent the ideas in the work from falling into the public domain when the software is widely distributed.

Copyright

Copyright is a statutory grant that protects creators of intellectual property from having their work copied by others for any purpose during the life of the author plus an additional 70 years after the author's death. For corporate-owned works, copyright protection lasts for 95 years after their initial creation. Congress has extended copyright protection to books, periodicals, lectures, dramas, musical compositions, maps, drawings, artwork of any kind, and motion pictures. The intent behind copyright laws has been to encourage creativity and authorship by ensuring that creative people receive the financial and other benefits of their work. Most industrial nations have their own copyright laws, and there are several international conventions and bilateral agreements through which nations coordinate and enforce their laws.

In the mid-1960s, the Copyright Office began registering software programs, and in 1980, Congress passed the Computer Software Copyright Act, which clearly provides protection for software program code and copies of the original sold in commerce; it sets forth the rights of the purchaser to use the software while the creator retains legal title.

Copyright protects against copying entire programs or their parts. Damages and relief are readily obtained for infringement. The drawback to copyright protection is that the underlying ideas behind a work are not protected, only their manifestation in a work. A competitor can use your software, understand how it works, and build new software that follows the same concepts without infringing on a copyright.

Look-and-feel copyright infringement lawsuits are precisely about the distinction between an idea and its expression. For instance, in the early 1990s, Apple Computer sued Microsoft Corporation and Hewlett-Packard for infringement of the expression of Apple's Macintosh interface, claiming that the defendants copied the expression of overlapping windows. The defendants countered that the idea of overlapping windows can be expressed only in a single way and, therefore, was not protectable under the merger doctrine of copyright law. When ideas and their expression merge, the expression cannot be copyrighted.

In general, courts appear to be following the reasoning of a 1989 case—*Brown Bag Software v. Symantec Corp*—in which the court dissected the elements of software alleged to be infringing. The court found that similar concept, function, general functional features (e.g., drop-down menus), and colors are not protected by copyright law (*Brown Bag Software v. Symantec Corp.*, 1992).

Patents

A **patent** grants the owner an exclusive monopoly on the ideas behind an invention for 20 years. The congressional intent behind patent law was to ensure that inventors of new machines, devices, or methods receive the full financial and other rewards of their labor and yet make widespread use of the invention possible by providing detailed diagrams for those wishing to use the idea under license from the patent's owner. The granting of a patent is determined by the United States Patent and Trademark Office and relies on court rulings.

The key concepts in patent law are originality, novelty, and invention. The Patent Office did not accept applications for software patents routinely until a 1981 Supreme Court decision that held that computer programs could be part of a patentable process. Since that time, hundreds of patents have been granted, and thousands await consideration.

The strength of patent protection is that it grants a monopoly on the underlying concepts and ideas of software. The difficulty is passing stringent criteria of nonobviousness (e.g., the work must reflect some special understanding and contribution), originality, and novelty as well as years of waiting to receive protection.

In what some call the patent trial of the century, in 2011, Apple sued Samsung for violating its patents for iPhones, iPads, and iPods. On August 24, 2012, a California jury in federal district court delivered a decisive victory to Apple and a stunning defeat to Samsung. The jury awarded Apple $1 billion in damages. The decision established criteria for determining just how close a competitor can come to an industry-leading and standard-setting product like Apple's iPhone before it violates the design and utility patents of the leading firm. The same court ruled that Samsung could not sell its new tablet computer (Galaxy 10.1) in the United States. In a later patent dispute, Samsung won an infringement case against Apple. In June 2013, the United States International Trade Commission issued a ban for a handful of older iPhone and iPad devices because they violated Samsung patents from years ago. In 2014, Apple sued Samsung again, claiming infringement of five patents. The patents cover hardware and software techniques for handling photos, videos, and lists used on the popular Galaxy 5. Apple sought $2 billion in damages. In 2015, the U.S. Court of Appeals reaffirmed that Samsung had copied specific design patents, but dropped the damages Apple was granted to $930 million. In 2016 the case moved to the Supreme Court to determine whether Samsung will have to turn over all its profits from the offending phones or just those profits that derived from the infringing elements in the phones.

To make matters more complicated, Apple has been one of Samsung's largest customers for flash memory processors, graphic chips, solid-state drives, and display parts that are used in Apple's iPhones, iPads, iPod Touch devices, and MacBooks. The Samsung and Apple patent cases are indicative of the complex relationships among the leading computer firms.

Challenges to Intellectual Property Rights

Contemporary information technologies, especially software, pose severe challenges to existing intellectual property regimes and, therefore, create significant ethical, social, and political issues. Digital media differ from books, periodicals, and other media in terms of ease of replication; ease of transmission; ease of alteration; compactness—making theft easy; and difficulties in establishing uniqueness.

The proliferation of digital networks, including the Internet, has made it even more difficult to protect intellectual property. Before widespread use of networks, copies of software, books, magazine articles, or films had to be stored on physical media, such as paper, computer disks, or videotape, creating some hurdles to distribution. Using networks, information can be more widely reproduced and distributed. The BSA Global Software Survey conducted by International Data Corporation and The Software Alliance (also known as BSA) reported that the rate of global software piracy was 39 percent in 2015 (The Software Alliance, 2016).

The Internet was designed to transmit information freely around the world, including copyrighted information. You can easily copy and distribute virtually anything to millions of people worldwide, even if they are using different types of computer systems. Information can be illicitly copied from one place and distributed through other systems and networks even though these parties do not willingly participate in the infringement.

Individuals have been illegally copying and distributing digitized music files on the Internet for several decades. File-sharing services such as Napster and, later, Grokster, Kazaa, Morpheus, Megaupload, and The Pirate Bay sprang up to help users locate and swap digital music and video files, including those protected by copyright. Illegal file sharing became so widespread that it threatened the viability of the music recording industry and, at one point, consumed 20 percent of Internet bandwidth. The recording industry won several legal battles for shutting these services down, but it has not been able to halt illegal file sharing entirely. The motion picture and cable television industries are waging similar battles. Several European nations have worked with U.S. authorities to shut down illegal sharing sites, with mixed results.

As legitimate online music stores such as the iTunes Store expanded, some forms of illegal file sharing have declined. Technology has radically altered the prospects for intellectual property protection from theft, at least for music, videos, and television shows (less so for software). The Apple iTunes Store legitimated paying for music and entertainment and created a closed environment from which music and videos could not be easily copied and widely distributed unless played on Apple devices. Amazon's Kindle also protects the rights of publishers and writers because its books cannot be copied to the Internet and distributed. Streaming of Internet radio, on services such as Pandora and Spotify, and Hollywood movies (at sites such as Hulu and Netflix) also inhibits piracy because the streams cannot be easily recorded on separate devices, and videos can be downloaded so easily. Despite these gains in legitimate online music platforms, Apple's iTunes based on downloads of singles and streaming services' unwillingness to pay labels and artists a reasonable fee for playing have resulted in a 50 percent decline in record industry revenues since 2000 and the loss of thousands of jobs.

The **Digital Millennium Copyright Act (DMCA)** of 1998 also provides some copyright protection. The DMCA implemented a World Intellectual Property Organization Treaty that makes it illegal to circumvent technology-based protections of copyrighted materials. Internet service providers (ISPs) are required to take down sites of copyright infringers they are hosting when the ISPs are notified of the problem. Microsoft and other major software and information content firms are represented by the Software and Information Industry Association (SIIA), which lobbies for new laws and enforcement of existing laws to protect intellectual property around the world. The SIIA runs an antipiracy hotline for individuals to report piracy activities, offers educational programs to help organizations combat software piracy, and has published guidelines for employee use of software.

4-4 How have information systems affected laws for establishing accountability and liability and the quality of everyday life?

Along with privacy and property laws, new information technologies are challenging existing liability laws and social practices for holding individuals and institutions accountable. If a person is injured by a machine controlled, in part, by software, who should be held accountable and, therefore, held liable? Should a social network site like Facebook or Twitter be held liable and accountable for the posting of pornographic material or racial insults, or should they be held harmless against any liability for what users post (as is true of common carriers, such as the telephone system)? What about the Internet? If you outsource your information processing to the cloud, and the cloud provider fails to provide adequate service, what can you do? Cloud providers often claim the software you are using is the problem, not the cloud servers.

Computer-Related Liability Problems

In late 2013 hackers obtained credit card, debit card, and additional personal information about 70 to 110 million customers of Target, one of the largest U.S. retailers. Target's sales took an immediate hit from which it has still not completely recovered. Target says it has spent over $60 million to strengthen its systems. In 2015, Target agreed to pay $10 million to customers and $19 million to MasterCard. It has paid an even greater price through the loss of sales and trust. A survey of U.K. retailers found that 70 percent had their customer files hacked, most notably the hack of Carphone Warehouse involving 2.4 million customers (Rigby, 2015).

Who is liable for any economic harm caused to individuals or businesses whose credit cards were compromised? Is Target responsible for allowing the breach to occur despite efforts it did make to secure the information? Or is this just a cost of doing business in a credit card world where customers and businesses have insurance policies to protect them against losses? Customers, for instance, have a maximum liability of $50 for credit card theft under federal banking law.

Are information system managers responsible for the harm that corporate systems can do? Beyond IT managers, insofar as computer software is part of a machine, and the machine injures someone physically or economically, the producer of the software and the operator can be held liable for damages. Insofar as the software acts like a book, storing and displaying information, courts have been reluctant to hold authors, publishers, and booksellers liable for contents (the exception being instances of fraud or defamation); hence, courts have been wary of holding software authors liable for software.

In general, it is very difficult (if not impossible) to hold software producers liable for their software products that are considered to be like books, regardless of the physical or economic harm that results. Historically, print publishers of books and periodicals have not been held liable because of fears that liability claims would interfere with First Amendment rights guaranteeing freedom of expression. The kind of harm software failures causes is rarely fatal and typically inconveniences users but does not physically harm them (the exception being medical devices).

What about software as a service? ATMs are a service provided to bank customers. If this service fails, customers will be inconvenienced and perhaps harmed economically if they cannot access their funds in a timely manner. Should liability protections be extended to software publishers and operators of defective financial, accounting, simulation, or marketing systems?

Software is very different from books. Software users may develop expectations of infallibility about software; software is less easily inspected than a book, and it is more difficult to compare with other software products for quality; software claims to perform a task rather than describe a task, as a book does; and people come to depend on services essentially based on software. Given the centrality of software to everyday life, the chances are excellent that liability law will extend its reach to include software even when the software merely provides an information service.

Telephone systems have not been held liable for the messages transmitted because they are regulated common carriers. In return for their right to provide telephone service, they must provide access to all, at reasonable rates, and achieve acceptable reliability. Likewise, cable networks are considered private networks not subject to regulation, but broadcasters using the public air waves are subject to a wide variety of federal and local constraints on content and facilities. In the United States, with few exceptions, websites are not held liable for content posted on their sites regardless of whether it was placed there by the website owners or users.

System Quality: Data Quality and System Errors

White Christmas turned into a blackout for millions of Netflix customers and social network users on December 24, 2012. The blackout was caused by the failure of Amazon's cloud computing service (AWS), which provides storage and computing power for all kinds of websites and services, including Netflix. The loss of service lasted for a day. Amazon's cloud computing services have had several subsequent outages, although not as long-lasting as the Christmas Eve outage. Outages at cloud computing services are rare but recurring. In 2016 cloud and data center outages occured across the globe, disrupting service at iTunes, Microsoft Azure, Twitter, Salesforce, and Nest (V3, 2016). These outages have called into question the reliability and quality of cloud services. Are these outages acceptable?

The debate over liability and accountability for unintentional consequences of system use raises a related but independent moral dimension: What is an acceptable, technologically feasible level of system quality? At what point should system managers say, "Stop testing, we've done all we can to perfect this software. Let's go live!" Individuals and organizations may be held responsible for avoidable and foreseeable consequences, which they have a duty to perceive and correct. The gray area is that some system errors are foreseeable and correctable only at very great expense, expense so great that pursuing this level of perfection is not feasible economically—no one could afford the product.

For example, although software companies try to debug their products before releasing them to the marketplace, they knowingly ship buggy products because the time and cost of fixing all minor errors would prevent these products from ever being released. What if the product was not offered on the marketplace? Would social welfare as a whole falter and perhaps even decline? Carrying this further, just what is the responsibility of a producer of computer services—should it withdraw the product that can never be perfect, warn the user, or forget about the risk (let the buyer beware)?

Three principal sources of poor system performance are (1) software bugs and errors, (2) hardware or facility failures caused by natural or other causes, and (3) poor input data quality. A Chapter 8 Learning Track discusses why zero defects in software code of any complexity cannot be achieved and why the seriousness of remaining bugs cannot be estimated. Hence, there is a technological barrier to perfect software, and users must be aware of the potential for catastrophic failure. The software industry has not yet arrived at testing standards for producing software of acceptable but imperfect performance.

Although software bugs and facility catastrophes are likely to be widely reported in the press, by far the most common source of business system failure is data quality. Few companies routinely measure the quality of their data, but individual organizations report data error rates ranging from 0.5 to 30 percent.

Quality of Life: Equity, Access, and Boundaries

The negative social costs of introducing information technologies and systems are beginning to mount along with the power of the technology. Many of these negative social consequences are not violations of individual rights or property crimes. Nevertheless, they can be extremely harmful to individuals, societies, and political institutions. Computers and information technologies potentially can destroy valuable elements of our culture and society even while they bring us benefits. If there is a balance of good and bad consequences of using information systems, who do we hold responsible for the bad consequences? Next, we briefly examine some of the negative social consequences of systems, considering individual, social, and political responses.

Balancing Power: Center Versus Periphery

An early fear of the computer age was that huge, centralized mainframe computers would centralize power in the nation's capital, resulting in a Big Brother society, as was suggested in George Orwell's novel *1984*. The shift toward highly decentralized client–server computing, coupled with an ideology of empowerment of Twitter and social media users, and the decentralization of decision making to lower organizational levels, up until recently reduced the fears of power centralization in government institutions. Yet much of the empowerment described in popular business magazines is trivial. Lower-level employees may be empowered to make minor decisions, but the key policy decisions may be as centralized as in the past. At the same time, corporate Internet behemoths such as Google, Apple, Yahoo, Amazon, and Microsoft have come to dominate the collection and analysis of personal private information of all citizens. Since the terrorist attacks against the United States on September 11, 2001, the U.S. federal government has greatly expanded its use of this private sector information under the authority of the Patriot Act of 2001 and subsequent and secret executive orders. Most European countries, including France, Germany, the UK, Hungary, and Poland, have passed legislation authorizing both mass and targeted surveillance programs (Council of Europe, 2016). In this sense, power has become more centralized in the hands of a few private oligopolies and large government agencies.

Rapidity of Change: Reduced Response Time to Competition

Information systems have helped to create much more efficient national and international markets. Today's more efficient global marketplace has reduced the normal social buffers that permitted businesses many years to adjust to competition. Time-based competition has an ugly side; the business you work for may not have enough time to respond to global competitors and may be wiped out in a year along with your job. We stand the risk of developing a just-in-time society with just-in-time jobs and just-in-time workplaces, families, and vacations. One impact of Uber (see Chapter 10) and other on-demand services firms is to create just-in-time jobs with no benefits or insurance for employees.

Maintaining Boundaries: Family, Work, and Leisure

Parts of this book were produced on trains and planes as well as on vacations and during what otherwise might have been family time. The danger to ubiquitous computing, telecommuting, nomad computing, mobile computing, and the do-anything-anywhere computing environment is that it is actually coming true. The traditional boundaries that separate work from family and just plain leisure have been weakened.

Although authors have traditionally worked just about anywhere, the advent of information systems, coupled with the growth of knowledge-work occupations, means that more and more people are working when traditionally they would have been playing or communicating with family and friends. The work umbrella now extends far beyond the eight-hour day into commuting time, vacation time, and leisure time. The explosive growth and use of smartphones have only heightened the sense of many employees that they are never away from work.

Although some people enjoy the convenience of working at home, the do-anything-anywhere computing environment can blur the traditional boundaries between work and family time.

© Hongqi Zhang/123RF

Even leisure time spent on the computer threatens these close social relationships. Extensive Internet and cell phone use, even for entertainment or recreational purposes, takes people away from their family and friends. Among middle school and teenage children, it can lead to harmful antisocial behavior, such as the recent upsurge in cyberbullying.

Dependence and Vulnerability

Today, our businesses, governments, schools, and private associations, such as churches, are incredibly dependent on information systems and are, therefore, highly vulnerable if these systems fail. Most critical systems involving national infrastructure, from electricity and water to hospitals and schools, are dependent on the Internet. Secondary schools, for instance, increasingly use and rely on educational software. Test results are often stored off campus. If these systems were to shut down, there is no backup educational structure or content that can make up for the loss of the system. With systems now as ubiquitous as the telephone system, it is startling to remember that there are no regulatory or standard-setting forces in place that are similar to telephone, electrical, radio, television, or other public utility technologies.

Computer Crime and Abuse

New technologies, including computers, create new opportunities for committing crime by creating new, valuable items to steal, new ways to steal them, and new ways to harm others. **Computer crime** is the commission of illegal acts by using a computer or against a computer system. Simply accessing a computer system without authorization or with intent to do harm, even by accident, is now a federal crime. The most frequent types of incidents comprise a greatest hits list of cybercrime: malware, phishing, network interruption, spyware, and denial of service attacks. (PwC, 2015). The true cost of all computer crime is unknown, but it is estimated to be in the billions of dollars. You can find a more detailed discussion of computer crime in Chapter 8.

Computer abuse is the commission of acts involving a computer that may not be illegal but are considered unethical. The popularity of the Internet and e-mail has turned one form of computer abuse—spamming—into a serious problem for both individuals and businesses. Originally, **spam** was junk e-mail an organization or individual sent to a mass audience of Internet users who had expressed no interest in the product or service being marketed. However, as cell phone use has mushroomed, spam was certain to follow. Identity and financial-theft cybercriminals are turning their attention to smartphones as users check e-mail, do online banking, pay bills, and reveal personal information. Cell phone spam usually comes in the form of SMS text messages, but increasingly, users are receiving spam in their Facebook Newsfeed and messaging service as well. Spammers tend to market pornography, fraudulent deals and services, outright scams, and other products not widely approved in most civilized societies. Some countries have passed laws to outlaw spamming or restrict its use. In the United States, it is still legal if it does not involve fraud and the sender and subject of the e-mail are properly identified.

Spamming has mushroomed because it costs only a few cents to send thousands of messages advertising wares to Internet users. The percentage of all e-mail that is spam was estimated at around 65 percent in 2015 (Kaspersky, 2015). Most spam originates from bot networks, which consist of thousands of captured PCs that can initiate and relay spam messages. Spam volume has declined somewhat since authorities took down the Rustock botnet in 2011. Spam costs for businesses are very high (estimated at more than $50 billion per year) because of the computing and network resources billions of unwanted e-mail messages and the time required to deal with them consume.

Spamming is more tightly regulated in Europe than in the United States. In 2002, the European Parliament passed a ban on unsolicited commercial messaging. Digital marketing can be targeted only to people who have given prior consent.

The U.S. CAN-SPAM Act of 2003, which went into effect in 2004, does not outlaw spamming but does ban deceptive e-mail practices by requiring commercial e-mail messages to display accurate subject lines, identify the true senders, and offer recipients an easy way to remove their names from e-mail lists. It also prohibits the use of fake return addresses. A few people have been prosecuted under the law, but it has had a negligible impact on spamming in large part because of the Internet's exceptionally poor security and the use of offshore servers and botnets. Most large-scale spamming has moved offshore to Russia and Eastern Europe where hackers control global botnets capable of generating billions of spam messages. The largest spam network in recent years was the Russian network Festi based in St. Petersburg. Festi is best known as the spam generator behind the global Viagra-spam industry, which stretches from Russia to Indian pharmaceutical firms selling counterfeit Viagra. Australia, South Africa, the European Union, Sweden, and Malaysia are among the countries that have anti-spam laws (ITU, 2016).

For a many years automobile manufacturers around the globe have tried to find ways of manipulating mileage and emissions tests to produce more favorable results on paper than what actually takes place on the road. The use of software for this purpose recently came to light with revelations that Volkswagen Group installed deceptive software in some of its diesel car models to violate the U.S. Clean Air Act.

INTERACTIVE SESSION: MANAGEMENT

Ethical Issues of Google Earth

Google Earth provides free satellite models of the earth. Originally developed by Keyhole Inc., a company funded by the Central Intelligence Agency (CIA), it was acquired by Google in 2004 and relaunched as Google Earth in 2005. Initially, Google Earth just provided locations of buildings and other structures, but gradually it widened its services to provide street maps in form of its Google Street View feature. In 2007, Google even started offering real-time traffic data. With such features, Google Earth has been able to uncover a variety of crimes such as:

- Catching thieves by identifying the images of the miscreants on Street View.
- Detecting other illegal activities, such as the Marijuana plantations in Oregon in 2013, which was grown three times beyond its permissible limits, or the detection of illegal logging of the rain forests in the Philippines.
- Finding tax evaders by using Google Earth to determine the true size of the properties of homeowners, as done by the Greek government in recent times.
- Spotting stolen or illegally dumped vehicles.
- Detecting drug-dealing gangs and identifying the areas in which they operate.

Although the advantages of Google Earth are many, it has not been without its share of ethical controversies. Some of the developing countries are concerned about the surveillance modes used by Google Earth. In such countries, where IT laws are less stringent, the threat of global terrorism has compounded. In 2005, when Google Earth started showing different places of the earth as full-color photographs, it was considered to be a boon for developing countries like India, which has severe traffic problems. This service could help users in these countries locate their destination easily and reduce traffic chaos. It could also give users two-dimensional images of far-flung areas, making them more accessible.

South Korea was probably one of the first countries to voice concerns against Google Earth. South Korea, which was then engaged in a war with North Korea, felt that the Google Earth images compromised their territory. The Austrian Nuclear Science and Technology Organization (ANSTO) also raised concern over the sensitive information provided by Google Earth. Similarly, in 2005, the Dutch legislators, Frans Weekers and Aleing Wolfson, asked, "Should the Dutch government consider taking measures (against Google Earth) and if not, why not"? There were security concerns raised in Iraq as well, as many thought that the Al-Qaida used Google Earth as an intelligence tool in its fight against the U.S. In 2007, all these concerns reached their crescendo when it was reported that terrorists are using Google Earth to target British bases in Basra. Meanwhile, India was also uneasy about the imaging conducted by Google Earth. In 2007, Indian President A.P.J. Abdul Kalam held a meeting with police officials to express concerns about the high-resolution images of the country's strategic sites on Google Earth.

Several countries are now contemplating the idea of launching their own service similar to that provided by Google Earth. In May 2008, the Indian Space Research Organization (ISRO) announced its plan to develop Bhuvan. In this tool, it was proposed that the high-security areas would be blurred out, so as to have more control over the content being displayed on the Internet. Moreover, the Bhuvan application could only be downloaded by registered users. A beta version of Bhuvan was released in 2009, and now it supports additional features such as providing flood and forest fire alerts, information about agricultural landslides, and so on. However, Bhuvan is not as sophisticated as Google Earth and has a lot of performance issues.

Imaging the entire planet is not an easy task, and it requires advanced technology and infrastructure. The countries that have tried to develop their own solution have realized the challenges of undertaking this project. As a workaround, some countries have demanded that Google take permission from the host country regarding the images that are safe to display and those that need to be camouflaged so that sensitive areas are not made public. But the problem here is: how does a government identify sensitive locations? For example, citizens might want places such as railway stations and bus stands to be mapped, while government might think that these are sensitive areas.

There have been several calls to ban Google Earth over the years. However, in this age of global information sharing, there have been debates as to whether that would be the right thing to do. Advocates such as Amit Karkhanis have filed a petition before the Mumbai High Court to ban Google Earth on the grounds that it is helping terrorists navigate their way to Mumbai via sea. However, such individuals have little legal evidence to substantiate their allegations. The satellites used for mapping do not cause noise, light, or air pollution, and hence, it is difficult to prove that the imaging causes any nuisance.

Apart from the apparent danger to national security posed by Google Earth, there has been some objection to Google mapping people's houses. Many argue that it is an invasion of privacy. There have also been accusations against Google for stealing personal information like name, address, passwords, and medical information from unsecured Wi-Fi networks.

The U.S. courts, however, have ruled that capturing the aerial view of someone's property does not amount to a trespass against that person: "We have said that the airspace is a public highway. Yet it is obvious that if the landowner is to have full enjoyment of the land, he must have exclusive control of the immediate reaches of the enveloping atmosphere. Otherwise buildings could not be erected, trees could not be planted, and even fences could not be run ... The landowner owns at least as much of the space above the ground as he can occupy or use in connection with the land."

Acknowledging the concerns raised by various governments, and especially the Indian government, Google Earth issued an official statement, which says, "Google has been talking and will continue to talk to the Indian government about any security concerns it may have regarding Google Earth. We are pleased to have initiated dialogue with the Indian government, the discussions have been substantive and constructive, but no agreements have been made ... We have committed to continue the dialogue." In the end, it is the openness or conservatism of individual governments that will determine to what extent its people are allowed to enjoy the benefits of a service like Google Earth.

Sources: Zhu, Yueqin, Jiantong Zhang and Liqiu Meng, "Ethical Concerns for Online Geoinformation Services". Retrieved from http://icaci.org/files/documents/ICC_proceedings/ICC2009/html/nonref/22_3.pdf. http://www.spatial.maine.edu/~onsrud/GSDI-Archive/gis_ethics.pdf. Doyle, Jack, "How Google lied over street spies: Watchdog relaunches inquiry into search engine's data trawl", *The Daily Mail* (2012). Retrieved from http://www.dailymail.co.uk/news/article-2158307/Google-facing-new-privacy-probe-Street-View-cars-data-theft-alleged-misled-watchdog.html. Strachan, Lindsey A., "Re-mapping Privacy Law: How the Google Maps Scandal Requires Tort Law Reform", *Richmond Journal of Law and Technology*, Vol. 15, Issue 4 (2011). Retrieved from http://jolt.richmond.edu/v17i4/article14.pdf. Banerjee, Debadyuti, "'Is My Laptop A Viable Tool To Invade Your Privacy?'—Such and Other Critical Legal Issues Generated By Google Earth", *Journal of International Commercial Law and Technology*, Vol. 5, Issue 4 (2010). Retrieved from http://www.jiclt.com/index.php/jiclt/article/viewFile/120/118. *Google Earth*. Retrieved from http://www.google.com/earth/explore/showcase/historical.html. Sui, Daniel and Michael Goodchild, "The convergence of GIS and social media: challenges for GIScience", *International Journal of Geographical Information Science* (2011). Retrieved from http://www.geog.ucsb.edu/~good/papers/516.pdf. *Bhuvan*. Retrieved from http://www.bhuvan.nrsc.gov.in/bhuvan_links.php#. Saxena, Anupam, "India's 'Google Earth' Bhuvan Upgraded: Disaster Services, Tourism Info, High Res", *Medianama* (2013). Retrieved from http://www.medianama.com/2013/01/223-bhuvan-new-datasets/. *National Remote Sensing Centre: Indian Space Research Organisation*. Retrieved from http://nrsc.gov.in/. "10 Crimes Caught On Google Earth", Yahoo! News. Retrieved on https://screen.yahoo.com/top-viral-videos/10-crimes-caught-google-earth-172002790.html

CASE STUDY QUESTIONS

1. Discuss the features of Google Earth and the benefits it offers.
2. What are the ethical concerns raised by the different countries against Google Earth? Do you think they are justified?
3. What are the various methods adopted to contemplate the ethical issues raised by Google Earth?
4. Do you think Google's response to such concerns is appropriate?

Employment: Trickle-Down Technology and Reengineering Job Loss

Reengineering work is typically hailed in the information systems community as a major benefit of new information technology. It is much less frequently noted that redesigning business processes has caused millions of mid-level factory managers and clerical workers to lose their jobs, along with millions of blue collar factory jobs. Several economists have sounded new alarms about information and computer technology threatening middle-class, white-collar jobs (in addition to blue-collar factory jobs). Erik Brynjolfsson and Andrew P. McAfee argue that the pace of automation has picked up in recent years because of a combination of technologies, including robotics, numerically controlled machines, computerized inventory control, pattern recognition, voice recognition, and online commerce. One result is that machines can now do a great many jobs heretofore reserved for humans, including tech support, call center work, X-ray examination, and even legal document review (Brynjolfsson and McAfee, 2011). These views contrast with earlier assessments by economists that both labor and capital would receive stable shares of income and that new technologies created as many or more new jobs as they destroyed old ones. However, there is no guarantee this will happen in the future, and the income wealth share of labor may continue to fall relative to capital, resulting in a loss of high-paying jobs and further declines in wages.

Other economists are much more sanguine about the potential job losses. In some cases, employment has grown or remained unchanged in industries where investment in IT capital is highest. These economists also believe that bright, educated workers who are displaced by technology will move to better jobs in fast-growth industries. Missing from this equation are unskilled, blue-collar workers and older, less well-educated middle managers. It is not clear that these groups can be retrained easily for high-quality, high-paying jobs.

Equity and Access: Increasing Racial and Social Class Cleavages

Does everyone have an equal opportunity to participate in the digital age? Will the social, economic, and cultural gaps that exist in the United States and other societies be reduced by information systems technology? Or will the cleavages be increased, permitting the better off to become even more better off relative to others?

These questions have not yet been fully answered because the impact of systems technology on various groups in society has not been thoroughly studied. What is known is that information, knowledge, computers, and access to these resources through educational institutions and public libraries are inequitably distributed along ethnic and social class lines, as are many other information resources. Although the gap in computer access is narrowing, higher-income families in each ethnic group are still more likely to have home computers and broadband Internet access than lower-income families in the same group. Moreover, the children of higher-income families are far more likely to use their Internet access to pursue educational goals, whereas lower-income children are much more likely to spend time on entertainment and games. This is called the "time-wasting" gap. Left uncorrected, this **digital divide** could lead to a society of information haves, computer literate and skilled, versus a large group of information have-nots, computer illiterate and unskilled.

Health Risks: RSI, CVS, and Cognitive Decline

A common occupational disease today is **repetitive stress injury (RSI)**. RSI occurs when muscle groups are forced through repetitive actions often with high-impact loads (such as tennis) or tens of thousands of repetitions under low-impact loads (such as working at a computer keyboard). The incidence of RSI is estimated to be as much as one-third of the labor force and accounts for one-third of all disability cases.

The single largest source of RSI is computer keyboards. The most common kind of computer-related RSI is **carpal tunnel syndrome (CTS)**, in which pressure on the median nerve through the wrist's bony structure, called a carpal tunnel, produces pain. The pressure is caused by constant repetition of keystrokes: in a single shift, a word processor may perform 23,000 keystrokes. Symptoms of CTS include numbness, shooting pain, inability to grasp objects, and tingling. Millions of workers have been diagnosed with CTS. It affects an estimated 3 percent to 6 percent of the workforce (LeBlanc and Cestia, 2011).

INTERACTIVE SESSION: ORGANIZATIONS

Are We Relying Too Much on Computers to Think for Us?

Does our ever-burgeoning dependence on computers foster complacency, suppressing our ability to marshal our mental faculties when required? Although computerization has undoubtedly mitigated malfunctions, work stoppages, and breakdowns, are we concurrently losing our ability to assess alternatives independently and make optimal choices?

At least one technology writer is sure this is exactly what is happening. Nicholas Carr's book, *The Glass Cage: Automation and Us*, lays out the case that our overreliance on computers has dulled our reflexes and eroded expertise. Two cognitive failures undermine performance. Complacency—overconfidence in the computer's ability—causes our attention to wander. Bias—overconfidence in the accuracy of the data we are receiving from the computer—causes us to disregard outside data sources, including conflicting sensory stimuli.

When pilots, soldiers, doctors, or even factory managers lose focus and lack situational awareness, they ignore both suspect data coming from the computer and the external cues that would refute it. The results can be catastrophic. In two instances in 2009, commercial airplane pilots misinterpreted the signals when their autopilot controls disconnected after receiving warnings that the aircraft would stall. Rather than pushing the yoke forward to gain velocity, both pilots heeded faulty control panel data while ignoring environmental cues and pulled back on the yoke, lifting the plane's nose and decreasing airspeed—the exact opposite of what was required. Loss of automation triggered confusion and panic. Sharply curtailed hands-on flight experience (on a typical passenger flight today, a human pilot mans the controls for just three minutes) resulted in stalled aircraft plunging to earth. Fifty died in Buffalo, New York; 228 perished in the Atlantic Ocean en route to Paris from Rio de Janeiro. The Federal Aviation Administration (FAA) is now pressing airlines to adopt stricter requirements for manual flying hours to offset the risks posed by complacency and bias.

Carr's critics point out that air travel is now safer than ever, with accidents and deaths steadily declining over decades and fatal airline crashes exceedingly rare. Carr concedes this point but still worries that pilots have come to rely so much on computers that they are forgetting how to fly. Andrew McAfee, a researcher at the MIT Sloan School of Management, points out that people have lamented the loss of skills due to technology for many centuries, but on balance, automation has made the world better off. There may be a high-profile crash, but he believes greater automation, not less, is the solution.

Although humans have historically believed that allocating tasks to machines liberates us from the mundane and enables us to pursue the extraordinary, computers have ushered in an altogether different era. Massive data compilation and complex analytical capabilities now mean that decision making, heretofore the sole province of the human brain, is increasingly being accomplished by computers. Offloading tasks to computers liberates us from complex thinking while requiring us to pursue mundane tasks such as inputting data, observing output, and absentmindedly awaiting equipment failure.

Complacency and bias-induced errors are piling up. For example, computer programs now highlight suspect spots on mammograms. With the compulsion to examine images scrupulously relieved, radiologists are now missing some early-stage tumors not flagged by the program. Australian researchers found that accountants at two international firms using advanced auditing software had a significantly weaker understanding of the different types of risk than did those at a firm using simpler software that required them to make risk assessment decisions themselves. Even the most rudimentary tasks, such as editing and spell checking, are now performed differently. Rather than actively participating, we are observers, waiting to be told to correct an error. Are such short-term efficiencies worth the long-term loss of knowledge and expertise?

What's more, software programs are shouldering ever more capabilities heretofore thought to be the exclusive domain of the human brain. Sensory assessment, environmental awareness, coordinated movement, and conceptual knowledge are included in programming that has enabled Google to begin testing its driverless cars on public roads. Some argue that this is precisely the direction in which we should be going: autonomous computers with no human oversight or intervention at all. The solution to pilot error during automation failures? A wholly autonomous autopilot. The solution to doctors' declining diagnostic skills due to complacency and bias? Cut doctors out of the equation altogether.

Carr sees two problems with this thinking. First, complex computer systems require complex interdependencies among databases, algorithms, sensors, software, and hardware. The more mutually dependent elements there are in a system, the greater the potential points of failure and the more difficult they are to find. Second, we have known for more than three decades that humans are spectacularly bad at precisely the job that increased computerization has relegated to them: passive observation. When not actively engaged, our minds tend to drift off to any topic other than the one we are supposed to be monitoring. What's more, because we now know that "use it or lose it" applies to flying airplanes, diagnosing illnesses, spell-checking, and everything in between, restricting humans to observation reduces experts to rookies, escalating the risk of improper responses to malfunctions.

One solution is to design programs that promote engagement and learning, for example, by returning control to the operator at frequent, but irregular, intervals or by ensuring that challenging tasks are included. If operators must perform and repeat complex manual and mental tasks, the generation effect will be reinforced. Unfortunately, introducing these changes necessarily includes software slowdown and productivity decline. Businesses are unlikely to value long-term expertise preservation and development over short-term profits. Who does this technology benefit in the long run?

Sources: Patrick Smith, "Why Pilots Still Matter," *New York Times*, April 10, 2015; Nicholas Carr, "All Can Be Lost: The Risk of Putting Our Knowledge in the Hands of Machines," *Atlantic*, October 23, 2013; John Preston, "Review of Nicholas Carr's *The Glass Cage: Where Automation Is Taking Us*," *Telegraph*, January 11, 2015; Daniel Menaker, " Review of Nicholas Carr's *The Glass Cage*," *New York Times Book Review*, November 7, 2014; John Jones, "The Technophobe's Dilemma: Nicholas Carr's *The Glass Cage*," *DML Central*, November 10, 2014; Maria Bustillos, "Nicholas Carr's Latest Anti-technology Rant, *The Glass Cage*," *LA Times*, September 19, 2014; Carol Callwaladr, "*The Glass Cage: Where Automation Is Taking Us* Review: On Course for Disaster," *Guardian*, January 19, 2015; Daniel J. Levitin, "Book Review: *The Glass Cage* by Nicholas Carr," *Wall Street Journal*, October 10, 2014.

CASE STUDY QUESTIONS

1. Identify the problem described in this case study. In what sense is it an ethical dilemma?
2. Should more tasks be automated? Why or why not? Explain your answer.
3. Can the problem of automation reducing cognitive skills be solved? Explain your answer.

RSI is avoidable. Designing workstations for a neutral wrist position (using a wrist rest to support the wrist), proper monitor stands, and footrests all contribute to proper posture and reduced RSI. Ergonomically correct keyboards are also an option. These measures should be supported by frequent rest breaks and rotation of employees to different jobs.

RSI is not the only occupational illness computers cause. Back and neck pain, leg stress, and foot pain also result from poor ergonomic designs of workstations. **Computer vision syndrome (CVS)** refers to any eyestrain condition related to display screen use in desktop computers, laptops, e-readers, smartphones, and handheld video games. CVS affects about 90 percent of people who spend three hours or more per day at a computer. Its symptoms, which are usually temporary, include headaches, blurred vision, and dry and irritated eyes.

In addition to these maladies, computer technology may be harming our cognitive functions or at least changing how we think and solve problems. Although the Internet has made it much easier for people to access, create, and use information, some experts believe that it is also preventing people from focusing and thinking clearly. They argue that exposure to computers reduces intelligence and actually makes people dumb. One MIT scholar believes exposure to computers discourages drawing and encourages looking up answers rather than engaging in real problem solving. Students, in this view, don't learn much surfing the web or answering e-mail when compared to listening, drawing, arguing, looking, playing outdoors, and exploring (Henry, 2011). The Interactive Session on Organizations describes a related concern: that automation is de-skilling people by removing opportunities to learn important tasks and impairing their ability to think on their own.

The computer has become part of our lives—personally as well as socially, culturally, and politically. It is unlikely that the issues and our choices will become easier as information technology continues to transform our world. The growth of the Internet and the information economy suggests that all the ethical and social issues we have described will be intensified further as we move further into the first digital century.

Repetitive stress injury (RSI) is a leading occupational disease today. The single largest cause of RSI is computer keyboard work.

Review Summary

4-1 *What ethical, social, and political issues are raised by information systems?*

Information technology is introducing changes for which laws and rules of acceptable conduct have not yet been developed. Increasing computing power, storage, and networking capabilities—including the Internet—expand the reach of individual and organizational actions and magnify their impacts. The ease and anonymity with which information is now communicated, copied, and manipulated in online environments pose new challenges to the protection of privacy and intellectual property. The main ethical, social, and political issues information systems raise center on information rights and obligations, property rights and obligations, accountability and control, system quality, and quality of life.

4-2 *What specific principles for conduct can be used to guide ethical decisions?*

Six ethical principles for judging conduct include the Golden Rule, Immanuel Kant's categorical imperative, the slippery slope rule, the utilitarian principle, the risk aversion principle, and the ethical no-free-lunch rule. These principles should be used in conjunction with an ethical analysis.

4-3 *Why do contemporary information systems technology and the Internet pose challenges to the protection of individual privacy and intellectual property?*

Contemporary data storage and data analysis technology enable companies to gather personal data from many sources easily about individuals and analyze these data to create detailed digital profiles about individuals and their behaviors. Data flowing over the Internet can be monitored at many points. Cookies and other web monitoring tools closely track the activities of website visitors. Not all websites have strong privacy protection policies, and they do not always allow for informed consent regarding the use of personal information. Traditional copyright laws are insufficient to protect against software piracy because digital material can be copied so easily and transmitted to many locations simultaneously over the Internet.

4-4 *How have information systems affected laws for establishing accountability and liability and the quality of everyday life?*

New information technologies are challenging existing liability laws and social practices for holding individuals and institutions accountable for harm done to others. Although computer systems have been sources of efficiency and wealth, they have some negative impacts. Computer errors can cause serious harm to individuals and organizations. Poor data quality is also responsible for disruptions and losses for businesses. Jobs can be lost when computers replace workers or tasks become unnecessary in reengineered business processes. The ability to own and use a computer may be exacerbating socioeconomic disparities among different racial groups and social classes. Widespread use of computers increases opportunities for computer crime and computer abuse. Computers can also create health and cognitive problems such as repetitive stress injury, computer vision syndrome, and the inability to think clearly and perform complex tasks.

Key Terms

Accountability, 136
Carpal tunnel syndrome (CTS), 159
Computer abuse, 155
Computer crime, 154
Computer vision syndrome (CVS), 161
Cookies, 143
Copyright, 147
Digital divide, 158
Digital Millennium Copyright Act (DMCA), 150
Due process, 136
Ethical no-free-lunch rule, 138
Ethics, 131
Fair Information Practices (FIP), 139
Golden Rule, 137
Immanuel Kant's categorical imperative, 137
Information rights, 132
Informed consent, 142
Intellectual property, 147
Liability, 136
Nonobvious relationship awareness (NORA), 135
Opt-in, 145
Opt-out, 145
Patent, 148
Privacy, 139
Profiling, 134
Repetitive stress injury (RSI), 159
Responsibility, 136
Risk aversion principle, 137
Safe harbor, 142
Slippery slope rule, 137
Spam, 155
Spyware, 144
Trade secret, 147
Utilitarian principle, 137
Web beacons, 144

Review Questions

4-1 What ethical, social, and political issues are raised by information systems?

- Define ethics and discuss the urgency to consider ethical issues in light of information systems.
- Explain the role of non-obvious relationship awareness in profiling and related privacy concerns.
- List the moral dimensions related to information systems.

4-2 What specific principles of conduct can be used to guide ethical decisions?

- Explain the responsibility, liability, accountability, and due processes involved in the ethical analysis of information systems.
- Discuss the implication of professional codes of conduct and ethics.

4-3 Why do contemporary information systems technology and the Internet pose challenges to the protection of an individual's privacy and intellectual property?

- List down the fair information practice principles provided by the FTC.

- Which directives make privacy protection in European countries more stringent than in the US?
- Which technologies are used by organizations to track web searches and how does Google use this information for advertising?
- How has the Internet led to the violation of intellectual property rights? What is the role of the Digital Millennium Copyright Act (DMCA) in curbing it?

4-4 How have information systems affected laws for establishing accountability and liability and the quality of everyday life?

- Explain why it is so difficult to hold software services liable for failure or injury.
- List and describe the principal causes of system quality problems.
- Define computer crime and computer abuse and describe their impacts on computer users.
- Define and describe computer vision syndrome and repetitive stress injury (RSI) and explain their relationship to information technology.

Discussion Questions

4-5 What is the digital divide and how do you think it should be dealt with?

4-6 Should companies be responsible for unemployment of their information systems cause? Why or why not?

4-7 Discuss the pros and cons of allowing companies to amass personal data for behavioral targeting.

Hands-On MIS Projects

The projects in this section give you hands-on experience in analyzing the privacy implications of using online data brokers, developing a corporate policy for employee web usage, using blog creation tools to create a simple blog, and analyzing web browser privacy.

Management Decision Problems

4-8 The Malaysian government is a major healthcare provider. The government plans to have 33 paperless public hospitals in Malaysia in the next few years. These paperless hospitals will be backed by information systems that will collect, process, and retrieve data. This will not only help to increase the operating efficiency of these hospitals but will also be environment-friendly. So far, the government has been successful in making two public hospitals paperless, and work to make 31 other hospitals paperless is in progress. Although the government has formulated a code of conduct for doctors to be good practitioners, there is no code in place for information ethics. There is an urgent need to regulate the collection, storage, and communication of medical data and patient information to prevent misuse. What concerns might patients have? What can hospitals do to prevent misuse? Given the scenario outlined above, what do you think should be part of an ethical code of conduct for securing the sensitive information gathered by healthcare service providers?

Achieving Operational Excellence: Creating a Simple Blog

Software skills: Blog creation
Business skills: Blog and web page design

4-9 In this project, you'll learn how to build a simple blog of your own design using the online blog creation software available at Blogger.com. Pick a sport, hobby, or topic of interest as the theme for your blog. Name the blog, give it a title, and choose a template for the blog. Post at least four entries to the blog, adding a label for each posting. Edit your posts if necessary. Upload an image, such as a photo from your hard drive or the web, to your blog. Add capabilities for other registered users, such as team members, to comment on your blog. Briefly describe how your blog could be useful to a company selling products or services related to the theme of your blog. List the tools available to Blogger that would make your blog more useful for business and describe the business uses of each. Save your blog and show it to your instructor.

Improving Decision Making: Analyzing Web Browser Privacy

Software Skills: Web browser software
Business Skills: Analyzing web browser privacy protection features

4-10 This project will help develop your Internet skills for using the privacy protection features of leading web browser software.

Examine the privacy protection features and settings for two leading web browsers such as Internet Explorer, Mozilla Firefox, or Google Chrome. Make a table comparing the features of two of these browsers in terms of functions provided and ease of use.

- How do these privacy protection features protect individuals?
- How do these privacy protection features affect what businesses can do on the Internet?
- Which does the best job of protecting privacy? Why?

Collaboration and Teamwork Project

Developing a Corporate Code of Ethics

4-11 With three or four of your classmates, develop a corporate ethics code on privacy that addresses both employee privacy and the privacy of customers and users of the corporate website. Be sure to consider e-mail privacy and employer monitoring of worksites as well as corporate use of information about employees concerning their off-the-job behavior (e.g., lifestyle, marital arrangements, and so forth). If possible, use Google Docs and Google Drive or Google Sites to brainstorm, organize, and develop a presentation of your findings for the class.

Business Problem-Solving Case

FACEBOOK PRIVACY: WHAT PRIVACY?

In less than a decade, Facebook has morphed from a small, niche networking site for mostly Ivy League college students into a publicly traded company with a market worth of $338 billion in 2016. Facebook boasts that it is free to join and always will be, so where's the money coming from to service 1.65 billion worldwide subscribers? Just like its fellow tech titan and rival Google, Facebook's revenue comes almost entirely from advertising. Facebook does not have a diverse array of hot new gadgets like Apple does, a global network of brick-and-mortar retail outlets like Walmart does, or a full inventory of software for sale. All Facebook has to sell is your personal information and the information of hundreds of millions of others with Facebook accounts.

Advertisers have long understood the value of Facebook's unprecedented trove of personal information. They can serve ads using highly specific details such as relationship status, location, employment status, favorite books, movies, or TV shows and a host of other categories. For example, an Atlanta woman who posts that she has become engaged might be offered an ad for a wedding photographer on her Facebook page. When advertisements are served to finely targeted subsets of users, the response is much more successful than traditional types of advertising.

A growing number of companies both big and small have taken notice. In 2015, Facebook generated $17.9 billion in revenue, 94 percent of which ($16.8 billion) was from selling ads and the remainder from selling games and virtual goods. Facebook's revenues in 2015 grew by 43 percent over the previous year, driven mostly by adding new users and showing 40 percent more ads than a year earlier. A major contributor to revenue growth in 2015 is ads sold in the mobile News Feed.

That was good news for Facebook, which is expected to continue to increase its revenue in coming years, but is it good news for you, the Facebook user? More than ever, companies such as Facebook and Google, which made approximately $67 billion in advertising revenue in 2015, are using your online activity to develop a frighteningly accurate picture of your life. Facebook's goal is to serve advertisements that are more relevant to you than anywhere else on the web, but the personal information it gathers about you both with and without your consent can also be used against you in other ways.

Facebook has a diverse array of compelling and useful features. Facebook's partnership with the Department of Labor helps connect job seekers and employers; Facebook has helped families find lost pets; Facebook allows active-duty soldiers to stay in touch with their families; it gives smaller companies a chance to further their e-commerce efforts and larger companies a chance to solidify their brands; and, perhaps most obviously, Facebook allows you to keep in touch with your friends, relatives, local restaurants, and in short, just about all things you are interested in more easily. These are the reasons so many people use Facebook—it provides value to users.

However, Facebook's goal is to get its users to share as much data as possible because the more Facebook knows about you, the more accurately it can serve relevant advertisements to you. Facebook CEO Mark Zuckerberg often says that people want the world to be more open and connected. It's unclear whether that is truly the case, but it is certainly true that Facebook wants the world to be more open and connected because it stands to make more money in that world. Critics of Facebook are concerned that the existence of a repository of personal data of the size that Facebook has amassed requires protections and privacy controls that extend far beyond those that Facebook currently offers.

Facebook wanting to make more money is understandable, but the company has a checkered past of privacy violations and missteps that raise doubts about whether it should be responsible for the personal data of hundreds of millions of people. There are no laws in the United States that give consumers the right to know what data companies like Facebook have compiled. You can challenge information in credit reports, but you can't even see what data Facebook has gathered about you, let alone try to change it. It's different in Europe: you can request Facebook to turn over a report of all the information it has about you.

More than ever, your every move, every click, on social networks is being used by outside entities to assess your interests and behavior and then pitch you an ad based on this knowledge. Law enforcement agencies use social networks to gather evidence on tax evaders and other criminals; employers use social networks to make decisions about prospective candidates for jobs; and data aggregators are gathering as much information about you as they can sell to the highest bidder. Facebook has admitted that it uses a software bug or code to track users across the Internet even if they are not using Facebook.

Think you own your face? Febook's newest privacy issue involves its facial recognition software used for photo tagging of users. This "tag suggestions" feature is automatically on when you sign up, and there is no user consent. A federal court in 2016 allowed a lawsuit to go forward contesting Facebook's right to photo tag without user consent. This feature is in violation of several state laws that seek to secure the privacy of biometric data.

A recent Consumer Reports study found that of 150 million Americans on Facebook, ever day, at least 4.8 million are willingly sharing information that could be used against them in some way. That includes plans to travel on a particular day, which burglars could use to time robberies, or Liking a page about a particular health condition or treatment, which insurers could use to deny coverage. Thirteen million users have never adjusted Facebook's privacy controls, which allow friends using Facebook applications to transfer your data unwittingly to a third party without your knowledge.

Credit card companies and similar organizations have begun engaging in weblining, taken from the phrase redlining, by altering their treatment of you based on the actions of other people with profiles similar to yours. Employers can assess your personality and behavior by using your Facebook likes. In one survey, 93 percent of people polled believe that Internet companies should be forced to ask for permission before using your personal information, and 72 percent want the ability to opt out of online tracking.

Why, then, do so many people share sensitive details of their life on Facebook? Often it's because users do not realize that their data are being collected and transmitted in this way. A Facebook user's friends are not notified if information about them is collected by that user's applications. Many of Facebook's features and services are enabled by default when they are launched without notifying users, and a study by Siegel + Gale found that Facebook's privacy policy is more difficult to comprehend than government notices or typical bank credit card agreements, which are notoriously dense. Did you know that whenever you log into a website using Facebook, Facebook shares some personal information with that site, and can track your movements in that site. Next time you visit Facebook, click Privacy Settings and see whether you can understand your options.

Facebook's value and growth potential are determined by how effectively it can leverage the personal data it aggregated about its users to attract advertisers. Facebook also stands to gain from managing and avoiding the privacy concerns its users and government regulators raise. For Facebook users who value the privacy of their personal data, this situation appears grim, but there are some signs that Facebook might become more responsible with its data collection processes, whether by its own volition or because it is forced to do so. As a publicly traded company, Facebook now invites more scrutiny from investors and regulators because, unlike in the past, its balance sheets, assets, and financial reporting documents are readily available.

In August 2012, Facebook settled a lawsuit with the Federal Trade Commission (FTC) in which it was barred from misrepresenting the privacy or security of users' personal information. Facebook was charged with deceiving its users by telling them they could keep their information on Facebook private but then repeatedly allowing it to be shared and made public. Facebook agreed to obtain user consent before making any change to that user's privacy preferences and to submit to biannual privacy audits by an independent firm for the next 20 years.

Privacy advocate groups such as the Electronic Privacy Information Center (EPIC) want Facebook to restore its more robust privacy settings from 2009 as well as to offer complete access to all data it keeps about its users. Facebook has also come under fire from EPIC for collecting information about users who are not even logged on to Facebook or may not even have accounts on Facebook. Facebook keeps track of activity on other sites that have Like buttons or recommendations widgets and records the time of your visit and your IP address when you visit a site with those features, regardless of whether you click them.

Although U.S. Facebook users have little recourse to access data that Facebook has collected on them, users from other countries have made inroads in this regard. In Europe, over 100,000 Facebook users have already requested their data, and European law requires Facebook to respond to these requests within 40 days. Government privacy regulators from France, Spain, Italy, Germany, Belgium, and the Netherlands have been actively investigating Facebook's privacy controls as the European Union pursues more stringent privacy protection legislation, In June 2015, Belgium's data-protection watchdog sued Facebook over privacy practices such as how Facebook tracks users across the web through Like and Share buttons on external websites. In 2016 an Austrian student's class-action suit against Facebook's privacy rules has been referred to the European Court of Justice. The suit alleges Facebook's privacy policies violate European data protection laws.

In January 2014, Facebook shut down its Sponsored Stories feature, which served advertisements in the user's news feed highlighting products and businesses that Facebook friends were using. Sponsored Stories had been one of the most effective forms of advertising on Facebook because they don't seem like advertisements at all to most users. However, this feature triggered many lawsuits, attempted settlements, and criticism from privacy groups, the FTC, and annoyed parents whose children's photos were being used throughout Facebook to sell products.

Although Facebook has shut down one of its more egregious privacy-invading features, the company's Data Use policies make it very clear that, as a condition of using the service, users grant the company wide latitude in using their information in advertising. This includes a person's name, photo, comments, and other information. Facebook's existing policies make clear that users are required to grant the company wide permission to use their personal information in advertising as a condition of using the service. This includes social advertising, by which your personal information is broadcast to your friends and, indeed, the entire Facebook service if the company sees fit. Although users can limit some uses, an advanced degree in Facebook data features is required.

Ad-based firms like Facebook, and hundreds of others, including Google, justify their collection of personal information by arguing that consumers, by virtue of using the service, implicitly know about the data collection efforts and the role of advertisers in paying for the service and must, therefore, believe they are receiving real economic value from ads. This line of reasoning received a blow when in June 2015, researchers at the Annenberg School of Communication at the University of Pennsylvania found that 65 percent of Americans feel they have lost control over their information to advertisers, 84 percent want to control their information, and 91 percent do not believe it is fair for companies to offer discounts or coupons in exchange for their personal information without their knowledge.

In June 2015, Facebook held its first ever privacy conference as part of a growing effort to convince users it really is concerned about privacy and aware of public criticism of the firm. It has hired more than 50 privacy experts focused on Facebook's privacy practices. Critics asked Facebook why it doesn't offer an ad-free service—like music streaming sites—for a monthly fee. Others wanted to know why Facebook does not allow users just to opt out of tracking. But these kinds of changes would be very difficult for Facebook because its business model depends entirely on the unfettered use of its users' personal private information, just like it declares in its data use policy. That policy declares very openly that if you use Facebook, you don't have any privacy with respect to any data you provide to it.

Sources: Samuel Gibbs, "WhatsApp, Facebook and Google Face Tough New Privacy Rules Under EC Proposal," *The Guardian*, January 10, 2017; Stephanie Bodoni, "Google, Facebook Face Tighter EU Grip With New Privacy Law," Bloomberg News, January 10, 2017; Hannah Kuchler and Duncan Robinson, "Facebook Privacy Case Referred to Europe's Top Court," *Financial Times*, September 16, 2016; "'Privacy Shield,' the New Deal Governing How Europe's User Data Is Sent to the US," *Reuters,* February 29, 2016; Katie Collins, "Facebook's Newest Privacy Problem: 'Faceprint' Data," *CNET,* May 16, 2016; United States District Court Northern District of California in Re Facebook Biometric Information Privacy Litigation. Case No. 15-cv-03747-JD Order Re Motion to Dismiss and Summary Judgment, May 6, 2016; Jessica Guynn, "Facebook to Face Privacy Lawsuit over Photo Tagging," *USA Today*, May 6, 2016; Natasha Singer, "Sharing Data, but Not Happily," *New York Times*, June 4, 2015; Sam Schechner and Natalia Drozdiak, "Belgium Takes Facebook to Court over Privacy, User Tracking," *Wall Street Journal*, June 16, 2015; Deepa Seethharaman, "At Facebook Summit, Little Consensus on Privacy," *New York Times*, June 4, 2015; Zeynep Tufecki, "Let Me Pay for Facebook," *New York Times*, June, 4, 2015; IBM, "IBM and Facebook Team Up to Deliver Personalized Brand Experiences through People-Based Marketing," press release, May 6, 2015; Lisa Fleisher, "Admitting Tracking Bug, Facebook Defends European Privacy Practices," *Wall Street Journal*, April 9, 2015; Facebook, Inc., SEC Form 10K filed with the Securities and Exchange Commission for the fiscal year ending December 31, 2014, January 29, 2015; Anna North, "How Your Facebook Likes Could Cost You a Job," *New York Times*, January 20, 2015; Natasha Singer, "Didn't Read Those Terms of Service? Here's What You Agreed to Give Up," *New York Times*, April 28, 2014.

CASE STUDY QUESTIONS

4-12 Perform an ethical analysis of Facebook. What is the ethical dilemma presented by this case?

4-13 What is the relationship of privacy to Facebook's business model?

4-14 Describe the weaknesses of Facebook's privacy policies and features. What people, organization, and technology factors have contributed to those weaknesses?

4-15 Will Facebook be able to have a successful business model without invading privacy? Explain your answer. Could Facebook take any measures to make this possible?

Chapter 4 References

Aeppel, Timothy. "What Clever Robots Mean for Jobs." *Wall Street Journal* (February 24, 2015).

Belanger, France and Robert E. Crossler. "Privacy in the Digital Age: A Review of Information Privacy Research in Information Systems." *MIS Quarterly* 35, No. 4 (December 2011).

Bernstein, Amy and Anand Raman. "The Great Decoupling: An Interview with Erik Brynjolfsson and Andrew McAfee." *Harvard Business Review* (June 2015).

Bernstein, Ethan, Saravanan Kesavan, and Bradley Staats. "How to Manage Scheduling Software Fairly." *Harvard Business Review* (December 2014).

Bertolucci, Jeff. "Big Data Firm Chronicles Your Online, Offline Lives." *Information Week* (May 7, 2013).

Bilski v. Kappos, 561 US (2010).

Brown Bag Software vs. Symantec Corp. 960 F2D 1465 (Ninth Circuit, 1992).

Brynjolfsson, Erik and Andrew McAfee. *Race Against the Machine*. Digital Frontier Press (2011).

Chan, Jason, Anindya Ghose, and Robert Seamans. "The Internet and Racial Hate Crimes: Offline Spillovers from Online Access." *MIS Quarterly* 40, No. 2 (June 2016).

Clemons, Eric K. and Joshua S. Wilson. "Family Preferences Concerning Online Privacy, Data Mining, and Targeted Ads: Regulatory Implications." *Journal of Management Information Systems* 32, No. 2 (2015).

Council of Europe, "European Court of Human Rights Case Law." Thematic Fact Sheet, rm.coe.int (February 2016).

Culnan, Mary J. and Cynthia Clark Williams. "How Ethics Can Enhance Organizational Privacy." *MIS Quarterly* 33, No. 4 (December 2009).

Davenport, Thomas H. and Julia Kirby. "Beyond Automation." *Harvard Business Review* (June 2015).

European Parliament. "Directive 2009/136/EC of the European Parliament and of the Council of November 25, 2009." European Parliament (2009).

Federal Trade Commission. "Protecting Consumer Privacy in an Era of Rapid Change." Washington, DC. (2012).

Goldfarb, Avi and Catherine Tucker. "Why Managing Consumer Privacy Can Be an Opportunity." *MIT Sloan Management Review* 54, No. 3 (Spring 2013).

Henry, Patrick. "Why Computers Make Us Stupid." *Slice of MIT* (March 6, 2011).

Hsieh, J. J. Po-An, Arun Rai, and Mark Keil. "Understanding Digital Inequality: Comparing Continued Use Behavioral Models of the Socio-Economically Advantaged and Disadvantaged." *MIS Quarterly* 32, No. 1 (March 2008).

Hutter, Katja, Johann Fuller, Julia Hautz, Volker Bilgram, and Kurt Matzler. "Machiavellianism or Morality: Which Behavior Pays Off In Online Innovation Contests?" *Journal of Management Information Systems* 32, No. 3 (2015).

ITU. "ITU Survey on Anti-Spam Legislation Worldwide." International Telecommunication Union, www.itu.int (2016).

Kaspersky Lab. "Spam and Phishing Statistics Report Q1-2015." (2015).

Kosseff, Joseph. "Twenty Privacy Bills to Watch in 2014." (January 15, 2014).

Laudon, Kenneth C. and Carol Guercio Traver. *E-Commerce 2016: Business, Technology, Society (12th ed.)*. Upper Saddle River, NJ: Prentice-Hall (2017).

Laudon, Kenneth C. *Dossier Society: Value Choices in the Design of National Information Systems*. New York: Columbia University Press (1986).

Leblanc, K. E., and W. Cestia. "Carpal Tunnel Syndrome." *American Family Physician, 83*, No. 8 (2011).

Lee, Dong-Joo, Jae-Hyeon Ahn, and Youngsok Bang. "Managing Consumer Privacy Concerns in Personalization: A Strategic Analysis of Privacy Protection." *MIS Quarterly* 35, No. 2 (June 2011).

MacCrory, Frank, George Westerman, Erik Brynjolfsson, and Yousef Alhammadi. "Racing with and Against the Machine: Changes in Occupational Skill Composition in an Era of Rapid Technological Advance." (2014).

PwC. "US State of Cybercrime Survey 2015." (June 2015),

Pew Research Center. "The State of Privacy in America." (January 20, 2016).

Rigby, Chloe. "How Can Ecommerce and Multichannel Retailers Respond to the Carphone Warehouse Data Breach?" Internetretailing.com (August 11, 2015).

Robinson, Francis. "EU Unveils Web-Privacy Rules." *Wall Street Journal* (January 26, 2012).

Smith, H. Jeff. "The Shareholders vs. Stakeholders Debate." *MIS Sloan Management Review* 44, No. 4 (Summer 2003).

Sojer, Manuel, Oliver Alexy, Sven Kleinknecht, and Joachim Henkel. "Understanding the Drivers of Unethical Programming Behavior: The Inappropriate Reuse of Internet-Accessible Code." *Journal of Management Information Systems* 31, No. 3 (Winter 2014).

Tarafdar. Monideepa, John D'Arcy, Ofir Turel, and Ashish Gupta. "The Dark Side of Information Technology." *MIT Sloan Management Review* 56, No. 2 (Winter 2015).

The Software Alliance. "BSA Global Software Survey 2016." (May 2016).

United States Department of Health, Education, and Welfare. *Records, Computers, and the Rights of Citizens.* Cambridge: MIT Press (1973).

U.S. Senate. "Do-Not-Track Online Act of 2011." Senate 913 (May 9, 2011).

U.S. Sentencing Commission. "Sentencing Commission Toughens Requirements for Corporate Compliance Programs." (April 13, 2004).

V3. "Top 10 Cloud Outages from Twitter and iTunes to Azure and AWS," http://www.v3.co.uk (accessed November 2016).

PART **TWO**

Information Technology Infrastructure

PART TWO provides the technical foundation for understanding information systems by examining hardware, software, database, and networking technologies along with tools and techniques for security and control. This part answers questions such as: What technologies do businesses today need to accomplish their work? What do I need to know about these technologies to make sure they enhance the performance of the firm? How are these technologies likely to change in the future? What technologies and procedures are required to ensure that systems are reliable and secure?

CHAPTER

5 IT Infrastructure and Emerging Technologies

Learning Objectives

After reading this chapter, you will be able to answer the following questions:

5-1 What is IT infrastructure, and what are the stages and drivers of IT infrastructure evolution?

5-2 What are the components of IT infrastructure?

5-3 What are the current trends in computer hardware platforms?

5-4 What are the current computer software platforms and trends?

5-5 What are the challenges of managing IT infrastructure and management solutions?

CHAPTER CASES

EasyJet Flies High with Cloud Computing
Establishing Global Classrooms through WebEx
Building Virtualization Infrastructure at NTT
BYOD: Business Opportunity or Big Headache?

EasyJet Flies High with Cloud Computing

EasyJet is the largest airline in the United Kingdom and the second-largest short-haul airline carrier in the world (behind Ryanair) with more than 800 domestic and international routes in 32 countries. Based in Luton, England, EasyJet has expanded rapidly since its founding in 1995, propelled by a series of acquisitions as well as fulfilling an important market need for low-cost airline services. EasyJet carries more than 70 million passengers per year. Obviously, having a reliable and robust system for booking and managing reservations while keeping costs low is a key business requirement.

EasyJet's customers, like those of other airlines, like the idea of being able to select their seats on a given flight when they made their reservations online. However, EasyJet's existing reservation system did not have the capability to add this new feature, which required investing in an additional computer center and modifying its IT infrastructure.

EasyJet's IT department found a better solution. It retained the core reservation system as is and hosted the seat allocation service in the cloud using Microsoft's Azure cloud service. EasyJet had tried other public cloud computing platforms, but Microsoft's offered a better integration of on-premises and cloud services. EasyJet had used the Microsoft Azure cloud service to build services that communicate wirelessly at airports without running up major airport charges for new services desks.

Microsoft's Azure cloud enabled EasyJet's information system developers to write their own software program code for seat allocation and use as much or as little processing power as needed to test the service. It then turned out to be much faster and cost-effective to have the public cloud actually host the new seat allocation service rather than use EasyJet's internal IT infrastructure.

EasyJet is adopting a hybrid cloud strategy. It is not moving its entire IT infrastructure to

© CPC Collection/Alamy Stock Photo

the cloud, only specific functions that its internal IT infrastructure can't easily handle. The new capabilities are integrated with the company's existing IT Infrastructure. By enhancing its systems by adding new features in the cloud, the company is able to get more value out of its earlier IT investments, which amounted to many millions of dollars.

When an EasyJet customer books a reservation, EasyJet's information systems integrate three different technologies. EasyJet's web servers handle the process of customers entering their desired travel dates and destinations for flight bookings. The company's reservation system residing in a different computer center presents data on alternative times and prices of flights for customers to choose from. Finally, the aircraft diagram where users can select their seats is fully hosted on Microsoft's Azure cloud service. The entire experience appears seamless to users.

By enhancing its systems to offer allocated seating, EasyJet was able to increase customer satisfaction by 5 percent and add 7 percent to its revenue growth according to the company's 2013 annual earnings report. In the following two years, the company increased customer conversion to its website by 13 percent. Selecting seats and boarding flights have become much more pleasant.

EasyJet's management believes that good customer experience combined with low prices clearly differentiates the company from competitors. The business benefits of offering online seat selection using cloud computing services have made it possible for EasyJet to continue this strategy because it can keep operating costs low while offering customers top-notch services in searching for and booking flights. Airlines on average spend 2 percent of their revenue on IT infrastructure; EasyJet spends only half a percent of its revenue on IT.

What if the new seat allocation system enhancement had failed to improve customer service and revenue? EasyJet could have easily turned off the cloud service for online seat selection if it so chose. It is much easier to eliminate a cloud service than to remove the functionality from the company's core internal system.

Sources: "Leading European Airline Improves Service and Scalability with Hybrid Cloud Solution," www.microsoft.com, accessed February 9, 2016; www.easyjet.com, accessed May 1, 2016; Clare McDonald, "How EasyJet Uses Digital to Drive Competitive Advantage," *Computer Weekly*, October 13, 2015; and "EasyJet Raises Customer Satisfaction with Hybrid IT," *Computer Weekly*, September 23–29, 2014.

The experience of EasyJet illustrates the importance of information technology infrastructure in running a business today. The right technology at the right price will improve organizational performance. EasyJet was saddled with an outdated IT infrastructure that was far too costly and unwieldy for adding new services, such as online passenger seat selection, that were being offered by competitors. This caused EasyJet to lose customers and prevented the company from operating as efficiently and effectively as it could have.

The chapter-opening case diagram calls attention to important points raised by this case and this chapter. As a low-cost carrier, EasyJet is under pressure

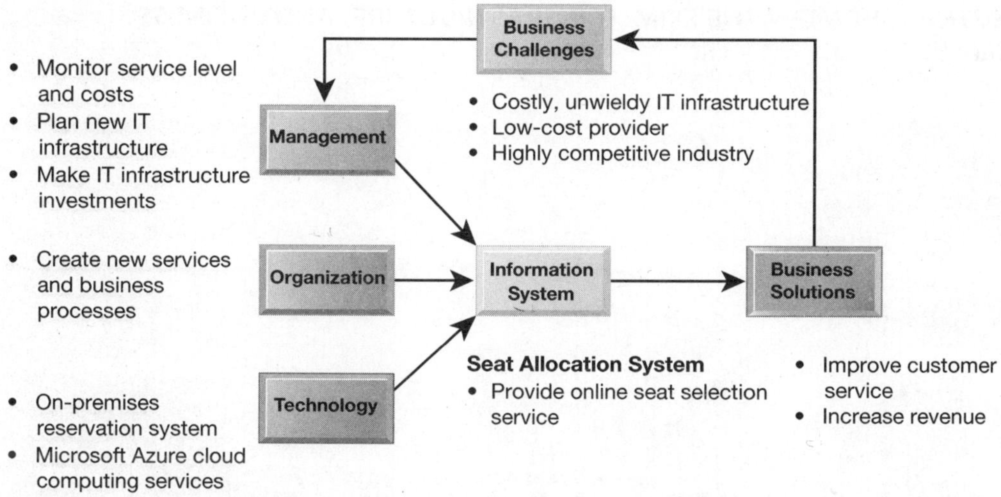

to keep costs down, but it still must offer services such as online seat selection that are provided by competing airlines. Management had to find a low-cost solution that enabled the company to remain competitive. It decided to develop and run the new seat selection service on Microsoft's Azure cloud computing platform, where the hardware is located in remote computing centers accessed via the Internet. The seat selection capability is integrated with EasyJet's internal reservation system, which is maintained on premises. This is an example of a hybrid cloud strategy, where an organization maintains part of its IT infrastructure itself and part using cloud computing services. Using cloud computing for part of its IT infrastructure enables EasyJet to expand and offer new services at very affordable prices. The company pays for only the computing capacity it actually uses on an as-needed basis and did not have to make extensive and costly new infrastructure investments.

Here are some questions to think about: How did EasyJet's hardware and software technology affect the company's ability to operate? What were the business benefits of using cloud computing?

5-1 What is IT infrastructure, and what are the stages and drivers of IT infrastructure evolution?

In Chapter 1, we defined *information technology (IT) infrastructure* as the shared technology resources that provide the platform for the firm's specific information system applications. An IT infrastructure includes investment in hardware, software, and services—such as consulting, education, and training—that are shared across the entire firm or across entire business units in the firm. A firm's IT infrastructure provides the foundation for serving customers, working with vendors, and managing internal firm business processes (see Figure 5.1).

Supplying firms worldwide with IT infrastructure (hardware and software) in 2016 is estimated to be a $3.5 trillion industry when telecommunications,

FIGURE 5.1 CONNECTION BETWEEN THE FIRM, IT INFRASTRUCTURE, AND BUSINESS CAPABILITIES

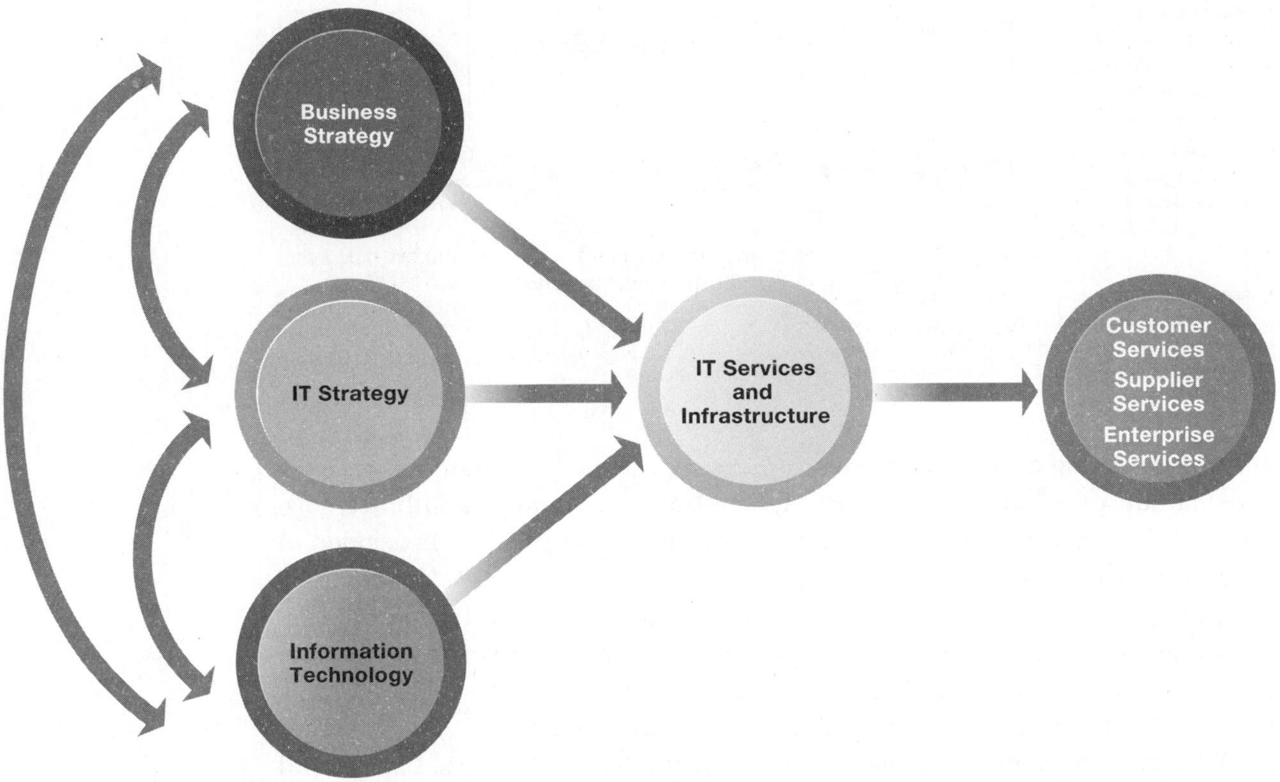

The services a firm is capable of providing to its customers, suppliers, and employees are a direct function of its IT infrastructure. Ideally, this infrastructure should support the firm's business and information systems strategy. New information technologies have a powerful impact on business and IT strategies as well as the services that can be provided to customers.

networking equipment, and telecommunications services (Internet, telephone, and data transmission) are included. Investments in infrastructure account for between 25 and 50 percent of information technology expenditures in large firms, led by financial services firms where IT investment is well over half of all capital investment.

Defining IT Infrastructure

An IT infrastructure consists of a set of physical devices and software applications that are required to operate the entire enterprise. But IT infrastructure also includes a set of firmwide services budgeted by management and composed of both human and technical capabilities. These services include the following:

- Computing platforms used to provide computing services that connect employees, customers, and suppliers into a coherent digital environment, including large mainframes, midrange computers, desktop and laptop computers, and mobile handheld and remote cloud computing services

- Telecommunications services that provide data, voice, and video connectivity to employees, customers, and suppliers
- Data management services that store and manage corporate data and provide capabilities for analyzing the data
- Application software services, including online software services, that provide enterprise-wide capabilities such as enterprise resource planning, customer relationship management, supply chain management, and knowledge management systems that are shared by all business units
- Physical facilities management services that develop and manage the physical installations required for computing, telecommunications, and data management services
- IT management services that plan and develop the infrastructure, coordinate with the business units for IT services, manage accounting for the IT expenditure, and provide project management services
- IT standards services that provide the firm and its business units with policies that determine which information technology will be used, when, and how
- IT education services that provide training in system use to employees and offer managers training in how to plan for and manage IT investments
- IT research and development services that provide the firm with research on potential future IT projects and investments that could help the firm differentiate itself in the marketplace

This "service platform" perspective makes it easier to understand the business value provided by infrastructure investments. For instance, the real business value of a fully loaded personal computer operating at 3.5 gigahertz that costs about $1,000 and a high-speed Internet connection is hard to understand without knowing who will use it and how it will be used. When we look at the services provided by these tools, however, their value becomes more apparent: The new PC makes it possible for a high-cost employee making $100,000 a year to connect to all the company's major systems, including collaboration systems, and the public Internet. The high-speed Internet service saves this employee about an hour per day in reduced wait time for Internet information. Without this PC and Internet connection, the value of this one employee to the firm might be cut in half.

Evolution of IT Infrastructure

The IT infrastructure in organizations today is an outgrowth of more than 50 years of evolution in computing platforms. There have been five stages in this evolution, each representing a different configuration of computing power and infrastructure elements (see Figure 5.2). The five eras are general-purpose mainframe and minicomputer computing, personal computers, client/server networks, enterprise computing, and cloud and mobile computing.

Technologies that characterize one era may also be used in another time period for other purposes. For example, some companies still run traditional mainframe systems or use mainframe computers as servers supporting large websites and corporate enterprise applications.

FIGURE 5.2 ERAS IN IT INFRASTRUCTURE EVOLUTION

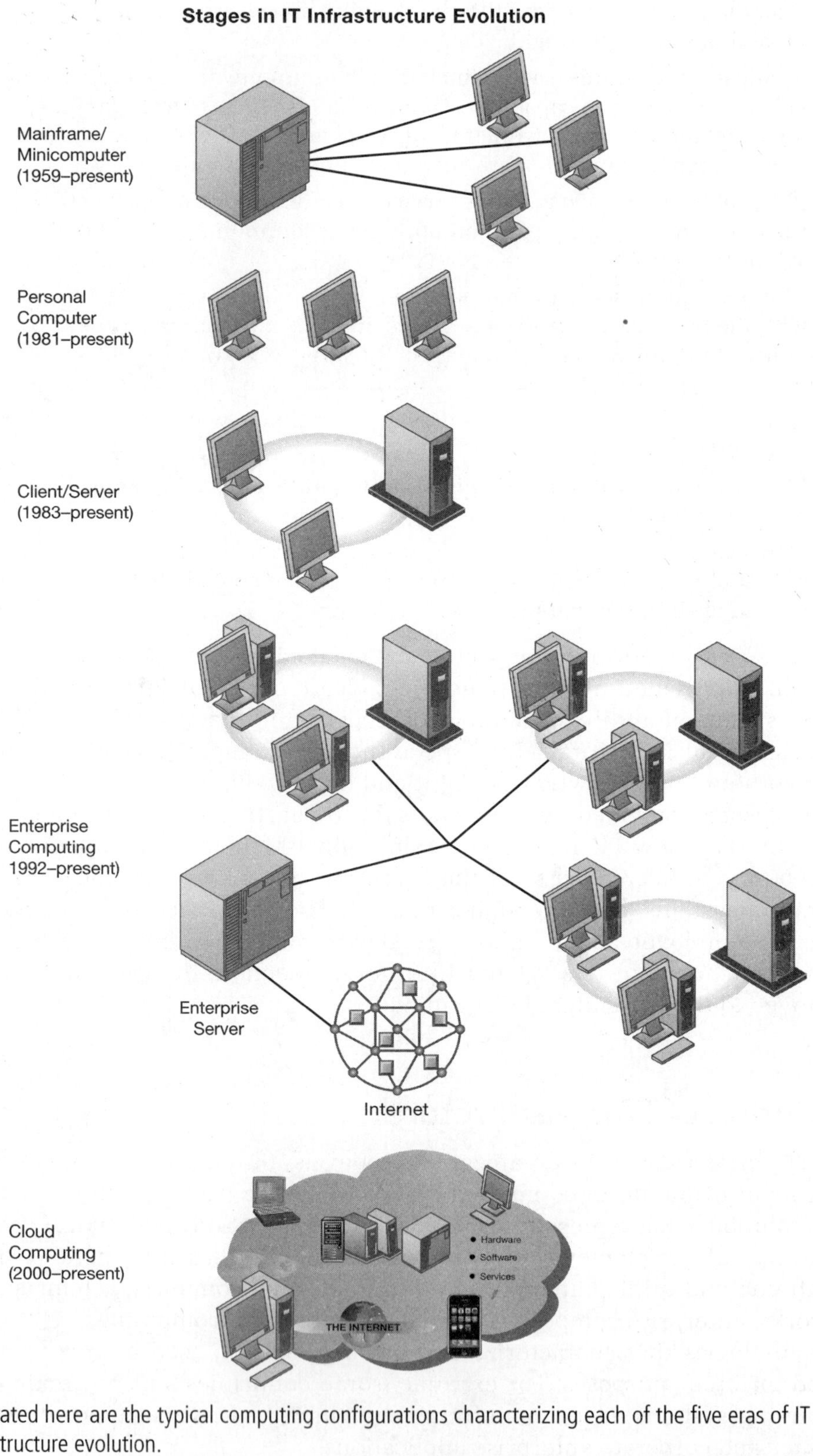

Illustrated here are the typical computing configurations characterizing each of the five eras of IT infrastructure evolution.

General-Purpose Mainframe and Minicomputer Era (1959 to Present)

The introduction of the IBM 1401 and 7090 transistorized machines in 1959 marked the beginning of widespread commercial use of **mainframe** computers. In 1965, the mainframe computer truly came into its own with the introduction of the IBM 360 series. The 360 was the first commercial computer that could provide time sharing, multitasking, and virtual memory in more advanced models. IBM has dominated mainframe computing from this point on. Mainframe computers became powerful enough to support thousands of online remote terminals connected to the centralized mainframe using proprietary communication protocols and proprietary data lines.

The mainframe era was a period of highly centralized computing under the control of professional programmers and systems operators (usually in a corporate data center), with most elements of infrastructure provided by a single vendor, the manufacturer of the hardware and the software.

This pattern began to change with the introduction of **minicomputers** produced by Digital Equipment Corporation (DEC) in 1965. DEC minicomputers (PDP-11 and later the VAX machines) offered powerful machines at far lower prices than IBM mainframes, making possible decentralized computing, customized to the specific needs of individual departments or business units rather than time sharing on a single huge mainframe. In recent years, the minicomputer has evolved into a midrange computer or midrange server and is part of a network.

Personal Computer Era (1981 to Present)

Although the first truly personal computers (PCs) appeared in the 1970s (the Xerox Alto, the MITS Altair 8800, and the Apple I and II, to name a few), these machines had only limited distribution to computer enthusiasts. The appearance of the IBM PC in 1981 is usually considered the beginning of the PC era because this machine was the first to be widely adopted by American businesses. At first using the DOS operating system, a text-based command language, and later the Microsoft Windows operating system, the **Wintel PC** computer (Windows operating system software on a computer with an Intel microprocessor) became the standard desktop personal computer. Worldwide PC shipments have declined more than 10 percent because of the popularity of tablets and smartphones, but the PC is still a popular tool for business. About 289 million new PCs were sold worldwide in 2015 (Gartner, Inc., 2016). Approximately 87 percent are thought to run a version of Windows, and about 4 percent run a version of Mac OS. The Wintel dominance as a computing platform is receding as iPhone and Android device sales increase. About 2 billion people worldwide own smartphones, and most of these users access the Internet with their mobile devices.

Proliferation of PCs in the 1980s and early 1990s launched a spate of personal desktop productivity software tools—word processors, spreadsheets, electronic presentation software, and small data management programs—that were very valuable to both home and corporate users. These PCs were stand-alone systems until PC operating system software in the 1990s made it possible to link them into networks.

Client/Server Era (1983 to Present)

In **client/server computing**, desktop or laptop computers called **clients** are networked to powerful **server** computers that provide the client computers with a variety of services and capabilities. Computer processing work is split between these two types of machines. The client is the user point of entry, whereas the server typically processes and stores shared data, serves up web pages, or manages network activities. The term *server* refers to both the software application and the physical computer on which the network software runs. The server could be a mainframe, but today, server computers typically are more powerful versions of personal computers, based on inexpensive chips and often using multiple processors in a single computer box or in server racks.

The simplest client/server network consists of a client computer networked to a server computer, with processing split between the two types of machines. This is called a *two-tiered client/server architecture*. Whereas simple client/server networks can be found in small businesses, most corporations have more complex, **multitiered** (often called **N-tier**) **client/server architectures** in which the work of the entire network is balanced over several different levels of servers, depending on the kind of service being requested (see Figure 5.3).

For instance, at the first level, a **web server** will serve a webpage to a client in response to a request for service. Web server software is responsible for locating and managing stored webpages. If the client requests access to a corporate system (a product list or price information, for instance), the request is passed along to an **application server**. Application server software handles all application operations between a user and an organization's back-end business systems. The application server may reside on the same computer as the web server or on its own dedicated computer. Chapters 6 and 7 provide more detail on other pieces of software that are used in multitiered client/server architectures for e-commerce and e-business.

FIGURE 5.3 A MULTITIERED (N-TIER) CLIENT/SERVER NETWORK

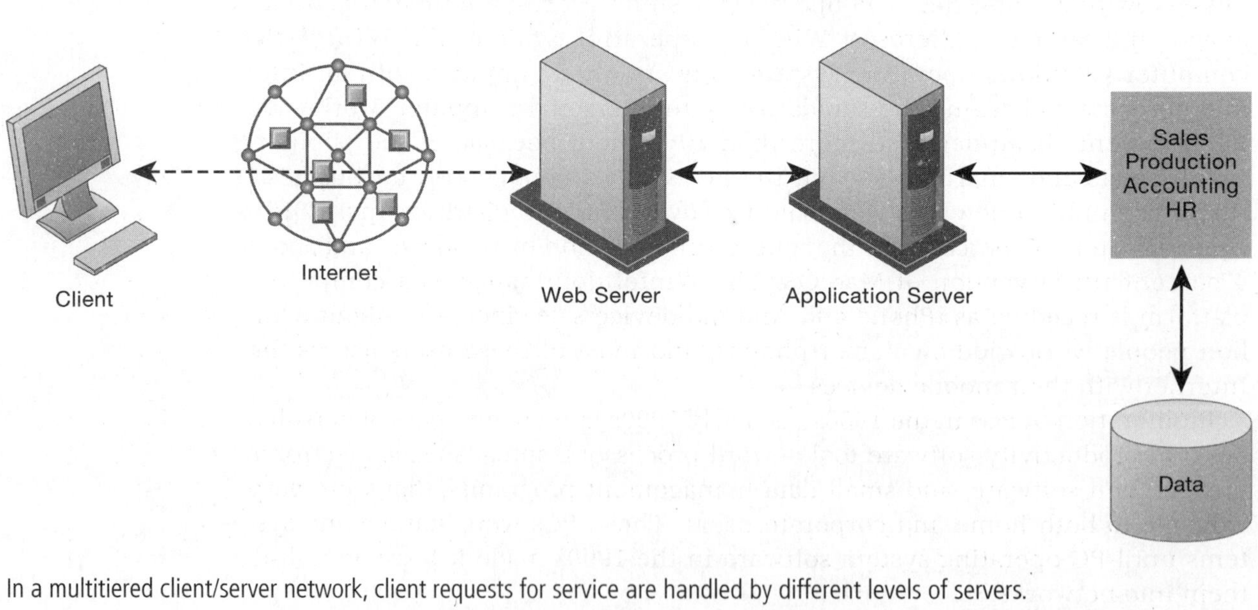

In a multitiered client/server network, client requests for service are handled by different levels of servers.

Client/server computing enables businesses to distribute computing work across a series of smaller, inexpensive machines that cost much less than centralized mainframe systems. The result is an explosion in computing power and applications throughout the firm.

Novell NetWare was the leading technology for client/server networking at the beginning of the client/server era. Today, Microsoft is the market leader with its **Windows** operating systems (Windows Server, Windows 10, Windows 8, and Windows 7).

Enterprise Computing Era (1992 to Present)

In the early 1990s, firms turned to networking standards and software tools that could integrate disparate networks and applications throughout the firm into an enterprise-wide infrastructure. As the Internet developed into a trusted communications environment after 1995, business firms began seriously using the *Transmission Control Protocol/Internet Protocol (TCP/IP)* networking standard to tie their disparate networks together. We discuss TCP/IP in detail in Chapter 7.

The resulting IT infrastructure links different pieces of computer hardware and smaller networks into an enterprise-wide network so that information can flow freely across the organization and between the firm and other organizations. It can link different types of computer hardware, including mainframes, servers, PCs, and mobile devices, and it includes public infrastructures such as the telephone system, the Internet, and public network services. The enterprise infrastructure also requires software to link disparate applications and enable data to flow freely among different parts of the business, such as enterprise applications (see Chapters 2 and 9) and web services (discussed in Section 5-4).

Cloud and Mobile Computing Era (2000 to Present)

The growing bandwidth power of the Internet has pushed the client/server model one step further, toward what is called the "cloud computing model." **Cloud computing** refers to a model of computing that provides access to a shared pool of computing resources (computers, storage, applications, and services) over the network, often the Internet. These "clouds" of computing resources can be accessed on an as-needed basis from any connected device and location.

Cloud computing is now the fastest growing form of computing. According to the International Data Corporation (IDC), worldwide spending on public cloud services is growing at a 19.4 percent compound annual growth rate, nearly six times the rate of overall IT spending growth—from nearly $70 billion in 2015 to more than $141 billion in 2019 (International Data Corporation, 2016).

Thousands or even hundreds of thousands of computers are located in cloud data centers, where they can be accessed by desktop computers, laptop computers, tablets, entertainment centers, smartphones, and other client machines linked to the Internet. Amazon, Google, IBM, and Microsoft operate huge, scalable cloud computing centers that provide computing power, data storage, and high-speed Internet connections to firms that want to maintain their IT infrastructures remotely. Firms such as Google, Microsoft, SAP, Oracle, and Salesforce.com sell software applications as services delivered over the Internet.

We discuss cloud and mobile computing in more detail in Section 5-3. The Learning Tracks include a table titled "Comparing Stages in IT Infrastructure Evolution," which compares each era on the infrastructure dimensions introduced.

Technology Drivers of Infrastructure Evolution

The changes in IT infrastructure we have just described have resulted from developments in computer processing, memory chips, storage devices, telecommunications and networking hardware and software, and software design that have exponentially increased computing power while exponentially reducing costs. Let's look at the most important developments.

Moore's Law and Microprocessing Power

In 1965, Gordon Moore, the director of Fairchild Semiconductor's Research and Development Laboratories, wrote in *Electronics* magazine that since the first microprocessor chip was introduced in 1959, the number of components on a chip with the smallest manufacturing costs per component (generally transistors) had doubled each year. This assertion became the foundation of **Moore's Law**. Moore later reduced the rate of growth to a doubling every two years.

There are at least three variations of Moore's Law, none of which Moore ever stated: (1) the power of microprocessors doubles every 18 months, (2) computing power doubles every 18 months, and (3) the price of computing falls by half every 18 months.

Figure 5.4 illustrates the relationship between number of transistors on a microprocessor and millions of instructions per second (MIPS), a common measure of processor power. Figure 5.5 shows the exponential decline in the cost of transistors and rise in computing power. For instance, in 2016, you could buy an Intel i7 quad-core processor chip with 2.5 billion transistors for about one ten-millionth of a dollar per transistor.

Exponential growth in the number of transistors and the power of processors coupled with an exponential decline in computing costs may not be able to continue much longer. Chip manufacturers continue to miniaturize components. Today's transistors should no longer be compared to the size of a human hair but rather to the size of a virus. Within the next five years or so, chip makers may reach the physical limits of semiconductor size. At that point they may need to use alternatives to fashioning chips from silicon or finding other ways to make computers more powerful (Markoff, 2016).

Chip manufacturers can shrink the size of transistors down to the width of several atoms by using nanotechnology. **Nanotechnology** uses individual atoms and molecules to create computer chips and other devices that are thousands of times smaller than current technologies permit. Chip manufacturers are trying to develop a manufacturing process to produce nanotube processors economically. Stanford University scientists have built a nanotube computer.

The Law of Mass Digital Storage

A second technology driver of IT infrastructure change is the Law of Mass Digital Storage. The amount of digital information is roughly doubling every

FIGURE 5.4 MOORE'S LAW AND MICROPROCESSOR PERFORMANCE

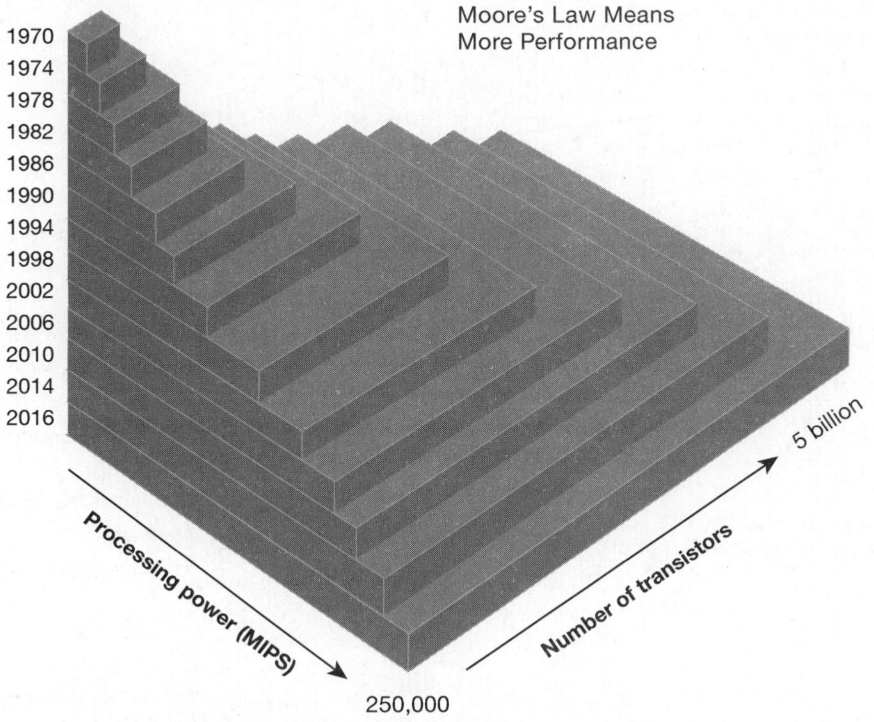

Packing more than 5 billion transistors into a tiny microprocessor has exponentially increased processing power. Processing power has increased to more than 250,000 MIPS (about 2.6 billion instructions per second).

Source: Authors' estimate.

year Lyman and Varian, 2003). Fortunately, the cost of storing digital information is falling at an exponential rate of 100 percent a year. Figure 5.6 shows that the number of megabytes that can be stored on magnetic media for $1 from 1950 to the present roughly doubled every 15 months. In 2016, a 500 gigabyte hard disk drive sells at retail for about $50.

Metcalfe's Law and Network Economics

Moore's Law and the Law of Mass Digital Storage help us understand why computing resources are now so readily available. But why do people want more computing and storage power? The economics of networks and the growth of the Internet provide some answers.

Robert Metcalfe—inventor of Ethernet local area network technology—claimed in 1970 that the value or power of a network grows exponentially as a function of the number of network members. Metcalfe and others point to the *increasing returns to scale* that network members receive as more and more people join the network. As the number of members in a network grows linearly, the value of the entire system grows exponentially and continues to grow as members increase. Demand for information technology has been driven by the social and business value of digital networks, which rapidly multiply the number of actual and potential links among network members.

FIGURE 5.5 FALLING COST OF CHIPS

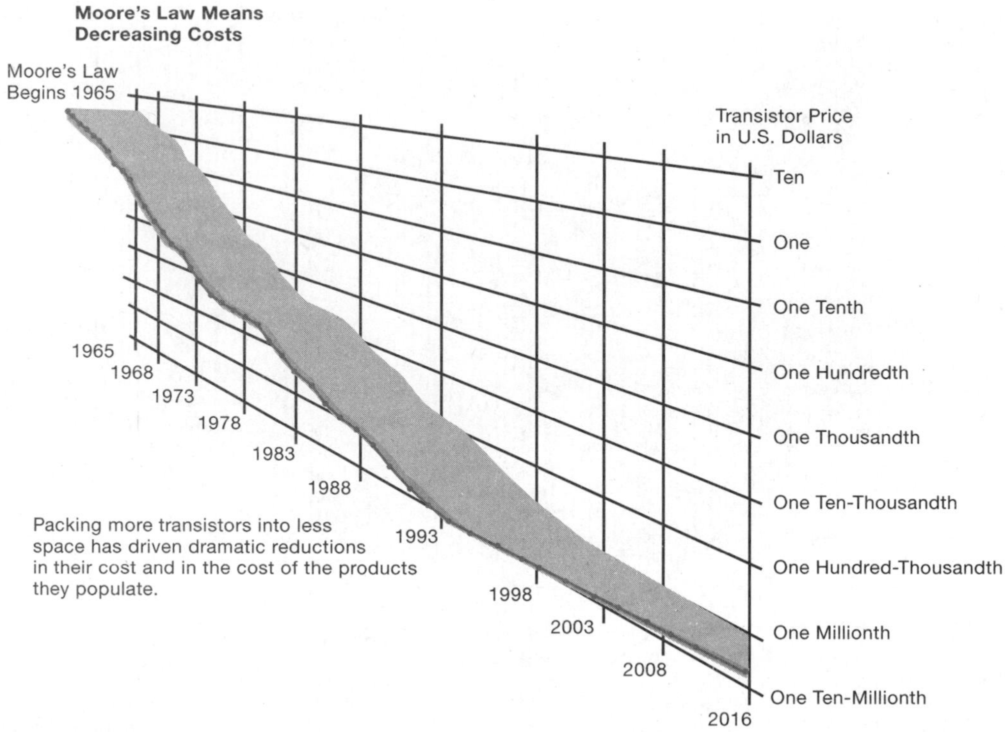

Source: Authors' estimate.

Nanotubes are tiny tubes about 10,000 times thinner than a human hair. They consist of rolled-up sheets of carbon hexagons and have potential use as minuscule wires or in ultrasmall electronic devices and are very powerful conductors of electrical current.

FIGURE 5.6 THE AMOUNT OF STORAGE PER DOLLAR RISES EXPONENTIALLY, 1950–2016

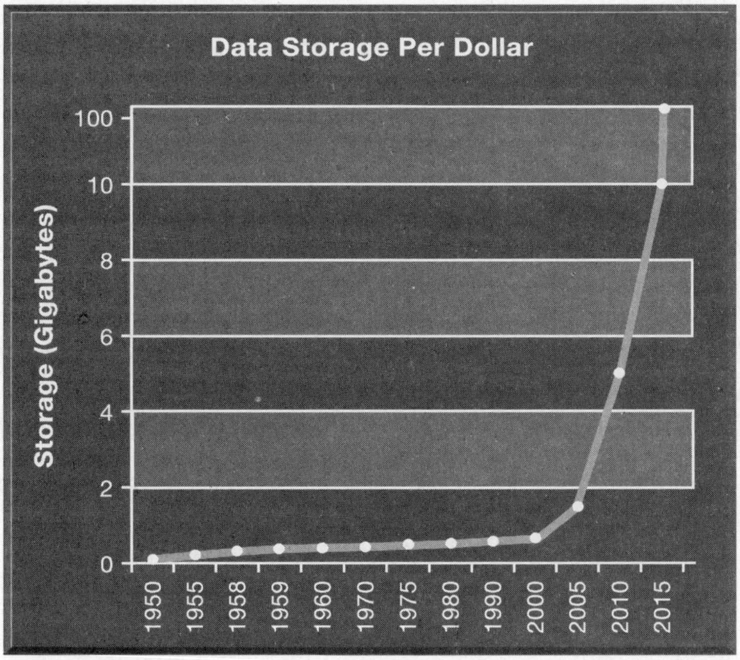

Cloud storage services like Google Drive provide 100 gigabytes of storage for $1.99 per month.
Source: Authors' estimates.

Declining Communications Costs and the Internet

A fourth technology driver transforming IT infrastructure is the rapid decline in the costs of communication and the exponential growth in the size of the Internet. Today there are more than 3.5 billion Internet users worldwide (Internetlivestats.com, 2016). Figure 5.7 illustrates the exponentially declining cost of communication both over the Internet and over telephone networks (which increasingly are based on the Internet). As communication costs fall toward a very small number and approach zero, utilization of communication and computing facilities explode.

To take advantage of the business value associated with the Internet, firms must greatly expand their Internet connections, including wireless connectivity, and greatly expand the power of their client/server networks, desktop clients, and mobile computing devices. There is every reason to believe these trends will continue.

Standards and Network Effects

Today's enterprise infrastructure and Internet computing would be impossible—both now and in the future—without agreements among manufacturers and widespread consumer acceptance of **technology standards**. Technology standards are specifications that establish the compatibility of products and the ability to communicate in a network.

FIGURE 5.7 EXPONENTIAL DECLINES IN INTERNET COMMUNICATIONS COSTS

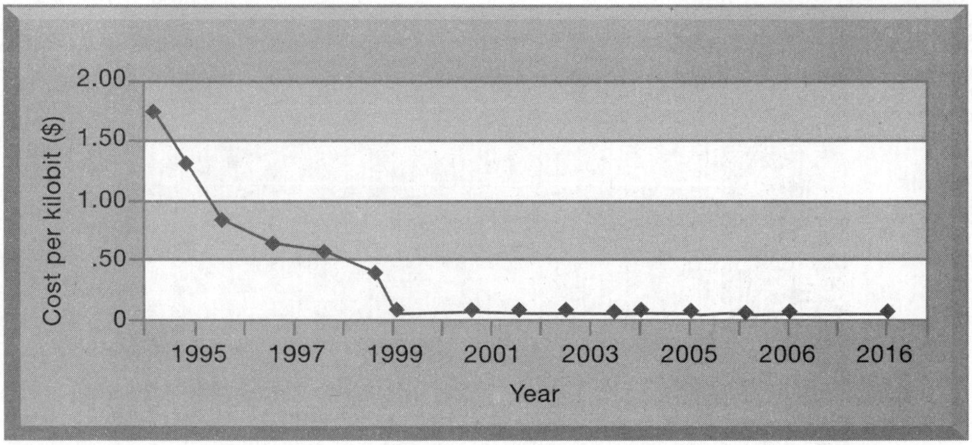

Verizon FiOS (fiber to the home) delivers 1 kilobit of data for a retail price less than 2 thousandths of a penny.

Source: Authors.

Technology standards unleash powerful economies of scale and result in price declines as manufacturers focus on the products built to a single standard. Without these economies of scale, computing of any sort would be far more expensive than is currently the case. Table 5.1 describes important standards that have shaped IT infrastructure.

Beginning in the 1990s, corporations started moving toward standard computing and communications platforms. The Wintel PC with the Windows operating system and Microsoft Office desktop productivity applications became the standard desktop and mobile client computing platform. (It now shares the spotlight with other standards, such as Apple's iOS and Macintosh operating systems and the Android operating system.) Widespread adoption of Unix-Linux as the enterprise server operating system of choice made possible the replacement of proprietary and expensive mainframe infrastructures. In telecommunications, the Ethernet standard enabled PCs to connect together in small local area networks (LANs; see Chapter 7), and the TCP/IP standard enabled these LANs to be connected into firmwide networks, and ultimately, to the Internet.

5-2 What are the components of IT infrastructure?

IT infrastructure today is composed of seven major components. Figure 5.8 illustrates these infrastructure components and the major vendors within each component category. These components constitute investments that must be coordinated with one another to provide the firm with a coherent infrastructure.

In the past, technology vendors supplying these components offered purchasing firms a mixture of incompatible, proprietary, partial solutions that

TABLE 5.1 SOME IMPORTANT STANDARDS IN COMPUTING

STANDARD	SIGNIFICANCE
American Standard Code for Information Interchange (ASCII) (1958)	Made it possible for computer machines from different manufacturers to exchange data; later used as the universal language linking input and output devices such as keyboards and mice to computers. Adopted by the American National Standards Institute in 1963.
Common Business Oriented Language (COBOL) (1959)	An easy-to-use software language that greatly expanded the ability of programmers to write business-related programs and reduced the cost of software. Sponsored by the Defense Department in 1959.
Unix (1969–1975)	A powerful multitasking, multiuser, portable operating system initially developed at Bell Labs (1969) and later released for use by others (1975). It operates on a wide variety of computers from different manufacturers. Adopted by Sun, IBM, HP, and others in the 1980s, it became the most widely used enterprise-level operating system.
Transmission Control Protocol/Internet Protocol (TCP/IP) (1974)	Suite of communications protocols and a common addressing scheme that enables millions of computers to connect together in one giant global network (the Internet). Later, it was used as the default networking protocol suite for local area networks and intranets. Developed in the early 1970s for the U.S. Department of Defense.
Ethernet (1973)	A network standard for connecting desktop computers into local area networks that enabled the widespread adoption of client/server computing and local area networks and further stimulated the adoption of personal computers.
IBM/Microsoft/Intel Personal Computer (1981)	The standard Wintel design for personal desktop computing based on standard Intel processors and other standard devices, Microsoft DOS, and later Windows software. The emergence of this standard, low-cost product laid the foundation for a 25-year period of explosive growth in computing throughout all organizations around the globe. Today, more than 1 billion PCs power business and government activities every day.
World Wide Web (1989–1993)	Standards for storing, retrieving, formatting, and displaying information as a worldwide web of electronic pages incorporating text, graphics, audio, and video enables creation of a global repository of billions of webpages.

could not work with other vendor products. Increasingly, vendor firms have been forced to cooperate in strategic partnerships with one another in order to keep their customers. For instance, a hardware and services provider such as IBM cooperates with all the major enterprise software providers, has strategic relationships with system integrators, and promises to work with whichever data management products its client firms wish to use (even though it sells its own database management software called DB2).

Another big change is that companies are moving more of their IT infrastructure to the cloud or to outside services, owning and managing much less on their premises. According to International Data Corporation, by 2020, business spending on cloud infrastructure will account for roughly half of the total computing resources budget. Firms' IT infrastructures will increasingly be an amalgam of components and services that are partially owned, partially rented or licensed, partially located on site, and partially supplied by external vendors or cloud services.

FIGURE 5.8 THE IT INFRASTRUCTURE ECOSYSTEM

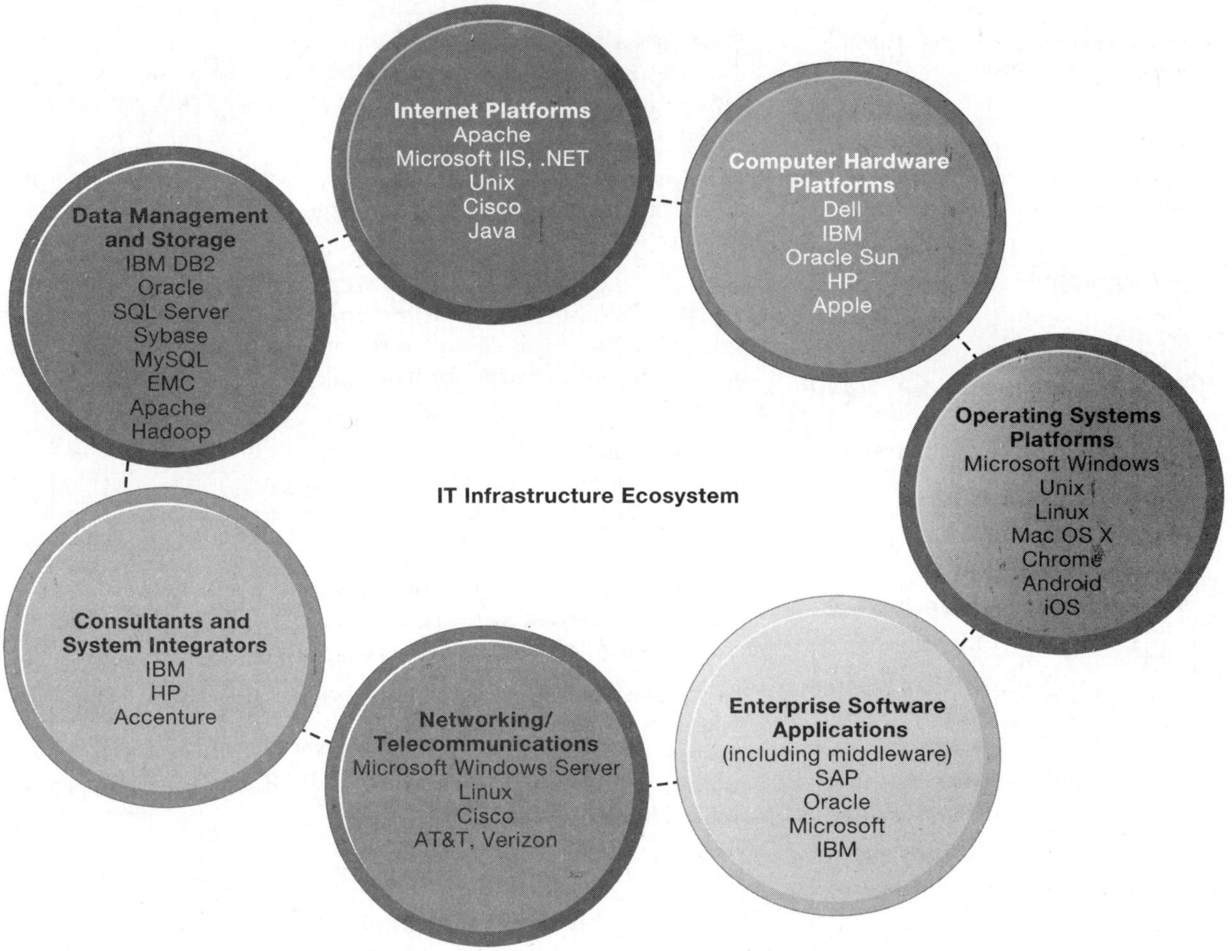

There are seven major components that must be coordinated to provide the firm with a coherent IT infrastructure. Listed here are major technologies and suppliers for each component.

Computer Hardware Platforms

Firms worldwide are expected to spend $626 billion on computer hardware devices in 2016, including mainframes, servers, PCs, tablets, and smartphones. All these devices constitute the computer hardware platform for corporate (and personal) computing worldwide.

Most business computing takes place using microprocessor "chips" manufactured or designed by Intel Corporation and, to a lesser extent, AMD Corporation. Intel and AMD processors are often referred to as "i86" processors because the original IBM PCs used an Intel 8086 processor and all the Intel (and AMD) chips that followed are downward compatible with this processor. (For instance, you should be able to run a software application designed 10 years ago on a new PC you bought yesterday.)

The computer platform changed dramatically with the introduction of mobile computing devices, from the iPod in 2001 to the iPhone in 2007 and the iPad in 2010. Worldwide, 2 billion people use smartphones. You can think of these devices as a second computer hardware platform, one that is consumer device–driven.

The computers with Intel microprocessors in the first computer hardware platform use complex instruction set computing (CISC) with several thousand instructions built into the chip. This requires a considerable number of transistors per processor, consumes power, and generates heat. Mobile devices in the second computer hardware platform are not required to perform as many tasks as computers in the first computer hardware platform. They are able to use reduced instruction set computing (RISC), which contains a smaller set of instructions, consumes less power, and generates less heat. RISC processors for mobile devices are manufactured by a wide range of firms, including Apple, Samsung, and Qualcomm, using an architecture designed by ARM Holdings.

Mainframes have not disappeared. They continue to be used to reliably and securely handle huge volumes of transactions, for analyzing very large quantities of data, and for handling large workloads in cloud computing centers. The mainframe is still the digital workhorse for banking and telecommunications networks that are often running software programs that are older and require a specific hardware platform. Currently, mainframes process 30 billion business transactions per day, and 80 percent of the world's corporate data also originates on the mainframe (ITBusinessEdge.com, 2015).

However, the number of providers has dwindled to one: IBM. IBM has also repurposed its mainframe systems so they can be used as giant servers for enterprise networks and corporate websites. A single IBM mainframe can run thousands of instances of Linux or Windows Server software and is capable of replacing thousands of smaller servers (see the discussion of virtualization in Section 5-3).

Operating System Platforms

The leading operating systems for corporate servers are Microsoft Windows Server, **Unix**, and **Linux**, an inexpensive and robust open source relative of Unix. Microsoft Windows Server is capable of providing enterprise-wide operating system and network services and appeals to organizations seeking Windows-based IT infrastructures. Unix and Linux are scalable, reliable, and much less expensive than mainframe operating systems. They can also run on many different types of processors. The major providers of Unix operating systems are IBM, HP, and Oracle-Sun, each with slightly different and partially incompatible versions.

At the client level, 81 percent of PCs use some form of the Microsoft Windows **operating system** (such as Windows 10, Windows 8, or Windows 7) to manage the resources and activities of the computer. However, there is now a much greater variety of client operating systems than in the past, with new operating systems for computing on handheld mobile digital devices or cloud-connected computers.

Google's **Chrome OS** provides a lightweight operating system for cloud computing using a web-connected computer. Programs are not stored on the user's computer but are used over the Internet and accessed through the Chrome web browser. User data reside on servers across the Internet. **Android** is an open source operating system for mobile devices such as smartphones and tablet computers developed by the Open Handset Alliance led by Google. It has become the most popular smartphone platform worldwide, competing with iOS, Apple's mobile operating system for the iPhone, iPad, and iPod Touch. Android is installed on more than half the tablets, smartphones, and portable computers in use globally.

Conventional client operating system software is designed around the mouse and keyboard but increasingly is becoming more natural and intuitive by using touch technology. **iOS**, the operating system for the phenomenally popular Apple iPad, iPhone, and iPod Touch, features a **multitouch** interface, where users employ one or more fingers to manipulate objects on a screen without a mouse or keyboard. Microsoft's **Windows 10** and Windows 8, which run on tablets as well as PCs, have multitouch capabilities, as do many Android devices.

Enterprise Software Applications

Firms worldwide are expected to spend about $321 billion in 2016 on software for enterprise applications that are treated as components of IT infrastructure. We introduced the various types of enterprise applications in Chapter 2, and Chapter 9 provides a more detailed discussion of each.

The largest providers of enterprise application software are SAP and Oracle. Also included in this category is middleware software supplied by vendors such as IBM and Oracle for achieving firmwide integration by linking the firm's existing application systems. Microsoft is attempting to move into the lower ends of this market by focusing on small and medium-sized businesses.

Data Management and Storage

Enterprise database management software is responsible for organizing and managing the firm's data so that they can be efficiently accessed and used. Chapter 6 describes this software in detail. The leading database software providers are IBM (DB2), Oracle, Microsoft (SQL Server), and Sybase (Adaptive Server Enterprise). MySQL is a Linux open source relational database product now owned by Oracle Corporation, and Apache Hadoop is an open source software framework for managing very large data sets (see Chapter 6). The physical data storage market for large-scale systems is dominated by EMC Corporation.

Networking/Telecommunications Platforms

Companies worldwide are expected to spend $1.44 trillion for telecommunications services in 2016 (Gartner, Inc., 2016). Windows Server is predominantly used as a local area network operating system, followed by Linux and Unix. Large, enterprise-wide area networks use some variant of Unix. Most local area networks, as well as wide area enterprise networks, use the TCP/IP protocol suite as a standard (see Chapter 7).

Cisco and Juniper Networks are leading networking hardware providers. Telecommunications platforms are typically provided by telecommunications/telephone services companies that offer voice and data connectivity, wide area networking, wireless services, and Internet access. Leading telecommunications service vendors include AT&T and Verizon. This market is exploding with new providers of cellular wireless, high-speed Internet, and Internet telephone services.

Internet Platforms

Internet platforms include hardware, software, and management services to support a firm's website, including web hosting services, routers, and cabling or wireless equipment. A **web hosting service** maintains a large web server, or series of servers, and provides fee-paying subscribers with space to maintain their websites.

The Internet revolution created a veritable explosion in server computers, with many firms collecting thousands of small servers to run their Internet operations. There has been a steady push to reduce the number of server computers by increasing the size and power of each and by using software tools that make it possible to run more applications on a single server. The Internet hardware server market has become increasingly concentrated in the hands of IBM, Dell, Oracle, and HP, as prices have fallen dramatically.

The major web software application development tools and suites are supplied by Microsoft (Microsoft Visual Studio and the Microsoft .NET family of development tools), Oracle-Sun (Sun's Java is the most widely used tool for developing interactive web applications on both the server and client sides), and a host of independent software developers, including Adobe (Creative Suite). Chapter 7 describes the components of the firm's Internet platform in greater detail.

Consulting and System Integration Services

Today, even a large firm does not have the staff, the skills, the budget, or the necessary experience to deploy and maintain its entire IT infrastructure. Implementing a new infrastructure requires (as noted in Chapters 13 and 14) significant changes in business processes and procedures, training and education, and software integration. Leading consulting firms providing this expertise include Accenture, IBM Global Business Services, HP, Infosys, and Wipro Technologies.

Software integration means ensuring the new infrastructure works with the firm's older, so-called legacy systems and ensuring the new elements of the infrastructure work with one another. **Legacy systems** are generally older transaction processing systems created for mainframe computers that continue to be used to avoid the high cost of replacing or redesigning them. Replacing these systems is cost prohibitive and generally not necessary if these older systems can be integrated into a contemporary infrastructure.

5-3 What are the current trends in computer hardware platforms?

The exploding power of computer hardware and networking technology has dramatically changed how businesses organize their computing power, putting more of this power on networks and mobile handheld devices. We look at seven hardware trends: the mobile digital platform, consumerization of IT and BYOD, quantum computing, virtualization, cloud computing, green computing, and high-performance/power-saving processors.

The Mobile Digital Platform

Chapter 1 pointed out that new mobile digital computing platforms have emerged as alternatives to PCs and larger computers. The iPhone and Android smartphones have taken on many functions of PCs, including transmitting data, surfing the web, transmitting e-mail and instant messages, displaying digital content, and exchanging data with internal corporate systems. The new mobile platform also includes small, lightweight netbooks optimized for wireless communication and Internet access, **tablet computers** such as the iPad, and digital e-book readers such as Amazon's Kindle with some web access capabilities.

Smartphones and tablet computers are increasingly used for business computing as well as for consumer applications. For example, senior executives at General Motors are using smartphone applications that drill down into vehicle sales information, financial performance, manufacturing metrics, and project management status.

Wearable computing devices are a recent addition to the mobile digital platform. These include smartwatches, smart glasses, smart ID badges, and activity trackers.

Consumerization of IT and BYOD

The popularity, ease of use, and rich array of useful applications for smartphones and tablet computers have created a groundswell of interest in allowing employees to use their personal mobile devices in the workplace, a phenomenon popularly called *"bring your own device" (BYOD)*. **BYOD** is one aspect of the **consumerization of IT**, in which new information technology that first emerges in the consumer market spreads into business organizations. Consumerization of IT includes not only mobile personal devices but also business uses of software services that originated in the consumer marketplace as well, such as Google and Yahoo search, Gmail, Google Apps, Dropbox, and even Facebook and Twitter.

Consumerization of IT is forcing businesses to rethink the way they obtain and manage information technology equipment and services. Historically, at least in large firms, the IT department was responsible for selecting and managing the information technology and applications used by the firm

INTERACTIVE SESSION: TECHNOLOGY

Establishing Global Classrooms through WebEx

Synopsys Electronics Education and Research (Seer) Akademi, an academic initiative of the Worldwide University Program of Nasdaq-listed Synopsys Inc, offers undergraduate and postgraduate degrees in VLSI (very large-scale integration) and embedded systems across rural India. The start-up was pioneered by California-based entrepreneur, Srikanth Jadcherla, who worked as an executive at Synopsys, an electronic design automation company. He is now the chairman and CEO of Seer Akademi. The institute deploys a non-traditional architecture of education, which is pending for a patent. This unique model of imparting education combines classroom curriculum conducted by local and online faculty, skill-based learning, and practical application of learning in state-of-the-art labs. The theory to practice ratio is 35 to 65, unlike any other course offered in India.

Since the institute targets rural students, providing quality and research-oriented education regardless of location with a lack of qualified facilitators is a key challenge. In addition, poor research in electronics in India and the time required for students to travel from remote rural locations to attend classes also pose problem for the institute. Although India has the largest population in the world under the age of 14 that is waiting to be organized into a potential soucrce of electronics expertise, these challenges inhibit their growth. One feasible solution that Jadcherla could think of was Web-conferencing.

Web-conferencing enables real-time face-to-face conversations through a Web browser at any place, and at any time. It requires wireless devices with internet connectivity, an audio connection, and an optional webcam. However, rural areas have limited bandwidth and students are not well-versed in the concept of collaborative online learning. Therefore, it was imperative that the solution offered not only a robust and reliable platform, but was also easy to use. Jadcherla evaluated several available products and decided to go with Cisco's WebEx technology. WebEx has been designed to minimize the amount of data transmitted over the network and works well in areas with low bandwidth or areas prone to network congestion. WebEx's use of internet data varies with the type of files shared. For example, if students view slides over the network, no or very little network traffic is generated, compared to video conferencing. Its several easy-to-use features include online collaboration tools such as discussion forums, document sharing, calendar, and so on. It allows for the creation of virtual teams and online sharing of content.

Using this technology, Seer Akademi has been able to setup global classrooms through which students in rural India can collaborate with professors located across the world. Instructors can share their desktops imparting real-time lectures on chip design and electronic processes from remote locations. WebEx provides tools for facilitators to markup documents as they are shared and take notes. Compared to the interactive whiteboard technology, the WebEx interface is far more superior in terms of ease of use. It also costs a lot less than other similar technology. WebEx is compatible with a range of mobile devices. "In 2009, the remote town of Nandyal was completely cut off from the rest of the world due to flooding, but the students there did not want to miss class. So a group of them gathered around an Apple iPhone and attended the WebEx session that way," says Jadcherla.

From offering certification courses, Seer Akademi has now moved to full-time degree programmes in microelectronics. Students who graduate from this institute are deemed skilled to get a higher degree in their field or placed in leading firms as well as innovative start-ups such as Broadcom, Synopsys, AMD, Blaze, and so on.

With the success of its pedagogy-laden engineering education, Jadcherla hopes that the model will be followed in engineering colleges across the world and expects his institute to grow 14 times in the coming years. According to the estimates of the India Electronics and Semiconductor Association, by 2020, the country will face around 2.8 million shortage of manpower in electronics. Jadcherla has, therefore, entered into joint ventures with other groups to set up advanced electronics labs and incubation centers. Besides, he also hopes to build a microelectronics laboratory that will give students hands-on experience with real-world electronics engineering technologies.

Currently the institute operates from offices in Hyderabad and Bangalore and has eight regional centers. It is looking forward to expand to places like Vietnam, Malaysia, Dubai, and other South Asian and Middle Eastern countries.

Sources: Benefits of WebEx, WebEx.com, accessed on December 21, 2015 (http://www.webex.co.in, Navigation > Home > Overview > Web Conferencing); http://www.cisco.com, (Navigation > Home > English-US > Products > Collateral Conferencing > Seer Academy Case Study), as accessed on 02 December 2015 at 2pm IST; Mobile Meetings, WebEx.com, accessed on December 21, 2015 (http://www.webex.co.in, (Navigation > Overview > Mobile Meetings).

CASE STUDY QUESTIONS

1. Discuss how Srikanth Jadcherla's vision of spreading engineering education to rural India has materialized by the application of technology?
2. Identify the features of Cisco's WebEx technology.
3. Discuss the challenges faced by Jadcherla before the implementation of Web conferencing. How did Cisco help him overcome these challenges?

and its employees. It furnished employees with desktops or laptops that were able to access corporate systems securely. The IT department maintained control over the firm's hardware and software to ensure that the business was being protected and that information systems served the purposes of the firm and its management. Today, employees and business departments are playing a much larger role in technology selection, in many cases demanding that employees be able to use their own personal computers, smartphones, and tablets to access the corporate network. It is more difficult for the firm to manage and control these consumer technologies and make sure they serve the needs of the business. The chapter-ending case study explores some of these management challenges created by BYOD and IT consumerization.

Quantum Computing

Quantum computing is an emerging technology with the potential to dramatically boost computer processing power to find answers to problems that would take conventional computers many years to solve. **Quantum computing** uses the principles of quantum physics to represent data and perform operations on these data. While conventional computers handle bits of data either as 0 or 1 but not both, quantum computing can process bits as 0, 1, or both simultaneously. A quantum computer would gain enormous processing power through this ability to be in multiple states at once, allowing it to solve some scientific and business problems millions of times faster than can be done today. IBM has made quantum computing available to the general public through IBM Cloud. Google's Alphabet and Lockheed Martin currently use quantum platforms (Follow, 2016).

Virtualization

Virtualization is the process of presenting a set of computing resources (such as computing power or data storage) so that they can all be accessed in ways that are not restricted by physical configuration or geographic location. Virtualization enables a single physical resource (such as a server or a storage device) to appear to the user as multiple logical resources. For example, a server or mainframe can be configured to run many instances of an operating system (or different operating systems) so that it acts like many different machines. Each virtual server "looks" like a real physical server to software programs, and multiple virtual servers can run in parallel on a single machine. VMware is the leading virtualization software vendor for Windows and Linux servers.

Server virtualization is a common method of reducing technology costs by providing the ability to host multiple systems on a single physical machine. Most servers run at just 15 to 20 percent of capacity, and virtualization can boost server utilization rates to 70 percent or higher. Higher utilization rates translate into fewer computers required to process the same amount of work, reduced data center space to house machines, and lower energy usage. Virtualization also facilitates centralization and consolidation of hardware administration.

Virtualization also enables multiple physical resources (such as storage devices or servers) to appear as a single logical resource, as in **software-defined storage (SDS)**, which separates the software for managing data storage from storage hardware. Using software, firms can pool and arrange multiple storage infrastructure resources and efficiently allocate them to meet specific application needs. SDS enables firms to replace expensive storage hardware with lower-cost commodity hardware and cloud storage hardware. There is less under- or over-utilization of storage resources (Letschin, 2016).

Cloud Computing

It is now possible for companies and individuals to perform all of their computing work using a virtualized IT infrastructure in a remote location, as is the case with cloud computing. Cloud computing is a model of computing in which computer processing, storage, software, and other services are provided as a shared pool of virtualized resources over a network, primarily the Internet. These "clouds" of computing resources can be accessed on an as-needed basis from any connected device and location. Figure 5.9 illustrates the cloud computing concept.

The U.S. National Institute of Standards and Technology (NIST) defines cloud computing as having the following essential characteristics (Mell and Grance, 2009):

- **On-demand self-service:** Consumers can obtain computing capabilities such as server time or network storage as needed automatically on their own.
- **Ubiquitous network access:** Cloud resources can be accessed using standard network and Internet devices, including mobile platforms.
- **Location-independent resource pooling:** Computing resources are pooled to serve multiple users, with different virtual resources dynamically assigned

FIGURE 5.9 CLOUD COMPUTING PLATFORM

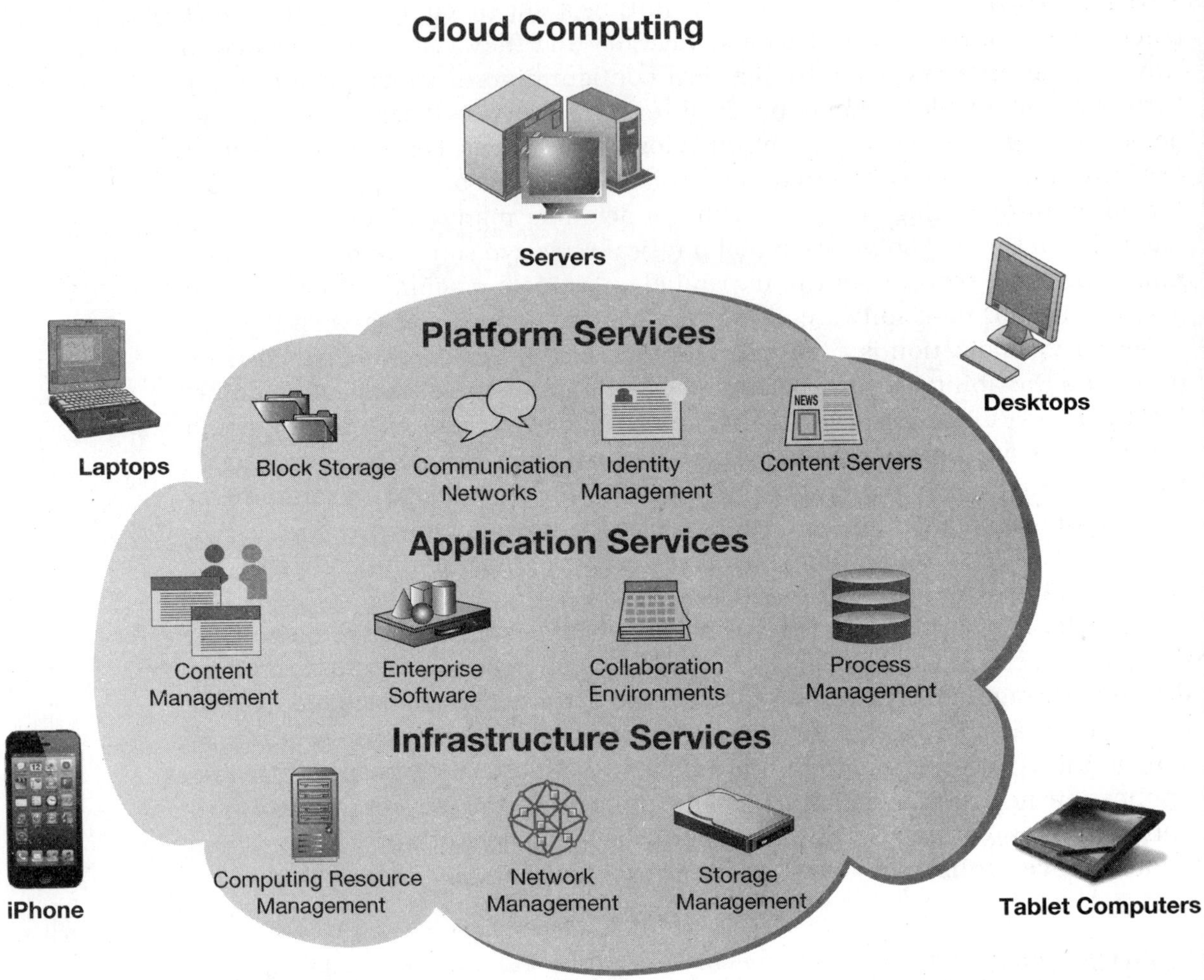

In cloud computing, hardware and software capabilities are a pool of virtualized resources provided over a network, often the Internet. Businesses and employees have access to applications and IT infrastructure anywhere, at any time, and on any device.

according to user demand. The user generally does not know where the computing resources are located.

- **Rapid elasticity:** Computing resources can be rapidly provisioned, increased, or decreased to meet changing user demand.
- **Measured service:** Charges for cloud resources are based on amount of resources actually used.

Cloud computing consists of three different types of services:

- **Infrastructure as a service (IaaS):** Customers use processing, storage, networking, and other computing resources from cloud service providers to

FIGURE 5.10 AMAZON WEB SERVICES

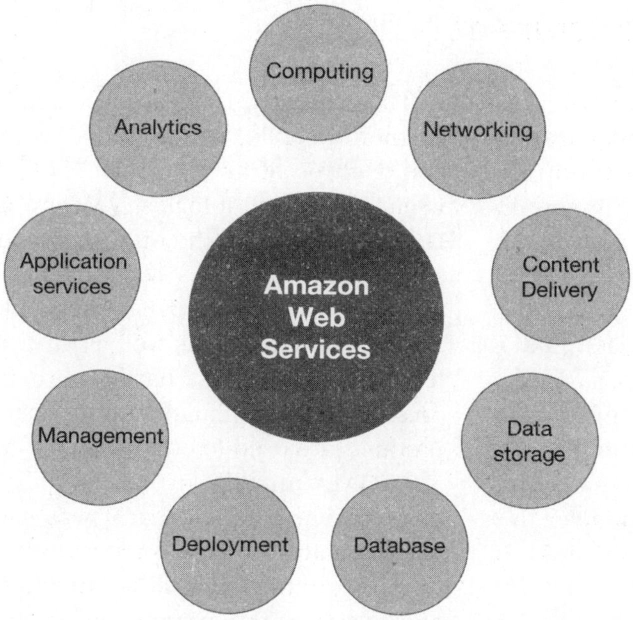

Amazon Web Services (AWS) is a collection of web services that Amazon provides to users of its cloud platform. AWS is the largest provider of cloud computing services In the United States.

run their information systems. For example, Amazon uses the spare capacity of its IT infrastructure to provide a broadly based cloud environment selling IT infrastructure services. These include its Simple Storage Service (S3) for storing customers' data and its Elastic Compute Cloud (EC2) service for running their applications. Users pay only for the amount of computing and storage capacity they actually use. Figure 5.10 shows the range of services Amazon Web Services offers.

- **Software as a service (SaaS):** Customers use software hosted by the vendor on the vendor's cloud infrastructure and delivered as a service over a network. Leading **software as a service (SaaS)** examples are Google Apps, which provides common business applications online, and Salesforce.com, which leases customer relationship management and related software services over the Internet. Both charge users an annual subscription fee, although Google Apps has a pared-down free version. Users access these applications from a web browser, and the data and software are maintained on the providers' remote servers.
- **Platform as a service (PaaS):** Customers use infrastructure and programming tools supported by the cloud service provider to develop their own applications. For example, IBM offers a Bluemix service for software development and testing on the IBM cloud. Another example is Salesforce.com's Force.com, which allows developers to build applications that are hosted on its servers as a service.

INTERACTIVE SESSION: ORGANIZATIONS

Building Virtualization Infrastructure at NTT

NTT Data has been providing IT infrastructure services since its inception in 1967. It is headquartered in Tokyo and runs business operations in 42 countries. NTT Data (originally a part of Nippon Telegraph and Telephone Public Corporation) is a part of the bigger NTT Group of Companies encompassing NTT Communications Corporation, NTT, NTT East, NTT West, Dimension Data Plc., and NTT DOCOMO. NTT DATA India started its operations in the 1990s. Across India, it caters to more than 1,000 enterprise clients, generating over $300 million annually. It has a workforce of 12,500 applicants and data center professionals. It's seven data centers, spread over five million square feet area and four cities in India. It has strategic partnership with leading firms like SAP, Oracle, Microsoft, HP, EMC, and the likes.

NTT DATA India offers a diverse portfolio of services in consulting, staffing, outsourcing, cloud services, infrastructure, testing, business intelligence, and so on. The firm had deployed a fleet of servers from various companies such as IBM, Sun Microsystems, and other leading firms. It has a primary data center in Bangalore and server rooms spread in three to four other locations in India. These servers are used for offshore software development, to support critical enterprise applications and in-house tools, and for product demonstration to customers. This server sprawl led to numerous issues at the firm. NTT was struggling with power issues, cooling, and real-estate costs. Whenever a team at NTT required a new application server, a process of procurement was carried out which was both tedious and expensive. This procurement delay became more pronounced when the number of incoming requests became very high. As a result, NTT started procuring high-end desktops which could act as servers; and at a certain point of time, it was using 300 high-end desktops as servers to create a testing environment. An added problem was that only limited capacity of each desktop could be utilized (a fraction of CPU resources), as each desktop was dedicated to a single project. This was adding to both organizational costs and environmental footprint, owing to overcrowded rack of servers which consumed tremendous amount of power and generated a lot of heat.

The company, Dell, which is one of the application partner of NTT Data, offered server virtualization on two or three of its servers at NTT, through VMware vSphere 3.5 technologies. VMware is a subsidiary of Dell Technologies, and offers cloud and virtualization software and services. VMware has desktop servers which run on operating systems like MS Windows, Linux, and Mac OS, as well as on enterprise software hypervisor which is a hardware that can run directly on servers without an operating system. Both of these products are used to create and run virtual machines. NTT DATA initially virtualized only two of the three blade servers of Dell that it was using to run client demonstrations. However, this puts constraint on resources of the physical server which acts as the host and can slow down applications and server performance. So, in order to create the required additional capacity, another product, EMC Corporation (now as Dell EMC), an entry level storage, was also deployed.

EMC, which has now been acquired by Dell Technologies, is a leader in IT storage hardware solutions for data backup and recovery. The firm soon saw the benefits of virtualization and conducted a thorough evaluation of its use for all of its servers used for non-critical activities. NTT DATA implemented VMware vSphere virtualization technology for other servers as well, and it was able to considerably reduce real estate investment for data center maintenance. Its seven data centers comprising three to four server rooms spread in four cities in India were reduced to just one rack which accommodated blade servers and one rack which had storage equipment at each location. They upgraded to the latest versions of VMware vSphere technology within two or three weeks of its release.

Next, NTT DATA wished to transform the way in which virtualization was offered to its users and clients (provided on demand). They wanted to completely automate the process of providing virtualization. By this time, VMware was available as a cloud service in the form of VMware vCloud suite, and its cloud based infrastructure-as-a-service model had matured as well. This suite allows the clients to build and manage private or hybrid clouds based on vSphere technologies.

This implies that all the server virtualization capabilities of vSphere were now available as a cloud service through the vCloud suite. Although initially, firms looked at alternatives such as creation of self-service portals where on-demand virtualization could be procured by the users, they realized that their requirements were completely fulfilled by VMware vCloud suite. So, by the end of 2015, they had executed some functions using vCloud suite to test its performance and were preparing to roll out a private cloud for complete operations. The private cloud was developed in close association with VMware sales team, service professionals, and operations team at NTT DATA. As a result, network provision was automated and operational costs were reduced. This benefited the clients as well as those who were now able to independently develop, deploy, and test their applications and migrate them to different data centers. This was immensely beneficial in 2011, when earthquake and tsunami triggered in Pacific coast of Tohoku (Japan) had hit several areas in Japan, and NTT was able to migrate its applications to other data centers ahead of (brown-outs) from the affected areas.

To identify potential areas of application of virtualization in future, they developed metrics to compare savings derived from virtualization and use it as a cloud service. As a result, they could compute per unit cost of infrastructure resources – memory, processing, and storage. Based on the findings from these metrics, they were able to develop a business case for future use of virtualization as infrastructure resources. Meanwhile NTT DATA also implemented VMware IT Business Management suite, after comprehensive evaluation for four months. This product analyzes and provides details of IT related costs on a private cloud. With this, NTT DATA was able to implement trend analysis where they could view past usage and forecast usage over the next few months. This also allowed them to compute any requirements for additional capacity and start an investment for the same. The firm now looks forward to delivering greater value to its clients and users through such technologies.

Sources: As accessed on 11 September 2015 at 2pm IST—Retrieved from http://www.vmware.com, please read: VMWare NTT Customer Case Study; Retrieved from http://www.cxotoday.com, please read the story: How NTT Data Gets Smarter with Server Visualization; Retrieved from http://www.vmware.com, (Navigation > Home > India > Products > VCloud Suite); Retrieved from http://india.nttdata.com, (Navigation > Home > About Us > NTT Data India); Retrieved from http://india.nttdata.com, (Navigation > Home > About Us > NTT Data Corporate Profile); Retrieved from http://computer.howstuffworks.com, (Navigation > Home > Server Visualization); "How to Tap the Power of the Mainframe." ITBusinessEdge.com.

CASE STUDY QUESTIONS

1. Discuss the infrastructure challenges faced by NTT DATA.
2. How has virtualization helped NTT DATA overcome the infrastructure challenges?
3. What was the need for implementing cloud virtualization at NTT DATA? How did they evaluate this solution?

Chapter 2 discussed Google Docs, Google Apps, and related software services for desktop productivity and collaboration. These are among the most popular software services for consumers, although they are increasingly used in business. Salesforce.com is a leading software service for business. Salesforce provides customer relationship management (CRM) and other application software solutions as software services leased over the Internet. Its sales and service clouds offer applications for improving sales and customer service. A marketing cloud enables companies to engage in digital marketing interactions with customers through e-mail, mobile, social, web, and connected products. Salesforce.com also provides a community cloud platform for online collaboration and engagement and an analytics cloud platform to deploy sales, service, marketing, and custom analytics apps.

Salesforce.com is also a leading example of platform as a service (PaaS). Its Force.com is an application development platform where customers can develop their own applications for use within the broader Salesforce network. Force.com provides a set of development tools and IT services that enable users to customize their Salesforce.com customer relationship management applications or to build entirely new applications and run them in the cloud on Salesforce.com's data center infrastructure. Salesforce opened up Force.com to other independent software developers and listed their programs on its AppExchange, an online marketplace for third-party applications that run on the Force.com platform.

A cloud can be private or public. A **public cloud** is owned and maintained by a cloud service provider, such as Amazon Web Services, and made available to the general public or industry group. Public cloud services are often used for websites with public information and product descriptions, one-time large computing projects, developing and testing new applications, and consumer services such as online storage of data, music, and photos. Google Drive, Dropbox, and Apple iCloud are leading examples of these consumer public cloud services.

A **private cloud** is operated solely for an organization. It may be managed by the organization or a third party and may be hosted either internally or externally. Like public clouds, private clouds are able to allocate storage, computing power, or other resources seamlessly to provide computing resources on an as-needed basis. Companies that want flexible IT resources and a cloud service model while retaining control over their own IT infrastructure are gravitating toward these private clouds. (Review the chapter-opening case on EasyJet and the Interactive Session on Organizations).

Because organizations using public clouds do not own the infrastructure, they do not have to make large investments in their own hardware and software. Instead, they purchase their computing services from remote providers and pay only for the amount of computing power they actually use (utility computing) or are billed on a monthly or annual subscription basis. The term **on-demand computing** has also been used to describe such services.

Cloud computing has some drawbacks. Unless users make provisions for storing their data locally, the responsibility for data storage and control is in the hands of the provider. Some companies worry about the security risks related to entrusting their critical data and systems to an outside vendor that also works with other companies. Companies expect their systems to be available 24/7 and do not want to suffer any loss of business capability if cloud infrastructures malfunction. Nevertheless, the trend is for companies to shift more of their computer processing and storage to some form of cloud infrastructure. Startups and small companies with limited IT resources and budgets will find public cloud services especially helpful.

Large firms are most likely to adopt a **hybrid cloud** computing model where they use their own infrastructure for their most essential core activities and adopt public cloud computing for less-critical systems or for additional processing capacity during peak business periods. Table 5.2 compares the three cloud computing models. Cloud computing will gradually shift firms from having a fixed infrastructure capacity toward a more flexible infrastructure, some of it owned by the firm and some of it rented from giant computer centers owned by computer hardware vendors. You can find out more about cloud computing in the Learning Tracks for this chapter.

TABLE 5.2 CLOUD COMPUTING MODELS COMPARED

TYPE OF CLOUD	DESCRIPTION	MANAGED BY	USES
Public cloud	Third-party service offering computing, storage, and software services to multiple customers and that is available to the public	Third-party service providers	Companies without major privacy concerns Companies seeking pay-as-you go IT services Companies lacking IT resources and expertise
Private cloud	Cloud infrastructure operated solely for a single organization and hosted either internally or externally.	In-house IT or private third-party host	Companies with stringent privacy and security requirements Companies that must have control over data sovereignty
Hybrid cloud	Combination of private and public cloud services that remain separate entities	In-house IT, private host, third-party providers	Companies requiring some in-house control of IT that are also willing to assign part of their IT infrastructures to a public cloud

Green Computing

By curbing hardware proliferation and power consumption, virtualization has become one of the principal technologies for promoting green computing. **Green computing**, or **green IT**, refers to practices and technologies for designing, manufacturing, using, and disposing of computers, servers, and associated devices such as monitors, printers, storage devices, and networking and communications systems to minimize impact on the environment.

According to Green House Data, the world's data centers use as much energy as the output of 30 nuclear power plants, which amounts to 1.5 percent of all energy use in the world. Reducing computer power consumption has been a very high "green" priority. A corporate data center can easily consume over 100 times more power than a standard office building. All this additional power consumption has a negative impact on the environment and corporate operating costs. Data centers are now being designed with energy efficiency in mind, using state-of-the art air-cooling techniques, energy-efficient equipment, virtualization, and other energy-saving practices. Large companies like Microsoft, Google, Facebook, and Apple are starting to reduce their carbon footprint with clean energy–powered data centers with power-conserving equipment and extensive use of wind and hydropower.

High-Performance and Power-Saving Processors

Another way to reduce power requirements and hardware sprawl is to use more efficient and power-saving processors. Contemporary microprocessors now feature multiple processor cores (which perform the reading and execution of computer instructions) on a single chip. A **multicore processor** is an integrated circuit to which two or more processor cores have been attached for enhanced performance, reduced power consumption, and more efficient simultaneous processing of multiple tasks. This technology enables two or more processing engines with reduced power requirements and heat dissipation to perform tasks faster than a resource-hungry chip with a single processing core. Today you'll find PCs with dual-core, quad-core, six-core, and eight-core processors and servers with 16-core processors.

Intel and other chip manufacturers are working on microprocessors that minimize power consumption, which is essential for prolonging battery life in small mobile digital devices. Highly power-efficient microprocessors, such as the A9 and A10 processors used in Apple's iPhone and iPad and Intel's Atom processor, are used in lightweight smartphones and tablets, intelligent cars, and healthcare devices. The Apple processors have about one-fiftieth of the power consumption of a laptop dual-core processor. Intel introduced a line of ultrasmall, low-power microprocessors called Quark that can be used in wearable devices and skin patches or even swallowed to gather medical data.

5-4 What are the current computer software platforms and trends?

There are four major themes in contemporary software platform evolution:

- Linux and open source software
- Java, HTML, and HTML5
- Web services and service-oriented architecture
- Software outsourcing and cloud services

Linux and Open Source Software

Open source software is software produced by a community of several hundred thousand programmers around the world. According to the leading open source professional association, OpenSource.org, open source software is free and can be modified by users. Works derived from the original code must also be free, and the software can be redistributed by the user without additional licensing. Open source software is by definition not restricted to any specific operating system or hardware technology, although most open source software is currently based on a Linux or Unix operating system.

The open source movement has demonstrated that it can produce commercially acceptable, high-quality software. Popular open source software tools include the Linux operating system, the Apache HTTP web server, the Mozilla Firefox web browser, and the Apache OpenOffice desktop productivity suite. Google's Android mobile operating system and Chrome web browser are based on open source tools. You can find out more out more about the Open Source Definition from the Open Source Initiative and the history of open source software in the Learning Tracks for this chapter.

Linux

Perhaps the most well-known open source software is Linux, an operating system related to Unix. Linux was created by the Finnish programmer Linus Torvalds and first posted on the Internet in August 1991. Linux applications are embedded in cell phones, smartphones, tablet computers and consumer electronics. Linux is available in free versions downloadable from the Internet or in low-cost commercial versions that include tools and support from vendors such as Red Hat.

Although Linux is not used in many desktop systems, it is a leading operating system for servers, mainframe computers, and supercomputers. IBM, HP, Intel, Dell, and Oracle have made Linux a central part of their offerings to corporations. Linux has profound implications for corporate software platforms—cost reduction, reliability and resilience, and integration—because Linux works on all the major hardware platforms from mainframes to servers to clients.

Software for the Web: Java, HTML, and HTML5

Java is an operating system-independent, processor-independent, object-oriented programming language created by Sun Microsystems that has become the leading interactive programming environment for the web. The Java platform has migrated into mobile phones, smartphones, automobiles, music players, game machines, and set-top cable television systems serving interactive content and pay-per-view services. Java software is designed to run on any computer or computing device, regardless of the specific microprocessor or operating system the device uses. For each of the computing environments in which Java is used, a Java Virtual Machine interprets Java programming code for that machine. In this manner, the code is written once and can be used on any machine for which there exists a Java Virtual Machine.

Java developers can create small applet programs that can be embedded in webpages and downloaded to run on a web browser. A **web browser** is an easy-to-use software tool with a graphical user interface for displaying webpages and for accessing the web and other Internet resources. Microsoft's Internet Explorer, Mozilla Firefox, Google Chrome, and Apple Safari browsers are examples. At the enterprise level, Java is being used for more complex e-commerce and e-business applications that require communication with an organization's back-end transaction processing systems.

HTML and HTML5

Hypertext Markup Language (HTML) is a page description language for specifying how text, graphics, video, and sound are placed on a webpage and for creating dynamic links to other webpages and objects. Using these links, a user need only point at a highlighted keyword or graphic, click on it, and immediately be transported to another document.

HTML was originally designed to create and link static documents composed largely of text. Today, however, the web is much more social and interactive, and many webpages have multimedia elements—images, audio, and video. Third-party plug-in applications like Flash, Silverlight, and Java have been required to integrate these rich media with webpages. However, these add-ons require additional programming and put strains on computer processing. The next evolution of HTML, called **HTML5**, solves this problem by making it possible to embed images, audio, video, and other elements directly into a document without processor-intensive add-ons. HTML5 makes it easier for webpages to function across different display devices, including mobile devices as well as desktops, and it will support the storage of data offline for apps that run over the web. Other popular programming tools for web applications include Ruby and Python. Ruby is an object-oriented programming language known for speed and ease of use in building web applications, and Python (praised for its clarity) is being used for building cloud computing applications. Major websites such as Google, Facebook, Amazon, and Twitter use Python and Ruby as well as Java.

Web Services and Service-Oriented Architecture

Web services refer to a set of loosely coupled software components that exchange information with each other using universal web communication standards and languages. They can exchange information between two different systems regardless of the operating systems or programming languages on which the systems are based. They can be used to build open standard web-based applications linking systems of two different organizations, and they can also be used to create applications that link disparate systems within a single company. Different applications can use web services to communicate with each other in a standard way without time-consuming custom coding.

The foundation technology for web services is **XML**, which stands for **Extensible Markup Language**. This language was developed in 1996 by the World Wide Web Consortium (W3C, the international body that oversees the development of the web) as a more powerful and flexible markup language than hypertext markup language (HTML) for webpages. Whereas HTML is limited to describing how data should be presented in the form of webpages, XML can perform presentation, communication, and storage of data. In XML, a number is not simply a number; the XML tag specifies whether the number represents a price, a date, or a ZIP code. Table 5.3 illustrates some sample XML statements.

By tagging selected elements of the content of documents for their meanings, XML makes it possible for computers to manipulate and interpret their data automatically and perform operations on the data without human intervention. Web browsers and computer programs, such as order processing or enterprise resource planning (ERP) software, can follow programmed rules for applying and displaying the data. XML provides a standard format for data exchange, enabling web services to pass data from one process to another.

TABLE 5.3 EXAMPLES OF XML

PLAIN ENGLISH	XML
Subcompact	<AUTOMOBILETYPE="Subcompact">
4 passenger	<PASSENGERUNIT="PASS">4</PASSENGER>
$16,800	<PRICE CURRENCY="USD">$16,800</PRICE>

Web services communicate through XML messages over standard web protocols. Companies discover and locate web services through a directory. Using web protocols, a software application can connect freely to other applications without custom programming for each different application with which it wants to communicate. Everyone shares the same standards.

The collection of web services that are used to build a firm's software systems constitutes what is known as a service-oriented architecture. A **service-oriented architecture (SOA)** is set of self-contained services that communicate with each other to create a working software application. Business tasks are accomplished by executing a series of these services. Software developers reuse these services in other combinations to assemble other applications as needed.

Virtually all major software vendors provide tools and entire platforms for building and integrating software applications using web services. IBM includes web service tools in its WebSphere e-business software platform, and Microsoft has incorporated web services tools in its Microsoft .NET platform.

Dollar Rent A Car's systems use web services for its online booking system with Southwest Airlines's website. Although both companies' systems are based on different technology platforms, a person booking a flight on Southwest.com can reserve a car from Dollar without leaving the airline's website. Instead of struggling to get Dollar's reservation system to share data with Southwest's information systems, Dollar used Microsoft .NET web services technology as an intermediary. Reservations from Southwest are translated into web services protocols, which are then translated into formats that can be understood by Dollar's computers.

Other car rental companies have linked their information systems to airline companies' websites before. But without web services, these connections had to be built one at a time. Web services provide a standard way for Dollar's computers to "talk" to other companies' information systems without having to build special links to each one. Dollar is now expanding its use of web services to link directly to the systems of a small tour operator and a large travel reservation system as well as a wireless website for cell phones and smartphones. It does not have to write new software code for each new partner's information systems or each new wireless device (see Figure 5.11).

Software Outsourcing and Cloud Services

Today, many business firms continue to operate legacy systems that continue to meet a business need and that would be extremely costly to replace. But they will purchase or rent most of their new software applications from external sources. Figure 5.12 illustrates the rapid growth in external sources of software for U.S. firms.

There are three external sources for software: software packages from a commercial software vendor, outsourcing custom application development to an external vendor, (which may or may not be offshore), and cloud-based software services and tools.

Software Packages and Enterprise Software

We have already described software packages for enterprise applications as one of the major types of software components in contemporary IT infrastructures.

FIGURE 5.11 HOW DOLLAR RENT A CAR USES WEB SERVICES

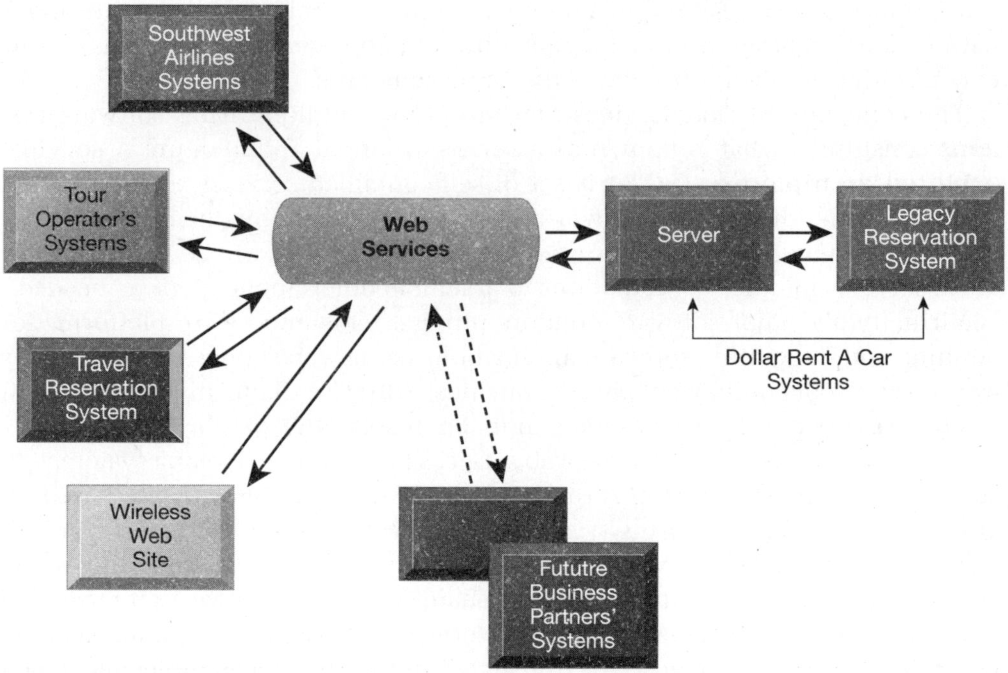

Dollar Rent A Car uses web services to provide a standard intermediate layer of software to "talk" to other companies' information systems. Dollar Rent A Car can use this set of web services to link to other companies' information systems without having to build a separate link to each firm's systems.

A **software package** is a prewritten commercially available set of software programs that eliminates the need for a firm to write its own software programs for certain functions, such as payroll processing or order handling.

Enterprise application software vendors such as SAP and Oracle-PeopleSoft have developed powerful software packages that can support the primary business processes of a firm worldwide from warehousing, customer relationship management, and supply chain management to finance and human resources. These large-scale enterprise software systems provide a single, integrated, worldwide software system for firms at a cost much less than they would pay if they developed it themselves. Chapter 9 discusses enterprise systems in detail.

Software Outsourcing

Software **outsourcing** enables a firm to contract custom software development or maintenance of existing legacy programs to outside firms, which often operate offshore in low-wage areas of the world. For example, UK communications regulator Ofcom recently signed a £23 million, six-year contract to outsource application and infrastructure management to NIIT Technologies. NIIT Technologies is an Indian firm specializing in application development and maintenance, infrastructure management, and business process management. NIIT provides Ofcom with a service desk, data center services, and application management and project management services (Flinders, 2016).

FIGURE 5.12 CHANGING SOURCES OF FIRM SOFTWARE

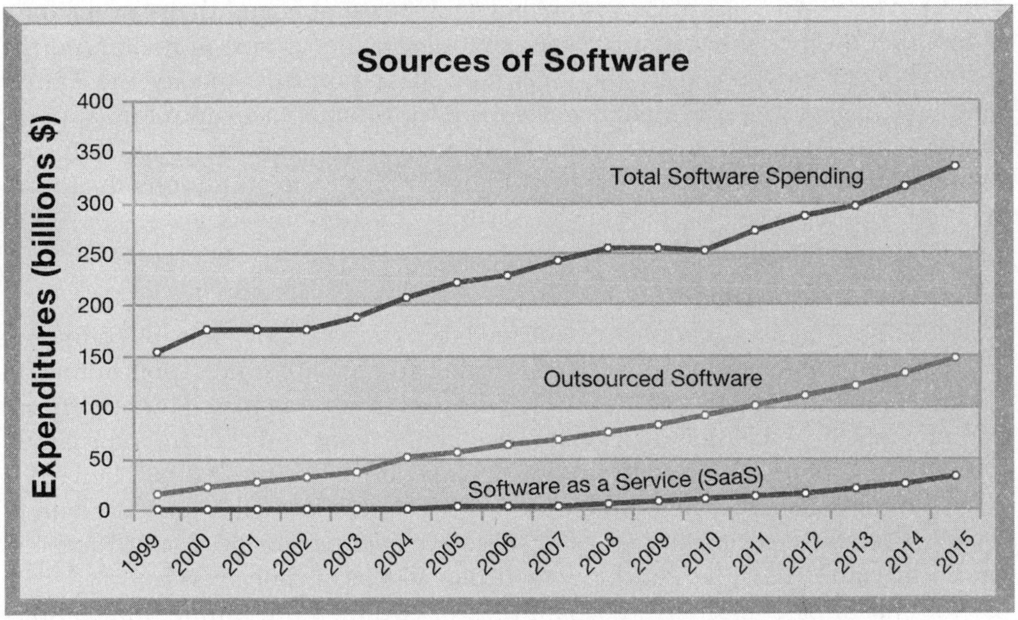

In 2015, U.S. firms spent and estimated $334 billion on software. About 44% of that originated outside the firm, provided by a variety of vendors. About 10% ($33 billion) was provided by SaaS vendors as an online cloud-based service.

Sources: BEA National Income and Product Accounts, 2016; authors' estimates.

Offshore software outsourcing firms have primarily provided lower-level maintenance, data entry, and call center operations, although more sophisticated and experienced offshore firms, particularly in India, have been hired for new-program development. However, as wages offshore rise and the costs of managing offshore projects are factored in (see Chapter 13), some work that would have been sent offshore is returning to domestic companies.

Cloud-Based Software Services and Tools

In the past, software such as Microsoft Word or Adobe Illustrator came in a box and was designed to operate on a single machine. Today, you're more likely to download the software from the vendor's website or to use the software as a cloud service delivered over the Internet.

Cloud-based software and the data it uses are hosted on powerful servers in data centers and can be accessed with an Internet connection and standard web browser. In addition to free or low-cost tools for individuals and small businesses provided by Google or Yahoo, enterprise software and other complex business functions are available as services from the major commercial software vendors. Instead of buying and installing software programs, subscribing companies rent the same functions from these services, with users paying either on a subscription or per-transaction basis. A leading example is of software as a service (SaaS) is Salesforce.com, described earlier in this chapter, which provides on-demand software services for customer relationship management.

In order to manage their relationship with an outsourcer or technology service provider, firms need a contract that includes a **service level agreement (SLA)**. The SLA is a formal contract between customers and their service providers that defines the specific responsibilities of the service provider and the level of service expected by the customer. SLAs typically specify the nature and level of services provided, criteria for performance measurement, support options, provisions for security and disaster recovery, hardware and software ownership and upgrades, customer support, billing, and conditions for terminating the agreement. We provide a Learning Track on this topic.

Mashups and Apps

The software you use for both personal and business tasks today may be composed of interchangeable components that integrate freely with other applications on the Internet. Individual users and entire companies mix and match these software components to create their own customized applications and to share information with others. The resulting software applications are called **mashups**. The idea is to take different sources and produce a new work that is greater than the sum of its parts. You have performed a mashup if you've ever personalized your Facebook profile or your blog with a capability to display videos or slide shows.

Web mashups combine the capabilities of two or more online applications to create a kind of hybrid that provides more customer value than the original sources alone. For instance, ZipRealty uses Google Maps and data provided by online real estate database Zillow.com to display a complete list of multiple listing service (MLS) real estate listings for any ZIP code specified by the user.

Apps are small specialized software programs (application software) that are designed for mobile devices like smartphones and tablets. They are downloaded from app stores like Apple's App Store and Google Play. Google refers to its online services as apps, including the Google Apps suite of desktop productivity tools. Windows 10 refers to all of its desktop software programs as apps. But when we talk about apps today, most of the attention goes to the apps that have been developed for mobile devices like smartphones and tablets. It is these apps that turn smartphones and tablets into general-purpose computing tools. First appearing in 2008, in 2016 there are hundreds of millions of apps for the iOS and Android mobile operating systems. The use of apps now exceeds the use of mobile browsers, which are much slower and cumbersome for accessing mobile software.

Apps provide a streamlined non-browser pathway for users to perform a number of tasks, ranging from reading the newspaper to shopping, searching, personal health monitoring, playing games, and buying. They increasingly are used by managers as gateways to their firm's enterprise systems. Because so many people are now accessing the Internet from their mobile devices, some say that apps are "the new browsers." Apps are also starting to influence the design and function of traditional websites as consumers are attracted to the look and feel of apps and their speed of operation.

Many apps are free or purchased for a small charge, much less than conventional software, which further adds to their appeal. There are already more than 2 million apps for the Apple iPhone and iPad platform and a similar number that run on devices using Google's Android operating system. Apple reports that more than 100 billion apps have been downloaded by users. The success of these mobile platforms depends in large part on the quantity and the quality of the apps they provide. Apps tie the customer to a specific hardware platform: As the user adds more and more apps to his or her mobile phone, the cost of switching to a competing mobile platform rises.

At the moment, the most commonly downloaded apps are games, news and weather, maps/navigation, social networking, music, and video/movies. But there are also serious apps for business users that make it possible to create and edit documents, connect to corporate systems, schedule and participate in meetings, track shipments, and dictate voice messages. Most large online retailers have apps for consumers for researching and buying goods and services online.

5-5 What are the challenges of managing IT infrastructure and management solutions?

Creating and managing a coherent IT infrastructure raises multiple challenges: dealing with platform and technology change (including cloud and mobile computing), management and governance, and making wise infrastructure investments.

Dealing with Platform and Infrastructure Change

As firms grow, they often quickly outgrow their infrastructure. As firms shrink, they can get stuck with excessive infrastructure purchased in better times. How can a firm remain flexible if investments in IT infrastructure are fixed-cost purchases and licenses? How well does the infrastructure scale? **Scalability** refers to the ability of a computer, product, or system to expand to serve a large number of users without breaking down. New applications, mergers and acquisitions, and changes in business volume all affect computer workload and must be considered when planning hardware capacity.

Firms using mobile computing and cloud computing platforms will require new policies and procedures for managing these platforms. They will need to inventory all of their mobile devices in business use and develop policies and tools for tracking, updating, and securing them and for controlling the data and applications that run on them. Firms using cloud computing and SaaS will need to fashion new contractual arrangements with remote vendors to make sure that the hardware and software for critical applications are always available when needed and that they meet corporate standards for information security. It is up to business management to determine acceptable levels of computer response time and availability for the firm's mission-critical systems to maintain the level of business performance that is expected.

Management and Governance

A long-standing issue among information system managers and CEOs has been the question of who will control and manage the firm's IT infrastructure.

Chapter 2 introduced the concept of IT governance and described some issues it addresses. Other important questions about IT governance are: Should departments and divisions have the responsibility of making their own information technology decisions, or should IT infrastructure be centrally controlled and managed? What is the relationship between central information systems management and business unit information systems management? How will infrastructure costs be allocated among business units? Each organization will need to arrive at answers based on its own needs.

Making Wise Infrastructure Investments

IT infrastructure is a major investment for the firm. If too much is spent on infrastructure, it lies idle and constitutes a drag on the firm's financial performance. If too little is spent, important business services cannot be delivered and the firm's competitors (who spent the right amount) will outperform the under-investing firm. How much should the firm spend on infrastructure? This question is not easy to answer.

A related question is whether a firm should purchase and maintain its own IT infrastructure components or rent them from external suppliers, including those offering cloud services. The decision either to purchase your own IT assets or rent them from external providers is typically called the *rent-versus-buy* decision.

Cloud computing is a low-cost way to increase scalability and flexibility, but firms should evaluate this option carefully in light of security requirements and impact on business processes and workflows. In some instances, the cost of renting software adds up to more than purchasing and maintaining an application in-house. Yet there are many benefits to using cloud services including significant reductions in hardware, software, human resources, and maintenance costs. Moving to cloud computing allows firms to focus on their core businesses rather than technology issues. As the reliability of cloud computing has improved greatly in the last decade, in 2016 some Fortune 500 firms are planning to move the majority of their computing platforms to cloud services.

Total Cost of Ownership of Technology Assets

The actual cost of owning technology resources includes the original cost of acquiring and installing hardware and software as well as ongoing administration costs for hardware and software upgrades, maintenance, technical support, training, and even utility and real estate costs for running and housing the technology. The **total cost of ownership (TCO)** model can be used to analyze these direct and indirect costs to help firms determine the actual cost of specific technology implementations. Table 5.4 describes the most important TCO components to consider in a TCO analysis.

When all these cost components are considered, the TCO for a PC might run up to three times the original purchase price of the equipment. Gains in productivity and efficiency from equipping employees with mobile computing devices must be balanced against increased costs from integrating these devices into the firm's IT infrastructure and from providing technical support. Other cost components include fees for wireless airtime, end-user training, help desk support, and software for special applications. Costs are higher if the mobile

TABLE 5.4 TOTAL COST OF OWNERSHIP (TCO) COST COMPONENTS

INFRASTRUCTURE COMPONENT	COST COMPONENTS
Hardware acquisition	Purchase price of computer hardware equipment, including computers, terminals, storage, and printers
Software acquisition	Purchase or license of software for each user
Installation	Cost to install computers and software
Training	Cost to provide training for information systems specialists and end users
Support	Cost to provide ongoing technical support, help desks, and so forth
Maintenance	Cost to upgrade the hardware and software
Infrastructure	Cost to acquire, maintain, and support related infrastructure, such as networks and specialized equipment (including storage backup units)
Downtime	Cost of lost productivity if hardware or software failures cause the system to be unavailable for processing and user tasks
Space and energy	Real estate and utility costs for housing and providing power for the technology

devices run many different applications or need to be integrated into back-end systems such as enterprise applications.

Hardware and software acquisition costs account for only about 20 percent of TCO, so managers must pay close attention to administration costs to understand the full cost of the firm's hardware and software. It is possible to reduce some of these administration costs through better management. Many large firms are saddled with redundant, incompatible hardware and software because their departments and divisions have been allowed to make their own technology purchases.

In addition to switching to cloud services, these firms could reduce their TCO through greater centralization and standardization of their hardware and software resources. Companies could reduce the size of the information systems staff required to support their infrastructure if the firm minimizes the number of different computer models and pieces of software that employees are allowed to use. In a centralized infrastructure, systems can be administered from a central location and troubleshooting can be performed from that location.

Competitive Forces Model for IT Infrastructure Investment

Figure 5.13 illustrates a competitive forces model you can use to address the question of how much your firm should spend on IT infrastructure.

Market demand for your firm's services. Make an inventory of the services you currently provide to customers, suppliers, and employees. Survey each group, or hold focus groups to find out if the services you currently offer are meeting the needs of each group. For example, are customers complaining of slow responses to their queries about price and availability? Are employees complaining about the difficulty of finding the right information for their jobs? Are suppliers complaining about the difficulties of discovering your production requirements?

FIGURE 5.13 COMPETITIVE FORCES MODEL FOR IT INFRASTRUCTURE

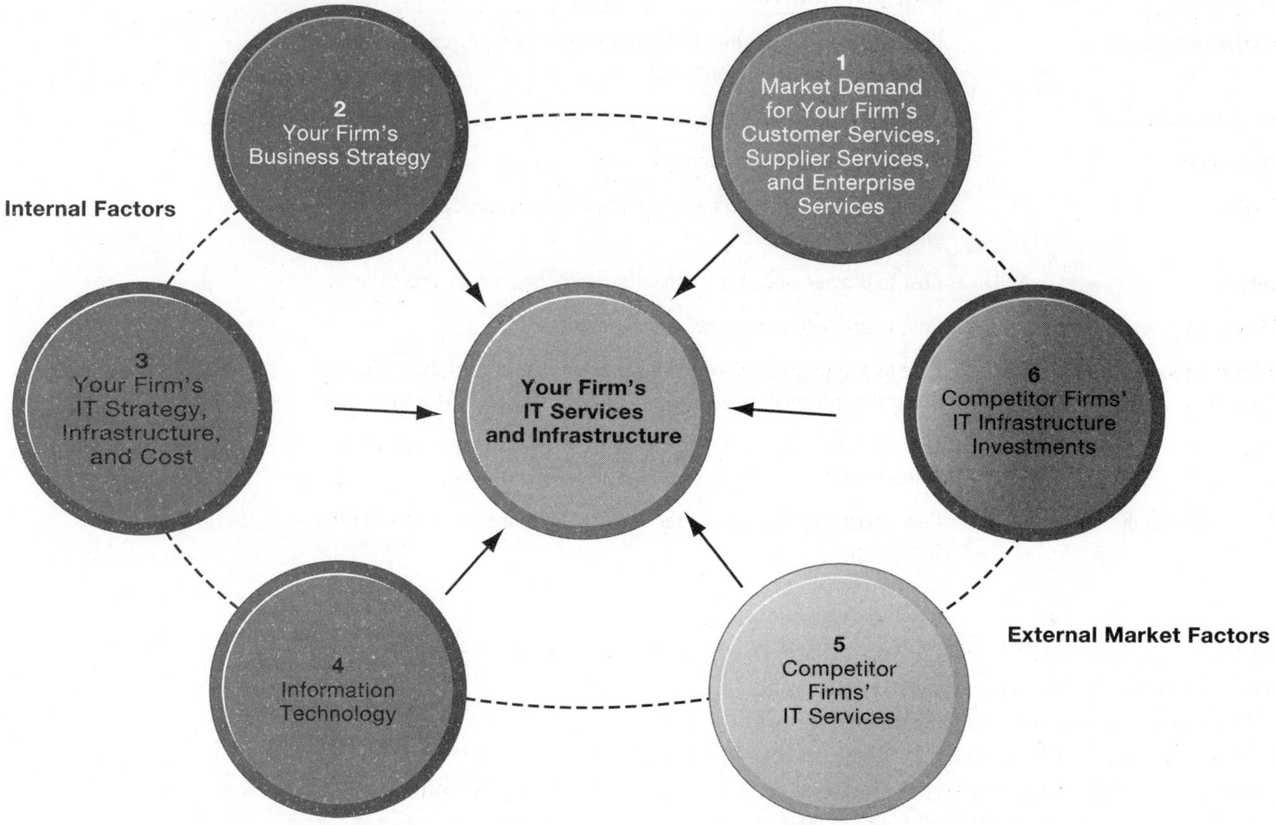

There are six factors you can use to answer the question "How much should our firm spend on IT infrastructure?"

Your firm's business strategy. Analyze your firm's five-year business strategy and try to assess what new services and capabilities will be required to achieve strategic goals.

Your firm's IT strategy, infrastructure, and cost. Examine your firm's information technology plans for the next five years and assess its alignment with the firm's business plans. Determine the total IT infrastructure costs. You will want to perform a TCO analysis. If your firm has no IT strategy, you will need to devise one that takes into account the firm's five-year strategic plan.

Information technology assessment. Is your firm behind the technology curve or at the bleeding edge of information technology? Both situations are to be avoided. It is usually not desirable to spend resources on advanced technologies that are still experimental, often expensive, and sometimes unreliable. You want to spend on technologies for which standards have been established and IT vendors are competing on cost, not design, and where there are multiple suppliers. However, you do not want to put off investment in new technologies or allow competitors to develop new business models and capabilities based on the new technologies.

Competitor firm services. Try to assess what technology services competitors offer to customers, suppliers, and employees. Establish quantitative and qualitative measures to compare them to those of your firm. If your firm's service levels fall short, your company is at a competitive disadvantage. Look for ways your firm can excel at service levels.

Competitor firm IT infrastructure investments. Benchmark your expenditures for IT infrastructure against your competitors. Many companies are quite public about their innovative expenditures on IT. If competing firms try to keep IT expenditures secret, you may be able to find IT investment information in public companies' SEC Form 10-K annual reports to the federal government when those expenditures affect a firm's financial results.

Your firm does not necessarily need to spend as much as or more than your competitors. Perhaps it has discovered much less expensive ways of providing services, and this can lead to a cost advantage. Alternatively, your firm may be spending far less than competitors and experiencing commensurate poor performance and losing market share.

Review Summary

5-1 *What is IT infrastructure, and what are the stages and drivers of IT infrastructure evolution?*

IT infrastructure is the shared technology resources that provide the platform for the firm's specific information system applications. IT infrastructure includes hardware, software, and services that are shared across the entire firm.

The five stages of IT infrastructure evolution are: the mainframe era, the personal computer era, the client/server era, the enterprise computing era, and the cloud and mobile computing era. Moore's Law deals with the exponential increase in processing power and decline in the cost of computer technology, stating that every 18 months the power of microprocessors doubles and the price of computing falls in half. The Law of Mass Digital Storage deals with the exponential decrease in the cost of storing data, stating that the number of kilobytes of data that can be stored on magnetic media for $1 roughly doubles every 15 months. Metcalfe's Law states that a network's value to participants grows exponentially as the network takes on more members. The rapid decline in costs of communication and growing agreement in the technology industry to use computing and communications standards are also driving an explosion of computer use.

5-2 *What are the components of IT infrastructure?*

Major IT infrastructure components include computer hardware platforms, operating system platforms, enterprise software platforms, networking and telecommunications platforms, database management software, Internet platforms, and consulting services and systems integrators.

5-3 *What are the current trends in computer hardware platforms?*

Increasingly, computing is taking place on a mobile digital platform. Quantum computing is an emerging technology that could dramatically boost processing power through the ability to be in more than one state at the same time. Consumerization of IT is the business use of information technology that originated in the consumer market. Virtualization organizes computing resources so that their use is not restricted by physical configuration or geographic location. In cloud computing, firms and individuals obtain computing power and software as services over a network, including the Internet, rather than purchasing and installing the hardware and software on their own computers. A multicore processor is a microprocessor to which two or more processing cores have been attached for enhanced performance. Green computing includes practices and technologies for producing, using, and disposing of information technology hardware to minimize negative impact on the environment.

5-4 *What are the current computer software platforms and trends?*

Open source software is produced and maintained by a global community of programmers and is often downloadable for free. Linux is a powerful, resilient open source operating system that can run on multiple hardware platforms and is used widely to run web servers. Java is an operating system– and hardware-independent programming language that is the leading interactive programming environment for the web. HTML5 makes it possible to embed images, audio, and video directly into a web document without add-on programs. Web services are loosely coupled software components based on open web standards that work with any application software and operating system. They can be used as components of web-based applications linking the systems of two different organizations or to link disparate systems of a single company. Companies are purchasing their new software applications from outside sources, including software packages, by outsourcing custom application development to an external vendor (that may be offshore), or by renting online software services (SaaS). Mashups combine two different software services to create new software applications and services. Apps are software applications that run on mobile devices and are delivered over the Internet.

5-5 *What are the challenges of managing IT infrastructure and management solutions?*

Major challenges include dealing with platform and infrastructure change, infrastructure management and governance, and making wise infrastructure investments. Solution guidelines include using a competitive forces model to determine how much to spend on IT infrastructure and where to make strategic infrastructure investments, and establishing the total cost of ownership (TCO) of information technology assets. The total cost of owning technology resources includes not only the original cost of computer hardware and software but also costs for hardware and software upgrades, maintenance, technical support, and training. Many firms are turning to cloud computing in an effort to reduce their IT platform costs.

Key Terms

Android, 190
Application server, 180
Apps, 208
BYOD, 192
Chrome OS, 190
Clients, 180
Client/server computing, 180
Cloud computing, 181
Consumerization of IT, 192
Extensible Markup Language (XML), 204
Green computing (green IT), 201
HTML (Hypertext Markup Language), 203
HTML5, 204
Hybrid cloud, 200
Hypertext Markup Language (HTML), 203
iOS, 190
Java, 203
Legacy systems, 191
Linux, 189
Mainframe, 179
Mashup, 208
Minicomputers, 179
Moore's Law, 182
Multicore processor, 202
Multitiered (N-tier) client/server architecture, 180
Multitouch, 190
Nanotechnology, 182
On-demand computing, 200
Open source software, 202
Operating system, 189
Outsourcing, 206
Private cloud, 200
Public cloud, 200
Quantum computing, 194
Scalability, 209
Service level agreement (SLA), 208
Server, 180
Service-oriented architecture (SOA), 205
Software as a service (SaaS), 197
Software package, 206
Software-defined storage (SDS), 195
Tablet computers, 192
Technology standards, 185
Total cost of ownership (TCO), 210
Unix, 189
Virtualization, 195
Web browser, 203
Web hosting service, 191
Web server, 180
Web services, 204
Windows, 181
Windows 10, 190
Wintel PC, 179

Review Questions

5-1 What is IT infrastructure, and what are the stages and drivers of IT infrastructure evolution?

- Define IT infrastructure from both a technology and a services perspective.
- List each of the eras in IT infrastructure evolution and describe its distinguishing characteristics.
- Define and describe the following: web server, application server, multitiered client/server architecture.
- Describe Moore's Law and the Law of Mass Digital Storage.
- Describe how network economics, declining communications costs, and technology standards affect IT infrastructure.

5-2 What are the components of IT infrastructure?

- What do you understand by IT infrastructure ecosystem? Why does it need to be maintained?

5-3 What are the current trends in computer hardware platforms?

- List and describe the difference between cloud computing, green computing, and quantum computing.
- List some business applications of mobile digital platforms, BYOD, virtualization, and high speed processors.

5-4 What are the current computer software platforms and trends?

- Define and describe open source software and Linux and explain their business benefits.
- Define Java and HTML5 and explain why they are important.
- Define and describe web services and the role played by XML.
- Name and describe the three external sources for software.
- Define and describe software mashups and apps.

5-5 What are the challenges of managing IT infrastructure and management solutions?

- How does scalability and make-versus-buy dilemma pose a challenge to the management of IT infrastructure? Explain.
- List and describe the factors which can be used by firms to decide on the amount of expenses that can be made on IT infrastructure.

Discussion Questions

5-6 Why is selecting computer hardware and software for the organization an important management decision? What management, organization, and technology issues should be considered when selecting computer hardware and software?

5-7 Why would some organizations choose a private cloud or hybrid cloud over a public cloud?

5-8 What are the advantages and disadvantages of cloud computing?

Hands-On MIS Projects

The projects in this section give you hands-on experience in developing solutions for managing IT infrastructures and IT outsourcing, using spreadsheet software to evaluate alternative desktop systems, and using web research to budget for a sales conference.

Management Decision Problems

5-9 Hischornklinik Group is a leading private medical clinic group in Germany. It relies on information systems to operate 14 hospitals, as well as hundreds of specialist institutes. Demand for additional servers and storage technology is growing by 20 percent each year. Hischornklinik was setting up a separate server for every application, and its servers and other computers were running a number of different operating systems, including several versions of UNIX and Windows. Hischornklinik had to manage technologies from many different vendors, including Hewlett-Packard (HP), Sun Microsystems, Microsoft, and IBM. Assess the impact of this situation on business performance. What factors and management decisions must be considered when developing a solution to this problem?

5-10 Qantas Airways, Australia's leading airline, faces cost pressures from high fuel prices and lower levels of global airline traffic. To remain competitive, the airline must find ways to keep costs low while providing a high level of customer service. Qantas had a 30-year-old data center. Management had to decide whether to replace its IT infrastructure with newer technology or outsource it. What factors should be considered by Qantas management when deciding whether to outsource? If Qantas decides to outsource, list and describe points that should be addressed in a service level agreement.

Improving Decision Making: Using Web Research to Budget for a Sales Conference

Software skills: Internet-based software
Business skills: Researching transportation and lodging costs

5-11 The Foremost Composite Materials Company is planning a two-day sales conference for October 19–20, starting with a reception on the evening of October 18. The conference consists of all-day meetings that the entire sales force, numbering 120 sales representatives and their 16 managers, must attend. Each sales representative requires his or her own room, and the company needs two common meeting rooms, one large enough to hold the entire sales force plus a few visitors (200) and the other able to hold half the force. Management has set a budget of $175,000 for the representatives' room rentals. The company would like to hold the conference in either Miami or Marco Island, Florida, at a Hilton- or Marriott-owned hotel.

Use the Hilton and Marriott websites to select a hotel in whichever of these cities that would enable the company to hold its sales conference within its budget and meet its sales conference requirements. Then locate flights arriving the afternoon prior to the conference. Your attendees will be coming from Los Angeles (51), San Francisco (30), Seattle (22), Chicago (19), and Pittsburgh (14). Determine costs of each airline ticket from these cities. When you are finished, create a budget for the conference. The budget will include the cost of each airline ticket, the room cost, and $70 per attendee per day for food.

Collaboration and Teamwork Project

Evaluating Server and Mobile Operating Systems

5-12 Form a group with three or four of your classmates. Choose server or mobile operating systems to evaluate. You might research and compare the capabilities and costs of Linux versus UNIX or the most recent version of the Windows operating system for servers. Alternatively, you could compare the capabilities of the Android mobile operating system with iOS for the iPhone. If possible, use Google Docs and Google Drive or Google Sites to brainstorm, organize, and develop a presentation of your findings for the class.

BYOD: Business Opportunity or Big Headache?

CASE STUDY

Just about everyone who has a smartphone wants to be able to bring it to work and use it on the job. And why not? Employees using their own smartphones would allow companies to enjoy all the same benefits of a mobile workforce without spending their own money to purchase these devices. Smaller companies are able to go mobile without making large investments in devices and mobile services. According to Gartner, Inc., by 2017, 50 percent of employers will require employees to supply their own mobile devices for the workplace. BYOD is becoming the "new normal."

But ... wait a minute. Half of all enterprises believe that BYOD represents a growing problem for their organizations, according to a number of studies. Although BYOD can improve employee job satisfaction and productivity, it also can cause a number of problems if not managed properly. Support for personally owned devices is more difficult than it is for company-supplied devices, the cost of managing mobile devices can increase, and protecting corporate data and networks becomes more difficult. Research conducted by the Aberdeen Group found that on average, an enterprise with 1,000 mobile devices spends an extra $170,000 per year when it allows BYOD. So it's not that simple.

BYOD requires a significant portion of corporate IT resources dedicated to managing and maintaining a large number of devices within the organization. In the past, companies tried to limit business smartphone use to a single platform. This made it easier to keep track of each mobile device and to roll out software upgrades or fixes because all employees were using the same devices or, at the very least, the same operating system. Today, the mobile digital landscape is much more complicated, with a variety of devices and operating systems on the market that do not have well-developed tools for administration and security. Android has 80 percent of the worldwide smartphone market, but it is more difficult to use for corporate work than Apple mobile devices using the iOS operating system. IOS is considered a closed system and runs only on a limited number of different Apple mobile devices. In contrast, Android's fragmentation makes it more difficult and costly for corporate IT to manage. There are about 25,000 different models of Android-based devices available around the world, according to a report by OpenSignal, which researches wireless networks and devices. Android's huge consumer market share attracts many hackers. Android is also vulnerable because it has an open source architecture and comes in multiple versions.

If employees are allowed to work with more than one type of mobile device and operating system, companies need an effective way to keep track of all the devices employees are using. To access company information, the company's networks must be configured to receive connections from that device. When employees make changes to their personal phone, such as switching cellular carriers, changing their phone number, or buying a new mobile device altogether, companies will need to quickly and flexibly ensure that their employees are still able to remain productive. Firms need a system that keeps track of which devices employees are using, where the device is located, whether it is being used, and what software it is equipped with. For unprepared companies, keeping track of who gets access to what data could be a nightmare.

With the large variety of phones and operating systems available, providing adequate technical support for every employee could be difficult. When employees are not able to access critical data or encounter other problems with their mobile devices, they will need assistance from the information systems department. Companies that rely on desktop computers tend to have many of the same computers with the same specs and operating systems, making tech support that much easier. Mobility introduces a new layer of variety and complexity to tech support that companies need to be prepared to handle.

There are significant concerns with securing company information accessed with mobile devices. If a device is stolen or compromised, companies need ways to ensure that sensitive or confidential information isn't freely available to anyone. Mobility puts assets and data at greater risk than if they were only located within company walls and on company machines. Marble Security Labs analyzed 1.2 million Android and iOS apps and found that the consumer apps on mobile devices did not adequately protect business information. Companies often use technologies that allow them to wipe data from devices remotely or encrypt data so that if the device is stolen, it cannot be used. You'll find a detailed discussion of mobile security issues in Chapter 8.

Management at Michelin North America believes BYOD will make the business more flexible and productive. Initially, all 4,000 mobile devices used by the company were company-owned and obsolete, with a large number of traditional cell phones that could only be used for voice transmission and messaging. Only 90 employees were allowed access to e-mail on mobile devices, and fewer than 400 were allowed access to calendars on these devices. Service costs were high, and the business received little value from its mobility program. Management had identified significant business benefits from increasing mobility in sales, customer support, and operations.

In mid-2011, the company created a team composed of executives and representatives from the IT, human resources, finance, and legal departments as well as the business units to share in the development, rollout, and management of a new mobile strategy for corporate-owned and personal mobile devices. The team decided to transition the mobility business model from corporate-owned to personal-liable.

According to Gartner, Inc. consultants, about half of organizations with a formal BYOD program compensate their employees for the amount of time they use their personal devices on their jobs using stipends, reimbursements, or allowances. Handling employee reimbursement for using personal devices for corporate purposes has proved to be one of the most problematic aspects of BYOD mobile programs. Although most companies use expense reports or payroll stipends to reimburse employees for BYOD, these methods have drawbacks. Expense reports are an administrative burden for both the employee and the employer, and payroll stipends can have tax consequences for both as well.

For some companies, the best option is to make direct payments to wireless carriers to reimburse employees for the expense they incur when they use their own wireless devices for company business. The employer provides funds to the wireless carrier, which then applies a credit to the employee's account. When the employee's bill arrives, the employee pays the amount owed less the credit amount that was funded by the employer.

Michelin opted for a managed service from Cass Information Systems that enables the company to make payments directly to wireless carriers. Cass Information Systems is a leading provider of transportation, utility, waste, and telecom expense management and related business intelligence services. A single employee portal handles enrollment of corporate and BYOD devices and provides tracking and reporting of all ongoing mobile and related inventory and expenses. The portal can automatically register employees, verify user eligibility, ensure policy acknowledgment, and distribute credits directly to employees' wireless accounts for the amount of service they used for their jobs.

Since implementing its version of BYOD, Michelin North America increased the number of mobile-enabled employees to 7,000. Employee efficiency, productivity, and satisfaction have improved from updating the mobile technology and functionality available to employees and giving them choices in mobile devices and wireless carrier plans, The program is cost-neutral. Michelin has obtained new vendor discounts across all wireless vendors in the United States and Canada and has reduced the cost of deploying each mobile device by more than 30 percent.

Iftekhar Khan, IT director at Toronto's Chelsea Hotel, remains less sanguine. He believes BYOD might work for his company down the road but not in the immediate future. Khan notes that the hospitality industry and many others still want employees to use corporate-owned devices for any laptop, tablet, or smartphone requiring access to the corporate network. His business has sensitive information and needs that level of control. Although the hotel might possibly save money with BYOD, it's ultimately all about productivity.

Management at Rosendin Electric, a Silicon Valley electrical contractor, worried that BYOD would become a big headache. Rosendin has thousands of employees and deploys hundreds of smartphones, more than 400 iPads, and a few Microsoft Surface tablets. These mobile devices have greatly enhanced the company's productivity by enabling employees to order equipment and supplies on the spot at a job site or check on-site to see whether ordered items have arrived. However, CIO Sam Lamonica does not believe BYOD would work for this company. He worries employees would be too careless using apps, cloud, and technology devices. (An Aruba Networks study of 11,500 workers in 23 countries found that 60 percent share their work and personal devices with others regularly, nearly 20 percent don't have passwords on devices, and 31 percent have lost data due to misuse of a mobile device.)

Lamonica feels more confident about equipping employees with company-owned devices because they can be more easily managed and secured. Rosendin uses MobileIron mobile device management (MDM) software for its smartphones and tablets. If a device is lost or stolen, the MDM software is able to wipe the devices remotely. Because MobileIron allows Rosendin to separate and isolate business apps and data from personal apps and data, the company allows employees to use certain consumer apps and store personal photos on company-owned tablets. Rosendin has found that employees of companies that are able to personalize company-owned iPads are more likely to treat them as prized possessions, and this has helped lower the number of devices that become broken or lost. The company has the right to wipe the devices if they are lost.

Rosendin's mobile security is not iron-clad. An employee might be able to put company data in his or her personal Dropbox account instead of the company-authorized Box account. However, MobileIron is able to encrypt data before it gets into a Dropbox account, and this lowers the risk. With company-owned and managed devices, Rosendin still benefits from volume discounts from wireless carriers and does not have to do the extra work involved in reimbursing employees when they use their own devices for work.

Sources: Ryan Patrick, "Is a BYOD Strategy Best for Business?" IT World Canada, March 22, 2016; "5 BYOD Management Case Studies," Sunviewsoftware.com, accessed May 5, 2016; Aruba Networks, "Enterprise Security Threat Level Directly Linked to User Demographics, Industry and Geography," *Business Wire,* April 14, 2015; Alan F., "Open Signal: 24,093 Unique and Different Android-Powered Devices Are Available," Phonearena.com, August 5, 2015; Tom Kaneshige, "Why One CIO Is Saying 'No' to BYOD," *CIO,* June 24, 2014; "CIO Meets Mobile Challenges Head-On," *CIO,* July 7, 2014; and "Cass BYOD: How Michelin Became a Mobile-First Enterprise," Cass Information Systems Inc., 2014.

CASE STUDY QUESTIONS

5-13 What are the advantages and disadvantages of allowing employees to use their personal smartphones for work?

5-14 What management, organization, and technology factors should be addressed when deciding whether to allow employees to use their personal smartphones for work?

5-15 Compare the BYOD experiences of Michelin North America and Rosendin Electric. Why did BYOD at Michelin work so well?

5-16 Allowing employees to use their own smartphones for work will save the company money. Do you agree? Why or why not?

Chapter 5 References

Andersson, Henrik, James Kaplan, and Brent Smolinski. "Capturing Value from IT Infrastructure Innovation." *McKinsey Quarterly* (October 2012).

Babcock, Charles. "Cloud's Thorniest Question: Does It Pay Off?" *Information Week* (June 4, 2012).

Benlian, Alexander, Marios Koufaris, and Thomas Hess. "Service Quality in Software-as-a-Service: Developing the SaaS-Qual Measure and Examining Its Role in Usage Continuance." *Journal of Management Information Systems* 28, No. 3 (Winter 2012).

Carr, Nicholas. *The Big Switch.* New York: Norton (2008).

Clark, Don. "Moore's Law Shows Its Age.." *Wall Street Journal* (April 17, 2015).

Choi, Jae, Derek L. Nazareth, and Hemant K. Jain. "Implementing Service-Oriented Architecture in Organizations." *Journal of Management Information Systems* 26, No. 4 (Spring 2010).

David, Julie Smith, David Schuff, and Robert St. Louis. "Managing Your IT Total Cost of Ownership." *Communications of the ACM* 45, No. 1 (January 2002).

Fitzgerald, Brian. "The Transformation of Open Source Software." *MIS Quarterly* 30, No. 3 (September 2006).

Flinders, Karl. "Ofcom Outsources IT Management to Indian Xervices Supplier NIIT." *Computer Weekly* (January 12, 2016).

Follow, Jaewon Kang. "IBM Bets on Next-Gen Technologies as It Tries to Stave Off Rivals." TheStreet.com (May 5, 2016).

Gantz, John and David Reinsal. "Extracting Value from Chaos." IDC (June 2011).

Gartner, Inc. "Gartner Says Worldwide IT Spending Is Forecast to Decline 0.5 Percent in 2016." *Business Wire* (April 7, 2016).

"How to Tap the Power of the Mainframe." ITBusinessEdge.com, accessed September 11, 2015.

International Data Corporation. "Worldwide Public Cloud Services Spending Forecast to Double by 2019, According to IDC." (January 21, 2016).

"Internet Users." Internetlivestats.com, accessed May 2, 2016.

Kauffman, Robert J. and Julianna Tsai. "The Unified Procurement Strategy for Enterprise Software: A Test of the 'Move to the Middle' Hypothesis." *Journal of Management Information Systems* 26, No. 2 (Fall 2009).

Letschin, Michael. "Six Trends that Will Change How You Think About Data Storage." *Information Management* (February 8, 2016).

Lyman, Peter and Hal R. Varian. "How Much Information 2003?" University of California at Berkeley School of Information Management and Systems (2003).

Markoff, John. "Moore's Law Running Out of Room, Tech Looks for a Successor," *New York Times* (May 4, 2016).

McCafferty, Dennis. "Eight Interesting Facts About Java." *CIO Insight* (June 16, 2014).

Mell, Peter and Tim Grance. "The NIST Definition of Cloud Computing" Version 15. NIST (October 17, 2009).

Moore, Gordon. "Cramming More Components Onto Integrated Circuits," *Electronics* 38, No. 8 (April 19, 1965).

Mueller, Benjamin, Goetz Viering, Christine Legner, and Gerold Riempp. "Understanding the Economic Potential of Service-Oriented Architecture." *Journal of Management Information Systems* 26, No. 4 (Spring 2010).

Netmarketshare. "Desktop Operating System Market Share April 2016." www.netmarketshare.com, accessed May 1, 2016.

Ray, Tierman. "Watch Out Intel, Here Comes Facebook." *Barrons* (October 31, 2015).

Schuff, David and Robert St. Louis. "Centralization vs. Decentralization of Application Software." *Communications of the ACM* 44, No. 6 (June 2001).

Stango, Victor. "The Economics of Standards Wars." *Review of Network Economics* 3, Issue 1 (March 2004).

Susarla, Anjana, Anitesh Barua, and Andrew B. Whinston. "A Transaction Cost Perspective of the 'Software as a Service' Business Model." *Journal of Management Information Systems* 26, No. 2 (Fall 2009).

Taft, Darryl K. "Application Development: Java Death Debunked: 10 Reasons Why It's Still Hot." *eWeek* (February 22, 2012).

Torode, Christine, Linda Tucci, and Karen Goulart. "Managing the Next-Generation Data Center." *Modern Infrastructure CIO Edition* (January 2013).

Weill, Peter and Marianne Broadbent. *Leveraging the New Infrastructure.* Cambridge, MA: Harvard Business School Press (1998).

Weitzel, Tim. *Economics of Standards in Information Networks.* Heidelberg, New York: Physica-Verlag (2004).

CHAPTER

6 Foundations of Business Intelligence: Databases and Information Management

Learning Objectives

After reading this chapter, you will be able to answer the following questions:

6-1 What are the problems of managing data resources in a traditional file environment?

6-2 What are the major capabilities of database management systems (DBMS), and why is a relational DBMS so powerful?

6-3 What are the principal tools and technologies for accessing information from databases to improve business performance and decision making?

6-4 Why are information policy, data administration, and data quality assurance essential for managing the firm's data resources?

CHAPTER CASES

BAE Systems
The Gym Database
Societe Generale Builds an Intelligent System to Manage Information Flow
Lego's Enterprise Software Spurs Growth

BAE Systems

BAE Systems (BAE) is the United Kingdom's largest manufacturing company and one of the largest commercial aerospace and defence organizations in Europe. Its high-technology, information-driven products and services range from one of the world's most capable multi-role combat fighters, the Eurofighter Typhoon, to the Jetstream family of commercial aircraft, to the provision of information technology (IT) and information systems (IS) for e-business to develop and implement logistics, IT, and e-capability services. With sales, manufacturing, and support sites throughout the world, including the United Kingdom, Europe, the United States, and Australia, BAE employs 83,000 people in 40 countries and generated more than €23.8 billion in annual revenue in 2015.

© Graham Taylor/Shutterstock

Although BAE has consolidated its competitive position in established markets, and continues to expand into new markets in the Middle East and Asia, its performance in the aircraft part of the business was being impeded by legacy information systems that support the computer-aided design (CAD) and computer-aided manufacturing (CAM) of its aircraft. The distributed nature of BAE's design and manufacturing sites meant that storing and analyzing accurate sets of operational data describing the complex components of the various aircraft types to produce aircraft assembly reports for the production lines became increasingly challenging and resource-consuming.

Accessing the data from the many systems was a complex task involving many technical challenges. As the aircraft business of BAE grew, so did the likelihood of delays in producing the aircraft assembly reports and other operations data sets necessary for aircraft production management decision-making. In the worst case, the production of aircraft on the assembly line would stop until accurate information was available, with consequent schedule and cost implications. BAE's CAD/CAM staff were storing and analyzing data sets sourced from five major aircraft design and manufacturing sites spread throughout the United Kingdom, each host to thousands of staff involved in the design and manufacturing process, so that assembly reports and other operations data could be produced. There were numerous occasions when paper drawings with annotations containing component design and manufacturing information were used to reconcile ambiguities and inconsistencies in the assembly reports. These data ambiguities and inconsistencies gave rise to a sense of uncertainty in the assembly reports produced.

What BAE needed was a single repository for CAD/CAM data that would also facilitate the integration of data held in its legacy systems. The company decided to replace its legacy systems with an enterprise-wide knowledge management system that would bring the design and manufacturing data into a single database that could be concurrently accessed by the design and manufacturing engineers. BAE implemented Siemens' Teamcenter product lifecycle management software and Dassault Systemes' CATIA CAD/CAM software. Teamcenter can also be configured to take advantage of recent developments in cloud computing using Microsoft's Azure, IBM's SmartCloud Enterprise+, and Amazon Web Services.

Bringing together Siemens' Teamcenter and Dassault Systemes' CATIA has given BAE Systems powerful integrated data management tools. The Teamcenter database includes tools for component markup and rollup capabilities, allowing users to visualize the effect of component design changes and configuration selections in real-time.

The new solution has produced significant cost savings at BAE in terms of its design and manufacturing data management and storage while boosting performance. With fewer legacy systems and data files to manage, BAE has been able to meet quality, time, and cost requirements by being able to produce complete and accurate aircraft component definitions and configurations. BAE has used Teamcenter to enlarge its business model to include "through-life" maintenance and repair for aircraft.

Sources: "BAE Systems Annual Report 2015," baesystems.com, March 25, 2016; "BAE Systems Military Air Solutions: Case Study: Teamcenter Supports Aircraft Through 50-year Lifecycle," 2015 Siemens Product Lifecycle Management Software Inc., 2015; "CMI-CATIA Teamcenter Integration," T-Systems, April 13, 2015, https://servicenet.t-systems.de; "BAE Systems Half-Yearly Report and Presentation 2015," www.baesystems.com, accessed December 21, 2015; "Teamcenter Supports Aircraft Through 50-year Cycle: BAE Systems Military Air Solutions," www.plm.automation.siemens.com, accessed November 8, 2012.

The experience of BAE Systems illustrates the importance of data management. Business performance depends on the accuracy and reliability of its data. The company has grown its business, but both operational CAD/CAM efficiency and production management decision making were impeded by data stored in legacy systems that were difficult to access. How businesses store, organize, and manage their data has a huge impact on organizational effectiveness.

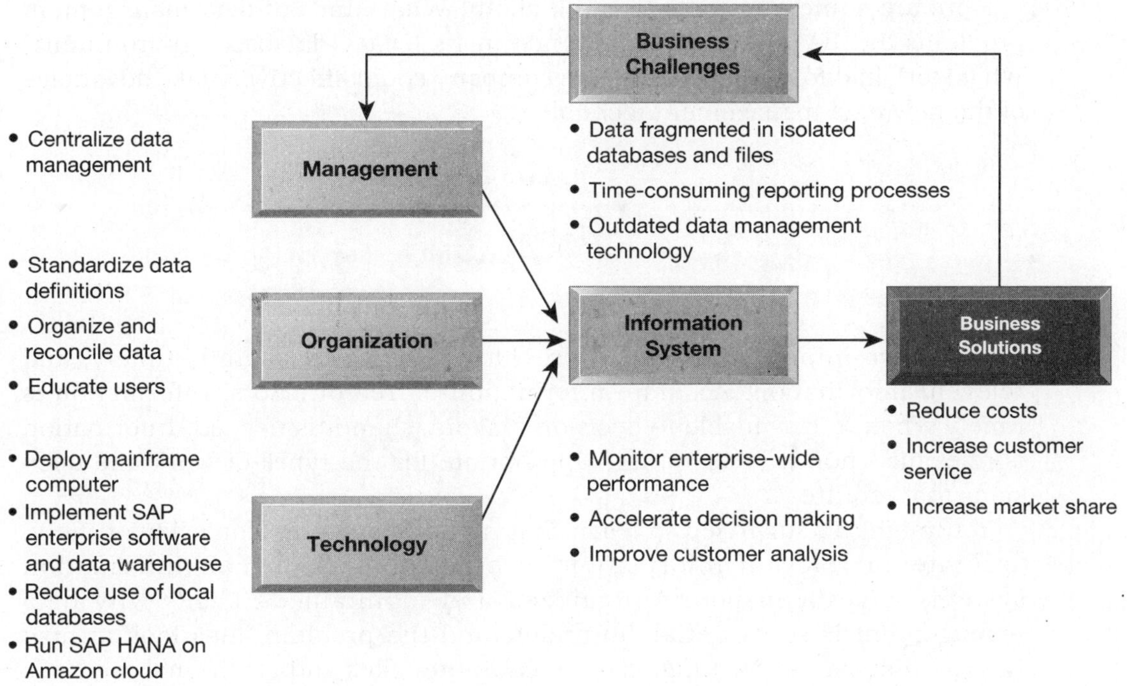

The chapter-opening diagram calls attention to important points raised by this case and this chapter. BAE Systems management decided that the firm needed to improve the management of its data. Pieces of data about design components, manufactured components, and their final assembly had been stored in many large legacy systems that made it extremely difficult for the data to be retrieved and correctly unified so that it could be used in the production line assembly of aircraft components. The data were often redundant and inconsistent, limiting their usefulness. Management was unable to obtain an enterprise-view of the company.

In the past, BAE Systems had used manual paper processes to reconcile its inconsistent and redundant data and to assemble data for management reporting. This solution was extremely time-consuming and costly, and prevented the company's information technology department from performing higher-value work. A more appropriate solution was to install new hardware and software to create an enterprise-wide repository for business information that would support a more streamlined set of business applications. The new software included enterprise software that was integrated with an up-to-date database management system that could supply data for enterprise-wide reporting. The company had to reorganize its data into a standard company-wide format, eliminate redundancies, and establish rules, responsibilities, and procedures for updating and using the data.

A state-of-the-art database management system suite of software helps BAE Systems boost efficiency by making it easier to locate and assemble data for management reporting and for processing day-to-day CAD/CAM transactions for final aircraft component assembly. The data are more accurate and reliable, and costs for managing and storing the data have been considerably reduced.

Here are some questions to think about: What kinds of data management problems did BAE Systems experience in its legacy database environment? What work had to be done before the company could effectively take advantage of the new data management technology?

6-1 What are the problems of managing data resources in a traditional file environment?

An effective information system provides users with accurate, timely, and relevant information. Accurate information is free of errors. Information is timely when it is available to decision makers when it is needed. Information is relevant when it is useful and appropriate for the types of work and decisions that require it.

You might be surprised to learn that many businesses don't have timely, accurate, or relevant information because the data in their information systems have been poorly organized and maintained. That's why data management is so essential. To understand the problem, let's look at how information systems arrange data in computer files and traditional methods of file management.

File Organization Terms and Concepts

A computer system organizes data in a hierarchy that starts with bits and bytes and progresses to fields, records, files, and databases (see Figure 6.1). A **bit** represents the smallest unit of data a computer can handle. A group of bits, called a **byte**, represents a single character, which can be a letter, a number, or another symbol. A grouping of characters into a word, a group of words, or a complete number (such as a person's name or age) is called a **field**. A group of related fields, such as the student's name, the course taken, the date, and the grade, comprises a **record**; a group of records of the same type is called a **file**.

For example, the records in Figure 6.1 could constitute a student course file. A group of related files makes up a database. The student course file illustrated in Figure 6.1 could be grouped with files on students' personal histories and financial backgrounds to create a student database.

A record describes an entity. An **entity** is a person, place, thing, or event on which we store and maintain information. Each characteristic or quality describing a particular entity is called an **attribute**. For example, Student_ID, Course, Date, and Grade are attributes of the entity COURSE. The specific values that these attributes can have are found in the fields of the record describing the entity COURSE.

Problems with the Traditional File Environment

In most organizations, systems tended to grow independently without a companywide plan. Accounting, finance, manufacturing, human resources, and

FIGURE 6.1 THE DATA HIERARCHY

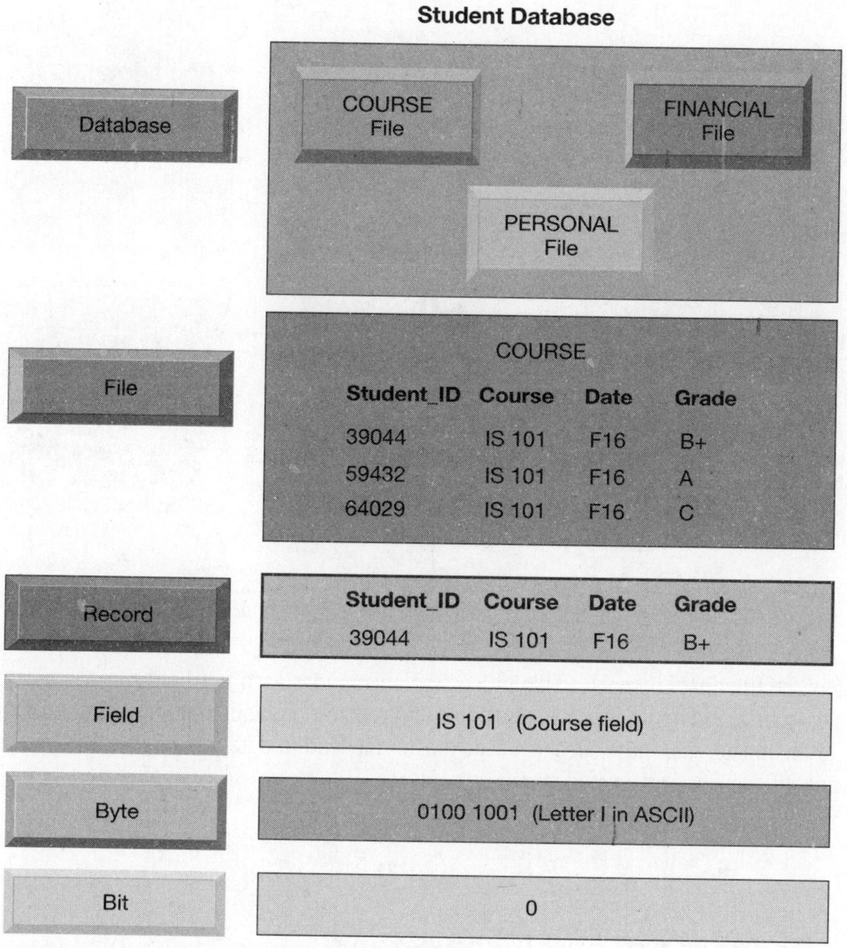

A computer system organizes data in a hierarchy that starts with the bit, which represents either a 0 or a 1. Bits can be grouped to form a byte to represent one character, number, or symbol. Bytes can be grouped to form a field, and related fields can be grouped to form a record. Related records can be collected to form a file, and related files can be organized into a database.

sales and marketing all developed their own systems and data files. Figure 6.2 illustrates the traditional approach to information processing.

Each application, of course, required its own files and its own computer program to operate. For example, the human resources functional area might have a personnel master file, a payroll file, a medical insurance file, a pension file, a mailing list file, and so forth, until tens, perhaps hundreds, of files and programs existed. In the company as a whole, this process led to multiple master files created, maintained, and operated by separate divisions or departments. As this process goes on for 5 or 10 years, the organization is saddled with hundreds of programs and applications that are very difficult to maintain and manage. The resulting problems are data redundancy and inconsistency, program-data dependence, inflexibility, poor data security, and an inability to share data among applications.

FIGURE 6.2 TRADITIONAL FILE PROCESSING

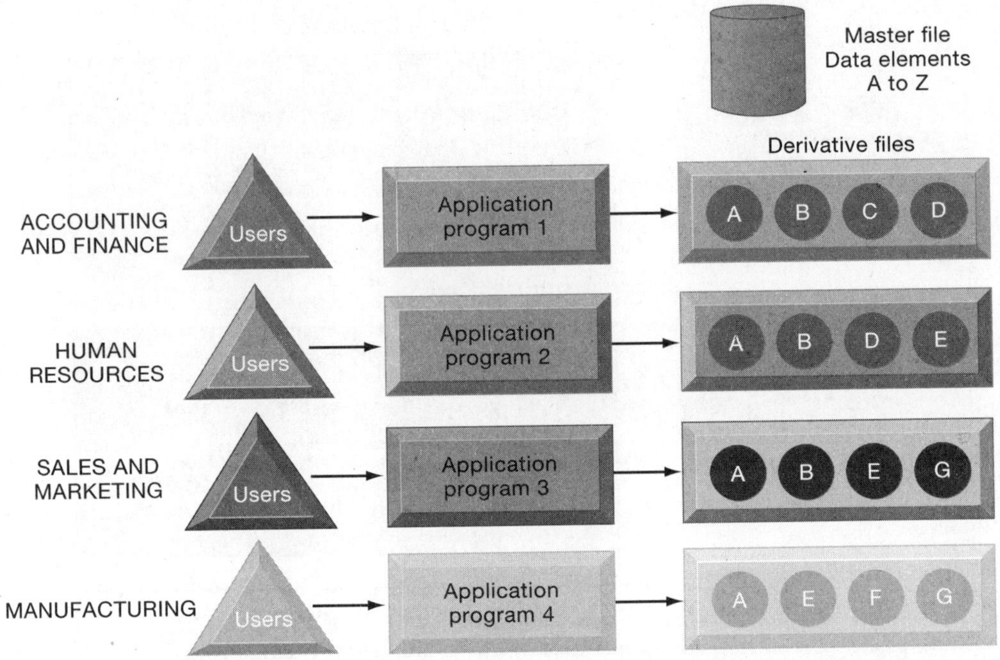

The use of a traditional approach to file processing encourages each functional area in a corporation to develop specialized applications. Each application requires a unique data file that is likely to be a subset of the master file. These subsets of the master file lead to data redundancy and inconsistency, processing inflexibility, and wasted storage resources.

Data Redundancy and Inconsistency

Data redundancy is the presence of duplicate data in multiple data files so that the same data are stored in more than one place or location. Data redundancy occurs when different groups in an organization independently collect the same piece of data and store it independently of each other. Data redundancy wastes storage resources and also leads to **data inconsistency**, where the same attribute may have different values. For example, in instances of the entity COURSE illustrated in Figure 6.1, the Date may be updated in some systems but not in others. The same attribute, Student_ID, may also have different names in different systems throughout the organization. Some systems might use Student_ID and others might use ID, for example.

Additional confusion might result from using different coding systems to represent values for an attribute. For instance, the sales, inventory, and manufacturing systems of a clothing retailer might use different codes to represent clothing size. One system might represent clothing size as "extra large," whereas another might use the code "XL" for the same purpose. The resulting confusion would make it difficult for companies to create customer relationship management, supply chain management, or enterprise systems that integrate data from different sources.

Program-Data Dependence

Program-data dependence refers to the coupling of data stored in files and the specific programs required to update and maintain those files such that changes in programs require changes to the data. Every traditional computer program has to describe the location and nature of the data with which it works. In a traditional file environment, any change in a software program could require a change in the data accessed by that program. One program might be modified from a five-digit to a nine-digit ZIP code. If the original data file were changed from five-digit to nine-digit ZIP codes, then other programs that required the five-digit ZIP code would no longer work properly. Such changes could cost millions of dollars to implement properly.

Lack of Flexibility

A traditional file system can deliver routine scheduled reports after extensive programming efforts, but it cannot deliver ad hoc reports or respond to unanticipated information requirements in a timely fashion. The information required by ad hoc requests is somewhere in the system but may be too expensive to retrieve. Several programmers might have to work for weeks to put together the required data items in a new file.

Poor Security

Because there is little control or management of data, access to and dissemination of information may be out of control. Management may have no way of knowing who is accessing or even making changes to the organization's data.

Lack of Data Sharing and Availability

Because pieces of information in different files and different parts of the organization cannot be related to one another, it is virtually impossible for information to be shared or accessed in a timely manner. Information cannot flow freely across different functional areas or different parts of the organization. If users find different values of the same piece of information in two different systems, they may not want to use these systems because they cannot trust the accuracy of their data.

6-2 What are the major capabilities of database management systems (DBMS), and why is a relational DBMS so powerful?

Database technology cuts through many of the problems of traditional file organization. A more rigorous definition of a **database** is a collection of data organized to serve many applications efficiently by centralizing the data and controlling redundant data. Rather than storing data in separate files for each application, data appear to users as being stored in only one location. A single database services multiple applications. For example, instead of a corporation storing employee data in separate information systems and separate files for personnel, payroll, and benefits, the corporation could create a single common human resources database.

Database Management Systems

A **database management system (DBMS)** is software that permits an organization to centralize data, manage them efficiently, and provide access to the stored data by application programs. The DBMS acts as an interface between application programs and the physical data files. When the application program calls for a data item, such as gross pay, the DBMS finds this item in the database and presents it to the application program. Using traditional data files, the programmer would have to specify the size and format of each data element used in the program and then tell the computer where they were located.

The DBMS relieves the programmer or end user from the task of understanding where and how the data are actually stored by separating the logical and physical views of the data. The *logical view* presents data as they would be perceived by end users or business specialists, whereas the *physical view* shows how data are actually organized and structured on physical storage media.

The database management software makes the physical database available for different logical views required by users. For example, for the human resources database illustrated in Figure 6.3, a benefits specialist might require a view consisting of the employee's name, social security number, and health insurance coverage. A payroll department member might need data such as the employee's name, social security number, gross pay, and net pay. The data for all these views are stored in a single database, where they can be more easily managed by the organization.

FIGURE 6.3 HUMAN RESOURCES DATABASE WITH MULTIPLE VIEWS

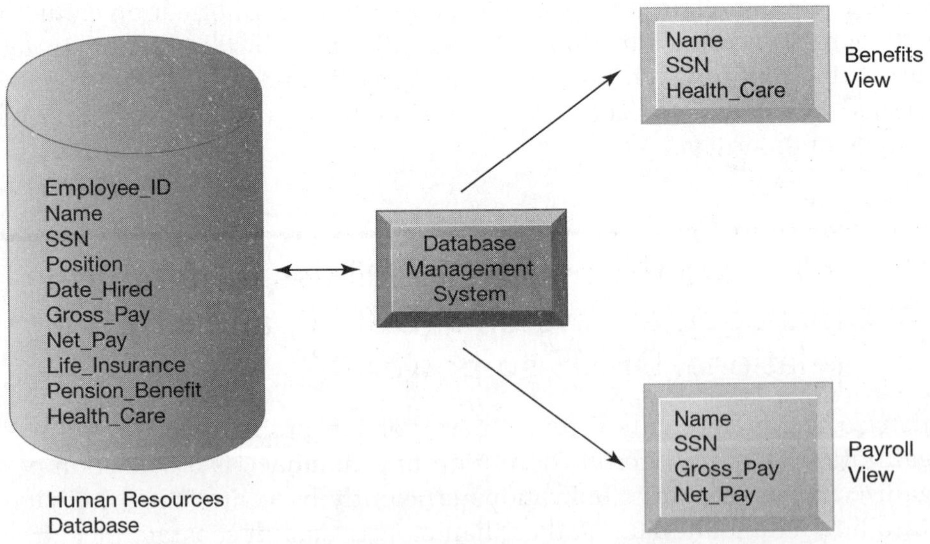

A single human resources database provides many different views of data, depending on the information requirements of the user. Illustrated here are two possible views, one of interest to a benefits specialist and one of interest to a member of the company's payroll department.

How a DBMS Solves the Problems of the Traditional File Environment

A DBMS reduces data redundancy and inconsistency by minimizing isolated files in which the same data are repeated. The DBMS may not enable the organization to eliminate data redundancy entirely, but it can help control redundancy. Even if the organization maintains some redundant data, using a DBMS eliminates data inconsistency because the DBMS can help the organization ensure that every occurrence of redundant data has the same values. The DBMS uncouples programs and data, enabling data to stand on their own. The description of the data used by the program does not have to be specified in detail each time a different program is written. Access and availability of information will be increased and program development and maintenance costs reduced because users and programmers can perform ad hoc queries of the database for many simple applications without having to write complicated programs. The DBMS enables the organization to centrally manage data, their use, and security. Data sharing throughout the organization is easier because the data are presented to users as being in a single location rather than fragmented in many different systems and files.

Relational DBMS

Contemporary DBMS use different database models to keep track of entities, attributes, and relationships. The most popular type of DBMS today for PCs as well as for larger computers and mainframes is the **relational DBMS**. Relational databases represent data as two-dimensional tables (called relations). Tables may be referred to as files. Each table contains data on an entity and its attributes. Microsoft Access is a relational DBMS for desktop systems, whereas DB2, Oracle Database, and Microsoft SQL Server are relational DBMS for large mainframes and midrange computers. MySQL is a popular open source DBMS.

Let's look at how a relational database organizes data about suppliers and parts (see Figure 6.4). The database has a separate table for the entity SUPPLIER and a table for the entity PART. Each table consists of a grid of columns and rows of data. Each individual element of data for each entity is stored as a separate field, and each field represents an attribute for that entity. Fields in a relational database are also called columns. For the entity SUPPLIER, the supplier identification number, name, street, city, state, and ZIP code are stored as separate fields within the SUPPLIER table and each field represents an attribute for the entity SUPPLIER.

The actual information about a single supplier that resides in a table is called a row. Rows are commonly referred to as records, or in very technical terms, as **tuples**. Data for the entity PART have their own separate table.

The field for Supplier_Number in the SUPPLIER table uniquely identifies each record so that the record can be retrieved, updated, or sorted. It is called a **key field**. Each table in a relational database has one field that is designated as its **primary key**. This key field is the unique identifier for all the information in any row of the table and this primary key cannot be duplicated. Supplier_Number is the primary key for the SUPPLIER table and Part_Number is the primary key for the PART table. Note that Supplier_Number appears in both the SUPPLIER and PART tables. In the SUPPLIER table, Supplier_Number is the primary key. When

FIGURE 6.4 RELATIONAL DATABASE TABLES

SUPPLIER

Columns (Attributes, Fields)

Supplier_Number	Supplier_Name	Supplier_Street	Supplier_City	Supplier_State	Supplier_Zip
8259	CBM Inc.	74 5th Avenue	Dayton	OH	45220
8261	B. R. Molds	1277 Gandolly Street	Cleveland	OH	49345
8263	Jackson Composites	8233 Micklin Street	Lexington	KY	56723
8444	Bryant Corporation	4315 Mill Drive	Rochester	NY	11344

Rows (Records, Tuples)

Key Field (Primary Key)

PART

Part_Number	Part_Name	Unit_Price	Supplier_Number
137	Door latch	22.00	8259
145	Side mirror	12.00	8444
150	Door molding	6.00	8263
152	Door lock	31.00	8259
155	Compressor	54.00	8261
178	Door handle	10.00	8259

Primary Key **Foreign Key**

A relational database organizes data in the form of two-dimensional tables. Illustrated here are tables for the entities SUPPLIER and PART showing how they represent each entity and its attributes. Supplier_Number is a primary key for the SUPPLIER table and a foreign key for the PART table.

the field Supplier_Number appears in the PART table, it is called a **foreign key** and is essentially a lookup field to look up data about the supplier of a specific part.

Operations of a Relational DBMS

Relational database tables can be combined easily to deliver data required by users, provided that any two tables share a common data element. Suppose we wanted to find in this database the names of suppliers who could provide us with part number 137 or part number 150. We would need information from two tables: the SUPPLIER table and the PART table. Note that these two files have a shared data element: Supplier_Number.

In a relational database, three basic operations, as shown in Figure 6.5, are used to develop useful sets of data: select, join, and project. The *select* operation creates a subset consisting of all records in the file that meet stated criteria.

FIGURE 6.5 THE THREE BASIC OPERATIONS OF A RELATIONAL DBMS

PART

Part_Number	Part_Name	Unit_Price	Supplier_Number
137	Door latch	22.00	8259
145	Side mirror	12.00	8444
150	Door molding	6.00	8263
152	Door lock	31.00	8259
155	Compressor	54.00	8261
178	Door handle	10.00	8259

Select Part_Number = 137 or 150

SUPPLIER

Supplier_Number	Supplier_Name	Supplier_Street	Supplier_City	Supplier_State	Supplier_Zip
8259	CBM Inc.	74 5th Avenue	Dayton	OH	45220
8261	B. R. Molds	1277 Gandolly Street	Cleveland	OH	49345
8263	Jackson Components	8233 Micklin Street	Lexington	KY	56723
8444	Bryant Corporation	4315 Mill Drive	Rochester	NY	11344

Join by Supplier_Number

Part_Number	Part_Name	Supplier_Number	Supplier_Name
137	Door latch	8259	CBM Inc.
150	Door molding	8263	Jackson Components

Project selected columns

The select, join, and project operations enable data from two different tables to be combined and only selected attributes to be displayed.

Select creates, in other words, a subset of rows that meet certain criteria. In our example, we want to select records (rows) from the PART table where the Part_Number equals 137 or 150. The *join* operation combines relational tables to provide the user with more information than is available in individual tables. In our example, we want to join the now-shortened PART table (only parts 137 or 150 will be presented) and the SUPPLIER table into a single new table.

The *project* operation creates a subset consisting of columns in a table, permitting the user to create new tables that contain only the information required. In our example, we want to extract from the new table only the following columns: Part_Number, Part_Name, Supplier_Number, and Supplier_Name.

Capabilities of Database Management Systems

A DBMS includes capabilities and tools for organizing, managing, and accessing the data in the database. The most important are its data definition language, data dictionary, and data manipulation language.

DBMS have a **data definition** capability to specify the structure of the content of the database. It would be used to create database tables and to define the characteristics of the fields in each table. This information about the database would be documented in a data dictionary. A **data dictionary** is an automated or manual file that stores definitions of data elements and their characteristics.

Microsoft Access has a rudimentary data dictionary capability that displays information about the name, description, size, type, format, and other properties of each field in a table (see Figure 6.6). Data dictionaries for large corporate

FIGURE 6.6 ACCESS DATA DICTIONARY FEATURES

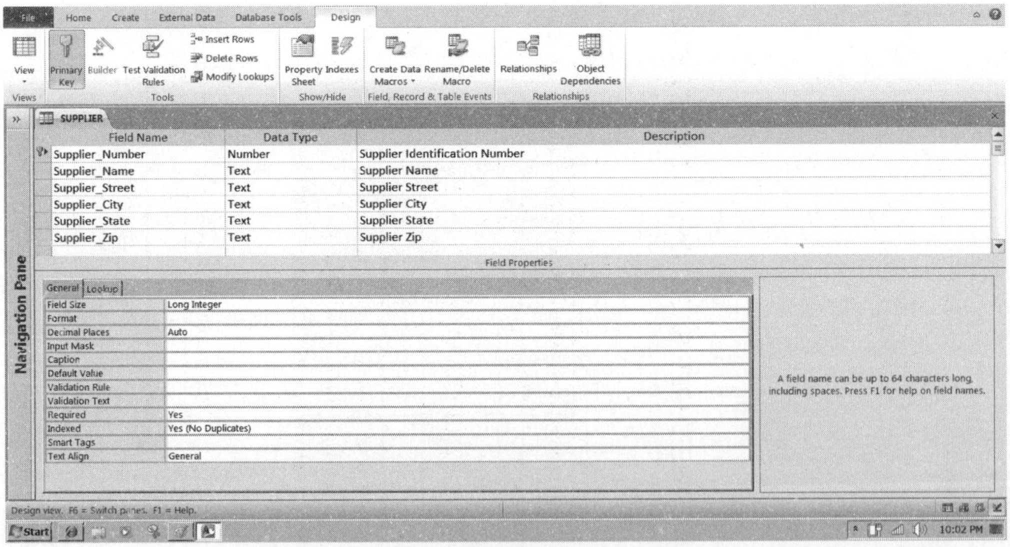

Microsoft Access has a rudimentary data dictionary capability that displays information about the size, format, and other characteristics of each field in a database. Displayed here is the information maintained in the SUPPLIER table. The small key icon to the left of Supplier_Number indicates that it is a key field.

Source: Microsoft Access 2016, Professional Office Version, © Microsoft Corporation 2016, as accessed on Windows 8 OS.

FIGURE 6.7 EXAMPLE OF AN SQL QUERY

```
SELECT PART.Part_Number, PART.Part_Name, SUPPLIER.Supplier_Number,
SUPPLIER.Supplier_Name
FROM PART, SUPPLIER
WHERE PART.Supplier_Number = SUPPLIER.Supplier_Number AND
Part_Number = 137 OR Part_Number = 150;
```

Illustrated here are the SQL statements for a query to select suppliers for parts 137 or 150. They produce a list with the same results as Figure 6.5.

databases may capture additional information, such as usage, ownership (who in the organization is responsible for maintaining the data), authorization, security, and the individuals, business functions, programs, and reports that use each data element.

Querying and Reporting

DBMS includes tools for accessing and manipulating information in databases. Most DBMS have a specialized language called a **data manipulation language** that is used to add, change, delete, and retrieve the data in the database. This language contains commands that permit end users and programming specialists to extract data from the database to satisfy information requests and develop applications. The most prominent data manipulation language today is **Structured Query Language**, or **SQL**. Figure 6.7 illustrates the SQL query that would produce the new resultant table in Figure 6.5. You can find out more about how to perform SQL queries in our Learning Tracks for this chapter.

Users of DBMS for large and midrange computers, such as DB2, Oracle, or SQL Server, would employ SQL to retrieve information they needed from the database. Microsoft Access also uses SQL, but it provides its own set of user-friendly tools for querying databases and for organizing data from databases into more polished reports.

In Microsoft Access, you will find features that enable users to create queries by identifying the tables and fields they want and the results and then selecting the rows from the database that meet particular criteria. These actions in turn are translated into SQL commands. Figure 6.8 illustrates how the same query as the SQL query to select parts and suppliers would be constructed using the Microsoft Access query-building tools.

Microsoft Access and other DBMS include capabilities for report generation so that the data of interest can be displayed in a more structured and polished format than would be possible just by querying. Crystal Reports is a popular report generator for large corporate DBMS, although it can also be used with Access. Access also has capabilities for developing desktop system applications. These include tools for creating data entry screens, reports, and developing the logic for processing transactions.

Designing Databases

To create a database, you must understand the relationships among the data, the type of data that will be maintained in the database, how the data will be

FIGURE 6.8 AN ACCESS QUERY

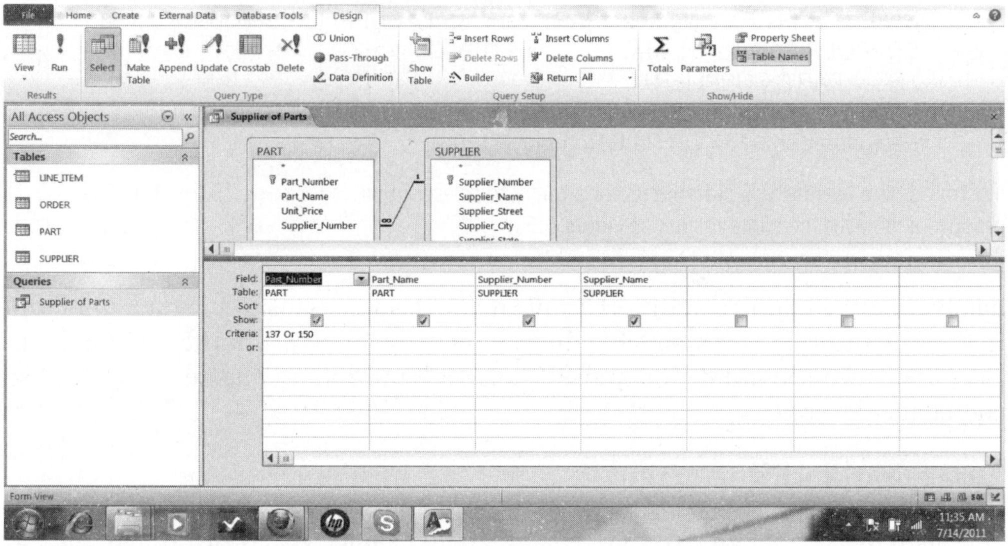

Illustrated here is how the query in Figure 6.7 would be constructed using Microsoft Access query-building tools. It shows the tables, fields, and selection criteria used for the query.

Source: Microsoft Access 2016, Professional Office Version, © Microsoft Corporation 2016, as accessed on Windows 8 OS.

used, and how the organization will need to change to manage data from a companywide perspective. The database requires both a conceptual design and a physical design. The conceptual, or logical, design of a database is an abstract model of the database from a business perspective, whereas the physical design shows how the database is actually arranged on direct-access storage devices.

Normalization and Entity-Relationship Diagrams

The conceptual database design describes how the data elements in the database are to be grouped. The design process identifies relationships among data elements and the most efficient way of grouping data elements together to meet business information requirements. The process also identifies redundant data elements and the groupings of data elements required for specific application programs. Groups of data are organized, refined, and streamlined until an overall logical view of the relationships among all the data in the database emerges.

To use a relational database model effectively, complex groupings of data must be streamlined to minimize redundant data elements and awkward many-to-many relationships. The process of creating small, stable, yet flexible and adaptive data structures from complex groups of data is called **normalization**. Figures 6.9 and 6.10 illustrate this process.

In the particular business modeled here, an order can have more than one part, but each part is provided by only one supplier. If we build a relation called ORDER with all the fields included here, we would have to repeat the name and address of the supplier for every part on the order, even though the order is for parts from a single supplier. This relationship contains what are called repeating

FIGURE 6.9 AN UNNORMALIZED RELATION FOR ORDER

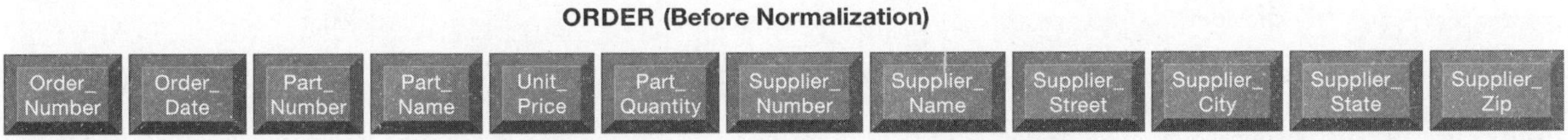

An unnormalized relation contains repeating groups. For example, there can be many parts and suppliers for each order. There is only a one-to-one correspondence between Order_Number and Order_Date.

data groups because there can be many parts on a single order to a given supplier. A more efficient way to arrange the data is to break down ORDER into smaller relations, each of which describes a single entity. If we go step by step and normalize the relation ORDER, we emerge with the relations illustrated in Figure 6.10. You can find out more about normalization, entity-relationship diagramming, and database design in the Learning Tracks for this chapter.

Relational database systems try to enforce **referential integrity** rules to ensure that relationships between coupled tables remain consistent. When one table has a foreign key that points to another table, you may not add a record to the table with the foreign key unless there is a corresponding record in the linked table. In the database we examined earlier in this chapter, the foreign key Supplier_Number links the PART table to the SUPPLIER table. We may not add a new record to the PART table for a part with Supplier_Number 8266 unless there is a corresponding record in the SUPPLIER table for Supplier_Number 8266. We must also delete the corresponding record in the PART table if we delete the record in the SUPPLIER table for Supplier_Number 8266. In other words, we shouldn't have parts from nonexistent suppliers!

Database designers document their data model with an **entity-relationship diagram**, illustrated in Figure 6.11. This diagram illustrates the relationship between the entities SUPPLIER, PART, LINE_ITEM, and ORDER. The boxes represent entities. The lines connecting the boxes represent relationships. A

FIGURE 6.10 NORMALIZED TABLES CREATED FROM ORDER

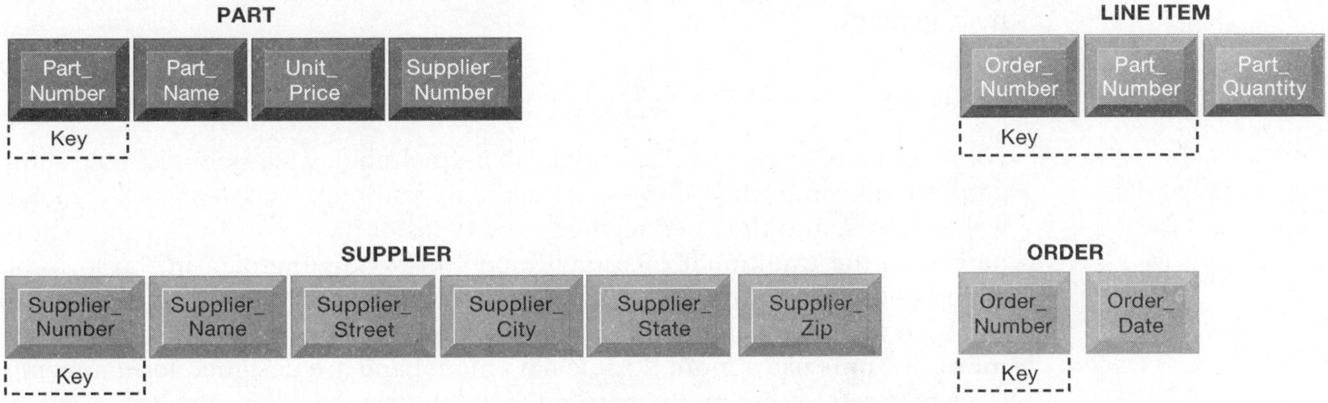

After normalization, the original relation ORDER has been broken down into four smaller relations. The relation ORDER is left with only two attributes, and the relation LINE_ITEM has a combined, or concatenated, key consisting of Order_Number and Part_Number.

FIGURE 6.11 AN ENTITY-RELATIONSHIP DIAGRAM

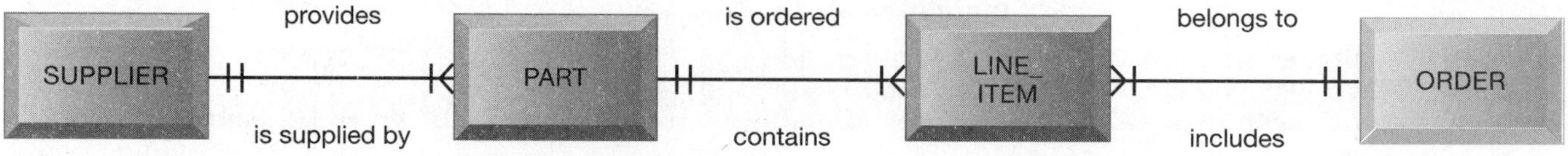

This diagram shows the relationships between the entities SUPPLIER, PART, LINE_ITEM, and ORDER that might be used to model the database in Figure 6.10.

line connecting two entities that ends in two short marks designates a one-to-one relationship. A line connecting two entities that ends with a crow's foot topped by a short mark indicates a one-to-many relationship. Figure 6.11 shows that one ORDER can contain many LINE_ITEMs. (A PART can be ordered many times and appear many times as a line item in a single order.) Each PART can have only one SUPPLIER, but many PARTs can be provided by the same SUPPLIER.

It can't be emphasized enough: If the business doesn't get its data model right, the system won't be able to serve the business well. The company's systems will not be as effective as they could be because they'll have to work with data that may be inaccurate, incomplete, or difficult to retrieve. Understanding the organization's data and how they should be represented in a database is perhaps the most important lesson you can learn from this course.

For example, Famous Footwear, a shoe store chain with more than 800 locations in 49 states, could not achieve its goal of having "the right style of shoe in the right store for sale at the right price" because its database was not properly designed for rapidly adjusting store inventory. The company had an Oracle relational database running on a midrange computer, but the database was designed primarily for producing standard reports for management rather than for reacting to marketplace changes. Management could not obtain precise data on specific items in inventory in each of its stores. The company had to work around this problem by building a new database where the sales and inventory data could be better organized for analysis and inventory management.

Non-relational Databases and Databases in the Cloud

For more than 30 years, relational database technology has been the gold standard. Cloud computing, unprecedented data volumes, massive workloads for web services, and the need to store new types of data require database alternatives to the traditional relational model of organizing data in the form of tables, columns, and rows. Companies are turning to "NoSQL" non-relational database technologies for this purpose. **Non-relational database management systems** use a more flexible data model and are designed for managing large data sets across many distributed machines and for easily scaling up or down. They are useful for accelerating simple queries against large volumes of structured and unstructured data, including web, social media, graphics, and other forms of data that are difficult to analyze with traditional SQL-based tools.

There are several different kinds of NoSQL databases, each with its own technical features and behavior. Oracle NoSQL Database is one example, as is Amazon's SimpleDB, one of the Amazon Web Services that run in the cloud. SimpleDB provides a simple web services interface to create and store multiple data sets, query data easily, and return the results. There is no need to predefine a formal database structure or change that definition if new data are added later.

For example, MetLife used the MongoDB open source NoSQL database to quickly integrate disparate data on more than 100 million customers and deliver a consolidated view of each. MetLife's database brings together data from more than 70 separate administrative systems, claims systems, and other data sources, including semi-structured and unstructured data, such as images of health records and death certificates. The NoSQL database is able to use structured, semi-structured, and unstructured information without requiring tedious, expensive, and time-consuming database mapping.

Cloud Databases

Amazon and other cloud computing vendors provide relational database services as well. Amazon Relational Database Service (Amazon RDS) offers MySQL, SQL Server, Oracle Database, PostgreSQL, MariaDB, or Amazon Aurora DB (compatible with MySQL) as database engines. Pricing is based on usage. Oracle has its own Database Cloud Services using its relational Oracle Database, and Microsoft Windows SQL Azure Database is a cloud-based relational database service based on Microsoft's SQL Server DBMS. Cloud-based data management services have special appeal for web-focused start-ups or small to medium-sized businesses seeking database capabilities at a lower price than in-house database products.

In addition to public cloud-based data management services, companies now have the option of using databases in private clouds. For example, Sabre Holdings, the world's largest software as a service (SaaS) provider for the aviation industry, has a private database cloud that supports more than 100 projects and 700 users. A consolidated database spanning a pool of standardized servers running Oracle Database provides database services for multiple applications.

6-3 What are the principal tools and technologies for accessing information from databases to improve business performance and decision making?

Businesses use their databases to keep track of basic transactions, such as paying suppliers, processing orders, keeping track of customers, and paying employees. But they also need databases to provide information that will help the company run the business more efficiently and help managers and employees make better decisions. If a company wants to know which product is the most popular or who is its most profitable customer, the answer lies in the data.

The Challenge of Big Data

Most data collected by organizations used to be transaction data that could easily fit into rows and columns of relational database management systems. We are now witnessing an explosion of data from web traffic, e-mail messages, and social media content (tweets, status messages), as well as machine-generated data from sensors (used in smart meters, manufacturing sensors, and electrical meters) or from electronic trading systems. These data may be unstructured or semi-structured and thus not suitable for relational database products that organize data in the form of columns and rows. We now use the term **big data** to describe these data sets with volumes so huge that they are beyond the ability of typical DBMS to capture, store, and analyze.

Big data doesn't refer to any specific quantity but usually refers to data in the petabyte and exabyte range—in other words, billions to trillions of records, all from different sources. Big data are produced in much larger quantities and much more rapidly than traditional data. For example, a single jet engine is capable of generating 10 terabytes of data in just 30 minutes, and there are more than 25,000 airline flights each day. Even though "tweets" are limited to 140 characters each, Twitter generates more than 8 terabytes of data daily. According to the International Data Center (IDC) technology research firm, data are more than doubling every two years, so the amount of data available to organizations is skyrocketing.

Businesses are interested in big data because they can reveal more patterns and interesting relationships than smaller data sets, with the potential to provide new insights into customer behavior, weather patterns, financial market activity, or other phenomena. For example, Shutterstock, the global online image marketplace, stores 24 million images, adding 10,000 more each day. To find ways to optimize the buying experience, Shutterstock analyzes its big data to find out where its website visitors place their cursors and how long they hover over an image before making a purchase.

Big data is also finding many uses in the public sector. Major cities in Europe and Europol are using Big Data to identify criminals and terrorists (Aline, 2016).

However, to derive business value from these data, organizations need new technologies and tools capable of managing and analyzing nontraditional data along with their traditional enterprise data. They also need to know what questions to ask of the data and limitations of big data. Capturing, storing, and analyzing big data can be expensive, and information from big data may not necessarily help decision makers. It's important to have a clear understanding of the problem big data will solve for the business. The chapter-ending case explores these issues.

INTERACTIVE SESSION: MANAGEMENT

The Gym Database

FitPro, a gymnasium and healthcare center, is a premium club spread across different locations in India. It provides differential workout routines to members including weight training, cardio-vascular routines, and aerobics and relaxation sessions. According to the current process flow, members need to schedule visits to the gym and trainers are assigned based on their availability at the time of the visit. The staff at the gym makes a manual entry in a spreadsheet against the member's name, reporting the time of the visit and the services availed. A new spreadsheet is generated daily to maintain these records. To prevent any unauthorized entry or threat to the patrons' private details, a password-based access to the computer is the only protection in place.

Due to a large number of members at the gym, the current system of recordkeeping was deemed inefficient. The management had no way of identifying the members who frequently visited the gym. Such information would be useful for the management because they could then tailor packages for tourists and communicate their offers via SMS or email. Since there was no centralized access for the members, the gym could not assign trainers to those who came in at odd hours. The members frequently complained of their inability to track the status of their health and fitness routines. Information could not be easily extracted from spreadsheets. As a result, receipts of payments could not be acknowledged on time. The gym wished to design a Web site that members could access 24/7, schedule workouts at flexible hours, and use their accounts to view their past history of sessions at the gym. The need for a central database could not be more pronounced at this stage. Hence, the gym's management hired an analyst who proposed the structure depicted in Figure 6.12.

The figure depicts the various end-users of the gym database: the employees, members, healthcare professionals, equipment suppliers, and so on. To build a database, it is necessary to design tables keeping in mind the business requirements of the club. Entities, and the relationships among them, need to

FIGURE 6.12 PROPOSED STRUCTURE OF THE GYM'S CENTRAL DATABASE

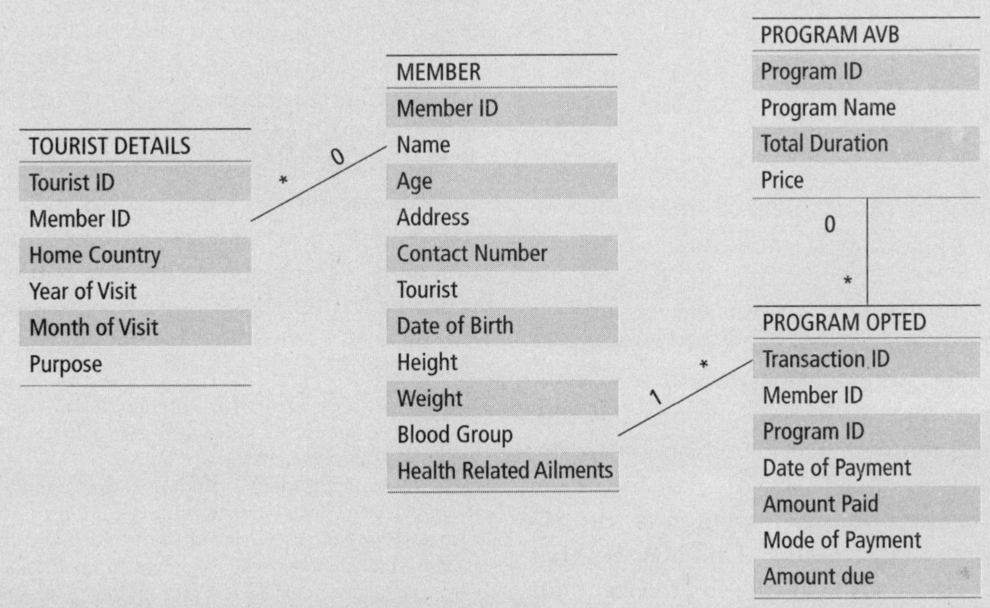

FIGURE 6.13 A PARTIAL VIEW OF THE DATABASE

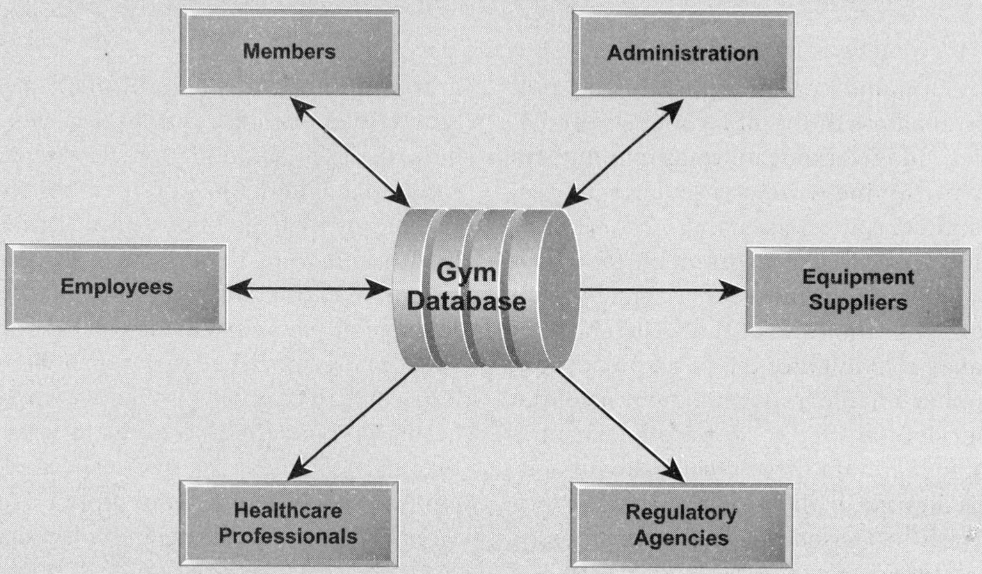

be determined at the outset. The analyst listed the following entities for the database design:

1. Region of operation
2. Member data
3. Employee data
4. Exercise routine
5. Program available
6. Program opted
7. Receipts
8. Payroll
9. Equipment
10. Employee schedule
11. Suppliers

Since the gym provides a variety of programs, each member's detail of the chosen program is saved as a separate entity under 'Program opted'. The employees at the gym are broadly categorized as staff (S) and trainers (T) under 'Employee type'. Figure 6.13 shows a partial view of the database for FitPro.

The relationship between the member and program opted has been depicted using the 1...* notation. This implies a one-to-many relationship. Each member is assigned a unique ID which is the primary key for the database table. This ensures that data duplicity does not occur. To identify the frequent travelers, the 'Member' entity takes two values: Y and N. If the answer is Y, information such as home country, year of visit, and so on, are recorded in a separate table. The relationship between member and tourist is depicted as 0...*, that is, it is a zero-to-many relationship. This is because not all members are tourists; but for each member who is a tourist, there can be several records for the different time periods at which they might have visited the gym. Similarly, there is a 0...* relationship between programs available and program opted. There might be programs that no member has opted for yet. The table also contains the payment details of the members, which can be used to alert the management if an account is overdue.

Using a well-designed database ensures that the records are clear of human error and data redundancy. Normalizing data entities removes information silos. The database also aids in the generation of reports for different end-users, whose levels of access can be easily controlled by the administration.

Sources: As accessed on 31 December 2015 at 3pm IST—"Enterprise Manager Concepts". Retrieved from http://docs.oracle.com; Kroenke, David and Randall J. Boyle, *Using MIS*, 8/e, Prentice Hall (2015); Shah, Megha, "India's sexiest gyms", *Live Well* (2015); Retrieved from http://www.gqindia.com; http://www.fitnessfirst.com.sg; *GymMaster*. Retrieved from http://www.gymmaster.co.nz; "Database Design Basics". Retrieved from http://office.microsoft.com.

CASE STUDY QUESTIONS

1. Identify the relationships among the various entities of the gym database system.
2. Develop a database design by specifying primary and foreign keys for the FitPro gym.
3. What are the possible information discrepancies that can occur in the system? How can the design ensure governance?
4. Analyze the technical, organizational, scheduling, and financial feasibility by listing major operational and developmental costs of the database design.

Business Intelligence Infrastructure

Suppose you wanted concise, reliable information about current operations, trends, and changes across the entire company. If you worked in a large company, the data you need might have to be pieced together from separate systems, such as sales, manufacturing, and accounting, and even from external sources, such as demographic or competitor data. Increasingly, you might need to use big data. A contemporary infrastructure for business intelligence has an array of tools for obtaining useful information from all the different types of data used by businesses today, including semi-structured and unstructured big data in vast quantities. These capabilities include data warehouses and data marts, Hadoop, in-memory computing, and analytical platforms. Some of these capabilities are available as cloud services.

Data Warehouses and Data Marts

The traditional tool for analyzing corporate data for the past two decades has been the data warehouse. A **data warehouse** is a database that stores current and historical data of potential interest to decision makers throughout the company. The data originate in many core operational transaction systems, such as systems for sales, customer accounts, and manufacturing, and may include data from website transactions. The data warehouse extracts current and historical data from multiple operational systems inside the organization. These data are combined with data from external sources and transformed by correcting inaccurate and incomplete data and restructuring the data for management reporting and analysis before being loaded into the data warehouse.

The data warehouse makes the data available for anyone to access as needed, but the data cannot be altered. A data warehouse system also provides a range of ad hoc and standardized query tools, analytical tools, and graphical reporting facilities.

Companies often build enterprise-wide data warehouses, where a central data warehouse serves the entire organization, or they create smaller, decentralized warehouses called data marts. A **data mart** is a subset of a data warehouse in which a summarized or highly focused portion of the organization's data is placed in a separate database for a specific population of users. For example, a company might develop marketing and sales data marts to deal with customer information.

Hadoop

Relational DBMS and data warehouse products are not well suited for organizing and analyzing big data or data that do not easily fit into columns and rows used in their data models. For handling unstructured and semi-structured data in vast quantities, as well as structured data, organizations are using **Hadoop**. Hadoop is an open source software framework managed by the Apache Software Foundation that enables distributed parallel processing of huge amounts of data across inexpensive computers. It breaks a big data problem down into sub-problems, distributes them among up to thousands of inexpensive computer processing nodes, and then combines the result into a smaller data set that is easier to analyze. You've probably used Hadoop to find the best airfare on the Internet, get directions to a restaurant, do a search on Google, or connect with a friend on Facebook.

Hadoop consists of several key services, including the Hadoop Distributed File System (HDFS) for data storage and MapReduce for high-performance parallel data processing. HDFS links together the file systems on the numerous nodes in a Hadoop cluster to turn them into one big file system. Hadoop's MapReduce was inspired by Google's MapReduce system for breaking down processing of huge data sets and assigning work to the various nodes in a cluster. HBase, Hadoop's non-relational database, provides rapid access to the data stored on HDFS and a transactional platform for running high-scale real-time applications.

Hadoop can process large quantities of any kind of data, including structured transactional data, loosely structured data such as Facebook and Twitter feeds, complex data such as web server log files, and unstructured audio and video data. Hadoop runs on a cluster of inexpensive servers, and processors can be added or removed as needed. Companies use Hadoop for analyzing very large volumes of data as well as for a staging area for unstructured and semi-structured data before they are loaded into a data warehouse. Yahoo uses Hadoop to track users' behavior so it can modify its home page to fit their interests. Life sciences research firm NextBio uses Hadoop and HBase to process data for pharmaceutical companies conducting genomic research. Top database vendors such as IBM, Hewlett-Packard, Oracle, and Microsoft have their own Hadoop software distributions. Other vendors offer tools for moving data into and out of Hadoop or for analyzing data within Hadoop.

In-Memory Computing

Another way of facilitating big data analysis is to use **in-memory computing**, which relies primarily on a computer's main memory (RAM) for data storage. (Conventional DBMS use disk storage systems.) Users access data stored in system primary memory, thereby eliminating bottlenecks from retrieving and reading data in a traditional, disk-based database and dramatically shortening query response times. In-memory processing makes it possible for very large sets of data, amounting to the size of a data mart or small data warehouse, to reside entirely in memory. Complex business calculations that used to take hours or days are able to be completed within seconds, and this can even be accomplished using handheld devices.

The previous chapter describes some of the advances in contemporary computer hardware technology that make in-memory processing possible, such as powerful high-speed processors, multicore processing, and falling computer memory prices. These technologies help companies optimize the use of memory and accelerate processing performance while lowering costs.

Leading commercial products for in-memory computing include SAP HANA and Oracle Exalytics. Each provides a set of integrated software components, including in-memory database software and specialized analytics software, that run on hardware optimized for in-memory computing work.

Analytic Platforms

Commercial database vendors have developed specialized high-speed **analytic platforms** using both relational and non-relational technology that are optimized for analyzing large data sets. Analytic platforms such as IBM PureData System for Analytics, feature preconfigured hardware-software systems that are specifically designed for query processing and analytics. For example, IBM PureData System for Analytics features tightly integrated database, server, and storage components that handle complex analytic queries 10 to 100 times faster than traditional systems. Analytic platforms also include in-memory systems and NoSQL non-relational database management systems. Analytic platforms are now available as cloud services.

Figure 6.14 illustrates a contemporary business intelligence infrastructure using the technologies we have just described. Current and historical data are

FIGURE 6.14 CONTEMPORARY BUSINESS INTELLIGENCE INFRASTRUCTURE

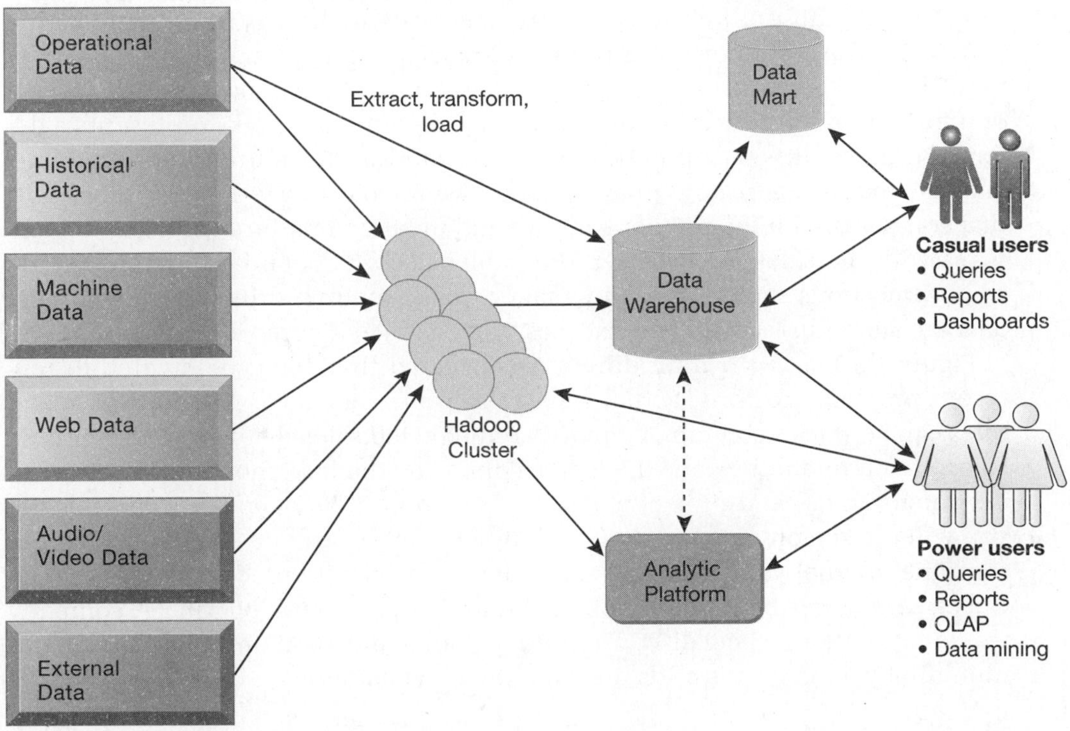

A contemporary business intelligence infrastructure features capabilities and tools to manage and analyze large quantities and different types of data from multiple sources. Easy-to-use query and reporting tools for casual business users and more sophisticated analytical toolsets for power users are included.

extracted from multiple operational systems along with web data, machine-generated data, unstructured audio/visual data, and data from external sources that have been restructured and reorganized for reporting and analysis. Hadoop clusters pre-process big data for use in the data warehouse, data marts, or an analytic platform or for direct querying by power users. Outputs include reports and dashboards as well as query results. Chapter 12 discusses the various types of BI users and BI reporting in greater detail.

Analytical Tools: Relationships, Patterns, Trends

Once data have been captured and organized using the business intelligence technologies we have just described, they are available for further analysis using software for database querying and reporting, multidimensional data analysis (OLAP), and data mining. This section will introduce you to these tools, with more detail about business intelligence analytics and applications in Chapter 12.

Online Analytical Processing (OLAP)

Suppose your company sells four different products—nuts, bolts, washers, and screws—in the East, West, and Central regions. If you wanted to ask a fairly straightforward question, such as how many washers sold during the past quarter, you could easily find the answer by querying your sales database. But what if you wanted to know how many washers sold in each of your sales regions and compare actual results with projected sales?

To obtain the answer, you would need **online analytical processing (OLAP)**. OLAP supports multidimensional data analysis, enabling users to view the same data in different ways using multiple dimensions. Each aspect of information—product, pricing, cost, region, or time period—represents a different dimension. So, a product manager could use a multidimensional data analysis tool to learn how many washers were sold in the East in June, how that compares with the previous month and the previous June, and how it compares with the sales forecast. OLAP enables users to obtain online answers to ad hoc questions such as these in a fairly rapid amount of time, even when the data are stored in very large databases, such as sales figures for multiple years.

Figure 6.15 shows a multidimensional model that could be created to represent products, regions, actual sales, and projected sales. A matrix of actual sales can be stacked on top of a matrix of projected sales to form a cube with six faces. If you rotate the cube 90 degrees one way, the face showing will be product versus actual and projected sales. If you rotate the cube 90 degrees again, you will see region versus actual and projected sales. If you rotate 180 degrees from the original view, you will see projected sales and product versus region. Cubes can be nested within cubes to build complex views of data. A company would use either a specialized multidimensional database or a tool that creates multidimensional views of data in relational databases.

Data Mining

Traditional database queries answer such questions as "How many units of product number 403 were shipped in February 2016?" OLAP, or multidimensional

FIGURE 6.15 MULTIDIMENSIONAL DATA MODEL

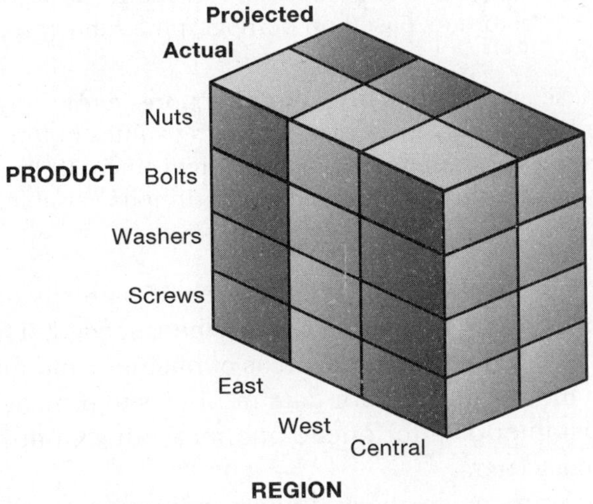

This view shows product versus region. If you rotate the cube 90 degrees, the face that will show is product versus actual and projected sales. If you rotate the cube 90 degrees again, you will see region versus actual and projected sales. Other views are possible.

analysis, supports much more complex requests for information, such as "Compare sales of product 403 relative to plan by quarter and sales region for the past two years." With OLAP and query-oriented data analysis, users need to have a good idea about the information for which they are looking.

Data mining is more discovery-driven. Data mining provides insights into corporate data that cannot be obtained with OLAP by finding hidden patterns and relationships in large databases and inferring rules from them to predict future behavior. The patterns and rules are used to guide decision making and forecast the effect of those decisions. The types of information obtainable from data mining include associations, sequences, classifications, clusters, and forecasts.

- *Associations* are occurrences linked to a single event. For instance, a study of supermarket purchasing patterns might reveal that, when corn chips are purchased, a cola drink is purchased 65 percent of the time, but when there is a promotion, cola is purchased 85 percent of the time. This information helps managers make better decisions because they have learned the profitability of a promotion.
- In *sequences*, events are linked over time. We might find, for example, that if a house is purchased, a new refrigerator will be purchased within two weeks 65 percent of the time, and an oven will be bought within one month of the home purchase 45 percent of the time.
- *Classification* recognizes patterns that describe the group to which an item belongs by examining existing items that have been classified and by inferring a set of rules. For example, businesses such as credit card or telephone companies worry about the loss of steady customers. Classification helps discover the characteristics of customers who are likely to leave and can provide a model to help managers predict who those customers are so that the managers can devise special campaigns to retain such customers.

- *Clustering* works in a manner similar to classification when no groups have yet been defined. A data mining tool can discover different groupings within data, such as finding affinity groups for bank cards or partitioning a database into groups of customers based on demographics and types of personal investments.
- Although these applications involve predictions, *forecasting* uses predictions in a different way. It uses a series of existing values to forecast what other values will be. For example, forecasting might find patterns in data to help managers estimate the future value of continuous variables, such as sales figures.

These systems perform high-level analyses of patterns or trends, but they can also drill down to provide more detail when needed. There are data mining applications for all the functional areas of business and for government and scientific work. One popular use for data mining is to provide detailed analyses of patterns in customer data for one-to-one marketing campaigns or for identifying profitable customers.

Caesars Entertainment, formerly known as Harrah's Entertainment, is the largest gaming company in the world. It continually analyzes data about its customers gathered when people play its slot machines or use its casinos and hotels. The corporate marketing department uses this information to build a detailed gambling profile, based on a particular customer's ongoing value to the company. For instance, data mining lets Caesars know the favorite gaming experience of a regular customer at one of its riverboat casinos along with that person's preferences for room accommodations, restaurants, and entertainment. This information guides management decisions about how to cultivate the most profitable customers, encourage those customers to spend more, and attract more customers with high revenue-generating potential. Business intelligence improved Caesars's profits so much that it became the centerpiece of the firm's business strategy.

Text Mining and Web Mining

Unstructured data, most in the form of text files, is believed to account for more than 80 percent of useful organizational information and is one of the major sources of big data that firms want to analyze. E-mail, memos, call center transcripts, survey responses, legal cases, patent descriptions, and service reports are all valuable for finding patterns and trends that will help employees make better business decisions. **Text mining** tools are now available to help businesses analyze these data. These tools are able to extract key elements from unstructured big data sets, discover patterns and relationships, and summarize the information.

Businesses might turn to text mining to analyze transcripts of calls to customer service centers to identify major service and repair issues or to measure customer sentiment about their company. **Sentiment analysis** software is able to mine text comments in an e-mail message, blog, social media conversation, or survey form to detect favorable and unfavorable opinions about specific subjects.

For example, discount brokers use analytic software to analyze hundreds of thousands of its customer interactions each month. The software analyzes customer service notes, e-mails, survey responses, and online discussions to discover signs of dissatisfaction that might cause a customer to stop using the company's services. The software is able to automatically identify the various "voices" customers use to express their feedback (such as a positive, negative, or conditional voice) to pinpoint a person's intent to buy, intent to leave, or reaction to a specific product or marketing message. Brokers use this information to take corrective actions such as stepping up direct broker communication with the customer and trying to quickly resolve the problems that are making the customer unhappy.

The web is another rich source of unstructured big data for revealing patterns, trends, and insights into customer behavior. The discovery and analysis of useful patterns and information from the World Wide Web are called **web mining**. Businesses might turn to web mining to help them understand customer behavior, evaluate the effectiveness of a particular website, or quantify the success of a marketing campaign. For instance, marketers use the Google Trends service, which tracks the popularity of various words and phrases used in Google search queries, to learn what people are interested in and what they are interested in buying.

Web mining looks for patterns in data through content mining, structure mining, and usage mining. Web content mining is the process of extracting knowledge from the content of webpages, which may include text, image, audio, and video data. Web structure mining examines data related to the structure of a particular website. For example, links pointing to a document indicate the popularity of the document, while links coming out of a document indicate the richness or perhaps the variety of topics covered in the document. Web usage mining examines user interaction data recorded by a web server whenever requests for a website's resources are received. The usage data records the user's behavior when the user browses or makes transactions on the website and collects the data in a server log. Analyzing such data can help companies determine the value of particular customers, cross-marketing strategies across products, and the effectiveness of promotional campaigns.

The chapter-ending case describes organizations' experiences as they use the analytical tools and business intelligence technologies we have described to grapple with "big data" challenges.

Databases and the Web

Have you ever tried to use the web to place an order or view a product catalog? If so, you were using a website linked to an internal corporate database. Many companies now use the web to make some of the information in their internal databases available to customers and business partners.

Suppose, for example, a customer with a web browser wants to search an online retailer's database for pricing information. Figure 6.16 illustrates how that customer might access the retailer's internal database over the web. The user accesses the retailer's website over the Internet using a web browser on his or her client PC or mobile device. The user's web browser software requests data from the organization's database, using HTML commands to communicate with the web server. Apps provide even faster access to corporate databases.

FIGURE 6.16 LINKING INTERNAL DATABASES TO THE WEB

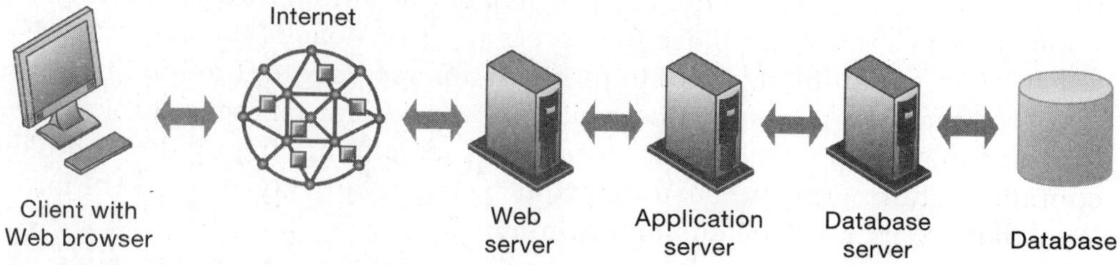

Users access an organization's internal database through the web using their desktop PC browsers or mobile apps.

Because many back-end databases cannot interpret commands written in HTML, the web server passes these requests for data to software that translates HTML commands into SQL so the commands can be processed by the DBMS working with the database. In a client/server environment, the DBMS resides on a dedicated computer called a **database server**. The DBMS receives the SQL requests and provides the required data. Middleware transfers information from the organization's internal database back to the web server for delivery in the form of a web page to the user.

Figure 6.16 shows that the middleware working between the web server and the DBMS is an application server running on its own dedicated computer (see Chapter 5). The application server software handles all application operations, including transaction processing and data access, between browser-based computers and a company's back-end business applications or databases. The application server takes requests from the web server, runs the business logic to process transactions based on those requests, and provides connectivity to the organization's back-end systems or databases. Alternatively, the software for handling these operations could be a custom program or a CGI script. A CGI script is a compact program using the *Common Gateway Interface (CGI)* specification for processing data on a web server.

There are a number of advantages to using the web to access an organization's internal databases. First, web browser software is much easier to use than proprietary query tools. Second, the web interface requires few or no changes to the internal database. It costs much less to add a web interface in front of a legacy system than to redesign and rebuild the system to improve user access.

Accessing corporate databases through the web is creating new efficiencies, opportunities, and business models. ThomasNet.com provides an up-to-date online directory of more than 700,000 suppliers of industrial products, such as chemicals, metals, plastics, rubber, and automotive equipment. Formerly called Thomas Register, the company used to send out huge paper catalogs with this information. Now it provides this information to users online via its website and has become a smaller, leaner company.

Other companies have created entirely new businesses based on access to large databases through the web. One is the social networking service Facebook, which helps users stay connected with each other and meet new people.

Facebook features "profiles" with information on 1.6 billion active users with information about themselves, including interests, friends, photos, and groups with which they are affiliated. Facebook maintains a very large database to house and manage all of this content. There are also many web-enabled databases in the public sector to help consumers and citizens access helpful information.

6-4 Why are information policy, data administration, and data quality assurance essential for managing the firm's data resources?

Setting up a database is only a start. In order to make sure that the data for your business remain accurate, reliable, and readily available to those who need them, your business will need special policies and procedures for data management.

Establishing an Information Policy

Every business, large and small, needs an information policy. Your firm's data are an important resource, and you don't want people doing whatever they want with them. You need to have rules on how the data are to be organized and maintained and who is allowed to view the data or change them.

An **information policy** specifies the organization's rules for sharing, disseminating, acquiring, standardizing, classifying, and inventorying information. Information policy lays out specific procedures and accountabilities, identifying which users and organizational units can share information, where information can be distributed, and who is responsible for updating and maintaining the information. For example, a typical information policy would specify that only selected members of the payroll and human resources department would have the right to change and view sensitive employee data, such as an employee's salary or social security number, and that these departments are responsible for making sure that such employee data are accurate.

If you are in a small business, the information policy would be established and implemented by the owners or managers. In a large organization, managing and planning for information as a corporate resource often require a formal data administration function. **Data administration** is responsible for the specific policies and procedures through which data can be managed as an organizational resource. These responsibilities include developing an information policy, planning for data, overseeing logical database design and data dictionary development, and monitoring how information systems specialists and end-user groups use data.

You may hear the term **data governance** used to describe many of these activities. Promoted by IBM, data governance deals with the policies and processes for managing the availability, usability, integrity, and security of the data employed in an enterprise with special emphasis on promoting privacy, security, data quality, and compliance with government regulations.

A large organization will also have a database design and management group within the corporate information systems division that is responsible for defining and organizing the structure and content of the database and maintaining the database. In close cooperation with users, the design group establishes the physical database, the logical relations among elements, and the access rules and security procedures. The functions it performs are called **database administration**.

Ensuring Data Quality

A well-designed database and information policy will go a long way toward ensuring that the business has the information it needs. However, additional steps must be taken to ensure that the data in organizational databases are accurate and remain reliable.

What would happen if a customer's telephone number or account balance were incorrect? What would be the impact if the database had the wrong price for the product you sold or your sales system and inventory system showed different prices for the same product? Data that are inaccurate, untimely, or inconsistent with other sources of information lead to incorrect decisions, product recalls, and financial losses. Gartner, Inc. reported that more than 25 percent of the critical data in large Global 1000 companies' databases is inaccurate or incomplete, including bad product codes and product descriptions, faulty inventory descriptions, erroneous financial data, incorrect supplier information, and incorrect employee data. Some of these data quality problems are caused by redundant and inconsistent data produced by multiple systems feeding a data warehouse. For example, the sales ordering system and the inventory management system might both maintain data on the organization's products. However, the sales ordering system might use the term *Item Number* and the inventory system might call the same attribute *Product Number*. The sales, inventory, or manufacturing systems of a clothing retailer might use different codes to represent values for an attribute. One system might represent clothing size as "medium," whereas the other system might use the code "M" for the same purpose. During the design process for the warehouse database, data describing entities, such as a customer, product, or order, should be named and defined consistently for all business areas using the database.

Think of all the times you've received several pieces of the same direct mail advertising on the same day. This is very likely the result of having your name maintained multiple times in a database. Your name may have been misspelled or you used your middle initial on one occasion and not on another or the information was initially entered onto a paper form and not scanned properly into the system. Because of these inconsistencies, the database would treat you as different people! We often receive redundant mail addressed to Laudon, Lavdon, Lauden, or Landon.

If a database is properly designed and enterprise-wide data standards established, duplicate or inconsistent data elements should be minimal. Most data quality problems, however, such as misspelled names, transposed numbers, or incorrect or missing codes, stem from errors during data input. The incidence of such errors is rising as companies move their businesses to the web and allow customers and suppliers to enter data into their websites that directly update internal systems.

Before a new database is in place, organizations need to identify and correct their faulty data and establish better routines for editing data once their database is in operation. Analysis of data quality often begins with a **data quality**

audit, which is a structured survey of the accuracy and level of completeness of the data in an information system. Data quality audits can be performed by surveying entire data files, surveying samples from data files, or surveying end users for their perceptions of data quality.

Data cleansing, also known as *data scrubbing*, consists of activities for detecting and correcting data in a database that are incorrect, incomplete, improperly formatted, or redundant. Data cleansing not only corrects errors but also enforces consistency among different sets of data that originated in separate information systems. Specialized data-cleansing software is available to automatically survey data files, correct errors in the data, and integrate the data in a consistent companywide format.

Data quality problems are not just business problems. They also pose serious problems for individuals, affecting their financial condition and even their jobs. For example, inaccurate or outdated data about consumers' credit histories maintained by credit bureaus can prevent creditworthy individuals from obtaining loans or lower their chances of finding or keeping a job.

A small minority of companies allow individual departments to be in charge of maintaining the quality of their own data. However, best data administration practices call for centralizing data governance, standardization of organizational data, data quality maintenance, and accessibility to data assets.

The Interactive Session on Management illustrates Societe Generale's experience with managing data as a resource. As you read this case, try to identify the policies, procedures, and technologies that were required to improve data management at this company.

INTERACTIVE SESSION: MANAGEMENT

Societe Generale Builds an Intelligent System to Manage Information Flow

Societe Generale is France's largest bank and the third largest bank in the European Union. In 2016 the bank reported revenues of €25 billion, and a net income of €4 billion. Societe Generale has offices in 76 countries and more than 33 million customers across the globe. Like many banks in Europe, Societe Generale is still struggling from the near collapse of the global financial system in 2008, and is burdened by a large volume of underperforming and non-performing loans and financial instruments. Extremely low interest rates in the past four years have also reduced the bank's traditional source of revenues, which is lending money to consumers and firms alike.

Like many large money-center banks in Europe and the U.S., Societe Generale has adopted a universal banking model, a one-stop shop for whatever its clients want. It operates in three banking segments: retail banking for consumers, international banking to service corporate clients, and investment banking for wealthy clients and other sources of capital like pension funds, insurance firms, and sovereign offshore funds.

As a global universal bank, Societe Generale sells hundreds of financial products to its customers, and this in turn generates tens of millions of daily transactions including account deposits, checks, credit card charges, ATM cash dispensing, financial instrument trades, and local payments. These transactions are stored in over 1,500 files (generally along product lines). These 1,500 files are sent each day to its "back office" operations group for storage and processing. Ultimately, the information in the files is used to update the bank's operational database applications that maintain the general ledger and sub-ledgers. In this sense, banks such as Societe Generale are industrial-scale information processing factories that are required to deliver bank services and products to customers with minimal errors.

But before the main databases are updated, the information streaming into the back office needs to be verified. Why does this basic information need to be verified? As it turns out, the data is often "dirty": record count and the amounts recorded can change as information flows between and across systems. Duplicate files are sometimes created, and sometimes the files needed for a business process are not present. A third problem is ensuring the correct information is being produced for downstream applications and the general ledger system in particular. Sometimes, files and records are out of sequence or incomplete, and that causes a downstream application to close down. There are hundreds of downstream applications relying on the transaction data.

In the past, the process of verification was handled manually by hundreds of employees checking files and records, dealing with errors, omissions, and system error messages on the fly, as they occurred. Given the critical nature of the verification process and the size and complexity of the task, Societe Generale senior management decided to find an automated solution that would capture the knowledge of its employees and then apply that knowledge to the verification process, which would operate in real time. What Societe Generale needed was an "intelligent system" to take over the work of many employees, or at least reduce the burden and the inherent chance for errors.

After evaluating several vendors, the chose Infogix, a French-based database firm that specializes in running data-intensive business environments. The Infogix Enterprise Data Platform monitors incoming transactions, provides balancing and reconciliation and identifies and predicts fraud and customer behavior. The Infogix Platform is a rule-based system allowing development of complex business rules for validating integrity. To implement this system, Infogix had to identify the rules and procedures that humans follow can when verifying the data, and then implement those rules in computer code. The firm identified over 220 business rules that employees had invented over many years of experience.

With the Infogix platform in operation, transactions are verified several times a day, enabling the bank to validate the accuracy of millions of transactions and about 1,500 files daily. The cost of verification and data management has been drastically reduced along with error rates and system shut downs. Humans are still needed to handle new situations or critical errors the system cannot decide. In the event of critical errors that disrupt the operation of important bank systems, the bank's production support team swings into action and, using the tools available on the Infogix platform, are able to solve the problem in much less time than with the manual system. Since automating the transaction process, the bank has reassigned employees to other tasks or to backing up the automated system.

Sources: David Jolly, "Société Générale Profit Rises Despite Weakness in Investment Banking," *New York Times*, May 4, 2016; "Societe Generale Group Results Full Year 2016," Annual Report, societegenerale.com, March 15, 2017; "Enhancing the Accuracy of Front-to-Back Office Information Flow," Infogix.com, 2016; Noemie Bisserbe, "Société Générale Shares Plunge After Profit Warning," Agence France-Presse, February 11, 2016.

CASE STUDY QUESTIONS

1. Why did Societe Generale's managers decide to develop an automated transaction processing system?
2. Why did managers decide they needed an "intelligent system?" In what way was the new system "intelligent?"
3. What is the role of human decision makers in the new system?
4. Why did managers select the Infogix platform?

Review Summary

6-1 *What are the problems of managing data resources in a traditional file environment?*

Traditional file management techniques make it difficult for organizations to keep track of all of the pieces of data they use in a systematic way and to organize these data so that they can be easily accessed. Different functional areas and groups were allowed to develop their own files independently. Over time, this traditional file management environment creates problems such as data redundancy and inconsistency, program-data dependence, inflexibility, poor security, and lack of data sharing and availability. A database management system (DBMS) solves these problems with software that permits centralization of data and data management so that businesses have a single consistent source for all their data needs. Using a DBMS minimizes redundant and inconsistent files.

6-2 *What are the major capabilities of DBMS, and why is a relational DBMS so powerful?*

The principal capabilities of a DBMS include a data definition capability, a data dictionary capability, and a data manipulation language. The data definition capability specifies the structure and content of the database. The data dictionary is an automated or manual file that stores information about the data in the database, including names, definitions, formats, and descriptions of data elements. The data manipulation language, such as SQL, is a specialized language for accessing and manipulating the data in the database.

The relational database has been the primary method for organizing and maintaining data in information systems because it is so flexible and accessible. It organizes data in two-dimensional tables called relations with rows and columns. Each table contains data about an entity and its attributes. Each row represents a record, and each column represents an attribute or field. Each table also contains a key field to uniquely identify each record for retrieval or manipulation. Relational database tables can be combined easily to deliver data required by users, provided that any two tables share a common data element. Non-relational databases are becoming popular for managing types of data that can't be handled easily by the relational data model. Both relational and non-relational database products are available as cloud computing services.

Designing a database requires both a logical design and a physical design. The logical design models the database from a business perspective. The organization's data model should reflect its key business processes and decision-making requirements. The process of creating small, stable, flexible, and adaptive data structures from complex groups of data when designing a relational database is termed normalization. A well-designed relational database will not have many-to-many relationships, and all attributes for a specific entity will only apply to that entity. It will try to enforce referential integrity rules to ensure that relationships between coupled tables remain consistent. An entity-relationship diagram graphically depicts the relationship between entities (tables) in a relational database.

6-3 *What are the principal tools and technologies for accessing information from databases to improve business performance and decision making?*

Contemporary data management technology has an array of tools for obtaining useful information from all the different types of data used by businesses today, including semi-structured and unstructured big data in vast quantities. These capabilities include data warehouses and data marts, Hadoop, in-memory computing, and analytical platforms. OLAP represents relationships among data as a multidimensional structure, which can be visualized as cubes of data and cubes within cubes of data, enabling more sophisticated data analysis. Data mining analyzes large pools of data, including the contents of data warehouses, to find patterns and rules that can be used to predict future behavior and guide decision making. Text mining tools help businesses analyze large unstructured data sets consisting of text. Web mining tools focus on analysis of useful patterns and information from the Web, examining the structure of websites and activities of website users as well as the contents of webpages. Conventional databases can be linked via middleware to the web or a web interface to facilitate user access to an organization's internal data.

6-4 *Why are information policy, data administration, and data quality assurance essential for managing the firm's data resources?*

Developing a database environment requires policies and procedures for managing organizational data as well as a good data model and database technology. A formal information policy governs the maintenance, distribution, and use of information in the organization. In large corporations, a formal data administration function is responsible for information policy as well as for data planning, data dictionary development, and monitoring data usage in the firm.

Data that are inaccurate, incomplete, or inconsistent create serious operational and financial problems for businesses because they may create inaccuracies in product pricing, customer accounts, and inventory data and lead to inaccurate decisions about the actions that should be taken by the firm. Firms must take special steps to make sure they have a high level of data quality. These include using enterprise-wide data standards, databases designed to minimize inconsistent and redundant data, data quality audits, and data cleansing software.

Key Terms

Analytic platform, 245
Attribute, 226
Big data, 240
Bit, 226
Byte, 226
Data administration, 251
Data cleansing, 253
Data definition, 234
Data dictionary, 234
Data governance, 251
Data inconsistency, 228
Data manipulation language, 235
Data mart, 243
Data mining, 247
Data quality audit, 252
Data redundancy, 228
Data warehouse, 243
Database, 229
Database administration, 252
Database management system (DBMS), 230
Database server, 250
Entity, 226
Entity-relationship diagram, 237
Field, 226
File, 226
Foreign key, 232
Hadoop, 244
In-memory computing, 244
Information policy, 251
Key field, 231
Non-relational database management systems, 238
Normalization, 236
Online analytical processing (OLAP), 246
Primary key, 231
Program-data dependence, 229
Record, 226
Referential integrity, 237
Relational DBMS, 231
Sentiment analysis, 248
Structured Query Language (SQL), 235
Text mining, 248
Tuple, 231
Web mining, 249

Review Questions

6-1 What are the problems of managing data resources in a traditional file environment?

- How do computer systems organize data in a hierarchy? Explain with an example.
- What constitutes a database? Discuss the role of an entity and discuss its attributes.
- What do you understand by traditional file processing approach in firms?

6-2 What are the major capabilities of Database Management Systems (DBMS), and why is a relational DBMS so powerful?

- Define a database and a database management system.
- Name and briefly describe the capabilities of a DBMS.

- Define a relational DBMS and explain how it organizes data.
- Explain the importance of data manipulation languages.
- Explain why non-relational databases are useful.
- Define and describe normalization and referential integrity and explain how they contribute to a well-designed relational database.
- Define and describe an entity-relationship diagram and explain its role in database design.

6-3 What are the principal tools and technologies for accessing information from databases to improve business performance and decision-making?

- Why are businesses interested in big data? What challenges does it pose?
- Discuss the role of business intelligence infrastructure in obtaining useful information from different data types by businesses.
- Explain business benefits of multidimensional data analysis and the tool that supports it.
- How is data mining discovery driven? What are its popular areas of application?
- How can businesses benefit from text mining and Web mining? Discuss with examples.
- List the advantages of using the Web to access the internal database of an organization.

6-4 Why are information policy, data administration, and data quality assurance essential for managing the firm's data resources?

- Define information policy. How does establishing it varies with the size of business? Discuss.
- How can data quality problems be addressed in the firm?

Discussion Questions

6-5 Imagine that you are the owner of a small business. How might you use sentiment analysis to improve your performance?

6-6 To what extent should end users be involved in the selection of a database management system and database design?

6-7 What are the consequences of an organization not having an information policy?

Hands-On MIS Projects

The projects in this section give you hands-on experience in analyzing data quality problems, establishing companywide data standards, creating a database for inventory management, and using the web to search online databases for overseas business resources.

Management Decision Problems

6-8 Iko Instruments Group, a global supplier of measurement, analytical, and monitoring instruments and services based in the Netherlands, had a new data warehouse designed to analyze customer activity to improve service and marketing. However, the data warehouse was full of inaccurate and redundant data. The data in the warehouse came from numerous transaction processing systems in the United States, Europe, Asia, and other locations around the world. The team that designed the warehouse had assumed that sales groups in all these areas would enter customer names, telephone numbers, and addresses the same way. In fact, companies in different countries were using multiple ways of entering quote, billing, shipping, contact information and other data. Assess the potential business impact of these data quality problems. What decisions have to be made and steps taken to reach a solution?

Improving Decision Making: Searching Online Databases for Overseas Business Resources

Software skills: Online databases
Business skills: Researching services for overseas operations

6-9 This project develops skills in searching web-enabled databases with information about products and services in faraway locations.

Your company, Caledonian Furniture, is located in Cumbernauld, Scotland, and manufactures office furniture of various types. You are considering opening a facility to manufacture and sell your products in Australia. You would like to contact organizations that offer many services necessary for you to open your Australian office and manufacturing facility, including lawyers, accountants, import-export experts, and telecommunications equipment and support firms. Access the following online databases to locate companies that you would like to meet with during your upcoming trip: Australian Business Register, AustraliaTrade Now (australiatradenow.com), and the Nationwide Business Directory of Australia (www.nationwide.com.au). If necessary, use search engines such as Yahoo! and Google.

- List the companies you would contact on your trip to determine whether they can help you with these and any other functions you think are vital to establishing your office.
- Rate the databases you used for accuracy of name, completeness, ease of use, and general helpfulness.

Collaboration and Teamwork Project

Identifying Entities and Attributes in an Online Database

6-10 With your team of three or four other students, select an online database to explore, such as AOL Music, iGo.com, or the Internet Movie Database. Explore one of these websites to see what information it provides. Then list the entities and attributes that the company running the website must keep track of in its databases. Diagram the relationship between the entities you have identified. If possible, use Google Docs and Google Drive or Google Sites to brainstorm, organize, and develop a presentation of your findings for the class.

Lego's Enterprise Software Spurs Growth

CASE STUDY

The Lego Group, headquartered in Billund, Denmark, is one of the largest toy manufacturers in the world. Lego's main products have been the bricks and figures that children have played with for generations. The Danish company has experienced sustained growth since its founding in 1932, and for most of its history its major manufacturing facilities were located in Denmark.

In 2003, Lego was facing tough competition from imitators and manufacturers of electronic toys. In an effort to reduce costs, the group decided to initiate a gradual restructuring process that continues today. In 2006, the company announced that a large part of its production would be outsourced to the electronics manufacturing service company Flextronics, which has plants in Mexico, Hungary, and the Czech Republic. The decision to outsource production came as a direct consequence of an analysis of Lego's total supply chain. To reduce labor costs, manually intensive processes were outsourced, keeping only the highly skilled workers in Billund. Lego's workforce was gradually reduced from 8,300 employees in 2003 to approximately 4,200 in 2010. Additionally, production had to be relocated to places closer to its natural markets. As a consequence of all these changes, Lego transformed itself from a manufacturing firm to a market-oriented company that is capable of reacting fast to changing global demand.

Lego's restructuring process, coupled with double-digit sales growth in the past few years, has led to the company's expansion abroad and made its work-force more international. These changes presented supply chain and human resources (HR) challenges to the company. The supply chain had to be reengineered to simplify production without reducing quality. Improved logistics planning allowed Lego to work more closely with retailers, suppliers, and the new outsourcing companies. At the same time, the HR department needed to play a more strategic role inside the company. HR was now responsible for implementing effective policies aimed at retaining and recruiting the most qualified employees from a diversity of cultural backgrounds.

Adapting company operations to these changes required a flexible and robust IT infrastructure with business intelligence capabilities that could help management perform better forecasting and planning. As part of the solution, Lego chose to move to SAP business suite software. SAP AG, a German company that specializes in enterprise software solutions, is one of the leading software companies in the world. SAP's software products include a variety of applications designed to efficiently support all of a company's essential functions and operations. Lego chose to implement SAP's Supply Chain Management (SCM), Product Lifecycle Management (PLM), and Enterprise Resources Planning (ERP) modules.

The SCM module includes essential features such as supply chain monitoring and analysis as well as forecasting, planning, and inventory optimization. The PLM module enables managers to optimize development processes and systems. The ERP module includes, among other applications, the Human Capital Management (HCM) application for personnel administration and development.

SAP's business suite is based on a flexible three-tier client–server architecture that can easily be adapted to the new service-oriented architecture (SOA) available in the latest versions of the software. In the first tier, a client interface—a browser-type graphical user interface (GUI) running on a laptop, desktop, or mobile device—submits users' requests to the application servers. The applications servers (the second tier in the system) receive and process clients' requests. In turn, these application servers send the processed requests to the database system (the third tier), which consists of one or more relational databases. SAP's business suite supports databases from different vendors, including those offered by Oracle, Microsoft, MySQL, and others. The relational databases contain tables that store data on Lego's products, daily operations, the supply chain, and thousands of employees. Managers can easily use the SAP query tool to obtain reports from the databases because it does not require any technical skill. Additionally, the distributed architecture enables authorized personnel to have direct access to the database system from the company's various locations, including those in Europe, North America, and Asia.

SAP's ERP-HCM module includes advanced features such as "Talent Manager" as well as those for handling employee administration, reporting, and travel and time management. These features allow Lego's HR personnel to select the best candidates, schedule their training, and create a stimulus plan to retain them. It is also possible to include performance measurements and get real-time insight into HR trends. Using these advanced features, together with tools from other software vendors, Lego's managers are able to track employees' leadership potential, develop their careers, and forecast the recruiting of new employees with certain skills.

The investments that The Lego Group has made in information systems and business re-design have paid off handsomely. In 2014 the Group increased sales by 13 percent to €3.8 billion against €3.3 billion the year before. Operating profit increased 15 percent to €1.26 billion. Full-time employees increased to 11,755 as the company expanded production in Asia. In 2015, sales surged by 25 percent.

Reflecting its growing emphasis on developing a global company and its substantial investment in global information systems both in the supply chain and the distribution chain, The Lego Group in 2014 showed strong, long-term growth in all regions. In Europe, America, and Asia, sales growth has been in the double digits for over five years despite the fact that the Global Great Recession (2008 to 2013) led to flat sales of toys worldwide. In the Asian region, growth in Lego sales varied from market to market. China's growth in consumer sales of more than 50 percent was the most significant in the region. This supports The Lego Group's ambitions to further globalize the company and make Asia a significant contributor to future growth.

In May 2014 The Lego Group opened its first factory in China, located in Jiaxing, and a new office in Shanghai, which is one of five main offices globally for The Lego Group. The executives at Lego believe there is huge potential in Asia, and have decided to learn more about the Asian market and build capabilities in the region. The new factory and office represent a significant expansion of the Lego physical presence in the region. According to executives, in combination with their existing office in Singapore, the Shanghai office and the new factory enable strategically important functions to be located close to their customers as well as children and parents in China and Asia.

The decision to place a Lego factory in China is a direct consequence of The Lego Group's ambition to have production placed close to core markets. This same philosophy has led to expansions of the Lego factory in the Czech Republic, and an entirely new factory was opened in Nyiregyhaza, Hungary, in March 2014. These factories, along with the parent factory in Denmark, serve the European markets. To serve the Americas faster and with customized products, the company expanded its Lego factory in Monterrey, Mexico.

Executives believe the global approach to information systems and production facilities enables the company to deliver Lego products to retailers and ultimately to children all over the world very fast, offering world-class service to consumers. In 2014, in addition to its growth across a variety of markets, *The LEGO Movie* was also released to overwhelmingly positive reviews, bolstering the company's brand and allowing it to develop a new array of products based on the movie's themes. The movie led to shortages of Lego bricks for Christmas 2015.

The Lego Group is primed to continue its growth throughout 2016 and beyond using its organizational flexibility and the concepts it has honed for years. The company is responding to its customers and releasing new versions of some of its most popular sets of toys, including its Bionicle series of block sets. So far, Lego has built an impressive worldwide presence, block by block.

Sources: Bob Ferrari, "A New CEO for LEGO with an Operations and Supply Chain Management Background," Theferrarigroup.com, December15, 2016; John Kell, "Lego Says 2015 Was Its 'Best Year Ever,' With Huge Sales Jump," Fortune.com, March 1, 2016; "The LEGO Group Annual Report 2015," Lego.com, 2016; Mary O'Connor, "LEGO Puts the RFID Pieces Together," *RFID Journal*, http://www.rfidjournal.com accessed December 21, 2015; Henrik Amsinck, "LEGO: Building Strong Customer Loyalty Through Personalized Engagements," http://events.sap.com/ accessed December 20, 2015; Gregory Schmidt, "Lego's Success Leads to Competitors and Spinoffs," *New York Times*, November 20, 2015; Niclas Rolander, "China Shock Can't Halt Lego Executive Chasing 'Fantastic' Growth," Bloombergbusiness.com, September 2, 2015; Rebecca Kanthor, "New Lego Facility in China to Start Production This Year," *Plastics News*, May 15, 2015; "Now Lego's Business Rules Are on the Table," *Economic Engineering*, 2015; "The Lego Group Annual Report 2014," The Lego Group, April 2015; Roar Trangbaek, "New London Office Supports Lego Group Strategy to Reach Children Globally, Newsroom, www.lego.com, November 2014; "How Lego Became World's Hottest Toy Company," *Economist*, March 9, 2013; "Lego, the Toy of the Century Had to Reinvent the Supply-Chain to Save the Company," *Supply Chain Digest*, September 25, 2007, www.scdigest.com/, accessed November 16, 2010.

CASE STUDY QUESTIONS

6-11 Explain the role of the database in SAP's three-tier system.

6-12 Explain why distributed architectures are flexible.

6-13 Identify some of the business intelligence features included in SAP's business software suite.

6-14 What are the main advantages and disadvantages of having multiple databases in a distributed architecture? Explain.

Case contributed by Daniel Ortiz Arroyo, Aalborg University.

Chapter 6 References

Aiken, Peter, Mark Gillenson, Xihui Zhang, and David Rafner. "Data Management and Data Administration. Assessing 25 Years of Practice." *Journal of Database Management* (July-September 2011).

Aline, Robert. "Big Data Revolutionises Europe's Fight Against Terrorism," www.euractiv.com, June 23, 2016.

Barton, Dominic and David Court. "Making Advanced Analytics Work for You." *Harvard Business Review* (October 2012).

Beath, Cynthia, Irma Becerra-Fernandez, Jeanne Ross, and James Short. "Finding Value in the Information Explosion." *MIT Sloan Management Review* 53, No. 4 (Summer 2012).

Bughin, Jacques, John Livingston, and Sam Marwaha. "Seizing the Potential for Big Data." *McKinsey Quarterly* (October 2011).

Caserta, Joe and Elliott Cordo. "Data Warehousing in the Era of Big Data." *Big Data Quarterly* (January 19, 2016).

Clifford, James, Albert Croker, and Alex Tuzhilin. "On Data Representation and Use in a Temporal Relational DBMS." *Information Systems Research* 7, No. 3 (September 1996).

DataInformed. "The Database Decision: Key Considerations to Keep in Mind." Wellesley Information Services (2015).

Davenport, Thomas H. *Big Data at Work: Dispelling the Myths, Uncovering the Opportunities.* Boston, MA: Harvard Business School Press (2014).

Eckerson, Wayne W. "Analytics in the Era of Big Data: Exploring a Vast New Ecosystem." TechTarget (2012).

_________."Data Quality and the Bottom Line." The Data Warehousing Institute (2002).

Experian Information Solutions. "The 2016 Global Data Management Benchmark Report." (2016).

Henschen, Doug. "MetLife Uses NoSQL for Customer Service Breakthrough." *Information Week* (May 13, 2013).

Hoffer, Jeffrey A., Ramesh Venkataraman, and Heikki Toppi. *Modern Database Management* (12th ed.). Upper Saddle River, NJ: Prentice-Hall (2016).

Horst, Peter and Robert Dubroff. "Don't Let Big Data Bury Your Brand." *Harvard Business Review* (November 2015).

Jordan, John. "The Risks of Big Data for Companies." *Wall Street Journal* (October 20, 2013).

Kroenke, David M. and David Auer. *Database Processing: Fundamentals, Design, and Implementation* (14th ed.). Upper Saddle River, NJ: Prentice-Hall (2016).

Lee, Yang W. and Diane M. Strong. "Knowing-Why About Data Processes and Data Quality." *Journal of Management Information Systems* 20, No. 3 (Winter 2004).

Loveman, Gary. "Diamonds in the Datamine." *Harvard Business Review* (May 2003).

Marcus, Gary and Ernest Davis. "Eight (No, Nine!) Problems with Big Data." *New York Times* (April 6, 2014).

Martens, David and Foster Provost. "Explaining Data-Driven Document Classifications." *MIS Quarterly* 38, No. 1 (March 2014).

McAfee, Andrew and Erik Brynjolfsson. "Big Data: The Management Revolution." *Harvard Business Review* (October 2012).

McKinsey Global Institute. "Big Data: The Next Frontier for Innovation, Competition, and Productivity." McKinsey & Company (2011).

Morrow, Rich. "Apache Hadoop: The Swiss Army Knife of IT." Global Knowledge (2013).

Mulani, Narendra. "In-Memory Technology: Keeping Pace with Your Data." *Information Management* (February 27, 2013).

O'Keefe, Kate. "Real Prize in Caesars Fight: Data on Players." *Wall Street Journal* (March 19, 2015).

Redman, Thomas. *Data Driven: Profiting from Your Most Important Business Asset.* Boston: Harvard Business Press (2008).

Redman, Thomas C. "Data's Credibility Problem" *Harvard Business Review* (December 2013).

Ross, Jeanne W., Cynthia M. Beath, and Anne Quaadgras. "You May Not Need Big Data After All." *Harvard Business Review* (December 2013).

TechTarget Inc. "Identifying and Meeting the Challenges of Big Data." (2016).

Wallace, David J. "How Caesar's Entertainment Sustains a Data-Driven Culture." *DataInformed* (December 14, 2012).

Zoumpoulis, Spyros, Duncan Simester, and Theos Evgeniou, "Run Field Experiments to Make Sense of Your Big Data." *Harvard Business Review* (November 12, 2015).

CHAPTER

7 Telecommunications, the Internet, and Wireless Technology

Learning Objectives

After reading this chapter, you will be able to answer the following questions:

7-1 What are the principal components of telecommunications networks and key networking technologies?

7-2 What are the different types of networks?

7-3 How do the Internet and Internet technology work, and how do they support communication and e-business?

7-4 What are the principal technologies and standards for wireless networking, communication, and Internet access?

CHAPTER CASES

Wireless Technology Makes Dundee Precious Metals Good as Gold
The Global Battle over Net Neutrality
Monitoring Employees on Networks: Unethical or Good Business?
RFID Enabled Weighbridge Automation

Wireless Technology Makes Dundee Precious Metals Good as Gold

Dundee Precious Metals (DPM) is a Canadian-based, international mining company engaged in the acquisition, exploration, development and mining, and processing of precious metal properties. One of the company's principal assets is the Chelopech copper and gold mine east of Sofia, Bulgaria; the company also has a gold mine in southern Armenia and a smelter in Namibia.

The price of gold and other metals has fluctuated wildly, and Dundee was looking for a way to offset lower gold prices by making its mining operations more efficient. However, mines are very complex operations, and there are special challenges with communicating and coordinating work underground.

© Caro/Alamy

Management decided to implement an underground wireless Wi-Fi network that allows electronic devices to exchange data wirelessly at the Chelopech mine to monitor the location of equipment, people, and ore throughout the mine's tunnels and facilities. The company deployed several hundred Cisco Systems Inc. high-speed wireless access points (in waterproof, dustproof, and crush-resistant enclosures), extended-range antennas, communications boxes with industrial switches connected to 90 kilometers of fiber optic lines that snake through the mine, emergency boxes on walls for Linksys Voice over Internet Protocol (VoIP) phones, protected vehicle antennas that can withstand being knocked against a mine ceiling, and custom walkie-talkie software. Dundee was able to get access points that normally have a range of 200 meters to work at a range of 600 to 800 meters in a straight line or 400 to 600 meters around a curve.

Another part of the solution was to use AeroScout Wi-Fi radio frequency identification (RFID) technology to track workers, equipment, and vehicles. About 1,000 AeroScout Wi-Fi RFID tags are worn by miners or mounted on vehicles and equipment, transmitting data about vehicle rock loads and mechanical status, miner locations, and the status of doors and ventilation fans over the mine's Wi-Fi network. AeroScout's Mobile View software can display a real-time visual representation of the location of people and items. The software can determine where loads came from, where rock should be sent, and where empty vehicles should go next. Data about any mishap or slowdown, such as a truck that made an unscheduled stop or a miner who is behind schedule, are transmitted to Dundee's surface crew so that appropriate action can be taken.

The Mobile View interface is easy to use and provides a variety of reports and rules-based alerts. By using this wireless technology to track the location of equipment and workers underground, Dundee has been able to decrease equipment downtime and use resources more efficiently. Dundee also uses the data from the underground wireless network for its Dassault Systemes' Geovia mine management software and IBM mobile planning software.

Before implementing AeroScout, Dundee kept track of workers by noting who had turned in their cap lamps at the end of their shift. AeroScout has automated this process, enabling staff in the control room to determine the location of miners quickly.

It is also essential for workers driving equipment underground to be able to communicate closely with the mine's control room. In the past, workers used a radio checkpoint system to relay their location. The new wireless system enables control room staff workers actually to see the location of machinery so they can direct traffic more effectively, quickly identify problems, and respond more rapidly to emergencies.

Thanks to wireless technology, Dundee has been able to reduce costs and increase productivity while improving the safety of its workers. Communication costs have dropped 20 percent. According to Dundee CEO Rick Howes, the $10 million project, along with new crushing and conveyor systems, helped lower production costs to $40 a ton from $60. In 2013, Chelopech ore production topped two million tons, a 12 percent increase over the previous year.

Sources: Clint Boulton, "Mining Sensor Data to Run a Better Gold Mine," *Wall Street Journal*, February 17, 2015, and "Tags to Riches: Mining Company Tracks Production with Sensors," *Wall Street Journal*, February 18, 2015, www.dundeeprecious.com, accessed April 29, 2015; Eric Reguly, "Dundee's Real-Time Data Innovations Are as Good as Gold," *The Globe and Mail*, December 1, 2013; and Howard Solomon, "How a Canadian Mining Company Put a Wi-Fi Network Underground," *IT World Canada*, December 3, 2013.

The experience of Dundee Precious Metals illustrates some of the powerful capabilities and opportunities contemporary networking technology provides. The company uses wireless networking, RFID technology, and AeroScout MobileView software to automate tracking of workers, equipment, and ore as they move through its Chelopech underground mine.

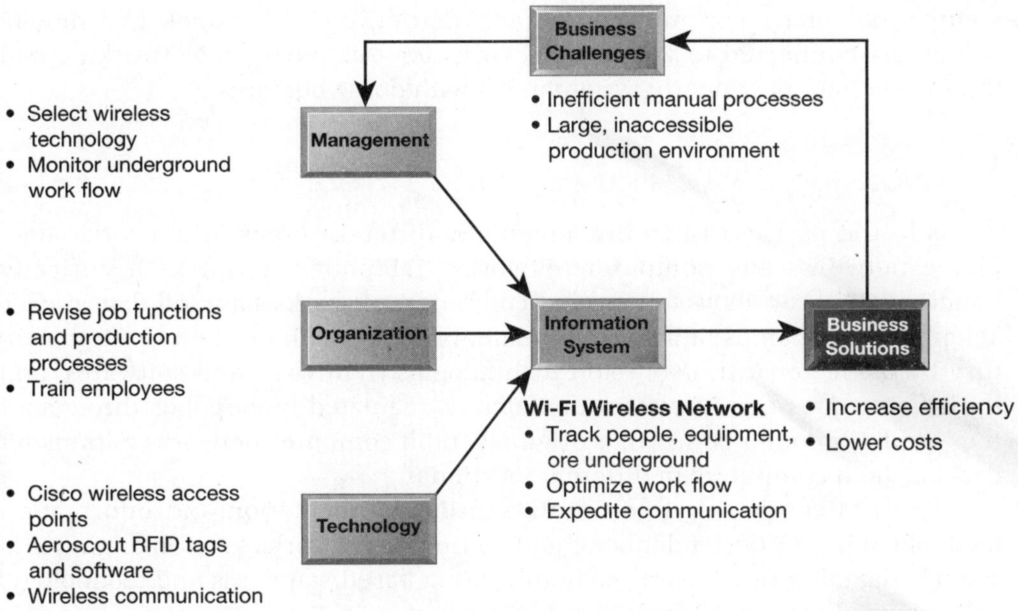

The chapter-opening diagram calls attention to important points this case and this chapter raise. The Dundee Precious Metals production environment in its Chelopech mine is difficult to monitor because it is underground yet requires intensive oversight and coordination to make sure that people, materials, and equipment are available when and where they are needed underground and that work is flowing smoothly. Tracking components manually or using older radio identification methods was slow, cumbersome, and error-prone. Dundee was also under pressure to cut costs because the price of gold had dropped and precious metals typically have wild price fluctuations.

Management decided that wireless Wi-Fi technology and RFID tagging provided a solution and arranged for the deployment of a wireless Wi-Fi network throughout the entire underground Chelopech production facility. The network made it much easier to track and supervise mining activities from above ground.

Here are some questions to think about: Why did wireless technology play such a key role in this solution? Describe how the new system changed the production process at the Chelopech mine.

7-1 What are the principal components of telecommunications networks and key networking technologies?

If you run or work in a business, you can't do without networks. You need to communicate rapidly with your customers, suppliers, and employees. Until about 1990, businesses used the postal system or telephone system with voice or fax for communication. Today, however, you and your employees use computers, e-mail, text messaging, the Internet, mobile phones, and mobile computers connected to wireless networks for this purpose. Networking and the Internet are now nearly synonymous with doing business.

Networking and Communication Trends

Firms in the past used two fundamentally different types of networks: telephone networks and computer networks. Telephone networks historically handled voice communication, and computer networks handled data traffic. Telephone companies built telephone networks throughout the twentieth century by using voice transmission technologies (hardware and software), and these companies almost always operated as regulated monopolies throughout the world. Computer companies originally built computer networks to transmit data between computers in different locations.

Thanks to continuing telecommunications deregulation and information technology innovation, telephone and computer networks are converging into a single digital network using shared Internet-based standards and technology. Telecommunications providers today, such as AT&T and Verizon, offer data transmission, Internet access, mobile phone service, and television programming as well as voice service. Cable companies, such as Cablevision and Comcast, offer voice service and Internet access. Computer networks have expanded to include Internet telephone and video services.

Both voice and data communication networks have also become more powerful (faster), more portable (smaller and mobile), and less expensive. For instance, the typical Internet connection speed in 2000 was 56 kilobits per second, but today more than 80 percent of EU households have high-speed **broadband** connections provided by telephone and cable TV companies running at 1 to 15 million bits per second. The cost for this service has fallen exponentially, from 25 cents per kilobit in 2000 to a tiny fraction of a cent today.

Increasingly, voice and data communication, as well as Internet access, are taking place over broadband wireless platforms such as mobile phones, mobile handheld devices, and PCs in wireless networks. More than half the Internet users in the United States use smartphones and tablets to access the Internet.

What is a Computer Network?

If you had to connect the computers for two or more employees in the same office, you would need a computer network. In its simplest form, a network consists of two or more connected computers. Figure 7.1 illustrates the major hardware, software, and transmission components in a simple network: a client computer and a dedicated server computer, network interfaces, a connection medium, network operating system software, and either a hub or a switch.

Each computer on the network contains a network interface device to link the computer to the network. The connection medium for linking network components can be a telephone wire, coaxial cable, or radio signal in the case of cell phone and wireless local area networks (Wi-Fi networks).

The **network operating system (NOS)** routes and manages communications on the network and coordinates network resources. It can reside on every

FIGURE 7.1 COMPONENTS OF A SIMPLE COMPUTER NETWORK

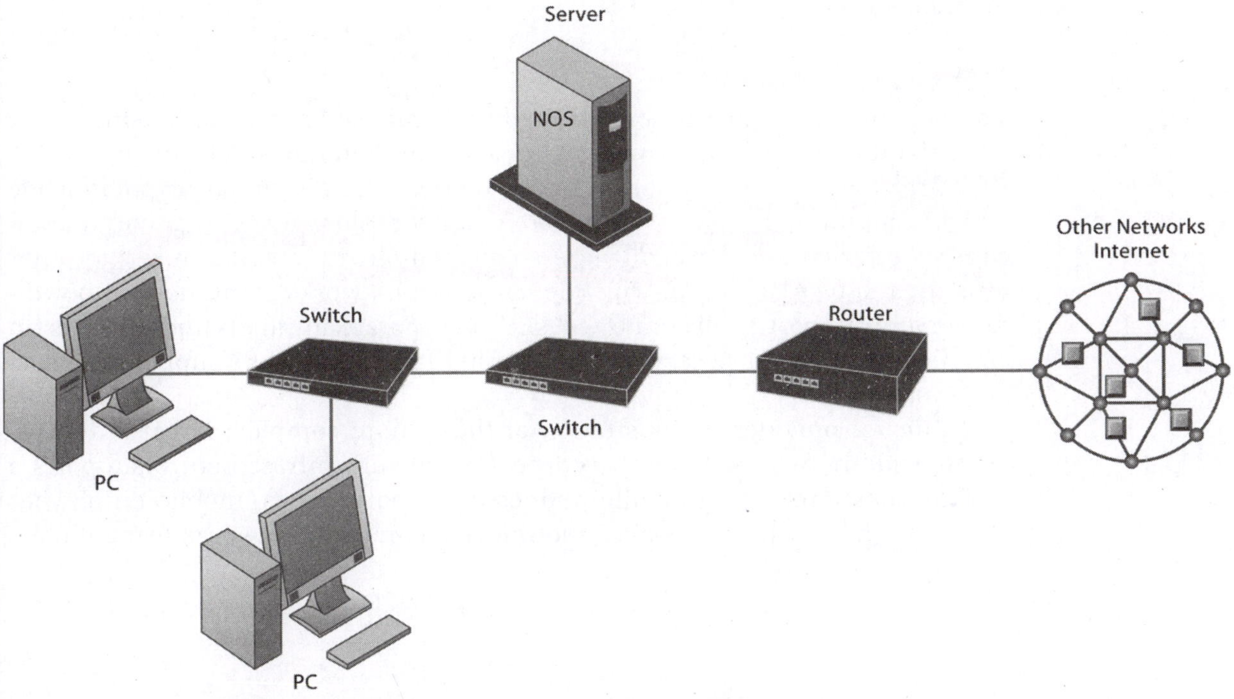

Illustrated here is a simple computer network consisting of computers, a network operating system (NOS) residing on a dedicated server computer, cable (wiring) connecting the devices, switches, and a router.

computer in the network or primarily on a dedicated server computer for all the applications on the network. A server is a computer on a network that performs important network functions for client computers, such as displaying web pages, storing data, and storing the network operating system (hence controlling the network). Microsoft Windows Server, Linux, and Novell Open Enterprise Server are the most widely used network operating systems.

Most networks also contain a switch or a hub acting as a connection point between the computers. **Hubs** are simple devices that connect network components, sending a packet of data to all other connected devices. A **switch** has more intelligence than a hub and can filter and forward data to a specified destination on the network.

What if you want to communicate with another network, such as the Internet? You would need a router. A **router** is a communications processor that routes packets of data through different networks, ensuring that the data sent get to the correct address.

Network switches and routers have proprietary software built into their hardware for directing the movement of data on the network. This can create network bottlenecks and makes the process of configuring a network more complicated and time-consuming. **Software-defined networking (SDN)** is a new networking approach in which many of these control functions are managed by one central program, which can run on inexpensive commodity servers that are separate from the network devices themselves. This is especially helpful in a cloud computing environment with many pieces of hardware because it allows a network administrator to manage traffic loads in a flexible and more efficient manner.

Networks in Large Companies

The network we've just described might be suitable for a small business, but what about large companies with many locations and thousands of employees? As a firm grows, its small networks can be tied together into a corporate-wide networking infrastructure. The network infrastructure for a large corporation consists of a large number of these small local area networks linked to other local area networks and to firmwide corporate networks. A number of powerful servers support a corporate website, a corporate intranet, and perhaps an extranet. Some of these servers link to other large computers supporting back-end systems.

Figure 7.2 provides an illustration of these more complex, larger scale corporate-wide networks. Here the corporate network infrastructure supports a mobile sales force using mobile phones and smartphones, mobile employees linking to the company website, and internal company networks using mobile

FIGURE 7.2 CORPORATE NETWORK INFRASTRUCTURE

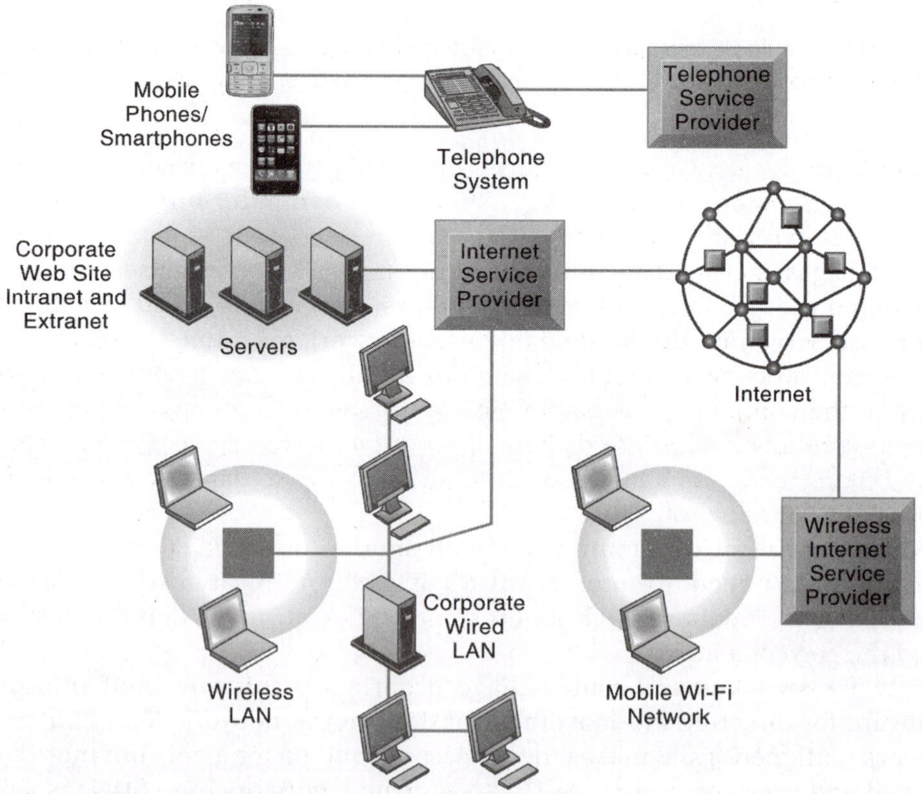

Today's corporate network infrastructure is a collection of many networks from the public switched telephone network, to the Internet, to corporate local area networks linking workgroups, departments, or office floors.

wireless local area networks (Wi-Fi networks). In addition to these computer networks, the firm's infrastructure may include a separate telephone network that handles most voice data. Many firms are dispensing with their traditional telephone networks and using Internet telephones that run on their existing data networks (described later).

As you can see from this figure, a large corporate network infrastructure uses a wide variety of technologies—everything from ordinary telephone service and corporate data networks to Internet service, wireless Internet, and mobile phones. One of the major problems facing corporations today is how to integrate all the different communication networks and channels into a coherent system that enables information to flow from one part of the corporation to another and from one system to another.

Key Digital Networking Technologies

Contemporary digital networks and the Internet are based on three key technologies: client/server computing, the use of packet switching, and the development of widely used communications standards (the most important of which is Transmission Control Protocol/Internet Protocol, or TCP/IP) for linking disparate networks and computers.

Client/Server Computing

Client/server computing, introduced in Chapter 5, is a distributed computing model in which some of the processing power is located within small, inexpensive client computers and resides literally on desktops or laptops or in handheld devices. These powerful clients are linked to one another through a network that is controlled by a network server computer. The server sets the rules of communication for the network and provides every client with an address so others can find it on the network.

Client/server computing has largely replaced centralized mainframe computing in which nearly all the processing takes place on a central large mainframe computer. Client/server computing has extended computing to departments, workgroups, factory floors, and other parts of the business that could not be served by a centralized architecture. It also makes it possible for personal computing devices such as PCs, laptops, and mobile phones to be connected to networks such as the Internet. The Internet is the largest implementation of client/server computing.

Packet Switching

Packet switching is a method of slicing digital messages into parcels called packets, sending the packets along different communication paths as they become available and then reassembling the packets once they arrive at their destinations (see Figure 7.3). Prior to the development of packet switching, computer networks used leased, dedicated telephone circuits to communicate with other computers in remote locations. In circuit-switched networks, such as the telephone system, a complete point-to-point circuit is assembled, and then communication can proceed. These dedicated circuit-switching techniques were expensive and wasted available communications capacity—the circuit was maintained regardless of whether any data were being sent.

FIGURE 7.3 PACKET-SWITCHED NETWORKS AND PACKET COMMUNICATIONS

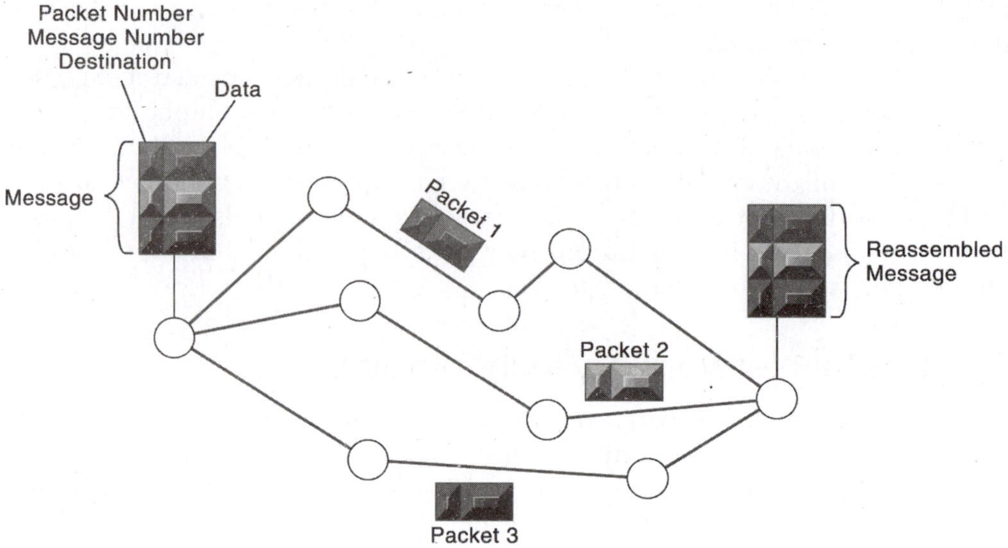

Data are grouped into small packets, which are transmitted independently over various communications channels and reassembled at their final destination.

Packet switching makes much more efficient use of the communications capacity of a network. In packet-switched networks, messages are first broken down into small fixed bundles of data called packets. The packets include information for directing the packet to the right address and for checking transmission errors along with the data. The packets are transmitted over various communications channels by using routers, each packet traveling independently. Packets of data originating at one source will be routed through many paths and networks before being reassembled into the original message when they reach their destinations.

TCP/IP and Connectivity

In a typical telecommunications network, diverse hardware and software components need to work together to transmit information. Different components in a network communicate with each other by adhering to a common set of rules called protocols. A **protocol** is a set of rules and procedures governing transmission of information between two points in a network.

In the past, diverse proprietary and incompatible protocols often forced business firms to purchase computing and communications equipment from a single vendor. However, today, corporate networks are increasingly using a single, common, worldwide standard called **Transmission Control Protocol/Internet Protocol (TCP/IP)**. TCP/IP was developed during the early 1970s to support U.S. Department of Defense Advanced Research Projects Agency (DARPA) efforts to help scientists transmit data among different types of computers over long distances.

TCP/IP uses a suite of protocols, the main ones being TCP and IP. TCP refers to the Transmission Control Protocol, which handles the movement of data

FIGURE 7.4 THE TRANSMISSION CONTROL PROTOCOL/INTERNET PROTOCOL (TCP/IP) REFERENCE MODEL

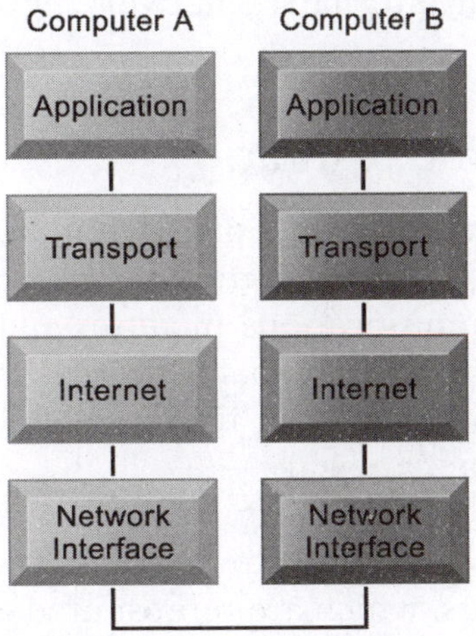

This figure illustrates the four layers of the TCP/IP reference model for communications.

between computers. TCP establishes a connection between the computers, sequences the transfer of packets, and acknowledges the packets sent. IP refers to the Internet Protocol (IP), which is responsible for the delivery of packets and includes the disassembling and reassembling of packets during transmission. Figure 7.4 illustrates the four-layered Department of Defense reference model for TCP/IP, and the layers are described as follows.

1. Application layer. The Application layer enables client application programs to access the other layers and defines the protocols that applications use to exchange data. One of these application protocols is the Hypertext Transfer Protocol (HTTP), which is used to transfer web page files.
2. Transport layer. The Transport layer is responsible for providing the Application layer with communication and packet services. This layer includes TCP and other protocols.
3. Internet layer. The Internet layer is responsible for addressing, routing, and packaging data packets called IP datagrams. The Internet Protocol is one of the protocols used in this layer.
4. Network Interface layer. At the bottom of the reference model, the Network Interface layer is responsible for placing packets on and receiving them from the network medium, which could be any networking technology.

Two computers using TCP/IP can communicate even if they are based on different hardware and software platforms. Data sent from one computer to the other passes downward through all four layers, starting with the sending computer's Application layer and passing through the Network Interface layer. After the data reach the recipient host computer, they travel up the layers and are reassembled into a format the receiving computer can use. If the receiving computer finds a damaged packet, it asks the sending computer to retransmit it. This process is reversed when the receiving computer responds.

7-2 What are the different types of networks?

Let's look more closely at alternative networking technologies available to businesses.

Signals: Digital Versus Analog

There are two ways to communicate a message in a network: an analog signal or a digital signal. An *analog signal* is represented by a continuous waveform that passes through a communications medium and has been used for voice communication. The most common analog devices are the telephone handset, the speaker on your computer, or your iPod earphone, all of which create analog waveforms that your ear can hear.

A *digital signal* is a discrete, binary waveform rather than a continuous waveform. Digital signals communicate information as strings of two discrete states: one bits and zero bits, which are represented as on-off electrical pulses. Computers use digital signals and require a modem to convert these digital signals into analog signals that can be sent over (or received from) telephone lines, cable lines, or wireless media that use analog signals (see Figure 7.5). **Modem** stands for modulator-demodulator. Cable modems connect your computer to the Internet by using a cable network. DSL modems connect your computer to the Internet using a telephone company's landline network. Wireless modems perform the same function as traditional modems, connecting your computer to a wireless network that could be a cell phone network or a Wi-Fi network.

Types of Networks

There are many kinds of networks and ways of classifying them. One way of looking at networks is in terms of their geographic scope (see Table 7.1).

Local Area Networks

If you work in a business that uses networking, you are probably connecting to other employees and groups via a local area network. A **local area network (LAN)** is designed to connect personal computers and other digital devices within a half-mile or 500-meter radius. LANs typically connect a few computers

FIGURE 7.5 FUNCTIONS OF THE MODEM

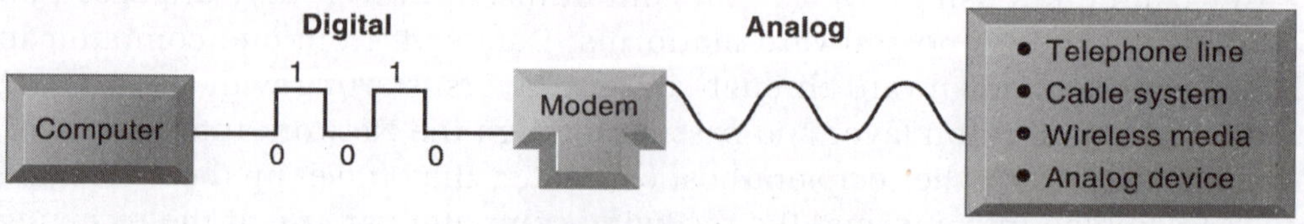

A modem is a device that translates digital signals into analog form (and vice versa) so that computers can transmit data over analog networks such as telephone and cable networks.

TABLE 7.1 TYPES OF NETWORKS

TYPE	AREA
Local area network (LAN)	Up to 500 meters (half a mile); an office or floor of a building
Campus area network (CAN)	Up to 1,000 meters (a mile); a college campus or corporate facility
Metropolitan area network (MAN)	A city or metropolitan area
Wide area network (WAN)	A regional, transcontinental, or global area

in a small office, all the computers in one building, or all the computers in several buildings in close proximity. LANs also are used to link to long-distance wide area networks (WANs, described later in this section) and other networks around the world, using the Internet.

Review Figure 7.1, which could serve as a model for a small LAN that might be used in an office. One computer is a dedicated network, providing users with access to shared computing resources in the network, including software programs and data files.

The server determines who gets access to what and in which sequence. The router connects the LAN to other networks, which could be the Internet, or another corporate network, so that the LAN can exchange information with networks external to it. The most common LAN operating systems are Windows, Linux, and Novell.

Ethernet is the dominant LAN standard at the physical network level, specifying the physical medium to carry signals between computers, access control rules, and a standardized set of bits that carry data over the system. Originally, Ethernet supported a data transfer rate of 10 megabits per second (Mbps). Newer versions, such as Gigabit Ethernet, support a data transfer rate of 1 gigabit per second (Gbps).

The LAN illustrated in Figure 7.1 uses a client/server architecture by which the network operating system resides primarily on a single server, and the server provides much of the control and resources for the network. Alternatively, LANs may use a **peer-to-peer** architecture. A peer-to-peer network treats all processors equally and is used primarily in small networks with 10 or fewer users. The various computers on the network can exchange data by direct access and can share peripheral devices without going through a separate server.

Larger LANs have many clients and multiple servers, with separate servers for specific services such as storing and managing files and databases (file servers or database servers), managing printers (print servers), storing and managing e-mail (mail servers), or storing and managing web pages (web servers).

Metropolitan and Wide Area Networks

Wide area networks (WANs) span broad geographical distances—entire regions, states, continents, or the entire globe. The most universal and powerful WAN is the Internet. Computers connect to a WAN through public networks, such as the telephone system or private cable systems, or through leased lines

TABLE 7.2 PHYSICAL TRANSMISSION MEDIA

TRANSMISSION MEDIUM	DESCRIPTION	SPEED
Twisted pair wire (CAT 5)	Strands of copper wire twisted in pairs for voice and data communications. CAT 5 is the most common 10 Mbps LAN cable. Maximum recommended run of 100 meters.	10–100+ Mbps
Coaxial cable	Thickly insulated copper wire, which is capable of high-speed data transmission and less subject to interference than twisted wire. Currently used for cable TV and for networks with longer runs (more than 100 meters).	Up to 1 Gbps
Fiber-optic cable	Strands of clear glass fiber, transmitting data as pulses of light generated by lasers. Useful for high-speed transmission of large quantities of data. More expensive than other physical transmission media and harder to install; often used for network backbone.	15 Mbps to 6+ Tbps
Wireless transmission media	Based on radio signals of various frequencies and includes both terrestrial and satellite microwave systems and cellular networks. Used for long-distance, wireless communication and Internet access.	Up to 600+ Mbps

or satellites. A **metropolitan area network (MAN)** is a network that spans a metropolitan area, usually a city and its major suburbs. Its geographic scope falls between a WAN and a LAN.

Transmission Media and Transmission Speed

Networks use different kinds of physical transmission media, including twisted pair wire, coaxial cable, fiber-optic cable, and media for wireless transmission. Each has advantages and limitations. A wide range of speeds is possible for any given medium, depending on the software and hardware configuration. Table 7.2 compares these media.

Bandwidth: Transmission Speed

The total amount of digital information that can be transmitted through any telecommunications medium is measured in bits per second (bps). One signal change, or cycle, is required to transmit one or several bits; therefore, the transmission capacity of each type of telecommunications medium is a function of its frequency. The number of cycles per second that can be sent through that medium is measured in **hertz**—one hertz is equal to one cycle of the medium.

The range of frequencies that can be accommodated on a particular telecommunications channel is called its **bandwidth**. The bandwidth is the difference between the highest and lowest frequencies that can be accommodated on a single channel. The greater the range of frequencies, the greater the bandwidth and the greater the channel's transmission capacity.

7-3 How do the Internet and Internet technology work, and how do they support communication and e-business?

The Internet has become an indispensable personal and business tool—but what exactly is the Internet? How does it work, and what does Internet technology have to offer for business? Let's look at the most important Internet features.

What is the Internet?

The Internet is the world's most extensive public communication system. It's also the world's largest implementation of client/server computing and Internetworking, linking millions of individual networks all over the world. This global network of networks began in the early 1970s as a U.S. Department of Defense network to link scientists and university professors around the world.

Most homes and small businesses connect to the Internet by subscribing to an Internet service provider. An **Internet service provider (ISP)** is a commercial organization with a permanent connection to the Internet that sells temporary connections to retail subscribers. EarthLink, NetZero, AT&T, and Time Warner are ISPs. Individuals also connect to the Internet through their business firms, universities, or research centers that have designated Internet domains.

There is a variety of services for ISP Internet connections. Connecting via a traditional telephone line and modem, at a speed of 56.6 kilobits per second (Kbps), used to be the most common form of connection worldwide, but broadband connections have largely replaced it. Digital subscriber line, cable, satellite Internet connections, and T lines provide these broadband services.

Digital subscriber line (DSL) technologies operate over existing telephone lines to carry voice, data, and video at transmission rates ranging from 385 Kbps all the way up to 40 Mbps, depending on usage patterns and distance. **Cable Internet connections** provided by cable television vendors use digital cable coaxial lines to deliver high-speed Internet access to homes and businesses. They can provide high-speed access to the Internet of up to 50 Mbps, although most providers offer service ranging from 1 Mbps to 6 Mbps. Where DSL and cable services are unavailable, it is possible to access the Internet via satellite, although some satellite Internet connections have slower upload speeds than other broadband services.

T1 and T3 are international telephone standards for digital communication. They are leased, dedicated lines suitable for businesses or government agencies requiring high-speed guaranteed service levels. **T1 lines** offer guaranteed delivery at 1.54 Mbps, and T3 lines offer delivery at 45 Mbps. The Internet does not provide similar guaranteed service levels but, simply, best effort.

Internet Addressing and Architecture

The Internet is based on the TCP/IP networking protocol suite described earlier in this chapter. Every computer on the Internet is assigned a unique **Internet Protocol (IP) address**, which currently is a 32-bit number represented by four strings of numbers ranging from 0 to 255 separated by periods. For instance, the IP address of www.microsoft.com is 207.46.250.119.

When a user sends a message to another user on the Internet, the message is first decomposed into packets using the TCP protocol. Each packet contains its destination address. The packets are then sent from the client to the network server and from there on to as many other servers as necessary to arrive at a specific computer with a known address. At the destination address, the packets are reassembled into the original message.

The Domain Name System

Because it would be incredibly difficult for Internet users to remember strings of 12 numbers, the **Domain Name System (DNS)** converts domain names to IP addresses. The **domain name** is the English-like name that corresponds to the unique 32-bit numeric IP address for each computer connected to the Internet. DNS servers maintain a database containing IP addresses mapped to their corresponding domain names. To access a computer on the Internet, users need only specify its domain name.

DNS has a hierarchical structure (see Figure 7.6). At the top of the DNS hierarchy is the root domain. The child domain of the root is called a top-level domain, and the child domain of a top-level domain is called a second-level domain. Top-level domains are two- and three-character names you are familiar with from surfing the web, for example, .com, .edu, .gov, and the various country codes such as .ca for Canada or .it for Italy. Second-level domains have two parts, designating a top-level name and a second-level name—such as buy.com, nyu.edu, or amazon.ca. A host name at the bottom of the hierarchy designates a specific computer on either the Internet or a private network.

FIGURE 7.6 THE DOMAIN NAME SYSTEM

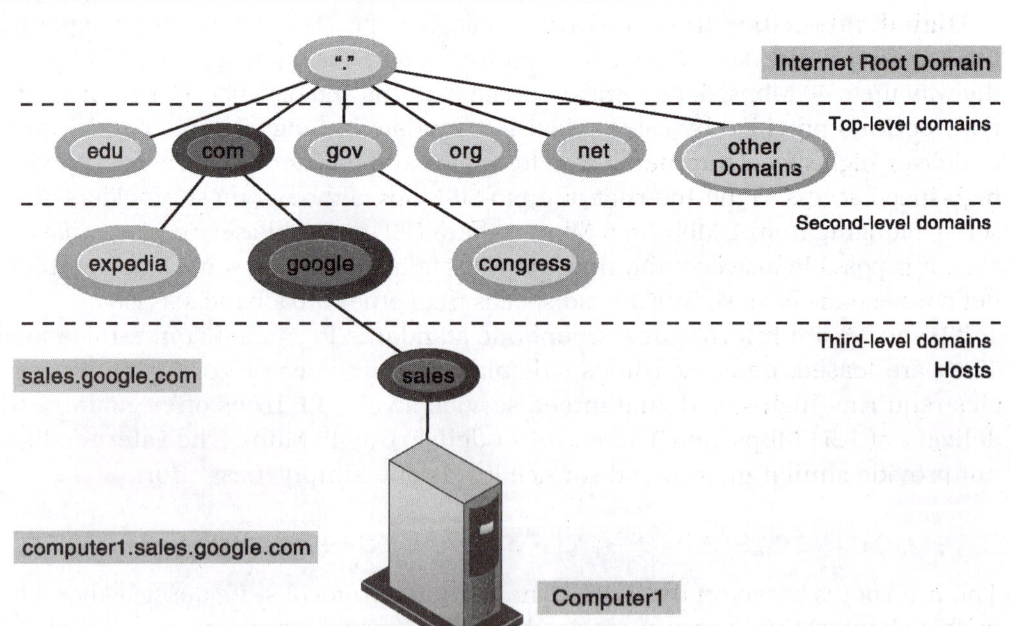

Domain Name System is a hierarchical system with a root domain, top-level domains, second-level domains, and host computers at the third level.

The following list shows the most common domain extensions currently available and officially approved. Countries also have domain names such as .uk, .au, and .fr (United Kingdom, Australia, and France, respectively), and there is a new class of internationalized top-level domains that use non-English characters. In the future, this list will expand to include many more types of organizations and industries.

.com	Commercial organizations/businesses
.edu	Educational institutions
.gov	U.S. government agencies
.mil	U.S. military
.net	Network computers
.org	Any type of organization
.biz	Business firms
.info	Information providers

Internet Architecture and Governance

Internet data traffic is carried over transcontinental high-speed backbone networks that generally operate in the range of 155 Mbps to 2.5 Gbps (see Figure 7.7). These trunk lines are typically owned by long-distance telephone

FIGURE 7.7 INTERNET NETWORK ARCHITECTURE

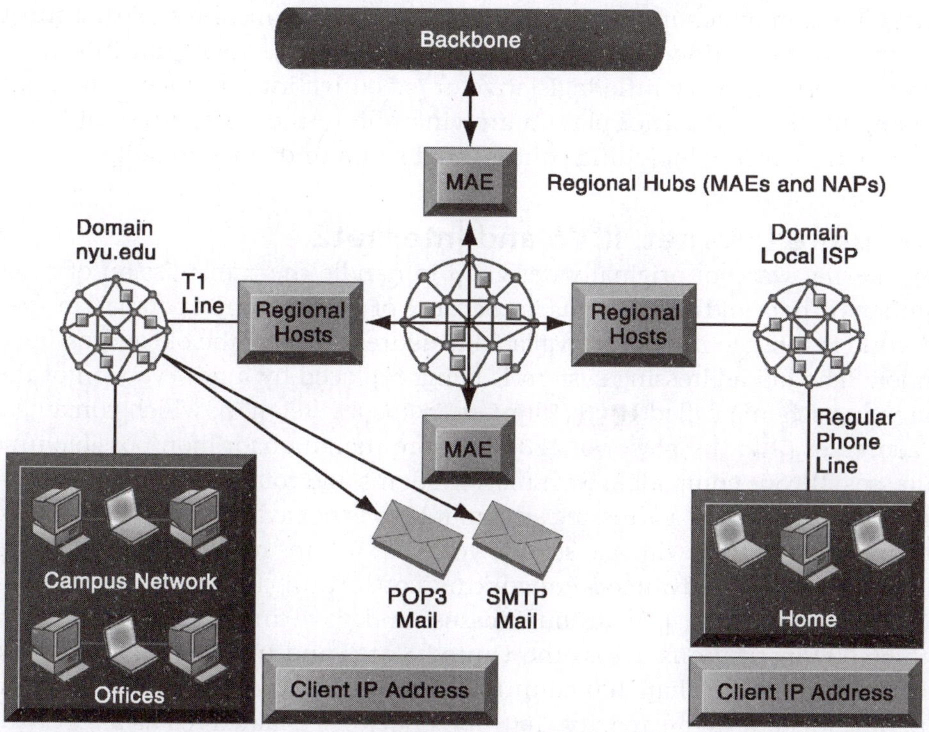

The Internet backbone connects to regional networks, which in turn provide access to Internet service providers, large firms, and government institutions. Network access points (NAPs) and metropolitan area exchanges (MAEs) are hubs where the backbone intersects regional and local networks and where backbone owners connect with one another.

companies (called *network service providers*) or by national governments. Local connection lines are owned by regional telephone and cable television companies in the United States and in other countries that connect retail users in homes and businesses to the Internet. The regional networks lease access to ISPs, private companies, and government institutions.

Each organization pays for its own networks and its own local Internet connection services, a part of which is paid to the long-distance trunk line owners. Individual Internet users pay ISPs for using their service, and they generally pay a flat subscription fee, no matter how much or how little they use the Internet. A debate is now raging on whether this arrangement should continue or whether heavy Internet users who download large video and music files should pay more for the bandwidth they consume. The Interactive Session on Organizations explores this topic by examining the pros and cons of net neutrality.

No one owns the Internet, and it has no formal management. However, worldwide Internet policies are established by a number of professional organizations and government bodies, including the Internet Architecture Board (IAB), which helps define the overall structure of the Internet; the Internet Corporation for Assigned Names and Numbers (ICANN), which manages the domain name system; and the World Wide Web Consortium (W3C), which sets Hypertext Markup Language and other programming standards for the web.

These organizations influence government agencies, network owners, ISPs, and software developers with the goal of keeping the Internet operating as efficiently as possible. The Internet must also conform to the laws of the sovereign nation-states in which it operates as well as to the technical infrastructures that exist within the nation-states. Although in the early years of the Internet and the web there was very little legislative or executive interference, this situation is changing as the Internet plays a growing role in the distribution of information and knowledge, including content that some find objectionable.

The Future Internet: IPV6 and Internet2

The Internet was not originally designed to handle the transmission of massive quantities of data and billions of users. Because of sheer Internet population growth, the world is about to run out of available IP addresses using the old addressing convention. The old addressing system is being replaced by a new version of the IP addressing schema called **IPv6** (Internet Protocol version 6), which contains 128-bit addresses (2 to the power of 128), or more than a quadrillion possible unique addresses. IPv6 is compatible with most modems and routers sold today, and IPv6 will fall back to the old addressing system if IPv6 is not available on local networks. The transition to IPv6 will take several years as systems replace older equipment.

Internet2 is an advanced networking consortium representing more than 500 U.S. universities, private businesses, and government agencies working with 66,000 institutions across the United States and international networking partners from more than 100 countries. To connect these communities, Internet2 developed a high-capacity, 100 Gbps network that serves as a test bed for leading-edge technologies that may eventually migrate to the public Internet, including large-scale network performance measurement and management tools, secure identity and access management tools, and capabilities such as scheduling high-bandwidth, high-performance circuits.

INTERACTIVE SESSION: ORGANIZATIONS

The Global Battle over Net Neutrality

What kind of Internet user are you? Do you primarily use the Net to do a little e-mail and online banking? Or are you online all day, watching YouTube videos, downloading music files, or playing online games? Do you use your iPhone to stream TV shows and movies on a regular basis? If you're a power Internet or smartphone user, you are consuming a great deal of bandwidth. Could hundreds of millions of people like you start to slow the Internet down?

Video streaming on Netflix has accounted for 32 percent of all bandwidth use in the United States and Google's YouTube for 19 percent of web traffic at peak hours. If user demand overwhelms network capacity, the Internet might not come to a screeching halt, but users could face sluggish download speeds and video transmission. Heavy use of iPhones in urban areas such as New York and San Francisco has degraded service on the AT&T wireless network. AT&T had reported that 3 percent of its subscriber base accounted for 40 percent of its data traffic.

Internet service providers (ISPs) assert that network congestion is a serious problem and that expanding their networks would require passing on burdensome costs to consumers. These companies believe differential pricing methods, which include data caps and metered use—charging based on the amount of bandwidth consumed—are the fairest way to finance necessary investments in their network infrastructures. However, metering Internet use is not widely accepted because of an ongoing debate about net neutrality.

Net neutrality is the idea that Internet service providers must allow customers equal access to content and applications, regardless of the source or nature of the content. Presently, the Internet is neutral; all Internet traffic is treated equally on a first-come, first-served basis by Internet backbone owners. However, this arrangement prevents telecommunications and cable companies from charging differentiated prices based on the amount of bandwidth consumed by the content being delivered over the Internet.

The strange alliance of net neutrality advocates includes MoveOn.org; the Electronic Frontier Foundation; the Christian Coalition; the American Library Association; data-intensive web businesses such as Netflix, Amazon, and Google; major consumer groups; and a host of bloggers and small businesses. Net neutrality advocates argue that differentiated pricing would impose heavy costs on heavy bandwidth users such as YouTube, Skype, and other innovative services, preventing high-bandwidth start-up companies from gaining traction. Net neutrality supporters also argue that without net neutrality, ISPs that are also cable companies, such as Comcast, might block online streaming video from Netflix or Hulu to force customers to use the cable company's on-demand movie rental services.

Network owners believe regulation to enforce net neutrality will impede competitiveness by discouraging capital expenditure for new networks and curbing their networks' ability to cope with the exploding demand for Internet and wireless traffic. U.S. Internet service lags behind many other nations in overall speed, cost, and quality of service, adding credibility to this argument. Moreover, with enough options for Internet access, dissatisfied consumers could simply switch to providers who enforce net neutrality and allow unlimited Internet use.

In the United States the Internet has recently been declared a public utility, and therefore subject to regulation of the Federal Communications Commission (FCC), which regulates the land telephone system. Public utilities are required to provide service on an equal footing to all users.

The new rules are intended to ensure that no content is blocked and that the Internet cannot be divided into pay-to-play fast lanes for Internet and media companies that can afford them and slow lanes for everyone else. Outright blocking of content, slowing of transmissions, and the creation of so-called fast lanes were prohibited. The FCC stated that it favors a light touch rather than the heavy-handed regulations to which the old regulated telephone companies were subjected. One provision requiring "just and reasonable" conduct allows the FCC to decide what is acceptable on a case-by-case basis. The new rules apply to mobile data service for smartphones and tablets in addition to wired lines. The order also includes provisions to protect consumer privacy and ensure that Internet service is available to people with disabilities and in remote areas.

In Europe, telecommunications carriers are subject to the European Parliament, which in 2015 adopted net neutrality legislation that required Internet service providers to treat all web traffic equally. In 2016 the Body of European Regulators for Electronic Communications (BEREC) issued regulations that prohibited ISPs from blocking or slowing down of Internet traffic, except where necessary for maintenance and security.

In 2015, United States Telecom Association, an industry trade group, filed a lawsuit to overturn the government's net neutrality rules. AT&T, the National Cable & Telecommunications Association, and CTIA, which represents wireless carriers, filed similar legal challenges. Pro-net neutrality forces have asked the FCC to look at "zero-rating" practices, in which certain services, like Spotify and Netflix, are exempt from data caps in a customer's data plan. The battle over net neutrality is not yet over

In Europe, telecommunications carriers are subject to the European Parliament, which in 2015 adopted net neutrality legislation that required internet service providers to treat all web traffic equally. In 2016, the Body of European Regulators for Electronic Communications (BEREC) issued regulations that prohibited ISPs from blocking or slowing down of Internet traffic except where necessary for maintenance and security.

In Europe, major ISPs including Deutsche Telekom, Nokia, Vodafone, and BT promise to launch 5G networks in every country in the European Union by 2020 if authorities hold off on implementing the new rules. Otherwise, 5G networks will take a much longer time, they argue.

Sources: Amar Toor, "Europe's Net Neutrality Guidelines Seen as a Victory for the Open Web," *The Verge*, August 30, 2016; BEREC, "All You Need to Know About Net Neutrality Rules in the EU," berec.europa.eu, 2016; David Meyer, "Here's Why Europe's Net Neutrality Advocates Are Celebrating," *Fortune*, August 30, 2016; John D. McKinnon and Brett Kendall, "FCC's Net-Neutrality Rules Upheld by Appeals Court," *Wall Street Journal*, June 14, 2016; Darren Orf, "The Next Battle for Net Neutrality Is Getting Bloody," *Gizmodo*, May 25, 2016; Stephanie Milot, "GOP Moves to Gut Net Neutrality, FCC Budget," *PC Magazine*, February 26, 2016; Rebecca Ruiz, "FCC Sets Net Neutrality Rules," *New York Times*, March 12, 2015; Rebecca Ruiz and Steve Lohr, "F.C.C. Approves Net Neutrality Rules, Classifying Broadband Internet Service as a Utility," *New York Times*, February. 26, 2015; Robert M. McDowell, "The Turning Point for Internet Freedom," *Wall Street Journal*, January 19, 2015; Ryan Knutson, "AT&T Sues to Overturn FCC's Net Neutrality Rules," *Wall Street Journal*, April 14, 2015.

CASE STUDY QUESTIONS

1. What is net neutrality? Why has the Internet operated under net neutrality up to this point?
2. Who's in favor of net neutrality? Who's opposed? Why?
3. What would be the impact on individual users, businesses, and government if Internet providers switched to a tiered service model for transmission over landlines as well as wireless?
4. It has been said that net neutrality is the most important issue facing the Internet since the advent of the Internet. Discuss the implications of this statement.
5. Are you in favor of legislation enforcing network neutrality? Why or why not?

Internet Services and Communication Tools

The Internet is based on client/server technology. Individuals using the Internet control what they do through client applications on their computers, such as web browser software. The data, including e-mail messages and web pages, are stored on servers. A client uses the Internet to request information from a particular web server on a distant computer, and the server sends the requested

TABLE 7.3 MAJOR INTERNET SERVICES

CAPABILITY	FUNCTIONS SUPPORTED
E-mail	Person-to-person messaging; document sharing
Chatting and instant messaging	Interactive conversations
Newsgroups	Discussion groups on electronic bulletin boards
Telnet	Logging on to one computer system and doing work on another
File Transfer Protocol (FTP)	Transferring files from computer to computer
World Wide Web	Retrieving, formatting, and displaying information (including text, audio, graphics, and video) by using hypertext links

information back to the client over the Internet. Client platforms today include not only PCs and other computers but also smartphones and tablets.

Internet Services

A client computer connecting to the Internet has access to a variety of services. These services include e-mail, chatting and instant messaging, electronic discussion groups, **Telnet**, **File Transfer Protocol (FTP)**, and the web. Table 7.3 provides a brief description of these services.

Each Internet service is implemented by one or more software programs. All the services may run on a single server computer, or different services may be allocated to different machines. Figure 7.8 illustrates one way these services can be arranged in a multitiered client/server architecture.

FIGURE 7.8 CLIENT/SERVER COMPUTING ON THE INTERNET

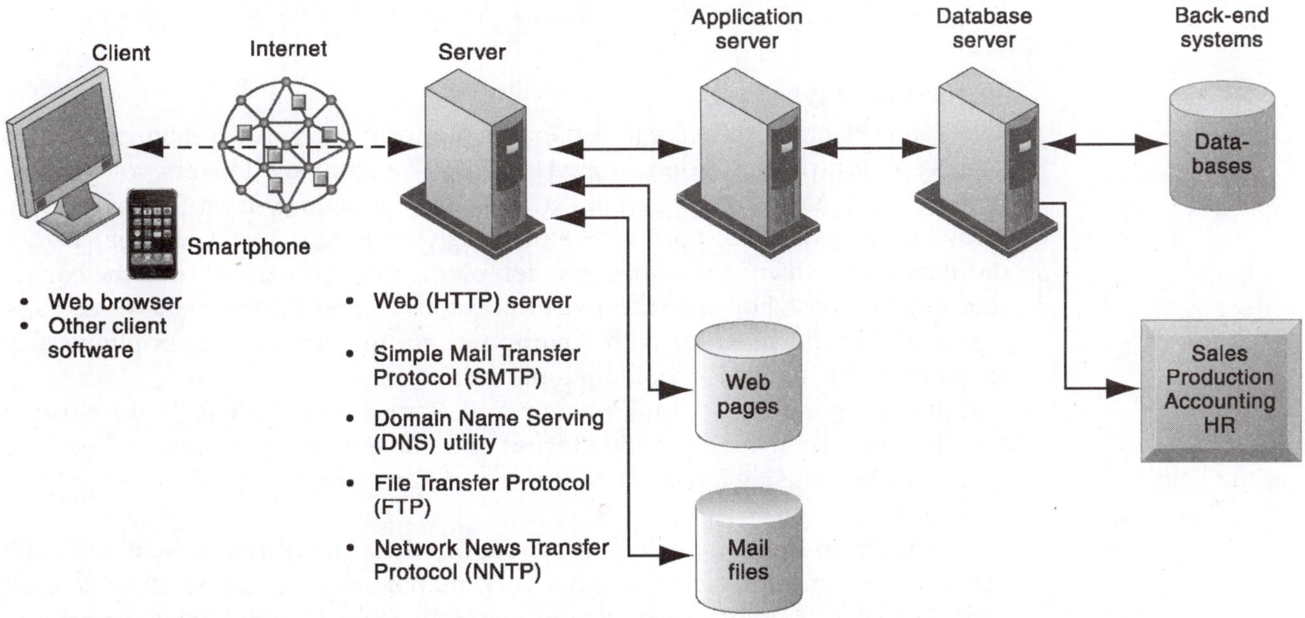

Client computers running web browsers and other software can access an array of services on servers over the Internet. These services may all run on a single server or on multiple specialized servers.

E-mail enables messages to be exchanged from computer to computer, with capabilities for routing messages to multiple recipients, forwarding messages, and attaching text documents or multimedia files to messages. Most e-mail today is sent through the Internet. The cost of e-mail is far lower than equivalent voice, postal, or overnight delivery costs, and e-mail messages arrive anywhere in the world in a matter of seconds.

Chatting enables two or more people who are simultaneously connected to the Internet to hold live, interactive conversations. **Chat** systems now support voice and video chat as well as written conversations. Many online retail businesses offer chat services on their websites to attract visitors, to encourage repeat purchases, and to improve customer service.

Instant messaging is a type of chat service that enables participants to create their own private chat channels. The instant messaging system alerts the user whenever someone on his or her private list is online so that the user can initiate a chat session with other individuals. Instant messaging systems for consumers include Yahoo! Messenger, Google Hangouts, AOL Instant Messenger, and Facebook Chat. Companies concerned with security use proprietary communications and messaging systems such as IBM Sametime.

Newsgroups are worldwide discussion groups posted on Internet electronic bulletin boards on which people share information and ideas on a defined topic such as radiology or rock bands. Anyone can post messages on these bulletin boards for others to read.

Employee use of e-mail, instant messaging, and the Internet is supposed to increase worker productivity, but the accompanying Interactive Session on Management shows that this may not always be the case. Many company managers now believe they need to monitor and even regulate their employees' online activity, but is this ethical? Although there are some strong business reasons companies may need to monitor their employees' e-mail and web activities, what does this mean for employee privacy?

Voice over IP

The Internet has also become a popular platform for voice transmission and corporate networking. **Voice over IP (VoIP)** technology delivers voice information in digital form using packet switching, avoiding the tolls charged by local and long-distance telephone networks (see Figure 7.9). Calls that would ordinarily be transmitted over public telephone networks travel over the corporate network based on the Internet protocol, or the public Internet. Voice calls can be made and received with a computer equipped with a microphone and speakers or with a VoIP-enabled telephone.

Cable firms such as Time Warner and Cablevision provide VoIP service bundled with their high-speed Internet and cable offerings. Skype offers free VoIP worldwide using a peer-to-peer network, and Google has its own free VoIP service.

Although up-front investments are required for an IP phone system, VoIP can reduce communication and network management costs by 20 to 30 percent. For example, VoIP saves Virgin Entertainment Group $700,000 per year in long-distance bills. In addition to lowering long-distance costs and eliminating monthly fees for private lines, an IP network provides a single voice-data

INTERACTIVE SESSION: MANAGEMENT

Monitoring Employees on Networks: Unethical or Good Business?

The Internet has become an extremely valuable business tool, but it's also a huge distraction for workers on the job. Employees are wasting valuable company time by surfing inappropriate websites (Facebook, shopping, sports, etc.), sending and receiving personal e-mail, talking to friends via online chat, and downloading videos and music. A series of studies have found that employees spend between one and three hours per day at work surfing the web on personal business. A company with 1,000 workers using the Internet could lose up to $35 million in productivity annually from just an hour of daily web surfing by workers.

Many companies have begun monitoring employee use of e-mail and the Internet, sometimes without their knowledge. Many tools are now available for this purpose, including Spector CNE Investigator, OsMonitor, IMonitor, Work Examiner, Mobistealth, and Spytech. These products enable companies to record online searches, monitor file downloads and uploads, record keystrokes, keep tabs on e-mails, create transcripts of chats, or take certain screenshots of images displayed on computer screens. Instant messaging, text messaging, and social media monitoring are also increasing. Although U.S. companies have the legal right to monitor employee Internet and e-mail activity while they are at work, is such monitoring unethical, or is it simply good business?

Managers worry about the loss of time and employee productivity when employees are focusing on personal rather than company business. Too much time on personal business translates into lost revenue. Some employees may even be billing time they spend pursuing personal interests online to clients, thus overcharging them.

If personal traffic on company networks is too high, it can also clog the company's network so that legitimate business work cannot be performed. GMI Insurance Services, which serves the U.S. transportation industry, found that employees were downloading a great deal of music and streaming video and storing them on company servers. GMI's server backup space was being eaten up.

When employees use e-mail or the web (including social networks) at employer facilities or with employer equipment, anything they do, including anything illegal, carries the company's name. Therefore, the employer can be traced and held liable. Management in many firms fear that racist, sexually explicit, or other potentially offensive material accessed or traded by their employees could result in adverse publicity and even lawsuits for the firm. An estimated 27 percent of *Fortune* 500 organizations have had to defend themselves against claims of sexual harassment stemming from inappropriate e-mail. Even if the company is found not to be liable, responding to lawsuits could run up huge legal bills. Companies also fear leakage of confidential information and trade secrets through e-mail or social networks. Another survey conducted by the American Management Association and the ePolicy Institute found that 14 percent of the employees polled admitted they had sent confidential or potentially embarrassing company e-mails to outsiders.

U.S. companies have the legal right to monitor what employees are doing with company equipment during business hours. The question is whether electronic surveillance is an appropriate tool for maintaining an efficient and positive workplace. Some companies try to ban all personal activities on corporate networks—zero tolerance. Others block employee access to specific websites or social sites, closely monitor e-mail messages, or limit personal time on the web.

GMI Insurance implemented Veriato Investigator and Veriato 360 software to record and analyze the Internet and computer activities of each GMI employee. The Veriato software is able to identify which websites employees visit frequently, how much time employees spend at these sites, whether employees are printing out or copying confidential documents to take home on a portable USB storage device, and whether there are any inappropriate communication conversations taking place. GMI and its sister company, CCS, had an acceptable use policy (AUP) in place prior to monitoring, providing rules about what employees are allowed and not allowed to do with the organization's computing resources. However, GMI's AUP was nearly impossible to enforce until implementation of the Veriato employee monitoring software. To deal with music and video downloads, GMI additionally developed a "software download policy," which must be reviewed and signed by employees. Management at both GMI and CCS believe employee productivity increased by 15 to 20 percent as a result of using the Veriato monitoring software.

A number of firms have fired employees who have stepped out of bounds. A Proofpoint survey found that one in five large U.S. companies had fired an employee for violating e-mail policies. Among managers who fired employees for Internet misuse, the majority did so because the employees' e-mail contained sensitive, confidential, or embarrassing information.

No solution is problem-free, but many consultants believe companies should write corporate policies on employee e-mail, social media, and web use. The policies should include explicit ground rules that state, by position or level, under what circumstances employees can use company facilities for e-mail, blogging, or web surfing. The policies should also inform employees whether these activities are monitored and explain why.

IBM now has "social computing guidelines" that cover employee activity on sites such as Facebook and Twitter. The guidelines urge employees not to conceal their identities, to remember that they are personally responsible for what they publish, and to refrain from discussing controversial topics that are not related to their IBM role.

The rules should be tailored to specific business needs and organizational cultures. For example, investment firms will need to allow many of their employees access to other investment sites. A company dependent on widespread information sharing, innovation, and independence could very well find that monitoring creates more problems than it solves.

Sources: Susan M. Heathfield, "Surfing the Web at Work," About.com, May 27, 2016; Veriato, "Veriato 'Golden' for GMI Insurance Services," 2016; "Office Slacker Stats," www.staffmonitoring.com, accessed May 28, 2016; "How Do Employers Monitor Internet Usage at Work?" wisegeek.org, accessed April 15, 2016;"Could HR Be Snooping on Your Emails and Web Browsing? What Every Worker Should Know," Philly.com, March 30, 2015; "How Do Employers Monitor Internet Usage at Work?" wisegeek.org, accessed April 15, 2015; Dune Lawrence, "Companies Are Tracking Employees to Nab Traitors," *Bloomberg*, March 23, 2015; and "Should Companies Monitor Their Employees' Social Media?" *Wall Street Journal*, May 11, 2014.

CASE STUDY QUESTIONS

1. Should managers monitor employee e-mail and Internet usage? Why or why not?
2. Describe an effective e-mail and web use policy for a company.
3. Should managers inform employees that their web behavior is being monitored? Or should managers monitor secretly? Why or why not?

infrastructure for both telecommunications and computing services. Companies no longer have to maintain separate networks or provide support services and personnel for each type of network.

Unified Communications

In the past, each of the firm's networks for wired and wireless data, voice communications, and videoconferencing operated independently of each other and had to be managed separately by the information systems department. Now, however, firms can merge disparate communications modes into a single universally accessible service using unified communications technology. **Unified communications** integrates disparate channels for voice communications, data communications, instant messaging, e-mail, and electronic conferencing

FIGURE 7.9 HOW VOICE OVER IP WORKS

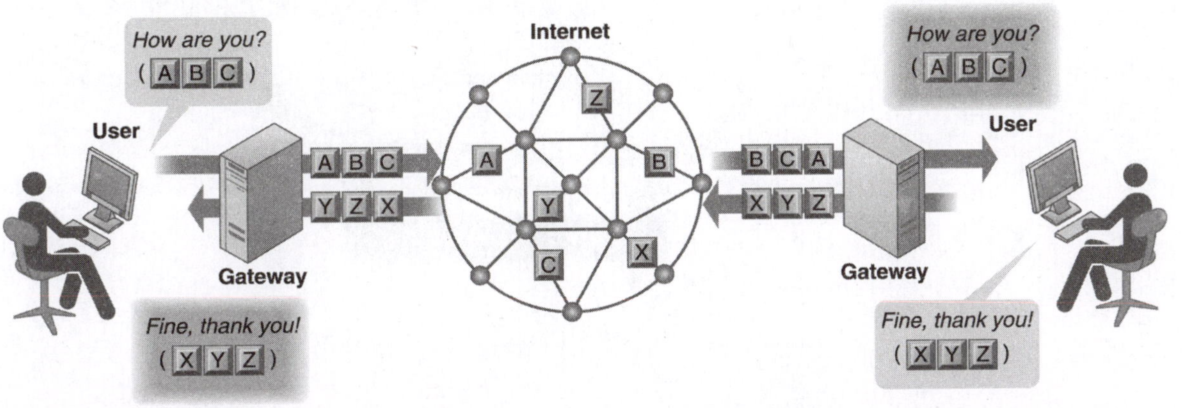

A VoIP phone call digitizes and breaks up a voice message into data packets that may travel along different routes before being reassembled at the final destination. A processor nearest the call's destination, called a gateway, arranges the packets in the proper order and directs them to the telephone number of the receiver or the IP address of the receiving computer.

into a single experience by which users can seamlessly switch back and forth between different communication modes. Presence technology shows whether a person is available to receive a call.

CenterPoint Properties, a major Chicago area industrial real estate company, used unified communications technology to create collaborative websites for each of its real estate deals. Each website provides a single point for accessing structured and unstructured data. Integrated presence technology lets team members e-mail, instant message, call, or videoconference with one click.

Virtual Private Networks

What if you had a marketing group charged with developing new products and services for your firm with members spread across the United States? You would want them to be able to e-mail each other and communicate with the home office without any chance that outsiders could intercept the communications. In the past, one answer to this problem was to work with large private networking firms that offered secure, private, dedicated networks to customers, but this was an expensive solution. A much less expensive solution is to create a virtual private network within the public Internet.

A **virtual private network (VPN)** is a secure, encrypted, private network that has been configured within a public network to take advantage of the economies of scale and management facilities of large networks, such as the Internet (see Figure 7.10). A VPN provides your firm with secure, encrypted communications at a much lower cost than the same capabilities offered by traditional non-Internet providers that use their private networks to secure communications. VPNs also provide a network infrastructure for combining voice and data networks.

Several competing protocols are used to protect data transmitted over the public Internet, including Point-to-Point Tunneling Protocol (PPTP). In a process

FIGURE 7.10 A VIRTUAL PRIVATE NETWORK USING THE INTERNET

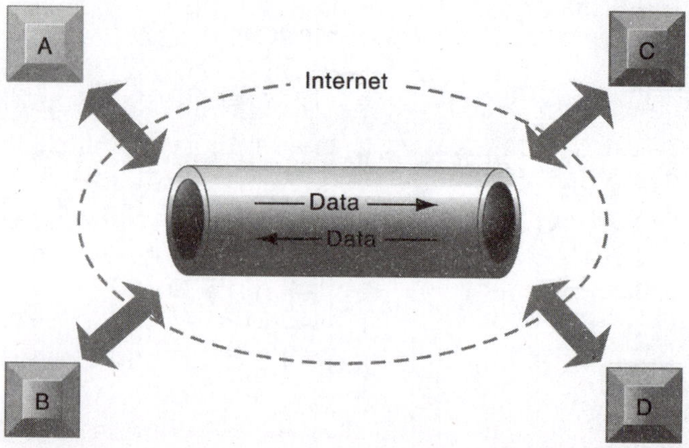

This VPN is a private network of computers linked using a secure tunnel connection over the Internet. It protects data transmitted over the public Internet by encoding the data and wrapping them within the Internet protocol. By adding a wrapper around a network message to hide its content, organizations can create a private connection that travels through the public Internet.

called *tunneling*, packets of data are encrypted and wrapped inside IP packets. By adding this wrapper around a network message to hide its content, business firms create a private connection that travels through the public Internet.

The Web

The web is the most popular Internet service. It's a system with universally accepted standards for storing, retrieving, formatting, and displaying information by using a client/server architecture. Web pages are formatted using hypertext with embedded links that connect documents to one another and that also link pages to other objects, such as sound, video, or animation files. When you click a graphic and a video clip plays, you have clicked a hyperlink. A typical **website** is a collection of web pages linked to a home page.

Hypertext

Web pages are based on a standard Hypertext Markup Language (HTML), which formats documents and incorporates dynamic links to other documents and pictures stored in the same or remote computers (see Chapter 5). Web pages are accessible through the Internet because web browser software operating your computer can request web pages stored on an Internet host server by using the **Hypertext Transfer Protocol (HTTP)**. HTTP is the communications standard that transfers pages on the web. For example, when you type a web address in your browser, such as http://www.sec.gov, your browser sends an HTTP request to the sec.gov server requesting the home page of sec.gov.

HTTP is the first set of letters at the start of every web address, followed by the domain name, which specifies the organization's server computer that is storing the document. Most companies have a domain name that is the same as or closely related to their official corporate name. The directory path and document name are two more pieces of information within the web address that help the browser track down the requested page. Together, the address is called a **uniform resource locator (URL)**. When typed into a browser, a URL tells the browser software exactly where to look for the information. For example, in the URL http://www.megacorp.com/content/features/082610.html, *http* names the protocol that displays web pages, www.megacorp.com is the domain name, content/features is the directory path that identifies where on the domain web server the page is stored, and 082610.html is the document name and the name of the format it is in. (It is an HTML page.)

Web Servers

A web server is software for locating and managing stored web pages. It locates the web pages a user requests on the computer where they are stored and delivers the web pages to the user's computer. Server applications usually run on dedicated computers, although they can all reside on a single computer in small organizations.

The most common web server in use today is Apache HTTP Server, followed by Microsoft Internet Information Services (IIS). Apache is an open source product that is free of charge and can be downloaded from the web.

Searching for Information on the Web

No one knows for sure how many web pages there really are. The surface web is the part of the web that search engines visit and about which information is recorded. For instance, Google indexed an estimated 60 trillion pages in 2016, and this reflects a large portion of the publicly accessible web page population. But there is a deep web that contains an estimated 1 trillion additional pages, many of them proprietary (such as the pages of *Wall Street Journal Online*, which cannot be visited without a subscription or access code) or that are stored in protected corporate databases. Searching for information on Facebook is another matter. With more than 1.6 billion members, each with pages of text, photos, and media, the population of web pages is larger than many estimates. However, Facebook is a closed web, and its pages are not completely searchable by Google or other search engines.

Search Engines Obviously, with so many web pages, finding specific ones that can help you or your business, nearly instantly, is an important problem. The question is, how can you find the one or two pages you really want and need out of billions of indexed web pages? **Search engines** attempt to solve the problem of finding useful information on the web nearly instantly and, arguably, they are the killer app of the Internet era. Today's search engines can sift through HTML files; files of Microsoft Office applications; PDF files; and audio, video, and image files. There are hundreds of search engines in the world, but the vast majority of search results come from Google, Yahoo, and Microsoft's Bing (see Figure 7.11). While we typically think of Amazon as an online store, it is also a powerful product search engine.

Web search engines started out in the early 1990s as relatively simple software programs that roamed the nascent web, visiting pages and gathering information about the content of each page. The first search engines were simple

FIGURE 7.11 TOP WEB SEARCH ENGINES IN THE UNITED STATES

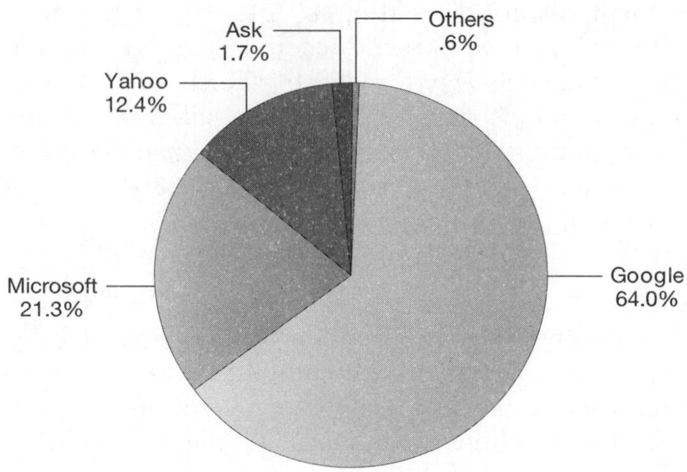

Google is the most popular search engine, handling about 64 percent of web searches in the United States and about 90 percent in Europe. Sources: Based on data from comScore Inc., February 2016.

keyword indexes of all the pages they visited, leaving users with lists of pages that may not have been truly relevant to their search.

In 1994, Stanford University computer science students David Filo and Jerry Yang created a hand-selected list of their favorite web pages and called it "Yet Another Hierarchical Officious Oracle," or Yahoo. Yahoo was not initially a search engine but rather an edited selection of websites organized by categories the editors found useful. Currently, Yahoo relies on Microsoft's Bing for search results.

In 1998, Larry Page and Sergey Brin, two other Stanford computer science students, released their first version of Google. This search engine was different. Not only did it index each web page's words but it also ranked search results based on the relevance of each page. Page patented the idea of a page ranking system (called *PageRank System*), which essentially measures the popularity of a web page by calculating the number of sites that link to that page as well as the number of pages to which it links. The premise is that popular web pages are more relevant to users. Brin contributed a unique web crawler program that indexed not only keywords on a page but also combinations of words (such as authors and the titles of their articles). These two ideas became the foundation for the Google search engine. Figure 7.12 illustrates how Google works.

Mobile Search With the growth of mobile smartphones and tablet computers, and with about 210 million Americans accessing the Internet via mobile devices, the nature of e-commerce and search is changing. Mobile search from smartphones and tablets made up more than 50 percent of all searches in 2016 and will expand rapidly in the next few years. Google, Amazon, and Yahoo have developed new search interfaces to make searching and shopping from smartphones more convenient. Google revised its search algorithm to favor sites that look good on smartphone screens. Although smartphones are widely used to shop, actual purchases typically take place on laptops or desktops, followed by tablets.

FIGURE 7.12 HOW GOOGLE WORKS

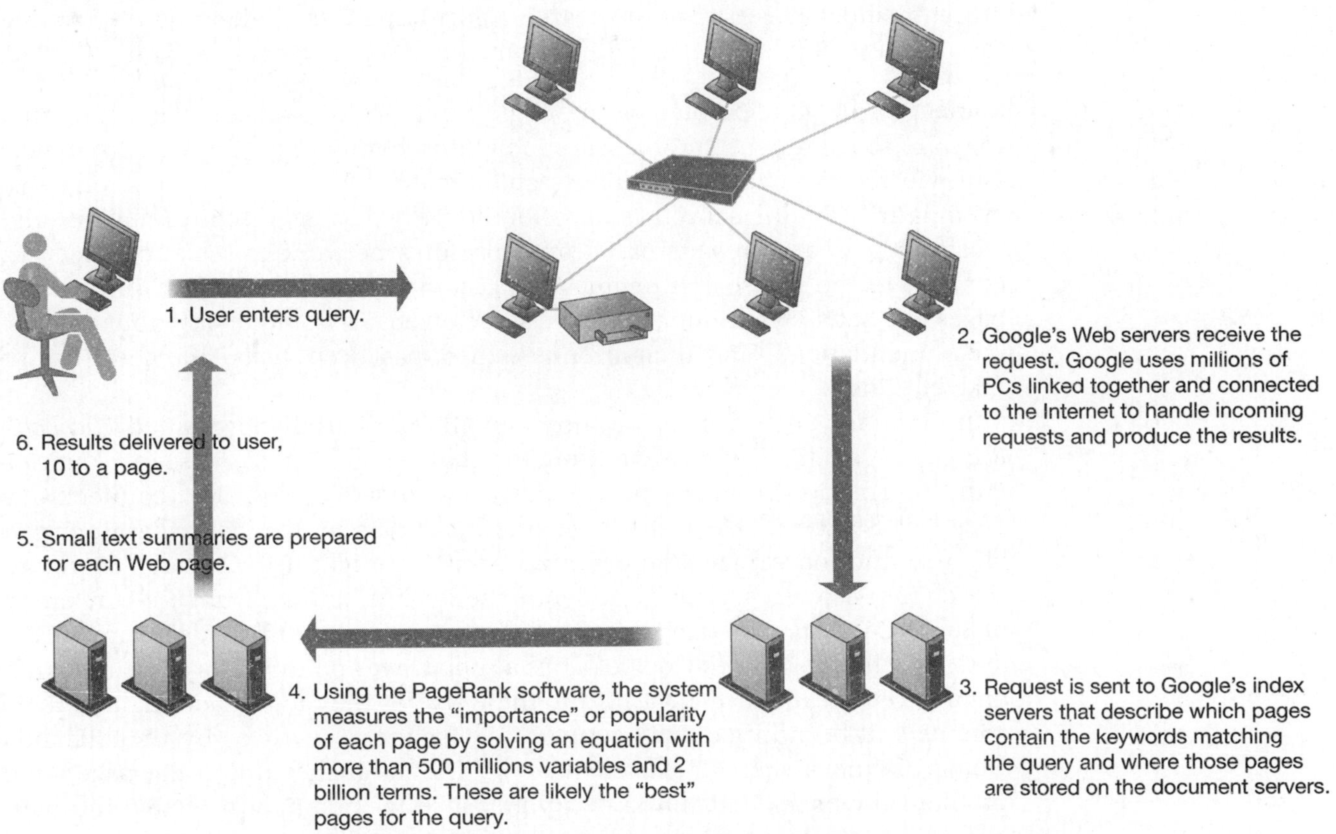

The Google search engine is continuously crawling the web, indexing the content of each page, calculating its popularity, and storing the pages so that it can respond quickly to user requests to see a page. The entire process takes about half a second.

Semantic Search Another way for search engines to become more discriminating and helpful is to make search engines capable of understanding what we are really looking for. Called **semantic search**, the goal is to build a search engine that could really understand human language and behavior. Google and other search engine firms are attempting to refine search engine algorithms to capture more of what the user intended and the meaning of a search. In September 2013, Google introduced its Hummingbird search algorithm. Rather than evaluate each word separately in a search, Google's semantically informed Hummingbird tries to evaluate an entire sentence, focusing on the meaning behind the words. For instance, if your search is a long sentence like "Google annual report selected financial data 2015," Hummingbird should be able to figure out that you really want Google's SEC Form 10K report filed with the Securities and Exchange Commission on March 31, 2016.

Google searches also take advantage of Knowledge Graph, an effort of the search algorithm to anticipate what you might want to know more about as you search on a topic. Results of the knowledge graph appear on the right of the screen and contain more information about the topic or person you are searching on. For example, if you search "Lake Tahoe," the search engine will return basic facts about Tahoe (altitude, average temperature, and local fish), a map, and hotel accommodations. Google has made **predictive search** part of most search results. This part of the search algorithm guesses what you are looking for and suggests search terms as you type your search words.

Social Search One problem with Google and mechanical search engines is that they are so thorough. Enter a search for "ultra computers" and, in 0.2 seconds, you will receive over 300 million responses! Search engines are not very discriminating. **Social search** is an effort to provide fewer, more relevant, and trustworthy search results based on a person's network of social contacts. In contrast to the top search engines that use a mathematical algorithm to find pages that satisfy your query, a social search website would review your friends' recommendations (and their friends'), their past web visits, and their use of Like buttons.

In January 2013, Facebook launched Graph Search (now called *Facebook Search*), a social network search engine that responds to user search queries with information from the user's social network of friends and connections. Facebook Search relies on the huge amount of data on Facebook that is, or can be, linked to individuals and organizations. You might use Facebook Search to search for Boston restaurants that your friends like, alumni from the University of South Carolina who like Lady Gaga, or pictures of your friends before 2012.

Google has developed Google +1 as a social layer on top of its existing search engine. Users can place a +1 next to the websites they found helpful, and their friends will be notified automatically. Subsequent searches by their friends would list the +1 sites recommended by friends higher up on the page. One problem with social search is that your close friends may not have intimate knowledge of topics you are exploring, or they may have tastes you don't appreciate. It's also possible your close friends don't have any knowledge about what you are searching for.

Visual Search and the Visual Web Although search engines were originally designed to search text documents, the explosion of photos and videos on the Internet created a demand for searching and classifying these visual objects. Facial recognition software can create a digital version of a human face. In 2012, Facebook introduced facial recognition software combined with tagging to create a new feature called *Tag Suggest*. The software creates a digital facial print, similar to a fingerprint. Users can put their own tagged photo on their timeline and their friends' timelines. Once a person's photo is tagged, Facebook can pick that person out of a group photo and identify for others who is in the photo. You can also search for people on Facebook by using their digital image to find and identify them. Facebook is now using artificial intelligence technology to make its facial recognition capabilities more accurate.

Searching photos, images, and video has become increasingly important as the web becomes more visual. The **visual web** refers to websites such as Pinterest, where pictures replace text documents, where users search pictures, and where pictures of products replace display ads for products. Pinterest is a social networking site that provides users (as well as brands) with an online board to which they can pin interesting pictures. One of the fastest-growing websites in history, Pinterest had 270 million monthly visitors worldwide in 2016. Instagram is another example of the visual web. Instagram is a photo and video sharing site that allows users to take pictures, enhance them, and share them with friends on other social sites such as Facebook, Twitter, and Google+. In 2016, Instagram had 400 million monthly active users.

Intelligent Agent Shopping Bots Chapter 11 describes the capabilities of software agents with built-in intelligence that can gather or filter information and perform other tasks to assist users. **Shopping bots** use intelligent agent software for searching the Internet for shopping information. Shopping bots such as MySimon or PriceGrabber can help people interested in making a purchase filter and retrieve information about products of interest, evaluate competing products according to criteria the users have established, and negotiate with vendors for price and delivery terms. Many of these shopping agents search the web for pricing and availability of products specified by the user and return a list of sites that sell the item along with pricing information and a purchase link.

Search Engine Marketing Search engines have become major advertising platforms and shopping tools by offering what is now called **search engine marketing**. Searching for information is one of the web's most popular activities; 70 percent of American adult Internet users will use a search engine at least once a day in 2016, generating about 20 billion queries a month. In addition, 180 million smartphone users will generate another 12 billion monthly searches. Worldwide, there are over 6 billion search engine requests daily. In Europe 90 percent of the searches are done with Google, and in the United States about 67 percent are Google searches. With this huge audience, search engines are the foundation for the most lucrative form of online marketing and advertising—search engine marketing. When users enter a search term on Google, Bing, Yahoo, or any of the other sites serviced by these search engines, they receive two types of listings: sponsored links, for which advertisers have paid to be listed (usually at the top of the search results page), and unsponsored, organic search results. In addition, advertisers can purchase small text boxes on the side of search results pages. The paid, sponsored advertisements are the fastest growing form of Internet advertising and are powerful new marketing tools that precisely match consumer interests with advertising messages at the right moment. Search engine marketing monetizes the value of the search process. In 2016, search engine marketing is expected to generate $28 billion in revenue, nearly half of all online advertising ($67 billion). About 90 percent of Google's revenue of $74 billion in 2015 came from online advertising, and 90 percent of that ad revenue came from search engine marketing (Google, 2016).

Because search engine marketing is so effective (it has the highest click-through rate and the highest return on ad investment), companies seek to optimize their websites for search engine recognition. The better optimized the page is, the higher a ranking it will achieve in search engine result listings. **Search engine optimization (SEO)** is the process of improving the quality and volume of web traffic to a website by employing a series of techniques that help a website achieve a higher ranking with the major search engines when certain keywords and phrases are put into the search field. One technique is to make sure that the keywords used in the website description match the keywords likely to be used as search terms by prospective customers. For example, your website is more likely to be among the first ranked by search engines if it uses the keyword *lighting* rather than *lamps* if most prospective customers are searching for *lighting*. It is also advantageous to link your website to as many other websites as possible because search engines evaluate such links to determine the popularity of a web page and how it is linked to other content on the web.

Search engines can be gamed by scammers who create thousands of phony website pages and link them or link them to a single retailer's site in an attempt to fool Google's search engine. Firms can also pay so-called link farms to link to their site. Google changed its search algorithm in 2012 to deal with this problem. Code named *Penguin*, the revised algorithm examines the quality of links more carefully with the intent of down-ranking sites that have a suspicious pattern of sites linking to them. Penguin is updated annually.

In general, search engines have been very helpful to small businesses that cannot afford large marketing campaigns. Because shoppers are looking for a specific product or service when they use search engines, they are what marketers call hot prospects—people who are looking for information and often intending to buy. Moreover, search engines charge only for click-throughs to a site. Merchants do not have to pay for ads that don't work, only for ads that receive a click. Consumers benefit from search engine marketing because ads for merchants appear only when consumers are looking for a specific product. Thus, search engine marketing saves consumers cognitive energy and reduces search costs (including the cost of transportation needed to search for products physically). One study estimated the global value of search to both merchants and consumers to be more than $800 billion, with about 65 percent of the benefit going to consumers in the form of lower search costs and lower prices (McKinsey & Company, 2011).

Web 2.0

Today's websites don't just contain static content—they enable people to collaborate, share information, and create new services and content online. These second-generation interactive Internet-based services are referred to as **Web 2.0**. If you have pinned a photo on Pinterest, posted a video to YouTube, created a blog, or added an app to your Facebook page, you've used some of these Web 2.0 services.

Web 2.0 has four defining features: interactivity, real-time user control, social participation (sharing), and user-generated content. The technologies and services behind these features include cloud computing, software mashups and apps, blogs, RSS, wikis, and social networks. We have already describd cloud computing, mashups, and apps in Chapter 5 and introduced social networks in Chapter 2.

A **blog**, the popular term for a weblog, is a personal website that typically contains a series of chronological entries (newest to oldest) by its author and links to related web pages. The blog may include a *blogroll* (a collection of links to other blogs) and *trackbacks* (a list of entries in other blogs that refer to a post on the first blog). Most blogs allow readers to post comments on the blog entries as well. The act of creating a blog is often referred to as blogging. Blogs can be hosted by a third-party service such as Blogger.com, TypePad.com, and Xanga.com, and blogging features have been incorporated into social networks such as Facebook and collaboration platforms such as IBM Notes. WordPress is a leading open source blogging tool and content management system. **Microblogging**, used in Twitter, is a type of blogging that features short posts of 140 characters or fewer.

Blog pages are usually variations on templates provided by the blogging service or software. Therefore, millions of people without HTML skills of any kind can post their own web pages and share content with others. The totality of blog-related websites is often referred to as the **blogosphere**. Although blogs have become popular personal publishing tools, they also have business uses (see Chapters 2 and 10).

If you're an avid blog reader, you might use RSS to keep up with your favorite blogs without constantly checking them for updates. **RSS**, which stands for Really Simple Syndication or Rich Site Summary, pulls specified content from websites and feeds it automatically to users' computers. RSS reader software gathers material from the websites or blogs that you tell it to scan and brings new information from those sites to you. RSS readers are available through websites such as Google and Yahoo, and they have been incorporated into the major web browsers and e-mail programs.

Blogs allow visitors to add comments to the original content, but they do not allow visitors to change the original posted material. **Wikis**, in contrast, are collaborative websites on which visitors can add, delete, or modify content, including the work of previous authors. Wiki comes from the Hawaiian word for *quick*. Wiki software typically provides a template that defines layout and elements common to all pages, displays user-editable software program code, and then renders the content into an HTML-based page for display in a web browser. Some wiki software allows only basic text formatting, whereas other tools allow the use of tables, images, or even interactive elements, such as polls or games. Most wikis provide capabilities for monitoring the work of other users and correcting mistakes.

Because wikis make information sharing so easy, they have many business uses. The U.S. Department of Homeland Security's National Cyber Security Center (NCSC) deployed a wiki to facilitate information sharing with other federal agencies on threats, attacks, and responses and as a repository for technical and standards information. Pixar Wiki is a collaborative community wiki for publicizing the work of Pixar Animation Studios. The wiki format allows anyone to create or edit an article about a Pixar film.

Social networking sites enable users to build communities of friends and professional colleagues. Members typically create a profile—a web page for posting photos, videos, audio files, and text—and then share these profiles with others on the service identified as their friends or contacts. Social networking sites are highly interactive, offer real-time user control, rely on user-generated content, and are broadly based on social participation and sharing of content and opinions. Leading social networking sites include Facebook, Twitter (with more than 1.6 billion and 310 million monthly active users, respectively, in 2016), and LinkedIn (for professional contacts).

For many, social networking sites are the defining Web 2.0 application and one that has radically changed how people spend their time online; how people communicate and with whom; how business people stay in touch with customers, suppliers, and employees; how providers of goods and services learn about their customers; and how advertisers reach potential customers. The large social networking sites are also application development platforms where members can create and sell software applications to other members of the community. Facebook alone has more than 1 million external developers who created more than 9 million applications for gaming, video sharing, and communicating with friends and family. In 2016 Facebook supported 3.5 billion app installations. We talk more about business applications of social networking in Chapters 2 and 10, and you can find social networking discussions in many other chapters of this book. You can also find a more detailed discussion of Web 2.0 in our Learning Tracks.

Web 3.0 and the Future Web

The future of the Internet, so-called Web 3.0, is already visible. The key features of **Web 3.0** are more tools for individuals to make sense out of the trillions of pages on the Internet, or the millions of apps available for smartphones and a visual, even three-dimensional (3D) Web where you can walk through pages in a 3D environment. (Review the discussion of semantic search and visual search earlier in this chapter.)

Even closer in time is a pervasive web that controls everything from a city's traffic lights and water usage, to the lights in your living room, to your car's rear view mirror, not to mention managing your calendar and appointments. This is referred to as the **Internet of Things** and is based on billions of Internet-connected sensors throughout our physical world. Objects, animals, or people are provided with unique identifiers and the ability to transfer data over a network without requiring human-to-human or human-to-computer interaction. Firms such as General electric, IBM, HP, and Oracle, and hundreds of smaller start-ups, are exploring how to build smart machines, factories, and cities through extensive use of remote sensors and fast cloud computing. A related Web 3.0 development is the emerging Internet of People (IoP) based on sensors attached to clothing and personal effects that monitor physical states and locations of individuals. We provide more detail on this topic in the following section.

The App Internet is another element in the future web. The growth of apps within the mobile platform is astounding. More than 80 percent of mobile minutes in the United States are generated through apps, only 20 percent using browsers. Apps give users direct access to content and are much faster than loading a browser and searching for content.

Other complementary trends leading toward a future Web 3.0 include more widespread use of cloud computing and software as a service (SaaS) business models, ubiquitous connectivity among mobile platforms and Internet access devices, and the transformation of the web from a network of separate siloed applications and content into a more seamless and interoperable whole. These more modest visions of the future Web 3.0 are more likely to be realized in the near term.

7-4 What are the principal technologies and standards for wireless networking, communication, and Internet access?

Welcome to the wireless revolution! Cell phones, smartphones, tablets, and wireless-enabled personal computers have morphed into portable media and computing platforms that let you perform many of the computing tasks you used to do at your desk, and a whole lot more. We introduced smartphones in our discussions of the mobile digital platform in Chapters 1 and 5. **Smartphones** such as the iPhone, Android phones, and BlackBerry combine the functionality of a cell phone with that of a mobile laptop computer with Wi-Fi capability. This makes it possible to combine music, video, Internet access, and telephone service in one device. A large part of the Internet is becoming a mobile, access-anywhere, broadband service for the delivery of video, music, and web search.

Cellular Systems

In 2015, more than 1.5 billion cell phones were sold worldwide. In the United States, there are 351 million cell phone subscriptions, and 190 million people have smartphones. About 193 million people access the web by using their phone (eMarketer, 2015). Smartphones, not the desktop PC, are now responsible for more than half of all Internet searches.

Digital cellular service uses several competing standards. In Europe and much of the rest of the world outside the United Sates, the standard is Global System for Mobile Communications (GSM). GSM's strength is its international roaming capability. There are GSM cell phone systems in the United States, including T-Mobile and AT&T.

A competing standard in the United States is Code Division Multiple Access (CDMA), which is the system Verizon and Sprint use. CDMA was developed by the military during World War II. It transmits over several frequencies, occupies the entire spectrum, and randomly assigns users to a range of frequencies over time, making it more efficient than GSM.

Earlier generations of cellular systems were designed primarily for voice and limited data transmission in the form of short text messages. Today wireless carriers offer 3G and 4G networks. **3G networks**, with transmission speeds ranging from 144 Kbps for mobile users in, say, a car, to more than 2 Mbps for stationary users, offer fair transmission speeds for e-mail, browsing the web, and online shopping but are too slow for videos. **4G networks** have much higher speeds: 100 megabits/second download and 50 megabits upload speed, with more than enough capacity for watching high-definition video on your smartphone. Long Term Evolution (LTE) and mobile Worldwide Interoperability for Microwave Access (WiMax—see the following section) are the current 4G standards.

Wireless Computer Networks and Internet Access

An array of technologies provides high-speed wireless access to the Internet for PCs and mobile devices. These new high-speed services have extended

Internet access to numerous locations that could not be covered by traditional wired Internet services and have made ubiquitous computing, anywhere, anytime, a reality.

Bluetooth

Bluetooth is the popular name for the 802.15 wireless networking standard, which is useful for creating small **personal area networks (PANs)**. It links up to eight devices within a 10-meter area using low-power, radio-based communication and can transmit up to 722 Kbps in the 2.4-GHz band.

Wireless phones, pagers, computers, printers, and computing devices using Bluetooth communicate with each other and even operate each other without direct user intervention (see Figure 7.13). For example, a person could direct a notebook computer to send a document file wirelessly to a printer. Bluetooth connects wireless keyboards and mice to PCs or cell phones to earpieces without wires. Bluetooth has low power requirements, making it appropriate for battery-powered handheld computers or cell phones.

Although Bluetooth lends itself to personal networking, it has uses in large corporations. For example, FedEx drivers use Bluetooth to transmit the delivery data captured by their handheld computers to cellular transmitters, which forward the data to corporate computers. Drivers no longer need to spend time docking their handheld units physically in the transmitters, and Bluetooth has saved FedEx $20 million per year.

FIGURE 7.13 A BLUETOOTH NETWORK (PAN)

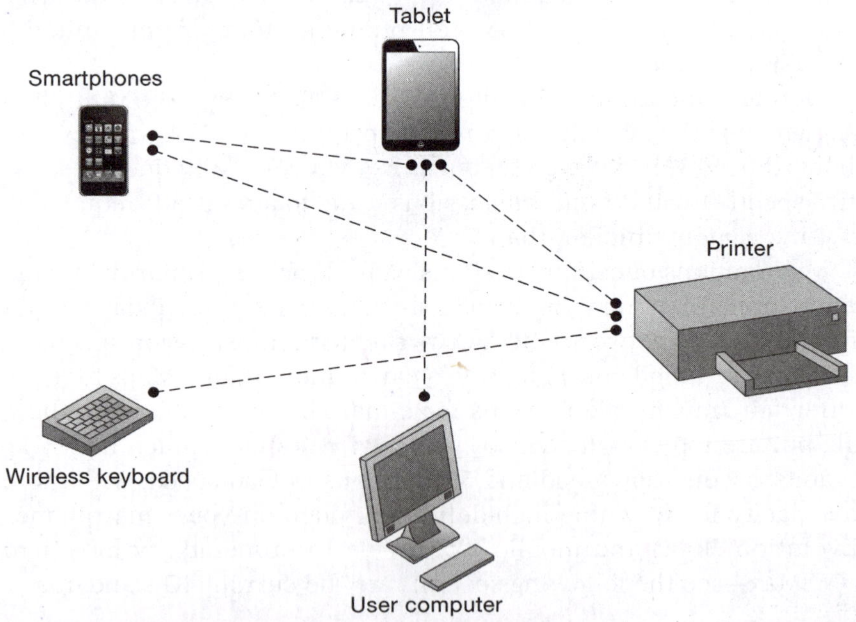

Bluetooth enables a variety of devices, including cell phones, smartphones, wireless keyboards and mice, PCs, and printers, to interact wirelessly with each other within a small, 30-foot (10-meter) area. In addition to the links shown, Bluetooth can be used to network similar devices to send data from one PC to another, for example.

Wi-Fi and Wireless Internet Access

The 802.11 set of standards for wireless LANs and wireless Internet access is also known as **Wi-Fi**. The first of these standards to be widely adopted was 802.11b, which can transmit up to 11 Mbps in the unlicensed 2.4-GHz band and has an effective distance of 30 to 50 meters. The 802.11g standard can transmit up to 54 Mbps in the 2.4-GHz range. 802.11n is capable of transmitting over 100 Mbps. Today's PCs and netbooks have built-in support for Wi-Fi, as do the iPhone, iPad, and other smartphones.

In most Wi-Fi communication, wireless devices communicate with a wired LAN using access points. An access point is a box consisting of a radio receiver/transmitter and antennas that links to a wired network, router, or hub.

Figure 7.14 illustrates an 802.11 wireless LAN that connects a small number of mobile devices to a larger wired LAN and to the Internet. Most wireless devices are client machines. The servers that the mobile client stations need to use are on the wired LAN. The access point controls the wireless stations and acts as a bridge between the main wired LAN and the wireless LAN. The access point also controls the wireless stations.

FIGURE 7.14 AN 802.11 WIRELESS LAN

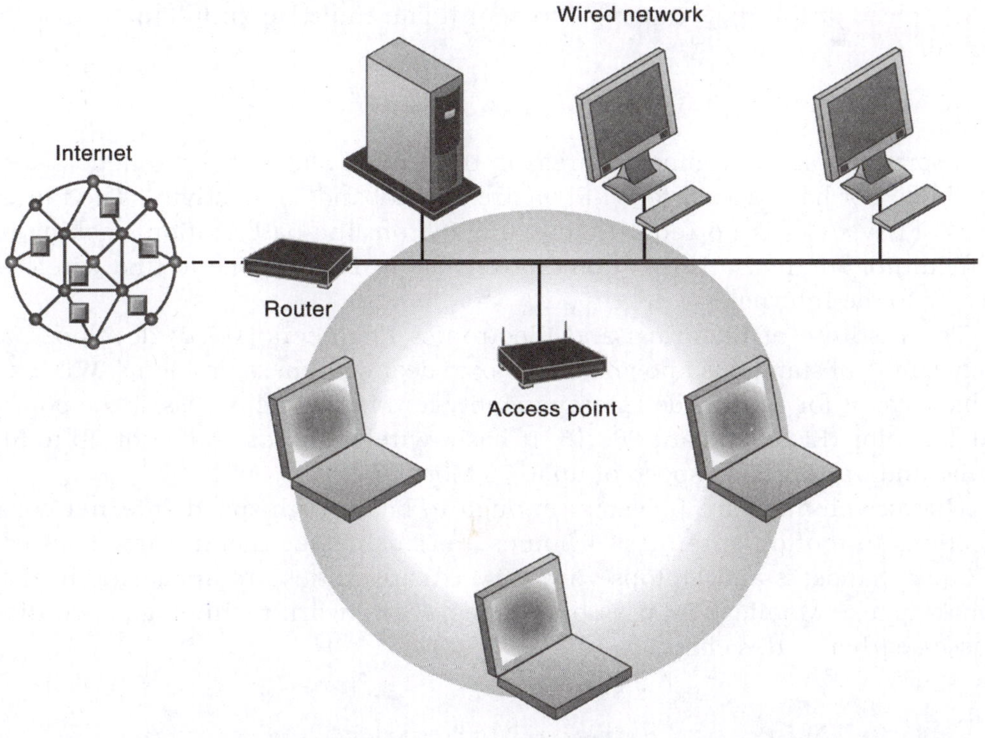

Mobile laptop computers equipped with network interface cards link to the wired LAN by communicating with the access point. The access point uses radio waves to transmit network signals from the wired network to the client adapters, which convert them to data that the mobile device can understand. The client adapter then transmits the data from the mobile device back to the access point, which forwards the data to the wired network.

The most popular use for Wi-Fi today is for high-speed wireless Internet service. In this instance, the access point plugs into an Internet connection, which could come from a cable service or DSL telephone service. Computers within range of the access point use it to link wirelessly to the Internet.

Hotspots are locations with one or more access points providing wireless Internet access and are often in public places. Some hotspots are free or do not require any additional software to use; others may require activation and the establishment of a user account by providing a credit card number over the web.

Businesses of all sizes are using Wi-Fi networks to provide low-cost wireless LANs and Internet access. Wi-Fi hotspots can be found in hotels, airport lounges, libraries, cafes, and college campuses to provide mobile access to the Internet. Dartmouth College is one of many campuses where students now use Wi-Fi for research, course work, and entertainment.

Wi-Fi technology poses several challenges, however. One is Wi-Fi's security features, which make these wireless networks vulnerable to intruders. We provide more detail about Wi-Fi security issues in Chapter 8.

Another drawback of Wi-Fi networks is susceptibility to interference from nearby systems operating in the same spectrum, such as wireless phones, microwave ovens, or other wireless LANs. However, wireless networks based on the 802.11n standard solve this problem by using multiple wireless antennas in tandem to transmit and receive data and technology called MIMO (multiple input multiple output) to coordinate multiple simultaneous radio signals.

WiMax

A surprisingly large number of areas in the United States and throughout the world do not have access to Wi-Fi or fixed broadband connectivity. The range of Wi-Fi systems is no more than 300 feet from the base station, making it difficult for rural groups that don't have cable or DSL service to find wireless access to the Internet.

The Institute of Electrical and Electronics Engineers (IEEE) developed a new family of standards known as WiMax to deal with these problems. **WiMax**, which stands for Worldwide Interoperability for Microwave Access, is the popular term for IEEE Standard 802.16. It has a wireless access range of up to 31 miles and transmission speed of up to 75 Mbps.

WiMax antennas are powerful enough to beam high-speed Internet connections to rooftop antennas of homes and businesses that are miles away. Cellular handsets and laptops with WiMax capabilities are appearing in the marketplace. Mobile WiMax is one of the 4G network technologies we discussed earlier in this chapter.

RFID and Wireless Sensor Networks

Mobile technologies are creating new efficiencies and ways of working throughout the enterprise. In addition to the wireless systems we have just described, radio frequency identification systems and wireless sensor networks are having a major impact.

Radio Frequency Identification (RFID) and Near Field Communication (NFC)

Radio frequency identification (RFID) systems provide a powerful technology for tracking the movement of goods throughout the supply chain. RFID systems use tiny tags with embedded microchips containing data about an item and its location to transmit radio signals over a short distance to RFID readers. The RFID readers then pass the data over a network to a computer for processing. Unlike bar codes, RFID tags do not need line-of-sight contact to be read.

The RFID tag is electronically programmed with information that can uniquely identify an item plus other information about the item such as its location, where and when it was made, or its status during production. The reader emits radio waves in ranges anywhere from 1 inch to 100 feet. When an RFID tag comes within the range of the reader, the tag is activated and starts sending data. The reader captures these data, decodes them, and sends them back over a wired or wireless network to a host computer for further processing (see Figure 7.15). Both RFID tags and antennas come in a variety of shapes and sizes.

In inventory control and supply chain management, RFID systems capture and manage more detailed information about items in warehouses or in production than bar coding systems. If a large number of items are shipped together, RFID systems track each pallet, lot, or even unit item in the shipment. This technology may help companies such as Walmart improve receiving and storage operations by improving their ability to see exactly what stock is stored in warehouses or on retail store shelves. Macy's, described in the chapter-opening case, uses RFID technology to track individual items for sale on store shelves.

Walmart has installed RFID readers at store receiving docks to record the arrival of pallets and cases of goods shipped with RFID tags. The RFID reader reads the tags a second time just as the cases are brought onto the sales floor

FIGURE 7.15 HOW RFID WORKS

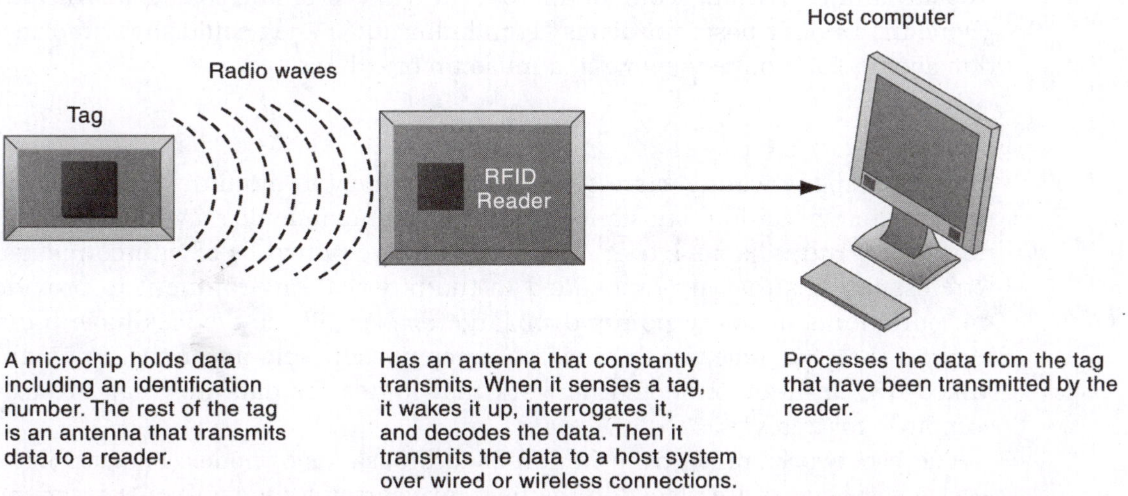

RFID uses low-powered radio transmitters to read data stored in a tag at distances ranging from 1 inch to 100 feet. The reader captures the data from the tag and sends them over a network to a host computer for processing.

from backroom storage areas. Software combines sales data from Walmart's point-of-sale systems and the RFID data regarding the number of cases brought out to the sales floor. The program determines which items will soon be depleted and automatically generates a list of items to pick in the warehouse to replenish store shelves before they run out. This information helps Walmart reduce out-of-stock items, increase sales, and further shrink its costs.

The cost of RFID tags used to be too high for widespread use, but now it starts at around 7 cents per tag in the United States. As the price decreases, RFID is starting to become cost-effective for many applications.

In addition to installing RFID readers and tagging systems, companies may need to upgrade their hardware and software to process the massive amounts of data produced by RFID systems—transactions that could add up to tens or hundreds of terabytes.

Software is used to filter, aggregate, and prevent RFID data from overloading business networks and system applications. Applications often need to be redesigned to accept large volumes of frequently generated RFID data and to share those data with other applications. Major enterprise software vendors now offer RFID-ready versions of their supply chain management applications.

Tap-and-go services like Apple Pay or Google Wallet use an RFID-related technology called **near field communication (NFC)**. NFC is a short-range wireless connectivity standard that uses electromagnetic radio fields to enable two compatible devices to exchange data when brought within a few centimeters of each other. A smartphone or other NFC-compatible device sends out radio frequency signals that interact with an NFC tag found in compatible card readers or smart posters. The signals create a current that flows through the NFC tag, allowing the device and the tag to communicate with one another. In most cases the tag is passive and only sends out information while the other device (such as a smartphone) is active and can both send and receive information. (There are NFC systems where both components are active.)

NFC is used in wireless payment services, to retrieve information, and even to exchange videos or information with friends on the go. You could share a website link by passing your phone over a friend's phone, while waving the phone in front of a poster or display containing an NFC tag could show information about what you're viewing at a museum or exhibit.

Wireless Sensor Networks

If your company wanted state-of-the art technology to monitor building security or detect hazardous substances in the air, it might deploy a wireless sensor network. **Wireless sensor networks (WSNs)** are networks of interconnected wireless devices that are embedded in the physical environment to provide measurements of many points over large spaces. These devices have built-in processing, storage, and radio frequency sensors and antennas. They are linked into an interconnected network that routes the data they capture to a computer for analysis.

These networks range from hundreds to thousands of nodes. Because wireless sensor devices are placed in the field for years at a time without any maintenance or human intervention, they must have very low power requirements and batteries capable of lasting for years.

FIGURE 7.16 A WIRELESS SENSOR NETWORK

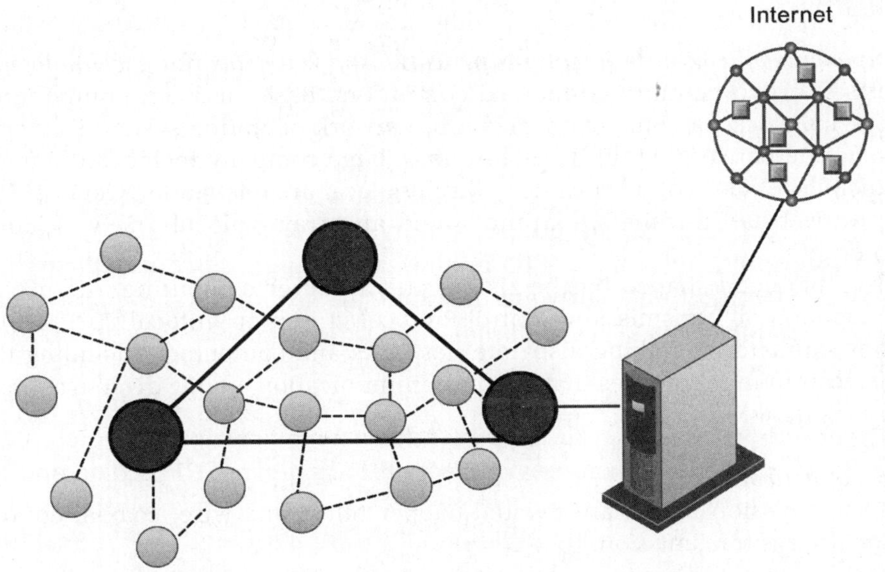

The small circles represent lower-level nodes, and the larger circles represent high-end nodes. Lower-level nodes forward data to each other or to higher-level nodes, which transmit data more rapidly and speed up network performance.

Figure 7.16 illustrates one type of wireless sensor network, with data from individual nodes flowing across the network to a server with greater processing power. The server acts as a gateway to a network based on Internet technology.

Wireless sensor networks are valuable for uses such as monitoring environmental changes; monitoring traffic or military activity; protecting property; efficiently operating and managing machinery and vehicles; establishing security perimeters; monitoring supply chain management; or detecting chemical, biological, or radiological material.

Output from RFID systems and wireless networks is fueling the Internet of Things (IoT), introduced earlier in this chapter, in which machines such as jet engines, power plant turbines, or agricultural sensors constantly gather data and send the data over the Internet for analysis. The data might signal the need to take action such as replacing a part that's close to wearing out, restocking a product on a store shelf, starting the watering system for a soybean field, or slowing down a turbine. Over time, more and more everyday physical objects will be connected to the Internet and will be able to identify themselves to other devices, creating networks that can sense and respond as data changes. Macy's Pick to the Last Unit system, described in the chapter opening case, is an example of an IoT application. According to the McKinsey Global Institute, up to 50 billion devices connected to the Internet could add \$3.9 trillion to \$11.1 trillion a year of new economic value to business and society by 2025 (Manyika et al., 2015). You'll find more examples of the Internet of Things in Chapters 2 and 12.

Review Summary

7-1 *What are the principal components of telecommunications networks and key networking technologies?*

A simple network consists of two or more connected computers. Basic network components include computers, network interfaces, a connection medium, network operating system software, and either a hub or a switch. The networking infrastructure for a large company includes the traditional telephone system, mobile cellular communication, wireless local area networks, videoconferencing systems, a corporate website, intranets, extranets, and an array of local and wide area networks, including the Internet.

Contemporary networks have been shaped by the rise of client/server computing, the use of packet switching, and the adoption of Transmission Control Protocol/ Internet Protocol (TCP/IP) as a universal communications standard for linking disparate networks and computers, including the Internet. Protocols provide a common set of rules that enable communication among diverse components in a telecommunications network.

7-2 *What are the different types of networks?*

The principal physical transmission media are twisted copper telephone wire, coaxial copper cable, fiber-optic cable, and wireless transmission.

Local area networks (LANs) connect PCs and other digital devices within a 500-meter radius and are used today for many corporate computing tasks. Wide area networks (WANs) span broad geographical distances, ranging from several miles to continents and are often private networks that are independently managed. Metropolitan area networks (MANs) span a single urban area.

Digital subscriber line (DSL) technologies, cable Internet connections, and T1 lines are often used for high-capacity Internet connections.

7-3 *How do the Internet and Internet technology work, and how do they support communication and e-business?*

The Internet is a worldwide network of networks that uses the client/server model of computing and the TCP/IP network reference model. Every computer on the Internet is assigned a unique numeric IP address. The Domain Name System (DNS) converts IP addresses to more user-friendly domain names. Worldwide Internet policies are established by organizations and government bodies such as the Internet Architecture Board (IAB) and the World Wide Web Consortium (W3C).

Major Internet services include e-mail, newsgroups, chatting, instant messaging, Telnet, FTP, and the web. Web pages are based on Hypertext Markup Language (HTML) and can display text, graphics, video, and audio. Website directories, search engines, and RSS technology help users locate the information they need on the web. RSS, blogs, social networking, and wikis are features of Web 2.0. The future Web 3.0 will feature more semantic search, visual search, prevalence of apps, and interconnectedness of many different devices (Internet of Things).

Firms are also starting to realize economies by using VoIP technology for voice transmission and virtual private networks (VPNs) as low-cost alternatives to private WANs.

7-4 *What are the principal technologies and standards for wireless networking, communication, and Internet access?*

Cellular networks are evolving toward high-speed, high-bandwidth, digital packet-switched transmission. Broadband 3G networks are capable of transmitting data at speeds ranging from 144 Kbps to more than 2 Mbps. 4G networks capable of transmission speeds of 100 Mbps are starting to be rolled out.

Major cellular standards include Code Division Multiple Access (CDMA), which is used primarily in the United States, and Global System for Mobile Communications (GSM), which is the standard in Europe and much of the rest of the world.

Standards for wireless computer networks include Bluetooth (802.15) for small personal area networks (PANs), Wi-Fi (802.11) for local area networks (LANs), and WiMax (802.16) for metropolitan area networks (MANs).

Radio frequency identification (RFID) systems provide a powerful technology for tracking the movement of goods by using tiny tags with embedded data about an item and its location. RFID readers read the radio signals transmitted by these tags and pass the data over a network to a computer for processing. Wireless sensor networks (WSNs) are networks of interconnected wireless sensing and transmitting devices that are embedded in the physical environment to provide measurements of many points over large spaces.

Key Terms

Review Questions

7-1 What are the principal components of telecommunications, networks, and key networking technologies?

- Discuss the evolution of networks in firms, from telephone and computer networks to single digital network and corporate wide networks.
- Describe the advantages of each of these key digital networking technologies over their traditional counterparts.

7-2 What are the different types of networks?

- Define digital signals and functions of modems.

- List and describe the different transmission media in networks.

7-3 How does the Internet and Internet technology work, and how do they support communication and e-business?

- Define the Internet. How does it work and how does it provide business value?
- Explain the workings of the Domain Name System (DNS) and IP addressing system work.
- List and describe the principal Internet services.
- Define and describe HTTP. Explain its importance to the Web.
- List and describe alternative ways of locating information on the Web.
- Describe how online search technologies are used for marketing.

7-4 What are the principal technologies and standards for wireless networking, communications, and Internet access?

- Illustrate the use of bluetooth to create a personal area network.
- Discuss the applications and limitations of Wi-Fi. How does Wi-Max overcome the challenges?
- Explain the use of RFID in inventory management and SCM. Also, describe the applications of Near-Field Communication (NFC).
- How does Wireless Sensor Network (WSN) aid in monitoring building security? Explain the ways in which these technologies are fueling growth of IoT.

Discussion Questions

7-5 It has been said that within the next few years, smartphones will become the single-most important digital device we own. Discuss the implications of this statement.

7-6 Should all major retailing and manufacturing companies switch to RFID? Why or why not?

7-7 What are some of the issues to consider in determining whether search engine optimization would provide your business with a competitive advantage?

Hands-On MIS Projects

The projects in this section give you hands-on experience evaluating and selecting communications technology, using spreadsheet software to improve selection of telecommunications services, and using web search engines for business research.

Management Decision Problems

7-8 Your company supplies ceramic floor tiles to Leroy Merlin, Bricorama, and other home improvement stores in France. You have been asked to start using radio frequency identification tags on each case of tiles you ship to help your customers improve the management of your products and those of other suppliers in their warehouses. Use the web to identify the cost of hardware, software, and networking components for an RFID system for your company. What factors should be considered? What are the key decisions that have to be made in determining whether your firm should adopt this technology?

7-9 BD sells medical devices and instrument systems to hospitals, health clinics, medical offices, and laboratories in over 50 countries. The company employs over 30,000 people around the world, including account managers, customer service and support representatives, and warehouse staff. Management is considering adopting a system for unified communications. What factors should be considered? What are the key decisions that have to be made in determining whether to adopt this technology? Use the Web, if necessary, to find out more about unified communications and its costs.

Improving Decision Making: Using Spreadsheet Software to Evaluate Wireless Services

Software skills: Spreadsheet formulas, formatting
Business skills: Analyzing telecommunications services and costs

7-10 In this project, you'll use the web to research alternative wireless services and use spreadsheet software to calculate wireless service costs for a sales force.

You would like to equip your sales force of 35, based in Dublin, Ireland, with mobile phones that have capabilities for voice transmission, text messaging, Internet access, and taking and sending photos. Use the web to select two wireless providers that offer nationwide voice and data service as well as good service in your home area. Examine the features of the mobile handsets and wireless plans offered by each of these vendors. Assume that each of the 35 salespeople will need to spend three hours per weekday between 8 a.m. and 6 p.m. on mobile voice communication, send 30 text messages per weekday, use 1 gigabyte of data per month, and send five photos per week. Use your spreadsheet software to determine the wireless service and handset that will offer the best pricing per user over a two-year period. For the purposes of this exercise, you do not need to consider corporate discounts.

Achieving Operational Excellence: Using Web Search Engines for Business Research

Software skills: Web search tools
Business skills: Researching new technologies

7-11 This project will help develop your Internet skills in using web search engines for business research.

Use Google and Bing to obtain information about ethanol as an alternative fuel for motor vehicles. If you wish, try some other search engines as well. Compare the volume and quality of information you find with each search tool. Which tool is the easiest to use? Which produced the best results for your research? Why?

Collaboration and Teamwork Project

Evaluating Smartphones

7-12 Form a group with three or four of your classmates. Compare the capabilities of Apple's iPhone with a smartphone from another vendor with similar features. Your analysis should consider the purchase cost of each device, the wireless networks where each device can operate, plan and handset costs, and the services available for each device. You should also consider other capabilities of each device, including available software, security features, and the ability to integrate with existing corporate or PC applications. Which device would you select? On what criteria would you base your selection? If possible, use Google Docs and Google Drive or Google Sites to brainstorm, organize, and develop a presentation of your findings for the class.

RFID Enabled Weighbridge Automation

CASE STUDY

A weighbridge, also referred to as truck scales, is a means to measure the load carried by huge vehicles such as trucks. This weight information is required by the state government to levy and collect taxes on goods transported. It is also required to ensure safety of the roads by checking that the weight carried in the truck is within permissible limits. The industries heavily rely on this process where vehicles are used for transportation and need to be tracked when they enter and exit a site, which is why weighbridges continue to play a dominant role. They serve as a critical control point for managing vehicles in such industries. Radio frequency identification device (RFID) is a dominant technology deployed for such vehicle management, providing the firm with an accurate and reliable date, besides being a secure and convenient solution. These industries use RFID to partially or completely automate vehicle management and tracking process.

The weight carried by a truck is primarily determined by two measurements—axle weight and gross weight. Axle weight is the amount of weight carried by each axle (a truck may have two or more axles), while gross weight is the combined amount of weight carried by all the axles. The weighbridges are made of steel, concrete, or both. A large set of scales are mounted underneath these bridges permanently, and different technologies are applied for computing the weight carried by trucks. Some of the commonly used technologies are load-cell systems, bending plate systems, and piezoelectric systems. The basic principle for all these technologies is same; when the truck passes over the bridge, it exerts pressure on the scales leading to compression, and this compression is either converted to stress, electric current, or voltage. Depending on the technology deployed, the resulting stress, voltage, or current is used for weight computation. Now, manpower is required to track the weight at a weighbridge. Generally four to five people may be involved at one scale–one for tracking the details of the truck which enters the weighbridge, one for generating a receipt for the weight, truck driver, and one individual who ensures that the truck is in proper place for weight calculation. Automation of this process, either complete or partial, leads to saving time and cost for both the parties. This is especially applicable in industries where heavy materials are transported in bulk everyday through trucks and individual scaling of each item is very difficult which restricts the number of trucks transporting the firm's goods each day.

One such scenario is of Bhushan Power and Steel Limited (BPSL), a leading steel processing industry based in India with an annual turnover exceeding ₹12,000 crore. This firm has state-of-the-art plants manufacturing products which covers the entire value chain of steel, starting from coal mining. It has deployed RFID-based weighbridge automated system to monitor the vehicles carrying the raw materials and finished goods from its manufacturing facilities. This solution was deployed to overcome numerous challenges which the firm was facing everyday. First, the trucks entering the plant queued for their turn for weight measurement; then, they are needed to register by a manual entry of truck and driver details, after which the load computation is done. Afterwards, the gate slip with weight details is also generated manually. All these processes used to be done manually, before the introduction of RIFD-based weighbridge. Furthermore, these details were manually entered into the ERP system for receipt generation, billing, and further processing. These processes being manual were prone to error due to human intervention and also opened avenues for fraudulent activities. Additionally, average log size is becoming smaller across the world and, therefore, individual scaling of each log is not only a tedious process but also a cost intensive task. Log scaling has wide applications in multiple industries such as in coal mining and steel industry, as this forms the basis for processing of raw material required for manufacturing of multiple products, such as the ones manufactured at BPSL plants. Besides this, weight is a benchmark for sale and purchase of products in the steel industry as well. Hence, it becomes imperative for BPSL to implement a weight management system which is both accurate and reliable and whose credibility is dependable across the value chain. When weightload computation is done manually, the truck is first weighed empty and then after loading of goods; the difference in the two values

FIGURE 7.17 IMAGES OF THE TRUCK CAPTURED FROM FOUR SIDES

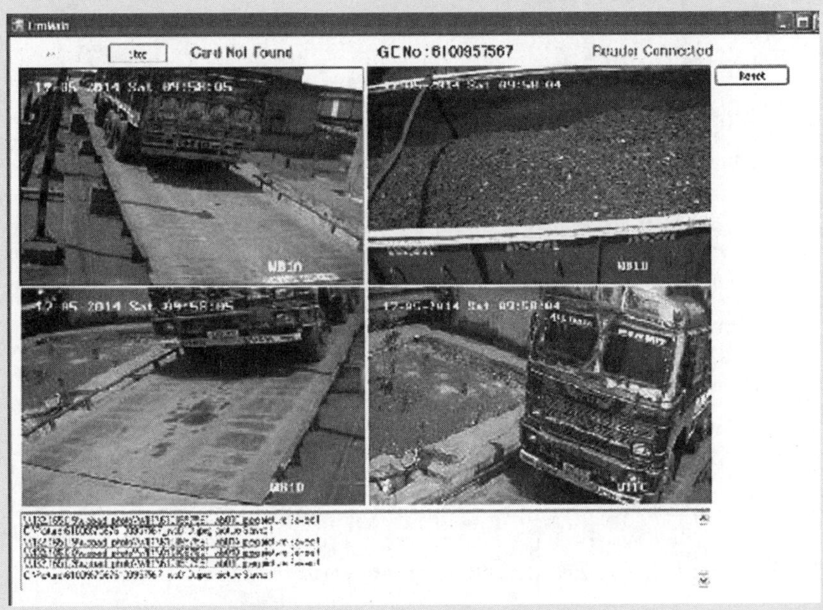

Source: © 2016 Microsoft Corporation, as captured by Author on Windows 8 OS.

generates the actual weight carried by the truck. In this method, manual inaccuracy can be introduced in computing inaccurate gross weights or erronoeuos computation can be made while calculating the difference between tare weight (unloaded or empty truck) and loaded truck. In addition to this, when hundreds of vehicles move in and out of a plant carrying goods, an automated efficient monitoring system is required which not only aids in vehicle identification but also works as an easy load computation.

To overcome these problems, the RFID solution deployed at BPSL was procured from Eco Tracksys, an RFID system integration and solution design provider, headquartered in Delhi. Eco Tracksys proposed the implementation of two solutions at BPSL – AVIS (Automated Vehicle Identification System) and WASS (Weighbridge Automation and Security Solution). For weight computation, they recommended the installation of passive RFID sensors or readers and IP cameras at the weighbridge. As part of the solution, an industrial plant at BPSL was equipped with eight weighbridges, each of which having a RFID reader and three cameras totalling to eight RFID readers and 24 cameras at a plant. All the authorized truck drivers at BPSL were issued identification cards with passive RFID tag which contained their individual details. The card was designed to perform well even in harsh environments wherein they were prone to dirt, humidity, etc. Before entering the weighbridge, the driver passed the card with RFID tag to a guard standing at the entrance of the weighbridge. The guard showed the card to RFID reader which was mounted at each weighbridge. Upon display of card, cameras installed at the weighbridge were triggered to capture images of the truck from all four sides, as shown in Figure 7.17.

This entire RFID system is integrated with SAP-based software system which uses the details captured from RFID system to generate bills, reports, and revenue information, providing higher cost and time efficiency to BPSL. Once the images are successfully captured, gate number (termed as GE) and the weight computed are automatically entered in the SAP system, along with the vehicle and truck driver details. This way, a gate pass can be generated for both incoming and outgoing material. (see Figure 7.18) Now to eliminate the errors introduced manually as discussed before, the same process is repeated at another weighbridge, and tare weights are also computed twice. This way net weights and gross weights are cross-verified and any residual error is automatically adjusted by the SAP system.

AVIS monitors the entry and exit of vehicles and vehicle movement at BPSL plants through RFID-based system. RFID readers are also installed at the boundaries of the plant premises, from where the vehicle's movement in or out of the plant occurs. This solution

FIGURE 7.18 GATE SLIP GENERATED BY THE SAP SYSTEM INTEGRATED WITH RFID SYSTEM

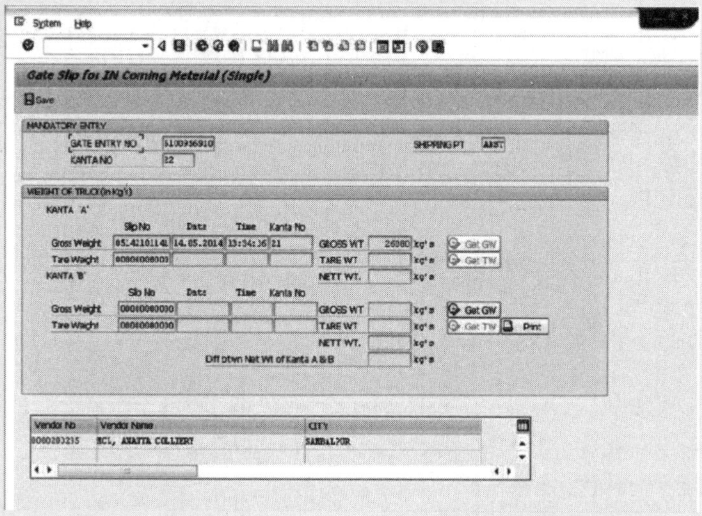

Source: © 2016 Microsoft Corporation, as captured by Author on Windows 8 OS.

not only eliminates any human dependency for tracking vehicle movement, but also looks for unauthorized vehicle entry, checks inaccurate in/out entries, aids in speed control of vehicles, and reduces the waiting time for vehicle entry and exit to zero.

The benefits fetched by this solution for BPSL in terms of return on investment (ROI) are immense. As per the company's figures, on an average 1,500 trucks pass through the industry in a day, with each truck carrying approximately 16 tonnes of material. The automation of weighbridge lead to a saving of around 2 percent of the total cost per month which earlier accounted to theft for lack of proper system for weight computation and tracking. On an average, each day the company was able to process only 1,000 trucks, with rest of them waiting for their turn. The use of RFID-based system has decreased the processing time for each truck resulting in an increase of 500 trucks being processed additionally each day. The firm is also able to save on manpower. Earlier eight weighbridges required eight individuals amounting to expenses in terms of salary of ₹10,000 for each per month. This has reduced to only two people for eight weighbridges, after RFID automation. The amount saved with RFID automation is approximately 60 times more than the amount saved per month by manual weight computation. This solution also eliminated redundancy in the system by removing the need to re-enter a truck's license plate number each time it is on the weighbridge. In this manner, the deployment of RFID solution has not only enhanced efficiency of operations at the firm, but it has also eliminated human intervention preventing theft and financial losses to the company. The solution is also environment-friendly as emissions from vehicles are reduced due to decreased waiting time at the entry and exit points at the weighbridge. This solution has the potential to be used for complete automation, that is, completely unmanned weighbridges, which is an area BPSL is seeking to explore.

Sources: Retrieved from http://science.howstuffworks.com/engineering/civil/question626.htm; Retrieved from http://www.weighbridges.com.au/howitworks.htm; Retrieved from http://amzbizsol.in/index.php/products-services/weight-bridge-automation; Retrieved from http://ecotracksys.com/solutions/weighbridge-automation/; Retrieved from https://www.loadscan.com/truck-measures-explained/; Retrieved from http://ecotracksys.com/solutions/vehicle-tracking-system/; Retrieved from http://glocon.co.in/weighbridge-automation-solutions/add-on-rfid/.

CASE STUDY QUESTIONS

7-13 What do you understand by a weighbridge? How does the weighbridge function?

7-14 Discuss the need at BPSL to automate weighbridge functions using RFID.

7-15 How did the company deploy the RFID-based solution? What was the role of RFID in eliminating the problems that they were facing?

7-16 Discuss the benefits that BPSL witnessed by deploying RFID-based solution at BPSL.

Chapter 7 References

Barr, Alistair. "Mobile Devices Upend Google Search." *Wall Street Journal* (February 25, 2016).

Chiang, I. Robert and Jhih-Hua Jhang-Li. "Delivery Consolidation and Service Competition Among Internet Service Providers." *Journal of Management Information Systems* 34 No. 3 (Winter 2014).

Deichmann, Johannes, Matthias Roggendorf, and Dominik Wee. "Preparing IT Systems and Organizations for the Internet of Things." McKinsey & Company (2015).

eMarketer, "It's 2015. What Does Mobile Mean Now?" (February 18, 2015).

Google, Inc. "SEC Form 10k for the Fiscal Year Ending December 31, 2015" (February 11, 2016).

IBM Global Technology Services. "Software-Defined Networking in the New Business Frontier." (July 2015).

Iyer, Bala. "To Project the Trajectory of the Internet of Things, Look to the Software Industry." *Harvard Business Review* (February 25, 2016).

Manjoo, Farhad. "Google Mighty Now, but Not Forever." *New York Times* (February 11, 2015).

Manyika, James, Michael Chui, Peter Bisson, Jonathan Woetzel, Richard Dobbs, Jacques Bughin, and Dan Aharon. "Unlocking the Potential of the Internet of Things." McKinsey Global Institute (2015).

McKinsey & Company. "The Impact of Internet Technologies: Search." (July 2011).

National Telecommunications and Information Agency. "NTIA Announces Intent to Transition Key Internet Domain Name Functions." (March 14, 2014).

Panko, Raymond R. and Julia Panko. *Business Data Networks and Security* 10e. Upper Saddle River, NJ: Prentice-Hall (2015).

Reisinger, Don. "How Mark Zuckerberg Is Shaping the Future of Facebook, Social Media." *eWeek* (May 16, 2016).

Winkler, Rolfe. "Getting More Than Just Words in a Google Search Result." *Wall Street Journal* (Aug. 18, 2014).

Wittman, Art. "Here Comes the Internet of Things" *Information Week* (July 22, 2013).

Wyatt, Edward. "U.S. to Cede Its Oversight of Addresses on Internet." *New York Times* (March 14, 2014).

CHAPTER

8 Securing Information Systems

Learning Objectives

After reading this chapter, you will be able to answer the following questions:

8-1 Why are information systems vulnerable to destruction, error, and abuse?

8-2 What is the business value of security and control?

8-3 What are the components of an organizational framework for security and control?

8-4 What are the most important tools and technologies for safeguarding information resources?

CHAPTER CASES

Hackers Attack Singapore's Telecom Infrastructure
SAS Helping SEBI Check Equities-Trading Malpractices
BYOD: A Security Nightmare?
Securing Information: The HSBC Way

Hackers Attack Singapore's Telecom Infrastructure

In October 2016, Singapore experienced an unprecedented attack on its Internet infrastructure when Starhub, one of the nation's three telecom companies, faced a massive distributed denial of service (DDoS) attack, forcing users offline. A DDoS attack forces an online service to become unavailable by overwhelming it with traffic from compromised computers called botnets by infecting them with malicious software. Owners of these computers, a small cluster or in the millions, do not even know that their computers are compromised and being used for such attacks.

According to Starhub, the scale and complexity of the attacks were unprecedented. That is because instead of computers it was malware-infected broadband routers and webcams that were involved in the attacks that overwhelmed the company's broadband service. Ironically, these devices were all bought by the customers themselves.

The attack on Singapore's telecommunications company raises the specter of more and bigger DDoS attacks in the future, especially in financial hubs such as Singapore and Hong Kong. In fact, the Singapore attack was likely related to the biggest global cyber-attack in Internet history, carried out with the malware Mirai, which searches the Internet for vulnerable devices and hijacks

© Brian Jackson/123RF

them. To make matters worse, Mirai's source code is published online, making the software available to practically anyone today.

Starhub addressed the problem in the short term by sending technicians to the affected customers to "clean up" their devices by upgrading the software. At the same time, the Cyber Security Agency of Singapore (CSA) and Info-comm Media Development Authority (IMDA) advised members of the public to adopt sound cyber-hygiene practices to secure their devices. For the long run, Singapore is launching a new national cyber-security strategy outlining a multi-tiered cyber-security response plan. A new Cybersecurity Act is also in the pipeline. Singapore's Communications and Information Minister Dr. Yaacob Ibrahim urged businesses to also take responsibility, adding that governments alone cannot address the problem and that everyone should make cybersecurity a priority. In the same way, Malaysia has expressed its concerns about rising cyberattacks using smart devices. It has urged consumers to regularly change the default passwords of their devices and companies to prepare themselves using penetration testing.

Mirai isn't the first malware of its kind, and neither are DDoS attacks a new phenomenon, but together they demonstrate the growing insecurity of the Internet of Things (IoT). The IoT is a platform to connect smart devices to the Internet, including everything from toasters to home appliances. The problem is that these IoT devices, unlike computers, have little security built in, and most ship with well-known default passwords, no passwords, or easily hackable passwords. Further, most IoT companies do not have the resources to push out mass security updates, and so vulnerable devices are never fixed.

The Starhub attack was a watershed moment because it was considered the beginning of a new era of cyberattacks orchestrated through everyday devices. This completely changes the security landscape because of the enormous technical challenge of securing already-compromised devices. The only solution is to disconnect and "brick" the vulnerable devices, rendering unusable millions of webcams, thermostats, and other everyday devices which consumers use!

It is clear that the new era of connected and smart devices will fuel more security attacks and the only way to address this challenge is through a multi-pronged approach involving government regulations, new industry standards, and user education. Singapore is working to strengthen its infrastructure and processes.

Case contributed by Neerja Sethi and Vijay Sethi, Nanyang Technological University

Sources: "DDoS Attack on Starhub First of Its Kind on Singapore's Telco Infrastructure: CSA, IMDA," channelnewsasia.com, October 26, 2016, accessed December 26, 2016; "DDoS Attacks: What You Need to Know," Today Online, October 28, 2016, www.todayonline.com, accessed December 26, 2016; "DDOS Via Smart Devices Is Next Global Cyber Threat, Warns Malaysian Hacker: Exclusive," cio-asia.com, November 15, 2016, accessed January 6, 2017; "Cyber Risks to Intensify in 2017 with Increased Cyber Espionage, Data Integrity Attacks, According to Stroz Friedberg's 2017 Cybersecurity Predictions Report," prnewswire.com, January 5, 2017, accessed January 6, 2017.

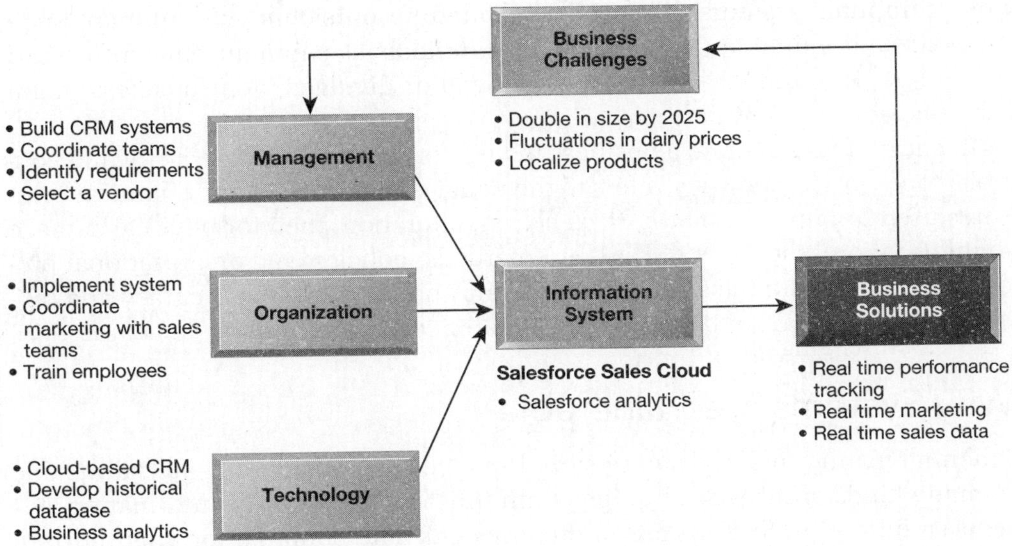

The problems created by the DDoS cyberattack resulting from break-ins into everyday "smart" devices illustrate some of the reasons businesses and consumers need to pay attention to all aspects of information system security. These attacks made the Internet—a critical tool for global business—even more vulnerable. From a security standpoint, as networks expand, hackers gain greater reach and access to increasingly vicious malware.

The chapter-opening diagram calls attention to important points raised by this case and this chapter. Smart devices are simple, easy to use, and do not have the same high level of security built in. Even though most institutions have installed state-of-the-art firewalls and updated software to protect their organizational systems, such as PCs and servers, they fail to pay attention to increasingly connected devices such as webcams and routers, which have very weak security. Thus, despite many strong security safeguards to protect the telecom and Internet infrastructure, criminals were able to compromise the weakest link in the system to launch DDoS attacks.

Here are some questions to think about: What security vulnerabilities were exploited by the hackers? What management, organizational, and technological factors contributed to these security weaknesses? What was the business impact of these problems?

8-1 Why are information systems vulnerable to destruction, error, and abuse?

Can you imagine what would happen if you tried to link to the Internet without a firewall or antivirus software? Your computer would be disabled in a few seconds, and it might take you many days to recover. If you used the computer to run your business, you might not be able to sell to your customers or place orders with your suppliers while it was down. And you might find that your computer system had been penetrated by outsiders, who perhaps stole or destroyed valuable data, including confidential payment data from your customers. If too much data were destroyed or divulged, your business might never be able to recover!

In short, if you operate a business today, you need to make security and control a top priority. **Security** refers to the policies, procedures, and technical measures used to prevent unauthorized access, alteration, theft, or physical damage to information systems. **Controls** are methods, policies, and organizational procedures that ensure the safety of the organization's assets, the accuracy and reliability of its records, and operational adherence to management standards.

Why Systems are Vulnerable

When large amounts of data are stored in electronic form, they are vulnerable to many kinds of threats. Through communications networks, information systems in different locations are interconnected. The potential for unauthorized access, abuse, or fraud is not limited to a single location but can occur at any access point in the network. Figure 8.1 illustrates the most common threats against contemporary information systems. They can stem from technical, organizational, and environmental factors compounded by poor management decisions. In the multitier client/server computing environment illustrated here, vulnerabilities exist at each layer and in the communications between the layers. Users at the client layer can cause harm by introducing errors or by accessing systems without authorization. It is possible to access data flowing over networks, steal valuable data during transmission, or alter data without authorization. Radiation may disrupt a network at various points as well. Intruders can launch denial-of-service attacks or malicious software to disrupt

FIGURE 8.1 CONTEMPORARY SECURITY CHALLENGES AND VULNERABILITIES

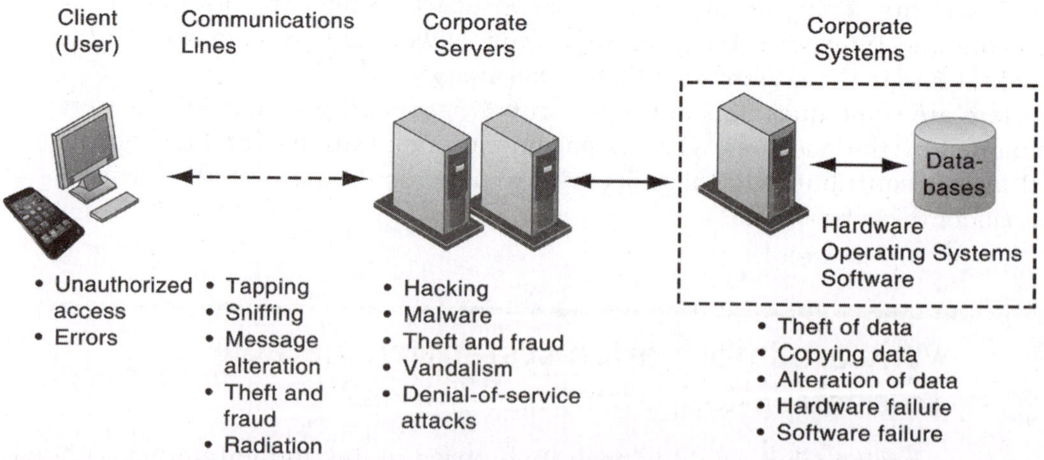

The architecture of a web-based application typically includes a web client, a server, and corporate information systems linked to databases. Each of these components presents security challenges and vulnerabilities. Floods, fires, power failures, and other electrical problems can cause disruptions at any point in the network.

the operation of websites. Those capable of penetrating corporate systems can steal, destroy, or alter corporate data stored in databases or files.

Systems malfunction if computer hardware breaks down, is not configured properly, or is damaged by improper use or criminal acts. Errors in programming, improper installation, or unauthorized changes cause computer software to fail. Power failures, floods, fires, or other natural disasters can also disrupt computer systems.

Domestic or offshore partnering with another company contributes to system vulnerability if valuable information resides on networks and computers outside the organization's control. Without strong safeguards, valuable data could be lost, destroyed, or fall into the wrong hands, revealing important trade secrets or information that violates personal privacy.

The popularity of handheld mobile devices for business computing adds to these woes. Portability makes cell phones, smartphones, and tablet computers easy to lose or steal. Smartphones share the same security weaknesses as other Internet devices and are vulnerable to malicious software and penetration from outsiders. Smartphones that corporate employees use often contain sensitive data such as sales figures, customer names, phone numbers, and e-mail addresses. Intruders may also be able to access internal corporate systems through these devices.

Internet Vulnerabilities

Large public networks, such as the Internet, are more vulnerable than internal networks because they are virtually open to anyone. The Internet is so huge that when abuses do occur, they can have an enormously widespread impact. When the Internet becomes part of the corporate network, the organization's information systems are even more vulnerable to actions from outsiders.

Telephone service based on Internet technology (see Chapter 7) is more vulnerable than the switched voice network if it does not run over a secure private network. Most Voice over IP (VoIP) traffic over the Internet is not encrypted. Hackers can intercept conversations or shut down voice service by flooding servers supporting VoIP with bogus traffic.

Vulnerability has also increased from widespread use of e-mail, instant messaging (IM), and peer-to-peer (P2P) file-sharing programs. E-mail may contain attachments that serve as springboards for malicious software or unauthorized access to internal corporate systems. Employees may use e-mail messages to transmit valuable trade secrets, financial data, or confidential customer information to unauthorized recipients. Popular IM applications for consumers do not use a secure layer for text messages, so they can be intercepted and read by outsiders during transmission over the Internet. Instant messaging activity over the Internet can in some cases be used as a back door to an otherwise secure network. Sharing files over P2P networks, such as those for illegal music sharing, may also transmit malicious software or expose information on either individual or corporate computers to outsiders.

Wireless Security Challenges

Is it safe to log on to a wireless network at an airport, library, or other public location? It depends on how vigilant you are. Even the wireless network in your home is vulnerable because radio frequency bands are easy to scan. Both Bluetooth and Wi-Fi networks are susceptible to hacking by eavesdroppers. Local area networks (LANs) using the 802.11 standard can be easily penetrated by outsiders armed with laptops, wireless cards, external antennae, and hacking software. Hackers use these tools to detect unprotected networks, monitor network traffic, and, in some cases, gain access to the Internet or to corporate networks.

Wi-Fi transmission technology was designed to make it easy for stations to find and hear one another. The service set identifiers (SSIDs) that identify the access points in a Wi-Fi network are broadcast multiple times and can be picked up fairly easily by intruders' sniffer programs (see Figure 8.2). Wireless networks in many locations do not have basic protections against **war driving**, in which eavesdroppers drive by buildings or park outside and try to intercept wireless network traffic.

An intruder who has associated with an access point by using the correct SSID is capable of accessing other resources on the network. For example, the intruder could use the Windows operating system to determine which other users are connected to the network, access their computer hard drives, and open or copy their files.

FIGURE 8.2 WI-FI SECURITY CHALLENGES

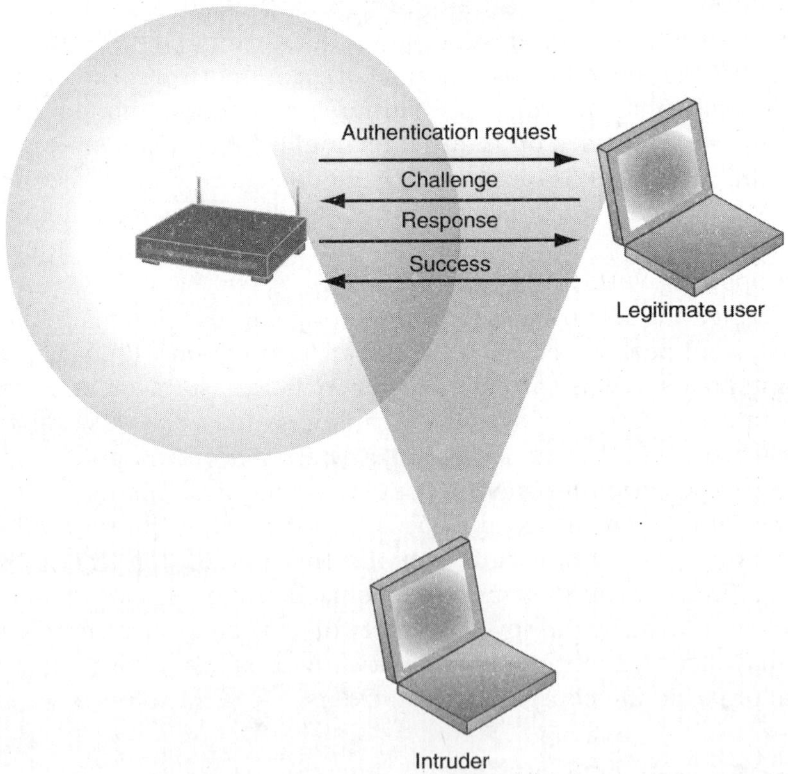

Many Wi-Fi networks can be penetrated easily by intruders using sniffer programs to obtain an address to access the resources of a network without authorization.

Intruders also use the information they have gleaned to set up rogue access points on a different radio channel in physical locations close to users to force a user's radio network interface controller (NIC) to associate with the rogue access point. Once this association occurs, hackers using the rogue access point can capture the names and passwords of unsuspecting users.

Malicious Software: Viruses, Worms, Trojan Horses, and Spyware

Malicious software programs are referred to as **malware** and include a variety of threats such as computer viruses, worms, and Trojan horses. (See Table 8.1.) A **computer virus** is a rogue software program that attaches itself to other software programs or data files to be executed, usually without user knowledge or permission. Most computer viruses deliver a payload. The payload may be relatively benign, such as instructions to display a message or image, or it may be highly destructive—destroying programs or data, clogging computer memory, reformatting a computer's hard drive, or causing programs to run improperly. Viruses typically spread from computer to computer when humans take an action, such as sending an e-mail attachment or copying an infected file.

Most recent attacks have come from **worms**, which are independent computer programs that copy themselves from one computer to other computers over a network. Unlike viruses, worms can operate on their own without attaching to other computer program files and rely less on human behavior to spread from computer to computer. This explains why computer worms spread much

TABLE 8.1 EXAMPLES OF MALICIOUS CODE

NAME	TYPE	DESCRIPTION
Cryptolocker	Ransomware/ Trojan	Hijacks users' photos, videos, and text documents; encrypts them with virtually unbreakable asymmetric encryption; and demands ransom payment for them
Conficker	Worm	First detected in November 2008 and still a problem. Uses flaws in Windows software to take over machines and link them into a virtual computer that can be commanded remotely. Had more than 5 million computers worldwide under its control. Difficult to eradicate.
Sasser.ftp	Worm	First appeared in May 2004. Spread over the Internet by attacking random IP addresses. Causes computers to continually crash and reboot and infected computers to search for more victims. Affected millions of computers worldwide and caused an estimated $14.8 billion to $18.6 billion in damages.
ILOVEYOU	Virus	First detected on May 3, 2000. Script virus written in Visual Basic script and transmitted as an attachment to e-mail with the subject line ILOVEYOU. Overwrites music, image, and other files with a copy of itself and did an estimated $10 billion to $15 billion in damage.

more rapidly than computer viruses. Worms destroy data and programs as well as disrupt or even halt the operation of computer networks.

Worms and viruses are often spread over the Internet from files of downloaded software; from files attached to e-mail transmissions; or from compromised e-mail messages, online ads, or instant messaging. Viruses have also invaded computerized information systems from infected disks or infected machines. Especially prevalent today are **drive-by downloads**, consisting of malware that comes with a downloaded file that a user intentionally or unintentionally requests.

Hackers can do to a smartphone just about anything they can do to any Internet device: request malicious files without user intervention, delete files, transmit files, install programs running in the background to monitor user actions, and potentially convert the smartphone to a robot in a botnet to send e-mail and text messages to anyone. With smartphones outselling PCs and increasingly used as payment devices, they are becoming a major avenue for malware.

According to IT security experts, mobile devices now pose the greatest security risks, outpacing those from larger computers. By the end of 2015, McAfee Labs had collected more than 6 million samples of mobile malware (Snell, 2016). Android, which is the world's leading mobile operating system, is the platform targeted by most hackers. Mobile device viruses pose serious threats to enterprise computing because so many wireless devices are now linked to corporate information systems (see the Interactive Session on Technology in Section 8-4).

Blogs, wikis, and social networking sites such as Facebook, Twitter, and LinkedIn have emerged as new conduits for malware. Members are more likely to trust messages they receive from friends, even if this communication is not legitimate. One malware scam in spring 2015 appeared to be a video link from a friend saying something like, "This is awesome." If the recipient clicked the link. a pop-up window appeared and prompted that person to click an Adobe Flash Player update to continue. Instead of downloading the player, the malware took over the user's computer, looking for bank account numbers, medical records, and other personal data (Thompson, 2015).

Security risks are bound to increase from the mushrooming number of Internet-linked devices within companies and across the Internet. The Internet of Things (IoT) introduces a wide range of new security challenges to IoT devices themselves, their platforms and operating systems, their communications, and even the systems to which they're connected. Additional security tools will be required to protect IoT devices and platforms from both information attacks and physical tampering, to encrypt their communications, and to address new challenges such as attacks that drain batteries. Many IoT devices such as sensors have simple processors and operating systems that may not support sophisticated security approaches.

Panda Security reported that it had identified and neutralized more than 84 million new malware samples throughout 2015 and that it had detected 230,000 new malware samples each day. More than 27 percent of all malware samples ever recorded were created in that one year alone (Panda Security, 2016).

More than 51 percent of the infections Panda found were Trojan horses. A **Trojan horse** is a software program that appears to be benign but then does something other than expected. The Trojan horse is not itself a virus because it does not replicate, but it is often a way for viruses or other malicious code to be introduced into a computer system. The term *Trojan horse* is based on the huge wooden horse the Greeks used to trick the Trojans into opening the gates to their fortified city during the Trojan War. Once inside the city walls, Greek soldiers hidden in the horse revealed themselves and captured the city.

An example of a modern-day Trojan horse is the Zeus Trojan. It is often used to steal login credentials for banking by surreptitiously capturing people's keystrokes as they use their computers. Zeus is spread mainly through drive-by downloads and phishing, and recent variants are hard for anti-malware tools to detect.

SQL injection attacks have become a major malware threat. SQL injection attacks take advantage of vulnerabilities in poorly coded web application software to introduce malicious program code into a company's systems and networks. These vulnerabilities occur when a web application fails to validate properly or filter data a user enters on a web page, which might occur when ordering something online. An attacker uses this input validation error to send a rogue SQL query to the underlying database to access the database, plant malicious code, or access other systems on the network. Large web applications have hundreds of places for inputting user data, each of which creates an opportunity for an SQL injection attack.

Malware known as **ransomware** is proliferating on both desktop and mobile devices. Ransomware tries to extort money from users by taking control of their computers or displaying annoying pop-up messages. One nasty example, CryptoLocker, encrypts an infected computer's files, forcing users to pay hundreds of dollars to regain access. You can get ransomware from downloading an infected attachment, clicking a link inside an e-mail, or visiting the wrong website.

Some types of **spyware** also act as malicious software. These small programs install themselves surreptitiously on computers to monitor user web-surfing activity and serve up advertising. Thousands of forms of spyware have been documented.

Many users find such spyware annoying, and some critics worry about its infringement on computer users' privacy. Some forms of spyware are especially nefarious. **Keyloggers** record every keystroke made on a computer to steal serial numbers for software, to launch Internet attacks, to gain access to e-mail accounts, to obtain passwords to protected computer systems, or to pick up personal information such as credit card or bank account numbers. The Zeus Trojan described earlier uses keylogging. Other spyware programs reset web browser home pages, redirect search requests, or slow performance by taking up too much memory.

Hackers and Computer Crime

A **hacker** is an individual who intends to gain unauthorized access to a computer system. Within the hacking community, the term *cracker* is typically used to denote a hacker with criminal intent, although in the public press, the terms *hacker* and *cracker* are used interchangeably. Hackers gain unauthorized access by finding weaknesses in the security protections websites and computer systems employ, often taking advantage of various features of the Internet that make it an open system and easy to use. Hacker activities have broadened beyond mere system intrusion to include theft of goods and information as well as system damage and **cybervandalism**, the intentional disruption, defacement, or even destruction of a website or corporate information system.

Spoofing and Sniffing

Hackers attempting to hide their true identities often spoof, or misrepresent, themselves by using fake e-mail addresses or masquerading as someone else. **Spoofing** may also involve redirecting a web link to an address different from the intended one, with the site masquerading as the intended destination. For example, if hackers redirect customers to a fake website that looks almost exactly like the true site, they can then collect and process orders, effectively stealing business as well as sensitive customer information from the true site. We will provide more detail about other forms of spoofing in our discussion of computer crime.

A **sniffer** is a type of eavesdropping program that monitors information traveling over a network. When used legitimately, sniffers help identify potential network trouble spots or criminal activity on networks, but when used for criminal purposes, they can be damaging and very difficult to detect. Sniffers enable hackers to steal proprietary information from anywhere on a network, including e-mail messages, company files, and confidential reports.

Denial-of-Service Attacks

In a **denial-of-service (DoS) attack**, hackers flood a network server or web server with many thousands of false communications or requests for services to crash the network. The network receives so many queries that it cannot keep up with them and is thus unavailable to service legitimate requests. A **distributed denial-of-service (DDoS)** attack uses numerous computers to inundate and overwhelm the network from numerous launch points.

Although DoS attacks do not destroy information or access restricted areas of a company's information systems, they often cause a website to shut down, making it impossible for legitimate users to access the site. For example, in November 2016 a large scale DDoS attack took down the servers of the European Commission website. For a period of several hours the EC staff was unable to work. Service was restored the following day. Often DDoS attacks are used to divert attention from the operation of other malware. The EC reports that no files were corrupted or information stolen.

For busy e-commerce sites, these attacks are costly; while the site is shut down, customers cannot make purchases. Especially vulnerable are small and midsize businesses whose networks tend to be less protected than those of large corporations.

Perpetrators of DDoS attacks often use thousands of zombie PCs infected with malicious software without their owners' knowledge and organized into a **botnet**. Hackers create these botnets by infecting other people's computers with bot malware that opens a back door through which an attacker can give instructions. The infected computer then becomes a slave, or zombie, serving a master computer belonging to someone else. When hackers infect enough computers, they can use the amassed resources of the botnet to launch DDoS attacks, phishing campaigns, or unsolicited spam e-mail.

Ninety percent of the world's spam and 80 percent of the world's malware are delivered by botnets. For example, a new version of the Pushdo spamming botnet was detected in spring 2015. Computers in more than 50 countries were infected. Pushdo has existed since 2007 despite numerous attempts to shut it down. The latest version has been pushing malware that steals login credentials and accesses online banking systems. At one time, Pushdo-infected computers sent as many as 7.7 billion spam messages per day (Kirk, 2015).

Computer Crime

Most hacker activities are criminal offenses, and the vulnerabilities of systems we have just described make them targets for other types of **computer crime** as well. Computer crime is defined by the U.S. Department of Justice as "any violations of criminal law that involve a knowledge of computer technology for their perpetration, investigation, or prosecution." Table 8.2 provides examples of the computer as both a target and an instrument of crime.

No one knows the magnitude of the computer crime problem—how many systems are invaded, how many people engage in the practice, or the total economic damage. According to the Ponemon Institute's 2015 Annual Cost of Cyber Crime Study, the average annualized cost of cybercrime for U.S. companies benchmarked was $15 million per year (Ponemon Institute,

TABLE 8.2 EXAMPLES OF COMPUTER CRIME

COMPUTERS AS TARGETS OF CRIME
Breaching the confidentiality of protected computerized data
Accessing a computer system without authority
Knowingly accessing a protected computer to commit fraud
Intentionally accessing a protected computer and causing damage negligently or deliberately
Knowingly transmitting a program, program code, or command that intentionally causes damage to a protected computer
Threatening to cause damage to a protected computer
COMPUTERS AS INSTRUMENTS OF CRIME
Theft of trade secrets
Unauthorized copying of software or copyrighted intellectual property, such as articles, books, music, and video
Schemes to defraud
Using e-mail or messaging for threats or harassment
Intentionally attempting to intercept electronic communication
Illegally accessing stored electronic communications, including e-mail and voice mail
Transmitting or possessing child pornography by using a computer

2015). Many companies are reluctant to report computer crimes because the crimes may involve employees, or the company fears that publicizing its vulnerability will hurt its reputation. The most economically damaging kinds of computer crime are DoS attacks, activities of malicious insiders, and web-based attacks.

Identity Theft

With the growth of the Internet and electronic commerce, identity theft has become especially troubling. **Identity theft** is a crime in which an imposter obtains key pieces of personal information, such as social security numbers, driver's license numbers, or credit card numbers, to impersonate someone else. The information may be used to obtain credit, merchandise, or services in the name of the victim or to provide the thief with false credentials.

Identity theft has flourished on the Internet, with credit card files a major target of website hackers. According to the 2016 Identity Fraud Study by Javelin Strategy & Research, 13.1 million consumers lost $15 billion to identity fraud in 2015 (Javelin, 2016). E-commerce sites are wonderful sources of customer personal information—name, address, and phone number. Armed with this information, criminals can assume new identities and establish new credit for their own purposes.

One increasingly popular tactic is a form of spoofing called **phishing**. Phishing involves setting up fake websites or sending e-mail messages that look like those of legitimate businesses to ask users for confidential personal data. The e-mail message instructs recipients to update or confirm records by providing social security numbers, bank and credit card information, and other confidential data either by responding to the e-mail message, by entering the information at a bogus website, or by calling a telephone number. eBay, PayPal, Amazon.com, Walmart, and a variety of banks have been among the top spoofed companies. In a more targeted form of phishing called *spear phishing*, messages appear to come from a trusted source, such as an individual within the recipient's own company or a friend.

Phishing techniques called evil twins and pharming are harder to detect. **Evil twins** are wireless networks that pretend to offer trustworthy Wi-Fi connections to the Internet, such as those in airport lounges, hotels, or coffee shops. The bogus network looks identical to a legitimate public network. Fraudsters try to capture passwords or credit card numbers of unwitting users who log on to the network.

Pharming redirects users to a bogus web page, even when the individual types the correct web page address into his or her browser. This is possible if pharming perpetrators gain access to the Internet address information Internet service providers (ISPs) store to speed up web browsing and the ISP companies have flawed software on their servers that allows the fraudsters to hack in and change those addresses.

According to the Ponemon Institute's 2015 Cost of a Data Breach Study, the average cost of a breach to a company was $3.5 million (Ponemon, 2015). Moreover, brand damage can be significant, albeit hard to quantify. In addition to the data breaches described in the opening and ending case studies for this chapter, Table 8.3 describes other major data breaches.

TABLE 8.3 MAJOR DATA BREACHES

DATA BREACH	DESCRIPTION
Anthem Health Insurance	In February 2015 hackers stole the personal information on more than 80 million customers of the giant health insurer, including names, birthdays, medical IDs, social security numbers, and income data. No medical or credit information was stolen. This was the largest healthcare breach ever recorded
Sony	In November 2014 hackers stole more than 100 terabytes of corporate data, including trade secrets, e-mail, personnel records, and copies of films for future release. Malware erased data from Sony's corporate systems, leading to hundreds of millions of dollars in losses as well as a tarnished brand image. Sony was hacked earlier in April 2011 when intruders obtained personal information, including credit, debit, and bank account numbers, from more than 100 million PlayStation Network users and Sony Online Entertainment users.
Home Depot	Hacked in 2014 with a malicious software program that plundered store registers while disguising itself as antivirus software. Fifty-six million credit card accounts were compromised, and 53 million customer e-mail addresses were stolen.
Target	Malware surreptitiously installed on security and payment systems in late 2013 stole credit card numbers and identifying data for 40 million Target customers and e-mail addresses of 70 million customers.
eBay	Cyberattack on eBay servers during February and March 2014 compromised database containing customer names, encrypted passwords, e-mail addresses, physical addresses, phone numbers, and birthdates; 145 million people were affected.

The U.S. Congress addressed the threat of computer crime in 1986 with the Computer Fraud and Abuse Act, which makes it illegal to access a computer system without authorization. Most states have similar laws, and nations in Europe have comparable legislation. For example, in July 2013 the European Parliament adopted a cybercrime Directive aimed at outlawing attacks against websites and networks, including the use of DDoS attacks, Botnets, illegal interception of messages, and falsely obtaining passwords. Congress passed the National Information Infrastructure Protection Act in 1996 to make malware distribution and hacker attacks to disable websites federal crimes.

U.S. legislation, such as the Wiretap Act, Wire Fraud Act, Economic Espionage Act, Electronic Communications Privacy Act, CAN-SPAM Act, and Protect Act of 2003 (prohibiting child pornography), covers computer crimes involving intercepting electronic communication, using electronic communication to defraud, stealing trade secrets, illegally accessing stored electronic communications, using e-mail for threats or harassment, and transmitting or possessing child pornography.

Click Fraud

When you click an ad displayed by a search engine, the advertiser typically pays a fee for each click, which is supposed to direct potential buyers to its products. **Click fraud** occurs when an individual or computer program fraudulently clicks an online ad without any intention of learning more about the advertiser or making a purchase. Click fraud has become a serious problem at Google and other websites that feature pay-per-click online advertising.

Some companies hire third parties (typically from low-wage countries) to click a competitor's ads fraudulently to weaken them by driving up their marketing costs. Click fraud can also be perpetrated with software programs doing the clicking, and botnets are often used for this purpose. Search engines such as Google attempt to monitor click fraud and have made some changes to curb it.

Global Threats: Cyberterrorism and Cyberwarfare

The cyber criminal activities we have described—launching malware, DoS attacks, and phishing probes—are borderless. Attack servers for malware are now hosted in more than 200 countries and territories. The most popular sources of malware attacks include the United States, India, Germany, South Korea, China, Netherlands, United Kingdom, and Russia. The global nature of the Internet makes it possible for cybercriminals to operate—and to do harm—anywhere in the world.

Internet vulnerabilities have also turned individuals and even entire nation-states into easy targets for politically motivated hacking to conduct sabotage and espionage. **Cyberwarfare** is a state-sponsored activity designed to cripple and defeat another state or nation by penetrating its computers or networks to cause damage and disruption. Cyberwarfare also includes defending against these types of attacks.

Cyberwarfare is more complex than conventional warfare. Although many potential targets are military, a country's power grids, financial systems, and communications networks can also be crippled. Non-state actors such as terrorists or criminal groups can mount attacks, and it is often difficult to tell who is responsible. Nations must constantly be on the alert for new malware and other technologies that could be used against them, and some of these technologies developed by skilled hacker groups are openly for sale to interested governments.

Preparations for cyberwarfare attacks have become much more widespread, sophisticated, and potentially devastating. Between 2011 and 2015, foreign hackers stole source code and blueprints to the oil and water pipelines and power grid of the United States and infiltrated the Department of Energy's networks 150 times (Perlroth, 2015). Over the years, hackers have stolen plans for missile tracking systems, satellite navigation devices, surveillance drones, and leading-edge jet fighters.

A 2015 report documented 29 countries with formal military and intelligence units dedicated to offensive cyberwarfare. Their cyberarsenals include collections of malware for penetrating industrial, military, and critical civilian infrastructure controllers, e-mail lists and text for phishing attacks on important targets, and algorithms for DoS attacks. U.S. cyberwarfare efforts are concentrated in the United States Cyber Command, which coordinates and directs the operations and defense of Department of Defense information networks and prepares for military cyberspace operations. Cyberwarfare poses a serious threat to the infrastructure of modern societies, since their major financial, health, government, and industrial institutions rely on the Internet for daily operations.

Internal Threats: Employees

We tend to think the security threats to a business originate outside the organization. In fact, company insiders pose serious security problems. Employees have access to privileged information, and in the presence of sloppy internal security procedures, they are often able to roam throughout an organization's systems without leaving a trace.

Studies have found that user lack of knowledge is the single greatest cause of network security breaches. Many employees forget their passwords to access computer systems or allow coworkers to use them, which compromises the system. Malicious intruders seeking system access sometimes trick employees into revealing their passwords by pretending to be legitimate members of the company in need of information. This practice is called **social engineering**.

Both end users and information systems specialists are also a major source of errors introduced into information systems. End users introduce errors by entering faulty data or by not following the proper instructions for processing data and using computer equipment. Information systems specialists may create software errors as they design and develop new software or maintain existing programs.

Software Vulnerability

Software errors pose a constant threat to information systems, causing untold losses in productivity and sometimes endangering people who use or depend on systems. Growing complexity and size of software programs, coupled with demands for timely delivery to markets, have contributed to an increase in software flaws or vulnerabilities. On April 29, 2015, American Airlines had to delay 40 flights due to faulty software on iPads pilots use to look at airport maps and navigational documents. The problem was fixed by having the pilots delete the malfunctioning app and reinstall it (Bajaj, 2015).

A major problem with software is the presence of hidden **bugs** or program code defects. Studies have shown that it is virtually impossible to eliminate all bugs from large programs. The main source of bugs is the complexity of decision-making code. A relatively small program of several hundred lines will contain tens of decisions leading to hundreds or even thousands of paths. Important programs within most corporations are usually much larger, containing tens of thousands or even millions of lines of code, each with many times the choices and paths of the smaller programs.

Zero defects cannot be achieved in larger programs. Complete testing simply is not possible. Fully testing programs that contain thousands of choices and millions of paths would require thousands of years. Even with rigorous testing, you would not know for sure that a piece of software was dependable until the product proved itself after much operational use.

Flaws in commercial software not only impede performance but also create security vulnerabilities that open networks to intruders. Each year security firms identify thousands of software vulnerabilities in Internet and PC software. A recent example is the Heartbleed bug, which is a flaw in OpenSSL, an open-source encryption technology that an estimated two-thirds of web servers use. Hackers could exploit the bug to access visitors' personal data as well as a site's encryption keys, which can be used to collect even more protected data.

Especially troublesome are **zero-day vulnerabilities**, which are holes in the software unknown to its creator. Hackers then exploit this security hole before the vendor becomes aware of the problem and hurries to fix it. This type of vulnerability is called zero day because the author of the software has zero days after learning about it to patch the code before it can be exploited in an attack. Sometimes security researchers spot the software holes but, more often, they remain undetected until an attack has occurred.

To correct software flaws once they are identified, the software vendor creates small pieces of software called **patches** to repair the flaws without disturbing the proper operation of the software. It is up to users of the software to track these vulnerabilities, test, and apply all patches. This process is called *patch management*.

Because a company's IT infrastructure is typically laden with multiple business applications, operating system installations, and other system services, maintaining patches on all devices and services a company uses is often time-consuming and costly. Malware is being created so rapidly that companies have very little time to respond between the time a vulnerability and a patch are announced and the time malicious software appears to exploit the vulnerability.

8-2 What is the business value of security and control?

Companies have very valuable information assets to protect. Systems often house confidential information about individuals' taxes, financial assets, medical records, and job performance reviews. They also can contain information on corporate operations, including trade secrets, new product development plans, and marketing strategies. Government systems may store information on weapons systems, intelligence operations, and military targets. These information assets have tremendous value, and the repercussions can be devastating if they are lost, destroyed, or placed in the wrong hands. Systems that are unable to function because of security breaches, disasters, or malfunctioning technology can have permanent impacts on a company's financial health. Some experts believe that 40 percent of all businesses will not recover from application or data losses that are not repaired within three days.

Inadequate security and control may result in serious legal liability. Businesses must protect not only their own information assets but also those of customers, employees, and business partners. Failure to do so may open the firm to costly litigation for data exposure or theft. An organization can be held liable for needless risk and harm created if the organization fails to take appropriate protective action to prevent loss of confidential information, data corruption, or breach of privacy. For example, Target had to pay $39 million to several U.S. banks servicing Mastercard that were forced to reimburse Target customers millions of dollars when those customers lost money due to a massive 2013 hack of Target's payment systems affecting 40 million people. Target also paid $67 million to Visa for the data hack and $10 million to settle a class-action lawsuit brought by Target customers. A sound security and control framework that protects business information assets can thus produce a high return on investment. Strong security and control also increase employee productivity and lower operational costs.

Legal and Regulatory Requirements for Electronic Records Management

U.S. government regulations are forcing companies to take security and control more seriously by mandating the protection of data from abuse, exposure, and unauthorized access. Firms face new legal obligations for the retention and storage of electronic records as well as for privacy protection.

If you work in the healthcare industry, your firm will need to comply with the Health Insurance Portability and Accountability Act (HIPAA) of 1996. **HIPAA** outlines medical security and privacy rules and procedures for simplifying the administration of healthcare billing and automating the transfer of healthcare data between healthcare providers, payers, and plans. It requires members of the healthcare industry to retain patient information for six years and ensure the confidentiality of those records. It specifies privacy, security, and electronic transaction standards for healthcare providers handling patient information, providing penalties for breaches of medical privacy, disclosure of patient records by e-mail, or unauthorized network access.

If you work in a firm providing financial services, your firm will need to comply with the Financial Services Modernization Act of 1999, better known as the **Gramm-Leach-Bliley Act** after its congressional sponsors. This act requires financial institutions to ensure the security and confidentiality of customer data. Data must be stored on a secure medium, and special security measures must be enforced to protect such data on storage media and during transmittal.

If you work in a publicly traded company, your company will need to comply with the Public Company Accounting Reform and Investor Protection Act of 2002, better known as the **Sarbanes-Oxley Act** after its sponsors Senator Paul Sarbanes of Maryland and Representative Michael Oxley of Ohio. This act was designed to protect investors after the financial scandals at Enron, WorldCom, and other public companies. It imposes responsibility on companies and their management to safeguard the accuracy and integrity of financial information that is used internally and released externally. One of the Learning Tracks for this chapter discusses Sarbanes-Oxley in detail.

Sarbanes-Oxley is fundamentally about ensuring that internal controls are in place to govern the creation and documentation of information in financial statements. Because information systems are used to generate, store, and transport such data, the legislation requires firms to consider information systems security and other controls required to ensure the integrity, confidentiality, and accuracy of their data. Each system application that deals with critical financial reporting data requires controls to make sure the data are accurate. Controls to secure the corporate network, prevent unauthorized access to systems and data, and ensure data integrity and availability in the event of disaster or other disruption of service are essential as well.

Electronic Evidence and Computer Forensics

Security, control, and electronic records management have become essential for responding to legal actions. Much of the evidence today for stock fraud, embezzlement, theft of company trade secrets, computer crime, and many civil cases is in digital form. In addition to information from printed or typewritten pages, legal cases today increasingly rely on evidence represented as digital data stored on portable storage devices, CDs, and computer hard disk drives as well as in e-mail, instant messages, and e-commerce transactions over the Internet. E-mail is currently the most common type of electronic evidence.

In a legal action, a firm is obligated to respond to a discovery request for access to information that may be used as evidence, and the company is required by law to produce those data. The cost of responding to a discovery request can be enormous if the company has trouble assembling the required data or the data have been corrupted or destroyed. Courts now impose severe financial and even criminal penalties for improper destruction of electronic documents.

An effective electronic document retention policy ensures that electronic documents, e-mail, and other records are well organized, accessible, and neither retained too long nor discarded too soon. It also reflects an awareness of how to preserve potential evidence for computer forensics. **Computer forensics** is the scientific collection, examination, authentication, preservation, and analysis of data held on or retrieved from computer storage media in such a way that the information can be used as evidence in a court of law. It deals with the following problems.

- Recovering data from computers while preserving evidential integrity
- Securely storing and handling recovered electronic data
- Finding significant information in a large volume of electronic data
- Presenting the information to a court of law

Electronic evidence may reside on computer storage media in the form of computer files and as *ambient data*, which are not visible to the average user. An example might be a file that has been deleted on a PC hard drive. Data that a computer user may have deleted on computer storage media can often be recovered through various techniques. Computer forensics experts try to recover such hidden data for presentation as evidence.

An awareness of computer forensics should be incorporated into a firm's contingency planning process. The CIO, security specialists, information systems staff, and corporate legal counsel should all work together to have a plan in place that can be executed if a legal need arises. You can find out more about computer forensics in the Learning Tracks for this chapter.

8-3 What are the components of an organizational framework for security and control?

Even with the best security tools, your information systems won't be reliable and secure unless you know how and where to deploy them. You'll need to know where your company is at risk and what controls you must have in place to protect your information systems. You'll also need to develop a security policy and plans for keeping your business running if your information systems aren't operational.

Information Systems Controls

Information systems controls are both manual and automated and consist of general and application controls. **General controls** govern the design, security, and use of computer programs and the security of data files in general throughout the organization's information technology infrastructure. On the whole, general controls apply to all computerized applications and consist of a combination of hardware, software, and manual procedures that create an overall control environment.

General controls include software controls, physical hardware controls, computer operations controls, data security controls, controls over the systems development process, and administrative controls. Table 8.4 describes the functions of each of these controls.

Application controls are specific controls unique to each computerized application, such as payroll or order processing. They include both automated and manual procedures that ensure that only authorized data are completely and accurately processed by that application. Application controls can be classified as (1) input controls, (2) processing controls, and (3) output controls.

Input controls check data for accuracy and completeness when they enter the system. There are specific input controls for input authorization, data conversion, data editing, and error handling. *Processing controls* establish that data are complete and accurate during updating. *Output controls ensure* that the results of computer processing are accurate, complete, and properly distributed. You can find more detail about application and general controls in our Learning Tracks.

Information systems controls should not be an afterthought. They need to be incorporated into the design of a system and should consider not only

TABLE 8.4 GENERAL CONTROLS

TYPE OF GENERAL CONTROL	DESCRIPTION
Software controls	Monitor the use of system software and prevent unauthorized access and use of software programs, system software, and computer programs.
Hardware controls	Ensure that computer hardware is physically secure and check for equipment malfunction. Organizations that are critically dependent on their computers also must make provisions for backup or continued operation to maintain constant service.
Computer operations controls	Oversee the work of the computer department to ensure that programmed procedures are consistently and correctly applied to the storage and processing of data. They include controls over the setup of computer processing jobs and backup and recovery procedures for processing that ends abnormally.
Data security controls	Ensure that valuable business data files maintained internally or by an external hosting service are not subject to unauthorized access, change, or destruction while they are in use or in storage.
Implementation controls	Audit the systems development process at various points to ensure that the process is properly controlled and managed.
Administrative controls	Formalize standards, rules, procedures, and control disciplines to ensure that the organization's general and application controls are properly executed and enforced.

how the system will perform under all possible conditions but also the behavior of organizations and people using the system.

Risk Assessment

Before your company commits resources to security and information systems controls, it must know which assets require protection and the extent to which these assets are vulnerable. A risk assessment helps answer these questions and determine the most cost-effective set of controls for protecting assets.

A **risk assessment** determines the level of risk to the firm if a specific activity or process is not properly controlled. Not all risks can be anticipated and measured, but most businesses will be able to acquire some understanding of the risks they face. Business managers working with information systems specialists should try to determine the value of information assets, points of vulnerability, the likely frequency of a problem, and the potential for damage. For example, if an event is likely to occur no more than once a year, with a maximum of a $1000 loss to the organization, it is not wise to spend $20,000 on the design and maintenance of a control to protect against that event. However, if that same event could occur at least once a day, with a potential loss of more than $300,000 a year, $100,000 spent on a control might be entirely appropriate.

INTERACTIVE SESSION: MANAGEMENT

SAS Helping SEBI Check Equities-Trading Malpractices

The Securities and Exchange Board of India (SEBI) regulates the securities market in India. It was formed in 1992 with the passing of the SEBI Act in the Indian parliament. Its main mandate is to protect the interest of investors and promote the development of a regulated securities market. Since its inception, SEBI has played a key role in the development of the capital market in India by boosting confidence for both institutional and retail investors. Today, SEBI regulates the primary and secondary markets, mutual funds, brokers as well as wealth management businesses in the country.

SEBI is charged with the task of dealing with unfair trade practices and curbing illegal activities in the the securities market. It does so with guidance from the Fraudulent and Unfair Trade Practices (FUTP) regulations issued in 2013. In 2014, incidents of insider trading or front running had been reported. Front-running implies use of personal information by individuals to trade shares prior to a large order of equities. For example, in June 2014, at least 70 entities were under the scanner for insider trading in the shares of Larsen and Turbo Finance. In another incident, top executives of DLF Limited, the realty company, were banned for indulging in unfair trade practices. Considering the recent increase in such activities, SEBI has brought front-running under the ambit of the FUTP. Entities that fail to register with SEBI also come under FUTP.

Increasing regulations and scrutiny require a robust surveillance and analytics system to detect malpractices. As a first step towards this, SEBI, with the aid of SAS, developed its own enterprise data warehouse. Every day, SEBI records more than 200 million transactions. On the whole, it collects 25GB of data per day, a figure that is likely to reach 80GB in a couple of years. The system is designed to track and analyze the collected data. Based on that, the surveillance engine generates alerts so that investigations can be conducted on a case-by-case basis. Researchers generally cull data from third-party sources, such as telephone records, print data, or other unconventional data sources. Such an analysis would have been impossible without a data warehouse. Besides, data needs to be integrated from disparate exchanges across the country. The SAS utilizes its enterprise data integration server for cleansing, standardizing, and removing duplicate data, thereby building a single-entity view of market participants. The current data warehouse has 473 tables and two data marts. It collects transaction data from stock exchanges such as NSE, BSE, USE, as well as depositories such as NSDL and CDSL. The system is able to generate an average of 300 reports each day. The warehouse supports the execution of SQL queries and about five to six tables are typically scanned for each query.

Once the data is loaded from the exchanges into the warehouse in the desired format, aggregates are computed and stored in the database itself. With the help of SAS analytics, fraud can be detected on a daily, weekly, monthly, fortnightly, or quarterly basis. With the implementation of SAS, the SEBI officials are able to get hold of uniform and formatted data, ready for investigation, on the very next day. As a result, SEBI can quickly spot malpractices and act on them. The SAS analytics tool combines multiple detection methods such as business rules, predictive analytics, and entity link analytics for faster detection of fraud. The entity link analysis feature tracks associations between the different entities. This is done on the assumption that if any one entity in the linked network is found to be fraudulent, the possibility of the other linked entities being fraudulent are also high. More the number of associations, more is the likelihood of committing fraud. This tool helps uncover hidden relationships or suspicious associations among customers, market participants, and so on. Since all reports of incidents are stored in a centralized database, past cases can easily be retrived.

Another feature, the SAS scoring accelerator, enables SEBI in the parallel processing of data. The scoring accelerator executes core statistical and analytical functions within the warehouse itself, rather than moving the data to another application. This helps prevent data inconsistency and promotes better governance of data. Since this process is automated, it requires very little human attention or intervention.

Using SAS analytics, SEBI can use analyst recommendations, blogs, and annual reports to understand the impact of social media on investor behavior. In addition to studying the behavior of market participants, it can generate the relationships between them and link them with reported frauds.

In using SAS, SEBI's main aim is to increase the conviction ratio. In 2013 and 2014, 108 new cases were taken up for investigation and 120 cases were completed. Of the 108 cases, market manipulation and price rigging accounted for 60 percent of the cases, insider trading, 12 percent, and takeover violations, 5.6 percent.

Going further, SEBI would like to build analytical models using the SAS Enterprise Miner to identify prevalent malpractices in the market, with special focus on insider trading, front-running, pump-and-dump, and circular trading. The pump-and-dump schemes are generally targeted at small, microcap companies. In such schemes, misleading statements about the lucrativeness of a company's shares are issued by a few miscreants. This leads to a heavy buying of the shares by investors and fraudsters alike, which leads to a consequent hike in share price. This is called pumping. Fraudsters then dump their stocks after making handsome profits, leading to a fall in share price and a loss of investors' money. Circular trading is carried out among a group of traders who have prior knowledge of certain shares. The SAS Enterprise Miner conducts a predictive and descriptive modeling of data. With the help of a user-friendly graphical interface, the mined data can be navigated. These models enable SEBI to uncover frauds in a more efficient manner. SEBI is now also trying to increase its data warehouse capacity and upgrade its analytical tools to accommodate the surge in data to twice the current load.

Sources: "Protecting investors from unscrupulous traders". Retrieved from http://www.sas.com/en_us/customers/securities-and-exchange-board-india.html; "SAS to help SEBI in probing suspicious transactions", *The Business Line* (2011). Retrieved from http://www.thehindubusinessline.com/markets/sas-to-help-sebi-in-probing-suspicious-transactions/article2388290.ece; "SEBI speeds investigations, builds confidence with SAS", *Business Wire* (2011). Retrieved from http://www.businesswire.com/news/home/20110822006092/en/Securities-Exchange-Board-India-SEBI-Speeds-Investigations#.VMdbxen9ku4; Zachariah, Reena, "Sebi to bring front-running under fraudulent and unfair trade practices regulations", *The Economic Times* (2013). Retrieved from http://articles.economictimes.indiatimes.com/2013-08-12/news/41332696_1_sebi-board-futp-securities-market-regulator-sebi; "Securities and Exchange Board of India (Prohibition of Fraudulent and Unfair Trade Practices Relating to Securities Market) Regulations, 2003". Retrieved from http://www.sebi.gov.in/acts/futpfinal.html; "Fraudulent and Unfair Trade Practices", *Money Control*. Retrieved from http://www.moneycontrol.com/news-topic/fraudulent-and-unfair-trade-practices/; Ninan, Oommen A., "SEBI bars DLF, six top executives from markets for 3 years", *The Hindu* (2014). Retrieved from http://www.thehindu.com/business/markets/sebi-bars-dlf-six-top-executives-from-markets-for-3-years/article6497041.ece; "Response to the Queries Raised by Bidders for Dwbis Capacity Augmentation". Retrieved from http://www.sebi.gov.in/cms/sebi_data/tenderdocs/1418705499261.pdf; "SEBI decides to upgrade software for fraud detection". *The Economic Times (2014). Retrieved from* http://articles.economictimes.indiatimes.com/2014-11-28/news/56540483_1_data-centres-insider-trading-market-regulator; "SEBI's Request for Proposal for Augmentation of Data Warehouse Capacity and Business Intelligence Report Capacity" (2014). Retrieved from http://www.sebi.gov.in/cms/sebi_data/tenderdocs/1416991959030.pdf.

CASE STUDY QUESTIONS

1. From your understanding of the case, discuss the role of SEBI. Also discuss the need for analytics at SEBI.

2. Why was an enterprise data warehouse (EDW) required at SEBI? List the sources of data and the different ways in which EDW is utilized at SEBI.

3. Discuss the features of SAS analytics that are used by the SEBI for fraud detection and prevention.

4. Discuss the advantages of using analytics to convict fraudsters.

TABLE 8.5 ONLINE ORDER PROCESSING RISK ASSESSMENT

EXPOSURE	PROBABILITY OF OCCURRENCE (%)	LOSS RANGE/ AVERAGE ($)	EXPECTED ANNUAL LOSS ($)
Power failure	30%	$5000–$200,000 ($102,500)	$30,750
Embezzlement	5%	$1000–$50,000 ($25,500)	$1275
User error	98%	$200–$40,000 ($20,100)	$19,698

Table 8.5 illustrates sample results of a risk assessment for an online order processing system that processes 30,000 orders per day. The likelihood of each exposure occurring over a one-year period is expressed as a percentage. The next column shows the highest and lowest possible loss that could be expected each time the exposure occurred and an average loss calculated by adding the highest and lowest figures and dividing by two. The expected annual loss for each exposure can be determined by multiplying the average loss by its probability of occurrence.

This risk assessment shows that the probability of a power failure occurring in a one-year period is 30 percent. Loss of order transactions while power is down could range from $5000 to $200,000 (averaging $102,500) for each occurrence, depending on how long processing is halted. The probability of embezzlement occurring over a yearly period is about 5 percent, with potential losses ranging from $1000 to $50,000 (and averaging $25,500) for each occurrence. User errors have a 98 percent chance of occurring over a yearly period, with losses ranging from $200 to $40,000 (and averaging $20,100) for each occurrence.

After the risks have been assessed, system builders will concentrate on the control points with the greatest vulnerability and potential for loss. In this case, controls should focus on ways to minimize the risk of power failures and user errors because anticipated annual losses are highest for these areas.

Security Policy

After you've identified the main risks to your systems, your company will need to develop a security policy for protecting the company's assets. A **security policy** consists of statements ranking information risks, identifying acceptable security goals, and identifying the mechanisms for achieving these goals. What are the firm's most important information assets? Who generates and controls this information in the firm? What existing security policies are in place to protect the information? What level of risk is management willing to accept for each of these assets? Is it willing, for instance, to lose customer credit data once every 10 years? Or will it build a security system for credit card data that can withstand the once-in-a-hundred-year disaster? Management must estimate how much it will cost to achieve this level of acceptable risk.

The security policy drives other policies determining acceptable use of the firm's information resources and which members of the company have access to its information assets. An **acceptable use policy (AUP)** defines acceptable uses of the firm's information resources and computing equipment, including desktop and laptop computers, wireless devices, telephones, and the Internet. A good AUP defines unacceptable and acceptable actions for every user and specifies consequences for noncompliance.

Security policy also includes provisions for identity management. **Identity management** consists of business processes and software tools for identifying the valid users of a system and controlling their access to system resources. It includes policies for identifying and authorizing different categories of system users, specifying what systems or portions of systems each user is allowed to access, and the processes and technologies for authenticating users and protecting their identities.

Figure 8.3 is one example of how an identity management system might capture the access rules for different levels of users in the human resources function. It specifies what portions of a human resource database each user is permitted to access, based on the information required to perform that person's job. The database contains sensitive personal information such as employees' salaries, benefits, and medical histories.

The access rules illustrated here are for two sets of users. One set of users consists of all employees who perform clerical functions, such as inputting employee data into the system. All individuals with this type of profile can

FIGURE 8.3 **ACCESS RULES FOR A PERSONNEL SYSTEM**

SECURITY PROFILE 1

User: Personnel Dept. Clerk

Location: Division 1

Employee Identification Codes with This Profile: 00753, 27834, 37665, 44116

Data Field Restrictions	Type of Access
All employee data for Division 1 only	Read and Update
• Medical history data	None
• Salary	None
• Pensionable earnings	None

SECURITY PROFILE 2

User: Divisional Personnel Manager

Location: Division 1

Employee Identification Codes with This Profile: 27321

Data Field Restrictions	Type of Access
All employee data for Division 1 only	Read Only

These two examples represent two security profiles or data security patterns that might be found in a personnel system. Depending on the security profile, a user would have certain restrictions on access to various systems, locations, or data in an organization.

update the system but can neither read nor update sensitive fields, such as salary, medical history, or earnings data. Another profile applies to a divisional manager, who cannot update the system but who can read all employee data fields for his or her division, including medical history and salary. We provide more detail about the technologies for user authentication later on in this chapter.

Disaster Recovery Planning and Business Continuity Planning

If you run a business, you need to plan for events, such as power outages, floods, earthquakes, or terrorist attacks, that will prevent your information systems and your business from operating. **Disaster recovery planning** devises plans for the restoration of disrupted computing and communications services. Disaster recovery plans focus primarily on the technical issues involved in keeping systems up and running, such as which files to back up and the maintenance of backup computer systems or disaster recovery services.

For example, MasterCard maintains a duplicate computer center in Kansas City, Missouri, to serve as an emergency backup to its primary computer center in St. Louis. Rather than build their own backup facilities, many firms contract with disaster recovery firms such as SunGard Availability Services and Acronis. These disaster recovery firms provide hot sites housing spare computers at locations around the country where subscribing firms can run their critical applications in an emergency. For example, Champion Technologies, which supplies chemicals used in oil and gas operations, can switch its enterprise systems from Houston to a SunGard data center in Scottsdale, Arizona, in two hours.

Business continuity planning focuses on how the company can restore business operations after a disaster strikes. The business continuity plan identifies critical business processes and determines action plans for handling mission-critical functions if systems go down. For example, Deutsche Bank, which provides investment banking and asset management services in 74 countries, has a well-developed business continuity plan that it continually updates and refines. It maintains full-time teams in Singapore, Hong Kong, Japan, India, and Australia to coordinate plans addressing loss of facilities, personnel, or critical systems so that the company can continue to operate when a catastrophic event occurs. Deutsche Bank's plan distinguishes between processes critical for business survival and those critical to crisis support and is coordinated with the company's disaster recovery planning for its computer centers.

Business managers and information technology specialists need to work together on both types of plans to determine which systems and business processes are most critical to the company. They must conduct a business impact analysis to identify the firm's most critical systems and the impact a systems outage would have on the business. Management must determine the maximum amount of time the business can survive with its systems down and which parts of the business must be restored first.

The Role of Auditing

How does management know that information systems security and controls are effective? To answer this question, organizations must conduct comprehensive and systematic audits. An **information systems audit** examines the firm's overall security environment as well as controls governing individual information systems. The auditor should trace the flow of sample transactions through the system and perform tests, using, if appropriate, automated audit software. The information systems audit may also examine data quality.

Security audits review technologies, procedures, documentation, training, and personnel. A thorough audit will even simulate an attack or disaster to test the response of the technology, information systems staff, and business employees.

The audit lists and ranks all control weaknesses and estimates the probability of their occurrence. It then assesses the financial and organizational impact of each threat. Figure 8.4 is a sample auditor's listing of control weaknesses for a loan system. It includes a section for notifying management of such weaknesses and for management's response. Management is expected to devise a plan for countering significant weaknesses in controls.

FIGURE 8.4 SAMPLE AUDITOR'S LIST OF CONTROL WEAKNESSES

Function: Loans **Location: Peoria, IL**	**Prepared by: J. Ericson** **Date: June 16, 2016**		**Received by: T. Benson** **Review date: June 28, 2016**	
Nature of Weakness and Impact	Chance for Error/Abuse		Notification to Management	
	Yes/No	Justification	Report date	Management response
User accounts with missing passwords	Yes	Leaves system open to unauthorized outsiders or attackers	5/10/16	Eliminate accounts without passwords
Network configured to allow some sharing of system files	Yes	Exposes critical system files to hostile parties connected to the network	5/10/16	Ensure only required directories are shared and that they are protected with strong passwords
Software patches can update production programs without final approval from Standards and Controls group	No	All production programs require management approval; Standards and Controls group assigns such cases to a temporary production status		

This chart is a sample page from a list of control weaknesses that an auditor might find in a loan system in a local commercial bank. This form helps auditors record and evaluate control weaknesses and shows the results of discussing those weaknesses with management as well as any corrective actions management takes.

8-4 What are the most important tools and technologies for safeguarding information resources?

Businesses have an array of technologies for protecting their information resources. They include tools for managing user identities, preventing unauthorized access to systems and data, ensuring system availability, and ensuring software quality.

Identity Management and Authentication

Midsize and large companies have complex IT infrastructures and many systems, each with its own set of users. Identity management software automates the process of keeping track of all these users and their system privileges, assigning each user a unique digital identity for accessing each system. It also includes tools for authenticating users, protecting user identities, and controlling access to system resources.

To gain access to a system, a user must be authorized and authenticated. **Authentication** refers to the ability to know that a person is who he or she claims to be. Authentication is often established by using **passwords** known only to authorized users. An end user uses a password to log on to a computer system and may also use passwords for accessing specific systems and files. However, users often forget passwords, share them, or choose poor passwords that are easy to guess, which compromises security. Password systems that are too rigorous hinder employee productivity. When employees must change complex passwords frequently, they often take shortcuts, such as choosing passwords that are easy to guess or keeping their passwords at their workstations in plain view. Passwords can also be sniffed if transmitted over a network or stolen through social engineering.

New authentication technologies, such as tokens, smart cards, and biometric authentication, overcome some of these problems. A **token** is a physical device, similar to an identification card, that is designed to prove the identity of a single user. Tokens are small gadgets that typically fit on key rings and display passcodes that change frequently. A **smart card** is a device about the size of a credit card that contains a chip formatted with access permission and other data. (Smart cards are also used in electronic payment systems.) A reader device interprets the data on the smart card and allows or denies access.

Biometric authentication uses systems that read and interpret individual human traits, such as fingerprints, irises, and voices to grant or deny access. Biometric authentication is based on the measurement of a physical or behavioral trait that makes each individual unique. It compares a person's unique characteristics, such as the fingerprints, face, or retinal image, against a stored profile of these characteristics to determine any differences between these characteristics and the stored profile. If the two profiles match, access is granted. Fingerprint and facial recognition technologies are just beginning to be used for security applications, with many PC laptops (and some smartphones) equipped

© Destinacigdem/123RF

This smartphone has a biometric fingerprint reader for fast yet secure access to files and networks. New models of PCs and smartphones are starting to use biometric identification to authenticate users.

with fingerprint identification devices and several models with built-in webcams and face recognition software.

The steady stream of incidents in which hackers have been able to access traditional passwords highlights the need for more secure means of authentication. **Two-factor authentication** increases security by validating users through a multistep process. To be authenticated, a user must provide two means of identification, one of which is typically a physical token, such as a smartcard or chip-enabled bank card, and the other of which is typically data, such as a password or personal identification number (PIN). Biometric data, such as fingerprints, iris prints, or voice prints, can also be used as one of the authenticating mechanisms. A common example of two-factor authentication is a bank card; the card itself is the physical item, and the PIN is the data that go with it.

Firewalls, Intrusion Detection Systems, and Antivirus Software

Without protection against malware and intruders, connecting to the Internet would be very dangerous. Firewalls, intrusion detection systems, and antivirus software have become essential business tools.

Firewalls

Firewalls prevent unauthorized users from accessing private networks. A firewall is a combination of hardware and software that controls the flow of

FIGURE 8.5 A CORPORATE FIREWALL

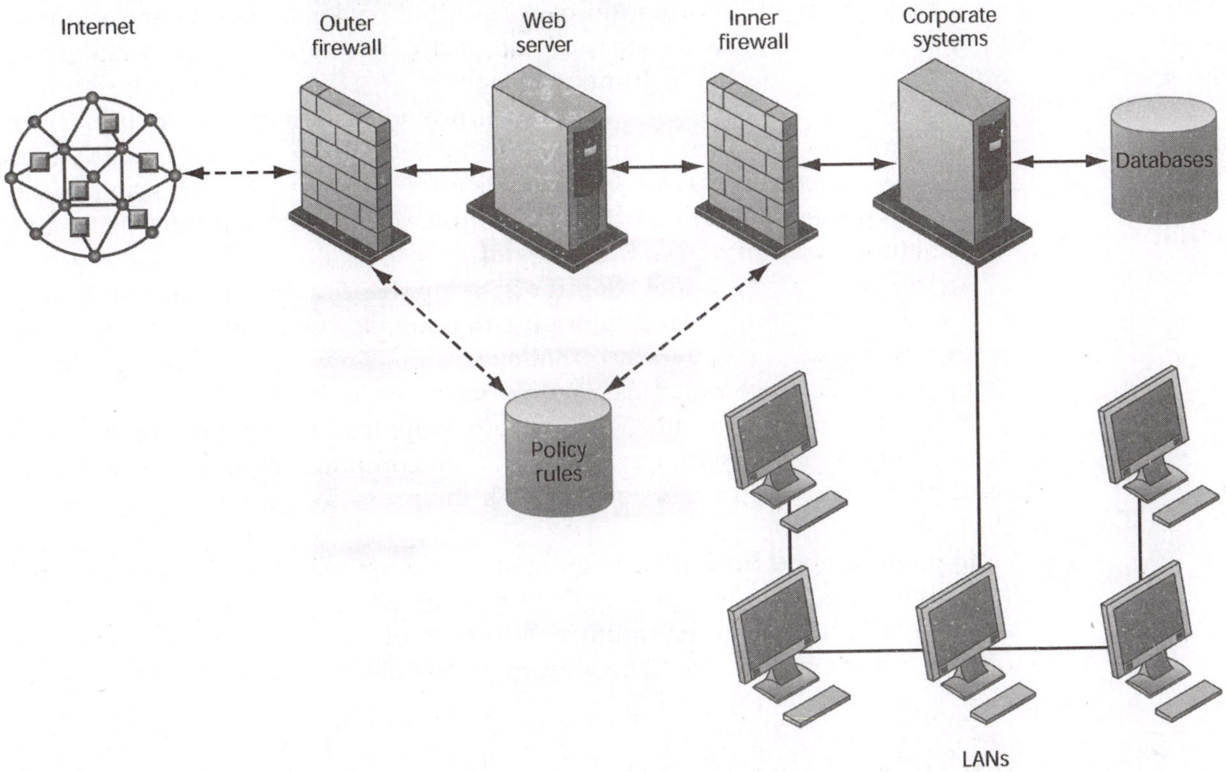

The firewall is placed between the firm's private network and the public Internet or another distrusted network to protect against unauthorized traffic.

incoming and outgoing network traffic. It is generally placed between the organization's private internal networks and distrusted external networks, such as the Internet, although firewalls can also be used to protect one part of a company's network from the rest of the network (see Figure 8.5).

The firewall acts like a gatekeeper that examines each user's credentials before it grants access to a network. The firewall identifies names, IP addresses, applications, and other characteristics of incoming traffic. It checks this information against the access rules that the network administrator has programmed into the system. The firewall prevents unauthorized communication into and out of the network.

In large organizations, the firewall often resides on a specially designated computer separate from the rest of the network, so no incoming request directly accesses private network resources. There are a number of firewall screening technologies, including static packet filtering, stateful inspection, Network Address Translation, and application proxy filtering. They are frequently used in combination to provide firewall protection.

Packet filtering examines selected fields in the headers of data packets flowing back and forth between the trusted network and the Internet, examining individual packets in isolation. This filtering technology can miss many types of attacks.

Stateful inspection provides additional security by determining whether packets are part of an ongoing dialogue between a sender and a receiver. It sets up state tables to track information over multiple packets. Packets are accepted or rejected based on whether they are part of an approved conversation or attempting to establish a legitimate connection.

Network Address Translation (NAT) can provide another layer of protection when static packet filtering and stateful inspection are employed. NAT conceals the IP addresses of the organization's internal host computer(s) to prevent sniffer programs outside the firewall from ascertaining them and using that information to penetrate internal systems.

Application proxy filtering examines the application content of packets. A proxy server stops data packets originating outside the organization, inspects them, and passes a proxy to the other side of the firewall. If a user outside the company wants to communicate with a user inside the organization, the outside user first communicates with the proxy application, and the proxy application communicates with the firm's internal computer. Likewise, a computer user inside the organization goes through the proxy to talk with computers on the outside.

To create a good firewall, an administrator must maintain detailed internal rules identifying the people, applications, or addresses that are allowed or rejected. Firewalls can deter, but not completely prevent, network penetration by outsiders and should be viewed as one element in an overall security plan.

Intrusion Detection Systems

In addition to firewalls, commercial security vendors now provide intrusion detection tools and services to protect against suspicious network traffic and attempts to access files and databases. **Intrusion detection systems** feature full-time monitoring tools placed at the most vulnerable points or hot spots of corporate networks to detect and deter intruders continually. The system generates an alarm if it finds a suspicious or anomalous event. Scanning software looks for patterns indicative of known methods of computer attacks such as bad passwords, checks to see whether important files have been removed or modified, and sends warnings of vandalism or system administration errors. The intrusion detection tool can also be customized to shut down a particularly sensitive part of a network if it receives unauthorized traffic.

Antivirus and Antispyware Software

Defensive technology plans for both individuals and businesses must include anti-malware protection for every computer. **Antivirus software** prevents, detects, and removes malware, including computer viruses, computer worms, Trojan horses, spyware, and adware. However, most antivirus software is effective only against malware already known when the software was written. To remain effective, the antivirus software must be continually updated. Even then it is not always effective because some malware can evade antivirus detection. Organizations need to use additional malware detection tools for better protection.

Unified Threat Management Systems

To help businesses reduce costs and improve manageability, security vendors have combined into a single appliance various security tools, including firewalls, virtual private networks, intrusion detection systems, and web content filtering and anti-spam software. These comprehensive security management products are called **unified threat management (UTM)** systems. UTM products are available for all sizes of networks. Leading UTM vendors include Fortinent, Sophos, and Check Point, and networking vendors such as Cisco Systems and Juniper Networks provide some UTM capabilities in their products.

Securing Wireless Networks

The initial security standard developed for Wi-Fi, called Wired Equivalent Privacy (WEP), is not very effective because its encryption keys are relatively easy to crack. WEP provides some margin of security, however, if users remember to enable it. Corporations can further improve Wi-Fi security by using it in conjunction with virtual private network (VPN) technology when accessing internal corporate data.

In June 2004, the Wi-Fi Alliance industry trade group finalized the 802.11i specification (also referred to as Wi-Fi Protected Access 2 or WPA2) that replaces WEP with stronger security standards. Instead of the static encryption keys used in WEP, the new standard uses much longer keys that continually change, making them harder to crack.

Encryption and Public Key Infrastructure

Many businesses use encryption to protect digital information that they store, physically transfer, or send over the Internet. **Encryption** is the process of transforming plain text or data into cipher text that cannot be read by anyone other than the sender and the intended receiver. Data are encrypted by using a secret numerical code, called an encryption key, that transforms plain data into cipher text. The message must be decrypted by the receiver.

Two methods for encrypting network traffic on the web are SSL and S-HTTP. **Secure Sockets Layer (SSL)** and its successor, Transport Layer Security (TLS), enable client and server computers to manage encryption and decryption activities as they communicate with each other during a secure web session. **Secure Hypertext Transfer Protocol (S-HTTP)** is another protocol used for encrypting data flowing over the Internet, but it is limited to individual messages, whereas SSL and TLS are designed to establish a secure connection between two computers.

The capability to generate secure sessions is built into Internet client browser software and servers. The client and the server negotiate what key and what level of security to use. Once a secure session is established between the client and the server, all messages in that session are encrypted.

Two methods of encryption are symmetric key encryption and public key encryption. In symmetric key encryption, the sender and receiver establish a secure Internet session by creating a single encryption key and sending it to

FIGURE 8.6 PUBLIC KEY ENCRYPTION

A public key encryption system can be viewed as a series of public and private keys that lock data when they are transmitted and unlock the data when they are received. The sender locates the recipient's public key in a directory and uses it to encrypt a message. The message is sent in encrypted form over the Internet or a private network. When the encrypted message arrives, the recipient uses his or her private key to decrypt the data and read the message.

the receiver so both the sender and receiver share the same key. The strength of the encryption key is measured by its bit length. Today, a typical key will be 56 to 256 bits long (a string of from 56 to 256 binary digits) depending on the level of security desired. The longer the key, the more difficult it is to break the key. The downside is that the longer the key, the more computing power it takes for legitimate users to process the information.

The problem with all symmetric encryption schemes is that the key itself must be shared somehow among the senders and receivers, which exposes the key to outsiders who might just be able to intercept and decrypt the key. A more secure form of encryption called **public key encryption** uses two keys: one shared (or public) and one totally private as shown in Figure 8.6. The keys are mathematically related so that data encrypted with one key can be decrypted using only the other key. To send and receive messages, communicators first create separate pairs of private and public keys. The public key is kept in a directory, and the private key must be kept secret. The sender encrypts a message with the recipient's public key. On receiving the message, the recipient uses his or her private key to decrypt it.

Digital certificates are data files used to establish the identity of users and electronic assets for protection of online transactions (see Figure 8.7). A digital certificate system uses a trusted third party, known as a certificate authority (CA), to validate a user's identity. There are many CAs in the United States and around the world, including Symantec, GoDaddy, and Comodo.

The CA verifies a digital certificate user's identity offline. This information is put into a CA server, which generates an encrypted digital certificate containing owner identification information and a copy of the owner's public key. The certificate authenticates that the public key belongs to the designated owner. The CA makes its own public key available either in print or perhaps on the Internet. The recipient of an encrypted message uses the CA's public key to decode the digital certificate attached to the message, verifies it was issued by the CA, and then obtains the sender's public key and identification information contained in the certificate. By using this information, the recipient can send an encrypted reply. The digital certificate system would enable, for example, a

FIGURE 8.7 DIGITAL CERTIFICATES

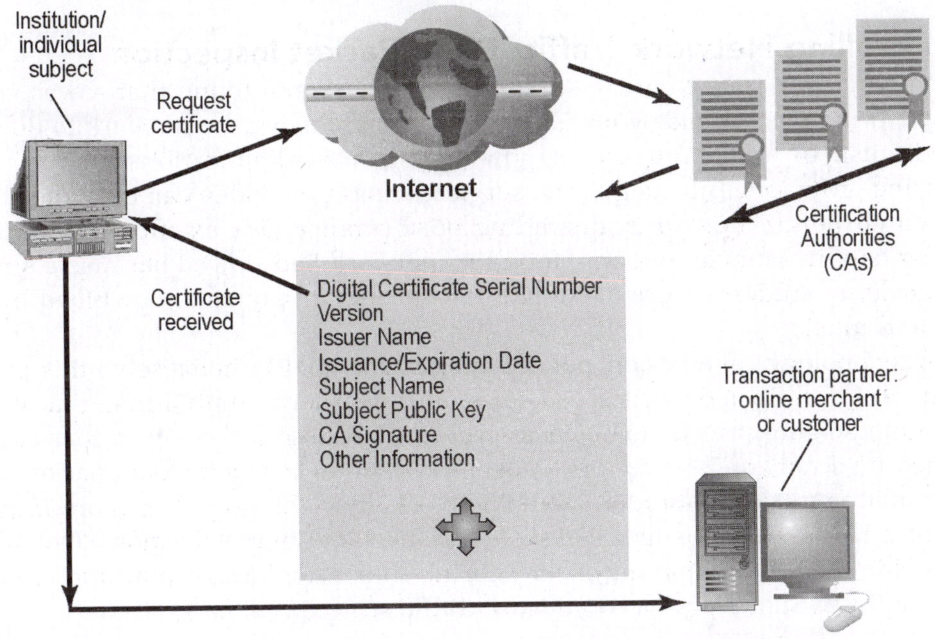

Digital certificates help establish the identity of people or electronic assets. They protect online transactions by providing secure, encrypted, online communication.

credit card user and a merchant to validate that their digital certificates were issued by an authorized and trusted third party before they exchange data. **Public key infrastructure (PKI)**, the use of public key cryptography working with a CA, is now widely used in e-commerce.

Ensuring System Availability

As companies increasingly rely on digital networks for revenue and operations, they need to take additional steps to ensure that their systems and applications are always available. Firms such as those in the airline and financial services industries with critical applications requiring online transaction processing have traditionally used fault-tolerant computer systems for many years to ensure 100 percent availability. In **online transaction processing**, transactions entered online are immediately processed by the computer. Multitudinous changes to databases, reporting, and requests for information occur each instant.

Fault-tolerant computer systems contain redundant hardware, software, and power supply components that create an environment that provides continuous, uninterrupted service. Fault-tolerant computers use special software routines or self-checking logic built into their circuitry to detect hardware failures and automatically switch to a backup device. Parts from these computers can be removed and repaired without disruption to the computer or downtime. **Downtime** refers to periods of time in which a system is not operational.

Controlling Network Traffic: Deep Packet Inspection

Have you ever tried to use your campus network and found that it was very slow? It may be because your fellow students are using the network to download music or watch YouTube. Bandwith-consuming applications such as file-sharing programs, Internet phone service, and online video can clog and slow down corporate networks, degrading performance. For example, Ball State University in Muncie, Indiana, found its network had slowed because a small minority of students were using P2P file-sharing programs to download movies and music.

A technology called **deep packet inspection (DPI)** helps solve this problem. DPI examines data files and sorts out low-priority online material while assigning higher priority to business-critical files. Based on the priorities established by a network's operators, it decides whether a specific data packet can continue to its destination or should be blocked or delayed while more important traffic proceeds. Using a DPI system from Allot Communications, Ball State was able to cap the amount of file-sharing traffic and assign it a much lower priority. Ball State's preferred network traffic sped up.

Security Outsourcing

Many companies, especially small businesses, lack the resources or expertise to provide a secure high-availability computing environment on their own. They can outsource many security functions to **managed security service providers (MSSPs)** that monitor network activity and perform vulnerability testing and intrusion detection. SecureWorks, AT&T, Verizon, IBM, Perimeter eSecurity, and Symantec are leading providers of MSSP services.

Security Issues for Cloud Computing and the Mobile Digital Platform

Although cloud computing and the emerging mobile digital platform have the potential to deliver powerful benefits, they pose new challenges to system security and reliability. We now describe some of these challenges and how they should be addressed.

Security in the Cloud

When processing takes place in the cloud, accountability and responsibility for protection of sensitive data still reside with the company owning that data. Understanding how the cloud computing provider organizes its services and manages the data is critical.

Cloud computing is highly distributed. Cloud applications reside in large remote data centers and server farms that supply business services and data management for multiple corporate clients. To save money and keep costs low, cloud computing providers often distribute work to data centers around the globe where work can be accomplished most efficiently. When you use the cloud, you may not know precisely where your data are being hosted.

The dispersed nature of cloud computing makes it difficult to track unauthorized activity. Virtually all cloud providers use encryption, such as SSL, to secure the data they handle while the data are being transmitted. However, if the data are stored on devices that also store other companies' data, it's important to ensure that these stored data are encrypted as well. According to research from Alert Logic, there has been a 45 percent year-over-year increase in attacks on the cloud. DDoS attacks are especially harmful because they render cloud services unavailable to legitimate customers.

Companies expect their systems to be running 24/7. Cloud providers still experience occasional outages, but their reliability has increased to the point where a number of large companies are using cloud services for part of their IT infrastructures. Most keep their critical systems in-house.

Cloud users need to confirm that regardless of where their data are stored, they are protected at a level that meets their corporate requirements. They should stipulate that the cloud provider store and process data in specific jurisdictions according to the privacy rules of those jurisdictions. Cloud clients should find how the cloud provider segregates their corporate data from those of other companies and ask for proof that encryption mechanisms are sound. It's also important to know how the cloud provider will respond if a disaster strikes, whether the provider will be able to restore your data completely, and how long this should take. Cloud users should also ask whether cloud providers will submit to external audits and security certifications. These kinds of controls can be written into the service level agreement (SLA) before signing with a cloud provider. The Cloud Security Alliance (CSA) has created industrywide standards for cloud security, specifying best practices to secure cloud computing.

Securing Mobile Platforms

If mobile devices are performing many of the functions of computers, they need to be secured like desktops and laptops against malware, theft, accidental loss, unauthorized access, and hacking attempts. The Interactive Session on Technology describes these mobile vulnerabilities in greater detail and their implications for both individuals and businesses.

Mobile devices accessing corporate systems and data require special protection. Companies should make sure that their corporate security policy includes mobile devices, with additional details on how mobile devices should be supported, protected, and used. They will need mobile device management tools to authorize all devices in use; to maintain accurate inventory records on all mobile devices, users, and applications; to control updates to applications; and to lock down or erase lost or stolen devices so they can't be compromised. Data loss prevention technology can identify where critical data are saved, who is accessing the data, how data are leaving the company, and where the data are going. Firms should develop guidelines stipulating approved mobile platforms and software applications as well as the required software and procedures for remote access of corporate systems. The organization's mobile security policy should forbid employees from using unsecured, consumer-based applications for transferring and storing corporate documents and files or sending such documents and files to oneself by e-mail without encryption.

Companies should encrypt communication whenever possible. All mobile device users should be required to use the password feature found in every smartphone. Mobile security products are available from Kaspersky, Symantec, Trend Micro, and McAfee.

Ensuring Software Quality

In addition to implementing effective security and controls, organizations can improve system quality and reliability by employing software metrics and rigorous software testing. Software metrics are objective assessments of the system in the form of quantified measurements. Ongoing use of metrics allows the information systems department and end users to measure the performance of the system jointly and identify problems as they occur. Examples of software metrics include the number of transactions that can be processed in a specified unit of time, online response time, the number of payroll checks printed per hour, and the number of known bugs per hundred lines of program code. For metrics to be successful, they must be carefully designed, formal, objective, and used consistently.

Early, regular, and thorough testing will contribute significantly to system quality. Many view testing as a way to prove the correctness of work they have done. In fact, we know that all sizable software is riddled with errors, and we must test to uncover these errors.

Good testing begins before a software program is even written, by using a *walkthrough*—a review of a specification or design document by a small group of people carefully selected based on the skills needed for the particular objectives being tested. When developers start writing software programs, coding walkthroughs can also be used to review program code. However, code must be tested by computer runs. When errors are discovered, the source is found and eliminated through a process called *debugging*. You can find out more about the various stages of testing required to put an information system into operation in Chapter 13. Our Learning Tracks also contain descriptions of methodologies for developing software programs that contribute to software quality.

INTERACTIVE SESSION: TECHNOLOGY

BYOD: A Security Nightmare?

Bring your own device has become a huge trend, with half of employees with mobile computing tools at workplaces worldwide using their own devices. This figure is expected to increase even more in the years to come. But while use of the iPhone, iPad, and other mobile computing devices in the workplace is growing, so are security problems. Quite a few security experts believe that smartphones and other mobile devices now pose one of the most serious security threats for organizations today.

Whether mobile devices are company-assigned or employee-owned, they are opening up new avenues for accessing corporate data that need to be closely monitored and protected. Sensitive data on mobile devices travel, both physically and electronically, from the office to home and possibly other off-site locations. According to a February 2016 Ponemon Institute study of 588 U.S. IT and security professionals, 67 percent of those surveyed reported that it was certain or likely that an employee's mobile access to confidential corporate data had resulted in a data breach. Unfortunately, only 41 percent of respondents said their companies had policies for accessing corporate data from mobile devices.

More than half of security breaches occur when devices are lost or stolen. That puts all of the personal and corporate data stored on the device, as well as access to corporate data on remote servers, at risk. Physical access to mobile devices may be a greater threat than hacking into a network because less effort is required to gain entry. Experienced attackers can easily circumvent passwords or locks on mobile devices or access encrypted data. Moreover, many smartphone users leave their phones totally unprotected to begin with or fail to keep the security features of their devices up-to-date. In the Websense and the Ponemon Institute's Global Study on Mobility Risks, 59 percent of respondents reported that employees circumvented or disabled security features such as passwords and key locks.

Another worry today is large-scale data leakage caused by use of cloud computing services. Employees are increasingly using public cloud services such as Google Drive or Dropbox for file sharing and collaboration. Valiant Entertainment, Cenoric Projects, Vita Coco, and BCBGMAXAZRIAGROUP are among the companies allowing employees and freelance contractors to use Dropbox for Business to post and share files. There are also many instances where employees are using Dropbox to store and exchange files without their employers' approval. In early 2015 Dropbox had to patch a security flaw that allowed cyberattackers to steal new information uploaded to accounts through compromised third-party apps that work with Dropbox services on Android devices. There's very little a company can do to prevent employees who are allowed to use their smartphones from downloading corporate data so they can work on those data remotely.

Text messaging and other mobile messaging technologies are being used to deliver all kinds of scam campaigns, such as adult content and rogue pharmacy, phishing, and banking scams, and text messages have been a propagation medium for Trojan horses and worms. A malicious source is now able to send a text message that will open in a mobile browser by default, which can be readily utilized to exploit the recipient.

To date, deliberate hacker attacks on mobile devices have been limited in scope and impact, but this situation is worsening. Android is now the world's most popular operating system for mobile devices with 81 percent of the global market, and most mobile malware is targeted at the Android platform. When corporate and personal data are stored on the same device, mobile malware unknowingly installed by the user could find its way onto the corporate network.

Apple uses a closed "walled garden" model for managing its apps and reviews each one before releasing it on its App Store. Android application security has been weaker than that for Apple devices, but it is improving. Android application security uses sandboxing, which confines apps, minimizing their ability to affect one another or manipulate device features without user permission. Google removes any apps that break its rules against malicious activity from Google Play, its digital distribution platform that serves as the official app store for the Android operating system. Google also vets the backgrounds of developers. Recent Android security enhancements include assigning varying levels of trust to each app, dictating what kind of data an app can access inside its confined domain, and providing a more robust way to store cryptographic credentials used to access sensitive information and resources.

Google Play now provides security scanning of all applications before they are available to download, ongoing security checks for as long as the application is available, and a Verify Apps service for mobile device protection for apps installed outside of Google Play. However, these Android improvements are largely only for people who use a phone or tablet running a newer version of Android and restrict their app downloads to Google's own Play store.

Companies need to develop mobile security strategies that strike the right balance between improving worker productivity and effective information security. Aetna's Chief Security Officer (CSO) Jim Routh says there is a certain minimum level of mobile security he requires regardless of whether a device is company- or personally owned. Aetna has about 6,000 users equipped with mobile devices that are either personally owned or issued by the company. Each device has mandatory protection that provides an encrypted channel to use in unsecured Wi-Fi networks and alerts the user and the company if a malicious app is about to be installed on the device.

Colin Minihan, director of security and best practices at VMWare AirWatch, believes that understanding users and their needs helps a mobile security strategy progress further. VmAirWatch categorizes similar groups of users and devises a specific plan of action for each group, choosing the right tools for the job.

According to Patrick Hevesi, Nordstrom's former director of security, if users need access to critical corporate data that must be protected, the firm should probably allow only fully managed, fully controlled, approved types of devices. Users who only want mobile tools for e-mail and contacts can more easily bring their own devices. The key questions to ask are called the "three Ws": Who needs access? What do they need to access? What is the security posture of the device?

Sources: Michael Heller, "Mobile Security Strategy Matures with BYOD," and Kathleen Richards, "CISOs Battle to Control Mobile Risk in the Workplace," *Information Security Magazine,* June 1, 2016; Nathan Olivarez-Giles, "Android's Security Improves—for the Few," *Wall Street Journal,* April 21, 2016; Ponemon Institute, "The Economic Risk of Confidential Data on Mobile Devices in the Workplace," February, 2016; McAfee Inc., "Mobile Threat Report: What's on the Horizon for 2016," 2016; Charlie Osborne, "Dropbox Patches Android Security Flaw," *Zero Day,* March 11, 2015; Edel Creely, "5 BYOD Security Implications and How to Overcome Them," Trilogy Technologies, May 26, 2015; Tony Kontzer, "Most of Your Mobile Apps Have Been Hacked," *Baseline,* January 16, 2015; and Ponemon Institute, Global Study on Mobility Risks (February 2012).

CASE STUDY QUESTIONS

1. It has been said that a smartphone is a computer in your hand. Discuss the security implications of this statement.
2. What kinds of security problems do mobile computing devices pose?
3. What management, organizational, and technology issues must be addressed by smartphone security?
4. What steps can individuals and businesses take to make their smartphones more secure?

Review Summary

8-1 *Why are information systems vulnerable to destruction, error, and abuse?*
Digital data are vulnerable to destruction, misuse, error, fraud, and hardware or software failures. The Internet is designed to be an open system and makes internal corporate systems more vulnerable to actions from outsiders. Hackers can unleash denial-of-service (DoS) attacks or penetrate corporate networks, causing serious system disruptions. Wi-Fi networks can easily be penetrated by intruders using sniffer programs to obtain an address to access the resources of the network. Computer viruses and worms can disable systems and websites. The dispersed nature of cloud computing makes it difficult to track unauthorized activity or to apply controls from afar. Software presents problems because software bugs may be impossible to eliminate and because software vulnerabilities can be exploited by hackers and malicious software. End users often introduce errors.

8-2 *What is the business value of security and control?*
Lack of sound security and control can cause firms relying on computer systems for their core business functions to lose sales and productivity. Information assets, such as confidential employee records, trade secrets, or business plans, lose much of their value if they are revealed to outsiders or if they expose the firm to legal liability. Laws, such as HIPAA, the Sarbanes-Oxley Act, and the Gramm-Leach-Bliley Act, require companies to practice stringent electronic records management and adhere to strict standards for security, privacy, and control. Legal actions requiring electronic evidence and computer forensics also require firms to pay more attention to security and electronic records management.

8-3 *What are the components of an organizational framework for security and control?*
Firms need to establish a good set of both general and application controls for their information systems. A risk assessment evaluates information assets, identifies control points and control weaknesses, and determines the most cost-effective set of controls. Firms must also develop a coherent corporate security policy and plans for continuing business operations in the event of disaster or disruption. The security policy includes policies for acceptable use and identity management. Comprehensive and systematic information systems auditing helps organizations determine the effectiveness of security and controls for their information systems.

8-4 *What are the most important tools and technologies for safeguarding information resources?*
Firewalls prevent unauthorized users from accessing a private network when it is linked to the Internet. Intrusion detection systems monitor private networks for suspicious network traffic and attempts to access corporate systems. Passwords, tokens, smart cards, and biometric authentication are used to authenticate system users. Antivirus software checks computer systems for infections by viruses and worms and often eliminates the malicious software; antispyware software combats intrusive and harmful spyware programs. Encryption, the coding and scrambling of messages, is a widely used technology for securing electronic transmissions over unprotected networks. Digital certificates combined with public key encryption provide further protection of electronic transactions by authenticating a user's identity. Companies can use fault-tolerant computer systems to make sure that their information systems are always available. Use of software metrics and rigorous software testing help improve software quality and reliability.

Key Terms

Acceptable use policy (AUP), 333
Antivirus software, 340
Application controls, 329
Authentication, 337
Biometric authentication, 337
Botnet, 320
Bugs, 325
Business continuity planning, 335
Click fraud, 324
Computer crime, 321
Computer forensics, 328
Computer virus, 317
Controls, 314
Cybervandalism, 320
Cyberwarfare, 324
Deep packet inspection (DPI), 344
Denial-of-service (DoS) attack, 320
Digital certificates, 342
Disaster recovery planning, 335
Distributed denial-of-service (DDoS) attack, 320
Downtime, 344
Drive-by download, 318
Encryption, 341
Evil twin, 322
Fault-tolerant computer systems, 343
Firewall, 338
General controls, 329
Gramm-Leach-Bliley Act, 327
Hacker, 319
HIPAA, 327
Identity management, 334
Identity theft, 322
Information systems audit, 336
Intrusion detection systems, 340
Keyloggers, 319
Malware, 317
Managed security service providers (MSSPs), 344
Online transaction processing, 343
Password, 337
Patches, 326
Pharming, 322
Phishing, 322
Public key encryption, 342
Public key infrastructure (PKI), 343
Ransomware, 319
Risk assessment, 330
Sarbanes-Oxley Act, 327
Secure Hypertext Transfer Protocol (S-HTTP), 341
Secure Sockets Layer (SSL), 341
Security, 314
Security policy, 333
Smart card, 337
Sniffer, 320
Social engineering, 325
Spoofing, 320
Spyware, 319
SQL injection attack, 319
Token, 337
Trojan horse, 318
Two-factor authentication, 338
Unified threat management (UTM), 341
War driving, 316
Worms, 317
Zero-day vulnerabilities, 326

Review Questions

8-1 Why are information systems vulnerable to destruction, error, and abuse?

- Define security and control. Why information systems are vulnerable to security issues?
- List and describe some major malware threats to businesses today.
- Distinguish between hacker and cracker. Explain different hacker activities to damage systems with examples.
- List and describe examples of computer crime where the computer has been used as a target and instrument of crime. Which of these do the highest damage?
- Define click frauds and cyberwarfare. Discuss some tactics of identity thefts.
- How do employees and software specialist introduce errors in information systems?
- How does software remain vulnerable despite rigorous testing and patching? Explain the reasons.

8-2 What is the business value of security and control?

- Discuss the need to incorporate computer forensics into firm's contingency planning.
- What are the implications of inadequate security and control? Discuss variations in government regulations with industry.

8-3 What are the components of an organizational framework for security and control?

- Explain the need for implementation of controls to protect information systems.
- What is the need for implementing controls for specific applications?
- What is the need for risk assessment in a firm? Discuss the role of managers and information system specialists in carrying out the same.
- Define disaster recovery planning and business continuity planning. Why do firms need to conduct business impact analysis for the same?
- How is information systems audit carried out in organizations? Discuss.

8-4 What are the most important tools and technologies for safeguarding information resources?

- Name and describe three authentication methods.
- Describe the roles of firewalls, intrusion detection systems, and antivirus software in promoting security.
- Explain the mechanism through which encryption protects information.
- Describe the role of encryption and digital certificates in a public key infrastructure.
- Describe the techniques which companies use to ensure system availability.
- Identify and describe the security problems that cloud computing poses.
- Describe measures for improving software quality and reliability.

Discussion Questions

8-5 Security isn't simply a technology issue; it's a business issue. Discuss.

8-6 If you were developing a business continuity plan for your company, where would you start? What aspects of the business would the plan address?

8-7 Suppose your business had an e-commerce website where it sold goods and accepted credit card payments. Discuss the major security threats to this website and their potential impact. What can be done to minimize these threats?

Hands-On MIS Projects

The projects in this section give you hands-on experience analyzing security vulnerabilities, using spreadsheet software for risk analysis, and using web tools to research security outsourcing services.

Management Decision Problems

8-8 Reloaded Games is an online games platform that powers leading massively multiplayer online games. The Reloaded platform serves more than 30 million users. The games can accommodate millions of players at once and are played simultaneously by people all over the world. Prepare a security analysis for this Internet-based business. What kinds of threats should it anticipate? What would be their impact on the business? What steps can it take to prevent damage to its websites and continuing operations?

Improving Decision Making: Evaluating Security Outsourcing Services

Software skills: Web browser and presentation software
Business skills: Evaluating business outsourcing services

8-9 This project will help develop your Internet skills in using the web to research and evaluate security outsourcing services.

You have been asked to help your company's management decide whether to outsource security or keep the security function within the firm. Search the web to find information to help you decide whether to outsource security and to locate security outsourcing services.

- Present a brief summary of the arguments for and against outsourcing computer security for your company.
- Select two firms that offer computer security outsourcing services and compare them and their services.
- Prepare an electronic presentation for management, summarizing your findings. Your presentation should make the case of whether your company should outsource computer security. If you believe your company should outsource, the presentation should identify which security outsourcing service you selected and justify your decision.

Collaboration and Teamwork Project

Evaluating Security Software Tools

8-10 With a group of three or four students, use the web to research and evaluate security products from two competing vendors, such as for antivirus software, firewalls, or antispyware software. For each product, describe its capabilities, for what types of businesses it is best suited, and its cost to purchase and install. Which is the best product? Why? If possible, use Google Docs and Google Drive or Google Sites to brainstorm, organize, and develop a presentation of your findings for the class.

Securing Information: The HSBC Way

CASE STUDY

Hongkong and Shanghai Banking Corporation Limited (HSBC) was set up in India in the year 1853 as Mercantile Bank. It soon opened branches in London, Chennai, Singapore, and Hong Kong. In 1959, it was acquired by Shanghai Banking Corporation Limited, which laid the foundation for the HSBC group. The HSBC group develops and applies advanced technology to deliver their banking and financial services in a convenient and efficient manner. Some of the technology-driven services the bank provides include:

- ATMs
- Phone banking
- Trade and corporate banking with real-time access to a centralized information database
- Inter-city transactions through online connections among all branches
- Treasury dealing system
- Debit and credit cards
- Domestic and international VISA, MasterCard, and co-branded cards
- Internet banking
- Internet payment gateway

Even though electronic banking services are convenient from the customer's point of view, they pose transactional and operational challenges for the bank. Hackers are a major threat. They can break into confidential information and illegally transfer money. The attackers can also can utilize user information from various sources, join the dots to get a complete picture of the victim's profile, and pose as the user to perform illegal transactions on their behalf. This is called social engineering. All these risks make it important for banks to have effective policies, procedures, and controls in place to tackle these challenges. Cyber attacks and information security threats are of increasing concern in India. HSBC recognizes the importance of security in Internet transactions and has incorporated the following security measures:

- Robust authentication processes
- Protection against key-logging and denial-of-service attacks
- Two-factor authentication using security devices or smart cards to generate one-time passwords
- Encrypted sessions between the customer and the bank (SSL v3 128 bit)
- Protection of sensitive information in transit and storage to ensure confidentiality of customer data
- Industry-standard security mechanisms to protect the infrastructure
- Regular independent reviews of system security
- Robust and regularly reviewed information security policies
- Comprehensive contingency and back-up arrangements
- Round-the-clock security monitoring and centralized incident management teams
- Audit trails for administrative and transactional activities

HSBC was one of the first banks in India to introduce the two-stage authentication system to boost the security of online transactions. In addition to authenticating the user with the usual user ID and password, an additional passcode is required. This passcode is sent to a security device, which needs to be entered to complete an online transaction. This two-step verification is very useful in certain sensitive transactions like account transfers to non-registered accounts, bill payment to merchants, setting up of direct debit authorizations to designated merchants, and updating personal details.

The two-factor authentication system is also mandated by the Reserve Bank of India, the central body controlling financial activities in India. To further enhance the security of transactions, HSBC sends SMS notifications to users on completion of transactions, especially for transfers to non-registered third-party accounts and electronic bill payments. The user information is not stored on any disc or Internet-facing Web server. The Web servers are physically separated from back-office databases that hold transactional data.

Another threat that banks face is that of MitM (man in the middle) attacks. These are caused due to the downloading of malware on part of the users. MitM attackers can fraudulently conduct transactions on behalf of the user. HSBC's policy of not sending any confidential information to customers by e-mail minimizes the chances of phishing. The bank's secure portal uses the 'https' protocol to establish a secured session. HSBC uses a 128-bit secure socket layer to encrypt the information sent and received. The session is set to time out after a certain period of inactivity. All these things work together to make the electronic banking experience safe and secure for the user as well as for the bank.

Sources: Carse, David, "The Regulatory Framework of E-banking", *Hong Kong Monetary Authority* (1999). Retrieved from http://www.hkma.gov.hk/eng/key-information/speech-speakers/dcarse/speech_081099b.shtml; "Bank Profile and History". Retrieved from https://bank.hangseng.com/1/2/about-us/corporate-info/bank-profile; "Terms and Conditions". Retrieved from http://www.hangseng.com/hsb/eng/ref/bib/pdf/e_bank_tnc.pdf; "New Security Device—Frequently Asked Questions". Retrieved from http://www.hangseng.com.cn/1/PA_esf-ca-app-content/content/pws/business/pdfs/TransactionDataSigning_FAQ_HACN_Eng.pdf; "e-Banking Security". Retrieved from https://bank.hangseng.com/1/2/e-services/e-banking-security/ebanking-security; "Hong Kong tightens online banking security", *ZDNet* (2005). Retrieved from http://www.zdnet.com/hong-kong-tightens-online-banking-security-2039240308/; Zhen, Simon, "HSBC to Provide Free Security Device for Safer Online Banking", *My Bank Tracker* (2014). Retrieved from http://www.mybanktracker.com/news/2014/02/12/hsbc-provide-free-security-device-safer-online-banking/.

CASE STUDY QUESTIONS

8-11 Discuss the need for securing electronic banking at HSBC.

8-12 Discuss the two-stage verification process adopted by HSBC.

8-13 Discuss some other steps taken by HSBC to protect its electronic banking transactions.

Chapter 8 References

Bajaj, Vikas. "The Perils of Automated Flight." *New York Times* (April 30, 2015).

Boss, Scott R., Dennis F. Galletta, Paul Benjamin Lowry, Gregory D. Moody, and Peter Polak. "What Do Systems Users Have to Fear? Using Fear Appeals to Engender Threats and Fear that Motivate Protective Security Behaviors. MIS Quarterly 39, No. 4 (December 2015).

Boyle, Randall J. and Raymond R. Panko. *Corporate Computer Security* (4th ed.). Upper Saddle River, NJ: Prentice-Hall (2015).

Chen, Yan and Fatemeh Mariam Zahedi. "Individuals' Internet Security Perceptions and Behaviors: Polycontextual Contrasts Between the United States and China" *MIS Quarterly* 40, No. 1 (March 2016).

Chen, Yan, K. Ram Ramamurthy, and Kuang-Wei Wen. "Organizations' Information Security Policy Compliance: Stick or Carrot Approach?" *Journal of Management Information Systems* 29, No. 3 (Winter 2013).

CSA Top Threats Working Group. "The Treacherous Twelve: CSA's Cloud Computing Top Threats in 2016." Cloud Security Alliance (February 2016).

FireEye. "Out of Pocket: A Comprehensive Mobile Threat Assessment of 7 Million iOS and Android Apps." (February 2015).

Focus Research. "Devastating Downtime: The Surprising Cost of Human Error and Unforeseen Events." (October 2010).

Galbreth, Michael R. and Mikhael Shor. "The Impact of Malicious Agents on the Enterprise Software Industry." *MIS Quarterly* 34, No. 3 (September 2010).

Hui, Kai Lung, Wendy Hui and Wei T. Yue. "Information Security Outsourcing with System Interdependency and Mandatory Security Requirement." *Journal of Management Information Systems* 29, No. 3 (Winter 2013).

Javelin Strategy & Research. "2016 Identity Fraud Study." (February 2, 2016).

Kaplan, James, Chris Rezek, and Kara Sprague. "Protecting Information in the Cloud." *McKinsey Quarterly* (January 2013).

Karlovsky, Brian. "FireEye Names Malware's Favorite Targets, Sources." *Australian Reseller News* (March 2, 2014).

Kirk, Jeremy. "Pushdo Spamming Botnet Gains Strength Again." IDG News Service (April 20, 2015).

Osterman Research. "The Risks of Social Media and What Can Be Done to Manage Them." Commvault (June 2011).

Paletta, Damian, Danny Yadron, and Jennifer Valentino-Devries. "Cyberwar Ignites a New Arms Race." *Wall Street Journal* (October 11, 2015).

Panda Security. "PandaLabs 2015 Annual Report." (January 28, 2016).

Panko, Raymond R. and Julie L. Panko. *Business Data Networks and Security*. Upper Saddle River, NJ: Pearson (2015).

Perlroth, Nicole. "Online Attacks on Infrastructure Are Increasing at a Worrying Pace," *New York Times* (October 1, 2015).

Ponemon Institute. "2015 Cost of Cybercrime Study: United States" (October 9, 2015).

________. "2015 Cost of Data Breach Study: United States" (2015).

________. "The Cost of Malware Containment" (January 2015).

Poremba, Sue Marquette. "Hackers Targeting the Cloud at Higher Rates Than Ever." *IT Business Edge* (October 15, 2015).

Posey, Clay, Tom L. Roberts, and Paul Benjamin Lowry. "The Impact of Organizational Commitment on Insiders' Motivation to Protect Organizational Information Assets." *Journal of Management Information Systems* 32 No. 4 (2015).

Reisinger, Don. "Android Security Remains a Glaring Problem: 10 Reasons Why." *eWeek* (March 2, 2014).

Ribeiro, John. "Hacker Group Targets Skype Social Media Accounts," *Computer World* (January 2, 2014).

Sadeh, Norman M. "Phish Isn't Spam." *Information Week* (June 25, 2012).

Samuel, Alexandra. "Online Security as Herd Immunity." *Harvard Business Review* (March 13, 2014).

Scharr, Jill. "Fake Instagram 'Image Viewers' Are Latest Malware Fad." *Tom's Guide* (May 8, 2014).

Schwartz, Matthew J. "Android Trojan Looks, Acts Like Windows Malware." *Information Week* (June 7, 2013).

Sen, Ravi and Sharad Borle. "Estimating the Contextual Risk of Data Breach: An Empirical Approach." *Journal of Management Information Systems* 32, No. 2 (2015).

Sengupta, Somini. "Machines That Know You Without Using a Password." *New York Times* (September 10, 2013).

Snell, Bruce. "Mobile Threat Report." McAfee Inc. (2016).

Solutionary. "Solutionary Security Engineering Research Team Unveils Annual Global Threat Intelligence Report." (March 12, 2013).

Spears, Janine L. and Henri Barki. "User Participation in Information Systems Security Risk Management." *MIS Quarterly* 34, No. 3 (September 2010).

Temizkan, Orcun, Ram L. Kumar, Sungjune Park, and Chandrasekar Subramaniam. "Patch Release Behaviors of Software Vendors in Response to Vulnerabilities: An Empirical Analysis. " *Journal of Management Information Systems* 28, No. 4 (Spring 2012).

Thompson, Jadiann. "Scam Alert: Two Clicks on Facebook Could Leak All Your Personal Info to an International Scammer." Kshb.com (April 30, 2015).

Vance, Anthony, Paul Benjamin Lowry, and Dennis Eggett. "Using Accountability to Reduce Access Policy Violations in Information Systems." *Journal of Management Information Systems* 29, No. 4 (Spring 2013).

Verizon. "2016 Data Breach Investigations Report." (2016).

Wakida, Clayton. "Anonymous Accused of Hacking TMT Web Site." KMTV.com (April 27, 2015).

Wang, Jingguo, Manish Gupta, and H. Raghav Rao. "Insider Threats in a Financial Institution: Analysis of Attack-Proneness of Information Systems Applications." *MIS Quarterly* 39, No. 1 (March 2015).

Young, Carl S. "The Enemies of Data Security: Convenience and Collaboration." *Harvard Business Review* (February 11, 2015).

Zhao, Xia, Ling Xue, and Andrew B. Whinston. "Managing Interdependent Information Security Risks: Cyberinsurance, Managed Security Services, and Risk Pooling Arrangements." *Journal of Management Information Systems* 30, No. 1 (Summer 2013).

PART **THREE**

Key System Applications for the Digital Age

PART THREE examines the core information system applications businesses are using today to improve operational excellence and decision making. These applications include enterprise systems; systems for supply chain management, customer relationship management, and knowledge management; e-commerce applications; and business intelligence systems. This part answers questions such as: How can enterprise applications improve business performance? How do firms use e-commerce to extend the reach of their businesses? How can systems improve decision making and help companies make better use of their knowledge assets?

CHAPTER

9 Achieving Operational Excellence and Customer Intimacy: Enterprise Applications

Learning Objectives

After reading this chapter, you will be able to answer the following questions:

9-1 How do enterprise systems help businesses achieve operational excellence?

9-2 How do supply chain management systems coordinate planning, production, and logistics with suppliers?

9-3 How do customer relationship management systems help firms achieve customer intimacy?

9-4 What are the challenges that enterprise applications pose, and how are enterprise applications taking advantage of new technologies?

CHAPTER CASES

Alimentation Couche-Tard Competes Using Enterprise Systems
Optimizing Operations at QuarkCity: A Move Away from Legacy Systems
McDonald's Serving Hot and Fresh
Customer Relationship Management Helps Celcom Become Number One

Alimentation Couche-Tard Competes Using Enterprise Systems

When Alimentation Couche-Tard purchased Statoil Fuel and Retail (SFR) in April 2012, it was the Canadian convenience store giant's most ambitious acquisition to date (€2.058 billion). SFR, a division of Statoil, the Norwegian State Oil Company, had been spun off from its parent in October 2010. The purchase added 2,300 retail fuel stations—most full-service with a convenience store—throughout North America and expanded Couche-Tard's reach to eight European countries—Norway, Sweden, Denmark, Poland, Estonia, Latvia, Lithuania, and Russia. In 2016 the firm had 12,000 sites and employed over 105,000 people.

© trondur/123rf.com

SFR operates in both the B2C (sales to consumers) and B2B (sales to other businesses) sectors. Fuel products including gasoline blends, diesel fuels, biofuels, and LPG (liquefied petroleum gas) generate 70 percent of its business. The full-service retail stations offer product lines that differ according to operator and location factors. Some prefer a product mix that concentrates on auto supplies and services while others focus on food-related products, beverages, and even fast-food. SFR's 12 terminals, 38 depots, and 400 road tankers provide bulk sales to commercial customers, including bus and car rental companies, road construction crews, and independent resellers.

Couche-Tard welcomed both the opportunities and the challenges of its acquisition. Immediate synergies between Couche-Tard and SFR could not completely cover the remaining expenses from SFR's split from Statoil, rebranding efforts, and the replacement of an antiquated IT infrastructure and enterprise resource planning (ERP) system. The old system used different processes in each country and market, resulting in over 5,000 custom software objects for the IT department to manage in addition to massive operational inefficiencies.

SFR needed to maximize supply chain efficiency for its three closely related value chains—the fuel value chain, the grocery value chain, and the lubricants value chain. All corporate functions that provided shared services to the value chains had to be standardized and workplace activities coordinated for its 18,500 employees. Finally, SFR managers wanted an advanced pricing method for fuel sales to maximize profits in its core low-margin business.

Oracle's JD Edwards EnterpriseOne enterprise resource planning system was chosen as the basic platform, and a Web services interface was developed within the ERP system to convert all data into a single format. This common source of master data now drives all transactions throughout the supply chains as well as financial and other reports generated by the Oracle Business Intelligence Suite. Stock availability and average sales at each service station feed a real-time planning program that projects expected demand and feeds the data to a third-party distribution planning system. Onboard computers convey product types and quantities to tanker drivers at terminals and delivery locations. Fuel restocking, delivery, and confirmation occur automatically.

To coordinate workplace activities, Oracle Fusion Middleware integrates data management and communication across social, mobile, and cloud technologies and among multiple systems and regions. Called the "Connect Project," the software coordinates dozens of interfaces throughout the supply chain, implements a consistent fuel pricing structure, and manages multiple complicated excise taxes and regulations.

In 2014 Statoil began a migration from Oracle database software to SAP's Business Planning and Consolidation Application. As a result, in 2015 Statoil achieved financial consolidation six times faster than before, data processing speeds increased fifteen times, and opening and closing periods for work status is now eight times faster than before.

In 2015 Couche-Tard re-branded its SFR retail stores to Circle K stores. Today it's one of the largest global players in the convenience store market space with over 12,000 sites in Canada, the U.S., Asia, and Europe, and employs more than 100,000 people. In 2016 the company announced it's largest ever acquisition of Texas-based CST Brands, which will bring it an additional 2,000 locations in the south and southwest U.S. states. The firm's prior investments in enterprise systems enable it to manage a sprawling global network of convenience stores. The company's executives promise to double the size of the firm once more in the next five years. Not bad for a company that started in 1980 with a single store in Quebec.

Sources: "Alimentation Couche Tard Inc. Is Severely Undervalued," by Joey Frenette, The Motley Fool, Fool.com, March 1, 2017; "Couche-Tard's Alain Bouchard Has a Bold Vision: 'We Will Double the Size of This Company Again'", by Karl Moore, businessfinancialpost.com, December 8, 2016; "After Shareholder Rebuff Last Year, Couche-Tard Gets Its Focus Back with Largest-Ever Acquisition," by Barry Crutchley, businessfinancialpost.com, August 22, 2016;

"Annual Report 2016," Alimentation Couche-Tard Inc., http://corpo.couche-tard.com; Alyn Bailey, "Statoil Fuel & Retail the World's First SAP to Oracle JD Edwards Migration," http://www.pcubed.com/bulletins, accessed January 2, 2016; "Statoil: Accelerating Planning and Financial Close Cycles with SAP® EPM powered by SAP HANA® and SAP MaxAttentionTM," dam.sap.com/28274_Statoil_BTS.htm, accessed January 2, 2016; Jade Vachon, "Statoil Switches from an Oracle DB to the SAP HANA Platform with SAP MaxAttention," SAP.com, February 21, 2014.

Couche-Tard and Statoil's efforts to standardize and integrate corporate functions into the supply chain and coordinate workplace activity illustrate the impact of ERP systems on supply chain management (SCM). Couche-Tard did not have a single source of business data nor uniform methods for handling many critical SCM functions. Inventory holding costs were unnecessarily high, the IT department was strained, and lack of coordination was negatively impacting workplace productivity.

The chapter-opening diagram calls attention to important points raised by this case and this chapter. All transactions throughout Couche-Tard's supply chains are now in a common and consistent format that feeds directly into its reporting software. The integrated ERP environment enables real-time planning based on stock availability and average sales at each service station, and a real-time fuel value chain can now accommodate variable demand from both consumer and business customers.

Benchmarks against which to assess future results by country, terminal, or market are being developed using the advanced pricing method developed by the Connect team. On the B2B side, managers will be able to quickly assess the effects of pricing structures and even sales reps will be able to evaluate the effects of purchasing terms.

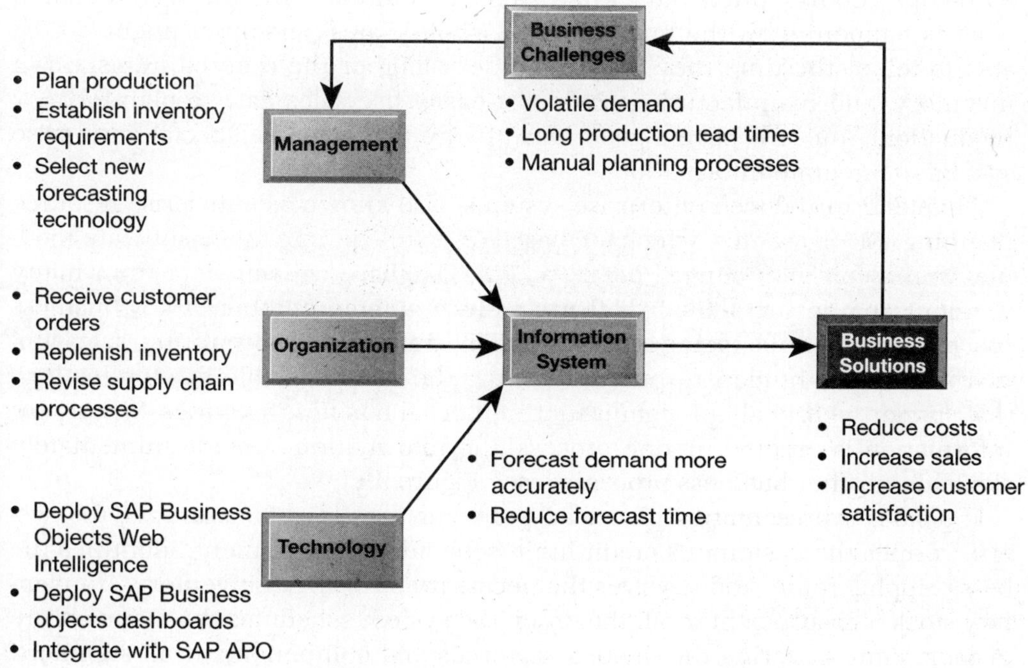

Here are some questions to think about: How did Couche-Tard's lack of standardized processes affect its business operations? How were Couche-Tard's employees and supply chain management affected by the adoption of standardized interfaces? Why did Couche-Tard retain its legacy systems instead of replacing them entirely?

9-1 How do enterprise systems help businesses achieve operational excellence?

Around the globe, companies are increasingly becoming more connected, both internally and with other companies. If you run a business, you'll want to be able to react instantaneously when a customer places a large order or when a shipment from a supplier is delayed. You may also want to know the impact of these events on every part of the business and how the business is performing at any point in time, especially if you're running a large company. Enterprise systems provide the integration to make this possible. Let's look at how they work and what they can do for the firm.

What are Enterprise Systems?

Imagine that you had to run a business based on information from tens or even hundreds of databases and systems, none of which could speak to one another. Imagine your company had 10 major product lines, each produced in separate factories and each with separate and incompatible sets of systems controlling production, warehousing, and distribution.

At the very least, your decision making would often be based on manual hard-copy reports, often out of date, and it would be difficult to understand what is happening in the business as a whole. Sales personnel might not be able to tell at the time they place an order whether the ordered items are in inventory, and manufacturing could not easily use sales data to plan for new production. You now have a good idea of why firms need a special enterprise system to integrate information.

Chapter 2 introduced enterprise systems, also known as enterprise resource planning (ERP) systems, which are based on a suite of integrated software modules and a common central database. The database collects data from many divisions and departments in a firm and from a large number of key business processes in manufacturing and production, finance and accounting, sales and marketing, and human resources, making the data available for applications that support nearly all an organization's internal business activities. When new information is entered by one process, the information is made immediately available to other business processes (see Figure 9.1).

If a sales representative places an order for tire rims, for example, the system verifies the customer's credit limit, schedules the shipment, identifies the best shipping route, and reserves the necessary items from inventory. If inventory stock is insufficient to fill the order, the system schedules the manufacture of more rims, ordering the needed materials and components from suppliers.

FIGURE 9.1 HOW ENTERPRISE SYSTEMS WORK

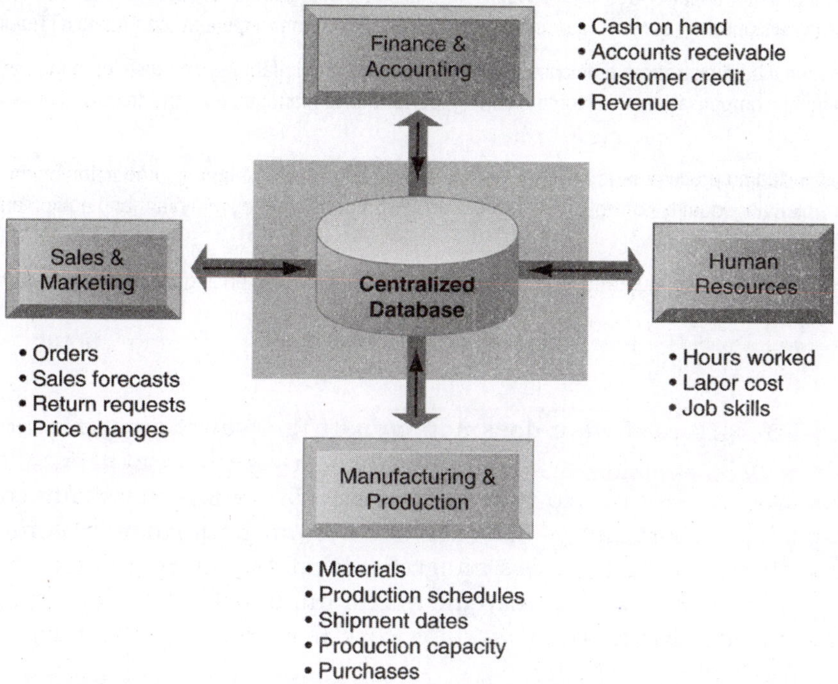

Enterprise systems feature a set of integrated software modules and a central database by which business processes and functional areas throughout the enterprise can share data.

Sales and production forecasts are immediately updated. General ledger and corporate cash levels are automatically updated with the revenue and cost information from the order. Users can tap into the system and find out where that particular order is at any minute. Management can obtain information at any point in time about how the business was operating. The system can also generate enterprise-wide data for management analyses of product cost and profitability.

Enterprise Software

Enterprise software is built around thousands of predefined business processes that reflect best practices. Table 9.1 describes some of the major business processes that enterprise software supports.

Companies implementing this software first have to select the functions of the system they wish to use and then map their business processes to the predefined business processes in the software. (One of our Learning Tracks shows how SAP enterprise software handles the procurement process for a new piece of equipment.) Configuration tables provided by the software manufacturer enable the firm to tailor a particular aspect of the system to the way it does business. For example, the firm could use these tables to select whether it wants to track revenue by product line, geographical unit, or distribution channel.

TABLE 9.1 BUSINESS PROCESSES SUPPORTED BY ENTERPRISE SYSTEMS

Financial and accounting processes, including general ledger, accounts payable, accounts receivable, fixed assets, cash management and forecasting, product-cost accounting, cost-center accounting, asset accounting, tax accounting, credit management, and financial reporting
Human resources processes, including personnel administration, time accounting, payroll, personnel planning and development, benefits accounting, applicant tracking, time management, compensation, workforce planning, performance management, and travel expense reporting
Manufacturing and production processes, including procurement, inventory management, purchasing, shipping, production planning, production scheduling, material requirements planning, quality control, distribution, transportation execution, and plant and equipment maintenance
Sales and marketing processes, including order processing, quotations, contracts, product configuration, pricing, billing, credit checking, incentive and commission management, and sales planning

If the enterprise software does not support the way the organization does business, companies can rewrite some of the software to support the way their business processes work. However, enterprise software is unusually complex, and extensive customization may degrade system performance, compromising the information and process integration that are the main benefits of the system. If companies want to reap the maximum benefits from enterprise software, they must change the way they work to conform to the business processes defined by the software.

To implement a new enterprise system, Tasty Baking Company identified its existing business processes and then translated them into the business processes built into the SAP ERP software it had selected. To ensure that it obtained the maximum benefits from the enterprise software, Tasty Baking Company deliberately planned for customizing less than 5 percent of the system and made very few changes to the SAP software itself. It used as many tools and features that were already built into the SAP software as it could. SAP has more than 3,000 configuration tables for its enterprise software.

Leading enterprise software vendors include SAP, Oracle, IBM, Infor Global Solutions, and Microsoft. Versions of enterprise software packages are designed for small and medium-sized businesses and on-demand software services running in the cloud (see the chapter-opening case and Section 9-4).

Business Value of Enterprise Systems

Enterprise systems provide value by both increasing operational efficiency and providing firmwide information to help managers make better decisions. Large companies with many operating units in different locations have used enterprise systems to enforce standard practices and data so that everyone does business the same way worldwide.

Coca-Cola, for instance, implemented a SAP enterprise system to standardize and coordinate important business processes in 200 countries. Lack of standard, companywide business processes prevented the company from using its worldwide buying power to obtain lower prices for raw materials and from reacting rapidly to market changes. Crocs used ERP for similar purposes, as described in the Chapter 15 ending case study.

Enterprise systems help firms respond rapidly to customer requests for information or products. Because the system integrates order, manufacturing, and delivery data, manufacturing is better informed about producing only what customers have ordered, procuring exactly the right number of components or raw materials to fill actual orders, staging production, and minimizing the time that components or finished products are in inventory.

Alcoa, the world's leading producer of aluminum and aluminum products with operations spanning 31 countries and more than 200 locations, had initially been organized around lines of business, each of which had its own set of information systems. Many of these systems were redundant and inefficient. Alcoa's costs for executing requisition-to-pay and financial processes were much higher, and its cycle times were longer than those of other companies in its industry. (Cycle time refers to the total elapsed time from the beginning to the end of a process.) The company could not operate as a single worldwide entity.

After implementing enterprise software from Oracle, Alcoa eliminated many redundant processes and systems. The enterprise system helped Alcoa reduce requisition-to-pay cycle time by verifying receipt of goods and automatically generating receipts for payment. Alcoa's accounts payable transaction processing dropped 89 percent. Alcoa was able to centralize financial and procurement activities, which helped the company reduce nearly 20 percent of its worldwide costs.

Enterprise systems provide much valuable information for improving management decision making. Corporate headquarters has access to up-to-the-minute data on sales, inventory, and production and uses this information to create more accurate sales and production forecasts. Enterprise software includes analytical tools to use data the system captures to evaluate overall organizational performance. Enterprise system data have common standardized definitions and formats that are accepted by the entire organization. Performance figures mean the same thing across the company. Enterprise systems allow senior management to find out easily at any moment how a particular organizational unit is performing, determine which products are most or least profitable, and calculate costs for the company as a whole.

For example, Alcoa's enterprise system includes functionality for global human resources management that shows correlations between investment in employee training and quality, measures the companywide costs of delivering services to employees, and measures the effectiveness of employee recruitment, compensation, and training.

9-2 How do supply chain management systems coordinate planning, production, and logistics with suppliers?

If you manage a small firm that makes a few products or sells a few services, chances are you will have a small number of suppliers. You could coordinate your supplier orders and deliveries by using just a telephone and fax machine.

But if you manage a firm that produces more complex products and services, you will have hundreds of suppliers, and each of your suppliers will have its own set of suppliers. Suddenly, you will need to coordinate the activities of hundreds or even thousands of other firms to produce your products and services. Supply chain management (SCM) systems, which we introduced in Chapter 2, are an answer to the problems of supply chain complexity and scale.

The Supply Chain

A firm's **supply chain** is a network of organizations and business processes for procuring raw materials, transforming these materials into intermediate and finished products, and distributing the finished products to customers. It links suppliers, manufacturing plants, distribution centers, retail outlets, and customers to supply goods and services from source through consumption. Materials, information, and payments flow through the supply chain in both directions.

Goods start out as raw materials and, as they move through the supply chain, are transformed into intermediate products (also referred to as components or parts) and, finally, into finished products. The finished products are shipped to distribution centers and from there to retailers and customers. Returned items flow in the reverse direction from the buyer back to the seller.

Let's look at the supply chain for Nike sneakers as an example. Nike designs, markets, and sells sneakers, socks, athletic clothing, and accessories throughout the world. Its primary suppliers are contract manufacturers with factories in China, Thailand, Indonesia, Brazil, and other countries. These companies fashion Nike's finished products.

Nike's contract suppliers do not manufacture sneakers from scratch. They obtain components for the sneakers—the laces, eyelets, uppers, and soles—from other suppliers and then assemble them into finished sneakers. These suppliers in turn have their own suppliers. For example, the suppliers of soles have suppliers for synthetic rubber, suppliers for chemicals used to melt the rubber for molding, and suppliers for the molds into which to pour the rubber. Suppliers of laces have suppliers for their thread, for dyes, and for the plastic lace tips.

Figure 9.2 provides a simplified illustration of Nike's supply chain for sneakers; it shows the flow of information and materials among suppliers, Nike, Nike's distributors, retailers, and customers. Nike's contract manufacturers are its primary suppliers. The suppliers of soles, eyelets, uppers, and laces are the secondary (Tier 2) suppliers. Suppliers to these suppliers are the tertiary (Tier 3) suppliers.

The *upstream* portion of the supply chain includes the company's suppliers, the suppliers' suppliers, and the processes for managing relationships with them. The *downstream* portion consists of the organizations and processes for distributing and delivering products to the final customers. Companies that manufacture, such as Nike's contract suppliers of sneakers, also manage their own *internal supply chain processes* for transforming materials, components, and services their suppliers furnish into finished products or intermediate products (components or parts) for their customers and for managing materials and inventory.

FIGURE 9.2 NIKE'S SUPPLY CHAIN

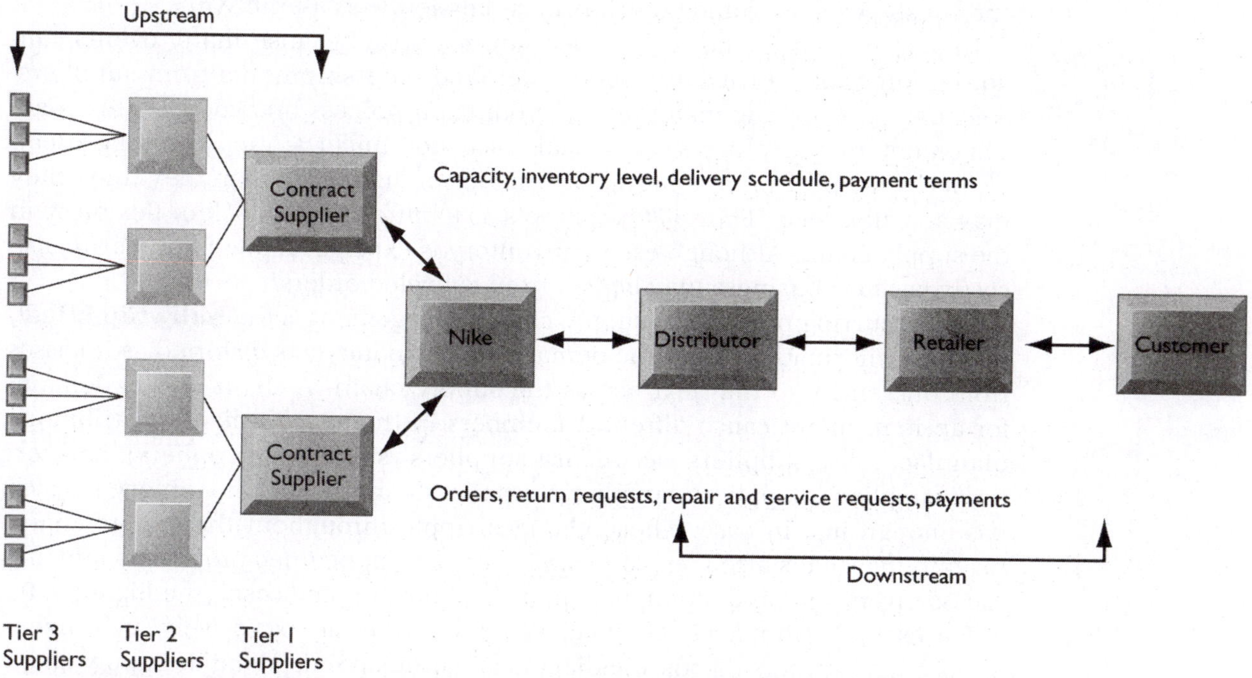

This figure illustrates the major entities in Nike's supply chain and the flow of information upstream and downstream to coordinate the activities involved in buying, making, and moving a product. Shown here is a simplified supply chain, with the upstream portion focusing only on the suppliers for sneakers and sneaker soles.

The supply chain illustrated in Figure 9.2 has been simplified. It only shows two contract manufacturers for sneakers and only the upstream supply chain for sneaker soles. Nike has hundreds of contract manufacturers turning out finished sneakers, socks, and athletic clothing, each with its own set of suppliers. The upstream portion of Nike's supply chain actually comprises thousands of entities. Nike also has numerous distributors and many thousands of retail stores where its shoes are sold, so the downstream portion of its supply chain is also large and complex.

Information Systems and Supply Chain Management

Inefficiencies in the supply chain, such as parts shortages, underused plant capacity, excessive finished goods inventory, or high transportation costs, are caused by inaccurate or untimely information. For example, manufacturers may keep too many parts in inventory because they do not know exactly when they will receive their next shipments from their suppliers. Suppliers may order too few raw materials because they do not have precise information on demand. These supply chain inefficiencies waste as much as 25 percent of a company's operating costs.

If a manufacturer had perfect information about exactly how many units of product customers wanted, when they wanted them, and when they could be produced, it would be possible to implement a highly efficient **just-in-time strategy**. Components would arrive exactly at the moment they were needed, and finished goods would be shipped as they left the assembly line.

In a supply chain, however, uncertainties arise because many events cannot be foreseen—uncertain product demand, late shipments from suppliers, defective parts or raw materials, or production process breakdowns. To satisfy customers, manufacturers often deal with such uncertainties and unforeseen events by keeping more material or products in inventory than they think they may actually need. The *safety stock* acts as a buffer for the lack of flexibility in the supply chain. Although excess inventory is expensive, low fill rates are also costly because business may be lost from canceled orders.

One recurring problem in supply chain management is the **bullwhip effect**, in which information about the demand for a product gets distorted as it passes from one entity to the next across the supply chain. A slight rise in demand for an item might cause different members in the supply chain—distributors, manufacturers, suppliers, secondary suppliers (suppliers' suppliers), and tertiary suppliers (suppliers' suppliers' suppliers)—to stockpile inventory so each has enough just in case. These changes ripple throughout the supply chain, magnifying what started out as a small change from planned orders and creating excess inventory, production, warehousing, and shipping costs (see Figure 9.3).

For example, Procter & Gamble (P&G) found it had excessively high inventories of its Pampers disposable diapers at various points along its supply chain because of such distorted information. Although customer purchases in stores were fairly stable, orders from distributors spiked when P&G offered aggressive price promotions. Pampers and Pampers' components accumulated in warehouses along the supply chain to meet demand that did not actually exist. To eliminate this problem, P&G revised its marketing, sales, and supply chain processes and used more accurate demand forecasting.

The bullwhip effect is tamed by reducing uncertainties about demand and supply when all members of the supply chain have accurate and up-to-date information. If all supply chain members share dynamic information about inventory levels, schedules, forecasts, and shipments, they have more precise knowledge about how to adjust their sourcing, manufacturing, and distribution plans. Supply chain management systems provide the kind of information that helps members of the supply chain make better purchasing and scheduling decisions.

Supply Chain Management Software

Supply chain software is classified as either software to help businesses plan their supply chains (supply chain planning) or software to help them execute the supply chain steps (supply chain execution). **Supply chain planning systems** enable the firm to model its existing supply chain, generate demand forecasts for products, and develop optimal sourcing and manufacturing plans. Such systems help companies make better decisions such as determining how much of a specific product to manufacture in a given time period; establishing inventory levels for raw materials, intermediate products, and finished goods; determining where to store finished goods; and identifying the transportation mode to use for product delivery.

FIGURE 9.3 THE BULLWHIP EFFECT

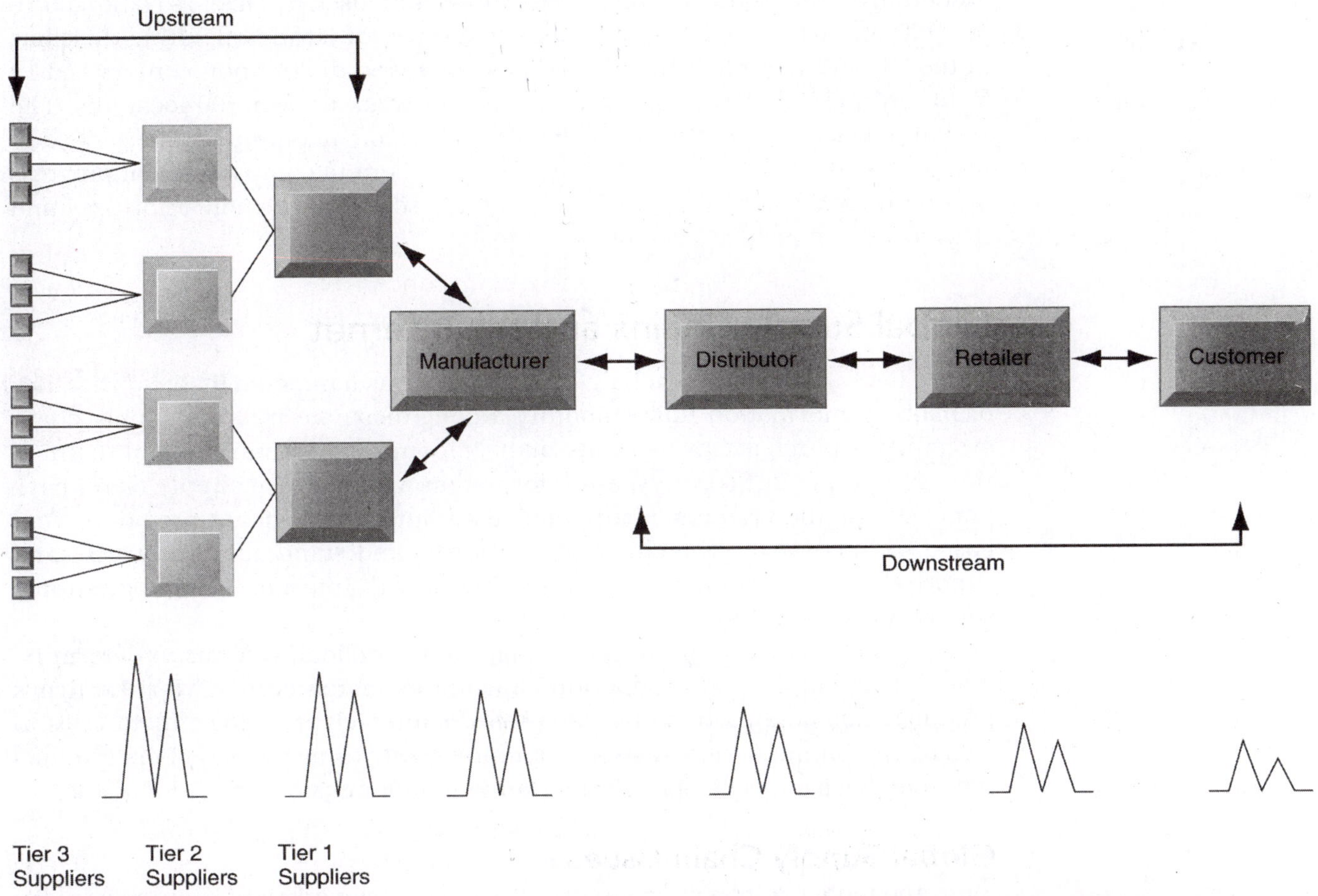

Inaccurate information can cause minor fluctuations in demand for a product to be amplified as one moves further back in the supply chain. Minor fluctuations in retail sales for a product can create excess inventory for distributors, manufacturers, and suppliers.

For example, if a large customer places a larger order than usual or changes that order on short notice, it can have a widespread impact throughout the supply chain. Additional raw materials or a different mix of raw materials may need to be ordered from suppliers. Manufacturing may have to change job scheduling. A transportation carrier may have to reschedule deliveries. Supply chain planning software makes the necessary adjustments to production and distribution plans. Information about changes is shared among the relevant supply chain members so that their work can be coordinated. One of the most important—and complex—supply chain planning functions is **demand planning**, which determines how much product a business needs to make to satisfy all its customers' demands. JDA Software, SAP, and Oracle all offer supply chain management solutions.

Supply chain execution systems manage the flow of products through distribution centers and warehouses to ensure that products are delivered to the right locations in the most efficient manner. They track the physical status of goods, the management of materials, warehouse and transportation operations, and financial information involving all parties. An example of a supply chain execution system is the delivery execution system used by Nestlé's National Primary Transport, an integrated transport service for Nestlé operating divisions in the UK and Ireland. The operation covers seven distribution centers and 12 factories, making around 3,500 deliveries per week to over 500 locations. The system takes data feeds from Nestlé UK's transport planning, vehicle scheduling, and yard management systems and uses them to compare actual progress of a delivery against the plan in the vehicle schedule. It then prioritizes and flags loads that need attention.

Global Supply Chains and the Internet

Before the Internet, supply chain coordination was hampered by the difficulties of making information flow smoothly among disparate internal supply chain systems for purchasing, materials management, manufacturing, and distribution. It was also difficult to share information with external supply chain partners because the systems of suppliers, distributors, or logistics providers were based on incompatible technology platforms and standards. Enterprise and supply chain management systems enhanced with Internet technology supply some of this integration.

A manager uses a web interface to tap into suppliers' systems to determine whether inventory and production capabilities match demand for the firm's products. Business partners use web-based supply chain management tools to collaborate online on forecasts. Sales representatives access suppliers' production schedules and logistics information to monitor customers' order status.

Global Supply Chain Issues

More and more companies are entering international markets, outsourcing manufacturing operations, and obtaining supplies from other countries as well as selling abroad. Their supply chains extend across multiple countries and regions. There are additional complexities and challenges to managing a global supply chain.

Global supply chains typically span greater geographic distances and time differences than domestic supply chains and have participants from a number of countries. Performance standards may vary from region to region or from nation to nation. Supply chain management may need to reflect foreign government regulations and cultural differences.

The Internet helps companies manage many aspects of their global supply chains, including sourcing, transportation, communications, and international finance. Today's apparel industry, for example, relies heavily on outsourcing to contract manufacturers in China and other low-wage countries. Apparel companies are starting to use the web to manage their global supply chain and production issues. (Review the discussion of Li & Fung in Chapter 3.)

In addition to contract manufacturing, globalization has encouraged outsourcing warehouse management, transportation management, and related operations to third-party logistics providers, such as UPS Supply Chain Solutions and Schneider National. These logistics services offer web-based software to give their customers a better view of their global supply chains. Customers can check a secure website to monitor inventory and shipments, helping them run their global supply chains more efficiently.

Demand-Driven Supply Chains: From Push to Pull Manufacturing and Efficient Customer Response

In addition to reducing costs, supply chain management systems facilitate efficient customer response, enabling the workings of the business to be driven more by customer demand. (We introduced efficient customer response systems in Chapter 3.)

Earlier supply chain management systems were driven by a push-based model (also known as build-to-stock). In a **push-based model**, production master schedules are based on forecasts or best guesses of demand for products, and products are pushed to customers. With new flows of information made possible by web-based tools, supply chain management more easily follows a pull-based model. In a **pull-based model**, also known as a demand-driven or build-to-order model, actual customer orders or purchases trigger events in the supply chain. Transactions to produce and deliver only what customers have ordered move up the supply chain from retailers to distributors to manufacturers and eventually to suppliers. Only products to fulfill these orders move back down the supply chain to the retailer. Manufacturers use only actual order demand information to drive their production schedules and the procurement of components or raw materials, as illustrated in Figure 9.4. Walmart's continuous replenishment system described in Chapter 3 is an example of the pull-based model.

The Internet and Internet technology make it possible to move from sequential supply chains, where information and materials flow sequentially from company to company, to concurrent supply chains, where information flows in many directions simultaneously among members of a supply chain network.

FIGURE 9.4 PUSH- VERSUS PULL-BASED SUPPLY CHAIN MODELS

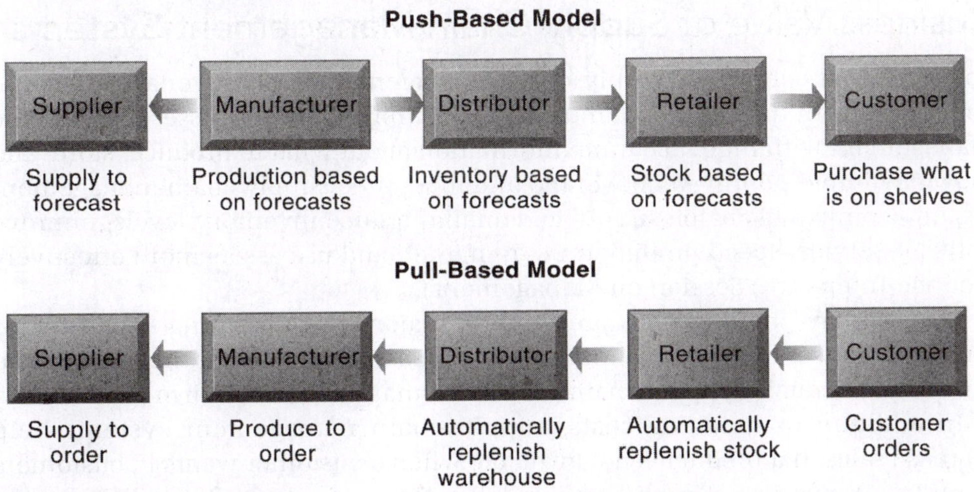

The difference between push- and pull-based models is summarized by the slogan "Make what we sell, not sell what we make."

FIGURE 9.5 THE EMERGING INTERNET-DRIVEN SUPPLY CHAIN

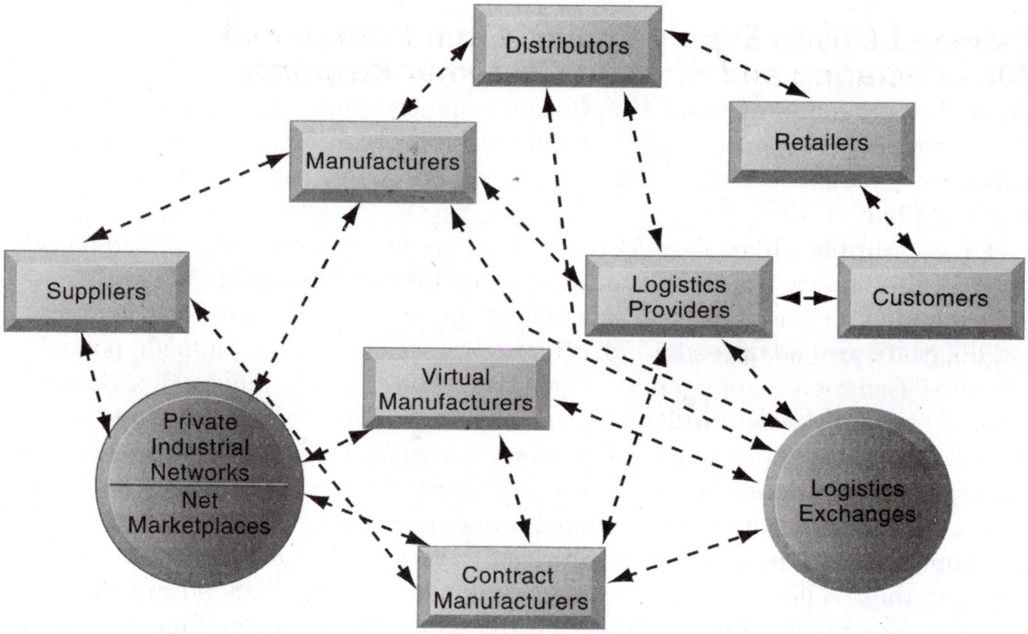

The emerging Internet-driven supply chain operates like a digital logistics nervous system. It provides multidirectional communication among firms, networks of firms, and e-marketplaces so that entire networks of supply chain partners can immediately adjust inventories, orders, and capacities.

Complex supply networks of manufacturers, logistics suppliers, outsourced manufacturers, retailers, and distributors can adjust immediately to changes in schedules or orders. Ultimately, the Internet will enable a digital logistics nervous system for supply chains (see Figure 9.5).

Business Value of Supply Chain Management Systems

You have just seen how supply chain management systems enable firms to streamline both their internal and external supply chain processes and provide management with more accurate information about what to produce, store, and move. By implementing a networked and integrated supply chain management system, companies match supply to demand, reduce inventory levels, improve delivery service, speed product time to market, and use assets more effectively (see the Interactive Session on Management).

Total supply chain costs represent the majority of operating expenses for many businesses and in some industries approach 75 percent of the total operating budget. Reducing supply chain costs has a major impact on firm profitability.

In addition to reducing costs, supply chain management systems help increase sales. If a product is not available when a customer wants it, customers often try to purchase it from someone else. More precise control of the supply chain enhances the firm's ability to have the right product available for customer purchases at the right time.

INTERACTIVE SESSION: TECHNOLOGY

Optimizing Operations at QuarkCity: A Move Away from Legacy Systems

QuarkCity India Private Limited was incorporated in October 2003 to design, study, develop, own, operate, buy, sell, or lease infrastructure projects and facilities. QuarkCity works on land acquisition, project development, and construction and management services. It recently shifted from legacy information systems to the more advanced enterprise resource planning (ERP) system. The older system involved working with Tally for accounting, Quark Commerce Software (QCMS) for purchasing, and MRP-II for material requirement planning.

The main problem with these systems was that data could not be integrated across departments in a consistent manner. For example, Tally worked independently, performing tasks related to financial transactions alone. Due to a lack of integration with any other software, the flow of information was restricted and other departments needed to manually request for information.

QCMS was a customized software only for material procurement. It could not handle service or job-order requirements, nor could it allow for the generation and approval of purchase orders. It could not record or report on returns and rejections from suppliers. Moreover, only a single unit of measurement (that is, pieces) could be used for each material. The system was not designed for multilevel approvals of purchase orders. Local taxation policies such as the excise duty or sales tax clauses were not incorporated in the purchase order formats. The purchase order, once approved, could not be amended if the need arose. There was no facility for tracking budgets against actual revenue items or capital items. Rates as well as quantities needed to be entered in absolute numbers and not in decimals.

The material requirement planning (MRP) system also had its limitations. For example, the activity codification system had no provision for checking activity codes and consumption of items. The inventory management system did not reflect the sub-stores, while the scrap management system did not codify entities properly.

In face of all these challenges posed by legacy systems, QuarkCity implemented the Oracle ERP functional suite. This helped the company avoid all issues related to data redundancy and inconsistency. Since the ERP data was centralized, updates made to any of the entries were immediately available to all the departments. The flow of information within the organization improved. For example, the purchase order requested by one department could be automatically sent to the concerned persons for approval. The inventory department could check against the same purchase order while inspecting and receiving the delivered material. The receipt of the items purchased could then be used as a basis for invoice generation and to record the transaction in the general ledger by the finance team. Moreover, the ERP could define each activity in various projects with its exact start and completion dates. This ensured that projects were completed on time, resulting in improved decision-making capabilities, productivity, and efficiency at the firm.

All the processes at QuarkCity are now managed by the ERP system, right from the procurement of materials, to their costs and consumption. Since the cost structure of each material is accurately known, it helps QuarkCity optimally utilize its resources to earn maximum profits. Besides, the ERP system tracks and controls all procurement activities, schedules production processes, and finally generates information that helps QuarkCity manage its inventory better. The ERP processes the information very quickly, which enables timely reporting of the numbers. Though the industry's standard percentage of cement and steel wastage is approximately 5 percent, the implementation of this system has reduced the wastage below this level. The firm's project and material management capabilities have also seen a marked improvement.

The inventory that sits in one's own warehouse just adds to the costs of the firm. Inventory levels can be reduced effectively by managing the lead time required for ordering the material. The ERP system at QuarkCity makes it possible to forecast demand of the material and help the firm in its timely purchase. Using the min/max formula for order planning, the ERP system alerts the managers when the quantity of material reaches its minimum level. With the real-estate business growing by leaps and bounds, there is a need for quality work in this sector. QuarkCity has been able to successfully navigate its difficulties with legacy systems to implement a modern management information system that has ultimately allowed it to improve the quality of its business.

Sources: Appelton, E. L., "How to Survive ERP", *Datamation,* Vol. 43, No. 3, pp. 50–53 (1997); Bancroft N., *Implementing SAP R/3,* Manning Publications (1996); N. Bancroft , H. Seip and A. Sprengel, *Implementing SAP R/,* Manning Publications (1998); Bowman I., "ERP 'Coned Off' Expect Delays", *Manufacturing-Computer-Solutions,* Vol. 3, No. 1, pp. 32–33 (1997); Caldwell B., "GTE Goes Solo on SAP R/3", *Informationweek,* No. 685, p. 150 (1998); B. Hecht, "Choose the Right ERP Software", *Datamation,* Vol. 43, No. 3, pp. 50–53 (1997); Holland , Light and Gibson, "A Critical Success Factors Model for Enterprise Resource Planning Implementation", *Proceedings of the 7th European Conference on Information Systems,* pp. 273–287 (1999); McKie S., "Packaged apps for the masses", *DBMS,* Vol. 10, No. 11, pp. 64–6 and 68 (1997); Piszczalski M., "Lessons learned from Europe's SAP users", *Production,* Vol. 109, No. 1, pp. 54–56 (1997); Ross J.W., *The ERP Revolution: Surviving Versus Thriving* (1998).

CASE STUDY QUESTIONS

1. Discuss the problems associated with the three legacy systems that were earlier in use at QuarkCity.
2. Discuss how these problems were solved by the implementation of the ERP software.
3. Visit www.sap.com and study the various applications of the SAP tool for managing business organizations.

9-3 How do customer relationship management systems help firms achieve customer intimacy?

You've probably heard phrases such as "the customer is always right" or "the customer comes first." Today these words ring truer than ever. Because competitive advantage based on an innovative new product or service is often very short lived, companies are realizing that their most enduring competitive strength may be their relationships with their customers. Some say that the basis of competition has switched from who sells the most products and services to who "owns" the customer and that customer relationships represent a firm's most valuable asset.

What is Customer Relationship Management?

What kinds of information would you need to build and nurture strong, long-lasting relationships with customers? You'd want to know exactly who your customers are, how to contact them, whether they are costly to service and sell to, what kinds of products and services they are interested in, and how much money they spend on your company. If you could, you'd want to make sure you knew each of your customers well, as if you were running a small-town store. And you'd want to make your good customers feel special.

In a small business operating in a neighborhood, it is possible for business owners and managers to know their customers well on a personal, face-to-face basis, but in a large business operating on a metropolitan, regional, national, or even global basis, it is impossible to know your customer in this intimate way.

In these kinds of businesses, there are too many customers and too many ways that customers interact with the firm (over the web, the phone, e-mail, blogs, and in person). It becomes especially difficult to integrate information from all these sources and deal with the large number of customers.

A large business's processes for sales, service, and marketing tend to be highly compartmentalized, and these departments do not share much essential customer information. Some information on a specific customer might be stored and organized in terms of that person's account with the company. Other pieces of information about the same customer might be organized by products that were purchased. In this traditional business environment, there is no convenient way to consolidate all this information to provide a unified view of a customer across the company.

This is where customer relationship management systems help. Customer relationship management (CRM) systems, which we introduced in Chapter 2, capture and integrate customer data from all over the organization, consolidate the data, analyze the data, and then distribute the results to various systems and customer touch points across the enterprise. A **touch point** (also known as a contact point) is a method of interaction with the customer, such as telephone, e-mail, customer service desk, conventional mail, Facebook, Twitter, website, wireless device, or retail store. Well-designed CRM systems provide a single enterprise view of customers that is useful for improving both sales and customer service (see Figure 9.6).

Good CRM systems provide data and analytical tools for answering questions such as these: What is the value of a particular customer to the firm

FIGURE 9.6 CUSTOMER RELATIONSHIP MANAGEMENT (CRM)

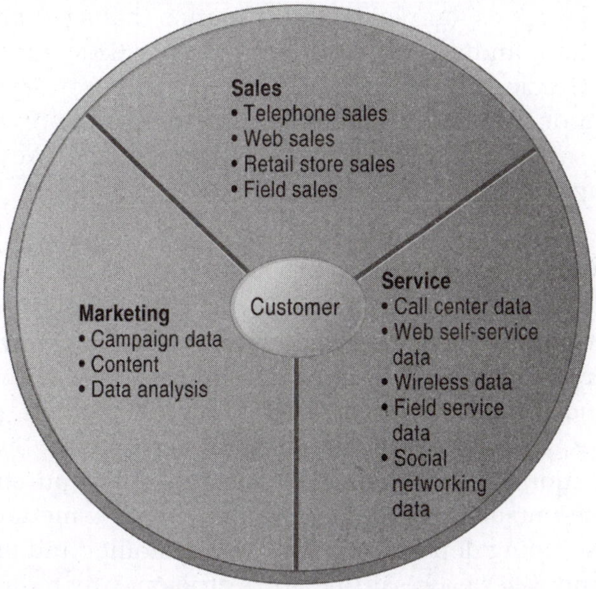

CRM systems examine customers from a multifaceted perspective. These systems use a set of integrated applications to address all aspects of the customer relationship, including customer service, sales, and marketing.

over his or her lifetime? Who are our most loyal customers? Who are our most profitable customers? What do these profitable customers want to buy? Firms use the answers to these questions to acquire new customers, provide better service and support to existing customers, customize their offerings more precisely to customer preferences, and provide ongoing value to retain profitable customers.

Customer Relationship Management Software

Commercial CRM software packages range from niche tools that perform limited functions, such as personalizing websites for specific customers, to large-scale enterprise applications that capture myriad interactions with customers, analyze them with sophisticated reporting tools, and link to other major enterprise applications, such as supply chain management and enterprise systems. The more comprehensive CRM packages contain modules for **partner relationship management (PRM)** and **employee relationship management (ERM)**.

PRM uses many of the same data, tools, and systems as customer relationship management to enhance collaboration between a company and its selling partners. If a company does not sell directly to customers but rather works through distributors or retailers, PRM helps these channels sell to customers directly. It provides a company and its selling partners with the ability to trade information and distribute leads and data about customers, integrating lead generation, pricing, promotions, order configurations, and availability. It also provides a firm with tools to assess its partners' performances so it can make sure its best partners receive the support they need to close more business.

ERM software deals with employee issues that are closely related to CRM, such as setting objectives, employee performance management, performance-based compensation, and employee training. Major CRM application software vendors include Oracle, SAP, Salesforce.com, and Microsoft Dynamics CRM.

Customer relationship management systems typically provide software and online tools for sales, customer service, and marketing. We briefly describe some of these capabilities.

Sales Force Automation

Sales force automation (SFA) modules in CRM systems help sales staff increase productivity by focusing sales efforts on the most profitable customers, those who are good candidates for sales and services. SFA modules provide sales prospect and contact information, product information, product configuration capabilities, and sales quote generation capabilities. Such software can assemble information about a particular customer's past purchases to help the salesperson make personalized recommendations. SFA modules enable sales, marketing, and shipping departments to share customer and prospect information easily. SFA increases each salesperson's efficiency by reducing the cost per sale as well as the cost of acquiring new customers and retaining old ones. SFA modules also provide capabilities for sales forecasting, territory management, and team selling.

Customer Service

Customer service modules in CRM systems provide information and tools to increase the efficiency of call centers, help desks, and customer support staff. They have capabilities for assigning and managing customer service requests.

One such capability is an appointment or advice telephone line. When a customer calls a standard phone number, the system routes the call to the correct service person, who inputs information about that customer into the system only once. When the customer's data are in the system, any service representative can handle the customer relationship. Improved access to consistent and accurate customer information helps call centers handle more calls per day and decrease the duration of each call. Thus, call centers and customer service groups achieve greater productivity, reduced transaction time, and higher quality of service at lower cost. The customer is happier because he or she spends less time on the phone restating his or her problem to customer service representatives.

CRM systems may also include web-based self-service capabilities: The company website can be set up to provide inquiring customers personalized support information as well as the option to contact customer service staff by phone for additional assistance.

Marketing

CRM systems support direct-marketing campaigns by providing capabilities for capturing prospect and customer data, for providing product and service information, for qualifying leads for targeted marketing, and for scheduling and tracking direct-marketing mailings or e-mail (see Figure 9.7). Marketing

FIGURE 9.7 HOW CRM SYSTEMS SUPPORT MARKETING

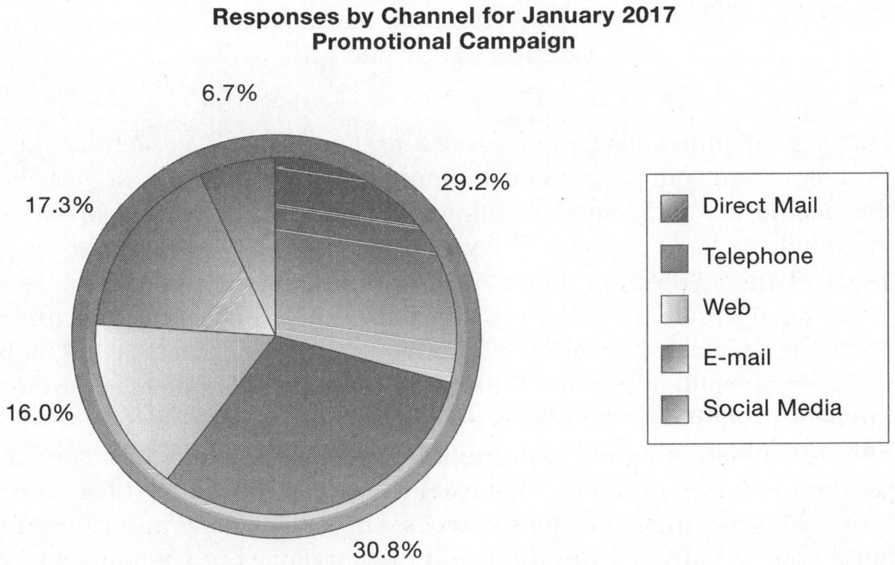

Customer relationship management software provides a single point for users to manage and evaluate marketing campaigns across multiple channels, including e-mail, direct mail, telephone, the web, and social media.

FIGURE 9.8 CRM SOFTWARE CAPABILITIES

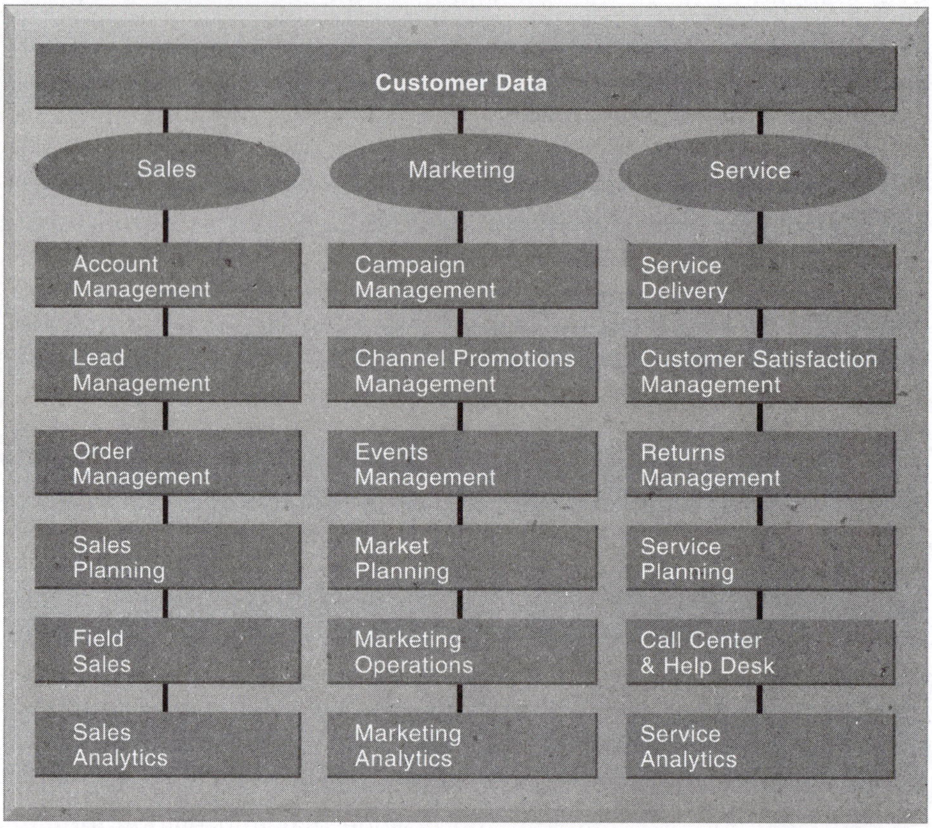

The major CRM software products support business processes in sales, service, and marketing, integrating customer information from many sources. Included is support for both the operational and analytical aspects of CRM.

modules also include tools for analyzing marketing and customer data, identifying profitable and unprofitable customers, designing products and services to satisfy specific customer needs and interests, and identifying opportunities for cross-selling.

Cross-selling is the marketing of complementary products to customers. (For example, in financial services, a customer with a checking account might be sold a money market account or a home improvement loan.) CRM tools also help firms manage and execute marketing campaigns at all stages, from planning to determining the rate of success for each campaign.

Figure 9.8 illustrates the most important capabilities for sales, service, and marketing processes found in major CRM software products. Like enterprise software, this software is business-process driven, incorporating hundreds of business processes thought to represent best practices in each of these areas. To achieve maximum benefit, companies need to revise and model their business processes to conform to the best-practice business processes in the CRM software.

FIGURE 9.9 CUSTOMER LOYALTY MANAGEMENT PROCESS MAP

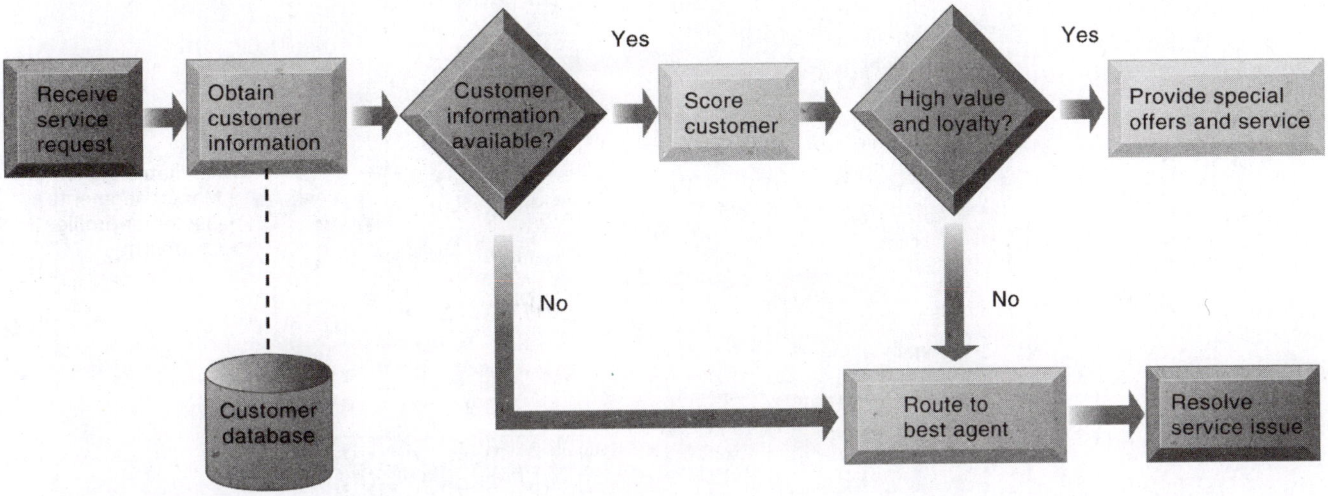

This process map shows how a best practice for promoting customer loyalty through customer service would be modeled by customer relationship management software. The CRM software helps firms identify high-value customers for preferential treatment.

Figure 9.9 illustrates how a best practice for increasing customer loyalty through customer service might be modeled by CRM software. Directly servicing customers provides firms with opportunities to increase customer retention by singling out profitable long-term customers for preferential treatment. CRM software can assign each customer a score based on that person's value and loyalty to the company and provide that information to help call centers route each customer's service request to agents who can best handle that customer's needs. The system would automatically provide the service agent with a detailed profile of that customer that includes his or her score for value and loyalty. The service agent would use this information to present special offers or additional service to the customer to encourage the customer to keep transacting business with the company. You will find more information on other best-practice business processes in CRM systems in our Learning Tracks.

Operational and Analytical CRM

All of the applications we have just described support either the operational or analytical aspects of customer relationship management. **Operational CRM** includes customer-facing applications, such as tools for sales force automation, call center and customer service support, and marketing automation. **Analytical CRM** includes applications that analyze customer data generated by operational CRM applications to provide information for improving business performance.

Analytical CRM applications are based on data from operational CRM systems, customer touch points, and other sources that have been organized in data warehouses or analytic platforms for use in online analytical processing (OLAP), data mining, and other data analysis techniques (see Chapter 6).

FIGURE 9.10 ANALYTICAL CRM

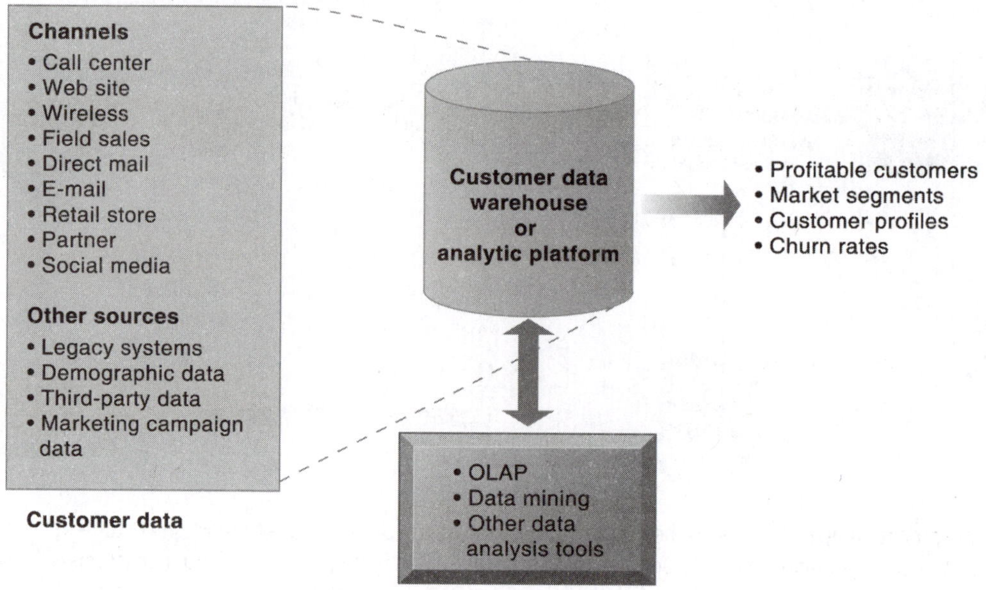

Analytical CRM uses a customer data warehouse or analytic platform and tools to analyze customer data collected from the firm's customer touch points and from other sources.

Customer data collected by the organization might be combined with data from other sources, such as customer lists for direct-marketing campaigns purchased from other companies or demographic data. Such data are analyzed to identify buying patterns, to create segments for targeted marketing, and to pinpoint profitable and unprofitable customers (see Figure 9.10).

Another important output of analytical CRM is the customer's lifetime value to the firm. **Customer lifetime value (CLTV)** is based on the relationship between the revenue produced by a specific customer, the expenses incurred in acquiring and servicing that customer, and the expected life of the relationship between the customer and the company.

Business Value of Customer Relationship Management Systems

Companies with effective customer relationship management systems realize many benefits, including increased customer satisfaction, reduced direct-marketing costs, more effective marketing, and lower costs for customer acquisition and retention. Information from CRM systems increases sales revenue by identifying the most profitable customers and segments for focused marketing and cross-selling.

Customer churn is reduced as sales, service, and marketing respond better to customer needs. The **churn rate** measures the number of customers who stop using or purchasing products or services from a company. It is an important indicator of the growth or decline of a firm's customer base.

INTERACTIVE SESSION: ORGANIZATIONS

McDonald's Serving Hot and Fresh

McDonald's is a world leading fast-food restaurants chain, operating through 33,000 restaurants in 118 countries and serving more than 67 million customers each day. In India, McDonald's first opened its outlets in Delhi and Mumbai within a month apart in 1996. In India, it was a pioneer in introducing the concept of quick service restaurants, and many global brands followed suit. As of now, it has a major presence in India, operating in 40 cities with 250 restaurants, and serving 650,000 customers daily. The changing Indian landscape has brought about changes in the lifestyle of the youth in the country, thereby presenting a promising future for such fast-food chains in India. The fast-food industry, at present, consists of 47 billion customers. This is expected to grow three fold by 2022 yielding ₹25,000 crore, at a compounded annual growth rate of 25 percent. The unique proposition of McDonald's is its limited menu offered at all its restaurants; therefore, it can compete on the speed of operations. We enjoy our McDonald's burger fresh and hot, but we might not have ever wondered about the processes that are followed to deliver our orders in limited time. The answer is the remarkable supply chain of the company, which is also sometimes referred to as the cold chain. Nine different ingredients are used to make a burger, which are procured from 35 suppliers across the country through a massive supply chain network of the firm. The current strength of the employees at all McDonald's chains across India is 9,000, including restaurant staff. And amazingly, its supply chain is managed by just five people across the country, which totals to only eight if quality assurance people are also included.

The story of McDonald's supply chain started way back in 1989, six years prior to the first opening of its restaurant in India. Besides pioneering the concept of quick service restaurants, McDonald's is also a pioneer in establishing the cold chain for the distribution of farm and dairy products in the country. In 1989, the firm sent its expert teams to conduct an in-depth analysis of Indian logistics industry, and assess reliability of the transportation sector. In a span of seven years, the firm established its supply chain which is an optimal supply chain despite weak infrastructure in the country. "We spent seven years to develop the supply chain. The first McDonald's team came to India way back in 1989," said S.D. Saravanan, Product Manager, National Supply Chain, McDonald's India.

The supply chain at McDonald's is 100 percent outsourced, lean with no back-up staff, and no-frills. It has one distribution agent, Radhakrishna Foodland Private Limited (RFPL), which acts as a hub for all its vendors. McDonald's India has four distribution centers across the country—Noida, Mumbai, Kolkata, and Bangalore. Each distribution center is a cold storage which maintains a fleet of refrigerated trucks for transportation of goods to 250 restaurants operated by the fast-food giant. This operates like a hub and spoke architecture where distribution center is the hub and restaurants are the spokes. "This centralized distribution system is unique to McDonald's. We have to ensure that the integrity of the product is maintained throughout the cold chain," said H. Shriram, General Manager, Distribution Center, RFPL. The firm maintains controlled temperature at each of its distribution center through special equipments. The fleet of chilled trucks are also maintained in the range of 1 to 4 degree celsius. Reefer trucks are maintained at -18 to -22 degree for contingency like in the event of power failure at restaurants.

All the food to prepare a burger reaches from suppliers to distribution centers through this fleet of reefer trucks. There are two tiers of suppliers. Tier 2 suppliers are responsible for raw food production like growing lettuce, potato, poultry, etc. They deliver these raw food items to Tier 1 suppliers who process these into patties, pies, nuggets, and vegetables. Some of the Tier 1 suppliers are Vista Processed Foods and Kitran Foods. McCain Foods India Private Limited is another Tier 1 supplier which supplies french fries, potato wedges, etc. There are 14 Tier 1 and 26 Tier 2 suppliers. Figure 9.11 presents an overview of McDonald's supply chain.

Another unique aspect of McDonald's supply chain is that it does not maintain any legally signed

FIGURE 9.11 AN OVERVIEW OF MCDONALD'S SUPPLY CHAIN

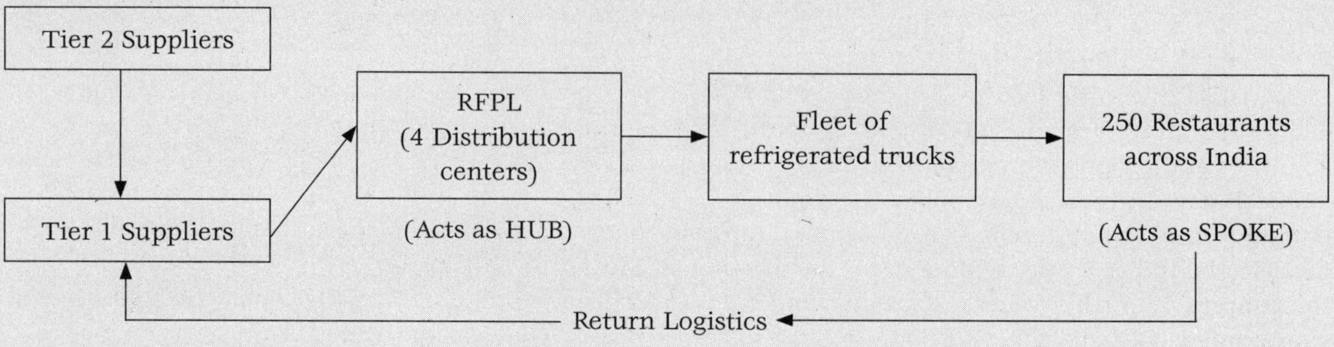

agreements with any of its suppliers. It's a simple handshake relationship based on mutual faith. It has a clear policy of one supplier for one product.

McDonald's insists on these suppliers to maintain standardization. All the Tier 2 suppliers train the local farmers to ensure products such as potatoes, peas, and lettuce are grown to a particular specification. For example, if peas exceed a particular size, they would pop out of the patties and burn. In this manner, McDonald's is also delivering technology to its suppliers by introducing new farming practices. For example, Trikaya Agriculture, one of McDonald's Tier 2 suppliers, is assisted by the firm to produce iceberg lettuce throughout the year, including in rain-shadow areas. This crop is harvested within 45 days, early in the morning, and stored in a vacuum of pre-cooled rooms at Trikaya's post-harvest facilities. McDonald's also practices Hazard Analysis Critical Control Point or HACCP certification, an industry level certification which ensures food quality from all its suppliers. Through joint ventures with each of its suppliers, it maintains the quality of its products by implementing HACCP systems and conducting random checks. Jose Azavedo, CEO, Vista & Kitran, which is a McDonald's supplier of ready-to-cook patties, affirms the same saying, "We have developed a supplier chain to get fresh vegetables and chicken. We test everything that comes into our plant." The plant at Vista and Kitran has a HACCP control system for quality assurance and stores the manufactured patties at a temperature of -26 degree celsius. According to industry level specifications at McDonald's, 3.5 lakh liters of milk is required everyday to produce freshly processed cheese. Other safety practices that all its suppliers adhere to are Suppliers Quality Management Systems (SQMS) and Distributor Quality Maintenance Program (DQMP). Independent auditors trained in these programs audit McDonald's plants and warehouses, and impart scores based on their assessment.

Another interesting aspect is the management of inventory and demand forecasting. A concept called pull supply is utilized along the supply chain. Each restaurant issues orders to distribution center which in turn routes it to suppliers who then produce it; this is also termed as 'made to order.' Usually 3 days to 1 week forecast is given by each restaurant to the distribution center, which enables planning of three month rolling forecast for suppliers who can then plan for their production schedules. So, the suppliers do not need to maintain surplus stocks, and fill rate is almost always 99.8 percent. RFPL manages all the items in this way for McDonald's, except those which are perishable in a day such as buns. Coca-Cola is also directly received at the restaurants as it has its own efficient distribution channel. Also, to optimally utilize vehicle capacity, goods from other vendors are transported through trucks. After carefully monitoring the time a truck leaves a distribution center and reaches restaurant and the time taken in offloading, each restaurant gets a 30-minute timeframe to complete the delivery.

Although there is legally no signed service-level agreement of McDonald's with its distribution partner RKFL, it evaluates its performance against key performance indicators defined on several factors like administration efficiency, warehouse efficiency, overtime, truck utilization, etc.

In a nutshell, McDonald's supply chain is optimally handled with the least number of employees on payroll, and despite being totally an outsourced chain, its control is commendable. It is not only delivering the best to customers, it has also been delivering immense benefits to its suppliers by imparting new technology and practices.

Sources: As accessed on 31 December 2015 at 4pm IST—Retrieved from http://www.globalthen.com, please read: Indian Fast Food Industry; Retrieved from http://www.crisil.com, (Navigation > Home > Research > CRISIL > QSR); Retrieved from http://www.mcdonaldsindia.com, please read: 'Supply Chain Management' on Home page; Retrieved from http://www.mcdonaldsindia.com; Retrieved from http://indianresearchjournals.com, (Navigation > Home > APJMMR January 10, 2013).

CASE STUDY QUESTIONS

1. Discuss the process followed by McDonald's to establish supply chain in India.
2. Discuss the role and advantages of centralized distribution system and tiering of suppliers at McDonald's.
3. How does McDonald's ensures that standards are maintained across its suppliers?
4. Explain the concepts of 'pull supply' and 'made to order' in the context of this case.

9-4 What are the challenges that enterprise applications pose, and how are enterprise applications taking advantage of new technologies?

Many firms have implemented enterprise systems and systems for supply chain and customer relationship management because they are such powerful instruments for achieving operational excellence and enhancing decision making. But precisely because they are so powerful in changing the way the organization works, they are challenging to implement. Let's briefly examine some of these challenges as well as new ways of obtaining value from these systems.

Enterprise Application Challenges

Promises of dramatic reductions in inventory costs, order-to-delivery time, more efficient customer response, and higher product and customer profitability make enterprise systems and systems for SCM and CRM very alluring. But to obtain this value, you must clearly understand how your business has to change to use these systems effectively.

Enterprise applications involve complex pieces of software that are very expensive to purchase and implement. It might take a large Fortune 500 company several years to complete a large-scale implementation of an enterprise system or a system for SCM or CRM. According to a 2015 survey of 562 companies conducted by Panorama Consulting Solutions, the average cost of an ERP project was $6.1 million. Projects took an average of 15.7 months to complete, and 53 percent of the projects delivered 50 percent or less of the expected benefits. Approximately 58 percent of these projects exceeded their planned budgets, and 65 percent experienced schedule overruns (Panorama Consulting Solutions, 2015). Changes in project scope and additional customization work add to implementation delays and costs.

Enterprise applications require not only deep-seated technological changes but also fundamental changes in the way the business operates. Companies must make sweeping changes to their business processes to work with the software. Employees must accept new job functions and responsibilities. They must learn how to perform a new set of work activities and understand how the information they enter into the system can affect other parts of the company. This requires new organizational learning and should also be factored into ERP implementation costs.

SCM systems require multiple organizations to share information and business processes. Each participant in the system may have to change some of its processes and the way it uses information to create a system that best serves the supply chain as a whole.

Some firms experienced enormous operating problems and losses when they first implemented enterprise applications because they didn't understand how much organizational change was required. For example, Kmart had trouble getting products to store shelves when it first implemented i2 Technologies (now JDA Software) SCM software. The i2 software did not work well with Kmart's promotion-driven business model, which created sharp spikes in demand for products. Overstock.com's order tracking system went down for a full week when the company replaced a homegrown system with an Oracle enterprise system. The company rushed to implement the software and did not properly synchronize the Oracle software's process for recording customer refunds with its accounts receivable system. The chapter-ending case shows how rushed implementation of enterprise applications contributed to Target Canada's business failure.

Enterprise applications also introduce switching costs. When you adopt an enterprise application from a single vendor, such as SAP, Oracle, or others, it is very costly to switch vendors, and your firm becomes dependent on the vendor to upgrade its product and maintain your installation.

Enterprise applications are based on organization-wide definitions of data. You'll need to understand exactly how your business uses its data and how the data would be organized in a CRM, SCM, or ERP system. CRM systems typically require some data cleansing work.

Enterprise software vendors are addressing these problems by offering pared-down versions of their software and fast-start programs for small and medium-sized businesses and best-practice guidelines for larger companies. Companies are also achieving more flexibility by using cloud applications for functions not addressed by the basic enterprise software so that they are not constrained by a single do-it-all type of system.

Companies adopting enterprise applications can also save time and money by keeping customizations to a minimum. For example, Kennametal, a $2 billion metal-cutting tools company, had spent $10 million over 13 years maintaining an ERP system with more than 6,400 customizations. The company replaced it with a plain-vanilla, uncustomized version of SAP enterprise software and changed its business processes to conform to the software.

Next-Generation Enterprise Applications

Today, enterprise application vendors are delivering more value by becoming more flexible, web-enabled, mobile, and capable of integration with other systems. Stand-alone enterprise systems, customer relationship management systems, and SCM systems are becoming a thing of the past. The major enterprise software vendors have created what they call *enterprise solutions, enterprise suites*, or e-business suites to make their CRM, SCM, and ERP systems work closely with each other and link to systems of customers and suppliers. SAP Business Suite, Oracle E-Business Suite, and Microsoft Dynamics Suite (aimed at midsized companies) are examples, and they now use web services and service-oriented architecture (SOA) (see Chapter 5).

SAP's next-generation enterprise applications incorporate SOA standards and can link SAP's own applications and web services developed by independent software vendors. Oracle also has included SOA and business process management capabilities in its Fusion middleware products. Businesses can use these tools to create platforms for new or improved business processes that integrate information from multiple applications.

Next-generation enterprise applications also include open source and cloud solutions as well as more functionality available on mobile platforms. Open source products such as Compiere, Apache Open for Business (OFBiz), and Openbravo do not offer as many capabilities as large commercial enterprise software but are attractive to companies such as small manufacturers because of their low cost.

For small- and medium-sized businesses, SAP offers cloud-based versions of its Business One and Business ByDesign enterprise software solutions (see the chapter-opening case study). Cloud-based enterprise systems are also offered by smaller vendors such as NetSuite and Plex Systems, but they are not as popular as cloud-based CRM products. The undisputed global market leader in cloud-based CRM systems is Salesforce.com, with more than 100,000 customers. Salesforce.com delivers its service through Internet-connected computers or mobile devices, and it is widely used by small, medium, and large enterprises. As cloud-based products mature, more companies will be choosing to run all or part of their enterprise applications in the cloud on an as-needed basis. Several Fortune 500 firms are planning to move most of their enterprise software to cloud based platforms in the next five years where they will not incur the costs of maintaining their own hardware, and the software will be charged on a metered basis.

Social CRM and Business Intelligence

CRM software vendors are enhancing their products to take advantage of social networking technologies. These social enhancements help firms identify new ideas more rapidly, improve team productivity, and deepen interactions with customers (see Chapter 10). Using **social CRM** tools, businesses can better engage with their customers by, for example, analyzing their sentiments about their products and services.

Social CRM tools enable a business to connect customer conversations and relationships from social networking sites to CRM processes. The leading CRM vendors now offer such tools to link data from social networks into their CRM software. SAP, Salesforce.com and Oracle CRM products now feature technology to monitor, track, and analyze social media activity in Facebook, LinkedIn, Twitter, YouTube, and other sites. Business intelligence and analytics software vendors such as SAS also have capabilities for social media analytics (with several measures of customer engagement across a variety of social networks) along with campaign management tools for testing and optimizing both social and traditional web-based campaigns.

Salesforce.com connected its system for tracking leads in the sales process with social-listening and social-media marketing tools, enabling users to tailor their social-marketing dollars to core customers and observe the resulting comments. If an ad agency wants to run a targeted Facebook or Twitter ad, these capabilities make it possible to aim the ad specifically at people in the client's lead pipeline who are already being tracked in the CRM system. Users will be able to view tweets as they take place in real time and perhaps uncover new leads. They can also manage multiple campaigns and compare them all to figure out which ones generate the highest click-through rates and cost per click.

Business Intelligence in Enterprise Applications

Enterprise application vendors have added business intelligence features to help managers obtain more meaningful information from the massive amounts of data these systems generate. SAP now makes it possible for its enterprise applications to use HANA in-memory computing technology so that they are capable of much more rapid and complex data analysis. Included are tools for flexible reporting, ad hoc analysis, interactive dashboards, what-if scenario analysis, and data visualization. Rather than requiring users to leave an application and launch separate reporting and analytics tools, the vendors are starting to embed analytics within the context of the application itself. They are also offering complementary analytics products such as SAP BusinessObjects and Oracle Business Intelligence Enterprise Edition.

The major enterprise application vendors offer portions of their products that work on mobile handhelds. You can find out more about this topic in our Learning Track on Wireless Applications for Customer Relationship Management, Supply Chain Management, and Healthcare.

Review Summary

9-1 *How do enterprise systems help businesses achieve operational excellence?*

Enterprise software is based on a suite of integrated software modules and a common central database. The database collects data from and feeds the data into numerous applications that can support nearly all of an organization's internal business activities. When one process enters new information, the information is made available immediately to other business processes.

Enterprise systems support organizational centralization by enforcing uniform data standards and business processes throughout the company and a single unified technology platform. The firmwide data that enterprise systems generate help managers evaluate organizational performance.

9-2 ***How do supply chain management systems coordinate planning, production, and logistics with suppliers?***

Supply chain management (SCM) systems automate the flow of information among members of the supply chain so they can use it to make better decisions about when and how much to purchase, produce, or ship. More accurate information from supply chain management systems reduces uncertainty and the impact of the bullwhip effect.

Supply chain management software includes software for supply chain planning and for supply chain execution. Internet technology facilitates the management of global supply chains by providing the connectivity for organizations in different countries to share supply chain information. Improved communication among supply chain members also facilitates efficient customer response and movement toward a demand-driven model.

9-3 ***How do customer relationship management systems help firms achieve customer intimacy?***

Customer relationship management (CRM) systems integrate and automate customer-facing processes in sales, marketing, and customer service, providing an enterprise-wide view of customers. Companies can use this customer knowledge when they interact with customers to provide them with better service or sell new products and services. These systems also identify profitable or unprofitable customers or opportunities to reduce the churn rate.

The major customer relationship management software packages provide capabilities for both operational CRM and analytical CRM. They often include modules for managing relationships with selling partners (partner relationship management) and for employee relationship management.

9-4 ***What are the challenges that enterprise applications pose, and how are enterprise applications taking advantage of new technologies?***

Enterprise applications are difficult to implement. They require extensive organizational change, large new software investments, and careful assessment of how these systems will enhance organizational performance. Enterprise applications cannot provide value if they are implemented atop flawed processes or if firms do not know how to use these systems to measure performance improvements. Employees require training to prepare for new procedures and roles. Attention to data management is essential.

Enterprise applications are now more flexible, web-enabled, and capable of integration with other systems, using web services and service-oriented architecture (SOA). They also have open source and on-demand versions and can run in cloud infrastructures or on mobile platforms. CRM software has added social networking capabilities to enhance internal collaboration, deepen interactions with customers, and use data from social networking sites. Open source, mobile, and cloud versions of some of these products are becoming available.

Key Terms

Analytical CRM, 377
Bullwhip effect, 366
Churn rate, 378
Cross-selling, 376
Customer lifetime value (CLTV), 378
Demand planning, 367
Employee relationship management (ERM), 374
Enterprise software, 361
Just-in-time strategy, 366
Operational CRM, 377
Partner relationship management (PRM), 374
Pull-based model, 369
Push-based model, 369
Sales force automation (SFA), 374
Social CRM, 383
Supply chain, 364
Supply chain execution systems, 367
Supply chain planning systems, 366
Touch point, 373

Review Questions

9-1 How do enterprise systems help businesses achieve operational excellence?

- Explain the business processes supported by enterprise systems and their working.
- How are enterprise systems aiding managers in making better decisions? Discuss with examples.

9-2 How do supply chain management systems coordinate planning, production, and logistics with suppliers?

- Distinguish between upstream and downstream portion of supply chain.
- What is just-in-time strategy? Why is it not possible to implement the same despite of SCM information systems?
- Define demand planning. How does supply chain management software support the same?
- How are global supply chains concurrent supply chains and why it is said to operate like a digital logistics nervous system? Discuss.
- Draw a comparison between traditional supply chain management system model and contemporary SCM models. How are they different and what are the business benefits of the same?

9-3 How do customer relationship management systems help firms achieve customer intimacy?

- Define touch point. Which aspects of customer relationship, customer relationship management systems address?
- Discuss the capabilities of different commercial and comprehensive customer relationship management software packages that are available in the market.
- Which business processes are supported by customer relationship management software? Illustrate the way CRM software can be modeled to increase customer loyalty.
- Discuss the role of analytical CRM in CLTV and reducing customer churn.

9-4 What are the challenges that enterprise applications pose? How are enterprise applications taking advantage of new technologies?

- List and describe the challenges enterprise applications pose.
- Explain the ways in which these challenges can be addressed.
- How are enterprise applications taking advantage of SOA, cloud computing, and open-source software? Describe.
- Define social CRM and explain the manner in which customer relationship management systems are using social networking.

Discussion Questions

9-5 Supply chain management is less about managing the physical movement of goods and more about managing information. Discuss the implications of this statement.

9-6 Why do more than half of enterprise application projects exceed budgets, deliver less than expected benefits, or experience overruns?

9-7 Which enterprise application should a business install first: ERP, SCM, or CRM? Explain your answer.

Hands-On MIS Projects

The projects in this section give you hands-on experience analyzing business process integration, suggesting supply chain management and customer relationship management applications, using database software to manage customer service requests, and evaluating supply chain management business services.

Management Decision Problems

9-8 Mercedes-Benz Retail Group UK Ltd., with a network of 18 retail sites, nine used car sites, and seven smart centers across London, Birmingham, and Manchester, wanted to learn more about its customers. How could CRM and PRM systems help solve this problem?

9-9 Office Depot sells a wide range of office supply products and services in the United States and internationally. The company tries to offer a wider range of office supplies at lower cost than other retailers by using just-in-time replenishment and tight inventory control systems. It uses information from a demand forecasting system and point-of-sale data to replenish its inventory in its 1,600 retail stores. Explain how these systems help Office Depot minimize costs and discuss any other benefits they provide. Identify and describe other supply chain management applications that would be especially helpful to Office Depot.

Improving Decision Making: Using Database Software to Manage Customer Service Requests

Software skills: Database design; querying and reporting
Business skills: Customer service analysis

9-10 In this exercise, you'll use database software to develop an application that tracks customer service requests and analyzes customer data to identify customers meriting priority treatment.

Prime Service is a large service company that provides maintenance and repair services for close to 1,200 commercial businesses in New York, New Jersey, and Connecticut. Its customers include businesses of all sizes. Customers with service needs call into its customer service department with requests for repairing heating ducts, broken windows, leaky roofs, broken water pipes, and other problems. The company assigns each request a number and writes down the service request number, the identification number of the customer account, the date of the request, the type of equipment requiring repair, and a brief description of the problem. The service requests are handled on a first-come-first-served basis. After the service work has been completed, Prime calculates the cost of the work, enters the price on the service request form, and bills the client. This arrangement treats the most important and profitable clients—those with accounts of more than $70,000—no differently from its clients with small accounts. Management would like to find a way to provide its best customers with better service. It would also like to know which types of service problems occur most frequently so that it can make sure it has adequate resources to address them.

Prime Service has a small database with client account information. Use database software to design a solution that would enable Prime's customer service representatives to identify the most important customers so that they could receive priority service. Your solution will require more than one table. Populate your database with at least 10 service requests. Create several reports that would be of interest to management, such as a list of the highest—and lowest—priority accounts and a report showing the most frequently occurring service problems. Create a report listing service calls that customer service representatives should respond to first on a specific date.

Achieving Operational Excellence: Evaluating Supply Chain Management Services

Software skills: Web browser and presentation software
Business skills: Evaluating supply chain management services

9-11 In addition to carrying goods from one place to another, some trucking companies provide supply chain management services and help their customers manage their information. In this project, you'll use the web to research and evaluate two of these business services. Investigate the websites of two companies, UPS Logistics and Schneider Logistics, to see how these companies' services can be used for supply chain management. Then respond to the following questions:

- What supply chain processes can each of these companies support for its clients?
- How can customers use the websites of each company to help them with supply chain management?
- Compare the supply chain management services these companies provide. Which company would you select to help your firm manage its supply chain? Why?

Collaboration and Teamwork Project

Analyzing Enterprise Application Vendors

9-12 With a group of three or four other students, use the web to research and evaluate the products of two vendors of enterprise application software. You could compare, for example, the SAP and Oracle enterprise systems, the supply chain management systems from JDA Software and SAP, or the customer relationship management systems of Oracle and Salesforce.com. Use what you have learned from these companies' websites to compare the software products you have selected in terms of business functions supported, technology platforms, cost, and ease of use. Which vendor would you select? Why? Would you select the same vendor for a small business (50–300 employees) as well as for a large one? If possible, use Google Docs and Google Drive or Google Sites to brainstorm, organize, and develop a presentation of your findings for the class.

Customer Relationship Management Helps Celcom Become Number One

CASE STUDY

Celcom Axiata Berhad (Celcom) is the oldest mobile telecommunications company in Malaysia and also its largest, with an unrivaled reputation for quality and reliability. Nevertheless, maintaining its competitive edge has been a struggle. In 2006 Celcom dropped to third place among Malaysian cellular providers. Since then, management has worked feverishly to turn the company around, and Celcom has regained the top spot in its market. This turnaround required new technology and business processes for managing the customer experience.

To become number one in the Malaysian market again, Celcom's senior management knew that the company had to build better networks and market more aggressively. But the real key to success lay in improving the customer experience. According to Suresh Sidhu, Celcom's chief corporate and operations officer, there will always be a competitor who can beat you on price or even out-innovate you. But it's much harder for a competitor to disrupt a strong, positive relationship with customers. Celcom believes it's the market's best differentiator.

The Malaysia telecommunications market is quite mature, with few opportunities to acquire new customers. Customer retention is essential, as is luring customers away from competitors. Malaysia's customer base of 14 million is large and diverse, which requires multiple approaches to interacting with them. Older customers prefer in-person service from Celcom dealers or retail outlets, while sophisticated young urban users prefer to do business online. All want reliable mobile service.

Celcom was saddled with a siloed information technology architecture and business processes that could not provide a complete view of customers. For instance, customer data from one system such as billing were not easily available to other systems such as inventory. This is a common problem for mobile providers because carriers have traditionally counted customers by looking at SIM (subscriber identity modules in mobile phones) IDs. However, many customers have multiple devices and SIMs for personal and work uses. Celcom needed systems that could identify and serve each customer rather than that person's SIMs. Otherwise, Celcom service representatives would waste valuable company and customer time making sense of a customer's multiple SIM IDs scattered among various records in the system. The company wanted to be able to see a customer as a specific person, not a SIM or a number.

Celcom's solution involved changes to the company's technology, processes, and people. At the core is an Oracle-based business support system (BSS) that consolidated customer records, centralized inventory management, and sped up business processes. This system consolidates customer information into a single view of the customer to improve customer service across online, call center, and retail channels. The Oracle implementation included new customer portal sites and retail stores as well as an Oracle Siebel call center system and Oracle inventory management and Communications Order and Service Management applications.

The BSS project team asked approximately 700 Celcom employees in customer service, retail, marketing, and other divisions to list the top 10 experiences that users and dealers wanted, such as fast activation, less paperwork, and always having the most popular phones in stock. The BSS transformation team then developed technical and business process requirements based on these top 10 lists and compared offerings from several vendors.

Celcom chose Oracle as the primary technology provider for the new customer experience management system. The company wanted the most complete suite of customer relationship management (CRM) tools that would support multichannel and cross-channel marketing efforts. Oracle seemed the best fit and had the most functionality built in without requiring additional modifications.

Celcom's transformation plan entailed retaining some of Celcom's existing systems, and the Celcom team liked Oracle Communications' modularity and interoperability as well as its cross-channel capabilities. Oracle Communications is a cross-channel product suite that provides a variety of services, including broadband data, wireless data, and mobile voice services. It helps communications services providers such as Celcom manage and integrate customer interactions across multiple channels to improve customer support, reduce problem resolution time, customize marketing to narrow market segments, and expedite time-to-market for new products and services. Celcom understood the importance of cross-channel customer experiences and wanted to make this differentiate the company among its competitors. Celcom's systems solution enables customer interactions to seamlessly traverse its retail shop, online shop, call center, and partner/dealer channels.

The BSS provides a single customer record, regardless of how many services (mobile, landline, and data) and devices a customer purchases; it is populated with data from various touchpoints. By consolidating customer data into a unified customer record, Celcom can offer tailored promotions offers in real time that fit a customer's individual history. Celcom's holistic view of a customer includes family relationships, which has special significance when marketing in Asia. The company is able to see every aspect of service each customer uses, which makes cross-marketing and up-selling more efficient.

Celcom completed the BSS implementation in just 18 months, replacing 17 separate systems with one seven-module Oracle system.

Celcom officials explicitly tried to get employees invested in the new system to ensure it aligned with the business. The company enlisted project directors from both business and IT departments. Representatives from sales and marketing chaired the technology selection committees to ensure that people outside of IT were making the case for the project. Top management, including sales and marketing department heads and Celcom's CEO, are part of a steering committee for customer experience management that meets every two weeks.

Celcom's integrated systems make it possible for call center representatives to respond much more rapidly to customer queries. In the past, customer agents needed to toggle between two to five screens to do their work. Now they work with just a single screen, which increases efficiency. Using fewer screens cuts average call-handling time by 15 to 20 percent. BSS includes a new tablet-based app for Celcom dealers that makes signing a customer up for a new mobile phone completely paperless. New phone activation time has been cut from two hours to two minutes. Fewer activations require manual follow-up. Celcom dealers and customers are happier.

Inventory of mobile handsets at Celcom facilities and dealer stores is now centralized and managed using BSS. Dealers can see what Celcom has in stock, and Celcom inventory managers can monitor the stock on dealer shelves. More detailed inventory control helps Celcom move more products because it can ship fast-selling units to dealers before shortages occur or have marketers target promotions in regions where the company wants to move specific products. This would have been impossible before. Salespeople are beginning to use big data collected in BSS to better manage sales by region.

Celcom is now much closer to achieving its brand vision: pleasing its customers and exceeding their expectations.

Sources: Jessica Sirkin, "Oracle Implementation at Celcom Brings IT, Business Together," searchoracle.techtarget.com, accessed January 17, 2016; www.celcom.com, accessed January 18, 2016; Fred Sandsmark, "Customers First," *Profit Magazine*, May 2014; and Oracle Corporation, "Celcom Transforms Its Customer Experience with Industry Leading Oracle Communications Suite," March 31, 2014.

CASE STUDY QUESTIONS

9-13 What was the problem at Celcom described in this case? What management, organization, and technology factors contributed to this problem?

9-14 What was Celcom's business strategy, and what was the role of customer relationship management in that strategy?

9-15 Describe Celcom's solution to its problem. What management, organization, and technology issues had to be addressed by the solution?

9-16 How effective was this solution? How did it affect the way Celcom ran its business and its business performance?

Chapter 9 References

Bozarth, Cecil, and Robert B. Handfield. *Introduction to Operations and Supply Chain Management* (4th ed.). (Upper Saddle River, NJ: Prentice-Hall, 2016.)

Cole, Brenda. "Cloud ERP Users Say Up, Up and Away." *Business Information* (February 2014).

D'Avanzo, Robert, Hans von Lewinski, and Luk N. Van Wassenhove. "The Link Between Supply Chain and Financial Performance." *Supply Chain Management Review* (November 1, 2003).

Davenport, Thomas H. *Mission Critical: Realizing the Promise of Enterprise Systems.* (Boston: Harvard Business School Press, 2000.)

Davenport, Thomas H., Leandro Dalle Mule, and John Lucke. "Know What Your Customers Want Before They Do." *Harvard Business Review* (December 2011).

Essex, David. "Tomorrow's ERP Raises New Hopes, Fears." *Business Information* (February 2014).

Hitt, Lorin, D. J. Wu, and Xiaoge Zhou. "Investment in Enterprise Resource Planning: Business Impact and Productivity Measures." *Journal of Management Information Systems* 19, No. 1 (Summer 2002).

Hu, Michael and Sean T. Monahan. "Sharing Supply Chain Data in the Digital Era." *MIT Sloan Management Review* (Fall 2015).

Kanaracus, Chris. "ERP Software Project Woes Continue to Mount, Survey Says." *IT World* (February 20, 2013).

Kimberling, Eric. "5 Lessons from Successful CRM Implementations." Panorama-consulting.com (January 28, 2015).

Klein, Richard, and Arun Rai. "Interfirm Strategic Information Flows in Logistics Supply Chain Relationships." *MIS Quarterly* 33, No. 4 (December 2009).

Laudon, Kenneth C. "The Promise and Potential of Enterprise Systems and Industrial Networks." Working paper, The Concours Group. Copyright Kenneth C. Laudon (1999).

Lee, Hau, L., V. Padmanabhan, and Seugin Whang. "The Bullwhip Effect in Supply Chains." *Sloan Management Review* (Spring 1997).

Liang, Huigang, Nilesh Sharaf, Quing Hu, and Yajiong Xue. "Assimilation of Enterprise Systems: The Effect of Institutional Pressures and the Mediating Role of Top Management." *MIS Quarterly* 31, No. 1 (March 2007).

Liang, Huigang, Zeyu Peng, Yajiong Xue, Xitong Guo, and Nengmin Wang. "Employees' Exploration of Complex Systems: An Integrative View." *Journal of Management Information Systems* 32, No. 1 (2015).

Maklan, Stan, Simon Knox, and Joe Peppard. "When CRM Fails." *MIT Sloan Management Review* 52, No. 4 (Summer 2011).

Malik, Yogesh, Alex Niemeyer, and Brian Ruwadi. "Building the Supply Chain of the Future." *McKinsey Quarterly* (January 2011).

Mehta, Krishna. "Best Practices for Developing a Customer Lifetime Value Program." *Information Management* (July 28, 2011).

Morrison, Tod. "Custom ERP No Longer in Vogue." *Business Information* (February 2014).

Maurno, Dann Anthony. "The New Word on ERP." *CFO Magazine* (July 25, 2014).

Oracle Corporation. "Alcoa Implements Oracle Solution 20% Below Projected Cost, Eliminates 43 Legacy Systems." www.oracle.com, accessed August 21, 2005.

Panorama Consulting Solutions. "2015 ERP Report." (2015).

Rai, Arun, Paul A. Pavlou, Ghiyoung Im, and Steve Du. "Interfirm IT Capability Profiles and Communications for Cocreating Relational Value: Evidence from the Logistics Industry." *MIS Quarterly* 36, No. 1 (March 2012).

Rai, Arun, Ravi Patnayakuni, and Nainika Seth. "Firm Performance Impacts of Digitally Enabled Supply Chain Integration Capabilities." *MIS Quarterly* 30, No. 2 (June 2006).

Ranganathan, C., and Carol V. Brown. "ERP Investments and the Market Value of Firms: Toward an Understanding of Influential ERP Project Variables." *Information Systems Research* 17, No. 2 (June 2006).

Sarker, Supreteek, Saonee Sarker, Arvin Sahaym, and Bjørn-Andersen. "Exploring Value Cocreation in Relationships Between an ERP Vendor and its Partners: A Revelatory Case Study." *MIS Quarterly* 36, No. 1 (March 2012).

Seldon, Peter B., Cheryl Calvert, and Song Yang. "A Multi-Project Model of Key Factors Affecting Organizational Benefits from Enterprise Systems." *MIS Quarterly 34,* No. 2 (June 2010).

Strong, Diane M., and Olga Volkoff. "Understanding Organization-Enterprise System Fit: A Path to Theorizing the Information Technology Artifact." *MIS Quarterly* 34, No. 4 (December 2010).

SupplyChainBrain. "Trends in Enterprise Resource Planning Cloud Technology." (February 25, 2015).

Sussin, Jenny. "Top Use Cases and Benefits of Social for CRM in 2015." Gartner, Inc. (February 12, 2015).

Sykes, Tracy Ann, Viswanath Venkatesh, and Jonathan L. Johnson. "Enterprise System Implementation and Employee Job Performance: Understanding the Role of Advice Networks." *MIS Quarterly* 38, No. 1 (March 2014).

Tate, Wendy L., Diane Mollenkopf, Theodore Stank, and Andrea Lago da Silva. "Integrating Supply and Demand." *MIT Sloan Management Review* (Summer 2015).

Tian, Feng, and Sean Xin Xu. "How Do Enterprise Resource Planning Systems Affect Firm Risk? Post-Implementation Impact." *MIS Quarterly* 39, No. 1 (March 2015).

"Top 5 Reasons ERP Implementations Fail and What You Can Do About It." Ziff Davis (2013).

"Trends in Enterprise Resource Planning Cloud Technology." *SupplyChainBrain* (February 25, 2015).

Van Caeneghem, Alexander and Jean-Marie Becquevort. "Turning on ERP Systems Can Turn Off People." *CFO* (February 5, 2016).

Wong, Christina W.Y., Lai, Kee-Hung, and Cheng, T.C.E. "Value of Information Integration to Supply Chain Management: Roles of Internal and External Contingencies." *Journal of Management Information Systems* 28, No. 3 (Winter 2012).

CHAPTER

10 E-commerce: Digital Markets, Digital Goods

Learning Objectives

After reading this chapter, you will be able to answer the following questions:

10-1 What are the unique features of e-commerce, digital markets, and digital goods?

10-2 What are the principal e-commerce business and revenue models?

10-3 How has e-commerce transformed marketing?

10-4 How has e-commerce affected business-to-business transactions?

10-5 What is the role of m-commerce in business, and what are the most important m-commerce applications?

10-6 What issues must be addressed when building an e-commerce presence?

CHAPTER CASES

Uber Storms Europe: Europe Strikes Back
Zomato Scripting Success With E-Com
Social Media Analytics in Indian Politics
Paytm Cashing on Demonetization

Uber Storms Europe: Europe Strikes Back

Uber, the so-called "ride hailing service" (otherwise known as a taxi service) is headquartered in San Francisco and was founded in 2009 by Travis Kalanick and Garrett Camp. Uber is the posterchild (along with Airbnb) for the on-demand economy, a place where independent contractors respond to online requests for service. Uber's various services for transporting people rely on a smartphone app to hail a ride provided by an independent contractor (a driver) who is not an employee of the company. Drivers are self-employed and not under the direct control of Uber as employees would be. They may or may not be licensed or trained. The drivers supply their own car, pay for the gas, maintenance, insurance, and even their own cell phones. They take a cut of the fare, which used to be 20 percent or less, but in 2016 is moving to 25 percent. Voila: a taxi company with no taxis or employees, and an Internet platform for hooking up cars with people looking for a ride. One more thing: Uber provides rides for 30 to 50 percent less than regulated taxis and also changes its fares depending on demand. It's called "surge pricing."

© FocusTechnology/Alamy Stock Photo

By 2016, Uber had more than 162,000 drivers working in 200 cities and 55 countries generating revenue of $10 billion and earnings (after paying its drivers) of $2 billion. More than 100,000 people use Uber on a regular basis. However, Uber's over-the-top success has created its own set of challenges.

Uber has taken many American cities by storm and largely succeeded. Not that there hasn't been plenty of opposition from local taxi businesses who have paid hundreds of thousands of dollars in many cities for official medallions licensing them to pick up and transport passengers. Local governments have also resisted Uber, fearing the loss of tax revenue and threats to public safety and health posed by unskilled and uninsured drivers whose cars may not pass inspection. Nevertheless, in most cases, Uber has prevailed over local opposition, based in part on public support for an expanded and higher-quality taxi service using mobile technology, and support from Uber drivers who see the company as providing opportunity for a decent living. Uber has been very successful in using social media and online marketing campaigns to organize opposition to local politicians who oppose it. The result is that Uber has not been banned from any U.S. city, although in some cities like New York Uber is required to obtain a license to operate, and drivers and cars need to be certified by the city. In 2016, there were 60,000 Uber drivers in New York City and 30,000 taxi drivers. The price of an official taxi medallion has fallen from $1.3 million in 2013 to $640,000 in 2016, down 50 percent in a few years. The largest taxi cab owner in the United States, with thousands of cars and drivers working for him, declared that "Uber was the nastiest, most morally corrupt company ever."

In Europe Uber has generated much stronger opposition, including some outright bans in certain cities. In 2014 a Berlin court banned some of Uber's services following complaints from the Berlin Taxi Association that the service did not comply with local licensing rules. A court in Brussels outlawed Uber because it did not have the correct approvals. The EU commissioner in charge of Europe's Digital Agenda criticized such moves as anti-technology and simply protecting a taxi cartel from competition. In November 2015 courts in Frankfurt re-instated one of the most severe legal restrictions on Uber in the world for its failure to train drivers and insure cars. Uber's pricing is one unspoken cause of resistance to its services: Uber's fares are typically 30 percent less than local taxis. The company withdrew its UberPop service in Frankfurt but is allowed to operate its UberBlack and UberTaxi services because they use licensed drivers.

Meanwhile, in 2015, investigators raided Uber's offices in Paris as part of an investigation into the legality of Uber services in France. In 2014 France passed legislation that requires all drivers carrying paying passengers to have a license and insurance. Most UberPop drivers in Europe have neither. Uber has also pulled out of Hamburg, Dusseldorf, and Amsterdam. In Paris and Madrid opposition has often been violent. London is considering changes in its regulations that would disrupt Uber. Uber has run up against a different culture than it faces in the United States. As one taxi driver in Germany explained, "It's not part of our German culture to flaunt the laws and regulations and not treat Uber drivers like employees but rather as contractors with no rights.

Sources: Mark Scottman, "Uber's No-Holds-Barred Expansion Strategy Fizzles in Germany," *New York Times*, January 3, 2016; Simon Van Zuylen-Wood, "The Struggles of New York City's Taxi King," Bloomberg.com, August 27, 2015; Melissa Eddymarch, "An Uber Service Is Banned in Germany Again," *New York Times*, March 18, 2015; Mark Scott, "Uber Faces Rebukes in Europe," *New York Times*, April 17, 2014.

Uber exemplifies two major trends in e-commerce today. This e-commerce business is powered by the near-ubiquitous use of mobile smartphones, and it is one of so-called on-demand companies such as Lyft (Uber's primary competitor), Airbnb (rooms for rent), Handy and Homejoy

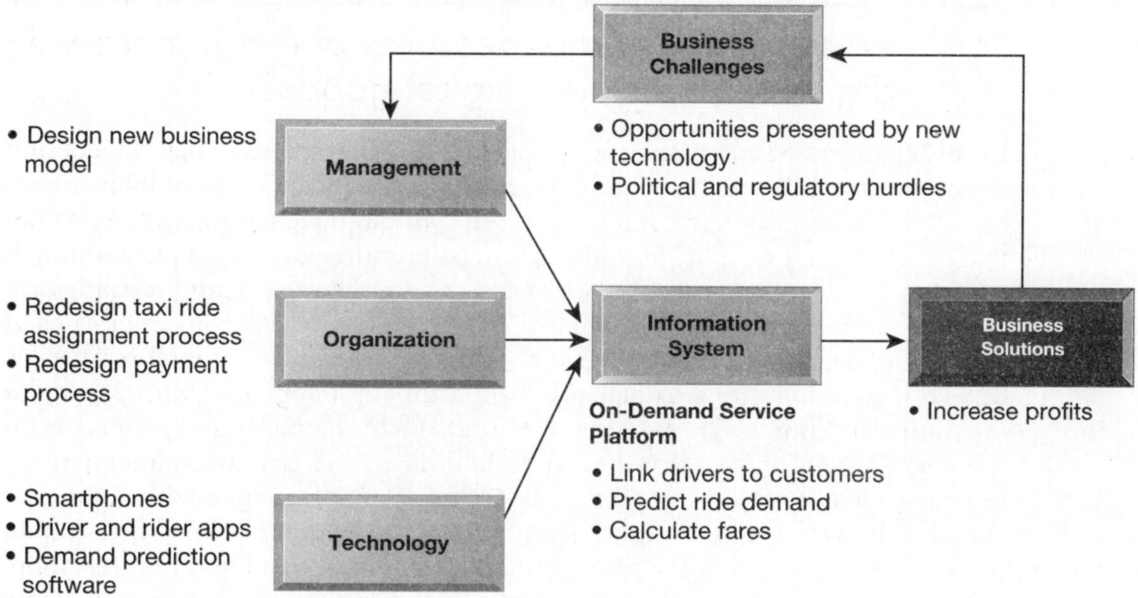

(both part-time household helpers), Instacart (grocery shoppers), and Washio (clothes washing). These on-demand firms don't sell goods; instead, they have built a platform by which people who want a service—such as a taxi—can find a provider to fill the demand. On-demand firms are currently considered the hottest business model in e-commerce, and they are disrupting major industries.

The chapter-opening diagram calls attention to important points this case and this chapter raise. The business challenge facing Uber is how to create a profitable company based on a new, on-demand business model. Uber's management decided to base its business on the use of wireless smartphones and apps that link buyers and sellers of taxi transportation services. The business earns revenue by charging users' credit cards for fares and giving a percentage of each fare to the driver, and it can charge prices that vary dynamically with demand. Uber has a lower cost structure than traditional cab companies because it does not have to pay employee wages or benefits, auto insurance, fuel, and licensing fees. Participating drivers pay for their own cars, fuel, and insurance. Under certain conditions, if demand is high, Uber can be more expensive than taxis, but it has disrupted the taxi industry because it offers a reliable, fast, convenient alternative to traditional taxi companies that book rides using the telephone, a central dispatcher using antiquated radio communications, or potential customers standing on street corners trying to hail a cab. Uber's growth is skyrocketing, but the company has to contend with many competitors and political and regulatory opposition from workers and the industries it is disrupting. It is still too early to tell whether Uber and other on-demand businesses will succeed.

Here are some questions to think about: Do you think Uber's business model is viable? Why or why not? How do you feel about using Uber compared with a regulated taxi?

10-1 What are the unique features of e-commerce, digital markets, and digital goods?

In 2017, purchasing goods and services online by using smartphones, tablets, and desktop computers will be ubiquitous. In 2017, an estimated 217 million Americans will shop online, and 185 million will purchase something online, as did millions of others worldwide. Although most purchases still take place through traditional channels, e-commerce continues to grow rapidly and to transform the way many companies do business. In 2017, e-commerce consumer sales of goods, services, travel, and online content, about 12 percent of total retail sales of $5.6 trillion, are growing at 15 percent annually (compared with 3 percent for traditional retailers) (eMarketer, 2016a). E-commerce has expanded from the desktop and home computer to mobile devices, from an isolated activity to a new social commerce, and from a *Fortune* 1000 commerce with a national audience to local merchants and consumers whose location is known to mobile devices. At the top 100 e-commerce retail sites, more than half of online shoppers arrive from their smartphones, although most continue to purchase using a PC or tablet. The key words for understanding this new e-commerce in 2017 will be "social, mobile, local."

E-commerce Today

E-commerce refers to the use of the Internet and the web to transact business. More formally, e-commerce is about digitally enabled commercial transactions between and among organizations and individuals. For the most part, this refers to transactions that occur over the Internet and the web. Commercial transactions involve the exchange of value (e.g., money) across organizational or individual boundaries in return for products and services.

E-commerce began in 1995 when one of the first Internet portals, Netscape.com, accepted the first ads from major corporations and popularized the idea that the web could be used as a new medium for advertising and sales. No one envisioned at the time what would turn out to be an exponential growth curve for e-commerce retail sales, which doubled and tripled in the early years. E-commerce grew at double-digit rates until the recession of 2008–2009, when growth slowed to a crawl, and revenues flattened (see Figure 10.1), not bad considering that traditional retail sales were shrinking by 5 percent annually. Since then, offline retail sales have increased only a few percentage points a year, whereas online e-commerce has been a stellar success.

The very rapid growth in e-commerce in the early years created a market bubble in e-commerce stocks. Like all bubbles, the dot-com bubble burst (in March 2001). A large number of e-commerce companies failed during this process. Yet for many others, such as Amazon, eBay, Expedia, and Google, the results have been more positive: soaring revenues, fine-tuned business models that produce profits and rising stock prices. By 2006, e-commerce revenues returned to solid growth, and have continued to be the fastest-growing form of retail trade in the United States, Europe, and Asia.

FIGURE 10.1 THE GROWTH OF E-COMMERCE

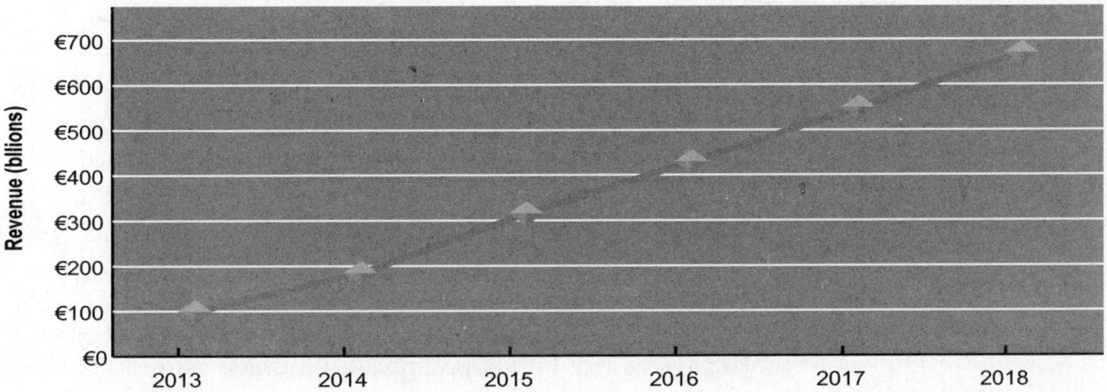

Retail e-commerce revenues grew 15–25 percent per year until the recession of 2008–2009, when they slowed measurably. In 2016, e-commerce revenues grew at an estimated 15 percent annually.

Sources: Based on data from eMarketer, "US Retail Ecommerce Sales, 2014–2020," 2016; eMarketer, "US Digital Travel Sales, 2014–2020," 2016; and eMarketer chart, "US Mobile Downloads and In-App Revenues, 2013–2016," 2016.

- Online consumer sales will grow to an estimated $669 billion in 2017, an increase of more than 15 percent over 2016 (including travel services and digital downloads), with 185 million people purchasing online and an additional 217 million shopping and gathering information but not purchasing (eMarketer, 2016a). The Internet influences more than $1.3 trillion in retail commerce that takes places in physical stores.
- The number of individuals of all ages online in the United States is expected to grow to 270 million in 2017, up from 147 million in 2004. In the world, more than 3.3 billion people are now connected to the Internet. Growth in the overall Internet population has spurred growth in e-commerce (Internet World Stats, 2016).
- Approximately 96 million households will have broadband access to the Internet in 2017, representing about 78 percent of all households.
- About 223 million Americans will access the Internet by using a smartphone. Mobile e-commerce has begun a rapid growth based on apps, ringtones, downloaded entertainment, and location-based services. Mobile e-commerce will account for about $170 billion in 2017, 25 percent of all e-commerce, and about 50 percent of all retail e-commerce. In a few years, mobile phones and tablets will be the most common Internet access device. Currently, more than 80 percent of all mobile phone users access the Internet by using their phones (eMarketer, 2016b).
- B2B e-commerce (use of the Internet for business-to-business commerce and collaboration among business partners) expanded to more than $7 trillion. Table 10.1 highlights these new e-commerce developments.

The New E-commerce: Social, Mobile, Local

One of the biggest changes is the extent to which e-commerce has become more social, mobile, and local. Online marketing once consisted largely of creating a corporate website, buying display ads on Yahoo, purchasing ad words on Google,

TABLE 10.1 THE GROWTH OF E-COMMERCE

BUSINESS TRANSFORMATION
E-commerce remains the fastest-growing form of commerce when compared to physical retail stores, services, and entertainment. Social, mobile, and local commerce have become the fastest-growing forms of e-commerce.
The breadth of e-commerce offerings grows, especially in the services economy of social networking, travel, entertainment, retail apparel, jewelry, appliances, and home furnishings.
The online demographics of shoppers broaden to match that of ordinary shoppers.
Pure e-commerce business models are refined further to achieve higher levels of profitability, whereas traditional retail brands, such as Walmart, Sears, JCPenney, L.L.Bean, and Macy's, use e-commerce to retain their dominant retail positions. Walmart, the world's largest retailer, has decided to get serious about e-commerce and take on Amazon with a more than $1 billion investment in its e-commerce efforts (see the chapter-ending case study).
Small businesses and entrepreneurs continue to flood the e-commerce marketplace, often riding on the infrastructures created by industry giants, such as Amazon, Apple, and Google, and increasingly taking advantage of cloud-based computing resources.
Mobile e-commerce has taken off in the United States with location-based services and entertainment downloads, including e-books, movies, music, and television shows. Mobile e-commerce will generate more than $170 billion in 2017.
TECHNOLOGY FOUNDATIONS
Wireless Internet connections (Wi-Fi, WiMax, and 4G smartphones) grow rapidly.
Powerful smartphones and tablet computers provide access to music, web surfing, and entertainment as well as voice communication. Podcasting and streaming take off as media for distribution of video, radio, and user-generated content.
Mobile devices expand to include wearable computers such as Apple Watch and Fitbit trackers.
The Internet broadband foundation becomes stronger in households and businesses as transmission prices fall.
Social networking apps and sites such as Facebook, Twitter, LinkedIn, Instagram, and others seek to become a major new platform for e-commerce, marketing, and advertising. Facebook has 1.65 billion users worldwide and 222 million in the United States (Facebook, 2016). One hundred ninety million Americans use social networks, about 70 percent of the Internet user population.
Internet-based models of computing, such as smartphone apps, cloud computing, software as a service (SaaS), and database software greatly reduce the cost of e-commerce websites.
NEW BUSINESS MODELS EMERGE
More than 70 percent of the Internet population has joined an online social network, created blogs, and shared photos and music. Together, these sites create an online audience as large as that of television that is attractive to marketers. In 2017, social networking will account for an estimated 28 percent of online time. Social sites have become the primary gateway to the Internet in news, music, and, increasingly, products.
The traditional advertising industry is disrupted as online advertising grows twice as fast as TV and print advertising; Google, Yahoo, and Facebook display nearly 1 trillion ads a year.
On-demand service e-commerce sites such as Uber and Airbnb extend the market creator business model to new areas of economy.

(Continued)

TABLE 10.1 THE GROWTH OF E-COMMERCE (Continued)

NEW BUSINESS MODELS EMERGE
Newspapers and other traditional media adopt online, interactive models but are losing advertising revenues to the online players despite gaining online readers. The *New York Times* adopts a paywall for its online edition and succeeds in capturing over 1 million subscribers, growing at 15 percent annually. Book publishing thrives because of the growth in e-books and the continuing appeal of traditional books.
Online entertainment business models offering television, movies, music, and games grow with cooperation among the major copyright owners in Hollywood and New York and with Internet distributors such as Apple, Amazon, Google, YouTube, and Facebook. Increasingly, the online distributors are moving into movie and TV production.

and sending e-mail messages. The workhorse of online marketing was the display ad. It still is, but it's increasingly being replaced by video ads, which are far more effective. Display ads from the very beginning of the Internet were based on television ads, where brand messages were flashed before millions of users who were not expected to respond immediately, ask questions, or make observations. If the ads did not work, the solution was often to repeat the ad. The primary measure of success was how many eyeballs (unique visitors) a website produced and how many impressions a marketing campaign generated. (An impression was one ad shown to one person.) Both of these measures were carryovers from the world of television, which measures marketing in terms of audience size and ad views.

From Eyeballs to Conversations: Conversational Commerce

After 2007, all this changed with the rapid growth of Facebook and other social sites, the explosive growth of smartphones beginning with Apple iPhone, and the growing interest in local marketing. What's different about the new world of social-mobile-local e-commerce are the dual and related concepts of conversations and engagement. In the popular literature, this is often referred to as conversational commerce. Marketing in this new period is based on firms engaging in multiple online conversations with their customers, potential customers, and even critics. Your brand is being talked about on the web and social media (that's the conversation part), and marketing your firm, building, and restoring your brands requires you to locate, identify, and participate in these conversations. Social marketing means all things social: listening, discussing, interacting, empathizing, and engaging. The emphasis in online marketing has shifted from a focus on eyeballs to a focus on participating in customer-oriented conversations. In this sense, social marketing is not simply a new ad channel but a collection of technology-based tools for communicating with shoppers. The leading social commerce platforms are Facebook, Instagram, and Pinterest.

In the past, firms could tightly control their brand messaging and lead consumers down a funnel of cues that ended in a purchase. That is not true of social marketing. Consumer purchase decisions are increasingly driven by the conversations, choices, tastes, and opinions of their social network. Social marketing is all about firms participating in and shaping this social process.

From the Desktop to the Smartphone

Traditional online marketing (browser-based, search, display ads, video ads, e-mail, and games) still constitutes the majority (63 percent) of all online marketing ($77 billion), but it's growing much more slowly than social-mobile-local marketing. The marketing dollars are following customers and shoppers from the PC to mobile devices.

Social, mobile, and local e-commerce are connected. As mobile devices become more powerful, they are more useful for accessing Facebook and other social sites. As mobile devices become more widely adopted, customers can use them to find local merchants, and merchants can use them to alert customers in their neighborhood of special offers.

Why E-commerce is Different

Why has e-commerce grown so rapidly? The answer lies in the unique nature of the Internet and the web. Simply put, the Internet and e-commerce technologies are much richer and more powerful than previous technology revolutions such as radio, television, and the telephone. Table 10.2 describes the unique features of the Internet and web as a commercial medium. Let's explore each of these unique features in more detail.

Ubiquity

In traditional commerce, a marketplace is a physical place, such as a retail store, that you visit to transact business. E-commerce is ubiquitous, meaning that it is available just about everywhere all the time. It makes it possible to shop from your desktop, at home, at work, or even from your car, using smartphones. The result is called a **marketspace**—a marketplace extended beyond traditional boundaries and removed from a temporal and geographic location.

From a consumer point of view, ubiquity reduces **transaction costs**—the costs of participating in a market. To transact business, it is no longer necessary for you to spend time or money traveling to a market, and much less mental effort is required to make a purchase.

Global Reach

E-commerce technology permits commercial transactions to cross cultural and national boundaries far more conveniently and cost effectively than is true in traditional commerce. As a result, the potential market size for e-commerce merchants is roughly equal to the size of the world's online population (estimated to be more than 3 billion).

In contrast, most traditional commerce is local or regional—it involves local merchants or national merchants with local outlets. Television, radio stations, and newspapers, for instance, are primarily local and regional institutions with limited, but powerful, national networks that can attract a national audience but not easily cross national boundaries to a global audience.

Universal Standards

One strikingly unusual feature of e-commerce technologies is that the technical standards of the Internet and, therefore, the technical standards for conducting

TABLE 10.2 EIGHT UNIQUE FEATURES OF E-COMMERCE TECHNOLOGY

E-COMMERCE TECHNOLOGY DIMENSION	BUSINESS SIGNIFICANCE
Ubiquity. Internet/web technology is available everywhere: at work, at home, and elsewhere by desktop and mobile devices. Mobile devices extend service to local areas and merchants.	The marketplace is extended beyond traditional boundaries and is removed from a temporal and geographic location. Marketspace is created; shopping can take place anytime, anywhere. Customer convenience is enhanced, and shopping costs are reduced.
Global Reach. The technology reaches across national boundaries, around the earth.	Commerce is enabled across cultural and national boundaries seamlessly and without modification. The marketspace includes, potentially, billions of consumers and millions of businesses worldwide.
Universal Standards. There is one set of technology standards, namely Internet standards.	With one set of technical standards across the globe, disparate computer systems can easily communicate with each other.
Richness. Video, audio, and text messages are possible.	Video, audio, and text marketing messages are integrated into a single marketing message and consumer experience.
Interactivity. The technology works through interaction with the user.	Consumers are engaged in a dialogue that dynamically adjusts the experience to the individual and makes the consumer a participant in the process of delivering goods to the market.
Information Density. The technology reduces information costs and raises quality.	Information processing, storage, and communication costs drop dramatically, whereas currency, accuracy, and timeliness improve greatly. Information becomes plentiful, cheap, and more accurate.
Personalization/Customization. The technology allows personalized messages to be delivered to individuals as well as to groups.	Personalization of marketing messages and customization of products and services are based on individual characteristics.
Social Technology. The technology supports content generation and social networking.	New Internet social and business models enable user content creation and distribution and support social networks.

e-commerce are universal standards. All nations around the world share them and enable any computer to link with any other computer regardless of the technology platform each is using. In contrast, most traditional commerce technologies differ from one nation to the next. For instance, television and radio standards differ around the world, as does cellular telephone technology.

The universal technical standards of the Internet and e-commerce greatly lower **market entry costs**—the cost merchants must pay simply to bring their goods to market. At the same time, for consumers, universal standards reduce **search costs**—the effort required to find suitable products.

Richness

Information **richness** refers to the complexity and content of a message. Traditional markets, national sales forces, and small retail stores have great richness; they can provide personal, face-to-face service, using aural and visual cues when making a sale. The richness of traditional markets makes them powerful selling or commercial environments. Prior to the development of the web, there was a trade-off between richness and reach; the larger the audience reached, the less rich the message. The web makes it possible to deliver rich messages with text, audio, and video simultaneously to large numbers of people.

Interactivity

Unlike any of the commercial technologies of the twentieth century, with the possible exception of the telephone, e-commerce technologies are interactive, meaning they allow for two-way communication between merchant and consumer and peer-to-peer communication among friends. Television, for instance, cannot ask viewers any questions or enter conversations with them, and it cannot request customer information to be entered on a form. In contrast, all these activities are possible on an e-commerce website or mobile app. Interactivity allows an online merchant to engage a consumer in ways similar to a face-to-face experience but on a massive, global scale.

Information Density

The Internet and the web vastly increase **information density**—the total amount and quality of information available to all market participants, consumers, and merchants alike. E-commerce technologies reduce information collection, storage, processing, and communication costs while greatly increasing the currency, accuracy, and timeliness of information.

Information density in e-commerce markets make prices and costs more transparent. **Price transparency** refers to the ease with which consumers can find out the variety of prices in a market; **cost transparency** refers to the ability of consumers to discover the actual costs merchants pay for products.

There are advantages for merchants as well. Online merchants can discover much more about consumers than in the past. This allows merchants to segment the market into groups that are willing to pay different prices and permits the merchants to engage in **price discrimination**—selling the same goods, or nearly the same goods, to different targeted groups at different prices. For instance, an online merchant can discover a consumer's avid interest in expensive, exotic vacations and then pitch high-end vacation plans to that consumer at a premium price, knowing this person is willing to pay extra for such a vacation. At the same time, the online merchant can pitch the same vacation plan at a lower price to a more price-sensitive consumer. Information density also helps merchants differentiate their products in terms of cost, brand, and quality.

Personalization/Customization

E-commerce technologies permit **personalization**. Merchants can target their marketing messages to specific individuals by adjusting the message to a person's clickstream behavior, name, interests, and past purchases. The technology also permits **customization**—changing the delivered product or service based on a user's preferences or prior behavior. Given the interactive nature of e-commerce technology, much information about the consumer can be gathered in the marketplace at the moment of purchase. With the increase in information density, a great deal of information about the consumer's past purchases and behavior can be stored and used by online merchants.

The result is a level of personalization and customization unthinkable with traditional commerce technologies. For instance, you may be able to shape what you see on television by selecting a channel, but you cannot change the content of the channel you have chosen. In contrast, online news outlets such as the *Wall Street Journal Online* allow you to select the type of news stories you want to see first and gives you the opportunity to be alerted when certain events happen.

Social Technology: User Content Generation and Social Networking

In contrast to previous technologies, the Internet and e-commerce technologies have evolved to be much more social by allowing users to create and share with their friends (and a larger worldwide community) content in the form of text, videos, music, or photos. By using these forms of communication, users can create new social networks and strengthen existing ones.

All previous mass media in modern history, including the printing press, use a broadcast model (one-to-many) in which content is created in a central location by experts (professional writers, editors, directors, and producers), and audiences are concentrated in huge numbers to consume a standardized product. The new Internet and e-commerce empower users to create and distribute content on a large scale and permit users to program their own content consumption. The Internet provides a unique many-to-many model of mass communications.

Key Concepts in E-commerce: Digital Markets and Digital Goods in a Global Marketplace

The location, timing, and revenue models of business are based in some part on the cost and distribution of information. The Internet has created a digital marketplace where millions of people all over the world can exchange massive amounts of information directly, instantly, and free. As a result, the Internet has changed the way companies conduct business and increased their global reach.

The Internet reduces information asymmetry. An **information asymmetry** exists when one party in a transaction has more information that is important for the transaction than the other party. That information helps determine their relative bargaining power. In digital markets, consumers and suppliers can see the prices being charged for goods, and in that sense, digital markets are said to be more transparent than traditional markets.

For example, before automobile retailing sites appeared on the web, there was significant information asymmetry between auto dealers and customers. Only the auto dealers knew the manufacturers' prices, and it was difficult for consumers to shop around for the best price. Auto dealers' profit margins depended on this asymmetry of information. Today's consumers have access to a legion of websites providing competitive pricing information, and three-fourths of U.S. auto buyers use the Internet to shop around for the best deal. Thus, the web has reduced the information asymmetry surrounding an auto purchase. The Internet has also helped businesses seeking to purchase from other businesses reduce information asymmetries and locate better prices and terms.

Digital markets are very flexible and efficient because they operate with reduced search and transaction costs, lower **menu costs** (merchants' costs of changing prices), greater price discrimination, and the ability to change prices dynamically based on market conditions. In **dynamic pricing**, the price of a product varies depending on the demand characteristics of the customer or the supply situation of the seller. For instance, online retailers from Amazon to Walmart change prices on many products based on time of day, demand for the product, and users' prior visits to their sites. Using big data analytics, some online firms can adjust prices at the individual level based on behavioral targeting parameters such as whether the consumer is a price haggler (who will receive a lower price offer) versus a person who accepts offered prices and does not search for lower prices. Prices can also vary by ZIP code, with higher prices set for poor sections of a community. Uber, along with other ride services, uses surge pricing to adjust prices of a ride based on demand (which always rises during storms and major conventions).

These new digital markets can either reduce or increase switching costs, depending on the nature of the product or service being sold, and they might cause some extra delay in gratification due to shipping times. Unlike a physical market, you can't immediately consume a product such as clothing purchased over the web (although immediate consumption is possible with digital music downloads and other digital products).

Digital markets provide many opportunities to sell directly to the consumer, bypassing intermediaries such as distributors or retail outlets. Eliminating intermediaries in the distribution channel can significantly lower purchase transaction costs. To pay for all the steps in a traditional distribution channel, a product may have to be priced as high as 135 percent of its original cost to manufacture.

Figure 10.2 illustrates how much savings result from eliminating each of these layers in the distribution process. By selling directly to consumers or reducing the number of intermediaries, companies can raise profits while charging

FIGURE 10.2 THE BENEFITS OF DISINTERMEDIATION TO THE CONSUMER

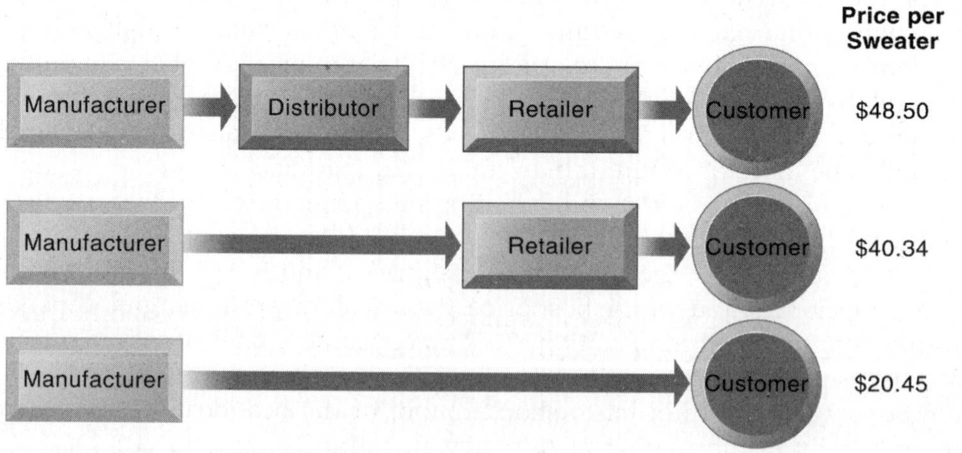

The typical distribution channel has several intermediary layers, each of which adds to the final cost of a product, such as a sweater. Removing layers lowers the final cost to the customer.

TABLE 10.3 DIGITAL MARKETS COMPARED WITH TRADITIONAL MARKETS

	DIGITAL MARKETS	TRADITIONAL MARKETS
Information asymmetry	Asymmetry reduced	Asymmetry high
Search costs	Low	High
Transaction costs	Low (sometimes virtually nothing)	High (time, travel)
Delayed gratification	High (or lower in the case of a digital good)	Lower: purchase now
Menu costs	Low	High
Dynamic pricing	Low cost, instant	High cost, delayed
Price discrimination	Low cost, instant	High cost, delayed
Market segmentation	Low cost, moderate precision	High cost, less precision
Switching costs	Higher/lower (depending on product characteristics)	High
Network effects	Strong	Weaker
Disintermediation	More possible/likely	Less possible/unlikely

lower prices. The removal of organizations or business process layers responsible for intermediary steps in a value chain is called **disintermediation**. E-commerce has also given rise to a completely new set of new intermediaries such as Amazon, eBay, PayPal, and Blue Nile. Therefore, disintermediation differs from one industry to another.

Disintermediation is affecting the market for services. Airlines and hotels operating their own reservation sites online earn more per ticket because they have eliminated travel agents as intermediaries. Table 10.3 summarizes the differences between digital markets and traditional markets.

Digital Goods

The Internet digital marketplace has greatly expanded sales of **digital goods**—goods that can be delivered over a digital network. Music tracks, video, Hollywood movies, software, newspapers, magazines, and books can all be expressed, stored, delivered, and sold as purely digital products. For the most part, digital goods are intellectual property, which is defined as "works of the mind." Intellectual property is protected from misappropriation by copyright, patent, trademark, and trade secret laws (see Chapter 4). Today, all these products are delivered as digital streams or downloads while their physical counterparts decline in sales.

In general, for digital goods, the marginal cost of producing another unit is about zero (it costs nothing to make a copy of a music file). However, the cost of producing the original first unit is relatively high—in fact, it is nearly the total cost of the product because there are few other costs of inventory and distribution. Costs of delivery over the Internet are very low, marketing costs often remain the same, and pricing can be highly variable. On the Internet, the merchant can change prices as often as desired because of low menu costs.

The impact of the Internet on the market for these kinds of digital goods is nothing short of revolutionary, and we see the results around us every day. Businesses dependent on physical products for sales—such as bookstores, music stores, book publishers, music labels, and film studios—face the possibility of declining sales and even destruction of their businesses. Newspapers and magazines subscriptions to hard copies are declining, while online readership and subscriptions are expanding.

Total record label industry revenues have fallen 50 percent from $14 billion in 1999 to about $6.9 billion in 2016, due almost entirely to the rapid decline in CD album sales and the growth of digital music services (both legal and illegal music piracy). On the plus side, the Apple iTunes Store has sold more than 35 billion songs for 99 cents each since opening in 2003, providing the industry with a digital distribution model that has restored some of the revenues lost to digital music channels. Since iTunes, illegal downloading has been cut in half, and legitimate online music sales (both downloads and streaming) are estimated to be approximately $4.5 billion in 2016. As cloud streaming services expand, illegal downloading will decline further. Digital music sales account for more than 70 percent of all music revenues. Yet the music labels make only about 32 cents from a single track download and only 0.5 cents for a streamed track (with the hope that sales of downloaded tracks or CDs will result). Although the record labels make revenue from ownership of the song (both words and music), the artists who perform the music make virtually nothing from streamed music.

Hollywood has not been similarly disrupted by digital distribution platforms, in part because it is more difficult to download high-quality, pirated copies of full-length movies and because of the availability of low-cost, high-quality legal movies. To avoid the fate of the music industry, Hollywood has struck lucrative distribution deals with Netflix, Google, Hulu, Amazon, and Apple, making it convenient to download and pay for high-quality movies and television series. These arrangements are not enough to compensate entirely for the loss in DVD sales, which fell 50 percent from 2006 to 2015, although this is changing rapidly as online distributors such as Netflix pay millions for high-quality Hollywood content. In 2017, for the first time, consumers will view more and pay more for web-based movie downloads, rentals, and streams than for DVDs or related physical products. As with television series, the demand for feature-length Hollywood movies appears to be expanding in part because of the growth of smartphones and tablets, making it easier to watch movies in more locations. In addition, the surprising resurgence of music videos, led by the VEVO website, is attracting millions of younger viewers on smartphones and tablets.

Online movies began a growth spurt in 2010 as broadband services spread throughout the country. In 2017, about 126 million Internet users are expected to view movies, about one-half of the adult Internet audience. Although this rapid growth will not continue forever, there is little doubt that the Internet is becoming a movie distribution and television channel that rivals cable television, and someday may replace cable television entirely. Table 10.4 describes digital goods and how they differ from traditional physical goods.

TABLE 10.4 HOW THE INTERNET CHANGES THE MARKETS FOR DIGITAL GOODS

	DIGITAL GOODS	TRADITIONAL GOODS
Marginal cost/unit	Zero	Greater than zero, high
Cost of production	High (most of the cost)	Variable
Copying cost	Approximately zero	Greater than zero, high
Distributed delivery cost	Low	High
Inventory cost	Low	High
Marketing cost	Variable	Variable
Pricing	More variable (bundling, random pricing games)	Fixed, based on unit costs

10-2 What are the principal e-commerce business and revenue models?

E-commerce has grown from a few advertisements on early web portals in 1995 to more than 12 percent of all retail sales in 2017 (an estimated $669 billion), surpassing the mail-order catalog business. E-commerce is a fascinating combination of business models and new information technologies. Let's start with a basic understanding of the types of e-commerce and then describe e-commerce business and revenue models.

Types of E-commerce

There are many ways to classify electronic commerce transactions—one is by looking at the nature of the participants. The three major electronic commerce categories are business-to-consumer (B2C) e-commerce, business-to-business (B2B) e-commerce, and consumer-to-consumer (C2C) e-commerce.

- **Business-to-consumer (B2C)** electronic commerce involves retailing products and services to individual shoppers. Amazon, Walmart, and iTunes are examples of B2C commerce. BarnesandNoble.com, which sells books, software, and music to individual consumers, is an example of B2C e-commerce.
- **Business-to-business (B2B)** electronic commerce involves sales of goods and services among businesses. Elemica's website for buying and selling chemicals and energy is an example of B2B e-commerce.
- **Consumer-to-consumer (C2C)** electronic commerce involves consumers selling directly to consumers. For example, eBay, the giant web auction site, enables people to sell their goods to other consumers by auctioning their merchandise off to the highest bidder or for a fixed price. eBay acts as a middleman by creating a digital platform for peer-to-peer commerce. Craigslist is the most widely used platform consumers use to buy from and sell directly to others.

Another way of classifying electronic commerce transactions is in terms of the platforms participants use in a transaction. Until recently, most e-commerce transactions took place using a desktop PC connected to the Internet over a wired network. Several wireless mobile alternatives have such as smartphones and tablet computers. The use of handheld wireless devices for purchasing goods and services from any location is termed **mobile commerce** or **m-commerce**. All three types of e-commerce transactions can take place using m-commerce technology, which we discuss in detail in Section 10.3.

E-commerce Business Models

Changes in the economics of information described earlier have created the conditions for entirely new business models to appear, while destroying older business models. Table 10.5 describes some of the most important Internet business models that have emerged. All, in one way or another, use the Internet (including apps on mobile devices) to add extra value to existing products and services or to provide the foundation for new products and services.

TABLE 10.5 INTERNET BUSINESS MODELS

CATEGORY	DESCRIPTION	EXAMPLES
E-tailer	Sells physical products directly to consumers or to individual businesses.	Amazon Blue Nile
Transaction broker	Saves users money and time by processing online sales transactions and generating a fee each time a transaction occurs.	ETrade.com Expedia
Market creator	Provides a digital environment where buyers and sellers can meet, search for products, display products, and establish prices for those products; can serve consumers or B2B e-commerce, generating revenue from transaction fees.	eBay Priceline.com Exostar Elemica
Content provider	Creates revenue by providing digital content, such as news, music, photos, or video, over the web. The customer may pay to access the content, or revenue may be generated by selling advertising space.	WSJ.com GettyImages.com iTunes.com Games.com
Community provider	Provides an online meeting place where people with similar interests can communicate and find useful information.	Facebook Google+ Twitter
Portal	Provides initial point of entry to the web along with specialized content and other services.	Yahoo Bing Google
Service provider	Provides applications such as photo sharing, video sharing, and user-generated content as services; provides other services such as online data storage and backup.	Google Apps Photobucket.com Dropbox

Portal

Portals are gateways to the web and are often defined as those sites that users set as their home page. Some definitions of a portal include search engines such as Google and Bing even if few make these sites their home page. Portals such as Yahoo, Facebook, MSN, and AOL offer powerful web search tools as well as an integrated package of content and services such as news, e-mail, instant messaging, maps, calendars, shopping, music downloads, video streaming, and more all in one place. The portal business model now provides a destination site where users start their web searching and linger to read news, find entertainment, meet other people, and, of course, be exposed to advertising, which provides the revenues to support the portal. Facebook is a very different kind of portal based on social networking. Portals generate revenue primarily by attracting very large audiences, charging advertisers for display ad placement (similar to traditional newspapers), collecting referral fees for steering customers to other sites, and charging for premium services. In 2017, portals (not including Google or Bing) will generate an estimated $37 billion in display ad revenues. Although there are hundreds of portal/search engine sites, the top four portals (Yahoo, Facebook, MSN, and AOL) gather more than 95 percent of the Internet portal traffic because of their superior brand recognition.

E-tailer

Online retail stores, often called **e-tailers**, come in all sizes, from giant Amazon with 2015 revenues of more than $107 billion, to tiny local stores that have websites. An e-tailer is similar to the typical bricks-and-mortar storefront, except that customers only need to connect to the Internet to check their inventory and place an order. Altogether, online retail (the sale of physical goods online) will generate about $457 billion in revenues in 2017. The value proposition of e-tailers is to provide convenient, low-cost shopping 24/7; large selections; and consumer choice. Some e-tailers, such as Walmart.com or Staples.com, referred to as bricks-and-clicks, are subsidiaries or divisions of existing physical stores and carry the same products. Others, however, operate only in the virtual world, without any ties to physical locations. Amazon, BlueNile.com, and Drugstore.com are examples of this type of e-tailer. Several other variations of e-tailers—such as online versions of direct-mail catalogs, online malls, and manufacturer-direct online sales—also exist.

Content Provider

Although e-commerce began as a retail product channel, it has increasingly become a global content channel. *Content* is defined broadly to include all forms of intellectual property. **Intellectual property** refers to tangible and intangible products of the mind for which the creator claims a property right. Content providers distribute information content—such as digital video, music, photos, text, and artwork—over the web. The value proposition of online content providers is that consumers can conveniently find a wide range of content online and purchase this content inexpensively to be played or viewed on multiple computer devices or smartphones.

Providers do not have to be the creators of the content (although sometimes they are, like Disney.com) and are more likely to be Internet-based distributors of content produced and created by others. For example, Apple sells music tracks at its iTunes Store, but it does not create or commission new music.

The phenomenal popularity of the iTunes Store, and Apple's Internet-connected devices such as the iPhone, iPod, and iPad, have enabled new forms of digital content delivery from podcasting to mobile streaming. **Podcasting** is a method of publishing audio or video broadcasts through the Internet, allowing subscribing users to download audio or video files onto their personal computers, smartphones, tablets, or portable music players. **Streaming** is a publishing method for music and video files that flows a continuous stream of content to a user's device without being stored locally on the device.

Estimates vary, but total online content will generate about around $24 billion in 2017, one of the fastest-growing e-commerce segments, growing at an estimated 18 percent annual rate.

Transaction Broker

Sites that process transactions for consumers normally handled in person, by phone, or by mail are transaction brokers. The largest industries using this model are financial services and travel services. The online transaction broker's primary value propositions are savings of money and time and providing an extraordinary inventory of financial products and travel packages in a single location. Online stock brokers and travel booking services charge fees that are considerably less than traditional versions of these services. Fidelity Financial Services and Expedia are the largest online financial and travel service firms based on a transaction broker model.

Market Creator

Market creators build a digital environment in which buyers and sellers can meet, display products, search for products, and establish prices. The value proposition of online market creators is that they provide a platform where sellers can easily display their wares and purchasers can buy directly from sellers. Online auction markets such as eBay and Priceline are good examples of the market creator business model. Another example is Amazon's Merchants platform (and similar programs at eBay), where merchants are allowed to set up stores on Amazon's website and sell goods at fixed prices to consumers. The so-called on-demand economy (mistakenly referred to often as the sharing economy), exemplified by Uber (described in the chapter-opening case) and Airbnb, is based on the idea of a market creator building a digital platform where supply meets demand; for instance, spare auto or room rental capacity finds individuals who want transportation or lodging. Crowdsource funding markets such as Kickstarter.com and Mosaic Inc. bring together private equity investors and entrepreneurs in a funding marketplace. Both are examples of B2B financial market places.

Service Provider

Whereas e-tailers sell products online, service providers offer services online. Photo sharing and online sites for data backup and storage all use a service provider business model. Software is no longer a physical product with a CD in a box but, increasingly, software as a service (SaaS) that you subscribe to online rather than purchase from a retailer, such as Office 365. Google has led the way in developing online software service applications such as Google Apps, Google Sites, Gmail, and online data storage services. Salesforce.com is a major provider of cloud-based software for customer management (see Chapter 5).

Community Provider (Social Networks)

Community providers are sites that create a digital online environment where people with similar interests can transact (buy and sell goods); share interests, photos, videos; communicate with like-minded people; receive interest-related information; and even play out fantasies by adopting online personalities called *avatars*. Social networking sites Facebook, Google+, Tumblr, Instagram, LinkedIn, and Twitter and hundreds of other smaller, niche sites such as Sportsvite all offer users community-building tools and services. Social networking sites have been the fastest-growing websites in recent years, often doubling their audience size in a year.

E-commerce Revenue Models

A firm's **revenue model** describes how the firm will earn revenue, generate profits, and produce a superior return on investment. Although many e-commerce revenue models have been developed, most companies rely on one, or some combination, of the following six revenue models: advertising, sales, subscription, free/freemium, transaction fee, and affiliate.

Advertising Revenue Model

In the **advertising revenue model**, a website generates revenue by attracting a large audience of visitors who can then be exposed to advertisements. The advertising model is the most widely used revenue model in e-commerce, and arguably, without advertising revenues, the web would be a vastly different experience from what it is now because people would be asked to pay for access to content. Content on the web—everything from news to videos and opinions—is free to visitors because advertisers pay the production and distribution costs in return for the right to expose visitors to ads. Companies will spend an estimated $77.3 billion on online advertising in 2017 (in the form of a paid message on a website, paid search listing, video, app, game, or other online medium, such as instant messaging). About $53 billion of this will be for mobile ads. Mobile ads will account for 68 percent of all digital advertising. In the past five years, advertisers have increased online spending and cut outlays on traditional channels such as radio and newspapers. In 2017, online advertising will grow at 15 percent and constitute about 38 percent of all advertising in the United States (eMarketer, 2016d).

Websites with the largest viewership or that attract a highly specialized, differentiated viewership and are able to retain user attention (stickiness) can charge higher advertising rates. Yahoo, for instance, derives nearly all its revenue from display ads (banner ads), video ads, and, to less extent, search engine text ads. Ninety-five percent of Google's revenue derives from advertising, including selling keywords (AdWord), selling ad spaces (AdSense), and selling display ad spaces to advertisers (DoubleClick). Facebook displayed one-third of the trillion display ads shown on all sites in 2016. Facebook's users spend an average of over 6 hours a week on the site, far longer than any of the other portal sites. In contrast, Americans spend an average of five hours watching television each day (eMarketer, 2016e).

Sales Revenue Model

In the **sales revenue model**, companies derive revenue by selling goods, information, or services to customers. Companies such as Amazon (which sells books, music, and other products), LLBean.com, and Gap.com all have sales revenue models. Content providers make money by charging for downloads of entire files such as music tracks (iTunes Store) or books or for downloading music and/or video streams (Hulu.com TV shows). Apple has pioneered and strengthened the acceptance of micropayments. **Micropayment systems** provide content providers with a cost-effective method for processing high volumes of very small monetary transactions (anywhere from 25 cents to $5.00 per transaction). The largest micropayment system on the web is Apple's iTunes Store, which has more than 800 million customers worldwide who purchase individual music tracks for 99 cents and feature length movies for various prices. A Learning Track is available with more detail on micropayment and other e-commerce payment systems, including Bitcoin.

Subscription Revenue Model

In the **subscription revenue model**, a website offering content or services charges a subscription fee for access to some or all of its offerings on an ongoing basis. Content providers often use this revenue model. For instance, the online version of *Consumer Reports* provides access to premium content, such as detailed ratings, reviews, and recommendations, only to subscribers, who have a choice of paying a $7.99 to 12.99 monthly subscription fee or a $30.00 annual fee. Netflix is one of the most successful subscriber sites with more that 75 million customers worldwide in 2016. The *New York Times* had about 1.3 million online paid subscribers, and the *Wall Street Journal* about 1 million in 2016. To be successful, the subscription model requires the content to be perceived as differentiated, having high added value, and not readily available elsewhere or easily replicated. Companies successfully offering content or services online on a subscription basis include Match.com and eHarmony (dating services), Ancestry.com and Genealogy.com (genealogy research), and Microsoft Xbox Live.

Free/Freemium Revenue Model

In the **free/freemium revenue model**, firms offer basic services or content for free and charge a premium for advanced or special features. For example, Google offers free applications but charges for premium services. Pandora, the subscription radio service, offers a free service with limited play time and advertising and a premium service with unlimited play. Spotify music service also uses a freemium business model. The idea is to attract very large audiences with free services and then convert some of this audience to pay a subscription for premium services. One problem with this model is converting people from being free loaders into paying customers. "Free" can be a powerful model for losing money. None of the freemium music streaming sites have earned a profit to date. Nevertheless, they are finding that free service with ad revenue is more profitable than the paid subscriber part of their business.

Transaction Fee Revenue Model

In the **transaction fee revenue model**, a company receives a fee for enabling or executing a transaction. For example, eBay provides an online auction marketplace and receives a small transaction fee from a seller if the seller is successful in selling an item. E*Trade, an online stockbroker, receives transaction fees each time it executes a stock transaction on behalf of a customer. The transaction revenue model enjoys wide acceptance in part because the true cost of using the platform is not immediately apparent to the user.

Affiliate Revenue Model

In the **affiliate revenue model**, websites (called *affiliate websites*) send visitors to other websites in return for a referral fee or percentage of the revenue from any resulting sales. Referral fees are also referred to as lead generation fees. For example, MyPoints makes money by connecting companies to potential customers by offering special deals to its members. When members take advantage of an offer and make a purchase, they earn points they can redeem for free products and services, and MyPoints receives a referral fee. Community feedback sites such as Epinions and Yelp receive much of their revenue from steering potential customers to websites where they make a purchase. Amazon uses affiliates that steer business to the Amazon website by placing the Amazon logo on their blogs. Personal blogs often contain display ads as part of affiliate programs. Some bloggers are paid directly by manufacturers, or receive free products, for speaking highly of products and providing links to sales channels.

10-3 How has e-commerce transformed marketing?

Although e-commerce and the Internet have changed entire industries and enabled new business models, no industry has been more affected than marketing and marketing communications.

The Internet provides marketers with new ways of identifying and communicating with millions of potential customers at costs far lower than traditional media, including search engine marketing, data mining, recommender systems, and targeted e-mail. The Internet enables **long tail marketing**. Before the Internet, reaching a large audience was very expensive, and marketers had to focus on attracting the largest number of consumers with popular hit products, whether music, Hollywood movies, books, or cars. In contrast, the Internet allows marketers to find potential customers inexpensively for products where demand is very low. For instance, the Internet makes it possible to sell independent music profitably to very small audiences. There's always some demand for almost any product. Put a string of such long tail sales together and you have a profitable business.

The Internet also provides new ways—often instantaneous and spontaneous—to gather information from customers, adjust product offerings, and increase

TABLE 10.6 ONLINE MARKETING AND ADVERTISING FORMATS (BILLIONS)

MARKETING FORMAT	2015 REVENUE	DESCRIPTION
Search engine	$30	Text ads targeted at precisely what the customer is looking for at the moment of shopping and purchasing. Sales oriented.
Display ads	$33	Banner ads (pop-ups and leave-behinds) with interactive features; increasingly behaviorally targeted to individual web activity. Brand development and sales. Includes social media and blog display ads.
Video	$9.8	Fastest-growing format, engaging and entertaining; behaviorally targeted, interactive. Branding and sales.
Classified	$3.1	Job, real estate, and services ads; interactive, rich media, and personalized to user searches. Sales and branding.
Rich media	$7.6	Animations, games, and puzzles. Interactive, targeted, and entertaining. Branding orientation.
Lead generation	$2.1	Marketing firms that gather sales and marketing leads online and then sell them to online marketers for a variety of campaign types. Sales or branding orientation.
Sponsorships	$1.8	Online games, puzzles, contests, and coupon sites sponsored by firms to promote products. Sales orientation.
E-mail	$.3	Effective, targeted marketing tool with interactive and rich media potential. Sales oriented.

customer value. Table 10.6 describes the leading marketing and advertising formats used in e-commerce.

Behavioral Targeting

Many e-commerce marketing firms use **behavioral targeting** techniques to increase the effectiveness of banners, rich media, and video ads. Behavioral targeting refers to tracking the clickstreams (history of clicking behavior) of individuals on thousands of websites to understand their interests and intentions and expose them to advertisements that are uniquely suited to their online behavior. Marketers and most researchers believe this more precise understanding of the customer leads to more efficient marketing (the firm pays for ads only to those shoppers who are most interested in their products) and larger sales and revenues. Unfortunately, behavioral targeting of millions of web users also leads to the invasion of personal privacy without user consent. When consumers lose trust in their web experience, they tend not to purchase anything. Backlash is growing against the aggressive uses of personal information as consumers seek out safer havens for purchasing and messaging. Snapchat offers disappearing messages, and even Facebook has retreated by making its default for new posts "for friends only."

Popular websites have hundreds of beacon programs on their home pages, which collect data about visitors' behavior and report that behavior to their databases. There the information is often sold to data brokers, firms that collect billions of data elements on every U.S. consumer and household, frequently combining online with offline purchase information. The data brokers in turn sell this information to advertisers who want to place ads on web pages. A recent Federal Trade Commission report about nine data brokers found that one data broker's database had information on 1.4 billion consumer transactions and more than 700 billion aggregated data elements. Another data broker had 3,000 data measures for nearly every consumer in the United States (FTC, 2014).

Behavioral targeting takes place at two levels: at individual websites or from within apps and on various advertising networks that track users across thousands of websites. All websites collect data on visitor browser activity and store it in a database. They have tools to record the site that users visited prior to coming to the website, where these users go when they leave that site, the type of operating system they use, browser information, and even some location data. They also record the specific pages visited on the particular site, the time spent on each page of the site, the types of pages visited, and what the visitors purchased (see Figure 10.3). Firms analyze this information about customer interests and behavior to develop precise profiles of existing and potential customers. In addition, most major websites have hundreds of tracking programs on their home pages, which track your clickstream behavior across the web by following you from site to site and re-target ads to you by showing you the same

FIGURE 10.3 WEBSITE VISITOR TRACKING

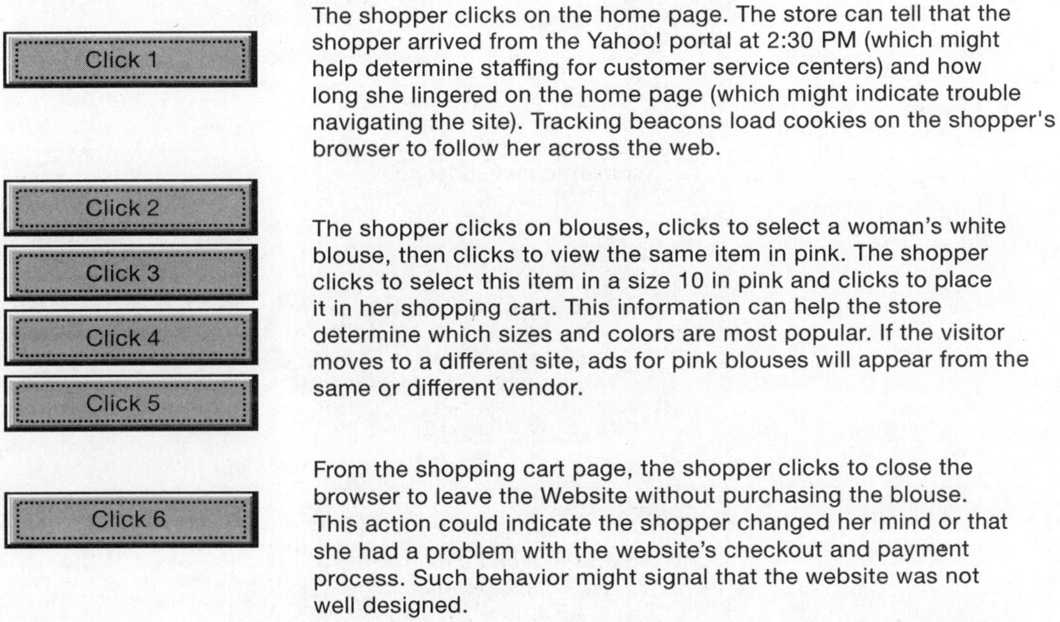

E-commerce websites and advertising platforms like Google's DoubleClick have tools to track a shopper's every step through an online store and then across the web as shoppers move from site to site. Close examination of customer behavior at a website selling women's clothing shows what the store might learn at each step and what actions it could take to increase sales.

ads on different sites. The leading online advertising networks are Google's DoubleClick, Yahoo's RightMedia, and AOL's Ad Network. Ad networks represent publishers who have space to sell and advertisers who want to market online. The lubricant of this trade is information about millions of web shoppers, which helps advertisers target their ads to precisely the groups and individuals they desire.

This information enables firms to understand how well their website is working, create unique personalized web pages that display content or ads for products or services of special interest to each user, improve the customer's experience, and create additional value through a better understanding of the shopper (see Figure 10.4). By using personalization technology to modify the web pages presented to each customer, marketers achieve some of the benefits of using individual salespeople at dramatically lower costs. For instance, General Motors will show a Chevrolet banner ad to women emphasizing safety and utility, whereas men will receive ads emphasizing power and ruggedness.

It's a short step from ad networks to programmatic ad buying. Ad networks create real-time bidding platforms (RTB) where marketers bid in an automated environment for highly targeted slots available from web publishers. Here, ad platforms can predict how many targeted individuals will view the ads, and ad buyers can estimate how much this exposure is worth to them.

FIGURE 10.4 WEBSITE PERSONALIZATION

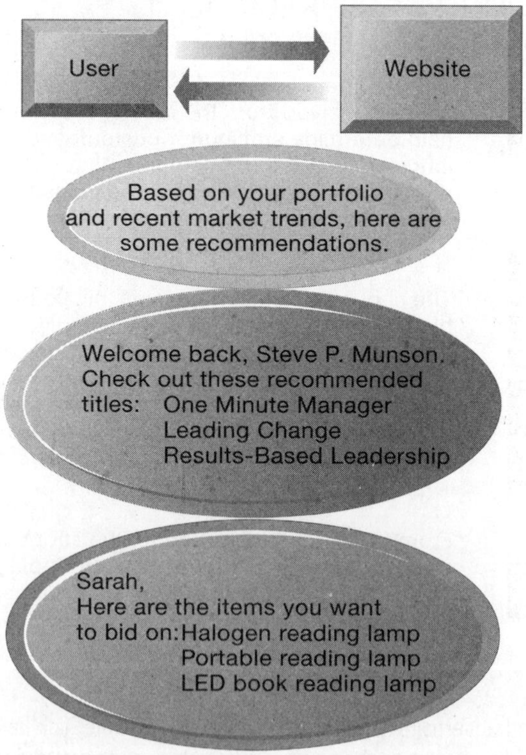

Firms can create unique personalized web pages that display content or ads for products or services of special interest to individual users, improving the customer experience and creating additional value.

What if you are a large national advertising company with many clients trying to reach millions of consumers? What if you were a large global manufacturer trying to reach potential consumers for your products? With millions of websites, working with each one would be impractical. Advertising networks solve this problem by creating a network of several thousand of the most popular websites millions of people visit, tracking the behavior of these users across the entire network, building profiles of each user, and then selling these profiles to advertisers in a real-time bidding environment. Popular websites download dozens of web tracking cookies, bugs, and beacons, which report user online behavior to remote servers without the users' knowledge. Looking for young, single consumers with college degrees, living in the Northeast, in the 18- to 34-age range who are interested in purchasing a European car? Not a problem. Advertising networks can identify and deliver thousands of people who fit this profile and expose them to ads for European cars as they move from one website to another. Estimates vary, but behaviorally targeted ads are generally 10 times more likely to produce a consumer response than a randomly chosen banner or video ad (see Figure 10.5). So-called advertising exchanges use this same technology to auction access to people with very specific profiles to advertisers in a few milliseconds. In 2016, about 50 percent of online display ads are targeted ads developed by programmatic ad buys, and the rest depend on the context of the pages shoppers visit—the estimated demographics of visitors, or so-called blast-and-scatter advertising—which is placed randomly on any available page with minimal targeting, such as time of day or season.

FIGURE 10.5 HOW AN ADVERTISING NETWORK SUCH AS DOUBLECLICK WORKS

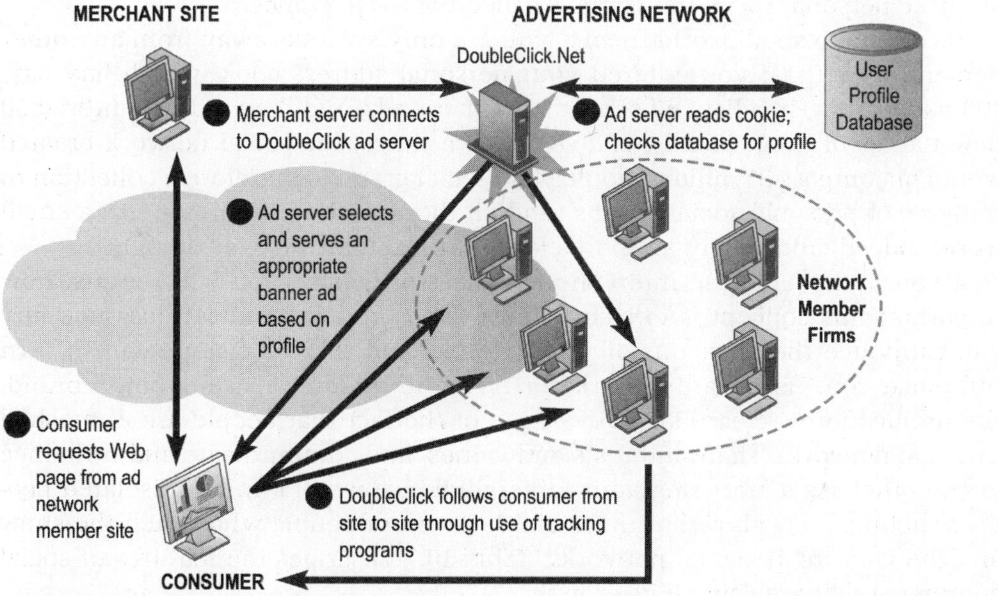

Advertising networks and their use of tracking programs have become controversial among privacy advocates because of their ability to track individual consumers across the Internet.

It's another short step to **native advertising**. Native advertising involves placing ads in social network newsfeeds or within traditional editorial content, such as a newspaper article. This is also referred to as organic advertising, where content and advertising are in very close proximity or integrated together.

Two-thirds (68 percent) of Internet users disapprove of search engines and websites tracking their online behavior to aim targeted ads at them. Twenty-eight percent of those surveyed approve of behavioral targeting because they believe it produces more relevant ads and information. A majority of Americans want a Do Not Track option in browsers that will stop websites from collecting information about their online behavior. More than 50 percent are very concerned about the wealth of personal data online; 86 percent have taken steps to mask their online behavior; 25 percent of web users use ad-blocking software. Next to hackers, Americans try to avoid advertisers pursuing them while online, and 64 percent block cookies to make tracking more difficult (Rainie and Duggan, 2016).

Social E-Commerce and Social Network Marketing

Social e-commerce is commerce based on the idea of the digital **social graph**, a mapping of all significant online social relationships. The social graph is synonymous with the idea of a social network used to describe offline relationships. You can map your own social graph (network) by drawing lines from yourself to the 10 closest people you know. If they know one another, draw lines between these people. If you are ambitious, ask these 10 friends to list and draw in the names of the 10 people closest to them. What emerges from this exercise is a preliminary map of your social network. Now imagine if everyone on the Internet did the same and posted the results to a very large database with a website. Ultimately, you would end up with Facebook or a site like it. The collection of all these personal social networks is called the *social graph*.

According to small world theory, you are only six links away from any other person on earth. If you entered your personal address book, which has, say, 100 names in it, in a list and sent it to your friends, and they in turn entered 50 new names of their friends, and so on, five times, the social network created would encompass 31 billion people! The social graph is therefore a collection of millions of personal social graphs (and all the people in them). So, it's a small world indeed, and we are all more closely linked than we ever thought.

If you understand the interconnectedness of people, you will see just how important this concept is to e-commerce: The products and services you buy will influence the decisions of your friends, and their decisions will in turn influence you. If you are a marketer trying to build and strengthen a brand, the implication is clear: Take advantage of the fact that people are enmeshed in social networks, share interests and values, and communicate and influence one another. As a marketer, your target audience is not a million isolated people watching a TV show but the social network of people who watch the show and the viewers' personal networks. Table 10.7 describes the features of social commerce that are driving its growth.

In 2017, one of the fastest-growing media for branding and marketing is social media. Companies will spend an estimated $16.5 billion in 2017 using

TABLE 10.7 FEATURES OF SOCIAL COMMERCE

SOCIAL COMMERCE FEATURE	DESCRIPTION
Newsfeed	A stream of notifications from friends and advertisers that social users find on their home pages.
Timelines	A stream of photos and events in the past that create a personal history for users, one that can be shared with friends.
Social sign-on	Websites allow users to sign into their sites through their social network pages on Facebook or another social site. This allows websites to receive valuable social profile information from Facebook and use it in their own marketing efforts.
Collaborative shopping	An environment where consumers can share their shopping experiences with one another by viewing products, chatting, or texting. Friends can chat online about brands, products, and services.
Network notification	An environment where consumers can share their approval (or disapproval) of products, services, or content or share their geolocation, perhaps a restaurant or club, with friends. Facebook's ubiquitous Like button is an example, as are Twitter's tweets and followers.
Social search (recommendations)	An environment where consumers can ask their friends for advice on purchases of products, services, and content. Although Google can help you find things, social search can help you evaluate the quality of things by listening to the evaluations of your friends or their friends. For instance, Amazon's social recommender system can use your Facebook social profile to recommend products.

social networks such as Facebook to reach millions of consumers who spend hours a day on the Facebook site. Facebook accounts for 74 percent of all social marketing in the United States. Expenditures for social media marketing are much smaller than for television, magazines, and even newspapers, but this will change in the future. Social networks in the offline world are collections of people who voluntarily communicate with one another over an extended period of time. Online social networks, such as Facebook, LinkedIn, Twitter, Tumblr, and Google+, along with other sites with social components, are websites that enable users to communicate with one another, form group and individual relationships, and share interests, values, and ideas. Individuals establish online profiles with text and photos, creating an online profile of how they want others to see them, and then invite their friends to link to their profile. The network grows by word of mouth and through e-mail links. Facebook, with 258 million U.S. monthly visitors, receives most of the public attention given to social networking, but the other top four social sites are also growing, though at slower rates than in the past. Facebook user growth has slowed in the United States. LinkedIn growth slowed in 2015 to 40 percent, and it had 119 million visitors a month in 2016. Twitter grew to reach 118 million active users, with stronger offshore growth than in the United States. Pinterest hit the top 50 websites with 63 million. According to ComScore, about 28 percent of the total time spent online in the United States was spent on social network sites, and it is the most common online activity (ComScore, 2016). The fastest-growing smartphone applications are social network apps; nearly half of smartphone users visit social sites daily. More than 60 percent of all visits to Facebook in 2016 came from smartphones.

At **social shopping** sites such as Pinterest and Kaboodle, you can swap shopping ideas with friends. Facebook offers the Like button and Google the +1 button to let your friends know you admire a product, service, or content and, in some cases, purchase something online. Facebook processes around 4.5 billion Likes a day. Online communities are also ideal venues to employ viral marketing techniques. Online viral marketing is like traditional word-of-mouth marketing except that the word can spread across an online community at the speed of light and go much further geographically than a small network of friends.

The Wisdom of Crowds

Creating sites where thousands, even millions, of people can interact offers business firms new ways to market and advertise and to discover who likes (or hates) their products. In a phenomenon called the **wisdom of crowds**, some argue that large numbers of people can make better decisions about a wide range of topics or products than a single person or even a small committee of experts.

Obviously, this is not always the case, but it can happen in interesting ways. In marketing, the wisdom of crowds concept suggests that firms should consult with thousands of their customers first as a way of establishing a relationship with them and, second, to understand better how their products and services are used and appreciated (or rejected). Actively soliciting the comments of your customers builds trust and sends the message to your customers that you care what they are thinking and that you need their advice.

Beyond merely soliciting advice, firms can be actively helped in solving some business problems by using **crowdsourcing**. For instance, BMW launched a crowdsourcing project to enlist the aid of customers in designing an urban vehicle for 2025. Kickstarter.com is arguably one of the most famous e-commerce crowdfunding sites where visitors invest in start-up companies. Other examples include Caterpillar working with customers to design better machinery, IKEA for designing furniture, and Pepsico using Super Bowl viewers to build an online video.

Marketing through social media is still in its early stages, and companies are experimenting in hopes of finding a winning formula. Social interactions and customer sentiment are not always easy to manage, presenting new challenges for companies eager to protect their brands.

10-4 How has e-commerce affected business-to-business transactions?

The trade between business firms (business-to-business commerce, or B2B) represents a huge marketplace. The total amount of B2B trade in the United States in 2015 was estimated to be about $14.6 trillion, with B2B e-commerce

INTERACTIVE SESSION: TECHNOLOGY

Zomato Scripting Success With E-Com

Founded in the year 2008 as FoodieBay by Deepinder Goyal (who is the CEO of the firm at present) and Pankaj Chaddah, Zomato was rechristened to its current name in the year 2010. An online restaurant search and discovery service provider, Zomato has a major presence in 23 countries. Its core features include provision of information and reviews of restaurants through its portal, scanned menus, photos, and geocoded coordinates for restaurants. It also allows the users to create their own network of foodies for personalized recommendations. The firm has been fortunate enough to receive substantial funding from investors with Info Edge India being a prominent one. At the same time, it has been able to spread its wings globally through some major acquisitions.

In India, food oriented online commerce services have never received substantial market response. And Zomato, which is one of the biggest online food giant operating in India, too took a dip when its net loss amounted to ₹590 crore in the 2015–16 fiscal. However, it is worth mentioning that despite the losses, its position was far better than its competitors, and Zomato was able to quickly revive from the losses as seen from the following numbers: Zomato saw a surge in the number of orders per day (2 million in 2017 as compared to 0.5 million in 2016). The firm's CEO, Deepinder Goyal, believes that constant effort towards improving its product with less room for error is the key to growth maintenance of the food giant. This holistic experience of restaurant discovery and dining provides them with an edge in competition.

Zomato's business model is worth an insight because that enables it to survive any crisis in the food industry, or the Indian economy for that matter. A core feature of Zomato's business model is restaurant advertising which accounts for approximately 75 percent of its revenue. While other competitors cave-in to business owners from a variety of segments, Zomato is focused on restaurateurs specifically based in the country of operation. For these business owners, Zomato acts as highly targeted advertising platform allowing the customers to effectively interact through its portal with the owners to build their dining options. Zomato has an extensive database of 1.4 million restaurants across 23 different countries, and it allows the customers to read menus, make table bookings, and order food for delivery by accessing this database through its online portal. Although, there are other players offering similar services such as OpenTable, Just Eat, and Deliveroo who have been doing this for years, Zomato stands apart because of its low overheads and a forward-thinking customer acquisition model. Goyal adds that his customer acquisition costs are considerably lower than the competitors who spend up to $15 per customer; in comparison, Zomato spends an average of just $0.04 per customer. After a customer places his first online order, it adds to the profitability of the firm as at this moment Zomato breaks even on its costs with the customer. Additionally, Zomato has a large registered user base (19 million registered users till March 2016), so it charges relatively high for a banner space on its mobile application.

The company promises fresh data to its customers. The data is refreshed every three months; hence, it remains relevant and updated. For this purpose, Zomato has maintained its own team of foot soldiers who go to each restaurant and maintain their data. This feet-on-street model sure differentiates the firm from the rest, and although the process is too intensive, the management believes this to be its strength. The collection of first-hand information from cafes, bars, and restaurants allows the presence of rich content on their website, and this is what (real-time refreshed data) attracts the customers back to Zomato. Another feature added on its portal is the ability of the users to review and give their opinions about a food space that they recently visited. The users are also encouraged to build and share the stories of their food experiences which make the site more social and helps to gain popularity.

A number of acquisitions made by the firm have allowed it an unprecedented diversification. For example, acquisition of food delivery start-up, Runnr, in 2017 has let it diversify in food delivery services, an area Zomato had overlooked in the past. With this,

Zomato has also launched a new service called Zomato Valet which focuses on food delivery from high-value restaurants who don't deliver on their own. The main motive is to seek bulk orders for food delivery, such as, on some special occasion when the average order value is expected to be high. The delivery for the same would be fulfilled through a hybrid delivery model implying that parent company alone where the order has been placed would not deliver the complete order. As in the case of Zomato, almost 93 percent of Zomato's order fulfilment occurs through the restaurants themselves where the orders have been placed, while the remaining 7 percent is fulfilled by third-party logistics firms that have been roped in. The firm made a major acquisition for $52 million in an all cash-deal to acquire Urbanspoon and thus made an entry into the biggest market of all, the United States of America. Urbanspoon has a strong presence on mobile applications in the US, Australia, Canada, New Zealand, Ireland, and UK, which allows Zomato to make foray into these markets as well. The firm also tied up with Ola for the year 2017 to let their customers use either firm's application to order their offering or to make payments. For example, Zomato app users can book Ola rides through the other's app, while users can pay for Zomato online orders using Ola Money. A Zomato micro-app has also been launched for Ola Play which provides many features of Zomato to Ola Play customers. A similar tie-up of the firm with Uber lasted for a year till 2016. Lately, the two have become rivals, following the launch of Uber Eats, an online food ordering company, in India.

In 2015, Zomato also acquired MapleGraph (which had built MaplePOS), a cloud-based point-of-sale (POS) system for restaurants. This has been renamed to Zomato Base, and it is an Android-based POS system which is customizable. With this acquisition, inventory management at the firm has been automated, and it also allows payment through debit and credit cards via an in-built payment solution. Besides this, Zomato Base also includes features for menu management, recipe management, CRM module, data analytics, printing of electronic receipts, etc. What really differentiates Zomato is the use of technology in not just building customer base but also in fostering relationships with restaurant owners. The food-tech company leverages technology to business owners to facilitate their services and aid in their growth. It is also creating a marketplace for these restaurateurs to purchase products such as cutlery or restaurant related technological solutions, and also aids in licensing and choice of vendors. This aims to provide a one-stop platform for complete operation of a restaurant. Zomato is planning a massive rollout of this feature and aiming to eventually become an integrated platform for interaction between business owners and customers.

Another product which is being offered by the firm is that of online table reservation and management under the name Zomato Book. The response towards the product is extremely variable depending on the country of operation as culture influences user behavior. For example, in markets such as London and Dubai where users are accustomed to advanced table reservation, the product is a success. While in India, efforts are being made by the company to promote the feature and gain customer attention. Another feather in the Zomato's cap is the 'Name and Shame' feature. When Zomato finds a restaurant guilty of obtaining reviews unethically, it displays a yellow badge against that restaurant (which stays on the portal for 30 days); this badge serves as a warning to consumers before they browse through the review. Although this has fetched mixed response from both consumers and owners, the firm plans to continue with this feature.

Zomato Treats, the latest concept launched in June 2017, treats subscribed users with free desserts. Users who have been loyal to the firm are invited for a low-fee Zomato Treats membership; each time they place an order with the partnering restaurant, they receive a complimentary dessert for free. The firm has seen increased repeat usage that is a 25 percent increase in order frequency from the users who have already received the free dessert through this program. The company is working on increasing revenue profitability and reduction in inefficiency. Even in its international operations, Zomato is focusing on a few key markets and slowly expanding to reduce cash burn. And the company is a firm believer in the use of technology to sustain growth and reap profits.

Sources: As accessed on 31 December 2015 at 5pm IST—http://trak.in, please read: Zomato-Maple POS Acquisition, Zomato Base; http://tech.economictimes.indiatimes.com, please read: Zomato Base: Marketplace Restaurant Owners; https://m.yourstory.com, please read: Zomato Acquires Maple Graph, Launches Zomato Base; https://www.idealsvdr.com, please read: Indian Unicorm: Zomato; https://m.yourstory.com, please read: Zomato Yelp!; http://economictimes.indiatimes.com, please read: How Zomato Managed to Survive the Carnage in The Food Tech Sector; http://www.thehindubusinessline.com, please read: Doing Food Delivery Aline is Not Sustainable: Zomato CEO.

CASE STUDY QUESTIONS

1. Give detailed insight into the core feature of Zomato's business model which is restaurant advertising.
2. How does data add to Zomato's competitive advantage? Discuss the role of feet-on-street model in the same.
3. How have acquisitions facilitated in flourishing Zomato's online ordering business?
4. Discuss with examples some of the key features of Zomato's e-commerce services. How do they differentiate the firm from its competitors?

(online B2B) contributing about $6.2 trillion of that amount (U.S. Bureau of the Census, 2015; authors' estimates). By 2019, B2B e-commerce is expected to grow to about $8.6 trillion in the United States. The process of conducting trade among business firms is complex and requires significant human intervention; therefore, it consumes significant resources. Some firms estimate that each corporate purchase order for support products costs them, on average, at least $100 in administrative overhead. Administrative overhead includes processing paper, approving purchase decisions, spending time using the telephone and fax machines to search for products and arrange for purchases, arranging for shipping, and receiving the goods. Across the economy, this adds up to trillions of dollars annually spent for procurement processes that could be automated. If even just a portion of inter-firm trade were automated, and parts of the entire procurement process were assisted by the Internet, literally trillions of dollars might be released for more productive uses, consumer prices potentially would fall, productivity would increase, and the economic wealth of the nation would expand. This is the promise of B2B e-commerce. The challenge of B2B e-commerce is changing existing patterns and systems of procurement and designing and implementing new Internet-based B2B solutions.

Electronic Data Interchange (EDI)

B2B e-commerce refers to the commercial transactions that occur among business firms. Increasingly, these transactions are flowing through a variety of Internet-enabled mechanisms. About 80 percent of online B2B e-commerce is still based on proprietary systems for **Electronic Data Interchange (EDI)**. EDI enables the computer-to-computer exchange between two organizations of standard transactions such as invoices, bills of lading, shipment schedules, or purchase orders. Transactions are automatically transmitted from one information system to another through a network, eliminating the printing and handling of paper at one end and the inputting of data at the other. Each major industry in the United States and much of the rest of the world has EDI standards that define the structure and information fields of electronic documents for that industry.

EDI originally automated the exchange of documents such as purchase orders, invoices, and shipping notices. Although many companies still use EDI for document automation, firms engaged in just-in-time inventory replenishment and continuous production use EDI as a system for continuous replenishment. Suppliers have online access to selected parts of the purchasing firm's

FIGURE 10.6 ELECTRONIC DATA INTERCHANGE (EDI)

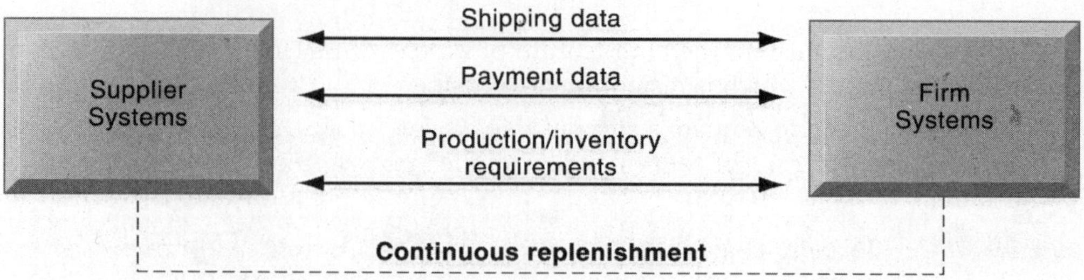

Companies use EDI to automate transactions for B2B e-commerce and continuous inventory replenishment. Suppliers can automatically send data about shipments to purchasing firms. The purchasing firms can use EDI to provide production and inventory requirements and payment data to suppliers.

production and delivery schedules and automatically ship materials and goods to meet prespecified targets without intervention by firm purchasing agents (see Figure 10.6).

Although many organizations still use private networks for EDI, they are increasingly web-enabled because Internet technology provides a much more flexible and low-cost platform for linking to other firms. Businesses can extend digital technology to a wider range of activities and broaden their circle of trading partners.

Procurement, for example, involves not only purchasing goods and materials but also sourcing, negotiating with suppliers, paying for goods, and making delivery arrangements. Businesses can now use the Internet to locate the lowest-cost supplier, search online catalogs of supplier products, negotiate with suppliers, place orders, make payments, and arrange transportation. They are not limited to partners linked by traditional EDI networks.

New Ways of B2B Buying and Selling

The Internet and web technology enable businesses to create electronic storefronts for selling to other businesses using the same techniques as used for B2C commerce. Alternatively, businesses can use Internet technology to create extranets or electronic marketplaces for linking to other businesses for purchase and sale transactions.

Private industrial networks typically consist of a large firm using a secure website to link to its suppliers and other key business partners (see Figure 10.7). The buyer owns the network, and it permits the firm and designated suppliers, distributors, and other business partners to share product design and development, marketing, production scheduling, inventory management, and unstructured communication, including graphics and e-mail. Another term for a private industrial network is a **private exchange**.

An example is VW Group Supply, which links the Volkswagen Group and its suppliers. VW Group Supply handles 90 percent of all global purchasing for Volkswagen, including all automotive and parts components.

Net marketplaces, which are sometimes called e-hubs, provide a single, digital marketplace based on Internet technology for many buyers and sellers (see Figure 10.8). They are industry-owned or operate as independent

FIGURE 10.7 A PRIVATE INDUSTRIAL NETWORK

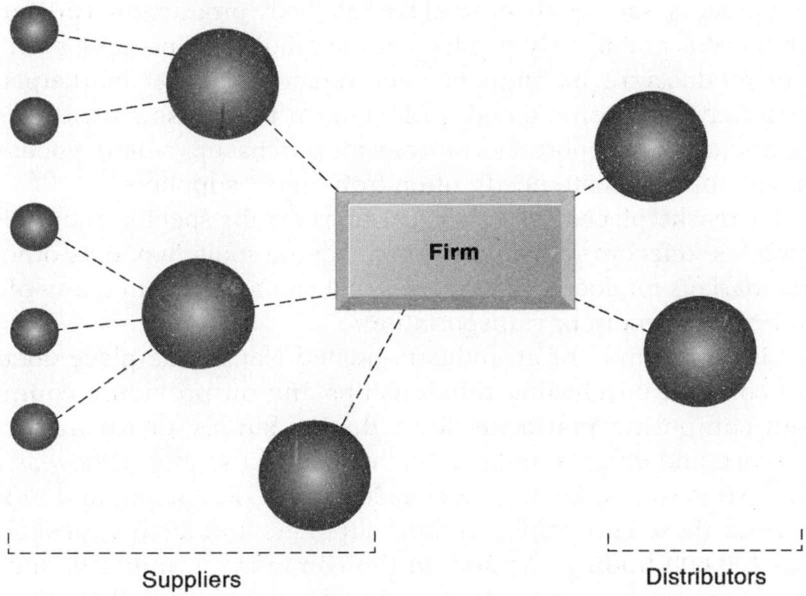

A private industrial network, also known as a private exchange, links a firm to its suppliers, distributors, and other key business partners for efficient supply chain management and other collaborative commerce activities.

intermediaries between buyers and sellers. Net marketplaces generate revenue from purchase and sale transactions and other services provided to clients. Participants in Net marketplaces can establish prices through online negotiations, auctions, or requests for quotations, or they can use fixed prices.

FIGURE 10.8 A NET MARKETPLACE

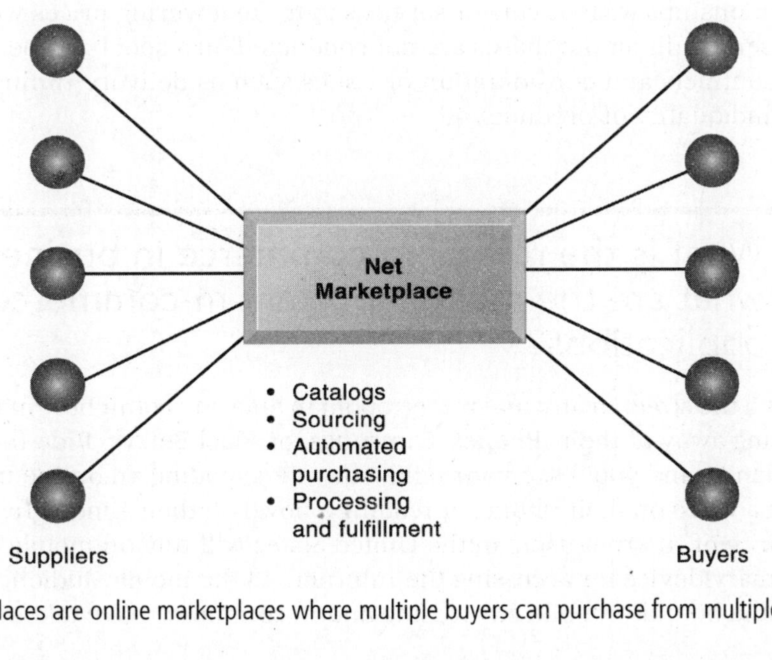

Net marketplaces are online marketplaces where multiple buyers can purchase from multiple sellers.

There are many types of Net marketplaces and ways of classifying them. Some sell direct goods and some sell indirect goods. **Direct goods** are goods used in a production process, such as sheet steel for auto body production. **Indirect goods** are all other goods not directly involved in the production process, such as office supplies or products for maintenance and repair. Some Net marketplaces support contractual purchasing based on long-term relationships with designated suppliers, and others support short-term spot purchasing, where goods are purchased based on immediate needs, often from many suppliers.

Some Net marketplaces serve vertical markets for specific industries, such as automobiles, telecommunications, or machine tools, whereas others serve horizontal markets for goods and services that can be found in many industries, such as office equipment or transportation.

Exostar is an example of an industry-owned Net marketplace, focusing on long-term contract purchasing relationships and on providing common networks and computing platforms for reducing supply chain inefficiencies. This aerospace and defense industry-sponsored Net marketplace was founded jointly by BAE Systems, Boeing, Lockheed Martin, Raytheon, and Rolls-Royce plc to connect these companies to their suppliers and facilitate collaboration. More than 100,000 trading partners in the commercial, military, and government sectors use Exostar's sourcing, e-procurement, and collaboration tools for both direct and indirect goods.

Exchanges are independently owned third-party Net marketplaces that connect thousands of suppliers and buyers for spot purchasing. Many exchanges provide vertical markets for a single industry, such as food, electronics, or industrial equipment, and they primarily deal with direct inputs. For example, Go2Paper enables a spot market for paper, board, and craft among buyers and sellers in the paper industries from more than 75 countries.

Exchanges proliferated during the early years of e-commerce, but many have failed. Suppliers were reluctant to participate because the exchanges encouraged competitive bidding that drove prices down and did not offer any long-term relationships with buyers or services to make lowering prices worthwhile. Many essential direct purchases are not conducted on a spot basis because they require contracts and consideration of issues such as delivery timing, customization, and quality of products.

10-5 What is the role of m-commerce in business, and what are the most important m-commerce applications?

Walk down the street in any major metropolitan area and count how many people are pecking away at their iPhones, Samsungs, or BlackBerrys. Ride the trains or fly the planes, and you'll see your fellow travelers reading an online newspaper, watching a video on their phone, or reading a novel on their Kindle. In five years, the majority of Internet users in the United States will rely on mobile devices as their primary device for accessing the Internet. As the mobile audience expands in leaps and bounds, mobile advertising and m-commerce have taken off.

FIGURE 10.9 MOBILE RETAIL COMMERCE REVENUES

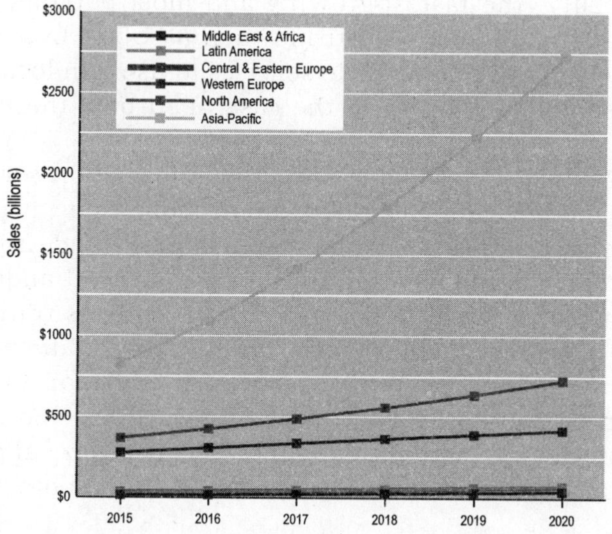

Mobile e-commerce is the fastest-growing type of B2C e-commerce and represented about 33 percent of all e-commerce in 2016.

Sources: Data from e-Marketer chart, "US Retail Mcommerce Sales, 2013-2019," May 2015.

In 2017, m-commerce constituted about 37 percent of all e-commerce, with about $170 billion in annual revenues generated by retail goods and services, apps, advertising, music, videos, ring tones, movies, television, and location-based services such as local restaurant locators and traffic updates. However, m-commerce is the fastest-growing form of e-commerce, expanding at a rate of 50 percent or more per year, and is estimated to grow to $300 billion by 2020 (see Figure 10.9) (eMarketer, 2016c)

The main areas of growth in mobile e-commerce are mass market retailing such as Amazon ($16.8 billion) and Apple (about $14 billion); sales of digital content such as music, TV shows, movies, and e-books (about $6 billion); and in-app sales to mobile devices (about $7 billion) (eMarketer, 2016d). These estimates do not include mobile advertising or location-based services. On-demand firms such as Uber (described in the chapter-opening case) and Airbnb are location-based services, but they are certainly examples of mobile commerce as well.

Location-Based Services and Applications

Location-based services include geosocial, geoadvertising, and geoinformation services. Seventy-four percent of smartphone owners use location-based services. What ties these activities together and is the foundation for mobile commerce is the global positioning system (GPS)–enabled map services available on smartphones. A **geosocial service** can tell you where your friends are meeting. **Geoadvertising services** can tell you where to find the nearest Italian restaurant, and **geoinformation services** can tell you the price of a house you are looking at or about special exhibits at a museum you are passing. In 2017, the fastest-growing and most popular location-based services are on-demand economy firms such as Uber, Lyft, Airbnb, Instacart, and hundreds more that provide services to users in local areas and are based on the user's location (or, in the case of Airbnb, the user's intended travel location).

Waze is an example of a popular, social geoinformation service. Waze is a GPS-based map and navigational app for smartphones, now owned by Google. Waze locates the user's car on a digital map using GPS and, like other navigation programs, collects information on the user's speed and direction continuously. What makes Waze different is that it collects traffic information from users who submit accident reports, speed traps, landmarks, street fairs, protests, and even addresses. Waze uses this information to come up with suggested alternative routes, travel times, and warnings and can even make recommendations for gas stations along the way. The Waze app is used extensively by Uber and Lyft drivers and more than 25 million other drivers in the United States.

Foursquare and new offerings by Facebook and Google are examples of geosocial services. Geosocial services help you find friends, or your friends to find you, by checking in to the service, announcing your presence in a restaurant or other place. Your friends are instantly notified. About 20 percent of smartphone owners use geosocial services.

Foursquare provides a location-based social networking service to 60 million registered individual users, who may connect with friends, update their location, and provide reviews and tips for enjoying a location. Points are awarded for checking in at designated venues. Users choose to post their check-ins on their accounts on Twitter, Facebook, or both. Users also earn badges by checking in at locations with certain tags, for check-in frequency, or for the time of check-in. More than 500,000 local merchants worldwide use the merchant platform for marketing.

Connecting people to local merchants in the form of geoadvertising is the economic foundation for mobile commerce. Geoadvertising sends ads to users based on their GPS locations. Smartphones report their locations back to Google and Apple. Merchants buy access to these consumers when they come within range of a merchant. For instance, Kiehl Stores, a cosmetics retailer, sent special offers and announcements to customers who came within 100 yards of their store.

Other Mobile Commerce Services

Banks and credit card companies have developed services that let customers manage their accounts from their mobile devices. JPMorgan Chase and Bank of America customers can use their cell phones to check account balances, transfer funds, and pay bills. Apple Pay for the iPhone 6 and Apple Watch, along with other Android and Windows smartphone models, allows users to charge items to their credit card accounts with a swipe of their phone. (See our Learning Track on mobile payment systems.)

INTERACTIVE SESSION: TECHNOLOGY

Social Media Analytics in Indian Politics

India, the world's largest democracy, holds the Lok Sabha (or parliamentary) elections every five years. With over 500 constituencies going to vote, it is fair to say that this is the most grandiose event in which the entire country participates. What made the General Elections of 2014 more special was the fact that out of the 800 million eligible voters, over a 100 million were first-time voters and 23 million were between 18 and 19 years of age. India, which has the second-largest population in the world, has the third-largest Internet-user base of 238 million people. Contrary to the popular belief that Internet usage is restricted to the Indian metros, the use of social media is rapidly spreading beyond the top eight cities. One-third of the users now reside in towns having a population of under five lakh people, while 25% of them live in cities with a population of less than two lakh people. This has had widespread consequences for the political campaign strategies during the General Elections of 2014.

Narendra Modi, the prime ministerial candidate for the National Democratic Alliance (NDA) led by the Bharatiya Janata Party (BJP), was one of the first political leaders to use Twitter in order to reach the masses. Modi joined Twitter in January 2009, and all the other BJP leaders were also encouraged to interact with voters through this social media platform. However, there was a need to professionally manage all the social media content, and to do this, the party appointed Arvind Gupta as its national technology head.

Prior to the elections, a centralized IT cell was formed in New Delhi comprising a team of 40 professionals from premier institutes of technology and management education, IITs and IIMs, respectively. They worked tirelessly to manage BJP's social media content. In addition, volunteers were brought in to click photos at Modi's rallies and post them on social networks. For better coordination between the volunteers and the IT cell at New Delhi, a WhatsApp group of 150 people was created. The party explored every online opportunity to engage with voters, be it Google Plus, Hangouts, Twitter, or Facebook. Taglines like "*Abki bar Modi sarkar*" became viral on Facebook, Twitter, and Instagram. Facebook pages such as "I want Narendra Modi as next PM of India" and "I support Narendra Modi" were created to attract voters and gauge their mood. Trending hashtags like #NaMo and #SelfieWithModi became the main topics of discussion. The IT cell regularly posted images, videos, and details about Modi's upcoming rallies. They also ran analytics on the huge data collected from social networking sites so as to increase the impact of Modi's speeches at the rallies.

Gupta laid emphasis on the need for analytics in managing such a huge campaign because he felt that this tool could help shape the campaign. For example, in October 2013, speaking at a youth function in New Delhi, Modi commented, "I am known to be a Hindutva leader. My image does not permit to say so, but I dare to say. My real thought is: *pehle shauchalaya, phir devalaya* (toilet first, temple later)." Analytics results showed that 45% of the social media users saw this statement in a favorable light. This gave Modi's team a clue that this could become one of the leading issues of the election. To spread this message further, the core IT team started engaging more users on social networking sites and found that now 68% of the people agreed with Modi's statement. After the elections, Modi started the Swachh Bharat Abhiyan on Gandhi Jayanti in New Delhi.

The Aam Aadmi Party (AAP), established in 2012 and headed by Arvind Kejriwal, also used social networking sites extensively to campaign for the elections. The main aim of the party was to share its honest opinion about important issues with the masses, spread awareness about party movements, display a common voice that would be coherent with the party's offline objectives, and connect with the youth. Consequently, Twitter hashtags like #VoteForAAP were strategically used by the party to gain political ground. In response to the rising digital popularity of the competitor, Modi, AAP created hashtags like #KejriwalAtKanpur to counter the leading one #NaMoInLucknow. Other hashtags such as #Internship4AAP and #Donate4CleanPoltics also ended up trending on Twitter. Rahul Jain, the director of digital marketing and sales at Social Rajneeti, an online reputation management and political promotions firm, said, "Aam Aadmi Party has been instrumental in shaping the revolutionary Indian politics since 2014 and has taken a prime position among the leading parties in the General Election of 2014. On social media, the party gets every aspect right from communication to uploading effective, thought-provoking videos and closely connecting with their audience through Google Hangouts." With the growing effectiveness of online campaigns, it comes as no surprise that political parties like the Congress, which didn't deploy as much time and effort on social media to engage with the tech-savvy, eligible young voters, lost the General Elections in 2014.

Sources: Rajan, Nandagopal, "SMW: Social media has changed political discourse like never before", *Financial Express* (2014). Retrieved from http://computer.financialexpress.com/events/smw-social-media-has-changed-political-discourse-like-never-before/3703; http://www.cioandleader.com/news/38911/google-launches-candidates-tool-lok-sabha-elections-2014; "Social Media & Lok Sabha Elections: A study finds that Facebook users may be the new votebank Indian politicians have to now worry about", IRIS Knowledge Foundation and Internet and Mobile Association of India. Retrieved from http://www.esocialsciences.org/General/A2013412184534_19.pdf; Daxina Pathak, "A Study on Use of Social Networking sites during Lok Sabha Elections-2014 by the Bhartiya Janta Party", *Altius Shodh Journal of Management & Commerce* (http://www.altius.ac.in/pdf/53.pdf); Surjit Kaur and Manpreet Kaur, "Impact of Social Media on Politics", *GIAN JYOTI E-JOURNAL*, Volume 3, Issue 4, Oct-Dec 2013 (http://www.gjimt.ac.in); "Social Media Played a Key Role in Lok Sabha Polls: Rajnath Singh", *NDTV* (2014). Retrieved from http://www.ndtv.com; "Social Media: The Game Changer of Lok Sabha Elections 2014", *Centrac*. Retrieved from http://centerac.com/2014; "The role of social media in 2014 Lok Sabha elections", IBNLive (2014). Retrieved from http://ibnlive.in.com; "Build toilets first and temples later, Narendra Modi says", The Times of India (2013). Retrieved from http://timesofindia.indiatimes.com; Kumar, Vikram, "Inside the BJP's war room where a team of 40 experts keeps an eye on the latest voting trends", *Daily Mail* (2014). Retrieved from http://www.dailymail.co.uk; Chopra, Raahil, "'Big data is like teenage sex': BJP's Arvind Gupta", *CampaignIndia* (2014). Retrieved from http://www.campaignindia.in; "Social Media Strategy Review: Aam Aadmi Party", *Social Samosa* (2014). Retrieved from http://www.socialsamosa.com.

CASE STUDY QUESTIONS

1. What are the factors that led to the widespread adoption of social media in India?
2. How did BJP utilize social media and analytics for its political campaign in 2014?
3. Which other political party used social media and how?

The mobile advertising market is the fastest-growing online ad platform, racking up $52 billion in ad revenue in 2017 and growing at 21 percent annually. Ads eventually move to where the eyeballs are, and increasingly that means mobile phones and, to less extent, tablets. Google is the largest mobile advertising market, posting about $10 billion in mobile ads, with Facebook number two with $4.9 billion. Yahoo displays ads on its mobile home page for companies such as Pepsico, Procter & Gamble, Hilton, Nissan, and Intel. Google is displaying ads linked to cell phone searches by users of the mobile version of its search engine; Microsoft offers banner and text advertising on its MSN Mobile portal in the United States. Ads are embedded in games, videos, and other mobile applications.

Shopkick is a mobile application that enables retailers such as Best Buy, Sports Authority, and Macy's to offer coupons to people when they walk into their stores. The Shopkick app automatically recognizes when the user has entered a partner retail store and offers a new virtual currency called kick-bucks, which can be redeemed for Facebook credits, iTunes gift cards, travel vouchers, DVDs, or immediate cashback rewards at any of the partner stores.

Fifty-five percent of online retailers now have m-commerce websites—simplified versions of their websites that enable shoppers to use cell phones to shop and place orders. Clothing retailers Lilly Pulitzer and Armani Exchange, Home Depot, Amazon, Walmart, and 1-800-Flowers are among those companies with apps for m-commerce sales. In 2016, more than half of m-commerce sales occurred within apps rather than mobile web browsers.

10-6 What issues must be addressed when building an e-commerce presence?

Building a successful e-commerce presence requires a keen understanding of business, technology, and social issues as well as a systematic approach. Today, an e-commerce presence is not just a corporate website but also includes a social network site on Facebook, a Twitter feed, and smartphone apps where customers can access your services. Developing and coordinating all these customer venues can be difficult. A complete treatment of the topic is beyond the scope of this text, and students should consult books devoted to just this topic (Laudon and Traver, 2016). The two most important management challenges in building a successful e-commerce presence are (1) developing a clear understanding of your business objectives and (2) knowing how to choose the right technology to achieve those objectives.

Develop an E-Commerce Presence Map

E-commerce has moved from being a PC-centric activity on the web to a mobile and tablet-based activity. Currently, a majority of Internet users in the United States use smartphones and tablets to shop for goods and services, look up prices, enjoy entertainment, and access social sites, less so to make purchases. Your potential customers use these various devices at different times during the day and involve themselves in different conversations, depending what they are doing—touching base with friends, tweeting, or reading a blog. Each of these is a touch point where you can meet the customer, and you have to think about how you develop a presence in these different virtual places. Figure 10.10 provides a roadmap to the platforms and related activities you will need to think about when developing your e-commerce presence.

Figure 10.10 illustrates four kinds of e-commerce presence: websites, e-mail, social media, and offline media. You must address different platforms for each of these types. For instance, in the case of website presence, there are three platforms: traditional desktop, tablets, and smartphones, each with different capabilities. Moreover, for each type of e-commerce presence, there are related activities you will need to consider. For instance, in the case of

FIGURE 10.10 E-COMMERCE PRESENCE MAP

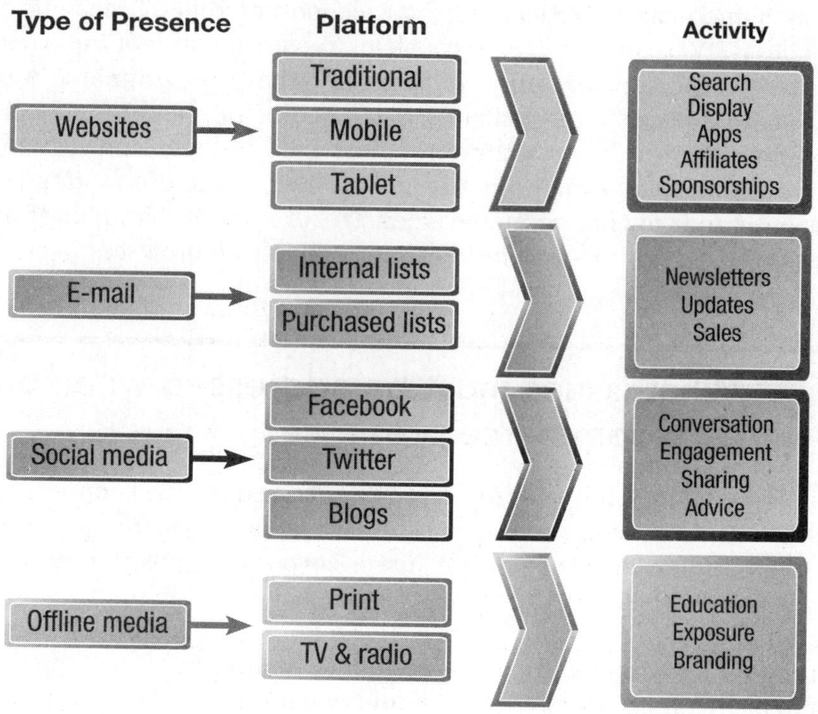

An e-commerce presence requires firms to consider the four types of presence, with specific platforms and activities associated with each.

websites, you will want to engage in search engine marketing, display ads, affiliate programs, and sponsorships. Offline media, the fourth type of e-commerce presence, is included here because many firms use multiplatform or integrated marketing by which print ads refer customers to websites.

TABLE 10.8 E-COMMERCE PRESENCE TIMELINE

PHASE	ACTIVITY	MILESTONE
Phase 1: Planning	Envision web presence; determine personnel.	Web mission statement
Phase 2: Website development	Acquire content; develop a site design; arrange for hosting the site.	Website plan
Phase 3: Web Implementation	Develop keywords and metatags; focus on search engine optimization; identify potential sponsors.	A functional website
Phase 4: Social media plan	Identify appropriate social platforms and content for your products and services.	A social media plan
Phase 5: Social media implementation	Develop Facebook, Twitter, and Pinterest presence.	Functioning social media presence
Phase 6: Mobile plan	Develop a mobile plan; consider options for porting your website to smartphones.	A mobile media plan

Develop a Timeline: Milestones

Where would you like to be a year from now? It's very helpful for you to have a rough idea of the time frame for developing your e-commerce presence when you begin. You should break your project down into a small number of phases that could be completed within a specified time. Table 10.8 illustrates a one-year timeline for the development of an e-commerce presence for a start-up company devoted to fashions for teenagers. You can also find more detail about developing an e-commerce website in the Learning Tracks for this chapter.

Review Summary

10-1 *What are the unique features of e-commerce, digital markets, and digital goods?*

E-commerce involves digitally enabled commercial transactions between and among organizations and individuals. Unique features of e-commerce technology include ubiquity, global reach, universal technology standards, richness, interactivity, information density, capabilities for personalization and customization, and social technology. E-commerce is becoming increasingly social, mobile, and local.

Digital markets are said to be more transparent than traditional markets, with reduced information asymmetry, search costs, transaction costs, and menu costs along with the ability to change prices dynamically based on market conditions. Digital goods, such as music, video, software, and books, can be delivered over a digital network. Once a digital product has been produced, the cost of delivering that product digitally is extremely low.

10-2 *What are the principal e-commerce business and revenue models?*

E-commerce business models are e-tailers, transaction brokers, market creators, content providers, community providers, service providers, and portals. The principal e-commerce revenue models are advertising, sales, subscription, free/freemium, transaction fee, and affiliate.

10-3 *How has e-commerce transformed marketing?*

The Internet provides marketers with new ways of identifying and communicating with millions of potential customers at costs far lower than traditional media. Crowdsourcing using the wisdom of crowds helps companies learn from customers to improve product offerings and increase customer value. Behavioral targeting techniques increase the effectiveness of banner, rich media, and video ads. Social commerce uses social networks and social network sites to improve targeting of products and services.

10-4 *How has e-commerce affected business-to-business transactions?*

B2B e-commerce generates efficiencies by enabling companies to locate suppliers, solicit bids, place orders, and track shipments in transit electronically. Net marketplaces provide a single, digital marketplace for many buyers and sellers. Private industrial networks link a firm with its suppliers and other strategic business partners to develop highly efficient and responsive supply chains.

10-5 *What is the role of m-commerce in business, and what are the most important m-commerce applications?*

M-commerce is especially well suited for location-based applications such as finding local hotels and restaurants, monitoring local traffic and weather, and providing personalized location-based marketing. Mobile phones and handhelds are being used for mobile bill payment, banking, securities trading, transportation schedule updates, and downloads of digital content such as music, games, and video clips. M-commerce requires wireless portals and special digital payment systems that can handle micropayments. The GPS capabilities of smartphones make geoadvertising, geosocial, and geoinformation services possible.

10-6 *What issues must be addressed when building an e-commerce presence?*
Building a successful e-commerce presence requires a clear understanding of the business objectives to be achieved and selection of the right platforms, activities, and timeline to achieve those objectives. An e-commerce presence includes not only a corporate website but also a presence on Facebook, Twitter, and other social networking sites and smartphone apps.

Key Terms

Advertising revenue model, 411
Affiliate revenue model, 413
Behavioral targeting, 414
Business-to-business (B30B), 407
Business-to-consumer (B30C), 407
Community providers, 411
Consumer-to-consumer (C30C), 407
Cost transparency, 402
Crowdsourcing, 420
Customization, 402
Digital goods, 405
Direct goods, 426
Disintermediation, 405
Dynamic pricing, 404
Electronic Data Interchange (EDI), 423
E-tailer, 409
Exchanges, 426
Free/freemium revenue model, 412
Geoadvertising services, 427
Geoinformation services, 428
Geosocial services, 427
Indirect goods, 426
Information asymmetry, 403
Information density, 402
Intellectual property, 409
Location-based services, 427
Long tail marketing, 413
Market creator, 410
Market entry costs, 401
Marketspace, 400
Menu costs, 404
Micropayment systems, 412
Mobile commerce (m-commerce), 408
Native advertising, 418
Net marketplaces, 424
Personalization, 402
Podcasting, 410
Price discrimination, 402
Price transparency, 402
Private exchange, 424
Private industrial networks, 424
Revenue model, 411
Richness, 401
Sales revenue model, 412
Search costs, 401
Social graph, 418
Social shopping, 420
Streaming, 410
Subscription revenue model, 412
Transaction costs, 400
Transaction fee revenue model, 413
Wisdom of crowds, 420

Review Questions

10-1 What are the unique features of e-commerce, digital markets, and digital goods?

- Name and describe four business trends and three technology trends shaping e-commerce today.
- List and describe the eight unique features of e-commerce.
- Define a digital market and digital goods. Describe their distinguishing features.

10-2 What are the principal e-commerce business and revenue models?

- List and describe the major classifications of e-commerce.
- Explain in detail the manner in which e-commerce has changed the conventional business models.

10-3 How has e-commerce transformed marketing?
- How have social networking and the wisdom of crowds helped companies improve their marketing? Explain.
- Define behavioral targeting. How does it work at individual websites and on advertising networks?

10-4 How has e-commerce affected business-to-business transactions?
- Define EDI and B2B e-commerce. How has EDI facilitated business transaction?
- List and describe different electronic marketplaces used for B2B transactions with relevant examples.

10-5 What is the role of m-commerce in business? What are the most important m-commerce applications?
- Define geosocial, geoadvertising, and geoinformaiton services. What are their applications?

10-6 What issues must be addressed while building an e-commerce presence?
- List and describe the activities and platforms for each e-commerce presence.

Discussion Questions

10-7 How does the Internet change consumer and supplier relationships?

10-8 The Internet may not make corporations obsolete, but the corporations will have to change their business models. Do you agree? Why or why not?

10-9 How have social technologies changed e-commerce?

Hands-On MIS Projects

The projects in this section give you hands-on experience developing e-commerce strategies for businesses, using spreadsheet software to research the profitability of an e-commerce company, and using web tools to research and evaluate e-commerce hosting services.

Management Decision Problems

10-10 Columbiana is a small, independent island in the Caribbean that has many historical buildings, forts, and other sites along with rain forests and striking mountains. A few first-class hotels and several dozen less expensive accommodations lie along its beautiful white-sand beaches. The major airlines have regular flights to Columbiana, as do several small airlines. Columbiana's government wants to increase tourism and develop new markets for the country's tropical agricultural products. How can a web presence help? What Internet business model would be appropriate? What functions should the web presence perform?

10-11 Explore the Web sites of the following companies: Eurosparkle, Promod, Kingfisher plc, and ebookers.com. Determine which of these Web sites would benefit most from adding a company-sponsored blog to the Web site. List the business benefits of the blog. Specify the intended audience for the blog. Decide who in the company should author the blog, and select some topics for the blog.

Improving Decision Making: Using Spreadsheet Software to Analyze a Dot-Com Business

Software skills: Spreadsheet downloading, formatting, and formulas
Business skills: Financial statement analysis

10-12 Pick one e-commerce company on the Internet—for example, Ashford, Yahoo, or Priceline. Study the web pages that describe the company and explain its purpose and structure. Use the web to find articles that comment on the company. Then visit the Securities and Exchange Commission's website at www.sec.gov to access the company's 10-K (annual report) form showing income statements and balance sheets. Select only the sections of the 10-K form containing the desired portions of financial statements that you need to examine and download them into your spreadsheet. Create simplified spreadsheets of the company's balance sheets and income statements for the past three years.

- Is the company a dot-com success, borderline business, or failure? What information provides the basis of your decision? Why? When answering these questions, pay special attention to the company's three-year trends in revenues, costs of sales, gross margins, operating expenses, and net margins.
- Prepare an overhead presentation (with a minimum of five slides), including appropriate spreadsheets or charts, and present your work to your professor and classmates.

Achieving Operational Excellence: Evaluating E-Commerce Hosting Services

Software skills: Web browser software
Business skills: Evaluating e-commerce hosting services

10-13 This project will help develop your Internet skills in evaluating commercial services for hosting an e-commerce site for a small start-up company.

You would like to set up a website to sell towels, linens, pottery, and tableware from Portugal and are examining services for hosting small business Internet storefronts. Your website should be able to take secure credit card payments and calculate shipping costs and taxes. Initially, you would like to display photos and descriptions of 40 products. Visit eHost.com, GoDaddy, and iPage and compare the range of e-commerce hosting services they offer to small businesses, their capabilities, and their costs. Examine the tools they provide for creating an e-commerce site. Compare these services and decide which you would use if you were actually establishing a web store. Write a brief report indicating your choice and explaining the strengths and weaknesses of each service.

Collaboration and Teamwork Project

Performing a Competitive Analysis of E-commerce Sites

10-14 Form a group with three or four of your classmates. Select two businesses that are competitors in the same industry and that use their websites for electronic commerce. Visit these websites. You might compare, for example, the websites for Pandora and Spotify, Amazon and BarnesandNoble.com, or E*Trade and Scottrade. Prepare an evaluation of each business's website in terms of its functions, user friendliness, and ability to support the company's business strategy. Which website does a better job? Why? Can you make some recommendations to improve these websites? If possible, use Google Docs and Google Drive or Google Sites to brainstorm, organize, and develop a presentation of your findings for the class.

Paytm Cashing on Demonetization

CASE STUDY

Demonetization is the act of stripping a currency unit of its status as a legal tender. The government of different countries use this as a measure to combat inflation, corruption, counterfeiting, and to reduce cash dependency in an economy. In India, demonetization has been implemented many times (in 1946, 1978, and 2016), however, the highest impact was felt in the year 2016. On 8 November 2016, the central government announced the demonetization of ₹500 and ₹1000 notes with immediate effect and provided a two-month period for the country (till the end of year) to replace these with newly launched ₹500 and ₹2000 notes. These notes accounted for 86 percent of the country's cash and 78 percent of the cash-based transaction in India. Although the intent of the government was eradication of counterfeiting and black money, prevention of tax evasion, and promoting a cashless economy, it created a sense of chaos among the citizens of the country. With reduced cash-in-hand, there were longer queues at ATMs and banks, and consumer spending and investment spending plummeted. The unorganized sector which mainly operates on cash also took the hit. Amongst all this, people started seeking alternate payment options such as using debit and credit cards, or mobile payments. While 'Digital India' still seems a far fetched story, demonetization has definitely pushed the sleeping nation towards being cashless. According to the Reserve Bank of India (RBI), digital payments and transaction have doubled and quadrupuled in both volume and value since demonetization came into effect. Transactions through debit cards crossed one-billion mark in January 2017, compared to 817 million transactions last year, inspiring the banks to deploy one million additional POS terminals within a span of three months.

The government is also steering the growth of smartphone-based transactions by launching the Unified Payments Interface (UPI) and government's own smartphone app Bharat Interface for Money (BHIM). UPI aids in electronic fund transfer from user's smartphones without entering bank account or net banking information. The interface lets the user send and receive money from smartphones by using only their mobile phone number or a Virtual Payment Address (VPA) uniquely issued to each user. Many banks have launched their own apps using this UPI interface. Prior to demonetization, total transactions using smartphone applications (mobile wallets) were only 100,000 (as on October 2016). By March 2017, these transactions grew up to 6.4 million. These wallet services are also termed as Pre-Paid Instruments or PPIs, and private players too have been actively playing their part in India. These PPIs have seen a 350 percent increase in transactions on an average in the first quarter of 2017 as compared to 2016, while the value of transactions also rose significantly. The transactions on mobile banking also saw a 30 percent increase as per the figures available with the RBI. It is seen that mobile payment is emerging as one of the most preferred methods for online payments, in addition to the use of debit and credit cards.

Now, a mobile wallet is basically a virtual wallet. The user first needs to download the mobile wallet service provider's application such as Paytm and MobiKwik in their smartphone. Then, the users register by creating a wallet ID, and they receive a password after successful registration. This account now becomes their online mobile wallet where money can be loaded by linking it with their bank account, through online banking, or credit/debit cards. Another alternative is to ask one's friends to transfer money from their wallet into the user's wallet. Just as a user keeps one's membership cards, loyalty cards, credit cards, and other useful information in a wallet, the digital wallet also allows to store personal information in a secure area, protected through passwords. One of the dominating mobile service provider in India is Paytm which is headquartered in Noida. It became operational in 2014 when it received its license from the RBI. Its positioning as the most used mobile service provider owes to fact that Paytm is available at 850,000 stores and petrol pumps and has a presence in more than 1,200 cities in India. Each month, Paytm aids in the processing of 30 million orders and logistics operations. Demonetization led to a sudden increase in the company's customer base. As of January 2017, it added 20 million new customers post demonetization, putting the total user base at 170 million. The transactions at Paytm grew to more than 7 million per day, higher than the average daily use of credit and debit cards in India.

To take advantage of this opportunity, Paytm released full front page advertisements in newspapers congratulating the Indian leadership at the government on its move of demonetization. Further, it rolled out marketing campaigns containing the tagline '*Ab ATM nahi, Paytm Karo*' (Now don't use ATM, use Paytm). Paytm also created a Twitter tag #PaytmKaro which trended for quite a while. Besides this, it also created print advertisements containing the tagline '*Paytm Karo*' to target daily-wage workers like electrician or plumbers. The advertisements have been quite a hit among the masses. Such was the impact that even local vegetable hawkers who visit different colonies to sell their produce accepted and made payments using Paytm. In metro cities like Delhi, Paytm became a household name. Within a few days, company registered 700 percent increase in overall traffic and 1000 percent growth in the amount of money added to Paytm. The number of app downloads too increased by 300 percent.

It has been strategically moving ahead to expand and maintain its customer base. It reached out to the least penetrated parts of the country through effective campaigning. Paytm understood that the factor which restricts the growth of mobile wallets in such regions in India is due to the lack of education and awareness among people about the use of smartphones and their features. However, Paytm took this up as a challenge and launched a community program called Paytm Pro where people were chosen as leaders from villages across the country to teach others about the digital payment solutions and the use of smartphones. "In order to add more momentum to the traction, we are making the app available in regional languages and expanding merchant acquisition network in smaller towns," said Deepak Abbott, Senior Vice President at Paytm. To promote the drive, Paytm also announced scholarships and certificates and exciting gifts like motorcycles, laptops, etc. for users who made efforts to promote digital inclusion in the country. As a result of this initiative, the revenue contribution from such towns which had a population of less than one lakh people increased to about 20 percent of the total revenue by January, 2017, compared to only 2 percent last year.

The company is also increasing its merchant network by targeting to widen its presence from 450 districts to 650 districts by the end of 2017. As on February 2017, the number of Paytm merchants is 4.5 million, and it is targeting to increase it to 10 million by the end of 2017. The merchants can start using Paytm at zero extra cost by just filling a form online, and those merchants who are Know Your Customer (KYC) enabled, the firm also waived off transaction fee it charged for money transfer. Paytm has also defined new quality standards for its sellers to enhance user experience. As part of this policy, the sellers at Paytm now need to provide brand authorization letters, submit their registration numbers, location of the shop, photos, and GST identification number. In an aggressive move, it removed 85,000 sellers who did not meet these standards.

To keep up with the growth plans, another initiative taken by the company is the provision of Paytm Mall QR code solution. The QR code is basically an encoding which contains information about the product it is displayed on. For example, for merchant information, the merchant's mobile wallet details may be contained in QR codes. This solution allows the users to pay offline. After verification of documents of each business user and KYC collected from the same, a unique QR code is issued to the business. The consumers simply scan the QR code using a specialized app on their smartphones and make and receive payments or browse the products and place instant order. Same technique is also used for making payments at shops and malls. The user scans the QR code of the merchant/seller and then simply transfers the money in the account.

The launch of Paytm Payments Bank is another milestone in Paytm's plans to solidify its presence. This venture is backed by investments from Asian technology giants such as SoftBank Corp and Alibaba Group Holding Limited. The difference between Paytm Payments Bank and a conventional bank is that it cannot lend money but can accept and maintain deposits from customers. The target segment of this bank is those customers in India who do not have access to conventional banking, although they use mobile phones and data services. The plan of the bank is to open 31 branches initially and reach out to 3,000 customers in its first year of operation. The current offerings of mobile wallets too could be merged into the payments bank. As per the company's statements, the bank will offer 4 percent interest rate on savings account, and there are no minimum balance requirements. In addition, all online transactions would be free for all users.

Paytm's success comes with its own set of hurdles and challenges. Paytm's TV advertisement released a week after announcement of demonetization which received a lot of flak from masses since the advertisement asked the Indian consumers to stop being melodramatic, and use Paytm instead. Consumers did not take it in the right note as they have been standing for hours in serpentine queues to access money. The firm relaunched the advertisement with a revised tagline a day later. Paytm also got itself involved in a political tussle following front-page advertisements congratulating the Indian leadership for the move of demonetization. Although the firm has no political affiliation, this was not taken lightly by the opposition parties who took to multiple platforms to express their criticism. In the first few months following demonetization, Paytm also faced a lot of technical glitches and outages, as a result of which consumers faced time-outs on the site. This was due to the sudden spike of traffic on its mobile application. Although the firm added additional capacity and new servers, the problem did not resolve immediately.

The firm also faces stiff competition from other players in the Indian market such as PayUMoney, Mobikwik, Citrus, and Airtel Money to name a few. Oxigen is the oldest electronic wallet, while it entered into the mobile wallet services in 2014. Mobikwik was launched in 2009, and it allows the users to share money over social networks and messaging platforms such as WhatsApp, Facebook, Twitter, and Google+. A special feature of Mobikwik is that it has hired a fleet of people who collect cash from users based in Gurugram and load the money into their Mobikwik wallets. PayUMoney, another Gurugram-based firm, has an award winning payment gateway technology platform. Its distinguishing features are benefits on its apps such as one-touch checkouts, discounts, cashbacks, and instant refunds on canceled orders. Others are Vodafone M-Pesa which is restricted for use to Vodafone users; Airtel Money which doesn't allow the customers to withdraw cash but supports several other functions like recharge, money transfer, bill payments, payments for online shopping, etc. The e-wallets are fast becoming indispensable to Indian users who can forget to carry cash, but not mobiles.

Sources: http://www.investopedia.com, please read: Demonetization; http://www.forbesindia.com, please read: in the Economic Policy Blog: Demonetization–The Long and Short of It; http://economictimes.indiatimes.com, please read: Digital Payments–India's New Currency Debit Card Transactions Surge over 1 Billion; https://m.yourstory.com, please read: Digital–India Post Demonetization and PayTM Launched Niche Bank; https://qz.com, please read: PayTM is Paying a Price for Its Sudden Stardom; http://www.tutorialspoint.com, please read: Mobile Wallets in India.

CASE STUDY QUESTIONS

10-15 What were the hurdles caused by demonetization to Indian people? How did the mobile application help overcome the same?

10-16 List the distinguishing features of Paytm as a mobile wallet. How does a mobile wallet work?

10-17 What initiatives were taken by Paytm to tap into the Indian market in the wake of demonetization?

10-18 Describe some challenges faced by Paytm as discussed in the text.

Chapter 10 References

Adomavicius, Gediminas, Jesse Bockstedt, and Shawn P. Curley. "Bundling Effects on Variety Seeking for Digital Information Goods." *Journal of Management Information Systems* 31, No. 4 (Spring 2015).

Brynjolfsson, Erik, Yu Hu, and Michael D. Smith. "Consumer Surplus in the Digital Economy: Estimating the Value of Increased Product Variety at Online Booksellers." *Management Science* 49, No. 11 (November 2003).

Brynjolfsson, Erik, Yu Jeffrey Hu, and Mohammad S. Rahman. "Competing in the Age of Multichannel Retailing." *MIT Sloan Management Review* (May 2013).

Butler, Brian S., Patrick J. Bateman, Peter H. Gray, and E. Ilana Diamant. "An Attraction-Selection-Attrition Theory of Online Community Size and Resilience." *MIS Quarterly* 38, No. 3 (September 2014).

Chandlee, Blake and Gerald C. (Jerry) Kane. "How Facebook Is Delivering Personalization on a Whole New Scale." *MIT Sloan Management Review* 55, No. 4 (August 5, 2014).

Chen, Jianquing and Jan Stallaert. "An Economic Analysis of Online Advertising Using Behavioral Targeting." *MIS Quarterly* 38, No. 2 (June 2014).

comScore Inc. "ComScore 2013 US Digital Future in Focus." [Nick Mulligan] (April 2, 2014).

Doyle, Cathy. "US Mobile StatPack."eMarketer (March 2016).

eMarketer. "E-Commerce Sales, 2014–2020," Chart (June 2016b).

eMarketer. "US Retail Sales to Near $5 Trillion in 2016," Report (December 2016e).

eMarke'er. "US Mobile Commerce Update 2016," Report, eMarketer (May 2016d).

eMarketer. "Digital Ad Spending United States," 2014–2018, Chart (2016a).

eMarketer. "US Ad Spending: Estimates for 2016," Report, eMarketer (March 2016c).

Federal Trade Commission. "Data Brokers: A Call for Transparency and Accountability," Federal Trade Commission (May 2014).

Fang, Yulin, Israr Qureshi, Heshan Sun, Patrick McCole, Elaine Ramsey, and Kai H. Lim. "Trust, Satisfaction, and Online Repurchase Intention: The Moderating Role of Perceived Effectiveness of E-Commerce Institutional Mechanisms." *MIS Quarterly* 38, No. 2 (June 2014).

Gast, Arne and Michele Zanini. "The Social Side of Strategy." *McKinsey Quarterly* (May 2012).

Ghoshal, Abhijeet, Subodha Kumar, and Vijay Mookerjee. "Impact of Recommender System on Competition Between Personalizing and Non-Personalizing Firms." *Journal of Management Information Systems* 31, No. 4 (Spring 2015).

Gupta, Sunil. "For Mobile Devices, Think Apps, Not Ads." *Harvard Business Review* (March 2013).

Hinz, Oliver, Il-Horn Hann, and Martin Spann. "Price Discrimination in E-Commerce? An Examination of Dynamic Pricing in Name-Your-Own Price Markets." *MIS Quarterly* 35, No. 1 (March 2011).

Holt, Douglas. "Branding in the Age of Social Media." *Harvard Business Review* (March 2016).

Hoofnagle, Chris Jay, Jennifer M. Urban, and Su Li. "Privacy and Modern Advertising: Most US Internet Users Want 'Do Not Track' to Stop Collection of Data About Their Online Activities." Berkeley Consumer Privacy Survey. BCLT Research Paper (October 8, 2012).

Im, Il, Jongkun Jun, Wonseok Oh, and Seok-Oh Jeong. "Deal-Seeking Versus Brand-Seeking: Search Behaviors and Purchase Propensities in Sponsored Search Platforms." *MIS Quarterly* 40, No. 1 (March 2016).

Internet Retailer. "Mobile Commerce Top 400 2015." (2015).

Internet World Stats. "Internet Users in the World." Internetworldstats.com (2016).

Kumar, V. and Rohan Mirchandan "Increasing the ROI of Social Media Marketing." *MIT Sloan Management Review* 54, No. 1 (Fall 2012).

Laudon, Kenneth C. and Carol Guercio Traver. *E-commerce: Business, Technology, Society*, 12th ed. Upper Saddle River, NJ: Prentice-Hall (2016).

Li, Xitong. "Could Deal Promotion Improve Merchants' Online Reputations? The Moderating Role of Prior Reviews." *Journal of Management Information Systems* 33, No.1 (2016).

Liu, Charles Zhechao, Yoris A Au., and Hoon Seok Choi. "Effects of Freemium Strategy in the Mobile App Market: An Empirical Study of Google Play." *Journal of Management Information Systems* 31, No. 3 (Winter 2014).

Oestreicher-Singer, Gal and Arun Sundararajan. "Recommendation Networks and the Long Tail of Electronic Commerce." *MIS Quarterly* 36, No. 1 (March 2012).

Oh, Hyelim, Animesh Animesh, and Alain Pinsonneault. "Free Versus For-a-Fee: The Impact of a Paywall on the Pattern and Effectiveness of Word-of-Mouth via Social Media." *MIS Quarterly* 40, No. 1 (March 2016).

Orlikowski, Wanda and Susan V. Scott. "The Algorithm and the Crowd: Considering the Materiality of Service Innovation." *MIS Quarterly* 39, No.1 (March 2015).

Pew Internet and American Life Project. "Americans' Attitudes About Privacy, Security, and Surveillance." (May 20, 2015a).

Pew Internet and American Life Project. "Americans' Privacy Strategies Post-Snowden." (March 16, 2015b).

Rainie, Lee and Maeve Duggan. "Privacy and Information Sharing." Pew Research Center (January, 2016).

Reynolds, Tracy. "NRF Forecasts Retail Sales to Grow 3.1 Percent in 2016." National Retail Federation (February 10, 2016).

Rigby, Darrell K. "Digital Physical Mashups." *Harvard Business Review* (September 2014).

Schulze, Christian, Lisa Schöler, and Bernd Skier. "Customizing Social Media Marketing." *MIT Sloan Management Review* (Winter 2015).

Shuk, Ying Ho and David Bodoff. "The Effects of Web Personalization on User Attitude and Behavior: An Integration of the Elaboration Likelihood Model and Consumer Search Theory." *MIS Quarterly* 38, No. 2 (June 2014).

Susarla, Anjana, Jeong-Ha Oh, and Young Tan. "Influentials, Imitables, or Susceptibles? Virality and Word-of-Mouth Conversations in Online Social Networks." *Journal of Management Information Systems* 33, No.1 (2016).

Urban, Glen L. and Fareena Sultan. "The Case for 'Benevolent' Mobile Apps." *MIT Sloan Management Review* (Winter 2015).

U.S. Bureau of the Census. "E-Stats. 2014." http://www.census.gov/econ/index.html (May 22, 2014).

Xiaojuan Ou, Carol, Paul A. Pavlou, and Robert M. Davison. "Swift Guanxi in Online Marketplaces: The Role of Computer-Mediated Communication Technologies." *MIS Quarterly* 38, No. 1 (March 2014).

Yin, Dezhi, Samuel D. Bond, and Han Zhang. "Anxious or Angry? Effects of Discrete Emotions on the Perceived Helpfulness of Online Reviews." *MIS Quarterly* 38, No. 2 (June 2014).

Zhang, Zan, Guofang Nan, Minqiang Li, and Yong Tan. "Duopoly Pricing Strategy for Information Products with Premium Service: Free Product or Bundling?" *Journal of Management Information Systems* 33, No. 1 (2016).

Zhou, Wenqi and Wenjing Duan. "Do Professional Reviews Affect Online User Choices Through User Reviews? An Empirical Study." *Journal of Management Information Systems* 33, No. 1 (2016).

CHAPTER

11 Managing Knowledge

Learning Objectives

After reading this chapter, you will be able to answer the following questions:

11-1 What is the role of knowledge management systems in business?

11-2 What types of systems are used for enterprise-wide knowledge management, and how do they provide value for businesses?

11-3 What are the major types of knowledge work systems, and how do they provide value for firms?

11-4 What are the business benefits of using intelligent techniques for knowledge management?

CHAPTER CASES

Connecting Unisys Globally Through Social Collaboration Information Systems

KMS Empowering Capella University

Will Robots Replace People in Manufacturing?

Knowledge Management and Collaboration at Tata Consulting Services

Connecting Unisys Globally Through Social Collaboration Information Systems

Unisys Corporation has global presence in more than 100 countries, including India. The company provides a range of IT, software, and technology services to commercial organizations and government agencies throughout the world. In its 140 years of existence, the firm has had approximately 23,000 employees. As a service firm, the harnessing and sharing of intellectual capital are vital to its operations. A quick response to customer queries is essential when it comes to tapping market opportunities. However, the management at Unisys felt that the lack of platforms to share knowledge among its employees limited the firm's ability to leverage its expertise to respond to the dynamic business environment.

It was discovered that the company had multiple information silos within its system, which prevented enterprise-wide sharing of knowledge. The model of communication was traditional and top-down. There was no way for employees to find and connect with subject-matter experts. Unisys wished to achieve true enterprise collaboration through an information system to sort out all these problems. This vision was shared by the company's CEO, Ed Coleman, who had already leveraged the value of social media for brand promotion and reaching out to customers. The firm then decided to once again adopt social media to empower its employees and increase their efficiency in the workplace.

© Shawn Hempel/Shutterstock

This model, however, had to be implemented with care. Unisys first started by conducting leadership interviews to understand how the adoption of social business could add value to their enterprise. Through this, areas were identified where social technology could deliver value to customers and provide improved capabilities. An advisory council of stakeholders across the organization was formed that could address potential barriers to implementation. Based on the recommendations of the advisory council, Unisys redesigned its intranet, Inside Unisys, by adding a new feature called NewsGator.

NewsGator is a social engine that enables employees to create their individual profiles and 'follow' colleagues to build valuable networks. Other features included transparent newsfeeds and blogs, which enables the employees to communicate and learn through sharing. To facilitate the adoption of social business, Unisys launched strategic communities at different levels of the firm, which were termed as the hub for social collaboration. 'Organic communities' were given the task of developing expertise through interaction with like-minded people. 'Business unit communities' were responsible for the disbursal of the latest news and alerts among employees. 'Role-based communities' and 'industry or vertical communities' were Unisys-sponsored communities of excellence. They primarily dealt with the development and dissemination of essential knowledge in sales, delivery, and market trends. 'Areas of strength communities' were authoritative communities that leveraged knowledge in Unisys' key solutions and offerings. Additionally, employees could crowd-source ideas into communities, which led the firm to innovations. The company hard aligned its employees to their business unit communities, so that they could push important news and information through these communities. The employees could also subscribe to other communities, which updated them with information in their areas of interest. This was also integrated into a new hire orientation program to increase their engagement and facilitate in quick on-boarding. From time to time, the firm also launched targeted role-based awareness campaigns to educate and train employees on the usage of enterprise collaboration.

The results of adopting this system were enormous. Within the first 18 months of implementation, 91 percent of the targeted base of 16,000 employees adopted this system. In its global workforce, it stood at 78 percentage. All members of the senior leadership of Unisys used this system and promoted social collaboration within their organizations. Thirteen strategic communities and 120 organic communities have been developed since. Social exchanges on newsfeed and blogs are populated with high-value business content. This rapid adoption of social technologies has fuelled the innovative culture at Unisys, increased workplace efficiency, facilitated employee development, and improved the market agility and customer service. This has also increased the efficiency of virtual teams, which comprises remote, home-based employees, who can feel connected to their business environment through Unisys' social tools and processes.

Sources: 'Unisys Case Study: Best Practices in Socially Enabling a Global Workforce' (2013). Retrieved from http://www.apqc.org; 'Unisys Unified Social Business Overview' (2014). Retrieved from https://www.youtube.com; Kass, Kelly, 'From Silos to Social: How Unisys socially-enabled its global enterprise'. Retrieved from https://www.simply-communicate.com; *Unisys*. Retried from http://www.unisys.com; 'Great Intranets: Unisys'. Retrieved from http://www.prescientdigital.com; Lightman, Stefanie, NewsGator's Free Adoption Framework Gains Momentum', *Sitrion* (2013). Retrieved from http://www.sitrion.com.

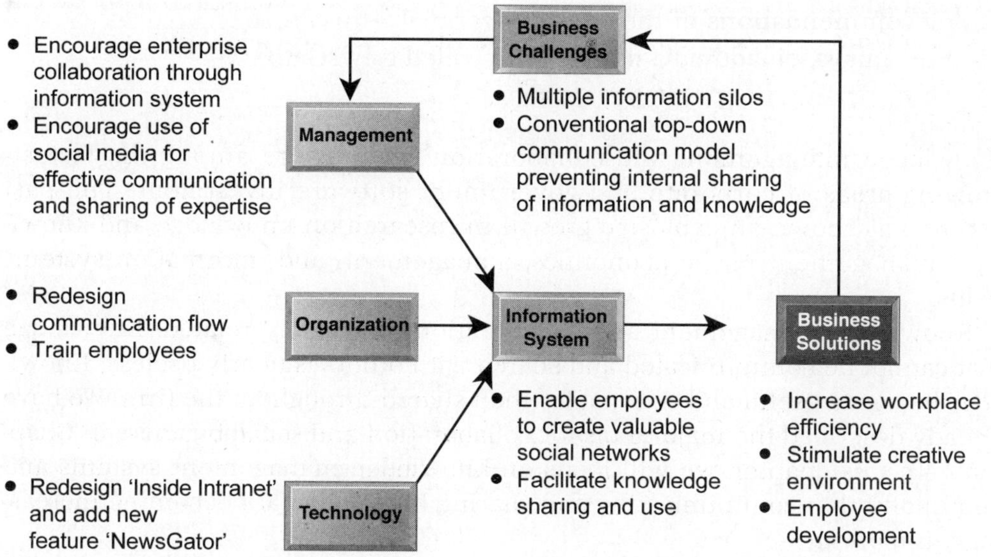

The experience of Unisys described in this case shows how business performance can benefit from new communication media to facilitate acquisition and the sharing of knowledge. Facilitating access to knowledge, and harnessing and using that knowledge to improve business processes are vital to the success and survival of all areas of business.

The chapter-opening diagram calls for attention to the important points raised by this case and this chapter. Constant communication and sharing of expertise among its employees are essential tools for any firm, especially if it is offering innovative services and solutions. However, Unisys had multiple information silos within its system, which prevented the enterprise-wide sharing of knowledge. The model of communication was the conventional top-down one. There was no way for employees to find and connect with subject-matter experts to resolve problems. There was an urgent need to achieve true enterprise collaboration through an information system. To achieve enterprise-wide collaboration, Unisys decided to change its internal communication system by using social media to empower employees and increase efficiency in the workplace. Unisys redesigned its Intranet, Inside Unisys, with the aim to provide a platform where the employees can interact with each other. The result was addition of a key feature in the company's intranet, known as NewsGator. Thanks to this new social media platform, employees can create their profiles and 'follow' other colleagues to build a valuable network. Other features of this platform are transparent newsfeeds and blogs which enabled the employees to communicate and learn through sharing. However, realizing the fact that adoption of new technology in the form of social media based interaction requires cultural changes in the organizational mindset, and to facilitate the adoption of social business, Unisys launched strategic communities at different levels of the firm. This was done to help employees easily adopt the new channel of communication.

Here are some questions to think about: Why are constant communication and sharing of expertise among its employees so important for a firm offering innovative services and solutions? How does Unisys's new social engine, NewsGator, make it easier for employees and managers to use and share knowledge?

11-1 What is the role of knowledge management systems in business?

Knowledge management and collaboration systems are among the fastest-growing areas of corporate and government software investment. The past decade has shown an explosive growth in research on knowledge and knowledge management in the economics, management, and information systems fields.

Knowledge management and collaboration are closely related. Knowledge that cannot be communicated and shared with others is nearly useless. Knowledge becomes useful and actionable when shared throughout the firm. We have already described the major tools for collaboration and social business in Chapter 2. In this chapter, we will focus on knowledge management systems and be mindful that communicating and sharing knowledge are becoming increasingly important.

We live in an information economy in which the major source of wealth and prosperity is the production and distribution of information and knowledge. An estimated 37 percent of the U.S. labor force consists of knowledge and information workers, the largest single segment of the labor force. About 55 percent of the gross domestic product (GDP) of the United States is generated by the knowledge and information sectors (U.S. Department of Labor, 2016). The European Union labor force exhibits similar patterns of rising employment for knowledge and information workers (Eurostate, 2016).

Knowledge management has become an important theme at many large business firms as managers realize that much of their firm's value depends on the firm's ability to create and manage knowledge. Studies have found that a substantial part of a firm's stock market value is related to its intangible assets, of which knowledge is one important component, along with brands, reputations, and unique business processes. Well-executed knowledge-based projects have been known to produce extraordinary returns on investment, although the impacts of knowledge-based investments are difficult to measure (Gu and Lev, 2001).

Important Dimensions of Knowledge

There is an important distinction between data, information, knowledge, and wisdom. Chapter 1 defines **data** as a flow of events or transactions captured by an organization's systems that, by itself, is useful for transacting but little else. To turn data into useful *information*, a firm must expend resources to organize data into categories of understanding, such as monthly, daily, regional, or store-based reports of total sales. To transform information into **knowledge**, a firm must expend additional resources to discover patterns, rules, and contexts where the knowledge works. Finally, **wisdom** is thought to be the collective and individual experience of applying knowledge to the solution of problems. Wisdom involves where, when, and how to apply knowledge.

Knowledge is both an individual attribute and a collective attribute of the firm. Knowledge is a cognitive, even a physiological, event that takes place

TABLE 11.1 IMPORTANT DIMENSIONS OF KNOWLEDGE

KNOWLEDGE IS A FIRM ASSET
Knowledge is an intangible asset.
The transformation of data into useful information and knowledge requires organizational resources.
Knowledge is not subject to the law of diminishing returns as are physical assets but instead experiences network effects as its value increases as more people share it.
KNOWLEDGE HAS DIFFERENT FORMS
Knowledge can be either tacit or explicit (codified).
Knowledge involves know-how, craft, and skill.
Knowledge involves knowing how to follow procedures.
Knowledge involves knowing why, not simply when, things happen (causality).
KNOWLEDGE HAS A LOCATION
Knowledge is a cognitive event involving mental models and maps of individuals.
There is both a social and an individual basis of knowledge.
Knowledge is "sticky" (hard to move), situated (enmeshed in a firm's culture), and contextual (works only in certain situations).
KNOWLEDGE IS SITUATIONAL
Knowledge is conditional; knowing when to apply a procedure is just as important as knowing the procedure (conditional).
Knowledge is related to context; you must know how to use a certain tool and under what circumstances.

inside people's heads. It is also stored in libraries and records, shared in lectures, and stored by firms in the form of business processes and employee know-how. Knowledge residing in the minds of employees that has not been documented is called **tacit knowledge**, whereas knowledge that has been documented is called **explicit knowledge**. Knowledge can reside in e-mail, voice mail, graphics, and unstructured documents as well as structured documents. Knowledge is generally believed to have a location, either in the minds of humans or in specific business processes. Knowledge is "sticky" and not universally applicable or easily moved. Finally, knowledge is thought to be situational and contextual. For example, you must know when to perform a procedure as well as how to perform it. Table 11.1 reviews these dimensions of knowledge.

We can see that knowledge is a different kind of firm asset from, say, buildings and financial assets; that knowledge is a complex phenomenon; and that there are many aspects to the process of managing knowledge. We can also recognize that knowledge-based core competencies of firms—the two or three things that an organization does best—are key organizational assets. Knowing how to do things effectively and efficiently in ways that other organizations cannot duplicate is a primary source of profit and competitive advantage that cannot be purchased easily by competitors in the marketplace.

For instance, having a unique build-to-order production system constitutes a form of knowledge and perhaps a unique asset that other firms cannot copy easily. With knowledge, firms become more efficient and effective in their use of scarce resources. Without knowledge, firms become less efficient and less effective in their use of resources and ultimately fail.

Organizational Learning and Knowledge Management

Like humans, organizations create and gather knowledge using a variety of organizational learning mechanisms. Through collection of data, careful measurement of planned activities, trial and error (experiment), and feedback from customers and the environment in general, organizations gain experience. Organizations that learn adjust their behavior to reflect that learning by creating new business processes and by changing patterns of management decision making. This process of change is called **organizational learning**. Arguably, organizations that can sense and respond to their environments rapidly will survive longer than organizations that have poor learning mechanisms.

The Knowledge Management Value Chain

Knowledge management refers to the set of business processes developed in an organization to create, store, transfer, and apply knowledge. Knowledge management increases the ability of the organization to learn from its environment and to incorporate knowledge into its business processes. Figure 11.1 illustrates the four value-adding steps in the knowledge management value chain. Each stage in the value chain adds value to raw data and information as they are transformed into usable knowledge.

In Figure 11.1, information systems activities are separated from related management and organizational activities, with information systems activities on the top of the graphic and organizational and management activities below. One apt slogan of the knowledge management field is "Effective knowledge management is 80 percent managerial and organizational and 20 percent technology."

In Chapter 1, we define *organizational and management capital* as the set of business processes, culture, and behavior required to obtain value from investments in information systems. In the case of knowledge management, as with other information systems investments, supportive values, structures, and behavior patterns must be built to maximize the return on investment in knowledge management projects. In Figure 11.1, the management and organizational activities in the lower half of the diagram represent the investment in organizational capital required to obtain substantial returns on the information technology (IT) investments and systems shown in the top half of the diagram.

Knowledge Acquisition

Organizations acquire knowledge in a number of ways, depending on the type of knowledge they seek. The first knowledge management systems sought to build corporate repositories of documents, reports, presentations, and best

FIGURE 11.1 THE KNOWLEDGE MANAGEMENT VALUE CHAIN

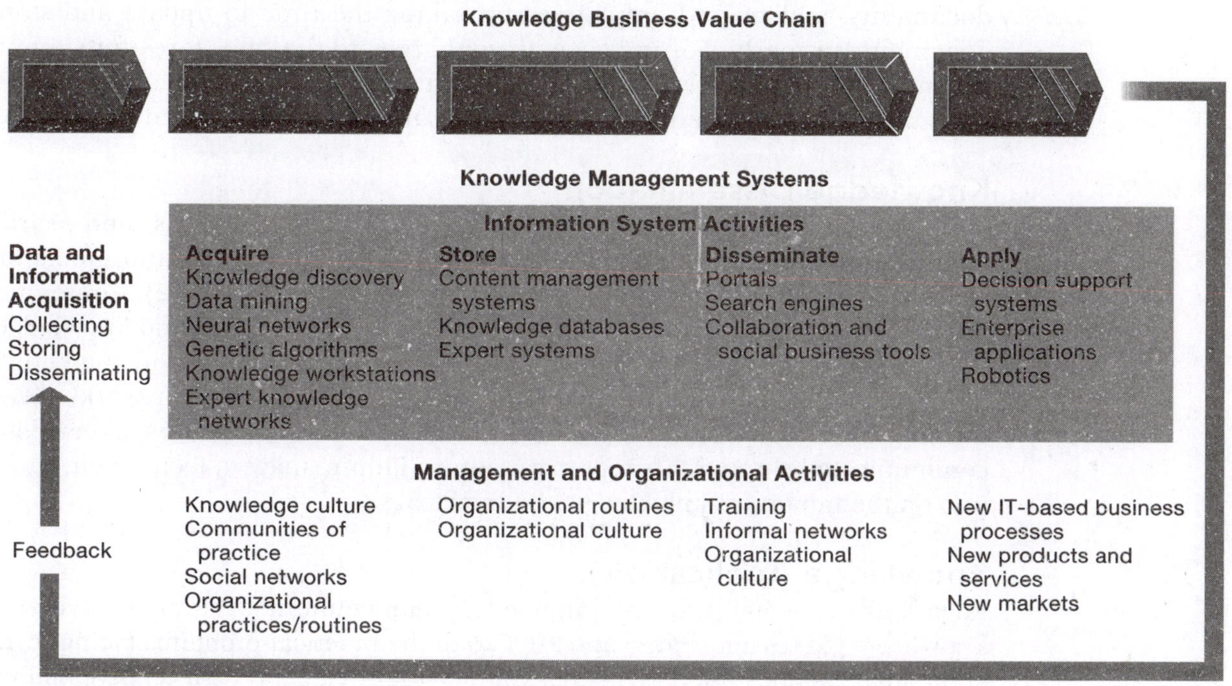

Knowledge management today involves both information systems activities and a host of enabling management and organizational activities.

practices. These efforts have been extended to include unstructured documents (such as e-mail). In other cases, organizations acquire knowledge by developing online expert networks so that employees can "find the expert" in the company who is personally knowledgeable.

In still other cases, firms must create new knowledge by discovering patterns in corporate data or by using knowledge workstations where engineers can discover new knowledge. These various efforts are described throughout this chapter. A coherent and organized knowledge system also requires systematic data from the firm's transaction processing systems that track sales, payments, inventory, customers, and other vital data as well as data from external sources such as news feeds, industry reports, legal opinions, scientific research, and government statistics.

Knowledge Storage

Once they are discovered, documents, patterns, and expert rules must be stored so they can be retrieved and used by employees. Knowledge storage generally involves the creation of a database. Document management systems that digitize, index, and tag documents according to a coherent framework are large databases adept at storing collections of documents. Expert systems also help corporations preserve the knowledge that is acquired by incorporating that knowledge into organizational processes and culture. Each of these is discussed later in this chapter and in the following chapter.

Management must support the development of planned knowledge storage systems, encourage the development of corporate-wide schemas for indexing documents, and reward employees for taking the time to update and store documents properly. For instance, it would reward the sales force for submitting names of prospects to a shared corporate database of prospects where all sales personnel can identify each prospect and review the stored knowledge.

Knowledge Dissemination

Portals, e-mail, instant messaging, wikis, social business tools, and search engine technology have added to an existing array of collaboration tools for sharing calendars, documents, data, and graphics (see Chapter 2). Contemporary technology seems to have created a deluge of information and knowledge. How can managers and employees discover, in a sea of information and knowledge, that which is really important for their decisions and their work? Here, training programs, informal networks, and shared management experience communicated through a supportive culture help managers focus their attention on the important knowledge and information.

Knowledge Application

Regardless of what type of knowledge management system is involved, knowledge that is not shared and applied to the practical problems facing firms and managers does not add business value. To provide a return on investment, organizational knowledge must become a systematic part of management decision making and become situated in systems for decision support (described in Chapter 12). Ultimately, new knowledge must be built into a firm's business processes and key application systems, including enterprise applications for managing key internal business processes and relationships with customers and suppliers. Management supports this process by creating—based on new knowledge—new business practices, new products and services, and new markets for the firm.

Building Organizational and Management Capital: Collaboration, Communities of Practice, and Office Environments

In addition to the activities we have just described, managers can help by developing new organizational roles and responsibilities for the acquisition of knowledge, including the creation of chief knowledge officer executive positions, dedicated staff positions (knowledge managers), and communities of practice. **Communities of practice (COPs)** are informal social networks of professionals and employees within and outside the firm who have similar work-related activities and interests. The activities of these communities include self-education and group education, conferences, online newsletters, and day-to-day sharing of experiences and techniques to solve specific work problems. Many organizations, such as IBM, the U.S. Federal Highway Administration, and the World Bank, have encouraged the development of thousands of online communities of practice. These communities of practice depend greatly on software environments that enable collaboration and communication.

COPs can make it easier for people to reuse knowledge by pointing community members to useful documents, creating document repositories, and filtering information for newcomers. COPs members act as facilitators, encouraging contributions and discussion. COPs can also reduce the learning curve for new employees by providing contacts with subject matter experts and access to a community's established methods and tools. Finally, COPs can act as a spawning ground for new ideas, techniques, and decision-making behavior.

Types of Knowledge Management Systems

There are essentially three major types of knowledge management systems: enterprise-wide knowledge management systems, knowledge work systems, and intelligent techniques. Figure 11.2 shows the knowledge management system applications for each of these major categories.

Enterprise-wide knowledge management systems are general-purpose firmwide efforts to collect, store, distribute, and apply digital content and knowledge. These systems include capabilities for searching for information, storing both structured and unstructured data, and locating employee expertise within the firm. They also include supporting technologies such as portals, search engines, collaboration and social business tools, and learning management systems.

The development of powerful networked workstations and software for assisting engineers and scientists in the discovery of new knowledge has led to the creation of knowledge work systems such as computer-aided design (CAD), visualization, simulation, and virtual reality systems. **Knowledge work systems (KWS)** are specialized systems built for engineers, scientists, and other

FIGURE 11.2 MAJOR TYPES OF KNOWLEDGE MANAGEMENT SYSTEMS

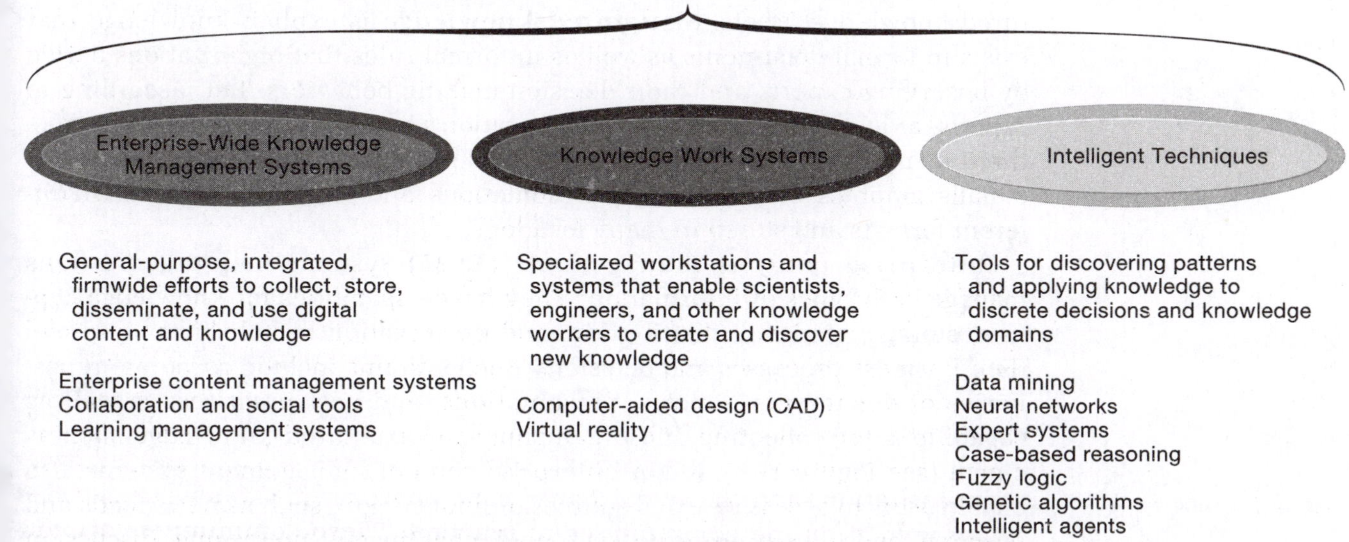

There are three major categories of knowledge management systems, and each can be broken down further into more specialized types of knowledge management systems.

knowledge workers charged with discovering and creating new knowledge for a company. We discuss knowledge work applications in detail in Section 11.3.

Knowledge management also includes a diverse group of **intelligent techniques**, such as data mining, expert systems, neural networks, fuzzy logic, genetic algorithms, and intelligent agents. These techniques have different objectives, from a focus on discovering knowledge (data mining and neural networks) to distilling knowledge in the form of rules for a computer program (expert systems and fuzzy logic) to discovering optimal solutions for problems (genetic algorithms). Section 11.4 provides more detail about these intelligent techniques.

11-2 What types of systems are used for enterprise-wide knowledge management, and how do they provide value for businesses?

Firms must deal with at least three kinds of knowledge. Some knowledge exists within the firm in the form of structured text documents (reports and presentations). Decision makers also need knowledge that is semistructured, such as e-mail, voice mail, chat room exchanges, videos, digital pictures, brochures, or bulletin board postings. In still other cases, there is no formal or digital information of any kind, and the knowledge resides in the heads of employees. Much of this knowledge is tacit knowledge that is rarely written down. Enterprise-wide knowledge management systems deal with all three types of knowledge.

Enterprise Content Management Systems

Businesses today need to organize and manage both structured and semistructured knowledge assets. **Structured knowledge** is explicit knowledge that exists in formal documents as well as in formal rules that organizations derive by observing experts and their decision-making behaviors. But, according to experts, at least 80 percent of an organization's business content is semistructured or unstructured—information in folders, messages, memos, proposals, e-mails, graphics, electronic slide presentations, and even videos created in different formats and stored in many locations.

Enterprise content management (ECM) systems help organizations manage both types of information. They have capabilities for knowledge capture, storage, retrieval, distribution, and preservation to help firms improve their business processes and decisions. Such systems include corporate repositories of documents, reports, presentations, and best practices, as well as capabilities for collecting and organizing semistructured knowledge such as e-mail (see Figure 11.3). Major enterprise content management systems also enable users to access external sources of information, such as news feeds and research, and to communicate via e-mail, chat/instant messaging, discussion groups, and videoconferencing. They are starting to incorporate blogs, wikis, and other enterprise social networking tools. Open Text Corporation, EMC

FIGURE 11.3 AN ENTERPRISE CONTENT MANAGEMENT SYSTEM

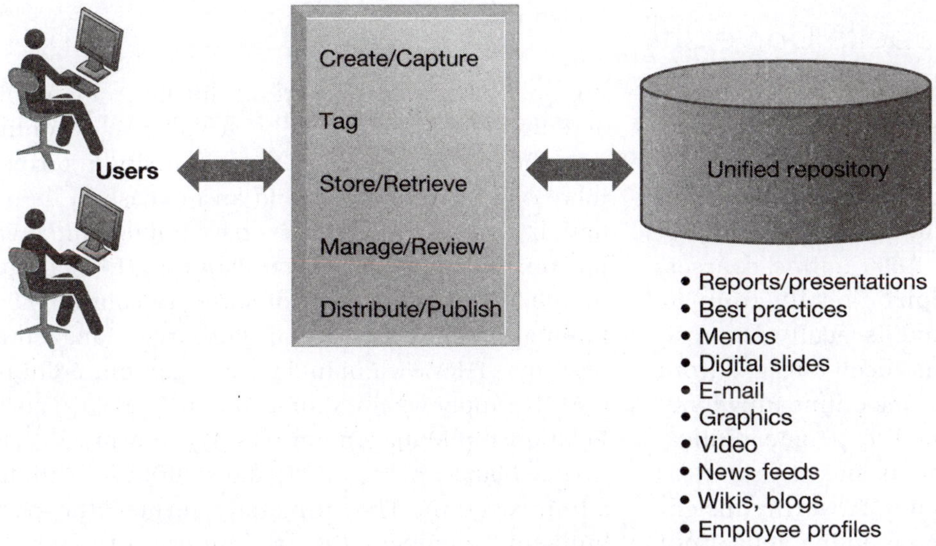

An enterprise content management system has capabilities for classifying, organizing, and managing structured and semistructured knowledge and making it available throughout the enterprise.

(Documentum), IBM, and Oracle Corporation are leading vendors of enterprise content management software. The Interactive Session on Organizations describes how the Capella University is benefited from Knowledge Management System ECM technology.

A key problem in managing knowledge is the creation of an appropriate classification scheme, or **taxonomy**, to organize information into meaningful categories so that it can be easily accessed. Once the categories for classifying knowledge have been created, each knowledge object needs to be "tagged," or classified, so that it can be easily retrieved. Enterprise content management systems have capabilities for tagging, interfacing with corporate databases and content repositories, and creating enterprise knowledge portals that provide a single point of access to information resources.

Firms in publishing, advertising, broadcasting, and entertainment have special needs for storing and managing unstructured digital data such as photographs, graphic images, video, and audio content. For example, Coca-Cola must keep track of all the images of the Coca-Cola brand that have been created in the past at all of the company's worldwide offices to prevent both redundant work and variation from a standard brand image. **Digital asset management systems** help companies classify, store, and distribute these digital objects.

Locating and Sharing Expertise

Some of the knowledge businesses need is not in the form of a digital document but instead resides in the memory of individual experts in the firm. Contemporary enterprise content management systems, along with the systems

INTERACTIVE SESSION: ORGANIZATIONS

KMS Empowering Capella University

Capella University is an institute for higher learning, owned by the Capella Education Company based in Minneapolis, Minnesota. The university largely delivers its education programs online which encompasses graduate, undergraduate, and certificate programs administered through 1,600 online courses. The university sees admissions globally from 61 countries other than the US, and its faculty (approximately 1,500 in number) too has been engaged from six different countries. It is the first online university to be recognized by the Council for Higher Education Accreditation (CHEA) for its success on measuring student learning outcomes. A worthy insight of the university is that due to an online delivery of courses, most of its students are working adults and more than 70 percent are pursuing postgraduate or doctoral degree. In light of the changing landscape of work and learning, where skill sets need to be acquired relatively quickly, Capella University has been continuously innovating. It has an innovative program called FlexPath, which is a direct assessment program allowing the students to complete a course at their own pace and assess their outcomes intermittently rather than periodically. Another innovation is Right Skill, a built-in partnership with CareerBuilder which provides the university with labor data indicating the areas where there is a dearth of labor and then the university designs and delivers programs to upskill the candidates to fill in that demand/supply gap. The university also engages with employers to train employees in certain verticals.

All these innovations and the nature of the online programs at the university brought about its own set of challenges. A basic requirement of an institute which delivers a bulk of its courses online is that of a web based system where faculty and students can access the university programs and experience university life through that portal. In addition, all the billing related activities, selection of courses, grading, submission of assignments, and recording of attendance needs to be done through the portal itself since that is the only means of communication between the university and the student. This makes the web based system highly complex which should not only be able to support all the above mentioned activities but should also be scalable to accommodate the growing needs of the university in terms of increased funcitonalities and an increase in the student base. Initially, the university implemented PeopleSoft Enterprise Resource Planning (ERP) system in 2007, which is a suite of software solutions containing modules for Human Resource Management Systems (HRMS), Financial Management Solutions (FMS), Supply Chain Management (SCM), Customer Relationship Management (CRM), Enterprise Performance Management (EPM) and solutions for student administration. The university termed the portal built on PeopleSoft ERP as iGuide. Although this suite provided immense benefits to the university, it could not keep up with the increase in the number of students, portfolio of courses offered, wider varieties of services and functionalities which made the current solution a pain in the neck. A major limitation of PeopleSoft was that it wasn't too flexible to accommodate new features rapidly, didn't support social media tools, lacked content management, and migration tool. The content management tool was essential since in its absence, all the editing had to be performed manually and a separate team of professionals were required to migrate the data onto the portal from different sources. Another challenge was an existence of disparate systems at the university to manage different activities such as Open Source Student Information System for managing student data, Shibboleth for user registration and account login, another system for student portfolio, another one for billing, grading and so on, all of which were incompatible with each other. As a result, the university administration as well as students had to access different portals to seek different information. Also, the content reusability was an issue. Besides this, the documents too were not stored in one location and different systems maintained different versions of the same document.

Therefore, Capella decided to look for a new solution which would be able to integrate all of its current technologies, eradicate existing problems, provide unified experience to users, and be scalable and flexible. Jason Scherschligt, Manager of Online User Experience at Capella admitted that the university needed a portal which was reliable, scalable, very flexible, accommodated new features rapidly and included Content Management System (CMS) and social media tools. The university also wished to enrich iGuide to create a virtual feel of the university for the students. It was decided by the university to enhance the core functionalities of ERP to create a richer web based experience for the users, and implement a complete knowledge management system which included a learning management system, a content management system, web portal, and document management system. For this purpose, it hired the services of CIGNEX Datamatics, which became a subsidiary of an Indian company Datamatics Global Services in 2011 and is an open source service provider of enterprise grade solutions, platforms, products and services. Through the services of CIGNEX Datamatics, an organization can leverage the open source technologies for their business purposes. It has been a global leader in content management, big data analytics, e-commerce solutions and so on.

CIGNEX Datamatics shortlisted the following combination of open source and proprietary technologies for solving the business challenges at the university namely, Liferay for portal development, Moodle for learning management system, and Alfresco for document management.

Liferay is an enterprise that makes open source software to create a personalized digital experience for its clients. It supports intranet capabilities with tools for collaboration such as communicators to share files among employees making their tasks easier, which can be accessed on any mobile device as well, and on interactive interfaces connected to back-end systems. In addition to this, it provides a role based access to the portal and offers the users various communities where they can share the space to discuss ideas, opinions, and content.

A remarkable feature of Liferay is its adherence to open standards which made it compatible with PeopleSoft ERP and hence they were easily integrated. Capella had chosen Liferay after throrough evalution of the same on over forty different criterias such as flexibility, architecture, interface, content, use and so on. By using the community and networking tools at Liferay, learners at the university were able to build their own professional profiles, and academic and professional networks. A striking feature of Liferay is offering a personalized course dashboard for every learner which displays academic activity from online course room called the Blackboard in real-time. The administrators can also use the group function of the technology aiding them to create groups in schools based on similar courses, interest areas, regions and so on. The Drag-and-Drop feature of the portal can be used to drag and drop courses taken by a candidate onto his webpage by creating a personalized Degree Completion Plan dynamically for the student. This also lets the student view his academic progress on demand. The new web portal is fully functional in all of Capella's schools and supports more than 40,000 users and staff. The users have developed over 100,000 friendly relations using networking tools of the site. In a survey carried out by the university, 90 percent of the students preferred the new portal over the previous one. The students find the new architecture user-friendly and more student oriented with easy navigation and quick access to data.

Moodle is an open source learning management system which is in use by more than 60,000 websites in 200 plus countries, supporting around 50 million users. The reason for Moodle being so popular is the plethora of features it supports including modules for course registrations, assignment submission, discussion forums, grading, quizzes, calendars, administration, tracking and analytics. CIGNEX Datamatics has developed approximately 110 solutions customizing Moodle learning management system. Moodle supports more than 120 languages which makes it a lucrative option for learning in different countries. It is also easily compatible with multiple devices and browsers and provides anytime-anywhere access. It was easily integrated with existing systems and a total of 19 learning solutions at the university were replaced by a single standardized platform which had low maintenance costs.

Alfresco is an open source document management solution which allows the university to maintain all the important documents at one place under a unified control. Earlier, the chaos was created due to storage of document at multiple places and a lack of document versioning. These limited the content reusability. However, Alfresco software enabled to locate all the data at one place for easier tracking, sharing and reuse, while also ensuring that the right information flowed at the right place at the right time. Alfresco also supports search features with instant search suggestions, speeding up the process of locating the relevant content. The data is stored and grouped based on what they contain rather than the location of the storage, which facilitates for easier search. It also allows for authenticated access to documents from any mobile device and any location. An important business benefit for Capella was that Alfresco automates repetitive tasks, so attendance record accumulation and interpretation was automated, thus saving the time of people doing the same manually. Similarly, grading and alerts generation for pending assignments too has been automated using Alfresco.

Capella is now thinking of implementing additional features like faculty content and tools, built-in alerts and indicators, enhanced partner pages to include corporate partnerships and so on. The additional benefits of implementing open source platforms were 50 percent savings in license, maintenance and support. Besides, integrated content management portal is scalable, which supports concurrent users (users accessing the system at the same time) in thousands, and is flexible.

Sources: http://s2.q4cdn.com, please read: the White Paper by Gilligan–Written Testimony; https://www.liferay.com, please read: the Customer Study on Capella University; http://www.capellauniversity.org; http://www.cignex.com, please navigate to 'Solutions Learning Management'; http://www.cignex.com, please read: Case Study: Reducing Cost Open Source Adoption; http://www.cignex.com, please navigate to Cignex Datamatics Expertise; https://www.slideshare.net, please search: 'Alfresco', then navigate to Alfresco in an Hour–Document Management, Web Content Management and Collaboration; https://www.alfresco.com, navigate to 'Capabilities', then read 'Document Management'; https://moodle.com/stories.

CASE STUDY QUESTIONS

1. Why is there a need for knowledge management system at a university which delivers online courses?
2. Discuss the components of knowledge management system at a university which delivers online courses.
3. Explain the features of Liferay and its business benefits to Capella Univeriusty.
4. Elaborate on the features of learning management system and document management system as highlighted in the case.

for collaboration and social business introduced in Chapter 2, have capabilities for locating experts and tapping their knowledge. These include online directories of corporate experts and their profiles with details about their job experience, projects, publications, and educational degrees, and repositories of expert-generated content. Specialized search tools make it easier for employees to find the appropriate expert in a company. For knowledge resources outside the firm, social networking and social business tools enable users to bookmark web pages of interest, tag these bookmarks with keywords, and share the tags and web page links with other people.

Learning Management Systems

Companies need ways to keep track of and manage employee learning and to integrate it more fully into their knowledge management and other corporate systems. A **learning management system (LMS)** provides tools for the management, delivery, tracking, and assessment of various types of employee learning and training.

Contemporary LMS support multiple modes of learning, including streaming videos, webinar classes, live instruction in classes or online, and group learning in online forums and chat sessions. The LMS consolidates mixed-media training, automates the selection and administration of courses, assembles and delivers learning content, and measures learning effectiveness.

Businesses run their own learning management systems, but they are also turning to publicly available **massive open online courses (MOOCs)** to educate their employees. A MOOC is an online course made available via the web to very large numbers of participants. Companies view MOOCs as a new way to design and deliver online learning where learners can collaborate with each other, watch short videos, and participate in threaded discussion groups. Firms such as Microsoft, AT&T, and Tenaris have developed their own MOOCs, while others such as Bank of America and Qualcomm are adapting publicly available MOOCs aligned with their core competencies (Meister, 2015). In Europe, MOOCs are not widely used by business firms yet and are considered mostly relevant to higher education institutions seeking to expand access to university courses (EADTU, 2015). In the near future, MOOCs will play a larger role in corporate training worldwide (Korn, 2014).

11-3 What are the major types of knowledge work systems, and how do they provide value for firms?

The enterprise-wide knowledge systems we have just described provide a wide range of capabilities that can be used by many if not all the workers and groups in an organization. Firms also have specialized systems for knowledge workers to help them create new knowledge and to ensure that this knowledge is properly integrated into the business.

Knowledge Workers and Knowledge Work

Knowledge workers, which we introduced in Chapter 1, include researchers, designers, architects, scientists, and engineers who primarily create knowledge and information for the organization. Knowledge workers usually have high levels of education and memberships in professional organizations and are often asked to exercise independent judgment as a routine aspect of their work. For example, knowledge workers create new products or find ways of improving existing ones. Knowledge workers perform three key roles that are critical to the organization and to the managers who work within the organization:

- Keeping the organization current in knowledge as it develops in the external world—in technology, science, social thought, and the arts
- Serving as internal consultants regarding the areas of their knowledge, the changes taking place, and opportunities
- Acting as change agents, evaluating, initiating, and promoting change projects

Requirements of Knowledge Work Systems

Most knowledge workers rely on office systems, such as word processors, voice mail, e-mail, videoconferencing, and scheduling systems, which are designed to increase worker productivity in the office. However, knowledge workers also require highly specialized knowledge work systems with powerful graphics, analytical tools, and communications and document management capabilities.

These systems require sufficient computing power to handle the sophisticated graphics or complex calculations necessary for such knowledge workers as scientific researchers, product designers, and financial analysts. Because knowledge workers are so focused on knowledge in the external world, these systems also must give the worker quick and easy access to external databases. They typically feature user-friendly interfaces that enable users to perform needed tasks without having to spend a great deal of time learning how to use the system. Knowledge workers are highly paid—wasting a knowledge worker's time is simply too expensive. Figure 11.4 summarizes the requirements of knowledge work systems.

Knowledge workstations often are designed and optimized for the specific tasks to be performed; for example, a design engineer requires a different workstation setup than a financial analyst. Design engineers need graphics with enough power to handle three-dimensional (3-D) CAD systems. However, financial analysts are more interested in access to a myriad number of external databases and large databases for efficiently storing and accessing massive amounts of financial data.

FIGURE 11.4 REQUIREMENTS OF KNOWLEDGE WORK SYSTEMS

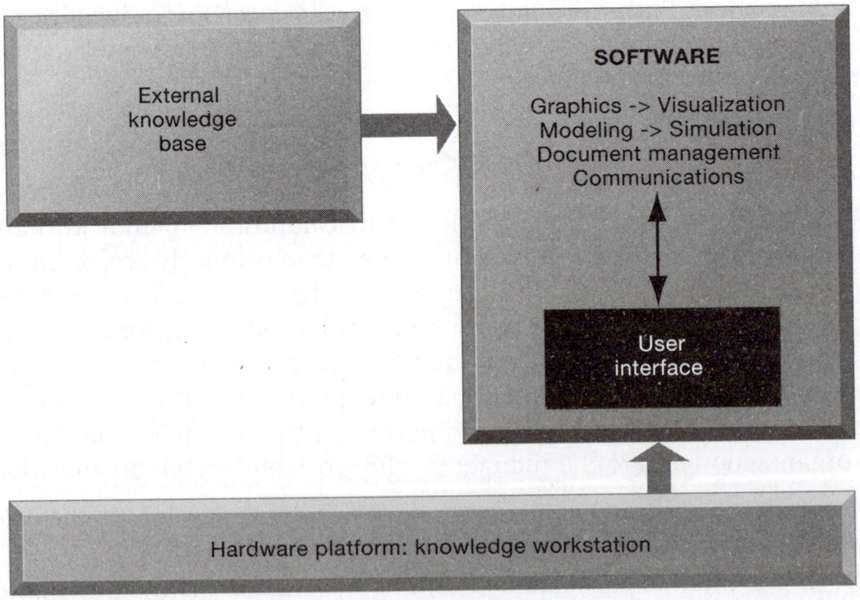

Knowledge work systems require strong links to external knowledge bases in addition to specialized hardware and software.

Examples of Knowledge Work Systems

Major knowledge work applications include CAD systems and virtual reality systems for simulation and modeling. **Computer-aided design (CAD)** automates the creation and revision of designs, using computers and sophisticated graphics software. Using a more traditional physical design methodology, each design modification requires a mold to be made and a prototype to be tested physically. That process must be repeated many times, which is a very expensive and time-consuming process. Using a CAD workstation, the designer need only make a physical prototype toward the end of the design process because the design can be easily tested and changed on the computer. The ability of CAD software to provide design specifications for the tooling and manufacturing processes also saves a great deal of time and money while producing a manufacturing process with far fewer problems.

For example, Dieguez Fridman, an award-winning Buenos Aires–based architectural design firm, uses AutoCAD software to provide the 3D conceptual design tools it needs to realize its ideas. For a retail interior design project for high-end fashion retailer Ayres, Dieguez Fridman architects used AutoCAD to develop a conceptual design for the client. The architects shared their ideas with each other, collaborating to choose the best ideas. After further refinement in AutoCAD, the firm transferred the digital design files into Autodesk 3ds Max Design software to help develop a photo-like rendering for Ayres. Viewing the design in 3D helped the client to visualize the interplay of space and light created by the complex forms featured in the design (Autocad, 2016).

CAD systems are able to supply data for **3-D printing**, also known as additive manufacturing, which uses machines to make solid objects, layer by layer, from specifications in a digital file. Unlike traditional techniques, by which objects are cut or drilled from molds, resulting in wasted materials, 3-D printing lets workers model an object on a computer and print it out with plastic, metal, or composite materials. 3-D printing is currently used for prototyping, custom manufacturing, and fashioning items with small production runs. Today's 3-D printers can handle materials including plastic, titanium, and human cartilage and produce fully functional components including batteries, transistors, prosthetic devices, LEDs, and other complex mechanisms, and there are now 3-D printing services that run over the cloud, such as that offered by Staples.

Virtual reality (VR) systems have visualization, rendering, and simulation capabilities that go far beyond those of conventional CAD systems. They use interactive graphics software to create computer-generated simulations that are so close to reality that users almost believe they are participating in a real-world situation. In many virtual reality systems, the user dons special clothing, headgear, and equipment, depending on the application. The clothing contains sensors that record the user's movements and immediately transmit that information back to the computer. For instance, to walk through a virtual reality simulation of a house, you would need garb that monitors the movement of your feet, hands, and head. You also would need goggles containing video screens and sometimes audio attachments and feeling gloves so that you can be immersed in the computer feedback. In the chapter-opening case, users of Cadillac's VR dealer system wear special VR headsets and headphones that make them feel they are seeing and listening to a real-world car.

Lloyds Banking Group is starting to use virtual reality to test applicants for its leadership programs in situations it would be unable to create under normal interview and test conditions. Lloyds receives 20,000 applications a year for 14 graduate leadership programs. Management believes virtual reality can help it learn more about the strengths and capabilities of candidates for information technology positions. Candidates will have complete freedom of movement within a 360-degree virtual world and will be able to move virtual objects using tracked motion controls (Flinders, 2016).

Augmented reality (AR) is a related technology for enhancing visualization. AR provides a live direct or indirect view of a physical real-world environment whose elements are augmented by virtual computer-generated imagery. The user is grounded in the real physical world, and the virtual images are merged with the real view to create the augmented display. The digital technology provides additional information to enhance the perception of reality, making the surrounding real world of the user more interactive and meaningful. The yellow first-down markers shown on televised football games are examples of augmented reality as are medical procedures like image-guided surgery, where data acquired from computerized tomography (CT) and magnetic resonance imaging (MRI) scans or from ultrasound imaging are superimposed on the patient in the operating room. Other industries where AR has caught on include military training, engineering design, robotics, and consumer design.

Virtual reality applications developed for the web use a standard called **Virtual Reality Modeling Language (VRML)**. VRML is a set of specifications for interactive, 3-D modeling on the web that can organize multiple media types, including animation, images, and audio to put users in a simulated real-world environment. VRML is platform independent, operates over a desktop computer, and requires little bandwidth.

11-4 What are the business benefits of using intelligent techniques for knowledge management?

Artificial intelligence and database technology provide a number of intelligent techniques that organizations can use to capture individual and collective knowledge and to extend their knowledge base. Expert systems, case-based reasoning, and fuzzy logic are used for capturing tacit knowledge. Neural networks and data mining are used for **knowledge discovery**. They can discover underlying patterns, categories, and behaviors in large data sets that could not be discovered by managers alone or simply through experience. Genetic algorithms are used for generating solutions to problems that are too large and complex for human beings to analyze on their own. Intelligent agents can automate routine tasks to help firms search for and filter information for use in electronic commerce, supply chain management, and other activities.

Data mining, which we introduced in Chapter 6, helps organizations capture undiscovered knowledge residing in large databases, providing managers with new insight for improving business performance. It has become an important tool for management decision making, and we provide a detailed discussion of data mining for management decision support in Chapter 12.

The intelligent techniques discussed in this chapter are based on **artificial intelligence (AI)** technology, which consists of computer-based systems (both hardware and software) that attempt to emulate human behavior. Such systems would be able to learn languages, accomplish physical tasks (robotics), use a perceptual apparatus that informs physical behavior and language, and emulate human expertise and decision making.

AI applications play an important role in contemporary knowledge management, but they do not exhibit the breadth, complexity, originality, and generality of human intelligence. Existing AI systems do not come up with new and novel solutions to problems. AI systems extend the powers of humans but in no way substitute for them or capture much of their intelligence. Briefly, existing systems lack the common sense and generality of naturally intelligent human beings. Human intelligence is vastly more complex than the most sophisticated computer programs and covers a much broader range of activities than is currently possible with so-called artificially intelligent devices. The Interactive Session on Technology on robots in manufacturing discusses some of these issues as does the chapter-ending case study on IBM's Watson.

Capturing Knowledge: Expert Systems

Expert systems are an intelligent technique for capturing tacit knowledge in a very specific and limited domain of human expertise. These systems capture the knowledge of skilled employees in the form of a set of rules in a software system that can be used by others in the organization. The set of rules in the expert system adds to the memory, or stored learning, of the firm.

Expert systems lack the breadth of knowledge and the understanding of fundamental principles of a human expert. They typically perform very limited tasks that can be performed by professionals in a few minutes or hours, such as diagnosing a malfunctioning machine or determining whether to grant credit for a loan. Problems that cannot be solved by human experts in the same short period of time are far too difficult for an expert system. However, by capturing human expertise in limited areas, expert systems can provide benefits, helping organizations make high-quality decisions with fewer people. Today, expert systems are used in business in discrete, highly structured decision-making situations.

How Expert Systems Work

Human knowledge must be modeled or represented in a way that a computer can process. Expert systems model human knowledge as a set of rules that

INTERACTIVE SESSION: TECHNOLOGY

Will Robots Replace People in Manufacturing?

For the past four decades, robots have been incorporated into manufacturing assembly lines in Europe, Japan, and the United States. These industrial robots—with mechanical arms that can be programmed to weld, paint, and pick up and place objects with predictable regularity—have not taken over many tasks performed by humans. The biggest users of robotic technology have been automobile manufacturing plants, where robots do heavy lifting, welding, applying glue, and painting. People still do most of the final assembly of cars, especially when installing small parts or wiring that needs to be guided into place.

For most manufacturing work, it has been less expensive to use manual labor than it is to own, operate, and maintain a robotics system, given the tasks that robots can perform. But this is changing. Robots have become smaller, more mobile, more collaborative and more adaptable, and their uses are widening. New robot models can work alongside humans without endangering them and help assemble all types of objects, as large as aircraft engines and as small and delicate as smartphones. They can also sense whether parts are being assembled correctly.

Robots are becoming easier to operate. Companies no longer need a software engineer to write program code to get a robot to perform a task. With some of today's robots, you can simply push a button, turn the robot's arm, and move it through the operation you want it to perform. The robot learns by doing.

A Renault SA plant in Cleon, France, now uses robots made by Universal Robots AS of Denmark to drive screws into engines, especially those that go into places people find hard to access. The robots have reach of more than 50 inches and six rotating joints to do the work. They also verify that parts are properly fastened and check to make sure the correct part is being used. The Renault robots weigh only about 64 pounds each so they can easily be moved around to different locations as needed. They are also "collaborative," designed to work in proximity to people. Using sonar, cameras, or other technologies, these robots can sense where people are and slow down or stop to avoid hurting them.

These new-style robots are moving into other industries as well. ABB Ltd of Switzerland and others have recently introduced robots to help assemble consumer-electronics items. The robots were designed to work close to people and handle small parts. JCB Laboratories is using robots at its Wichita, Kansas, plant to pick up syringes, fill them with medications, and snap on caps. The robots work five to six times faster than people.

This new generation of robots promises to bring major changes to the factory floor and perhaps the global competitive landscape. The Boston Consulting Group predicts that by 2025 the share of tasks performed by robots will rise from a global average of about 10 percent across all manufacturing industries to about 25 percent. In some industries, more than 40 percent of manufacturing tasks will be performed by robots. There will be dramatic productivity gains in many industries around the world (potentially boosting output per worker by 30 percent) and shifts in competitiveness among manufacturing countries.

Does this mean that robots will take over the production line? Unlikely. They still lack the flexibility, delicacy, and insight provided by humans. For example, today's collaborative robots often have to slow down or stop whenever people veer into their paths, disrupting production. Sales have been disappointing for Baxter, a two-armed collaborative robot from Rethink, which is used primarily for simple tasks such as moving materials, picking up parts, and packing or unpacking boxes. The robot's speed is restricted by safety considerations. For all their recent advances, robots still can't duplicate a human being's fine motor skills in manipulating materials and small parts. Robots still have trouble dealing with soft or floppy material, such as cloth or bundles of electrical wire.

Although robots are good at reliably and repeatedly performing defined tasks, they're not good at adapting. Mercedes-Benz had to cut back on its use of robots on the production line because the level of customization demanded by its customers requires a level of flexibility and dexterity that only humans can provide. Today's Mercedes customer wants to configure his or her own car, choosing among customization options such as carbon-fiber trim, four types of tire valve caps, and heated and cooled cup holders for 30 different models. Robots can't deal with the amount of variation in options that Mercedes cars have today.

Mercedes has found that if manufacturing focuses around a skilled crew of workers, it can shift a production line in a weekend. It would take weeks to reprogram robots and shift assembly patterns, and during that downtime, production would be at a standstill. Going forward, robots won't completely disappear from the Mercedes factory floor, but they'll be smaller and more flexible, operating alongside human workers. BMW AG and Volkswagen AG's Audi are also testing lightweight, sensor-equipped robots safe enough to work alongside people. Auto manufacturers are under continuing pressure to upgrade their models more frequently than the traditional seven-year cycle.

As robots become more widespread, manufacturing tasks performed by humans will become higher-level and more complex. Workers will be expected to supervise and perhaps even program robots, and there will be fewer low-level manufacturing jobs. Workers will need more sophisticated skills to succeed in tomorrow's manufacturing plants.

Sources: Bloomberg, "Why Mercedes Is Halting Robots' Reign on the Production Line," *Industry Week*, February 25, 2016; Harold L. Sirkin, Michael Zinser, and Justin Rose, "The Robotics Revolution: The Next Great Leap in Manufacturing," *BCG Perspectives*, September 23, 2015; "Industries and Economies Leading the Robotics Revolution," *BCG Perspectives*, September 23, 2015; and James R. Hagerty, "Meet the New Generation of Robots for Manufacturing," *Wall Street Journal*, June 2, 2015.

CASE STUDY QUESTIONS

1. Why have robots caught on in manufacturing? What knowledge to they require?
2. Can robots replace human workers in manufacturing? Explain your answer.
3. If you were considering introducing robots in your manufacturing plant, what management, organization, and technology issues would you need to address?

collectively are called the **knowledge base**. The rules are obtained by carefully interviewing one or several "experts" who have a thorough command of the knowledge base for the system or by documenting business rules found in manuals, books, or reports. Expert systems have from 200 to many thousands of these rules, depending on the complexity of the problem. These rules are much more interconnected and nested than in a traditional software program (see Figure 11.5).

The strategy used to search through the knowledge base is called the **inference engine**. Two strategies are commonly used: forward chaining and backward chaining (see Figure 11.6).

In **forward chaining**, the inference engine begins with the information entered by the user and searches the rule base to arrive at a conclusion. The strategy is to fire, or carry out, the action of the rule when a condition is true. In Figure 11.6, beginning on the left, if the user enters a client's name with income greater than $100,000, the engine will fire all rules in sequence from left to right. If the user then enters information indicating that the same client owns real estate, another pass of the rule base will occur and more rules will fire. Processing continues until no more rules can be fired.

In **backward chaining**, the strategy for searching the rule base starts with a hypothesis and proceeds by asking the user questions about selected facts

FIGURE 11.5 RULES IN AN EXPERT SYSTEM

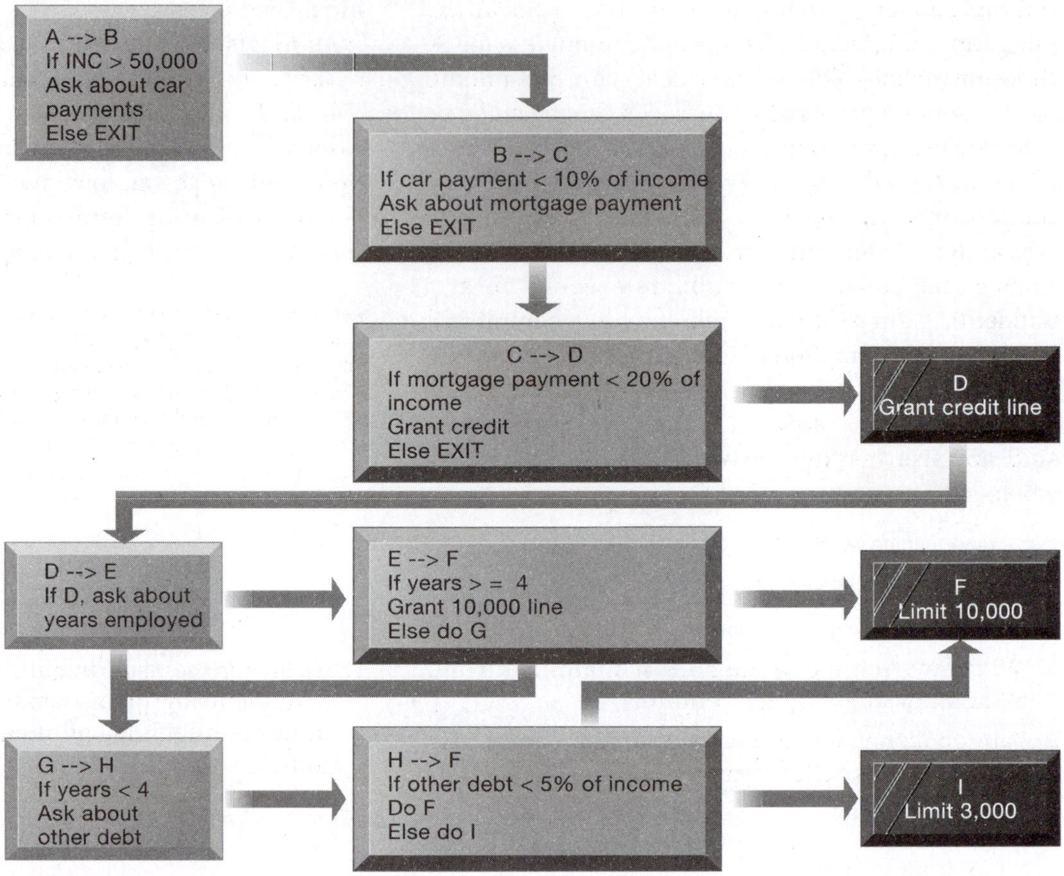

An expert system contains a number of rules to be followed. The rules are interconnected, the number of outcomes is known in advance and is limited, there are multiple paths to the same outcome, and the system can consider multiple rules at a single time. The rules illustrated are for simple credit-granting expert systems.

until the hypothesis is either confirmed or disproved. In our example, in Figure 11.6, ask the question "Should we add this person to the prospect database?" Begin on the right of the diagram and work toward the left. You can see that the person should be added to the database if a sales representative is sent, term insurance is granted, or a financial adviser visits the client.

Examples of Successful Expert Systems

Expert systems provide businesses with an array of benefits including improved decisions, reduced errors, reduced costs, reduced training time, and higher levels of quality and service. Con-Way Transportation built an expert system called Line-haul to automate and optimize planning of overnight shipment routes for its nationwide freight-trucking business. The expert system captures the business rules that dispatchers follow when assigning drivers, trucks, and trailers to transport 50,000 shipments of heavy freight each night

FIGURE 11.6 INFERENCE ENGINES IN EXPERT SYSTEMS

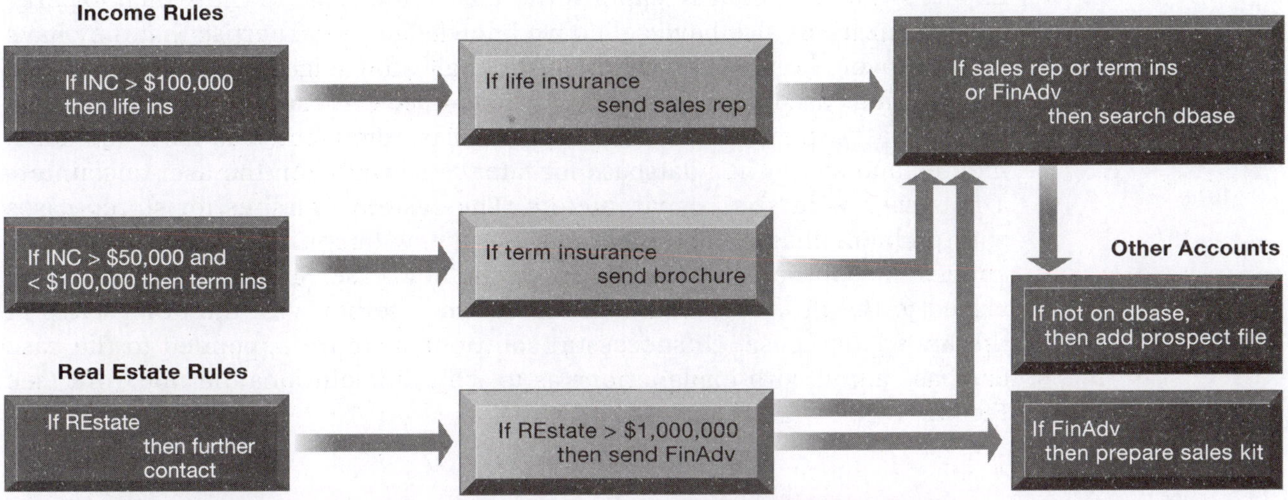

An inference engine works by searching through the rules and "firing" those rules that are triggered by facts gathered and entered by the user. Basically, a collection of rules is similar to a series of nested IF statements in a traditional software program; however, the magnitude of the statements and degree of nesting are much greater in an expert system.

across 25 states and Canada and then plots their routes. Line-haul runs on a Sun computer platform and uses data on daily customer shipment requests, available drivers, trucks, trailer space, and weight stored in an Oracle database. The expert system uses thousands of rules and 100,000 lines of program code written in C + + to crunch the numbers and create optimum routing plans for 95 percent of daily freight shipments. Con-Way dispatchers tweak the routing plan provided by the expert system and relay final routing specifications to field personnel responsible for packing the trailers for their nighttime runs. Con-Way recouped its $3 million investment in the system within two years by reducing the number of drivers, packing more freight per trailer, and reducing damage from rehandling. The system also reduces dispatchers' arduous nightly tasks.

Although expert systems lack the robust and general intelligence of human beings, they can provide benefits to organizations if their limitations are well understood. Only certain classes of problems can be solved using expert systems. Virtually all successful expert systems deal with problems of classification in limited domains of knowledge where there are relatively few alternative outcomes and these possible outcomes are all known in advance. Expert systems are much less useful for dealing with unstructured problems typically encountered by managers.

Many expert systems require large, lengthy, and expensive development efforts. Hiring or training more experts may be less expensive than building an expert system. Typically, the environment in which an expert system operates is continually changing so that the expert system must also continually change. Some expert systems, especially large ones, are so complex that in a few years the maintenance costs equal the development costs.

Organizational Intelligence: Case-Based Reasoning

Expert systems primarily capture the tacit knowledge of individual experts, but organizations also have collective knowledge and expertise that they have built up over the years. This organizational knowledge can be captured and stored using case-based reasoning. In **case-based reasoning (CBR)**, descriptions of past experiences of human specialists, represented as cases, are documented and stored in a database for later retrieval when the user encounters a new case with similar parameters. The system searches for stored cases with problem characteristics similar to the new one, finds the closest fit, and applies the solutions of the old case to the new case. Successful solutions are tagged to the new case and both are stored together with the other cases in the knowledge base. Unsuccessful solutions also are appended to the case database along with explanations as to why the solutions did not work (see Figure 11.7).

FIGURE 11.7 HOW CASE-BASED REASONING WORKS

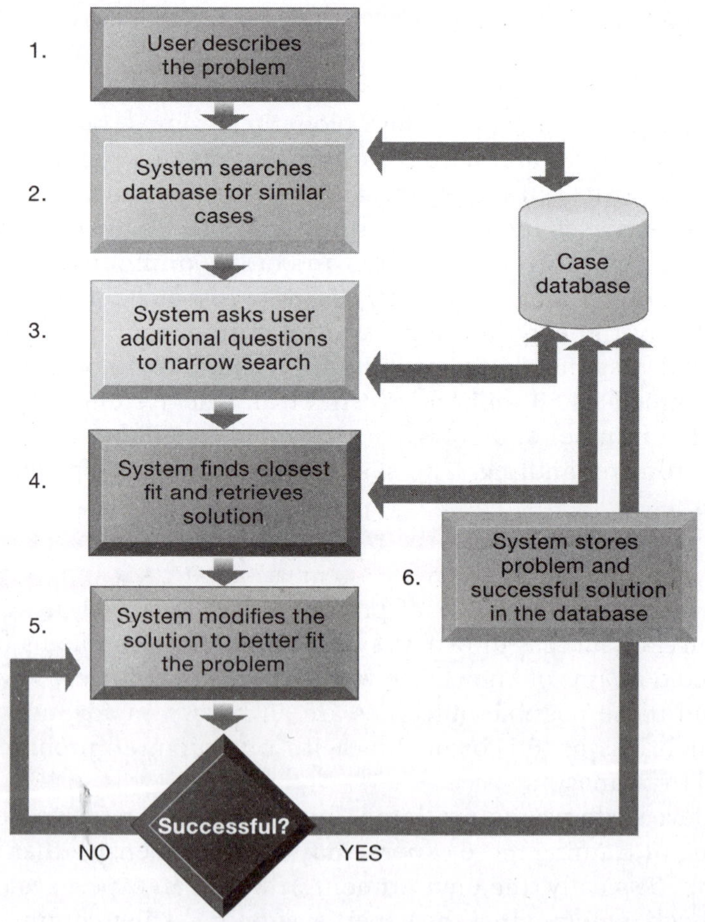

Case-based reasoning represents knowledge as a database of past cases and their solutions. The system uses a six-step process to generate solutions to new problems encountered by the user.

Expert systems work by applying a set of IF-THEN-ELSE rules extracted from human experts. Case-based reasoning, in contrast, represents knowledge as a series of cases, and this knowledge base is continuously expanded and refined by users. You'll find case-based reasoning in diagnostic systems in medicine or customer support where users can retrieve past cases whose characteristics are similar to the new case. The system suggests a solution or diagnosis based on the best-matching retrieved case.

Fuzzy Logic Systems

Most people do not think in terms of traditional IF-THEN rules or precise numbers. Humans tend to categorize things imprecisely using rules for making decisions that may have many shades of meaning. For example, a man or a woman can be *strong* or *intelligent*. A company can be *large, medium,* or *small* in size. Temperature can be *hot, cold, cool,* or *warm*. These categories represent a range of values.

Fuzzy logic is a rule-based technology that can represent such imprecision by creating rules that use approximate or subjective values. It can describe a particular phenomenon or process linguistically and then represent that description in a small number of flexible rules. Organizations can use fuzzy logic to create software systems that capture tacit knowledge where there is linguistic ambiguity.

Let's look at the way fuzzy logic would represent various temperatures in a computer application to control room temperature automatically. The terms (known as *membership functions*) are imprecisely defined so that, for example, in Figure 11.8, cool is between 45 degrees and 70 degrees, although the temperature is most clearly cool between about 60 degrees and 67 degrees. Note that *cool* is overlapped by *cold* or *norm*. To control the room environment using

FIGURE 11.8 FUZZY LOGIC FOR TEMPERATURE CONTROL

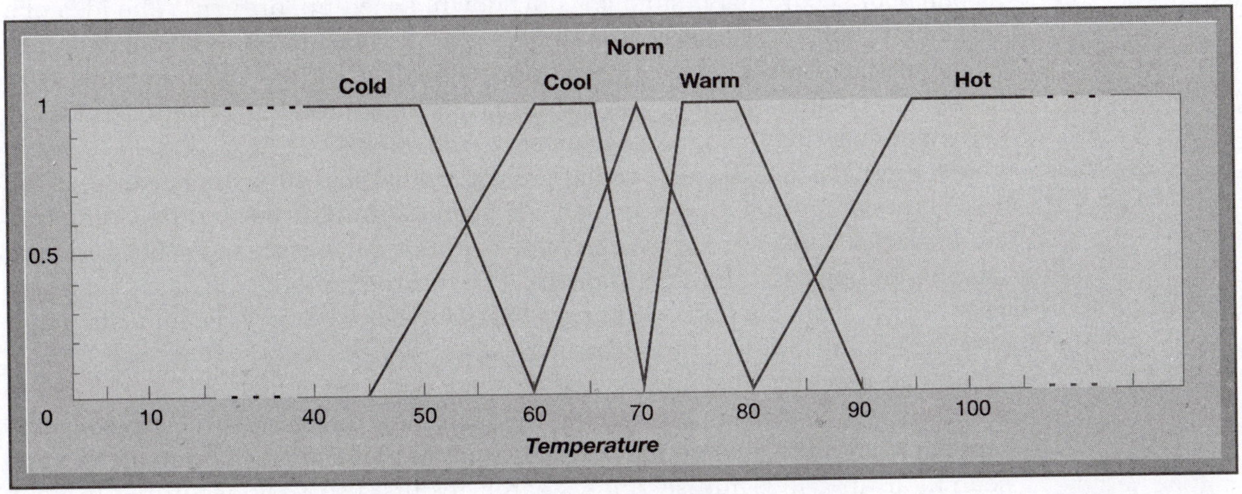

The membership functions for the input called temperature are in the logic of the thermostat to control the room temperature. Membership functions help translate linguistic expressions such as warm into numbers that the computer can manipulate.

this logic, the programmer would develop similarly imprecise definitions for humidity and other factors, such as outdoor wind and temperature. The rules might include one that says: "If the temperature is *cool* or *cold* and the humidity is low while the outdoor wind is high and the outdoor temperature is low, raise the heat and humidity in the room." The computer would combine the membership function readings in a weighted manner and, using all the rules, raise and lower the temperature and humidity.

Fuzzy logic provides solutions to problems requiring expertise that is difficult to represent in the form of crisp IF-THEN rules. In Japan, Sendai's subway system uses fuzzy logic controls to accelerate so smoothly that standing passengers need not hold on. Mitsubishi Heavy Industries in Tokyo has been able to reduce the power consumption of its air conditioners by 20 percent by implementing control programs in fuzzy logic. The autofocus device in cameras is only possible because of fuzzy logic. In these instances, fuzzy logic allows incremental changes in inputs to produce smooth changes in outputs instead of discontinuous ones, making it useful for consumer electronics and engineering applications.

Management also has found fuzzy logic useful for decision making and organizational control. A Wall Street firm created a system that selects companies for potential acquisition using the language stock traders understand. A fuzzy logic system has been developed to detect possible fraud in medical claims submitted by health care providers anywhere in the United States.

Machine Learning

Machine learning is the study of how computer programs can improve their performance without explicit programming. Why does this constitute learning? A machine that learns is a machine that, like a human being, can recognize patterns in data, and change its behavior based on its recognition of patterns, experience, or prior learnings (a database). For instance, a car-driving robot should be able to recognize the presence of other cars and objects (people), and change its behavior accordingly (stop, go, slow down, speed up, or turn). The idea of a self-taught, self-correcting, computer program is not new, and has been a part of the artificial intelligence field at least since the 1970s. Up until the 1990s, however, machine learning was not very capable of producing useful devices or solving interesting business problems.

Machine learning has expanded greatly in the past 10 years because of the growth in computing power available to scientists and firms and its falling cost along with advances in the design of algorithms, databases, and robots (see the chapter-ending case on IBM's Watson). The Internet and the big data (see Chapter 6) made available on the Internet have proved to be very useful testing and proving grounds for machine learning.

We use machine learning every day but don't recognize it. Every Google search is resolved using algorithms that rank the billions of web pages based on your query and change the results based on any changes you make in your search, all in a few milliseconds. Search results also vary according to your prior searches and the items you clicked on. Every time you buy something on Amazon, its recommender engine will suggest other items you might be interested in based on patterns in your prior consumption, behavior on other websites, and the purchases of others who are "similar" to you. Every time you visit Netflix, a recommender system will come up with movies you might be interested in based on a similar set of factors.

Neural Networks

Neural networks are used for solving complex, poorly understood problems for which large amounts of data have been collected. They find patterns and relationships in massive amounts of data that would be too complicated and difficult for a human being to analyze. Neural networks discover this knowledge by using hardware and software that parallel the processing patterns of the biological or human brain. Neural networks "learn" patterns from large quantities of data by sifting through data, searching for relationships, building models, and correcting over and over again the model's own mistakes.

A neural network has a large number of sensing and processing nodes that continuously interact with each other. Figure 11.9 represents one type of neural network comprising an input layer, an output layer, and a hidden processing layer. Humans "train" the network by feeding it a set of training data for which the inputs produce a known set of outputs or conclusions. This helps the computer learn the correct solution by example. As the computer is fed more data, each case is compared with the known outcome. If it differs, a correction is calculated and applied to the nodes in the hidden processing layer. These steps are repeated until a condition, such as corrections being less than a certain amount, is reached. The neural network in Figure 11.9 has learned how to identify a fraudulent credit card purchase. Also, self-organizing neural networks can be trained by exposing them to large amounts of data and allowing them to discover the patterns and relationships in the data.

FIGURE 11.9 HOW A NEURAL NETWORK WORKS

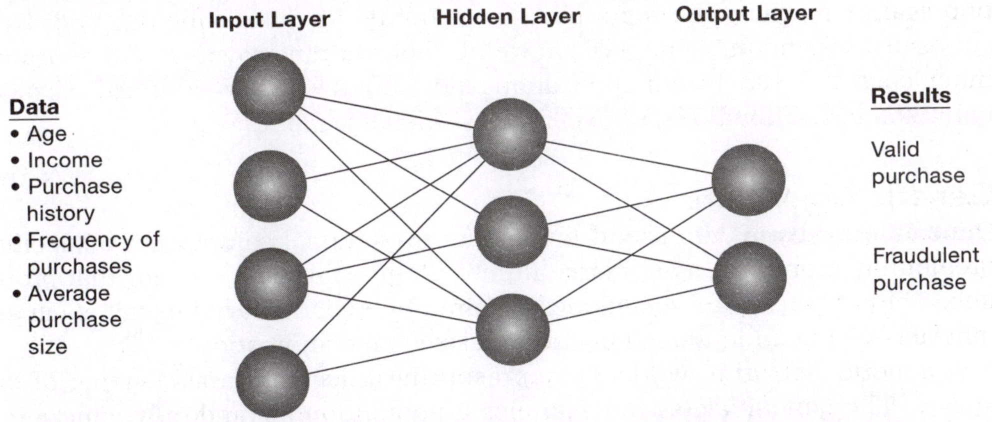

A neural network uses rules it "learns" from patterns in data to construct a hidden layer of logic. The hidden layer then processes inputs, classifying them based on the experience of the model. In this example, the neural network has been trained to distinguish between valid and fraudulent credit card purchases.

A Google research team headed by Stanford University computer scientist Andrew Y. Ng and Google fellow Jeff Dean recently created a neural network with more than a billion connections that could identify cats. The network used an array of 16,000 processors and was fed random thumbnails of images, each extracted from a collection of 10 million YouTube videos. The neural network taught itself to recognize cats without human help in identifying specific features during the learning process. Google believes this neural network has promising applications in image search, speech recognition, and machine language translation. IBM has developed an energy-efficient processor chip that relies on a dense web of transistors similar to the brain's neural network. It is still in experimental mode, with great promise for pattern recognition (Markoff, 2012, 2013).

Whereas expert systems seek to emulate or model a human expert's way of solving problems, neural network builders claim that they do not program solutions and do not aim to solve specific problems. Instead, neural network designers seek to put intelligence into the hardware in the form of a generalized capability to learn. In contrast, the expert system is highly specific to a given problem and cannot be retrained easily.

Neural network applications in medicine, science, and business address problems in pattern classification, prediction, financial analysis, and control and optimization. In medicine, neural network applications are used for screening patients for coronary artery disease, for diagnosing patients with epilepsy and Alzheimer's disease, and for performing pattern recognition of pathology images. The financial industry uses neural networks to discern patterns in large pools of data that might help predict the performance of equities, corporate bond ratings, or corporate bankruptcies. Visa International uses a neural network to help detect credit card fraud by monitoring all Visa transactions for sudden changes in the buying patterns of cardholders.

There are many puzzling aspects of neural networks. Unlike expert systems, which typically provide explanations for their solutions, neural networks cannot always explain why they arrived at a particular solution. Moreover, they cannot always guarantee a completely certain solution, arrive at the same solution again with the same input data, or guarantee the best solution. They are very sensitive and may not perform well if their training covers too little or too much data. In most current applications, neural networks are best used as aids to human decision makers instead of substitutes for them.

Genetic Algorithms

Genetic algorithms are useful for finding the optimal solution for a specific problem by examining a very large number of possible solutions for that problem. They are based on techniques inspired by evolutionary biology, such as inheritance, mutation, selection, and crossover (recombination).

A genetic algorithm works by representing information as a string of 0s and 1s. The genetic algorithm searches a population of randomly generated strings of binary digits to identify the right string representing the best possible solution for the problem. As solutions alter and combine, the worst ones are discarded and the better ones survive to go on to produce even better solutions.

FIGURE 11.10 THE COMPONENTS OF A GENETIC ALGORITHM

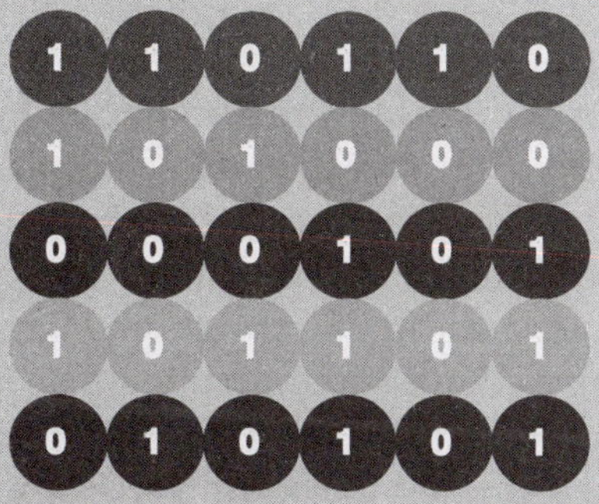

	Length	Width	Weight	Fitness
1	Long	Wide	Light	55
2	Short	Narrow	Heavy	49
3	Long	Narrow	Heavy	36
4	Short	Medium	Light	61
5	Long	Medium	Very light	74

A population of chromosomes | **Decoding of chromosomes** | **Evaluation of chromosomes**

This example illustrates an initial population of "chromosomes," each representing a different solution. The genetic algorithm uses an iterative process to refine the initial solutions so that the better ones, those with the higher fitness, are more likely to emerge as the best solution.

In Figure 11.10, each string corresponds to one of the variables in the problem. One applies a test for fitness, ranking the strings in the population according to their level of desirability as possible solutions. After the initial population is evaluated for fitness, the algorithm then produces the next generation of strings, consisting of strings that survived the fitness test plus offspring strings produced from mating pairs of strings, and tests their fitness. The process continues until a solution is reached.

Genetic algorithms are used to solve problems that are very dynamic and complex, involving hundreds or thousands of variables or formulas. The problem must be one where the range of possible solutions can be represented genetically and criteria can be established for evaluating fitness. Genetic algorithms expedite the solution because they are able to evaluate many solution alternatives quickly to find the best one. For example, General Electric engineers used genetic algorithms to help optimize the design for jet turbine aircraft engines, where each design change required changes in up to 100 variables. The supply chain management software from JDA Software uses genetic algorithms to optimize production-scheduling models incorporating hundreds of thousands of details about customer orders, material and resource availability, manufacturing and distribution capability, and delivery dates.

Intelligent Agents

Intelligent agent technology helps businesses navigate through large amounts of data to locate and act on information that is considered important. **Intelligent agents** are software programs that work without direct human intervention to carry out specific tasks for an individual user, business process, or software application. The agent uses a built-in or learned knowledge base to accomplish tasks or make decisions on the user's behalf, such as deleting junk e-mail, scheduling appointments, or traveling over interconnected networks to find the cheapest airfare to California.

There are many intelligent agent applications today in operating systems, application software, e-mail systems, mobile computing software, and network tools. For example, the wizards found in Microsoft Office software tools have built-in capabilities to show users how to accomplish various tasks, such as formatting documents or creating graphs, and to anticipate when users need assistance. Chapter 7 describes how intelligent agent shopping bots can help consumers find products they want and assist them in comparing prices and other features.

Although some intelligent agents are programmed to follow a simple set of rules, others are capable of learning from experience and adjusting their behavior. Siri, an application on Apple's iOS operating system for the iPhone and iPad, is an example. Siri is an intelligent personal assistant that uses voice recognition technology to answer questions, make recommendations, and perform actions. The software adapts to the user's individual preferences over time and personalizes results, performing tasks such as finding nearby restaurants, purchasing movie tickets, getting directions, scheduling appointments, and sending messages. Siri understands natural speech, and it asks the user questions if it needs more information to complete a task. Google Now, Microsoft's Cortana, and Amazon's Echo are other intelligent agent tools for consumers with similar capabilities.

Chatbots (chatterbots) are software agents designed to simulate a conversation with one or more human users via textual or auditory methods. They try to understand what you type or say and respond by answering questions or executing tasks. Chatbots are typically used in systems for customer service or information acquisition. For example, Facebook has integrated chatbots into its Messenger messaging app so that an outside company with a Facebook brand page can interact with Facebook users through the chat program. A Facebook user could, for example, browse for a pair of lightweight running shoes on Messenger by texting a message to begin a conversation with Spring, a mobile shopping app. Spring would ask the user for his or her preferred price range for the shoes and display small selections of what it thinks the user might like.

Many complex phenomena can be modeled as systems of autonomous agents that follow relatively simple rules for interaction. **Agent-based modeling** applications have been developed to model the behavior of consumers, stock markets, and supply chains and to predict the spread of epidemics.

Procter & Gamble (P&G) used agent-based modeling to improve coordination among different members of its supply chain in response to changing business conditions (see Figure 11.11). It modeled a complex supply chain as a group of semiautonomous "agents" representing individual supply chain components, such as trucks, production facilities, distributors, and retail stores.

FIGURE 11.11 INTELLIGENT AGENTS IN P&G'S SUPPLY CHAIN NETWORK

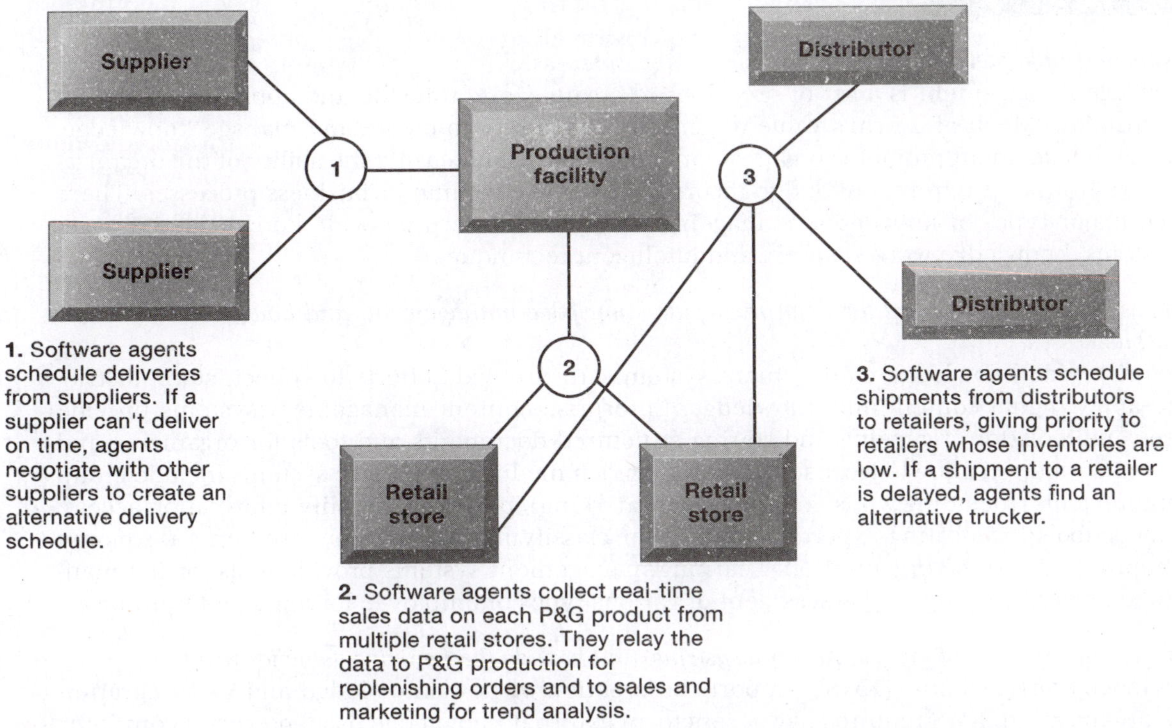

Intelligent agents are helping P&G shorten the replenishment cycles for products such as a box of Tide.

Using intelligent agent models, P&G discovered that trucks should often be dispatched before being fully loaded. Although transportation costs would be higher using partially loaded trucks, the simulation showed that retail store stockouts would occur less often, thus reducing the amount of lost sales, which would more than make up for the higher distribution costs. Agent-based modeling has saved P&G $300 million annually on an investment of less than 1 percent of that amount.

Hybrid AI Systems

Genetic algorithms, fuzzy logic, neural networks, and expert systems can be integrated into a single application to take advantage of the best features of these technologies. Such systems are called **hybrid AI systems**. Hybrid applications in business are growing. In Japan, Hitachi, Mitsubishi, Ricoh, Sanyo, and others are starting to incorporate hybrid AI in products such as home appliances, factory machinery, and office equipment. Matsushita has developed a "neurofuzzy" washing machine that combines fuzzy logic with neural networks.

Review Summary

11-1 *What is the role of knowledge management systems in business?*

Knowledge management is a set of processes to create, store, transfer, and apply knowledge in the organization. Much of a firm's value depends on its ability to create and manage knowledge. Knowledge management promotes organizational learning by increasing the ability of the organization to learn from its environment and to incorporate knowledge into its business processes. There are three major types of knowledge management systems: enterprise-wide knowledge management systems, knowledge work systems, and intelligent techniques.

11-2 *What types of systems are used for enterprise-wide knowledge management, and how do they provide value for businesses?*

Enterprise-wide knowledge management systems are firmwide efforts to collect, store, distribute, and apply digital content and knowledge. Enterprise content management systems provide databases and tools for organizing and storing structured documents and tools for organizing and storing semistructured knowledge, such as e-mail or rich media. Often these systems include group collaboration tools (including wikis and social bookmarking), portals to simplify information access, search tools, tools for locating experts, and tools for classifying information based on a taxonomy that is appropriate for the organization. Learning management systems provide tools for the management, delivery, tracking, and assessment of various types of employee learning and training.

11-3 *What are the major types of knowledge work systems, and how do they provide value for firms?*

Knowledge work systems (KWS) support the creation of new knowledge and its integration into the organization. KWS require easy access to an external knowledge base; powerful computer hardware that can support software with intensive graphics, analysis, document management, and communications capabilities; and a user-friendly interface. Computer-aided design (CAD) systems, augmented reality applications, and virtual reality systems, which create interactive simulations that behave like the real world, require graphics and powerful modeling capabilities.

11-4 *What are the business benefits of using intelligent techniques for knowledge management?*

Artificial intelligence lacks the flexibility, breadth, and generality of human intelligence, but it can be used to capture, codify, and extend organizational knowledge. Expert systems capture tacit knowledge from a limited domain of human expertise and express that knowledge in the form of rules. Expert systems are most useful for problems of classification or diagnosis. Case-based reasoning represents organizational knowledge as a database of cases that can be continually expanded and refined.

Fuzzy logic is a software technology for expressing knowledge in the form of rules that use approximate or subjective values. Fuzzy logic has been used for controlling physical devices and is starting to be used for limited decision-making applications.

Machine learning refers to the ability of computer programs to automatically learn and improve with experience. Neural networks consist of hardware and software that attempt to mimic the thought processes of the human brain. Neural networks are notable for their ability to learn without programming and to recognize patterns that cannot be easily described by humans. They are being used in science, medicine, and business to discriminate patterns in massive amounts of data.

Genetic algorithms develop solutions to particular problems using genetically based processes such as fitness, crossover, and mutation. Genetic algorithms are beginning to be applied to problems involving optimization, product design, and monitoring industrial systems where many alternatives or variables must be evaluated to generate an optimal solution.

Intelligent agents are software programs with built-in or learned knowledge bases that carry out specific tasks for an individual user, business process, or software application. Intelligent agents can be programmed to navigate through large amounts of data to locate useful information and in some cases act on that information on behalf of the user.

Key Terms

3-D printing, 459
Agent-based modeling, 472
Artificial intelligence (AI), 461
Augmented reality (AR), 460
Backward chaining, 463
Case-based reasoning (CBR), 466
Chatbot, 472
Communities of practice (COPs), 450
Computer-aided design (CAD), 459
Data, 446
Digital asset management systems, 453
Enterprise content management (ECM), 452
Enterprise-wide knowledge management systems, 451
Expert systems, 461
Explicit knowledge, 447
Forward chaining, 463
Fuzzy logic, 467
Genetic algorithms, 470
Hybrid AI systems, 473
Inference engine, 463
Intelligent agents, 471
Intelligent techniques, 452
Knowledge, 446
Knowledge base, 463
Knowledge discovery, 460
Knowledge management, 448
Knowledge work systems (KWS), 451
Learning management system (LMS), 456
Machine learning, 468
Massive open online course (MOOC), 457
Neural networks, 469
Organizational learning, 448
Structured knowledge, 452
Tacit knowledge, 447
Taxonomy, 453
Virtual Reality Modeling Language (VRML), 460
Virtual reality (VR), 459
Wisdom, 446

Review Questions

11-1 What is the role of knowledge management systems in business?

- Discuss the characteristics of knowledge which makes it different from other firm's assets.
- Define COPs and describe how do they aid in knowledge management in organizations?
- Describe the major types of knowledge management systems and applications for each of these categories.
- Define organizational learning and discuss organizational capital investments required in KM value chain.

11-2 What type of systems are used for enterprise-wide knowledge management, and how do they provide value for business?

- Differentiate between structured and semi-structured knowledge. How does the enterprise content management system aid organizations in managing both?
- List and describe knowledge management system used to manage digital data and experts' knowledge?

11-3 What are the major types of knowledge work systems? How do they provide value for firms?

- Define knowledge workers, their key roles and also discuss why do they need knowledge work systems.
- List and describe major knowledge work applications and also discuss their business benefits.

11-4 What are the business benefits of using intelligent techniques for knowledge management?

- Define artificial intelligence. Explain its role in knowledge management.
- Define an expert system, describe how it works, and explain its value to business.
- Define case-based reasoning and explain how it differs from an expert system.
- Define fuzzy logic and describe the types of decisions fuzzy logic systems make.
- Define machine learning and give some examples.
- Define and describe intelligent agents and give an example of a type of intelligent agent.

Discussion Questions

11-5 Knowledge management is a business process, not a technology. Discuss.

11-6 Describe various ways that knowledge management systems could help firms with sales and marketing or with manufacturing and production.

11-7 Your company wants to do more with knowledge management. Describe the steps it should take to develop a knowledge management program and select knowledge management applications.

Hands-On MIS Projects

The projects in this section give you hands-on experience designing a knowledge portal, identifying opportunities for knowledge management, creating a simple expert system, and using intelligent agents to research products for sale on the web.

Hands-On MIS Projects. Management Decision Problems

11-8 U.S. Pharma Corporation is headquartered in New Jersey but has research sites in Germany, France, the United Kingdom, Switzerland, and Australia. Research and development of new pharmaceuticals is key to ongoing profits, and U.S. Pharma researches and tests thousands of possible drugs. The company's researchers need to share information with others within and outside the company, including the U.S. Food and Drug Administration, the World Health Organization, and the International Federation of Pharmaceutical Manufacturers & Associations. Also critical is access to health information sites, such as the U.S. National Library of Medicine, and to industry conferences and professional journals. Design a knowledge portal for U.S. Pharma's researchers. Include in your design specifications relevant internal systems and databases, external sources of information, and internal and external communication and collaboration tools. Design a home page for your portal.

11-9 Canadian Tire is one of Canada's largest companies, with 50,000 employees and 1,100 stores and gas bars (gas stations) across Canada selling sports, leisure, home products, apparel, and financial services as well as automotive and petroleum products. The retail outlets are independently owned and operated. Canadian Tire has been using daily mailings and thick product catalogs to inform its dealers about new products, merchandise setups, best practices, product ordering, and problem resolution, and it is looking for a better way to provide employees with human resources and administrative documents. Describe the problems created by this way of doing business and how knowledge management systems might help.

Improving Decision Making: Building a Simple Expert System for Retirement Planning

Software skills: Spreadsheet formulas and IF function or expert system tool
Business skills: Benefits eligibility determination

11-10 Expert systems typically use a large number of rules. This project has been simplified to reduce the number of rules, but it will give you experience working with a series of rules to develop an application.

When employees at your company retire, they are given cash bonuses. These cash bonuses are based on the length of employment and the retiree's age. To receive a bonus, an employee must be at least 50 years of age and have worked for the company for more than five years. The following table summarizes the criteria for determining bonuses.

LENGTH OF EMPLOYMENT	BONUS
<5 years	No bonus
5–10 years	20 percent of current annual salary

LENGTH OF EMPLOYMENT	BONUS
11–15 years	30 percent of current annual salary
16–20 years	40 percent of current annual salary
21–25 years	50 percent of current annual salary
26 or more years	100 percent of current annual salary

Using the information provided, build a simple expert system. Find a demonstration copy of an expert system software tool on the web that you can download. Alternatively, use your spreadsheet software to build the expert system. (If you are using spreadsheet software, we suggest using the IF function so you can see how rules are created.)

Improving Decision Making: Using Intelligent Agents for Comparison Shopping

Software skills: Web browser and shopping bot software
Business skills: Product evaluation and selection

11-11 This project will give you experience using shopping bots to search online for products, find product information, and find the best prices and vendors. Select a digital camera you might want to purchase, such as the Canon PowerShot SX530 or the Olympus Tough TG-4. Visit MySimon (www.mysimon.com), BizRate.com (www.bizrate.com), and Google Shopping to do price comparisons for you. Evaluate these shopping sites in terms of their ease of use, number of offerings, speed in obtaining information, thoroughness of information offered about the product and seller, and price selection. Which site or sites would you use, and why? Which camera would you select, and why? How helpful were these sites for making your decision?

Collaboration and Teamwork Project

Rating Enterprise Content Management Systems

11-12 With a group of classmates, select two enterprise content management (ECM) products, such as those from Oracle, Open Text, IBM, or EMC Documentum. Compare their features and capabilities. To prepare your analysis, use articles from computer magazines and the websites of the ECM software vendors. If possible, use Google Docs and Google Drive or Google Sites to brainstorm, organize, and develop a presentation of your findings for the class.

Knowledge Management and Collaboration at Tata Consulting Services

CASE STUDY

Tata Consultancy Services (TCS) is an IT-services, business-solutions, and outsourcing organization that offers a portfolio of IT and IT-enabled services to clients all over the globe in horizontal, vertical, and geographical domains. A part of the Tata Group, India's largest industrial conglomerate, TCS has over 108,000 IT consultants in 47 countries.

The concept of knowledge management (KM) was introduced in TCS in 1995 and a dedicated KM team called "Corporate GroupWare" was formed in 1998. In mid-1999, this group launched the KM-pilot, which was implemented subsequently by a team comprising the steering committee, corporate GroupWare implanters, branch champions, application owners, and the infrastructure group.

At that time, KM in TCS covered nearly every function, from quality assurance to HR management. While its 50 offices in India were linked through dedicated communication lines, overseas offices were connected through the Net and the Lotus Notes Domino Servers. The employees could access the knowledge repository that resided on the corporate and branch servers through the intranet with a browser front-end or a Notes client. The knowledge repository, also called KBases, contained a wide range of information about processes, line of business, line of technology, and projects.

Though the formal KM efforts started in TCS in the late 1990s, the informal, closely knit communities of practices (CoPs) had existed at TCS since the 1980s, when it had around a thousand employees. The earliest "group" was based on the migration of technologies. Later, teams were formed for mainframe, Unix, and databases. The groups, consisting of one or two experts in their respective fields, began formal documentation practices, with the members writing down the best practices. Recollecting the group practices in the initial days, K. Ananth Krishnan, a technology consultant at that time, recounted that in the mid-1980s, problems and solutions were documented and there were over 1,500 case studies dealing with mainframes. Similarly, 40 case studies dealing with overall system quality were reviewed as early as 1993.

The next step was to create process asset libraries (PALs). These contained information related to technology, processes, and case studies for project leaders, which were made available to all development centers through the intranet.

Then Ultimatix, a Web-based electronic knowledge management (EKM) portal, which made the knowledge globally available, was developed. The PAL library and KBases, which were hosted on the intranet, were merged with Ultimatix, which had sub-portals for a quality management system, software productivity improvement, training materials, and tools information. There were EKM administrators for each practice and subject group with defined responsibilities, such as editing the documents and approving them for publication. Commenting on the success of CoP, Krishnan maintained that between January 2003 and June 2003, CoP members had exchanged around 10,000 document transactions relating to industry practices and 21,000 service practices via Ultimatix. The telecom CoP alone had 6,000 transactions, excluding the intranet-based community activities.

To encourage employee conversations, TCS took considerable care in the architecture of its development centers located across the country. Reflecting on the new design of one of its development centers in Sholinganallur, Chennai, CFO S. Mahalingam commented that the center is made up of modules, each dedicated to one particular technology or a client or an industry practice. These structures lead to garden terraces where employees gather during their break for informal conversations and to brainstorm the solutions to many problems.

TCS also launched a number of training programs such as the Initial Learning Program, targeted at new employees; the Continuous Learning Program for experienced employees; and the Leadership Development Program for employees with more than five years' experience. The integrated competency and learning management systems (iCALMS) that were deployed globally across all TCS offices promoted a culture of learning and growth in the organization. Equipped with data about competency definitions, role definitions, and online/classroom learning objectives, it helped the consultants to enhance their skills in a customized manner. To gain cross-industry experience, TCS regularly rotated people across various functions and within other Tata Group companies. Employees were also encouraged to join outside bodies like the IEEE and to go in for certifications.

Knowmax, a knowledge management system, developed using Microsoft sharepoint portal server in 2007, gave TCS consultants access to nearly 40 years of experience and best practices, arranged by type of engagement, the technology in use, and customer requirements. It supported more than 60 knowledge assets and was accessible via Ultimatix to all TCS associates. Any associate could contribute to the K-Bank and knowledge officers were made responsible for maintaining the quality of content.

To maintain the work–life balance of its employees, TCS initiated Propel sessions, which brought together employees with similar interests to conduct various activities such as reading books. Held every quarter through conferences and camps, this initiative also spurred knowledge transfer among the employees. The knowledge sharing at the project level was done through the LiveMeeting application, where all the project meetings were recorded and stored in the project repository. Team members who missed the meeting and any new members in the team could listen to the recorded sessions, and this enabled them to catch up with the rest of the team. Furthermore, Knowledge Transition sessions conducted weekly by a subject matter expert helped the team to learn from the experience of the experts. A "Tip of the Day" mail, comprising technical, conceptual, or human skills tips, was also shared within the organization almost daily.

Though Ultimatix, launched in 2002, digitized the entire organization from end to end and improved the business processes' efficiency, it still couldn't tap the knowledge of employees effectively. To improve collaboration among employees, Project Infinity was launched in 2007; this involved a number of technologies including IBM's Sametime, QuickPlace, Lotus Domino Collaboration tools, Avaya VOIP telephony, and Polycom IP videoconferencing.

As a result of adopting Infinity, collaboration of overseas and local offices improved as instant messaging (IM) got rid of cultural and pronunciation differences that could occur on the phone. Furthermore, corporate communications were able to run a 24-hour internal news broadcast to all TCS offices in the world. In addition, travel and telecommunications costs were reduced by 40 percent and 6 percent respectively.

In 2015, TCS remained India's largest software exporter, and became the first company to surpass $90 billion in market capitalization. In 2015, TCS continued to report solid financial figures, generating $15.5 billion in revenue with over 319,000 employees. Clearly knowledge management tools are a key strategic resource at TCS, and are the source of new services that the company can market to other firms seeking knowledge management systems. The future for TCS continues to look bright going forward.

Sources: TCS, "Case Study: A Global Professional Services Firm Successfully Optimizes Its Knowledge Management Function and Accrues Cost Savings Worth USD 400,000," Tata Consulting Services, TCS.com, 2015; Jolly Marikan, "Case Study: Knowledge Management and Collaboration at Tata Consulting Services," Jollymarikan.blogspot.com, October 12, 2015; N. Hainisani, "Knowledge Management and Collaboration at TATA Consulting Services," Malaysian Graduate School of Entrepreneurship and Business, University of Malaysia Kelantan, May 15, 2015; "Strong Customer Additions, Holistic Growth Helps TCS Take Market Leadership in FY15," press release, TCS, April 16, 2015; Dhanya Thoppil, "Tata Consultancy Services Manages Its Size to Stay Agile," *Wall Street Journal*, July 27, 2014; Sankaranarayanan G., "Building Communities, the TCS Way," expressitpeople.com, September 2003; Kavita Kaur, "Give and Take," india-today.com, January 2000; Sunil Shah, "Network Wonder: Collaborative Tools Help TCS Grow," cio.com, July 2007; Shivani Shinde, "TCS Sees Synergy in Gen X Tools," rediff.com, July 2008.

CASE STUDY QUESTIONS

11-13 Analyze the knowledge management efforts at TCS using the knowledge management value chain model. Which tools or activities were used for managing tacit knowledge and which ones are used for explicit knowledge?

11-14 Describe the growth of knowledge management systems at TCS. How have these systems helped TCS in its business?

11-15 Describe the collaboration tools used at TCS. What benefits did TCS reap from these tools?

11-16 How did Web 2.0 tools help TCS to manage knowledge and collaboration among its employees?

Case contributed by Neerja Sethi and Vijay Sethi, Nanyang Technological University

Chapter 11 References

Alavi, Maryam and Dorothy Leidner. "Knowledge Management and Knowledge Management Systems: Conceptual Foundations and Research Issues," *MIS Quarterly 25*, No. 1(March 2001).

Althuizen, Niek and Berend Wierenga. "Supporting Creative Problem Solving with a Case-Based Reasoning System." *Journal of Management Information Systems* 31. No. 1 (Summer 2014).

Althuizen, Niek and Astrid Reichel. "The Effects of IT-Enabled Cognitive Stimulation Tools on Creative Problem Solving: A Dual Pathway to Creativity." *Journal of Management Information Systems* 33, No. 1 (2016).

Autocad. "Dieguez Fridman Arquitectos Creates Award-winning Conceptual Designs in 3D Using AutoCAD Software." www.autocad.com, accessed January 5, 2016.

Burtka, Michael. "Generic Algorithms." *The Stern Information Systems Review* 1, No. 1 (Spring 1993).

Clark, Don. "IBM Unveils Chip Simulating Brain Functions." *Wall Street Journal* (August 7, 2014).

Davenport, Thomas H. and Julia Kirby. "Just How Smart Are Smart Machines?" *MIT Sloan Management Review* 57, No. 3 (Spring 2016).

Davenport, Thomas H., and Lawrence Prusak. *Working Knowledge: How Organizations Manage What They Know*. Boston, MA: Harvard Business School Press (1997).

Davenport, Thomas H., Laurence Prusak, and Bruce Strong. "Putting Ideas to Work." *Wall Street Journal* (March 10, 2008).

Davenport, Thomas H., Robert J. Thomas, and Susan Cantrell. "The Mysterious Art and Science of Knowledge-Worker Performance." *MIT Sloan Management Review* 44, No. 1 (Fall 2002).

Dhar, Vasant and Roger Stein. *Intelligent Decision Support Methods: The Science of Knowledge Work*. Upper Saddle River, NJ: Prentice Hall (1997).

EADTU (The European Association of Distance Teaching Universities). "MOOCs in Europe," Papers HOME Conference, Rome (November 2015).

El Najdawi, M. K., and Anthony C. Stylianou. "Expert Support Systems: Integrating AI Technologies." *Communications of the ACM* 36, No. 12 (December 1993).

Flinders, Karl. "Lloyds Bank to Use Virtual Reality to Test Applicants for Graduate Programme." *Computer Weekly* (October 13, 2016).

Gelernter, David. "Machines That Will Think and Feel." *Wall Street Journal* (March 18, 2016).

Gu, Feng and Baruch Lev. "Intangible Assets. Measurements, Drivers, Usefulness." (2001). http://pages.stern.nyu.edu/~blev/.

Holland, John H. "Genetic Algorithms." *Scientific American* (July 1992).

Housel, Tom and Arthur A. Bell. *Measuring and Managing Knowledge*. New York: McGraw-Hill (2001).

"How Machines Learn and You Win." *Harvard Business Review* (November 2015).

Iyengar, Kishen, Jeffrey R. Sweeney, and Ramiro Montealegre. "Information Technology Use as a Learning Mechanism: The Impact of IT Use on Knowledge Transfer Effectiveness, Absorptive Capacity, and Franchisee Performance." *MIS Quarterly* 39, No. 3 (September 2015).

Kim, Seung Hyun, Tridas Mukhopadhyay, and Robert E. Kraut. "When Does Repository KMS Use Lift Performance? The Role of Alternative Knowledge Sources and Task Environments?" *MIS Quarterly* 40, No. 1 (March 2016).

Korn, Melissa. "Corporate Training Gets an Online Refresh: MOOC Providers Find New Earnings Opportunities in Offering Web Courses to Companies." *Wall Street Journal* (October 1, 2014).

Leonard-Barton, Dorothy and Walter Swap. "Deep Smarts." *Harvard Business Review* (September 1, 2004).

Leonardi, Paul M. "Ambient Awareness and Knowledge Acquisition: Using Social Media to Learn 'Who Knows What' and 'Who Knows Whom'." *MIS Quarterly* 39, No. 4 (December 2015).

Lev, Baruch. "Sharpening the Intangibles Edge." *Harvard Business Review* (June 1, 2004).

Lim, Shi Ying, Sirkka L. Jarvenpaa, and Holly J Lanham. "Barriers to Interorganizational Knowledge Transfer in Post-Hospital Care Transitions: Review and Directions for Information Systems Research." *Journal of Management Information Systems* 32, No. 3 (2015).

Lohr, Steve. "The Promise of Artificial Intelligence Unfolds in Small Steps." New York Times, February 28, 2016.

Malone, Thomas W., Robert Laubacher, and Chrysanthos Dellarocas. "The Collective Intelligence Genome." *MIT Sloan Management Review* 51, No. 3 (Spring 2010).

Markoff, John. "Brainlike Computers, Learning from Experience." *New York Times* (December 28, 2013).

Markoff, John. "How Many Computers to Identify a Cat? 16,000." *New York Times* (June 26, 2012).

Markus, M. Lynne, Ann Majchrzak, and Less Gasser. "A Design Theory for Systems That Support Emergent Knowledge Processes." *MIS Quarterly* 26, No. 3 (September 2002).

McCarthy, John. "Generality in Artificial Intelligence." *Communications of the ACM* (December 1987).

Mehra, Amit, Nishtha Langer, Ravi Bapna, and Ram Gopal. "Estimating Returns to Training in the Knowledge Economy: A Firm-Level Analysis of Small and Medium Enterprises." *MIS Quarterly* 38, No. 3 (September 2014).

Meister, Jeanne. "MOOCs Emerge as Disruptors to Corporate Learning." *Forbes* (June 10, 2015).

Nurmohamed, Zafred, Nabeel Gillani, and Michael Lenox. "New Use for MOOCs: Real-World Problem-Solving." *Harvard Business Review* (July 2013).

Orlikowski, Wanda J. "Knowing in Practice: Enacting a Collective Capability in Distributed Organizing." *Organization Science* 13, No. 3 (May–June 2002).

Pyle, Dorian and Cristina San Jose. "An Executive's Guide to Machine Learning." *McKinsey Quarterly* (June 2015).

Sadeh, Norman, David W. Hildum, and Dag Kjenstad. "Agent-Based E-supply Chain Decision Support." *Journal of Organizational Computing and Electronic Commerce* 13, No. 3 & 4 (2003).

Singer, Natasha. "The Virtual Anatomy, Ready for Dissection." *New York Times* (January 7, 2012).

"Smarter, Smaller, Safer Robots." *Harvard Business Review* (November 2015).

U.S. Department of Labor, Occupational Employment Statistics. "May 2015 National Occupational Employment and Wage Estimates." Bureau of Labor Statisics (2016).

Weill, Peter, Thomas Malone, and Thomas G. Apel. "The Business Models Investors Prefer." *MIT Sloan Management Review* 52, No. 4 (Summer 2011).

Zadeh, Lotfi A. "Fuzzy Logic, Neural Networks, and Soft Computing." *Communications of the ACM* 37, No. 3 (March 1994).

Zadeh, Lotfi A. "The Calculus of Fuzzy If/Then Rules." *AI Expert* (March 1992).

Zeying Wan, Deborah Compeau, and Nicole Haggerty. "The Effects of Self- Regulated Learning Processes on E-Learning Outcomes in Organizational Settings." *Journal of Management Information Systems* 29, No. 1 (Summer 2012).

Zhao, Li, Brian Detlor, and Catherine E. Connelly. "Sharing Knowledge in Social Q&A Sites: The Unintended Consequences of Extrinsic Motivation." *Journal of Management Information Systems* 33, No. 1 (2016).

CHAPTER

12 Enhancing Decision Making

Learning Objectives

After reading this chapter, you will be able to answer the following questions:

12-1 What are the different types of decisions, and how does the decision-making process work?

12-2 How do information systems support the activities of managers and management decision making?

12-3 How do business intelligence and business analytics support decision making?

12-4 How do different decision-making constituencies in an organization use business intelligence, and what is the role of information systems in helping people working in a group make decisions more efficiently?

CHAPTER CASES

Roche: Changing Medical Care with Mobile Technology and Big Data
Singapore Sports Institute Uses Analytics for SEA Games
Britain's National Health Service Jettisons Choose and Book System
GE Bets on the Internet of Things and Big Data Analytics

Roche: Changing Medical Care with Mobile Technology and Big Data

Imagine a world where instead of calling the doctor for a checkup, routine exam, or mild illness, the doctor called you instead. Imagine a healthcare system that monitored your body's vital signs in real time: heart rate, blood pressure, activity levels, and dietary intake. Imagine receiving notices on your smartphone with recommendations for changes in diet and exercise or, better yet, congratulations from your doctor for successfully managing your health!

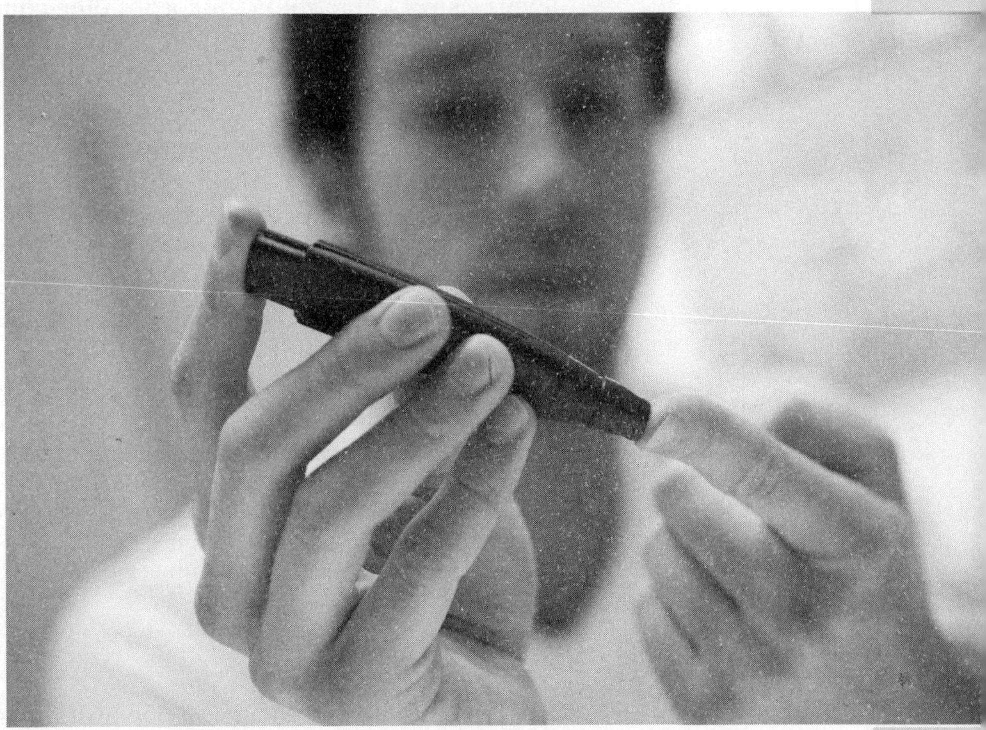

© bikeriderlondon/Shutterstock

Welcome to the future world of connected healthcare! This new model of healthcare delivery is powered by sensors attached to your body, wirelessly connected to your smartphone, which monitors and displays your health functions and makes personal recommendations. The data in turn is sent to a health monitoring facility, staffed by nurses and doctors standing by at their own desktop displays, who in real-time monitor your health using cloud servers, Big Data software analytics, and smartphone connections to their "patients."

The connected healthcare model is the future of healthcare in advanced and developing countries for three powerful reasons. In advanced countries healthcare is typically the largest industry: in the U.S. healthcare consumes 17 percent of GDP, in Europe around 10 percent, and in the global economy about 8 percent. Healthcare is growing globally at twice the rate of inflation and driving budgets increases which are not sustainable in the long-term. Proponents believe that connected healthcare could reduce healthcare costs by 40 percent! Populations are aging and requiring more healthcare than in the past. The technology is available and inexpensive. The Internet of Things (IoT) technologies (sensors, wireless communication, cloud databases, massive storage facilities, and analytic software)—honed in manufacturing to monitor everything from planes, trains, and cars, to home appliances—are inexpensive, increasingly powerful, and have already been extended to the Internet-of-People (IoP) in the form of activity monitors, driverless cars, and smartphones which record many user activities.

A good example of the connected healthcare model is the AccuCheck View from Roche Diabetes Care, Inc. F. Hoffman-LaRoche is a Swiss-based global healthcare company with headquarters in Basel, Switzerland. There are over 450 million adults in the world with diabetes, four times the number in 1980. The greatest increase is in Type 2 diabetes, which is related to diet, primarily the consumption of sugars and simple carbohydrates, leading to overweight and obesity.

Teaming up with the enterprise software company SAP, Roche in 2015 introduced a line of products that helps diabetic patients monitor their blood glucose levels using a handheld glucose meter connected wirelessly to a smartphone app developed by SAP. Called AccuCheck View, Roche's new package combines a blood glucose monitor, a wearable fitness tracker, a mobile SAP app, SAP's HANA cloud platform, and related SAP Big Bata analytics software. The integrated package can measure a patient's vital signs and blood sugar level in relation to their physical activity level and dietary intake in real-time. The data is sent automatically to healthcare providers who can monitor the patient remotely. The aggregated data is used by SAP analytic software to identify patterns in large populations for use later in medical decision making and treatment. The goal is to help diabetes patients make better decisions about their diets and exercise, and to improve the decision making of healthcare providers using body sensors, real-time monitoring, and Big Data analytics.

Sources: David Squires and Chloe Anderson, "U.S. Health Care from a Global Perspective: Spending, Use of Services, Prices, and Health in 13 Countries," The Commonwealth Fund, New York, 2017; "Global Report on Diabetes," World Health Organization, 2016; "SAP Leonardo Innovation Portfolio & Customer Use Cases," SAP 2015; Christine Donato, "Roche Diagnostics Prevents Diabetes with Connected Care," SAP Community, April 27, 2015.

AccuCheck from Roche is a powerful illustration of how information systems improve decision making, in this case, the decision making of patients as well as their health providers. Healthcare costs are soaring worldwide, and there is an on-going diabetes epidemic, both of which are likely to get worse, not better, with aging populations in developed countries. Existing business models of healthcare delivery employ very sophisticated technologies to help cure patients of diseases, but technologies for managing their healthcare have not changed in decades. The connected care business and organizational model inverts the traditional model: instead of going to the doctor's office when people become ill, instead the doctor's office is with patients 24/7 using hand-held diagnostic tools, smartphone apps, and cloud-based databases.

The chapter-opening diagram calls attention to important points raised by this case and this chapter. Firms like Roche are responding to the business opportunity to address exploding health costs worldwide, aging populations, and a diabetes epidemic. To develop AccuCheck, Roche management needed

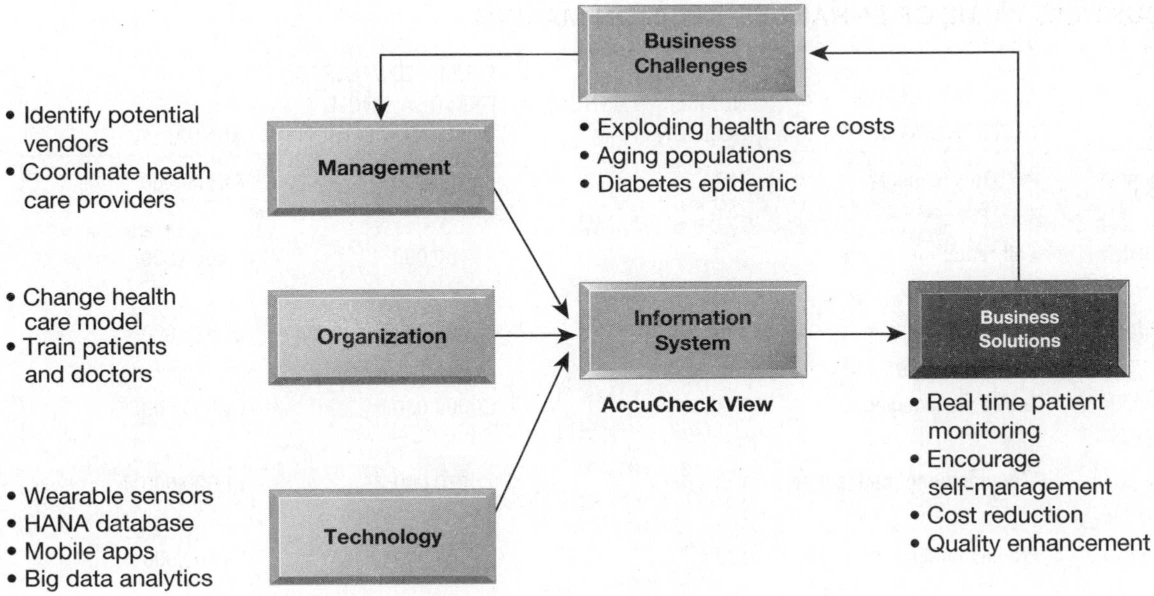

to partner with an experienced database and technology firm like SAP, and to develop outreach programs to doctors, hospitals, and patients. The organizational and business model of healthcare itself needed to change, and providers needed training in how to use the new technologies. The technologies to develop the system were widely available: home diagnostic tools (where Roche is a leader), the SAP HANA database, mobile apps, and Big Data analytics. The resulting system enhances the ability of patients to make better health decisions everyday and helps providers of care make better decisions about their patients in a real-time environment.

12-1 What are the different types of decisions, and how does the decision-making process work?

Decision making in businesses used to be limited to management. Today, lower-level employees are responsible for some of these decisions, as information systems make information available to lower levels of the business. But what do we mean by better decision making? How does decision making take place in businesses and other organizations? Let's take a closer look.

Business Value of Improved Decision Making

What does it mean to the business to make better decisions? What is the monetary value of improved decision making? Table 12.1 attempts to measure the monetary value of improved decision making for a small UK manufacturing firm with €280 million in annual revenue and 140 employees. The firm has identified a number of key decisions where new system investments might

TABLE 12.1 BUSINESS VALUE OF ENHANCED DECISION MAKING

EXAMPLE DECISION	DECISION MAKER	NUMBER OF ANNUAL DECISIONS	ESTIMATED VALUE TO FIRM OF A SINGLE IMPROVED DECISION	ANNUAL VALUE
Allocate support to most valuable customers	Accounts manager	12	€100,000	€1,200,000
Predict call center daily demand	Call center management	4	€150,000	€600,000
Decide parts inventory levels daily	Inventory manager	365	€5,000	€1,825,000
Identify competitive bids from major suppliers	Senior management	1	€2,000,000	€2,000,000
Schedule production to fill orders	Manufacturing manager	150	€10,000	€1,500,000
Allocate labor to complete a job	Production floor manager	100	€4,000	€400,000

improve the quality of decision making. The table provides selected estimates of annual value (in the form of cost savings or increased revenue) from improved decision making in selected areas of the business.

We can see from Table 12.1 that decisions are made at all levels of the firm and that some of these decisions are common, routine, and numerous. Although the value of improving any single decision may be small, improving hundreds of thousands of "small" decisions adds up to a large annual value for the business.

Types of Decisions

Chapters 1 and 2 showed that there are different levels in an organization. Each of these levels has different information requirements for decision support and responsibility for different types of decisions (see Figure 12.1). Decisions are classified as structured, semi-structured, and unstructured.

Unstructured decisions are those in which the decision maker must provide judgment, evaluation, and insight to solve the problem. Each of these decisions is novel, important, and nonroutine, and there is no well-understood or agreed-on procedure for making them.

Structured decisions, by contrast, are repetitive and routine, and they involve a definite procedure for handling them so that they do not have to be treated each time as if they were new. Many decisions have elements of both types of decisions and are **semi-structured**, where only part of the problem has a clear-cut answer provided by an accepted procedure. In general, structured decisions are more prevalent at lower organizational levels, whereas unstructured problems are more common at higher levels of the firm.

Senior executives face many unstructured decision situations, such as establishing the firm's 5- or 10-year goals or deciding new markets to enter. Answering

FIGURE 12.1 INFORMATION REQUIREMENTS OF KEY DECISION-MAKING GROUPS IN A FIRM

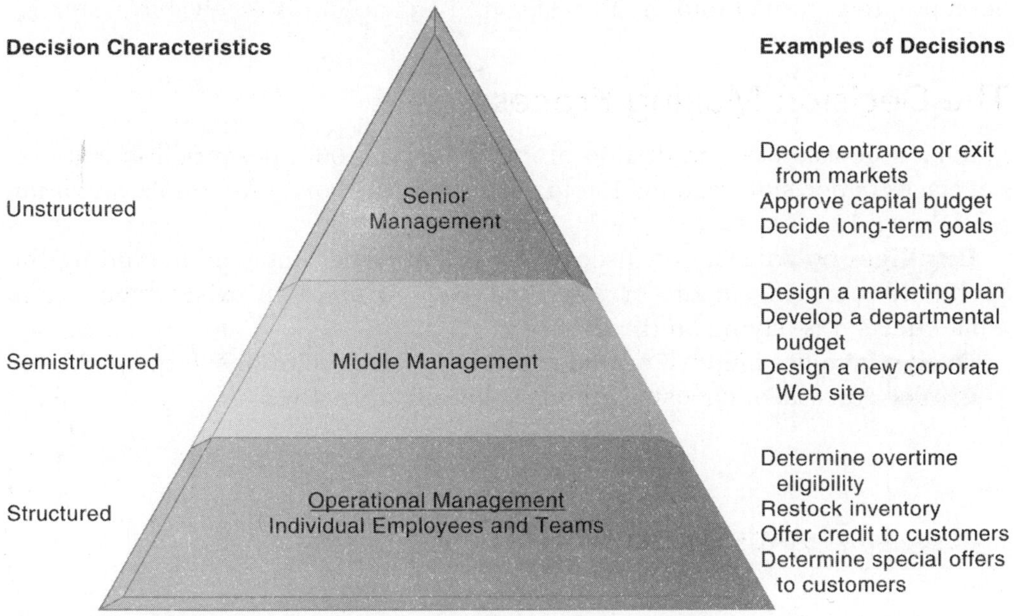

Senior managers, middle managers, operational managers, and employees have different types of decisions and information requirements.

the question "Should we enter a new market?" would require access to news, government reports, and industry views as well as high-level summaries of firm performance. However, the answer would also require senior managers to use their own best judgment and poll other managers for their opinions.

Middle managers face more structured decision scenarios, but their decisions may include unstructured components. A typical middle-level management decision might be "Why is the reported order fulfillment report showing a decline over the past six months at a distribution center in Dubai?" This middle manager will obtain a report from the firm's enterprise system or distribution management system on order activity and operational efficiency at the Dubai distribution center. This is the structured part of the decision. But before arriving at an answer, this middle manager will have to interview employees and gather more unstructured information from external sources about local economic conditions or sales trends.

Operational management and rank-and-file employees tend to make more structured decisions. For example, a supervisor on an assembly line has to decide whether an hourly paid worker is entitled to overtime pay. If the employee worked more than eight hours on a particular day, the supervisor would routinely grant overtime pay for any time beyond eight hours that was clocked on that day.

A sales account representative often has to make decisions about extending credit to customers by consulting the firm's customer database that contains credit information. If the customer met the firm's prespecified criteria for granting credit, the account representative would grant that customer credit to make a purchase. In both instances, the decisions are highly structured and are routinely made thousands of times each day in most large firms. The answer has been preprogrammed into the firm's payroll and accounts receivable systems.

The Decision-Making Process

Making a decision is a multistep process. Simon (1960) described four different stages in decision making: intelligence, design, choice, and implementation (see Figure 12.2).

Intelligence consists of discovering, identifying, and understanding the problems occurring in the organization—why a problem exists, where, and what effects it is having on the firm.

Design involves identifying and exploring various solutions to the problem.

Choice consists of choosing among solution alternatives.

FIGURE 12.2 STAGES IN DECISION MAKING

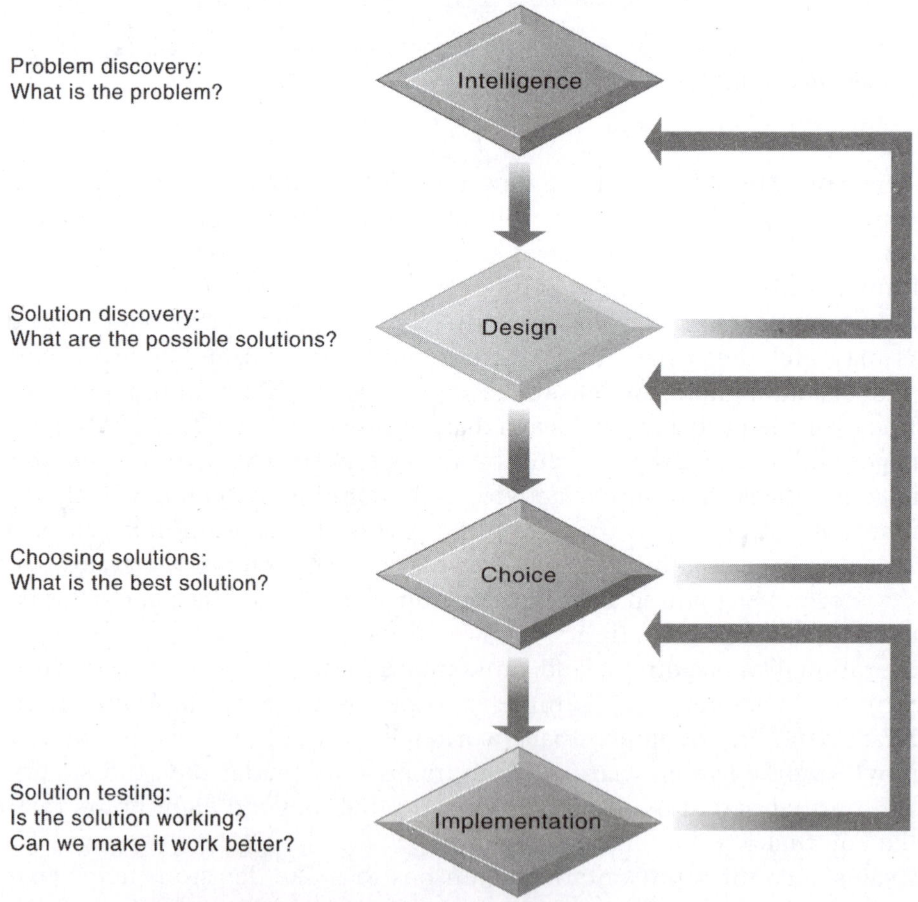

The decision-making process is broken down into four stages.

Implementation involves making the chosen alternative work and continuing to monitor how well the solution is working.

What happens if the solution you have chosen doesn't work? Figure 12.2 shows that you can return to an earlier stage in the decision-making process and repeat it if necessary. For instance, in the face of declining sales, a sales management team may decide to pay the sales force a higher commission for making more sales to spur on the sales effort. If this does not produce sales increases, managers would need to investigate whether the problem stems from poor product design, inadequate customer support, or a host of other causes that call for a different solution.

12-2 How do information systems support the activities of managers and management decision making?

The premise of this book and this chapter is that systems to support decision making produce better decision making by managers and employees, above-average returns on investment for the firm, and ultimately higher profitability. However, information systems cannot improve every decision taking place in an organization. Let's examine the role of managers and decision making in organizations to see why this is so.

Managerial Roles

Managers play key roles in organizations. Their responsibilities range from making decisions, to writing reports, to attending meetings, to arranging birthday parties. We are able to better understand managerial functions and roles by examining classical and contemporary models of managerial behavior.

The **classical model of management**, which describes what managers do, was largely unquestioned for the more than 70 years since the 1920s. Henri Fayol and other early writers first described the five classical functions of managers as planning, organizing, coordinating, deciding, and controlling. This description of management activities dominated management thought for a long time, and it is still popular today.

The classical model describes formal managerial functions but does not address exactly what managers do when they plan, decide things, and control the work of others. For this, we must turn to the work of contemporary behavioral scientists who have studied managers in daily action. **Behavioral models** argue that the actual behavior of managers appears to be less systematic, more informal, less reflective, more reactive, and less well organized than the classical model would have us believe.

Observers find that managerial behavior actually has five attributes that differ greatly from the classical description. First, managers perform a great deal of work at an unrelenting pace—studies have found that managers engage in more than 600 different activities each day, with no break in their pace. Second, managerial activities are fragmented; most activities last for less than nine minutes, and only 10 percent of the activities exceed one hour in duration. Third, managers prefer current, specific, and ad hoc information (printed information often will be too old). Fourth, they prefer oral forms of communication to written forms because oral media provide greater flexibility, require less effort, and bring a faster response. Fifth, managers give high priority to maintaining a diverse and complex web of contacts that acts as an informal information system and helps them execute their personal agendas and short- and long-term goals.

Analyzing managers' day-to-day behavior, Henry Mintzberg found that it could be classified into 10 managerial roles. **Managerial roles** are expectations of the activities that managers should perform in an organization. Mintzberg found that these managerial roles fell into three categories: interpersonal, informational, and decisional.

Interpersonal Roles

Managers act as figureheads for the organization when they represent their companies to the outside world and perform symbolic duties, such as giving out employee awards, in their **interpersonal role**. Managers act as leaders, attempting to motivate, counsel, and support subordinates. Managers also act as liaisons between various organizational levels; within each of these levels, they serve as liaisons among the members of the management team. Managers provide time and favors, which they expect to be returned.

Informational Roles

In their **informational role**, managers act as the nerve centers of their organizations, receiving the most concrete, up-to-date information and redistributing it to those who need to be aware of it. Managers are therefore information disseminators and spokespersons for their organizations.

Decisional Roles

Managers make decisions. In their **decisional role**, they act as entrepreneurs by initiating new kinds of activities, they handle disturbances arising in the organization, they allocate resources to staff members who need them, and they negotiate conflicts and mediate between conflicting groups.

Table 12.2, based on Mintzberg's role classifications, is one look at where systems can and cannot help managers. The table shows that information systems are now capable of supporting most, but not all, areas of managerial life.

Real-World Decision Making

We now see that information systems are not helpful for all managerial roles. And in those managerial roles where information systems might improve decisions, investments in information technology do not always produce positive results. There are three main reasons: information quality, management filters, and organizational culture (see Chapter 3).

Information Quality

High-quality decisions require high-quality information. Table 12.3 describes information quality dimensions that affect the quality of decisions.

TABLE 12.2 MANAGERIAL ROLES AND SUPPORTING INFORMATION SYSTEMS

ROLE	BEHAVIOR	SUPPORT SYSTEMS
INTERPERSONAL ROLES		
Figurehead		Telepresence systems
Leader	Interpersonal	Telepresence, social networks, Twitter
Liaison		Smartphones, social networks
INFORMATIONAL ROLES		
Nerve center		Management information systems, executive support system
Disseminator	Information	Texting, e-mail, social networks
Spokesperson	processing	Webinars, telepresence
DECISIONAL ROLES		
Entrepreneur	Decision	None exist
Disturbance handler	making	None exist
Resource allocator		Business intelligence, decision-support system
Negotiator		None exist

Sources: Authors and Mintzberg, 1971.

If the output of information systems does not meet these quality criteria, decision making will suffer. Chapter 6 describes how corporate databases and files have varying levels of inaccuracy and incompleteness, which in turn will degrade the quality of decision making.

Management Filters

Even with timely, accurate information, managers often make bad decisions. Managers (like all human beings) absorb information through a series of filters to make sense of the world around them. Cognitive scientists, behavioral economists, and

TABLE 12.3 INFORMATION QUALITY DIMENSIONS

QUALITY DIMENSION	DESCRIPTION
Accuracy	Do the data represent reality?
Integrity	Are the structure of data and relationships among the entities and attributes consistent?
Consistency	Are data elements consistently defined?
Completeness	Are all the necessary data present?
Validity	Do data values fall within defined ranges?
Timeliness	Are data available when needed?
Accessibility	Are the data accessible, comprehensible, and usable?

recently neuro-economists have found that managers, like other humans, are poor at assessing risk, are risk averse, perceive patterns where none exist, and make decisions based on intuition, feelings, and the framing of the problem as opposed to empirical data (Kahneman, 2011; Tversky and Kahneman, 1986).

For instance, Wall Street firms such as Bear Stearns and Lehman Brothers imploded in 2008 because they underestimated the risk of their investments in complex mortgage securities, many of which were based on subprime loans that were more likely to default. The computer models they and other financial institutions used to manage risk were based on overly optimistic assumptions and overly simplistic data about what might go wrong. Management wanted to make sure that their firms' capital was not all tied up as a cushion against defaults from risky investments, preventing them from investing it to generate profits. So the designers of these risk management systems were encouraged to measure risks in a way that minimized their risk. Some trading desks also oversimplified the information maintained about the mortgage securities to make them appear as simple bonds with higher ratings than were warranted by their underlying components. The rating firms went along with their clients' wishes and provided high quality ratings to low quality bonds.

Organizational Inertia and Politics

Organizations are bureaucracies with limited capabilities and competencies for acting decisively. When environments change and businesses need to adopt new business models to survive, strong forces within organizations resist making decisions calling for major change. Decisions taken by a firm often represent a balancing of the firm's various interest groups rather than the best solution to the problem.

Studies of business restructuring find that firms tend to ignore poor performance until threatened by outside takeovers, and they systematically blame poor performance on external forces beyond their control—such as economic conditions (the economy), foreign competition, and rising prices—rather than blaming senior or middle management for poor business judgment. When the external business environment is positive and firm performance improves, managers typically credit themselves for the improved performance rather than the positive environment.

High-Velocity Automated Decision Making

Today, many decisions made by organizations are not made by managers—or any humans. For instance, when you enter a query into Google's search engine, Google has to decide which URLs to display in about half a second on average (500 milliseconds). High-frequency traders at electronic stock exchanges execute their trades in under 30 milliseconds.

The class of decisions that are highly structured and automated is growing rapidly. What makes this kind of automated high-speed decision making possible are computer algorithms that precisely define the steps to be followed to produce a decision, very large databases, very high-speed processors, and software optimized to the task. In these situations, humans (including managers) are eliminated from the decision chain because they are too slow.

This also means organizations in these areas are making decisions faster than what managers can monitor or control. The past few years have seen a series of breakdowns in computerized trading systems, including one on August 1, 2012, when a software error caused Knight Capital to enter millions of faulty trades in less than an hour. The trading glitch created wild surges and plunges in nearly 150 stocks and left Knight with $440 million in losses. In high-velocity decision environments, the intelligence, design, choice, and implementation parts of the decision-making process are captured by the software's algorithms. The humans who wrote the software have already identified the problem, designed a method for finding a solution, defined a range of acceptable solutions, and implemented the solution. Obviously, with humans out of the loop, great care needs to be taken to ensure the proper operation of these systems to prevent significant harm.

12-3 How do business intelligence and business analytics support decision making?

Chapter 2 introduced you to the different types of systems used for supporting management decision making. At the foundation of all of these decision support systems are a business intelligence and business analytics infrastructure that supplies the data and the analytic tools for supporting decision making.

What is Business Intelligence?

Business intelligence (BI) is a term used by hardware and software vendors and information technology consultants to describe the infrastructure for warehousing, integrating, reporting, and analyzing data that come from the business environment, including big data. The foundation infrastructure collects, stores, cleans, and makes relevant information available to managers. Think databases, data warehouses, data marts, Hadoop, and analytic platforms, which we described in Chapter 6. *Business analytics (BA)* is also a vendor-defined term that focuses more on tools and techniques for analyzing and understanding data. Think online analytical processing (OLAP), statistics, models, and data mining, which we also introduced in Chapter 6.

Business intelligence and analytics are essentially about integrating all the information streams produced by a firm into a single, coherent enterprise-wide set of data and then using modeling, statistical analysis tools and data mining tools to make sense out of all these data so managers can make better decisions and plans. eHarmony, described in the chapter-opening case, is using business intelligence and analytics to make some very fine-grained decisions about matching potential couples based on personality traits.

It is important to remember that business intelligence and analytics are products defined by technology vendors and consulting firms. Leading providers of these products include Oracle, SAP, IBM, Microsoft, and SAS. A number of BI and BA products now have cloud and mobile versions.

FIGURE 12.3 BUSINESS INTELLIGENCE AND ANALYTICS FOR DECISION SUPPORT

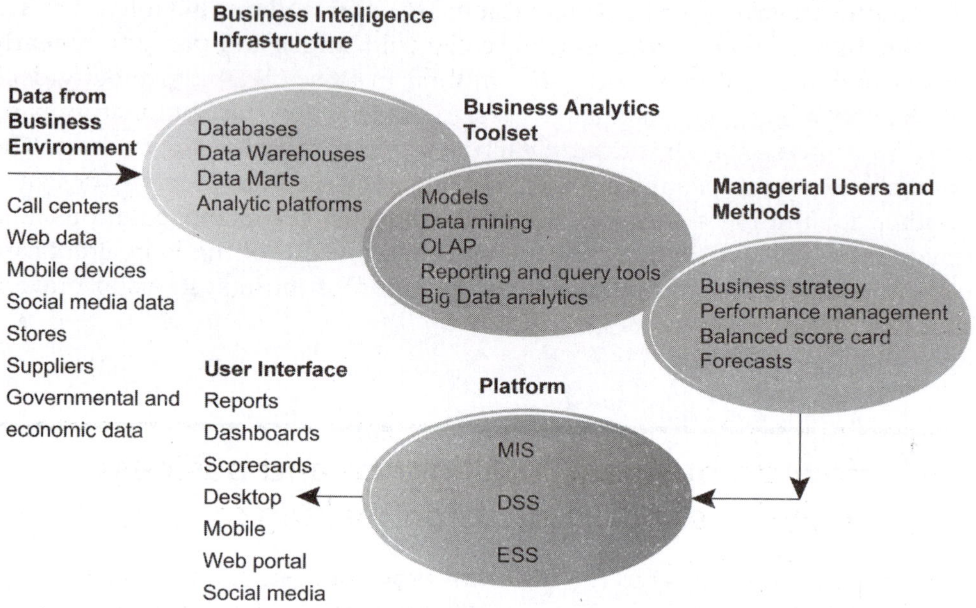

Business intelligence and analytics require a strong database foundation, a set of analytic tools, and an involved management team that can ask intelligent questions and analyze data.

The Business Intelligence Environment

Figure 12.3 gives an overview of a business intelligence environment, highlighting the kinds of hardware, software, and management capabilities that the major vendors offer and that firms develop over time. There are six elements in this business intelligence environment:

- **Data from the business environment:** Businesses must deal with both structured and unstructured data from many different sources, including big data. The data need to be integrated and organized so that they can be analyzed and used by human decision makers.
- **Business intelligence infrastructure:** The underlying foundation of business intelligence is a powerful database system that captures all the relevant data to operate the business. The data may be stored in transactional databases or combined and integrated into an enterprise-data warehouse or series of interrelated data marts.
- **Business analytics toolset:** A set of software tools are used to analyze data and produce reports, respond to questions posed by managers, and track the progress of the business using key indicators of performance.
- **Managerial users and methods:** Business intelligence hardware and software are only as intelligent as the human beings who use them. Managers impose order on the analysis of data using a variety of managerial methods that define strategic business goals and specify how progress will be measured. These include business performance management and balanced scorecard approaches focusing on key performance indicators and industry strategic analyses

focusing on changes in the general business environment, with special attention to competitors. Without strong senior management oversight, business analytics can produce a great deal of information, reports, and online screens that focus on the wrong matters and divert attention from the real issues.

- **Delivery platform—MIS, DSS, ESS:** The results from business intelligence and analytics are delivered to managers and employees in a variety of ways, depending on what they need to know to perform their jobs. MIS, DSS, and ESS, which we introduced in Chapter 2, deliver information and knowledge to different people and levels in the firm—operational employees, middle managers, and senior executives. In the past, these systems could not share data and operated as independent systems. Today, one suite of hardware and software tools in the form of a business intelligence and analytics package is able to integrate all this information and bring it to managers' desktop or mobile platforms.
- **User interface:** Businesspeople are no longer tied to their desks and desktops. They often learn quicker from a visual representation of data than from a dry report with columns and rows of information. Today's business analytics software suites feature **data visualization** tools, such as rich graphs, charts, dashboards, and maps. They also are able to deliver reports on iPhones, iPads, and other mobile handhelds as well as on the firm's web portal. BA software is adding capabilities to post information on Twitter, Facebook, or internal social media to support decision making in an online group setting rather than in a face-to-face meeting.

Business Intelligence and Analytics Capabilities

Business intelligence and analytics promise to deliver correct, nearly real-time information to decision makers, and the analytic tools help them quickly understand the information and take action. There are six analytic functionalities that BI systems deliver to achieve these ends:

- **Production reports:** These are predefined reports based on industry-specific requirements (see Table 12.4).

TABLE 12.4 EXAMPLES OF BUSINESS INTELLIGENCE PREDEFINED PRODUCTION REPORTS

BUSINESS FUNCTIONAL AREA	PRODUCTION REPORTS
Sales	Forecast sales; sales team performance; cross-selling; sales cycle times
Service/call center	Customer satisfaction; service cost; resolution rates; churn rates
Marketing	Campaign effectiveness; loyalty and attrition; market basket analysis
Procurement and support	Direct and indirect spending; off-contract purchases; supplier performance
Supply chain	Backlog; fulfillment status; order cycle time; bill of materials analysis
Financials	General ledger; accounts receivable and payable; cash flow; profitability
Human resources	Employee productivity; compensation; workforce demographics; retention

- **Parameterized reports:** Users enter several parameters as in a pivot table to filter data and isolate impacts of parameters. For instance, you might want to enter region and time of day to understand how sales of a product vary by region and time. If you were Starbucks, you might find that customers in the East buy most of their coffee in the morning, whereas in the Northwest customers buy coffee throughout the day. This finding might lead to different marketing and ad campaigns in each region. (See the discussion of pivot tables in Section 12.4.)
- **Dashboards/scorecards:** These are visual tools for presenting performance data defined by users.
- **Ad hoc query/search/report creation:** These allow users to create their own reports based on queries and searches.
- **Drill down:** This is the ability to move from a high-level summary to a more detailed view.
- **Forecasts, scenarios, models:** These include the ability to perform linear forecasting and what-if scenario analysis and analyze data using standard statistical tools.

Predictive Analytics

An important capability of business intelligence analytics is the ability to model future events and behaviors, such as the probability that a customer will respond to an offer to purchase a product. **Predictive analytics** use statistical analysis, data mining techniques, historical data, and assumptions about future conditions to predict future trends and behavior patterns. Variables that can be measured to predict future behavior are identified. For example, an insurance company might use variables such as age, gender, and driving record as predictors of driving safety when issuing auto insurance policies. A collection of such predictors is combined into a predictive model for forecasting future probabilities with an acceptable level of reliability.

Predictive analytics are being incorporated into numerous business intelligence applications for sales, marketing, finance, fraud detection, and health care. One of the most well-known applications is credit scoring, which is used throughout the financial services industry. When you apply for a new credit card, scoring models process your credit history, loan application, and purchase data to determine your likelihood of making future credit payments on time.

For instance, ZEAL Network SE (formerly Tipp24 AG), which offers online lottery-based games, analyzes billions of transactions and hundreds of customer attributes. It uses predictive analytics to target customers and personalize marketing messages on the fly. To provide the right lotto offer to the right customers at the right time, ZEAL Network built predictive models based on a wide range of customer data, including who is playing which games, when they are playing them, and where. Once the company understands the interests and playing behavior of each customer, it directs specific offers and marketing campaigns to the customer segments that would be most interested. Predictive analytics has also helped ZEAL predict which customers are at risk of becoming inactive and which inactive customers are likely to become active again (SAP, 2017).

Big Data Analytics

Predictive analytics are starting to use big data from both private and public sectors, including data from social media, customer transactions, and output from sensors and machines. In e-commerce, many online retailers have capabilities for making personalized online product recommendations to their website visitors to help stimulate purchases and guide their decisions about what merchandise to stock. However, most of these product recommendations have been based on the behaviors of similar groups of customers, such as those with incomes under € 50,000 or whose ages are between 18 and 25 years. Now some retailers are starting to analyze the tremendous quantities of online and in-store customer data they collect along with social media data to make these recommendations more individualized. These efforts are translating into higher customer spending and customer retention rates. Table 12.5 provides examples of companies using big data analytics.

In the public sector, big data analytics have been driving the movement toward "smart cities," which make intensive use of digital technology to make better decisions about running cities and serving their residents. Public record-keeping has produced warehouses full of property transfers, tax records, corporate filings, environmental compliance audits, restaurant inspections, building maintenance reports, mass transit appraisals, crime data, health department stats, public education records, utility reviews, and more. Municipalities are adding more data captured through sensors, location data from mobile phones, and targeted smartphone apps. Predictive modeling programs now inform public policy decisions on utility management, transportation operation, healthcare

TABLE 12.5 WHAT BIG DATA ANALYTICS CAN DO

Barclays	Analyzes transactional big data to develop customized products for customers. For example, a "smart business" application for small and medium-sized businesses enables them to see patterns in anonymized data generated by the bank's other customers. A hairdresser in Birmingham could see what hairdressers in other locations are spending on electricity.
Vestas Wind Systems	Improves wind turbine placement for optimal energy output using IBM BigInsights software and an IBM "Firestorm" supercomputer to analyze 2.8 petabytes of structured and unstructured data such as weather reports, tidal phases, geospatial and sensor data, satellite images, deforestation maps, and weather modeling research. The analysis, which used to take weeks, can now be completed in less than one hour.
Hunch.com	Analyzes massive database with data from customer purchases, social networks, and signals from around the web to produce a "taste graph" that maps users with their predicted affinity to products, services, and websites. The taste graph includes predictions about 500 million people, 200 million objects (videos, gadgets, books), and 30 billion connections between people and objects. Helps eBay develop more finely customized recommendations on items to offer.
Germany World Cup soccer team	Big data analytics helped it win the 2014 World Cup. The German team analyzed very large amounts of video and numeric data about individual player and team performance for itself and competing teams and then used what it had learned to improve how it played. .

delivery, and public safety. What's more, the ability to evaluate how changes in one service affect the operation and delivery of other services enables holistic problem solving that could only be dreamed of a generation ago.

Operational Intelligence and Analytics

Many decisions deal with how to run the business of these cities on a day-to-day basis. These are largely operational decisions, and this type of business activity monitoring is called **operational intelligence**. An example of operational intelligence is the use of data generated by sensors on trains and equipment by SNCF, which operates France's rail services, including France's high-speed rail network. The railway network consists of about 32,000 km (20,000 miles) of route and about 14,000 trains run daily. The sensors monitor data about train speed, engine and train car functioning, and track conditions. SNCF is able to analyze these data to reduce failures and improve the reliability of trains, signals and tracks. Engineers can connect to running trains in real time, enabling the company to figure out if a component is likely to fail, which could lead to a train being taken out of service (Saran, 2016). The chapter-ending case describes how General Electric (GE) is using operational intelligence to monitor and analyze the performance of generators, jet engines, locomotives, and oil-refining gear and to connect these devices to the cloud.

The Internet of Things is creating huge streams of data from web activities, smartphones, sensors, gauges, and monitoring devices that can be used for operational intelligence about activities inside and outside the organization. Software for operational intelligence and analytics enables organizations to analyze these streams of big data as they are generated in real time. Companies can set trigger alerts on events or have them fed into live dashboards to help managers with their decisions.

Another example of operational intelligence is the use of real-time data in the 28th South East Asian (SEA) Games held in Singapore in 2015 as described in the Interactive Session on Technology. This case also looks at the use of big data analytics in SEA Games. As you read this case, try to determine the extent to which information technology is replacing human decision makers or making them even more important.

Location Analytics and Geographic Information Systems

Data and decisions are also based on location data. BI analytics include **location analytics**, the ability to gain business insight from the location (geographic) component of data, including location data from mobile phones, output from sensors or scanning devices, and data from maps. For example, location analytics might help a marketer determine which people to target with mobile ads about nearby restaurants and stores or quantify the impact of mobile ads on in-store visits. Location analytics would help a utility company view and measure outages and their associated costs as related to customer location to help prioritize marketing, system upgrades, and customer service efforts. UPS's package tracking and delivery-routing systems described in Chapter 1 use location analytics.

Geographic information systems (GIS) provide tools to help decision makers visualize problems that benefit from mapping. GIS software ties location

INTERACTIVE SESSION: TECHNOLOGY

Singapore Sports Institute Uses Analytics for SEA Games

Established in 2011, the Singapore Sports Institute (SSI) is a specialist institute for sports science, medicine, and technology with the aim of becoming a world-class sports institute to transform sporting talent into champions. In August 2014, SSI created the High Performance Sports (HPS) Analytics, Technology, and Education Department with the objective of leveraging analytics for sporting excellence in Singapore. The department provides video and data analysis of Team Singapore athletes' performance during both practice and competitions, and it aims to educate the Singapore National Sports Associations (NSAs) on how to use the technology in sports.

During training and competitions, athletes' activities are captured using the Dartfish video platform and then analyzed at the SSI based on input from coaches and NSAs. The analysis is conducted using specialized software called SimulCam and StroMotion to compare an athlete's performance with others or to pinpoint deficiencies and shortcomings via the process of tagging. Tagging is a way to identify and categorize sports activities that impact performance. Activities are categorized in four ways: creation, such as kick, tackle, or turnover; categorization, covering offense or defense, team or individual play; identification of the specific players involved; and description, which includes the place where the shot was taken, the outcome, etc. The tagging files and video analysis are uploaded on a secure cloud platform to be shared with athletes and coaches. Coaches can also download the videos and discuss specific portions of the game with their athletes by using the relevant tags rather than watching the whole game. Similarly, athletes can watch the videos to better prepare themselves for practice or actual competitions.

The HPS Analytics Team used this system in 2015 during the 28th Southeast Asian (SEA) Games, which were held in Singapore. The department's key objectives were to build a video management system and a video repository of Singapore athletes as well as other top athletes from the region. Through the video management system, the department aimed to integrate and streamline the processes of capturing video footage of athletes, analyzing the videos, and finally sharing the analysis with coaches, athletes, and other stakeholders.

Before the games started, the team created a "Pre-Games Report" with an analysis of Team Singapore's chances of winning medals in different sports; it even made an analysis of individual athletes based on their performance relative to their competitors over a 12-month period. The HPS Analytics team also worked closely with Team Singapore athletes and coaches to develop tagging templates that were then used to analyze the videos. The videos were collected via the broadcast feed, analyzed, and then uploaded online in as short a period as possible. For example, as soon as an athlete's event was over, the video would be processed and uploaded to an online video platform that only coaches and athletes could access, via web browser or Dartfish's mobile app. In total, the team processed 1,297 videos with 745 hours of footage covering 19 different sports. These videos became part of the video database, and to enable an efficient retrieval of videos, each video was marked with relevant keywords and metadata.

In addition to the video analysis, the HPS team also produced daily reports of Team Singapore's performance and sent them to key stakeholders and senior management. The team also provided hourly information on Team Singapore's results as well as the medal count. These details were also updated in Qlik, an online business intelligence and data visualization platform. End-of-the-day reports showed Team Singapore's performance against their targets as well as a comparison with historical results. For example, for the women's discus throw, officials could not only monitor the distance thrown but also the athlete's rankings over the years and comparisons with regional discus throwers. In addition, the reports allowed the officials to drill down to key information related to individual athletes, such as the level of support provided and whether the athlete was new or experienced.

Analytics made a huge impact on the success of Team Singapore, which received 84 gold, 73 silver, and 102 bronze medals, placing Singapore second behind Thailand. In addition, HPS received numerous accolades, especially from NSAs, who experienced first-hand the power of analytics and thus became more amenable to working with HPS to implement their own video management and analytics systems.

Sources: Channel NewsAsia. "SEA Games: Team Singapore Breaks Records in Best Performance Yet," Channel NewsAsia, June 16, 2015, www.channelnewsasia.com, accessed December 22, 2016; S. Ian, "The Science Behind Team Singapore," Yahoo Sports Website, February 15, 2016, sg.sports.yahoo.com, accessed December 22, 2016; Sport Singapore, "SSI HPS Analytics," Sport Singapore Website, April 2015, www.sportsingapore.gov.sg, accessed December 22, 2016; Sport Singapore, "Singapore Sports Institute—Building the Foundation for Team Singapore's Success," Sport Singapore Website, October 30, 2015, www.myactivesg.com, accessed December 22, 2016; N. Tan, "Getting a Winning Edge with Help of Data Analytics," Today, May 14, 2016, www.todayonline.com, accessed December 22, 2016; "Case Study: Analytics at the 28th South East Asian (SEA) Games 2015," in G. Fried and C. Mumcu (eds.), *Sport Analytics: A Data-driven Approach to Sport Business and Management* (Routledge 2017).

CASE STUDY QUESTIONS

1. What technologies are used by SSI? What is their purpose?
2. To what extent was technology responsible for Team Singapore's success at the SEA games? Explain.
3. Search the web for SimulCam and StroMotion. How can these tools be used for video analysis?
4. Search the web for the role of big data in the German team's 2014 World Cup victory and compare it with Team Singapore's success at the SEA Games.

Case contributed by Neerja Sethi and Vijay Sethi, Nanyang Technological University

data about the distribution of people or other resources to points, lines, and areas on a map. Some GIS have modeling capabilities for changing the data and automatically revising business scenarios.

GIS might be used to help state and local governments calculate response times to natural disasters and other emergencies, to help banks identify the best location for new branches or ATM terminals, or to help police forces pinpoint locations with the highest incidence of crime.

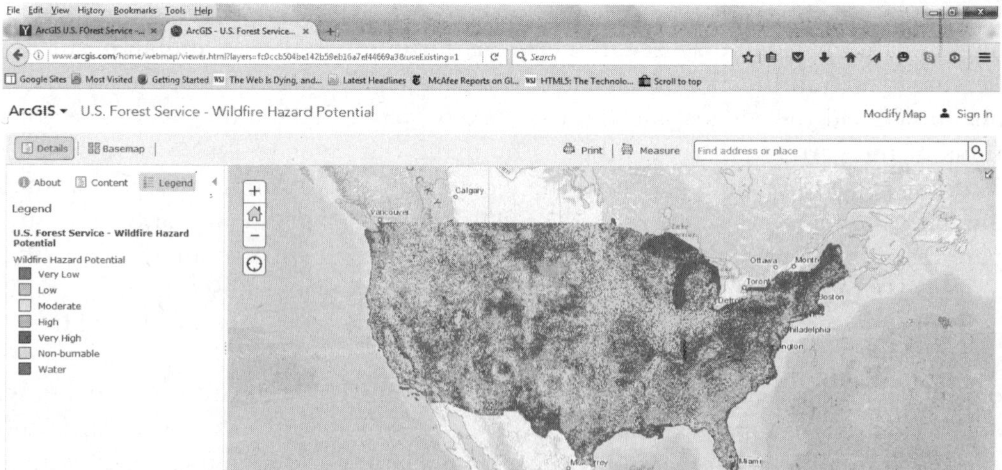

The U.S. Forest Service and Fire Modeling Institute created this map of Wildfire Hazard Potential (WHP) to assess wildfire risk and for prioritization of fuels management needs across large landscapes.

INTERACTIVE SESSION: MANAGEMENT

Britain's National Health Service Jettisons Choose and Book System

When senior cardiologist Duncan Dymond complained in 2010 that patients were arriving at his hospital at incorrect times and, far worse, in need of a different specialist, it was neither the beginning nor the end of problems with the Choose and Book system. Installed in 2004 as part of a £200 million IT modernization of Great Britain's National Health Service (NHS), the patient booking system was supposed to enable patients to select a hospital for an outpatient appointment from a range of options, primarily with the help and direction of their general practitioner (GP). A letter with a referral number and a secure code was then generated so that the patient could either go online or call a central booking service to confirm the appointment. Initial contact could also occur directly through the national appointments line or at the HealthSpace website. The goals were threefold: to speed up the referral process, eliminate costly paperwork, and encourage patient participation to stem losses of up to £225 million annually from 1.6 million patient no-shows.

Implementation was sluggish and plagued with glitches. One early problem was that many hospital Patient Administration Systems (PAS) and GP clinical computer systems were not compatible. Choose and Book served as the liaison between the two systems; thus, both had to be compliant. The objective to book 90 percent of all referrals by December 2006 was never met. Four years later, even though Choose and Book had been installed in 94 percent of all GP surgeries, it was used to book just 54 percent of appointments. Even a three-year £100 million incentive program to encourage physician adoption failed to sway doctors who had witnessed patients unnecessarily traveling to distant hospitals and referral letters rebuffed when patients sought confirmation.

Designers also focused on building provider choice into the service. This turned out to be a solution in search of a problem. According to the NHS Alliance, a coalition of healthcare providers, managers, and patients dedicated to improving care and providing a voice to patients, the ability to choose physicians and facilities from a wide range of options was never a chief concern. Instead, patients were looking for swift referrals to their local hospital. In rural areas, choice was considerably limited anyway, and older patients, in particular, simply found the array of choices confusing, difficult to navigate, and time-consuming to select.

Although many doctors were fans, system misfires created a significant population of disgruntled caregivers who refused to use Choose and Book. Glitches included appointment letters gone astray, last-minute cancellations, costs incurred for phone calls to the booking line in some locations, and treatment delays due to lack of visit categorization—either urgent or routine—not incorporated because cases requiring immediate treatment bypassed the queuing system.

By 2014, Choose and Book's cost had ballooned to £356 million. It did provide reliable referrals for more than half of first-time outpatients and was used—at least to some degree—by more than 90 percent of providers. However, when a study by the Public Accounts Committee (PAC) reported that use by both doctors and patients had dropped and that waiting times for elective care had shown no improvement, Choose and Book's days were numbered. The system had never been able to function optimally because not all available outpatient appointments were listed. Members of Parliament (MPs) were fatigued by nearly a decade of patchwork fixes and frustrated that projected annual savings of up to £51 million had never materialized.

The discrete replacement of Choose and Book by a new system of unstipulated—and perhaps greater—cost underscores both the mission and the challenges of the NHS. Launched in 1948, the comprehensive health system is funded by tax dollars and administered by the Department of Health (DH). All British citizens are afforded care from their first newborn exam to their end-of-life care, with many services free of charge. NHS England covers 53 million citizens. Another 10.2 million people are covered by NHS divisions in Northern Ireland, Wales, and Scotland.

The most pressing and urgent challenge the NHS faces is the often lengthy waiting time to receive care, which can sometimes yield dire consequences.

Healthcare for all, regardless of wealth, is a core value of British society. A 2013 Commonwealth Fund study of national healthcare systems ranked NHS first for quality of care, safety, coordination of care, patient-centered care, and cost. On timeliness of care, the UK ranked third.

With timeliness of care as the overriding goal, the NHS planned to launch in England a new e-Referral Service in spring 2015. Director of Strategic Systems and Technology Beverley Bryant expects significantly reduced paperwork and fewer data errors, along with an accelerated referral process because patients monitor and manage their own hospital appointments. Several ideas to encourage adoption are being explored, including making physician participation mandatory and developing an incentive program that incorporates penalties as well as rewards. The goal is to improve upon or eliminate the flaws of Choose and Book—for example, moving away from the hybrid electronic/paper environment that has proved burdensome for hospitals. The switch to all digital will occur by 2019.

Sources: National Health Service, "NHS e-Referral Service Best Practice Guidelines," NHS, October 2016; Warwick Ashford, "NHS to Scrap £356m Outpatient Booking System," ComputerWeekly.com, May 12, 2014; www.chooseandbook.nhs.uk, accessed February 22, 2015; Toby Helm and Dennis Campbell, "NHS Hit by New Tech Failure as It Scraps Patient Booking System," *The Observer*, May 10, 2014; "About the National Health Service (NHS)," nhs.uk/NHSEngland, accessed August 10, 2014; Caroline Baldwin, "New NHS e-Referral Service to Use Agile and Open Technologies," ComputerWeekly.com, May 13, 2014; "NHS e-Referral Service Vision," systems.hscic.gov.uk, accessed August 10, 2014; "NHS to Stop Choose and Book Outpatient Appointments System and Replace It with New IT System," UK News, May 11, 2014; and Mark Gould, "Claims That NHS Choose and Book System Puts Choice Before Quality," *The Guardian*, March 23, 2010.

CASE STUDY QUESTIONS

1. Clarify and describe the problems of the NHS Choose and Book System. What people, organization, and technology factors were responsible for those problems?

2. To what extent was Choose and Book a failure? Explain your answer.

3. What was the economic and social impact of Choose and Book?

4. Describe the steps that should have been taken to make Choose and Book more successful.

Management Strategies for Developing BI and BA Capabilities

There are two different strategies for adopting BI and BA capabilities for the organization: one-stop integrated solutions versus multiple best-of-breed vendor solutions. The hardware firms (IBM, HP, and now Oracle, which owns Sun Microsystems) want to sell your firm integrated hardware/software solutions that tend to run only on their hardware (the totally integrated solution). It's called "one-stop shopping." The software firms (SAP, SAS, and Microsoft) encourage firms to adopt the "best-of-breed" software that runs on any machine they want. In this strategy, you adopt the best database and data warehouse solution, and select the business intelligence and analytics package from whatever vendor you believe is best.

The first solution carries the risk that a single vendor provides your firm's total hardware and software solution, making your firm dependent on its pricing power. However, it offers the advantage of dealing with a single vendor who can deliver on a global scale. The second solution offers greater flexibility and independence, but with the risk of potential difficulties integrating the software to the hardware platform, as well as to other software. Vendors always claim their software is "compatible" with other software, but the reality is that it can be very difficult to integrate software from different vendors.

Regardless of which strategy your firm adopts, all BI and BA systems lock the firm into a set of vendors and switching is very costly. Once you train thousands of employees across the world on using a particular set of tools, it is extremely difficult to switch. When you adopt these systems, you are in essence taking in a new partner.

12-4 How do different decision-making constituencies in an organization use business intelligence, and what is the role of information systems in helping people working in a group make decisions more efficiently?

Earlier in this text and in this chapter, we described the different information constituencies in business firms—from senior managers to middle managers, analysts, and operational employees. This also holds true for BI and BA systems (see Figure 12.4). More than 80 percent of the audience for BI consists of casual users who rely largely on production reports. Senior executives tend to use BI to monitor firm activities using visual interfaces like dashboards and scorecards. Middle managers and analysts are much more likely to be immersed in the data and software, entering queries and slicing and dicing the data along different dimensions. Operational employees will, along with customers and suppliers, be looking mostly at prepackaged reports.

FIGURE 12.4 BUSINESS INTELLIGENCE USERS

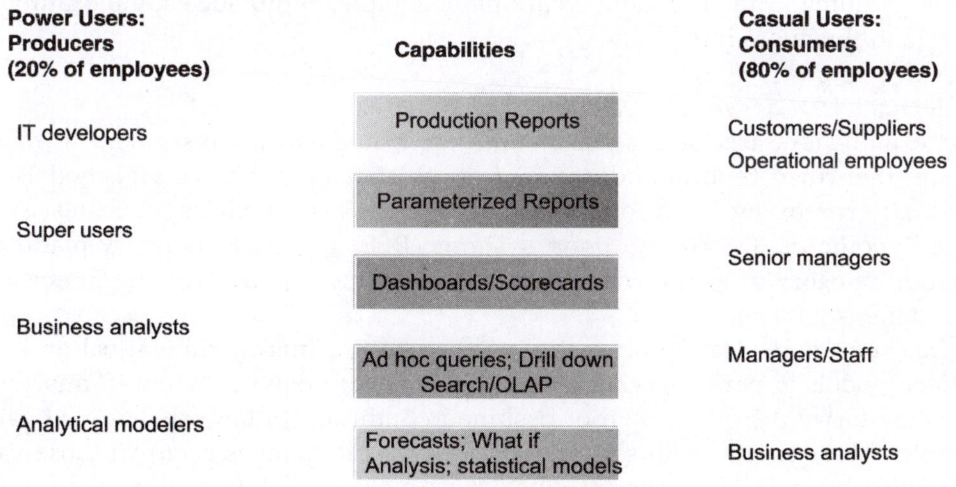

Casual users are consumers of BI output, while intense power users are the producers of reports, new analyses, models, and forecasts.

TABLE 12.6 EXAMPLES OF MIS APPLICATIONS

COMPANY	MIS APPLICATION
Plan International	Headquartered in Surrey, UK, with operations in over 70 countries. Human resources MIS tracks the location, skills, and job experience of all of its 10,000 workers and identifies which people have the appropriate skills and experience in medical aid, child protection, education, and shelter management to provide the necessary services for various types of emergencies..
Black & Veatch	Web-based MIS tracks construction costs for its projects in many different locations. This global company has approximately 10,000 professionals working out of more than 110 offices worldwide.
Dubai Islamic Bank	MIS reports on customer eligibility for loans. Uses data about balances in the customer's banking account and how the customer's business works to determine whether the customer can cover the amount of the loan in the future. Output from this MIS guides management decisions about whether to approve or reject the loan application.

Decision Support for Operational And Middle Management

Operational and middle management are generally charged with monitoring the performance of key aspects of the business, ranging from the downtime of machines on a factory floor to the daily or even hourly sales at franchise food stores to the daily traffic at a company's website. Most of the decisions these managers make are fairly structured. Management information systems (MIS), which we introduced in Chapter 2, are typically used by middle managers to support this type of decision making. Increasingly, middle managers receive these reports online and are able to interactively query the data to find out why events are happening. Managers at this level often turn to exception reports, which highlight only exceptional conditions, such as when the sales quotas for a specific territory fall below an anticipated level or employees have exceeded their spending limits in a dental care plan. Table 12.6 provides some examples of MIS for business intelligence.

Support for Semi-structured Decisions

Some managers are "super users" and keen business analysts who want to create their own reports and use more sophisticated analytics and models to find patterns in data, to model alternative business scenarios, or to test specific hypotheses. Decision-support systems (DSS) are the BI delivery platform for this category of users, with the ability to support semi-structured decision making.

DSS rely more heavily on modeling than MIS, using mathematical or analytical models to perform what-if or other kinds of analysis. "What-if" analysis, working forward from known or assumed conditions, allows the user to vary certain values to test results to predict outcomes if changes occur in those values. What happens if we raise product prices by 5 percent or increase the advertising budget by $1 million? **Sensitivity analysis** models ask what-if questions repeatedly to predict a range of outcomes when one or more variables are

FIGURE 12.5 SENSITIVITY ANALYSIS

Total fixed costs	19000					
Variable cost per unit	3					
Average sales price	17					
Contribution margin	14					
Break-even point	1357					
			Variable Cost per Unit			
Sales	1357	2	3	4	5	6
Price	14	1583	1727	1900	2111	2375
	15	1462	1583	1727	1900	2111
	16	1357	1462	1583	1727	1900
	17	1267	1357	1462	1583	1727
	18	1188	1267	1357	1462	1583

This table displays the results of a sensitivity analysis of the effect of changing the sales price of a necktie and the cost per unit on the product's break-even point. It answers the question "What happens to the break-even point if the sales price and the cost to make each unit increase or decrease?"

changed multiple times (see Figure 12.5). Backward sensitivity analysis helps decision makers with goal seeking: If I want to sell 1 million product units next year, how much must I reduce the price of the product?

Chapter 6 described multidimensional data analysis and OLAP as key business intelligence technologies. Spreadsheets have a similar feature for multidimensional analysis called a **pivot table**, which manager "super users" and analysts employ to identify and understand patterns in business information that may be useful for semi-structured decision making.

Figure 12.6 illustrates a Microsoft Excel pivot table that examines a large list of order transactions for a company selling online management training videos and books. It shows the relationship between two dimensions: the sales region and the source of contact (web banner ad or e-mail) for each customer order. It answers the question: Does the source of the customer make a difference in addition to region? The pivot table in this figure shows that most customers come from the West and that banner advertising produces most of the customers in all the regions.

In the past, much of this modeling was done with spreadsheets and small stand-alone databases. Today these capabilities are incorporated into large enterprise BI systems where they are able to analyze data from large corporate databases. BI analytics include tools for intensive modeling, some of which we described earlier. Such capabilities help insurance companies identify the best customers for their products. Using widely available insurance industry data, insurance firms can identify small groups of customers, or "cells," such as motorcycle riders of ages 30 and above with college educations, credit scores over a certain level, and no accidents. For each "cell," these firms perform a regression analysis to identify factors most closely correlated with the insurance losses that are typical for this group. It then sets prices for each cell and uses simulation software to test whether this pricing arrangement will enable the company to make a profit. These analytic techniques make it possible for insurance firms to profitably insure

FIGURE 12.6 A PIVOT TABLE THAT EXAMINES CUSTOMER REGIONAL DISTRIBUTION AND ADVERTISING SOURCE

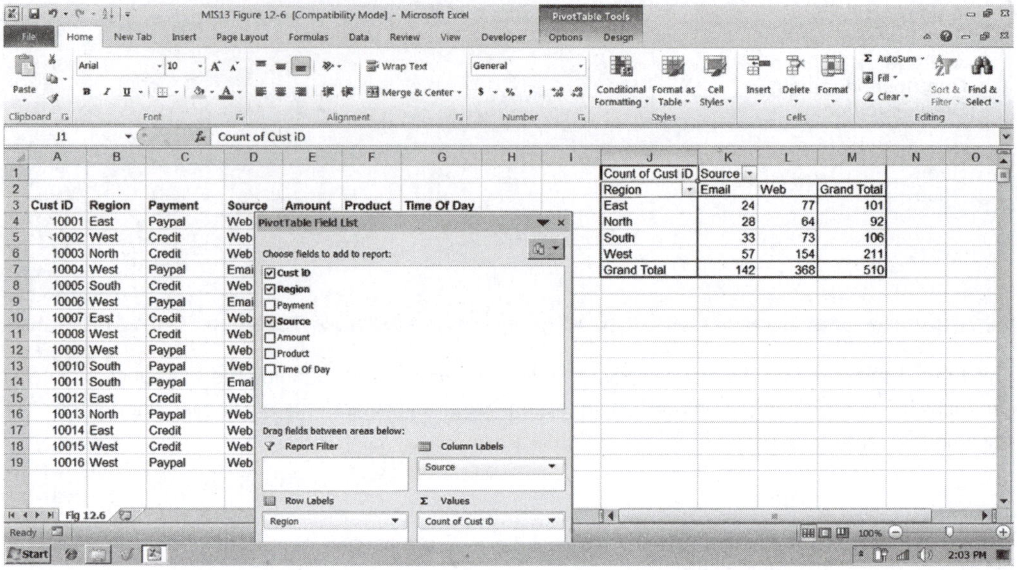

In this pivot table, we are able to examine where an online training company's customers come from in terms of region and advertising source.

customers in traditionally high-risk categories that other insurers would have rejected.

Decision Support for Senior Management: Balanced Scorecard and Enterprise Performance Management Methods

The purpose of executive support systems (ESS), introduced in Chapter 2, is to help C-level executive managers focus on the really important performance information that affects the overall profitability and success of the firm. There are two parts to developing ESS. First, you will need a methodology for understanding exactly what is "the really important performance information" for a specific firm that executives need, and second, you will need to develop systems capable of delivering this information to the right people in a timely fashion.

Currently, the leading methodology for understanding the really important information needed by a firm's executives is called the **balanced scorecard method** (Kaplan and Norton, 1992, 2004). The balanced scorecard is a framework for operationalizing a firm's strategic plan by focusing on measurable outcomes on four dimensions of firm performance: financial, business process, customer, and learning and growth (Figure 12.7).

Performance on each dimension is measured using **key performance indicators (KPIs)**, which are the measures proposed by senior management for understanding how well the firm is performing along any given dimension.

FIGURE 12.7 THE BALANCED SCORECARD FRAMEWORK

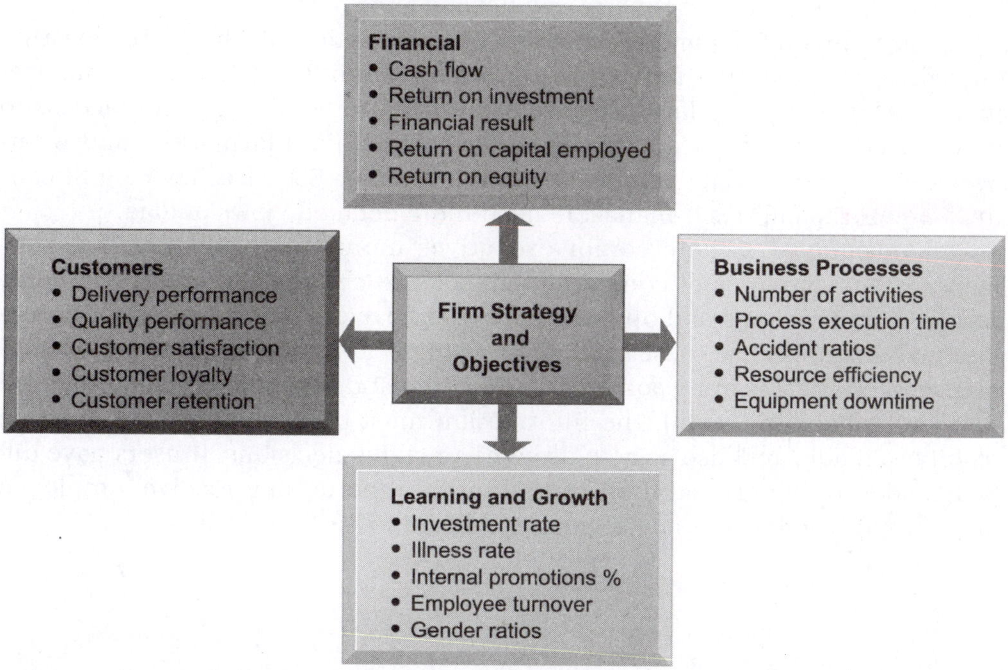

In the balanced scorecard framework, the firm's strategic objectives are operationalized along four dimensions: financial, business process, customer, and learning and growth. Each dimension is measured using several KPIs.

For instance, one key indicator of how well an online retail firm is meeting its customer performance objectives is the average length of time required to deliver a package to a consumer. If your firm is a bank, one KPI of business process performance is the length of time required to perform a basic function like creating a new customer account.

The balanced scorecard framework is thought to be "balanced" because it causes managers to focus on more than just financial performance. In this view, financial performance is past history—the result of past actions—and managers should focus on the things they are able to influence today, such as business process efficiency, customer satisfaction, and employee training. Once a scorecard is developed by consultants and senior executives, the next step is automating a flow of information to executives and other managers for each of the key performance indicators. There are literally hundreds of consulting and software firms that offer these capabilities, which are described below. Once these systems are implemented, they are often referred to as ESS.

Another closely related popular management methodology is **business performance management (BPM)**. Originally defined by an industry group in 2004 (led by the same companies that sell enterprise and database systems like Oracle, SAP, and IBM), BPM attempts to systematically translate a firm's strategies (e.g., differentiation, low-cost producer, market share growth, and scope of operation) into operational targets. Once the strategies and targets are identified, a set of KPIs are developed that measure progress toward the targets.

The firm's performance is then measured with information drawn from the firm's enterprise database systems. BPM uses the same ideas as the balanced scorecard but with a stronger strategy flavor.

Corporate data for contemporary ESS are supplied by the firm's existing enterprise applications (enterprise resource planning, supply chain management, and customer relationship management). ESS also provide access to news services, financial market databases, economic information, and whatever other external data senior executives require. ESS also have significant **drill-down** capabilities if managers need more detailed views of data.

Well-designed ESS help senior executives monitor organizational performance, track activities of competitors, recognize changing market conditions, and identify problems and opportunities. Employees lower down in the corporate hierarchy also use these systems to monitor and measure business performance in their areas of responsibility. For these and other business intelligence systems to be truly useful, the information must be "actionable"—it must be readily available and also easy to use when making decisions. If users have difficulty identifying critical metrics within the reports they receive, employee productivity and business performance will suffer.

Group Decision-Support Systems (GDSS)

The systems we have just described focus primarily on helping you make a decision acting alone. However, what if you are part of a team and need to make a decision as a group? You would use a special category of systems called group decision-support systems for this purpose.

Group decision-support systems (GDSS) are interactive computer-based systems that facilitate the solution of unstructured problems by a set of decision makers working together as a group in the same location or in different locations. Originally, GDSS required dedicated conference rooms with special hardware and software tools for documenting and ranking ideas. GDSS capabilities have evolved along with the power of desktop PCs, the explosion of mobile computing, and the rapid expansion of bandwidth on Wi-Fi and cellular networks. Dedicated rooms for collaboration can be replaced with much less expensive and flexible virtual collaboration rooms that can connect mobile employees with colleagues in the office sitting at desktops in a high-quality video and audio environment. We introduced some of these contemporary collaboration environments in Chapter 2.

Cisco's Collaboration Meeting Rooms Hybrid (CMR) allows groups of employees to meet using any device via WebEx video software, which does not require any special network connections, special displays, or complex software. The software to run CMR can be hosted on company servers or in the cloud. This allows even customers to participate in group meetings. The meetings can be scheduled by employees whenever needed. CMR can handle up to 500 participants in a meeting, but that is quite rare. Skype began deploying a similar cloud-based collaboration environment called Skype for Business to support online meetings, sharing of documents, audio, and video. Skype for Business is integrated into Microsoft Office 365, which will make Skype for Business an integral part of office life in the near future.

Review Summary

12-1 *What are the different types of decisions, and how does the decision-making process work?*

The different levels in an organization (strategic, management, operational) have different decision-making requirements. Decisions can be structured, semi-structured, or unstructured, with structured decisions clustering at the operational level of the organization and unstructured decisions at the strategic level. Decision making can be performed by individuals or groups and includes employees as well as operational, middle, and senior managers. There are four stages in decision making: intelligence, design, choice, and implementation.

12-2 *How do information systems support the activities of managers and management decision making?*

Early classical models of managerial activities stress the functions of planning, organizing, coordinating, deciding, and controlling. Contemporary research looking at the actual behavior of managers has found that managers' real activities are highly fragmented, variegated, and brief in duration and that managers shy away from making grand, sweeping policy decisions.

Information technology provides new tools for managers to carry out both their traditional and newer roles, enabling them to monitor, plan, and forecast with more precision and speed than ever before and to respond more rapidly to the changing business environment. Information systems have been most helpful to managers by providing support for their roles in disseminating information, providing liaisons between organizational levels, and allocating resources. However, information systems are less successful at supporting unstructured decisions. Where information systems are useful, information quality, management filters, and organizational culture can degrade decision making.

12-3 *How do business intelligence and business analytics support decision making?*

Business intelligence and analytics promise to deliver correct, nearly real-time information to decision makers, and the analytic tools help them quickly understand the information and take action. A business intelligence environment consists of data from the business environment, the BI infrastructure, a BA toolset, managerial users and methods, a BI delivery platform (MIS, DSS, or ESS), and the user interface. There are six analytic functionalities that BI systems deliver to achieve these ends: predefined production reports, parameterized reports, dashboards and scorecards, ad hoc queries and searches, the ability to drill down to detailed views of data, and the ability to model scenarios and create forecasts.

12-4 *How do different decision-making constituencies in an organization use business intelligence, and what is the role of information systems in helping people working in a group make decisions more efficiently?*

Operational and middle management are generally charged with monitoring the performance of their firm. Most of the decisions they make are fairly structured. Management information systems (MIS) producing routine production reports are typically used to support this type of decision making. For making unstructured decisions, middle managers and analysts will use decision-support systems (DSS) with powerful analytics and modeling tools, including spreadsheets and pivot tables. Senior executives making unstructured decisions use dashboards and visual interfaces displaying key performance information affecting the overall profitability, success, and strategy of the firm. The balanced scorecard and business performance management are two methodologies used in designing executive support systems (ESS). Group decision-support systems (GDSS) help people working together in a group arrive at decisions more efficiently.

Key Terms

Balanced scorecard method, 506
Behavioral models, 489
Business performance management (BPM), 507
Choice, 488
Classical model of management, 489
Data visualization, 495
Decisional role, 490
Design, 488
Drill down, 508
Geographic information systems (GIS), 498
Group decision-support systems (GDSS), 508
Implementation, 489
Informational role, 490
Intelligence, 488
Interpersonal role, 490
Key performance indicators (KPIs), 506
Managerial roles, 490
Location analytics, 498
Operational intelligence, 498
Pivot table, 505
Predictive analytics, 496
Semi-structured decisions, 486
Sensitivity analysis, 504
Structured decisions, 486
Unstructured decisions, 486

Review Questions

12-1 What are the different types of decisions? How does the decision-making process work?

- How does the information requirements of key decision-making groups in an organization differ? Discuss with the help of examples.
- Explain the characteristics of three different types of decisions and their business values.
- How is decision making a multi-step process? Discuss with the help of examples.

12-2 How do information systems support the activities of managers and management decision making?

- List and describe the three major categories of managerial roles as identified by Mintzberg. What are their business implications?
- Identify dimensions of information quality which impact quality of organizational decisions.

12-3 How do business intelligence and business analytics support decision making?

- Define operational intelligence, location analytics, and geographic information system.
- Explain with examples the business intelligence applications of predictive and big data analytics.
- Which analytic functionalities of BI systems help deliver correct, real-time information to decision makers? Discuss.
- How do BI and BA infrastructure support decision making in organizations?

12-4 How do different decision-making constituencies in an organization use business intelligence? What is the role of information systems in helping people working in a group make decisions more efficiently?

- List each of the major decision-making constituencies in an organization and describe the types of decisions each makes.
- Define and describe the balanced scorecard method and business performance management.
- Define a group decision-support system (GDSS) and explain how it differs from a DSS.

Discussion Questions

12-5 As a manager or user of information systems, what would you need to know to participate in the design and use of a DSS or an ESS? Why?

12-6 What types of businesses might benefit from location analytics and geographic information systems? Which might not benefit?

12-7 How much can business intelligence and business analytics help companies refine their business strategy? Explain your answer.

Hands-On MIS Projects

The projects in this section give you hands-on experience identifying opportunities for DSS, using a spreadsheet pivot table to analyze sales data, and using online retirement planning tools for financial planning.

Management Decision Problems

12-8 Dealerships for Subaru and other automobile manufacturers keep records of the mileage of cars they sell and service. Mileage data are used to remind customers of when they need to schedule service appointments, but they are used for other purposes as well. What kinds of decisions does this piece of data support at the local level and at the corporate level? What would happen if this piece of data were erroneous, for example, showing mileage of 130,000 instead of 30,000? How would it affect decision making? Assess its business impact.

12-9 Applebee's is the largest casual dining chain in the world, with more than 1,800 locations throughout the United States and also in 20 other countries. The menu features beef, chicken, and pork items as well as burgers, pasta, and seafood. Applebee's CEO wants to make the restaurant more profitable by developing menus that are tastier and contain more items that customers want and are willing to pay for despite rising costs for gasoline and agricultural products. How might business intelligence help management implement this strategy? What pieces of data would Applebee's need to collect? What kinds of reports would be useful to help management make decisions on how to improve menus and profitability?

Improving Decision Making: Using a Web-Based DSS for Retirement Planning

Software skills: Internet-based software
Business skills: Financial planning

12-10 This project will help develop your skills in using web-based DSS for financial planning.

The websites for CNN Money and Kiplinger feature web-based DSS for financial planning and decision making. Select either site to plan for retirement. Use your chosen site to determine how much you need to save to have enough income for your retirement. Assume that you are 50 years old and single and plan to retire in 17 years. You have $100,000 in savings. Your current annual income is $85,000. Your goal is to be able to generate an annual retirement income of $60,000, including social security benefit payments.

Use the website you have selected to determine how much money you need to save to help you achieve your retirement goal. If you need to calculate your estimated social security benefit, use the Quick Calculator at the Social Security Administration website

Critique the site—its ease of use, its clarity, the value of any conclusions reached, and the extent to which the site helps investors understand their financial needs and the financial markets.

Collaboration and Teamwork Project

Investigating Data-Driven Analytics in Sports

12-11 With three or four of your classmates, select a sport, such as football, baseball, basketball, or soccer. Use the web to research how the sport uses data and analytics to improve team performance or increase ticket sales to events. If possible, use Google Docs and Google Drive or Google Sites to brainstorm, organize, and develop a presentation of your findings for the class.

GE Bets on the Internet of Things and Big Data Analytics

CASE STUDY

General Electric (GE) is one of the world's largest industrial companies with products ranging from turbines to jet engines to medical equipment, but it may not be much longer. The company is transitioning to a much more technology-centric business strategy and business model. GE is selling off its division that makes refrigerators and microwave ovens along with most of GE Capital financial services to focus on electric power generators, jet engines, locomotives, and oil-refining gear and software to connect these devices to the cloud. Leading software companies such Oracle, SAP, and Microsoft have traditionally been focused on providing technology for the back office. In contrast, GE is putting its money on the technology that controls and monitors industrial machines as well as software-powered, cloud-based services for analyzing and deriving value from the data. GE hopes this strategy will turn it into a major software company.

GE is using sensor-generated data from industrial machines to help customers monitor equipment performance, prevent breakdowns, and assess the machines' overall health. This new technology is opening new opportunities for GE customers while also helping to transform GE from a traditional manufacturer to a modern digital business. GE has committed $1 billion to installing sensors on gas turbines, jet engines, and other machines; connecting them to the cloud; and analyzing the resulting data to identify ways to improve machine productivity and reliability. In other words, GE is betting its future on software and the Internet of Things (IoT).

In a number of industries, improving the productivity of existing assets by even a single percentage point can generate significant benefits. This is true of the oil and gas sector, where average recovery rate of an oil well is 35 percent. That means 65 percent of a well's potential is left in the earth because available technology makes it too expensive to extract. If technology can help oil extraction companies raise the recovery rate from 35 to 36 percent, the world's output will increase by 80 billion barrels—the equivalent of three years of global supply.

The oil and gas industry is also deeply affected by unplanned downtime, when equipment cannot operate because of a malfunction. A single unproductive day on a platform can cost a liquified natural gas (LNG) facility as much as $25 million, and an average midsized LNG facility experiences about five down days a year. That's $125 to $150 million lost. Minimizing downtime is critical, especially considering declining revenues from lower energy prices. GE sees a $1 billion opportunity for its IoT software.

The foundation for all of GE's Industrial Internet (IoT) applications is Predix, a software platform launched in 2015 to collect data from industrial sensors and analyze the information in the cloud. Predix can run on any cloud infrastructure. The platform has open standards and protocols that allow customers to more easily and quickly connect their machines to the Industrial Internet. The platform can accommodate the size and scale of industrial data for every customer at current levels of use, but it also has been designed to scale up as demand grows. Predix can offer apps developed by other companies as well as GE, is available for on-premises or cloud-based deployment, and can be extended by customers with their own data sources, algorithms, and code. Customers may develop their own custom applications for the Predix platform. GE is also building a developer community to create apps that can be hosted on Predix. Predix is not limited to industrial applications. It could be used for analyzing data in healthcare systems, for example. GE now has a Health Cloud running on Predix. Data security is embedded at all platform application layers, and this is essential for companies linking their operations to the Internet.

GE currently uses Predix to monitor and maintain its own industrial products, such as wind turbines, jet engines, and hydroelectric turbine systems. Predix is able to provide GE corporate customers' machine operators and maintenance engineers with real-time information to schedule maintenance checks, improve machine efficiency, and reduce downtime. Helping customers collect and use this operational data proactively would lower costs in GE service agreements. When GE agrees to provide service for a customer's machine, it often comes with a performance guarantee. Proactive identification of potential issues that also takes the cost out of shop visits helps the customer and helps GE.

In early 2013, GE began to use Predix to analyze data across its fleet of machines. By identifying what made one machine more efficient or downtime-prone than another, GE could more tightly manage its operations. For example, by using high-performance analytics, GE learned that some of its jet aircraft engines were beginning to require more frequent unscheduled maintenance. A single engine's operating data will only tell you there's a problem with that engine. But by collecting massive amounts of data and analyzing the data across its entire fleet of machines, GE was able to cluster engine data by operating environment. The company found that the hot and harsh environments in the Middle East and China caused engines to clog, heat up, and lose efficiency, so they required more maintenance. GE found that engines had far fewer of these problems if they were washed more frequently. Fleet analytics helped GE increase engine lifetime and reduce engine maintenance. The company thinks it can save its customers an average of $7 million of jet airplane fuel annually because their engines will be more efficient. Predix's robust data and analytics platform made it possible for GE to use data across every GE engine all over the world and cluster fleet data.

Predix is starting to provide solutions for GE customers. Irish Power is an early Predix user. The company adopted GE's predictive analytics tool suite Reliability Excellence based on the Predix platform. Irish Power started out by using operational data analytics to improve the efficiency of its Whitegate plant, a 445-megawatt gas combined-cycle power plant located 25 miles east of the city of Cork, Ireland. Irish Power plans to roll out a module for process optimization and will connect plant performance to the real-time energy marketplace. These analytics help Irish Power and customers identify ways of lowering production costs, increasing plant capability, and improving system reliability. Applying analytics built on the Predix platform can enable GE to offer customers like Irish Power anomaly detection or enable cost savings by reducing the need for preventative maintenance thanks to the visibility of the operational data GE can now provide.

British oil and gas company BP plc had been using its own software to monitor conditions in its oil wells. Recently, however, BP management decided to get out of the software business and became a GE customer. By the end of 2015, BP equipped 650 of its thousands of oil wells with GE sensors linked to Predix. Each well was outfitted with 20 to 30 sensors to measure pressure and temperature, transmitting 500,000 data points to the Predix cloud every 15 seconds. BP hopes to use the data to predict well flows and the useful life of each well and ultimately to obtain an enterprise-wide view of its oil fields' performance.

GE identified pipeline risk management as a major challenge for the oil and gas industry. There are 2 million miles of transmission pipe throughout the globe, moving liquid oil or gas from its point of extraction to refining, processing, or market. About 55 percent of transmission pipeline in the United States was installed before 1970. Pipeline spills are not frequent, but when they occur, they cause serious economic and environmental damage as well as bad publicity for pipeline operators and energy companies. Pipeline operators are always anxious to know where their next rupture will be, but they typically lacked the data to measure pipeline fitness. Operators had no way of integrating multiple sources of data into one place so they could see and understand the risk in their pipelines.

GE developed a pipeline-management software suite for accessing, managing, and integrating critical data for the safe management of pipelines, including a risk assessment tool to monitor aging infrastructure. GE's risk-assessment solution combines internal and external factors (such as flooding) to provide an accurate, up-to-the minute visual representation of where risk exists in a pipeline. This risk assessment tool enables pipeline operators to see how recent events affect their risk and make real-time decisions about where field service crews should be deployed along the pipeline. The risk assessment tool visualization and analytics capabilities run on Predix.

GE is also pulling data from weather systems and dig-reporting services to provide a more comprehensive view of a pipeline network. Weather has a sizable impact on risk for pipelines in areas prone to seismic activity, waterways, and washouts.

Checking weather patterns along thousands of miles of pipe for rain or flood zones, and integrating those data with other complex pipeline data sets is very difficult to perform manually. But by bringing all relevant together data in one place, GE gives pipeline operators easier access to information to help them address areas with the greatest potential impact.

GE expects customers to benefit immediately from having all of their data integrated. But it wants them to be able to do more. In addition to being able to examine all current risk, pipeline operators would benefit from a "what-if" calculation tool to model hypothetical scenarios, such as assessing the impact of adjusting operating pressures or addressing particular areas of corrosive pipe. GE would give them the tools for a color-coded view of how those actions affect pipeline risk.

In addition, GE wants to go beyond helping its customers manage the performance of their GE machines to managing the data on all of the machines in their entire operations. Many customers use GE equipment alongside of equipment from competitors. The customer cares about running the whole plant, not just GE turbines, for example, and 80 percent of the equipment in these facilities is not from GE. If, for example, if an oil and gas customer has a problem with a turbo compressor, a heat exchanger upstream from that compressor may be the source of the problem, so analyzing data from the turbo compressor will only tell part of the story. Customers therefore want GE to analyze non-GE equipment and help them keep their entire plant running. GE is in discussions with some customers about managing sensor data from all of the machine assets in their operation.

If a customer purchases a piece of GE equipment such as a gas turbine or aircraft engine, GE often enters into a 10- to 15-year contractual services agreement that allows GE to connect to and monitor that machine, perform basic maintenance and diagnostics, and provide scheduled repairs. GE receives a bonus payment for keeping the equipment running at a specified threshold. GE may now be able to apply such outcome-based pricing to coverage of non-GE machines.

GE CEO Jeffrey Immelt wants GE to become a top 10 software company by 2020. In order to do this, GE needs to sell vast amounts of applications and Predix-based analytics. Although few businesses have the capital or infrastructure to operate a platform for integrating and analyzing their IoT data, GE faces competition from many sources. Amazon, Google, IBM, and Microsoft are all getting into Internet of Things platforms, and dozens of start-ups have similar ambitions. The biggest question is whether other large industrial companies will turn to GE or to another cloud platform to manage their information. And if you're a manufacturer of some size and sophistication, will you allow GE to "own" the data on your business, or will you manage and analyze the data yourself?

Sources: Laura Winig, "GE's Big Bet on Data and Analytics," *MIT Sloan Management Review,* February 2016; Devin Leonard and Rick Clough, "How GE Exorcised the Ghost of Jack Welch to Become a 124-Year-Old Startup," *Bloomberg Businessweek,* March 21, 2016; www.ge.com, accessed May 19, 2016; Holly Lugassy,"GE Leverages Pivotal Cloud Foundry to Build Predix, First Cloud for Industry," CloudFoundry.org, May 11, 2016; Kurt Marko, "AWS IoT Platform Connects Devices to Cloud Services," techtarget.com, accessed May 24, 2016; Cliff Saran, "GE Predictive Analytics Optimises Irish Power Electricity Production," *Computer Weekly,* July 13, 2015; Charles Babcock, "GE Predix Cloud: Industrial Support for Machine Data," *Information Week,* August 6, 2015; and "GE: IoT Makes Power Plants $50M More Valuable," *Information Week,* September 29, 2015.

CASE STUDY QUESTIONS

12-12 How is GE changing its business strategy and business model? What is the role of information technology in GE's business?

12-13 On what business functions and level of decision making is GE focusing?

12-14 Describe three kinds of decisions that can be supported using Predix. What is the value to the firm of each of those decisions? Explain.

12-15 To what extent is GE becoming a software company? Explain your answer.

12-16 Do you think GE will become one of the top 10 U.S. software companies? Why or why not?

Chapter 12 References

Bell, Peter C. "Sustaining an Analytics Advantage." *MIT Sloan Management Review* (Spring 2015).

Bhandari, Rishi, Marc Singer, and Hiek van der Scheer. "Using Marketing Analytics to Drive Superior Growth." McKinsey & Co. (June 2014).

Chen, Daniel Q., David S. Preston, and Morgan Swink. "How the Use of Big Data Analytics Affects Value Creation in Supply Chain Management." *Journal of Management Information Systems* 32, No. 4 (2015).

Clark, Thomas D., Jr., Mary C. Jones, and Curtis P. Armstrong. "The Dynamic Structure of Management Support Systems: Theory Development, Research Focus, and Direction." *MIS Quarterly* 31, No. 3 (September 2007).

Davenport, Thomas H. "Analytics 3.0." *Harvard Business Review* (December 2013).

________ *Big Data at Work: Dispelling the Myths, Uncovering the Opportunities*. Harvard Business Review Press (2014).

Davenport, Thomas H. and Jill Dyche. "Big Data in Big Companies." International Institute of Analytics (May 2013).

Davenport, Thomas H., Jeanne G. Harris, and Robert Morison. *Analytics at Work: Smarter Decisions, Better Results*. Boston: Harvard Business Press (2010).

De la Merced, Michael J. and Ben Protess. "A Fast-Paced Stock Exchange Trips over Itself." *New York Times* (March 23, 2012)

Dennis, Alan R., Jay E. Aronson, William G. Henriger, and Edward D. Walker III. "Structuring Time and Task in Electronic Brainstorming." *MIS Quarterly* 23, No. 1 (March 1999).

Fogarty, David and Peter C. Bell. "Should You Outsource Analytics?" *MIT Sloan Management Review* (Winter 2014).

Gallupe, R. Brent, Geraldine DeSanctis, and Gary W. Dickson. "Computer-Based Support for Group Problem-Finding: An Experimental Investigation." *MIS Quarterly* 12, No. 2 (June 1988).

Grau, Jeffrey. "How Retailers Are Leveraging 'Big Data' to Personalize Ecommerce." *eMarketer* (2012).

Harris, Jeanne G. and Vijay Mehrotra. "Getting Value from Your Data Scientists." *MIT Sloan Management Review* (Fall 2014).

Hurst, Cameron with Michael S. Hopkins and Leslie Brokaw. "Matchmaking with Math: How Analytics Beats Intuition to Win Customers." *MIT Sloan Management Review* 52, No. 2 (Winter 2011).

Jensen, Matthew, Paul Benjamin Lowry, Judee K. Burgoon, and Jay Nunamaker. "Technology Dominance in Complex Decision Making." *Journal of Management Information Systems* 27, No. 1 (Summer 2010).

Kahneman, Daniel. *Thinking, Fast and Slow*. New York: Farrar, Straus and Giroux (2011).

Kaplan, Robert S. and David P. Norton. "The Balanced Scorecard: Measures That Drive Performance." *Harvard Business Review* (January–February 1992).

Kaplan, Robert S. and David P. Norton. *Strategy Maps: Converting Intangible Assets into Tangible Outcomes*. Boston: Harvard Business School Press (2004).

Kiron, David, Pamela Kirk Prentice, and Renee Boucher Ferguson. "Raising the Bar with Analytics." *MIT Sloan Management Review* (Winter 2014).

Lauricella, Tom and Scott Patterson. "With Knight Wounded, Traders Ask If Speed Kills." *Wall Street Journal* (August 2, 2012).

LaValle, Steve, Eric Lesser, Rebecca Shockley, Michael S. Hopkins and Nina Kruschwitz. "Big Data, Analytics, and the Path from Insights to Value." *MIT Sloan Management Review* 52, No. 2 (Winter 2011).

Leidner, Dorothy E., and Joyce Elam. "The Impact of Executive Information Systems on Organizational Design, Intelligence, and Decision Making." *Organization Science* 6, No. 6 (November–December 1995).

Luca, Michael, Jon Kleinberg, and Sendhil Mullainathan. "Algorithms Need Managers, Too." *Harvard Business Review* (January–February 2016).

Marchand, Donald A. and Joe Peppard. "Why IT Fumbles Analytics." *Harvard Business Review* (January–February 2013).

Mintzberg, Henry."Managerial Work: Analysis from Observation." Management Science 18 (October 1971).

Nichols, Wes. "Advertising Analytics 2.0." *Harvard Business Review* (March 2013).

"The New Science of Sales Performance." *Harvard Business Review Analytic Services* (March 5, 2015).

Parenteau, Josh, Rita L. Sallam, Cindi Howson, Joao Tapadinhas, Kurt Schlegel, and Thomas W. Oestreich. "Magic Quadrant for Business Intelligence and Analytics Platforms." Gartner, Inc. (February 4, 2016).

Ransbotham, Sam, David Kiron, and Pamela Kirk Prentice. "Minding the Analytics Gap." *MIT Sloan Management Review* (Spring 2015).

Simon, H. A. *The New Science of Management Decision*. New York: Harper & Row (1960).

Tversky, Amos and Daniel Kahneman. "Rational Choice and the Framing of Decisions." *Journal of Business* (1986).

PART **FOUR**

Building and Managing Systems

PART FOUR shows how to use the knowledge acquired in earlier chapters to analyze and design information system solutions to business problems. This part answers questions such as these: How can I develop a solution to an information system problem that provides genuine business benefits? How can the firm adjust to the changes introduced by the new system solution? What alternative approaches are available for building system solutions?

CHAPTER

13 Building Information Systems

Learning Objectives

After reading this chapter, you will be able to answer the following questions:

13-1 How does building new systems produce organizational change?

13-2 What are the core activities in the systems development process?

13-3 What are the principal methodologies for modeling and designing systems?

13-4 What are alternative methods for building information systems?

13-5 What are new approaches for system building in the digital firm era?

CHAPTER CASES

Angostura Builds a Mobile Sales System
Centralization of Operations at Tata Power
Developing Mobile Apps: What's Different
ConAgra's Recipe for a Better Human Resources System

Angostura Builds a Mobile Sales System

House of Angostura (also known as Angostura Limited), headquartered in Laventille, Trinidad, is one of the Caribbean's leading rum producers and the world market leader for bitters used in many cocktails. Angostura has 330 full-time employees and annual revenue of approximately $100 million.

Angostura still takes care of local distribution of its products in Trinidad and Tobago, with a team of 16 sales representatives taking orders out in the field. Although this arrangement worked well in the past, the process was heavily manual, tedious, and time-consuming and sometimes produced inaccurate orders.

Each day, the 16 sales reps in the field had to copy the orders on paper and return to the office to hand off the order forms to a customer service representative, who would then manually input the order data into Angostura's SAP enterprise resource planning (ERP) system. Because the orders were handwritten, information could be read and entered incorrectly, which could result in the wrong goods being sent to a customer. Such inaccurate orders were often returned, creating more paperwork and higher costs. Angostura also used manual processes for reporting and tracking invoices and accounts receivable information, which could create additional delays and errors.

The sales representatives were also working with data on product availability that might be out of date. If the sales reps were away from the office, they would not be able to tell whether an order could actually be fulfilled. They would have to call Angostura's warehouse to find out if an order was possible.

In 2012 Angostura's management decided that the sales process needed to be more streamlined and efficient and that it should use mobile technology. The company identified a set of detailed information requirements for the improved sales process and spent more than a year evaluating system solutions from five mobile vendors. One important requirement was that the application should be able to automatically update the availability of purchased products from the company's overall inventory and integrate with the firm's back-end SAP ERP system. Another requirement was that the mobile system be able to operate offline so that a sales representative could still input an order on a mobile device even if there was no online connectivity. Once online, the device could then send the order through to the ERP system.

The vendor selected was the one that could best develop the mobile application to the company's specifications and stay within the budget established by management. In 2013 Angostura partnered with IDS Scheer and itCampus consultants to develop a mobile sales solution running on Apple iPads. The solution includes an offline customer database, product catalog, customer-specific pricing, order entry, order preview, and integration with Bluetooth printers. It was quickly created using SAP NetWeaver Gateway technology to connect various devices and platforms to SAP software. A pilot application was ready for testing that June, and the entire application went live January 2014.

Each of Angostura's 16 sales representatives was issued an iPad that includes not only the order application but other mobile apps to make the sales process more efficient, such as email, Google Maps, and a video and PDF document uploader to display the Angostura product line. The sales application integrates with the corporate ERP system, providing the sales reps with up-to-date information on the availability of products in the warehouse.

With the Angostura Mobile Sales App, an order can be created in less than 30 seconds, depending on the size of the order, making the ordering process two times faster. There is a 20 percent time savings per salesperson because the sales reps now have the ability to send orders through as they place them rather than waiting until they return to the office. The amount of time customer service representatives would typically spend on data entry—which was considerable—has been reduced by 75 percent, freeing up time for more useful tasks. Returned orders have been reduced by 30 percent.

Sources: Natalie Miller, "Generations-Old Company with a Modern Twist on Sales," SAP Insider Profiles, January 2016; www.angostura.com, accessed February 10, 2016; and IDS Scheer Consulting Group, "Angostura's iPad-Based SAP Mobile Sales Solution," 2014.

Angostura's experience illustrates some of the steps required to design and build new information systems. Building a new system for mobile sales orders entailed analyzing the organization's problems with existing systems, assessing information requirements, selecting appropriate technology, and redesigning business processes and jobs. Management had to oversee the systems-building effort and evaluate benefits and costs. The information requirements were incorporated into the design of the new system, which represented a process of planned organizational change.

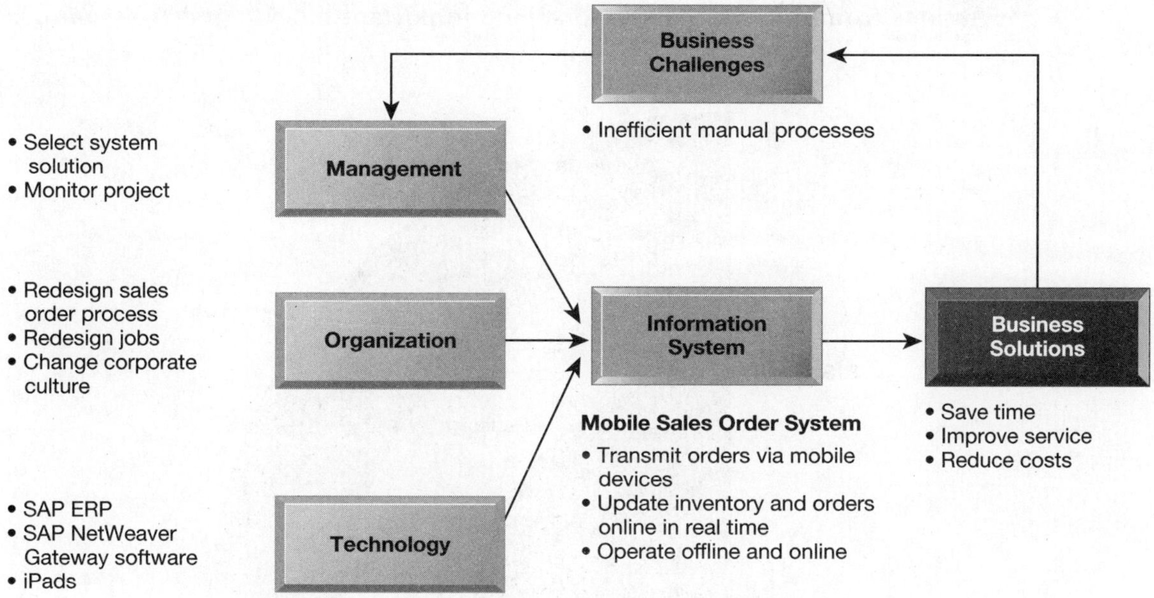

The chapter-opening case calls attention to important points raised by this case and this chapter. Angostura's ability to handle sales orders was hampered by outdated and inefficient manual processes, which raised costs, slowed down work, and limited the company's ability to serve its customers.

The solution was to redesign the sales order process to use mobile devices and software and allow orders to be entered through iPads and transmitted to the firm's back-end ERP system. Angostura's information requirements were incorporated into the system design. The solution encompassed not just the application of new technology but changes to corporate culture, business processes, and job functions. Angostura's sales operations have become much more efficient and cost-saving.

Here are some questions to think about: How did Angostura's Mobile Sales App meet its information requirements? How effective a solution was Angostura's Mobile Sales App? Why? How much did the new system change the way Angostura ran its business?

13-1 How does building new systems produce organizational change?

Building a new information system is one kind of planned organizational change. The introduction of a new information system involves much more than new hardware and software. It also includes changes in jobs, skills, management, and organization. When we design a new information system, we are redesigning the organization. System builders must understand how a system will affect specific business processes and the organization as a whole.

FIGURE 13.1 ORGANIZATIONAL CHANGE CARRIES RISKS AND REWARDS

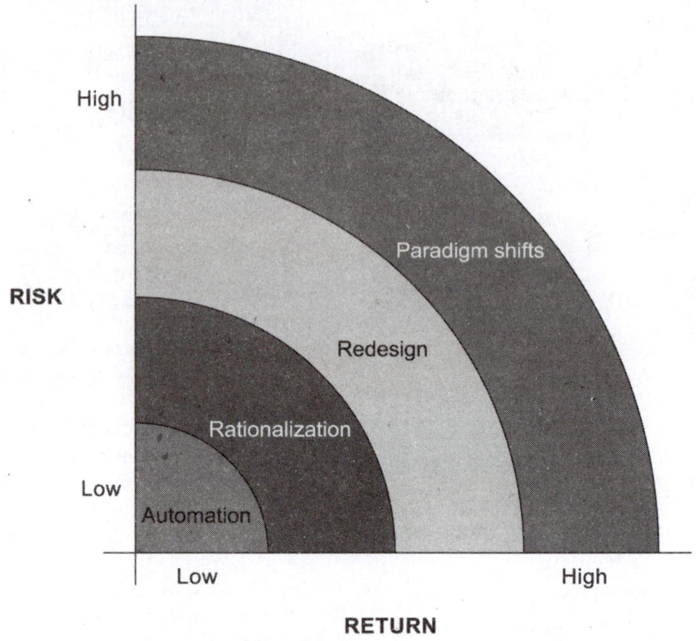

The most common forms of organizational change are automation and rationalization. These relatively slow-moving and slow-changing strategies present modest returns but little risk. Faster and more comprehensive change—such as redesign and paradigm shifts—carries high rewards but offers substantial chances of failure.

Systems Development and Organizational Change

Information technology can promote various degrees of organizational change, ranging from incremental to far-reaching. Figure 13.1 shows four kinds of structural organizational change that are enabled by information technology: (1) automation, (2) rationalization, (3) business process redesign, and (4) paradigm shifts. Each carries different risks and rewards.

The most common form of IT-enabled organizational change is **automation**. The first applications of information technology involved assisting employees with performing their tasks more efficiently and effectively. Calculating paychecks and payroll registers, giving bank tellers instant access to customer deposit records, and developing a nationwide reservation network for airline ticket agents are all examples of early automation.

A deeper form of organizational change—one that follows quickly from early automation—is **rationalization of procedures**. Automation frequently reveals new bottlenecks in production and makes the existing arrangement of procedures and structures painfully cumbersome. Rationalization of procedures is the streamlining of standard operating procedures. For example, Angostura's new mobile order system is effective not only because it uses computer technology but also because the company simplified its business processes for this function. Fewer manual steps are required.

Rationalization of procedures is often found in programs for making a series of continuous quality improvements in products, services, and operations, such as total quality management (TQM) and six sigma. **Total quality management (TQM)** makes achieving quality an end in itself and the responsibility of all people and functions within an organization. TQM derives from concepts developed by American quality experts such as W. Edwards Deming and Joseph Juran, but it was popularized by the Japanese. **Six sigma** is a specific measure of quality, representing 3.4 defects per million opportunities. Most companies cannot achieve this level of quality but use six sigma as a goal for driving ongoing quality improvement programs.

A more powerful type of organizational change is **business process redesign**, in which business processes are analyzed, simplified, and redesigned. Business process redesign reorganizes workflows, combining steps to cut waste and eliminate repetitive, paper-intensive tasks. (Sometimes the new design eliminates jobs as well.) It is much more ambitious than rationalization of procedures, requiring a new vision of how the process is to be organized.

A widely cited example of business process redesign is Ford Motor Company's invoiceless processing, which reduced head count in Ford's North American Accounts Payable organization of 500 people by 75 percent. Accounts payable clerks used to spend most of their time resolving discrepancies between purchase orders, receiving documents, and invoices. Ford redesigned its accounts payable process so that the purchasing department enters a purchase order into an online database that can be checked by the receiving department when the ordered items arrive. If the received goods match the purchase order, the system automatically generates a check for accounts payable to send to the vendor. There is no need for vendors to send invoices.

Rationalizing procedures and redesigning business processes are limited to specific parts of a business. New information systems can ultimately affect the design of the entire organization by transforming how the organization carries out its business or even the nature of the business. For instance, the long-haul trucking and transportation firm Schneider National used new information systems to change its business model. Schneider created a new business managing logistics for other companies. This more radical form of business change is called a **paradigm shift**. A paradigm shift involves rethinking the nature of the business and the nature of the organization.

Paradigm shifts and business process redesign often fail because extensive organizational change is so difficult to orchestrate (see Chapter 14). Why, then, do so many corporations contemplate such radical change? Because the rewards are equally high (see Figure 13.1). In many instances, firms seeking paradigm shifts and pursuing reengineering strategies achieve stunning, order-of-magnitude increases in their returns on investment (or productivity). Some of these success stories, and some failure stories, are included throughout this book.

Business Process Redesign

Like Angostura, described in the chapter-opening case, many businesses today are trying to use information technology to improve their business processes. Some of these systems entail incremental process change, but others require more far-reaching redesign of business processes. To deal with these changes, organizations are turning to business process management. **Business process management (BPM)** provides a variety of tools and methodologies to analyze existing processes, design new processes, and optimize those processes. BPM is never concluded because process improvement requires continual change. Companies practicing business process management go through the following steps:

1. **Identify processes for change:** One of the most important strategic decisions that a firm can make is not deciding how to use computers to improve business processes but understanding what business processes need improvement. When systems are used to strengthen the wrong business model or business processes, the business can become more efficient at doing what it should not do. As a result, the firm becomes vulnerable to competitors who may have discovered the right business model. Considerable time and cost may also be spent improving business processes that have little impact on overall firm performance and revenue. Managers need to determine what business processes are the most important and how improving these processes will help business performance.
2. **Analyze existing processes:** Existing business processes should be modeled and documented, noting inputs, outputs, resources, and the sequence of activities. The process design team identifies redundant steps, paper-intensive tasks, bottlenecks, and other inefficiencies.

Figure 13.2 illustrates the "as-is" process for purchasing a book from a physical bookstore. Consider what happens when a customer visits a physical bookstore

FIGURE 13.2 AS-IS BUSINESS PROCESS FOR PURCHASING A BOOK FROM A PHYSICAL BOOKSTORE

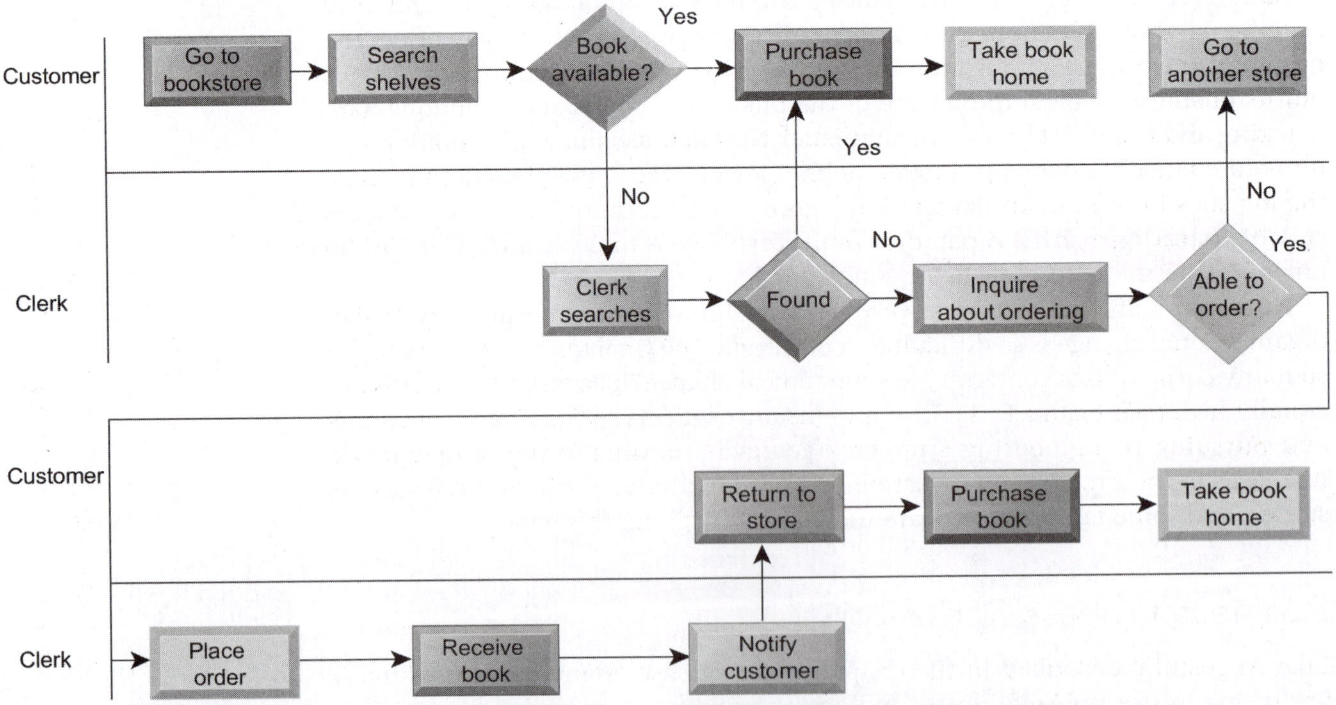

Purchasing a book from a physical bookstore requires many steps to be performed by both the seller and the customer.

and searches its shelves for a book. If he or she finds the book, that person takes it to the checkout counter and pays for it via credit card, cash, or check. If the customer is unable to locate the book, he or she must ask a bookstore clerk to search the shelves or check the bookstore's inventory records to see if it is in stock. If the clerk finds the book, the customer purchases it and leaves. If the book is not available locally, the clerk inquires about ordering it for the customer from the bookstore's warehouse or from the book's distributor or publisher. Once the ordered book arrives at the bookstore, a bookstore employee telephones the customer with this information. The customer would have to go to the bookstore again to pick up the book and pay for it. If the bookstore is unable to order the book for the customer, the customer would have to try another bookstore. You can see that this process has many steps and might require the customer to make multiple trips to the bookstore.

3. Design the new process: Once the existing process is mapped and measured in terms of time and cost, the process design team will try to improve the process by designing a new one. A new streamlined "to-be" process will be documented and modeled for comparison with the old process.

Figure 13.3 illustrates how the book-purchasing process can be redesigned by taking advantage of the Internet. The customer accesses an online bookstore over the Internet from his or her computer. He or she searches the bookstore's online catalog for the book he or she wants. If the book is available, the customer orders the book online, supplying credit card and shipping address information, and the book is delivered to the customer's home. If the online bookstore does not carry the book, the customer selects another online bookstore and searches for the book again. This process has far fewer steps than that for purchasing the book in a physical bookstore, requires much less effort on the part of the customer, and requires less sales staff for customer service. The new process is therefore much more efficient and time-saving.

The new process design needs to be justified by showing how much it reduces time and cost or enhances customer service and value. Management first measures the time and cost of the existing process as a baseline. In our example,

FIGURE 13.3 REDESIGNED PROCESS FOR PURCHASING A BOOK ONLINE

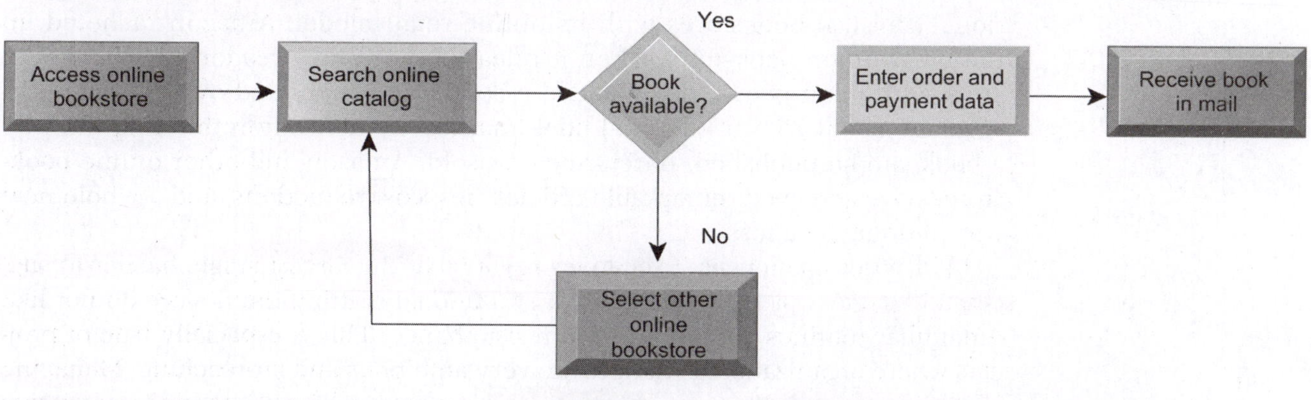

Using Internet technology makes it possible to redesign the process for purchasing a book so that it requires fewer steps and consumes fewer resources.

the time required for purchasing a book from a physical bookstore might range from 15 minutes (if the customer immediately finds what he or she wants) to 30 minutes if the book is in stock but has to be located by sales staff. If the book has to be ordered from another source, the process might take one or two weeks and another trip to the bookstore for the customer. If the customer lives far away from the bookstore, the time to travel to the bookstore would have to be factored in. The bookstore will have to pay the costs for maintaining a physical store and keeping the book in stock, for sales staff on site, and for shipment costs if the book has to be obtained from another location.

The new process for purchasing a book online might only take several minutes, although the customer might have to wait several days or a week to have the book delivered and will have to pay a shipping charge. But the customer saves time and money by not having to travel to the bookstore or make additional visits to pick up the book. Booksellers' costs are lower because they do not have to pay for a physical store location or for local inventory.

4. **Implement the new process:** Once the new process has been thoroughly modeled and analyzed, it must be translated into a new set of procedures and work rules. New information systems or enhancements to existing systems may have to be implemented to support the redesigned process. The new process and supporting systems are rolled out into the business organization. As the business starts using this process, problems are uncovered and addressed. Employees working with the process may recommend improvements.
5. **Continuous measurement:** Once a process has been implemented and optimized, it needs to be continually measured. Why? Processes may deteriorate over time as employees fall back on old methods, or they may lose their effectiveness if the business experiences other changes.

Although many business process improvements are incremental and ongoing, there are occasions when more radical change must take place. Our example of a physical bookstore redesigning the book-purchasing process so that it can be carried out online is an example of this type of radical, far-reaching change. When properly implemented, business process redesign produces dramatic gains in productivity and efficiency and may even change the way the business is run. In some instances, it drives a "paradigm shift" that transforms the nature of the business itself.

This actually happened in book retailing when Amazon challenged traditional physical bookstores with its online retail model. Amazon racheted up the pressure on bookstores when it released the Kindle reader for e-books. In 2015, 84 million people downloaded e-books, and generated over $4 billion in revenue, about 25% of the total book market. By radically rethinking the way a book can be published, purchased and sold, Amazon and other online bookstores have achieved remarkable efficiencies, cost reductions, and a whole new way of doing business.

BPM poses challenges. Executives report that the largest single barrier to successful business process change is organizational culture. Employees do not like unfamiliar routines and often try to resist change. This is especially true of projects where organizational changes are very ambitious and far-reaching. Managing change is neither simple nor intuitive, and companies committed to extensive process improvement need a good change management strategy (see Chapter 14).

Tools for Business Process Management

More than 100 software firms provide tools for various aspects of BPM, including IBM, Oracle, and TIBCO. These tools help businesses identify and document processes requiring improvement, create models of improved processes, capture and enforce business rules for performing processes, and integrate existing systems to support new or redesigned processes. BPM software tools also provide analytics for verifying that process performance has been improved and for measuring the impact of process changes on key business performance indicators.

Some BPM tools document and monitor business processes to help firms identify inefficiencies using software to connect with each of the systems a company uses for a particular process to identify trouble spots. Another category of tools automate some parts of a business process and enforce business rules so that employees perform that process more consistently and efficiently.

For example, American National Insurance Company, which offers life insurance, medical insurance, property casualty insurance, and investment services, used Pega BPM workflow software to streamline customer service processes across four business groups. The software built rules to guide customer service representatives through a single view of a customer's information that was maintained in multiple systems. By eliminating the need to juggle multiple applications simultaneously to handle customer and agent requests, the improved process increased customer service representative workload capacity by 192 percent.

A third category of tools helps businesses integrate their existing systems to support process improvements. They automatically manage processes across the business, extract data from various sources and databases, and generate transactions in multiple related systems.

13-2 What are the core activities in the systems development process?

New information systems are an outgrowth of a process of organizational problem solving. A new information system is built as a solution to some type of problem or set of problems the organization perceives it is facing. The problem may be one in which managers and employees realize that the organization is not performing as well as expected or that the organization should take advantage of new opportunities to perform more successfully.

The activities that go into producing an information system solution to an organizational problem or opportunity are called **systems development**. Systems development is a structured kind of problem solved with distinct activities. These activities consist of systems analysis, systems design, programming, testing, conversion, and production and maintenance.

Figure 13.4 illustrates the systems development process. The systems development activities depicted usually take place in sequential order. But some of the activities may need to be repeated or some may take place simultaneously depending on the approach to system building that is being employed (see Section 13-4).

FIGURE 13.4 THE SYSTEMS DEVELOPMENT PROCESS

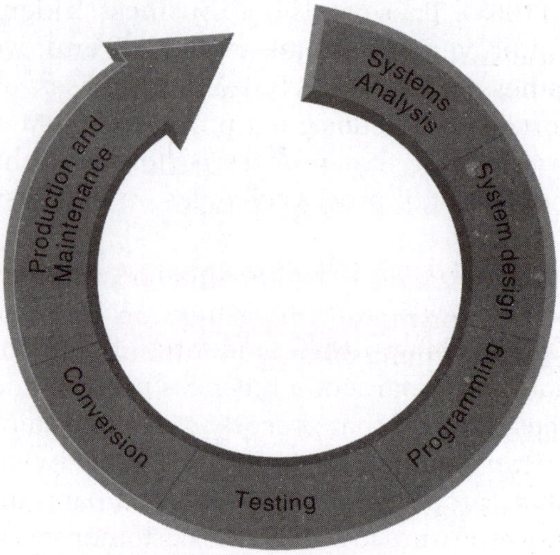

Building a system can be broken down into six core activities.

Systems Analysis

Systems analysis is the analysis of a problem that a firm tries to solve with an information system. It consists of defining the problem, identifying its causes, specifying the solution, and identifying the information requirements that must be met by a system solution.

The systems analyst creates a road map of the existing organization and systems, identifying the primary owners and users of data along with existing hardware and software. The systems analyst then details the problems of existing systems. By examining documents, work papers, and procedures, observing system operations, and interviewing key users of the systems, the analyst can identify the problem areas and objectives a solution would achieve. Often, the solution requires building a new information system or improving an existing one.

The systems analysis also includes a **feasibility study** to determine whether that solution is feasible, or achievable, from a financial, technical, and organizational standpoint. The feasibility study determines whether the proposed system is expected to be a good investment, whether the technology needed for the system is available and can be handled by the firm's information systems specialists, and whether the organization can handle the changes introduced by the system.

Normally, the systems analysis process identifies several alternative solutions that the organization can pursue and assess the feasibility of each. A written systems proposal report describes the costs and benefits, and the advantages and disadvantages, of each alternative. It is up to management to determine which mix of costs, benefits, technical features, and organizational impacts represents the most desirable alternative.

Establishing Information Requirements

Perhaps the most challenging task of the systems analyst is to define the specific information requirements that must be met by the chosen system solution. At the most basic level, the **information requirements** of a new system involve identifying who needs what information, where, when, and how. Requirements analysis carefully defines the objectives of the new or modified system and develops a detailed description of the functions that the new system must perform. Faulty requirements analysis is a leading cause of systems failure and high systems development costs (see Chapter 14). A system designed around the wrong set of requirements will either have to be discarded because of poor performance or will need to undergo major modifications. Section 13-3 describes alternative approaches to eliciting requirements that help minimize this problem.

Some problems do not require an information system solution but instead need an adjustment in management, additional training, or refinement of existing organizational procedures. If the problem is information-related, systems analysis still may be required to diagnose the problem and arrive at the proper solution.

Systems Design

Systems analysis describes what a system should do to meet information requirements, and **systems design** shows how the system will fulfill this objective. The design of an information system is the overall plan or model for that system. Like the blueprint of a building or house, it consists of all the specifications that give the system its form and structure.

The systems designer details the system specifications that will deliver the functions identified during systems analysis. These specifications should address all of the managerial, organizational, and technological components of the system solution. Table 13.1 lists the types of specifications that would be produced during systems design.

Like houses or buildings, information systems may have many possible designs. Each design represents a unique blend of technical and organizational components. What makes one design superior to others is the ease and efficiency with which it fulfills user requirements within a specific set of technical, organizational, financial, and time constraints.

The Role of End Users

User information requirements drive the entire system-building effort. Users must have sufficient control over the design process to ensure that the system reflects their business priorities and information needs, not the biases of the technical staff. Working on design increases users' understanding and acceptance of the system. As we describe in Chapter 14, insufficient user involvement in the design effort is a major cause of system failure. However, some systems require more user participation in design than others, and Section 13-4 shows how alternative systems development methods address the user participation issue.

Completing the Systems Development Process

The remaining steps in the systems development process translate the solution specifications established during systems analysis and design into a fully

TABLE 13.1 SYSTEM DESIGN SPECIFICATIONS

OUTPUT	PROCESSING	DOCUMENTATION
Medium	Computations	Operations documentation
Content	Program modules	Systems documentation
Timing	Required reports	User documentation
INPUT	Timing of outputs	CONVERSION
Origins	MANUAL PROCEDURES	Data conversion rules
Flow	What activities	Testing method
Data entry	Who performs them	Conversion strategy
USER INTERFACE	When	TRAINING
Simplicity	How	Training techniques
Efficiency	Where	Training modules
Logic	CONTROLS	ORGANIZATIONAL CHANGES
Feedback	Input controls (characters, limit, reasonableness)	Task redesign
Errors	Processing controls (consistency, record counts)	Job design
DATABASE DESIGN	Output controls (totals, samples of output)	Process design
Logical data model	Procedural controls (passwords, special forms)	Organization structure design
Volume and speed requirements	SECURITY	Reporting relationships
File organization and design	Access controls	
Record specifications	Catastrophe plans	
	Audit trails	

operational information system. These concluding steps consist of programming, testing, conversion, production, and maintenance.

Programming

During the **programming** stage, system specifications that were prepared during the design stage are translated into software program code. Today, many organizations no longer do their own programming for new systems. Instead, they purchase the software that meets the requirements for a new system from external sources such as software packages from a commercial software vendor, software services from a software service provider, or outsourcing firms that develop custom application software for their clients (see Section 13-4).

Testing

Exhaustive and thorough **testing** must be conducted to ascertain whether the system produces the right results. Testing answers the question "Will the system produce the desired results under known conditions?" As Chapter 5 noted, some companies are starting to use cloud computing services for this work.

The amount of time needed to answer this question has been traditionally underrated in systems project planning (see Chapter 14). Testing is time-consuming: Test data must be carefully prepared, results reviewed, and corrections made in the system. In some instances, parts of the system may have to be redesigned. The risks resulting from glossing over this step are enormous.

Testing an information system can be broken down into three types of activities: unit testing, system testing, and acceptance testing. **Unit testing**, or program testing, consists of testing each program separately in the system. It is widely believed that the purpose of such testing is to guarantee that programs are error-free, but this goal is realistically impossible. Testing should be viewed instead as a means of locating errors in programs, focusing on finding all the ways to make a program fail. Once they are pinpointed, problems can be corrected.

System testing tests the functioning of the information system as a whole. It tries to determine whether discrete modules will function together as planned and whether discrepancies exist between the way the system actually works and the way it was conceived. Among the areas examined are performance time, capacity for file storage and handling peak loads, recovery and restart capabilities, and manual procedures.

Acceptance testing provides the final certification that the system is ready to be used in a production setting. Systems tests are evaluated by users and reviewed by management. When all parties are satisfied that the new system meets their standards, the system is formally accepted for installation.

The systems development team works with users to devise a systematic test plan. The **test plan** includes all of the preparations for the series of tests we have just described.

Figure 13.5 shows an example of a test plan. The general condition being tested is a record change. The documentation consists of a series of test plan screens maintained on a database (perhaps a PC database) that is ideally suited to this kind of application.

FIGURE 13.5 A SAMPLE TEST PLAN TO TEST A RECORD CHANGE

Procedure	Address and Maintenance "Record Change Series"		Test Series 2		
	Prepared By:	Date:	Version:		
Test Ref.	**Condition Tested**	**Special Requirements**	**Expected Results**	**Output On**	**Next Screen**
2.0	Change records				
2.1	Change existing record	Key field	Not allowed		
2.2	Change nonexistent record	Other fields	"Invalid key" message		
2.3	Change deleted record	Deleted record must be available	"Deleted" message		
2.4	Make second record	Change 2.1 above	OK if valid	Transaction file	V45
2.5	Insert record		OK if valid	Transaction file	V45
2.6	Abort during change	Abort 2.5	No change	Transaction file	V45

When developing a test plan, it is imperative to include the various conditions to be tested, the requirements for each condition tested, and the expected results. Test plans require input from both end users and information systems specialists.

Conversion

Conversion is the process of changing from the old system to the new system. Four main conversion strategies can be employed: the parallel strategy, the direct cutover strategy, the pilot study strategy, and the phased approach strategy.

In a **parallel strategy**, both the old system and its potential replacement are run together for a time until everyone is assured that the new one functions correctly. This is the safest conversion approach because, in the event of errors or processing disruptions, the old system can still be used as a backup. However, this approach is very expensive, and additional staff or resources may be required to run the extra system.

The **direct cutover strategy** replaces the old system entirely with the new system on an appointed day. It is a very risky approach that can potentially be more costly than running two systems in parallel if serious problems with the new system are found. There is no other system to fall back on. Dislocations, disruptions, and the cost of corrections may be enormous.

The **pilot study strategy** introduces the new system to only a limited area of the organization, such as a single department or operating unit. When this pilot version is complete and working smoothly, it is installed throughout the rest of the organization, either simultaneously or in stages.

The **phased approach strategy** introduces the new system in stages, either by functions or by organizational units. If, for example, the system is introduced by function, a new payroll system might begin with hourly workers who are paid weekly, followed six months later by adding salaried employees (who are paid monthly) to the system. If the system is introduced by organizational unit, corporate headquarters might be converted first, followed by outlying operating units four months later.

Moving from an old system to a new one requires that end users be trained to use the new system. Detailed **documentation** showing how the system works from both a technical and end-user standpoint is finalized during conversion time for use in training and everyday operations. Lack of proper training and documentation contributes to system failure, so this portion of the systems development process is very important.

Production and Maintenance

After the new system is installed and conversion is complete, the system is said to be in **production**. During this stage, the system will be reviewed by both users and technical specialists to determine how well it has met its original objectives and to decide whether any revisions or modifications are in order. In some instances, a formal **post-implementation audit** document is prepared. After the system has been fine-tuned, it must be maintained while it is in production to correct errors, meet requirements, or improve processing efficiency. Changes in hardware, software, documentation, or procedures to a production system to correct errors, meet new requirements, or improve processing efficiency are termed **maintenance**.

Approximately 20 percent of the time devoted to maintenance is used for debugging or correcting emergency production problems. Another 20 percent is concerned with changes in data, files, reports, hardware, or system software.

TABLE 13.2 SYSTEMS DEVELOPMENT

CORE ACTIVITY	DESCRIPTION
Systems analysis	Identify problem(s) Specify solutions Establish information requirements
Systems design	Create design specifications
Programming	Translate design specifications into program code
Testing	Perform unit testing Perform systems testing Perform acceptance testing
Conversion	Plan conversion Prepare documentation Train users and technical staff
Production and maintenance	Operate the system Evaluate the system Modify the system

But 60 percent of all maintenance work consists of making user enhancements, improving documentation, and recoding system components for greater processing efficiency. The amount of work in the third category of maintenance problems could be reduced significantly through better systems analysis and design practices. Table 13.2 summarizes the systems development activities.

13-3 What are the principal methodologies for modeling and designing systems?

There are alternative methodologies for modeling and designing systems. Structured methodologies and object-oriented development are the most prominent.

Structured Methodologies

Structured methodologies have been used to document, analyze, and design information systems for many decades. **Structured** refers to the fact that the techniques are step by step, with each step building on the previous one. Structured methodologies are top-down, progressing from the highest, most abstract level to the lowest level of detail—from the general to the specific.

Structured development methods are process-oriented, focusing primarily on modeling the processes, or actions that capture, store, manipulate, and distribute data as the data flow through a system. These methods separate data from processes. A separate programming procedure must be written every time someone wants to take an action on a particular piece of data. The procedures act on data that the program passes to them.

FIGURE 13.6 DATA FLOW DIAGRAM FOR MAIL-IN UNIVERSITY REGISTRATION SYSTEM

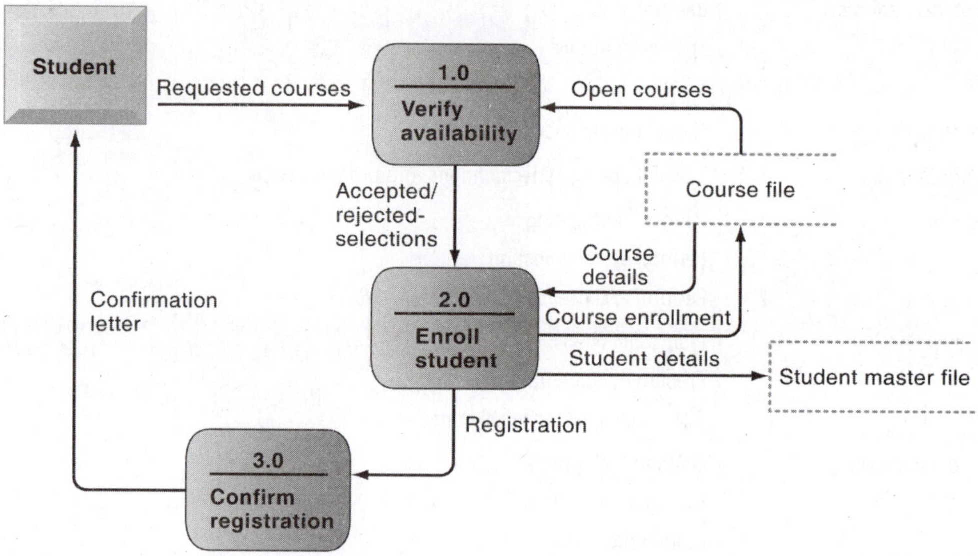

The system has three processes: Verify availability (1.0), Enroll student (2.0), and Confirm registration (3.0). The name and content of each of the data flows appear adjacent to each arrow. There is one external entity in this system: the student. There are two data stores: the student master file and the course file.

The primary tool for representing a system's component processes and the flow of data between them is the **data flow diagram (DFD)**. The data flow diagram offers a logical graphic model of information flow, partitioning a system into modules that show manageable levels of detail. It rigorously specifies the processes or transformations that occur within each module and the interfaces that exist between them.

Figure 13.6 shows a simple data flow diagram for a mail-in university course registration system. The rounded boxes represent processes, which portray the transformation of data. The square box represents an external entity, which is an originator or receiver of information located outside the boundaries of the system being modeled. The open rectangles represent data stores, which are either manual or automated inventories of data. The arrows represent data flows, which show the movement between processes, external entities, and data stores. They contain packets of data with the name or content of each data flow listed beside the arrow.

This data flow diagram shows that students submit registration forms with their name, their identification number, and the numbers of the courses they wish to take. In process 1.0, the system verifies that each course selected is still open by referencing the university's course file. The file distinguishes courses that are open from those that have been canceled or filled. Process 1.0 then determines which of the student's selections can be accepted or rejected. Process 2.0 enrolls the student in the courses for which he or she has been accepted. It updates the university's course file with the student's name and identification number and recalculates the class size. If maximum enrollment has been reached, the course number is flagged as closed. Process 2.0 also updates the university's student master file with information about new students or changes in address. Process 3.0 then sends each student applicant a confirmation of registration letter listing the courses for which he or she is registered and noting the course selections that could not be fulfilled.

The diagrams can be used to depict higher-level processes as well as lower-level details. Through leveled data flow diagrams, a complex process can be broken down into successive levels of detail. An entire system can be divided into subsystems with a high-level data flow diagram. Each subsystem, in turn, can be divided into additional subsystems with second-level data flow diagrams, and the lower-level subsystems can be broken down again until the lowest level of detail has been reached.

Another tool for structured analysis is a data dictionary, which contains information about individual pieces of data and data groupings within a system (see Chapter 6). The data dictionary defines the contents of data flows and data stores so that systems builders understand exactly what pieces of data they contain. **Process specifications** describe the transformation occurring within the lowest level of the data flow diagrams. They express the logic for each process.

In structured methodology, software design is modeled using hierarchical structure charts. The **structure chart** is a top-down chart, showing each level of design, its relationship to other levels, and its place in the overall design structure. The design first considers the main function of a program or system, then breaks this function into subfunctions, and decomposes each subfunction until the lowest level of detail has been reached. Figure 13.7 shows a high-level structure chart for a payroll system. If a design has too many levels to fit onto one structure chart, it can be broken down further on more detailed structure charts. A structure chart may document one program, one system (a set of programs), or part of one program.

FIGURE 13.7 HIGH-LEVEL STRUCTURE CHART FOR A PAYROLL SYSTEM

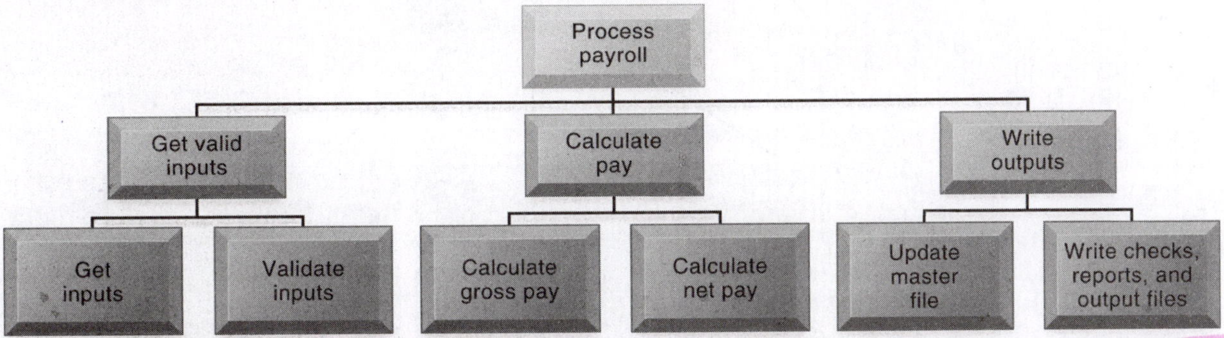

This structure chart shows the highest or most abstract level of design for a payroll system, providing an overview of the entire system.

Object-Oriented Development

Structured methods are useful for modeling processes but do not handle the modeling of data well. They also treat data and processes as logically separate entities, whereas in the real world such separation seems unnatural. Different modeling conventions are used for analysis (the data flow diagram) and for design (the structure chart).

Object-oriented development addresses these issues. Object-oriented development uses the **object** as the basic unit of systems analysis and design. An object combines data and the specific processes that operate on those data. Data encapsulated in an object can be accessed and modified only by the operations, or methods, associated with that object. Instead of passing data to procedures, programs send a message for an object to perform an operation that is already embedded in it. The system is modeled as a collection of objects and the relationships among them. Because processing logic resides within objects rather than in separate software programs, objects must collaborate with each other to make the system work.

Object-oriented modeling is based on the concepts of *class* and *inheritance*. Objects belonging to a certain class, or general category of similar objects, have the features of that class. Classes of objects in turn can inherit all the structure and behaviors of a more general class and then add variables and behaviors unique to each object. New classes of objects are created by choosing an existing class and specifying how the new class differs from the existing class instead of starting from scratch each time.

We can see how class and inheritance work in Figure 13.8, which illustrates the relationships among classes concerning employees and how they are paid.

FIGURE 13.8 CLASS AND INHERITANCE

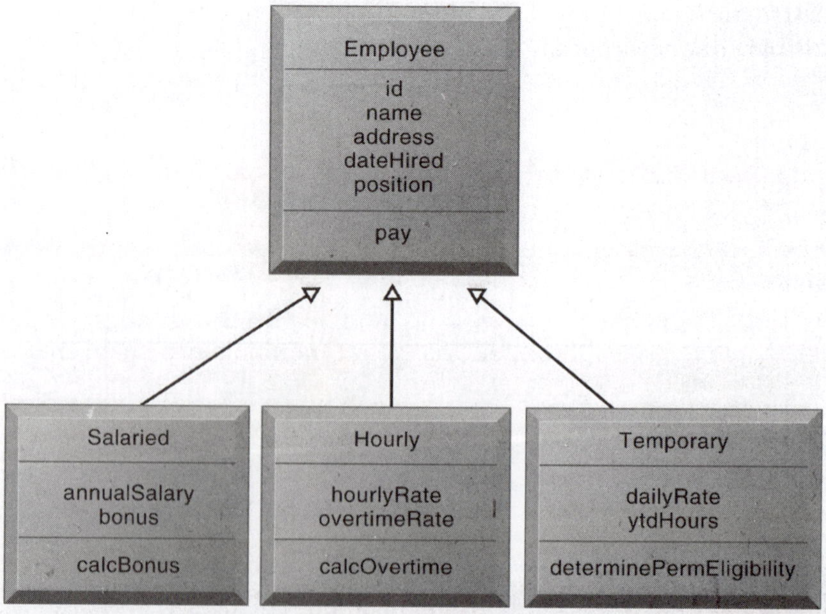

This figure illustrates how classes inherit the common features of their superclass.

Employee is the common ancestor, or superclass, for the other three classes. Salaried, Hourly, and Temporary are subclasses of Employee. The class name is in the top compartment, the attributes for each class are in the middle portion of each box, and the list of operations is in the bottom portion of each box. The features that are shared by all employees (ID, name, address, date hired, position, and pay) are stored in the Employee superclass, whereas each subclass stores features that are specific to that particular type of employee. Specific to hourly employees, for example, are their hourly rates and overtime rates. A solid line from the subclass to the superclass is a generalization path showing that the subclasses Salaried, Hourly, and Temporary have common features that can be generalized into the superclass Employee.

Object-oriented development is more iterative and incremental than traditional structured development. During analysis, systems builders document the functional requirements of the system, specifying its most important properties and what the proposed system must do. Interactions between the system and its users are analyzed to identify objects, which include both data and processes. The object-oriented design phase describes how the objects will behave and how they will interact with one another. Similar objects are grouped together to form a class, and classes are grouped into hierarchies in which a subclass inherits the attributes and methods from its superclass.

The information system is implemented by translating the design into program code, reusing classes that are already available in a library of reusable software objects, and adding new ones created during the object-oriented design phase. Implementation may also involve the creation of an object-oriented database. The resulting system must be thoroughly tested and evaluated.

Because objects are reusable, object-oriented development could potentially reduce the time and cost of writing software because organizations can reuse software objects that have already been created as building blocks for other applications. New systems can be created by using some existing objects, changing others, and adding a few new objects. Object-oriented frameworks have been developed to provide reusable, semicomplete applications that the organization can further customize into finished applications.

Computer-Aided Software Engineering

Computer-aided software engineering (CASE)—sometimes called *computer-aided systems engineering*—provides software tools to automate the methodologies we have just described to reduce the amount of repetitive work the developer needs to do. CASE tools also facilitate the creation of clear documentation and the coordination of team development efforts. Team members can share their work easily by accessing each other's files to review or modify what has been done. Modest productivity benefits can also be achieved if the tools are used properly.

CASE tools provide automated graphics facilities for producing charts and diagrams, screen and report generators, data dictionaries, extensive reporting facilities, analysis and checking tools, code generators, and documentation generators. In general, CASE tools try to increase productivity and quality by:

- Enforcing a standard development methodology and design discipline
- Improving communication between users and technical specialists

- Organizing and correlating design components and providing rapid access to them using a design repository
- Automating tedious and error-prone portions of analysis and design
- Automating code generation and testing and control rollout

CASE tools contain features for validating design diagrams and specifications. CASE tools thus support iterative design by automating revisions and changes and providing prototyping facilities. A CASE information repository stores all the information defined by the analysts during the project. The repository includes data flow diagrams, structure charts, entity-relationship diagrams, data definitions, process specifications, screen and report formats, notes and comments, and test results.

To be used effectively, CASE tools require organizational discipline. Every member of a development project must adhere to a common set of naming conventions and standards as well as to a development methodology. The best CASE tools enforce common methods and standards, which may discourage their use in situations where organizational discipline is lacking.

13-4 What are alternative methods for building information systems?

Systems differ in terms of their size and technological complexity and in terms of the organizational problems they are meant to solve. A number of systems-building approaches have been developed to deal with these differences. This section describes these alternative methods: the traditional systems life cycle, prototyping, application software packages, end-user development, and outsourcing.

Traditional Systems Life Cycle

The **systems life cycle** is the oldest method for building information systems. The life cycle methodology is a phased approach to building a system, dividing systems development into formal stages, as illustrated in Figure 13.9. Systems development specialists have different opinions on how to partition the systems-building stages, but they roughly correspond to the stages of systems development we have just described.

The systems life cycle methodology maintains a formal division of labor between end users and information systems specialists. Technical specialists, such as systems analysts and programmers, are responsible for much of the systems analysis, design, and implementation work; end users are limited to providing information requirements and reviewing the technical staff's work. The life cycle also emphasizes formal specifications and paperwork, so many documents are generated during the course of a systems project.

The systems life cycle is still used for building large complex systems that require a rigorous and formal requirements analysis, predefined specifications, and tight controls over the system-building process. However,

FIGURE 13.9 THE TRADITIONAL SYSTEMS DEVELOPMENT LIFE CYCLE

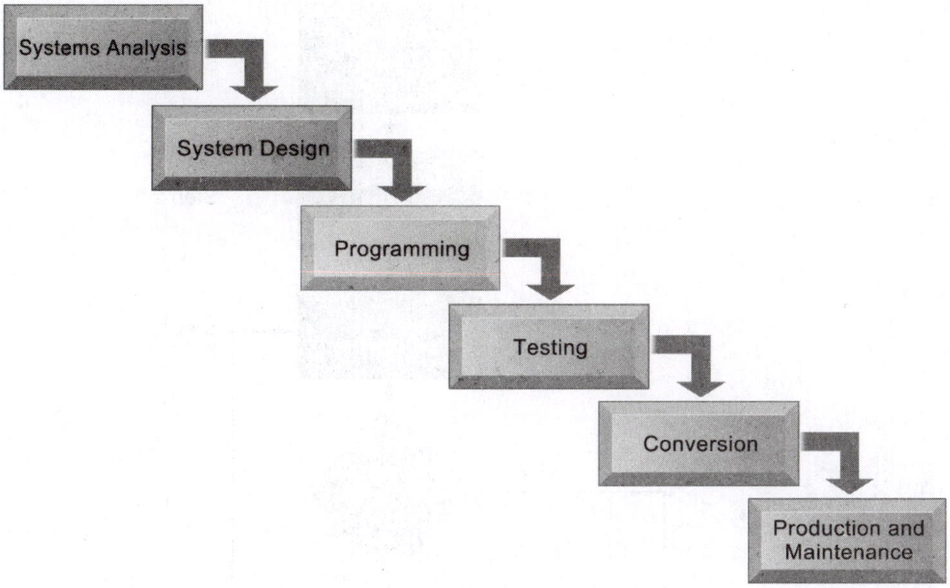

The systems development life cycle partitions systems development into formal stages, with each stage requiring completion before the next stage can begin.

the systems life cycle approach can be costly, time-consuming, and inflexible. Although systems builders can go back and forth among stages in the life cycle, the systems life cycle is predominantly a "waterfall" approach in which tasks in one stage are completed before work for the next stage begins. Activities can be repeated, but volumes of new documents must be generated and steps retraced if requirements and specifications need to be revised. This encourages freezing of specifications relatively early in the development process. The life cycle approach is also not suitable for many small desktop systems, which tend to be less structured and more individualized.

Prototyping

Prototyping consists of building an experimental system rapidly and inexpensively for end users to evaluate. By interacting with the prototype, users can get a better idea of their information requirements. The prototype endorsed by the users can be used as a template to create the final system.

The **prototype** is a working version of an information system or part of the system, but it is meant to be only a preliminary model. Once operational, the prototype will be further refined until it conforms precisely to users' requirements. Once the design has been finalized, the prototype can be converted to a polished production system.

The process of building a preliminary design, trying it out, refining it, and trying again has been called an **iterative** process of systems development because the steps required to build a system can be repeated over and over

FIGURE 13.10 THE PROTOTYPING PROCESS

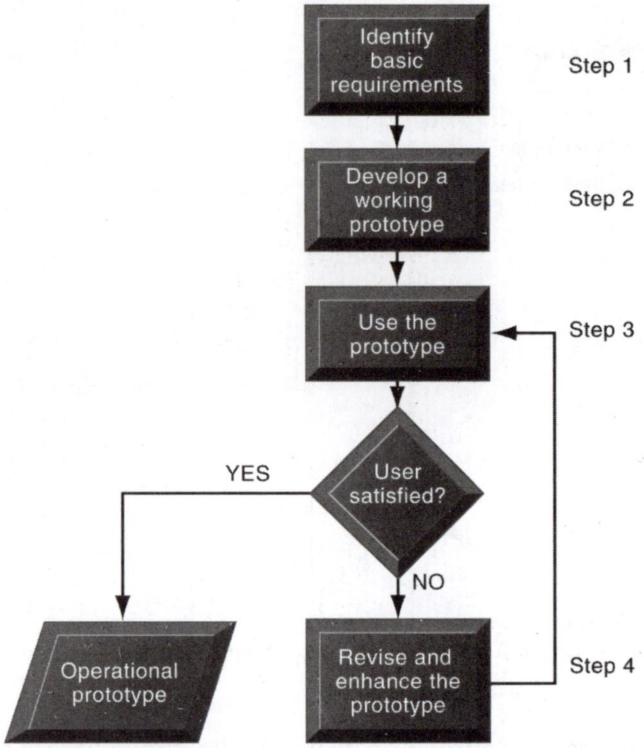

The process of developing a prototype can be broken down into four steps. Because a prototype can be developed quickly and inexpensively, systems builders can go through several iterations, repeating steps 3 and 4, to refine and enhance the prototype before arriving at the final operational one.

again. Prototyping is more explicitly iterative than the conventional life cycle, and it actively promotes system design changes. It has been said that prototyping replaces unplanned rework with planned iteration, with each version more accurately reflecting users' requirements.

Steps in Prototyping

Figure 13.10 shows a four-step model of the prototyping process, which consists of the following:

Step 1: *Identify the user's basic requirements*. The systems designer (usually an information systems specialist) works with the user only long enough to capture the user's basic information needs.

Step 2: *Develop an initial prototype*. The systems designer creates a working prototype quickly, using tools for rapidly generating software.

Step 3: *Use the prototype*. The user is encouraged to work with the system to determine how well the prototype meets his or her needs and to make suggestions for improving the prototype.

Step 4: *Revise and enhance the prototype*. The system builder notes all changes the user requests and refines the prototype accordingly. After the prototype has been revised, the cycle returns to Step 3. Steps 3 and 4 are repeated until the user is satisfied.

When no more iterations are required, the approved prototype then becomes an operational prototype that furnishes the final specifications for the application. Sometimes the prototype is adopted as the production version of the system.

Advantages and Disadvantages of Prototyping

Prototyping is most useful when there is some uncertainty about requirements or design solutions and often used for designing an information system's **end-user interface** (the part of the system with which end users interact, such as online display and data entry screens, reports, or web pages). Because prototyping encourages intense end-user involvement throughout the systems development life cycle, it is more likely to produce systems that fulfill user requirements.

However, rapid prototyping can gloss over essential steps in systems development. If the completed prototype works reasonably well, management may not see the need for reprogramming, redesign, or full documentation and testing to build a polished production system. Some of these hastily constructed systems may not easily accommodate large quantities of data or a large number of users in a production environment.

End-User Development

End-user development allows end users, with little or no formal assistance from technical specialists, to create simple information systems, reducing the time and steps required to produce a finished application. Using user-friendly query languages and reporting, website development, graphics, and PC software tools, end users can access data, create reports, and develop simple applications on their own with little or no help from professional systems analysts or programmers. A **query language** is a software tool that provides immediate online answers to questions that are not predefined, such as "Who are the highest-performing sales representatives?" Query languages are often tied to data management software (see Chapter 6).

For example, Yellow Pages (YP), a digital media and marketing solutions company serving 260,000 small and medium-sized Canadian businesses, used Information Builders WebFOCUS to build a user-friendly analytics application that helps customers measure return on their advertising dollars and track the success of their campaigns. The system, called YP Analytics, features a user-friendly dashboard to track interactions and measure key performance indicators focused on ROI and revenue. YP Analytics users can track important metrics such as visitors, visits, page views, and interactions/clicks as well as calls, in-shop walk-ins, digital contacts, and other performance indicators, and they can customize the outputs they want (Information Builders, 2015).

On the whole, end-user-developed systems can be completed more rapidly than those developed through the conventional systems life cycle. Allowing users to specify their own business needs improves requirements gathering and often leads to a higher level of user involvement and satisfaction with the system. However, end-user software tools still cannot replace conventional tools for some business applications because they cannot easily handle the processing of large numbers of transactions or applications with extensive procedural logic and updating requirements.

End-user computing also poses organizational risks because it occurs outside of traditional mechanisms for information systems management and control. When systems are created rapidly without a formal development methodology, testing and documentation may be inadequate. Control over data can be lost in systems outside the traditional information systems department. To help organizations maximize the benefits of end-user applications development, management should control the development of end-user applications by requiring cost justification of end-user information system projects and by establishing hardware, software, and quality standards for user-developed applications.

Application Software Packages, Software Services, and Outsourcing

Chapter 5 points out that much of today's software is not developed in-house but is purchased from external sources. Firms can rent the software from an online software service provider, they can purchase the software from a commercial vendor as a package to run in-house, or they can have a custom application developed by an outside outsourcing firm.

Application Software Packages and Cloud Software Services

Today many systems are based on commercially available application software packages or cloud software as a service (SaaS). For example, companies can choose to implement Oracle enterprise resource planning, supply chain management, or human capital management software in-house or pay to use this software running on the Oracle Cloud platform. Microsoft Office desktop productivity software comes in both desktop and cloud (Office 365) versions. Many applications are common to all business organizations—for example, payroll, accounts receivable, general ledger, or inventory control. For such universal functions with standard processes that do not change a great deal over time, a more generic system will fulfill the requirements of many organizations.

If a commercial software package or cloud software service can fulfill most of an organization's requirements, the company does not have to write its own software (see the Interactive Session on Organizations). The company can save time and money by using the prewritten, predesigned, pretested software programs from the software vendor. Package and SaaS vendors supply much of the ongoing maintenance and support for the system, including enhancements to keep the system in line with ongoing technical and business developments. When a package or SaaS solution is pursued, end users will be responsible for supplying the business information requirements for the system, and information systems specialists will provide technical requirements.

INTERACTIVE SESSION: ORGANIZATIONS

Centralization of Operations at Tata Power

Prior to 2002, Delhi was plagued with frequent power cuts and blackouts. There were regular power thefts, and each year, the government had to provide a subsidy of approximately ₹1,500 to the Delhi Vidyut Board (DVB). Subsidies, however, are not a long-term solution to cut losses. The electric supply situation in Delhi needed to improve. For this to happen, the power sector needed to become self-sufficient. To reform the DVB, the board was unbundled in 2002 into three divisions, one distribution company, one generation unit, and one transmission company. The Tata Power Delhi Distribution Limited (TPDDL), a joint venture between Tata Power and the government of the National Capital Territory of Delhi, was formed as a result of this unbundling. Even though it inherited losses from the DVB, the TPDDL now has an annual turnover of ₹5,979 crore. It has a registered consumer base of 14 lakh and operates over an area of 510 square kilometers in north and north-west Delhi. This turnaround has largely been accredited to the several IT initiatives undertaken by TPDDL after its formation.

At the time of its formation, the TPDDL was burdened with losses of approximately ₹10 crore a day. It received around 10,000 complaints each day regarding the lack of power supply. It had a backlog of 100,000 consumer complaints and 20,000 new connections. It employed a large workforce of over 5,000 employees, who were not skilled enough to deal with the situation. Consumer records were erroneous and ill-maintained, and there was no system of management for functions such as human resources, finance, and governance. There was no proper consumer service interface either.

Within a span of 10 years, TPDDL overhauled the entire system and reduced the Aggregate Technical and Commercial (AT&C) losses to less than 10 percent. The consumers now interact with the firm through a one-stop state-of-the-art integrated call center. The reliability of the power supply increased significantly because of these initiatives, and so did the profits. The company's operational performance is shown in Figure 13.11.

This change in the company's fortunes can be attributed to the adoption of innovative technology and the deployment of a skilled workforce. The company knew that it needed to re-engineer its business processes in order to bring in sustainability. The first step was to address the AT&C losses and find solutions to overcome them. The company soon discovered that these losses occurred due to thefts, unauthorized use of meters, tampering of meters by direct hooking, deficiencies in the metering process, slow or defective meters, or deficiencies in the billing process. Bills often did not get delivered correctly and went unpaid by customers. The company decided to replace the electromechanical meters with electronic meters to enable Automatic Meter Reading (AMR). This was done for all high-revenue customers who contributed at least 60% of the total revenue. A software was developed in-house for analyzing the data downloaded through AMR. Besides, a High-Voltage Distribution System (HVDS) was installed in more than 250 areas. This system prevented electrical losses owing to the fact that it is deployed nearer to load centers and covers a reduced number of customers. This way, faults can be localized. Since this system transmits power at a high voltage, it also eliminates the need for long low-tension lines.

Accounting of the energy at TPDDL has also been re-engineered to flow smoothly from the transmission level at the grids to the distribution level at the consumer premises. The company automated the grids within its distribution area to form "smart grids". It implemented the Supervisory Control and Data Acquisition system (SCADA), which connected all the automated grids together. These grids are remotely monitored from a SCADA master-control center at Pitampura in north-west Delhi. This enabled centralized control and monitoring of the entire electrical network. The company also used Geographic Information Systems (GIS) to map all its assets including transformers, buildings, poles, cables, and so on. For better connectivity and communication between the power grids and the commercial offices, a strong optical fiber cable was deployed. A distribution management system (DMS) was also installed to centrally monitor all distribution networks. Prior to the use of this system, the networks were managed manually.

FIGURE 13.11 SNAPSHOT OF TPDDL'S OPERATIONAL PERFORMANCE

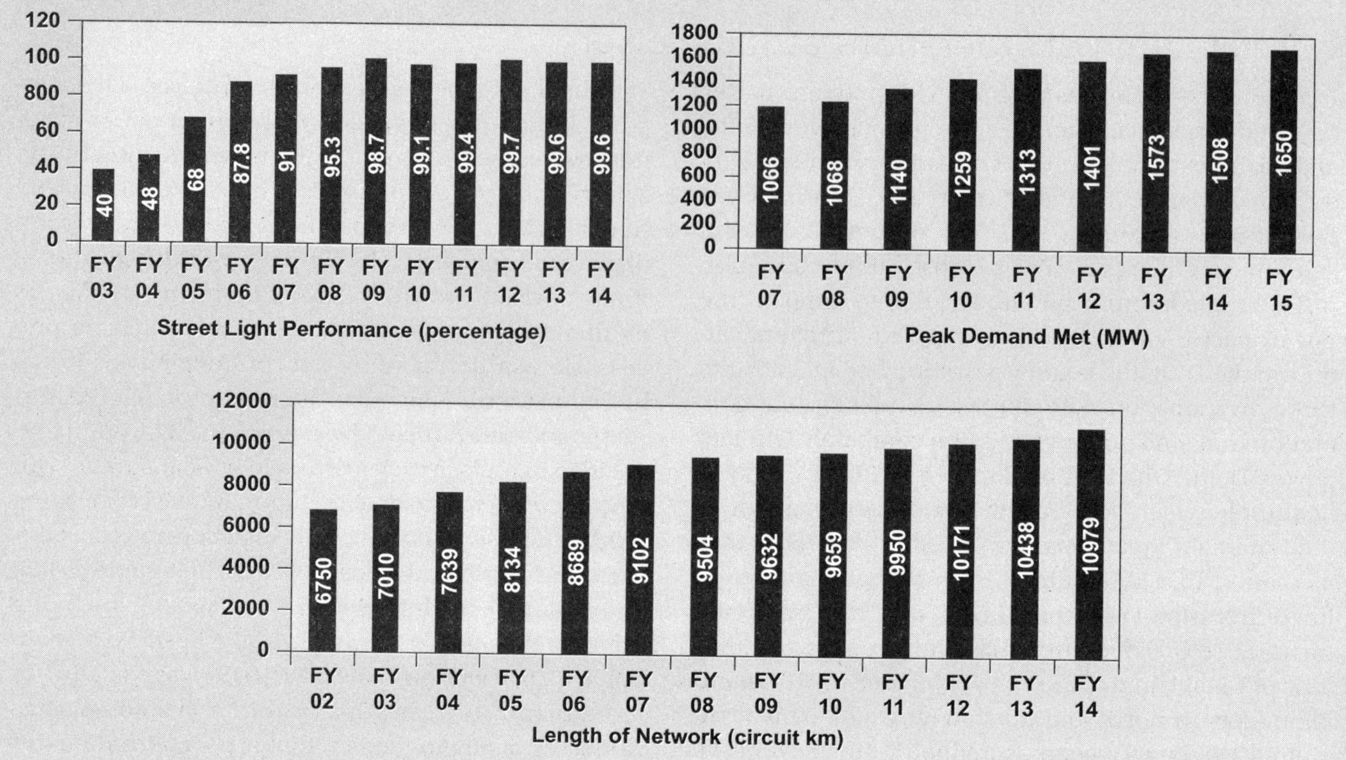

Source: Tata Power Delhi Distribution System, "TPDDL Excellence Journey," (2014); Retrieved from http://www.slideshare.net/TataPowerDDL/tpddl-excellence-journey

This meant that it was not possible to obtain any real-time network data. But with the presence of a DMS, network decisions can be taken by the control-center executives based on real-time network information. Centralization of operations and mapping through GIS has enabled quicker identification of fault locations and timely redressal of issues.

An Outage Management System (OMS) has also been deployed. It is an automation solution which aids in the prompt restoration of outages affecting the customers. The system provides geo-referenced network details to the field crew that is responsible for restoring power in the impacted area. The historical data collected by this system also helps the management predict power outages. The CRM is updated on any planned outage and consumers are intimated accordingly.

Further, the company also launched an SMS-based fault management system that uses the GSM technology to log the "no supply" complaints. This has led to a speedy redressal of issues. The system also has provisions for collecting customer feedback on the service provided. Apart from this system, Sampark Kendras with a seating capacity of 65 were also set up. Now, in each of the 12 districts where TPDDL distributes power, there is an online customer-care center with an individual customer-care executive for each district. Besides, the company now uploads the billing details of all subscribers on its official website, where consumers can view, print, and make online payments. TPDDL has also set up ATM-like kiosks in Delhi, where both cash and cheque payment towards electricity bills are accepted. These machines operate round the year, from 8 a.m. to 8 p.m.

An in-house CRM application, called Sambandh, serves a lot of different functions through its various modules. These are:

- The customer-care module, which is used for registering, tracking, and closing of customer complaints.
- The connection management module, which is responsible for new connections, reconnections, or disconnections.
- The meter management module that handles applications for meter installation, repair, removal, and replacement.
- The revenue collection module that takes care of the payments received from consumers in lieu of their electricity bills.
- The revenue recovery module that brings attention to the payment defaulters or subscribers with disconnected meters.
- The revenue disciplinary module, which is invaluable in legal cases such as theft or non-compliance with regulations.
- The record management module, which is used to manage records of customer requests.

All these systems are integrated with each other. Such is the magnitude of the impact of the reforms brought in by TPDDL that it is the only utility in the country to be empanelled by the Power Finance Corporation as an IT and SCADA consultant. The firm now provides project management and consultancy services to other states such as Haryana and Uttar Pradesh. With support from the U.S. Trade and Development Agency (USTDA), TPDDL is planning to embark on several new IT projects in the future. These include the use of business analytics, mobile workforce management, enterprise application integration, and demand response management.

Sources: *"Frequently Asked Questions regarding Tata Power-DDL's power distribution operations in Delhi". Retrieved from* http://www.ndpl.com/UploadedDocuments/FAQ%27s.pdf; *Ghosh, Arup, "Performance Improvement of the Distribution Segment (A Case Study of NDPL)" (2010). Retrieved from* http://www.iitk.ac.in/ime/anoops/for10/pdf/16%20-%20Y%20S%20Butola%20-%20Performance%20Improvement%20of%20the%20Distribution%20Segment%20A%20Case%20Study%20of%20NDPL.pdf; *"TPDDL Excellence Journey" (2014). Retrieved from* http://www.slideshare.net/TataPowerDDL/tpddl-excellence-journey; *"TPDDL Case Study" (2014). Retrieved from* http://www.slideshare.net/TataPowerDDL/tpddl-case-study.

CASE STUDY QUESTIONS

1. What was the need for the formation of TPDDL? Discuss the challenges faced by the company.
2. What was the role of business process re-engineering to overcome the AT&C losses that were handed down to TPDDL?
3. Discuss the role of IT in the centralization of operations at TPDDL and list advantages of doing so.
4. How did TPDDL use information technology to deliver better services to customers?

If an organization has unique requirements that the package does not address, many packages include capabilities for customization. **Customization** features allow a commercial software package or cloud-based software to be modified to meet an organization's unique requirements without destroying the integrity of the software. If a great deal of customization is required, additional programming and customization work may become so expensive and time-consuming that they negate many of the advantages of software packages and services.

When a system is developed using an application software package or a cloud software service, systems analysis will include a formal evaluation of the software package or service in which both end users and information systems specialists will participate. The most important evaluation criteria are the functions provided by the software, flexibility, user-friendliness, hardware requirements, database requirements, installation and maintenance efforts, documentation, vendor quality, and cost. The package or software service evaluation process often is based on a **request for proposal (RFP)**, which is a detailed list of questions submitted to software vendors.

When software from an external source is selected, the organization no longer has total control over the systems design process. Instead of tailoring the systems design specifications directly to user requirements, the design effort will consist of trying to mold user requirements to conform to the features of the package or software service. If the organization's requirements conflict with the way the package or software service works and this software cannot be customized, the organization will have to adapt to the package or software service and change its procedures.

Outsourcing

If a firm does not want to use its internal resources to build or operate information systems, it can outsource the work to an external organization that specializes in providing these services. Cloud computing and software as a service (SaaS) providers, which we described in Chapter 5, are one form of outsourcing. Subscribing companies use the software and computer hardware provided by the service as the technical platform for their systems. In another form of outsourcing, a company could hire an external vendor to design and create the software for its system, but that company would operate the system on its own computers. The outsourcing vendor might be domestic or in another country.

Domestic outsourcing is driven primarily by the fact that outsourcing firms possess skills, resources, and assets that their clients do not have. Installing a new supply chain management system in a very large company might require hiring an additional 30 to 50 people with specific expertise in supply chain management software, licensed from a vendor. Rather than hire permanent new employees, most of whom would need extensive training in the new software, and then release them after the new system is built, it makes more sense, and is often less expensive, to outsource this work for a 12-month period.

In the case of **offshore outsourcing**, the decision is much more cost-driven. A skilled programmer in India or Russia earns about $10,000–$30,000 per year compared with about $60,000–$120,000 per year for a comparable programmer in the United States. The Internet and low-cost communications technology have drastically reduced the expense and difficulty of coordinating the work of global teams in offshore locations. In addition to cost savings, many offshore outsourcing firms offer world-class technology assets and skills. Wage inflation outside the United States has recently eroded some of these advantages, and some jobs have moved back to the United States. Firms generally do not outsource the conception, systems analysis, and design of IT systems to offshore firms, but often do outsource programming, testing, maintenance, and daily operation of IT systems.

There is a very strong chance that at some point in your career, you'll be working with offshore outsourcers or global teams. Your firm is most likely to benefit from outsourcing if it takes the time to evaluate all the risks and to make sure outsourcing is appropriate for its particular needs. Any company that outsources its applications must thoroughly understand the project, including its requirements, method of implementation, anticipated benefits, cost components, and metrics for measuring performance.

Many firms underestimate costs for identifying and evaluating vendors of information technology services, for transitioning to a new vendor, for improving internal software development methods to match those of outsourcing vendors, and for monitoring vendors to make sure they are fulfilling their contractual obligations. Companies will need to allocate resources for documenting requirements, sending out RFPs, handling travel expenses, negotiating contracts, and project management. Experts claim it takes from three months to a full year to fully transfer work to an offshore partner and make sure the vendor thoroughly understands your business.

Outsourcing offshore incurs additional costs for coping with cultural differences that drain productivity and dealing with human resources issues, such as terminating or relocating domestic employees. All of these hidden costs undercut some of the anticipated benefits from outsourcing. Firms should be especially cautious when using an outsourcer to develop or to operate applications that give it some type of competitive advantage.

General Motors Corporation (GM) had outsourced 90 percent of its IT services, including its data centers and application development. The company recently decided to bring 90 percent of its IT infrastructure in-house, with only 10 percent managed by outsourcers. Lowering costs is important, but GM's primary reason for cutting back outsourcing is to take back control of its information systems, which it believes were preventing the company from responding quickly to competitive opportunities. Bringing information systems in-house will make it easier for GM standardize and streamline its systems and data centers. Figure 13.12

FIGURE 13.12 TOTAL COST OF OFFSHORE OUTSOURCING

TOTAL COST OF OFFSHORE OUTSOURCING				
Cost of outsourcing contract		€10,000,000		
Hidden Costs	Best Case	Additional Cost (€)	Worst Case	Additional Cost (€)
1. Vendor selection	0%	20,000	2%	200,000
2. Transition costs	2%	200,000	3%	300,000
3. Layoffs & retention	3%	300,000	5%	500,000
4. Lost productivity/cultural issues	3%	300,000	27%	2,700,000
5. Improving development processes	1%	100,000	10%	1,000,000
6. Managing the contract	6%	600,000	10%	1,000,000
Total additional costs		1,520,000		5,700,000
	Outstanding Contract (€)	Additional Cost (€)	Total Cost (€)	Additional Cost
Total cost of outsourcing (TCO) best case	10,000,000	1,520,000	11,520,000	15.2%
Total cost of outsourcing (TCO) worst case	10,000,000	5,700,000	15,700,000	57.0%

If a firm spends $10 million on offshore outsourcing contracts, that company will actually spend 15.2 percent in extra costs even under the best-case scenario. In the worst-case scenario, where there is a dramatic drop in productivity along with exceptionally high transition and layoff costs, a firm can expect to pay up to 57 percent in extra costs on top of the $10 million outlay for an offshore contract.

shows best- and worst-case scenarios for the total cost of an offshore outsourcing project. It shows how much hidden costs affect the total project cost. The best case reflects the lowest estimates for additional costs, and the worst case reflects the highest estimates for these costs. As you can see, hidden costs increase the total cost of an offshore outsourcing project by an extra 15 to 57 percent. Even with these extra costs, many firms will benefit from offshore outsourcing if they manage the work well.

13-5 What are new approaches for system building in the digital firm era?

In the digital firm environment, organizations need to be able to add, change, and retire their technology capabilities very rapidly to respond to new opportunities, including the need to provide applications for mobile platforms. Companies are starting to use shorter, more informal development processes that provide fast solutions. In addition to using software packages and online software services, businesses are relying more heavily on fast-cycle techniques such as rapid application development, joint application design, agile development, and reusable standardized software components that can be assembled into a complete set of services for e-commerce and e-business.

Rapid Application Development (RAD), Agile Development, and DevOps

Object-oriented software tools, reusable software, prototyping, and tools for automating program code generation are helping systems builders create working systems much more rapidly than they could using traditional systems-building methods and software tools. The term **rapid application development (RAD)** is used to describe this process of creating workable systems in a very short period of time with some flexibility to adapt as a project evolves. RAD also involves close teamwork among end users and information systems specialists as well as among the IT groups developing and operating the systems. Simple systems often can be assembled from prebuilt components. The process does not have to be sequential, and key parts of development can occur simultaneously.

Sometimes a technique called **joint application design (JAD)** is used to accelerate the generation of information requirements and to develop the initial systems design. JAD brings end users and information systems specialists together in an interactive session to discuss the system's design. Properly prepared and facilitated, JAD sessions can significantly speed up the design phase and involve users at an intense level.

Agile development focuses on rapid delivery of working software by breaking a large project into a series of small subprojects that are completed in short periods of time using iteration and continuous feedback. Each mini-project is worked on by a team as if it were a complete project. Improvement or addition of new functionality takes place within the next iteration as developers clarify requirements. This helps to minimize the overall risk and allows the project to adapt to changes more quickly. Agile methods emphasize face-to-face communication over written documents, encouraging people to collaborate and make decisions quickly and effectively.

DevOps

DevOps builds on agile development principles as an organizational strategy to create a culture and environment that further promote rapid and agile development practices. *DevOps* stands for "development and operations" and emphasizes close collaboration between the software developers who create applications and the IT operational staff who run and maintain the applications. Traditionally, in a large enterprise, an application development team would be in charge of gathering business requirements for an application, designing the application, and writing and testing the software. The operations team would run and maintain the software once it was put into production. Problems arise when the development team is unaware of operational issues that prevent the software from working as expected, requiring additional time and rework to fix the software.

DevOps tries to change this relationship by promoting better and more frequent communication and collaboration between systems development and operations groups and a fast and stable workflow throughout the entire application development life cycle. With this type of organizational change along with agile techniques, standardized processes, and more powerful automated software creation and testing tools, it is possible to release more reliable applications more rapidly and more frequently.

For example, Barclays Bank has adopted agile practices, including DevOps, for many areas of the business to speed innovation and respond to competitive pressure from new and varied entrants to the banking market, including mobile-only banks, as well as Apple and Google, who are entering the mobile payments area. DevOps and agile practices have helped Barclays reduce the time required for software updates as well as the complexity of software code written by its developers. Barclays is responsible for processing payments each day equivalent to 30 percent of the UK's gross domestic product, and using DevOps software development methods ensures its systems remain operational and competitive (Donnelly, 2016).

Component-Based Development and Web Services

We have already described some of the benefits of object-oriented development for building systems that can respond to rapidly changing business environments, including web applications. To further expedite software creation, groups of objects have been assembled to provide software components for common functions such as a graphical user interface or online ordering capability that can be combined to create large-scale business applications. This approach to software development is called **component-based development**, and it enables a system to be built by assembling and integrating existing software components. Increasingly, these software components are coming from cloud services. Businesses are using component-based development to create their e-commerce applications by combining commercially available components for shopping carts, user authentication, search engines, and catalogs with pieces of software for their own unique business requirements.

Web Services and Service-Oriented Computing

Chapter 5 introduced *web services* as loosely coupled, reusable software components using Extensible Markup Language (XML) and other open protocols and standards that enable one application to communicate with another with no custom programming required to share data and services. In addition to supporting internal and external integration of systems, web services can be used as tools for building new information system applications or enhancing existing systems. Because these software services use a universal set of standards, they promise to be less expensive and less difficult to weave together than proprietary components.

Web services can perform certain functions on their own, and they can also engage other web services to complete more complex transactions, such as checking credit, procurement, or ordering products. By creating software components that can communicate and share data regardless of the operating system, programming language, or client device, web services can provide significant cost savings in systems building while opening up new opportunities for collaboration with other companies.

Mobile Application Development: Designing for A Multiscreen World

Today, employees and customers expect, and even demand, to be able to use a mobile device of their choice to obtain information or perform a transaction anywhere and at any time. To meet these needs, companies will need to develop mobile websites, mobile apps, and native apps as well as traditional information systems.

Once an organization decides to develop mobile apps, it has to make some important choices, including the technology it will use to implement these apps (whether to write a native app or mobile web app) and what to do about a mobile website. A **mobile website** is a version of a regular website that is scaled down in content and navigation for easy access and search on a small mobile screen. (Access Amazon's website from your computer and then from your smartphone to see the difference from a regular website.)

A **mobile web app** is an Internet-enabled app with specific functionality for mobile devices. Users access mobile web apps through their mobile device's web browser. The web app resides primarily on a server, is accessed via the Internet, and doesn't need to be installed on the device. The same application can be used by most devices that can surf the web, regardless of their brand.

A **native app** is a standalone application designed to run on a specific platform and device. The native app is installed directly on a mobile device. Native apps can connect to the Internet to download and upload data, and they can also operate on these data even when not connected to the Internet. For example, an e-book reading app such as Kindle software can download a book from the Internet, disconnect from the Internet, and present the book for reading. Native mobile apps provide fast performance and a high degree of reliability. They are also able to take advantage of a mobile device's particular capabilities, such as its camera or touch features. However, native apps are expensive to develop because multiple versions of an app must be programmed for different mobile operating systems and hardware.

Developing applications for mobile platforms is quite different from development for PCs and their much larger screens. The reduced size of mobile devices makes using fingers and multitouch gestures much easier than typing and using keyboards. Mobile apps need to be optimized for the specific tasks they are to perform, they should not try to carry out too many tasks, and they should be designed for usability. The user experience for mobile interaction is fundamentally different from using a desktop or laptop PC. Saving resources—bandwidth, screen space, memory, processing, data entry, and user gestures—is a top priority.

When a full website created for the desktop shrinks to the size of a smartphone screen, it is difficult for the user to navigate through the site. The user must continually zoom in and out and scroll to find relevant material. Therefore, companies need to design websites specifically for mobile interfaces and create multiple mobile sites to meet the needs of smartphones, tablets, and desktop browsers. This equates to at least three sites with separate content, maintenance, and costs. Currently, websites know what device you are using because your browser will send this information to the server when you log on. Based on this information, the server will deliver the appropriate screen.

One solution to the problem of having multiple websites is to use **responsive web design**. Responsive web design enables websites to change layouts automatically according to the visitor's screen resolution, whether on a desktop, laptop, tablet, or smartphone. Responsive design uses tools such as flexible grid-based layouts, flexible images, and media queries to optimize the design for different viewing contexts. This eliminates the need for separate design and development work for each new device. HTML5, which we introduced in Chapter 5, is also used for mobile application development because it can support cross-platform mobile applications.

The Interactive Session on Technology describes how some companies have addressed the challenges of mobile development we have just identified.

INTERACTIVE SESSION: TECHNOLOGY

Developing Mobile Apps: What's Different

Just about all businesses today want to deploy mobile apps. Studies show that mobile consumers look at their phones an average of 1,500 times each week and spend 177 minutes on their phone per day. With every swipe, tap, and zoom, customers are coming to expect the same experience in all their dealings with businesses. Businesses today know they must respond, and they want mobile apps developed in a very short time frame. That's not so easy.

Developing successful mobile apps poses some unique challenges. The user experience on a mobile device is fundamentally different from that on a PC. There are special features on mobile devices such as location-based services that that give firms the potential to interact with customers in meaningful new ways. Firms need to be able to take advantage of those features while delivering an experience that is appropriate to a small screen. There are multiple mobile platforms to work with, including iOS, Android, and Windows 10, and a firm may need a different version of an application to run on each of these. System builders need to understand how, why, and where customers use mobile devices and how these mobile experiences change business interactions and behavior. You can't just port a website or desktop application to a smartphone or tablet. It's a different systems development process.

Alex and Ani learned this when developing mobile app for employees in its stores to help customers make selections and then complete the purchase transaction. Alex and Ani, founded in 2004, designs, produces, and sells high-quality, eco-friendly jewelry in the United States using artisanal techniques and is dedicated to helping its customers find inner peace and positive energy. Having customers in Alex and Ani stores wait in long checkout lines ran counter to the company's philosophy and brand image.

Working with Mobiquity, a developer of enterprise mobile solutions, Alex and Ani created a mobile point-of-sale and payment solution where Alex and Ani's Bangle Bartenders can swipe credit cards, scan bar codes, and print, allowing customers to sign and receive a copy of the credit card receipt at the time of purchase while they are in the store aisles. They do not have to wait in line for a cashier. The mobile app helps store sales staff to be more attentive to customers while reducing time to pay for purchases. This enhances the in-store customer experience, improves brand perception, and provides better customer service, thereby increasing sales revenues.

The starting point for developing a mobile app is to identify the mobile moments (occasions when someone would pull out a mobile device to get something done) where a mobile app would be especially helpful. Alex and Ani's chief technology officer Joe Lezon and head of retail operations Susan Soards mapped out the mobile moments where employees interact with customers. They then specified the context—the situation, preferences, and attitudes of customers and employees in these mobile moments. Lezon and Soards determined where physically in the store mobile moments occur, how long they last, the stage of the checkout process, what information is available, and customer expectations.

The second step is to design the mobile engagement. Businesspeople, designers, and app developers get together to decide how to engage a customer during mobile moments and which moments benefit both the customer and the company. A mobile app for moments that benefit both customers and the company is more likely to be successful. Alex and Ani had a small team draw pictures to design the mobile engagement, mapping out exactly how an employee would use an iPod Touch application and a credit card reader/printer linked directly to the company's point-of-sale system to engage customers. The design specifications included screen layouts, the sequence of events, and transactions needed at each step.

The third step is to engineer people, processes, and platforms to deliver the mobile experience. An effective mobile app often requires changing the firm's internal systems, such as those for inventory management, customers, and reservations. Changes such as new APIs and tuning the systems to respond more quickly to requests account for 80 percent of the cost of most mobile projects. (*API* stands for "application program interface," a set of routines, protocols, and tools for building software applications, specifying how software components should interact.) Alex and Ani connected their mobile app to the company's point-of-sale systems as well as to systems with detailed product information.

The fourth, final step is to monitor performance and improve outcomes. Alex and Ani analyzed its mobile retail application to determine how much the length of time for checkouts decreased and which customers completed transactions. The new mobile system gave Bangle Bartenders more time to spend with customers, eliminated customer lines, and helped increase holiday sales by more than 300 percent. Alex and Ani was able to increase the number of checkout points from four to 10 in most of its 28 U.S. stores.

Mobile apps should not be built for the sake of going mobile but for genuinely helping the company become more successful. The mobile app must be connected in a meaningful way to the systems that power the business. Chicago-based TTX, which provides rail cars and freight rail management services to the railroad industry, found that the most critical aspect of its mobile application development project was having a firm idea of what it was trying to accomplish with the app. In 2014 the company developed a mobile app to improve billing accuracy and boost the productivity of its maintenance crews in its 50 maintenance shops that operate along the railroads. The app took about six months to design and build in-house.

The purpose of the app was to improve record-keeping involved in TTX's maintenance work, which takes place in rough outdoor conditions where connectivity is spotty or nonexistent and is performed by employees who often wear gloves. Maintenance crews had used paper and pencil to record their notes on the rail car repairs. The mobile application was based on a Windows platform for a plastic-encased PC with a touchscreen. TTX CIO and Vice President Bruce Schinelli and his systems development team recognized that what the app needed to do was to replace pen and paper, and it had to work that well in the field. That early understanding of how the mobile app would provide value to the business drove the entire system design and implementation. Schinelli believes that if a company makes the wrong assumptions about the purpose of its mobile application, it will have to do a lot of rework. For TTX, the hard work was making sure its system builders knew exactly how the mobile app would work out in the field.

Sources: Mary K. Pratt, "As Mobile Apps for Employees Proliferate, CIOs Get Involved," searchCIO.com, accessed February 10, 2016; Alex and Ani, "Alex and Ani mPOS," www.mobiquity.com, accessed February 22, 2016; Linda Tucci, "Enterprise Mobile App Development: No Easy Answers," searchCIO.com, accessed February 22, 2016; and Brian Solis, "Mobile Is Eating the World," Sitecore Corporation, February 2016.

CASE STUDY QUESTIONS

1. What management, organization, and technology issues need to be addressed when building a mobile application?
2. How does user requirement definition for mobile applications differ from traditional systems analysis?
3. Describe how Alex and Ani's sales process before and after the mobile application was deployed.

Review Summary

13-1 *How does building new systems produce organizational change?*

Building a new information system is a form of planned organizational change. Four kinds of technology-enabled change are (1) automation, (2) rationalization of procedures, (3) business process redesign, and (4) paradigm shift, with far-reaching changes carrying the greatest risks and rewards. Many organizations are using business process management to redesign workflows and business processes in the hope of achieving dramatic productivity breakthroughs. Business process management is also useful for promoting total quality management (TQM), six sigma, and other initiatives for incremental process improvement.

13-2 *What are the core activities in the systems development process?*

The core activities in systems development are systems analysis, systems design, programming, testing, conversion, production, and maintenance. Systems analysis is the study and analysis of problems of existing systems and the identification of requirements for their solutions. Systems design provides the specifications for an information system solution, showing how its technical and organizational components fit together.

13-3 *What are the principal methodologies for modeling and designing systems?*

The two principal methodologies for modeling and designing information systems are structured methodologies and object-oriented development. Structured methodologies focus on modeling processes and data separately. The data flow diagram is the principal tool for structured analysis, and the structure chart is the principal tool for representing structured software design. Object-oriented development models a system as a collection of objects that combine processes and data. Object-oriented modeling is based on the concepts of class and inheritance.

13-4 *What are alternative methods for building information systems?*

The oldest method for building systems is the systems life cycle, which requires that information systems be developed in formal stages. The stages must proceed sequentially and have defined outputs; each requires formal approval before the next stage can commence. The systems life cycle is useful for large projects that need formal specifications and tight management control over each stage of systems building, but it is very rigid and costly.

Prototyping consists of building an experimental system rapidly and inexpensively for end users to interact with and evaluate. Prototyping encourages end-user involvement in systems development and iteration of design until specifications are captured accurately. The rapid creation of prototypes can result in systems that have not been completely tested or documented or that are technically inadequate for a production environment.

Using a software package or online software services (SaaS) reduces the amount of design, programming, testing, installation, and maintenance work required to build a system. Application software packages or SaaS are helpful if a firm does not have the internal information systems staff or financial resources to custom develop a system. To meet an organization's unique requirements, packages may require extensive modifications that can substantially raise development costs.

End-user development is the development of information systems by end users, either alone or with minimal assistance from information systems specialists. End user–developed systems can be created rapidly and informally using user-friendly software tools. However, end-user development may create information systems that do not necessarily meet quality assurance standards and that are not easily controlled by traditional means.

Outsourcing consists of using an external vendor to build (or operate) a firm's information systems instead of the organization's internal information systems staff. Outsourcing can save application development costs or enable firms to develop applications without an internal information systems staff. However, firms risk losing control over their information systems and becoming too dependent on external vendors. Outsourcing also entails hidden costs, especially when the work is sent offshore.

13-5 *What are new approaches for system building in the digital firm era?*

Companies are turning to rapid application design (RAD), joint application design (JAD), agile development, and reusable software components to accelerate the systems development process. RAD uses object-oriented software, visual programming, prototyping, and tools for very rapid creation of systems. Agile development breaks a large project into a series of small subprojects that are completed in short periods of time using iteration and continuous feedback. Component-based development expedites application development by grouping objects into suites of software components that can be combined to create large-scale business applications. DevOps emphasizes close collaboration between the software developers who create applications and the IT operational staff who run and maintain the applications. Web services provide a common set of standards that enable organizations to link their systems regardless of their technology platform through standard plug-and-play architecture. Mobile application development must pay attention to simplicity, usability, and the need to optimize tasks for tiny screens.

Key Terms

Acceptance testing, 531
Agile development, 548
Automation, 522
Business process management (BPM), 524
Business process redesign, 523
Component-based development, 549
Computer-aided software engineering (CASE), 537
Conversion, 532
Customization, 545
Data flow diagram (DFD), 534
DevOps, 549
Direct cutover strategy, 532
Documentation, 532
End-user development, 541
End-user interface, 541
Feasibility study, 528
Information requirements, 529
Iterative, 539
Joint application design (JAD), 548
Maintenance, 532
Mobile web app, 550
Mobile website, 550
Native app, 551
Object, 536
Object-oriented development, 536
Offshore outsourcing, 546
Paradigm shift, 523
Parallel strategy, 532
Phased approach strategy, 532
Pilot study strategy, 532
Post-implementation audit, 532
Process specifications, 535
Production, 532
Programming, 530
Prototype, 539
Prototyping, 539
Query languages, 541
Rapid application development (RAD), 548
Rationalization of procedures, 522
Request for proposal (RFP), 546
Responsive web design, 551
Six sigma, 523
Structure chart, 535
Structured, 533
Systems analysis, 528
Systems design, 529
Systems development, 527
Systems life cycle, 538
System testing, 531
Test plan, 531
Testing, 530
Total quality management (TQM), 523
Unit testing, 531

Review Questions

13-1 How does building new systems produce organizational change?

- How is the magnitude of IT-enabled organizational change related with risk and return? Discuss with the help of examples.
- Explain the manner in which BPM aids in both incremental process change and paradigm shifts.

13-2 What are the core activities in the systems development process?

- Distinguish between systems analysis and systems design. Describe the activities for each.
- Define information requirements and explain why they are difficult to determine correctly.

- Explain why the testing stage of systems development is so important. Name and describe the three stages of testing for an information system.
- Describe the role of programming, conversion, production, and maintenance in systems development.

13-3 What are the principal methodologies for building information systems?

- Describe data flow diagrams, structured charts, and CASE tools for modelling and designing IS.

13-4 What are the alternative methods for building information systems?

- Define the traditional systems life cycle. Describe its advantages and disadvantages for systems building.
- Define information system prototyping. Describe its benefits and limitations. List and describe the steps in the prototyping process.
- Define an application software package. Explain the advantages and disadvantages of developing information systems based on software packages.
- Define end-user development and describe its advantages and disadvantages. Name some policies and procedures for managing end-user development.
- Describe the advantages and disadvantages of using outsourcing for building information systems.

13-5 What are the new approaches for system building in the digital firm era?

- List and describe the contemporary approaches adopted by firms for system building in the digital era.
- Define component-based development, web services and their areas of application in system building.
- Discuss the challenges of mobile application development. How do the firms address these problem?

Discussion Questions

13-6 Why is selecting a systems development approach an important business decision? Who should participate in the selection process?

13-7 What are the benefits and risks of domestic outsourcing and offshore outsourcing?

13-8 What are the advantages of responsive web design compared to a native app or a mobile website?

Hands-On MIS Projects

The projects in this section give you hands-on experience analyzing business processes, designing and building a customer system for auto sales, and analyzing website information requirements.

Management Decision Problems

13-9 For an additional fee, a customer purchasing from the online appliance store Appliancesdirect.com in the UK, such as a washing machine, can purchase a three-year service contract. The contract provides free repair service and parts for the specified appliance using an authorized service provider. When a person with a Appliancesdirect service contract needs to repair an appliance, such as a washing machine, he or she calls the company's Repairs & Parts department to schedule an appointment. The department makes the appointment and gives the caller the date and approximate time of the appointment. The repair technician arrives during the designated time framework and diagnoses the problem. If the problem is caused by a faulty part, the technician either replaces the part if he is carrying the part with him or orders the replacement part. If the part is not in stock, it will order the part and give the customer an approximate time when the part will arrive. The part is shipped directly to the customer.

After the part has arrived, the customer must call Appliancesdirect to schedule a second appointment for a repair technician to replace the ordered part. This process is very lengthy. It may take two weeks to schedule the first repair visit, another two weeks to order and receive the required part, and another week to schedule a second repair visit after the ordered part has been received.

- Diagram the existing process.
- What is the impact of the existing process on Sears's operational efficiency and customer relationships?
- What changes could be made to make this process more efficient? How could information systems support these changes? Diagram the improved process.

13-10 Management at your agricultural chemicals corporation has been dissatisfied with production planning. Production plans are created using best guesses of demand for each product, which are based on how much of each product has been ordered in the past. If a customer places an unexpected order or requests a change to an existing order after it has been placed, there is no way to adjust production plans. The company may have to tell customers it can't fill their orders, or it may run up extra costs maintaining additional inventory to prevent stock-outs.

At the end of each month, orders are totaled and manually keyed into the company's production planning system. Data from the past month's production and inventory systems are manually entered into the firm's order management system. Analysts from the sales department and from the production department analyze the data from their respective systems to determine what the sales targets and production targets should be for the next month. These estimates are usually different. The analysts then get together at a high-level planning meeting to revise the production and sales targets to take into account senior management's goals for market share, revenues, and profits. The outcome of the meeting is a finalized production master schedule.

The entire production planning process takes 17 business days to complete. Nine of these days are required to enter and validate the data. The remaining days are spent developing and reconciling the production and sales targets and finalizing the production master schedule.

- Draw a diagram of the existing production planning process.
- Analyze the problems this process creates for the company.
- How could an enterprise system solve these problems? In what ways could it lower costs? Diagram what the production planning process might look like if the company implemented enterprise software.

Improving Decision Making: Using Database Software to Design a Customer System for Auto Sales

Software skills: Database design, querying, reporting, and forms
Business skills: Sales lead and customer analysis

13-11 This project requires you to perform a systems analysis and then design a system solution using database software.

Burrows Auto Dealers specializes in selling new vehicles from Toyota in Sheffield, England. The company advertises in local newspapers and is listed as an authorized dealer on the Toyota Web site and other major websites for auto buyers. The company benefits from a good local word-of-mouth reputation and name recognition.

Burrows does not believe it has enough information about its customers. It cannot easily determine which prospects have made auto purchases, nor can it identify which customer touch points have produced the greatest number of sales leads or actual sales so it can focus advertising and marketing more on the channels that generate the most revenue. Are purchasers discovering Burrows from newspaper ads, from word of mouth, or from the Web?

Prepare a systems analysis report detailing Burrows' problem and a system solution that can be implemented using PC database management software. Then use database software to develop a simple system solution.

Achieving Operational Excellence: Analyzing Website Design and Information Requirements

Software skills: Web browser software
Business skills: Information requirements analysis, website design

13-12 Visit the website of your choice and explore it thoroughly. Prepare a report analyzing the various functions provided by that website and its information requirements. Your report should answer these questions: What functions does the website perform? What data does it use? What are its inputs, outputs, and processes? What are some of its other design specifications? Does the website link to any internal systems or systems of other organizations? What value does this website provide the firm?

Collaboration and Teamwork Project

Preparing Website Design Specifications

13-13 With three or four of your classmates, select a system described in this text that uses the web. Review the website for the system you select. Use what you have learned from the website and the description in this book to prepare a report describing some of the design specifications for the system you select. If possible, use Google Docs and Google Drive or Google Sites to brainstorm, organize, and develop a presentation of your findings for the class.

ConAgra's Recipe for a Better Human Resources System

CASE STUDY

Do you have Chef Boyardee Ravioli or Orville Redenbacher popcorn in your pantry or Healthy Choice or Banquet chicken nuggets in your freezer? If so, you're one of the 99 percent of U.S. households that use ConAgra food products. ConAgra Foods Inc., headquartered in Omaha, Nebraska, is one of North America's largest food companies, providing quick, convenient meals, tasty treats, and snacks with brands such as Libbys, Banquet, LaChoy, Hunts, Healthy Choice, and Blue Bonnet. Thirty-two of ConAgra's brands account for more than $100 million in annual retail sales.

ConAgra relies on 33,000 employees to ensure that supermarket and grocery shelves are stocked with its products, and management considers its human resources to be an essential ingredient for its success. Like many forward-looking companies, ConAgra recognizes the importance of human resources to overall corporate success and the ability of the firm to have the right people in place as it pursues its business strategy. Technology is expected to play an even larger role going forward in helping the company recruit, retain, develop, and manage the workers it needs.

Until recently, ConAgra did not have the right technology in place to obtain maximum value from the talents and expertise of its salaried and hourly employees. It had a core system for basic human resources (HR) functions, but it also had disparate siloed systems for HR functions such as employee compensation, development, recruiting, succession planning, and talent review. These systems produced fragmented information and could not support companywide views of the employee or human resources processes. Some of these systems were based on commercial business software products, and others were homegrown. These systems worked well but only up to a point because they were not integrated. That meant that data from one system could not be combined easily with data from another for more insightful reporting and talent analysis or for obtaining a complete picture of employees. There was no central system to house and manage the data so HR staff often had to extract information from multiple systems and piece reports together manually. The company also had to pay for multiple information systems teams to support these systems.

That all changed in 2013 when the company decided to retire most of its existing HR systems and implement a comprehensive talent management system that was integrated with its on-premises core HR system. The talent management system consisted of integrated modules that ran on a cloud-based platform. ConAgra called the project to build the new talent management system "My Recipe."

A major objective of My Recipe was to store and share all workforce data in a single central, integrated cloud-based system. Another was to reduce data redundancies, complexity, and operational efficiencies by centralizing the data so they appeared to be coming from one source. Another was to provide user-friendly tools and processes that made it easier for managers and employees to have meaningful conversations about performance and career growth. Another requirement was the ability to provide a snapshot of ConAgra's current talent pool and show how it was developing to meet future business needs. Such a system was expected to better engage employees and managers, provide more useful data to HR staff, improve talent management, and increase productivity.

After a thorough vendor evaluation process, ConAgra narrowed the search to three vendors and then selected SuccessFactors. SuccessFactors is an SAP-owned global provider of cloud-based software for human capital management. Its human capital management application suite features a learning management system (LMS), performance management, recruiting software, applicant tracking software, succession planning, talent management, and HR analytics along with social business and collaboration tools to help organizations maximize employee growth and performance. Management believed SuccessFactors was superior because it provided an easy-to-use and customizable user interface that would support employee and management self-service using the system. SuccessFactors also integrated with other SAP products and third-party products.

ConAgra implemented My Recipe in three phases over a 15-month period. During the first phase, completed in mid-2013, ConAgra upgraded the overall user interface and implemented the SuccessFactors Learning and Succession & Development modules. In phase two, completed in late 2013, the firm implemented SAP SuccessFactors Workforce Analytics, Workforce Planning, Recruiting Marketing, and Recruiting Management modules. In the final phase, completed in mid-2014, ConAgra implemented a SuccessFactors Compensation module and an update to SuccessFactors Performance & Goals, including the functionality for performance rating calibration. (Calibration is a process for gaining greater consistency in how performance evaluation ratings are delivered.) The new SuccessFactors system replaced eight legacy human resource systems, substantially reduced the amount of HR data stored in manual files, and provided new tools for managers and employees to obtain information and reports directly from the system on their own.

The My Recipe team selected implementation target dates that coincide with the time of year the specified processes were typically performed. For example, the rollout of the SuccessFactors Succession & Development software was timed for when the company conducted its annual talent review. Rolling out the system in stages kept the project alive and relevant, and staff were able to easily understand how one module built upon the next. The project timelines also facilitated adoption of the system because users were exposed from early on to a one-stop shop for human resources and became increasingly interested in seeing the system completed. System log records show that the average HR user accesses some aspect of the SuccessFactors solution about 100 times per year. When ConAgra had fragmented HR systems, there was never that amount of manager and employee interactions with those systems.

Once fully implemented, My Recipe made it possible for ConAgra to capture, store and share succession planning, talent review, and other data that were previously inaccessible and impossible to share. It empowered employees to proactively track tasks, performance, career growth, and opportunities on their own, and it standardized HR business processes throughout the employee life cycle. The new system makes it possible for HR staff to focus on workforce planning issues instead of on tactical day-to-day employee management and recordkeeping. My Recipe also eliminated eight legacy HR systems and their associated administrative burdens and inefficiencies.

One of the new system improvements is the ability to link an employee's payroll records (which are processed in ConAgra's core HR system) to a tile on the SuccessFactors home screen, allowing employees to view their payroll records directly from My Recipe. Other home screen tiles, which can be easily customized, provide access to employee performance and career data in a way that is easy to understand. Ease of use is further promoted by built-in reminders. For instance, a manager viewing an employee's objectives might be alerted that the employee has an upcoming talent review. By centralizing employee data and making the data more easily available, the company is able to see how each employee fits into to individual, team, and companywide plans involving performance, succession, and development. In other words, the system makes it possible for human resources to operate more strategically and align ConAgra's workforce more precisely with the overall goals of the firm.

It was not easy to develop a fully integrated system with common companywide processes. ConAgra had to spend considerable time identifying and evaluating its existing processes and deciding which should be kept and which would need to be changed. The processes had to be mapped against the business processes supported by the SuccessFactors software. It was important to know what each of ConAgra's processes would look like when the SuccessFactors system was implemented and the new system ran in the cloud.

Another challenge was dealing with analytics and reporting. Reporting was difficult when ConAgra's systems were fragmented because it was so difficult to assemble the required data from so many different sources. When the company realized how much more useful and retrievable human resources data the new system would produce, the project was redirected to pay more attention to reporting and analytics and to make sure the system was designed to deliver the data required for this purpose.

ConAgra harnessed the expertise of PricewaterhouseCoopers (PwC) consultants for the implementation. They were able to quickly learn about ConAgra's needs and apply that knowledge along with their expertise to the project. For example, PwC made themselves experts in ConAgra's compensation structure and used that knowledge to configure the system accordingly. They also brought to bear their expertise in cloud systems projects.

How much has the new SuccessFactors system helped ConAgra? According to KC Bradley, ConAgra's Director of Talent Management, SuccessFactors has helped take HR to the next level at her firm. The system has helped facilitate conversations between managers and employees and has armed managers with information they can articulate to higher management about how each employee contributes to the organization's business goals and affects the bottom line. Everyone is now able to see if the right people are in place throughout the organization.

Sources: Ken Murphy, "ConAgra Foods Fine-Tunes Recipe for Enhanced HR," SAP Insider Profiles, October 1, 2015; www.conagra.com, accessed February 21, 2016; www.successfactors.com, accessed February 21,2016; and "ConAgra Foods: Food Leader Finds Right Recipe to Drive Change Management with SuccessFactors Solutions,"SAP, 2015.

CASE STUDY QUESTIONS

13-14 Analyze ConAgra's problems with its old systems. What management, organization, and technology factors were responsible for these problems? What was the business impact of these problems?

13-15 List and describe the information requirements of My Recipe.

13-16 What types of systems-building methods and tools did ConAgra use for building its system?

13-17 What steps did ConAgra take to make sure the My Recipe was successful?

13-18 What were the benefits of the new system? How did it change operational activities and decision making at ConAgra ? How successful was this system solution?

Chapter 13 References

"5 DevOps Trends Businesses Should Adopt this Year." Itbusinessedge.com, accessed March 31, 2016.

Armstrong, Deborah J. and Bill C. Hardgrove. "Understanding Mindshift Learning: The Transition to Object-Oriented Development." *MIS Quarterly* 31, No. 3 (September 2007).

Aron, Ravi, Eric K.Clemons, and Sashi Reddi. "Just Right Outsourcing: Understanding and Managing Risk." *Journal of Management Information Systems* 22, No. 1 (Summer 2005).

Ashrafi, Noushin and Hessam Ashrafi. *Object-Oriented Systems Analysis and Design*. Upper Saddle River, NY: Prentice-Hall (2009).

Baily, Martin N. and Diana Farrell. "Exploding the Myths of Offshoring." *McKinsey Quarterly* (July 2004).

Benaroch, Michael, Yossi Lichtenstein, and Lior Fink. "Contract Design Choices and the Balance of Ex Ante and Ex Post Transaction Costs in Software Development Outsourcing." *MIS Quarterly* 40 No. 1 (March 2016).

Bossert, Oliver, Chris Ip, and Irina Starikova. "Beyond Agile: Reorganizing IT for Faster Software Delivery." McKinsey & Company (2015).

Cao, Lan, Kannan Mohan, Balasubramaniam Ramesh, and Sumantra Sarkar. "Evolution of Governance: Achieving Ambidexterity in IT Outsourcing." *Journal of Management Information Systems* 30, No. 3 (Winter 2014).

DeMarco, Tom. *Structured Analysis and System Specification*. New York: Yourdon Press (1978).

Dibbern, Jess, Jessica Winkler, and Armin Heinzl. "Explaining Variations in Client Extra Costs between Software Projects Offshored to India." *MIS Quarterly* 32, No. 2 (June 2008).

Donnelly, Caroline. "Barclays Banks on Agile and DevOps to Tackle Competitive Threats in Fintech." *Computer Weekly* (July 1, 2016).

Edberg, Dana T., Polina Ivanova, and William Kuechler. "Methodology Mashups: An Exploration of Processes Used to Maintain Software." *Journal of Management Information Systems* 28, No. 4 (Spring 2012).

El Sawy, Omar A. *Redesigning Enterprise Processes for E-Business*. McGraw-Hill (2001).

Feeny, David, Mary Lacity, and Leslie P. Willcocks. "Taking the Measure of Outsourcing Providers." *MIT Sloan Management Review* 46, No. 3 (Spring 2005).

Gefen, David and Erran Carmel. "Is the World Really Flat? A Look at Offshoring in an Online Programming Marketplace." *MIS Quarterly* 32, No. 2 (June 2008).

Goo, Jahyun, Rajive Kishore, H. R. Rao, and Kichan Nam. "The Role of Service Level Agreements in Relational Management of Information Technology Outsourcing: An Empirical Study." *MIS Quarterly* 33, No. 1 (March 2009).

Hahn, Eugene D., Jonathan P. Doh, and Kraiwinee Bunyaratavej. "The Evolution of Risk in Information Systems Offshoring: The Impact of Home Country Risk, Firm Learning, and Competitive Dynamics." *MIS Quarterly* 33, No. 3 (September 2009).

Hammer, Michael and James Champy. *Reengineering the Corporation*. New York: HarperCollins (1993).

Hoehle, Hartmut and Viswanath Venkatesh. "Mobile Application Usability: Conceptualization and Instrument Development." *MIS Quarterly* 39, No. 2 (June 2015).

Information Builders. "Yellow Pages Uses WebFOCUS to Demonstrate ROI to Advertisers." www.informationbuilders.com, accessed March 30, 2015.

Ivari, Juhani, Rudy Hirscheim, and Heinz K. Klein. "A Dynamic Framework for Classifying Information Systems Development Methodologies and Approaches." *Journal of Management Information Systems* 17, No. 3 (Winter 2000–2001).

Kendall, Kenneth E. and Julie E. Kendall. *Systems Analysis and Design* (9th ed.). Upper Saddle River, NJ: Prentice Hall (2014).

Kindler, Noah B., Vasantha Krishnakanthan, and Ranjit Tinaikar. "Applying Lean to Application Development and Maintenance." *McKinsey Quarterly* (May 2007).

Kotlarsky, Julia, Harry Scarbrough, and Ilan Oshri. "Coordinating Expertise Across Knowledge Boundaries in Offshore-Outsourcing Projects: The Role of Codification." *MIS Quarterly* 38 No. 2 (June 2014).

Levina, Natalia and Jeanne W. Ross. "From the Vendor's Perspective: Exploring the Value Proposition in Information Technology Outsourcing." *MIS Quarterly* 27, No. 3 (September 2003).

Majchrzak, Ann, Cynthia M. Beath, and Ricardo A. Lim. "Managing Client Dialogues During Information Systems Design to Facilitate Client Learning." *MIS Quarterly* 29, No. 4 (December 2005).

Mani, Deepa, Anitesh Barua, and Andrew Whinston. "An Empirical Analysis of the Impact of Information Capabilities Design on Business Process Outsourcing Performance." *MIS Quarterly* 34, No. 1 (March 2010).

Mani, Deepa and Anitesh Barua. "The Impact of Firm Learning on Value Creation in Strategic Outsourcing Relationships." *Journal of Management Information Systems* 32 No. 1 (2015).

Mocker, Martin, Jeanne Ross, and Craig Hopkins." How USAA Architected Its Business for Life Event Integration." *MIS Quarterly Executive* 14, No. 4 (2015).

Nelson, H. James, Deborah J. Armstrong, and Kay M. Nelson. "Patterns of Transition: The Shift from Traditional to Object-Oriented Development." *Journal of Management Information Systems* 25, No. 4 (Spring 2009).

Overby, Stephanie. "The Hidden Costs of Offshore Outsourcing," *CIO Magazine* (September 1, 2003).

Ozer, Muammer and Doug Vogel. "Contextualized Relationship Between Knowledge Sharing and Performance in Software Development." *Journal of Management Information Systems* 32, No. 2 (2015).

Pollock, Neil and Sampsa Hyysalo. "The Business of Being a User: The Role of the Reference Actor in Shaping Packaged Enterprise System Acquisition and Development." *MIS Quarterly* 38, No. 2 (June 2014).

Saunders, Adam and Erik Brynjolfsson. "Valuing Information Technology Related Intangible Assets." *MIS Quarterly* 40 No. 1 (March 2016).

Sircar, Sumit, Sridhar P. Nerur, and Radhakanta Mahapatra. "Revolution or Evolution? A Comparison of Object-Oriented and Structured Systems Development Methods." *MIS Quarterly* 25, No. 4 (December 2001).

Su, Ning, Natalia Levina, and Jeanne W. Ross. "The Long-Tail Strategy for IT Outsourcing." *MIT Sloan Management Review* (Winter 2016).

Valacich, Joseph A. and Joey George. *Modern Systems Analysis and Design* (7th ed.). Upper Saddle River, NJ: Prentice-Hall (2014).

Yourdon, Edward and L. L. Constantine. *Structured Design*. New York: Yourdon Press (1978).

CHAPTER

14 Managing Projects

Learning Objectives

After reading this chapter, you will be able to answer the following questions:

14-1 What are the objectives of project management, and why is it so essential in developing information systems?

14-2 What methods can be used for selecting and evaluating information systems projects and aligning them with the firm's business goals?

14-3 How can firms assess the business value of information systems?

14-4 What are the principal risk factors in information systems projects, and how can they be managed?

CHAPTER CASES

Intuit Counts on Project Management
Can the National Health Service Go Paperless?
Reliance Installing the 4G Project in India
A Shaky Start for Healthcare.gov

Intuit Counts on Project Management

Intuit is a leading provider of financial management software and tools for consumers and business professionals such as TurboTax, QuickBooks, Quicken, and Mint.com. Selling these tools and providing customer service generate a great deal of valuable data. Intuit had no problem gathering and storing such data, but it did face hurdles deriving useful insights from all of its data. That's why Intuit launched the Intuit Analytics Cloud (IAC) project to turn lakes of data into pools of information.

In the past, Intuit had a number of data teams and multiple data silos maintained in isolation of each other. Despite many positive outcomes the arrangement produced within the enterprise or within the infrastructures for the individual products, Intuit was unable to utilize its data effectively for the entire organization or for all of its customers. Management wanted a more holistic approach so that the company could better use data to serve its customers and customers could have better experiences from the data and better insight about themselves.

The IAC project differed from the way projects were handled at Intuit in two major ways: first, Intuit's Analytics Cloud wasn't designed for a specific business use. Instead, it was supposed to be a general (holistic) platform serving the entire company for business units to use in any way they chose. Second, IAC was less structured than a traditional database so that the data could

© Lucadp/Fotolia

be used more flexibly. (In a traditional database, one designs and organizes the database before entering any data.) A data lake, such as IAC, is quite the opposite, dumping data into a big Hadoop repository without designing a data model beforehand. This approach provides tools for people to analyze the data along with a high-level definition of what data exists in the lake. People build various views into the data as they go along.

The Intuit IAC project required cooperation across the entire company because it incorporated all of the company's enterprise data, its product data, and third-party data into a single platform. IAC project leaders moved a number of functional teams from the data engineering group to production work for the project.

The project team was very sensitive to deadlines and the project budget. One of the key steps was breaking down the project into easy-to-handle pieces. Organizing a large project into "bite-sized" pieces makes it possible to deliver demonstrable results as the project progresses. The IAC project was a multi-year endeavor, and a "big bang" approach wasn't operationally or politically feasible. Creating a series of smaller deliverables rather than a single large end product made the project more manageable for the project teams. Additionally, executives authorizing project expenditures would be pleased by a series of demonstrable results as well. The success of the smaller project "bites" meant that project leaders didn't have to work hard to convince business unit leaders to participate in the project. Intuit's IAC project has been so successful that internal business units are jostling to use the new enterprise analytics cloud.

Sources: www.intuit.com, accessed January 16, 2016; Curtis Franklin Jr.,"Intuit CIO: Changing the Way Projects Are Managed," *Information Week*, December 17, 2015; Vindu Goel, "Intuit Sheds Its PC Roots and Rises as a Cloud Software Company," *New York Times*, April 10, 2016; and Robert L. Mitchell, "Eight Big Trends in Big Data Analytics," *Computerworld*, October 23, 2014.

One of the principal challenges posed by information systems is ensuring they deliver genuine business benefits. There is a very high failure rate among information systems projects because organizations have incorrectly assessed their business value or because firms have failed to manage the organizational change surrounding the introduction of new technology. Projects to build or improve information systems require special managerial and organizational techniques to make them effective.

Intuit's management realized this when it undertook its Intuit Analytics Cloud (IAC) project. The new technology involved changes to important business processes (and use of data) as well as new software. Intuit succeeded with this project because its management clearly understood that strong project management and attention to organizational issues were essential to success.

The chapter-opening diagram calls attention to important points raised by this case and this chapter. Intuit's future growth called for more intensive companywide use of internal and external data. Outdated file organization and legacy systems made internal operations inefficient, preventing the company

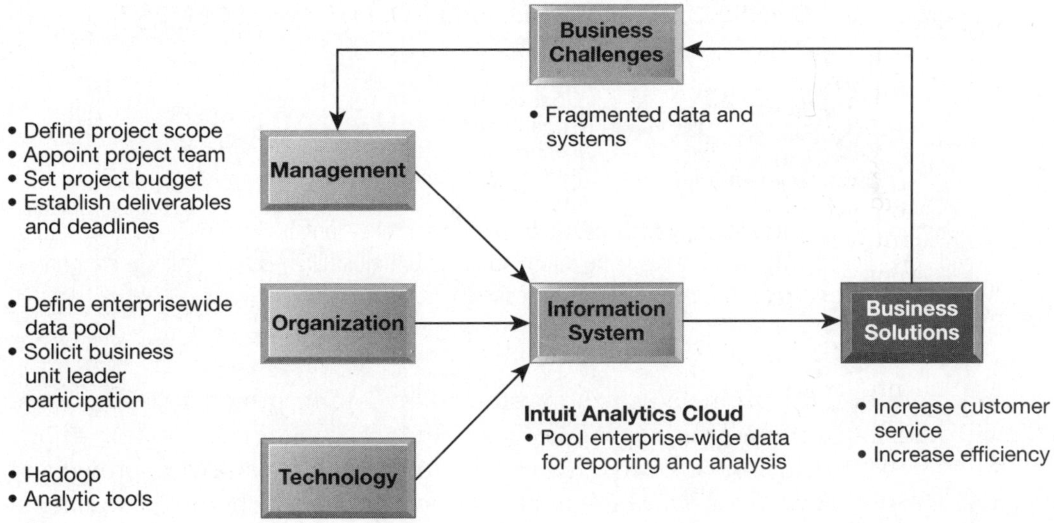

from providing the high level of service to customers that management desired. Management wisely assembled a project team and established desired outcomes and deadlines. It chose to break this very large project down into manageable chunks, each with a deliverable, which made the project more manageable and also garnered support from top management and from the business units that wanted to use the IAC.

Here are some questions to think about: Why was this project successful? Why was it important to break down the project into smaller chunks?

14-1 What are the objectives of project management, and why is it so essential in developing information systems?

There is a very high failure rate among information systems projects. In nearly every organization, information systems projects take much more time and money to implement than originally anticipated, or the completed system does not work properly. When an information system does not meet expectations or costs too much to develop, companies may not realize any benefit from their information system investment, and the system may not be able to solve the problems for which it was intended. The development of a new system must be carefully managed and orchestrated, and the way a project is executed is likely to be the most important factor influencing its outcome. That's why it's essential to have some knowledge about managing information systems projects and the reasons why they succeed or fail.

Runaway Projects and System Failure

How badly are projects managed? On average, private sector projects are underestimated by half in terms of budget and time required to deliver the

FIGURE 14.1 CONSEQUENCES OF POOR PROJECT MANAGEMENT

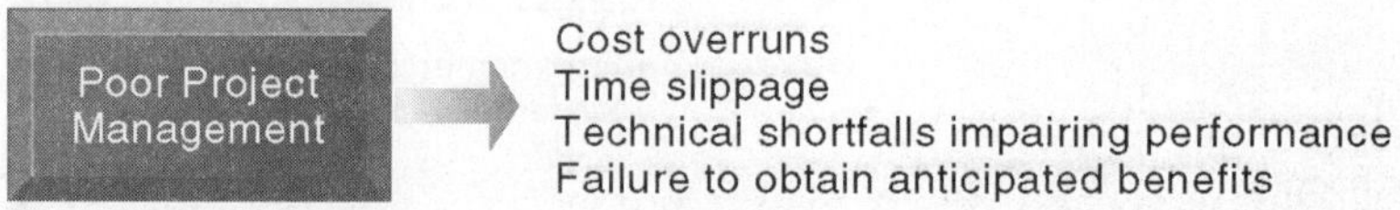

Without proper management, a systems development project takes longer to complete and most often exceeds the allocated budget. The resulting information system most likely is technically inferior and may not be able to demonstrate any benefits to the organization.

complete system promised in the system plan. Many projects are delivered with missing functionality (promised for delivery in later versions). A joint study by McKinsey and Oxford University found that large software projects on average run 66 percent over budget and 33 percent over schedule; as many as 17 percent of projects turn out so badly that they can threaten the existence of the company (Chandrasekaran, Gudlavalleti, and Kaniyar, 2014). Between 30 and 40 percent of all software projects are "runaway" projects that far exceed the original schedule and budget projections and fail to perform as originally specified.

As illustrated in Figure 14.1, a systems development project without proper management will most likely suffer these consequences:

- Costs that vastly exceed budgets
- Unexpected time slippage
- Technical performance that is less than expected
- Failure to obtain anticipated benefits

The systems produced by failed information projects are often not used in the way they were intended or are not used at all. Users often have to develop parallel manual systems to make these systems work. According to a 2015 report by 1E, which develops software solutions for managing and reducing IT costs, 37 percent of all software installed is not being used, wasting $30 billion in the United States alone (1E, 2016).

The actual design of the system may fail to capture essential business requirements or improve organizational performance. Information may not be provided quickly enough to be helpful, it may be in a format that is impossible to digest and use, or it may represent the wrong pieces of data.

The way in which nontechnical business users must interact with the system may be excessively complicated and discouraging. A system may be designed with a poor user interface. The **user interface** is the part of the system with which end users interact. For example, an online input form or data entry screen may be so poorly arranged that no one wants to submit data or request information. System outputs may be displayed in a format that is too difficult to comprehend.

Websites may discourage visitors from exploring further if the web pages are cluttered and poorly arranged, if users cannot easily find the information they are seeking, or if it takes too long to access and display the web page on the user's computer.

Additionally, the data in the system may have a high level of inaccuracy or inconsistency. The information in certain fields may be erroneous or ambiguous, or it may not be organized properly for business purposes. Information required for a specific business function may be inaccessible because the data are incomplete.

Project Management Objectives

A **project** is a planned series of related activities for achieving a specific business objective. Information systems projects include the development of new information systems, enhancement of existing systems, or upgrade or replacement of the firm's information technology (IT) infrastructure.

Project management refers to the application of knowledge, skills, tools, and techniques to achieve specific targets within specified budget and time constraints. Project management activities include planning the work, assessing risk, estimating resources required to accomplish the work, organizing the work, acquiring human and material resources, assigning tasks, directing activities, controlling project execution, reporting progress, and analyzing the results. As in other areas of business, project management for information systems must deal with five major variables: scope, time, cost, quality, and risk.

Scope defines what work is or is not included in a project. For example, the scope of a project for a new order processing system might be to include new modules for inputting orders and transmitting them to production and accounting but not any changes to related accounts receivable, manufacturing, distribution, or inventory control systems. Project management defines all the work required to complete a project successfully and should ensure that the scope of a project does not expand beyond what was originally intended.

Time is the amount of time required to complete the project. Project management typically establishes the amount of time required to complete major components of a project. Each of these components is further broken down into activities and tasks. Project management tries to determine the time required to complete each task and establish a schedule for completing the work.

Cost is based on the time to complete a project multiplied by the cost of human resources required to complete the project. Information systems project costs also include the cost of hardware, software, and work space. Project management develops a budget for the project and monitors ongoing project expenses.

Quality is an indicator of how well the end result of a project satisfies the objectives specified by management. The quality of information systems projects usually boils down to improved organizational performance and decision making. Quality also considers the accuracy and timeliness of information produced by the new system and ease of use.

Risk refers to potential problems that would threaten the success of a project. These potential problems might prevent a project from achieving its objectives by increasing time and cost, lowering the quality of project outputs, or preventing the project from being completed altogether. Section 14.4 describes the most important risk factors for information systems.

14-2 What methods can be used for selecting and evaluating information systems projects and aligning them with the firm's business goals?

Companies typically are presented with many different projects for solving problems and improving performance. There are far more ideas for systems projects than there are resources. Firms will need to select from this group the projects that promise the greatest benefit to the business. Obviously, the firm's overall business strategy should drive project selection. How should managers choose among all the options?

Management Structure for Information Systems Projects

Figure 14.2 shows the elements of a management structure for information systems projects in a large corporation. It helps ensure that the most important projects are given priority.

At the apex of this structure is the corporate strategic planning group and the information system steering committee. The corporate strategic planning group is responsible for developing the firm's strategic plan, which may require the development of new systems. Often, this group will have developed objective

FIGURE 14.2 MANAGEMENT CONTROL OF SYSTEMS PROJECTS

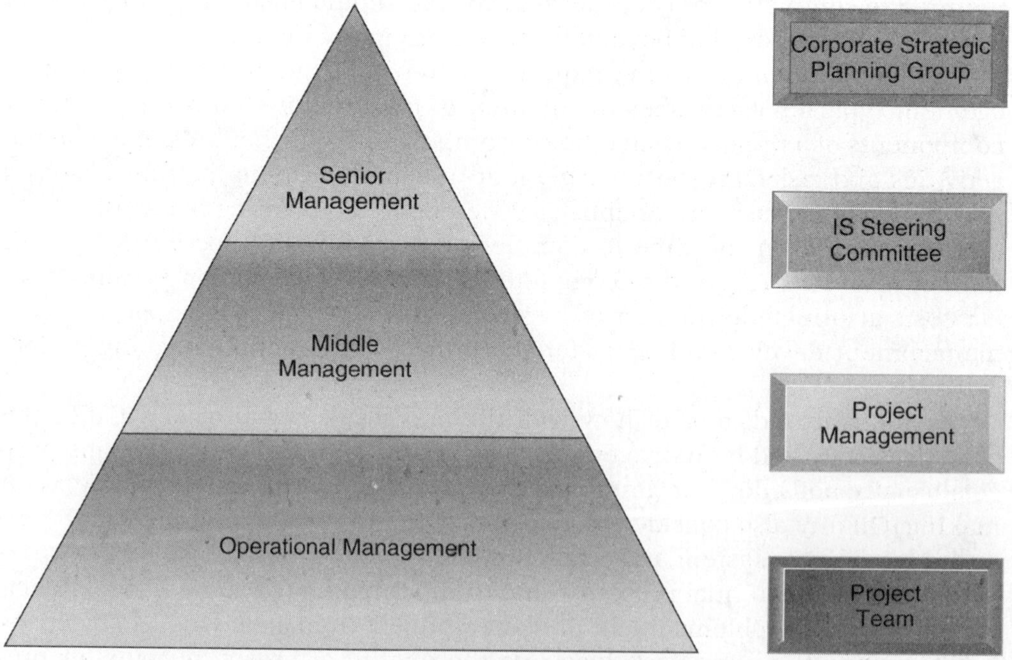

Each level of management in the hierarchy is responsible for specific aspects of systems projects, and this structure helps give priority to the most important systems projects for the organization.

measures of firm performance (called *key performance indicators*, introduced in Chapter 12) and choose to support IT projects that can make a substantial improvement in one or several key performance indicators. These performance indicators are reviewed and discussed by the firm's board of directors.

The information systems steering committee is the senior management group with responsibility for systems development and operation. It is composed of department heads from both end-user and information systems areas. The steering committee reviews and approves plans for systems in all divisions, seeks to coordinate and integrate systems, and occasionally becomes involved in selecting specific information systems projects. This group also has a keen awareness of the key performance indicators decided on by higher-level managers and the board of directors.

The project team is supervised by a project management group composed of information systems managers and end-user managers responsible for overseeing several specific information systems projects. The project team is directly responsible for the individual systems project. It consists of systems analysts, specialists from the relevant end-user business areas, application programmers, and perhaps database specialists. The mix of skills and the size of the project team depend on the specific nature of the system solution.

Linking Systems Projects to The Business Plan

In order to identify the information systems projects that will deliver the most business value, organizations need to develop an **information systems plan** that supports their overall business plan and in which strategic systems are incorporated into top-level planning. The plan serves as a road map indicating the direction of systems development (the purpose of the plan), the rationale, the state of current systems, new developments to consider, the management strategy, the implementation plan, and the budget (see Table 14.1).

The plan contains a statement of corporate goals and specifies how information technology will support the attainment of those goals. The report shows how general goals will be achieved by specific systems projects. It identifies specific target dates and milestones that can be used later to evaluate the plan's progress in terms of how many objectives were actually attained in the time frame specified in the plan. The plan indicates the key management decisions concerning hardware acquisition; telecommunications; centralization/decentralization of authority, data, and hardware; and required organizational change. Organizational changes are also usually described, including management and employee training requirements, recruiting efforts, changes in business processes, and changes in authority, structure, or management practice.

In order to plan effectively, firms will need to inventory and document all of their information system applications and IT infrastructure components. For projects in which benefits involve improved decision making, managers should try to identify the decision improvements that would provide the greatest additional value to the firm. They should then develop a set of metrics to quantify the value of more timely and precise information on the outcome of the decision. (See Chapter 12 for more detail on this topic.)

TABLE 14.1 INFORMATION SYSTEMS PLAN

1.	Purpose of the Plan
	Overview of plan contents
	Current business organization and future organization
	Key business processes
	Management strategy
2.	Strategic Business Plan Rationale
	Current situation
	Current business organization
	Changing environments
	Major goals of the business plan
	Firm's strategic plan
3.	Current Systems
	Major systems supporting business functions and processes
	Current infrastructure capabilities
	Hardware
	Software
	Database
	Telecommunications and Internet
	Difficulties meeting business requirements
	Anticipated future demands
4.	New Developments
	New systems projects
	Project descriptions
	Business rationale
	Applications' role in strategy
	New infrastructure capabilities required
	Hardware
	Software
	Database
	Telecommunications and Internet
5.	Management Strategy
	Acquisition plans
	Milestones and timing
	Organizational realignment
	Internal reorganization
	Management controls
	Major training initiatives
	Personnel strategy
6.	Implementation Plan
	Anticipated difficulties in implementation
	Progress reports

(Continued)

TABLE 14.1 INFORMATION SYSTEMS PLAN (Continued)

7.	Budget Requirements Requirements Potential savings Financing Acquisition cycle

Information Requirements and Key Performance Indicators

To develop an effective information systems plan, the organization must have a clear understanding of both its long- and short-term information requirements. A strategic approach to information requirements, strategic analysis, or critical success factors argues that an organization's information requirements are determined by a small number of key performance indicators (KPIs) of managers. KPIs are shaped by the industry, the firm, the manager, and the broader environment. For instance, KPIs for an automobile firm might be unit production costs, labor costs, factory productivity, rework and error rate, customer brand recognition surveys, J.D. Power quality rankings, employee job satisfaction ratings, and health costs. New information systems should focus on providing information that helps the firm meet these goals implied by key performance indicators.

Portfolio Analysis

Once strategic analyses have determined the overall direction of systems development, **portfolio analysis** can be used to evaluate alternative systems projects. Portfolio analysis inventories all of the organization's information systems projects and assets, including infrastructure, outsourcing contracts, and licenses. This portfolio of information systems investments can be described as having a certain profile of risk and benefit to the firm (see Figure 14.3) similar to a financial portfolio.

Each information systems project carries its own set of risks and benefits. (Section 14-4 describes the factors that increase the risks of systems projects.) Firms would try to improve the return on their portfolios of IT assets by balancing the risk and return from their systems investments. Although there is no ideal profile for all firms, information-intensive industries (e.g., finance) should have a few high-risk, high-benefit projects to ensure that they stay current with technology. Firms in non-information-intensive industries should focus on high-benefit, low-risk projects.

Most desirable, of course, are systems with high benefit and low risk. These promise early returns and low risks. Second, high-benefit, high-risk systems should be examined; low-benefit, high-risk systems should be totally avoided; and low-benefit, low-risk systems should be reexamined for the possibility of

FIGURE 14.3 A SYSTEM PORTFOLIO

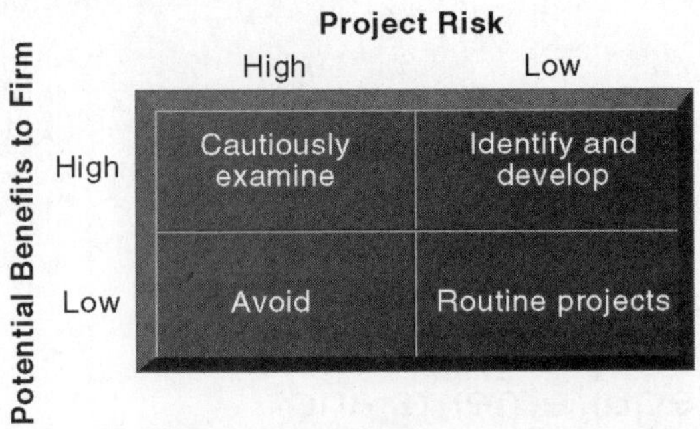

Companies should examine their portfolio of projects in terms of potential benefits and likely risks. Certain kinds of projects should be avoided altogether and others developed rapidly. There is no ideal mix. Companies in different industries have different profiles.

rebuilding and replacing them with more desirable systems having higher benefits. By using portfolio analysis, management can determine the optimal mix of investment risk and reward for their firms, balancing riskier high-reward projects with safer lower-reward ones. Firms where portfolio analysis is aligned with business strategy have been found to have a superior return on their IT assets, better alignment of IT investments with business objectives, and better organization-wide coordination of IT investments (Jeffrey and Leliveld, 2004).

Scoring Models

A **scoring model** is useful for selecting projects where many criteria must be considered. It assigns weights to various features of a system and then calculates the weighted totals. Using Table 14.2, the firm must decide among two alternative enterprise resource planning (ERP) systems. The first column lists the criteria that decision makers will use to evaluate the systems. These criteria are usually the result of lengthy discussions among the decision-making group. Often the most important outcome of a scoring model is not the score but agreement on the criteria used to judge a system.

Table 14.2 shows that this particular company attaches the most importance to capabilities for sales order processing, inventory management, and warehousing. The second column in Table 14.2 lists the weights that decision makers attached to the decision criteria. Columns 3 and 5 show the percentage of requirements for each function that each alternative ERP system can provide. Each vendor's score can be calculated by multiplying the percentage of requirements met for each function by the weight attached to that function. ERP System B has the highest total score.

As with all "objective" techniques, there are many qualitative judgments involved in using the scoring model. This model requires experts who understand the issues and the technology. It is appropriate to cycle through the scoring model several times, changing the criteria and weights, to see how sensitive the outcome is to reasonable changes in criteria. Scoring models are used most commonly to confirm, to rationalize, and to support decisions rather than as the final arbiters of system selection.

TABLE 14.2 EXAMPLE OF A SCORING MODEL FOR AN ERP SYSTEM

CRITERIA	WEIGHT	ERP SYSTEM A %	ERP SYSTEM A SCORE	ERP SYSTEM B %	ERP SYSTEM B SCORE
1.0 Order Processing					
1.1 Online order entry	4	67	268	73	292
1.2 Online pricing	4	81	324	87	348
1.3 Inventory check	4	72	288	81	324
1.4 Customer credit check	3	66	198	59	177
1.5 Invoicing	4	73	292	82	328
Total Order Processing			1,370		1,469
2.0 Inventory Management					
2.1 Production forecasting	3	72	216	76	228
2.2 Production planning	4	79	316	81	324
2.3 Inventory control	4	68	272	80	320
2.4 Reports	3	71	213	69	207
Total Inventory Management			1,017		1,079
3.0 Warehousing					
3.1 Receiving	2	71	142	75	150
3.2 Picking/packing	3	77	231	82	246
3.3 Shipping	4	92	368	89	356
Total Warehousing			741		752
Grand Total			3,128		3,300

14-3 How can firms assess the business value of information systems?

Even if a systems project supports a firm's strategic goals and meets user information requirements, it needs to be a good investment for the firm. The value of systems from a financial perspective essentially revolves around the issue of return on invested capital. Does a particular information system investment produce sufficient returns to justify its costs?

Information System Costs and Benefits

Table 14.3 lists some of the more common costs and benefits of systems. **Tangible benefits** can be quantified and assigned a monetary value. **Intangible benefits**, such as more efficient customer service or enhanced decision making, cannot be immediately quantified but may lead to quantifiable gains in the

TABLE 14.3 COSTS AND BENEFITS OF INFORMATION SYSTEMS

COSTS
Hardware
Telecommunications
Software
Services
Personnel
TANGIBLE BENEFITS (COST SAVINGS)
Increased productivity
Lower operational costs
Reduced workforce
Lower computer expenses
Lower outside vendor costs
Lower clerical and professional costs
Reduced rate of growth in expenses
Reduced facility costs
INTANGIBLE BENEFITS
Improved asset utilization
Improved resource control
Improved organizational planning
Increased organizational flexibility
More timely information
More information
Increased organizational learning
Legal requirements attained
Enhanced employee goodwill
Increased job satisfaction
Improved decision making
Improved operations
Higher client satisfaction
Better corporate image

long run. Transaction and clerical systems that displace labor and save space always produce more measurable, tangible benefits than management information systems, decision-support systems, and computer-supported collaborative work systems (see Chapters 2 and 11).

Chapter 5 introduced the concept of total cost of ownership (TCO), which is designed to identify and measure the components of information technology expenditures beyond the initial cost of purchasing and installing hardware and software. However, TCO analysis provides only part of the information needed to evaluate an information technology investment because it does not typically deal with benefits, cost categories such as complexity costs, and "soft" and strategic factors discussed later in this section.

Capital Budgeting for Information Systems

To determine the benefits of a particular project, you'll need to calculate all of its costs and all of its benefits. Obviously, a project where costs exceed benefits should be rejected. But even if the benefits outweigh the costs, additional financial analysis is required to determine whether the project represents a good return on the firm's invested capital. **Capital budgeting** models are one of several techniques used to measure the value of investing in long-term capital investment projects.

Capital budgeting methods rely on measures of cash flows into and out of the firm; capital projects generate those cash flows. The investment cost for information systems projects is an immediate cash outflow caused by expenditures for hardware, software, and labor. In subsequent years, the investment may cause additional cash outflows that will be balanced by cash inflows resulting from the investment. Cash inflows take the form of increased sales of more products (for reasons such as new products, higher quality, or increasing market share) or reduced costs in production and operations. The difference between cash outflows and cash inflows is used for calculating the financial worth of an investment. Once the cash flows have been established, several alternative methods are available for comparing different projects and deciding about the investment.

The principal capital budgeting models for evaluating IT projects are the payback method, the accounting rate of return on investment (ROI), net present value, and the internal rate of return (IRR). You can find out more about how these capital budgeting models are used to justify information system investments in the Learning Tracks for this chapter.

Limitations of Financial Models

The traditional focus on the financial and technical aspects of an information system tends to overlook the social and organizational dimensions of information systems that may affect the true costs and benefits of the investment. Many companies' information systems investment decisions do not adequately consider costs from organizational disruptions created by a new system, such as the cost to train end users, the impact that users' learning curves for a new system have on productivity, or the time managers need to spend overseeing new system-related changes. Intangible benefits such as more timely decisions from a new system or enhanced employee learning and expertise may also be overlooked in a traditional financial analysis.

14-4 What are the principal risk factors in information systems projects, and how can they be managed?

We have already introduced the topic of information system risks and risk assessment in Chapter 8. In this chapter, we describe the specific risks to information systems projects and show what can be done to manage them effectively.

Dimensions of Project Risk

Systems differ dramatically in their size, scope, level of complexity, and organizational and technical components. Some systems development projects are more likely to create the problems we have described earlier or to suffer delays because they carry a much higher level of risk than others. The level of project risk is influenced by project size, project structure, and the level of technical expertise of the information systems staff and project team.

- *Project size*. The larger the project—as indicated by the dollars spent, the size of the implementation staff, the time allocated for implementation, and the number of organizational units affected—the greater the risk. Very large-scale systems projects have a failure rate that is 50 to 75 percent higher than that for other projects because such projects are complex and difficult to control. The organizational complexity of the system—how many units and groups use it and how much it influences business processes—contributes to the complexity of large-scale systems projects just as much as technical characteristics, such as the number of lines of program code, length of project, and budget. In addition, there are few reliable techniques for estimating the time and cost to develop large-scale information systems.
- *Project structure*. Some projects are more highly structured than others. Their requirements are clear and straightforward, so outputs and processes can be easily defined. Users know exactly what they want and what the system should do; there is almost no possibility of the users changing their minds. Such projects run a much lower risk than those with relatively undefined, fluid, and constantly changing requirements; with outputs that cannot be fixed easily because they are subject to users' changing ideas; or with users who cannot agree on what they want.
- *Experience with technology*. The project risk rises if the project team and the information system staff lack the required technical expertise. If the team is unfamiliar with the hardware, system software, application software, or database management system proposed for the project, it is highly likely that the project will experience technical problems or take more time to complete because of the need to master new skills.

Although the difficulty of the technology is one risk factor in information systems projects, the other factors are primarily organizational, dealing with the complexity of information requirements, the scope of the project, and how many parts of the organization will be affected by a new information system. The Interactive Session on Management about the UK National Health Service's move toward paperless recordkeeping illustrates a project with some of these risks.

Change Management and the Concept of Implementation

The introduction or alteration of an information system has a powerful behavioral and organizational impact. Changes in the way that information is defined, accessed, and used to manage the organization's resources often lead to new distributions of authority and power. This internal organizational change breeds resistance and opposition and can lead to the demise of an otherwise good system.

INTERACTIVE SESSION: MANAGEMENT

Can the National Health Service Go Paperless?

The National Health Service (NHS) is the United Kingdom's publicly funded national healthcare system. Funded primarily by taxation, NHS provides free or low-cost healthcare to all legal residents of the United Kingdom. NHS services include hospitals, family doctors, specialists, dentists, chemists (pharmacists), opticians, and ambulance service. Medications are subsidized as well. Specific policies vary among England, Scotland, Wales, and Northern Ireland.

The UK Department of Health oversees the NHS. Patient records are maintained by healthcare providers, who must ensure confidentiality of patient data and compliance with regulatory standards. Like other healthcare systems, such as in the United States, patient records were primarily paper-based. Physician and hospital offices had shelves full of folders and papers devoted to the storage of medical records, making patient and treatment information very difficult to access or share. Just pulling the notes for NHS patients to be seen in the morning was a nightmare.

In January 2013 Health Secretary Jeremy Hunt called for making the NHS paperless by 2018 to save billions, improve services, and help meet the challenges of an aging population. Hunt and many others believe that patients should have compatible digital records so their health information can follow them around the health and social care system. Whether patients need a general practitioner (GP), hospital, or care home, the professionals involved in their treatment should be able to see their history at the touch of a button and share crucial information. Improved use of technology would allow health professionals to spend more time with patients and help patients take control of their own care, saving more than £4 billion.

Hunt announced the following goals:

- Paperless referrals: Instead of sending a letter to the hospital when referring a patient, the GP can send an e-mail instead.
- Secure linking of the electronic health and care records wherever they are held, so there is as complete a record as possible of the care someone receives.
- Ability of those records to be able to follow individuals, with their consent, to any part of the NHS or social care system.
- Ability of individuals to get online access to their own health records held by their GP by March 2015.
- Digital information fully available across NHS and social care services by April 2018 unless individuals opt out.

Paperless solutions can lead to a reduction in treatment/medication errors, quicker time to diagnosis, shorter time to treatment, more collaborative diagnostics (allowing a wider range of specialists to be involved), and better overall patient care.

However, many working in the NHS and private sectors—including those within the technology industry—believe that a paperless NHS is not achievable within a five-year time frame. This is an extremely ambitious target, and critics question how much this will really improve NHS services, if it's worth the cost of implementing new IT systems, and if it's even achievable.

According to S. A. Mathieson, an EHI Intelligence analyst, the English NHS is made up of several hundred organizations with greatly differing IT capabilities as well as thousands of independent GPs. All of them would have to acquire new software and hardware and convert their paper records to digital form. To make the new system effective, they would also have to change their procedures (business processes) to take advantage of the new technology. Answering patient phone calls, examining patients, and writing prescriptions will need to incorporate procedures for accessing and updating electronic medical records; paper-based records will have to be converted into electronic form, most likely with codes assigned for various treatment options and data structured to fit the record's format. Training can take up to 20 hours of a doctor's time, and doctors are extremely time-pressed. In order to get the system up and running, physicians themselves may have to enter some of the data, taking away time they could be spending with their patients. When the United States tried to implement electronic medical records in healthcare nationwide, many physicians complained about the time and effort required to make these changes. NHS has experienced some of this resistance.

The UK doctors' union, the British Medical Association (BMA), says there are several challenges to be overcome in order to make the NHS paperless and is skeptical about the extent of the benefits such a system can offer. According to the BMA, the biggest challenges to making the NHS paperless by 2018 are funding, resources, prioritization, and the choice of systems in secondary care. As well as ongoing hardware and software funding, sufficient resources will be required to support training of users and IT specialists to use the paperless system and to provide IT support and administrative support. Although there may potentially be some efficiencies, technology alone will not necessarily create very large cost savings.

Currently, 40 percent of a clinician's time is spent waiting for relevant information or making decisions based on information that is inaccurate or unreliable, and digitization needs to tackle these problems as well.

The House of Commons Public Accounts Committee warned that making the NHS paperless requires significant additional investments in IT and business transformation. Yet the Department of Health had not even set aside a specific budget for this purpose. The department said it was investing £1 billion (approximately $1.5 billion) in the paperless project—half from the central government and the rest from local health and care budgets.

A report by a Public Accounts Committee (PAC) recently said that changes made toward a digital NHS system "has not gone to plan," and some are saying it has been an "expensive waste of time." For any large organization, going paperless is a challenge, but when it is cash strapped and under intense public scrutiny and has a dismal history of IT failure (including unsuccessful earlier efforts to digitize patient records), the task looks like mission impossible, observes Michael Cross, news editor at *The Law Society Gazette.* Can the health service meet that deadline? Or will the NHS just end up with less paper than it did when the paperless project started?

Sources: Kat Hall, "NHS IT Projects Worth £5bn at 'High Risk' of Failure, Warns HSCIC," *The Register,* December 8, 2015; Clare McDonald, "What Is Standing in the Way of a Paperless NHS?" *Computer Weekly,* September 2015; S. A. Mathieson, "How Can IT Contribute to NHS Efficiency?" *Computer Weekly,* September 2015; Michael Cross, "NHS Chases a Paperless Tiger," *Raconteur*, April 29, 2014; Claire Read, "Barriers to a Paperless NHS: Are You Ready for Your Screen Test?" *HSJ,* March 14, 2014; Ben Rossi, "Going Paperless: The Clash Between IT Staff and NHS Trust Heads," *Information Age,* February 18, 2014; Department of Health and the Rt Hon Jeremy Hunt MP, "NHS Challenged to Go Paperless by 2018," www.gov.uk, accessed January 4, 2016; "The Paperless NHS...?" *Computacenter,* April 12, 2013.

CASE STUDY QUESTIONS

1. Why is paperless NHS a risky project? Identify the key risk factors.
2. What management, organization, and technology problems is the paperless NHS likely to encounter?
3. What steps should be taken to make the paperless NHS more successful?

A very large percentage of information systems projects stumble because the process of organizational change surrounding system building was not properly addressed. Successful system building requires careful **change management**.

The Concept of Implementation

To manage the organizational change surrounding the introduction of a new information system effectively, you must examine the process of implementation. **Implementation** refers to all organizational activities working toward the adoption, management, and routinization of an innovation, such as a new information system. In the implementation process, the systems analyst is a **change agent**. The analyst not only develops technical solutions but also redefines the configurations, interactions, job activities, and power relationships of various organizational groups. The analyst is the catalyst for the entire change process and is responsible for ensuring that all parties involved accept the changes created by a new system. The change agent communicates with users, mediates between competing interest groups, and ensures that the organizational adjustment to such changes is complete.

The Role of End Users

System implementation generally benefits from high levels of user involvement and management support. User participation in the design and operation of information systems has several positive results. First, if users are heavily involved in systems design, they have more opportunities to mold the system according to their priorities and business requirements and more opportunities to control the outcome. Second, they are more likely to react positively to the completed system because they have been active participants in the change process. Incorporating user knowledge and expertise leads to better solutions.

The relationship between users and information systems specialists has traditionally been a problem area for information systems implementation efforts. Users and information systems specialists tend to have different backgrounds, interests, and priorities. This is referred to as the **user-designer communications gap**. These differences lead to divergent organizational loyalties, approaches to problem solving, and vocabularies.

Information systems specialists, for example, often have a highly technical, or machine, orientation to problem solving. They look for elegant and sophisticated technical solutions in which hardware and software efficiency is optimized at the expense of ease of use or organizational effectiveness. Users prefer systems that are oriented toward solving business problems or facilitating organizational tasks. Often the orientations of both groups are so at odds that they appear to speak in different tongues.

These differences are illustrated in Table 14.4, which depicts the typical concerns of end users and technical specialists (information systems designers)

TABLE 14.4 THE USER DESIGNER COMMUNICATIONS GAP

USER CONCERNS	DESIGNER CONCERNS
Will the system deliver the information we need for our work?	What demands will this system put on our servers?
Can we access the data on our iPhones, BlackBerrys, tablets, and PCs?	What kind of programming demands will this place on our group?
What new procedures do we need to enter data into the system?	Where will the data be stored? What's the most efficient way to store them?
How will the operation of the system change employees' daily routines?	What technologies should we use to secure the data?

regarding the development of a new information system. Communication problems between end users and designers are a major reason why user requirements are not properly incorporated into information systems and why users are driven out of the implementation process.

Systems development projects run a very high risk of failure when there is a pronounced gap between users and technical specialists and when these groups continue to pursue different goals. Under such conditions, users are often driven away from the project. Because they cannot comprehend what the technicians are saying, users conclude that the entire project is best left in the hands of the information specialists alone.

Management Support and Commitment

If an information systems project has the backing and commitment of management at various levels, it is more likely to be perceived positively by both users and the technical information services staff. Both groups will believe that their participation in the development process will receive higher-level attention and priority. They will be recognized and rewarded for the time and effort they devote to implementation. Management backing also ensures that a systems project receives sufficient funding and resources to be successful. Furthermore, to be enforced effectively, all the changes in work habits and procedures and any organizational realignments associated with a new system depend on management backing. If a manager considers a new system a priority, the system will more likely be treated that way by his or her subordinates. According to the Project Management Institute, executive sponsors who are actively engaged is the leading factor in project success (Kloppenborg and Tesch, 2015; Project Management Institute, 2013).

Change Management Challenges for Business Process Reengineering, Enterprise Applications, and Mergers and Acquisitions

Given the challenges of innovation and implementation, it is not surprising to find a very high failure rate among enterprise application and business process reengineering (BPR) projects, which typically require extensive organizational change and which may require replacing old technologies and legacy systems that are deeply rooted in many interrelated business processes. A number of studies have indicated that 70 percent of all business process reengineering projects fail to deliver promised benefits. Likewise, a high percentage of enterprise applications fail to be fully implemented or to meet the goals of their users even after three years of work.

Many enterprise application and reengineering projects have been undermined by poor implementation and change management practices that failed to address employees' concerns about change. Dealing with fear and anxiety throughout the organization, overcoming resistance by key managers, and changing job functions, career paths, and recruitment practices have posed greater threats to reengineering than the difficulties companies faced visualizing and designing breakthrough changes to business processes. All of the enterprise applications require tighter coordination among different functional groups as well as extensive business process change (see Chapter 9).

Projects related to mergers and acquisitions have a similar failure rate. Mergers and acquisitions are deeply affected by the organizational characteristics of the merging companies as well as by their IT infrastructures. Combining the information systems of two different companies usually requires considerable organizational change and complex systems projects to manage. If the integration is not properly managed, firms can emerge with a tangled hodgepodge of inherited legacy systems built by aggregating the systems of one firm after another. Without a successful systems integration, the benefits anticipated from the merger cannot be realized, or, worse, the merged entity cannot execute its business processes effectively.

Controlling Risk Factors

Various project management, requirements gathering, and planning methodologies have been developed for specific categories of implementation problems. Strategies have also been devised for ensuring that users play appropriate roles throughout the implementation period and for managing the organizational change process. Not all aspects of the implementation process can be easily controlled or planned. However, anticipating potential implementation problems and applying appropriate corrective strategies can increase the chances for system success.

The first step in managing project risk involves identifying the nature and level of risk confronting the project. Implementers can then handle each project with the tools and risk management approaches geared to its level of risk. Not all risks are identifiable in advance, but with skilful project management, most are. Frequent communication and a culture of collaboration will help project teams adapt to unforeseen problems that arise (Browning and Ramasesh, 2015; Laufer et al., 2015; McFarlan, 1981).

Managing Technical Complexity

Projects with challenging and complex technology to master benefit from **internal integration tools**. The success of such projects depends on how well their technical complexity can be managed. Project leaders need both heavy technical and administrative experience. They must be able to anticipate problems and develop smooth working relationships among a predominantly technical team. The team should be under the leadership of a manager with a strong technical and project management background, and team members should be highly experienced. Team meetings should take place frequently. Essential technical skills or expertise not available internally should be secured from outside the organization.

Formal Planning and Control Tools

Large projects benefit from appropriate use of **formal planning tools** and **formal control tools** for documenting and monitoring project plans. The two most commonly used methods for documenting project plans are Gantt charts and PERT charts. A **Gantt chart** lists project activities and their corresponding start and completion dates. The Gantt chart visually represents the timing and duration of different tasks in a development project as well as their human resource requirements (see Figure 14.4). It shows each task as a horizontal bar whose length is proportional to the time required to complete it.

Although Gantt charts show when project activities begin and end, they don't depict task dependencies, how one task is affected if another is behind schedule, or how tasks should be ordered. That is where **PERT charts** are useful. *PERT* stands for "Program Evaluation and Review Technique," a methodology developed by the U.S. Navy during the 1950s to manage the Polaris submarine missile program. A PERT chart graphically depicts project tasks and their interrelationships. The PERT chart lists the specific activities that make up a project and the activities that must be completed before a specific activity can start, as illustrated in Figure 14.5.

The PERT chart portrays a project as a network diagram consisting of numbered nodes (either circles or rectangles) representing project tasks. Each node is numbered and shows the task, its duration, the starting date, and the completion date. The direction of the arrows on the lines indicates the sequence of tasks and shows which activities must be completed before the commencement of another activity. In Figure 14.5, the tasks in nodes 2, 3, and 4 are not dependent on each other and can be undertaken simultaneously, but each is dependent on completion of the first task. PERT charts for complex projects can be difficult to interpret, and project managers often use both techniques.

These project management techniques can help managers identify bottlenecks and determine the impact that problems will have on project completion times. They can also help systems developers partition projects into smaller, more manageable segments with defined, measurable business results. Standard control techniques can successfully chart the progress of the project against budgets and target dates, so deviations from the plan can be spotted.

Increasing User Involvement and Overcoming User Resistance

Projects with relatively little structure and many undefined requirements must involve users fully at all stages. Users must be mobilized to support one of many possible design options and to remain committed to a single design. **External integration tools** consist of ways to link the work of the implementation team to users at all organizational levels. For instance, users can become active members of the project team, take on leadership roles, and take charge of installation and training. The implementation team can demonstrate its responsiveness to users, promptly answering questions, incorporating user feedback, and showing their willingness to help.

Participation in implementation activities may not be enough to overcome the problem of user resistance to organizational change. Different users may be affected by the system in different ways. Whereas some users may welcome a new system because it brings changes they perceive as beneficial to them, others may resist these changes because they believe the shifts are detrimental to their interests.

If the use of a system is voluntary, users may choose to avoid it; if use is mandatory, resistance will take the form of increased error rates, disruptions, turnover, and even sabotage. Therefore, the implementation strategy must not only encourage user participation and involvement, but it must also address the issue of counterimplementation. **Counterimplementation** is a deliberate

FIGURE 14.4 A GANTT CHART

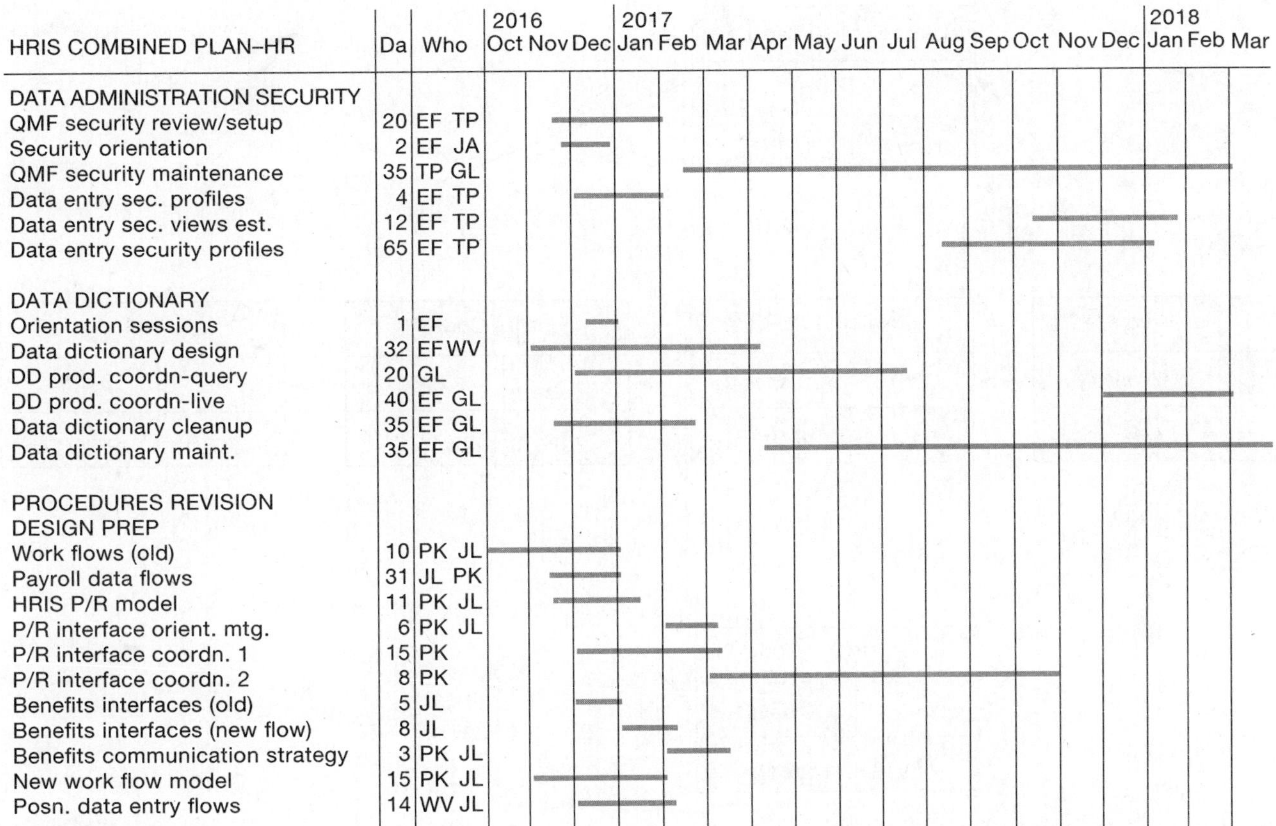

RESOURCE SUMMARY		Who	Oct 2016	Nov	Dec	Jan 2017	Feb	Mar	Apr	May	Jun	Jul	Aug	Sep	Oct	Nov	Dec	Jan 2018	Feb	Mar
Edith Farrell	5.0	EF	2	21	24	24	23	22	22	27	34	34	29	26	28	19	14			
Woody Vinton	5.0	WV	5	17	20	19	12	10	14	10	2							4	3	
Charles Pierce	5.0	CP		5	11	20	13	9	10	7	6	8	4	4	4	4	4			
Ted Leurs	5.0	TL		12	17	17	19	17	14	12	15	16	2	1	1	1	1			
Toni Cox	5.0	TC	1	11	10	11	11	12	19	19	21	21	21	17	17	12	9			
Patricia Knopp	5.0	PC	7	23	30	34	27	25	15	24	25	16	11	13	17	10	3	3	2	
Jane Lawton	5.0	JL	1	9	16	21	19	21	21	20	17	15	14	12	14	8	5			
David Holloway	5.0	DH	4	4	5	5	5	2	7	5	4	16	2							
Diane O'Neill	5.0	DO	6	14	17	16	13	11	9	4										
Joan Albert	5.0	JA	5	6			7	6	2	1				5	5	1				
Marie Marcus	5.0	MM	15	7	2	1	1													
Don Stevens	5.0	DS	4	4	5	4	5	1												
Casual	5.0	CASL		3	4	3			4	7	9	5	3	2						
Kathy Mendez	5.0	KM		1	5	16	20	19	22	19	20	18	20	11	2					
Anna Borden	5.0	AB					9	10	16	15	11	12	19	10	7	1				
Gail Loring	5.0	GL		3	6	5	9	10	17	18	17	10	13	10	10	7	17			
UNASSIGNED	0.0	X										9			236	225	230	14	13	
Co-op	5.0	CO		6	4				2	3	4	4	2	4	16			216	178	
Casual	5.0	CAUL								3	3	3								
TOTAL DAYS			49	147	176	196	194	174	193	195	190	181	140	125	358	288	284	237	196	12

The Gantt chart in this figure shows the task, person-days, and initials of each responsible person as well as the start and finish dates for each task. The resource summary provides a good manager with the total person-days for each month and for each person working on the project to manage the project successfully. The project described here is a data administration project.

FIGURE 14.5 A PERT CHART

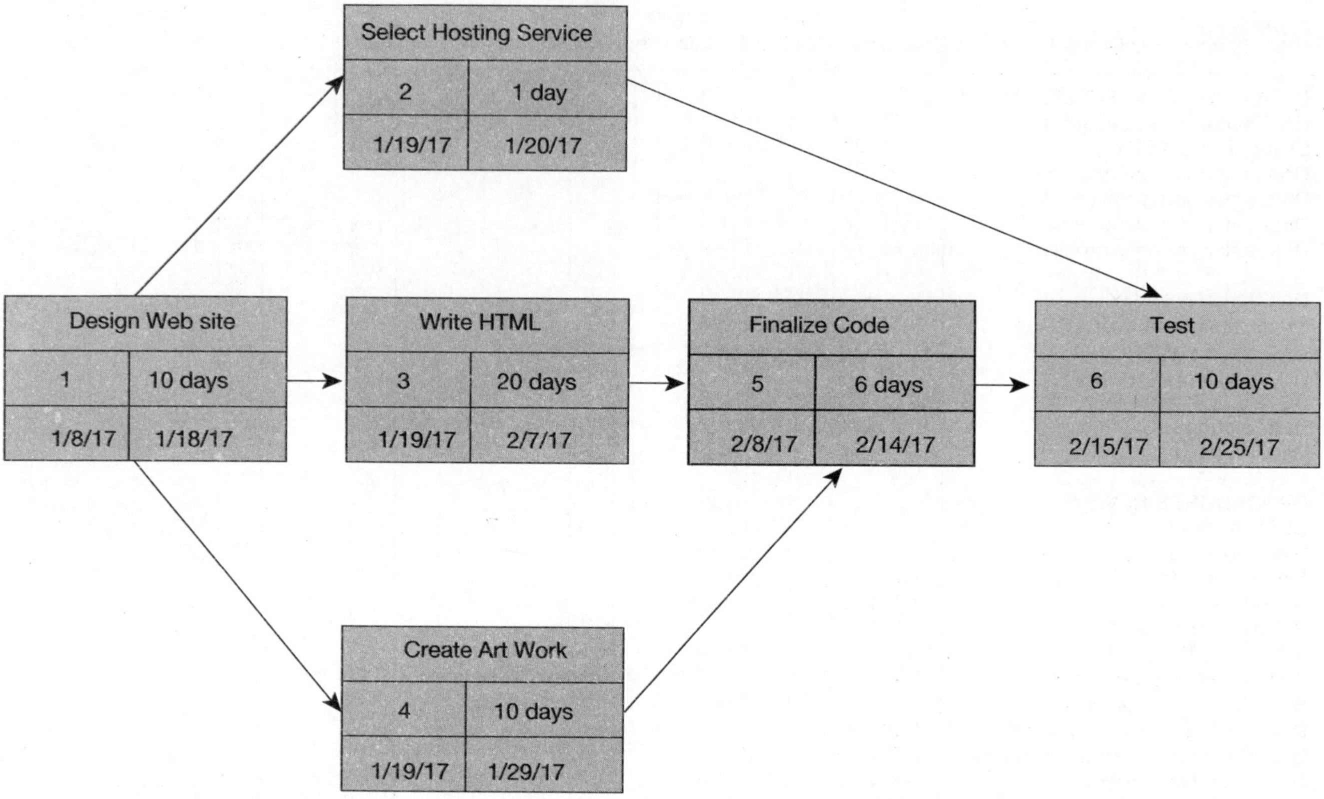

This is a simplified PERT chart for creating a small website. It shows the ordering of project tasks and the relationship of a task with preceding and succeeding tasks.

strategy to thwart the implementation of an information system or an innovation in an organization.

Strategies to overcome user resistance include user participation (to elicit commitment as well as to improve design), user education and training, management edicts and policies, and better incentives for users who cooperate. The new system can be made more user-friendly by improving the end-user interface. Users will be more cooperative if organizational problems are solved prior to introducing the new system. The Interactive Session on Organizations describes some of the challenges of developing mobile applications.

Designing for the Organization

Because the purpose of a new system is to improve the organization's performance, information systems projects must explicitly address the ways in which the organization will change when the new system is installed, including installation of mobile and web applications. In addition to procedural changes, transformations in job functions, organizational structure, power relationships, and the work environment should be carefully planned.

INTERACTIVE SESSION: ORGANIZATIONS

Reliance Installing the 4G Project in India

Reliance Jio Infocomm Limited (RJIL), a subsidiary of Reliance Industries Limited (RIL), is the first telecom company to obtain a pan-India unified operating license. The company commercially launched its 4G broadband services in 2015. The setting up of the network and hardware infrastructure for this project has cost the company ₹40,000 crore in investments. The firm managed to successfully acquire the Broadband Wireless Access (BWA) spectrum through an auction. It also entered into key agreements with several companies such as Tower Vision and Viom Networks for the use of their 8,400 and 42,000 towers, respectively. Contracts have also been signed with companies like Bharti Airtel for fiber utilization and infrastructure sharing, among other things.

There were several challenges that RJIL faced when it decided to embark on this journey. Three types of working processes were to be set up. The first involved negotiations with the infrastructure companies, which would provide the necessary towers, hardware, antennas, microwave, and so on. The second related to discussion with the networking companies, who would be responsible for the provisioning and installation of networking equipment. Finally, a customer-facing operator was needed to take the 4G service to market. Indus Towers, Viom Networks, and BSNL took care of Reliance's infrastructural needs; networking services were provided by Samsung; while Reliance Communications acted as the telecom operator that would provide the 4G service to the customers. Indus Towers is the largest provider of telecom towers in the world. It is a joint venture between the Bharti Group, the Aditya Birla Group, and the Vodafone Group. India is divided into 22 circles for telecom operations, and Indus has over one lakh towers in 15 of those circles. These towers can be used by any of the telecom players. This sharing of towers benefits not just the customer (by lowering the price of the service) but also reduces radiation damage on the environment.

Once the infrastructure partner hands over the site to RJIL, Samsung, the networking partner, steps in and surveys the site to determine whether the infrastructure is electronically viable. As part of the survey, the site engineers collect information such as the length of the cable required, height of the antenna, images of the infrastructure site, and so on. They also find a suitable location for installation as per the requirements of the client. All this information is then fed into a material information system, which generates an Excel-based survey report summarizing the findings. This report is then handed over to RJIL to be uploaded to its geographic information system to get a complete picture of the site. Once Samsung determines the readiness of the site for network installation, RJIL releases payment to the tower infrastructure provider.

An acceptance testing procedure is now conducted on the site. Here, images of the site extracted from the Geographic Information System (GIS) are uploaded to another software called SiteForge. This makes the real-time sharing of geo-tagged photos possible. Samsung now needs to determine the range of the towers. This is done through the process of linking, where the microwaves installed on each tower are linked to one another. Once this is accomplished (it usually takes 15 days), Samsung performs another survey to test the electromagnetic field, measure the bandwidth of antennas, test antenna radiation, determine the strength of the power transmitted and received, and so on. All this is done to assess the effect of radiation on nearby settlements. This information is again fed into SiteForge, which generates real-time statistics on the health of the network assets at the site. This information system then calculates the impact of the radiation using three techniques: the simple calculation method, the broadband method, and the narrowband method. The simple calculation method is employed first and the results are compared with an effective radiation limit as prescribed by the Department of Telecommunications (DOT). If the radiation limit at this stage exceeds the prescibed limit, the angle of the antenna is modified and the broadband method is applied. If this method also fails to provide results within the prescribed limit, changes are made to the site itself and the narrowband method of calculating radiation is used. Most sites are able to meet the expected radiation limits when tested with these three techniques. If the results still exceed the prescribed values, the site is declared harmful. Based on these findings, the DOT decides whether to give permission for integration or not.

The last step is to conduct a Single-Cell Function Test (SCFT) or a drive test. All the sites which receive permission from the DOT need to undergo this test, where the ability of the site to offer the promised Internet speed (which, in RJIL's case, is 50 Mbps) is determined. A stationary test is first conducted by uploading and downloading files. Then the field staff perform a moving test by driving anti-clockwise and clockwise around the site. When the site meets the speed requirements, it is handed over by Samsung to RJIL. The site is then deemed fit for the use of the customer.

Sources: "RJIL signs agreement with Indus Towers to launch 4G services", SmartCity.eletsonline.com. Retrieved from http://smartcity.eletsonline.com/rjil-signs-agreement-with-indus-towers-to-launch-4g-services/; "Reliance Jio Infocomm to launch 4G in 2015: Mukesh Ambani", *The Times of India* (2014). Retrieved from http://timesofindia.indiatimes.com/tech/tech-news/Reliance-Jio-Infocomm-to-launch-4G-in-2015-Mukesh-Ambani/articleshow/36763068.cms; "Core Members". Retrieved from http://www.coai.com/About-Us/Members/Core-Members/Reliance-Jio-Infocomm-Limited; "Looking back, looking forward". Retrieved from http://www.rcom.co.in/Rcom/aboutus/overview/overview_reliancegroup.html.

CASE STUDY QUESTIONS

1. What are the three processes involved in the setting up of any project in the telecom sector?
2. Discuss the role of information systems in conducting the environment-readiness survey on the tower site.
3. How is SiteForge used in the acceptance testing procedure?
4. What do you understand by drive test in the telecom sector?

Areas where users interface with the system require special attention, with sensitivity to ergonomics issues. **Ergonomics** refers to the interaction of people and machines in the work environment. It considers the design of jobs, health issues, and the end-user interface of information systems. Table 14.5 lists the organizational dimensions that must be addressed when planning and implementing information systems.

TABLE 14.5 ORGANIZATIONAL FACTORS IN SYSTEMS PLANNING AND IMPLEMENTATION

Employee participation and involvement
Job design
Standards and performance monitoring
Ergonomics (including equipment, user interfaces, and the work environment)
Employee grievance resolution procedures
Health and safety
Government regulatory compliance

Although systems analysis and design activities are supposed to include an organizational impact analysis, this area has traditionally been neglected. An **organizational impact analysis** explains how a proposed system will affect organizational structure, attitudes, decision making, and operations. To integrate information systems successfully with the organization, thorough and fully documented organizational impact assessments must be given more attention in the development effort.

Sociotechnical Design

One way of addressing human and organizational issues is to incorporate **sociotechnical design** practices into information systems projects. Designers set forth separate sets of technical and social design solutions. The social design plans explore different workgroup structures, allocation of tasks, and the design of individual jobs. The proposed technical solutions are compared with the proposed social solutions. The solution that best meets both social and technical objectives is selected for the final design. The resulting sociotechnical design is expected to produce an information system that blends technical efficiency with sensitivity to organizational and human needs, leading to higher job satisfaction and productivity.

Project Management Software Tools

Commercial software tools that automate many aspects of project management facilitate the project management process. Project management software typically features capabilities for defining and ordering tasks, assigning resources to tasks, establishing starting and ending dates to tasks, tracking progress, and facilitating modifications to tasks and resources. Many automate the creation of Gantt and PERT charts and provide communication, collaboration, and social tools.

Some of these tools are large sophisticated programs for managing very large projects, dispersed work groups, and enterprise functions. These high-end tools can manage very large numbers of tasks and activities and complex relationships. The most widely used project management tool today is Microsoft Project, but there are also lower-cost tools for smaller projects and small businesses, such as Zoho Projects and Teamwork Projects, which are available in the cloud as are some versions of Microsoft Project. Many project management applications are now cloud-based to enable project team members to access project management tools and their data wherever they are working. Huddle, Clarizen, and Citrix Podio are other examples (Reisinger, 2016).

While project management software helps organizations track individual projects, the resources allocated to them, and their costs, **project portfolio management software** helps organizations manage portfolios of projects and dependencies among them. Project portfolio management software helps managers compare proposals and projects against budgets and resource capacity levels to determine the optimal mix and sequencing of projects that best achieves the organization's strategic goals.

Review Summary

14-1 *What are the objectives of project management, and why is it so essential in developing information systems?*

Good project management is essential for ensuring that systems are delivered on time and on budget and provide genuine business benefits. Project management activities include planning the work, assessing the risk, estimating and acquiring resources required to accomplish the work, organizing the work, directing execution, and analyzing the results. Project management must deal with five major variables: scope, time, cost, quality, and risk.

14-2 *What methods can be used for selecting and evaluating information systems projects and aligning them with the firm's business goals?*

Organizations need an information systems plan that describes how information technology supports the attainment of their business goals and documents all their system applications and IT infrastructure components. Large corporations will have a management structure to ensure the most important systems projects receive priority. Key performance indicators, portfolio analysis, and scoring models can be used to identify and evaluate alternative information systems projects.

14-3 *How can firms assess the business value of information systems?*

To determine whether an information systems project is a good investment, one must calculate its costs and benefits. Tangible benefits are quantifiable, and intangible benefits that cannot be immediately quantified may provide quantifiable benefits in the future. Benefits that exceed costs should be analyzed using capital budgeting methods to make sure a project represents a good return on the firm's invested capital.

14-4 *What are the principal risk factors in information systems projects, and how can they be managed?*

The level of risk in a systems development project is determined by (1) project size, (2) project structure, and (3) experience with technology. IS projects are more likely to fail when there is insufficient or improper user participation in the systems development process, lack of management support, and poor management of the implementation process. There is a very high failure rate among projects involving business process reengineering, enterprise applications, and mergers and acquisitions because they require extensive organizational change.

Implementation refers to the entire process of organizational change surrounding the introduction of a new information system. User support and involvement and management support and control of the implementation process are essential, as are mechanisms for dealing with the level of risk in each new systems project. Project risk factors can be brought under some control by a contingency approach to project management. The risk level of each project determines the appropriate mix of external integration tools, internal integration tools, formal planning tools, and formal control tools to be applied.

Key Terms

Capital budgeting, 575
Change agent, 579
Change management, 578
Counterimplementation, 582
Ergonomics, 586
External integration tools, 582
Formal control tools, 581
Formal planning tools, 581
Gantt chart, 581
Implementation, 578
Information systems plan, 569
Intangible benefits, 573
Internal integration tools, 581
Organizational impact analysis, 587
PERT chart, 582
Portfolio analysis, 571
Project, 567
Project management, 567

Project portfolio management, 587
Scope, 567
Scoring model, 572
Sociotechnical design, 587
Tangible benefits, 573
User-designer communications gap, 579
User interface, 566

Review Questions

14-1 What are the objectives of project management? Explain its importance in developing information systems.

- Define 'runaway projects'. Why do they occur and what are the consequences?
- Define project, scope, cost, time, quality and risk in relation to projects. State some examples of IS projects.

14-2 What methods can be used for selecting and evaluating information systems projects and aligning them with the firm's business goals?

- Explain the need for defining management structure for managing information system projects.
- What is the need to link information systems plan to overall business plan and how is it done?
- List and describe the techniques used for selection of IS projects and their areas of application.

14-3 How can firms assess the business value of information systems?

- Explain how firms utilize capital budgeting models to assess business value of information systems.
- Discuss the limitations of financial models.

14-4 What are the principal risk factors in information systems projects, and how can they be managed?

- Identify and describe each of the principal risk factors in information systems projects.
- Define implementation and change agents and explain their importance to change management.
- Explain why eliciting support of management and end users is so essential for successful implementation of information systems projects.
- Explain why there is such a high failure rate for implementations involving enterprise applications, business process reengineering, and mergers and acquisitions.
- Identify and describe the strategies for controlling project risk.
- Identify the organizational considerations that should be addressed by project planning and implementation.
- Describe the roles of ergonomics, organizational impact analysis, and sociotechnical design in designing for the organization.

Discussion Questions

14-5 How much does project management impact the success of a new information system?

14-6 It has been said that most systems fail because systems builders ignore organizational behavior problems. Why might this be so?

14-7 What is the role of end users in information systems project management?

Hands-On MIS Projects

The projects in this section give you hands-on experience evaluating information systems projects, using spreadsheet software to perform capital budgeting analyses for new information systems investments, and using web tools to analyze the financing for a new home.

Management Decision Problems

14-8 The U.S. Census launched an IT project to arm its census takers in the field with high-tech handheld devices that would save taxpayer money by directly beaming population data to headquarters from census takers in the field. Census officials signed a $600 million contract with Harris Corporation in 2006 to build 500,000 devices but still weren't sure which features they wanted included in the units. Census officials did not specify the testing process to measure the performance of the handheld devices. As the project progressed, 400 change requests to project requirements were added. Two years and hundreds of millions of taxpayer dollars later, the handhelds were far too slow and unreliable to be used for the 2010 U.S. census. What could Census Bureau management and the Harris Corporation have done to prevent this outcome?

14-9 Caterpillar is the world's leading maker of earth-moving machinery and supplier of agricultural equipment. Caterpillar wants to end its support for its Dealer Business System (DBS), which it licenses to its dealers to help them run their businesses. The software in this system is becoming outdated, and senior management wants to transfer support for the hosted version of the software to Accenture Consultants so it can concentrate on its core business. Caterpillar never required its dealers to use DBS, but the system had become a de facto standard for doing business with the company. The majority of the 50 Cat dealers in North America use some version of DBS, as do about half of the 200 or so Cat dealers in the rest of the world. Before Caterpillar turns the product over to Accenture, what factors and issues should it consider? What questions should it ask? What questions should its dealers ask?

Improving Decision Making: Using Web Tools for Buying and Financing a Home

Software skills: Internet-based software
Business skills: Financial planning

14-10 This project will develop your skills using web-based software for searching for a home and calculating mortgage financing for that home.

You would like to purchase a home in Fort Collins, Colorado. Ideally, it should be a single-family house with at least three bedrooms and one bathroom that costs between $170,000 and $300,000 and financed with a 30-year fixed rate mortgage. You can afford a down payment that is 20 percent of the value of the house. Before you purchase a house, you would like to find out what homes are available in your price range, find a mortgage, and determine the amount of your monthly payment. Use the Realtor.com site to help you with the following tasks:

- Locate homes in Fort Collins, Colorado, that meet your specifications.
- Find a mortgage for 80 percent of the list price of the home. Compare rates from at least three sites (use search engines to find sites other than Yahoo).
- After selecting a mortgage, calculate your closing costs and the monthly payment.

When you are finished, evaluate the whole process. For example, assess the ease of use of the site and your ability to find information about houses and mortgages, the accuracy of the information you found, and the breadth of choice of homes and mortgages.

Collaboration and Teamwork Project

Identifying Implementation Problems

Form a group with three or four other students. Write a description of the implementation problems you might expect to encounter in one of the systems described in the Interactive Sessions or chapter-ending cases in this text. Write an analysis of the steps you would take to solve or prevent these problems. If possible, use Google Docs and Google Drive or Google Sites to brainstorm, organize, and develop a presentation of your findings for the class.

A Shaky Start for Healthcare.gov

CASE STUDY

The Patient Protection and Affordable Care Act, often called Obamacare, is considered the centerpiece of President Barack Obama's legacy. Essential to Obama's healthcare reform plan is Healthcare.gov, a health insurance exchange website that facilitates the sale of private health insurance plans to U.S. residents, assists people eligible to sign up for Medicaid, and has a separate marketplace for small businesses.

The site allows users to compare prices on health insurance plans in their states, to enroll in a plan they choose, and to find out whether they qualify for government healthcare subsidies. Users must sign up and create their own specific account first, providing some personal information, to receive detailed information about available healthcare plans in their area.

Healthcare.gov was launched on October 1, 2013, as promised, but visitors quickly encountered numerous technical problems. Software that assigned digital identities to enrollees and ensured that they saw only their own personal data was overwhelmed. Customers encountered cryptic error messages and could not log on to create accounts. Many users received quotes that were incorrect because the feature used prices based on just two age groups. It was estimated that only 1 percent of interested consumers were able to enroll through the site for the first week of operations, and many applications sent to insurers contained erroneous information. Thousands of enrollees for HealthCare.gov—at least one in five at the height of the problems—received inaccurate assignments to Medicaid or to private health plans. Some people were wrongly denied coverage.

Insurers received enrollment files from the federal exchange that were incomplete or inaccurate, as many as one in ten. The information includes who is enrolling and what subsidies they may receive. Some insurers reported being deluged with phone calls from people who believed they had signed up for a particular health plan, only to find that the company had no record of the enrollment. Enrollment problems with insurers persisted into November.

U.S. Chief Technology Officer Todd Park stated on October 6 that Healthcare.gov's glitches were caused by an unexpectedly high volume of users. Between 50,000 and 60,000 had been expected, but the site had to handle 250,000 simultaneous users. More than 8.1 million people visited Healthcare.gov between October 1, 2013, and October 4, 2013.

White House officials later admitted that Healthcare.gov's problems were not just caused by high traffic volume but also by software and system design issues. Stress tests performed by contractors a day before the launch date revealed that the site slowed substantially with only 1,100 simultaneous users, far fewer than the 50,000 to 60,000 that were anticipated. Technical experts found out that the site was riddled with hardware and software defects, amounting to more than 600 items that needed to be fixed.

A major contributor to these problems was the part of the system's design that required users to create individual accounts before shopping for health insurance. This meant that before users could shop for coverage, they must input personal data that would be exchanged among separate computer systems built or run by multiple vendors, including CGI Group, developer of Healthcare.gov; Quality Software Services; and credit-checker Experian PLC. If any part of this web of systems failed to work properly, users would be blocked from entering the exchange marketplace. A bottleneck had been created where these systems interacted with a software component called Oracle Identity Manager, supplied by Oracle Corporation, which was embedded in the government's identity-checking system. This problem might have been averted if the system allowed users to browse plans without first going through the complex registration process.

Problems, including pull-down menus that only worked intermittently and excruciatingly long wait times, persisted into the third week of operations. For some weeks in October, the site was down 60 percent of the time.

What happened to Healthcare.gov is another example of IT project management gone awry, which often happens with large technology projects, especially those for the U.S. federal government. There was no single leader overseeing the Healthcare.gov implementation. The U.S. Centers for Medicare and Medicaid Services (CMS) coordinated the development effort. However, CMS had a siloed management structure, and no single unit was designated to take charge of the entire project.

CMS parceled out the work for building and implementing the Healthcare.gov system to a number of outside contractors. The front end of the website (including the user interface) was developed by the start-up Development Seed. The back end (where all the heavy-duty processing of enrollment data and transactions with insurers takes place) was contracted to CGI Federal, a subsidiary of the Canadian multinational CGI Group, which received $231 million for the project. CGI then subcontracted much of its work to other companies. This is common in large government projects. Functions relating to digital identity authentication were contracted to Experian, the global information services company noted for its credit-checking expertise.

CMS set deadlines for the contractors, who were expected to attend meetings to hammer out the details of the specifications for the website, but the computer specialists skipped some of those sessions. Contractors for different parts of the system barely communicated with each other.

Some IT experts also criticized CMS's decision to use database software from a company called MarkLogic, which handles data management differently from more mainstream database management systems of companies such as IBM and Oracle. Work proceeded more slowly because so few people were familiar with MarkLogic, and MarkLogic continued to perform below expectations after the Healthcare.gov website was launched.

The website had not been thoroughly tested before it went live, so a number of software and hardware defects had not been detected. Testing of the system by insurers had been scheduled for July but didn't begin until the third week in September. CMS was responsible for user-testing the system during the final weeks.

Technology experts also faulted Healthcare.gov's developers for trying to go live with all parts of a large and very complex system all at once. It would have been better to roll out system functions gradually. CGI believed that a full-function Healthcare.gov with all the anticipated bells and whistles was an unrealistic target. Given the time required to complete and test the software, it was impossible to launch a full-function exchange by October 1, but government officials insisted that October 1 was not negotiable and had become impatient with CGI's pattern of excuses for missed deadlines. The Obama administration kept on modifying regulations and policies until summer 2013, which meant that contractors had to deal with changing requirements.

The Healthcare.gov enrollment system is very complex. It connects to other federal computer networks, including the Social Security Administration (SSA), Internal Revenue Service (IRS), Veterans Affairs (VA), the Office of Personnel Management, and the Peace Corps. It has to verify a considerable amount of personal information, including income and immigration status.

Vital components were never secured. There was insufficient access to a data center to prevent the website from crashing. No backup system for a website crash was created. The interaction between the data center where the information is stored and the system was so poorly configured that it had to be redesigned.

CMS had several warnings between March and July that the project was going off-track but didn't seek deep White House involvement or change the leadership structure, according to officials, congressional aides, and emails from the period. An administration report noted that inadequate management oversight and coordination among technical teams prevented real-time decision making and efficient responses to address the issues with the site.

The consulting firm McKinsey & Co. detailed the project's potential risks in a presentation between March 28 and April 8 to the top CMS official, Marilyn Tavenner, to Health and Human Services Secretary Kathleen Sebelius, and to White House Chief Technology Officer Todd Park. McKinsey's report anticipated many of the site's pitfalls and urged the administration to name a single project leader to streamline decision making. It also emphasized the importance of White House support for CMS to meet the October 1 launch date. Nevertheless, according to documents from the period and officials, the White House's minimal involvement in the project's details didn't change after the McKinsey report.

The White House assembled experts from government and industry, and they worked frantically to fix the system. The Obama administration appointed contractor Quality Software Services Inc. (QSSI) to coordinate the work involved in fixing the website. QSSI had worked earlier on the website's back-end. In January 2014, Accenture replaced CGI Group as the website's lead contractor.

Work on fixing the website continued through October and November 2013, and the website appeared to be working more smoothly. For the vast majority of users, Healthcare.gov was working more than 90 percent of the time. Response time (the time required for a web page to load) was reduced from eight seconds to less than one. The incidence of error messages preventing people from using the site went from 6 percent down to 0.75 percent, but by November 30, only 137,000 people had signed up for private health insurance, far fewer than the government had forecast. Healthcare.gov's problems also forced the Obama administration to delay by one year an online exchange for small business.

Reuters reported in mid-October 2013 that the total cost of building Healthcare.gov using contractors had tripled from an initial estimate of $93.7 million to about $292 million. Overall cost for building the website reached $500 million by October 2013. As of February 2014, the government had committed to paying $800 million for contracts for the site, and the full amount spent to date is still unknown.

By early 2014, Healthcare.gov was working much better but was not problem-free. Then HealthCare .gov went down shortly after midnight March 30, 2014, and remained unusable until a day later. Some of the hundreds of thousands of Americans trying to sign up for healthcare at the last minute of the enrollment period were unable to do so. Nevertheless, 8 million people signed up for healthcare that year.

Kathleen Sebelius resigned as Secretary for Health and Human Services on April 10, 2014, and was replaced by Sylvia Mathews Burwell on June 9 of that year. On July 30, 2014, the U.S. Government Accountability Office (GAO) released a nonpartisan study finding that the Healthcare.gov website was developed without effective planning or oversight practices. These findings were supported by another report issued by the Inspector General of the Department of Health and Human Services in January 2015. The Inspector General's investigation found that the federal government failed to probe fully the past performance of CGI before awarding its contract and had neglected to put a cap on contractor billings.

After a bumpy debut, HealthCare.gov appeared in 2015 to be running smoothly. There have been a few minor, short-lived technical glitches. The Obama administration was able to boast that enrollment of 11 million people in healthcare plans for 2015 surpassed the president's goals.

Sources: Louise Radnofsky, "Poor Oversight, Work Marred Health Care Site's Launch," *Wall Street Journal*, January 20, 2015; Alex Barinka,"Healthcare.gov Bug Plagues Obamacare Just before Deadline," *Bloomberg*, February 14, 2015; Amy Nordrum, "Obama's Healthcare.gov Website Isn't Consumer-Friendly Enough, Experts Say," *International Business Times*, February 18, 2015; Spencer E. Ante and Louise Radnofsky, "New Technical Woes Hobble Health-Insurance Sign-Ups at Zero Hour," *Wall Street Journal*, March 31, 2014; "How HealthCare.gov Was Supposed to Work and How It Didn't," *New York Times*, December 2, 2013; Sheryl Gay Stolberg and Michael D. Shear, "Inside the Race to Rescue a Health Care Site, and Obama," *New York Times*, November 30, 2013; Gautham Nagesh, "Health Website Problems Weren't Flagged in Time," *Wall Street Journal*, December 2, 2013; Christopher Weaver and Louise Radnofsky, "Healthcare.gov's Flaws Found, Fixes Eyed," *Wall Street Journal*, October 10, 2013, and "Federal Health Site Stymied by Lack of Direction," *Wall Street Journal*, October 28, 2013; and Eric Lipton, Jan Austen, and Sharon LaFraniere, "Tension and Flaws before Health Website Crash," *New York Times*, November 22, 2013.

CASE STUDY QUESTIONS

14-11 Why was the Healthcare.gov project so important?

14-12 Evaluate the key risk factors in this project.

14-13 Describe the steps that should have been taken to prevent a negative outcome in this project.

Chapter 14 References

1E. "The Real Cost of Unused Software." www.1E.com, accessed February 5, 2016.

Appan, Radha and Glenn J. Browne. "The Impact of Analyst-Induced Misinformation on the Requirements Elicitation Process." *MIS Quarterly* 36, No 1 (March 2012).

Banker, Rajiv. "Value Implications of Relative Investments in Information Technology." Department of Information Systems and Center for Digital Economy Research, University of Texas at Dallas, January 23, 2001.

Barki, Henri, Suzanne Rivard, and Jean Talbot. "An Integrative Contingency Model of Software Project Risk Management." *Journal of Management Information Systems* 17, No. 4 (Spring 2001).

Bloch, Michael, Sen Blumberg, and Jurgen Laartz. "Delivering Large-Scale IT Projects on Time, on Budget, and on Value." *McKinsey Quarterly* (October 2012).

Brock, Jon Tamim Saleh and Sesh Iyer. "Large-Scale IT Projects: From Nightmare to Value Creation." Boston Consulting Group (May 20, 2015).

Browning, Tyson, R. and Ranga V. Ramasesh. "Reducing Unwelcome Surprises in Project Management." *MIT Sloan Management Review* (Spring 2015).

Brynjolfsson, Erik and Lorin M. Hitt. "Information Technology and Organizational Design: Evidence from Micro Data." (January 1998).

Ditmore, Jim. "Why Do Big IT Projects Fail So Often?" *Information Week* (October 29, 2013).

Dubravka Cecez-Kecmanovic, Karlheinz Kautz, and Rebecca Abrahall. "Reframing Success and Failure of Information Systems: A Performative Perspective." *MIS Quarterly* 38, No. 2 (June 2014).

Chandrasekaran, Sriram, Sauri Gudlavalleti, and Sanjay Kaniyar. "Achieving Success in Large Complex Software Projects." *McKinsey Quarterly* (July 2014).

Clement, Andrew and Peter Van den Besselaar. "A Retrospective Look at PD Projects." *Communications of the ACM* 36, No. 4 (June 1993).

Delone, William H. and Ephraim R. McLean. "The Delone and McLean Model of Information Systems Success: A Ten-Year Update. *Journal of Management Information Systems* 19, No. 4 (Spring 2003).

Flyvbjerg, Bent and Alexander Budzier. "Why Your IT Project May Be Riskier Than You Think." *Harvard Business Review* (September 2011).

He Jun and William R. King. "The Role of User Participation In Information Systems Development: Implications from a Meta-Analysis." *Journal of Management Information Systems* 25, No. 1 (Summer 2008).

Hitt, Lorin, D. J. Wu, and Xiaoge Zhou. "Investment in Enterprise Resource Planning: Business Impact and Productivity Measures." *Journal of Management Information Systems* 19, No. 1 (Summer 2002).

Housel, Thomas J., Omar El Sawy, Jianfang Zhong, and Waymond Rodgers. "Measuring the Return on e-Business Initiatives at the Process Level: The Knowledge Value-Added Approach." ICIS (2001).

Jeffrey, Mark and Ingmar Leliveld. "Best Practices in IT Portfolio Management." *MIT Sloan Management Review* 45, No. 3 (Spring 2004).

Jiang, James J., Jamie Y. T. Chang, Houn-Gee Chen, Eric T. G. Wang, and Gary Klein. "Achieving IT Program Goals with Integrative Conflict Management." *Journal of Management Information Systems* 31, No. 1 (Summer 2014).

Karhade, Prasanna, Michael J. Shaw, and Ramanath Subramanyam. "Patterns in Information Systems Portfolio Prioritization: Evidence from Decision Tree Induction." *MIS Quarterly* 39, No.2 (June 2015).

Keen, Peter W. "Information Systems and Organizational Change." *Communications of the ACM* 24 (January 1981).

Keil, Mark, H. Jeff Smith, Charalambos L. Iacovou, and Ronald L. Thompson. "The Pitfalls of Project Status Reporting." *MIT Sloan Management Review* 55, No. 3 (Spring 2014).

Keil, Mark, Joan Mann, and Arun Rai. "Why Software Projects Escalate: An Empirical Analysis and Test of Four Theoretical Models." *MIS Quarterly* 24, No. 4 (December 2000).

Kim, Hee Woo and Atreyi Kankanhalli. "Investigating User Resistance to Information Systems Implementation: A Status Quo Bias Perspective." *MIS Quarterly* 33, No. 3 (September 2009).

Kloppenborg, Timothy J. and Debbie Tesch. "How Executive Sponsors Influence Project Success." *MIT Sloan Management Review* (Spring 2015).

Kolb, D. A. and A. L. Frohman. "An Organization Development Approach to Consulting." *Sloan Management Review* 12 (Fall 1970).

Lapointe, Liette and Suzanne Rivard. "A Multilevel Model of Resistance to Information Technology Implementation." *MIS Quarterly* 29, No. 3 (September 2005).

Laudon, Kenneth C. "CIOs Beware: Very Large Scale Systems." Center for Research on Information Systems, New York University Stern School of Business, working paper (1989).

Laufer, Alexander, Edward J. Hoffman, Jeffrey S. Russell, and W. Scott Cameron. "What Successful Project Managers Do." *MIT Sloan Management Review* (Spring 2015).

Lee, Jong Seok, Mark Keil, and Vijay Kasi. "The Effect of an Initial Budget and Schedule Goal on Software Project Escalation." *Journal of Management Information Systems* 29, No. 1 (Summer 2012).

Li, Xitong and Madnick, Stuart E. "Understanding the Dynamics of Service-Oriented Architecture Implementation." *Journal of Management Information Systems* 32, No. 2 (2015).

Liang, Huigang, Zeyu Peng, Xue Zeyu, Guo Yajiong, and Wang Xitong. "Employees' Exploration of Complex Systems: An Integrative View." *Journal of Management Information Systems* 32 No. 1 (2015).

Liang, Huigang, Nilesh Sharaf, Qing Hu, and Yajiong Xue. "Assimilation of Enterprise Systems: The Effect of Institutional Pressures and the Mediating Role of Top Management." *MIS Quarterly* 31, No. 1 (March 2007).

Mastrogiacomo, Stefano, Stephanie Missonier, and Riccardo Bonazzi. "Talk Before It's Too Late: Reconsidering the Role of Conversation in Information Systems Project Management." *Journal of Management Information Systems* 31, No. 1 (Summer 2014).

McFarlan, F. Warren. "Portfolio Approach to Information Systems." *Harvard Business Review* (September–October 1981).

Mumford, Enid and Mary Weir. *Computer Systems in Work Design: The ETHICS Method.* New York: John Wiley (1979).

Polites, Greta L. and Elena Karahanna. "Shackled to the Status Quo: The Inhibiting Effects of Incumbent System Habit, Switching Costs, and Inertia on New System Acceptance." *MIS Quarterly* 36, No. 1 (March 2012).

Project Management Institute. *A Guide to the Project Management Body of Knowledge* (5th ed.). Newtown Square, PA: Project Management Institute (2013).

__________"The High Cost of Low Performance." (2016).

Ramasubbu, Narayan, Anandhi Bharadwaj, and Giri Kumar Tayi. "Software Process Diversity: Conceptualization, Measurement, and Analysis of Impact on Project Performance." *MIS Quarterly* 39, No. 4 (December 2015).

Reisinger, Don. "10 Cloud-Based Project Management Tools to Serve Every Company's Needs." *eWeek* (March 10, 2016).

Rivard, Suzanne and Liette Lapointe. "Information Technology Implementers' Responses to User Resistance: Nature and Effects." *MIS Quarterly* 36, No. 3 (September 2012).

Ross, Jeanne W. and Cynthia M. Beath. "Beyond the Business Case: New Approaches to IT Investment." *Sloan Management Review* 43, No. 2 (Winter 2002).

Ryan, Sherry D., David A. Harrison, and Lawrence L Schkade. "Information Technology Investment Decisions: When Do Cost and Benefits in the Social Subsystem Matter?" *Journal of Management Information Systems* 19, No. 2 (Fall 2002).

Schmidt, Roy, Kalle Lyytinen, Mark Keil, and Paul Cule. "Identifying Software Project Risks: An International Delphi Study." *Journal of Management Information Systems* 17, No. 4 (Spring 2001).

Schwalbe, Kathy. *Information Technology Project Management* (8th ed.). Cengage (2016).

Sharma, Rajeev and Philip Yetton. "The Contingent Effects of Training, Technical Complexity, and Task Interdependence on Successful Information Systems Implementation." *MIS Quarterly* 31, No. 2 (June 2007).

Smith, H. Jeff, Mark Keil, and Gordon Depledge. "Keeping Mum as the Project Goes Under." *Journal of Management Information Systems* 18, No. 2 (Fall 2001).

Sting, Fabian J., Christoph H. Loch, and Dirk Stempfhuber. "Accelerating Projects by Encouraging Help." *MIT Sloan Management Review* (Spring 2015).

Swanson, E. Burton. *Information System Implementation.* Homewood, IL: Richard D. Irwin (1988).

Sykes, Tracy Ann. "Support Structures and Their Impacts on Employee Outcomes: A Longitudinal Field Study of an Enterprise System Implementation." *MIS Quarterly* 39, No. 2 (June 2015).

Tornatsky, Louis G., J. D. Eveland, M. G. Boylan, W. A. Hetzner, E. C. Johnson, D. Roitman, and J. Schneider. *The Process of Technological Innovation: Reviewing the Literature.* Washington, DC: National Science Foundation (1983).

Vaidyanathan, Ganesh. *Project Management: Process, Technology and Practice.* Upper Saddle River, NJ: Prentice Hall (2013).

Wang, Eric T. G., Gary Klein, and James J. Jiang. "ERP Misfit: Country of Origin and Organizational Factors." *Journal of Management Information Systems* 23, No. 1 (Summer 2006).

Westerman, George. "IT Is from Venus, Non-IT Is from Mars." *Wall Street Journal* (April 2, 2012).

Xue, Yajion, Huigang Liang, and William R. Boulton. "Information Technology Governance in Information Technology Investment Decision Processes: The Impact of Investment Characteristics, External Environment, and Internal Context." *MIS Quarterly* 32, No. 1 (March 2008).

Yin, Robert K. "Life Histories of Innovations: How New Practices Become Routinized." *Public Administration Review* (January–February 1981).

Zhu, Kevin and Kenneth L. Kraemer. "E-Commerce Metrics for Net-Enhanced Organizations: Assessing the Value of e-Commerce to Firm Performance in the Manufacturing Sector." *Information Systems Research* 13, No. 3 (September 2002).

CHAPTER

15 Managing Global Systems

Learning Objectives

After reading this chapter, you will be able to answer the following questions:

15-1 What major factors are driving the internationalization of business?

15-2 What are the alternative strategies for developing global businesses?

15-3 What are the challenges posed by global information systems and management solutions for these challenges?

15-4 What are the issues and technical alternatives to be considered when developing international information systems?

CHAPTER CASES

The Bel Group: Laughing All the Way to Success
Indian E-commerce: Obstacles to Opportunity
One Organization, One Data, One Information: ONGC's Global System
Crocs Clambers to Global Efficiency

The Bel Group: Laughing All the Way to Success

The Bel Group is a global producer and distributor of cheese. Headquartered in Paris, it is best known for its small-portion cheese snacks packaged in branded packets. Born in Leon Bel's French cheese plant in 1921, The Laughing Cow is one of the Bel group's core brands together with Mini Babybel, Kiri, Leerdammer, and Boursin. The Group operates through numerous subsidiaries in Europe, the Americas, Asia, Turkey, and Africa, including a subsidiary in Egypt. As a multinational leader in the production of branded cheeses with a specialization in miniaturization, the group's strategy is to double in size by 2025. While the focus is primarily on dairy products, the company is exposed to fluctuations in dairy product prices and exchange rates, and achieving this ambitious target might prove challenging if it relies on organic growth alone. The acquisition of the MOM Group on 15 December 2016, however, now offers potential expansion into snacks, juices, and sweet desserts, so it could be acquisitions that will play a key role in achieving its future growth strategy.

© northshoot - Food/Alamy Stock Photo

The company markets its core brands in 130 countries as a healthy and fun eating experience, with children an important driver for sales. The challenge is to create a bond with the customer, and key products such as The Laughing Cow are localized in an attempt to build a new dairy generation. The formulas of its various cheeses are changed to meet local taste and regulatory requirements; for example, calcium and vitamin D are added for the Egyptian market, and a sweet strawberry flavor is added for South Korea and China. The core brands are active on a range of social media platforms, and the company entered into a strategic partnership with Facebook in July 2016 to gain a better understanding of its consumers and more effectively measure marketing campaign performance.

In addition to defending and growing established markets in Europe, untouched market potential exists in Africa, Asia, and South America. The ability to make a proper response as well as manage multinational relationships requires an efficient and effective customer relationship management (CRM) system. Customers now have instant access to the Internet via mobile technology, and companies must be able to adapt and provide new levels of responsiveness. CRM is not merely about managing existing customers' expectations, but also about acquiring new customers and building brand loyalty across a range of contact points.

The Bel Group identified the need for a single CRM system to coordinate sales and marketing teams across both the new and the more mature marketplaces. Each operating unit and sales office has specific market needs, but coordination is required to ensure market agility while enabling effective management of the diverse multilingual and cultural aspects of the business. A decision was taken to use Salesforce's Sales Cloud to provide a sales and marketing tool while enabling the enhancement of overall supply chain management. The system provides the company with scalability as well as with ease of use.

According to CIO Yves Gauguier, the Salesforce system can be customized, allowing for market developments, diverse negotiation, and sales promotion needs, with knowledge and expertise quickly shared across the Group, enabling faster communication. The system provides updates on progress toward its target, helps to measure the effectiveness of different marketing campaigns, and helps convert the data collected via the numerous data streams.

Case contributed by June Clarke, Sheffield Hallam University

Sources: www.groupe-bel.com, accessed January 13, 2017; "Salesforce Helps Bel Reach Its Growth Targets," www.salesforce.com, accessed January 13, 2017.

The Bel Group's efforts to create global customer relationship management systems highlight some of the issues that organizations need to consider if they want to operate worldwide. Like many large, multinational firms, Bel has subsidiaries and sales offices in a number of different countries. It also has an acquisitions strategy, meaning that potential differences in systems, business processes, and reporting standards have to be managed. Given the Group's product range and target audience, creating a bond with the customer and building customer understanding are vital to success.

In a mobile-enhanced world, speed of communication and customization across diverse contact points become essential. The company identified the

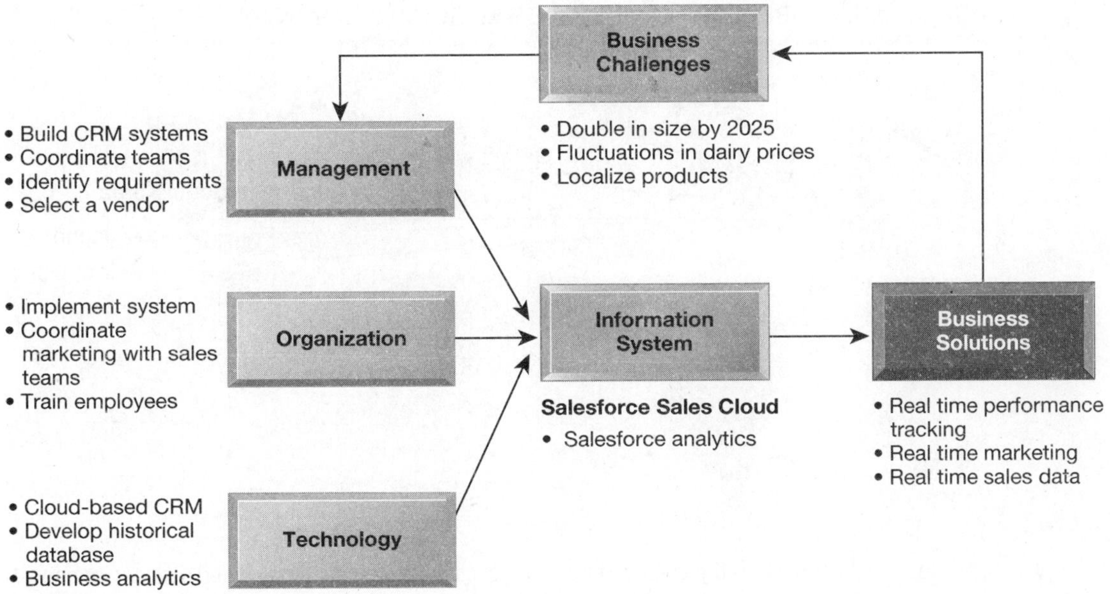

need for a scalable, easy-to-use system that would provide an effective measurement tool for different marketing campaigns in order to meet the varying needs of its target audiences.

The chapter-opening diagram calls attention to important points raised by this case and this chapter. To improve global management and customer-facing business processes, the Bel Group implemented a new global system based on Salesforce CRM software. Hosted in the cloud, it provides managers and employees with enterprise-wide information on campaigns, customers, and prospects around the globe. This helps the company manage diverse contact points more efficiently around the world and drives global growth.

Here are some questions to think about: How does information technology improve operations and decision making at the Bel Group? How would the company's new CRM system facilitate its business strategy? Why is it important to incorporate the impact of a social media presence as a measurement tool?

15-1 What major factors are driving the internationalization of business?

In earlier chapters, we describe the emergence of a global economic system and global world order driven by advanced networks and information systems. The new world order is sweeping away many national corporations, national industries, and national economies controlled by domestic politicians. Many localized firms will be replaced by fast-moving networked corporations that transcend national boundaries. The growth of international trade has radically altered domestic economies around the globe.

Consider the path to market for an iPhone, which is illustrated in Figure 15.1. The iPhone was designed by Apple engineers in the United States, sourced with

FIGURE 15.1 APPLE IPHONE'S GLOBAL SUPPLY CHAIN

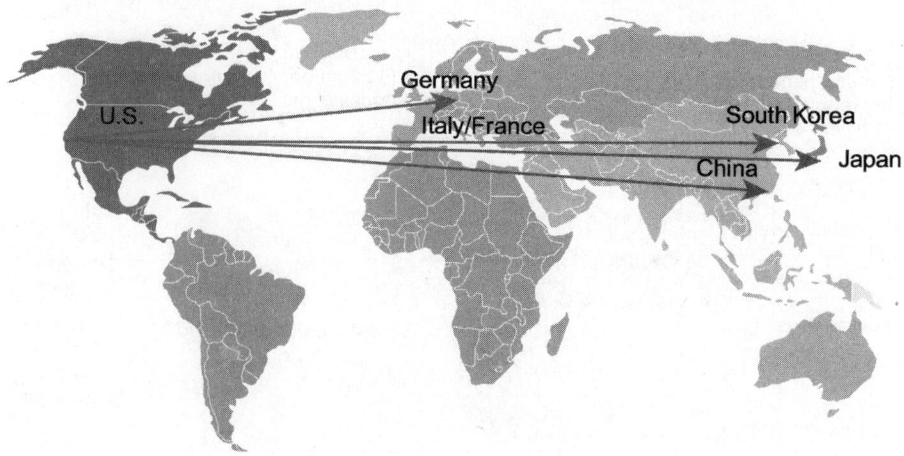

Apple designs the iPhone in the United States and relies on suppliers in the United States, Germany, Italy, France, Japan, and South Korea for other parts. Final assembly occurs in China.

more than 100 high-tech components from around the world, and assembled in China. Companies in Taiwan, South Korea, Japan, France, Italy, Germany, and the United States provided components such as the case, camera, processor, accelerator, gyroscope, electronic compass, power management chip, touch-screen controller, and high-definition display screen. Foxconn, a Chinese division of Taiwan's Hon Hai Group, is in charge of manufacturing and assembly.

Developing an International Information Systems Architecture

This chapter describes how to go about building an international information systems architecture suitable for your international strategy. An **international information systems architecture** consists of the basic information systems required by organizations to coordinate worldwide trade and other activities. Figure 15.2 illustrates the reasoning we follow throughout the chapter and depicts the major dimensions of an international information systems architectue.

The basic strategy to follow when building an international system is to understand the global environment in which your firm is operating. This means understanding the overall market forces, or business drivers, that are pushing your industry toward global competition. A **business driver** is a force in the environment to which businesses must respond and that influences the direction of the business. Likewise, examine carefully the inhibitors or negative factors that create *management challenges*—factors that could scuttle the development of a global business. Once you have examined the global environment, you will need to consider a corporate strategy for competing in that environment. How will your firm respond? You could ignore the global market and focus on domestic competition only, sell to the globe from a domestic base, or organize production and distribution around the globe. There are many in-between choices.

FIGURE 15.2 INTERNATIONAL INFORMATION SYSTEMS ARCHITECTURE

The major dimensions for developing an international information systems architecture are the global environment, the corporate global strategies, the structure of the organization, the management and business processes, and the technology platform.

After you have developed a strategy, it is time to consider how to structure your organization so it can pursue the strategy. How will you accomplish a division of labor across a global environment? Where will production, administration, accounting, marketing, and human resource functions be located? Who will handle the systems function?

Next, you must consider the management issues in implementing your strategy and making the organization design come alive. Key here will be the design of business processes. How can you discover and manage user requirements? How can you induce change in local units to conform to international requirements? How can you reengineer on a global scale, and how can you coordinate systems development?

The last issue to consider is the technology platform. Although changing technology is a key driving factor leading toward global markets, you need to have a corporate strategy and structure before you can rationally choose the right technology.

After you have completed this process of reasoning, you will be well on your way toward an appropriate international information systems portfolio capable of achieving your corporate goals. Let's begin by looking at the overall global environment.

The Global Environment: Business Drivers and Challenges

Table 15.1 lists the business drivers in the global environment that are leading all industries toward global markets and competition.

TABLE 15.1 THE GLOBAL ENVIRONMENT: BUSINESS DRIVERS AND CHALLENGES

GENERAL CULTURAL FACTORS	SPECIFIC BUSINESS FACTORS
Global communication and transportation technologies	Global markets
Development of global culture	Global production and operations
Emergence of global social norms	Global coordination
Political stability	Global workforce
Global knowledge base	Global economies of scale

The global business drivers can be divided into two groups: general cultural factors and specific business factors. Easily recognized general cultural factors have driven internationalization since World War II. Information, communication, and transportation technologies have created a *global village* in which communication (by telephone, television, radio, or computer network) around the globe is no more difficult and not much more expensive than communication down the block. The cost of moving goods and services to and from geographically dispersed locations has fallen dramatically.

The development of global communications has created a global village in a second sense: A **global culture** created by television, the Internet, and other globally shared media such as movies now permits different cultures and peoples to develop common expectations about right and wrong, desirable and undesirable, heroic and cowardly. The collapse of the Eastern bloc has accelerated the growth of a world culture enormously, increased support for capitalism and business, and reduced the level of cultural conflict in Europe considerably.

A last factor to consider is the growth of a global knowledge base. At the end of World War II, knowledge, education, science, and industrial skills were highly concentrated in North America, Western Europe, and Japan, with the rest of the world euphemistically called the *Third World*. This is no longer true. Latin America, China, India, southern Asia, and Eastern Europe have developed powerful educational, industrial, and scientific centers, resulting in a much more democratically and widely dispersed knowledge base.

These general cultural factors leading toward internationalization result in specific business globalization factors that affect most industries. The growth of powerful communications technologies and the emergence of world cultures lay the groundwork for *global markets*—global consumers interested in consuming similar products that are culturally approved. Coca-Cola, American sneakers (made in Korea but designed in Los Angeles), and Cable News Network (CNN) programming can now be sold in Latin America, Africa, and Asia.

Responding to this demand, global production and operations have emerged with precise online coordination between far-flung production facilities and central headquarters thousands of miles away. At Maersk, a major global shipping company based in Copenhagen, Denmark, shipping managers at Copenhagen and other locations can watch the loading of ships in Rotterdam online, check trim and ballast, and trace packages to specific ship locations as the activity proceeds. This is all possible through an international satellite link.

The new global markets and pressure toward global production and operation have called forth whole new capabilities for global coordination. Production, accounting, marketing and sales, human resources, and systems development (all the major business functions) can be coordinated on a global scale.

Frito-Lay, for instance, can develop a marketing sales force automation system in the United States and, once provided, may try the same techniques and technologies in Spain. Micromarketing—marketing to very small geographic and social units—no longer means marketing to neighborhoods in the United States but to neighborhoods throughout the world! Internet-based marketing means marketing to individuals and social networks throughout the world. These new levels of global coordination permit for the first time in history the location of business activity according to comparative advantage. Design should be located where it is best accomplished, as should marketing, production, and finance.

Finally, global markets, production, and administration create the conditions for powerful, sustained global economies of scale. Production driven by worldwide global demand can be concentrated where it can best be accomplished, fixed resources can be allocated over larger production runs, and production runs in larger plants can be scheduled more efficiently and precisely estimated. Lower-cost factors of production can be exploited wherever they emerge. The result is a powerful strategic advantage to firms that can organize globally. These general and specific business drivers have greatly enlarged world trade and commerce.

Not all industries are similarly affected by these trends. Clearly, manufacturing has been much more affected than services that still tend to be domestic and highly inefficient. However, the localism of services is breaking down in telecommunications, entertainment, transportation, finance, law, and general business. Clearly, those firms within an industry that can understand the internationalization of the industry and respond appropriately will reap enormous gains in productivity and stability.

Business Challenges

Although the possibilities of globalization for business success are significant, fundamental forces are operating to inhibit a global economy and to disrupt international business. Table 15.2 lists the most common and powerful challenges to the development of global systems.

At a cultural level, **particularism**, making judgments and taking action on the basis of narrow or personal characteristics, in all its forms (religious, nationalistic, ethnic, regionalism, geopolitical position) rejects the very concept of a shared global culture and rejects the penetration of domestic markets by foreign goods and services. Differences among cultures produce differences in social expectations, politics, and ultimately legal rules. In certain countries, such as the United States, consumers expect domestic name-brand products to be built domestically and are disappointed to learn that much of what they thought of as domestically produced is in fact foreign made.

Different cultures produce different political regimes. Among the many different countries of the world are different laws governing the movement of

TABLE 15.2 CHALLENGES AND OBSTACLES TO GLOBAL BUSINESS SYSTEMS

GLOBAL	SPECIFIC
Cultural particularism: Regionalism, nationalism, language differences	Standards: Different Electronic Data Interchange (EDI), e-mail, telecommunications standards
Social expectations: Brand-name expectations, work hours	Reliability: Phone networks not uniformly reliable
Political laws: Transborder data and privacy laws, commercial regulations	Speed: Different data transfer speeds, many slower than United States
	Personnel: Shortages of skilled consultants

information, information privacy of their citizens, origins of software and hardware in systems, and radio and satellite telecommunications. Even the hours of business and the terms of business trade vary greatly across political cultures. These different legal regimes complicate global business and must be considered when building global systems.

For instance, European countries have different laws concerning transborder data flow and privacy than those in the United States. **Transborder data flow** is defined as the movement of information across international boundaries in any form. In 1998 the European Union adopted a Data Protection Directive that broadened and standardized privacy protection in E.U. nations, and allowed for the transfer of personal data to systems located in the United States and under nations under a "safe harbor" provision. As long as systems in the United States met European privacy standards, the data could be transferred to and processed by U.S. systems. This agreement was replaced with a new agreement known as the E.U.-U.S. Privacy Shield in July 2016. Privacy Shield provides additional privacy protection for European citizens. Over 4,000 U.S. firms are registered with European privacy regulators allowing them to process personal information of European citizens in the United States. Privacy Shield also protects European citizens from certain surveillance activities of U.S. national security agencies. U.S. firms are changing their practices to ensure their systems comply with Privacy Shield.

Cultural and political differences profoundly affect organizations' business processes and applications of information technology. A host of specific barriers arise from the general cultural differences, everything from different reliability of phone networks to the shortage of skilled consultants.

National laws and traditions have created disparate accounting practices in various countries, which affects the ways profits and losses are analyzed. German companies generally do not recognize the profit from a venture until the project is completely finished and they have been paid. Conversely, British firms begin posting profits before a project is completed, when they are reasonably certain they will get the money.

These accounting practices are tightly intertwined with each country's legal system, business philosophy, and tax code. British, U.S., and Dutch firms share a predominantly Anglo-Saxon outlook that separates tax calculations from reports to shareholders to focus on showing shareholders how fast profits are growing. Continental European accounting practices are less oriented toward impressing investors, focusing rather on demonstrating compliance with strict rules and minimizing tax liabilities. These diverging accounting practices make it difficult for large international companies with units in different countries to evaluate their performance.

Language remains a significant barrier. Although English has become a kind of standard business language, this is truer at higher levels of companies and not throughout the middle and lower ranks. Software may have to be built with local language interfaces before a new information system can be successfully implemented.

Currency fluctuations can play havoc with planning models and projections. A product that appears profitable in Mexico or Japan may actually produce a loss because of changes in foreign exchange rates.

These inhibiting factors must be taken into account when you are designing and building international systems for your business. For example, companies trying to implement "lean production" systems spanning national boundaries typically underestimate the time, expense, and logistical difficulties of making goods and information flow freely across different countries.

State of the Art

One might think, given the opportunities for achieving competitive advantages as outlined previously and the interest in future applications, that most international companies have rationally developed marvelous international systems architectures. Nothing could be further from the truth. Most companies have inherited patchwork international systems from the distant past, often based on concepts of information processing developed in the 1960s—batch-oriented reporting from independent foreign divisions to corporate headquarters, manual entry of data from one legacy system to another, with little online control and communication. Corporations in this situation increasingly face powerful competitive challenges in the marketplace from firms that have rationally designed truly international systems. Still other companies have recently built technology platforms for international systems but have nowhere to go because they lack global strategy.

As it turns out, there are significant difficulties in building appropriate international architectures. The difficulties involve planning a system appropriate to the firm's global strategy, structuring the organization of systems and business units, solving implementation issues, and choosing the right technical platform. Let's examine these problems in greater detail.

15-2 What are the alternative strategies for developing global businesses?

Three organizational issues face corporations seeking a global position: choosing a strategy, organizing the business, and organizing the systems management area. The first two are closely connected, so we discuss them together.

TABLE 15.3 GLOBAL BUSINESS STRATEGY AND STRUCTURE

BUSINESS FUNCTION	DOMESTIC EXPORTER	MULTINATIONAL	FRANCHISER	TRANSNATIONAL
Production	Centralized	Dispersed	Coordinated	Coordinated
Finance/accounting	Centralized	Centralized	Centralized	Coordinated
Sales/marketing	Mixed	Dispersed	Coordinated	Coordinated
Human resources	Centralized	Centralized	Coordinated	Coordinated
Strategic management	Centralized	Centralized	Centralized	Coordinated

Global Strategies and Business Organization

Four main global strategies form the basis for global firms' organizational structure. These are domestic exporter, multinational, franchiser, and transnational. Each of these strategies is pursued with a specific business organizational structure (see Table 15.3). For simplicity's sake, we describe three kinds of organizational structure or governance: centralized (in the home country), decentralized (to local foreign units), and coordinated (all units participate as equals). Other types of governance patterns can be observed in specific companies (e.g., authoritarian dominance by one unit, a confederacy of equals, a federal structure balancing power among strategic units, and so forth).

The **domestic exporter** strategy is characterized by heavy centralization of corporate activities in the home country of origin. Nearly all international companies begin this way, and some move on to other forms. Production, finance/accounting, sales/marketing, human resources, and strategic management are set up to optimize resources in the home country. International sales are sometimes dispersed using agency agreements or subsidiaries, but even here, foreign marketing relies on the domestic home base for marketing themes and strategies. Caterpillar Corporation and other heavy capital-equipment manufacturers fall into this category of firm.

The **multinational** strategy concentrates financial management and control out of a central home base while decentralizing production, sales, and marketing operations to units in other countries. The products and services on sale in different countries are adapted to suit local market conditions. The organization becomes a far-flung confederation of production and marketing facilities in different countries. Many financial service firms, along with a host of manufacturers, such as General Motors, Chrysler, and Intel, fit this pattern.

Franchisers are an interesting mix of old and new. On the one hand, the product is created, designed, financed, and initially produced in the home country but for product-specific reasons must rely heavily on foreign personnel for further production, marketing, and human resources. Food franchisers such as McDonald's, Mrs. Fields Cookies, and KFC fit this pattern. McDonald's created a new form of fast-food chain in the United States and continues to rely largely on the United States for inspiration of new products, strategic management, and financing. Nevertheless, because the product must be produced locally—it is perishable—extensive coordination and dispersal of production, local marketing, and local recruitment of personnel are required.

Generally, foreign franchisees are clones of the mother country units, but fully coordinated worldwide production that could optimize factors of production is not possible. For instance, potatoes and beef can generally not be bought where they are cheapest on world markets but must be produced reasonably close to the area of consumption.

Transnational firms are the stateless, truly globally managed firms that may represent a larger part of international business in the future. Transnational firms have no single national headquarters but instead have many regional headquarters and perhaps a world headquarters. In a **transnational** strategy, nearly all the value-adding activities are managed from a global perspective without reference to national borders, optimizing sources of supply and demand wherever they appear, and taking advantage of any local competitive advantages. Transnational firms take the globe, not the home country, as their management frame of reference. The governance of these firms has been likened to a federal structure in which there is a strong central management core of decision making but considerable dispersal of power and financial muscle throughout the global divisions. Few companies have actually attained transnational status.

Information technology and improvements in global telecommunications are giving international firms more flexibility to shape their global strategies. Protectionism and a need to serve local markets better encourage companies to disperse production facilities and at least become multinational. At the same time, the drive to achieve economies of scale and take advantage of short-term local advantage moves transnationals toward a global management perspective and a concentration of power and authority. Hence, there are forces of decentralization and dispersal as well as forces of centralization and global coordination.

Global Systems to Fit the Strategy

Information technology and improvements in global telecommunications are giving international firms more flexibility to shape their global strategies. The configuration, management, and development of systems tend to follow the global strategy chosen. Figure 15.3 depicts the typical arrangements. By *systems* we mean the full range of activities involved in building and operating information systems: conception and alignment with the strategic business plan, systems development, and ongoing operation and maintenance. For the sake of simplicity, we consider four types of systems configuration. *Centralized systems* are those in which systems development and operation occur totally at the domestic home base. *Duplicated systems* are those in which development occurs at the home base but operations are handed over to autonomous units in foreign locations. *Decentralized systems* are those in which each foreign unit designs its own unique solutions and systems. *Networked systems* are those in which systems development and operations occur in an integrated and coordinated fashion across all units.

As can be seen in Figure 15.3, domestic exporters tend to have highly centralized systems in which a single domestic systems development staff develops

FIGURE 15.3 GLOBAL STRATEGY AND SYSTEMS CONFIGURATIONS

SYSTEM CONFIGURATION	Strategy			
	Domestic Exporter	Multinational	Franchiser	Transnational
Centralized	X			
Duplicated			X	
Decentralized	x	X	x	
Networked		x		X

The large Xs show the dominant patterns, and the small Xs show the emerging patterns. For instance, domestic exporters rely predominantly on centralized systems, but there is continual pressure and some development of decentralized systems in local marketing regions.

worldwide applications. Multinationals offer a direct and striking contrast: Here, foreign units devise their own systems solutions based on local needs with few if any applications in common with headquarters (the exceptions being financial reporting and some telecommunications applications). Franchisers have the simplest systems structure: Like the products they sell, franchisers develop a single system usually at the home base and then replicate it around the world. Each unit, no matter where it is located, has identical applications. Last, the most ambitious form of systems development is found in transnational firms: Networked systems are those in which there is a solid, singular global environment for developing and operating systems. This usually presupposes a powerful telecommunications backbone, a culture of shared applications development, and a shared management culture that crosses cultural barriers. The networked systems structure is the most visible in financial services where the homogeneity of the product—money and money instruments—seems to overcome cultural barriers.

Reorganizing the Business

How should a firm organize itself for doing business on an international scale? To develop a global company and information systems support structure, a firm needs to follow these principles:

1. Organize value-adding activities along lines of comparative advantage. For instance, marketing/sales functions should be located where they can best be performed for least cost and maximum impact; likewise with production, finance, human resources, and information systems.
2. Develop and operate systems units at each level of corporate activity—regional, national, and international. To serve local needs, there should be *host country systems units* of some magnitude. *Regional systems units* should handle telecommunications and systems development across national boundaries that take place within major geographic regions (European, Asian, American). *Transnational systems units* should be established to create the linkages across major

regional areas and coordinate the development and operation of international telecommunications and systems development (Roche, 1992).

3. Establish at world headquarters a single office responsible for development of international systems—a global chief information officer (CIO) position.

Many successful companies have devised organizational systems structures along these principles. The success of these companies relies not only on the proper organization of activities but also on a key ingredient—a management team that can understand the risks and benefits of international systems and that can devise strategies for overcoming the risks. We turn to these management topics next.

15-3 What are the challenges posed by global information systems and management solutions for these challenges?

Table 15.4 lists the principal management problems posed by developing international systems. It is interesting to note that these problems are the chief difficulties managers experience in developing ordinary domestic systems as well. But these are enormously complicated in the international environment.

A Typical Scenario: Disorganization on a Global Scale

Let's look at a common scenario. A traditional multinational consumer-goods company based in the United States and operating in Europe would like to expand into Asian markets and knows that it must develop a transnational strategy and a supportive information systems structure. Like most multinationals, it has dispersed production and marketing to regional and national centers while maintaining a world headquarters and strategic management in the United States. Historically, it has allowed each of the subsidiary foreign divisions to develop its own systems. The only centrally coordinated system is financial controls and reporting. The central systems group in the United States focuses only on domestic functions and production.

The result is a hodgepodge of hardware, software, and telecommunications. The e-mail systems between Europe and the United States are incompatible. Each production facility uses a different manufacturing resources planning system (or a different version of the same ERP system) and different marketing, sales, and human resource systems. Hardware and database platforms are wildly different. Communications between different sites are poor, given the high cost of European intercountry communications.

What do you recommend to the senior management leaders of this company, who now want to pursue a transnational strategy and develop an information systems architecture to support a highly coordinated global systems environment? Consider the problems you face by reexamining Table 15.4. The foreign divisions will resist efforts to agree on common user requirements; they

TABLE 15.4 MANAGEMENT CHALLENGES IN DEVELOPING GLOBAL SYSTEMS

Agreeing on common user requirements
Introducing changes in business processes
Coordinating applications development
Coordinating software releases
Encouraging local users to support global systems

have never thought about much other than their own units' needs. The systems groups in American local sites, which have been enlarged recently and told to focus on local needs, will not easily accept guidance from anyone recommending a transnational strategy. It will be difficult to convince local managers anywhere in the world that they should change their business procedures to align with other units in the world, especially if this might interfere with their local performance. After all, local managers are rewarded in this company for meeting local objectives of their division or plant. Finally, it will be difficult to coordinate development of projects around the world in the absence of a powerful telecommunications network and, therefore, difficult to encourage local users to take on ownership in the systems developed.

Global Systems Strategy

Figure 15.4 lays out the main dimensions of a solution. First, consider that not all systems should be coordinated on a transnational basis; only some core systems are truly worth sharing from a cost and feasibility point of view. **Core systems** support functions that are absolutely critical to the organization. Other systems should be partially coordinated because they share key elements, but they do not have to be totally common across national boundaries. For such systems, a good deal of local variation is possible and desirable. A final group of systems is peripheral, truly provincial, and needed to suit local requirements only.

Define the Core Business Processes

How do you identify core systems? The first step is to define a short list of critical core business processes. Business processes are defined and described in Chapter 2, which you should review. Briefly, business processes are sets of logically related tasks to produce specific business results, such as shipping out correct orders to customers or delivering innovative products to the market. Each business process typically involves many functional areas, communicating and coordinating work, information, and knowledge.

The way to identify these core business processes is to conduct a business process analysis. How are customer orders taken, what happens to them once they are taken, who fills the orders, and how are they shipped to the customers? What about suppliers? Do they have access to manufacturing resource planning systems so that supply is automatic? You should be able to identify

FIGURE 15.4 LOCAL, REGIONAL, AND GLOBAL SYSTEMS

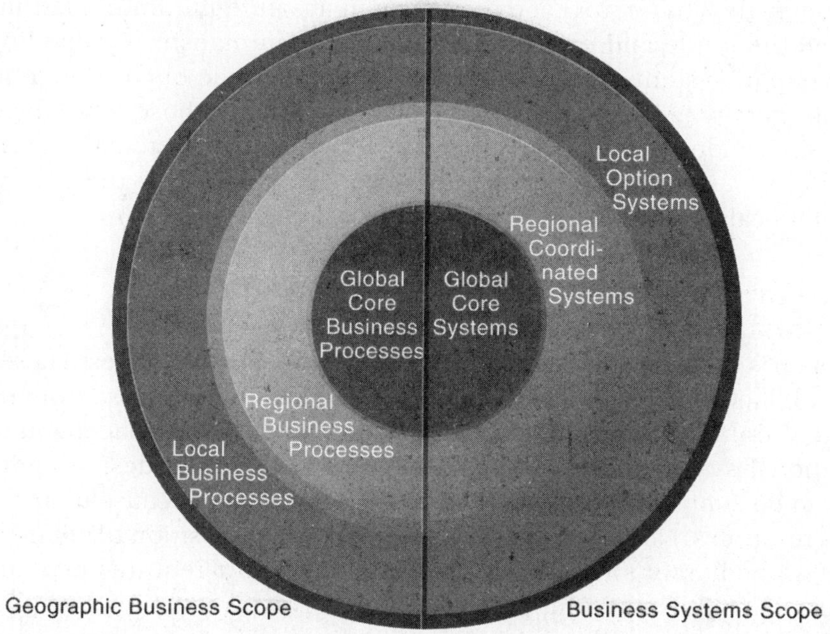

Agency and other coordination costs increase as the firm moves from local option systems toward regional and global systems. However, transaction costs of participating in global markets probably decrease as firms develop global systems. A sensible strategy is to reduce agency costs by developing only a few core global systems that are vital for global operations, leaving other systems in the hands of regional and local units.

Source: From *Managing Information Technology in Multinational Corporations* by Edward M. Roche, © 1993. Adapted by permission of Prentice Hall, Inc., Upper Saddle River, NJ.

and set priorities in a short list of 10 business processes that are absolutely critical for the firm.

Next, can you identify centers of excellence for these processes? Is the customer order fulfillment superior in the United States, manufacturing process control superior in Germany, and human resources superior in Asia? You should be able to identify some areas of the company, for some lines of business, where a division or unit stands out in the performance of one or several business functions.

When you understand the business processes of a firm, you can rank-order them. You then can decide which processes should be core applications, centrally coordinated, designed, and implemented around the globe and which should be regional and local. At the same time, by identifying the critical business processes, the really important ones, you have gone a long way to defining a vision of the future that you should be working toward.

Identify the Core Systems to Coordinate Centrally

By identifying the critical core business processes, you begin to see opportunities for transnational systems. The second strategic step is to conquer the core systems and define these systems as truly transnational. The financial and political costs of defining and implementing transnational systems are extremely high. Therefore, keep the list to an absolute minimum, letting experience be the guide and erring on the side of minimalism. By dividing off a small group of systems as absolutely critical, you divide opposition to a transnational strategy. At the same time, you can appease those who oppose the central worldwide coordination implied by transnational systems by permitting peripheral systems development to progress unabated with the exception of some technical platform requirements.

Choose an Approach: Incremental, Grand Design, Evolutionary

A third step is to choose an approach. Avoid piecemeal approaches. These surely will fail for lack of visibility, opposition from all who stand to lose from transnational development, and lack of power to convince senior management that the transnational systems are worth it. Likewise, avoid grand design approaches that try to do everything at once. These also tend to fail because of an inability to focus resources. Nothing gets done properly, and opposition to organizational change is needlessly strengthened because the effort requires extraordinary resources. An alternative approach is to evolve transnational applications incrementally from existing applications with a precise and clear vision of the transnational capabilities the organization should have in five years. This is sometimes referred to as the "salami strategy," or one slice at a time.

Make the Benefits Clear

What is in it for the company? One of the worst situations to avoid is to build global systems for the sake of building global systems. From the beginning, it is crucial that senior management at headquarters and foreign division managers clearly understand the benefits that will come to the company as well as to individual units. Although each system offers unique benefits to a particular budget, the overall contribution of global systems lies in four areas.

Global systems—truly integrated, distributed, and transnational systems—contribute to superior management and coordination. A simple price tag cannot be put on the value of this contribution, and the benefit will not show up in any capital budgeting model. It is the ability to switch suppliers on a moment's notice from one region to another in a crisis, the ability to move production in response to natural disasters, and the ability to use excess capacity in one region to meet raging demand in another.

A second major contribution is vast improvement in production, operation, and supply and distribution. Imagine a global value chain with global suppliers and a global distribution network. For the first time, senior managers can locate value-adding activities in regions where they are most economically performed.

Third, global systems mean global customers and global marketing. Fixed costs around the world can be amortized over a much larger customer base. This will unleash new economies of scale at production facilities.

Last, global systems mean the ability to optimize the use of corporate funds over a much larger capital base. This means, for instance, that capital in a surplus region can be moved efficiently to expand production of capital-starved regions; that cash can be managed more effectively within the company and put to use more effectively.

These strategies will not by themselves create global systems. You will have to implement what you strategize.

The Management Solution: Implementation

We now can reconsider how to handle the most vexing problems facing managers developing the global information systems architectures that were described in Table 15.4.

Agreeing on Common User Requirements

Establishing a short list of the core business processes and core support systems will begin a process of rational comparison across the many divisions of the company, develop a common language for discussing the business, and naturally lead to an understanding of common elements (as well as the unique qualities that must remain local).

Introducing Changes in Business Processes

Your success as a change agent will depend on your legitimacy, your authority, and your ability to involve users in the change design process. **Legitimacy** is defined as the extent to which your authority is accepted on grounds of competence, vision, or other qualities. The selection of a viable change strategy, which we have defined as evolutionary but with a vision, should assist you in convincing others that change is feasible and desirable. Involving people in change, assuring them that change is in the best interests of the company and their local units, is a key tactic.

Coordinating Applications Development

Choice of change strategy is critical for this problem. At the global level there is far too much complexity to attempt a grand design strategy of change. It is far easier to coordinate change by making small incremental steps toward a larger vision. Imagine a five-year plan of action rather than a two-year plan of action, and reduce the set of transnational systems to a bare minimum to reduce coordination costs.

Coordinating Software Releases

Firms can institute procedures to ensure that all operating units convert to new software updates at the same time so that everyone's software is compatible.

Encouraging Local Users to Support Global Systems

The key to this problem is to involve users in the creation of the design without giving up control over the development of the project to parochial interests. The overall tactic for dealing with resistant local units in a transnational company is cooptation. **Cooptation** is defined as bringing the opposition into the process of designing and implementing the solution without giving up control over the direction and nature of the change. As much as possible, raw power should be avoided. Minimally, however, local units must agree on a short list of transnational systems, and raw power may be required to solidify the idea that transnational systems of some sort are truly required.

How should cooptation proceed? Several alternatives are possible. One alternative is to permit each country unit the opportunity to develop one transnational application first in its home territory and then throughout the world. In this manner, each major country systems group is given a piece of the action in developing a transnational system, and local units feel a sense of ownership in the transnational effort. On the downside, this assumes the ability to develop high-quality systems is widely distributed and that a German team, for example, can successfully implement systems in France and Italy. This will not always be the case.

A second tactic is to develop new transnational centers of excellence, or a single center of excellence. There may be several centers around the globe that focus on specific business processes. These centers draw heavily from local national units, are based on multinational teams, and must report to worldwide management. Centers of excellence perform the initial identification and specification of business processes, define the information requirements, perform the business and systems analysis, and accomplish all design and testing. Implementation, however, and pilot testing are rolled out to other parts of the globe. Recruiting a wide range of local groups to transnational centers of excellence helps send the message that all significant groups are involved in the design and will have an influence.

Even with the proper organizational structure and appropriate management choices, it is still possible to stumble over technology issues. Choices of technology platforms, networks, hardware, and software are the final element in building transnational information systems architectures.

15-4 What are the issues and technical alternatives to be considered when developing international information systems?

Once firms have defined a global business model and systems strategy, they must select hardware, software, and networking standards along with key system applications to support global business processes. Hardware, software, and networking pose special technical challenges in an international setting.

One major challenge is finding some way to standardize a global computing platform when there is so much variation from operating unit to operating unit and from country to country. Another major challenge is finding specific software applications that are user-friendly and that truly enhance the productivity of international work teams. The universal acceptance of the Internet around the globe has greatly reduced networking problems. But the mere presence of the Internet does not guarantee that information will flow seamlessly throughout the global organization because not all business units use the same applications, and the quality of Internet service can be highly variable (just as with the telephone service). For instance, German business units may use an open source collaboration tool to share documents and communicate, which is incompatible with American headquarters teams, which use Microsoft solutions. Overcoming these challenges requires systems integration and connectivity on a global basis.

Computing Platforms and Systems Integration

The development of a transnational information systems architecture based on the concept of core systems raises questions about how the new core systems will fit in with the existing suite of applications developed around the globe by different divisions and different people and for different kinds of computing hardware. The goal is to develop global, distributed, and integrated systems to support digital business processes spanning national boundaries. Briefly, these are the same problems faced by any large domestic systems development effort. However, the problems are magnified in an international environment. Just imagine the challenge of integrating systems based on the Windows, Linux, Unix, or proprietary operating systems running on IBM, Oracle Sun, HP, and other hardware in many different operating units in many different countries!

Moreover, having all sites use the same hardware and operating system does not guarantee integration. Some central authority in the firm must establish data standards as well as other technical standards with which sites are to comply. For instance, technical accounting terms such as the beginning and end of the fiscal year must be standardized (review the earlier discussion of the cultural challenges to building global businesses) as well as the acceptable interfaces between systems, communication speeds and architectures, and network software.

Connectivity

Truly integrated global systems must have connectivity—the ability to link together the systems and people of a global firm into a single integrated network just like the phone system but capable of voice, data, and image transmissions. The Internet has provided an enormously powerful foundation for providing connectivity among the dispersed units of global firms. However, many issues remain. The public Internet does not guarantee any level of service (even in the United States). Few global corporations trust the security of the Internet and generally use private networks to communicate sensitive data and Internet virtual private networks (VPNs) for communications that require less security. Not all countries support even basic Internet service that requires obtaining reliable circuits, coordinating among different carriers and the regional telecommunications authority, and obtaining standard agreements for the level of telecommunications service provided. Table 15.5 lists the major challenges posed by international networks.

While private networks have guaranteed service levels and better security than the Internet, the Internet is the primary foundation for global corporate networks when lower security and service levels are acceptable. Companies can create global intranets for internal communication or extranets to exchange information more rapidly with business partners in their supply chains. They can use the public Internet to create global networks using VPNs from Internet service providers, which provide many features of a private network using the

TABLE 15.5 CHALLENGES OF INTERNATIONAL NETWORKS

Quality of service
Security
Costs and tariffs
Network management
Installation delays
Poor quality of international service
Regulatory constraints
Network capacity

public Internet (see Chapter 7). However, VPNs may not provide the same level of quick and predictable response as private networks, especially during times of the day when Internet traffic is very congested, and they may not be able to support large numbers of remote users.

The high cost of PCs and low incomes limit access to Internet service in many developing countries (see Figure 15.5). Where an Internet infrastructure exists in less-developed countries, it often lacks bandwidth capacity and is unreliable in part due to power grid issues. The purchasing power of most people in developing countries makes access to Internet services very expensive in local currencies. In the case of India, uneven Internet service and an undeveloped infrastructure for distributing and paying for goods have hampered the growth of e-commerce (see the Interactive Session on Organizations).

FIGURE 15.5 INTERNET POPULATION IN SELECTED COUNTRIES

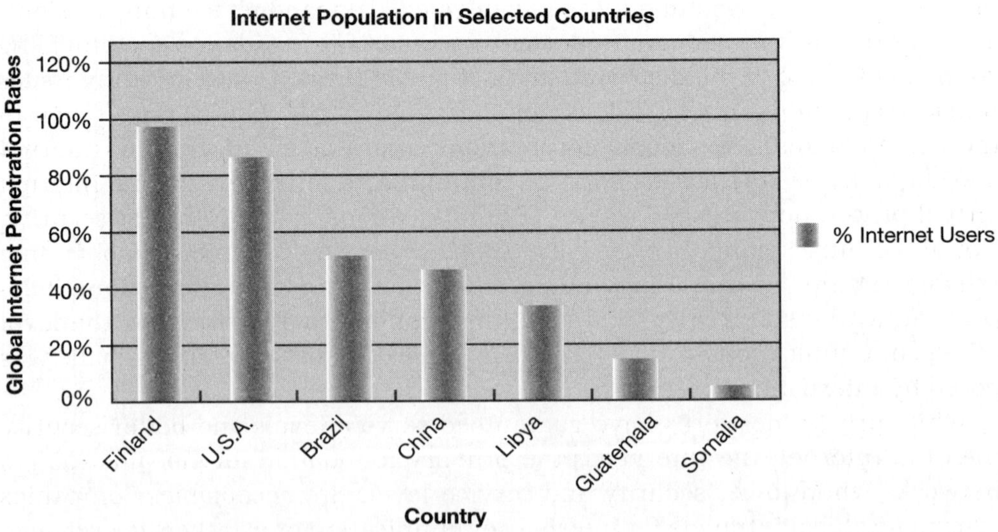

The percentage of the total population using the Internet in developing countries is much smaller than in the United States and Europe, but it is growing rapidly.

Source: Based on data from Internerworldstats.com, 2015; Pew Global Attitudes Project, 2015; and authors.

INTERACTIVE SESSION: ORGANIZATIONS

Indian E-commerce: Obstacles to Opportunity

After China, India has the world's second-largest number of Internet users, more than 400 million by the end of 2015. Rising smartphone ownership, with 4G networks rapidly replacing 3G in urban centers and slower, more affordable data plans in rural areas, has made this possible. Still, this represents only 32 percent of India's population of 1.25 billion. E-commerce in India is expected to surge in the next five years, but it faces some hefty challenges.

For example, a government initiative to lay fiber-optic cable and connect hundreds of thousands of villages to the national Internet backbone formulated in 2011 has stalled due to inaccessibility of remote areas, unwillingness of the large telecoms to invest (even with government financing) in non-lucrative sparsely populated areas, and red tape engendered by overlapping authority between governmental bodies in India's seven union territories, 29 states, and numerous districts and smaller administrative divisions.

Because standard infrastructure in India is primitive—including poor and even nonexistent roads and bridges—less than 5 percent of the planned million miles of cable had been completed by the end of 2015. What's more, India's electrical grid is woefully inadequate, many villages lack sufficient power lines, and electrical service is spotty at best. Bureaucratic right-of-way conflicts stalled work in 15 percent of villages scheduled to be connected, while a duct shortage and glitches with government-developed technology to connect the cables to their endpoints caused additional delays.

Prime Minister Narendra Modi is determined to hook up 600 million rural Indians, including schools, community centers, and hospitals, by 2019. Along with healthcare, educational, and other government services, he wants to ensure that online banking and e-commerce are universally available. Modi has tried to reduce intergovernmental body red tape and to curb corrupt state border officials, and he has also created the Committee on the National Fibre Optic Network to jump-start state government and private sector cooperation in both construction and maintenance and wrest control from state-owned giants.

The picture is mixed. In 2015, 94 percent of Internet usage was conducted by 276 million mobile phone users. Uber rival Ola, restaurant search site Zomato, and the What's App messaging service are rapidly gaining followers, but only 25 percent of urban dwellers and 5 percent of rural Indians have made an online purchase. Pending completion of Modi's broadband superhighway, growth will still be driven by falling smartphone and mobile data plan prices, with two-thirds of the projected 11 million new 2016 users accessing the Internet via portable device.

E-commerce travel sites are especially popular. MakeMytrip.com, Yatra.com, and Indian Railways' IRCTC website along with a number of smaller players account for 75 to 80 percent of all e-commerce purchases. Another top sector is digital downloads, including e-books, music, and content subscriptions, also traditionally a breakthrough sector. The remaining 20 percent of the business-to-consumer (B2C) e-commerce market is composed of durable goods, financial instruments such as online bill payment services and insurance products, and online classified ads, including job, dating, and matrimonial services driven by a growing middle class with rising disposable incomes.

The rush to capitalize on the projected $70 billion in online purchases by 2020 has been led by online giants Amazon and eBay. Amazon is following an unconventional path in India with Junglee.com, a transaction facilitator site that connects buyers and sellers while providing product and price comparison services, making it unambiguously a direct competitor to eBay India. eBay India was a pioneer, setting up shop in 2005. Credit card adoption is still in its infancy, and eBay had to pave the way in gaining consumer trust. The Indian iteration of PayPal, Paisa Pay, remits payment to the seller only after the buyer has received the item and refunds payment if the item is not shipped within three days. (Two days is the goal.) Coupons, a guarantee of full refund or replacement within 30 days if the buyer is not satisfied, and a Power Ship service have aided eBay's efforts. About 30,000 domestic and 15,000 worldwide sellers, mostly small, many artisans, and some from the poorest areas of the country, sell 16 products every minute to 128 million buyers in more than 30 countries. The key to this success was appreciating the unique nature of Indian consumers and tailoring the shopping experience and transaction flow to satisfy their needs.

Still, not all the kinks have been ironed out. Some states insist on requiring buyers to complete a form that must be sent to the seller before the product can ship. Less than 2 percent of Indian consumers own credit cards, so most e-commerce sites must offer a cash-on-delivery (COD) payment option. In 2015 60 to 70 percent of Indian e-commerce purchases were cash-on-delivery. About 45 percent of customers reject these COD orders at the point of delivery, making this a very expensive and probably unsustainable business model. Making matters worse, many e-tailers offer free shipping to acquire and retain customers. The national Indian poverty rate runs between 22 and 25 percent depending on how the rate is measured.

All retailers face steep costs for warehouses and logistics systems to overcome poor transportation infrastructure, bad roads, and traffic congestion. Until India's infrastructure catches up, the e-commerce war is likely to be won by those competitors with the best mobile app. On low-price smartphones feasible for most Indian consumers, many apps come preinstalled, and there is little space on the phone for additional app storage. In this emerging market, profits are yet to be realized, and market consolidation is ongoing. Developing a strong brand and effective customer service and, for some companies, cultivating a vibrant market niche will be the keys to survival.

Sources: Sean McLain and Newley Purnell, "India Startups Vie to Win E-Commerce Battle," *Wall Street Journal*, October 22, 2015; Joanna Sugden, "In 'Digital India,' a 15-Minute Wait for Email," *Wall Street Journal*, August 20, 2015; Sean McLain, "India to Become World's Second-Largest Internet User Base," *Wall Street Journal*, November 17, 2015; "The Quest for E-commerce Dominance in India," *Bloomberg News*, July 31, 2015; Arun Shroff, "E-Commerce in India: Trends, Opportunities and Challenges," India Advisory Board, February 1, 2013; Ramnath Subbu, "Indian E-commerce Market Is Nowhere Near Maturity—eBay India MD," *The Hindu*, April 21, 2014.

CASE STUDY QUESTIONS

1. Describe the technical, cultural, and organizational obstacles to e-commerce growth in India.
2. How do these factors hamper companies from doing business in India or setting up Indian e-commerce sites?
3. Will non-Indian companies like Amazon.com and eBay flourish in India? Explain.

In addition, many countries monitor transmissions. Governments in China, Singapore, Iran, and Saudi Arabia monitor Internet traffic and block access to websites considered morally or politically offensive. On the other hand, the rate of growth in the Internet population is far faster in Asia, Africa, and the Middle East than in North America and Europe, where the Internet population is growing slowly if at all. Therefore, in the future, Internet connectivity will be much more widely available and reliable in less-developed regions of the world, and it will play a significant role in integrating these economies with the world economy.

Software Localization

The development of core systems poses unique challenges for application software: How will the old systems interface with the new? Entirely new interfaces must be built and tested if old systems are kept in local areas (which is common). These interfaces can be costly and messy to build. If new software must be created, another challenge is to build software that can be realistically used by multiple business units from different countries given that business units are accustomed to their unique business processes and definitions of data.

Aside from integrating the new with the old systems, there are problems of human interface design and functionality of systems. For instance, to be truly useful for enhancing productivity of a global workforce, software interfaces must be easily understood and mastered quickly. Graphical user interfaces are ideal for this but presuppose a common language—often English. When international systems involve knowledge workers only, English may be the assumed international standard. But as international systems penetrate deeper into management and clerical groups, a common language may not be assumed and human interfaces must be built to accommodate different languages and even conventions. The entire process of converting software to operate in a second language is called **software localization**.

What are the most important software applications? Many international systems focus on basic transaction and management reporting systems. Increasingly, firms are turning to supply chain management and enterprise resource planning systems to standardize their business processes on a global basis and to create coordinated global supply chains and workforces (see the Interactive Session on Management). However, these cross-functional systems are not always compatible with differences in languages, cultural heritages, and business processes in other countries (Accenture, 2014;). Company units in countries that are not technically sophisticated may also encounter problems trying to manage the technical complexities of enterprise applications.

INTERACTIVE SESSION: MANAGEMENT

One Organization, One Data, One Information: ONGC's Global System

Oil and Natural Gas Corporation (ONGC) is one of India's most valuable companies, with a market capitalization of ₹2,32,000 crore. ONGC owns and operates more than 11,000 kilometers of gas pipelines in India. Realizing the importance of IT in managing its operations, the company embarked on a project called Information Consolidation for Efficiency in the year 2000, with an aim of creating an overarching set-up of "one organization, one data, one information". The target of the project was to achieve global standards in operations and introduce new business processes.

Oil exploration firms collect extensive data, which can be difficult to manage. A lot of the business decisions of such firms depend upon the results of this data. In order to ensure that its managers get an uninhibited view of all the collected information, the company chose to leverage state-of-the-art technologies like the supervisory control and data acquisition (SCADA), SAP Enterprise Resource Planning (ERP), and Exposure Prevention Information Network (EPINet) to further its goals. It was believed that these applications would make valuable information available on a real-time basis across the globe and eliminate the problem of data duplicity.

EPINet is a web-enabled data management system for geophysical as well as exploration and planning data. It provides multiple users, even those who work remotely, simultaneous access to all the assets, logs, drilling data related to exploration and planning, and so on. As a result, the managers at ONGC are now able to take speedy technical and business decisions.

Till the 1990s, all of the firm's exploration and planning data were stored in non-electronic physical forms like tapes and films. Moreover, these were held in different locations around the world with very little centralized access. In order to obtain the older data, manual indexing was done, which often led to the data being inaccurate or difficult to find. The information from oil well surveys was stored digitally, but since there was no common data store, each team saved it according to its individual preferences. This resulted in multiple versions of unedited data. The legacy system that ONGC used for material management, project monitoring, and maintenance planning often made access to data difficult. Managers weren't sure where to start looking for a piece of information that they needed to make important business decisions. Once the data was located, its collation, consolidation, and analysis proved to be difficult and time consuming. EPINet was judged to be a solution to all these challenges.

EPINet now manages both legacy and current data for the company. The outcome was an integrated exploration and planning database with single, validated exploration and planning database throughout ONGC. It also handles the analysis and interpretation of the data, while the web-based reporting feature allows all the current data on exploration and planning to flow directly into EPINet for centralized access. Moreover, this software is compliant with industry standards and best practices.

The firm's operations are global in nature and this calls for an IT solution that streamlines its business processes and integrates all the information along business lines. ONGC, with the help of the SAP ERP, went on to standardize more than 100 of its business processes for 13,000 users across all locations in less than 2.5 years time. The SAP R/3 ERP was implemented for the finance and HR activities. This led to the automation of several tasks related to payroll and administration. This ERP was then tested at oil-drilling platforms, which required that daily processes be run at specific times.

ONGC undertook another initiative to manage its global operations, this time with the help of the global automation company, ABB Limited. ONGC rolled out the enterprise-wide SCADA system to manage its onshore and offshore assets. This enabled the company officials to collect information about the business processes running at various locations. This solution was integrated with the EPINet software and the SAP ERP for a seamless experience.

Sources: "ONGC: Changing the face of the Upstream Oil and Gas Industry in India", https://library.e.abb.com/public/f53d01ec85d-7d8e9852571c4007859b2/ONGC%20success%20story.pdf ; Kumar, Sharath, "ONGC's innovative implementation of Wimax based BWA system", *Ciol* (2014). Retrieved from http://www.ciol.com/ongcs-innovative-implementation-wimax-bwa/; "ONGC India chooses ABB Industrial IT for offshore Fire and Gas System Upgrade at the WIN Platform" (2002). Retrieved from http://www.abb.co.in/cawp/seitp202/c1256c290031524bc1256c02002db8e3.aspx; Mittal, P.K. and Debashis Chatterjee, "EPINET In ONGC India: Transforming E&P Information Into Energy Intelligence", Society of Petroleum Engineers (2006). Retrieved from https://www.onepetro.org/conference-paper/SPE-99336-MS; "Business Process Re-engineering ONGC" (2009). Retrieved from http://www.slideshare.net/swapnilsaurav/business-process-reengineering-ongc.Kumar, C.R. &and M.P. Rao, M.P. (2013). "EPINET—G&G Information Resource Management in ONGC", 10th Biennial International Conference and Exposition, Kochi (2013); "Transforming Asia's largest oil and gas company". Retrieved from http://www.abb.co.in/cawp/seitp202/a22bc1ab5feefe4dc1257546003ad925.aspx.

CASE STUDY QUESTIONS

1. What were the challenges faced by ONGC which led to its adoption of EPINet?

2. Discuss the features of EPINet as a global IT solution.

3. Discuss how SCADA aids ONGC in managing its on-site and offshore assets.

4. How did the SAP ERP streamline the global business processes for the firm?

Electronic Data Interchange (EDI) systems and supply chain management systems are widely used by manufacturing and distribution firms to connect to suppliers on a global basis. Collaboration systems, e-mail, and videoconferencing are especially important worldwide collaboration tools for knowledge- and data-based firms, such as advertising firms, research-based firms in medicine and engineering, and graphics and publishing firms. Internet-based tools will be increasingly employed for such purposes.

Review Summary

15-1 *What major factors are driving the internationalization of business?*

The growth of inexpensive international communication and transportation has created a world culture with stable expectations or norms. Political stability and a growing global knowledge base that is widely shared also contribute to the world culture. These general factors create the conditions for global markets, global production, coordination, distribution, and global economies of scale.

15-2 *What are the alternative strategies for developing global businesses?*

There are four basic international strategies: domestic exporter, multinational, franchiser, and transnational. In a transnational strategy, all factors of production are coordinated on a global scale. However, the choice of strategy is a function of the type of business and product.

There is a connection between firm strategy and information systems design. Transnational firms must develop networked system configurations and permit considerable decentralization of development and operations. Franchisers almost always duplicate systems across many countries and use centralized financial controls. Multinationals typically rely on decentralized independence among foreign units with some movement toward development of networks. Domestic exporters typically are centralized in domestic headquarters with some decentralized operations permitted.

15-3 *What are the challenges posed by global information systems and management solutions for these challenges?*

Global information systems pose challenges because cultural, political, and language diversity magnifies differences in organizational culture and business processes and encourages proliferation of disparate local information systems that are difficult to integrate. Typically, international systems have evolved without a conscious plan. The remedy is to define a small subset of core business processes and focus on building systems to support these processes. Tactically, managers will have to co-opt widely dispersed foreign units to participate in the development and operation of these systems, being careful to maintain overall control.

15-4 *What are the issues and technical alternatives to be considered when developing international information systems?*

Implementing a global system requires an implementation strategy that considers both business design and technology platforms. The main hardware and telecommunications issues are systems integration and connectivity. The choices for integration are to go either with a proprietary architecture or with open systems technology. Global networks are extremely difficult to build and operate. Firms can build their own global networks or they can create global networks based on the Internet (intranets or virtual private networks). The main software issues concern building interfaces to existing systems and selecting applications that can work with multiple cultural, language, and organizational frameworks.

Key Terms

Business driver, 600
Cooptation, 613
Core systems, 610
Domestic exporter, 606
Franchisers, 606
Global culture, 602
International information systems architecture, 600
Legitimacy, 613
Multinational, 606
Particularism, 603
Software localization, 619
Transborder data flow, 604
Transnational, 607

Review Questions

15-1 What major factors are driving the internationalization of business?

- List and describe the five major dimensions for developing an international information systems architecture.
- Describe the five general cultural factors leading towards growth in the global business and the four specific business factors. Describe the interconnection among these factors.
- List and describe the major challenges to the development of global systems.
- Explain why some firms have not planned for the development of international systems.

15-2 What are the alternative strategies for developing global businesses?

- Discuss with examples the specific organization structure required to support global strategy.
- Explain the principles that a firm needs to follow to conduct business on an international scale.

15-3 What are the challenges posed by global information systems? Elaborate the management solutions for these challenges.

- List and describe the areas in which overall contribution of global systems can be identified.
- Discuss the tactics adopted by firms to deal with local resistant units in transnational companies.
- Define core systems. Explain their importance and the process of identifying core systems.
- Discuss how management challenges in developing domestic systems differ from international system building?

15-4 What are the issues and technical alternatives to be considered when developing international information systems?

- List and describe the challenges posed by international networks.
- Define software localization. Explain the role of system integration and connectivity in building global systems.

Discussion Questions

15-5 If you were a manager in a company that operates in many countries, what criteria would you use to determine whether an application should be developed as a global application or as a local application?

15-6 Describe the ways in which Internet can be used in international information systems.

Hands-On MIS Projects

The projects in this section give you a hands-on experience conducting international market research, analyzing international systems issues for an expanding business, and building a job posting database and web page for an international company.

Management Decision Problems

15-7 United Parcel Service (UPS) has been expanding its package delivery and logistics services in China, serving both multinational companies and local businesses. UPS drivers in China need to use UPS systems and tools such as its handheld Delivery Information Acquisition Device for capturing package delivery data. UPS wants to make its WorldShip, CampusShip, and other shipping-management services accessible to Chinese and multinational customers via the web. What are some of the international systems issues UPS must consider in order to operate successfully in China?

15-8 Your company manufactures and sells tennis racquets and would like to start selling outside the United States. You are in charge of developing a global web strategy, and the first countries you are thinking of targeting are Brazil, China, Germany, Italy, and Japan. Using the statistics in the *CIA World Factbook* and other online sources, which of these countries would you target first? What criteria did you use? What other considerations should you address in your web strategy? What features would you put on your website to attract buyers from the countries you target?

Achieving Operational Excellence: Building a Job Database and Web Page for an International Consulting Firm

Software skills: Database and web page design
Business skills: Human resources internal job postings

15-9 Companies with many overseas locations need a way to inform employees about available job openings in these locations. In this project you'll use database software to design a database for posting internal job openings and a web page for displaying this information.

KTP Consulting operates in various locations around the world. KTP specializes in designing, developing, and implementing enterprise systems for medium- to large-size companies. KTP offers its employees opportunities to travel, live, and work in various locations throughout the United States, Europe, and Asia. The firm's human resources department has a simple database that enables its staff to track job vacancies. When an employee is interested in relocating, she or he contacts the human resources department for a list of KTP job vacancies. KTP also posts its employment opportunities on the company's website.

What type of data should be included in the KTP job vacancies database? What information should not be included in this database? Based on your answers to these questions, build a job vacancies database for KTP. Populate the database with at least 20 records. You should also build a simple web page that incorporates job vacancy data from your newly created database. Submit a copy of the KTP database and web page to your professor.

Improving Decision Making: Conducting International Marketing and Pricing Research

Software skills: Internet-based software
Business skills: International pricing and marketing

15-10 In this project you'll use the web to research overseas distributors and customs regulations and use Internet-based software to calculate prices in foreign currencies.

You are in charge of marketing for a U.S. manufacturer of furniture that has decided to enter the international market. You want to test the market by contacting a European office furniture retailer to offer it a specific desk that you have to sell at about $125. Using the web, locate the information needed to locate and contact this firm and to find out how many euros you would get for the chair in the current market. One source for locating European companies is Europages. In addition, consider using a universal currency converter website, which determines the value of one currency expressed in other currencies. Obtain both the information needed to contact the firm and the price of your chair in its local currency. Then locate and obtain customs and legal restrictions on the products you will export from the United States and import into the country of the retailer you have selected. Finally, locate a company that will represent you as a customs agent and gather information on shipping costs.

Collaboration and Teamwork Project

Identifying Technologies for Global Business Strategies

15-11 With a group of students, identify an area of information technology and explore how this technology might be useful for supporting global business strategies. For instance, you might choose e-mail, smartphones, virtual private networks, enterprise systems, collaboration software, or the web. It will be necessary to identify a business scenario to discuss the technology. You might choose an automobile parts franchise or a clothing franchise, such as Express, as example businesses. Which applications would you make global, which core business processes would you choose, and how would the technology be helpful? If possible, use Google Docs and Google Drive or Google Sites to brainstorm, organize, and develop a presentation of your findings for the class.

Crocs Clambers to Global Efficiency

CASE STUDY

Crocs, Inc. is a world leader in innovative casual footwear for men, women and children. From the first mall kiosk in 2004, Crocs has grown to more than 500 branded retail locations around the world. It has outlets in more than 30 countries including Australia, New Zealand, China, Japan, South Korea, the United Kingdom, France, Germany, and the Netherlands but sells footwear in more than 90. The company now produces more than 300 four-season styles including boots, wedges, flip-flops, sandals, loafers, slippers, rain boots, and sneakers.

Rapid expansion from 2005 through 2007 was amplified by the acquisitions of footwear companies Ocean Minded and Bite Footwear, Dutch messenger bag company Tagger, South African third-party distributor Tidal Trade, and Jibbitz, a manufacturer of charms that snap into the holes of the classic clogs. Unsurprisingly, this resulted in a number of disparate IT systems. To keep pace with short-term growth, Crocs purchased best-of-breed systems in a variety of categories for order management, warehouse management, retail merchandising and reporting, and Electronic Data Interchange (EDI) functions. The problem with this approach is that while dedicated systems often perform better within their specialized niche, without an integrated system, enterprise-wide connectivity is compromised and maintenance needs exacerbated.

Regionally, this meant that highly customized systems evolved in order to integrate functions. This in turn meant that integration across regions became increasingly difficult if not impossible. Basic business functions such as closing the books required manually collating and reconciling spreadsheets from multiple countries and regions, punctuated by multiple phone calls and e-mails in pursuit of missing or incorrectly formatted data. Order entry began in numerous locales but had to proceed through three different systems before the order was placed. What's more, points of failure were unwieldy to locate.

By 2011, it became clear that Crocs's patchwork system was unsustainable. Cross-currency and multilanguage orders were unmanageable, and local or country-specific business regulations had to be managed manually. Crocs began scrutinizing and revamping its business processes and embarked on an enterprise-level IT project named Sunlight. Only after all vital business processes had been re-envisioned to support and serve the way the company did business did management begin searching for an enterprise resource planning (ERP) system to fit those needs. In this way, a companywide transformation was undertaken.

When management began to search for a solution to implement the standardized global processes it had outlined, SAP Apparel and Footwear was quickly chosen. It is one of a number of SAP Consumer Products solutions that tailor the SAP Enterprise Resource Planning (ERP) platform for specific industries. With its main goal of avoiding customizations uppermost, Crocs was further persuaded by the three-way size grid function and many other features custom-made for footwear sellers. Materials master data now store all size, color, and style information, reducing the number of SKUs (stock-keeping units) by an astonishing 40 percent. In fact, according to Dennis Sheldon, Senior Vice President of Global Distribution, the grid function in SAP Apparel and Footwear was instrumental in excising the surfeit of SKUs that had been driving the numerous system customizations at the regional level, shackling global integration. With shoe size, the key demand variable in the footwear industry, driving the grid, data requirements plummeted, business processes were streamlined, and at least 24 legacy systems were shed.

Phase one of the global rollout began in Australia in November 2012. The objectives were to modify the core product as minimally as possible, validate best practices, and discover areas in need of improvement while problems were confined to a single region. Phased ERP rollouts are often functional, rolling out modules for essential business functions (daily operations) enterprise-wide and gradually adding more modules and functionality. Alternatively, a rollout can be implemented by business unit, starting perhaps in the Human Resources department and then moving on to Accounting, Finance, and so on. For Crocs, neither of these approaches was tenable due to the fragmented state of its systems; thus, a phased global rollout was chosen.

SAP's general methodology for implementation of any project follows five steps. Phase I, Project Preparation, is the initial planning and preparation stage. Phase II is the Business Blueprint stage in which a detailed description of the business processes and system requirements is compiled producing the project structure and documentation that will be used in the next two phases.

A hierarchical structure of business scenarios, business processes, and process steps is created, and transactions are assigned to each process step. Phase III, Realization, is when all business process requirements are implemented and the system configuration is outlined at two levels: the baseline (major scope) configuration and the final (remaining scope) configuration. Phase IV is the Final Preparation stage in which testing, end-user training, system management, and cutover activities are performed and any unresolved critical issues are ironed out. Phase V is the Go Live & Support stage in which the project moves from a project-oriented, preproduction operation to a live production undertaking.

During the Business Blueprint phase, Crocs worked with an implementation partner, which helped it with development and data conversion. In total, the Blueprint, Realization, and Final Preparation stages took just 17 months, with Crocs's Australia division going live in April 2014.

Because Crocs also implemented a full suite of other SAP products, including SAP BusinessObjects (a Business Intelligence product), SAP BW (Business Warehouse), a B2B Internet sales application, SAP solutions for GRC (Governance, Risk, and Compliance), and SAP Business Planning and Consolidation to interface with the ERP system, it could use its Australian rollout to discover and implement any necessary modifications in a complete system before it proceeded to the next region, which it did within two months.

However, when Crocs took its Japan division (a six-times-larger business—$120 million as opposed to $20 million) live, it ran into language and cultural barriers that even advance training with a change management consulting firm could not forestall. Change management (CM) focuses on the human side of change—how to guide people through major organizational changes, including those brought about by information systems. Nevertheless, despite having to navigate several unforeseen cultural hurdles, the Japan rollout saw fewer data migration problems, and in short order, the company announced a target date of January 7, 2015, for its full global rollout.

To meet this goal, Crocs built regional "readiness" teams of subject matter experts (SMEs) from the different functional departments by immersing them in the training, development, and testing of the system. This eased adoption and bolstered the change management side of the equation. Often, companies will fly in IT department project managers and/or vendor project managers to train employees and oversee system implementation. Instead, Crocs made sure that known quantities familiar with local culture, business practices, and habits guided the process. These resident teams proved invaluable in troubleshooting and crisis management during the Go Live & Support phase.

With more than 100 of these "readiness" team leaders and SMEs on the ground and, equally as importantly, an enterprise-wide buy-in and broad understanding of the project goals, 1,400 users successfully finalized the launch across 32 countries, speaking 15 different languages and using 23 different currencies. What's more, Crocs could not have been more pleased that only 25 customizations were required, and those were to satisfy local legal and regulatory stipulations.

Crocs now administers the automation of purchasing, delivery tracking, inventory segmentation, chargebacks, and nearly every other aspect of the design, manufacture, and distribution of its footwear in SAP Apparel and Footwear. With business processes streamlined, sales are now outstanding for fewer days, and the fill, or demand satisfaction rate—percent of orders satisfied from inventory on hand—has significantly improved. Freight costs, nonproduction selling expenses, and SG&A (selling, general, and administrative) expenditures, which combine salaries, commissions, and travel expenses for executives and salespeople, advertising costs, and payroll expenses, have all been substantially reduced.

Perhaps even more noteworthy, whereas data were formerly regarded with a dubious eye, managers now have confidence in the numbers and can immediately proceed to data analysis. Order location, order status, and inventory availability are readily discernible, making order fulfillment both easier and faster.

In the year following implementation, Crocs kept a close eye on its users to make sure that they did not slip back into old habits, maintaining a strict prohibition on regionally based spreadsheets and insisting on meticulous conformance with revamped business processes. Analytics solutions working with SAP Apparel and Footwear are providing greater visibility into the business at the enterprise level. Operational efficiencies have provided improved control over Crocs's global supply chain from raw materials purchase to product delivery around the world. Its numerous design and style variations, seasonal offerings, and customer value-added services such as Jibbitz personalization generate very large quantities of data that can now be efficiently managed.

Though Crocs experienced a company shakeup in 2014 that included 70 jobs lost, 100 store closings, scaling back some of its newer, fashion-seeking styles to concentrate on its casual styles, and reducing investment in some smaller markets to concentrate on just six countries—the United States, the United Kingdom, Germany, South Korea, Japan, and China—its financial difficulties were not attributed to its IT investment. Rather, the slowdown was ascribed to changing customer tastes for a brand that has perennially suffered slings and arrows for its unattractive form.

Refocusing on its footwear's five key attributes—colorful, relaxed, comfortable, distinctive, and fun—Crocs was able to revive business back up to $9.7 million in 2015 (a 3.7 percent increase from the previous year) after Crocs had become a billion-dollar company in 2012.

Though some dissatisfaction with supply chain efficiency that resulted in poor customer service was noted by President and Principal Executive Officer Andrew Rees at the end of the third quarter of 2015, SAP Footwear and Apparel had only been up and running for those three quarters, and full functionality of the integrated analytics software had likely not yet been reached.

It is unlikely that without Crocs's forward-thinking commitment to revamping and streamlining its business processes, reducing costs, and improving order fulfillment efficiency the downturn of 2014 would have been navigated so seamlessly. The company was able to reduce its SKU count to simplify product development, forecasting, and inventory management. Crocs had identified reducing its direct-ship model as crucial. It had always permitted very low minimum order quantities and direct order placement with factories, but this was becoming unwieldy, creating needless complexity in the factory order management process. With its new systems, the company could now easily increase the minimum order quantity to industry standards enterprise-wide.

Crocs also decided to bring its value-added services more in line with industry standards to make it easier to package orders and move them through distribution centers. Once again, without an integrated global system, achieving this goal would have been significantly more problematic. Order location, order status, and inventory availability are all now easily obtainable, making global supply chain management easier. Finally, Crocs developed its management team, adding leaders from several key areas to ensure that its IT investment was used to its fullest potential. Project Sunlight should continue to reap benefits in 2016 and beyond.

Sources: www.company.crocs.com, accessed February 3, 2016; Ken Murphy, "Crocs Climbs New Business Heights," SAP Insider Profiles, July 6, 2015; Natalie Rinn, "Finding My Fun: A Thorough Examination of Crocs, the Most-Hated Shoe in America," racked.com, May 14, 2015; Jamie Grill-Goodman, "Crocs' E-commerce Business Grows Despite Inventory, Supply Chain Issues," Consumer Goods Technology, November 6, 2015; and "Crocs Discovers Multichannel Growth, Rolls Out ERP," *Retail Info Systems News*, February 26, 2013.

CASE STUDY QUESTIONS

15-12 What management problems typical of global systems was Crocs experiencing? What management, organization, and technology factors were responsible for those problems?

15-13 How did Crocs's new systems and use of SAP Apparel and Footwear support its business strategy? How effective was the solution chosen by the company?

15-14 How did Crocs's new systems improve operations and management decision making?

15-15 What influence does the global business environment have on Crocs, and how does that affect its choice of systems?

Chapter 15 References

Accenture. "Technology Not Widely Used in Global Companies' Emerging Market Supply Chains, Study Says." (September 16, 2014).

Bisson, Peter, Elizabeth Stephenson, and S. Patrick Viguerie. "Global Forces: An Introduction." *McKinsey Quarterly* (June 2010).

Burtch, Gordon, Anindya Ghose, and Sunil Watta. "Cultural Differences and Geography as Determinants of Online Prosocial Lending." *MIS Quarterly* 38, No. 3 (September 2014).

Davison, Robert. "Cultural Complications of ERP." *Communications of the ACM* 45, No. 7 (July 2002).

Deans, Candace P. and Michael J. Kane. *International Dimensions of Information Systems and Technology*. Boston, MA: PWS-Kent (1992).

Dewhurst, Martin, Jonathan Harris, and Suzanne Heywood. "The Global Company's Challenge." *McKinsey Quarterly* (June 2012).

Dou, Eva. "Timeline of China's Social Media Crackdowns." *Wall Street Journal* (August 8, 2014).

Ghislanzoni, Giancarlo, Risto Penttinen, and David Turnbull. "The Multilocal Challenge: Managing Cross-Border Functions." *McKinsey Quarterly* (March 2008).

Ives, Blake and Sirkka Jarvenpaa. "Applications of Global Information Technology: Key Issues for Management." *MIS Quarterly* 15, No. 1 (March 1991).

Ives, Blake, S. L. Jarvenpaa, and R. O. Mason. "Global Business Drivers: Aligning Information Technology to Global Business Strategy." *IBM Systems Journal* 32, No. 1 (1993).

King, William R. and Vikram Sethi. "An Empirical Analysis of the Organization of Transnational Information Systems." *Journal of Management Information Systems* 15, No. 4 (Spring 1999).

Kirsch, Laurie J. "Deploying Common Systems Globally: The Dynamic of Control." *Information Systems Research* 15, No. 4 (December 2004).

Krishna, S., Sundeep Sahay, and Geoff Walsham. "Managing Cross-Cultural Issues in Global Software Outsourcing." *Communications of the ACM* 47, No. 4 (April 2004).

Martinsons, Maris G. "ERP In China: One Package Two Profiles," *Communications of the ACM* 47, No. 7 (July 2004).

Meyer, Erin. "When Culture Doesn't Translate." *Harvard Business Review* (October 2015).

McKinsey & Company. "Lions Go Digital: The Internet's Transformative Potential in Africa. (November 2013).

Pew Research Global Attitudes Project. "Emerging Nations Embrace Internet, Mobile Technology." (February 13, 2014).

Quelch, John A. and Lisa R. Klein. "The Internet and International Marketing." *Sloan Management Review* (Spring 1996).

Roche, Edward M. *Managing Information Technology in Multinational Corporations*. New York: Macmillan (1992).

Su, Ning. "Cultural Sensemaking in Offshore Information Technology Service Suppliers: A Cultural Frame Perspective." *MIS Quarterly* 39, No. 4 (December 2015).

Tractinsky, Noam and Sirkka L. Jarvenpaa. "Information Systems Design Decisions in a Global Versus Domestic Context." *MIS Quarterly* 19, No. 4 (December 1995).

Waxer, Cindy."Cross-Border Data Blues." Computerworld Digital Magazine (May 2016).

Glossary

3-D printing Uses machines to make solid objects, layer by layer, from specifications in a digital file. Also known as additive manufacturing.

3G networks Cellular networks based on packet-switched technology with speeds ranging from 144 Kbps for mobile users to more than 2 Mbps for stationary users, enabling users to transmit video, graphics, and other rich media in addition to voice.

4G networks The next evolution in wireless communication is entirely packet switched and capable of providing between 1 Mbps and 1 Gbps speeds; up to 10 times faster than 3G networks.

acceptable use policy (AUP) Defines acceptable uses of the firm's information resources and computing equipment, including desktop and laptop computers, wireless devices, telephones, and the Internet, and specifies consequences for noncompliance.

acceptance testing Provides the final certification that the system is ready to be used in a production setting.

accountability The mechanisms for assessing responsibility for decisions made and actions taken.

advertising revenue model Website generating revenue by attracting a large audience.

affiliate revenue model An e-commerce revenue model in which websites are paid as "affiliates" for sending their visitors to other sites in return for a referral fee.

agency theory Economic theory that views the firm as a nexus of contracts among self-interested individuals who must be supervised and managed.

agent-based modeling Modeling complex phenomena as systems of autonomous agents that follow relatively simple rules for interaction.

agile development Rapid delivery of working software by breaking a large project into a series of small sub-projects that are completed in short periods of time using iteration and continuous feedback.

analytic platform Preconfigured hardware-software system that is specifically designed for high-speed analysis of large datasets.

analytical CRM Customer relationship management applications dealing with the analysis of customer data to provide information for improving business performance.

Android A mobile operating system developed by Android, Inc. (purchased by Google) and later the Open Handset Alliance as a flexible, upgradeable mobile device platform.

antivirus software Software designed to detect, and often eliminate, malware from an information system.

application controls: Specific controls unique to each computerized application that ensure that only authorized data are completely and accurately processed by that application.

application server Software that handles all application operations between browser-based computers and a company's back-end business applications or databases.

apps Small pieces of software that run on the Internet, on your computer, or on your cell phone and are generally delivered over the Internet.

artificial intelligence (AI) The effort to develop computer-based systems that can behave like humans, with the ability to learn languages, accomplish physical tasks, use a perceptual apparatus, and emulate human expertise and decision making.

attribute A piece of information describing a particular entity.

augmented reality (AR) A technology for enhancing visualization. Provides a live direct or indirect view of a physical real-world environment whose elements are augmented by virtual computer-generated imagery.

authentication The ability of each party in a transaction to ascertain the identity of the other party.

automation Using the computer to speed up the performance of existing tasks.

backward chaining A strategy for searching the rule base in an expert system that acts like a problem solver by beginning with a hypothesis and seeking out more information until the hypothesis is either proved or disproved.

balanced scorecard method Framework for operationalizing a firm's strategic plan by focusing on measurable financial, business process, customer, and learning and growth outcomes of firm performance.

bandwidth The capacity of a communications channel as measured by the difference between the highest and lowest frequencies that can be transmitted by that channel.

behavioral models Descriptions of management based on behavioral scientists' observations of what managers actually do in their jobs.

behavioral targeting Tracking the click-streams (history of clicking behavior) of individuals across multiple websites for the purpose of understanding their interests and intentions, and exposing them to advertisements which are uniquely suited to their interests.

benchmarking Setting strict standards for products, services, or activities and measuring organizational performance against those standards.

best practices The most successful solutions or problem-solving methods that have been developed by a specific organization or industry.

big data Data sets with volumes so huge that they are beyond the ability of typical relational DBMS to capture, store, and analyze. The data are often unstructured or semi-structured.

biometric authentication Technology for authenticating system users that compares a person's unique characteristics such as fingerprints, face, or retinal image against a stored set profile of these characteristics.

bit A binary digit representing the smallest unit of data in a computer system. It can only have one of two states, representing 0 or 1.

blog Popular term for "weblog," designating an informal yet structured website where individuals can publish stories, opinions, and links to other websites of interest.

blogosphere Totality of blog-related websites.

Bluetooth Standard for wireless personal area networks that can transmit up to 722 Kbps within a 10-meter area.

botnet A group of computers that have been infected with bot malware without users' knowledge, enabling a hacker to use the amassed resources of the computers to launch distributed denial-of-service attacks, phishing campaigns, or spam.

broadband High-speed transmission technology. Also designates a single communications medium that can transmit multiple channels of data simultaneously.

bugs Software program code defects.

bullwhip effect Distortion of information about the demand for a product as it passes from one entity to the next across the supply chain.

business continuity planning Planning that focuses on how the company can restore business operations after a disaster strikes.

business driver A force in the environment to which businesses must respond and that influences the direction of business.

business ecosystem Loosely coupled but interdependent networks of suppliers, distributors, outsourcing firms, transportation service firms, and technology manufacturers.

business functions Specialized tasks performed in a business organization, including manufacturing and production, sales and marketing, finance and accounting, and human resources.

business intelligence Applications and technologies to help users make better business decisions.

business model An abstraction of what an enterprise is and how the enterprise delivers a product or service, showing how the enterprise creates wealth.

business performance management (BPM) Attempts to systematically translate a firm's strategies (e.g., differentiation, low-cost producer, market share growth, and scope of operation) into operational targets.

business process management (BPM) An approach to business which aims to continuously improve and manage business processes.

business process redesign Type of organizational change in which business processes are analyzed, simplified, and redesigned.

business processes The unique ways in which organizations coordinate and organize work activities, information, and knowledge to produce a product or service.

business-to-business (B2B) electronic commerce Electronic sales of goods and services among businesses.

business-to-consumer (B2C) electronic commerce Electronic retailing of products and services directly to individual consumers.

BYOD Stands for "bring your own device,"and refers to employees using their own computing devices in the workplace.

byte A string of bits, usually eight, used to store one number or character in a computer system.

cable Internet connections Internet connections that use digital cable lines to deliver high-speed Internet access to homes and businesses.

capital budgeting The process of analyzing and selecting various proposals for capital expenditures.

carpal tunnel syndrome (CTS) Type of RSI in which pressure on the median nerve through the wrist's bony carpal tunnel structure produces pain.

case-based reasoning (CBR) Artificial intelligence technology that represents knowledge as a database of cases and solutions.

change agent In the context of implementation, the individual acting as the catalyst during the change process to ensure successful organizational adaptation to a new system or innovation.

change management Managing the impact of organizational change associated with an innovation, such as a new information system.

chat Live, interactive conversations over a public network.

chatbot Software agent designed to simulate a conversation with one or more human users via textual or auditory methods.

chief data officer (CDO) Responsible for enterprise-wide governance and utilization of information to maximize the value the organization can realize from its data.

chief information officer (CIO) Senior manager in charge of the information systems function in the firm.

chief knowledge officer (CKO) Senior executive in charge of the organization's knowledge management program.

chief privacy officer (CPO) Responsible for ensuring the company complies with existing data privacy laws.

chief security officer (CSO) Heads a formal security function for the organization and is responsible for enforcing the firm's security policy.

choice Simon's third stage of decision making, when the individual selects among the various solution alternatives.

Chrome OS Google's lightweight computer operating system for users who do most of their computing on the Internet; runs on computers ranging from netbooks to desktop computers.

churn rate Measurement of the number of customers who stop using or purchasing products or services from a company. Used as an indicator of the growth or decline of a firm's customer base.

classical model of management Traditional description of management that focused on its formal functions of planning, organizing, coordinating, deciding, and controlling.

click fraud Fraudulently clicking on an online ad in pay per click advertising to generate an improper charge per click.

client The user point-of-entry for the required function in client/server computing. Normally a desktop computer, workstation, or laptop computer.

client/server computing A model for computing that splits processing between clients and servers on a network, assigning functions to the machine most able to perform the function.

cloud computing Model of computing in which computer processing, storage, software, and other services are provided as a shared pool of virtualized resources over a network, primarily the Internet.

collaboration Working with others to achieve shared and explicit goals.

community provider A website business model that creates a digital online environment where people with similar interests can transact (buy and sell goods); share interests, photos, videos; communicate with like-minded people; receive interest-related information; and even play out fantasies by adopting online personalities called avatars.

communities of practice (COPs) Informal social networks of professionals and employees within and outside the firm who have similar work-related activities and interests and share their knowledge.

competitive forces model Model used to describe the interaction of external influences, specifically threats and opportunities, that affect an organization's strategy and ability to compete.

complementary assets Additional assets required to derive value from a primary investment.

component-based development Building large software systems by combining preexisting software components.

computer abuse The commission of acts involving a computer that may not be illegal but are considered unethical.

computer crime The commission of illegal acts through the use of a computer or against a computer system.

computer forensics The scientific collection, examination, authentication, preservation, and analysis of data held on or retrieved from computer storage media in such a way that the information can be used as evidence in a court of law.

computer hardware Physical equipment used for input, processing, and output activities in an information system.

computer literacy Knowledge about information technology, focusing on understanding of how computer-based technologies work.

computer software Detailed, preprogrammed instructions that control and coordinate the work of computer hardware components in an information system.

computer virus Rogue software program that attaches itself to other software programs or data files in order to be executed, often causing hardware and software malfunctions.

computer vision syndrome (CVS) Eyestrain condition related to computer display screen use; symptoms include headaches, blurred vision, and dry and irritated eyes.

computer-aided design (CAD) Information system that automates the creation and revision of designs using sophisticated graphics software.

computer-aided software engineering (CASE) Automation of step-by-step methodologies for software and systems development to reduce the amounts of repetitive work the developer needs to do.

consumer-to-consumer (C2C) Consumers selling goods and services electronically to other consumers.

consumerization of IT New information technology originating in the consumer market that spreads to business organizations.

controls All of the methods, policies, and procedures that ensure protection of the organization's assets, accuracy and reliability of its records, and operational adherence to management standards.

conversion The process of changing from the old system to the new system.

cookies Tiny file deposited on a computer hard drive when an individual visits certain websites. Used to identify the visitor and track visits to the website.

cooptation Bringing the opposition into the process of designing and implementing a solution without giving up control of the direction and nature of the change.

copyright A statutory grant that protects creators of intellectual property against copying by others for any purpose for a minimum of 70 years.

core competency Activity at which a firm excels as a world-class leader.

core systems Systems that support functions that are absolutely critical to the organization.

cost transparency The ability of consumers to discover the actual costs merchants pay for products.

counterimplementation A deliberate strategy to thwart the implementation of an information system or an innovation in an organization.

cross-selling Marketing complementary products to customers.

crowdsourcing Using large Internet audiences for advice, market feedback, new ideas, and solutions to business problems. Related to the "wisdom of crowds" theory.

culture The set of fundamental assumptions about what products the organization should produce, how and where it should produce them, and for whom they should be produced.

customer lifetime value (CLTV) Difference between revenues produced by a specific customer and the expenses for acquiring and servicing that customer minus the cost of promotional marketing over the lifetime of the customer relationship, expressed in today's dollars.

customer relationship management (CRM) Business and technology discipline that uses information systems to coordinate all of the business processes surrounding the firm's interactions with its customers in sales, marketing, and service.

customer relationship management systems Information systems that track all the ways in which a company interacts with its customers and analyze these interactions to optimize revenue, profitability, customer satisfaction, and customer retention.

customization The modification of a software package to meet an organization's unique requirements without destroying the package software's integrity.

customization In e-commerce, changing a delivered product or service based on a user's preferences or prior behavior.

cybervandalism Intentional disruption, defacement, or destruction of a website or corporate information system.

cyberwarfare State-sponsored activity designed to cripple and defeat another state or nation by damaging or disrupting its computers or networks.

data Streams of raw facts representing events occurring in organizations or the physical environment before they have been organized and arranged into a form that people can understand and use.

data administration A special organizational function for managing the organization's data resources, concerned with information policy, data planning, maintenance of data dictionaries, and data quality standards.

data cleansing Activities for detecting and correcting data in a database or file that are incorrect, incomplete, improperly formatted, or redundant. Also known as data scrubbing.

data definition DBMS capability that specifies the structure and content of the database.

data dictionary An automated or manual tool for storing and organizing information about the data maintained in a database.

data element A field.

data flow diagram (DFD) Primary tool for structured analysis that graphically illustrates a system's component process and the flow of data between them.

data governance Policies and processes for managing the availability, usability, integrity, and security of the firm's data.

data inconsistency The presence of different values for same attribute when the same data are stored in multiple locations.

data management technology Software governing the organization of data on physical storage media.

data manipulation language A language associated with a database management system that end users and programmers use to manipulate data in the database.

data mart A small data warehouse containing only a portion of the organization's data for a specified function or population of users.

data mining Analysis of large pools of data to find patterns and rules that can be used to guide decision making and predict future behavior.

data quality audit A survey and/or sample of files to determine accuracy and completeness of data in an information system.

data redundancy The presence of duplicate data in multiple data files.

data visualization Technology for helping users see patterns and relationships in large amounts of data by presenting the data in graphical form.

data warehouse A database, with reporting and query tools, that stores current and historical data extracted from various operational systems and consolidated for management reporting and analysis.

data workers People such as secretaries or bookkeepers who process the organization's paperwork.

database A group of related files.

database (rigorous definition) A collection of data organized to service many applications at the same time by storing and managing data so that they appear to be in one location.

database administration Refers to the more technical and operational aspects of managing data, including physical database design and maintenance.

database management system (DBMS) Special software to create and maintain a database and enable individual business applications to extract the data they need without having to create separate files or data definitions in their computer programs.

database server A computer in a client/server environment that is responsible for running a DBMS to process SQL statements and perform database management tasks.

decisional roles Mintzberg's classification for managerial roles where managers initiate activities, handle disturbances, allocate resources, and negotiate conflicts.

decision-support systems (DSS) Information systems at the organization's management level that combine data and sophisticated analytical models or data analysis tools to support semi-structured and unstructured decision making.

deep packet inspection (DPI) Technology for managing network traffic by examining data packets, sorting out low-priority data from higher priority business-critical data, and sending packets in order of priority.

demand planning Determining how much product a business needs to make to satisfy all its customers' demands.

denial-of-service (DoS) attack Flooding a network server or web server with false communications or requests for services in order to crash the network.

design Simon's second stage of decision making, when the individual conceives of possible alternative solutions to a problem.

DevOps Organizational strategy to create a culture and environment to promote rapid and agile development practices by emphasizing close collaboration between software developers and the IT operational staff.

digital asset management systems Classify, store, and distribute digital objects such as photographs, graphic images, video, and audio content.

digital certificate An attachment to an electronic message to verify the identity of the sender and to provide the receiver with the means to encode a reply.

digital dashboard Displays all of a firm's key performance indicators as graphs and charts on a single screen to provide one-page overview of all the critical measurements necessary to make key executive decisions.

digital divide Large disparities in access to computers and the Internet among different social groups and different locations.

digital firm Organization where nearly all significant business processes and relationships with customers, suppliers, and employees are digitally enabled, and key corporate assets are managed through digital means.

digital goods Goods that can be delivered over a digital network.

Digital Millennium Copyright Act (DMCA) Adjusts copyright laws to the Internet Age by making it illegal to make, distribute, or use devices that circumvent technology-based protections of copyrighted materials.

digital subscriber line (DSL) A group of technologies providing high-capacity transmission over existing copper telephone lines.

direct cutover strategy A risky conversion approach where the new system completely replaces the old one on an appointed day.

direct goods Goods used in a production process.

disaster recovery planning Planning for the restoration of computing and communications services after they have been disrupted.

disintermediation The removal of organizations or business process layers responsible for certain intermediary steps in a value chain.

disruptive technologies Technologies with disruptive impact on industries and businesses, rendering existing products, services, and business models obsolete.

distributed denial-of-service (DDoS) attack Numerous computers inundating and overwhelming a network from numerous launch points.

documentation Descriptions of how an information system works from either a technical or end-user standpoint.

domain name English-like name that corresponds to the unique 32-bit numeric Internet Protocol (IP) address for each computer connected to the Internet.

Domain Name System (DNS) A hierarchical system of servers maintaining a database enabling the conversion of domain names to their numeric IP addresses.

domestic exporter Form of business organization characterized by heavy centralization of corporate activities in the home county of origin.

downtime Period of time in which an information system is not operational.

drill down The ability to move from summary data to lower and lower levels of detail.

drive-by download Malware that comes with a downloaded file a user intentionally or unintentionally requests.

due process A process in which laws are well-known and understood and there is an ability to appeal to higher authorities to ensure that laws are applied correctly.

dynamic pricing Pricing of items based on real-time interactions between buyers and sellers that determine what a item is worth at any particular moment.

e-government Use of the Internet and related technologies to digitally enable government and public sector agencies' relationships with citizens, businesses, and other arms of government.

efficient customer response system System that directly links consumer behavior back to distribution, production, and supply chains.

electronic business (e-business) The use of the Internet and digital technology to execute all the business processes in the enterprise. Includes e-commerce as well as processes for the internal management of the firm and for coordination with suppliers and other business partners.

electronic commerce (e-commerce) The process of buying and selling goods and services electronically involving transactions using the Internet, networks, and other digital technologies.

electronic data interchange (EDI) The direct computer-to-computer exchange between two organizations of standard business transactions, such as orders, shipment instructions, or payments.

email The computer-to-computer exchange of messages.

employee relationship management (ERM) Software dealing with employee issues that are closely related to CRM, such as setting objectives, employee performance management, performance-based compensation, and employee training.

encryption The coding and scrambling of messages to prevent their being read or accessed without authorization.

end-user development The development of information systems by end users with little or no formal assistance from technical specialists.

end-user interface The part of an information system through which the end user interacts with the system, such as online screens and commands.

end users Representatives of departments outside the information systems group for whom applications are developed.

enterprise applications Systems that can coordinate activities, decisions, and knowledge across many different functions, levels, and business units in a firm. Include enterprise systems, supply chain management systems, and knowledge management systems.

enterprise content management (ECM) Help organizations manage structured and semi-structured knowledge, providing corporate repositories of documents, reports, presentations, and best practices and capabilities for collecting and organizing email and graphic objects.

enterprise software Set of integrated modules for applications such as sales and distribution, financial accounting, investment management, materials management, production planning, plant maintenance, and human resources that allow data to be used by multiple functions and business processes.

enterprise systems Integrated enterprise-wide information systems that coordinate key internal processes of the firm.

enterprise-wide knowledge management systems General-purpose, firmwide systems that collect, store, distribute, and apply digital content and knowledge.

entity A person, place, thing, or event about which information must be kept.

entity-relationship diagram A methodology for documenting databases illustrating the relationship between various entities in the database.

ergonomics The interaction of people and machines in the work environment, including the design of jobs, health issues, and the end-user interface of information systems.

e-tailer Online retail stores from the giant Amazon to tiny local stores that have websites where retail goods are sold.

ethical no-free-lunch rule Assumption that all tangible and intangible objects are owned by someone else, unless there is a specific declaration otherwise, and that the creator wants compensation for this work.

ethics Principles of right and wrong that can be used by individuals acting as free moral agents to make choices to guide their behavior.

evil twins Wireless networks that pretend to be legitimate to entice participants to log on and reveal passwords or credit card numbers.

exchange Third-party Net marketplace that is primarily transaction oriented and that connects many buyers and suppliers for spot purchasing.

executive support systems (ESS) Information systems at the organization's strategic level designed to address unstructured decision making through advanced graphics and communications.

expert system Knowledge-intensive computer program that captures the expertise of a human in limited domains of knowledge.

explicit knowledge Knowledge that has been documented.

Extensible Markup Language (XML) General-purpose language that describes the structure of a document and can perform presentation, communication, and storage of data, allowing data to be manipulated by the computer.

external integration tools Project management technique that links the work of the implementation team to that of users at all organizational levels.

extranet Private intranet that is accessible to authorized outsiders.

Fair Information Practices (FIP) A set of principles originally set forth in 1973 that governs the collection and use of information about individuals and forms the basis of most U.S. and European privacy laws.

fault-tolerant computer systems Systems that contain extra hardware, software, and power supply components that can back a system up and keep it running to prevent system failure.

feasibility study As part of the systems analysis process, the way to determine whether the solution is achievable, given the organization's resources and constraints.

feedback Output that is returned to the appropriate members of the organization to help them evaluate or correct input.

field A grouping of characters into a word, a group of words, or a complete number, such as a person's name or age.

File Transfer Protocol (FTP) Tool for retrieving and transferring files from a remote computer.

file A group of records of the same type.

firewall Hardware and software placed between an organization's internal network and an external network to prevent outsiders from invading private networks.

foreign key Field in a database table that enables users find related information in another database table.

formal control tools Project management technique that helps monitor the progress toward completion of a task and fulfillment of goals.

formal planning tools Project management technique that structures and sequences tasks, budgeting time, money, and technical resources required to complete the tasks.

forward chaining A strategy for searching the rule base in an expert system that begins with the information entered by the user and searches the rule base to arrive at a conclusion.

franchiser Form of business organization in which a product is created, designed, financed, and initially produced in the home country, but for product-specific reasons relies heavily on foreign personnel for further production, marketing, and human resources.

free/fremium revenue model An e-commerce revenue model in which a firm offers basic services or content for free while charging a premium for advanced or high-value features.

fuzzy logic Rule-based AI that tolerates imprecision by using nonspecific terms called membership functions to solve problems.

Gantt chart Visually representats the timing, duration, and resource requirements of project tasks.

general controls Overall control environment governing the design, security, and use of computer programs and the security of data files in general throughout the organization's information technology infrastructure.

genetic algorithms Problem-solving methods that promote the evolution of solutions to specified problems using the model of living organisms adapting to their environment.

geoadvertising services Delivering ads to users based on their GPS location.

geographic information system (GIS) System with software that can analyze and display data using digitized maps to enhance planning and decision-making.

geoinformation services Information on local places and things based on the GPS position of the user.

geosocial services Social networking based on the GPS location of users.

global culture The development of common expectations, shared artifacts, and social norms among different cultures and peoples.

Golden Rule Putting oneself in the place of others as the object of a decision.

Gramm-Leach-Bliley Act Requires financial institutions to ensure the security and confidentiality of customer data.

green computing (green IT) Refers to practices and technologies for designing, manufacturing, using, and disposing of computers, servers, and associated devices such as monitors, printers, storage devices, and networking and communications systems to minimize impact on the environment.

group decision-support system (GDSS) An interactive computer-based system to facilitate the solution to unstructured problems by a set of decision makers working together as a group.

hacker A person who gains unauthorized access to a computer network for profit, criminal mischief, or personal pleasure.

Hadoop Open source software framework that enables distributed parallel processing of huge amounts of data across many inexpensive computers.

hertz Measure of frequency of electrical impulses per second, with 1 Hertz equivalent to 1 cycle per second.

HIPAA Law outlining rules for medical security, privacy, and the management of healthcare records.

hotspot A specific geographic location in which an access point provides public Wi-Fi network service.

HTML5 Next evolution of HTML, which makes it possible to embed images, video, and audio directly into a document without add-on software.

hubs Very simple devices that connect network components, sending a packet of data to all other connected devices.

hybrid AI systems Integration of multiple AI technologies into a single application to take advantage of the best features of these technologies.

hybrid cloud Computing model where firms use both their own IT infrastructure and also public cloud computing services.

Hypertext Markup Language (HTML) Page description language for creating web pages.

Hypertext Transfer Protocol (HTTP) The communications standard used to transfer pages on the web. Defines how messages are formatted and transmitted.

identity management Business processes and software tools for identifying the valid users of a system and controlling their access to system resources.

identity theft Theft of key pieces of personal information, such as credit card or Social Security numbers, in order to obtain merchandise and services in the name of the victim or to obtain false credentials.

Immanuel Kant's categorical imperative A principle that states that if an action is not right for everyone to take it is not right for anyone.

implementation All the organizational activities surrounding the adoption, management, and routinization of an innovation, such as a new information system.

in-memory computing Technology for very rapid analysis and processing of large quantities of data by storing the data in the computer's main memory rather than in secondary storage.

indirect goods Goods not directly used in the production process, such as office supplies.

inference engine The strategy used to search through the rule base in an expert system; can be forward or backward chaining.

information Data that have been shaped into a form that is meaningful and useful to human beings.

information asymmetry Situation where the relative bargaining power of two parties in a transaction is determined by one party in the transaction possessing more information essential to the transaction than the other party.

information density The total amount and quality of information available to all market participants, consumers, and merchants.

information policy Formal rules governing the maintenance, distribution, and use of information in an organization.

information requirements A detailed statement of the information needs that a new system must satisfy; identifies who needs what information, and when, where, and how the information is needed.

information rights The rights that individuals and organizations have with respect to information that pertains to themselves.

information system Interrelated components working together to collect, process, store, and disseminate information to support decision making, coordination, control, analysis, and visualization in an organization.

information systems audit Identifies all the controls tht govern individual information systems and assesses their effectiveness.

information systems department The formal organizational unit that is responsible for the information systems function in the organization.

information systems literacy Broad-based understanding of information systems that includes behavioral knowledge about organizations and individuals using information systems as well as technical knowledge about computers.

information systems managers Leaders of the various specialists in the information systems department.

information systems plan A road map indicating the direction of systems development: the rationale, the current situation, the management strategy, the implementation plan, and the budget.

information technology (IT) All the hardware and software technologies a firm needs to achieve its business objectives.

information technology (IT) infrastructure Computer hardware, software, data, storage technology, and networks providing a portfolio of shared IT resources for the organization.

informational roles Mintzberg's classification for managerial roles where managers act as the nerve centers of their organizations, receiving and disseminating critical information.

informed consent Consent given with knowledge of all the facts needed to make a rational decision.

input The capture or collection of raw data from within the organization or from its external environment for processing in an information system.

instant messaging Chat service that allows participants to create their own private chat channels so that a person can be alerted whenever someone on his or her private list is online to initiate a chat session with that particular individual.

intangible benefits Benefits that are not easily quantified; they include more efficient customer service or enhanced decision making.

intellectual property Intangible property created by individuals or corporations that is subject to protections under trade secret, copyright, and patent law.

intelligence The first of Simon's four stages of decision making, when the individual collects information to identify problems occurring in the organization.

intelligent agent Software program that uses a built-in or learned knowledge base to carry out specific, repetitive, and predictable tasks for an individual user, business process, or software application.

intelligent techniques Technologies that aid human decision makers by capturing individual and collective knowledge, discovering patterns and behaviors in large quántities of data, and generating solutions to problems that are too large and complex for human beings to solve on their own.

internal integration tools Project management technique that ensures that the implementation team operates as a cohesive unit.

international information systems architecture The basic information systems required by organizations to coordinate worldwide trade and other activities.

Internet Global network of networks using universal standards to connect millions of different networks.

Internet of Things Pervasive web in which each object or machine has a unique identity and is able to use the Internet to link with other machines or send data. Also known as the Industrial Internet.

Internet Protocol (IP) address Four-part numeric address indicating a unique computer location on the Internet.

Internet service provider (ISP) A commercial organization with a permanent connection to the Internet that sells temporary connections to subscribers.

Internet2 Research network with new protocols and transmission speeds that provides an infrastructure for supporting high-bandwidth Internet applications.

interorganizational systems Information systems that automate the flow of information across organizational boundaries and link a company to its customers, distributors, or suppliers.

interpersonal roles Mintzberg's classification for managerial roles where managers act as figureheads and leaders for the organization.

intranet An internal network based on Internet and World Wide Web technology and standards.

intrusion detection system Tools to monitor the most vulnerable points in a network to detect and deter unauthorized intruders.

iOS Operating system for the Apple iPad, iPhone, and iPod Touch.

IPv6 New IP addressing system using 128-bit IP addresses. Stands for Internet Protocol version 6.

IT governance Strategy and policies for using information technology within an organization, specifying the decision rights and accountabilities to ensure that information technology supports the organization's strategies and objectives.

iterative A process of repeating over and over again the steps to build a system.

Java Programming language that can deliver only the software functionality needed for a particular task, such as a small applet downloaded from a network; can run on any computer and operating system.

joint application design (JAD) Process to accelerate the generation of information requirements by having end users and information systems specialists work together in intensive interactive design sessions.

just-in-time strategy Scheduling system for minimizing inventory by having components arrive exactly at the moment they are needed and finished goods shipped as soon as they leave the assembly line.

key field A field in a record that uniquely identifies instances of that record so that it can be retrieved, updated, or sorted.

key performance indicators Measures proposed by senior management for understanding how well the firm is performing along specified dimensions.

keylogger Spyware that records every keystroke made on a computer to steal personal information or passwords or to launch Internet attacks.

knowledge Concepts, experience, and insight that provide a framework for creating, evaluating, and using information.

knowledge base Model of human knowledge that is used by expert systems.

knowledge discovery Identification of novel and valuable patterns in large databases.

knowledge management The set of processes developed in an organization to create, gather, store, maintain, and disseminate the firm's knowledge.

knowledge management systems Systems that support the creation, capture, storage, and dissemination of firm expertise and knowledge.

knowledge workers People such as engineers or architects who design products or services and create knowledge for the organization.

knowledge work systems Information systems that aid knowledge workers in the creation and integration of new knowledge into the organization.

learning management system (LMS) Tools for the management, delivery, tracking, and assessment of various types of employee learning.

legacy system A system that has been in existence for a long time and that continues to be used to avoid the high cost of replacing or redesigning it.

legitimacy The extent to which one's authority is accepted on grounds of competence, vision, or other qualities.

liability The existence of laws that permit individuals to recover the damages done to them by other actors, systems, or organizations.

Linux Reliable and compactly designed operating system that is an offshoot of UNIX and that can run on many different hardware platforms and is available free or at very low cost. Used as alternative to UNIX.

local area network (LAN) A telecommunications network that requires its own dedicated channels and that encompasses a limited distance, usually one building or several buildings in close proximity.

location-based services GPS map services available on smartphones.

location analytics Ability to gain insights from the location (geographic) component of data, including loation data from mobile phones, output from sensors or scanning devices, and data from maps.

long tail marketing Refers to the ability of firms to profitably market goods to very small online audiences, largely because of the lower costs of reaching very small market segements (people who fall into the long tail ends of a Bell curve).

machine learning Study of how computer programs can improve their performance without explicit programming.

mainframe Largest category of computer, used for major business processing.

maintenance Changes in hardware, software, documentation, or procedures to a production system to correct errors, meet new requirements, or improve processing efficiency.

malware Malicious software programs such as computer viruses, worms, and Trojan horses.

managed security service provider (MSSP) Company that provides security management services for subscribing clients.

management information systems (MIS) Specific category of information system providing reports on organizational performance to help middle management monitor and control the business.

management information systems (MIS): The study of information systems focusing on their use in business and management.

managerial roles Expectations of the activities that managers should perform in an organization.

market creator An e-commerce business model in which firms provide a digital online environment where buyers and sellers can meet, search for products, and engage in transactions.

market entry costs The cost merchants must pay to bring their goods to market.

marketspace A marketplace extended beyond traditional boundaries and removed from a temporal and geographic location.

mashups Composite software applications that depend on high-speed networks, universal communication standards, and open source code.

mass customization The capacity to offer individually tailored products or services using mass production resources.

massive open online course (MOOC) Online course made available via the web to very large numbers of participants.

menu costs Merchants' costs of changing prices.

metropolitan area network (MAN) Network that spans a metropolitan area, usually a city and its major suburbs. Its geographic scope falls between a WAN and a LAN.

microblogging Blogging featuring very short posts, such as using Twitter.

micropayment systems Payment for a very small sum of money, often less than $10.

middle management People in the middle of the organizational hierarchy who are responsible for carrying out the plans and goals of senior management.

minicomputer Middle-range computer used in systems for universities, factories, or research laboratories.

mobile commerce (m-commerce) The use of wireless devices, such as smartphones or tablets to conduct both business-to-consumer and business-to-business e-commerce transactions over the Internet.

mobile web app Internet-enabled app with specific functionality for mobile devices that is accessed through a mobile device's web browser.

mobile website Version of a regular website that is scaled down in content and navigation for easy access and search on a small mobile screen.

modem A device for translating a computer's digital signals into analog form for transmission over analog networks or for translating analog signals back into digital form for reception by a computer.

Moore's Law Assertion that the number of components on a chip doubles each year.

multicore processor Integrated circuit to which two or more processors have been attached for enhanced performance, reduced power consumption, and more efficient simultaneous processing of multiple tasks.

multinational Form of business organization that concentrates financial management, and control out of a central home base while decentralizing production, sales and marketing.

multitiered (N-tier) client/server architecture Client/server network which the work of the entire network is balanced over several different levels of servers.

multitouch Interface that features the use of one or more finger gestures to manipulate lists or objects on a screen without using a mouse or keyboard.

nanotechnology Technology that builds structures and processes based on the manipulation of individual atoms and molecules.

native advertising Placing ads within social network newsfeeds or traditional editorial content, such as a newspaper article.

native app Standalone application designed to run on a specific platform and device and is installed directly on the mobile device

near field communication (NFC) Short-range wireless connectivity standard that uses electromagnetic radio fields to enable two compatible devices to exchange data when brought within a few centimeters of each other.

net marketplace A single digital marketplace based on Internet technology linking many buyers to many sellers.

network The linking of two or more computers to share data or resources, such as a printer.

network economics Model of strategic systems at the industry level based on the concept of a network where adding another participant entails zero marginal costs but can create much larger marginal gains.

network operating system (NOS) Special software that routes and manages communications on the network and coordinates network resources.

networking and telecommunications technology Physical devices and software that link various computer hardware components and transfer data from one physical location to another.

neural network Hardware or software that attempts to emulate the processing patterns of the biological brain.

non-relational database management system Database management system for working with large quantities of structured and unstructured data that would be difficult to analyze with a relational model.

nonobvious relationship awareness (NORA) Technology that can find obscure hidden connections between people or other entities by analyzing information from many different sources to correlate relationships.

normalization The process of creating small stable data structures from complex groups of data when designing a relational database.

object Software building block that combines data and the procedures acting on the data.

object-oriented development Approach to systems development that uses the object as the basic unit of systems analysis and design. The system is modeled as a collection of objects and the relationship between them.

offshore outsourcing Outsourcing systems development work or maintenance of existing systems to external vendors in another country.

on-demand computing Firms off-loading peak demand for computing power to remote, large-scale data processing centers, investing just enough to handle average processing loads and paying for only as much additional computing power as the market demands. Also called utility computing.

online analytical processing (OLAP) Capability for manipulating and analyzing large volumes of data from multiple perspectives.

online transaction processing Transaction processing mode in which transactions entered online are immediately processed by the computer.

open source software Software that provides free access to its program code, allowing users to modify the program code to make improvements or fix errors.

operating system Software that manages the resources and activities of the computer.

operational CRM Customer-facing applications, such as sales force automation, call center and customer service support, and marketing automation.

operational intelligence Business analytics that delivers insight into data, streaming events and business operations.

operational management People who monitor the day-to-day activities of the organization.

opt-in Model of informed consent permitting prohibiting an organization from collecting any personal information unless the individual specifically takes action to approve information collection and use.

opt-out Model of informed consent permitting the collection of personal information until the consumer specifically requests that the data not be collected.

organization (behavioral definition) A collection of rights, privileges, obligations, and responsibilities that are delicately balanced over a period of time through conflict and conflict resolution.

organization (technical definition) A stable, formal, social structure that takes resources from the environment and processes them to produce outputs.

organizational and management capital Investments in organization and management such as new business processes, management behavior, organizational culture, or training.

organizational impact analysis Study of the way a proposed system will affect organizational structure, attitudes, decision making, and operations.

organizational learning Creation of new standard operating procedures and business processes that reflect organizations' experience.

output The distribution of processed information to the people who will use it or to the activities for which it will be used.

outsourcing The practice of contracting computer center operations, telecommunications networks, or applications development to external vendors.

packet switching Technology that breaks messages into small, fixed bundles of data and routes them in the most economical way through any available communications channel.

paradigm shift Radical reconceptualization of the nature of the business and the nature of the organization.

parallel strategy A safe and conservative conversion approach where both the old system and its potential replacement are run together for a time until everyone is assured that the new one functions correctly.

particularism Making judgments and taking action on the basis of narrow or personal characteristics, in all its forms (religious, nationalistic, ethnic, regionalism, geopolitical position).

partner relationship management (PRM) Automation of the firm's relationships with its selling partners using customer data and analytical tools to improve coordination and customer sales.

password Secret word or string of characters for authenticating users so they can access a resource such as a computer system.

patch Small pieces of software to repair the software flaws without disturbing the proper operation of the software.

patent A legal document that grants the owner an exclusive monopoly on the ideas behind an invention for 20 years; designed to ensure that inventors of new machines or methods are rewarded for their labor while making widespread use of their inventions.

peer-to-peer Network architecture that gives equal power to all computers on the network; used primarily in small networks.

personal area network (PAN) Computer network used for communication among digital devices that are close to one person.

personalization Ability of merchants to target marketing messages to specific individuals by adjusting the message for a person's name, interests, and past purchases.

PERT chart Network diagram depicting project tasks and their interrelationships.

pharming Phishing technique that redirects users to a bogus web page, even when an individual enters the correct web page address.

phased approach Introduces the new system in stages either by functions or by organizational units.

phishing Form of spoofing involving setting up fake websites or sending email messages that resemble those of legitimate businesses that ask users for confidential personal data.

pilot study strategy A strategy to introduce the new system to a limited area of the organization until it is proven to be fully functional; only then can the conversion to the new system across the entire organization take place.

pivot table Spreadsheet tool for reorganizing and summarizing two or more dimensions of data in a tabular format.

platform Business providing information systems, technologies, and services that thousands of other firms in different industries use to enhance their own capabilities.

podcasting Publishing audio broadcasts via the Internet so that subscribing users can download audio files onto their personal computers or portable music players.

portal Web interface for presenting integrated personalized content from a variety of sources. Also refers to a website service that provides an initial point of entry to the web.

portfolio analysis An analysis of the portfolio of potential applications within a firm to determine the risks and benefits, and to select among alternatives for information systems.

post-implementation audit Formal review process conducted after a system has been placed in production to determine how well the system has met its original objectives.

predictive analytics The use of data mining techniques, historical data, and assumptions about future conditions to predict outcomes of events, such as the probability a customer will respond to an offer or purchase a specific product.

predictive search Part of a search alogrithm that predicts what a user query is looking as it is entered based on popular searches.

price discrimination Selling the same goods, or nearly the same goods, to different targeted groups at different prices.

price transparency The ease with which consumers can find out the variety of prices in a market.

primary activities Activities most directly related to the production and distribution of a firm's products or services.

primary key Unique identifier for all the information in any row of a database table.

privacy The claim of individuals to be left alone, free from surveillance or interference from other individuals, organizations, or the state.

private cloud A proprietary network or a data center that ties together servers, storage, networks, data, and applications as a set of virtualized services that are shared by users inside a company.

private exchange Another term for a private industrial network.

private industrial networks Web-enabled networks linking systems of multiple firms in an industry for the coordination of trans-organizational business processes.

process specifications Describe the logic of the processes occurring within the lowest levels of a data flow diagram.

processing The conversion, manipulation, and analysis of raw input into a form that is more meaningful to humans.

product differentiation Competitive strategy for creating brand loyalty by developing new and unique products and services that are not easily duplicated by competitors.

production The stage after the new system is installed and the conversion is complete; during this time the system is reviewed by users and technical specialists to determine how well it has met its original goals.

production or service workers People who actually produce the products or services of the organization.

profiling The use of computers to combine data from multiple sources and create electronic dossiers of detailed information on individuals.

program-data dependence The close relationship between data stored in files and the software programs that update and maintain those files. Any change in data organization or format requires a change in all the programs associated with those files.

programmers Highly trained technical specialists who write computer software instructions.

programming The process of translating the system specifications prepared during the design stage into program code.

project Planned series of related activities for achieving a specific business objective.

project management Application of knowledge, tools, and techniques to achieve specific targets within a specified budget and time period.

project portfolio management Helps organizations evaluate and manage portfolios of projects and dependencies among them.

protocol A set of rules and procedures that govern transmission between the components in a network.

prototype The preliminary working version of an information system for demonstration and evaluation purposes.

prototyping The process of building an experimental system quickly and inexpensively for demonstration and evaluation so that users can better determine information requirements.

public cloud A cloud maintained by an external service provider, accessed through the Internet, and available to the general public.

public key encryption Uses two keys: one shared (or public) and one private.

public key infrastructure (PKI) System for creating public and private keys using a certificate authority (CA) and digital certificates for authentication.

pull-based model Supply chain driven by actual customer orders or purchases so that members of the supply chain produce and deliver only what customers have ordered.

push-based model Supply chain driven by production master schedules based on forecasts or best guesses of demand for products, and products are "pushed" to customers.

quantum computing Use of principles of quantum physics to represent data and perform operations on the data, with the ability to be in many different states at once and to perform many different computations simultaneously.

query language Software tool that provides immediate online answers to requests for information that are not predefined.

radio frequency identification (RFID) Technology using tiny tags with embedded microchips containing data about an item and its location to transmit short-distance radio signals to special RFID readers that then pass the data on to a computer for processing.

ransomware Malware that extorts money from users by taking control of their computers or displaying annoying pop-up messages.

Rapid Application Development (RAD) Process for developing systems in a very short time period by using prototyping, state-of-the-art software tools and close teamwork among users and systems specialists.

rationalization of procedures The streamlining of standard operating procedures, eliminating obvious bottlenecks, so that automation makes operating procedures more efficient.

record A group of related fields.

referential integrity Rules to ensure that relationships between coupled database tables remain consistent.

relational DBMS A type of logical database model that treats data as if they were stored in two-dimensional tables. It can relate data stored in one table to data in another as long as the two tables share a common data element.

Repetitive stress injury (RSI) Occupational disease that occurs when muscle groups are forced through repetitive actions with high-impact loads or thousands of repetitions with low-impact loads.

Request for proposal (RFP) A detailed list of questions submitted to vendors of software or other services to determine how well the vendor's product can meet the organization's specific requirements.

responsibility Accepting the potential costs, duties, and obligations for the decisions one makes.

responsive web design Ability of a website to automatically change screen resolution and image size as a user switches to devices of different sizes, such as a laptop, tablet computer, or smartphone. Eliminates the need for separate design and development work for each new device.

revenue model A description of how a firm will earn revenue, generate profits, and produce a return on investment.

richness Measurement of the depth and detail of information that a business can supply to the customer as well as information the business collects about the customer.

risk assessment Determining the potential frequency of the occurrence of a problem and the potential damage if the problem were to occur. Used to determine the cost/benefit of a control.

Risk aversion principle Principle that one should take the action that produces the least harm or incurs the least cost.

router Specialized communications processor that forwards packets of data from one network to another network.

routines Precise rules, procedures and practices that have been developed to cope with expected situations.

RSS Technology using aggregator software to pull content from websites and feed it automatically to subscribers' computers.

safe harbor Private self-regulating policy and enforcement mechanism that meets the objectives of government regulations but does not involve government regulation or enforcement.

sales revenue model Selling goods, information, or services to customers as the main source of revenue for a company.

Sarbanes-Oxley Act Law passed in 2002 that imposes responsibility on companies and their management to protect investors by safeguarding the accuracy and integrity of financial information that is used internally and released externally.

scalability The ability of a computer, product, or system to expand to serve a larger number of users without breaking down.

scope Defines what work is and is not included in a project.

scoring model A quick method for deciding among alternative systems based on a system of ratings for selected objectives.

search costs The time and money spent locating a suitable product and determining the best price for that product.

search engine A tool for locating specific sites or information on the Internet.

search engine marketing Use of search engines to deliver in their results sponsored links, for which advertisers have paid.

search engine optimization (SEO) The process of changing a website's content, layout, and format in order to increase the ranking of the site on popular search engines and to generate more site visitors.

Secure Hypertext Transfer Protocol (S-HTTP) Protocol used for encrypting data flowing over the Internet; limited to individual messages.

Secure Sockets Layer (SSL) Enables client and server computers to manage encryption and decryption activities as they communicate with each other during a secure web session.

security Policies, procedures, and technical measures used to prevent unauthorized access, alteration, theft, or physical damage to information systems.

security policy Statements ranking information risks, identifying acceptable security goals, and identifying the mechanisms for achieving these goals.

semantic search Search technology capable of understanding human language and behavior.

semi-structured decisions Decisions in which only part of the problem has a clear-cut answer provided by an accepted procedure.

senior management People occupying the topmost hierarchy in an organization who are responsible for making long-range decisions.

sensitivity analysis Models that ask "what-if" questions repeatedly to determine the impact of changes in one or more factors on the outcomes.

sentiment analysis Mining text comments in an email message, blog, social media conversation, or survey form to detect favorable and unfavorable opinions about specific subjects.

server Computer specifically optimized to provide software and other resources to other computers over a network.

service level agreement (SLA) Formal contract between customers and their service providers that defines the specific responsibilities of the service provider and the level of service expected by the customer.

service-oriented architecture (SOA) Software architecture of a firm built on a collection of software programs that communicate with each other to perform assigned tasks to create a working software application

shopping bot Software with varying levels of built-in intelligence to help electronic commerce shoppers locate and evaluate products or service they might wish to purchase.

six sigma A specific measure of quality, representing 3.4 defects per million opportunities; used to designate a set of methodologies and techniques for improving quality and reducing costs.

smart card A credit-card-size plastic card that stores digital information and that can be used for electronic payments in place of cash.

smartphone Wireless phone with voice, text, and Internet capabilities.

sniffer Type of eavesdropping program that monitors information traveling over a network.

social business Use of social networking platforms, including Facebook, Twitter, and internal corporate social tools, to engage employees, customers, and suppliers.

social CRM Tools enabling a business to link customer conversatins, data, and relationships from social networking sites to CRM processes.

social engineering Tricking people into revealing their passwords by pretending to be legitimate users or members of a company in need of information.

social graph Map of all significant online social relationships, comparable to a social network describing offline relationships.

social networking sites Online community for expanding users' business or social contacts by making connections through their mutual business or personal connections.

social search Effort to provide more relevant and trustworthy search results based on a person's network of social contacts.

social shopping Use of websites featuring user-created web pages to share knowledge about items of interest to other shoppers.

sociotechnical design Design to produce information systems that blend technical efficiency with sensitivity to organizational and human needs.

sociotechnical view Seeing systems as composed of both technical and social elements.

Software as a service (SaaS) Services for delivering and providing access to software remotely as a web-based service.

software-defined networking (SDN) Using a central control program separate from network devices to manage the flow of data on a network.

software-defined storage (SDS) Software to manage provisioning and management of data storage independent of the underlying hardware.

software localization Process of converting software to operate in a second language.

software package A prewritten, precoded, commercially available set of programs that eliminates the need to write software programs for certain functions.

spam Unsolicited commercial email.

spoofing Tricking or deceiving computer systems or other computer users by hiding one's identity or faking the identity of another user on the Internet.

spyware Technology that aids in gathering information about a person or organization without their knowledge.

SQL injection attack Attacks against a website that take advantage of vulnerabilities in poorly coded SQL (a standard and common database software application) applications in order to introduce malicious program code into a company's systems and networks.

strategic transitions A movement from one level of sociotechnical system to another. Often required when adopting strategic systems that demand changes in the social and technical elements of an organization.

streaming A publishing method for music and video files that flows a continuous stream of content to a user's device without being stored locally on the device.

structure chart System documentation showing each level of design, the relationship among the levels, and the overall place in the design structure; can document one program, one system, or part of one program.

structured Refers to the fact that techniques are carefully drawn up, step by step, with each step building on a previous one.

structured decisions Decisions that are repetitive and routine and have a definite procedure for handling them.

structured knowledge Knowledge in the form of structured documents and reports.

Structured Query Language (SQL) The standard data manipulation language for relational database management systems.

subscription revenue model Website charging a subscription fee for access to some or all of its content or services on an ongoing basis.

supply chain Network of organizations and business processes for procuring materials, transforming raw materials into intermediate and finished products, and distributing the finished products to customers.

supply chain execution systems Systems to manage the flow of products through distribution centers and warehouses to ensure that products are delivered to the right locations in the most efficient manner.

supply chain management systems Information systems that automate the flow of information between a firm and its suppliers in order to optimize the planning, sourcing, manufacturing, and delivery of products and services.

supply chain planning systems Systems that enable a firm to generate demand forecasts for a product and to develop sourcing and manufacturing plans for that product.

support activities Activities that make the delivery of a firm's primary activities possible. Consist of the organization's infrastructure, human resources, technology, and procurement.

switch Device to connect network components that has more intelligence than a hub and can filter and forward data to a specified destination.

switching costs The expense a customer or company incurs in lost time and expenditure of resources when changing from one supplier or system to a competing supplier or system.

system testing Tests the functioning of the information system as a whole in order to determine if discrete modules will function together as planned.

systems analysis The analysis of a problem that the organization will try to solve with an information system.

systems analysts Specialists who translate business problems and requirements into information requirements and systems, acting as liaison between the information systems department and the rest of the organization.

systems design Details how a system will meet the information requirements as determined by the systems analysis.

systems development The activities that go into producing an information systems solution to an organizational problem or opportunity.

systems life cycle A traditional methodology for developing an information system that partitions the systems development process into formal stages that must be completed sequentially with a very formal division of labor between end users and information systems specialists.

T lines High-speed guaranteed service level data lines leased from communications providers, such as T-1 lines (with a transmission capacity of 1.544 Mbps).

tablet computer Mobile handheld computer that is larger than a mobile phone and operated primarily by touching a flat screen.

tacit knowledge Expertise and experience of organizational members that has not been formally documented.

tangible benefits Benefits that can be quantified and assigned a monetary value; they include lower operational costs and increased cash flows.

taxonomy Method of classifying things according to a predetermined system.

teams Formal groups whose members collaborate to achieve specific goals.

teamware Group collaboration software that is customized for teamwork.

technology standards Specifications that establish the compatibility of products and the ability to communicate in a network.

telepresence Telepresence is a technology that allows a person to give the appearance of being present at a location other than his or her true physical location.

Telnet Network tool that allows someone to log on to one computer system while doing work on another.

test plan Prepared by the development team in conjunction with the users; it includes all of the preparations for the series of tests to be performed on the system.

testing The exhaustive and thorough process that determines whether the system produces the desired results under known conditions.

text mining Discovery of patterns and relationships from large sets of unstructured data.

token Physical device similar to an identification card that is designed to prove the identity of a single user.

total cost of ownership (TCO) Designates the total cost of owning technology resources, including initial purchase costs, the cost of hardware and software upgrades, maintenance, technical support, and training.

total quality management (TQM) A concept that makes quality control a responsibility to be shared by all people in an organization.

touch point Method of firm interaction with a customer, such as telephone, email, customer service desk, conventional mail, or point-of-purchase.

trade secret Any intellectual work or product used for a business purpose that can be classified as belonging to that business, provided it is not based on information in the public domain.

transaction costs Costs incurred when a firm buys on the marketplace what it cannot make itself.

transaction cost theory Economic theory stating that firms grow larger because they can conduct marketplace transactions internally more cheaply than they can with external firms in the marketplace.

transaction fee revenue model An online e-commerce revenue model where the firm receives a fee for enabling or executing transactions.

transaction processing systems (TPS) Computerized systems that perform and record the daily routine transactions necessary to conduct the business; they serve the organization's operational level.

transborder data flow The movement of information across international boundaries in any form.

Transmission Control Protocol/Internet Protocol (TCP/IP) Dominant model for achieving connectivity among different networks. Provides a universally agreed-on method for breaking up digital messages into packets, routing them to the proper addresses, and then reassembling them into coherent messages.

transnational Truly global form of business organization with no national headquarters; value-added activities are managed from a global perspective without reference to national borders, optimizing sources of supply and demand and local competitive advantage.

Trojan horse A software program that appears legitimate but contains a second hidden function that may cause damage.

tuple A row or record in a relational database.

two-factor authentication Validating user identity with two means of identification, one of which is typically a physical token, and the other of which is typically data.

Unified communications Integrates disparate channels for voice communications, data communications, instant messaging, email, and electronic conferencing into a single experience where users can seamlessly switch back and forth between different communication modes.

unified threat management (UTM) Comprehensive security management tool that combines multiple security tools, including firewalls, virtual private networks, intrusion detection systems, and web content filtering and anti-spam software.

uniform resource locator (URL) The address of a specific resource on the Internet.

unit testing The process of testing each program separately in the system. Sometimes called program testing.

Unix Operating system for all types of computers, which is machine independent and supports multiuser processing, multitasking, and networking. Used in high-end workstations and servers.

unstructured decisions Nonroutine decisions in which the decision maker must provide judgment, evaluation, and insights into the problem definition; there is no agreed-upon procedure for making such decisions.

user interface The part of the information system through which the end user interacts with the system; type of hardware and the series of on-screen commands and responses required for a user to work with the system.

user-designer communications gap The difference in backgrounds, interests, and priorities that impede communication and problem solving among end users and information systems specialists.

utilitarian principle Principle that assumes one can put values in rank order of utility and understand the consequences of various courses of action.

value chain model Model that highlights the primary or support activities that add a margin of value to a firm's products or services where information systems can best be applied to achieve a competitive advantage.

value web Customer-driven network of independent firms who use information technology to coordinate their value chains to collectively produce a product or service for a market.

virtual company Organization using networks to link people, assets, and ideas to create and distribute products and services without being limited to traditional organizational boundaries or physical location.

virtual private network (VPN) A secure connection between two points across the Internet to transmit corporate data. Provides a low-cost alternative to a private network.

Virtual Reality Modeling Language (VRML) A set of specifications for interactive three-dimensional modeling on the World Wide Web.

virtual reality systems Interactive graphics software and hardware that create computer-generated simulations that provide sensations that emulate real-world activities.

virtualization Presenting a set of computing resources so that they can all be accessed in ways that are not restricted by physical configuration or geographic location.

visual web Refers to web linking visual sites such as Pinterest where pictures replace text socuents and where users search on pictures and visual characteristics.

Voice over IP (VoIP) Facilities for managing the delivery of voice information using the Internet Protocol (IP).

war driving Technique in which eavesdroppers drive by buildings or park outside and try to intercept wireless network traffic.

Web 2.0 Second-generation, interactive Internet-based services that enable people to collaborate, share information, and create new services online, including mashups, blogs, RSS, and wikis.

Web 3.0 Future vision of the web where all digital information is woven together with intelligent search capabilities.

web beacons Tiny objects invisibly embedded in email messages and web pages that are designed to monitor the behavior of the user visiting a website or sending email.

web browser An easy-to-use software tool for accessing the World Wide Web and the Internet.

web hosting service Company with large web server computers to maintain the websites of fee-paying subscribers.

web mining Discovery and analysis of useful patterns and information from the World Wide Web.

web server Software that manages requests for web pages on the computer where they are stored and that delivers the page to the user's computer.

web services Set of universal standards using Internet technology for integrating different applications from different sources without time-consuming custom coding. Used for linking systems of different organizations or for linking disparate systems within the same organization.

website All of the World Wide Web pages maintained by an organization or an individual.

Wi-Fi Stands for "wireless fidelity" and refers to the 802.11 family of wireless networking standards.

wide area network (WAN) Telecommunications network that spans a large geographical distance. May consist of a variety of cable, satellite, and microwave technologies.

wiki Collaborative website where visitors can add, delete, or modify content, including the work of previous authors.

WiMax Popular term for IEEE Standard 802.16 for wireless networking over a range of up to 31 miles with a data transfer rate of up to 75 Mbps. Stands for Worldwide Interoperability for Microwave Access.

Windows Microsoft family of operating systems for both network servers and client computers.

Windows 10 Most recent Microsoft Windows client operating system.

Wintel PC Any computer that uses Intel microprocessors (or compatible processors) and a Windows operating system.

wireless sensor networks (WSNs) Networks of interconnected wireless devices with built-in processing, storage, and radio frequency sensors and antennas that are embedded into the physical environment to provide measurements of many points over large spaces.

wisdom The collective and individual experience of applying knowledge to the solution of problems.

wisdom of crowds The belief that large numbers of people can make better decisions about a wide range of topics or products than a single person or even a small committee of experts.

World Wide Web A system with universally accepted standards for storing, retrieving, formatting, and displaying information in a networked environment.

worms Independent software programs that propagate themselves to disrupt the operation of computer networks or destroy data and other programs.

zero-day vulnerabilities Security vulnerabilities in software, unknown to the creator, that hackers can exploit before the vendor becomes aware of the problem.

Index

Name Index

Organizations Index

Subject Index

D

E

F

G

N

O

INTEGRATING BUSINESS WITH TECHNOLOGY

By completing the projects in this text, students will be able to demonstrate business knowledge, application software proficiency, and Internet skills.These projects can be used by instructors as learning assessment tools and by students as demonstrations of business, software, and problem-solving skills to future employers. Here are some of the skills and competencies students using this text will be able to demonstrate:

Business Application skills: Use of both business and software skills in real-world business applications. Demonstrates both business knowledge and proficiency in spreadsheet, database, and web page/blog creation tools.

Internet skills: Ability to use Internet tools to access information, conduct research, or perform online calculations and analysis.

Analytical, writing and presentation skills: Ability to research a specific topic, analyze a problem, think creatively, suggest a solution, and prepare a clear written or oral presentation of the solution, working either individually or with others in a group.

Business Application Skills

BUSINESS SKILLS	SOFTWARE SKILLS	CHAPTER
Finance and Accounting		
Financial statement analysis	Spreadsheet charts	Chapter 2*
	Spreadsheet formulas	Chapter 10
	Spreadsheet downloading and formatting	
Pricing hardware and software	Spreadsheet formulas	Chapter 5
Technology rent vs. buy decision Total Cost of Ownership (TCO) analysis	Spreadsheet formulas	Chapter 5*
Analyzing telecommunications services and costs	Spreadsheet formulas	Chapter 7
Risk assessment	Spreadsheet charts and formulas	Chapter 8
Retirement planning	Spreadsheet formulas and logical functions	Chapter 11
Capital budgeting	Spreadsheet formulas	Chapter 14
		Chapter 14*
Human Resources		
Employee training and skills tracking	Database design Database querying and reporting	Chapter 13*
Job posting database and Web page	Database design Web page design and creation	Chapter 15
Manufacturing and Production		
Analyzing supplier performance and pricing	Spreadsheet date functions Database functions Data filtering	Chapter 2
Inventory management	Importing data into a database Database querying and reporting	Chapter 6
Bill of materials cost sensitivity analysis	Spreadsheet data tables Spreadsheet formulas	Chapter 12*

Sales and Marketing

Sales trend analysis	Database querying and reporting	Chapter 1
Customer reservation system	Database querying and reporting	Chapter 3
Improving marketing decisions	Spreadsheet pivot tables	Chapter 12
Customer profiling	Database design Database querying and reporting	Chapter 6*
Customer service analysis	Database design Database querying and reporting	Chapter 9
Sales lead and customer analysis	Database design Database querying and reporting	Chapter 13
Blog creation and design	Blog creation tool	Chapter 4

Internet Skills

Using online software tools for job hunting and career development	Chapter 1
Using online interactive mapping software to plan efficient transportation routes	Chapter 2
Researching product information and evaluating websites for auto sales	Chapter 3
Analyzing web browser privacy protection	Chapter 4
Researching travel costs using online travel sites	Chapter 5
Searching online databases for products and services	Chapter 6
Using web search engines for business research	Chapter 7
Researching and evaluating business outsourcing services	Chapter 8
Researching and evaluating supply chain management services	Chapter 9
Evaluating e-commerce hosting services	Chapter 10
Using shopping bots to compare product price, features, and availability	Chapter 11
Using online software tools for retirement planning	Chapter 12
Analyzing website design and information requirements	Chapter 13
Researching real estate prices	Chapter 14
Researching international markets and pricing	Chapter 15

Analytical, Writing and Presentation Skills*

BUSINESS PROBLEM	CHAPTER
Management analysis of a business	Chapter 1
Value chain and competitive forces analysis	Chapter 3
Business strategy formulation	
Formulating a corporate privacy policy	Chapter 4
Employee productivity analysis	Chapter 7
Disaster recovery planning	Chapter 8
Locating and evaluating suppliers	Chapter 9
Developing an e-commerce strategy	Chapter 10
Identifying knowledge management opportunities	Chapter 11
Identifying international markets	Chapter 15

*Dirt Bikes Running Case on MyLab MIS